The authors

Consultant editor: Simon Osborne

Sarah Clarke is CPAG's solicitor.

Pamela Fitzpatrick is Director of Harrow Law Centre.

Carolyn George is a freelance trainer and writer on welfare rights.

Alison Gilles is a welfare rights worker at CPAG in Scotland.

Will Hadwen is a freelance trainer and consultant on welfare rights and related areas. She previously worked for Citizens Advice as a social security specialist.

Daphne Hall is a part-time welfare rights adviser at Bristol City Council, and a freelance trainer and writer on welfare rights.

Henri Krishna is a welfare rights worker at CPAG in Scotland.

Susan Mitchell is a freelance writer on welfare rights.

Paul Moorhouse is a part-time welfare rights worker for Central and South Sussex CAB, and a freelance trainer and writer.

Simon Osborne is a welfare rights worker at CPAG, based at CPAG in Scotland.

Judith Paterson is CPAG in Scotland's welfare rights co-ordinator.

Jon Shaw is a welfare rights worker at CPAG in Scotland.

Angela Toal is a welfare rights worker at CPAG in Scotland.

Paula Twigg works at the Mary Ward Legal Centre as the Advice Services Director.

Rebecca Walker is a part-time welfare rights worker at Pitsmoor CAB, and a freelance trainer and writer on welfare rights.

Martin Williams is a welfare rights worker at CPAG.

Mark Willis is a welfare rights worker at CPAG in Scotland.

Acknowledgements

The authors would like to thank Miranda Bayliss, Mark Brough, Barbara Donegan, Edward Graham, Barbara Gray, Arnie James, Lindsay Judge, Beth Lakhani, David Malcolm and Kelly Smith for their invaluable contribution.

We would also like to acknowledge the efforts of the many authors of previous editions of the *National Welfare Benefits Handbook*, the *Rights Guide to Non-Means-Tested Benefits* and the *Jobseeker's Allowance Handbook*, on which this book is based.

Thanks are due to Nicola Johnston and Alison Key for editing and managing the production of the book so efficiently, and to Kathleen Armstrong, Anne Ketley and Paula McDiarmid for proofreading the text. Particular thanks are due to Katherine Dawson for producing the index.

We would also like to thank, once again, staff at the Department for Work and Pensions, the Child Support Agency, HM Customs and Revenue, HM Courts and Tribunals Service and the Department for Education for their help and co-operation.

Thanks to the staff at KonnectSoft, David Lewis XML Associates and CPI William Clowes for keeping up with our schedules.

The law covered in this book was correct on 1 March 2012 and includes regulations laid up to this date.

Foreword

Welcome to the 2012/13 *Welfare Benefits and Tax Credits Handbook*, which I know is the essential guide to UK social security for so many practitioners. This *Handbook* has been produced against the backdrop of the government's ongoing welfare reform programme, which is, according to many, the most radical shake-up of the benefits system since Beveridge. Central to the reform agenda is the belief that the current system is too complex, and that this inhibits take up, potentially deters claimants from working and generates significant administrative costs. By integrating in- and out-of-work benefits with the introduction of universal credit in October 2013, the government aims to address all of these issues in one fell swoop.

However, as well as seeking to remove many of the perversities of the current benefits system, the government's welfare reform agenda also represents an assault on the core principles on which it has been based. Nowhere is this clearer than the proposed benefit cap, due to be implemented from April 2013, which will, for the first time in a generation, delink the level of benefits provided from assessed need.

Many of the key changes being implemented this year presage the much larger structural reforms to come. For example, contributory employment and support allowance will be withdrawn for the work-related activity group after one year, a period that we regard as far too short for most recipients to recover and reconnect with the workforce. Rather than supporting a system where risks are pooled, the government is moving towards an increasingly means-tested approach. The contributory principle, so central to Beveridge's conception of the welfare state, is being left to wither away.

Moreover, in this age of austerity, cutting the welfare benefits bill is a central priority for the government, and the adequacy of benefits is under more ferocious attack than ever before. Wherever we look, means tests are becoming increasingly stringent. The whole raft of changes to working tax credit being made this year – from the new working hours rule for couples to the cut in backdating from three months to one, the £2,500 disregard for in-year income falls to the scrapping of the 50-plus element – all conspire to reduce eligibility and limit the amounts working families receive to protect them from poverty.

Children's benefits are also taking a real hit in 2012/13. Child tax credit will not be uprated at above-inflation rates as promised in 2010, despite the fact that the government explicitly marked this policy as poverty-preventing when announced. The value of child benefit is frozen for the second year running, even though we know this is a critical component of poorer families' incomes. Finally, in 2013, child benefit will be withdrawn from higher rate taxpayers as the government continues its retreat from universalism.

Given the vital role that benefits and tax credits have played in reducing child poverty over the last decade, it comes as no surprise that child poverty rates are now expected to rise substantially in the near future. Analysis from the Institute for Fiscal Studies suggests that progress on child poverty has already stalled, and projects that the government's current programme of cuts will result in an additional 400,000 children living in poverty by 2015, and another 800,000 by 2020.

This multiplicity of changes to the benefits system is occurring at a time when the advice sector is shrinking in response to cuts at both national and local level. Yet without good advice, claimants will find it more difficult than ever to navigate the system and access their full entitlement. Many critical benefits decisions, such as an employment adviser sanctioning a jobseeker's allowance claimant or an evaluator issuing a work capability assessment, involve a high degree of discretion. Without expert assistance in such murky areas, claimants are inevitably going to be short-changed, often with grave consequences for the welfare of both themselves and their families.

The government is currently working out many of the practicalities for universal credit and other welfare reforms that will be implemented in subsequent years. On the positive side, it is investing significantly in delivery and implementation, a refreshing move as this aspect is often a poor relation to the more exciting task of policy development. However, universal credit will rely on many more people accessing their benefits online and, in turn, on the stability and functionality of the 'real time' information system passing earnings information from HM Revenue and Customs to the DWP. While the potential for an IT disaster to strike is great, we hope, for the sake of families across the country, that all runs smoothly.

With so many changes to the benefits and tax credits system being made this year, it would be wrong to describe 2012/13 as the lull before the storm. We know we have a critical job to do, both now and in subsequent years, to protect the incomes of the most vulnerable from further erosion. But equally important is the task of ensuring that the founding principles of our welfare system endure, and indeed flourish, into the future.

Alison Garnham

Chief Executive, CPAG

Welfare Benefits and Tax Credits Handbook

14th edition

Child Poverty Action Group

CPAG promotes action for the prevention and relief of poverty among children and families with children. To achieve this, CPAG aims to raise awareness of the causes, extent, nature and impact of poverty, and strategies for its eradication and prevention; bring about positive policy changes for families with children in poverty; and enable those eligible for income maintenance to have access to their full entitlement. If you are not already supporting us, please consider making a donation, or ask for details of our membership schemes, training courses and publications.

Published by Child Poverty Action Group
94 White Lion Street
London N1 9PF
Tel: 020 7837 7979
staff@cpag.org.uk
www.cpag.org.uk

A CIP record for this book is available from the British Library

ISBN: 978 1 906076 62 7

Child Poverty Action Group is a charity registered in England and Wales (registration number 294841) and in Scotland (registration number SC039339), and is a company limited by guarantee, registered in England (registration number 1993854). VAT number: 690 808117

Cover design by Devious Designs
Typeset by David Lewis XML Associates Ltd
Content management system by Konnect Soft (www.konnectsoft.com)
Printed by CPI Group (UK) Ltd, Croydon CR0 4YY
Cover photo by Ray Roberts/Photofusion

Contents

How to use this *Handbook*

This *Handbook* covers the rules for all welfare benefits and tax credits.

The basic structure of the benefit and tax credit systems is summarised in Chapter 1. This chapter explains the differences between the various types of benefits and tax credits. It includes a quick guide to the benefits and tax credits you can claim depending on your circumstances and a short A to Z of benefits and tax credits.

New this year is a section in the *Handbook* devoted to welfare reform. Part 2 looks ahead to the way the system is changing, and introduces the new universal credit and personal independence payment.

This *Handbook* also aims to give practical help in the areas where disputes are likely to arise between claimants and local authorities, the Department for Work and Pensions (DWP), HM Revenue and Customs or other government departments. If you are challenging a decision about your claim, it is helpful to refer to the relevant law and official guidance, and references are given in the notes at the end of each chapter.

In this *Handbook* the chapters are organised into eight parts. Part 1 outlines the benefit and tax credit systems. Part 2 gives an overview of welfare reform, including universal credit and personal independence payment. Broadly, all the information about individual benefits, in alphabetical order, is in Part 3, and all the benefit rules that apply to particular groups, or are common to all the benefits, are in Parts 4–6. Part 7 describes the two different tax credits, as well as the rules common to both. Part 8 outlines the immigration and residence rules that apply to both benefits and tax credits.

Each chapter begins with key facts so you can see at a glance the main features of the benefit or rules described in the chapter.

The notes are at the end of each chapter and are numbered in the order they appear in the text. The notes are in abbreviated form, in order to save space, and the relevant abbreviations are listed in Appendix 12.

For example, 'Reg 52(2) JSA Regs' is regulation 52(2) of the Jobseeker's Allowance Regulations 1996. The references are usually to Acts or regulations, but sometimes they are to caselaw (Upper Tribunal, social security commissioners' or court decisions) and guidance issued by the DWP. Appendix 2 and Appendix 3 suggest where to look for copies of the law and caselaw.

In the text, abbreviations are also used for most of the benefits in order to save space. There is a list of abbreviations used in the text on p. However, an abbreviated term is always given in full the first time it is used in a chapter or section.

The index contains entries in bold type, directing you to the general information on the subject or where the subject is covered more fully. Sub-entries under the bold headings are listed alphabetically and direct you to specific aspects of the subject.

The cross references in the text refer you to other information about the relevant topic.

The main subjects in each chapter are summarised in the contents pages at the front of this book. The main subject headings and page numbers are repeated at the beginning of each chapter.

Contents of this Handbook

Part 1 contains just one chapter introducing the main structure of the benefit and tax credit systems.

Part 2 describes the way the system is changing under welfare reform and outlines universal credit and personal independence payment.

Part 3 covers the rules for all the non-means-tested and means-tested benefits.

Part 4 describes the special rules that apply to certain groups of claimants.

Part 5 gives the general rules that apply to all, or most of, the benefits.

Part 6 describes the administration of benefits and how to challenge decisions made about benefits or complain if you have been treated unfairly.

Part 7 covers the rules for tax credits, describes how they are administered and explains how to challenge tax credit decisions.

Part 8 covers the immigration and residence rules that apply to benefits and tax credits.

The benefit and tax credit rates listed in the following sections and throughout this *Handbook* are those applying from April 2012.

Abbreviations

AA	attendance allowance
BL	budgeting loan
CA	carer's allowance
CAB	Citizens Advice Bureau
CCG	community care grant
CL	crisis loan
CSA	Child Support Agency
CRU	Compensation Recovery Unit
CTB	council tax benefit
CTC	child tax credit
DLA	disability living allowance
DWP	Department for Work and Pensions
EC	European Community
ECtHR	European Court of Human Rights
ECJ	European Court of Justice
EEA	European Economic Area
EO	employment officer
ESA	employment and support allowance
EU	European Union
EWC	expected week of childbirth
GP	general practitioner
HB	housing benefit
HMCTS	HM Courts and Tribunals Service
HMRC	HM Revenue and Customs
IB	incapacity benefit
ICA	invalid care allowance
IIDB	industrial injuries disablement benefit
IRS	Independent Review Service
IS	income support
JSA	jobseeker's allowance
MA	maternity allowance
MP	Member of Parliament
MS	Medical Service
NI	national insurance
NICO	National Insurance Contributions Office
PAYE	Pay As You Earn
PC	pension credit
PIP	personal independence payment
REA	reduced earnings allowance
SAAS	Student Awards Agency for Scotland
SAP	statutory adoption pay
SDA	severe disablement allowance
SF	social fund
SFI	social fund inspector
SFO	social fund officer
SLC	Student Loans Company
SMP	statutory maternity pay
SPP	statutory paternity pay
SSP	statutory sick pay
TCO	Tax Credit Office
UC	universal credit
WTC	working tax credit

Means-tested benefit rates

Income support/income-based jobseeker's allowance

Personal allowances		£pw
Single	Under 25	56.25
	25 or over	71.00
Lone parent	Under 18	56.25
	18 or over	71.00
Couple	Both under 18	56.25
	Both under 18, certain cases	84.95
	One under 18, one 18–24	56.25
	One under 18, one 25 or over	71.00
	One under 18, certain cases	111.45
	Both 18 or over	111.45
Premiums		
Carer		32.60
Disability	Single	30.35
	Couple	43.25
Enhanced disability	Single	14.80
	Couple	21.30
Severe disability	One qualifies	58.20
	Two qualify	116.40
Pensioner	Single (jobseeker's allowance only)	71.70
	Couple	106.45

Children (Pre-6 April 2004 claims with no child tax credit)

Child under 20 personal allowance	64.99
Family premium	17.40
Disabled child premium	56.63
Enhanced disability premium (child)	22.89

Capital limits	**Lower**	**Upper**
Standard	6,000	16,000
Care homes	10,000	16,000

Tariff income £1 per £250 between lower and upper limit

Pension credit

		£pw
Guarantee credit		
Standard minimum guarantee	Single	142.70
	Couple	217.90
Severe disability addition	One qualifies	58.20
	Two qualify	116.40
Carer addition		32.60
Savings credit		
Threshold	Single	111.80
	Couple	178.35
Maximum	Single	18.54
	Couple	23.73
Capital disregard		
Standard/care homes		10,000
No upper limit		
Deemed income £1 per £500 above disregard		

Income-related employment and support allowance

		Assessment phase	Main phase
Personal allowances			
Single	Under 25	56.25	71.00
	25 or over	71.00	71.00
Lone parent	Under 18	56.25	71.00
	18 or over	71.00	71.00
Couple	Both under 18 (max)	84.95	111.45
	Both 18 or over	111.45	111.45
Components			
Work-related activity		–	28.15
Support		–	34.05
Premiums			
Carer		32.60	32.60
Severe disability (one qualifies)		58.20	58.20
Severe disability premium (two qualify)		116.40	116.40
Enhanced disability	Single	14.80	14.80
	Couple	21.30	21.30
Pensioner	Single, no component	71.70	–
	Couple, no component	106.45	–
	Single, work-related activity component	–	43.55

		Assessment phase	£pw Main phase
	Couple, work-related activity component	–	78.30
	Single, support component	–	37.65
	Couple, support component	–	72.40

Capital limits

As for income support

Housing benefit and council tax benefit

Personal allowances

Single	Under 25	56.25
	Under 25 (on main phase ESA)	71.00
	25 or over	71.00
Lone parent	Under 18	56.25
	Under 18 (on main phase ESA)	71.00
	18 or over	71.00
Couple	Both under 18	84.95
	Both under 18 (claimant on main phase ESA)	111.45
	One or both 18 or over	111.45
Dependent children	Under 20	64.99
Over qualifying age for pension credit	Single under 65	142.70
	Single 65 or over	161.25
	Couple both under 65	217.90
	Couple one or both 65 or over	241.65

Components

Work-related activity		28.15
Support		34.05

Premiums

Carer		32.60
Disability	Single	30.35
	Couple	43.25
Disabled child		56.63
Enhanced disability	Single	14.80
	Couple	21.30
	Child	22.89
Severe disability	One qualifies	58.20
	Two qualify	116.40

		£pw
Family	Ordinary rate	17.40
	Some lone parents	22.20

Capital limits	Lower	Upper
Standard	6,000	16,000
Care home (housing benefit only)	10,000	16,000
Over qualifying age for pension credit	10,000	16,000

Tariff income £1 per £250 between lower and upper limit£1 per £500 for those over qualifying age for pension credit

No upper limit or tariff income for those on pension credit guarantee credit

Social fund payments

Maternity grant		500.00
Cold weather payment		25.00
Winter fuel payment (over qualifying age for pension credit)	Under 80	200.00
	80 or over	300.00
	Care home (under 80)	100.00
	Care home (80 or over)	150.00

Non-means-tested benefit rates

	£pw
Attendance allowance	
Higher rate	77.45
Lower rate	51.85
Bereavement benefits	
Bereavement payment (lump sum)	2,000
Bereavement allowance/widow's pension (55 or over)	105.95
Bereavement allowance/widow's pension (45–54)	31.79–98.53
Widowed parent's allowance/widowed mother's allowance	105.95
Carer's allowance	58.45
Adult dependant (some existing claimants only)	34.40
Child benefit	
Only/eldest child	20.30
Other child(ren)	13.40
Child dependant (some existing claimants only)	
Only/eldest child	8.10
Other child(ren)	11.35
Disability living allowance	
Care component	
Highest rate	77.45
Middle rate	51.85
Lowest rate	20.55
Mobility component	
Higher rate	54.05
Lower rate	20.55
Contributory employment and support allowance	
Assessment phase	
Under 25	56.25
25 or over	71.00

	£pw
Main phase	
16 or over	71.00
Work-related activity component	28.15
Support component	34.05
Guardian's allowance	15.55
Short-term incapacity benefit (under pension age)	
Lower rate	74.80
Higher rate	88.55
Adult dependant	44.85
Short-term incapacity benefit (over pension age)	
Lower rate	95.15
Higher rate	99.15
Adult dependant	55.45
Long-term incapacity benefit	99.15
Age addition (under 35)	11.70
Age addition (35–44)	5.90
Adult dependant	57.60
Industrial injuries disablement benefit	
Under 18 without dependants	20%: £19.38 to 100%: £96.90
Any other claimant	20%: £31.62 to 100%: £158.10
Contribution-based jobseeker's allowance	
Under 25	56.25
25 or over	71.00
Maternity allowance	
Standard rate	135.45
Retirement pension	
Category A	107.45
Adult dependant (some existing claimants only)	61.85
Category B (widow(er)/surviving civil partner)	107.45
Category B (spouse/civil partner)	64.40
Category D	64.40
Severe disablement allowance	69.00
Age addition (under 40)	11.70
Age addition (40–49)	5.90
Age addition (50–59)	5.90
Adult dependant	34.60

	£pw
Statutory maternity, paternity and adoption pay	
Standard rate	135.45
Statutory sick pay	85.85
National insurance contributions	
Lower earnings limit	107.00
Primary threshold	146.00
Employee's class 1 rate	12% of £146 to £817 2% above £817
Class 2 rate (self employed)	2.65

Tax credit rates

		£ per day	£ per year
Child tax credit			
Family element		1.50	545
Child element		7.37	2,690
Disabled child element		8.09	2,950
Severely disabled child element		3.26	1,190
Working tax credit			
Basic element		5.27	1,920
Couple element		5.35	1,950
Lone parent element		5.35	1,950
30-hour element		2.17	790
Disabled worker element		7.65	2,790
Severe disability element		3.27	1,190
Childcare element	70% of eligible weekly childcare costs :		
	One child		weekly maximum 175
	Two or more children		weekly maximum 300
Thresholds			
Income threshold	Working tax credit only or with child tax credit		6,420
	Child tax credit only		15,860
Taper			41%
Income decrease disregard			2,500
Income increase disregard			10,000

Part 1

Introduction

Chapter 1

Introduction

This chapter covers:

Key facts

- There are a large number of benefits. Some are means tested and some are non-means tested.
- There are two means-tested tax credits.
- It is worth getting help to ensure you are claiming all the benefits and tax credits to which you are entitled.
- Receipt of some means-tested benefits and tax credits acts as a 'passport' to other benefits, such as free school lunches, health benefits and social fund payments.

Future changes: April 2013 and after

Major changes are taking place that affect the benefits and tax credits system (see Chapter 2). Changes that will affect the information in this *Handbook* are shown at the start of each chapter. See CPAG's *Welfare Rights Bulletin* for updates.

1. The benefit and tax credit system

The government department responsible for the overall administration and policy work for most social security benefits, other than housing benefit (HB) and council tax benefit (CTB), is the **Department for Work and Pensions** (DWP). Tax credits, child benefit and guardian's allowance are dealt with by **HM Revenue and Customs** (HMRC). HB and CTB are administered by **local authorities**.

An executive agency of the DWP, called **Jobcentre Plus**, administers most benefit claims for people under state retirement age (referred to by the DWP as people of working age). The **Pension Service** deals with retirement pension and pension credit, and the **Disability and Carers Service** deals with disability benefits and carer's allowance. **Note:** these two agencies merged on 1 April 2008 to create the **Pension, Disability and Carers Service**. However, claimants still see the Pension Service and Disability and Carers Service as two distinct organisations and the contact details for each remain the same.

An executive agency of the Ministry of Justice, **HM Courts and Tribunals Service**, is responsible for administering benefit and tax credit appeals.

The main types of benefit and tax credit

Some benefits are paid only if you have limited income and capital. These benefits are known as **means-tested benefits** because there is an investigation into your means before you can be paid them (see ppxiii–xvi for a list). You do not have to satisfy any national insurance (NI) contribution conditions.

Child tax credit (CTC) and **working tax credit** are also means tested.

Some other benefits (known as 'passported' benefits) are payable if you qualify for particular means-tested benefits or tax credits (see p5). Some benefits are paid on a 'discretionary' basis even if you satisfy a means test – eg, social fund community care grants, budgeting loans and crisis loans.

Non-means-tested benefits do not involve a detailed investigation of your means (see ppxvii–xix for a list). You qualify if you satisfy certain basic conditions such as being available for work, disabled or bereaved. It may still be relevant to ask whether you have any earnings or an occupational pension because many of the benefits are designed to compensate for your loss of earnings, but normally your income or capital does not affect your entitlement. You have to satisfy the NI contribution conditions for some non-means-tested benefits (see Chapter 35).

Jobseeker's allowance (JSA) and employment and support allowance (ESA) are benefits that are both means tested and non-means tested.

- *Income-based* JSA and *income-related* ESA are means tested. A third type of JSA, *joint-claim* JSA, is a kind of income-based JSA, but has some special rules about claiming for certain couples.
- *Contribution-based* JSA and *contributory* ESA are non-means tested (although some pension and earnings-related income can reduce the amount you are paid). A third type of ESA, ESA in *youth* is similar to contributory ESA, but does not have NI contribution conditions.

If you qualify for the non-means-tested element of either JSA or ESA, you may also qualify for the means-tested elements if:

- you qualify for any of the premiums that can be added to your basic personal allowance (see Chapter 37); *or*
- you need help with your mortgage interest or other types of housing costs (see Chapter 38).

This *Handbook* also covers the rules for **statutory sick pay**, **statutory maternity pay**, **statutory paternity pay** and **statutory adoption pay**, which are not means tested and are paid by your employer rather than by the DWP or HMRC.

Passported benefits

Some benefits and tax credits act as a 'passport' to other benefits.

Passported benefit	*Passports*
Free school lunches	Income support Income-based jobseeker's allowance Income-related employment and support allowance Some recipients of child tax credit Guarantee credit of pension credit (England and Wales only)
Health benefits	Income support Income-based jobseeker's allowance Income-related employment and support allowance Some recipients of child tax credit Some recipients of working tax credit Guarantee credit of pension credit
Sure Start maternity grant	Income support Income-based jobseeker's allowance Income-related employment and support allowance Pension credit (either or both credits) Some recipients of child tax credit Some recipients of working tax credit
Social fund funeral expenses payment	Income support Income-based jobseeker's allowance Income-related employment and support allowance Pension credit (either or both credits) Some recipients of child tax credit Some recipients of working tax credit Housing benefit Council tax benefit
Social fund cold weather payment, community care grant and budgeting loan	Income support Income-based jobseeker's allowance Income-related employment and support allowance Pension credit (either or both credits)

2. Which benefits and tax credits should you claim

You may be entitled to a combination of non-means-tested benefits, means-tested benefits and tax credits. For example, you might receive retirement pension topped up by pension credit (PC). In addition, you might also qualify for child benefit and child tax credit (CTC) if you have children and for help with your rent (housing benefit – HB) and your council tax (council tax benefit – CTB). You should check to see:

- if you are entitled to any 'earnings replacement' benefits – these are non-means-tested benefits to compensate you for your inability to work, such as carer's allowance and retirement pension; *then*
- if you can get any non-means-tested benefits because of your circumstances – eg, because you are disabled or are looking after children; *and finally*
- whether you qualify for any means-tested benefits or tax credits to top up your benefit and other income. **Remember:**
  - Qualifying for some of the non-means-tested benefits means you qualify for some of the means-tested benefits at a higher rate. It is worth getting help to ensure you are claiming all the benefits to which you are entitled.
  - There is a limit on the length of time you can qualify for bereavement allowance and contribution-based jobseeker's allowance (JSA). From some time in 2012, the government says that unless you get the support component, there will also be a limit on the length of time you can qualify for contributory employment and support allowance (ESA). In all cases, if your entitlement to a non-means-tested benefit ends, you should claim means-tested benefits and tax credits if you are not already getting these.

See Appendix 2 for information about where you can go for advice and assistance. See the table on p7 for ideas of benefits you might claim, depending on your circumstances. You may find that more than one of the circumstances applies to you. Refer to each separate circumstance that applies.

Whatever your circumstances, you might get the following benefits/tax credits if you do not have enough money to live on. These can be paid on their own, or in addition to other benefits:

- income support (IS) or JSA if not in full-time paid work;
- income-related ESA if you have limited capability for work;
- working tax credit (WTC) if in full-time paid work;
- PC if in or out of full-time paid work.

Remember:

- When you claim, ask for your claim to be backdated if relevant.

- If getting one of the non-means-tested benefits you are claiming qualifies you for another benefit, claim the other benefit at the same time (see p1029).

Summaries of the rules for each benefit and tax credit are provided in the text following the table. Refer to the relevant chapters for full details.

Your circumstances	*Benefits/tax credits to which you may be entitled*
Bereaved	Bereavement payment
	Widowed parent's allowance
	Bereavement allowance
	Funeral expenses payment
Carer	Carer's allowance
Responsible for a child	Child tax credit
	Child benefit
	Guardian's allowance
	Statutory maternity pay
	Statutory paternity pay
	Statutory adoption pay
	Maternity allowance
	Health benefits
	Cold weather payment
Disabled	Disability living allowance
	Attendance allowance
	Industrial injuries benefits
	Cold weather payment
Incapable of work	Employment and support allowance
	Incapacity benefit (in limited circumstances)
	Statutory sick pay
	Severe disablement allowance (not for new claims)
	Cold weather payment
Have a mortgage	Income support
	Income-based jobseeker's allowance
	Income-related employment and support allowance
	Pension credit
	Council tax benefit
Not enough money to meet certain needs	Community care grant
	Budgeting loan
	Crisis loan
Pensioner	State retirement pension
	Pension credit
	Winter fuel payment
	Cold weather payment

Pregnant	Statutory maternity pay Maternity allowance Sure Start maternity grant Health benefits
Tenant	Housing benefit Council tax benefit
Unemployed or working part time and seeking work or more work	Jobseeker's allowance

Attendance allowance

Attendance allowance (AA) is not means tested and is for those aged 65 or over when they claim who need help with personal care (see Chapter 9).

If you get AA, your carer may qualify for carer's allowance (CA) (but before claiming, your carer should check whether this will affect any IS/income-based JSA/income-related ESA/HB/CTB or PC you or your partner may be getting).

Bereavement allowance

Bereavement allowance is paid for up to 52 weeks for people who were 45 or over but under pension age when their spouse or civil partner died.

Bereavement payment

Bereavement payment is a one-off lump-sum payment for people who were under pension age when their spouse or civil partner died or whose late spouse or civil partner was not entitled to state retirement pension (see Chapter 5).

Budgeting loan

You may get an interest-free loan to help you with specific categories of expenses. You must be in receipt of a qualifying benefit when you claim and throughout the previous 26 weeks (see Chapter 25).

Carer's allowance

CA is paid if you are providing care for 35 hours or more a week for a person to whom disability living allowance (DLA) care component at the middle or highest rate, or AA is payable (see Chapter 6).

Before you claim CA check whether this will affect the person for whom you are caring – if s/he gets a benefit that includes a severe disability premium or additional amount, this could be stopped if you claim CA (see Chapter 37).

Child benefit

Child benefit is paid to people who are responsible for a child or qualifying young person. It is not means tested and is paid whether you are in or out of work (see Chapter 7).

Child tax credit

CTC is paid to people who are responsible for a child or qualifying young person. It is means tested but is paid whether you are in or out of work (see Chapter 51).

Christmas bonus

You qualify for a Christmas bonus of £10 if you are entitled (or treated as entitled) to any of the qualifying benefits for at least part of the 'relevant week' (even if the benefit is paid later). The relevant week is usually the week beginning with the first Monday in December.

Qualifying benefits

AA, DLA, CA, disablement benefit (if it includes unemployability supplement or constant attendance allowance), contributory ESA which includes either the support or the work-related activity component, long-term incapacity benefit (IB), industrial death benefit for widows or widowers, mobility supplement, retirement pension, PC, severe disablement allowance (SDA), war disablement pension (if you are at least pension age – see p531), war widow's or surviving civil partner's pension, widowed mother's allowance, widowed parent's allowance or widow's pension.

You may also claim an extra bonus for your partner (a further £10) if s/he has not received a bonus in her/his own right, and:

- you are both at least pension age (see p531) and you are entitled, or may be treated as entitled, to an increase of one of the qualifying benefits in respect of her/him; *or*
- you are both at least the qualifying age for PC (see p509) and the only qualifying benefit you get is PC.

The bonus is not taxable and has no effect on other benefits or tax credits.

It is paid automatically. However, you should contact the DWP if you have not obtained your bonus within a year. Otherwise, your right is lost.

Cold weather payment

Social fund cold weather payments are paid during periods of very cold weather. They are paid automatically if you have been awarded IS, income-based JSA or income-related ESA that includes a qualifying premium/component or you have a child under five, or you have been awarded PC (see Chapter 26).

Community care grant

You may get a grant to help you live independently in the community, if there is exceptional pressure on you and your family and in some other situations. You have to be in receipt of a qualifying benefit when you claim (see Chapter 25).

Council tax benefit

If you are liable for council tax and are on a low income, you may get CTB. It is paid whether you are in or out of work (see Chapter 8).

If you are the only person liable for council tax on your home and you have an adult on a low income living with you, you might be able to get a type of CTB known as 'second adult rebate', no matter how much income or capital you have.

Crisis loan

A crisis loan may be payable if you have had an emergency or disaster and you do not have enough money to meet immediate short-term needs. A crisis loan may also be payable for rent in advance. You do not have to be in receipt of a benefit to get this loan but have to be likely to be able to repay it (see Chapter 25).

Disability living allowance

DLA is paid if you need help with your mobility, your personal care or both. You must be under 65 when you first claim (see Chapter 9). Both adults and children can qualify for DLA.

If you get DLA care component at the middle or highest rate, your carer may qualify for CA, but before claiming, your carer should check whether this will affect any IS/income-based JSA/income-related ESA/HB/CTB or PC you or your partner are getting.

Employment and support allowance

ESA is a benefit for people who have 'limited capability for work' because of ill health or a disability.

Contributory ESA is paid if you satisfy the national insurance (NI) contribution conditions, but you do not have to pass a means test. However, some earnings-related income can reduce the amount you are paid (see Chapter 10 and p898).

Income-related ESA is paid if you pass the means test, but you do not have to satisfy NI contribution conditions.

ESA in youth is neither contributory nor means tested but you must be aged under 20 (or in some circumstances aged under 25) when the period of limited capability for work began. **Note:** ESA in youth will be abolished for all new claims from 1 May 2012. See CPAG's *Welfare Rights Bulletin* for updates.

Some mortgage payments and other housing costs can be met by income-related ESA (see Chapter 38).

It is possible to receive contributory ESA (or ESA in youth) topped up with income-related ESA .

Funeral expenses payment

A social fund funeral expenses payment is paid to provide help with the cost of a funeral. To get one you must have been awarded a qualifying benefit (see Chapter 26).

Guardian's allowance

Guardian's allowance is paid to you if you are looking after a child who is effectively an orphan (see Chapter 12).

Health benefits

Health benefits include free prescriptions, sight tests and dental treatment. If you get a qualifying benefit, you have a 'passported' entitlement to health benefits. Alternatively, you may qualify on low-income grounds (see Chapter 13).

Healthy Start food vouchers and vitamins

If you are entitled to a qualifying benefit (or you are pregnant and under the age of 18), you are 'passported' to help under the Healthy Start scheme. Help includes food vouchers for milk, fresh and frozen fruit and vegetables as well as vitamins (see Chapter 13).

Housing benefit

If you have rent to pay and are on a low income, you may get HB. It is paid whether you are in or out of work (see Chapter 14).

Incapacity benefit

IB is a benefit for people who are incapable of work. You have to satisfy the NI contribution conditions to be paid IB unless you became incapable of work in youth (see Chapter 16). IB is not means tested (although some earnings-related income can reduce the amount you are paid – see p887).

In most cases, you cannot make a new claim for IB (see p337).

Income support

You have to fit into one of the groups of people who can claim IS (see Chapter 17). IS can be paid in addition to other benefits to top up your income to a certain level. Some mortgage payments and other housing costs can be met by IS (see Chapter 38).

Industrial injuries benefits

Industrial injuries benefits are paid if you are disabled as a result of being injured or contracting a disease at work (see Chapter 18).

Jobseeker's allowance

To qualify for JSA, you must show that you are available for and actively seeking work, and you must have a current jobseeker's agreement with Jobcentre Plus.

Contribution-based JSA is paid for 26 weeks if you satisfy the NI contribution conditions. It is not means tested but some earnings-related income can reduce the amount you are paid (see Chapter 19 and p896).

Income-based JSA is means tested and non-contributory. It is paid for as long as you satisfy the conditions of entitlement. It can be paid in addition to contribution-based JSA. Some mortgage payments and other housing costs can be met by income-based JSA (see Chapter 38).

Maternity allowance

If you are pregnant or have recently had a baby and you are not entitled to statutory maternity pay (SMP), you may qualify for maternity allowance (MA) – eg, if you are self-employed (see Chapter 21).

Pension credit

If you are at least the qualifying age for PC (see p509), you may qualify for the guarantee credit of PC to top up a low income. It is means tested. The savings credit of PC is paid to those aged 65 or over (or whose partner is 65 or over) and acts as a reward for making provisions for retirement, such as savings, above the basic state pension (see Chapter 22).

Some mortgage payments and other housing costs can be met by PC (see Chapter 38).

Severe disablement allowance

SDA is a benefit for people who are incapable of work. It was abolished for new claimants on 6 April 2001 but some claimants entitled before that date can continue to receive it (see Chapter 24).

State retirement pension

When you reach pension age (see p531) you may qualify for state retirement pension. It is based on the amount of your NI contributions (or your partner's in the case of a Category B pension) (see Chapter 23).

Statutory adoption pay

Statutory adoption pay is paid when a child is placed, or is expected to be placed, with you for adoption (see Chapter 27). You must be, or have been, an employee who satisfies the continuous employment and earnings conditions.

Statutory maternity pay

Statutory maternity pay (SMP) is paid if you are pregnant or have recently given birth (see Chapter 27). You must be, or have been, an employee who satisfies the continuous employment and earnings conditions.

If you are not entitled to SMP you may be eligible for MA – eg, if you are self-employed.

Statutory paternity pay

Statutory paternity pay (SPP) is paid if your partner has just given birth or you have adopted a child (see Chapter 27). There are two types of SPP – ordinary SPP and additional SPP. You must be, or have been, an employee who satisfies the continuous employment and earnings conditions.

Statutory sick pay

Statutory sick pay (SSP) is paid if you are incapable of work. It is paid to employees for the first 28 weeks of incapacity (see Chapter 28).

Sure Start maternity grant

Sure Start maternity grants are paid if you or a member of your family are pregnant or have recently given birth. In most cases, you cannot have any other children aged under 16. To get a grant, you or your partner must have been awarded a qualifying benefit (see Chapter 26).

Widowed parent's allowance

Widowed parent's allowance is paid to widows, widowers and surviving civil partners with children, and for widows or surviving civil partners who are pregnant (see Chapter 5).

Winter fuel payment

Social fund winter fuel payments are annual payments to provide help with fuel. They are paid to people who are at least the qualifying age for PC (see p509), regardless of their means (see Chapter 26).

Working tax credit

WTC is paid if you or your partner work sufficient hours a week and have a low income (see Chapter 52). It is means tested.

3. Financial help when starting work

If you or your partner start working full time, you might be entitled to some financial support to help your transition into work after a period of time on benefit.

If you or your partner start to work full time (16 hours or more a week) or increase your earnings and, as a result, stop claiming certain benefits, you might qualify for:

- **mortgage interest run-on** if you have a home loan or other housing costs (see p879);
- **extended payments of housing benefit and council tax benefit** if you pay rent or council tax (see pp286 and 130).

Jobcentre Plus administers a number of other types of financial support for those starting full-time work. In most cases, you must start to work at least 16 hours a week, having been receiving specified benefits or payments, or a combination of these (or, in some cases, having been on an employment scheme or programme), for a set period of time. The types of support are added to and changed from time to time, as are the qualifying rules. Check with your Jobcentre Plus office or employment scheme or programme provider to see what is available. Do this *before* you start work because you may have to apply for the financial support before your job starts. Some information is available at www.direct.gov.uk.

Employment schemes and programmes also provide help with costs such as childcare and training. For further details of the various financial incentives to move into full-time work, contact your local Jobcentre Plus office.

4. Other financial help

This *Handbook* is mainly concerned with information about social security benefits and tax credits. However, there is other financial help to which you may be entitled, especially if you are on a low income, have children, have an illness, disability or other special needs, or are an older person.

See the *Disability Rights Handbook*, published by Disability Alliance, for help for those with care needs.

Education benefits

Free school lunches

Children are entitled to free school lunches if their families receive:

- income support (IS), income-based jobseeker's allowance or income-related employment and support allowance (ESA);
- child tax credit (CTC), and have annual taxable income of £16,190 (in Scotland, £15,860) or less. However, this does not apply if the family is entitled to working tax credit (WTC) unless:
  - this is during the four-week 'WTC run-on' period (see p1304); *or*
  - in Scotland only, the WTC award is based on annual taxable income of £6,420 or less – ie, the family gets maximum WTC;
- in England and Wales only, guarantee credit of pension credit (PC). PC claimants in Scotland may qualify if they receive CTC, as above.

Also entitled are:

- 16–18-year-olds receiving the above benefits or tax credits in their own right;
- asylum seekers in receipt of support provided under Part VI of the Immigration and Asylum Act 1999.

In Scotland, free school lunches may be more widely available to Primary 1 to Primary 3 pupils – ie, for the first three years of primary school. It is worthwhile checking with your local authority.

Education maintenance allowance and 16 to 19 bursaries

Education maintenance allowances are means-tested payments for young people aged 16 to 19 from Wales and Scotland who stay on in further education. The payments are made direct to the young person and are conditional upon regular course attendance. The young person may receive a weekly allowance of up to £30 during term time depending on the household income. For further details, see www.emascotland.com or www.studentfinancewales.co.uk.

In England, you cannot apply for an education maintenance allowance after January 2011. Those already getting education maintenance allowances will continue to get them, but only until the end of the 2012/13 academic year.

16 to 19 bursaries are available for young people aged 16 to 19 who stay on in further education or training in England. These are available through your school, college or training provider. Certain young people in need (eg, care leavers, young people who get IS or who get both ESA and disability living allowance) can get the maximum bursary of £1,200 a year if their course is 30 hours a week or more. Discretionary bursaries are available to those in financial difficulty. See www.direct.gov.uk/en/educationandlearning/14to19/moneytolearn for further information.

Education maintenance allowances and 16 to 19 bursaries do not count as income for any benefits or tax credits the parent may be getting, so the young person can get these and the parent's child benefit and CTC are unaffected. They are also not affected by any income the young person has from part-time work.

Clothing grants

Local authorities can give grants for school uniforms and other school clothes. Each authority determines its own eligibility rules. Some school governing bodies or parents' associations also provide help with school clothing.

School transport

Local authorities must provide free transport to school for pupils under 16 where it is considered necessary to enable that pupil to get to the 'nearest suitable school'.

Other support for students

To find out what help is available to finance your studies, contact your local authority or college. Also see Chapter 29 and CPAG's *Student Support and Benefits Handbook* for England and Wales and *Benefits for Students in Scotland Handbook*.

Housing grants

Your local authority may be able to provide you with a grant to help with the cost of improving your home. The main types of grant available are:

- home improvement grants;
- disabled facilities grants.

You may be able to get assistance to repair, improve, maintain or adapt your home from a home improvement agency (a local not-for-profit organisation), sometimes called 'care and repair' or 'staying put' schemes. For information see www.foundations.uk.com/about_home_improvement_agencies, www.careandrepair.org.uk and www.careandrepairscotland.co.uk.

Home energy efficiency schemes

There are grants available for help with insulation and other energy efficiency measures in your home. Different schemes operate in England, Wales and Scotland. For further information, contact the Energy Savings Trust on freephone 0800 512 012 (for textphone users add 18001 as a prefix).

For more details, see CPAG's *Fuel Rights Handbook*.

Help from social services

Local authority social services departments have statutory duties to provide a range of practical and financial help to families, children, young people, older people, people with disabilities and asylum seekers.

If you are an asylum seeker, see Chapter 61.

Special funds for sick or disabled people

A range of help is available for people with an illness or disability to assist with things like paying for care services in their own home, equipment, holidays, furniture and transport needs, and for people with haemophilia or HIV contracted via haemophilia treatment.

For more information, see the *Disability Rights Handbook*, published by Disability Alliance.

Charities

There are many charities that provide various types of help to people in need. Your local authority social services department or local advice centre may know of appropriate charities that could assist you, or you can consult publications, such as *A Guide to Grants for Individuals in Need* and the *Charities Digest*, in your local library. The organisation turn2us has a website (www.turn2us.org.uk) with an A-Z of all the charities that can provide financial help. In many cases, applications for support can be made directly from the website.

Food banks

If you are experiencing severe financial hardship (eg, caused by debt, benefit delays or being ineligible for a crisis loan), you may be able to get vouchers for food which can be redeemed at a 'food bank' run by the Trussell Trust. One voucher can be exchanged for three days' food. Jobcentre Plus staff may be able to give out vouchers. Further information and details of where there are food banks is available at www.trusselltrust.org.

Part 2

Future changes: Welfare Reform Act 2012

Chapter 2

Welfare reform: overview

This chapter covers:

Note: at the time of writing, it is not known when all the changes outlined in this chapter will be implemented. If there is a provisional date set, this is indicated, but all these dates are subject to change. See CPAG's *Welfare Rights Bulletin* for updates.

Key facts

- The Welfare Reform Act 2012 will introduce radical changes to the benefits and tax credits system.
- A universal credit will replace most means-tested benefits.
- There will be increased conditionality and sanctions for not complying.
- Rules on the recovery of overpayments will be stricter and have more severe penalties.
- Disability living allowance for adults will be replaced by a new personal independence payment.

1. Universal credit and the abolition of current benefits

From October 2013, a new benefit for working-age claimants – universal credit (UC) – will replace all the following benefits:

- income support (IS);
- income-based jobseeker's allowance (JSA);
- income-related employment and support allowance (ESA);

- housing benefit (HB);
- child tax credit (CTC);
- working tax credit (WTC).

There will be no new claims for IS, income-based JSA or income-related ESA after October 2013, and no new claims for HB, CTC and WTC after April 2014. If you are already on one of these benefits, your claim will be transferred to UC by 2017. Once UC is fully established, all the above benefits will be abolished.[1] For more information on UC, see Chapter 4.

2. **Means-tested benefits**

Income support, jobseeker's allowance and employment and support allowance

Claimant commitment and sanctions

While they continue to exist, a 'claimant commitment' will be introduced as a condition of entitlement for income support (IS), jobseeker's allowance (JSA) and employment and support allowance (ESA). This is expected to be similar to that introduced for universal credit (UC) (see p50).[2] The claimant commitment will replace the current jobseeker's agreement for JSA and the work-related activity and support groups in ESA.

The level of sanctions for not complying with the claimant commitment will be brought in line with those for UC once this is introduced (see p50).[3] This is so that there will be equal treatment between claimants on UC and those who remain on IS, JSA or ESA pending transfer to UC.

These changes are likely to be introduced before UC is introduced, but it is not yet known when this will be.

Contributory employment and support allowance and employment and support allowance in youth

From 1 May 2012, contributory ESA will be limited to a maximum of 365 days' entitlement unless you are in the support group.[4] If, on 30 April 2012, you have already received at least 365 days of contributory ESA, including payments during the assessment phase, you will cease to do so. Any time spent in the support group will not count towards the 365 days; you will continue to receive ESA while you remain in the support group. See Chapter 10 for more details.

From 1 May 2012, ESA in youth will be abolished for new claimants.[5] Whatever your age, you will be required to meet either the contribution conditions for contributory ESA or the means test for income-related ESA. If you are in receipt of ESA in youth when the change is introduced, it will be limited to a total of 365 days if you are in the work-related activity group (including time already spent, both in the assessment phase and the main phase). Time spent in the support group will not count towards the 365 days.

Lone parents

To qualify for IS as a lone parent, your youngest child must be under five years old.[6] See Chapter 17 for more details. No date has been set for when this change will come into force.

Entitlement to work

In order to claim JSA or ESA you must be entitled to work in the UK.[7] This requirement is being introduced to prevent people who are not entitled to work in the UK from claiming contributory benefits. Similar provisions will apply to maternity allowance, statutory maternity pay, statutory paternity pay and statutory adoption pay.[8] This change will be implemented after UC has been introduced in October 2013, when JSA and ESA will only be contributory benefits for new claimants.

Pension credit

Entitlement to the carer addition in pension credit (PC) will no longer be linked to entitlement to carer's allowance (CA). It will be included in your applicable amount if you or your partner have 'substantial caring responsibilities'. What this means will be specified in regulations.[9] It is not yet known when this change will be brought into force.

Currently there is no capital limit for PC. The Welfare Reform Act 2012 will introduce a new capital limit.[10] As UC is introduced, housing benefit (HB) will be abolished and replaced by a housing credit in PC.[11] As HB has a capital limit for pensioners, this change allows the capital limit to continue to apply to the housing credit. This is likely to happen between October 2013 and 2017 as UC is introduced and HB is gradually abolished.

Housing benefit

From April 2013, changes will be made so that your liability to pay rent can be treated as less than it actually is, so you will not be able to claim HB to cover your full rental liability.[12]

If you are of working age and renting your home in the social rented sector, your HB may be restricted if you are considered to have more bedrooms than you need for the size of your household. Your rent liability will be reduced by 14 per cent for one spare bedroom and by 25 per cent for two or more spare bedrooms to create an 'appropriate maximum housing benefit'.[13] See Chapter 15 for more details on this.

From April 2013, local housing allowances (LHAs) will be fixed, either by adjusting them to rise in line with the Consumer Prices Index or by aligning them with the bottom 30 per cent of private sector rents, whichever is the lowest.[14] LHA rates will be frozen from April 2012 to prepare for this. See Chapter 15 for more details.

Council tax benefit

From April 2013, council tax benefit in its current form will be abolished. It will be replaced by 'localised support', administered by local authorities in England. The Scottish and Welsh governments are expected to put forward their own proposals. Individual authorities will decide how to manage the scheme, but the budget will be cut by 10 per cent and they are required to maintain the current level of support for pensioners. Support must also be provided for other vulnerable groups and the schemes must promote incentives to work.[15]

The social fund

From April 2013, community care grants and crisis loans, together with the Independent Review Service, will be abolished.[16] Community care grants and crisis loans (other than those paid pending a benefit claim being processed) will be replaced by 'locally administered assistance'. In England, individual local authorities will decide the best way of providing this, including the use of furniture reuse projects and foodbanks.[17] The Scottish and Welsh governments will decide the most appropriate arrangements for assistance.

Crisis loans made pending payment of a benefit or tax credit (known as 'alignment payments') will be replaced by 'short-term advances' administered by the DWP.[18]

Maternity and funeral payments will be added to the list of items for which you can claim a budgeting loan, although maternity grants and funeral payments will still be available from the regulated social fund (see Chapter 26).[19] This will come into force two months after the Welfare Reform Act has received Royal Assent – ie, from 8 May 2012. Budgeting loans will remain in place until UC is fully rolled out. UC claimants will have access to a system of 'budgeting advances' instead of budgeting loans.

3. Other benefits

Disability living allowance

From April 2013, disability living allowance (DLA) will be replaced by a new benefit called personal independence payment (PIP) for adults aged 16 to 65. A few claims for PIP will be started from this date to trial the scheme and then all new claims from June 2013 will be for PIP. If you are already receiving DLA on this date, you will be reassessed for PIP between autumn 2013 and 2016 either when your claim is due for renewal, when there is a change of circumstances or, if there is no renewal date, on a date initiated by the DWP.[20] For more information on PIP, see Chapter 3.

Industrial injuries benefits

Changes will be made to the Industrial Injuries Disablement Benefits Scheme, so that it also deals with injuries and accidents which were previously covered by the pre-1948 schemes.[21] Trainees and people under 18 will also be covered by this.[22] It is not yet known when this will be introduced.

Bereavement benefits

The government is proposing to reform bereavement benefits. This is currently under consultation and will not happen before 2014. If you are already in receipt of bereavement benefits, these will not be affected.

4. The benefit cap

From April 2013, if you or your partner are of working age, the total amount of benefits and tax credits you will be able to receive will be 'capped' at the level of the average earnings of working households in Great Britain.[23]

The cap will apply to the combined income you and your partner receive from universal credit, income support, jobseeker's allowance, employment and support allowance (ESA), housing benefit, child benefit, child tax credit, carer's allowance and industrial injuries benefits. It will not apply if you, or anyone in your household, receives working tax credit, disability living allowance, constant attendance allowance, or if you are a war widow.[24]

It is envisaged that the cap will be set at around £500 a week for couples and lone parents, and around £350 a week for a single person. Support for childcare and discretionary housing payments will not be affected by the cap, but it is not yet clear how localised support for council tax (see p24) will be treated.[25] Certain exemptions to the cap have been announced, including the following.[26]

- If you are in the support group for ESA, you will be exempt from the cap.
- If you have been in work for at least 12 months and you lose your job through no fault of your own, the cap will not apply for nine months.
- Transitional support will be available in the form of discretionary housing payments (see p294).

5. Overpayments, fraud and civil penalties

Recovery of overpayments

The Welfare Reform Act 2012 gives the DWP the power to recover any overpayments of universal credit, jobseeker's allowance and employment and support allowance, whatever the cause of the overpayment. The usual rules on recovery of social security benefits (see Chapter 43) will not apply from the point this rule is brought into force. It is not yet known when this will be. This will also be the case for overpayments of the housing credit in pension credit in prescribed circumstances.[27]

The Act also removes the six-year statute of limitations from the recovery of all social security overpayments (which restricts recovery to overpayments that were made within the previous six years) unless it is through proceedings in a court of law. Time limits will therefore not apply if, for example, recovery is carried out by deductions from current benefit. This applies to any proceedings started after the Welfare Reform Act received Royal Assent on 8 March 2012, regardless of when the overpayment arose.

Fraud

A new single Fraud Investigation Service will be introduced to take responsibility for investigating all suspected benefit fraud.[28] In addition, there will be a minimum penalty for any case of fraud, whether or not benefit has been overpaid. This will be £350 or 50 per cent of the amount overpaid, whichever is greater, up to a maximum of £2,000.[29]

If you are convicted of a first benefit offence, you can be sanctioned for 13 weeks (four weeks if you are merely cautioned or accept a penalty).[30] A second offence within five years will incur a 26-week sanction and a third offence (within five years of the second offence) will incur a three-year sanction.[31] See Chapter 44 for details. It is not yet known when these fraud measures will come into force.

Civil penalties

If there is no suggestion of fraud, but you fail to provide information without reasonable excuse or you negligently give incorrect information, you may be liable for a civil penalty of £50. See Chapter 44 for details. No date is set for this yet.

6. Appeals

Currently, if you disagree with a benefits or tax credits decision, you can choose to ask for a revision or go straight to an appeal. It is intended that, in future, you will only be allowed to appeal once a decision maker has considered whether to revise the decision. The date for this is not yet known.[32] See Chapter 46 for details.

7. Timetable for change

The following table shows the likely timetable for when the changes will come into force. All dates are subject to change.

Date	*Change*
At point of Royal Assent (8 March 2012)	The six-year statute of limitations on the recovery of overpayments other than through the courts is removed.
1 April 2012	Local housing allowance rates are frozen.
1 May 2012	Contributory employment and support allowance is limited to one year. Employment and support allowance in youth is abolished.
Two months after Royal Assent	Maternity and funeral expenses are included in the list of items for which you can get a budgeting loan.
April 2013	Local housing allowance rates are increased with the lower of the Consumer Prices Index or the increase in the lowest 30 per cent of market rents. The 'appropriate maximum housing benefit' for social sector rents is introduced. Council tax benefit is replaced by 'localised support'. Personal independence payment is introduced as a replacement for disability living allowance. Claims will be transferred between 2013 and 2016. Crisis loans and community care grants are abolished and replaced by 'localised support'. The 'benefit cap' is introduced.
October 2013	Universal credit is introduced. No new claims for income support, income-based jobseeker's allowance or income-related employment and support allowance.
April 2014	No new claims for housing benefit or tax credits. Claims will be transferred to universal credit between April 2014 and 2017. During this period, housing benefit is abolished and a housing credit is introduced in pension credit with a capital limit.
2014	Bereavement benefit reform.

Notes

1. **Universal credit and the abolition of current benefits**
   1 s33 WRA 2012

2. **Means-tested benefits**
   2 ss44, 49, 54, 57 and 59 WRA 2012
   3 s46 WRA 2012
   4 s51 WRA 2012
   5 s53 WRA 2012
   6 s58 WRA 2012
   7 ss61 and 62 WRA 2012
   8 s63 WRA 2012
   9 s74 WRA 2012
   10 s75 WRA 2012
   11 s34 WRA 2012
   12 s69(3) WRA 2012
   13 Welfare Reform Bill 2011, Explanatory Notes, para 325
   14 Welfare Reform Bill 2011, Explanatory Notes, para 325
   15 *Localising Support for Council Tax in England Consultation,* August 2011
   16 s70 WRA 2012
   17 *Local Support to Replace Community Care Grants and Crisis Loans for Living Expenses: a call for evidence,* DWP, February 2011
   18 s101 WRA 2012
   19 s71 WRA 2012

3. **Other benefits**
   20 *Managing Claims to Personal Independence Payment Policy Briefing Note,* DWP, 14 November 2011
   21 s64 WRA 2012
   22 ss65 and 66 WRA 2012

4. **The benefit cap**
   23 s96 WRA 2012
   24 *Impact Assessment for Household Benefit Cap,* DWP, 16 February 2011
   25 Welfare Reform Bill, House of Lords Grand Committee, Lords Hansard, 21 November 2011, col GC345
   26 House of Commons, *Hansard,* 1 February 2012, cols 875 and 876

5. **Overpayments, fraud and civil penalties**
   27 s102 WRA 2012
   28 s109 WRA 2012; Welfare Reform Bill 2011, Explanatory Notes, para 561
   29 ss110-11 WRA 2012
   30 s115 WRA 2012
   31 s116 WRA 2012

6. **Appeals**
   32 s99 WRA 2012

Chapter 3

Personal independence payment

This chapter covers:

Key facts

- Personal independence payment (PIP) is a new benefit for adults with disabilities who need help getting around and/or help with daily living activities. It is due to be introduced for new claims in some areas from April 2013, and across the country from summer 2013. Between autumn 2013 and the end of 2016, PIP will replace disability living allowance (DLA) for existing claimants aged at least 16 but under 65.
- PIP is a non-means-tested benefit.
- You do not have to have paid national insurance contributions to qualify.
- It is intended that existing DLA claimants between the ages of 16 and 64 will be transferred to PIP by the end of 2016.
- Children under 16 will still be able to claim DLA. Adults aged 65 or over will still be able to claim attendance allowance.
- You can qualify for PIP whether you are in or out of work.
- PIP will be administered and paid by the DWP.
- If you disagree with a PIP decision, you will be able to apply for a revision or supersession, or appeal against it. Rules on decisions, revisions and supersessions, and appeals are expected to be similar to those that currently apply to benefits.[1]

1. Who can claim personal independence payment

At the time of writing, it was expected that you will not be able to claim personal independence payment (PIP) if you are in receipt of disability living allowance (DLA – see p136).

PIP will be a single benefit with two separate components, a daily living component and a mobility component. Each component will be paid at two different rates, depending on the severity of your disability or health problem.

Provided you are not in receipt of DLA, you will qualify for PIP if you satisfy the 'basic conditions', and the 'disability conditions' for one or both of the two components.

The **'basic conditions'** are:

- you are aged 16 or over and under 65 (see p33);[2]
- you are not a 'person subject to immigration control' (see p1410 for how this currently applies to benefits);[3]
- you satisfy certain conditions relating to residence and presence in Great Britain.[4] At the time of writing, the details of these rules had not been published, but the government has suggested that they may *not* be the same as the current residence and presence tests for DLA.[5]

The **'disability conditions' for the daily living component** are:[6]

- for the standard rate, your ability to undertake 'daily living activities' (see below) is limited by your physical or mental condition; *or*
- for the enhanced rate, your ability to undertake 'daily living activities' (see below) is severely limited by your physical or mental condition, or you are terminally ill (see p33); *and*
- for either rate, you meet the 'required period condition' (see p32), unless you are terminally ill (see p33).

The meaning of **'daily living activities'** will be set out in regulations. At the time of writing, the draft regulations listed nine activities, including preparing food and drink, bathing and grooming, communicating and making financial decisions.

The **'disability conditions' for the mobility component** are:[7]

- for the standard rate, your ability to undertake 'mobility activities' (see p31) is limited by your physical or mental condition; *or*
- for the enhanced rate, your ability to undertake 'mobility activities' (see p31) is severely limited by your physical or mental condition; *and*
- for either rate, you meet the 'required period condition' (see p32), unless you are terminally ill (see p33).

At the time of writing, the two '**mobility activities**' were intended to be planning and following a journey, and moving around.

Even if you satisfy the disability conditions above, regulations may say that you are not entitled to the mobility component if, for most of the time, you are 'unable to benefit from enhanced mobility'.[8]

How you are assessed

Your ability to undertake activities will be assessed by a test, the details of which will be set out in regulations. You may be required to:[9]

- provide specified information or evidence relevant to your ability to undertake daily living or mobility activities; *and*
- attend and participate in a consultation with an approved assessor.

It is intended that the majority of claims will involve a face-to-face consultation with an independent assessor, who may also be responsible for gathering other evidence from you. S/he will then advise the DWP decision maker, who will make a decision on your claim.[10] The DWP plans to contract out the delivery of assessments, but at the time of writing, had yet to award the contract.

If you do not provide any information required to assess your entitlement to PIP (including if you do not attend and participate in a consultation if asked to do so) and you do not have a 'good reason' for your actions, a decision may be made that you do not qualify for PIP.[11]

At the time of writing, the regulations on the assessment for PIP were still in draft form.[12] However, the government intends the following.

- There will be a set number of 'daily living activities' and 'mobility activities'.
- Under each activity, there will be a list of statements (called '**descriptors**'), which describe different types and levels of help needed with the activity.
- Each descriptor will have a points score, and you are awarded the highest scoring descriptor that applies to you for each activity. Descriptors that describe a greater limitation in undertaking the activity will score more points. For example, you are likely to score more points if you need *assistance* to prepare a simple meal than if you can do so yourself with *prompting* from another person.
- Entitlement to a component will be determined by:
  - adding up the highest scoring descriptors that you satisfy for each activity relevant to that component; *and*
  - comparing your total score with a 'threshold' for entitlement to the standard and enhanced rates of the component. At the time of writing, this was set at eight points for the standard rate and 12 points for the enhanced rate, but had not been finally decided.

Aids and appliances

Many of the draft descriptors mention the ability to do something 'using an aid or appliance'. The current definition of this is something that improves, provides or replaces a function (including a prosthetic limb) – eg, a walking stick, modified cutlery or kitchen utensils needed because of your disability, or adaptations to your home such as grab rails in the shower and a shower seat. It does not include something normally used for an activity by someone without a disability.[13] The government intends that if you do not actually have an aid or appliance when you are assessed, it will only be taken into account if you could 'reasonably be expected' to use one.[14]

Fluctuating conditions

Because you will have to satisfy the disability conditions for a component throughout a one-year period (see below), the assessment will take account of changes in your condition. The intention is that the descriptor that is applied to you will be decided as follows.[15]

- If one descriptor applies to you for more than 50 per cent of the days in the year, that descriptor will be used.
- If two or more descriptors apply to you for more than 50 per cent of the days in the year, the one that applies on most days will be used.
- If neither of the above bullet points apply but the time during which you satisfy two or more descriptors totals more than 50 per cent of the days in the year, the descriptor that applies most often will be used.

When your entitlement is reassessed

The current intention is that it will be possible to reassess your entitlement to PIP at any time after it has been awarded.[16]

The required period

In general, you will have to satisfy the disability conditions for the daily living component or the mobility component throughout a one-year period. This is called the **'required period condition'**. You must have met the disability conditions for three months before the date you are awarded PIP and be expected to meet them for a further nine months after that date.[17]

There is no required period for either component if you claim PIP on the grounds that you have a terminal illness (p33).[18]

The current intention is to allow awards of PIP to be made up to three months in advance if you are expected to meet the disability conditions for over a year, but have not yet met them for three months on the date of your claim.[19]

2. The rules about your age

You must be aged 16 or over and under 65 to claim personal independence payment (PIP).[20] The upper age limit for claiming will increase to 66 between 2018 and 2020 in line with changes to pension age (see p531).[21]

The intention is that if you are receiving PIP when you reach 65, you will continue to receive it, as long as you continue to be entitled.[22]

The government intends that you will be able to renew an existing award of PIP if you are 65 or over, or reclaim it after a short gap in entitlement.[23] At the time of writing this *Handbook*, it was understood that the rules may be similar to those that currently apply to allow you to reclaim disability living allowance after the age of 65 in certain circumstances (see p155).[24]

3. The amount of benefit

The daily living component and the mobility component of personal independence payment will both be paid at two different rates. There will be a standard and enhanced rate of each component, depending on how severely your disability or health problem impacts on your daily living activities or mobility.

If you satisfy the conditions of entitlement for both components, you will receive both.

The amounts of the components have not yet been set.

4. Special benefit rules

Special rules will apply to:

- people who are terminally ill (see below);
- people in hospital (see p34);
- people in residential care (see p34);
- prisoners (see p34);
- people from abroad and 'people subject to immigration control' (see p30).

Terminal illness

You are regarded as 'terminally ill' if you have a progressive disease and can reasonably be expected to die within six months as a result of that disease.[25] If you claim personal independence payment (PIP) and you are terminally ill, you are automatically treated as satisfying the conditions for the enhanced rate of the daily living component. You do not have to serve the three-month qualifying period before you are entitled.[26] If you are terminally ill, you do not automatically get the PIP mobility component. You must satisfy the usual disability conditions, but there is no three-month qualifying period before you are entitled.[27]

Someone else can make a claim for PIP on behalf of a terminally ill person without her/his knowledge or authority.[28]

The rules on claims from people who are terminally ill may be similar to those that currently apply to disability living allowance (see p157), although no details on how claims on this basis will work in practice have yet been published.

People in hospital

Regulations may say that neither component of PIP is paid if you are in hospital and the cost of your care is met by public or local funds.[29] The intention is that PIP will be payable for your first 28 days in hospital only.[30]

People in residential care

Regulations may say that the daily living component of PIP is not payable if you live in a registered care home and the cost of your care is met by public or local funds.[31] The intention is that the daily living component will be payable for your first 28 days in residential care only.[32]

Prisoners

Generally, neither component of PIP will be payable if you are in prison or legal custody.[33] It is possible that PIP may be paid during short periods in custody, although at the time of writing, no plans had been published.[34]

5. Claims and backdating

Making a claim

The government intends that claims for personal independence payment (PIP) will be made online or by completing a paper claim form.[35]

Who should claim

A claim for PIP should be made by the person entitled to it. If you are unable to manage your own affairs, someone else (an 'appointee') can claim for you. A claim can also be made on behalf of someone who is terminally ill without her/his knowledge or permission (see p33).

Information to support your claim

You must provide any information required to support your claim. In particular, you may be required to provide information which is needed to help the decision maker decide whether you satisfy the disability conditions (see p30). If you do not provide this information without a good reason, your claim will be refused (see p31). The government intends that you will provide the information to support your claim yourself, but that the PIP claim form will be more straightforward than that used for disability living allowance (DLA).[36]

The date of your claim

Generally, once PIP is introduced (expected to be from April 2013 onwards), if you are not getting DLA, claim as soon as you think you might be entitled.

Claiming in advance

You may be able to claim PIP in advance if, at the time you make a claim, you do not satisfy the 'required period condition' (see p32).

Backdating your claim

You will not be able to backdate your claim for PIP, even if you would have qualified had you claimed sooner.[37]

Transfers from disability living allowance

When it is introduced, PIP will replace DLA for working-age adults. If you are already getting DLA when PIP is introduced, you will continue to receive it until the DWP decides to transfer your claim to PIP. The transfer process for all existing claimants between the ages of 16 and 64 is likely to begin in autumn 2013 and finish by the end of 2016.[38] It is intended that the process will be as follows.[39]

- If your award of DLA ends between these dates, you are likely to be assessed for transfer to PIP in the months before your DLA award is due to end.
- If you report a change in your circumstances that is relevant to your DLA entitlement, this may trigger the transfer process.
- If neither of the above apply, you will be contacted at some point between the above dates and the transfer will begin.

You will not have to a make a claim for PIP. You will be treated as having done so.

If you do not want to claim PIP, if you do not meet the conditions of entitlement, or if you refuse to take part in the transfer process, your DLA award will end.[40]

If you are nearing the age of 65 when PIP is introduced, you may be allowed to remain on DLA (see p136).

The law will allow the DWP to deal with claims flexibly shortly before and after PIP is introduced.[41] See CPAG's *Welfare Rights Bulletin* for updates.

6. Getting paid

It is expected that personal independence payment (PIP) will normally be paid directly into your bank account or building society account.

If you are eligible to use the Motability scheme and choose to do so (see p170), part of your PIP award may be paid directly to the scheme.

Awards of PIP will normally be made for a fixed period. It will be possible to be paid indefinitely in certain circumstances if it is unlikely that your level of needs will change in the future. How long an award is made for will depend on how likely your care or mobility needs are to change over time.

Change of circumstances

You must report any changes in your circumstances that might affect your entitlement to PIP. You must do so promptly, otherwise you might be overpaid (see below) or underpaid.

Overpayments and fraud

If you are paid more PIP than you are entitled to, this will be regarded as an overpayment and may be recovered from you. The government intends that overpayments of PIP will be recoverable under the same rules as those that currently apply to most DWP benefits.[42] See Chapter 43 for more details.

If you are considered to have acted 'knowingly', you may be considered to have committed an offence. If you are convicted of an offence or given a penalty instead of being prosecuted, your PIP may be stopped for a set period.[43] For more information about fraud and social security benefits, see Chapter 44.

7. Tax, tax credits and other benefits

Personal independence payment (PIP) will not be taxable.[44]

Tax credits

No details have been published on how PIP will affect tax credits.

Means-tested benefits

At the time of writing, the government intends that you will be able to claim PIP without it affecting the amount of universal credit (UC) that you receive.[45]

If you are claiming another means-tested benefit and have not yet been transferred to UC (see p49), it is possible that your entitlement to PIP will increase the amount of the means-tested benefit you receive (through additional premiums) in a similar way to disability living allowance (DLA – see p820).[46]

Non-means-tested benefits

As PIP replaces DLA for claimants between the ages of 16 and 64, you will not be able to receive both PIP and DLA at the same time. After the introduction of PIP, it is expected that you will be able to get DLA while you remain entitled, until you are assessed to see if you can be transferred to PIP.

If you have reached the age of 65 and are still receiving PIP, you will not be able to claim attendance allowance (AA).[47]

PIP may also overlap with other non-means-tested benefits.[48] It is likely that it will overlap with other benefits in a similar way to DLA and AA (see Chapter 9).

If you get PIP, someone else may be able to get carer's allowance (CA) for looking after you. At the time of writing, the intention was that both the standard and enhanced rate of the daily living component of PIP will allow someone to claim CA for looking after you.[49] See Chapter 6 for more information on CA.

Passports and other sources of help

You will qualify for a Christmas bonus if you receive PIP (see p9).[50]

If you get the mobility component of PIP, you may be entitled to other 'passported' benefits such as a 'blue badge' or exemption from road tax. Entitlement to the higher rate of DLA mobility component is currently used to assess this (see p169), but the government plans to develop new rules for PIP.[51]

Motability is a charity that runs a scheme to help you lease or buy a car if you are disabled. You can currently access it if you are entitled to the higher rate of DLA mobility component (see p170). At the time of writing, the intention was that PIP will give you access to the Motability scheme. However, the rules have not been decided for how the Motability scheme will link to entitlement to PIP.[52]

Notes

1 s8 SSA 1998, as amended by Sch 9 para 39 WRA 2012

1. Who can claim personal independence payment

2 s83 WRA 2012
3 s115(1) IAA 1999, as amended by Sch 9 para 44 WRA 2012
4 s77(3) WRA 2012
5 House of Commons Public Bill Committee, Welfare Reform Bill, 18th sitting, 10 May 2011, col 780
6 s78 WRA 2012
7 s79 WRA 2012
8 s79(7) WRA 2012
9 s80(4) WRA 2012
10 DWP, *Personal Independence Payment: Policy Briefing Note on Delivery – the operational approach*, 9 May 2011, paras 12-14
11 s80(5)(a) WRA 2012
12 The current version is available at: www.dwp.gov.uk/pip
13 Reg 2(1) PIPA Regs, draft
14 Reg 4(4)(d) PIPA Regs, draft
15 Reg 4(4)(c) PIPA Regs, draft
16 Reg 9 PIPA Regs, draft
17 s81(1) WRA 2012
18 s82(2) and (3) WRA 2012
19 Reg 13(1) PIPA Regs, draft

2. The rules about your age

20 DWP, *Personal Independence Payment: Policy Briefing Note on Young People*, 21 November 2011, para 2
21 s83(2) WRA 2012
22 DWP, *Personal Independence Payment: Policy Briefing Note on People Aged Over 65*, 9 May 2011, para 3
23 House of Commons Public Bill Committee, Welfare Reform Bill, 18th sitting, 10 May 2011, col 857
24 DWP, *Personal Independence Payment: Policy Briefing Note on People Aged Over 65*, 9 May 2011, para 9

4. Special benefit rules

25 s82(4) WRA 2012
26 s82(2) WRA 2012
27 s82(3) WRA 2012
28 s82(5) WRA 2012 and s1(3)(za) SSAA 1992, as inserted by Sch 9 para 8 WRA 2012
29 s86(1) and (2) WRA 2012
30 Welfare Reform Bill 2011, Explanatory Notes, para 381
31 s85 WRA 2012
32 Welfare Reform Bill 2011, Explanatory Notes, para 381
33 s87 WRA 2012
34 House of Lords Select Committee on Delegated Powers and Regulatory Reform, Welfare Reform Bill Memorandum from the DWP, para 312

5. Claims and backdating

35 DWP, *Personal Independence Payment: Policy Briefing Note on Delivery – the operational approach*, 9 May 2011, para 17
36 DWP, *Personal Independence Payment: Policy Briefing Note on Delivery – the operational approach*, 9 May 2011, para 18
37 s88(1) WRA 2012
38 DWP, *Personal Independence Payment: Frequently Asked Questions*, March 2012, question 7
39 DWP, *Personal Independence Payment: Policy Briefing Note on Managing Claims to Personal Independence Payment*, 14 November 2011, para 5
40 DWP, *Personal Independence Payment: Policy Briefing Note on Managing Claims to Personal Independence Payment*, 14 November 2011, para 2
41 Sch 10 WRA 2012

6. Getting paid

42 s71(11)(ad) SSAA 1992, as inserted by Sch 9 para 10 WRA 2012
43 s6A SSFA 2001, as amended by Sch 9 para 46 WRA 2012

7. Tax, tax credits and other benefits

44 s677(1) IT(EP)A 2003, as amended by Sch 9 para 49 WRA 2012
45 Welfare Reform Bill 2011, Explanatory Notes, para 50

46 ss159-160B SSAA 1992, as amended by Sch 9 paras 18-24 WRA 2012
47 s64 1 and 1A SSCBA 1992, as amended by Sch 9 para 5 WRA 2012
48 s73 SSAA 1992, as amended by Sch 9 para 11 WRA 2012
49 DWP, *Personal Independence Payment: Policy Briefing Note on Passporting from Personal Independence Payment*, 16 December 2011, para 7
50 s150(1)(bb) SSCBA 1992, as inserted by Sch 9 para 6 WRA 2012
51 DWP, *Personal Independence Payment: Policy Briefing Note on Passporting from Personal Independence Payment*, 16 December 2011, paras 15-19
52 DWP, *Personal Independence Payment: Policy Briefing Note on Passporting from Personal Independence Payment*, 16 December 2011, para 11

Chapter 4

Universal credit

This chapter covers:

Key facts

- Universal credit (UC) is a new benefit for people on a low income who are in or out of work (including those who are sick or a carer). It is due to be introduced in October 2013.
- UC is a means-tested benefit.
- From October 2013, UC will replace income support, income-based jobseeker's allowance and income-related employment and support allowance. Probably from April 2014, it will also replace housing benefit, child tax credit and working tax credit.
- When it is introduced, UC will initially be for new claimants only. Existing claimants of other means-tested benefits and tax credits will be transferred to UC between April 2014 and 2017.
- You do not have to have paid national insurance contributions to qualify.
- Most full-time students will not be entitled to UC.
- UC will be administered and paid by the DWP.
- If you disagree with a UC decision, you will be able to apply for a revision or supersession, or appeal against it. Rules on decisions, revisions and supersessions, and appeals are expected to be similar to those that currently apply to benefits.

1. Who can claim universal credit

You will qualify for universal credit (UC) if you satisfy both the 'basic conditions' and the 'financial conditions' (but see below for who cannot claim UC).

The '**basic conditions**' are:[1]

- you are aged 18 or over (in most cases) and you are under the qualifying age for pension credit (see p42);
- you are not 'receiving education' (see below);
- you satisfy the 'habitual residence test' and (probably, though this is not yet clear) the 'right to reside test' (see Chapter 62 for how these tests are currently applied to means-tested benefits), and are in Great Britain (see Chapters 62 and 63 for current rules on presence and temporary absence);
- you are not a 'person subject to immigration control' (see p1410 for how this currently applies to benefits);
- you have accepted a 'claimant commitment' (see p50).

The '**financial conditions**' are:[2]

- your income is not too high for you to qualify for a set minimum amount of UC;
- your savings and other capital are worth £16,000 or less.

For more details, see p43.

Who cannot claim universal credit

When it is introduced, UC will initially be for new claimants only. In general, if you are already getting income support (IS), income-related employment and support allowance (ESA), income-based jobseeker's allwance (JSA), housing benefit (HB), child tax credit (CTC) or working tax credit (WTC), you will not be able to get UC instead. These benefits will start to be abolished from October 2013, with existing claims transferred to UC from April 2014. It is understood that new claims for HB, CTC and WTC will be the last to end in April 2014.[3]

Rules will clarify if, for example, you can qualify for UC if you are getting HB, but not IS or income-related ESA.

Receiving education

Generally, you will not be able to claim UC if you are 'receiving education'. What this means has not yet been made clear, although it seems likely that most full-time students will be excluded from entitlement. However, there are expected to be exceptions to this.

The government intends 'to maintain and continue the support that is provided on an exceptional basis to people in education through the benefit system'.[4] However, it has not yet said how this will be done.

Currently, rules allow some students in full-time education to claim existing benefits and tax credits. Parents can claim tax credits for their children; lone parents and disabled students can claim IS or ESA and HB; young students in further education can claim HB to help with their rent and, if they are estranged from their parents, can also claim IS. UC will replace all of the benefits that provide this support. Regulations will set out which groups will be eligible for UC.

The claimant commitment

A basic condition of entitlement to UC is that you accept a 'claimant commitment'. This is an agreement that you will meet certain requirements.[5] The claimant commitment will set out what you must do to receive your UC award, and you will have to agree to this. If you do not, you may have a benefit sanction imposed on you. See p50 for further details.

2. The rules about your age

In most cases, you must be aged at least 18 or over to claim universal credit (UC). Provision is likely to be made for younger claimants in certain circumstances – eg, lone parents or young people who are estranged from their parents may be able to claim from age 16.[6]

You must be under the qualifying age for pension credit (PC – see p509).[7] If you are in a couple and just one of you is over the qualifying age for PC, you will be eligible for UC and will not be able to choose to claim PC instead.[8] The government has said that couples in this situation who are already on PC will not have to move to UC.[9]

3. Claiming for others

Universal credit (UC) includes amounts for yourself, your partner and children.

If you are single, you will claim as a single person (you will have to meet both the basic conditions and the financial conditions). If you are a member of a couple, you will normally make a joint claim with your partner.[10] There will be some exceptions to this.

Both members of a couple will normally have to meet the basic conditions and the financial conditions for a joint claim. There may be circumstances in which a couple may be entitled without both meeting the basic conditions.

You will count as a member of a couple if you are living together and you are married, or you are living together as if you were married. If you are of the same sex, you will count as a couple if you are living together and you are civil partners, or you are living together as if you were civil partners.[11] In some circumstances, to be set out in regulations, even though you are a member of a couple you will claim as a single person. For example, this may apply if you have a 'right to reside' in the UK but your partner does not.[12] For more information on the current rules on claiming as a couple, see p753.

In exceptional circumstances, it will be possible to get UC in a joint claim even though one of you does not meet the basic conditions. For example, if your partner has not agreed to a claimant commitment but you have, you will still be able to get UC, but the amount will be reduced.[13]

Your UC award will also include amounts for your children (see below).

4. The amount of benefit

Universal credit (UC) is a means-tested benefit. The amount you get depends on your family circumstances and on how much capital and income you have. As your income increases, your UC award will reduce.

Capital

If you have more than £16,000 capital, you will not be entitled to any UC.[14] If you have £16,000 or less, but more than £6,000, there will be assumed income ('tariff income') from that capital, which will affect your UC award – see p47. It is expected that the main rules on capital and how it is calculated will be similar to the current rules for means-tested benefits (see Chapter 41).

Calculating universal credit

Your UC is worked out in the following way.

- **Step 1:** calculate your maximum amount.
- **Step 2:** work out your earnings and how much can be ignored.
- **Step 3:** work out your other income and how much can be ignored.
- **Step 4:** calculate your total income.
- **Step 5:** calculate your UC entitlement.

Note: at the time this *Handbook* was written, the rules that will apply to these steps had not been finalised.

Step one: calculate your maximum amount

Your maximum UC is made up of the total of:

- a standard allowance – for a single claimant or a couple;
- an element for each child, with an increase for disabled and severely disabled children;
- an element for an ill or disabled adult who is too ill to work;
- an element for a carer;

- an element for housing costs;
- an element for childcare costs.

At the time this *Handbook* was written, it was thought likely that the following will apply.[15]

- The standard allowance will be set at jobseeker's allowance (JSA) rates.
- Elements for children (the 'child responsibility element') will depend on whether the child is aged under 16, or 16–19 and a 'qualifying young person' for child benefit purposes (see p94 for what this currently means). There will be a higher rate for the eldest or only child.
- The child responsibility element will be increased for a disabled child if s/he is entitled to disability living allowance (DLA) or has a severe visual impairment. There will be a higher addition for a child who is entitled to DLA care component at the highest rate or who is registered blind.
- There will be a 'limited capability for work element' for an ill or disabled adult with limited capability for work. See Chapter 11 for how this currently applies to employment and support allowance (ESA) – the test is expected to be the same.
- There will be a 'limited capability for work and work-related activity element' for an ill or disabled adult who has both limited capability for work and 'limited capability for work-related activity'. See p185 for how this currently applies to ESA – the test is expected to be the same. There will only be one element, even if both partners in a joint claim satisfy the condition.
- The 'carer element' will be included if you are caring for a severely disabled person for at least 35 hours a week without receiving any earnings for this.[16] You will not get this element if the limited capability for work and work-related activity element (see above) is also included for you, although you can if it is included for your partner.[17] The carer element will also not be included if it is already included because your partner cares for the same person, or if you already get it for caring for a different person, or if someone else gets carer's allowance (CA) for caring for the same person.
- Housing costs can be either rent or mortgage interest payments (see below).
- The element for childcare costs can be included if you are working, provided you are paying for 'formal childcare' – eg, a registered childminder, nursery or after-school club.[18] You will not be required to work a set number of hours. You will be able to get 70 per cent of your childcare costs, subject to a maximum of £760 per month for one child and £1,300 per month for two or more children.[19]

Housing costs

The government intends there to be a 'housing element', payable as part of UC. At the time this *Handbook* was written, the rules had not been finalised, but it is expected that a housing element will be included if your housing costs are for:

- rent, licences or similar payment ('Category A' payments). The rules on these will be broadly in line with the current local housing allowance rules for housing benefit (HB);
- a mortgage or loan taken out to buy a property or make essential repairs to a property ('Category B' payments). The rules on these (including the calculation using a standard interest rate) will be broadly in line with the current rules on such housing costs, but will not be payable for people in work;
- service charges ('Category C' payments). The general approach will be to include only those charges that are necessary for the occupation of the accommodation;
- certain other types of accommodation, such as tents, caravans and houseboats ('Category D' payments). At time of writing, the government was still considering whether and, if so, how to make these rules different from the ones that apply to HB.

You must be liable, or treated as liable, to make one or more of the above types of housing payment and you must occupy (or normally occupy) the accommodation as your home, or be treated as occupying it – eg, if you are temporarily absent or have left because of domestic violence.

You could potentially be eligible for an amount to be included for any, or all, of the Category A, B, C and D payments described above. In exceptional circumstances (eg, if you are considered to have an unreasonably high rent), your eligible housing costs may be restricted.

The amount you get to help with your rent will depend on how many people are in your family and on your circumstances.[20] If you are living in the private-rented sector, the amount you get to help with your housing costs is likely to be limited to reflect the lowest one-third of market rents available.[21] Other limitations, such as what size of property you need, will also be applied. There will be an overall ceiling on the amount of rent that UC will cover for a particular size of property.

The government will be able to limit the length of time housing costs can apply.[22] Amounts for mortgage interest are likely to apply only if you are not in full-time work, and are likely to be time-limited to two years.[23] It is not expected that the time limits will apply to you if your home is rented.

At the time of writing, rules on assumed contributions to housing costs from non-dependants were being considered.

Step 2: work out your earnings and how much can be ignored

At the time this *Handbook* was written, it was thought likely that the following rules will apply.

Your net earnings (after tax, national insurance and half of any contribution to an occupational pension scheme[24]) may affect your UC.[25] If you are self-employed, it is likely that you will be assumed to have earnings equivalent to the national minimum wage for the number of hours you work, even if your actual earnings are less.[26] If you are self-employed and your earnings are more than the minimum wage, your actual earnings will be used.

It is possible that income such as statutory sick pay may count as earnings rather than as a benefit.[27] If so, this will mean that it will be subject to disregards and the 'taper' (see below).

For some claimants there will be an earnings disregard. This is the amount of your earnings that you can keep before the amount of your UC is affected. There will be minimum weekly disregards, the amounts of which have not yet been set. The maximum weekly disregards are likely to be the following (although these amounts could be different by October 2013).[28]

Single person (no children)	£13.46
Couple (no children)	£57.96
Couple (with a child or children)	£139.42
Lone parent	£173.07
Disabled person	£134.61

Only the highest earnings disregard will apply to each household.

If your UC includes an amount for housing costs, the disregard will be reduced. The government intends that your disregard will be reduced by 1.5 times the amount of housing costs you receive.[29] However, the disregard will only be reduced to a minimum amount, which will depend on your circumstances. The government has said that the weekly minimum disregard will be approximately as follows (although these amounts could be different by October 2013).[30]

Couple	£10, plus £10 for the first child, and £5 each for the second and third child
Lone parent	£30, plus £10 for the first child, and £5 each for the second and third child
Disabled person	£40

Once you have worked out which disregard applies to you and how much of your earnings count, the maximum UC is reduced by a proportion of this figure. This is often called the **'taper'** – ie, the rate at which your UC will 'taper' away as your earnings increase. It is likely that the taper for UC will be 65 per cent.[31] This means that, as your earnings increase above the level that is disregarded, your UC will decrease by 65 pence for every extra pound you earn.

Step 3: work out your other income and how much can be ignored

If you have other income (eg, other benefits), this may affect your UC by reducing it pound for pound. At the time this *Handbook* was written, it was expected that such income will be listed in regulations, and if it is not listed, it will be disregarded. Some income, such as DLA, its replacement personal independence payment, and child benefit will be disregarded.[32] It is likely that other benefits, such as ESA and CA will be taken into account in full. Income such as an occupational pension will also count in full.[33] At the time this *Handbook* was written, it was expected that child maintenance payments will be disregarded.

Income from capital

If you and your partner have more than £16,000 capital, you will not be able to get UC. If you have £16,000 or less but more than £6,000, you will count as having an income of £1 a week for every £250 or part of £250 over £6,000.[34] For example, if you have capital of £7,400, you will be treated as having £6 a week income from this.

Step 4: calculate your total income

Add the income that is to be taken into account under Steps 2 and 3.

Step 5: calculate your universal credit entitlement

Deduct your total income to be taken into account (Step 4) from your maximum UC (Step 1).

Transitional protection

If you are already getting one of the benefits or tax credits that are to be abolished when UC is introduced (see p40), you will stay on that benefit or tax credit until the DWP transfers your claim to UC. This transfer process is due to begin in April 2014 and end by 2017.

If you are transferred to UC from one or more of the benefits or tax credits which are being abolished, transitional protection will ensure that the amount of UC you will get at the point of transfer will not be less than the amount you were previously receiving.[35] You will continue to receive the same level of benefit without any increases (provided your circumstances do not change) until the UC amounts catch up over time. You will only get this transitional protection if your claim is transferred for you, not if you are allowed to claim UC because of a change in circumstances. There will be rules setting out what kind of changes in circumstances will mean that you lose your transitional protection.

The benefit cap

The government intends to introduce a 'benefit cap', probably in 2013. The benefit cap will mean that your overall benefit entitlement will be capped at the level of average household earnings. Your benefit entitlement will include UC, as well as benefits like contributory ESA and contribution-based JSA (and probably child benefit), but not DLA, pension credit or retirement pension. For more information on the benefits cap, see p25.

5. **Special benefit rules**

At the time this *Handbook* was written, it was expected that special rules will apply to:

- people from abroad and 'people subject to immigration control' (see p41);
- people who are studying (see p41).

6. **Claims and backdating**

Making a claim

The government intends that claims for universal credit (UC) will be made:[36]

- online; *or*
- by telephone if you cannot claim online; *or*
- in person, if you really need to claim this way.

There will be provision to phase in the transfer of existing claimants to UC and the DWP will have flexibility to deal with new claims when UC is introduced – eg, by having provision for early claims and advance awards.[37]

Who should claim

If you are single, you claim on your own behalf. If you are a member of a couple, you will normally make a joint claim with your partner.[38] Provision will be made for some exceptions to this. For more on when you count as a couple, see p42.

Information to support your claim

You will need to provide all the information required for the claim, including details of your and your partner's income and savings and the circumstances of you, your partner and dependent children. If you are working, the DWP intends to use a new 'real-time information system' to gather information about your earnings. This is a new system, which will require your employer to send information to HM Revenue and Customs (HMRC) every time your wages are paid. The DWP will use this to reassess your UC award on a regular basis. So if your earnings are taxed through PAYE (Pay as You Earn), you will not need to report your earnings even when they change, though you will need to report any other income you have.

The date of your claim

In general, once UC is introduced, if you are not already getting benefit, you should claim as soon as you think you might be entitled.

Claiming in advance

You might be able to claim in advance. If you make your claim at a time when you are not yet entitled, but the DWP thinks you will become entitled shortly, it can make an advance award.[39] For example, this might help you if you have a low income which means that you are not entitled to UC at the start of your claim, but will be entitled when additions are made to your award some weeks later – eg, to help with mortgage interest payments.

Backdating your claim

The government has not yet said whether you will be able to backdate a claim for UC.

Transfers to universal credit

If you are already getting one of the benefits that are to be abolished when UC is introduced (see p55), you will stay on that benefit until the DWP decides to transfer your claim to UC. You will not be able to choose to claim UC instead. The transfer process is due to begin in April 2014 and end by 2017.

It is expected that the transfer process will be in three main stages.[40]

- From October 2013, if you have a change of circumstance (eg, you find a job or have your first child), this will trigger the end of your means-tested benefit or tax credits claim and you will be transferred to UC.
- From April 2014, existing claimants of means-tested benefits and tax credits whose circumstances have not changed will start to be transferred to UC. The DWP may concentrate on those households 'whose work behaviour is most likely to benefit' from the transfer. Most of these are expected to be transferred by about the end of 2015.
- From around the end of 2015, the remaining claimants of means-tested benefits and tax credits will be transferred to UC. This is expected to be complete by the end of 2017.

If you are nearing pension age, you might not be transferred to UC at all.[41] The details of this provision will be in rules that are still to be published.

When you transfer into the new system, you will not need to make a separate claim. The transfer will be automatic.

It is possible that you do not qualify for UC, despite having been entitled to an existing benefit. However, there will be provision to allow you to get UC, despite not qualifying. Rules on how this will be used were not finalised at the time this *Handbook* was written.

The DWP will have flexibility in how it deals with claims shortly before and after UC is introduced. For example, it is expected that:[42]

- if you claim backdated benefit starting from a date before UC is introduced, you can be awarded an existing benefit from the start of your claim and then UC from its introduction;
- if you try to claim UC before you are allowed to do so (eg, because you are in a group that is due to be transferred later), your claim can be treated as a claim for an existing benefit.

7. The claimant commitment

A basic condition of entitlement to universal credit (UC) is that you agree to a 'claimant commitment'.[43] This sets out your 'responsibilities' and, in particular, what work-related requirements apply to you (see below). The commitment should set out the sanction you will be given if you do not comply with the requirements in the commitment (see p52).

Work-related requirements

The key part of your claimant commitment is about 'work-related requirements'. These are imposed on you as a condition for claiming UC. The requirements are activities that you must carry out and may include:[44]

- attending work-focused interviews;
- preparing to return to work ('work preparation');
- looking for work and being available to start work ('work availability and work search').

The claimant commitment will be adjusted to some extent to reflect personal circumstances. For example, lone parents with children between five and 12 will only be expected to look for work that is compatible with school hours, carers will only be expected to look for work that is compatible with their caring requirements, and people with poor health may only be expected to work part time.[45] Some claimants will have no work-related requirements imposed. You may be subject to some requirements even if you are working.

No work-related requirements

You will not have *any* work-related requirements if:[46]

- you have 'regular and substantial caring responsibilities for a severely disabled person'; *or*
- you are the lone parent or the 'responsible carer' of a child under one; *or*
- you have both 'limited capability for work' (see Chapter 11) and 'limited capability for work-related activity' (see p185); *or*
- you are a recent victim of domestic violence (for 13 weeks); *or*
- you or your partner work, and your earnings or hours of work are relatively high or you do not receive much UC because of the level of your income. Rules

will set a 'conditionality threshold', which will be the gross taxable earnings for working full time at the national minimum wage. If your earnings are above this amount, you will not have any work-related requirements; *or*

- you are in one of the other groups who will be exempt. These groups had not been decided at the time this *Handbook* was written, but it is expected they will include people on maternity or paternity leave, people getting statutory sick pay, prisoners, people who have reached the qualifying age for pension credit and women who are least 24 weeks pregnant.

Work-focused interviews

Work-focused interviews are intended to provide advice, identify skills needs and encourage participation in activities to prepare you to return to work or look for work. If you are a lone parent or the 'responsible carer' of a child aged one to four, you will *only* have to take part in work-focused interviews (and will have no other work-related requirements). **Note:** the upper age of four was not confirmed at the time this *Handbook* was written.[47] Other groups (eg, foster carers) may also be specified by regulations.

Work preparation

In addition to attending work-focused interviews, you will also be required to prepare for a return to work (unless you only have to take part in work-focused interviews – see above) if you have 'limited capability for work', but do not have 'limited capability for work-related activity'.[48] Other groups may be specified by regulations. You may be required to undertake particular action, such as attending training, an employment programme or attending a work placement (including as part of 'mandatory work activity').

Work availability and work search

If you are not exempt from the work-related requirements or are required only to take part in work-focused interviews and work preparation, you are subject to *all* work-related requirements – ie, you must also be available for and actively looking for work. This means doing anything reasonable to find a job.[49] In general, you may be expected to be available for and looking for work regardless of type or salary as long as it pays at least the minimum wage, on a full-time basis and is within 90 minutes of your home. This may be varied to take into account personal circumstances.[50] For instance, at the time this *Handbook* was written, it was expected that you will not have to be available for and looking for work if you are a prisoner, on maternity or paternity leave or have self-certificated that you are unfit for work from a particular date.

To look for work, you may also have to spend a specific amount of time on the following activities:

- carrying out work searches;
- applying for particular jobs;

- maintaining an online profile;
- registering with an employment agency;
- seeking references.

You may be able to limit the work you will look for or accept by:
- the type of work;
- the number of hours or the times you can work;
- the wages;
- the location.

These limitations may be either temporary or permanent. You will also have to be willing and able to start work immediately, although this rule may be relaxed for some people.

Note: if you are subject to all the work-related requirements when you claim UC but, before your claim, you either gave up work or lost pay, or failed to take up a job and did not have 'good reason' for your actions, your UC may be subject to a higher level sanction (see p53).[51]

Sanctions

If you do not comply with the requirements of your claimant commitment, you may be subject to a sanction – ie, the amount of UC you are paid is reduced. A sanction will be applied if you fail to comply 'for no good reason', and (depending on the circumstances) it will last for up to three years. This also applies if you are required to be available and looking for work and, before you claimed UC, you either gave up work or lost pay (including through misconduct), or failed to take up a job without a good reason.[52]

You will be able to appeal against a decision applying a sanction – eg, if you want to argue that you do have good reasons for your actions.

At the time this *Handbook* was written, the rules on sanctions were not finalised. It is expected, however, that they will include the following.
- Sanctions will only apply if you did not have a 'good reason' for not complying with a requirement. **'Good reason'** will not be defined and will depend on the circumstances of your case.
- Most sanctions will be a loss of the standard personal allowance. If you are in a couple, 50 per cent of the standard allowance for a couple will be lost if only one of you has failed to comply.
- If you have no other income and get the maximum amount of UC, sanctions will not reduce your award to below the amount included for housing costs, children and disability.
- Sanctions will not reduce a UC award to less than zero, so you continue to retain your entitlement even if you are sanctioned.
- Sanctions will be applied monthly, calculated by multiplying a standard daily reduction by the number days left in the month. For claimants who have only

to attend work-focused interviews, sanctions will double for a second consecutive failure.

- Sanctions will apply at three levels of severity (see below).

Sanction levels

It is expected that rules will include the following.

- If you are subject to *all* the work-related requirements, **higher level sanctions** will apply if you:
  - do not attend a work placement;
  - do not apply for a particular vacancy;
  - do not take up an offer of paid work, including in a period before claiming (not specified at the time of writing);
  - stop work or lose pay (including as a result of misconduct, but not voluntary redundancy).
- If you are subject to *all* the work-related requirements, **medium level sanctions** will apply if you do not meet a requirement to look for all reasonable work or to be available for work.
- If you are subject to all the work-related requirements or only to work-focused interviews and work preparation, **lower level sanctions** will apply if you do not attend a work-focused interview or do not take a particular action as part of work preparation or work search.
- If you are subject only to work-focused interviews, a sanction of 20 per cent of the standard allowance for a single person will apply if you fail to participate in an interview (rising to 40 per cent for a repeat failure) and will continue to apply until you have participated.
- Higher level sanctions will apply for a three-month 'reduction period' for the first failure to comply; then for an additional six months for a repeat failure if this is within a year of the first; then for a maximum total of three years for another repeat failure within a year of that.
- Medium level sanctions will apply for four weeks; then for three months for a repeat failure if this is within a year of the first.
- Lower level sanctions will apply until you comply, and then for an additional week. If you have another failure to compy within a year, the sanction will continue for an additional two weeks after you comply, or four weeks for another failure.

8. **Getting paid**

Universal credit (UC) will normally be paid direct into your bank or building society account.

Your award will be assessed over a set period.[53] The government has said that UC will be paid monthly.[54]

If you find monthly payments difficult to budget for, it may be possible to be paid more often. The intention is that there will be a 'payments exception service' for this. This will be discretionary and you will need to show that you are in exceptional circumstances.[55]

The following will also apply.[56]

- Couples will be able to decide which partner will be paid the UC award. There will also be provision for the DWP to decide that the other partner should be paid instead, or to split payments in exceptional circumstances – eg, if there is hardship or the relationship has broken down.[57]
- Payments ('payments on account') will be made if there is a delay in deciding your UC claim. If there is a delay on only one part of your claim (eg, if there is still some information or evidence needed to decide how much housing costs to pay), you will be able to get the remainder of your UC award in the meantime as a payment on account.[58]
- Rules will provide for payments on account to be made in cases of need or in other specified situations.
- If you need a loan for an item you cannot afford, you will be able to ask for a payment on account (instead of a current social fund budgeting loan). Rules will set out the qualifying conditions, the maximum amount you can get and the repayment terms. The DWP plans for these advances to be available to claimants who have been on UC for 26 weeks.[59] You must be able to repay the loan, which will normally be done by deductions from your ongoing award of UC.
- There will be provision to make direct payments from UC to third parties – eg, the amount to cover your mortgage interest will be made directly to your mortgage lender.[60] If you rent your home, the government has said that the amount in your UC for your rent will be paid to you, not to your landlord, whether you rent from a local authority, housing association or private landlord. However, direct payments may be made to landlords in some circumstances.[61]

Change of circumstances

You must report changes in your circumstances that might affect your entitlement to UC. Rules may also specify certain changes that you are required to report, even though they do not affect your entitlement.[62]

It will be very important to report changes of circumstances promptly. Not only could you find that you are overpaid (see p55) or underpaid if you do not, it is also possible that you may be considered to have committed an offence or be subject to a 'civil penalty' (see p55).

You will have an online account for your UC award. This will allow you to check the information about your claim and payments, and to report changes in circumstances. If you cannot use the internet, there will be other ways to report changes in circumstances – eg, by telephone or face-to-face with an adviser.

The intention is that if you are working, you will not need to report changes in your earnings. The DWP will get this information automatically from HM Revenue and Customs through a new 'real-time' information system (see p48).

Overpayments and fraud

If you are paid more UC than you are entitled to, this will be regarded as an overpayment and may be recovered from you. At the time this *Handbook* was written, it was intended that an overpayment of UC will be recoverable from you even if you did not cause it – eg, it was caused solely by official error.[63] See Chapter 43 for how the rules currently apply.

If you are considered to have acted 'knowingly', you may be considered to have committed an offence. Alternatively, if you are considered to have acted negligently, you may be subject to a fine (a 'civil penalty'). See Chapter 44 for how these rules currently apply to benefits.

9. Tax, tax credits and other benefits

It is expected that universal credit (UC) will not be taxable.

Means-tested benefits and tax credits

The following benefits and tax credits will be abolished and replaced by UC for new claimants from October 2013:

- income support;
- income-based jobseeker's allowance (JSA);
- income-related employment and support allowance (ESA);
- housing benefit;
- working tax credit;
- child tax credit.

You will not be able to get the above benefits and tax credits at the same time as UC. If your partner is claiming one of these benefits, you will not be able to get UC at the same time. If you are already getting one of these benefits when UC is introduced in October 2013, you will be transferred to UC at a later date. This process is not expected to be completed until October 2017.

You will not be able to get pension credit at the same time as UC because of the rules about your age (see p42).

The government also intends to abolish council tax benefit (CTB) by April 2013. However, unlike other benefits which are being abolished, it will not be replaced by UC, and there will be no additional amount in UC to help you pay your council tax. Instead, local authorities in England and the Scottish and Welsh governments will set their own versions of CTB.

Non-means-tested benefits

After the introduction of UC, you will still be able to claim contribution-based JSA or contributory ESA. If you cannot get UC (eg, because your savings are too high), you will still be able to claim one of these benefits.

You may be entitled to contribution-based JSA or contributory ESA at the same time as UC, but you will not be able to receive both in full. This could mean the contributory JSA or contributory ESA counts as income for UC, leaving you with a top-up of UC. However, rules may say that, in certain cases, payment will be made entirely by UC instead.

You will still be able to claim bereavement benefits. You may be entitled to a bereavement benefit at the same time as UC, but it is likely that your UC will be reduced. Bereavement benefits will generally count as income for UC, but may be partially ignored to ensure widows and widowers are not worse off than in the current system.[64]

The government plans to abolish disability living allowance (DLA) for adults from April 2013 and replace it with personal independence payment (PIP – see Chapter 3). You will still be able to clam DLA for a disabled child (see p136). You will be able to get DLA or PIP and UC. DLA and PIP will be ignored as income for UC. There will be additional payments for disabled children in UC, which will remain linked to receipt of DLA.[65] There will be a higher rate payable for the most severely disabled children getting the highest rate of the care component.

You will be able to get carer's allowance (CA) at the same time as UC, but CA will count as income for UC and reduce your entitlement accordingly. Getting CA will probably mean that you are entitled to an additional amount as a carer in your UC. It will also probably mean that you are treated as a carer and will not be required to undertake any work-related activity.

The government has said that other non-means-tested benefits will remain outside UC, including:
- child benefit;
- statutory sick pay;
- statutory maternity/paternity/adoption pay;
- maternity allowance;
- industrial injuries benefits.

You will be able to claim the above benefits after the introduction of UC. It is expected that you will be able to receive them at the same time as UC, but you may not be able to get both in full. However, the interaction of such benefits with UC is not yet clear.

Passports and other sources of help

Some UC claimants will be entitled to other 'passported' benefits, such as free school lunches.[66] However, at the time this *Handbook* was written, the rules were not finalised.

Options under consideration for the future of passported benefits under UC include:

- replacing passported benefits with an additional cash amount in UC;
- keeping passported benefits as benefits in cash, vouchers or discounts, linked to receipt of UC and a certain level of income;
- withdrawing passported benefits gradually, rather than all at once, when you have a certain level of income.

Notes

1. **Who can claim universal credit**

1 s4 WRA 2012
2 s5 WRA 2012
3 DWP, *Universal Credit Policy Briefing Note 15*, 1 November 2011
4 House of Commons, *Hansard*, 29 March 2011, col 195
5 s14 WRA 2012

2. **The rules about your age**

6 s4(3) WRA 2012; Welfare Reform Bill 2011, Explanatory Notes, para 37
7 s4(4) WRA 2012
8 Sch 2 para 64 WRA 2012; Welfare Reform Bill 2011, Explanatory Notes, para 36
9 House of Commons, *Hansard*, 28 April 2011, col 553

3. **Claiming for others**

10 s2 WRA 2012
11 s40 WRA 2012
12 Welfare Reform Bill 2011, Explanatory Notes, para 33
13 Sch 3 para 1 WRA 2012; House of Lords Select Committee on Delegated Powers and Regulatory Reform, Welfare Reform Bill Memorandum from the DWP, para 99

4. **The amount of benefit**

14 DWP, *Universal Credit Policy Briefing Note 3*, 12 September 2011, para 1(c)
15 DWP, *Universal Credit Policy Briefing Note 1*, 12 September 2011
16 DWP, *Universal Credit Policy Briefing Note 7*, 12 September 2011, para 2(b)
17 DWP, *Universal Credit Policy Briefing Note 1*, 12 September 2011, para 3 (e)
18 Welfare Reform Bill 2011, Explanatory Notes, para 58
19 DWP, *Universal Credit Policy Briefing Note 10*, 10 October 2011
20 Welfare Reform Bill 2011, Explanatory Notes, para 55
21 DWP, *21st Century Welfare*, Cm 7913, July 2010, paras 29 and 30
22 s11(5)(b) WRA 2012
23 Welfare Reform Bill 2011, Explanatory Notes, para 56; House of Lords *Hansard*, 13 October 2011, col GC532
24 DWP, *Universal Credit Policy Briefing Note 3*, 12 September 2011, para 4(b)
25 *21st Century Welfare*, Cm 7913, DWP, July 2010 para 9
26 Sch 1 para 4(4) WRA 2012; DWP, *Universal Credit: welfare that works*, Cm 7957, November 2010, Annex 3, para 5
27 DWP, *Universal Credit Policy Briefing Note 3*, 12 September 2011, para 4(c)

28 DWP, *Universal Credit Policy Briefing Note 14*, 10 October 2011, para 3(k)
29 DWP, *Universal Credit Policy Briefing Note 14*, 10 October 2011, para 3(g)
30 DWP, *Universal Credit Policy Briefing Note 14*, 10 October 2011, para 3(i)
31 DWP, *Universal Credit Policy Briefing Note 14*, 10 October 2011, para 4(c)
32 Welfare Reform Bill 2011, Explanatory Notes, para 50
33 DWP, *21st Century Welfare*, Cm 7913, July 2010, Annex 3 para 7
34 DWP, *21st Century Welfare*, Cm 7913, July 2010, para 8
35 Sch 6 para 4(3) WRA 2012

6. **Claims and backdating**

36 DWP, *Universal Credit: welfare that works*, Cm 7957, November 2010, s4 paras 5 and 27
37 Sch 6 WRA 2012
38 s2 WRA 2012
39 s98 WRA 2012
40 DWP, *Universal Credit Policy Briefing Note 15*, November 2011
41 Welfare Reform Bill 2011, Explanatory Notes, Clause 37
42 Sch 6 para 2 WRA 2012; House of Lords Select Committee on Delegated Powers and Regulatory Reform Welfare Reform Bill Memorandum from the DWP, paras 175-81

7. **The claimant commitment**

43 ss4(1)(e) and 14 WRA 2012
44 s13 WRA 2012
45 DWP, *Universal Credit Policy Briefing Note 11*, October 2011
46 s19 WRA 2012; DWP, *Universal Credit Policy Briefing Note 11*, 10 October 2011
47 ss15 and 20 WRA 2012
48 ss16 and 21 WRA 2012
49 ss17, 18 and 22 WRA 2012
50 DWP, *Universal Credit Policy Briefing Note 12*, 10 October 2011
51 s26(4) WRA 2012
52 ss26 and 27 WRA 2012

8. **Getting paid**

53 s7 WRA 2012
54 'Jobseekers on benefits who need help to speak English will have to take up free language training', DWP Press Release, 13 September 2011
55 DWP, *Universal Credit Policy Briefing Note 2*, 12 September 2011
56 ss100 and 101 and Sch 2 paras 5 and 6 WRA 2012
57 House of Commons Public Bill Committee, Welfare Reform Bill, 22nd sitting, 17 May 2011, col 997
58 House of Commons Public Bill Committee, Welfare Reform Bill 22nd sitting, 17 May 2011, col 997
59 DWP, *Amendments to Payment on Account Provisions Equality Impact Assessment*, March 2011, paras 8 and 9
60 Sch 2 para 6 WRA 2012
61 House of Commons Public Bill Committee, Welfare Reform Bill, 9th sitting, 5 April 2011, col 362
62 s95(5) WRA 2012
63 s102 WRA 2012

9. **Tax, tax credits and other benefits**

64 Welfare Reform Bill, House of Commons Committee Stage Report, 8 June 2011, p16
65 DWP, *Universal Credit Policy Briefing Note 1*, 12 September 2011, para 3d
66 Sch 2 para 39 WRA 2012

Part 3

Benefits

Chapter 5

Bereavement benefits

This chapter covers:

Key facts

- Bereavement benefits are paid to widows, widowers or surviving civil partners.
- To qualify for a bereavement benefit, your late spouse or civil partner must have satisfied the national insurance (NI) contribution conditions or died as a result of an industrial accident or disease.
- There are three main bereavement benefits: a lump-sum **bereavement payment**, **widowed parent's allowance** for people with children or for pregnant women and **bereavement allowance** for people who were at least 45 when their spouse or civil partner died.
- Bereavement benefits are non-means-tested benefits.
- You can qualify for bereavement benefits whether you are in or out of work.
- You may qualify for means-tested benefits or tax credits while you get bereavement benefits.
- Widowed parent's allowance and bereavement allowance are affected by the overlapping benefit rules.
- Bereavement benefits are administered and paid by the DWP.
- If you disagree with a bereavement benefit decision, you can apply for a revision or supersession, or appeal against it (see Chapters 45 and 46).

Future changes: April 2013 and after

Major changes are taking place that affect the benefits and tax credits system (see Chapter 2).

- From April 2013, total benefit payments to many working-age households will be 'capped' (see p25). There will be limited exceptions, including households in which

someone is entitled to working tax credit or receives disability living allowance. It is not yet known whether bereavement benefits will be included in the capped amount.
- You will still be able to claim bereavement benefits when universal credit is introduced in October 2013.
- The government proposes to replace current bereavement benefits with a lump sum benefit, or possibly with a lump sum together with a weekly benefit payable for a year. The new benefit would have a single NI contribution condition, like that for bereavement payment, and would be introduced for new claimants only from 2014 at the earliest.

See CPAG's *Welfare Rights Bulletin* for updates.

1. Bereavement payment

A bereavement payment is a one-off, lump-sum payment that can be paid in addition to widowed parent's allowance or bereavement allowance.

Who can claim a bereavement payment

You qualify for a bereavement payment if:[1]

- you are either:
  - a widow or widower and your spouse died on or after 9 April 2001 (see p68 for the meaning of widow and widower); *or*
  - a surviving civil partner (see p68); *and*
- your late spouse or civil partner either:
  - satisfied the national insurance contribution conditions (see p792); *or*
  - died as the result of an industrial injury or disease (see p71); *and*
- when your spouse or civil partner died, you were either:
  - under pension age (see p531); *or*
  - pension age or over and your spouse or civil partner was not entitled to a Category A retirement pension when s/he died; *and*
- you claim within the time limits if you must make a claim (see below).

See p63 if you were living with someone else when your spouse or civil partner died.

Time limit

To qualify for a bereavement payment, you must make a claim within 12 months of your spouse's or civil partner's death.[2] However, there are exceptions to this rule.

- *If you were receiving* retirement pension on the date your spouse or civil partner died, the 12-month time limit does not apply as you do not need to make a claim in order to qualify for a bereavement payment.[3] This rule has applied since 30 October 2008.

- If your spouse or civil partner died before 30 October 2008 and you reached pension age before that date, the 12-month time limit may not apply (see p26 of CPAG's *Welfare Benefits and Tax Credits Handbook* 2011/12 for details). If you are in this situation and are refused a bereavement payment because you claimed more than 12 months after your spouse or civil partner died, seek advice.
- If you were not aware that your spouse or civil partner had died, the normal 12-month time limit can be extended (see p76).

Disqualification

Your entitlement to a bereavement payment is not affected if you marry or enter into a civil partnership after the death of your late spouse or civil partner. However, a bereavement payment is not paid to you if, at the time of your spouse's or civil partner's death, you were cohabiting with someone else (see p71).[4]

If your spouse or civil partner was not in Great Britain at the time s/he died, you cannot always qualify for a bereavement payment – see p1434 for details.[5]

The rules about your age

There is no lower age limit for entitlement to a bereavement payment. Anyone who is legally old enough to marry or form a civil partnership may qualify.

For the upper age limit for qualifying for a bereavement payment, see p62.

Claiming for others

No additions can be made to a bereavement payment for any of your dependants.

The amount of bereavement payment

A bereavement payment is a lump sum of £2,000.[6]

See p73 for details of how to claim a bereavement payment.

2. Widowed parent's allowance

Widowed parent's allowance is a weekly benefit. You cannot receive widowed parent's allowance and bereavement allowance at the same time, but you may qualify for bereavement allowance after your entitlement to widowed parent's allowance ends (see p66).

In addition to your widowed parent's allowance, you may also qualify for a bereavement payment (see p62).

Who can claim widowed parent's allowance

You qualify for widowed parent's allowance if:[7]

- you are either:
  - a widow or widower (see p68) whose spouse died on or after 9 April 2001; *or*
  - a surviving civil partner (see p69); *or*
  - a widower whose wife died before 9 April 2001 (if you are a widow whose husband died before this date, see p71); *and*
- you are under pension age (see p531); *and*
- your late spouse or civil partner either:
  - satisfied the national insurance (NI) contribution conditions (see p793); *or*
  - died as the result of an industrial injury or disease (see p71); *and*
- you are either:
  - entitled to child benefit (or treated as entitled to child benefit) for at least one eligible child (see below); *or*
  - a widow and you are pregnant by your late husband; *or*
  - a widow or a surviving civil partner and you were residing with your late husband or civil partner immediately before her/his death and you are pregnant as a result of artificial insemination by a donor or *in vitro* fertilisation which was carried out before her/his death.

Eligible child

The term 'child' in this chapter means both a 'child' and a 'qualifying young person'. The definitions of 'child' and 'qualifying young person' used for child benefit also apply to widowed parent's allowance (see p94).

A child only counts as an eligible child if *either*:[8]

- s/he is your and your late spouse's (or late civil partner's) son or daughter; *or*
- you were residing with your late spouse or civil partner immediately before s/he died and you were entitled, or treated as entitled (see p65), to child benefit for the child at that time; *or*
- immediately before s/he died, your late spouse or civil partner was entitled, or treated as entitled, to child benefit for the child.

If you and your spouse or civil partner were living apart at the time of her/his death, you can still be considered to have been residing with her/him if your separation was only intended to be temporary.[9]

Note: if the child does not live with you and you got an increase for a dependent child in your widowed parent's allowance, or in another non-means-tested benefit, on 5 April 2003, the child only counts as an eligible child if, in addition to one of the above applying, you contribute £15.55 a week to the cost of supporting her/him (on top of the contribution you must make to qualify for child benefit for her/him).[10]

Treated as entitled to child benefit

You or your late spouse or civil partner can be treated as entitled to child benefit for a child if you would have been entitled to it had you claimed it, and had the child not been abroad.[11]

In certain circumstances, if you were not residing with your late spouse or civil partner at the time of her/his death, your late spouse or civil partner can be treated as having been entitled to child benefit for a child. This may apply if, prior to your marriage or civil partnership, you were previously widowed or your civil partner had died. If you might need to rely on this rule, seek advice.[12]

Disqualification and suspension

Entitlement to widowed parent's allowance ends if you marry or enter into a civil partnership, and you are not able to requalify for it even if you subsequently get divorced or if your civil partnership is dissolved. It is suspended if you are cohabiting (see p71) but can be reinstated if you stop cohabiting.[13]

The rules about your age

There is no lower age limit for widowed parent's allowance. Anyone who is legally old enough to have married or formed a civil partnership may qualify. Widowed parent's allowance cannot be paid once you reach pension age (see p531), but you may then qualify for a Category A or B retirement pension (see p527).

Claiming for others

You claim widowed parent's allowance for yourself. You cannot claim an addition for a partner (see above for the effect of marriage, entering into a civil partnership and cohabitation on your entitlement to widowed parent's allowance). You also cannot normally claim an addition for children (but see below).

Increases for dependent children

If you were entitled to an increase in your widowed parent's allowance for a dependent child on 5 April 2003, you may be able to continue to receive it (see p745).[14]

The amount of widowed parent's allowance

Widowed parent's allowance is made up of:

- a basic widowed parent's allowance. The full weekly rate of this is £105.95 but it may be paid at a reduced rate if your late spouse's or civil partner's NI record was incomplete (see p66);
- an additional earnings-related payment based on your late spouse's or civil partner's earnings under the additional state pension scheme, if her/his NI

contribution record qualifies you for this (see p537). You may be entitled to this even if her/his contribution record is not sufficient for you to qualify for basic widowed parent's allowance.[15]

Reduction in the basic widowed parent's allowance

You get a reduced rate of basic widowed parent's allowance if your spouse's or civil partner's contribution record was incomplete (see p795).[16] You may be able to increase your entitlement by paying Class 3 contributions on your spouse's or civil partner's behalf (which you may do even though s/he has died contact HM Revenue and Customs' National Insurance Helpline on 0845 302 1479 or textphone 0845 915 3296 about this). See p776 for further details and p778 for certain time limits for making such payments.

3. Bereavement allowance

Bereavement allowance is a weekly benefit paid for up to 52 weeks. You cannot receive widowed parent's allowance and bereavement allowance at the same time, but you may qualify for bereavement allowance when your entitlement to widowed parent's allowance stops.

In addition to qualifying for bereavement allowance, you may also be entitled to a bereavement payment (see p62).

Who can claim bereavement allowance

You qualify for bereavement allowance if:[17]

- you are either:
  - a widow or widower and your spouse died on or after 9 April 2001 (see p68 for the meaning of widow and widower); *or*
  - a surviving civil partner (see p68); *and*
- you were at least 45 years old when your spouse or civil partner died; *and*
- you are under pension age (see p531); *and*
- not more than 52 weeks have passed since your spouse or civil partner died; *and*
- your late spouse or civil partner either:
  - satisfied the national insurance (NI) contribution conditions (see p793); *or*
  - died as the result of an industrial injury or disease (see p71).

Disqualification and suspension

Bereavement allowance stops if you marry or form a civil partnership and you cannot requalify for it, even if you subsequently get divorced or your civil partnership is dissolved. It is suspended while you are cohabiting but can be reinstated if you stop cohabiting (see p71).[18]

The rules about your age

You must be 45 or over at the time your spouse or civil partner died to qualify for bereavement allowance and the allowance is reduced if you were under 55 when s/he died (see below).

You cannot receive bereavement allowance if you are pension age or over (see p531). However, you may qualify for retirement pension based on your own or your late spouse's or civil partner's NI contributions (see Chapter 23).

Claiming for others

You claim bereavement allowance for yourself. You cannot get an addition for a partner (see p66 for the effect of marriage, entering into a civil partnership and cohabitation on your entitlement to bereavement allowance) or for a child (if you have a dependent child you may get widowed parent's allowance rather than bereavement allowance).

The amount of bereavement allowance

The full weekly rate of bereavement allowance is £105.95.[19]

Your bereavement allowance may be reduced, as described below, if:

- your late spouse's or civil partner's NI contribution record was incomplete; *or*
- you were under 55 when s/he died.

Your late spouse's or civil partner's contribution record

If your late spouse's or civil partner's NI contribution record was not complete, the amount of basic bereavement allowance you receive is reduced proportionately (see p795). You may be able to increase your entitlement by paying Class 3 contributions on your spouse's or civil partner's behalf (see p66).

Your age

Your bereavement allowance is reduced if you were under 55 when your spouse or civil partner died.[20] For each year, or part of a year, you were under 55, your bereavement allowance is reduced by 7 per cent. This percentage reduction remains the same for as long as you receive bereavement allowance.

If your spouse or civil partner had a complete NI contribution record, the amount you would receive is as follows.

Age when spouse or civil partner died	*Rate of bereavement allowance (£pw)*
54	98.53
53	91.12
52	83.70
51	76.28
50	68.87
49	61.45

48	54.03
47	46.62
46	39.20
45	31.79

4. **Definition of terms**

Who counts as a widow, widower or surviving civil partner

To qualify for bereavement benefits, you must be a widow, widower or surviving civil partner. If you have been bereaved more than once, your entitlement depends on the contribution record of your most recent spouse or civil partner.

If, following the death of your spouse or civil partner, you marry or enter into a civil partnership, you are no longer a widow, widower or a surviving civil partner and lose all entitlement to widowed parent's allowance and bereavement allowance based on your previous spouse's or civil partner's contribution record.[21]

If you are cohabiting, see p71.

Widows and widowers

You are a widow or widower if you were married to your spouse at the date of her/his death and the marriage was considered valid under UK law. See p70 for details about invalid marriages.

In Scotland (but not the rest of Great Britain), you can also be a widow or widower if you were married 'by cohabitation with habit and repute' (see below) even if you did not go through a formal wedding ceremony. However, this only applies if your cohabitation with habit and repute began before 4 May 2006.[22] If it began on or after 4 May 2006, you will not be treated as married and, therefore, will not count as a widow or widower if your partner dies (unless, in certain circumstances, you or your partner were domiciled in Scotland, married abroad and you have since realised the marriage was invalid – if so, seek advice).

There is no equivalent to the Scottish marriage by cohabitation with habit and repute in the rest of Great Britain.[23]

'Cohabitation with habit and repute'

To be considered married by cohabitation with habit and repute, your relationship must have been more than simply living together – there must have been something about it which meant that it could be inferred that you and your partner consented to marriage *and nothing* existed which would have prevented a valid marriage taking place – eg, either party already being married to someone else.[24] In addition, your relationship must have been such that other people generally believed that you were married.[25]

Surviving civil partners

You are a surviving civil partner if, at the time of your partner's death, you were civil partners and the civil partnership was valid under UK law. Civil partnerships were introduced in the UK from 5 December 2005. See p70 for details about invalid civil partnerships.

To count as civil partners, you must have been registered as such in the UK or, in certain circumstances, have registered a legal relationship abroad – ie, under the law of another country. If your civil partnership was registered abroad, at a place such as a British consulate or as a result of a connection to the armed forces, you may also count as civil partners.[26]

Separation, divorce and dissolution

If you were divorced when your ex-spouse died, or if your civil partnership had been dissolved when your ex-civil partner died, you are not a widow, widower or surviving civil partner.

In England and Wales, a divorce becomes effective only when the decree absolute is pronounced, and a civil partnership is dissolved only when a final dissolution order is issued. However, if you were in the process of obtaining a divorce or of dissolving your civil partnership and your spouse or civil partner died before the decree was made absolute, or before the final dissolution order was issued, you are still a widow, widower or surviving civil partner (and so may be entitled to bereavement benefits). This is the case even if you were judicially separated. In Scotland, you are not divorced until a decree of divorce is issued and your civil partnership is not dissolved until a decree of dissolution is granted.

Your entitlement to bereavement benefits will be affected if the DWP disputes the validity of an earlier divorce or dissolution of a civil partnership. In this circumstance, seek advice.

Polygamous marriages

If your marriage was polygamous, you are not normally entitled to bereavement benefits following the death of your spouse. This is because, as a general rule, the law in England, Wales and Scotland does not treat a man and a woman as legally married unless their marriage is a monogamous one.[27]

It is only if your marriage was *actually* polygamous when your spouse died that you do not normally qualify for bereavement benefits – ie, if, when s/he died, either you or your late spouse had another husband or wife. If your marriage was *formerly* polygamous, you can qualify – ie, if, when your late spouse died, any other spouses had already died or been divorced.

A marriage is only considered polygamous if the law of the country where the marriage takes place permits either party to have another wife or husband.[28]

If you are refused bereavement benefits because your marriage was or is polygamous, seek advice. The law on polygamous marriages is complex and it is possible that, even if you think your marriage is polygamous, it is not in law.

This depends on whether you were your spouse's first wife or husband and on where you and your spouse were 'domiciled' at the time of your marriage and any subsequent marriage. 'Domicile' is a difficult legal concept but, in very general terms, it means the country in which you have chosen to make your permanent home.[29] Domicile is not the same as 'presence' (see p1429), 'residence' (see p1430), 'ordinary residence' (see p1430) or nationality.

In particular, no one who is domiciled in England and Wales is allowed to contract a polygamous marriage anywhere in the world even if the local law allows it.[30]

Decision makers refer any questions about whether a marriage is to be treated as monogamous or polygamous to a special section of the DWP.

If the DWP considers that you were polygamously married because it disputes the validity of an earlier divorce, seek advice.

Example

At the time of their wedding, Shaznaz and her husband were domiciled in Pakistan and were married under Islamic law. After the wedding they came to live in England, made their permanent home here and had no intention of returning to live in Pakistan at any time. Later, her husband returned temporarily to Pakistan and married a second wife. As her husband was domiciled in England rather than Pakistan at the time of the second marriage, English law does not recognise the second marriage and, therefore, regards Shaznaz as her late husband's only wife. Provided she meets the other conditions of entitlement, she is entitled to bereavement benefits.[31] If her husband had re-acquired domicile in Pakistan at the time of his second marriage, and his second wife was still alive, both marriages would be polygamous, and neither wife could claim bereavement benefits.[32]

Void and voidable marriages and civil partnerships

Sometimes the law treats a marriage or civil partnership as invalid even though you have been through a marriage or registration ceremony.

A **void** marriage or civil partnership (eg, one where at least one of the partners was not eligible to marry or form a civil partnership) is invalid and from a legal point of view is treated as if it never existed (although for most practical purposes, it is necessary to confirm the position by getting a court order).[33]

A **voidable** marriage or civil partnership (eg, in England and Wales, a marriage that has not been consummated) can be annulled, and in England and Wales is treated as having been valid until a decree absolute of annulment is pronounced.[34]

Questions about the validity of marriages or civil partnerships can be deceptively difficult. The DWP has a special unit that decides questions in this area. If it claims that your marriage or civil partnership was invalid, seek advice.

Proving that your spouse or civil partner is dead

It is up to you to prove to the DWP decision maker that your spouse or civil partner is dead and that you were married or were civil partners when s/he died.

Normally this is straightforward (see p74 for the information expected). However, if your spouse or civil partner is missing and you think that s/he has died, it may be difficult to establish your entitlement to bereavement benefits. In these circumstances, you can request that a DWP decision maker determines whether your spouse or civil partner has died or can be presumed to have died.[35] If you are in this situation, seek advice. See p76 for details of backdating benefit if you were unaware of your spouse's or civil partner's death.

Cohabitation

A bereavement payment is not paid to you if you are cohabiting with someone else at the time of your spouse's or civil partner's death.

Your widowed parent's allowance or bereavement allowance is suspended if you are cohabiting, but becomes payable again if the cohabitation ends.[36]

In this chapter, 'cohabiting' means living with someone of the opposite sex as if you are husband and wife, or living with someone of the same sex as if you are civil partners. Deciding whether or not you are cohabiting may not be straightforward. For futher information, see p754.

If the DWP decides that you are cohabiting and you do not agree, you can challenge its decision (see Chapters 45 and 46).

Industrial accident or disease

The meaning of 'industrial accident or disease' is discussed on p368. To qualify for bereavement benefits, the industrial accident or disease must have been a cause of death, but it need not have been a direct cause or the only cause.[37]

5. Special benefit rules

Special rules apply to:

- widows whose husbands died before 9 April 2001 (see below);
- widowers whose wives died before 9 April 2001 (see p72);
- people who have obtained a gender recognition certificate (see p72);
- people who are abroad (see p1481);
- people who are in prison or detention (see p692).

Widows whose husbands died before 9 April 2001

If your husband died before 9 April 2001, you are not entitled to bereavement benefits but instead may qualify for widowed mother's allowance or widow's pension.

For an explanation of the main qualifying conditions for widows' benefits, see the 2000/01 edition of this *Handbook*. See pxvii for the current rates of widows' benefits.

If you satisfy the qualifying conditions, you can get **widowed mother's allowance** for as long as you have an eligible child, as there is no upper age limit. Just as for widowed parent's allowance, a 'child' is someone who counts as a child or qualifying young person for child benefit purposes, and it is the child benefit rules that are in force at the time for which payment is made or sought that are relevant.

If your entitlement to widowed mother's allowance ends, or if you are not entitled to widowed mother's allowance, you may qualify for a **widow's pension**. This can be paid until you reach 65 if you satisfy the qualifying conditions.

Widows' benefits and retirement pension

If your husband died before 9 April 2001 and you are over pension age, you may be entitled to both retirement pension and either widow's pension or widowed mother's allowance. Because of the overlapping benefit rules, you cannot receive both benefits in full at the same time but see p132 of CPAG's *Welfare Benefits Handbook* 2000/01 if you are in this position.

You may qualify for retirement pension on the basis of being a widow (see Chapter 23). Once you qualify, your entitlement continues even if you remarry or form a civil partnership. Therefore, it may be financially beneficial to delay marriage or the formation of a civil partnership until after pension age (see p528).

Widowers whose wives died before 9 April 2001

If your wife died before 9 April 2001, you may be in a less favourable position than a woman whose husband died before 9 April 2001. This is because a woman whose husband died before 9 April 2001 may qualify for widows' benefits but you cannot. Although you can claim widowed parent's allowance, this can only be paid until you reach 65. In contrast, a woman in the same position could claim widowed mother's allowance, which is payable after pension age if the other qualifying conditions are met.

The fact that there were no widowers' benefits equivalent to the widows' benefits available to women has been challenged on the basis that it breached the non-discrimination principle contained in the European Convention on Human Rights.[38] For a discussion of the decisions in these cases and their consequences, see CPAG's *Welfare Rights Bulletin 198*. If you are over pension age, you may qualify for a Category B retirement pension based on your late wife's national insurance contribution record (see p527).

People who have obtained a gender recognition certificate

If you have obtained a full gender recognition certificate, your entitlement to bereavement and widows' benefits may be affected. (An interim gender recognition certificate does not affect your benefit entitlement.) The following is a summary of some of the rules. If you are likely to be affected, seek advice.[39]

- As you must dissolve or annul any existing marriage or civil partnership in order to obtain a full gender recognition certificate, you are not entitled to bereavement benefits on the basis of your ex-spouse's or former civil partner's contribution record, if s/he subsequently dies.
- If you were still married or in a civil partnership at the time of your spouse's or civil partner's death, you may qualify for bereavement benefits even if, after the death, you obtain a full gender recognition certificate. However, on the issue of a full certificate any entitlement to:
  - widow's pension ends;
  - widowed mother's allowance ends, but instead you qualify for widowed parent's allowance.
- See pp526 and 1247 for how your pension age is affected. In some circumstances, your pension age can be changed without you obtaining a full certificate.[40]

6. **Claims and backdating**

The rules about claiming and backdating are in Chapter 42. This section gives the specific rules that apply to bereavement benefits. To be entitled to bereavement benefits, you must usually make a claim (but see below for an exception).

Making a claim

If you were receiving retirement pension when your spouse or civil partner died, you do not need to make a claim in order to qualify for a bereavement payment. However, it is advisable to ensure that the DWP is aware of the death by telephoning the Pension Service (see Appendix 1).

If this does not apply, you must make a claim to qualify for a bereavement payment – and to qualify for widowed parent's allowance or bereavement allowance you must always make a claim. Your claim can be made:[41]

- by telephoning the DWP's Bereavement Service (tel: 0845 606 0265 or 0845 606 0275 for Welsh speakers; textphone: 0845 606 0285). After giving information over the telephone you are sent a statement to approve and sign. You return this to the DWP office that deals with claims in your area; *or*
- in writing, normally on the approved form (see p74). Send your claim form to the DWP office which covers your local area. You can obtain the address by telephoning Jobcentre Plus (see p74). Alternatively, if you have reached the qualifying age for pension credit (PC – see p509), you may also be able to take or send your claim to a designated local authority or English county council office or other 'alternative office' (see p1018).

If you claim in writing, you must complete the form in accordance with the instructions (keep a copy of your claim in case queries arise). If you claim by telephone, you must provide all the information needed to decide the claim (see p1019).

In certain circumstances, the decision maker may accept a written application which is not on the approved form (see p1019). You can amend or withdraw your claim before a decision is made (see p1019).

Forms

The BB1 form is the approved claim form for bereavement payment, widowed parent's allowance and bereavement allowance. When you register the death you are normally given a Certificate of Registration of Death. If you complete the form on the certificate and send it to the DWP, you should be sent a BB1 form. Alternatively, get Form BB1 by telephoning Jobcentre Plus (tel: 0800 055 6688 or 0800 012 1888 for Welsh speakers; textphone: 0800 023 4888) or complete a BB1 form online (follow the link from www.direct.gov.uk/en/moneytaxandbenefits). The online form cannot be submitted electronically, but must be printed off, signed and sent by post.

Who should claim

You must normally claim bereavement benefits yourself. However, bereavement benefits can be claimed by another adult on your behalf if you are not able to act for yourself. This person is known as your 'appointee' (see p1016).

Information to support your claim

When you claim bereavement benefits, you must:

- satisfy the 'national insurance number requirement' (see p1023). However, you do not have to do so if you qualify for only a bereavement payment and are not required to make a claim to receive it (see p73);
- provide proof of your identity, if required (see p1024);
- supply the information requested either on the claim form if your claim is in writing, or over the telephone if it is a telephone claim. If you do not, your claim might be 'defective' – ie, not valid (see p1019). If requested, you must also provide additional information and evidence relevant to your claim. There is a time limit for doing so (see p1022).

You will normally be expected to provide proof of your spouse's or civil partner's death. When you register the death you usually get an extra certificate for social security purposes, called a Certificate of Registration of Death. You can complete the back of the Certificate and send it to the DWP as proof, or provide a death certificate. If your claim is made through the Bereavement Service (see p73), or if you have reported the death to a local office under the 'Tell Us Once' arrangements (see p1047), you may not need to send such proof of the death to the DWP. (If you do not have proof of whether your spouse or civil partner has died, see p71.) You will also normally be expected to provide your marriage or civil partnership certificate.[42] A commissioner's decision has given guidance on assessing evidence from countries where reliable documentary proof of life events such as marriage may not be available.[43]

The date of your claim

The date of your claim determines the date from when you are paid widowed parent's allowance or bereavement allowance (see p77) and whether you qualify for a bereavement payment (if you are required to make a claim in order to qualify for a bereavement payment – see p73). The date of your claim is normally:[44]

- if you claim by telephone (see p73), the date of your telephone call; *or*
- the date your written claim is received at a DWP or Jobcentre Plus office (but see below); *or*
- if you have reached the qualifying age for PC (see p509) and submit your claim to a designated local authority, English county council or other 'alternative office' (see p1018), the date it is received by that office.

If your claim is 'defective' as you did not give all the information needed on the telephone or your claim form was not completed correctly, or if you made a written claim which was not on the correct form, you may be asked to provide further information or to complete the correct form. Provided this additional information or form is received by the DWP within a month of the DWP first telling you of the defect or of the DWP supplying you with the correct form (or longer if the decision maker thinks that the delay is reasonable), your claim can be treated as having been made on the date that the initial claim was received.[45]

In some circumstances, you can claim before you qualify for bereavement benefits (see p76) or the date of your claim can be backdated (see p76).

See p76 if you claim late because you did not know that your spouse or civil partner had died.

If you claim the wrong benefit

The decision maker may treat a claim for retirement pension as a claim for bereavement benefits.[46] This may help you qualify for a bereavement payment (although see p73 for when you can qualify for a bereavement payment without making a claim). A claim for retirement pension may also allow you to get your widowed parent's allowance or bereavement allowance backdated for more than the normal three months (see p76). However, you cannot get widowed parent's allowance or bereavement allowance for any period when you are over pension age. See p1025 for details of interchanging claims in this way.

Claiming in advance

You can claim bereavement benefits up to three months before you expect to qualify. In most circumstances, you will not know of your need to claim benefit in advance, but this may be relevant if, for example, you know that you will no longer be cohabiting.[47]

Backdating your claim

A claim for a **bereavement payment** must usually be made within 12 months of your spouse's or civil partner's death, unless:

- you were not aware that your spouse or civil partner had died (see below); *or*
- you are not required to make a claim in order to qualify for a bereavement payment (see p73).

There is no time limit for claiming **widowed parent's allowance** or **bereavement allowance**, and payment of these benefits can be backdated for up to three months before the date you make your claim, if you satisfy the qualifying conditions over that period. You do not need to show reasons why your claim was late (see p1026). If you were not aware of your spouse's or civil partner's death, you may be able to get your claim backdated further (see below). However, it is important to remember that bereavement allowance is only payable for the 52-week period running from the date your spouse or civil partner died.

If you might have qualified for benefit earlier but did not claim because you were given the wrong information or were misled by the DWP, you could ask for compensation (see p1261) or complain to the Independent Case Examiner or Ombudsman through your MP (see pp1256 and 1260).

See p75 if you claimed retirement pension instead of bereavement benefits.

If you were unaware of your spouse's or civil partner's death

If you were not aware that your spouse or civil partner had died (eg, if s/he had been missing), the time limit for claiming a bereavement payment and the normal three-month time limit on backdating of widowed parent's allowance and bereavement allowance can be extended.

If you claim within 12 months of your spouse's or civil partner's death

From 11 April 2005 (or for civil partners, from 5 December 2005), if:[48]

- your spouse's or civil partner's death has been difficult to establish but s/he has been found to have died or is presumed by the DWP to have died (whether or not her/his body has been found or identified); *and*
- you claim bereavement benefit within 12 months of the death or presumed death,

your claim can be backdated to the date s/he died or is presumed to have died, as long as you meet the other conditions of entitlement over that period.

If it is more than 12 months since your spouse or civil partner died

The time limit for claiming may be extended further if it is more than 12 months since your spouse or civil partner died, or since the date that s/he is presumed to have died, and *either:*

- her/his body has not been found or identified (or if it has, you were not aware of this when you asked the DWP decision maker to decide whether s/he had died); *and*
- the decision maker has decided that your spouse or civil partner has died or can be presumed dead; *and*
- you claim within 12 months of that decision;

or

- your spouse's or civil partner's body has been found or identified and you learn this within 12 months of the discovery or identification; *and*
- you claim within 12 months of finding out about her/his death.

In the former situation, bereavement benefits can be backdated to the date of death as determined by the decision maker. In the latter situation, bereavement benefits can only be backdated for a maximum of two years. This is because you must claim within 12 months of finding out about your spouse's or civil partner's death and, in turn, you must have learnt about your spouse's or civil partner's death within 12 months of her/his body being identified.[49]

7. Getting paid

Payment of a bereavement payment (which is a lump-sum one-off payment), widowed parent's allowance or bereavement allowance is normally made by direct credit transfer into your bank (or similar) account (see p1039). If you are unable to open or manage an account, the DWP may agree to pay you by cheque or 'simple payment' (see p1040). If you cannot act for yourself, bereavement benefits can be paid to someone else on your behalf, called your 'appointee' (see p1016).

When are widowed parent's allowance and bereavement allowance paid?	The day you are paid depends on your national insurance number.
How often are widowed parent's allowance and bereavement allowance paid?	Normally fortnightly in arrears. However, the DWP may choose to pay you weekly in advance or in arrears or, if you agree, every four or 13 weeks in arrears.[50]

If the amount of benefit to which you are entitled is less than £5 a week, the DWP decision maker can decide how often you are paid, although you must be paid at least once a year.[51]

If you qualify for widowed parent's allowance or bereavement allowance, payments run from the date your entitlement starts (which is normally the date of your claim – see p75).[52]

If your entitlement to widowed parent's allowance or bereavement allowance ends and you are paid in arrears, your benefit should be paid up to (and including) the last day on which you qualify for that benefit. If you are paid in advance and your entitlement ends, payment of benefit continues up to, but not including, the following payday. However, if your entitlement ends on a payday, your benefit is paid up to, but not including, that day.[53] Payments can be made for part weeks at the beginning and, if you are paid in arrears, at the end of your claim. The daily rate is calculated as one-seventh of the weekly rate of benefit.[54]

Note:

- Your widowed parent's allowance or bereavement allowance might be paid at a reduced rate in certain circumstances (see pp66 and 67).
- You might not be paid widowed parent's allowance or bereavement allowance if you have been sanctioned for benefit offences (see p1106).
- If you have forgotten your PIN or if a cheque is lost or stolen, see p1043.
- If payment of your bereavement benefit is delayed, see p1262. You might be able to get an interim payment (see p1046). You may also be eligible for a crisis loan (see p564). If you wish to complain about how your claim has been dealt with, see p1255. You might be able to claim compensation (see p1261).
- If payment of your widowed parent's allowance or bereavement allowance is suspended, see p1043.
- If you are overpaid a bereavement benefit, you might have to repay it (see Chapter 43). If you have been accused of fraud, see Chapter 44.

Change of circumstances

You must report changes in your circumstances which might affect your benefit (see p1047). Report such changes promptly either by writing to or telephoning the office handling your claim (unless the DWP has decided that you can tell it about the change another way). In some cases, the decision maker might say you must report changes in writing.[55] In practice, it is *always* advisable to report the change in writing or to confirm a telephone conversation in writing and keep a copy of your letter in case of a dispute in the future. If the change is a birth or a death, you may be able to report it in other ways (see p1047).

If a change of circumstances affects your entitlement to widowed parent's allowance or bereavement allowance, before your benefit can be stopped or adjusted, the decision maker should first revise or supersede the earlier decision on your entitlement (see Chapter 45).[56] The date from which a new decision takes effect following such a supersession normally depends on whether or not it is advantageous to you and whether you reported the change in time (see p1141).

8. Tax, tax credits and other benefits

A bereavement payment is not taxable. Widowed parent's allowance and bereavement allowance are taxable apart from any increase to widowed parent's allowance for children.[57]

Tax credits

A bereavement payment is ignored when calculating your entitlement to working tax credit (WTC) and child tax credit (CTC). Widowed parent's allowance counts as pension income for WTC and CTC (it may be possible to ignore some of your pension income – see p1337 for details). Bereavement allowance counts in full as benefit income (see p1333).

Means-tested benefits

A bereavement payment is counted as capital for all means-tested benefits. Widowed parent's allowance and bereavement allowance (less any tax payable on them) count as income. However:

- £10 of your weekly widowed parent's allowance is ignored when calculating your entitlement to income support (IS – see Chapter 17),[58] income-based jobseeker's allowance (JSA – see Chapter 19),[59] income-related employment and support allowance (ESA – see Chapter 10)[60] and pension credit (PC – see Chapter 22);[61]
- an increase in your widowed parent's allowance paid for a child is ignored when calculating your entitlement to PC and income-related ESA, and may be ignored when calculating your entitlement to IS and income-based JSA (see pp920 and 948);
- when calculating your entitlement to housing benefit (HB – see Chapter 14) and council tax benefit (CTB – see Chapter 8), £15 of your weekly widowed parent's allowance is ignored.[62] However, if you are getting both widowed parent's allowance and only the savings credit of PC, the income used to calculate your HB and CTB is that used by the DWP to calculate your entitlement to PC (which includes only a £10 disregard from your widowed parent's allowance);
- bereavement allowance is counted in full as income when calculating your entitlement to IS, income-based JSA, income-related ESA, HB, CTB and PC.

If your partner was entitled to HB when s/he died and you claim HB within a month of her/his death, your HB claim can be treated as having been made on the date your partner died (see p276). The same rule applies for CTB. In some circumstances your HB or CTB claim can be backdated further (see pp277 and 129).

Non-means-tested benefits

Your entitlement to non-means-tested benefits is not affected by your entitlement to a bereavement payment.

Widowed parent's allowance and bereavement allowance are affected by the overlapping benefit rules and so you may not get these benefits in full if another earnings replacement benefit is being paid to you (see p1041).

If you receive an increase in your widowed parent's allowance for a child or young person and you also receive child benefit or guardian's allowance, see p1043 for details of how the overlapping benefit rules may affect you.

Once you reach pension age, you may qualify for a Category A or B retirement pension on the basis of your late spouse's or civil partner's national insurance (NI) contribution record (see p527).

When your bereavement benefit stops, you may qualify for NI credits for contributory ESA and JSA (see p786).[63]

Passports and other sources of help

If you are entitled to widowed parent's allowance, you are also entitled to a Christmas bonus (see p9).

In some circumstances, you may qualify for a social fund grant for funeral expenses (see p576).

For advice about preparing funerals and registering deaths, see www.direct.gov.uk. Alternatively, consult the DWP leaflet DWP1027, *What to Do After a Death in England or Wales,* or the Scottish Government Civil and Law Division leaflet, *What to Do After a Death in Scotland.*

Notes

1. Bereavement payment

1 ss36 and 60(2) and (3) SSCBA 1992; regs 3(da) and 19(3A) SS(C&P) Regs
2 Reg 19(3A) SS(C&P) Regs
3 Reg 3(da) SS(C&P) Regs
4 s36(2) SSCBA 1992
5 Reg 4(2B) SSB(PA) Regs
6 Sch 4 Part II SSCBA 1992

2. Widowed parent's allowance

7 ss39A and 60(2) and (3) SSCBA 1992
8 ss39A(3), 77(5) and 122(5) SSCBA 1992
9 Reg 2(4) SSB(PRT) Regs
10 Arts 2(3)(b) and 3(3) Welfare Reform Act 2007 (Commencement No.7, Transitional and Savings Provisions) Order 2008, No.2101
11 Reg 16ZA SS(WB&RP) Regs
12 Reg 16ZA(2) SS(WB&RP) Regs
13 s39A(4), (4A) and (5) SSCBA 1992
14 ss80(5) and 81 SSCBA 1992; art 3 TCA(No.3)O; regs 4A(4) and 4B SSB(Dep) Regs
15 Reg 6(2) SS(WB&RP) Regs
16 Reg 6 SS(WB&RP) Regs

3. Bereavement allowance

17 ss39B and 60(2) and (3) SSCBA 1992
18 s39B(4), (4A) and (5) SSCBA 1992
19 ss39C and 44 SSCBA 1992
20 s39C(5) SSCBA 1992

4. Definition of terms

21 ss39A(4) and (4A) and 39B(4) and (4A) SSCBA 1992
22 R(G) 5/83; s3 Family Law (Scotland) Act 2006; The Family Law (Scotland) Act 2006 (Commencement, Transitional Provisions and Savings) Order 2006, No.212
23 But see *CAO v Bath*, *The Times*, 28 October 1999 (CA), reported as R(G) 1/00; R(G) 2/70
24 R(G) 1/71
25 CSG/7/1995; CSG/681/2003; but see also CSG/648/2007
26 s1 CPA 2004
27 *Hyde v Hyde* [1866]; reg 2 SSFA(PM) Regs
28 Reg 1(2) SSFA(PM) Regs
29 R(S) 2/92
30 s11(3) MCA 1973
31 R(G) 1/95
32 R(G) 1/93; R(P) 2/06
33 R(G) 2/63
34 R(G) 1/73
35 paras 10470-96 DMG
36 ss39A(5) and 39B(5) SSCBA 1992
37 CI/142/1949; R(I) 14/51

5. Special benefit rules

38 *Willis v United Kingdom*, No.36042/97, 11 June 2002, unreported (ECtHR); *Runkee and White v United Kingdom*, Nos.42949/98 and 53134/99, 10 May 2007, unreported (ECtHR)
39 ss4 and 5 and Sch 5 paras 3-5 GRA 2004
40 *Richards v SSWP*, C-423/04 [2006] ECR, unreported; R(P) 1/07; *Grant v United Kingdom*, No.32570/03, 23 May 2006, unreported (ECtHR); CP/3485/2003; R(P) 1/09; R(P) 2/09; CSP 503/2007; *Timbrell v SSWP* [2010] EWCA Civ 701

6. Claims and backdating

41 s1 SSAA 1992; reg 4(1), (6A), (6B) and (11) SS(C&P) Regs
42 Reg 7(1) SS(C&P) Regs
43 CP/4062/2004; see also CP/891/2008
44 Reg 6(1) and (1ZA) SS(C&P) Regs
45 Regs 4(7), (7ZA), (8), (12) and (13) and 6(1) SS(C&P) Regs
46 Reg 9(1) and Sch 1 Part I SS(C&P) Regs
47 Reg 13 SS(C&P) Regs
48 Reg 19(3B) SS(C&P) Regs
49 CG/7235/1995

7. Getting paid

50 Reg 22A SS(C&P) Regs
51 Reg 22(2) SS(C&P) Regs
52 Reg 22B(1) SS(C&P) Regs
53 Regs 16(2C)and 22B(3) and (4) SS(C&P) Regs
54 Reg 22B(6) SS(C&P) Regs
55 Reg 32(1)-(1C) SS(C&P) Regs
56 Reg 17 SS(C&P) Regs

8. Tax, tax credits and other benefits

57 ss577-79, 661 and 676 IT(EP)A 2003
58 Reg 40 and Sch 9 para 16(h) IS Regs

59 Reg 103 and Sch 7 para 17(e) JSA Regs
60 Sch 8 para 17(i) ESA Regs
61 Sch IV para 7 SPC Regs
62 **HB** Reg 40 and Sch 5 para 16 HB Regs; reg 29 and Sch 5 paras 7 and 8 HB(SPC) Regs
CTB Reg 30 and Sch 4 para 17 CTB Regs; reg 19 and Sch 3 paras 7 and 8 CTB(SPC) Regs
63 Reg 8C SS(Cr) Regs

Chapter 6

Carer's allowance

This chapter covers:

Key facts

- Carer's allowance (CA) is paid to people who care for someone who is severely disabled.
- CA is a non-means-tested benefit.
- You do not have to have paid national insurance contributions to qualify.
- You can qualify for CA whether you are in or out of work, but you must not earn more than £100 in a week.
- CA can be paid in addition to other benefits and tax credits, but the overlapping benefit rules may apply. CA counts as income for means-tested benefits.
- CA is administered and paid by the DWP's Carer's Allowance Unit.
- If you disagree with a CA decision, you can apply for a revision or a supersession, or appeal against it (see Chapters 45 and 46).

Future changes: April 2013 and after

Major changes are taking place that affect the benefits and tax credits system (see Chapter 2).

- From April 2013, total benefit payments to many working-age households will be 'capped' (see p25). There will be limited exceptions, including households in which someone is entitled to working tax credit or receives disability living allowance. CA will be included in the capped amount.
- You will still be able to claim CA when universal credit (UC) is introduced in October 2013. CA is *not* being abolished.

– From October 2013, if you claim UC, this will include an extra amount if you get CA and you will only be expected to look for work that is compatible with your caring responsibilities.
– When personal independence payment is introduced (see Chapter 3), the government intends that you will be able to qualify for CA if the person for whom you care gets either level of the daily living component.

See CPAG's *Welfare Rights Bulletin* for updates.

1. Who can claim carer's allowance

You qualify for carer's allowance (CA) if:[1]

- you are caring for a 'severely disabled person' (see below for the meaning). You do not have to be the person's relative, nor do you have to live with her/him;
- the care you give is regular and substantial (see below);
- you are not gainfully employed (see p85);
- you are not in full-time education. The rules for what counts are on p650;
- you are aged 16 or over;
- you satisfy the residence conditions (see p1433);
- you are not a 'person subject to immigration control' (see p1410).[2]

Who counts as a severely disabled person

In this chapter, when we refer to a 'severely disabled person' we mean a person to whom either attendance allowance (AA) or the highest or middle rate of disability living allowance (DLA) care component, or constant attendance allowance in respect of an industrial or war disablement (see p380) is payable.[3]

Note:[4]

- Only one person can qualify for CA for caring for the same disabled person. If you cannot agree on who this should be, the DWP decides.
- Even if you care for two or more disabled people, you can only qualify for one award of CA.

Regularly and substantially caring

To qualify for CA you must be engaged in 'regularly and substantially' caring for a severely disabled person. You satisfy this requirement during any week in which you are (or are likely to be) engaged and regularly engaged in caring for her/him *for 35 hours or more*.[5] For CA, a week runs from Sunday to Saturday.[6] Caring can include supervision as well as assistance. If some of the time is spent preparing for the disabled person to come to stay with you or clearing up after her/his visit, this can also count towards the 35 hours.[7]

Note:

- You cannot average the hours in one week with those in another – eg, if you care 35 hours or more in some weeks and less than 35 in others.[8] You must care for at least 35 hours in the week in question.
- If you are caring for two or more disabled people, you can only qualify for CA if you are caring for at least one of them for 35 hours or more a week.[9] You cannot add together the hours you are caring for all of them to make up the 35.

Breaks from caring

Once you have been caring for a severely disabled person for a while, temporary breaks in your caring do not lead to the loss of your CA. If you have been providing care for at least 35 hours a week in 22 of the last 26 weeks (or for at least 14 of the last 26 weeks, and the reason you did not provide care for 22 weeks was that either you or the disabled person were in hospital or in a similar institution), you can still qualify for CA. Weeks before you claimed CA can be counted. Effectively, you can have a four-week break from caring in any period of six months, or a 12-week break if one of you was in hospital or in a similar institution (see p675 for what counts) for at least eight weeks.[10] Note, however, that CA stops if the AA, DLA or constant attendance allowance of the person for whom you are caring stops because s/he is in hospital or in a similar institution (see Chapter 30).[11]

If the person receiving care dies

If the person you care for dies, you continue to be entitled to CA for a further eight weeks, although you are no longer providing care, as long as you satisfy the other qualifying conditions. The eight weeks run from the Sunday following the death, or from the day of the death if this was a Sunday.[12]

Gainfully employed

You cannot qualify for CA if you are 'gainfully employed'. You count as gainfully employed in a week (and cannot qualify for CA in that week) if your earnings in the previous week (from employment and/or self-employment) were more than £100.[13] For the way earnings are calculated, see p890. Your earnings are ignored if you are working during a period when you are not actually caring for the severely disabled person – eg, because s/he is in hospital or you are on a four-week break from caring (see above).[14]

2. **The rules about your age**

You can claim carer's allowance (CA) if you are aged 16 or over.[15] There is no upper age limit.

Age rules before 1994 and 2002

There has been no upper age limit for CA since 28 October 2002.

Between 28 October 1994 and 28 October 2002, the upper age limit for invalid care allowance (ICA) (now called CA) was 65. Before 28 October 1994, the upper age limit discriminated against women and some affected women may still be able to claim now.

Before 28 October 2002, to qualify for ICA after your 65th birthday, you had to have been entitled to it before you were 65. When you then reached 65, some of the qualifying conditions were relaxed. You may be able to continue to qualify on this basis now.

See p46 of the *Welfare Benefits and Tax Credits Handbook* 2010/11 for further information.

3. Claiming for others

You claim carer's allowance (CA) for yourself. You cannot normally claim any additions for your partner or children.

Increases for dependent children and adults

If you were entitled to an increase in your CA for a dependent child on 5 April 2003, or for an increase in your CA for a spouse/civil partner or someone who cares for your child on 5 April 2010, you may be able to continue to receive it (see pp745 and 740).

4. The amount of benefit

Carer's allowance (CA) is paid at a weekly rate of £58.45.[16]

If you are still entitled to an increase in your CA for an adult or child dependant, see pp745 and 746 for the amounts.

5. Special benefit rules

Special rules may apply if:

- you have come from or are going abroad (see Chapters 61 to 64);
- you, or the person you are caring for, are in hospital (see p678);
- the person you are caring for goes into a care home or other similar accommodation (see p687);
- you, or the person you are caring for, is a prisoner (see p691).

6. Claims and backdating

The rules on claiming and backdating are in Chapter 42. This section tells you about the specific rules that apply to carer's allowance (CA).

If you are claiming a means-tested benefit, see p91 before claiming CA, as the effect of CA on your other benefits (and possibly those of the person for whom you care) means it is not always advisable for you to claim it.

Making a claim

A claim for CA must be made in writing. You can do this by completing:

- the approved form. Send it to the Carer's Allowance Unit, Palatine House, Lancaster Road, Preston PR1 1HB. You may also be able to make your claim by taking or sending it to an 'alternative office' (see p1018); *or*
- an online application form at www.dwp.gov.uk/carersallowance.

Whichever procedure you follow, keep a copy of your claim form in case queries arise.

You must provide any information or evidence required (see below). In certain circumstances, the DWP may accept a written application not on the approved form (see p1019). You can amend or withdraw your claim before a decision is made (see p1019).

Forms

Get Form DS700 (DS700(SP) if you get retirement pension) from your local Jobcentre Plus office, DWP office or telephone contact centre or from www.direct.gov.uk/en/caringforsomeone or the Carer's Allowance Unit on 0845 608 4321 (textphone 0845 604 5312; text relay 18001 0845 608 4321) or the Benefit Enquiry Line on 0800 882200 (textphone 0800 243355).

Who should claim

You must normally claim CA on your own behalf. However, CA can be claimed by another adult on your behalf if you are unable to act for yourself – called your 'appointee' (see p1016).

Before claiming, you should be aware of how CA affects your entitlement to means-tested benefits and the means-tested benefit entitlement of the person for whom you care (see p91).

Information to support your claim

When you claim CA, you must:

- satisfy the 'national insurance (NI) number requirement' (see p1023);

- provide proof of your identity, if required (see p1024);
- supply information and evidence required with the claim (see p1019), and additional information and evidence relevant to your claim (see p1022). There is a strict time limit for doing so.

The CA claim forms contain a declaration to be completed by the person for whom you care or the person acting for her/him. This asks for confirmation that you provide 35 hours' care a week and explains that her/his benefit may be affected if your claim is successful. Even if this declaration is not completed, the DWP should still make a decision on your claim, although failure to return it is likely to lead to a delay in the decision and, if it raises questions about the level of care you provide, may result in a refusal of your claim.

The date of your claim

The date of your claim is important as it determines the date from which you are awarded CA. In some cases, you can claim in advance (see below) and sometimes your claim can be backdated (see p89). If you want this to be done, make this clear when you claim or the DWP might not consider it.

Your **'date of claim'** is usually the date on which your completed claim form is received by the DWP or a designated 'alternative office' (see p1018).[17] However, if you make a claim for CA in writing, but not on the approved form, or if the claim form you submit is incomplete, you may be asked to provide further information or to complete the approved form properly. As long as this additional information or the form is returned within a month of its being sent back to you (or longer if the decision maker thinks it is reasonable – see p1019), the decision maker must treat your claim as made on the date your initial written claim or form was received.[18] If you submit your claim online, your date of claim is usually the date it is received, although a decision maker has the discretion to treat it as having been received on an earlier or later date than this.[19]

If you claim the wrong benefit

If you claim income support (IS) when you should have claimed CA (either in addition to or instead of IS), a decision maker can treat your IS claim as a claim for CA (see p1025).[20] This applies even if you claim IS 'on the grounds of disability' (see p351) on or after 27 October 2008. This rule may enable you to get round the strict time limits on backdating (see p89).

Claiming in advance

You can claim CA up to three months before you qualify.[21] This gives the DWP time to ensure you receive benefit as soon as you are entitled. The decision maker can award benefit from a future date if s/he believes you will satisfy all the CA qualifying conditions on that date. You may want to consider claiming in advance – eg, if you are currently earning more than £100 a week, but you plan to stop work or reduce your hours.

Backdating your claim

It is very important to claim in time. A claim for CA can usually only be backdated for a maximum of three months.[22] You must satisfy the qualifying conditions over that period. You do not have to show any reasons why your claim was late. The general rules on backdating are covered on p1026.

Your claim can be backdated for more than three months if:[23]

- you claim CA within three months of a decision to award a 'qualifying benefit' to the person for whom you care (including a decision made by the First-tier Tribunal, the Upper Tribunal or a court). Your CA is backdated to the first day of the benefit week in which the qualifying benefit is payable. However, if the decision awarding the qualifying benefit was made following a renewal claim where a fixed period award has ended or is due to end, your CA is backdated to the first day of the benefit week in which the renewal award became payable; *or*
- your CA stopped because the 'qualifying benefit' of the person for whom you care was reduced or stopped (including where a fixed-term award for the qualifying benefit came to an end) or where payment of the qualifying benefit stopped because the person for whom you care goes into hospital, or is being provided with accommodation in a care home or other similar accommodation (see p684). If you make a further claim within three months of the decision to reinstate the qualifying benefit, or of payment starting again, your CA is backdated to the date that your earlier claim ended or the date from which the qualifying benefit was re-awarded or became payable again, whichever is later.

A **'qualifying benefit'** is either attendance allowance, the middle or highest rate disability living allowance care component or constant attendance allowance.

If you might have qualified for benefit earlier but did not claim because you were given the wrong information by the DWP or because you were misled by it, you could ask for compensation (see p1261) or complain to the Ombudsman via your MP (see p1260).

7. Getting paid

Payment of carer's allowance (CA) is normally made by direct credit transfer into your bank (or similar) account.[24] If you are unable to open or manage an account, payment can be made by cheque or by 'simple payment' (see p1040). If you are unable to act for yourself, CA can be paid to someone else on your behalf – called your appointee (see p1016).

When is CA paid?	On a Monday (or Wednesday if the person for whom you care receives constant attendance allowance with an industrial injuries benefit or war pension).[25]
How often is CA paid?	Weekly in advance or four-weekly in arrears (13-weekly in arrears if you agree).[26]

Payments normally run from the first payday (ie, Monday or Wednesday) after the date of your claim, unless the date of your claim is on your payday, when they run from that day.

Note:

- CA awards can be made for a fixed or indefinite period.[27]
- Deductions can be made from your CA to repay certain loans (see p1054), and in some cases to pay child support maintenance (see p1054).
- You might not be paid CA if you have been sanctioned for benefit offences (see p1106).
- If you have forgotten your PIN or if a cheque is lost or stolen, see p1040.
- If payment of your CA is delayed, see p1262. You might be able to get an interim payment (see p1046). You may also be eligible for a crisis loan (see p564). If you wish to complain about how your claim has been dealt with, see p1255. You might be able to claim compensation (see p1261).
- If payment of your CA is suspended, see p1043.
- If you are overpaid CA, you might have to repay it (see Chapter 43). If you have been accused of fraud, see Chapter 44.

Change of circumstances

You must report changes in your circumstances that might affect your benefit (see p1047). You should do this promptly in writing or by telephone to the Carer's Allowance Unit (although in individual cases notification might be accepted in a form other than in writing or by telephone).[28] In some cases, however, the decision maker might say you must report changes in writing. You can also notify your change of circumstances online at www.dwp.gov.uk/carersallowance.[29]

Although you may be able to report changes of circumstances by telephone or some other means, it is always best to report changes in writing. Keep a copy of the letter you send in case problems arise.

When there has been a relevant change of circumstances, a decision maker looks at your claim again and makes a new decision. To find out the date from which the new decision takes effect, see p1141.

8. Tax, tax credits and other benefits

Carer's allowance (CA) is taxable.[30] However, increases for children (if you are still receiving them) are not taxable.

Tax credits

CA counts in full as income for child tax credit (CTC) and working tax credit (WTC). Remember, however, that you cannot get CA if you are in gainful employment (see p85).

Means-tested benefits

Before you claim CA, consider how your claim might affect your entitlement (and that of the person for whom you care) to means-tested benefits. If in doubt, seek advice.

- If you receive CA, you come within one of the groups of people who can claim income support (IS).
- CA counts in full as income for all means-tested benefits.
- If you are a member of a 'joint-claim couple' claiming income-based jobseeker's allowance (JSA), you are not required to satisfy the jobseeking conditions (see p434) if you are a carer who can claim IS (see p348). You may wish to consider claiming IS or pension credit (PC) instead of income-based JSA.
- If you receive CA (or are entitled but do not receive it because of the overlapping benefit rules – see p1041), a carer premium/additional amount is included in your IS, income-based JSA, income-related employment and support allowance (ESA), PC, housing benefit (HB) and council tax benefit (CTB).
- CA counts as qualifying income for the savings credit of PC.
- If the person for whom you care gets one of the means-tested benefits, a severe disability premium/additional amount may be included in her/his IS, income-based JSA, income-related ESA, PC, HB or CTB. If you are entitled to and receive CA, her/his entitlement to that premium/additional amount can be affected (see p835). Bear in mind that the severe disability premium/additional amount is worth more than the carer premium/additional amount.
- For IS, income-based JSA, income-related ESA and, if you are under the qualifying age for PC, HB and CTB, if you choose *not* to claim CA and the DWP decides that you failed to apply for it deliberately, you may be treated as if you receive it (but see p933).
- For all means-tested benefits, if you give up your claim for CA, you can be treated as if you receive it if the DWP decides that you deliberately deprived yourself of it in order to qualify for, or increase your entitlement to, benefit for yourself or your family (but see pp933 and 953).

Non-means-tested benefits

For each week you receive CA, you can get national insurance credits (see p784).

CA is subject to the overlapping benefit rules, which means that you may not be paid CA in full if another earnings-replacement benefit (eg, retirement pension) is paid to you (see p1041).

Passports and other sources of help

If you get CA (or would get it but for the overlapping benefit rules), you are entitled to a Christmas bonus (see p9). You may be able to get help, support and services from your local authority; ask your social services department for a carer's assessment.

Notes

1. **Who can claim carer's allowance**
   1 s70 SSCBA 1992; regs 5 and 9(1) SS(ICA) Regs
   2 s115 IAA 1999
   3 s70(2) SSCBA 1992; reg 3 SS(ICA) Regs
   4 s70(7) SSCBA 1992
   5 Reg 4(1) SS(ICA) Regs
   6 s122 SSCBA 1992
   7 CG/6/1990
   8 R(G) 3/91
   9 Reg 4(1A) SS(ICA) Regs
   10 Reg 4(2) SS(ICA) Regs
   11 *SSWP v Pridding* [2002] EWCA Civ 306
   12 s70(1A) SSCBA 1992
   13 Reg 8(1) SS(ICA) Regs
   14 Reg 8(2) SS(ICA) Regs

2. **The rules about your age**
   15 s70(3) SSCBA 1992

4. **The amount of benefit**
   16 Sch 4 SSCBA 1992

6. **Claims and backdating**
   17 Reg 6(1)(a) and (1ZA) SS(C&P) Regs
   18 Reg 6(1)(b) SS(C&P) Regs
   19 Reg 4ZC and Sch 9ZC para 4(1) and (2) SS(C&P) Regs
   20 Reg 9(1) and Sch 1 SS(C&P) Regs
   21 Reg 13 SS(C&P) Regs
   22 Reg 19 SS(C&P) Regs
   23 Reg 6(16)-(22), (33) and (34) SS(C&P) Regs

7. **Getting paid**
   24 Reg 21 SS(C&P) Regs
   25 Reg 22(3) and Sch 6 SS(C&P) Regs
   26 Reg 22(1) SS(C&P) Regs
   27 Reg 17 SS(C&P) Regs
   28 Reg 32 SS(C&P) Regs
   29 Reg 32ZA SS(C&P) Regs

8. **Tax, tax credits and other benefits**
   30 ss660, 661 and 676 IT(EP)A 2003

Chapter 7

Child benefit

This chapter covers:

Key facts

- You may be entitled to child benefit if you are responsible for a child or qualifying young person.
- You do not need to be the child's parent to qualify for child benefit for her/him and the child does not need to live with you.
- Child benefit is paid for each child for whom you are responsible, with a higher amount payable for your eldest eligible child.
- Child benefit is a non-means-tested benefit.
- You do not need to have paid national insurance contributions to qualify.
- You can qualify for child benefit whether you are in or out of work.
- Child benefit is administered and paid by HM Revenue and Customs.
- If you disagree with a child benefit decision, you can apply for a revision or a supersession, or appeal against it (see Chapters 45 and 46).

Future changes: April 2013 and after

Major changes are taking place that affect the benefits and tax credits system (see Chapter 2).

– From April 2013, total benefit payments to many working-age households will be 'capped' (see p25). There will be limited exceptions, including households in which someone is entitled to working tax credit or receives disability living allowance. Child benefit will be included in the capped amount.

– You will still be able to claim child benefit when universal credit is introduced in October 2013. Child benefit is *not* being abolished.

See CPAG's *Welfare Rights Bulletin* for updates.

1. Who can claim child benefit

You qualify for child benefit for a child if:[1]

- s/he counts as a 'child' or 'qualifying young person' (see below). **Note:** in the rest of this chapter the term 'child' is used for both child and qualifying young person; *and*
- you are responsible for the child because *either*:
  - the child lives with you (see p100); *or*
  - you contribute to the cost of supporting the child (see p101) at a rate of at least the amount of child benefit for that child; *and*
- you have priority over other potential claimants (see p102); *and*
- you and the child satisfy the presence and residence conditions (including for you if you claim child benefit on or after 1 May 2004, the 'right to reside' test – see pp1435 and 1448); *and*
- you are not a 'person subject to immigration control', although there are exceptions to this (see p1410).

Note: from January 2013 if you pay the higher rate of income tax, any child benefit you or your partner receive may be withdrawn from you through additional income tax (see p112).

See p104 for details of when child benefit will not be paid.

If your child has died, see p112.

Who counts as a 'child'

Anyone aged under 16 is a **'child'** for child benefit purposes. Provided you meet the other qualifying conditions, child benefit can be paid for them, whether they go to school or not.[2] Child benefit can then continue be paid for a child after s/he reaches 16 for as long as s/he counts as a 'qualifying young person'.

Who counts as a 'qualifying young person'

A **'qualifying young person'** is someone who:[3]

- is aged 16 and has left relevant education (see p95) or training. In this *circumstance* s/he can count as a qualifying young person up to and including 31 August after her/his 16th birthday unless her/his birthday is on 31 August when s/he will count as a qualifying young person up to and including the day after her/his 16th birthday. (**Note:** HM Revenue and

Customs (HMRC) states that a young person whose 16th birthday falls on 31 August is only a qualifying young person up to and including that day, but arguably, this is not correct)[4]; *or*

- is aged 16 or 17, has left education or training and meets the conditions for being a qualifying young person during an 'extension period' (see p96); *or*
- is aged 16 or over and under 20 and:
  - is on a course of full-time non-advanced education (see p97) or on a course of approved training (see p98) and the course of education or training is not provided as result of her/his employment; *and*
  - began, or was enrolled or accepted on, that course before reaching 19 (but see p96 if s/he is aged 19 and see p99 for the interruptions in education or training that can be ignored); *or*
- is aged 16 or over and under 20 (but see p96 if s/he is aged 19) and has either:
  - finished a course of full-time non-advanced education (see p97) and is enrolled or accepted on another such course; *or*
  - finished a course of full-time non-advanced education or approved training (see p98) and is enrolled or accepted on a course of approved training.

  Neither course must be provided as a result of her/his employment; *or*
- is aged 16 or over and under 20 (but see below if s/he is aged 19) and has left relevant education (see below) or approved training and has not passed the end of the week that includes her/his 'terminal date' (this is also referred to in this chapter as the 'terminal date rule' – see p98).

If more than one of the above grounds apply to your child, s/he counts as a qualifying young person until the last date that applies.[5]

If child benefit for your child stops because s/he no longer counts as a qualifying young person, but s/he later becomes a qualifying young person once more, you can get child benefit for her/him again if you make a new claim (but see p99 if there is just a temporary interruption in meeting the above conditions).

In the rest of this chapter we use the term 'child' to mean both young people aged under 16 and qualifying young people aged 16 or over. See p100 for who cannot count as a qualifying young person.

Relevant education

Relevant education is defined as education that is full time and non-advanced. For the meaning of non-advanced education, see p98. In deciding if your child is in relevant education, HMRC considers that the definition of 'full time' given on p97 applies, but this is not actually stated in the legislation.

19-year-olds

A 19-year-old counts as a qualifying young person (and so you may qualify for child benefit for her/him) if any one of the last three bullet points listed on p95 applies to her/him.

If a young person is due to start a new course of full-time non-advanced education or approved training *after* reaching 19 and arrangements for the course mean that s/he is not able to enrol on it before becoming 19:

- consider approaching the course provider to see if s/he can be accepted on the course before her/his 19th birthday, so that s/he counts as a qualifying young person while on the course. If you meet the other qualifying conditions, you will then normally get child benefit for her/him while s/he is on the course until the end of the week that includes the first terminal date falling after the course or training ends (unless s/he is 20 before that date – see p98);
- if the above is not possible, the child will not count as a qualifying young person while on the new course (but see below if your child has been in continuous education). However, provided s/he is under 20:
  - s/he can count as a qualifying young person from the date s/he is enrolled or accepted on the course until the date the new course starts; *and*
  - arguably, s/he can count as a qualifying young person for a period after s/he leaves such a course under the 'terminal date rule' (see p98).[6]

If you satisfy the other qualifying conditions, but are refused child benefit for a 19-year-old in these circumstances, seek advice.

Note: HMRC states that if a 19-year-old has been in *continuous* full-time non-advanced education, s/he is treated as having begun a course before reaching 19, even if s/he started it after reaching 19 and was not enrolled or accepted on the course before reaching 19.

The extension period

If a child is 16 or 17 and has left education or training, s/he continues to count as a qualifying young person, and so child benefit can continue to be paid for her/him, during an **'extension period'** if:[7]

- s/he is registered as available for work, education or training with the Careers Service or a specified body; *and*
- s/he is not in remunerative work – ie, s/he is not working for 24 hours a week or more for payment, or in expectation of payment; *and*
- s/he is not in education or training. If s/he is, see p94, as you may still qualify for child benefit; *and*
- you were entitled to child benefit for her/him immediately before the extension period started; *and*
- you apply in writing (or by another method – eg, by telephone – if HMRC accepts this) within three months of the date your child's education or training finished.

In this context, 'education' and 'training' are not defined and so may mean any kind of part-time or full-time education or training.

The extension period starts from the Monday after your child's course of education or training ends and lasts for 20 weeks from that date. If your child reaches 18 during the extension period, unless s/he counts as a qualifying young person on another ground (see p94), your child benefit for her/him will end from the first child benefit payday on or after s/he reaches 18.[8]

If your child's ability to satisfy the above conditions is interrupted, see p99.

See p104 for circumstances when child benefit will not be paid.

Full-time non-advanced education

A child aged 16 or over but under 20 counts as a qualifying young person if:[9]

- s/he is attending a full-time course of non-advanced education which s/he either started, or was enrolled or accepted on before reaching 19 (but see p96); *or*
- having previously been on a course of full-time non-advanced education, s/he is enrolled or accepted on another such course.

For either of these circumstances to apply:

- the course must not be provided as a result of your child's employment or because of an office s/he holds (but see p99); *and*
- the course must either be provided:
  - at a school or college; *or*
  - elsewhere (such as at home) but only if a decision maker approves the education and s/he was being educated in this way before reaching 16.

If your child finishes a course of full-time non-advanced education before s/he is 20, you may still qualify for child benefit for her/him until the end of the week that includes the first terminal date after her/his course ends (or until s/he is 20 if this is earlier – see p98). You may also still qualify for child benefit for her/him if s/he counts as a qualifying young person on another ground (see p94).[10]

See p99 if your child's education is interrupted.

Full-time education

For the purpose of defining full-time non-advanced education, a course of education counts as full time if it is for an average of more than 12 hours a week during term time, including tuition, supervised study, exams and practical work, but excluding meal breaks and unsupervised study.[11]

'Supervised' study requires the close proximity of a teacher or tutor to enforce discipline, and provide encouragement and help.[12]

Examples of non-advanced and advanced courses[13]

Non-advanced courses	*Advanced courses*
GCSEs	a university degree
AS and A levels	NVQ level 4
NVQ and SVQ level 3 and below	Higher National Diploma (HND) or Higher National Certificate (HNC)
International Baccalaureate	Diploma of Higher Education
Scottish National Qualifications (up to higher or advanced higher level)	a teaching qualification
BTEC and OCR Nationals	SVQ level 4 and above

Approved training

A child aged 16 or over but under 20, counts as a qualifying young person if:[14]

- s/he is on a course of approved training, which s/he either started or was enrolled or accepted on before s/he reached 19 (but see p96); *or*
- s/he was on a course of full-time non-advanced education or approved training and is now enrolled or accepted on a course of approved training.

For either of these circumstances to apply the courses must not be provided under a contract of employment (but see p99).

Approved training is any of the following training courses:[15]

- in England, Foundation Learning courses or Access to Apprenticeships;
- in Scotland, Get Ready for Work or Skillseekers;
- in Wales, Skillbuild, Skillbuild+, Traineeships or Foundation Apprenticeships.

See p99 if your child's training is interrupted.

If your child leaves approved training before reaching 20, you may still qualify for child benefit for her/him until the end of the week which includes the first 'terminal date' after s/he leaves (or until s/he reaches 20 if that is earlier – see p99). You may also still qualify for child benefit for her/him if she counts as a qualifying young person on another ground (see p94).[16]

The 'terminal date rule'

If your child leaves relevant education (see p95) or approved training before reaching 20, s/he continues to count as a qualifying young person until either:[17]

- her/his 'terminal date' if this falls on a Sunday or until the first Sunday after her/his 'terminal date' (see p99); *or*
- if s/he reaches 20 on or before that date:
  - the Sunday on which her/his 20th birthday falls (if it falls on a Sunday); *or*
  - the Sunday before her/his 20th birthday (if it falls on a Monday); *or*
  - the first Sunday after her/his 20th birthday (if it falls on any other day).

Your child's '**terminal date**' is the first of the following dates that falls after the date her/his relevant education or approved training finished:

- the last day in February; *or*
- 31 May; *or*
- 31 August; *or*
- 30 November.

Note:

- If, after leaving a course of relevant education, a child returns to sit an external examination in connection with this course, s/he is treated as still being in relevant education until the date of the last exam, provided that s/he was entered for the exam before leaving the course.[18]
- A child who has taken the Higher or Advanced Higher Certificate in Scotland is treated as being in relevant education until the date a comparable course in England or Wales would end, if this is later.[19] This is because exams are often taken earlier in Scotland than in England and Wales.
- A child cannot count as a qualifying young person on the grounds of being on a course of full-time non-advanced education or approved training (or on the grounds of being enrolled or accepted on such a course) if the course is provided as a result of her/his job. However, as long as s/he is under 20, it may be arguable that s/he can count as a qualifying young person from the date s/he leaves such a course under the terminal date rule. This is because the rules on terminal dates do not exclude young people whose course was provided under an employment contract (but see p104 if your child is working).

Interruptions

Any break in a child being able to satisfy the conditions for being a qualifying young person can be ignored:[20]

- for up to six months (whether or not the interruption began before or after the child was 16) if it is found to be 'reasonable' in the circumstances; *or*
- indefinitely if it is caused by the child having a physical or mental illness or disability and the length of the absence is found to be reasonable given the circumstances.

In practical terms, this means a child can still be considered to be a qualifying young person during the interruption.

HMRC states that this rule should only apply when there is an interruption in a child's ability to attend a course of education or training – eg, due to ill health, but arguably, the rule can also apply to 16/17-year-olds during the extension period.

However, an interruption cannot be ignored if, immediately after the interruption, a child starts, or is likely to start:[21]

- a training course which is not 'approved training'; *or*

- a course of advanced education; *or*
- education connected to her/his employment.

Who does not count as a qualifying young person

A 16–19-year-old cannot count as a qualifying young person, and so you cannot receive child benefit for her/him, if s/he receives in her/his own right:[22]

- income support (see Chapter 17);
- income-based jobseeker's allowance (see Chapter 19);
- employment and support allowance (see Chapter 10);
- working tax credit (see Chapter 52) or child tax credit (see Chapter 51);
- incapacity benefit paid on the basis of her/his incapacity for work in youth (see Chapter 16).

Responsible for a child

You are only entitled to child benefit for a child if you are responsible for her/him. You count as responsible for a child in any week in which you:[23]

- have the child living with you (see below); *or*
- contribute to the cost of providing for the child (see p101).

A child 'living with' you

To be living with you, the child 'must live in the same house or other residence as [you] and also be carrying on there with [you] a settled course of daily living'.[24] This does not mean the same as 'residing together' or 'presence under the same roof'.[25] A child may be 'living with' you even while away. There are special rules if your child is looked after by a local authority (see p106).

Absence from home

If the child is absent from home, s/he is still treated as living with you as long as s/he has not been away for more than 56 days in the last 16 weeks.[26] When calculating whether a child has been absent from home for 56 days, certain days of absence are ignored. These are days when the child is away only to:[27]

- receive education or training (HMRC states that this rule applies only if the child is away receiving full-time non-advanced education or approved training); *or*
- stay in certain forms of residential accommodation, if this is necessary only because of the child's disability or because her/his health would be 'significantly impaired or further impaired' were s/he not staying in the accommodation (but see p101); *or*
- receive inpatient treatment in a hospital or similar institution (but see below).

In the latter two situations a maximum of 12 consecutive weeks' absence can be ignored, unless you are regularly incurring expenditure in respect of the child, when the period of absence can be ignored indefinitely.[28] (If you are making visits, or giving the child pocket money, this condition is likely to be satisfied.) Two or more periods in hospital or residential accommodation separated by 28 days or less are treated as one when calculating the 12-week period.

If the child's absence is not solely for one of the three reasons listed above her/his days of absence cannot be ignored and s/he will not count as living with you if s/he has been away for more than 56 days in the last 16 weeks.

However, even if a child is not living with you, you may still qualify for child benefit for her/him if you are contributing to the cost of supporting the child.

See p1435 if your child is abroad.

Example

Amy's son was in hospital for 18 weeks. She regularly took him food, drinks and comics. On being discharged, he stayed with his grandmother for a month to convalesce before returning home. Amy is entitled to child benefit for her son while he was away. He is treated as still living with her while in hospital as she was regularly incurring expenditure for him. He also counts as still living with her while staying with his grandmother as he was not considered to be absent from home for more than 56 days in the previous 16 weeks. The period he was in hospital is ignored when calculating the 56-day period.

Contributing to the cost of supporting a child

If a child is not living with you, you can still qualify for child benefit if you contribute to the cost of supporting her/him. To satisfy this condition you must contribute at least the amount of child benefit payable for the child (see p105).[29]

Note:

- Contributions must be regular, although the odd hiccup may be ignored.[30]
- Payments in kind rather than cash may be accepted.[31]
- If you reside with your spouse or civil partner, any contribution made by one of you may be treated as a contribution by the other.[32]
- If you and another person(s) each contribute less than the amount of child benefit payable for the child, but your total contributions are at least equal to the amount of child benefit payable, one of you is treated as contributing the whole sum. If you do not agree on which one of you it is to be, HMRC decides.[33] If you qualify for child benefit on this basis, once benefit has been awarded, you alone must actually contribute at least the amount of child benefit paid for the child in order to continue to be entitled.

Priority between claimants

Potentially, it is possible for more than one person to be entitled to child benefit for the same child – eg, when a child is living with one parent and maintained by the other. However, only one person can be awarded child benefit for a particular child. There is an order of priority which governs who receives child benefit when two or more people have claimed it and would otherwise be entitled.[34]

No one is entitled to child benefit without making a claim and the priority rules do not apply unless at least two people have claimed child benefit for the same child and both of them would qualify for it.[35] In this situation, claimants take priority in the following order:[36]

- a person with whom the child lives (who has priority over a person who counts as responsible for a child only because s/he is contributing to the cost of supporting the child);
- a wife, where a husband and wife are residing together (see p104);
- a parent (including a step-parent and adoptive parent). In this context a 'parent' means a child's 'legal parent', not just her/his biological parent. So it can also include someone who has 'legal parental responsibility' because a court has made a residence order in her/his favour in respect of the child under the Children Act 1989;[37]
- the mother (including a stepmother) where the parents are unmarried and are residing together (see p104);
- in any other case, a person agreed by those entitled;
- if there is no agreement, a person selected by a decision maker at HMRC (in which case there is no appeal against the decision[38] – but see p1159).

Even if a new claim takes priority over an existing claim, child benefit continues to be paid on the existing claim for the three weeks following the week in which the new claim is made, unless the existing claimant withdraws her/his claim before this or stops being entitled to child benefit for another reason.[39] In addition, even if your claim has priority, you normally cannot receive child benefit for a period before you made your claim during which it has already been paid to someone else for the same child (see p111).

If you have claimed child benefit but you want someone who has equal or lower priority to you to receive it instead, contact the Child Benefit Office (see Appendix 1).[40]

It may be important to concede priority if you spend periods abroad, as entitlement to child benefit normally stops if you have been abroad for more than eight weeks (or 12 weeks in some circumstances – see p1482).

Separation and the priority rules

Problems can arise when there are competing child benefit claims for a child from a mother and father who have just separated. If the mother was receiving child benefit before the separation and the child continues to live with her, she continues to be entitled to child benefit. If instead the child goes to live with the father, a commissioner's decision indicates that, provided he has made a valid claim for child benefit, his claim should have priority if:[41]

- he and the mother are no longer considered to be residing together. If their separation is permanent this should normally be from the date that they separate (see p104); *or*
- the mother either withdraws her child benefit claim or elects that he receive it instead; *or*
- the child is no longer treated as living with her/his mother (normally after s/he has been away from her for 56 days – see p100).

The legislation appears to suggest that, if the father and mother are no longer considered to be residing together, then for any period when the child is still treated as living with her/his mother and so both parents remain potentially entitled to child benefit, HMRC decides who receives child benefit if the parents cannot agree (under the priority rules on p102). However, the above commissioner's decision conflicts with this view and for similar cases is binding (see p1211).

Note: even if the father's claim has priority, the mother will continue to be entitled to child benefit instead of him for the three weeks following the week in which he makes his claim, unless she either withdraws her claim before this, or she stops qualifying for child benefit for another reason. Also, the father cannot normally receive child benefit for a period before he made his claim during which it has already been paid to the mother (but see p111 for exceptions to this rule).

Shared care

When the care of a child is shared between two parents who are both entitled to child benefit but cannot agree on who should receive it, HMRC must exercise its discretion to decide to whom it is reasonable to pay the benefit. This will usually involve considering which parent has the greater responsibility of care. In reaching its decision, HMRC might consider issues such as the number of hours each parent has responsibility for the child each week, the terms of any court orders, where the child's possessions are kept, at which address the child is registered with schools and doctors, the contributions each parent makes towards the cost of bringing up the child (although this may not be conclusive if the resources of one parent are greater than the other), and the impact that the decision might have on each parent. These are just examples of what might be considered, as each case will depend on its circumstances.

In reaching its decision, HMRC is also entitled to take into account the existence of other children of the relationship for whom child benefit is paid. For example, the High Court held that where two parents had nearly equal responsibility for the care of their two children, it was not unreasonable for the decision maker to decide that each parent should receive child benefit in respect of one child.[42]

'Residing together'

Whether a couple are 'residing together' (or 'residing with' each other)[43] may be important because, for example, if a married couple are residing together, the wife's claim has priority over the husband's, and if an unmarried couple are residing together, the mother's claim has priority.

If you are married, in a civil partnership or are a parent of a child, you and your spouse/your civil partner/the other parent of your child are still treated as residing together, even if you are apart, if:[44]

- your absence from each other is not likely to be permanent; *or*
- the reason for the absence is only because one or both of you is receiving care or treatment as an inpatient in a hospital or a similar institution (either of which is for people with mental health problems), whether this is likely to be temporary or permanent.

Even if you have not lived together, you can be treated as residing together if your absence from each other is not likely to be permanent.[45]

It is possible to be absent from one another while you are living under the same roof if you are maintaining separate households.[46]

When child benefit is not paid

You cannot get child benefit for a child if:[47]

- s/he is married, in a civil partnership or cohabiting , unless the child's spouse, civil partner or partner is in relevant education or approved training, or unless the child is not residing with her/his spouse or civil partner (see above). However, the child's spouse, civil partner or partner can never be the claimant even in these circumstances. (S/he counts as cohabiting if s/he is living with her/his partner as if they are husband and wife, or civil partners);[48] *or*
- in certain circumstances, s/he works for 24 hours a week or more (see below); *or*
- s/he is a 16–19-year-old and is receiving certain benefits (see p100); *or*
- s/he has spent more than eight consecutive weeks either:
  - in prison or other custody; *or*
  - being looked after by the local authority (but see p106).

16–19-year-olds who work

If your child is under 16, your entitlement to child benefit for her/him is unaffected by any work that s/he does.

If your child is 16 or over and only counts as a qualifying young person under the 'terminal date' rule (see p98), child benefit is not payable for her/him if s/he works for 24 hours or more a week if the work is done for payment, or in the expectation of payment. Also, a 16/17-year-old who does such work cannot count as a qualifying young person on the grounds of being in an extension period (see p96).[49]

However, if your child is a qualifying young person on any of the other grounds listed on p94, any work s/he does should not affect your entitlement to child benefit.

2. The rules about your age

There is no upper or lower age limit for entitlement to child benefit.

3. Claiming for others

Child benefit can be claimed for each child for whom you are responsible. No increase in child benefit is paid for any other dependants you have.

4. The amount of benefit

Child benefit is payable at the following weekly rates.[50] The government has stated that child benefit will remain frozen at the current levels until April 2014.[51]

	£pw
Eldest eligible child	20.30
Other children (each)	13.40

The higher rate of child benefit is normally paid for the eldest (or only) child in a family.[52]

If you live with your partner and each of you has children from a previous relationship for whom you receive separate child benefit, you will not both receive the higher rate of child benefit. Instead, the higher rate is paid to the person who has the eldest child. (In this context, 'partner' means spouse, civil partner or someone with whom you are living as if you were husband and wife or civil partners.[53])

5. Special benefit rules

Special rules may apply if:

- your child is being looked after by a local authority, or is in prison or detention (see below);
- you or your child are going or coming from abroad (see pp1435 and 1482);
- you are subject to immigration control (see p1410);
- you are in prison (see p693).

Prison, detention or looked after by the local authority

Special rules apply if your child is:[54]

- being looked after by a local authority and is provided with accommodation under the Children Act 1989 or the Children (Scotland) Act 1995 and at least part of the cost of either the accommodation or the child's maintenance is being paid out of local authority or public funds (but see below); *or*
- subject to a supervision requirement and living in residential accommodation under s44 of the Social Work (Scotland) Act 1968. (**Note:** although the child benefit rules refer to s44, it has been repealed and a supervision requirement is now made under the Children (Scotland) Act 1995); *or*
- in prison or another form of detention such as a detention centre or young offenders' institution, as a result of criminal proceedings or non-payment of a penalty which was imposed on conviction.

If any of these circumstances apply to your child and have done so for at least one day a week in the last eight consecutive weeks, you cannot be entitled to child benefit for her/him after the eight-week period. However, there are some exceptions to this rule.

We refer to children in the situations above as being 'looked after by the local authority', 'subject to a supervision requirement' and 'in prison' respectively.

Exceptions

- You are not excluded from entitlement to child benefit for a child on the grounds that s/he is being looked after by the local authority if the child is placed in residential accommodation by the local authority solely because s/he has a disability or because her/his health would be significantly impaired or further impaired were s/he not in the accommodation.[55] In these circumstances, however, see p100.
- As child benefit only stops after the child has been looked after by the local authority, subject to a supervision requirement or in prison for at least one day a week in the last eight consecutive weeks, if the child ceases to be in one of these situations for at least a week (ie, from Monday to Sunday), the eight-week period should start again if s/he is subsequently looked after by the local authority, subject to a supervision requirement or placed in prison once more.
- You continue to get child benefit after the first eight weeks as long as the child 'ordinarily' lives with you throughout at least one whole day each week

(which, in practice means at least two nights – see below) even if s/he is not actually at home in that particular week.[56]

- After the first eight weeks' absence, even if the child continues to be looked after by the local authority, subject to a supervision requirement or in prison and does not 'ordinarily' live with you for at least one day a week, you still qualify for child benefit when the child comes to stay with you if s/he comes to stay for a week or more.[57]
- If the child is detained in a hospital or a similar institution because of mental health problems, s/he is treated as if she is in prison only if s/he was taken there from prison or another place of detention, and the date that s/he would have been expected to be released under her/his sentence has not passed. Otherwise, s/he is not considered to be in prison and so you can continue to get child benefit, provided you meet the normal qualifying conditions.[58]
- If the child has been detained in custody but, at the conclusion of criminal proceedings, is not sentenced to a term of imprisonment or detention, or detention and training, you are entitled to child benefit for her/him for the period of her/his earlier detention.[59]

A **'week'** means seven days beginning with a Monday.[60] A **'day'** means from midnight to midnight.[61] Because the child must live with you 'throughout' the day,[62] this means that, in practice, s/he has to stay with you for two nights to be regarded as living with you for one day.

Fostering and adoption

- *You* cannot qualify for child benefit for a child if, for any day in a week, the local authority has arranged for the child to be placed with you under placement, looking after or fostering arrangements and the local authority is paying you an allowance towards the cost of her/his accommodation or maintenance under ss22C(10) or 23 of the Children Act 1989 or reg 33 of the Looked After Children (Scotland) Regulations 2009.[63]
- *No one* can qualify for child benefit for a child if s/he has been placed for adoption in the house of her/his prospective adopters and the local authority is making a payment for the child's accommodation or maintenance under the above provisions.[64]

If these circumstances do not apply (eg, if the local authority is not making payments under the above provisions), the normal rules on entitlement apply, including the rules on children who are being looked after by the local authority described on p106 (and the exceptions to these rules described on p106).

Your entitlement to child benefit is not affected if you are looking after a child under private fostering arrangements.

6. Claims and backdating

The detailed rules about claiming and backdating are in Chapter 42. This section tells you about the specific rules that apply to child benefit.

Making a claim

A claim for child benefit should be made in writing. You can do this by completing:

- the approved form; *or*
- the approved online form at www.hmrc.gov.uk/forms/ch2-online.pdf which can be completed online, printed, signed and sent by post.

Send your claim to the Child Benefit Office (see Appendix 1). Alternatively, if your claim is made immediately following the birth of the child, you may be able to submit your claim through a specified local office under the 'Tell Us Once' scheme. Details should be available when you register the birth.

Keep a copy of your claim form in case queries arise. You must provide any information and evidence required (see below). HM Revenue and Customs (HMRC) has the discretion to accept claims made in another way. However, as it is unlikely to accept any claim not made in writing, it is always best to claim in writing, using the approved form whenever possible (see p1019).[65] You can amend or withdraw your claim before it is assessed (see p1019).

Forms

The approved form is Form CH2, which you can get from the Child Benefit Office (see Appendix 1) or from www.direct.gov.uk.

Who should claim

You must normally make a claim for child benefit yourself. However, child benefit can be claimed by another adult on your behalf if you are unable to act for yourself. This person is known as your 'appointee' (see p1016).

If someone else makes a claim on her/his own behalf for child benefit for the same child, you are only entitled to child benefit for that child if you have priority over the other claimant. See p102 for details of priority between claimants.

Information to support your claim

When you claim child benefit you must:

- satisfy the 'national insurance (NI) number requirement' (see p1023);
- provide proof of your identity, if required (see p1024);
- supply information requested on the claim form. If you do not, your claim might be 'defective' – ie, not valid (but see p1019). If requested, you must also

provide additional information and evidence relevant to your claim (see p1022). There is a time limit for doing so.

HMRC usually needs to see an original copy of your child's birth or adoption certificate. You can either send this to the Child Benefit Office or take it to your local HMRC enquiry centre or Jobcentre Plus office, where a copy can be made and verified and the verified copy can be sent to the Child Benefit Office.[66] If your claim is made through a local office under the 'Tell Us Once' scheme (see p108), you do not need to send your child's birth certificate to HMRC.

The date of your claim

The date of your claim is important as it determines the date from which you will be paid (see p110). The date of your claim is normally the date it is received at the Child Benefit Office. If HMRC has stated, in writing, that another office can receive child benefit claims (eg, in certain circumstances offices operating under the 'Tell Us Once' scheme – see p108), the date of claim can be the date the claim is received by that office.[67]

If the claim form you submit is not completed correctly or you make a written claim which is not on the approved form, you may be asked to provide further information or to complete the approved form. Provided this additional information or form is received by the Child Benefit Office (or by any other office that HMRC has stated in writing can receive it) within one month of it being sent back to you (or longer if the decision maker thinks the delay is reasonable), your claim is treated as made on the date the initial claim was received.[68]

In some circumstances, you can claim before you qualify for child benefit (see below), or the date of your claim can be backdated (see p110).

If you claim the wrong benefit

The decision maker has the discretion to treat a claim for guardian's allowance (see Chapter 12) as a claim for child benefit for the same child.[69] If your guardian's allowance claim is accepted as a claim for child benefit, your child benefit can be backdated for up to three months before the date you claimed guardian's allowance, if you satisfy the qualifying conditions for child benefit over that period. However, see p111 if someone else has been getting child benefit for the child. See p1025 for further details of interchanging claims in this way.[70]

Claiming in advance

If you do not qualify for child benefit when you make your claim but will qualify for it within the three months after your claim is made, the decision maker has the discretion to award child benefit in advance and can treat your date of claim as the date you start to qualify for child benefit.[71]

Backdating your claim

You should make a claim for child benefit within three months of becoming entitled to it. If you claim late, you can only receive up to three months' arrears (although there are special rules if you were getting child benefit and move between Great Britain and Northern Ireland or if you have been recognised as a refugee – see p1423).[72] You do not have to show any reason why your claim was late. However, if someone else who is also entitled to child benefit for the same child has already been receiving it, you are not entitled to arrears. Instead, if your claim takes priority (see p102), you will be paid child benefit from the fourth week after the week in which you claim, unless the other person withdraws her/his claim before this (but see p111 if someone else has already been paid child benefit for the same child).[73]

If you might have qualified for child benefit earlier but did not claim because you were given the wrong information or misled by the DWP or HMRC, you could ask for compensation (see p1261) or complain to the Ombudsman through your MP (see p1260).

See p109 for when a claim for another benefit can be treated as a claim for child benefit.

7. Getting paid

Child benefit is normally paid by direct credit transfer into your bank (or similar) account (see p1039). If you are unable to open or manage an account, HM Revenue and Customs (HMRC) may agree to make payments by cheque (see p1040). If you are unable to act for yourself, child benefit can be paid to someone else on your behalf (called your appointee – see p1016).

When is child benefit paid?	Normally on a Monday (or on a Tuesday), although the decision maker has discretion to choose any day of the week as your normal payday.
How often is child benefit paid?	Normally four-weekly: three weeks in arrears and one week in advance.[74]

In some circumstances, weekly payments of child benefit can be made – eg, if:[75]

- you are a lone parent; *or*
- you or your spouse/civil partner or partner are getting income-based jobseeker's allowance, income support, income-related employment and support allowance or pension credit. (Your partner is someone with whom you live as if you were husband and wife or civil partners); *or*
- the decision maker is satisfied that four-weekly payment 'is causing hardship'.

Child benefit is a weekly benefit, which means that it cannot be paid for periods of less than a week. If you qualify for child benefit, your benefit is paid from the Monday after the date of your claim (see p109), unless the date of your claim is a Monday, when payment should begin from that day.[76] As your date of claim can be backdated for up to three months, if you claim within three months of your child's birth and you satisfy the qualifying conditions, child benefit is normally paid from the Monday on which your child was born if s/he was born on a Monday, or from the Monday after her/his birth.

If you are making a claim for child benefit for a child and someone else is already getting child benefit for that child, you will only receive child benefit if your claim has priority over that of the existing claimant (see p102). In these circumstances, your benefit normally starts from the beginning of the fourth week after the week in which you claim, unless the existing claimant withdraws her/his claim before this or stops qualifying for child benefit for another reason. However, even if your claim has priority, you cannot get child benefit for a period before your claim was made if it has already been paid to someone else for the same child for that period, unless:[77]

- the decision maker (or, if the decision has been made following an appeal, the First-tier Tribunal or Upper Tribunal) has decided that the child benefit paid is recoverable because the person has failed to disclose or misrepresented a material fact (see p1069) and no appeal against that decision has been made within the time limit; *or*
- the child benefit has been repaid.

If your entitlement ends, payment of child benefit normally continues up to, but not including, the following Monday. However, if your entitlement ends on a Monday your benefit is normally paid up to, but not including, that day.

Note:

- Even if you have been sanctioned for benefit offences, you must be paid your child benefit.
- If you have forgotten your PIN or if a cheque is lost or stolen, see p1043.
- If payment of your child benefit is delayed (see p1262), you might be able to get an interim payment (see p1046). You may also be eligible for a crisis loan (see p564). If you wish to complain about how your claim has been dealt with, see Chapter 50. You might be able to claim compensation (see p1261).
- If payment of your child benefit is suspended, see p1043.
- If you are overpaid child benefit, you might have to repay it (see Chapter 43). If you have been accused of fraud, see Chapter 44.

Change of circumstances

You must report any change in your circumstances that might affect your benefit (see p1047).[78] Report such changes promptly by writing to the Child Benefit Office. If you have reported a change verbally or to another office that HMRC has specified in writing can receive such notifications, in some circumstances this may be sufficient.[79] However, in this situation it is advisable to make a note of the time and date of your conversation, the name of the person you informed and confirm your conversation promptly in writing to the Child Benefit Office, keeping a copy of your letter in case problems arise.

You can also report changes of circumstances online by using one of the forms available on HMRC's website (see Appendix 1).

Child benefit is normally awarded for an indefinite period (unless your circumstances are likely to change shortly after the award). In order for payment of child benefit to be stopped or adjusted, the decision on your entitlement must first be revised or superseded (see Chapter 45).[80] If, following a change in your circumstances, the decision on your claim is superseded and your entitlement to benefit is affected, the date from when the new decision takes effect depends on whether or not it is advantageous to you and whether you reported the change in time (see p1141 for further details).

If your child dies

If your child dies and you were entitled to child benefit for her/him in the week in which s/he died (or you would have been had s/he not died in the same week s/he was born), child benefit will continue to be paid for the following eight weeks, or until the Monday after s/he would have been 20, if this falls within the eight-week period. If your partner got child benefit for the child and s/he also dies, you are entitled to child benefit for the eight-week period. This only applies if you were living with your partner at the time s/he died. In this context, 'partner' means your spouse, civil partner or someone with whom you were living as husband and wife or as civil partners.[81]

8. Tax, tax credits and other benefits

Child benefit and higher rate taxpayers

The government has announced plans to tax some people's child benefit from January 2013. At the time of writing, details of these plans were being reconsidered. The following information is therefore likely to change.

Until January 2013, child benefit is not taxable.[82]

From January 2013, if you (or your partner, if you live with your partner) are a higher rate taxpayer, the government plans to withdraw your child benefit through additional income tax. If neither of you are higher rate taxpayers, your child benefit remains untaxed. (On 2012/13 rates, higher rate tax payers are usually those who earn £42,476 or more a year.)

If you or your partner are thinking of ending your child benefit claim because of this, this may affect any entitlement to credited national insurance (NI) contributions (see p779). See CPAG's *Welfare Rights Bulletin* for updates.

Tax credits

Child benefit is ignored when calculating your entitlement to tax credits.[83]

Means-tested benefits

Means-tested benefits can be paid in addition to child benefit.

Any child benefit you get is ignored when calculating your entitlement to income support (IS) and income-based jobseeker's allowance (JSA).[84] However, this is subject to an exception (see p919 for when child benefit is taken into account).[85]

Child benefit is ignored when calculating entitlement to employment and support allowance, pension credit, housing benefit and council tax benefit.[86]

Non-means-tested benefits

If you get an increase in a non-means-tested benefit for a child, the increase will be reduced if you also receive child benefit for that child paid at the rate for the eldest eligible child – ie, £20.30 (see p1043). Increases for children were abolished on 6 April 2003, but some people continue to receive them (see p745).

If you get child benefit for a child aged under 12 or, in some circumstances, if you reside with someone who does or are a family member providing care for the child, you can qualify for NI credits (see pp781 and 783). You may also be able to build up entitlement to additional state pension see p537).

Your entitlement to any other non-means-tested benefit is not affected by your entitlement to child benefit.

Passports and other sources of help

For details of the qualifying conditions for free school lunches, see p14.

Children and young people under 19 may qualify for health benefits (see Chapter 13). Young people between the ages of 16 and 19 who are in non-advanced education may qualify for financial help with their studies (see p15).

Notes

1. **Who can claim child benefit**

1 ss141, 142, 143, 144, and 146 SSCBA 1992; s115 IAA 1999; reg 23 CB Regs
2 s142(1) SSCBA 1992
3 s142(2) SSCBA 1992; regs 2-7 CB Regs
4 CBTM 07030; reg 4(3) CB Regs
5 Reg 2(2) CB Regs
6 As there is no requirement in the terminal date rules that a course must be started before the age of 19.
7 Reg 5 CB Regs
8 Reg 14 CB&GA(Admin) Regs; reg 5(3) CB Regs
9 Reg 3CB Regs
10 Regs 2(2), 3, 4, 5, 6 and 7 CB Regs
11 Reg 1(3) CB Regs
12 R(F) 1/93, but see also *Flemming v SSWP* [2002] EWCA Civ 641, reported as R(G) 2/02; *SSWP v Deane* [2010] EWCA Civ 699
13 Reg 1(3) CB Regs
14 Reg 3(2)(c), (d) and (4) CB Regs
15 Reg 1(3) CB Regs
16 Regs 2(2) and 7 CB Regs
17 Reg 7(1) and (2) CB Regs
18 Reg 7(2)2.1 CB Regs
19 Reg 7(2)1.3 CB Regs
20 Reg 6(2) and (3) CB Regs
21 Reg 6(4) CB Regs
22 Regs 2(4) and 8 CB Regs
23 s143 SSCBA 1992
24 R(F) 2/81
25 R(F) 2/79
26 s143(2) SSCBA 1992
27 s143(3) SSCBA 1992; reg 9 CB Regs
28 s143(3)(b) and (c) and (4) SSCBA 1992; reg 10 CB Regs
29 s143(1)(b) SSCBA 1992
30 R(U) 14/62
31 R(U) 3/66
32 Reg 11(4) CB Regs
33 Reg 11 CB Regs
34 s144(3) and Sch 10 SSCBA 1992
35 s13(1) SSAA 1992
36 Sch 10 SSCBA 1992
37 s147(3) SSCBA 1992; R(F)1/08
38 Sch 2 para 4 SSA 1998
39 Sch 10 para 1 SSCBA 1992
40 Regs 14 and 15 CB Regs
41 CF/1771/2003
42 *R (on the application of Ford) v Board of Inland Revenue* [2005] EWHC Admin 1109, 19 May 2005; see also *R (Chester) v Secretary of State for Social Security* [2001] EWHC Admin 1119, 7 December 2001, unreported
43 *Grove v Insurance Officer*, reported as an appendix to R(F) 4/85
44 s147(4) SSCBA 1992; regs 1(3) and 34 CB Regs
45 R(F) 4/85
46 R(F) 3/81
47 Sch 9 paras 1 and 3 SSCBA 1992; regs 8, 12, 13 and 16 CB Regs
48 But see *KW v HMRC (CHB)* [2011] UKUT 489 (AAC)
49 Regs 1(3), 5(2)(c) and 7(3) CB Regs

4. **The amount of benefit**

50 Reg 2(1) CB(R) Regs
51 *Budget Report*, June 2010, para 2.47
52 Reg 2(1) CB(R) Regs
53 Reg 2(2) CB(R) Regs

5. **Special benefit rules**

54 s147(2) and Sch 9 para 1 SSCBA 1992; regs 16-19 CB Regs
55 Regs 9 and 18(b) CB Regs
56 Reg 16(1)(b)(iv) CB Regs
57 Reg 16(1)(b)(i)-(iii) CB Regs
58 Reg 17(2)-(5) CB Regs
59 Regs 1(3) and 17(1) CB Regs
60 s147(1) SSCBA 1992
61 R(F) 3/85
62 Reg 16(2) CB Regs
63 Reg 16(3) CB Regs
64 Reg 16(4) and (5) CB Regs

6. **Claims and backdating**

65 Reg 5 CB&GA(Admin) Regs
66 Regs 3(2) and 5(5) CB&GA(AA) Regs
67 Reg 5(3) CB&GA(Admin) Regs
68 Reg 10 CB&GA(Admin) Regs
69 Reg 11 CB&GA(Admin) Regs
70 See also reg 9(2)and Sch 1 SS(C&P) Regs
71 Reg 12 CB&GA(Admin) Regs
72 Reg 6 CB&GA(Admin) Regs
73 Sch 10 para 1 SSCBA 1992

7. **Getting paid**

74 Reg 18(2) CB&GA(Admin) Regs
75 Regs 18(3), 19 and 20(1) and (2) CB&GA(Admin) Regs
76 Reg 13 CB&GA(Admin) Regs
77 Sch 10, para 1 SSCBA 1992; s13(2) SSAA 1992; reg 38 CB Regs; CF/2826/2007
78 Reg 23 CB&GA(Admin) Regs
79 For a change notified before 1 January 2010, see *WW v HMRC (CHB)* [2011] UKUT 11 (AAC)
80 Reg 15 CB&GA(Admin) Regs
81 s145A SSCBA 1992; reg 20 CB Regs

8. **Tax, tax credits and other benefits**

82 s677 IT(EP)A 2003
83 Reg 7 TC(DCI) Regs
84 Sch 9 para 5B IS Regs; Sch 7 para 6B JSA Regs
85 Reg 40 IS Regs; reg 103 JSA Regs; regs 1, 7 and 8 SS(WTCCTC)(CA) Regs
86 **ESA** Reg 104(2) and Sch 8 para 7(2) ESA Regs
PC Regs 9 and 15(1)(j) SPC Regs
HB Reg 40 and Sch 5 para 65 HB Regs; regs 27 and 29 HB(SPC) Regs
CTB Reg 30(2) and Sch 4 para 66 CTB Regs; regs 17 and 19(1)(j) CTB(SPC) Regs

8

Chapter 8

Council tax benefit

This chapter covers:

The rules for council tax benefit (CTB) are often the same as for housing benefit (HB). In this chapter, where the rules are the same or similar, reference is made to Chapter 14. Footnotes in that chapter contain references to both the HB and CTB legislation where applicable.

Key facts

- Council tax benefit (CTB) is paid to people with a low income who pay council tax.
- There are two types of CTB: **'main CTB'**, based on your council tax liability and your assumed needs and resources, and **'alternative maximum CTB'**, known as second adult rebate. This is not based on your needs or resources, but on the circumstances of certain other adults ('second adults') living with you.
- If you are eligible for both types of CTB, you are paid whichever is the higher.
- CTB is a means-tested benefit.
- You do not have to have paid national insurance contributions to qualify.
- You can qualify for CTB whether or not you are in or out of work.
- If you need extra financial assistance to meet housing costs (including council tax), you can claim discretionary housing payments to top up your CTB.
- CTB is administered and paid by local authorities, although it is a national scheme and the rules are mainly determined by DWP regulations.
- If you disagree with a CTB decision, you can apply for a revision or a supersession, or appeal against it (see Chapters 45 and 46).

Future changes: April 2013 and after

Major changes are taking place that affect the benefits and tax credits system (see Chapter 2).

- From April 2013, CTB will be localised – ie, local authorities will have their own schemes for help with council tax. This is likely to be in the form of a council tax discount.
- From April 2013, total benefit payments to many working-age households will be 'capped' (see p25). There will be limited exceptions, including households in which someone is entitled to working tax credit or receives disability living allowance. It is not yet known if the localised help with council tax will be included in the capped amount.

See CPAG's *Welfare Rights Bulletin* for updates.

1. Who can claim council tax benefit

You qualify for council tax benefit (CTB) if:[1]

- you are liable for council tax for the home where you are 'resident' (see p119); *and*
- you satisfy the 'right to reside test' and the 'habitual residence test' (see Chapter 62); *and*
- you are not a 'person subject to immigration control' (see p1410). There are exceptions to this rule.

In addition, you must satisfy extra rules. For main CTB, see below. For second adult rebate, see p118.

If you are at least the qualifying age for pension credit

The CTB rules for people who are at least the qualifying age for pension credit (PC – see p509) who are not (and whose partners are not) on income support (IS), income-based jobseeker's allowance (JSA) or income-related employment and support allowance (ESA) are different (and more generous) than those for other claimants. When you reach the qualifying age for PC, check to see if you qualify for CTB, even if you did not do so before that age. The different rules for income, capital and applicable amounts are covered in other chapters.

Main council tax benefit

To qualify for main CTB, in addition to satisfying the rules that apply to both types of CTB (see above):[2]

- your income must be low enough (see Chapter 40); *and*

- unless you or your partner are getting the guarantee credit of PC, your savings and other capital must be worth £16,000 or less (see Chapter 41). There is no capital limit if you or your partner are getting the guarantee credit of PC;[3] *and*
- you must not be a full-time student (although there are limited exceptions – see p647).[4] This rule does not apply if you are at least the qualifying age for PC (see p509) and neither you nor your partner are getting IS, income-based JSA or income-related ESA.

Second adult rebate

Second adult rebate is an alternative type of CTB, designed to help you if you share your home with anyone on a low income who does not share liability for council tax with you and who does not pay you rent (referred to as a second adult).

To qualify for a second adult rebate, in addition to satisfying the rules that apply to both types of CTB (see p117):[5]

- you must be the only person liable for the council tax on the home where you are 'resident' (with certain exceptions – see p119); *and*
- no one living in your home can be liable to pay you rent (for the exceptions, see p119); *and*
- you must have one or more 'second adults' (see below) living with you who are on a low income.

Note: second adult rebate is based on the circumstances of the 'second adult(s)' living with you. The whole of *your* income and capital is ignored when you claim second adult rebate. So you can get it even if *you* have a high income and/or capital worth more than £16,000.[6]

For second adult rebate it does not matter if you are a student.

Who counts as a second adult

You must have at least one 'second adult' residing with you to qualify for second adult rebate. In practice, second adults are mainly the same people as those treated as non-dependants for main CTB purposes (see p123). However, someone residing with you does *not* count as a second adult if s/he:[7]

- is aged under 18;[8] *or*
- has a 'status discount' (and is ignored for council tax purposes) – eg, full-time students and people who are severely mentally impaired;[9] *or*
- is your partner with whom you are jointly liable for council tax;[10] *or*
- is jointly liable to pay the council tax with you – eg, s/he is a joint owner or tenant. Although you cannot get second adult rebate for her/him, s/he may be able to claim CTB for her/his own share of the bill.[11]

No one who resides with you counts as a second adult (and you therefore cannot get second adult rebate) if you are:

- a member of a couple or polygamous marriage, unless both you and your partner (or in the case of a polygamous marriage, at least two of the members) have status discounts;[12] *or*
- living with one or more other people, all of whom are jointly liable for council tax with you (eg, as joint owners or tenants) and at least two of those who are jointly liable do *not* have status discounts.[13]

Residents liable to pay rent

You cannot qualify for second adult rebate if a second adult is liable to pay you rent for occupying your home. Any people paying you rent who do not count as second adults are ignored for these purposes.[14] Some local authorities say that you are not entitled to second adult rebate if *any* resident is liable to pay you rent. If this affects you, argue that if a person paying you rent does not come within the description of a second adult, s/he does not prevent you receiving second adult rebate.

Liability to pay council tax

See CPAG's *Council Tax Handbook* for the rules about who is liable to pay council tax. If you are jointly liable, this may affect the amount of main CTB or second adult rebate you receive (see pp123 and 128).

Where you are resident

For CTB purposes, you are a resident in the home where you have your 'sole or main residence'.[15] This is the same criterion as for liability for council tax, so any decision on your sole or main residence should be the same for CTB purposes.[16] Your main residence is the property that a reasonable onlooker with knowledge of the facts would regard as your home.[17]

Note: you cannot qualify for CTB if you are a prisoner on temporary release.[18]

Temporary absence from home

A property can count as your sole or main residence even if you spend substantial periods of time away from it, if you consider it to be the main place where you live.[19] However, if you are absent from home for more than a set temporary period, you cannot qualify for CTB.[20]

The rules about temporary absence from your home are broadly the same as those for housing benefit (HB) – see p254.

Council tax benefit for more than one home

Unlike for HB, there are no rules on when you can and cannot get CTB for more than one home. If you occupy more than one property as a home (eg, because you have a large family) and you are liable for council tax on both, argue that you are a resident in, and qualify for CTB for, both properties.[21] However, if you choose to split your time between two homes (eg, your normal home and a holiday home), you can only get CTB for the property that is your sole or main residence.

2. The rules about your age

You must be aged 18 or over to qualify for council tax benefit (CTB). If you are under 18 you cannot be liable for council tax, so you do not need to claim CTB.

If you are at least the qualifying age for pension credit (see p509) and neither you nor your partner are getting income support, income-based jobseeker's allowance or income-related employment and support allowance, more generous rules apply.

3. Claiming for others

You claim council tax benefit for your family (see Chapter 34).

4. The amount of benefit

Main council tax benefit (CTB) and second adult rebate are calculated differently. Second adult rebate can be paid instead of, but not as well as, main CTB. Whenever you claim CTB, the local authority must assess you for both types and award whichever is the greater – sometimes referred to as the 'best buy'.[22]

Note: you might get a reduced amount of CTB if it is restricted under the 'loss of benefit for benefit offences' rules (see p1106).

Calculating main council tax benefit

The amount of main council tax benefit (CTB) you get depends on:

- your 'applicable amount' (see Chapter 37). This is made up of personal allowances, as well as premiums and components for any special needs. It may include a transitional addition if you or your partner were transferred to contributory employment and support allowance (ESA) from income support (IS) 'on the grounds of disability', incapacity benefit (IB) or severe disablement allowance (SDA), or are appealing a decision not to transfer you to ESA (see p839);
- your 'maximum CTB' (see p122); *and*
- how much income and capital you have (see Chapters 40 and 41).

If you do not currently qualify for CTB, you may qualify when:

- the benefit rates go up every April; *or*

- you or your partner reach:
  - the qualifying age for pension credit (PC – see p509), if neither you nor your partner are on IS, income-based jobseeker's allowance (JSA) or income-related ESA. Your applicable amount is then higher and the income and capital rules are also more generous; *or*
  - 65. Your personal allowance is increased by the equivalent of the amount of the maximum savings credit of PC, whether or not you receive this, if neither you nor your partner are on IS, income-based JSA or income-related ESA.

In addition, if your income is currently too high for you to qualify for CTB, you might qualify once you or a member of your family becomes entitled to another benefit (a 'qualifying benefit'). See p128 for further information.

If you need extra financial assistance to meet your council tax, you might be entitled to discretionary housing payments (see p294).

Remember that if you or your partner:

- stop getting IS, income-based JSA, income-related or contributory ESA, IB or SDA because of starting work or increasing your hours or your earnings, you may be entitled to extended payments of CTB (see p130);
- stop getting IS, income-based JSA or income-related ESA because you are moving onto PC, you may be able to continue to receive CTB at the same rate for four weeks (see p130);
- have been incapable of work or have had limited capability for work but move into work or training, you might count as a 'welfare to work beneficiary' (see p738) or a 'work or training beneficiary' (see p214). This means you can retain entitlement to the disability premium, or work-related activity or support component, if you become incapable of work (or have limited capability for work) again within 104 weeks.

If you are on a means-tested benefit

Being on IS, income-based JSA, income-related ESA or the guarantee credit of PC is an automatic passport to maximum CTB (once you have made a claim). You do not need to work out applicable amounts, income or capital.[23] CTB equals maximum CTB.

For these purposes you are treated as being on:

- income-based JSA:[24]
  - when you satisfy the conditions of entitlement but are not being paid it because of a sanction (see Chapter 20) or because you failed to attend an interview as required (see p422);
  - on your waiting days (see p402); *and*
  - when it is not paid because of the 'loss of benefit' rules (see p1106);
- income-related ESA:[25]

- when you satisfy the conditions of entitlement, but are not being paid it because you are disqualified for the reasons on p178 or during a temporary absence abroad or because you are a prisoner; *and*
- on your waiting days (see p212).

You continue to be passported to full CTB entitlement if your entitlement to IS or income-based JSA ceased on or before 5 April 2003 because your help with housing costs no longer included charges for support services.[26] You must have been entitled to IS or income-based JSA on 31 March 2003.

If you are not on a means-tested benefit

If you are not on IS, income-based JSA, income-related ESA or the guarantee credit of PC, follow the steps below to calculate main CTB.

- **Step one:** check that your capital is not too high (see Chapter 41).
- **Step two:** work out your maximum CTB (see below).
- **Step three:** work out your applicable amount (see Chapter 37).
- **Step four:** work out your income (see Chapter 40 but also p652 if you are a student and p941 if you are getting the savings credit of PC).
- **Step five:** calculate CTB.
  - If your income is **less than or equal to your applicable amount**, CTB equals 'maximum CTB'.
  - If your income is **more than your applicable amount**, work out the difference. CTB equals 'maximum CTB' minus 20 per cent of the difference between your income and your applicable amount.[27]

Maximum council tax benefit

Maximum CTB is your net weekly liability for council tax after deducting:[28]

- any disability reduction, discount or transitional reduction;
- any non-dependant deductions (see p125).

Net weekly liability for council tax

Net weekly liability is assessed by dividing your annual council tax liability by the number of days in the financial year (365 or 366) and then multiplying this by seven.[29]

Example

Cara's net council tax liability is £810.

Divide this by 365 = £2.219178

Multiply this by 7. Cara's net weekly liability = £15.534246

DWP guidance recommends that the figures should not be rounded until the final annual amount of CTB is worked out, and that calculations should usually be done to six decimal places.[30] When notifying you of your CTB, a rounded figure can be specified.[31]

Joint liability

If you are a member of a couple and are jointly liable for council tax, one of you must claim CTB for both of you.[32] If you are also jointly liable with one or more other residents, you can claim on a two-person share of the bill. See p753 for who counts as a couple.

If you are (or count as) a single person and are jointly liable for council tax, the local authority calculates your maximum CTB by dividing the total net liability for council tax by the number of liable people. Any liable person who is a student not entitled to CTB is ignored.[33]

Example

Ravi, Maxine and Bill share a flat. They are jointly liable for a net annual council tax bill of £1,200. £1,200 divided by 3 = £400. Ravi and Maxine are a couple. Either of them can make a claim for CTB on £800 liability (a two-person share), with Bill making a separate claim on £400 liability (a one-person share).

Bill becomes a full-time student and is therefore excluded from entitlement to CTB. Ravi and Maxine can now claim CTB on the full £1,200 liability.

Under the council tax rules, a person who is jointly and severally liable for council tax can be held responsible for the full council tax liability while receiving CTB only on her/his share. Note, however, that students who share with non-students are not jointly and severally liable for council tax with the non-students.[34]

Deductions for non-dependants

If other people normally live with you in your home who are not part of your family for benefit purposes (see p751) and are not liable for council tax (called '**non-dependants**'), a set deduction is usually made from your CTB.[35] This is because it is assumed the non-dependant makes a contribution towards your outgoings, whether or not s/he does so. Examples of non-dependants are adult sons or daughters, or older relatives who share your home.

The rules for whether a person is a non-dependant are the same as for HB (see p265). However, the categories of people who are not non-dependants are slightly different.

People who are not non-dependants

The following people do *not* count as non-dependants and no non-dependant deduction is made for them, even if they normally live with you:[36]

- a member of your family for benefit purposes (see p751);

- a child or qualifying young person living with you who does not count as a member of your household (see p762) – eg, a foster child or someone placed with you prior to adoption;
- someone who is employed by a charitable or voluntary organisation as a resident carer for you or your partner and who you pay for the service. This can also apply if a public body pays on your behalf;
- someone who is jointly liable to pay council tax in respect of your home;
- someone who is liable to pay rent on a commercial basis to you or your partner. However, although no non-dependant deduction can be made for her/him, the rent s/he pays can count as your income (see pp924 and 950).

If the person comes within the last two categories above, s/he *does* count as your non-dependant if:[37]

- you or your partner are her/his landlord, s/he resides with you and s/he is:
  - a close relative of yours or your partner; *or*
  - the agreement to pay rent or council tax is not a commercial one.

  The meaning of these terms is the same as for HB (see p250); *or*
- you or your partner are her/his landlord and the agreement to pay rent or council tax has been created to take advantage of the CTB scheme. This does not apply if s/he had a legitimate liability to pay you or your partner within the eight weeks prior to entering into the agreement.

  For the meaning of 'taking advantage', see p252. **Note:** just because someone is taking advantage of the HB scheme does not mean that s/he is taking advantage of the CTB scheme. The local authority should consider the two schemes separately; *or*
- s/he is jointly liable with you for council tax on the home and within the last eight weeks was a non-dependant of one or more residents there who were liable for the tax. This does not apply if you can persuade the local authority that the liability to pay council tax was not made to take advantage of the CTB scheme.

When no non-dependant deduction is made

The rules on when no non-dependant deduction is made are the same as for HB (see p267) except that:[38]

- all non-dependants on IS, income-based JSA or income-related ESA (even where a work-related activity component or support component is included) are ignored, and not just those under 25; *and*
- no deduction is made for people with what are known as status discounts including:
  - people aged 18 or over for whom child benefit is payable and recent school and college leavers under 20;
  - student nurses, foreign language assistants, apprentices and certain foreign spouses or dependants of students;

- people who are 'severely mentally impaired' (see below);
- people in detention;
- certain carers; *and*
- members of visiting armed forces, members of international headquarters and defence organisations and their dependants;
- no non-dependant deduction is ever made for a full-time student – even if s/he works during the summer vacation.

A person counts as '**severely mentally impaired**' if a doctor has certified that s/he has a severe impairment of intelligence and social functioning which appears to be permanent.[39] S/he must also be entitled to a qualifying benefit.[40] See CPAG's *Council Tax Handbook* for further information.

The amount of deductions

If you have a non-dependant living with you who is 18 or over and for whom a deduction must be made, a fixed amount is deducted from your CTB, whatever s/he pays you. Unless your non-dependant is in full-time paid work, a £3.30 deduction is made each week. If your non-dependant is in full-time paid work, the amount of the deduction depends on her/his gross weekly income as follows.[41]

Circumstances of the non-dependant	*Deduction*
18 or over and in full-time paid work with a weekly gross income of:	
– £394 or more	£9.90
– £316–£393.99	£8.25
– £183–£315.99	£6.55
– Under £183	£3.30
Others aged 18 or over (for whom a deduction is made)	£3.30

The rules on full-time paid work are covered in Chapter 31.

Remember:

- a non-dependant who is not in (or treated as in) full-time paid work does not attract the higher levels of deduction even if her/his income is £183 or more;
- if someone is on IS, income-based JSA or income-related ESA (see p121) for more than three days in a benefit week, s/he does not count as in full-time paid work in that week. This means no deduction is made.[42]

Your CTB can be assessed using the income and capital of a non-dependant, instead of your own, if you are trying to take advantage of the CTB scheme (see p269).

Only one deduction is made for a non-dependant couple (or members of a polygamous marriage). The deduction made is the highest that would have been made if they were treated as individuals and based on their joint income, even if only one of them is in full-time paid work.[43]

If you share liability for council tax with others, the amount of the non-dependant deduction is divided equally between you, even if the others are not claiming CTB.[44] However, if the local authority thinks that the non-dependant deduction only belongs to one of you, the whole deduction is made from that person's CTB. If you are a member of a couple and share liability with someone, the non-dependant deduction is apportioned – eg, if you share with one other person, your CTB is reduced by two-thirds of the non-dependant deduction.

Extra benefit for war pensioners

The local authority has the power to pay extra CTB to people getting certain war pensions. See p269 for further information.

Calculating second adult rebate

The amount of second adult rebate you get is a percentage of your council tax liability (see p127), based on the gross income of the second adult. The percentages are:[45]

Income of second adult(s)	*Second adult rebate*
Second adult (or all second adults) on:	
IS/income-based JSA/income-related ESA/PC	25%
Second adult(s) total gross weekly income:	
– Under £180	15%
– £180–£234.99	7.5%
– £235 or more	Nil
Student dwellings	
Occupiers are either students excluded from entitlement to main CTB or on IS/income-based JSA/income-related ESA/PC. At least one must be a student and at least one on IS/income-based JSA/income-related ESA/PC.	100%

For the 100 per cent rebate, someone counts as a student excluded from entitlement to main CTB if s/he would be excluded if s/he were under the qualifying age for PC (see p509).[46]

Unless you qualify for a 100 per cent rebate, the maximum second adult rebate you can get is always 25 per cent of your council tax liability, even if you would have received a 50 per cent council tax discount, or would have been exempt from council tax altogether were it not for the presence of two or more second adults in your home.

Council tax liability used for a second adult rebate

Second adult rebate is based on your gross council tax liability, after any reductions for disability and, in the case of 100 per cent rebate, any discounts, have been applied.[47] **Note:** this is not the same figure as used for main CTB. However, the procedure for converting annual to weekly amounts is the same (see p122). If you have received a discount, it must be added back on to the net amount of council tax payable to arrive at the figure used in the second adult rebate calculation. This is only done for the purposes of the CTB calculation – in practice, you still receive your discount.

Assessment of second adult income

To obtain a second adult rebate, you must give the local authority details of the gross income of any second adults living with you. If there is more than one second adult, their combined gross income is used.[48]

Gross income includes the second adult's:

- earnings;
- non-earned income, including social security benefits;
- actual income from capital (as opposed to, for example, 'tariff income'). The capital itself is ignored.

Gross income does *not* include:[49]

- any income of a second adult on IS, income-based JSA, income-related ESA or PC;
- any attendance allowance or disability living allowance;
- certain payments from the MacFarlane Trusts, the Eileen Trust, MFET Ltd, the Skipton Fund, the Caxton Foundation, the London Bombings Relief Charitable Fund, the Fund and the Independent Living Fund (2006);
- the income of any person with a status discount (see p118), except if that person has a partner who is not ignored for discount purposes (in which case the gross income of both partners, less disregarded income, is taken into account).

A basic problem with second adult rebate is that it involves looking at the income of someone who may not always wish to give you that information. If you have difficulty establishing the income of your second adult(s), you may find that the local authority automatically assumes the highest income and that you are not entitled to CTB. If you cannot persuade your second adult(s) to give income details to you, s/he may be prepared to tell the local authority directly. Failing this, you could try finding out the going rate for the type of work s/he does, or social security benefits s/he receives, and ask the local authority to make a reasonable estimate based on that. The local authority should not assume the worst. It should assess what the likely level of your second adult's income is on the evidence available.[50]

Second adult rebates and jointly liable claimants

In contrast to main CTB, if there is more than one resident liable for council tax in your dwelling, any second adult rebate is always calculated on the (pre-discounted) liability for your dwelling as a whole. Unless you are jointly liable with your partner, every jointly liable person must make her/his own separate claim in order to get a share of the second adult rebate. Any second adult rebate is then split equally between all the jointly liable residents.[51] However, if you are jointly liable with your partner, one of you claims on behalf of both and receives the entire second adult rebate (or if you are sharing with other liable residents, a couple's share).[52]

5. Special benefit rules

Special rules may apply to:

- people subject to immigration control (see p1410);
- students (see p646);
- people in care homes and other similar accommodation (see p687);
- prisoners (see p694).

6. Claims and backdating

The rules for claiming council tax benefit (CTB) are the same as for housing benefit (HB) (see p270). The different rules for CTB are covered below. Remember that:

- you can claim CTB even if you have already paid your council tax bill in advance;
- if you are in arrears with your council tax bill, this does not affect your right to claim CTB. You may even be able to get your claim backdated (see p129);
- if you want to claim discretionary housing payments, you must claim separately. See p296 for further information.

Claiming in advance

The rules about advance claims for CTB are generally the same as for HB (see p276). You can also claim CTB up to eight weeks before you become liable for council tax. You are treated as having claimed on the day your liability begins.[53]

Council tax benefit after an award of a 'qualifying benefit'

You might not be currently entitled to CTB, but would be once you or a member of your family become entitled to another 'qualifying benefit' – eg, disability living allowance or carer's allowance. Alternatively, you might be entitled to a higher rate of benefit once the qualifying benefit is awarded. If you are already entitled to CTB when the qualifying benefit is awarded, see pp1132 and 1139. If you only qualify for CTB when the qualifying benefit is awarded, see p277.

Backdating your claim

The rules about late claims and backdated CTB are the same as for HB (see p277). In addition to other situations when you may have 'good cause' for a late claim, if you did not claim CTB because your name was not put on the council tax bill, argue that you have good cause because you did not realise you were liable for council tax as the local authority had failed (via the council tax bill) to inform you of this.

There is a special rule if your local authority has not set its council tax rate by the beginning of the financial year.[54] Provided you claim within one month of the council tax being set or imposed, your claim is backdated to 1 April, or the date you first became entitled to CTB if that is later.

Notice of the decision

You receive separate decision notices for HB and CTB. However, the information that must be included is the same (see p280) except that those items specifically relating to rent are excluded in a CTB decision notice and, instead, it must show your weekly council tax liability rounded to the nearest penny.[55] Among other things, it should also include:

- if you have been assessed for, and are entitled to, both main CTB and second adult rebate, the amount of benefit entitlement in each case and the fact that you can only be paid the higher amount;[56]
- if you have been assessed for a second adult rebate, the gross income of any second adult(s) used to determine the rate of CTB, including if any second adult is on income support, income-based jobseeker's allowance, income-related employment and support allowance or pension credit.[57]

7. Getting paid

Payment of council tax benefit (CTB) is normally made by reducing your annual council tax bill. The reduction is: your weekly benefit divided by seven and then multiplied by the number of days between your first day of entitlement and the following 31 March.

If you are jointly liable for council tax with one or more other residents, apart from your partner, remember that any CTB they receive is also credited to the same bill as your own. You need to take this into account when agreeing how any remaining balance of council tax liability should be shared between you.

If your CTB cannot be used to reduce your bill (eg, you have already paid it in full), payment can be made direct to you.[58] Usually you must ask for the money. If you do not, your CTB is likely to be credited against your next year's bill.[59] However, if you are no longer liable for council tax in an authority's area, it must send you any outstanding CTB within 14 days if possible.[60] Payment is normally made to you. If you are unable to act for yourself, payment can be made to someone else on your behalf – called your appointee (see p1016).[61]

There is no minimum entitlement to CTB. This means that you are paid CTB however low your entitlement is.

Your entitlement to CTB starts:[62]

- if you became liable for council tax in the first of the weeks for which you are claiming, from the Monday of that week; *or*
- in all other cases, from the Monday following your date of claim (or following the date from which you are claiming if your claim is backdated). See p275 for information about what counts as your date of claim. The rules are the same as for housing benefit (HB).

Note:

- Your CTB might be paid at a reduced rate if you have been sanctioned for benefit offences (see p1106).
- If payment of your CTB is delayed, see p289. If you wish to complain about how your claim has been dealt with, see p1258. You might be able to claim compensation (see p1261).
- If payment of your CTB is suspended, see p1043.
- If you are overpaid CTB, you might have to repay it (see Chapter 43). If you have been accused of fraud, see Chapter 44.

Continuing payments

There are two situations when your CTB can continue to be paid at the same rate even though your entitlement may otherwise have changed. If you stop claiming:

- income support (IS), income-based jobseeker's allowance (JSA) or income-related employment and support allowance (ESA) because you or your partner are moving onto pension credit (PC), you may be able to continue to receive CTB at the same rate for four weeks. The rules are the same as for HB (see p285);
- IS, income-based JSA, income-related or contributory ESA, incapacity benefit (IB) or severe disablement allowance (SDA) because you or your partner start work or increase your hours or earnings, you may be entitled to extended payments of CTB (see below).

Extended payments of council tax benefit

If you (or your partner) are on IS, income-based JSA, income-related or contributory ESA, IB or SDA and your entitlement ends because you (or your partner) start work, or increase your hours or pay in your current job, you may be entitled to continue to receive the same amount of CTB as you did before your entitlement ended. These extended payments of CTB are paid for up to four weeks. If you pay rent, you may also be entitled to extended payments of HB. For information about extended payments, see p286. The rules are the same as for HB.

Note: you have to report the change in your circumstances to the local authority (and the DWP). Although the change does not end your entitlement to CTB, at least until the end of the extended payment period, it could result in an overpayment of CTB from the end of that period. You could also be overpaid IS, JSA, ESA, IB or SDA and might have to repay it. You could be entitled to a higher rate of CTB than you were before your entitlement to IS, income-based JSA, ESA, IB or SDA ended. Report the change as soon as possible so it can be taken into account.

Amount of extended payments

The weekly amount of your extended payments of CTB is the higher of the amount of CTB:[63]

- you got in the last week before your entitlement to IS, income-based JSA, ESA, IB or SDA ceased; *or*
- to which you would be entitled based on your new circumstances; *or*
- if you are a member of a couple, to which your partner would be entitled based on her/his circumstances.

The rules on how long the payments last are the same as for extended payments of HB (see p287). **Note:** if your circumstances change during the four-week extended payment period, the weekly amount you get is then the highest of the above amounts.

If you were being paid discretionary housing payments (see p294), ask for these to continue for the extended payment period.

Payments on death

If a claimant dies, any outstanding CTB can be paid to her/his personal representative or, if there is none, to the next of kin aged 16 or over.[64] A written application for this must be sent to the local authority within 12 months of the death. The local authority may allow longer.

Change of circumstances

It is your duty to report any changes in circumstances which you might reasonably be expected to know might affect your right to, or the amount of, your CTB or payment of your benefit.[65] Do this promptly to the office handling your claim. You can do this in writing, although in individual cases notification may be accepted in a form other than in writing. In addition, you can report a change of circumstances by telephone if your local authority has published a telephone number for that purpose, or allows you to claim CTB by telephone (unless it says you must report it in writing). Note that if your local authority authorises it, you can report changes electronically – eg, by email.[66] However, it is always best to report a change in writing and to keep a copy in case of a dispute in the future.

There are exceptions to this rule.

- You may report a change in your circumstances to the DWP instead of the local authority, if the DWP has provided a telephone number for this purpose, and:[67]
  - you or your partner are getting IS or JSA; *and*
  - the change of circumstance is that you or your partner have started work; *and*
  - as a result of the change, entitlement to IS or JSA will end or, if you or your partner are getting contribution-based JSA, the amount will reduce.
- If the change is a birth or a death, there is a special rule (sometimes called 'Tell Us Once'). You can report such a change in person at a local authority (and, in England, a county council) office, if such an office has been specified for reporting these changes.[68] If the change is a death, you can notify it to the DWP by electronic communication or by telephone if a number has been specified for that purpose. Check with your local authority (eg, at the registrar's office) to see if it provides this service.

If you do not report a change promptly, any resulting overpayment may be recoverable from you (see Chapter 43). If you are considered deliberately to have acted falsely or dishonestly, you may also be guilty of an offence (see Chapter 44).

The rules are the same as for HB (see p290) except that:

- you do not need to notify any changes in rent for council tax purposes, nor do you have to tell the local authority the amount of council tax you pay;[69]
- if you are getting second adult rebate, you must give written notice of any changes in the number of adults living in your home and any changes to their gross income.[70]

There are additional changes you have to report if you are getting PC. The rules are the same as for HB (see p291).

When changes in circumstances take effect

The rules about when changes in circumstance take effect are generally the same as those for HB (see p292), but there are some differences. As with HB, normally, a change affects your CTB from the Monday after it occurs.[71] However, the following changes affect your benefit from the date they occur:[72]

- a change in the amount of your council tax;
- changes to the CTB regulations;
- becoming part of a couple;

- the death of, or separation from, your partner.

If two or more changes occur in the same week and each takes effect from a different date under the above rules, they are all taken into account from the date of the first change.[73]

8. Tax, tax credits and other benefits

Council tax benefit (CTB) is not taxable.

Tax credits

Working tax credit counts as income when working out your CTB. So does child tax credit, unless you are at least the qualifying age for pension credit (PC – see p509) and neither you nor your partner are getting income support (IS), income-based jobseeker's allowance (JSA) or income-related employment and support allowance (ESA).

Means-tested benefits

If you pay rent, you may be able to claim housing benefit (HB) as well as CTB. Entitlement to IS, income-based JSA, income-related ESA or the guarantee credit of PC acts as an automatic passport to maximum CTB (see p121) because all of your income and capital are ignored.

Non-means-tested benefits

Most non-means-tested benefits are taken into account as income when working out the amount of CTB you get. Attendance allowance, disability living allowance, guardian's allowance and child benefit are not taken into account. It can still be worth claiming non-means-tested benefits. If you, your partner or your child(ren) qualify for certain of these, you also qualify for certain premiums and components (see Chapter 37) and potentially a higher rate of CTB. If you think you might qualify, seek advice to see if you would be better off.

You may only qualify for CTB once you or a member of your family are awarded another benefit, known as a 'qualifying benefit'. You may be entitled to a higher rate of CTB once the qualifying benefit is awarded (see p128).

Passports and other sources of help

If you have been awarded CTB, you may qualify for a social fund funeral expenses payment (see Chapter 26).

Financial help on starting work

If you or your partner stop getting IS, income-based JSA, income-related or contributory ESA, incapacity benefit or severe disablement allowance because you start work, or your hours or earnings in your existing job increase, you may be entitled to extended payments of HB or CTB (see p130). You may also be able to get mortgage interest run-on (if you have a home loan – see p879). See p13 for information about other financial help you might get.

Notes

1. **Who can claim council tax benefit**

1 s131(1) and (3) SSCBA 1992
2 s131(1)(a) and (3)-(5) SSCBA 1992
3 Reg 16 CTB(SPC) Regs
4 Reg 45 CTB Regs
5 s131(1)(b), (3) and (6) SSCBA 1992
6 Sch 5 para 46(1) CTB Regs; reg 16 and Sch 4 para 26A CTB(SPC) Regs
7 s131(7) SSCBA 1992
8 s6(5) LGFA 1992
9 Sch 1 LGFA 1992
10 Reg 63(a) CTB Regs; reg 47(a) CTB(SPC) Regs
11 Reg 63(c) CTB Regs; reg 47(c) CTB(SPC) Regs
12 Reg 63(b) CTB Regs; reg 47(b) CTB(SPC) Regs
13 Reg 63(d) CTB Regs; reg 47(d) CTB(SPC) Regs
14 s131(6)(a) and (7) SSCBA 1992
15 s131(11) SSCBA 1992; s6(5) LGFA 1992; reg 2(1) CTB Regs; reg 2(1) CTB(SPC) Regs
16 R(H) 3/08
17 *Williams v Horsham District Council* [2004] unreported, EWCA Civ 39, 21 January 2004
18 Reg 8(5) and (6)(c) CTB Regs; reg 8(5) and (6)(c) CTB(SPC) Regs
19 *Ward v Kingston upon Hull MBC* [1993] RA 71 (QBD)
20 s131(3)(b) SSCBA 1992; reg 8 CTB Regs; reg 8 CTB(SPC) Regs
21 R(H) 3/08

4. **The amount of benefit**

22 s131(9) SSCBA 1992; CH/48/2006
23 Schs 4 para 4 and 5 para 5 CTB Regs; reg 16 CTB(SPC) Regs
24 Reg 2(4) CTB Regs; reg 2(4) CTB(SPC) Regs
25 Reg 2(4A) CTB Regs; reg 2(4A) CTB(SPC) Regs
26 Sch 4 para 6 CTB Regs; Sch 3 para 25 CTB(SPC) Regs
27 *IB v Barnsley MBC* [2009] UKUT 279 (AAC)
28 Reg 57(1) and (2) CTB Regs; reg 40(1) and (2) CTB(SPC) Regs
29 Reg 57(1) CTB Regs; reg 40(1) CTB(SPC) Regs
30 Annex B A5 GM
31 Sch 8 paras 9-10 CTB Regs; Sch 7 paras 9-10 CTB(SPC) Regs
32 Reg 57(4) CTB Regs; reg 40(4) CTB(SPC) Regs
33 Reg 57(3) CTB Regs; reg 40(3) CTB(SPC) Regs
34 **EW** ss6(4) and 9(2) LGFA 1992
S ss75 and 77 LGFA 1992
Both Sch 1 para 4(2) LGFA 1992
Note that the definition of student is different from that for CTB.
35 Regs 3 and 57(1) CTB Regs; regs 3 and 40(1) CTB(SPC) Regs
36 Reg 3(2) CTB Regs; reg 3(2) CTB(SPC) Regs
37 Reg 3(3) CTB Regs; reg 3(3) CTB(SPC) Regs
38 Reg 58(6)-(8) CTB Regs; reg 42(6)-(8) CTB(SPC) Regs

39 Sch 1(2) LGFA 1992
40 Reg 3 CT(DD)O
41 Reg 58(1), (2) and (9) CTB Regs; reg 42(1), (2) and (9) CTB(SPC) Regs
42 Reg 6(6) CTB Regs; reg 6(6) CTB(SPC) Regs
43 Reg 58(3) and (4) CTB Regs; reg 42(3) and (4) CTB(SPC) Regs
44 Reg 58(5) CTB Regs; reg 42(5) CTB(SPC) Regs
45 Reg 62 and Sch 2 para 1 CTB Regs; reg 46 and Sch 6 para 1 CTB(SPC) Regs
46 Sch 2 para 1(1)(b) CTB Regs; Sch 6 para 1(1)(b) CTB(SPC) Regs
47 Reg 62 and Sch 2 para 1(2) CTB Regs; reg 46 and Sch 6 para 1(2) CTB(SPC) Regs
48 Reg 62 and Sch 2 para 1 Table CTB Regs; reg 46 and Sch 6 para 1 Table CTB(SPC) Regs
49 Reg 62 and Sch 2 paras 1 (Table), 2 and 3 CTB Regs; reg 46 and Sch 6 paras 1 (Table), 2 and 3 CTB(SPC) Regs
50 CH/48/2006
51 Reg 62(2) CTB Regs; reg 46(2) CTB(SPC) Regs
52 Reg 62(3) CTB Regs; reg 46(3) CTB(SPC) Regs

6. **Claims and backdating**

53 Reg 69(10) CTB Regs; reg 53(10) CTB(SPC) Regs
54 Reg 69(11) CTB Regs; reg 53(11) CTB(SPC) Regs
55 Sch 8 paras 9(a) and 10(a) CTB Regs; Sch 7 paras 9(1)(a) and 10(a) CTB(SPC) Regs
56 Sch 8 paras 12(b), 14(b) and 15 CTB Regs; Sch 7 paras 12(b), 14(b) and 15 CTB(SPC) Regs
57 Sch 8 para 13(c) and (e) CTB Regs; Sch 7 para 13(c) and (e) CTB(SPC) Regs

7. **Getting paid**

58 Reg 77(1)(b) and (3) CTB Regs; reg 62(1)(b) and (3) CTB(SPC) Regs
59 Reg 77(3)(a)(ii) CTB Regs; reg 62(3)(a)(ii) CTB(SPC) Regs
60 Reg 77(3)(b) CTB Regs; reg 62(3)(b) CTB(SPC) Regs
61 Reg 78 CTB Regs; reg 63 CTB(SPC) Regs
62 Reg 64 CTB Regs; reg 48 CTB(SPC) Regs
63 Regs 60B and 61B CTB Regs; reg 44B CTB(SPC) Regs
64 Reg 80 CTB Regs; reg 65 CTB(SPC) Regs
65 Reg 74(1) CTB Regs; reg 59(1) CTB(SPC) Regs; reg 4 SS(NCC) Regs
66 Reg 74A and Sch 9 CTB Regs; reg 59A and Sch 8 CTB(SPC) Regs
67 Reg 74(7) CTB Regs; reg 59(10) CTB(SPC) Regs
68 Reg 74ZA CTB Regs; reg 59ZA CTB(SPC) Regs
69 Reg 74(3) CTB Regs; reg 59(3) CTB(SPC) Regs
70 Reg 74(5) CTB Regs; reg 59(5) CTB(SPC) Regs
71 Reg 67(1) CTB Regs; reg 50(1) CTB(SPC) Regs
72 Reg 67(2)-(6) CTB Regs; reg 50(2)-(6) CTB(SPC) Regs
73 Reg 67(7) CTB Regs; reg 50(7) CTB(SPC) Regs

Chapter 9

Disability living allowance and attendance allowance

This chapter covers:

Key facts

- Disability living allowance (DLA) is a benefit for people with disabilities who need help getting around and/or with supervision or attention needs who are under 65 when they claim.
- Attendance allowance (AA) is a benefit for people with disabilities who need help with attention or supervision needs who are aged 65 or over when they claim.
- DLA has two separate components, one for care and one for mobility. However, it is a single benefit for which you only have to make one claim. Each component can be paid at different rates.
- DLA and AA are non-means-tested benefits.
- You can qualify for DLA or AA whether or not you are in or out of work.
- You do not have to have paid national insurance contributions to qualify.
- DLA and AA can be paid in addition to other benefits and are disregarded as income for means-tested benefits and tax credits.
- DLA and AA are administered and paid by the DWP's Disability and Carers Service.
- If you disagree with a DLA or AA decision, you can apply for a revision or a supersession, or appeal against it (see Chapters 45 and 46).

Future changes: April 2013 and after

Major changes are taking place that affect the benefits and tax credits system (see Chapter 2).

- From April 2013, total benefit payments to many working-age households will be 'capped' (see p25). There will be limited exceptions, including households in which someone is entitled to working tax credit or receives DLA. DLA is *not* included in the capped amount.
- From April 2013 in some parts of the country and summer 2012 for the rest, DLA for new claimants aged between 16 and 65 will be replaced with a new personal independence payment. See Chapter 3 for more information.

See CPAG's *Welfare Rights Bulletin* for updates.

1. Disability living allowance mobility component

Disability living allowance (DLA) mobility component is for people who have difficulties with walking. There is a higher rate and a lower rate.

Who can claim

You qualify for DLA mobility component if:[1]

- you satisfy the residence conditions (see p1426);
- you are not a 'person subject to immigration control', although there are exceptions to this rule (see p1410);
- you satisfy the age rules (see p153) – ie:
  - for the *higher rate* you must be aged three or over, but under 65;
  - for the *lower rate* you must be aged five or over, but under 65;
- you are not in hospital (although sometimes DLA mobility component is paid in hospital – see p677);
- you are likely to be able, from time to time, to benefit from enhanced facilities for locomotion (see below);
- you satisfy the **'disability'** conditions – ie:
  - for the *higher rate*:
    - you have a disability from a physical cause that means you are unable, or virtually unable, to walk (see p138); *or*
    - you are both deaf and blind (see p140); *or*
    - you were born without feet, are a double amputee or otherwise without both legs or feet (see p141); *or*
    - you are 'severely mentally impaired', have severe behavioural problems, and qualify for the highest rate of DLA care component (see p141);
    - you are blind or severely visually impaired (see p142);

- for the *lower rate,* although you are able to walk, you are so severely disabled, physically or mentally, that, ignoring any ability to use familiar routes, you are unable to walk outdoors without guidance or supervision from another person most of the time (see p142).[2] There is also an extra test if you are claiming on behalf of a child under 16 (see p154);
- for *both rates* you must satisfy one of the disability conditions throughout the three months before the start of your award and be likely to satisfy it for the next six months (unless you are terminally ill – see p143). However, see p160 if a previous award had ended and you are reclaiming.

To 'benefit from enhanced facilities for locomotion'

To qualify for either rate of the DLA mobility component, you must be able to 'benefit from enhanced facilities for locomotion'. This means you must be able to make outdoor journeys. It is not essential that you are interested in or enjoy going out, provided it would be beneficial for you to do so.[3] For example, you can get DLA mobility component even if you have to be carried out to a car for a ride.

Disability conditions for the higher rate mobility component

'Unable or virtually unable to walk'

You are eligible for the higher rate if:

- you are unable to walk; *or*
- your ability to walk out of doors is so limited, as regards:
  - the distance over which; *and/or*
  - the speed at which; *and/or*
  - the length of time for which; *and/or*
  - the manner in which you can make progress on foot without severe discomfort,

  that you are virtually unable to walk; *or*
- the exertion required to walk would constitute a danger to your life or would be likely to lead to a serious deterioration in your health.[4]

Personal circumstances, such as the location of your home or job, should not be taken into account. It is not, for instance, relevant if you live a long way from your nearest bus stop,[5] or if you are no longer able to use public transport.

Physical disability

Your inability, or virtual inability, to walk must have a physical cause.[6] There can be a physical cause, such as pain or dizziness, even without a medically diagnosed origin. It does not matter if the original cause was mental so long as a current physical impairment impairs your walking. For example, someone with severe depression whose muscles have atrophied, making her/him virtually unable to walk, could qualify. The physical contribution to a combination of mental and physical factors must be more than minimal. Myalgic encephalomyelitis (ME), or chronic fatigue syndrome, should be accepted as having a physical origin unless there is evidence that your mobility restrictions are purely psychological. If your walking is impaired by weakness due to anorexia nervosa, the cause is physical.[7] Inability to make any progress on foot because of behavioural problems may qualify if the cause is physical – eg, Downs syndrome or autism, which are both accepted as disorders of development of the brain.[8]

Unable to walk

You are unable to walk if you cannot move your body along by alternate, weight-bearing steps of the feet.[9]

Prostheses, aids and medication

Your ability to walk is considered taking into account any prosthesis or artificial aid you use, or that would be suitable for you.[10] You may not qualify if you are able to walk with a stick or crutches. However, if you have one leg and no artificial limb suitable to use, you are regarded as 'unable to walk', even if you can get around on crutches.[11] If you have no feet, you qualify automatically (see p141).[12]

Your walking is assessed taking account of any medication you normally and reasonably use – eg, it may not be practical to carry a bulky nebuliser.[13] However, you should not be expected to undergo surgery, and if you do not take medicines or treatment due to alcoholism or your mental health your walking should be assessed as you are now, not how you might be if you accepted the treatment.[14]

Outdoors

The test is whether you can walk outdoors. Walking indoors, around a supermarket for instance, 'is not necessarily an indication' of your ability to walk out of doors.[15] It is relevant if you have problems with your balance on uneven pavements and roads, or if you have a lung or other condition which is made worse by wind or rain.[16]

Distance

The law does not require a specific distance to be used when determining your inability to walk, it is concerned with 'broad concepts, not... precise distances and times'.[17] In practice, you may be refused benefit if you state that you can walk more than 50 metres, although someone who can only walk this distance five or six times a week 'and then cannot repeat the walk... may well be virtually unable to walk'.[18] Your walking speed, the time it takes you to cover the distance and your manner of walking are also relevant, so give details about these on the form. Caselaw says that walking speeds of less than 60 metres per minute are slow, so if you cannot walk this fast without severe discomfort, you should say so.[19]

Without severe discomfort

Any walking you can achieve only with severe discomfort should be ignored when considering whether you are virtually unable to walk.[20] If, when you walk, you feel severe discomfort (eg, pain or breathlessness brought on by walking[21]), make this clear. You may be able to walk a distance without severe discomfort, a further distance that causes you severe discomfort, and then have to stop altogether. In this case it would be incorrect to decide that discomfort became severe only when you have to stop.[22] The correct test is 'how far the person can walk before severe discomfort is occasioned by going any further'. But further walking (ie, without severe discomfort) after a brief rest stop could be taken into account.[23]

If you are in severe discomfort before you start to walk, even if the pain gets no worse, you should count as virtually unable to walk so long as your disability affects the physical act of walking. For example, someone with an injured foot qualified in this way.[24] You do not, however, count as virtually unable to walk if something unconnected with walking causes the discomfort. For example, someone whose skin blistered in sunlight was held not to be virtually unable to walk even though he was in severe discomfort walking outdoors.[25]

The exertion required to walk

You can qualify for the higher rate mobility component if walking endangers your health. The 'exertion required to walk' must lead to a danger to life or a serious deterioration in health, either suddenly or progressively. If the deterioration is sudden, you must show that you would never recover, or recovery would take a significant period of time (eg, 12 months) or would require some form of medical intervention. So, a person with ME who needed a few days' rest after walking would not satisfy this test.[26]

Blind and deaf

You are treated as being unable to walk if:

- the degree of disablement resulting from your loss of vision is 100 per cent; *and*
- the degree of disablement resulting from your loss of hearing is 80 per cent on a scale where 100 per cent represents absolute deafness;[27] *and*
- the combined effects of the blindness and deafness mean that you are unable to walk to any intended or required destination while out of doors without the help of another person.[28]

The regulations do not specify how to assess the degree of disablement, but caselaw suggests that the industrial injury provisions should be used.[29] So 100 per cent disablement through 'loss of vision' means 'loss of sight to such an extent as to render the claimant unable to perform any work for which eyesight is essential'.[30] This is the definition used when someone is registered as blind.

If your level of hearing loss, averaged between both ears at 1, 2 and 3 kHz is at least 87 decibels, you will satisfy the 80 per cent disablement test.[31] You may be required to undertake a hearing test. The assessment of your hearing ability takes into account any hearing aid you use or could reasonably be expected to use.[32]

People without feet

If you do not have feet or legs (missing from the ankle or above) you are automatically treated as being unable to walk,[33] even if you can walk with prostheses.

Severe mental impairment and behavioural problems

This route to the higher rate DLA mobility component is for people with severe behavioural difficulties. You qualify if:

- you are 'severely mentally impaired' – ie, you have arrested or incomplete physical development of the brain, which results in severe impairment of intelligence and social functioning; *and*
- you display severe behavioural problems – ie:
  - you exhibit extreme disruptive behaviour; *and*
  - you regularly require someone else to intervene and physically restrain you to prevent you causing injury to yourself or others or damage to property; *and*
  - you are so unpredictable that another person has to be present and watching over you whenever you are awake;[34] *and*
- you qualify for the highest rate of DLA care component.[35]

If you do not meet all these elements of the severe mental impairment test (eg, if you cannot get the highest rate of the care component), you might still qualify for the higher rate mobility component on the grounds that you can be said to be virtually unable to walk (see p138) because your disability prevents you from walking effectively, causing so many refusals to walk that you can be said to be virtually unable to walk.[36]

Arrested or incomplete development

'Arrested or incomplete development' must occur before the brain reaches its final development. Medical opinion suggests this is at or before the age of 30. Someone with Alzheimer's disease, a degenerative condition which occurs after the brain has fully developed, would not qualify under this route.[37] In the case of an illness such as schizophrenia, you may qualify in this way, but the age at which your illness began is significant and you also need to have a severe impairment of intelligence *and* of social functioning.[38]

Severe impairment of intelligence

An IQ of 55 or less is generally accepted as a 'severe impairment of intelligence'. However, some people may have a higher IQ but be unable to apply it practically.[39] Your 'degree of judgement in relation to everyday living' should also be taken into account.[40] For example, an autistic child with no awareness of danger may have severely impaired intelligence even if her/his IQ is over 55.[41]

Physical restraint

Physical restraint may involve as little as a hand on the arm. You do not need to show that any force is used.[42] If the presence of those who watch over you is enough to prevent you from being disruptive altogether or a specially adapted environment allows you to be safely left alone, you may not pass the test. However, the decision maker must consider the need for intervention in all environments.[43]

Blind or severely visually impaired

You must have been certified blind or severely sight impaired and have combined visual accuity, in both eyes, on the 'Snellen Scale', while using appropriate corrective lenses if necessary, of:[44]

- less than 3/60; *or*
- 3/60 or more, but less than 6/60, if you have a complete loss of peripheral vision and a central visual field of no more than 10 degrees.

Disability condition for the lower rate mobility component

You qualify for the lower rate mobility component if you are 'so severely disabled physically or mentally' that you cannot walk outdoors 'without guidance or supervision from another person most of the time'.[45]

Any walking that you can do on familiar routes is ignored for the purposes of this test – but inability to walk, whether on familiar or unfamiliar routes, should be considered.[46] Qualification for the lower rate mobility component is based on an assessment of your need for supervision or guidance rather than physical difficulty walking, which might qualify you for the higher rate component.[47]

'Guidance' and 'supervision' overlap: some forms of assistance could be guidance or supervision (see p143).

Fear and anxiety

You can qualify for the lower rate on the basis of mental as well as physical disablement. If you have an anxiety disorder and you are so mentally disabled that you need the help of an escort to overcome your fear of going outside, you are likely to satisfy the 'guidance or supervision' requirement.[48] If no amount of reassurance can persuade you to go outside, you may not qualify.[49] However, if you can just manage a walk into your garden, this could be enough to qualify.[50]

Any fear or anxiety that stops you going out on your own must be a symptom of mental disability in order to count. Fear and anxiety arising from a physical disability, such as a rational fear of having to cope with incontinence while alone, is not sufficient, although you may still have a physical need for supervision.[51] If your physical disability causes you such fear or anxiety that you can be said to be mentally disabled, you may qualify.

Guidance

'Guidance' can take a number of different forms. It can mean physically leading or directing you, giving oral suggestions or persuasion, helping you avoid obstacles or places that upset you, or leading or persuading you when you become disorientated or have a panic attack. Even if your companion only intervenes occasionally, s/he could still be guiding 'most of the time' if you would otherwise not know when to change direction. A visually impaired person who uses a guide dog or a cane may still need guidance to follow directions, avoid obstacles or cross roads. A deaf person whose primary method of communication is sign language, may require guidance in unfamiliar places if s/he is unable to ask for or follow directions.[52] However, deaf people may not qualify if they can study maps, read street signs or communicate with passers by.[53]

Supervision

'Supervision' can also vary. It can be precautionary – accompanying and watching over you, in order to monitor your physical, mental or emotional state in case you need more positive assistance to continue walking. It can also be monitoring the route ahead for obstacles, dangers, places or situations which might upset you. Supervision can also be more active, such as encouraging, persuading or cajoling you, talking to you to take your mind off your fears,[54] or distracting you from possibly alarming situations through conversation.[55]

Unlike the 'continual supervision' condition for the DLA care component, supervision need not be required to prevent 'substantial danger'.[56] If you qualify for the care component because you require continual supervision, you may also qualify for the lower rate mobility component.[57] However, this is not automatic; your eligibility must be assessed on the mobility criteria alone.[58]

The supervision does not need to actually improve your walking ability, but should enable you to 'take advantage of the faculty of walking'. If you need to have someone with you, for example, to provide help in the event of fits or seizures or a severe asthma attack,[59] even though you have no difficulty getting about, you can qualify for the lower rate mobility component.[60]

Terminal illness

If you are terminally ill, you do not automatically qualify for the mobility component. However, where a claim is made specifically on the basis that you are terminally ill, you do not have to satisfy the three-month backward qualifying condition[61] and the forward test only has to be satisfied to the date of death (see p137).[62] Terminal illness is defined for the mobility component in the same way as for the care component (see p157).

2. Disability living allowance care component

Disability living allowance (DLA) care component is for people with attention or supervision needs.

Who can claim

You qualify for the DLA care component if:[63]

- you satisfy the residence conditions (see p1426);
- you are not a 'person subject to immigration control', although there are some exceptions (see p1410);
- you are under the age of 65 when you first claim (see p153);
- you are not in hospital (see p677) or residential care (see p683);
- you satisfy the '**disability**' conditions, for either:
  - the lowest rate of the care component (see below); *or*
  - the middle rate of the care component (see below); *or*
  - the highest rate of the care component (see p145); *or*
  - you are terminally ill (see p157);
- you have satisfied the disability condition throughout the three months immediately before your award begins (see p160 if you are reclaiming within two years) and you are likely to continue to satisfy the disability conditions for the next six months *or* you are terminally ill.

Children under 16 also have to satisfy an extra disability test (see p154).

Disability conditions for the lowest rate care component

You qualify for the lowest rate care component if:[64]

- you are 16 or over and you are so severely disabled, physically or mentally, that you cannot prepare a cooked main meal for yourself if you have the ingredients (the 'cooking test' – see p146); *or*
- you are so severely disabled, physically or mentally (see p147), that you require in connection with your bodily functions, attention from another person for a significant portion of the day, whether during a single period or a number of periods (see pp148 and 151).

Disability conditions for the middle rate care component

To qualify for the middle rate care component you must show that you are so severely disabled, physically or mentally, that you require (see p147):[65]

- frequent attention from another person throughout the day in connection with your bodily functions (see p148); *or*
- continual supervision throughout the day in order to avoid substantial danger to yourself or others (see p151); *or*

- prolonged or repeated attention at night (see p151) in connection with your bodily functions (see p148); *or*
- another person to be awake at night for a prolonged period or at frequent intervals to watch over you (see p153) in order to avoid substantial danger to yourself or others.

This means you must have either daytime or night-time attention or supervision needs.

Disability conditions for the highest rate care component

To qualify for the highest rate care component you must be so severely disabled, physically or mentally, that:

- you require frequent attention throughout the day in connection with your bodily functions, *or* continual supervision throughout the day to avoid substantial danger to yourself or others; *and*
- you require prolonged or repeated attention at night in connection with your bodily functions, *or* in order to avoid substantial danger to yourself or others, you require another person to be awake at night for a prolonged period or at frequent intervals to watch over you;[66] *or*
- you are terminally ill (see p157).[67]

This means you must have both daytime and night-time requirements, *or* you must be terminally ill.

'So severely disabled physically or mentally'

To qualify you must be 'so severely disabled physically or mentally' that you need attention or supervision. There is no requirement that you must have a specific medical condition – ie, one which has been named by a doctor. What is important is that you are so disabled (ie, have some functional incapacity or impairment) that you have care needs.[68] However, medical evidence can still be important to establish that you are disabled and what your care needs are.[69]

Problems sometimes arise if, for example, a child has behavioural problems that have not been attributed to a disability. In one case it was ruled that what is key is whether you have the physical or mental power to control the behaviour.[70] A previous case held, regarding children with enuresis, that immaturity (ie, unexceptional developmental delay) is not a disability,[71] but it is arguable that this no longer stands in light of this decision.

There is no extra test of severity; your disability is regarded as severe if you satisfy one of the disability tests.[72]

Care needs resulting from any medical condition caused or made worse by alcohol should be taken into account, whether or not you can control your drinking. The transitory effects of intoxication, such as incontinence or vomiting, can also be considered for the care component (and the lower rate, but not higher rate, mobility component) if the consumption of alcohol is because of a medical condition that means you cannot realistically stop drinking.[73]

The cooking test

You qualify for the lowest rate care component if you can show that you are so severely disabled, physically or mentally, that you cannot prepare a cooked main meal for yourself if you have the ingredients. This test does not apply to children under the age of 16.[74] The meal in question is a labour-intensive main meal for one person, freshly cooked on a traditional cooker (but note that the fact that you use a microwave is not proof that you cannot prepare a cooked main meal).[75] It is a hypothetical test about what you can reasonably do – it does not matter whether you actually do or do not cook,[76] or even have never learnt to do so.[77]

This is a broad test of your ability – it does not necessarily matter if there are some days when your ability is more or less than it is the rest of the time.[78]

You need to show that your disability makes you unable to perform the tasks that are needed to cook a main meal. You need to explain about your ability to plan a meal and to prepare and cook it – eg, to:

- peel and chop vegetables;
- use taps;
- use cooking utensils;
- use a cooker, but not necesssarily the oven;
- lift hot or heavy pans;
- drain vegetables;
- tell if food is cooked properly.

In order to cook a main meal, you must be able to manage both physical tasks (eg, lifting, carrying, bending, and using kitchen equipment) and mental tasks such as concentrating and planning.

- If you have a visual impairment, you should qualify if you are unable to read labels or cooking instructions, check whether vegetables have been adequately prepared and washed or see whether food is properly cooked.
- If you have a mental condition and so lack the motivation or concentration to cook, you should satisfy the test.[79]
- You may qualify if you can perform some of the individual cooking tasks (eg, chopping meat or vegetables) but overall you do not have the stamina to prepare an entire meal. For example, if you have chronic back pain and cannot stand for long periods, it may not be reasonable to expect you to prepare a meal and wait for it to cook while sitting down.[80]
- You may qualify if breathing difficulties in a hot, steamy kitchen or nausea stop you cooking.[81]

Kitchen aids and adaptations

There is some confusion about whether the availability of cooking aids and adaptations is a relevant consideration for the cooking test. This is a hypothetical test of what you can or cannot reasonably do, so you could argue that it is not appropriate, or reasonable, to consider whether your kitchen is, or could be, specially adapted.[82] It would certainly be incorrect to expect you to use a microwave to heat up convenience food.[83] However, cooking aids and adaptations may be taken into account if it is 'reasonable' to do so – eg, if you could readily obtain them, or whether you cook a 'sufficiently wide range of meals'.[84] If it is suggested you use a slotted spoon instead of draining vegetables from the pan, explain any difficulties you might still have lifting pans of water on and off the cooker. In another case it was ruled that, although a perching stool may be useful to relieve fatigue or discomfort, you still need to be sufficiently agile and mobile to cook a meal.[85]

Reasonableness

Only those who could 'reasonably' be expected to prepare a cooked main meal should be regarded as being able to do so. What is reasonable depends on the circumstances of your case. For example, if you have blackouts or seizures, it may be dangerous for you to cook. In one case, a person with haemophilia was judged to be at some risk and to experience some anxiety when cooking, but not to the extent that it was unreasonable for him to prepare a cooked main meal.[86]

Attention and supervision

'Requires'

To satisfy the attention or supervision conditions (see p144), you have to show that you 'require' this assistance from another person. The assistance must be 'reasonably required' rather than 'medically required'.[87] For example, if you are incontinent and need help changing your bedding, that help should count as 'reasonably required', even if not actually required to protect your skin.

Reasonably requires attention

Attention must be 'reasonably required to enable' you 'as far as reasonably possible to live a normal life'.[88] Having a social life, recreation, and cultural activities are part of normal life.[89] It is, therefore, reasonable for a blind person to have someone read newspapers, describe television pictures, or guide her/him during social outings. Similarly, it is reasonable for a person with learning disabilities to travel to, or take part in, social and recreational pursuits. What is reasonable should take into account your age and interests.[90]

Reasonably requires supervision

The requirement for supervision need only be reasonable. You are not expected to avoid every risk of harm in order to avoid the need for supervision. You can avoid most risks by staying in a chair all day but that may be totally unreasonable.[91] It is not reasonable to expect you to avoid all situations in which you might fall.[92]

When considering your need for continual supervision (see p151), you can argue that the fact that supervision is provided shows it is needed. Caselaw suggests that carers 'would be unlikely to exhaust themselves by providing it unnecessarily for years'.[93] If supervision is not provided because you live alone, you may be told that your choice is 'a strong indication that... [continual]... supervision is not required'.[94] But this always depends on the facts of your particular case. You may reasonably require supervision even if you do not receive it. Be very clear about the difficulties you have when your needs are not met, and about what help you think you need.[95]

Refusing medical treatment

Refusing medical treatment may affect the assessment. If treatment you have been offered by your doctor would remove the need for help, it may not be reasonably required. However, it may not be 'reasonably appropriate' for you to take the treatment – eg, because of the side effects.[96] It should be accepted as reasonable if your psychiatric condition causes you to refuse treatment, or you refuse invasive surgery.[97]

Attention

The attention you require must be in connection with **'bodily functions'**. These have been defined as the normal action of any organ of the body, or a number of organs acting together.[98] Thus, movement of the limbs is a bodily function that is used in walking. Eating is made up of the bodily functions of the jaw, mouth, stomach and bowels. Shopping or cleaning do not qualify because they are not normal actions or purposes of an organ or set of organs 'but merely things which a body can do if the relevant bodily functions... are working normally'.

The attention is in connection with the bodily function if it is a substitute method of providing what the bodily function would provide if it were not impaired.[99] For example, guiding a blind person so that s/he is able to walk outside should be treated as attention with the bodily function of 'seeing', rather than of 'walking'. A guide assists with 'seeing' by acting 'as the eyes' of a blind person.

'Attention' is 'a service of a close and intimate nature ... involving personal contact carried out in the presence of the disabled person'. The attention must normally to be given in the physical presence of the disabled person (see p149).[100] It must also be in connection with the bodily function. So helping someone to drink counts; carrying the drinks to where s/he is sitting does not.[101] Although attention must usually involve personal contact, it need not take the form of *physical* contact. Contact established by the spoken word may count if, for example, you are blind.[102] Thus, reading, describing or giving verbal instructions can be attention.

Similarly, if you would neglect yourself unless cajoled or stimulated to do routine tasks, you may require attention in the form of active stimulation.[103] Spoken reassurance counts as long as the carer is required to be physically in the same place as the disabled person. Reassurance provided over the telephone and other types of support not required to be given in the physical presence of the disabled person cannot qualify as attention,[104] although they may indicate a need for attention where help cannot be provided otherwise.[105]

Attention or supervision?

'**Attention**' involves a service of an 'active nature'[106] whereas '**supervision**' is passive and 'may be precautionary or anticipatory, yet never result in intervention'.[107] However, where supervision does lead to intervention, it becomes attention, so the two categories are never completely separate; if you need to be supervised because you are likely to fall and injure yourself, you receive attention when your carer gives you a steadying hand or warns you of an obstacle.[108] If attention is frequent, you qualify for the middle rate care component, even if the supervision is not 'continual' throughout the day. Sometimes an act can be both supervision and attention. It is, therefore, important to emphasise the full extent of your needs without trying to fit them neatly into either 'attention' or 'supervision' categories at the expense of leaving things out.

Communication

Communication is made up of a 'bundle' of bodily functions, including functions of the brain (such as language processing) or the senses (such as hearing). However, you need to identify what bodily function is impaired and what attention is needed from another person in connection with that bodily function.[109] If you are profoundly deaf, you may need an interpreter because you cannot hear spoken language,[110] or extra effort may be required to initiate a two-way conversation.[111]

Help to explain written information to someone with poor literacy skills as result of deafness[112] or a learning disability may also qualify.[113]

Domestic duties

Attention must normally be carried out in the presence of the disabled person.[114] A period of attention can also include incidental activities that could take place outside the presence of the claimant. For example, if a carer strips a soiled bed at night, the additional tasks of wringing out the sheets or hanging them up to dry could count as attention if done on the spot, as would cleaning a soiled carpet in the event of incontinence.[115] Taking the washing away or doing the cleaning at a different time would not qualify as attention.

Domestic tasks performed by a carer outside your presence, however, do not normally count as attention. It is different if you do your own domestic tasks with the help of a carer. If you are blind and someone helps you cook for yourself by reading cooking instructions to you, this is assistance with the bodily function of 'seeing' and can count as attention.[116] Similarly, if you have a learning disability and go shopping, you may need help to communicate your requirements. There is conflicting caselaw on whether assistance to perform domestic tasks yourself is attention that is reasonably required.[117] Argue that if, with help, you are able to shop or cook for yourself, this is part of what constitutes a 'normal life' (see definition of 'requires' on p147).[118]

Childcare

Help you have which enables you to look after your children can also count as attention.[119] For example, lifting or holding your baby for feeding is a sufficiently intimate service.[120] It will help if you can identify the bodily function in connection with which you need attention. Similarly, assisting you to take part in outdoor activities with your children allows you to lead a normal social life.[121] However, while help provided to you counts as attention, that given directly to your child does not.[122]

Special diets

Attention only counts if it needs to be given in the physical presence of the disabled person, so it will often be difficult to include help with food preparation. Arguably though, this type of help may, nonetheless, count as attention if it forms part of a broader sequence of care tasks. For example, the various parts of the process of regulating the blood sugar levels of a diabetic child, some of which require personal contact and some of which do not, should nonetheless *all* be treated as attention because they are integral elements of an overall regime.[123]

Night and day

Someone who needs help going to the toilet at 3am, when most people are asleep, clearly needs that help at night. Problems can arise when children or adults need supervision or attention in the late evening or early morning.

'Night' has been defined as 'that period of inactivity' which begins when 'the household, as it were, closes down for the night'.[124] The pattern of activities of each household needs to be taken into account. If a carer stays up into the small hours to help you but would otherwise go to bed earlier, that should count as night care.[125] Similarly, if a carer gets up early in the morning to help you rather than rise later with the rest of the household, that should count as night care.[126] If you live alone and go to bed unusually late or get up unusually early, your 'night' may be assumed to begin at a more average time of 11pm or to end at 7am.[127] The definition of 'night' for a child is the same as for an adult, so that attention given to a child in the evening before the adults have gone to bed counts only towards satisfying the day condition.[128]

'Attention... for a significant portion of the day'

If you can show that you need attention for a 'significant portion of the day' you qualify for the lowest rate care component.[129] A significant portion of the day can be either one period or a number of periods.

You may qualify for the lowest rate care component if you only need help for *part* of the day, rather than *throughout* the day (see below) – eg, you need help with activities connected with getting up, such as dressing and washing, at the beginning of the day and with activities connected with going to bed, such as undressing and washing, at the end of the day, but are otherwise able to care for yourself without help. Help at night does not count for the lower rate.[130]

The term **'a significant portion of the day'** is often taken to mean an hour or thereabouts.[131] However, if your carer spends less time than that in total but has to give help for a brief period on a number of small occasions, that might qualify.[132] If your carer does not have much time available or the help s/he gives is in spells of particularly concentrated activity, less than an hour's help may be enough. Factors like the amount, importance or effect of the attention, may be taken into account.[133]

Frequent attention throughout the day

To satisfy the day attention condition, you need to show that attention is required **frequently throughout the day**.[134] A frequent need might include help with toileting (eg, to reach the toilet, use a commode, or deal with zips), or help to walk in your own home. These are both examples of activities that most people normally engage in often. Most people who satisfy the 'frequency' condition do so by virtue of a range of different types of care needs. So it is the pattern of the needs across the day which is crucial. If you only need help at the beginning and end of the day, you are unlikely to satisfy the test. The help you need must be both **'frequent'**, meaning 'several times – not once or twice',[135] and required 'at intervals spread over the day'.[136] However, if the spread is uneven and you do not need help for lengthy periods, this should not necessarily disqualify you.[137]

Prolonged or repeated attention at night

The help that needs to be given in the night has to be either prolonged or repeated.[138] The DWP regards 20 minutes of attention as **'prolonged'**.[139] **'Repeated'** simply means twice or more.[140]

Because sleeping is a 'bodily function', soothing a child back to sleep counts as giving attention in connection with a bodily function.[141]

Continual supervision

You satisfy the **daytime supervision** condition if you require another person to provide 'continual supervision' throughout the day to avoid the risk of substantial danger, either to yourself or to others.[142] Supervision can be precautionary and anticipatory. It does not necessarily involve direct intervention. The supervision test consists of four parts.[143]

- **There must be a substantial danger to yourself or someone else as a result of your medical condition.** What constitutes a 'substantial danger' must be decided on the facts of each case. For example, if an elderly person falls, this is more likely to constitute a 'substantial danger' than if a younger person falls but only sustains minor bruises. What causes the fall may also be relevant. A person who loses consciousness would not be able to do anything to save her/himself.
- **The substantial danger must be one against which it is reasonable to guard.** This involves weighing the remoteness of the risk and the seriousness of the consequences should it arise. While the risk of a house catching fire may be remote, the consequences of leaving a disabled person who is unable to move alone in a house which did catch fire would be catastrophic. Similarly, the consequences of allowing a child to run out onto the road could be dire even though such an incident may be isolated.[144] Thus, it can be argued that you reasonably require continual supervision.[145] In assessing the likelihood of danger, the decision maker must look not only at what has happened in the past but at what may happen in the future.[146]
- **There must be a need for the supervision.** What should count as supervision is the level of supervision you 'reasonably require' (see p147). Although you may not receive much supervision (eg, if you live alone), you may still qualify if you can show you ought to be receiving it. If you have mental health problems, you may need supervision to help prevent you harming yourself. It is wrong to assume, without fully investigating your case, that if you really were at risk of harming yourself, you would be a hospital inpatient.[147] Further, if you are at risk of committing suicide, it would also be wrong to suggest that no amount of supervision would prevent a determined suicide attempt and supervision is, therefore, not required. The correct approach is to decide whether supervision would result in 'a real reduction in the risk of harm' to you.[148]
- **The supervision must be continual.** This is something less than 'continuous', but supervision which is required only occasionally or spasmodically is insufficient. If you can safely be left alone for a few hours, the supervision may not be continual.[149] If it is unavoidable that your carer leaves you alone for a period, you can still qualify if you can show that you are at risk during this time.If you are liable to epileptic fits without warning, you may need continual supervision, although attention for the period between the fits is not required.[150] Even if you have warning of the fits so that you can prevent yourself from falling, you may require continual supervision if you suffer from prolonged periods of confusion afterwards.[151]

Watching over

You satisfy the night-time supervision condition if you need someone to be awake to watch over you at night to avoid the risk of substantial danger to yourself or others.[152] The person watching over you has to be awake for a 'prolonged period' or 'at frequent intervals'. DWP guidance suggests a 'prolonged period' may mean 20 minutes or more[153] and the term 'at frequent intervals' means more than twice.

3. Attendance allowance

Attendance allowance (AA) is a benefit for people aged 65 and over with attention or supervision needs. There is a higher rate and a lower rate, the rules of which are similar to those for the highest and middle rates of the disability living allowance (DLA) care component respectively (see p144). Unlike DLA, AA does not have a mobility component.

Who can claim

You qualify for AA if:[154]

- you satisfy the residence conditions (see p1426);
- you are not a 'person subject to immigration control', although there are exceptions to this (see p1410);
- you are 65 or over when you first claim (see p155);
- you are not in hospital (see p677) or residential care (see p683);
- you satisfy the **'disability'** conditions – ie:
  - you meet one or more of the day or night conditions for the middle and highest rate of the DLA care component (see p144); *and*
  - you meet the condition(s) throughout a period of six months, ending within at least two years of the date on which your award begins; *or*
  - you are terminally ill (see p157).

The disability conditions

The disability conditions for AA are the same as those for the middle or highest rates of DLA care component. There is no equivalent in AA of the lowest rate care component. You get the lower rate of AA if you satisfy the disability conditions for the DLA middle rate care component (see p144). You get the higher rate of AA if you satisfy the disability conditions for the DLA highest rate care component (see p145).

4. The rules about your age

Disability living allowance (DLA) mobility component has lower and upper age limits. DLA care component has an upper age limit of 65.

Children aged under 16 must satisfy an additional test for the DLA care component and the lower rate mobility component. They cannot qualify for the lower rate care component by the 'cooking test' route.

You cannot claim attendance allowance (AA) if you are under 65.

Age limits for children

Children can get the higher rate DLA mobility component from age three onwards and the lower rate mobility component from age five.[155] The three months before the child reaches the age at which s/he can get the mobility component can form the qualifying period (see p144), enabling payment to be made from her/his birthday.

There is no lower age limit for DLA care component. However, a baby still has to meet the qualifying conditions for three months before the allowance becomes payable, unless s/he is terminally ill.

Children under the age of 16 cannot qualify for the lowest rate care component via the cooking test (see p146). A child can only qualify for lowest rate if s/he requires attention for a 'significant portion of the day' (see p151).

There is also an additional test for children for the lower rate mobility component and for the care component.

The additional tests for children

For the lower rate mobility component, in addition to the usual guidance or supervision condition (see p143) you must also show that *either*:

- the child requires substantially more guidance or supervision (see p142) than children of her/his age in normal physical and mental health; *or*
- children of the same age in normal physical and mental health would not require such guidance or supervision.[156]

Able-bodied children may only require adults to accompany them, whereas children with, for example, visual impairments or learning disabilities may need adults physically to hold or guide them, or to watch over them much more attentively (see p163 for tips on answering the mobility questions on the children's claim form). Similarly, a young deaf child may need someone to stay within touching distance, whereas a hearing child would not.[157]

This extra test does not apply to the higher rate mobility component.

For the DLA care component, you must show that *either*:

- the child has attention or supervision requirements 'substantially in excess of the normal requirements' of a child of the same age; *or*
- the child has substantial attention or supervision requirements which younger children in normal physical and mental health may also have, but which children of the same age and in normal physical and mental health would not have.[158] If this is due to 'developmental delay' see p145.

These extra tests do not apply if you are claiming DLA care component for a child who is terminally ill.[159]

As all young children require assistance throughout the day, it can be difficult to explain how you are providing attention, supervision or guidance that is 'substantially in excess' of what is normally required (see p163 for tips on filling out the children's claim form). It may be either because of the extra time you devote to these tasks, or 'by virtue of the quality or degree of attention or supervision which is required'.[160] For example, non-disabled children may need their food cut up, whereas disabled children may also need their food spooned into their mouths, or they may require you to be in the same room at all times, whereas you could supervise a non-disabled child from a different room.

The comparison should be with an 'average child' – ie, a child of average intelligence whose behaviour is neither particularly good nor bad.[161]

Aged over 65

You can claim AA if you are aged 65 or over. If you are approaching your 65th birthday, it is usually better to claim DLA since DLA has a mobility component and an additional lowest rate care component.

Normally, the upper age limit for claiming either rate of DLA mobility component is 65. You must make your claim and be sufficiently disabled to qualify before the date of your 65th birthday, but you need not have completed the three-month qualifying period by then.[162]

Although you must normally be under 65 to claim, once DLA is awarded it can be paid beyond the age of 65. You can renew an award, including a mobility component award or the lowest rate care component award that expires after age 65, but you must reclaim within a year of the previous award ending.[163] If your condition changes after you reach the age of 65, you cannot qualify for either rate of mobility component or the lowest rate care component for the first time.

However, you can be awarded either rate of mobility component or the lowest rate care component after reaching the age of 65 if you have an existing award of another component of DLA, and ask for a revision or supersession of that award after you are 65. You must show that you have satisfied the disability conditions for the new component since you were 64 or earlier.[164]

If your condition changes, you can move to the middle or highest rate care component. You must show that you have met the qualifying conditions for the middle or highest rate for six months before it can be awarded, not three months. This is because the rules about qualifying periods for those in receipt of DLA care component over the age of 65 are the same as for AA.[165] If it has been over a year since your previous award ended, you must claim AA instead of DLA.

5. The amount of benefit

Disability living allowance (DLA) mobility component is paid at two weekly rates:[166]

- the lower rate is £20.55;
- the higher rate is £51.85.

DLA care component is paid at three weekly rates:[167]

- the lowest rate is £20.55;
- the middle rate is £51.85;
- the highest rate is £77.45.

Attendance allowance (AA) is paid at two weekly rates:[168]

- the lower rate is £51.85;
- the higher rate is £77.45.

You are not credited with national insurance contributions by virtue of receiving DLA or AA.

6. Special benefit rules

Special rules may apply to:

- people on renal dialysis (see below);
- people who are terminally ill (see p157);
- people subject to immigration control (see p1410);
- people who have gone abroad (see p1480);
- people in care homes and other special accommodation (see p684);
- people in hospital and hospices (see p677);
- people in prison (see p692).

People on renal dialysis

If you are undergoing renal dialysis on a kidney machine, special rules may apply entitling you to the middle rate of disability living allowance (DLA) care component or the lower rate of attendance allowance (AA).[169]

To qualify, you need to have treatment regularly for two or more sessions a week. The dialysis must normally require the attendance or supervision of another person.

If you dialyse in hospital as an outpatient you must not have help from any member of the staff. Others who dialyse in hospital do not qualify by this special route but can count these spells of hospital dialysis towards the qualifying periods. This helps those who alternate between dialysis in hospital and at home to get AA or DLA care component more quickly for the times they dialyse at home. Even if you do not qualify under this route, you may qualify under the ordinary conditions.

People who are terminally ill

You are regarded as **'terminally ill'** if you have a progressive disease and can reasonably be expected to die within six months as a result of that disease.[170] This does not mean that it must be more likely than not that you will die within this period. It simply means that death within six months would not be unexpected.

If you are terminally ill, you are automatically treated as satisfying the conditions for the highest rate DLA care component and there is no requirement to satisfy the three-month qualifying period.[171] Similarly, the higher rate of AA is paid straight away without your having to serve the six-month qualifying period.[172] If you are terminally ill, you do not automatically get DLA mobility component. You must satisfy the usual disability conditions, but you do not need to serve the usual three-month qualifying period, and the 'forward test' only applies until your death.[173]

The DWP aims to deal with these claims within eight working days. They are referred to as 'claims under the special rules'.

The special rules apply only if your claim, or a revision or supersession request on an existing claim, expressly states that you are terminally ill.[174]

Someone else is allowed to make a claim, or apply for a revision or supersession, on behalf of a terminally ill person without her/his knowledge or authority.[175]

The DWP can supersede your award if your condition or prognosis improves so that you are no longer regarded as 'terminally ill'.

Awards are normally made for a fixed period of three years. If there is already a mobility award in place, the length of the special rules award may be adjusted to finish at the same time as the mobility award.

7. Claims and backdating

The rules about claiming and backdating are in Chapter 42. This sections tells you about the specific rules that apply to disability living allowance (DLA) and attendance allowance (AA).

Note: the success of a DLA or AA claim can often depend on how well you have completed the claim form. See p160 for further information.

Making a claim

A claim for DLA or AA must be in writing. You can do this by completing:

- the approved form. Send it to the disability benefits office covering your region or any DWP office. You may also be able to take or send it to an 'alternative

office' (see p1018). In practice, it is nearly always best to post the form to the disability benefits centre;
- an online application form at www.dwp.gov.uk/eservice.

Keep a copy of your claim form in case queries arise.

You must provide any information or evidence required (see p159). In certain circumstances, the DWP may accept a written application which is not on the approved form (see p1019).[176] You can amend or withdraw your claim before a decision is made (see p1019).

Claims for terminally ill people are made in a different way (see below).

Forms

Get Form AA1 (for AA) or DLA1 or DLA1 Child (for those under 16) (for DLA) from your local disability benefits centre or an 'alternative office', the Benefit Enquiry Line for people with disabilities on 0800 882200 (textphone 0800 243 355) or by sending in the tear-off coupon from leaflet AA5DCS (for AA) or DLA5DCS (for DLA).

When you request a form from the DWP or an alternative office, it should be date stamped. You have six weeks from the date of your request to return it.[177] Keep a record of the date you asked for the form. The DWP may complete a checklist to assess your 'potential benefit entitlement'. This is not part of the claim process and you should always be sent a claim pack.

Claim packs are also available from Citizens Advice Bureaux, other advice agencies and at www.direct.gov.uk/en/disabledpeople. These packs are not date stamped so you must send in the completed form as soon as possible to secure your date of claim. This is the date on which your form is received by the DWP (see p159).

Who should claim

A claim for DLA or AA is normally made by the disabled person her/himself. A claim for a child under 16 or a person unable to manage her/his own affairs is made by an appointee (see pp166 and 1016).

Claiming for terminally ill people

If a claim is being made on the basis that a person is terminally ill (see p157), it may be made without that person's knowledge or authority.

These claims are known as 'claims under the special rules'. People claiming under these rules need to provide Form DS1500, completed by their GP or consultant, detailing their medical condition. They do not need to fill in the parts of the claim form relating to their need for personal care. If they wish to claim DLA mobility component, they do need to answer the relevant questions.

It is possible for someone acting on behalf of a terminally ill person to request a revision or supersession of an unfavourable decision, and even to appeal without that person's knowledge or permission.[178]

When the decision maker receives the DS1500 s/he makes an assessment on whether the person meets the special rules. If s/he decides s/he does not, the person can claim in the normal way or appeal the decision.

Information to support your claim

When you claim DLA or AA, you must:

- satisfy the national insurance (NI) number requirement (see p1023). This does not apply if you are claiming DLA on behalf of a child under 16;[179]
- provide proof of your identity, if required (see p1024).

The date of your claim

The date of your claim is the date your request for a claim pack is received by the DWP or an 'alternative office', providing you return the properly completed form within six weeks of the date of your request.[180] If the DWP has issued a form without date-stamping it, write and explain when and where it was issued and ask to be paid from that date or six weeks before you sent it in.[181] There is also some discretion to extend the six-week deadline, so if you return the form late explain why.

If you are using a claim form issued by an advice agency or downloaded from the internet, your date of claim is the date your completed form is received by the DWP. If you submit a claim online, it is treated as having been made on the date it is accepted by the system.[182]

If you claim the wrong benefit

A claim for DLA can be treated as a claim for AA and *vice versa* (see p1025).[183] A claim for an increase of industrial injuries disablement benefit where constant attendance is needed can be treated as a claim for DLA or AA and *vice versa* (see p1025).[184]

Claiming in advance

A claim for DLA or AA can be made before you have satisfied the three-month qualifying period for DLA[185] (see pp137 and 144), the six-month qualifying period for AA[186] (see p153), or any other qualifying condition. Provided you claim no more than three months before you would qualify for DLA or six months before you would qualify for AA, a decision can be made on your claim in advance of your date of entitlement.

Renewal claims

DLA and AA can be awarded for fixed periods (see p166). Renewal claims can be invited up to six months before your old award expires. It is important that you send back your completed renewal claim form before your old award expires as no backdating is possible.

Decision makers normally treat your renewal claim as a new claim beginning on the day after your old award runs out.[187] However, they may use the information you give in the renewal claim to revise or supersede your existing award, in which case your entitlement may be changed earlier.[188] If you think you have a strong case for an increased award, return your renewal form early and ask for a revision or supersession. If this is not the case, it is advisable to return the form nearer the date your current award runs out.

Reclaiming under age 65

If your award has ended and you reclaim within two years (eg, because your condition has deteriorated), you do not have to serve the standard three-month qualifying period again, provided you meet all the other qualifying conditions for the rate you previously received. This is because the qualifying period is taken to be the last three months of your previous award.[189] If you reclaim a different rate, you do have to serve the standard qualifying period.

Reclaiming over age 65

If your DLA award ended after you reached 65 and you reclaim the same rate within one year, you can be paid without having to serve the standard qualifying period again.To reclaim another rate (see p155), you do have to serve the qualifying period again. If it has been over a year since your previous award ended, you must claim AA instead of DLA care, and you will not be able to reclaim DLA mobility.[190] The qualifying period is three months for DLA mobility or six months for DLA care, unless you already completed a three-month qualifying period by the time you turned 65.[191]

If your AA award has ended, you can reclaim the same rate within two years without having to serve the standard six-month qualifying period again.[192]

Completing the claim form

Make sure you get the correct form. There are two DLA claim packs – one for those under the age of 16 (DLA1 Child) and one for those aged 16 and over (DLA1) – and one AA claim pack (AA1).

If you find it difficult to complete the form, the DWP can help you complete it by telephone or, in some circumstances, can send a visiting officer to do so. Most advice agencies can also help you.

Attendance allowance claims

Try to include all the information that is relevant and use extra pages if necessary. You will find useful tips on completing the from in the section below on the DLA form for adults. However, problems you have with cooking a meal or walking out of doors may not be relevant to your claim for AA. Sometimes the decision maker will phone you to ask for further information. If you do not want to be phoned, write this clearly on the form.

Disability living allowance claims

The DLA claim form is long and has several pages on different aspects of care and mobility. Fill in all the pages that are relevant. If the same difficulties apply on more than one page, repeat the information or refer back to earlier in the form. There is space to include details of people who know about your difficulties – include carers and support workers as well as medical professionals.

The claim pack for adults

The DLA form asks you questions about your mobility problems, your supervision and attention needs, and your ability to cook a main meal. Do not worry if a lot of the questions do not apply to you. You can, for example, qualify for the lowest rate of the care component because of the problems you have cooking a main meal (see p146), which only takes up one page of the claim pack.

- **Give as much detail as you can**. Do not feel bound by the size of the boxes. If you need extra space to explain your situation, use a separate piece of paper. There is a statement to be completed by someone who knows you. If your doctor fills this in, s/he should not charge you. If you do not have anyone who can complete it, leave it blank.
- **Unmet care needs**. If you are not receiving any help from another person, it can be difficult to describe your attention or supervision needs. Many disabled people struggle to perform daily tasks on their own. If you do not have a carer, you should still describe your problems. Consider whether certain activities cause you pain, or make you dizzy, tired or breathless. If you take a long time to perform particular tasks, explain this. Also say if you are not able to perform a particular activity adequately – eg, if you cannot bend to reach your feet when washing.
- **Aids and adaptions**. If a decision maker thinks that you can use a particular aid or adaptation, s/he may decide you do not need attention or supervision. For example, if you have a commode, the decision maker may conclude you do not need someone to help you get to the toilet at night. Therefore, try to explain how useful any equipment actually is and whether you still need help from another person in spite of the equipment. If, for instance, you have had a bath rail fitted, but find it very difficult to climb in or out of a bath, explain this.

- **Frequency, variability and duration.** You are asked throughout the form to estimate how long you need help for, and how often. You should explain:
  - **how long you need help for**, if you need attention for a 'significant portion of the day' (see p151), or you need 'prolonged' attention at night (see p151);
  - **how often you need help**, to show that you need 'frequent attention throughout the day' (see p151) or 'watching over' repeatedly during the night (see p153);
  - **how many days a week you need help**, to estabish your overall needs, particularly if you have a variable or fluctuating condition. If your condition does not vary but you only receive help on certain days, still say that you need help seven days a week. It is the help you need, not the help you actually get, that counts. If you need attention or supervision or have difficulties walking most days of the week, your needs are taken into account. However, if you only have problems a few days a week, you will not necessarily be refused DLA.[193] In this case, explain fully the help you need on your 'bad' days but include the help you need on your 'good' days as well so that you give an overall picture.

  It can sometimes be helpful to keep a diary of your needs over a period of a week or more and send this in.
- **Walking outdoors.** The section on 'getting about outdoors' is for the higher rate of DLA mobility component. If walking causes you 'severe discomfort', you may be regarded as being virtually unable to walk (see p138).
  - You are asked to say how far you can walk before you feel discomfort and how long on average it takes you to walk this distance. If you are not sure how to answer this, get someone to walk outdoors with you to measure the distance you can walk without severe discomfort and the time it takes you to walk this far. It may help to give an example of the distance – eg, 'I can walk past five houses – about 40 metres'. Bear in mind that if you can walk a further distance without severe discomfort after a brief rest, it is the total distance that counts.
  - Explain what sort of discomfort you experience – eg, pain or breathlessness.
  - Describe your manner of walking – eg, you may have problems with balance, or you may walk with a limp, drag your feet, or shuffle.
  - If you need to stop to rest, try to explain how far you can walk before you need to stop, and for how long you need to rest.
- **Mental disabilities.** There is no specific section about your mental health. There is a section on 'communicating with other people', where you should mention problems caused by anxiety, intrusive thoughts or anger, or learning difficulties. Questions throughout the claim pack ask if you need encouraging or reminding to attend to your bodily functions. The section on 'the help you need when you go out' may also be appropriate if you need assistance to undertake social, leisure and recreational activities. At the end of the form there is a page to 'tell us anything else you think we should know'. It often

helps to summarise here your mental health problems and explain any other attention or supervision needs you have.

- **Sensory impairments.** The section on 'communicating with other people' applies to deaf claimants who may need an interpreter or other help with communicating or reading, or blind people who need to have newspapers or correspondence read to them (see p147). Blind people who need someone to tell them if they have stains on their clothes or if their hands are clean should explain these problems in the 'dressing' and 'washing' sections. It is important that people with sensory impairments complete the section on 'the help you need when you go out during the day or in the evening' to explain the help needed to undertake social and recreational activities. If you need extra help because you are working or studying, include this.

The claim pack for children

The claim pack for children is substantially different from the adult form. However, some issues, such as how to answer the questions on frequency, variability and duration of needs, are similar to those faced by people filling in the adult pack (see p161). Therefore, read the section on the adult claim pack, as well as this section, if you are completing a child's pack. The following issues are specific to claiming for children.

- **When the child is in bed at night.** Only the needs your child has after the rest of the household has gone to bed count as night-time needs (see p150).
- **Mobility.** Children can only qualify for DLA mobility component from the age of three, but problems with getting around may indicate care or supervision needs, so explain them somewhere on the claim form. It can be difficult to explain how a disabled child requires 'substantially more' guidance or supervision (see p154) outdoors in order to qualify for the lower rate mobility component (see p142). This is because most young children do not go out, at least in unfamiliar places, on their own. A child with a sensory impairment or learning disability may require much more direct or close supervision than a non-disabled child.[194] Whereas a non-disabled child may be allowed to walk in the presence of an adult, a disabled child may require an adult physically to hold or guide her/him. Also, a 'familiar route' to a non-disabled child may be a hazardous obstacle course to a child whose sight is impaired. It may help to make comparisons with siblings or classmates, perhaps a child with attention deficit disorder would need to be accompanied to school or to local shops, whereas a non-disabled child would be allowed to go alone.[195]
- **Extra attention or supervision.** When explaining about your child's 'extra' requirements, bear in mind that they must be 'substantially in excess' of that required by a non-disabled child (see p154). Disabled children may need extra help to develop daily living skills, language and social skills. For example, babies with sensory impairments may require more physical stimulation to aid parental bonding and develop communication skills. Children learn

spontaneously through play, but a disabled child may need help to use toys, or may need to be coaxed to explore her/his environment. Children with learning or sensory disabilities require extra help to develop daily living or language skills. They may also develop these skills later than non-disabled children. Similarly, you may let a non-disabled child play outdoors and instruct her/him not to cross roads. You may be able to supervise the child indirectly without having to watch her/him all the time. However, you may have to supervise directly a child with sensory impairments or behavioural problems, or confine him/her indoors.

- **About the child's development.** The questions on development are extremely important to show that disabled children need extra care or supervision. If you have no experience of bringing up children, you may not know exactly when a child should be crawling, walking, speaking and feeding her/himself. If you are not sure, ask your health visitor or paediatrician. For example, most children pick up and eat food by 8–12 months. Therefore, if you are still feeding a child after 12 months, you are providing attention that a non-disabled child of the same age would not need.
  When completing renewal forms, bear in mind that the decision maker may suppose that your child no longer needs the same help as s/he did when s/he was younger. However, it is wrong to assume that all disabled children develop in the same way. In one case, a child with photosensitive epilepsy watched television even though he was not supposed to. It could not be said that he was 'old enough to know better', as there was evidence that he persisted in doing things that were known to be bad for him.[196]
- **School-age children.** Disabled children, particularly those with sensory impairments or learning disabilities, usually require extra help with their school work. Extra help in the classroom or with homework can count towards a child's attention needs, provided you can show it is in connection with a bodily function (see p148).[197] Caselaw suggests that straightforward teaching would probably not be sufficiently intimate to qualify.[198] A statement of special educational needs may provide useful supporting evidence of the extra help needed with her/his studies.
- **Communicating.** Prelingual deaf children, whose first language is British Sign Language, may need help to understand or communicate in written or spoken English. Blind children will not only need help to understand written information, but may also need help to learn Braille. Children with behavioural problems may need help to express themselves or understand other people.

How your claim is dealt with

Claims are initially dealt with at a specified office dealing with your region. A decision maker can award DLA or AA on the basis of your claim form alone, but may choose to contact someone you have named on the form for more information. It is a good idea to include details of all the medical professionals and other people who know and understand your needs, and, if possible, enclose evidence from them. If the decision maker cannot get enough information, s/he may also arrange for you to be given a medical examination by a healthcare professional acting on behalf of the DWP, who will sometimes visit you at home.

If you refuse a medical examination 'without good cause', the decision maker has to decide your claim against you.[199]

The decision maker may telephone you to ask for further information. If you do not want to be telephoned, write this clearly on the claim form.

The DWP aims to deal with new claims for DLA within 39 working days and new claims for AA within 22 working days. Claims made under the 'special rules' for terminal illness (see p157) should be decided within eight working days.

Backdating your claim

It is very important to claim in time. A claim for DLA or AA cannot be backdated.[200]

If you might have qualified for benefit earlier but did not claim because you were given the wrong information or were misled by the DWP, you could ask for a compensation payment (see p1261) or complain to the Ombudsman through your MP (see p1260).

8. Getting paid

Payment of disability living allowance (DLA) or attendance allowance (AA) is normally made by direct credit transfer into your bank (or similar) account (see p1038).[201] If you are unable to open or manage an account, it may be possible to be paid by cheque or by 'simple payment' (see p1040). Payment can also be made to someone else on your behalf, called your 'appointee' (see p1016), if you are unable to act for yourself.

When are AA and DLA paid?	Normally on a Wednesday, but the Secretary of State can vary the payday.[202]
How often are AA and DLA paid?	Normally every four weeks in arrears. However: – AA and DLA can be paid at shorter intervals in individual cases.[203] – AA can be paid weekly in advance and DLA under the special rules for terminal illness can be paid weekly. If you leave hospital or a care home and expect to return within 28 days, DLA and AA can be paid at a daily rate for days at home.[204]

Note:
- If you are claiming other DWP benefits, DLA or AA may be paid in a single payment with them instead.

- The higher rate of DLA mobility component can be paid directly to Motability if you are purchasing a car through the scheme (see p170).
- Even if you have been sanctioned for benefit offences (see p1106) you must be paid your AA or DLA.
- If you have forgotten your PIN or if a cheque is lost or stolen, see p1043.
- If payment of your AA or DLA is delayed, see p1262. You might be able to get an interim payment (see p1046). You may also be eligible for a crisis loan (see p564). If you wish to complain about how your claim has been dealt with, see p1255. You might be able to claim compensation (see p1261).
- If payment of your DLA or AA is suspended, see p1043.
- If you have been overpaid DLA or AA, you might have to repay it (see Chapter 43). If you have been accused of fraud, see Chapter 44.

Length of awards

Awards of DLA or AA can be made for either fixed or indefinite periods.[205] The length of an award depends on how long a decision maker estimates your current needs may last. If you have an indefinite award, you will not have to make a renewal claim at any stage, but it is always open to the DWP to reduce or stop your award if it has grounds to revise or supersede it.

In practice, awards are usually made for at least six months because of the DLA requirement that you should satisfy the disability conditions for the next six months. However, there is no legal minimum length for an award.[206] If you think benefit should be awarded for longer, perhaps because your condition is such that your care or mobility needs will not decrease, you can consider asking for a revision (see p1126). Bear in mind that, if you challenge the length of your award, the rate of your award may also be reconsidered. If your award is for a limited period you will be invited to make a renewal claim up to six months before the award runs out (see p160). Special rules awards are made for three years (see p157).

Although DLA has two components, there can only be a single DLA award, consisting of one or both components. You can have an indefinite award of one component combined with a limited period award of the other. However, although components can be awarded for fixed periods starting at different times, both fixed award periods must be aligned to end on the same day.[207]

Payment to children

DLA for a child under the age of 16 is usually paid to an adult with whom s/he is living, whom the Secretary of State appoints to act on her/his behalf (often called an 'appointee'). This is normally the child's mother or father.[208] Children cannot make valid claims on their own behalf.[209]

The allowance can continue to be paid to the appointee in some circumstances when the child and appointee are not living together, including during a temporary separation of up to 12 weeks, or when the child is absent at a boarding school or in hospital (although other rules may mean that payment stops – see p675). DLA ceases to be paid to the appointee immediately when the child is in the care of a local authority or any similar arrangement, unless the arrangement is not intended to last for more than 12 weeks.[210]

Change of circumstances

It is your duty to report any change in your circumstances that might affect your right to, the amount of, or payment of your benefit (see p1047).[211] Do this promptly by writing to or telephoning the Disability Contact and Processing Unit (although in individual cases notification might be accepted in other forms such as online via the benefit update service – see p1015). In some cases, however, the decision maker might say you must report changes in writing. It is usually best to do this and keep a copy in case of a dispute in the future.

If your condition deteriorates so that you become eligible for a higher rate or another component, benefit can be backdated to the first payday after the end of the three-month (for DLA) or six-month (for AA) qualifying period, as long as you tell the DWP no later than a month after completing the qualifying period. If payment of (but not entitlement to) DLA or AA has stopped – eg, while you are in hospital or a care home, still notify the DWP so that the correct rate is paid when payment resumes. If you do not report a change of circumstances within the month, benefit can still be backdated if you do so within 13 months and there were 'special circumstances' that meant it was not practical to report the change earlier.[212]

If your condition improves so that you should drop down a rate, lose a component or lose benefit altogether, the new decision normally takes effect from the date you tell the DWP of the improvement, or from the date of the decision if the DWP changed it without your asking.[213] It would only take effect from an earlier date (and cause an overpayment) if you should have realised earlier that the change should have been reported. The DWP recognises that it is difficult for claimants to realise when a gradual improvement begins to affect benefit entitlement.[214]

'Right payment programme' and 'correctness programme'

The DWP checks existing DLA awards as part of a 'right payment programme'. AA recipients do not currently have their awards checked.

The programme applies to people on all rates of DLA, including those originally awarded DLA 'for life' or indefinitely. You are exempt if your award has been looked at in the last 12 months, if you have been awarded benefit under the 'special rules' (see p157) or if no DLA is being paid – eg, because you are in hospital (see Chapter 30).

The DWP contacts you by sending a postal questionnaire (DLA300). You have a duty to supply any information requested that may affect benefit entitlement.[215] If you do not respond, the DWP may notify you that your benefit may be suspended if you do not reply within a further month.[216] This one-month limit can be extended if necessary to arrange for someone to help you complete the questionnaire.[217] If, after your benefit has been suspended for a month, you still have not complied, your award can be terminated.[218]

As part of the initial investigation into an existing award, the DWP can require you to have a medical examination.[219] If you fail, without good cause, to have a medical examination on two consecutive occasions, your benefit can be suspended.[220] If, after your benefit has been suspended for one month, you still have not had a medical examination, your benefit can be terminated.[221]

Further checks on claimants who have been reported to the fraud hotline, but where there is not enough evidence to justify a fraud investigation, may be made under a 'correctness programme'. If you are being checked under this programme you will be sent Form DLA80.

9. Tax, tax credits and other benefits

Attendance allowance (AA) and disability living allowance (DLA) are not taxable.[222]

Tax credits

DLA and AA are ignored as income when calculating child tax credit (CTC) and working tax credit (WTC). A disabled child element is included in CTC for each child who gets DLA (any rate). If s/he gets the highest rate of the DLA care component, you may get a severe disabled child element in CTC. An award of AA or DLA at any rate counts as a qualifying benefit for the disabled worker element of WTC. If you or your partner get the highest rate care component or the higher rate of AA, a severe disability element is included in WTC.

Means-tested benefits

Neither AA nor any rate of DLA is taken into account as income when calculating any of the means-tested benefits. DLA and AA are paid on top of these benefits.

If you or your partner are entitled to AA or DLA, your income support (IS), income-based jobseeker's allowance (JSA), and, unless you have reached the qualifying age for state pension credit (PC), housing benefit (HB) and council tax benefit (CTB) include the disability premium (or for IS and JSA only, higher pensioner premium if either of you have reached the qualifying age for PC). If you or your partner are entitled to the highest rate of DLA care component and aged under the qualifying age for PC, you also get an enhanced disability premium, which is also paid with income-related ESA (see p827). A severe disability premium is included in IS, income-based JSA, income-related employment and support allowance (ESA), HB or CTB, or an addition for severe disability is included in the guarantee credit of PC if you receive AA or the highest or middle rate of the DLA care component and meet the other conditions for that premium. For further information, see p830.

If your child is entitled to DLA, HB/CTB includes a disabled child premium. If s/he gets the highest rate care component, HB/CTB includes an enhanced disability premium. These premiums are also included in IS and income-based JSA if you do not yet get CTC.

If you or your partner are entitled to AA or DLA care component, non-dependant deductions (see p869) are not made from any housing costs you claim – ie, HB, CTB and mortgage interest payments included in IS, income-based JSA, income-related ESA and the guarantee credit of PC.

Non-means-tested benefits

DLA and AA may be paid in addition to any other non-means-tested benefits except that:

- AA and DLA care overlap with constant attendance allowance under the industrial injuries scheme (see p380) or war pensions scheme;[223] *and*
- DLA mobility component overlaps with the war pensioners' mobility supplement payable under the war pensions scheme.[224]

If you are receiving the highest or middle rate DLA care component or AA and someone regularly looks after you, that person may be entitled to carer's allowance (CA – see Chapter 6). However, your entitlement to a severe disability premium (additonal amount) can be affected if s/he receives CA.

Passports and other sources of help

You qualify for a Christmas bonus if you receive AA or DLA at any rate (see p9).

If you get the higher rate of DLA mobility component, you or your carer can be exempt from paying road tax on a car used solely by you or for your purposes. Contact the Disability Contact and Processing Unit (see Appendix 1) for an application form.

If you get the higher rate mobility component, you should qualify for the blue badge scheme of parking concessions, which operates throughout Great Britain and the European Economic Area (with certain local variations). Contact your local authority for further information.

If any member of your household receives AA or DLA at any rate, you can get a grant for help with insulation and other energy efficiency measures in your home (see p16).

If you are getting the highest rate of DLA care component you may be eligible for money from the Independent Living Funds to finance care provision.

Motability

Motability is a charity that runs a scheme to help you lease or buy a car if you receive the higher rate of DLA mobility component for a period of 12 months or more (see p137).

DLA mobility component is paid directly to Motability.[225] You may also have to make extra payments. For further information, telephone 0845 456 4566 or visit www.motability.co.uk.

Notes

1. Disability living allowance mobility component

1 s73 SSCBA 1992
2 s73(1)(d) SSCBA 1992
3 CM/5/1986; *BP v SSWP* [2009] UKUT 90 (AAC)
4 Reg 12(1)(a) SS(DLA) Regs
5 R(M) 3/78
6 Reg 12(1)(a) SS(DLA) Regs; R(M) 2/78; R(DLA) 4/06
7 CDLA/2822/1999; CDLA/4329/1999; CDLA/1525/2008
8 R(M) 3/86; CSDLA/202/2007; CDLA/3839/2007; *DM v SSWP (DLA)* [2010] UKUT 375 (AAC)
9 R(M) 2/89; CDLA/97/2001; *Sanhu v SSWP* [2010] EWCA Civ 962
10 Reg 12(4) SS(DLA) Regs
11 R(M) 2/89
12 Reg 12(1)(b) SS(DLA) Regs
13 CDLA/3188/2002 ; *HJ v SSWP (DLA)* [2010] UKUT 307 (AAC)
14 R(M) 1/95; CSDLA/171/1998
15 *JK v SSWP (DLA)* [2010] UKUT 197 (AAC)
16 CM/208/1989; CSDLA/0444/2002
17 CDLA/3519/2008
18 *NR v SSWP (DLA)* [2010] UKUT 111 (AAC)
19 CDLA/1389/1997; CDLA/2195/2008
20 R(M) 1/81
21 R(M) 1/83
22 CM/267/93
23 CDLA/608/1994; R(DLA) 4/03
24 R(DLA) 4/04
25 *Hewitt and Diment v CAO* 29 June 1998 (CA), reported as R(DLA) 6/99
26 R(M) 1/98; CDLA/3941/2005 interpreted 'exertion' to mean the activity of walking 'however slight the exertion'.
27 Reg 12(2) SS(DLA) Regs
28 Reg 12(3) SS(DLA) Regs
29 R(DLA) 3/95
30 Sch 2 SS(GB) Regs
31 Reg 34(2) and Sch 3 Parts II & III SS(IIPD) Regs
32 Reg 12(2) SS(DLA) Regs
33 Reg 12(1)(b) SS(DLA) Regs
34 *JH v SSWP (DLA)* [2010] UKUT 456 (AAC)
35 s73(3) SSCBA 1992; reg 12(5) and (6) SS(DLA) Regs
36 R(M) 3/86; CSDLA/202/2007
37 R(DLA) 2/96
38 R(DLA) 3/98
39 *M (a child) v CAO* 29 October 1999 (CA), reported as R(DLA) 1/00
40 CDLA/95/1995
41 CDLA/3215/2001
42 CDLA/2054/1998
43 R(DLA) 7/02; R(DLA) 9/02; CDLA/3244/2001; CDLA/2955/2008; *SSWP v DM (DLA)* [2010] UKUT 318 (AAC)
44 s73 (1AB) SSCBA 1992; reg 12 (1A) SS(DLA) Regs
45 s73(1)(d) SSCBA 1992
46 R(DLA) 6/03
47 CDLA/42/1994
48 CDLA/42/1994; R(DLA) 3/04

49 There are conflicting decisions on whether a person who needs guidance or supervision, but cannot take advantage of the faculty of walking, can qualify. See CDLA/2364/1995 and CDLA/42/1994.
50 CDLA/2142/2005
51 Reg 12(7) and (8) SS(DLA) Regs; R(DLA) 3/04; CDLA/2409/2003; R(DLA) 6/05
52 R(DLA) 4/01
53 R(DLA) 4/01
54 R(DLA) 3/04
55 CDLA/42/1994
56 CDLA/42/1994
57 CDLA/42/1994; CDLA/3360/1995; CSDLA/591/1997; CDLA/2643/1998
58 R(DLA) 4/01
59 R(DLA) 6/05
60 R(DLA) 4/01
61 s73(12) SSCBA 1992
62 s73(9)(b)(ii) SSCBA 1992

2. **Disability living allowance care component**
63 s72 SSCBA 1992
64 s72(1)(a) SSCBA 1992
65 s72(1)(b) and (c) SSCBA 1992
66 s72(4)(a) SSCBA 1992
67 s72(5) SSCBA 1992
68 R(DLA) 3/06, tribunal of commissioners
69 CDLA/4475/04
70 R(DLA) 3/06, tribunal of commissioners
71 R(DLA) 1/05; see also *AC v SSWP* [2009] UKUT 83 (AAC)
72 R(DLA) 10/02 approved by R(DLA) 3/06, tribunal of commissioners
73 R(DLA) 6/06, tribunal of commissioners
74 s72(1A)(a) SSCBA 1992
75 CDLA/1215/2005; CDLA/2367/2004
76 *SSWP v Moyna* [2003] (HL), reported as R(DLA) 7/03
77 *R v Secretary of State for Social Security ex parte Armstrong* [1996] (CA)
78 *Moyna v SSWP* [2003] (HL), reported as R(DLA) 7/03
79 CSDLA/80/1996
80 CDLA/7374/1995; R(DLA) 8/02
81 CDLA/20/1994; CDLA/4214/2002; R(DLA) 1/08; CDLA/2991/2007
82 R(DLA) 2/95, which nonetheless allows for the use of 'certain devices to assist' which may form part of 'normal reasonable facilities' for cooking. However, CDLA/1212/2005 held, following R(DLA) 7/03 (cooking test is a notional test and a thought experiment), that it is not relevant to the tests whether a claimant does or does not have a microwave oven or other standard equipment.
83 CDLA/20/1994; R(DLA) 2/95 insists on a traditional cooker, but note CDLA/770/2000, which allows fresh food to be prepared in a microwave. See also CDLA/3778/2002.
84 CDLA/17329/1996 and CDLA/770/2000, both of which would appear to give more weight to the use of special cooking aids than R(DLA) 2/95; see CPAG's *Welfare Rights Bulletin 163*; *KS v SSWP (DLA)* [2011] UKUT 29 (AAC)
85 CDLA/1714/2005
86 R(DLA) 1/97
87 R(A) 3/86 and *Mallinson v Secretary of State for Social Security* 21 April 1994 (HL), reported as R(A) 3/94
88 *Secretary of State for Social Security v Fairey* (aka *Halliday*) 21 May 1997 (HL), reported as R(A) 2/98
89 *Secretary of State for Social Security v Fairey* (aka *Halliday*) 21 May 1997 (HL), reported as R(A) 2/98
90 *Secretary of State for Social Security v Fairey* (aka *Halliday*) 21 May 1997 (HL), reported as R(A) 2/98
91 R(A) 3/89
92 R(A) 5/90
93 R(A) 1/73
94 CDLA/899/1994
95 See for example, R(A) 3/86 and *R v Secretary of State for Social Services ex parte Connolly* [1986] 1 WLR 421 (CA)
96 CDLA/3925/1997; *HJ v SSWP (DLA)* [2010] UKUT 307 (AAC)
97 R(DLA) 10/02
98 *R v National Insurance Commissioner ex parte Secretary of State for Social Services* [1981] 1 WLR 1017 (CA), also reported as R(A) 2/80
99 *Mallinson v Secretary of State for Social Security* 21 April 1994 (HL), reported as R(A) 3/94
100 *R v National Insurance Commissioner ex parte Secretary of State for Social Services* [1981] 1 WLR 1017 (CA), also reported as R(A) 2/80; reg 10C SS (DLA) Regs
101 R(A) 1/06

102 *Mallinson v Secretary of State for Social Security* 21 April 1994 (HL), reported as R(A) 3/94
103 CA/177/1988; CDLA/14696/1996; R(DLA) 1/07, tribunal of commissioners
104 Reg 10C SS(DLA) Regs; reg 8BA SS(AA) Regs
105 CDLA/4333/2004
106 R(A) 3/74
107 R(A) 2/75
108 CA/86/1987
109 R(DLA) 1/07, tribunal of commissioners
110 *R v Social Security Commissioner ex parte Butler,* February 1984, unreported and *Secretary of State for Social Security v Fairey* (aka *Halliday*), 21 May 1997 (HL), reported as R(A) 2/98
111 *Fairey,* 15 June 1995 (CA); R(DLA) 1/02; R(DLA) 2/02; R(DLA) 3/02; *SSWP v PV (DLA)* [2010] UKUT 33 (AAC)
112 R(DLA) 2/02
113 CDLA/3607/2001
114 Reg 10C SS(DLA) Regs; *R v National Insurance Commissioner ex parte Secretary of State for Social Services* [1981] 1 WLR 1017 (CA), also reported as R(A) 2/80
115 *Cockburn v CAO and Another,* 21 May 1997 (HL), reported as R(A) 2/98; *Ramsden v SSWP,* 31 January 2003 (CA), reported as R(DLA) 2/03
116 CDLA/267/1994
117 CDLA/267/1994, CDLA/11652/1995, CDLA/3711/1995, CDLA/12381/1996, CDLA/16996/1996, CDLA/16129/1996 and CDLA/4352/1999 are useful, but conflict with CSDLA/281/1996 and CSDLA/314/1997. See CPAG's *Welfare Rights Bulletin 145* for an analysis of this issue.
118 *Secretary of State for Social Security v Fairey* (aka *Halliday*), 21 May 1997 (HL), reported as R(A) 2/98
119 CDLA/16129/1996, CDLA/16996/1996 and CDLA/4352/1999 are helpful, but conflict with CSDLA/314/1997
120 CDLA/4352/1999 and CDLA/5216/1998, the latter being more restrictive.
121 CDLA/4352/1999
122 CDLA/5216/1998
123 R(DLA) 1/98
124 *R v National Insurance Commissioner ex parte Secretary of State for Social Services* [1974] 1 WLR 1290 (DC), also reported as R(A) 4/74
125 CDLA/2852/2002
126 CDLA/997/2003
127 R(A) 1/04
128 R(A) 1/78
129 s72(1)(a)(i) SSCBA 1992
130 R(DLA) 8/02
131 CDLA/58/1993
132 CSDLA/29/1994
133 *Ramsden v SSWP,* 31 January 2003 (CA), reported as R(DLA) 2/03
134 **DLA** s72(1)(b) SSCBA 1992
AA s64 (2)(a) SSCBA 1992
135 *R v National Insurance Commissioner ex parte Secretary of State for Social Services* [1981] 1 WLR 1017 (CA), also reported as R(A) 2/80. However, see also R(DLA) 5/05.
136 CA/281/1989
137 CA/140/1985
138 **DLA** s72(1)(c)(i) SSCBA 1992
AA s64 (3)(b) SSCBA 1992
139 R(DLA) 5/05
140 *R v National Insurance Commissioner ex parte Secretary of State for Social Services* [1981] 1 WLR 1017 (CA), also reported as R(A) 2/80. However, see also R(DLA) 5/05.
141 R(A) 3/78
142 ss64(2)(b) and 72(1)(b)(ii) SSCBA 1992
143 R(A) 1/83
144 CA/15/1979, approved in R(A) 1/83
145 R(A) 2/89
146 CA/33/1984
147 R(A) 2/91
148 R(A) 3/92
149 R(A) 2/75
150 *Moran v Secretary of State for Social Services, The Times,* 14 March 1987 (CA), reported as R(A) 1/88
151 R(A) 5/81
152 **DLA** s72(1)(c)(ii) SSCBA 1992
AA s64 (3)(b) SSCBA 1992
153 para 61165 DMG

3. **Attendance allowance**
154 ss64, 65 and 66 SSCBA 1992; reg 3 SS(AA) Regs

4. **The rules about your age**
155 s73(1A) SSCBA 1992
156 s73(4A) SSCBA 1992
157 CDLA/2268/1999
158 s72(1A)(b) SSCBA 1992
159 s72 (5) SSCBA
160 CA/92/1992; CSDLA/76/1998; CDLA/4806/2002; CSDLA/91/2003; CDLA/4100/2004. See CPAG's *Welfare Rights Bulletin 147* for an analysis of the extra test for children.
161 CA/92/1992

162 s75(1) SSCBA 1992; reg 3 SS(DLA) Regs
163 Sch 1 para 1 SS(DLA) Regs; see also CSDLA/388/2000
164 Sch 1 para 1 (3) SS(DLA) Regs
165 Sch 1 para 3(2)(b) SS(DLA) Regs

5. **The amount of benefit**
166 Reg 4(1) SS(DLA) Regs
167 Reg 4(1) SS(DLA) Regs
168 Sch 4 III SSCBA 1992

6. **Special benefit rules**
169 Reg 5 SS(AA) Regs; reg 7 SS(DLA) Regs
170 s66(1) and (2) SSCBA 1992
171 s72(5) SSCBA 1992
172 s66(1) SSCBA 1992
173 s73(12) SSCBA 1992; s73(9)(b)(ii) SSCBA 1992
174 Regs 3(9)(b) and 6(6)(c) SS&CS(DA) Regs
175 ss66(2)(b) and 76(3) SSCBA 1992

7. **Claims and backdating**
176 Reg 4(1) SS(C&P) Regs
177 Reg 6(8), (8A) and (9) SS(C&P) Regs
178 Regs 3(9)(b), 6(6)(c) and 25(b) SS&CS(DA) Regs
179 Reg 1A SS(DLA) Regs
180 Reg 6(8), (8A) and (9) SS(C&P) Regs
181 Reg 6(8A) SS(C&P) Regs
182 Sch 9ZC para 4(3) SS(C&P) Regs
183 Reg 9(1) and Sch 1 SS(C&P) Regs
184 Reg 9(1) and Sch 1 SS(C&P) Regs
185 Reg 13A(1) SS(C&P) Regs
186 s65(6) SSCBA 1992
187 Reg 13C SS(C&P) Regs
188 CDLA/14895/1996
189 Regs 6 and 11 SS(DLA) Regs
190 Regs 6 and 11 and Sch 1 paras 3 and 5 SS(DLA) Regs
191 Reg 6(3) and (4) SS(DLA) Regs
192 Reg 3 SS(AA) Regs
193 R(A) 2/74; see also *Moyna v SSWP*, 31 July 2003 (HL), reported as R(DLA) 7/03
194 CDLA/2268/1999
195 CDLA/4806/2002
196 CDLA/339/1994
197 *SSWP v Hughes (a minor)*, reported as R(DLA) 1/04
198 CDLA/1983/2006
199 s19(3) SSA 1998
200 ss65(4) and 76(1) SSCBA 1992

8. **Getting paid**
201 Reg 21 SS(C&P) Regs
202 Reg 22(3) and Sch 6 SS(C&P) Regs
203 Reg 22 SS(C&P) Regs
204 Reg 25 SS(C&P) Regs
205 ss65(1)(a) and 71(3) SSCBA 1992
206 R(DLA) 11/02
207 s71(3) SSCBA 1992; CDLA/2887/2008
208 Reg 43 SS(C&P) Regs
209 CDLA/1326/1995
210 Reg 43 SS(C&P) Regs
211 Reg 32(1A) and (1B) SS(C&P) Regs
212 Reg 7(9) SS&CS(DA) Regs
213 s10(5) SSA 1998
214 Reg 7(2)(c) SS&CS(DA) Regs
215 Reg 32(1) SS(C&P) Regs
216 Reg 17 SS&CS(DA) Regs
217 Reg 17(4)(a)(ii) SS&CS(DA) Regs
218 Reg 18 SS&CS(DA) Regs
219 Reg 19(1) SS&CS(DA) Regs
220 Reg 19(2) SS&CS(DA) Regs
221 Reg 19(3) and (4) SS&CS(DA) Regs

9. **Tax, tax credits and other benefits**
222 s677 IT(EP)A 2003
223 Sch 1 para 5 SS(OB) Regs
224 Reg 42(1)(b)(ii) SS(C&P) Regs
225 Regs 44, 45 and 46 SS(C&P) Regs

Chapter 10

Employment and support allowance

This chapter covers:

Key facts

- Employment and support allowance (ESA) is a benefit for people who have 'limited capability for work' (ie, they are unable to work because of illness or disability) and who are not entitled to statutory sick pay.
- Entitlement to ESA is assessed by a test called the work capability assessment.
- There are two types of ESA: **contributory ESA**, which depends on your national insurance (NI) contribution record but is not means tested, and **income-related** ESA, which does not depend on your NI contribution record, but is means tested. **ESA in youth** is a form of contributory ESA for certain young people, which does not depend on your NI contribution record. However, ESA in youth will be abolished for new claimants from 1 May 2012.
- ESA is administered and paid by the DWP.
- If you disagree with an ESA decision, you can apply for a revision or supersession, or appeal against it (see Chapters 45 and 46). All parts of the decision may be looked at.

Future changes: April 2013 and after

Major changes are taking place that affect the benefits and tax credits system (see Chapter 2).

– From April 2013, total benefit payments to many working-age households will be 'capped' (see p25). There will be limited exceptions, including households in which someone is entitled to working tax credit or receives disability living allowance. ESA will be included in the capped amount.

– From October 2013, when universal credit (UC) is introduced, no new claims for income-related ESA will be allowed (although contributory ESA will continue). Claimants of income-related ESA will be transferred to UC between April 2014 and October 2017.

See CPAG's *Welfare Rights Bulletin* for updates.

1. Who can claim employment and support allowance

You qualify for employment and support allowance (ESA) if you:[1]

- have 'limited capability for work' (see p199); *and*
- are aged 16 or over but under pension age (see p531); *and*
- are in Great Britain (see p187 if you go abroad); *and*
- are not entitled in your own right to income support (IS) or jobseeker's allowance (JSA), and are not in a couple entitled to joint-claim JSA (see p413); *and*
- are not entitled to statutory sick pay (SSP); *and*
- satisfy the extra rules for contributory ESA (see below) or income-related ESA (see p177).

You are not usually entitled to ESA for the first three days of your claim (see p212). You cannot get ESA and certain other benefits at the same time (see p192). Most claimants of ESA (except those in the 'support group' – see p184) are required to take part in work-focused interviews and some can be required to undertake some 'work-related activity' (see p1031). **Note:** the government intends to introduce a requirement that you accept a 'claimant commitment'.[2] This will be a record of your 'responsibilities' in connection with your ESA award. See p1031 for more details and CPAG's *Welfare Rights Bulletin* for updates.

Extra rules for contributory employment and support allowance

To get contributory ESA, in addition to satisfying the basic rules of entitlement (see above), you must satisfy either the national insurance (NI) contribution conditions or the rules for ESA in youth (see p176).[3] If you are being transferred from incapacity benefit (IB) or severe disablement allowance (SDA) to a claim for ESA (see p193), you do not have to satisfy this requirement. **Note:** at the time this *Handbook* was written, the government intended to time-limit contributory ESA so that entitlement stops after one year (see p181).

Employment and support allowance in youth

Note: the government intends to abolish ESA in youth for new claimants from 1 May 2012.[4] If you are already getting it when it is abolished, it will stop after a year. Time in the 'support group' (see p184) will be ignored. If you lose entitlement but are then put in the support group, the government intends that it will not be possible to requalify. However, you may be able to get contributory ESA if you satisfy the usual rules including the NI contribution conditions. You may also be entitled to income-related ESA. At the time this *Handbook* was written, these rules were not finalised, but were expected to be introduced on 30 April 2012, so that new claims for ESA in youth will not be possible after that date. See CPAG's *Welfare Rights Bulletin* for updates.

You can get ESA in youth if, in addition to satisfying the basic rules of entitlement (see p175), you:[5]

- were aged under 20 (or in some circumstances aged under 25 – see below) when the 'period of limited capability for work' that applies to your claim for ESA began; *and*
- if aged under 19, are not in 'full-time education'; *and*
- have had 'limited capability for work' for a consecutive period (different periods cannot be linked) of at least 196 days (these may fall before your 16th birthday); *and*
- are not a 'person subject to immigration control' (see p1410); *and*
- satisfy rules on residence and/or presence in Great Britain (see Chapter 59).[6]

You are in **'full-time education'** if (as well as being aged under 19) you attend a course for 21 hours or more a week. In calculating the 21 hours, temporary interruptions are ignored. Also, only the instruction or tuition you receive which would be suitable for someone of your age who did not have a disability is counted.[7] It is arguable that both the course content and the method of teaching must be taken into account when deciding this.[8]

If you previously qualified for ESA on the basis of having limited capability for work in youth, but your entitlement ended, you may be able to requalify for ESA on the same basis if you have limited capability for work again, even if you are now over 20 or 25 (see below).

Under-25-year-olds

If you are under 25 when your limited capability for work starts, you can still qualify for ESA in youth if, in addition to the ESA in youth rules above:[9]

- you registered on a course of 'full-time advanced or secondary education' or 'training' (see p177 for definitions) at least three months before you became 20; *and*
- not more than one academic term passed between the date you registered on that course and when you attended it; *and*
- you started the course at least three months before you reached 20; *and*

- you stopped attending the course at some time after the start of the last two complete tax years (ie, 6 April–5 April) which fall before the benefit year (from the first Sunday in January) in which you claim ESA. You are treated as still attending during interruptions that are because of illness or domestic emergency.

Education and training

'**Full time**' includes part time if your disability prevents attendance on a full-time course, but otherwise is not defined, so arguably should have its ordinary and natural meaning and could include periods of unsupervised, as well as supervised, study.

'**Advanced education**' means a course for a degree, diploma of higher education, HND, HND of the Business and Technician Education Council or Scottish Qualifications Authority, a teaching qualification, or any other course which is above OND, a diploma of the Business and Technician Education Council or Scottish national qualification (higher or advanced level) or GCSE or A level.

'**Secondary education**' means a course below 'advanced education' and attending university, college or school or a place officially recognised as comparable or where the education is recognised as equivalent.

'**Training**' means training under s2(1) of the Employment and Training Act 1973 or s2(3) of the Enterprise and New Towns (Scotland) Act 1990, or any training on a course attended for 16 hours or more a week, the main purpose of which is the learning of occupational or vocational skills.[10]

Extra rules for income-related employment and support allowance

In addition to satisfying the basic rules of entitlement (see p175), you can get income-related ESA if:[11]

- your income is less than your applicable amount (see p182); *and*
- your capital is not over £16,000 (see Chapter 41);[12] *and*
- you are not entitled to pension credit (PC); *and*
- neither you nor your partner, if you are in a couple (see p753), are engaged in full-time work; *and*
- your partner is not entitled to income-related ESA, income-based JSA, IS or PC in her/his own right; *and*
- you are not receiving 'education' (unless you are entitled to disability living allowance (DLA), in which case you can still qualify for income-related ESA);[13] *and*
- you satisfy the 'right to reside' and 'habitual residence' tests (see Chapter 62);[14] *and*
- you are not a 'person subject to immigration control' (see p1410).[15]

'Full-time work' for you means *any* work for which you are paid or which is done in expectation of payment, unless it is work you are allowed to do while claiming, including 'permitted work' (see p200). For your partner, it is also work for which s/he is paid or which is done in expectation of payment. However, if s/he works under 24 hours a week, it is ignored. There are certain circumstances in which your partner may be treated as engaged in full-time work or treated as not engaged in it (see Chapter 31).[16] **Note**: when claiming ESA of any kind (including contributory ESA), consult the DWP before doing any work. Even if the work does not count as full-time work, the general rule is that unless it is allowed, any work you do will result in your losing all entitlement to ESA.

You are in **'education'** if you are a 'qualifying young person' (eg, you are aged under 20 and in full-time, non-advanced education or approved training – see p94) or you are on a course that is classed as full time.[17] The rules are very similar to those that apply to the definition of full-time courses for IS (see p640). Seek advice if you are unsure.

Rules on income and capital are generally similar to those for IS and other means-tested benefits – see Chapters 40 and 41 (but for ESA, earnings from 'permitted work' that are under the relevant earnings limit are ignored).[18]

Disqualification from benefit

You can be disqualified from receiving ESA for up to six weeks if you:[19]
- have 'limited capability for work' because of your own misconduct (but not if your limited capability for work is due to pregnancy or a sexually transmitted disease); *or*
- have failed without 'good cause' (see below) to accept medical treatment (excluding vaccination, inoculation or major surgery) recommended by a doctor treating you and which would be likely to overcome your limited capability for work; *or*
- have failed without 'good cause' (see below) to stop engaging in behaviour that would 'retard' your recovery; *or*
- are absent from your home without telling the DWP where you may be found without 'good cause' (see below).

'Good cause' is not defined. You will not be disqualified if you are considered to be a person in hardship – ie, if you are:[20]
- pregnant, or a member of your family is pregnant;
- a single claimant aged under 18, or a member of a couple and both of you are aged under 18;
- *responsible* for a child who lives with you, or your partner is;
- entitled to attendance allowance (AA) or the middle or highest rate care component of DLA, or your partner is;
- waiting for a decision on a claim for AA or DLA, or your partner is;

- a carer for someone who is entitled to AA or the middle or highest rate care component of DLA or who is waiting for a decision on a claim for AA or DLA, or your partner is;
- at least the qualifying age for PC (see p509), or your partner is;
- at risk of hardship (or a member of your family is at risk) if ESA is not paid to you, including if there is a 'substantial risk' that you will not have sufficient essential items such as food, clothing and heating.

Although you are not disqualified in these situations, your ESA is paid at a reduced rate. You will get 80 per cent of your basic allowance in contributory ESA, or 80 per cent of your personal allowance in income-related ESA.[21]

You can also be disqualified from receiving contributory ESA during any period in which you are:

- absent from Great Britain (see p1484); *or*
- a prisoner or detained in legal custody (see Chapter 30).

2. The rules about your age

To satisfy the basic rules for employment and support allowance (ESA), you must be aged at least 16 but under pension age (see p531).

For ESA in youth, you must have been aged under 20 (or in some circumstances under 25) when your 'period of limited capability for work' began (see p212).

3. Claiming for others

You claim contributory employment and support allowance (ESA) for yourself. You cannot claim any additions for your partner or children.

You claim income-related ESA for yourself and your partner, if you have one. The applicable amount that forms part of the calculation of your benefit includes a personal allowance for a couple (see p753 for when you count as a couple). It does not include amounts for children.[22] However, there are some situations in which you need to show that a child is part of your family for benefit purposes (see p759).

4. The amount of benefit

You are paid a limited amount of employment and support allowance (ESA) during an initial 'assessment phase'. In most cases, this is expected to last 13 weeks. Thereafter, you are paid more during the 'main phase'.

There are no age-related additions or additions for dependants.

The exact amount of ESA you are paid depends on:

- whether you are claiming contributory ESA or income-related ESA;
- whether you are in the 'assessment phase' or the 'main phase';
- which of the two possible additional components you get after the assessment phase. These are the 'support component' (see p184) and the 'work-related activity component' (see p185).

ESA is worked out as follows.

- In the assessment phase, for **contributory ESA** you get a basic allowance (see p180); for **income-related ESA**, the amount depends on your applicable amount and income (see p182).
- After the assessment phase is over (in the 'main phase' of ESA), you get an additional component. In contributory ESA, this is simply added to the basic allowance. In income-related ESA, this is added to your applicable amount and, as in the assessment phase, your income is subtracted from your applicable amount.
- Finally, you are entitled to just one award of ESA, but this may be made up of contributory ESA topped up with income-related ESA.[23] If contributory ESA is topped up by income-related ESA, the total amount of ESA payable is, in effect, the amount of entitlement to income-related ESA.

Note: if you have been transferred from incapacity benefit (IB), severe disablement allowance (SDA) or income support (IS) on disability grounds to an award of ESA, but your ESA would be less than your IB/SDA/IS, you are also entitled to a 'transitional addition' of ESA (see p193).

The assessment phase

The first weeks of your entitlement to ESA (contributory or income-related) are known as the **'assessment phase'**. During this phase, you usually get a lower amount of ESA. This phase normally ends after 13 weeks.[24] **Note:** if you are transferred from IB/SDA/IS on grounds of disability to ESA (see p193), you are treated as already having satisfied the assessment phase.

The assessment phase is the period during which the DWP gathers further information relevant to your claim. If the DWP has not yet determined whether you have limited capability for work, the assessment phase does not end until this has happened, in which case it may last longer than 13 weeks. If you are appealing against a finding that you do not have limited capability for work and are getting an award of ESA pending an appeal (see p210), the assessment phase does not usually end until the First-tier Tribunal has made its decision. However, if before your appeal is heard you experience a new condition or your condition significantly worsens, a new determination on your limited capability for work can be made and it is possible for the assessment phase to end.[25] You are not entitled to an additional component in your ESA until the assessment phase has ended, but if the assessment phase lasts longer than 13 weeks, the component is backdated to the 14th week of your claim.[26]

In some circumstances, your assessment phase is taken to begin on the first day of a period of previous entitlement to ESA (of either kind), so that some or all of the 13 weeks are taken to have been already served.[27] This happens if your current period of limited capability for work is linked to a previous one (see p213) in which you were entitled to ESA, but the assessment phase had not ended. In these circumstances, your assessment phase ends when your combined entitlement from the previous and current ESA claims amounts to 13 weeks. If, however, the assessment phase had ended in your earlier linked claim (or you were entitled to ESA for more than 13 weeks), the work-related activity component is payable from the start of your current claim. Alternatively, the support component is payable from the start of your current claim if you qualified for it in your earlier linked claim and are a 'work or training beneficiary' (p214).

Contributory employment and support allowance

During the **assessment phase** for contributory ESA, in most cases you are only entitled to a set rate of benefit, called the **'basic allowance'**.[28] This is £56.25 if you are under 25 or £71 if you are 25 or over. If you are terminally ill, you are also entitled to one of the additional components.

In the **'main phase'** of ESA, your basic allowance is paid at the same rate (£71), no matter what your age.

In addition to the basic allowance, you are also paid one of two possible additional components: the 'support component' or the 'work-related activity component' (see pp184 and 185). **Note:** if you have been transferred from IB or SDA to an award of ESA and are entitled to a 'transitional addition' (see p193), this is part of your basic allowance.[29]

Contributory ESA can be topped up with income-related ESA.

Your benefit may be reduced if you receive certain kinds of pension payments or a councillor's allowance (see p186).

Duration of contributory employment and support allowance

From 1 May 2012, contributory ESA is only paid for a limited period of 365 days. However, any time spent in the 'support group' (ie, because you are paid the support component on the basis of limited capability for work-related activity) is ignored. In effect, once you have had a year of contributory ESA in which you have not been entitled to the support component, you lose your entitlement to contributory ESA. You may, however, be entitled to income-related ESA. At the time this *Handbook* was written, the rules had not been finalised, but were expected to be introduced from 30 April 2012, and to include the following.[30]

- The time limit will apply to all new claims of contributory ESA.

- If you already getting contributory ESA on 1 May 2012, the time you have already spent on contributory ESA and getting the work-related activity component will be taken into account when calculating the one-year period – ie, if you have already had a year or more of contributory ESA, your entitlement will stop immediately.
- Time spent in the assessment phase will be taken into account when calculating the one-year period (excluding time in the support group).
- If you are transferred from IB/SDA to contributory ESA, your one-year period will be calculated from the date your award was converted to contributory ESA.
- You can only become entitled to contributory ESA again if:
  - you remain assessed or treated as having limited capability for work, and you become entitled to the support component; *or*
  - the tax years used to decide whether you satisfy the national insurance (NI) contribution conditions (see p789) are different from the ones that applied to your previous entitlement. To become entitled again, the two tax years must now include at least one tax year which is later than the later of the two tax years that applied to your previous entitlement. Note that if you continue to have limited capability for work, under the linking rules (see p213) your period of limited capability for work remains unbroken, meaning that the tax years will remain the same as those that applied to your previous entitlement.

See CPAG's *Welfare Rights Bulletin* for updates.

Example

Ravi is aged 24. He has worked since leaving school and has a full NI contribution record. He has had to leave his job because of ill health. He gets lowest rate care component of disability living allowance. He is not assessed as being in the support group.

ESA during assessment phase = £56.25 (basic allowance for someone aged under 25)

ESA during main phase = £99.15 (basic allowance of £71 *plus* work-related activity component of £28.15)

Income-related employment and support allowance

In most cases, there is an initial 'assessment phase' (normally 13 weeks).[31] The assessment phase is followed by a 'main phase'. The amount you get in both phases depends on your needs (your 'applicable amount') and how much income you have. Your applicable amount during the assessment phase is set at a lower level. In both phases, your applicable amount is compared with your income and, if your applicable amount is more, you get the difference as ESA. For more details on applicable amounts, see Chapter 37. For how your income is assessed, see Chapter 40.

Your applicable amount in the **assessment phase** consists of:[32]

- a personal allowance – the amount depends on whether or not you are under 25 or, in some cases, under 18 (see p815); *and*
- premiums – only the enhanced disability, severe disability, carer and pensioner premiums may apply (see p820); *and*
- housing costs (see Chapter 38).

When calculating your entitlement, your income is subtracted from your applicable amount and any remaining sum is your entitlement to income-related ESA. If you would not be entitled to ESA until either of the two additional components described below are added, you may be given an 'advance award' under which you will be paid from the point that the additional component is awarded, as long as you satisfy the other conditions.[33]

If you are terminally ill, you also have one of the two additional components added to your applicable amount during the assessment phase.

In the '**main phase**' one of the two additional components (a support component or work-related activity component) is added to your applicable amount.[34] The personal allowance is paid at the 'aged 25 and over' rate irrespective of your age. Your applicable amount in the main phase therefore consists of:

- a personal allowance paid at the aged 25 and over rate; *and*
- premiums – only the enhanced disability, severe disability, carer and pensioner premiums may apply (see p820); *and*
- either the support component or the work-related activity component; *and*
- housing costs (see Chapter 38).

Your income is subtracted from your applicable amount and any remaining sum is your entitlement to income-related ESA.

Note: if you have been transferred from IS to an award of income-related ESA and you are entitled to a 'transitional addition' (see p193), this is also included as part of your applicable amount – ie, it is a payment of income-related ESA. However unlike the rest of your applicable amount, the transitional addition is not affected by any changes in your income.[35]

Income-related ESA can top up contributory ESA. This can happen if the amount of entitlement to income-related ESA is greater than the amount of entitlement to contributory ESA. If this is the case, your ESA will consist of both contributory ESA and (the remainder of) income-related ESA.[36]

Example

Terry is aged 35 when he claims ESA. He lives with his wife, Julie, and six-year-old son, Ray. They get child benefit and child tax credit. Julie works 10 hours a week and earns £80 a week. Terry is not assessed as being in the support group. He has not paid enough NI contributions to get contributory ESA.

Assessment phase
Applicable amount = £111.45 (personal allowance for couple both aged 18 or over)
Income to be taken into account = £60 (child benefit and child tax credit ignored; £20 earnings disregard applies)
Terry's income-related ESA during assessment phase is £111.45 *minus* £60 = £51.45
Main phase
Applicable amount = £139.60 (personal allowance of £111.45 for couple both aged 18 or over *plus* work-related activity component of £28.15)
Income to be taken into account (as above) = £60
Terry's income-related ESA during the main phase is £139.60 *minus* £60 = £79.60.

Support component

The support component is one of the additional components that can be included as part of your entitlement to ESA.[37] If you get the support component, you are regarded as being in the '**support group**'. The support component is £34.05 a week. There is no couple rate.[38] In most cases, you are entitled to the support component if:

- the assessment phase has ended; *and*
- you are assessed as having 'limited capability for work-related activity' (see p185).

As well as being entitled to the support component, you do not have to take part in work-focused interviews or associated activity as a condition of getting benefit.[39] The intention is that where paper evidence (eg, medical evidence from your doctor) already shows that you should be in the support group, that decision will be made without your having to attend a medical examination.[40]

Note: if you are being transferred from IB/SDA/IS on grounds of disability to a claim for ESA (see p193), when calculating your ESA the support component or the work-related activity component (see p185) is included straight away. You can also be entitled to the support component before the assessment phase has ended if:[41]

- you are terminally ill (ie, you have a progressive disease, because of which your death can reasonably be expected within six months) and have either claimed ESA expressly on that ground, or asked for a revision or supersession and have said expressly that you are terminally ill (in this case you qualify for the support component automatically); *or*
- your period of limited capability for work is linked to an earlier period in which you were entitled to ESA, and the assessment phase in that period had ended or you were entitled to ESA for more than 13 weeks. In this case, if your previous ESA award included the support component, it can be included from the start of your new claim. However, unless you are a 'work or training beneficiary' (see p214), the component is not paid until the DWP has decided

that you are entitled to it again. You should get the work-related activity component in the meantime;[42] *or*

- your ESA entitlement has started within 12 weeks of your losing entitlement to IS, when your IS ended it included the disability premium, and the sole reason for your losing entitlement to IS was because you are a lone parent and the age of your youngest child no longer met the requirements (see p347). In this case, once you are entitled to the support component, it is included straight away.

Limited capability for work-related activity

In order to have limited capability for work-related activity, your mental or physical condition must be such that one or more statements (or 'descriptors') describing a severe limitation in certain activities (eg, walking, continence, maintaining personal hygiene, learning and communication) could be applied to you. For the activities and descriptors, see Appendix 11.

A descriptor will apply if it applies to you for the majority of the time(s) you try the activity described. You are assessed wearing any prosthesis and/or using any aid or appliance that you normally use. The DWP may retest you to find out if there has been a relevant change of circumstances, to see if a previous finding was wrong or mistaken, or if it is three months or more since your last test.[43] You may be required to complete a questionnaire and/or attend a medical examination. You will automatically qualify if:[44]

- you have a terminal illness; *or*
- you are receiving intravenous, intraperitoneal or intrathecal chemotherapy treatment, or recovering from that treatment or you are due to receive such treatment within six months after the DWP determines whether you have limited capability for work-related activity; *or*
- because of a specific disease or disablement there would be a substantial risk to your mental or physical health or to the mental or physical health of someone else if you were found not to have limited capability for work-related activity; *or*
- you are pregnant and there would be a serious risk of damage to your health or to your baby's health if you do not refrain from work-related activity.

Work-related activity component

A work-related activity component can be included as part of your entitlement to ESA.[45] If this is included, you are regarded as being in the **'work-related activity group'**. This also means that you are required to take part in work-focused interviews and possibly undertake some work-related activity (see p1031).

The work-related activity component is £28.15 a week. There is no couple rate.[46] You are entitled to the work-related activity component if:

- the assessment phase has ended (but see p186); *and*

- you are not assessed as having 'limited capability for work-related activity' – ie, you are not entitled to the support component; *and*
- you comply with the requirement to attend work-focused interviews and associated activity (see p1034). If you do not, you may have the component reduced and eventually removed completely.

Note: if you are being transferred from IB/SDA/IS on grounds of disability to ESA (see p193), when your ESA is calculated the support component or the work-related activity component is included straight away. You can also be entitled to the work-related activity component before the assessment phase has ended if your:[47]

- period of limited capability for work is linked to an earlier period in which you were entitled to ESA, and the assessment phase in that period had ended or you were entitled to ESA for more than 13 weeks;[48] *or*
- ESA entitlement has started within 12 weeks of your losing entitlement to IS, when your IS ended it included the disability premium, and the sole reason for your losing entitlement to IS was that you are a lone parent and your youngest child ceased to satisfy the age requirements (see p347).

When your employment and support allowance is reduced

In certain circumstances, your ESA may be reduced. For **contributory ESA**, this applies if you receive certain pension payments of over £85 a week and if you are a local councillor and your net allowances exceed £97.50.[49]

Pension payments that are taken into account for contributory ESA are periodic payments made under:[50]

- any personal, occupational or public service pension scheme; *and*
- any permanant health insurance policy arranged by your employer that provides payments in connection with ill health or disability after your employment ends. However, if you contributed more than 50 per cent of the pension premiums, the amount you receive from this kind of pension is ignored; *and*
- the Pension Protection Fund and the Financial Assistance scheme.

If the total amount of the gross pension payments you receive is more than £85 a week, your contributory ESA is reduced by half the pension payments above £85.

Other types of pension payments (including one-off lump-sum payments) are ignored. The following types of payment are also ignored:[51]

- arguably, any part of your pension paid directly to an ex-spouse or ex-civil partner by the pension scheme trustees under a court order, although the DWP may not accept this;[52]
- any payments you receive as a result of the death of the pension holder;
- any shortfall in your pension, where it cannot be paid in full because the pension scheme is in deficit or has insufficient funds;

- payments under a pension scheme for death as a result of military or war service under s639(2) of the Income Tax (Earnings and Pensions) Act 2003, or a guaranteed income payment.

Note: if you are transferred from IB to an award of ESA (see p193) and your pension payment was ignored immediately before the transfer, it will continue to be ignored in your ESA.[53] This includes if your IB was not reduced because you were entitled to the highest rate of disability living allowance care component, if you were transferred from SDA to long-term IB, and if you were transferred from invalidity benefit to long-term IB.

For more detail on how **councillor's allowances** affect contributory ESA, see p898.

For **either type of ESA**, your benefit may also be reduced if:

- the work-related activity component (see p185) applies to you and you do not comply with the requirement to attend work-focused interviews and associated activity (see p185); *or*
- you are a person in 'hardship' (see p178); *or*
- your ESA is restricted under the 'loss of benefit for benefit offences rule' (see p1106); *or*
- you are claiming ESA while appealing against a decision that you do not have 'limited capability for work' under the work capability assessment (see p210).

5. Special benefit rules

Special rules may apply to:

- people in prison or detention (see Chapter 30);
- people subject to immigration control (see p1410);
- people in care homes and other special accommodation (see p683);
- people going abroad. A basic rule of entitlement for employment and support allowance is that you are in Great Britain. However, you can remain entitled during a temporary absence in some circumstances provided you otherwise continue to satisfy the rules (see Chapter 63).[54]

6. Claims and backdating

The general rules on claiming and backdating are in Chapter 42. This section describes the specific rules for employment and support allowance (ESA). You must usually make a claim in order to become entitled. However, you do not have to make a claim if you have appealed against a decision that you do not have limited capability for work, the appeal has not yet been decided, and you wish to claim ESA while continuing with it.[55]

If you make a new claim for incapacity benefit (IB), income support (IS) on the grounds of disability or severe disablement allowance (SDA) for a period beginning on or after 27 October 2008, this is treated as a claim for ESA (but see pp337 and 351 for exceptions for IB and IS).[56]

In most cases (unless you are recognised as exempt straight away), you are required to attend a medical examination to assess whether you have 'limited capability for work' and 'limited capability for work-related activity'. Also, unless you are in the 'support group' (see p184), you are usually required to attend compulsory work-focused interviews and in some cases carry out work-related activity (see p1034).

Making a claim

A claim for ESA can be made:[57]

- by telephone. Phone a Jobcentre Plus contact centre (Monday–Friday, 8am–6pm, telephone: 0800 055 6688; textphone: 0800 023 4888). However, the DWP may require you to use a claim form; *or*
- in writing by completing the approved claim form. Send it to your local Jobcentre Plus office. If the DWP has arranged for a local authority to receive claims for ESA, you can also send it to a local authority housing benefit or council tax benefit office.

If you claim in writing, keep a copy of your claim form in case queries arise.

You must provide any information or evidence required (see p189). You can amend or withdraw your claim before a decision is made (see p1019).

Forms

Get Form ESA1 from your local Jobcentre Plus office, telephone contact centre, www.direct.gov.uk/en/disabledpeople or the Benefit Enquiry Line on 0800 882 200 (textphone 0800 243 355).

Who should claim

Usually, you must claim ESA on your own behalf, although if you are unable to act for yourself, an 'appointee' can claim on your behalf (see p1016). For income-related ESA, if you are a member of a couple you should choose which of you claims for you both (bearing in mind that to get ESA the claimant must satisfy the *entitlement* rules, including having limited capability for work). Whoever is the claimant can be switched later by the other member of the couple claiming income-related ESA and (if s/he is entitled) both you and your partner confirming in writing that you want the claim to be switched.[58]

If you are employed

If you are employed, you should normally be paid statutory sick pay (SSP – see Chapter 28) for the first 28 weeks of your limited capability for work. Note, however, that if you are a 'work or training beneficiary' (see p214) you are not entitled to SSP (see p618). If your employer thinks that you are not entitled to SSP or if your entitlement to SSP has run out, it should complete and give you Form SSP1 and you should claim ESA. You are normally expected to include Form SSP1 and a medical certificate with your claim. If your employer refuses your SSP claim on the grounds that you are not entitled to it, your claim for ESA can be backdated to the date of your SSP claim (see p190). If you disagree with your employer's decision not to pay SSP, you can refer the matter to HM Revenue and Customs (HMRC – see Chapter 47), but do not delay claiming ESA. If you have asked HMRC to decide whether you are entitled to SSP, tell the DWP this when you claim ESA.

Information to support your claim

When you claim ESA you must:

- satisfy the national insurance number requirement (see p1023);
- provide proof of your identity, if required (see p1024);
- supply information or evidence required on the claim form and additional information and evidence relevant to your claim – eg, medical evidence of your limited capability for work (see p1022). There is a strict time limit for doing so.

For the first seven days of your limited capability for work, the DWP should accept a self-certificate as medical evidence. After seven days, you need to provide a medical certificate from your doctor. If it is unreasonable to expect you to provide this, the DWP can accept other evidence if that is sufficient.[59]

You may be referred by the DWP for a medical assessment. If you fail to attend the medical without good cause, your claim can be refused.[60]

The date of your claim

Unless it is backdated (see p190), the date of your claim is usually the date of your telephone call, or the date your claim form is received at a DWP office (or a local authority office – see p188).[61] However, if you notify the DWP that you intend to send in a claim form and you send in a properly completed form within one month, your date of claim is the date of your notification of intent to claim. Remember that, in any case, your claim can be backdated for up to three months (see p190). If your claim (either by phone or claim form) is considered defective, the DWP must advise you of that. If you correct the defect within one month of the date the defect was last pointed out to you (or longer, if considered reasonable), your date of claim is still the date you first made the claim.[62]

If you claim the wrong benefit

If your employer has decided that you are not entitled to SSP and you claim ESA within three months of being notified in writing of this, your ESA claim is treated as having been made on the date of your SSP claim.[63]

A claim for maternity allowance (MA) can be treated as a claim for ESA.[64] If your MA claim is accepted as a claim for ESA, your ESA can be backdated for up to three months before the date you claimed MA if you satisfy the qualifying conditions during that period (see p1025).

Claiming in advance

In most cases, you can claim ESA up to three months before the date on which you qualify for it.[65] The exception is if, for income-related ESA, the reason you do not qualify is because you fail the habitual residence test (see p1431), in which case you cannot claim ESA in advance.

Backdating your claim

Your claim can be backdated for up to three months before the day you actually claim – ie, for the time in that period in which you were otherwise entitled to ESA. You should state from which date you are claiming in that period and ask for it to be backdated. You do not need special reasons for backdating.[66]

Starting work when your claim ends

If you start work, depending on the circumstances, you may be able to benefit from the rules for linking periods of limited capability for work should you later fall sick again (see p213). In such a case, if you have to claim ESA again within a 104-week linking period, or within a 12-week linking period, you can return to the same level of ESA that you were previously receiving.

7. Getting paid

Payment of employment and support allowance (ESA) is normally made by direct credit transfer into your bank (or similar) account (see p1039). If you are unable to open or manage an account, payment can be made by cheque or by 'simple payment' (see p1039).

Payment may be made to someone else on your behalf (your 'appointee' – see p1016) if you are unable to act for yourself.

When is ESA paid?	The day you are paid depends on your national insurance number.[67]
How often is ESA paid?	Normally fortnightly in arrears. ESA can be paid at different intervals, including at a daily rate of one-seventh of the weekly amount.[68]

Note:

- Your ESA might be paid at a reduced rate in some circumstances (see p186).
- Deductions can be made from your ESA to pay to third parties (see p1048).
- You might not be paid ESA, or it might be paid at a reduced rate, if you have been sanctioned for benefit offences (see p1106).
- If you have forgotten your PIN or if a cheque is lost or stolen, see p1040.
- If payment of your ESA is delayed, see p1262. You might be able to get an interim payment (see p1046). You may also be eligible for a crisis loan (see p564). If you wish to complain about how your claim has been dealt with, see p1262. You might be able to claim compensation (see p1261).
- If payment of your ESA is suspended, see p1043. This includes where you have failed to supply evidence of your limited capability for work.
- If you are overpaid ESA, you might have to repay it (see Chapter 43). If you have been accused of fraud, see Chapter 44.

Change of circumstances

You must report changes in your circumstances that might affect your benefit (see p1047). Report such changes promptly either by writing to or telephoning the office handling your claim – unless the DWP has decided you can tell it in another way. You can report changes online, if you are registered to do so with the government gateway. Check the information you have been sent for the correct office and contact the DWP if in doubt. In practice, it is always advisable to report the change in writing, in case of a dispute in the future. If you have a mortgage, the DWP can ask your lender about any changes in the amount you owe. If you have this information (eg, from an annual statement from your lender), you must also advise the DWP just in case your lender fails to do so. Make sure the DWP takes this information into account so you are not overpaid.

When your employment and support allowance is adjusted

The general rule is that your ESA is adjusted from the beginning of the week in which the change of circumstances takes effect.[69] However, there are exceptions to this general rule, including, for example, when you have notified the DWP that you are terminally ill, or when you have failed to notify it of a change regarding your limited capability for work that you should have (see p1141).[70]

8. Tax, tax credits and other benefits

Contributory employment and support allowance (ESA), including ESA in youth, is taxable; income-related ESA is not.[71] **Note:** if you have been transferred from incapacity benefit (IB) or severe disablement allowance (SDA) to contributory ESA (see p193), your contributory ESA is taxable (even if your IB/SDA was not). This includes any contributory ESA paid as a 'transitional addition'.[72]

Tax credits

If you are getting contributory ESA and your partner works, you may be entitled to working tax credit (WTC – see Chapter 49). ESA counts as a 'qualifying benefit' for the disability element of WTC (see p1311). Income-related ESA acts as a passport to the maximum rate of tax credits (see p1319).

Means-tested benefits

The rules on who can get ESA (see p175) mean you can only get some means-tested benefits and ESA together. Remember that contributory ESA can be topped up by income-related ESA.

You cannot claim ESA and income support (IS) in your own right at the same time.[73] If your partner gets IS in her/his own right, you cannot get income-related ESA.[74] If it is possible for you to claim either ESA or IS (eg, if, in addition to being ill or disabled, you are also a lone parent or a carer), you need to decide which benefit to claim. Seek advice about this, as it affects the amount of benefit you get and the sort of work-focused interviews you have to attend.

You cannot claim ESA and jobseeker's allowance (JSA) in your own right, including as part of a joint-claim couple, at the same time. You cannot get income-related ESA if your partner gets income-based JSA in her/his own right.[75] If your *partner* is entitled in her/his own right to income-based JSA (and it is not joint-claim JSA – eg, because you have a dependent child), you can get contributory ESA at the same time.

You cannot claim income-related ESA if you or your partner get pension credit.[76]

You can get ESA and housing benefit (HB) and/or council tax benefit (CTB) at the same time. If you do, you may be entitled to an additional component as part of your HB/CTB (see p837). If you are transferred from IB or SDA to contributory ESA (see p193) and do not get income-related ESA, you may get a transitional addition in your HB (see p840).

Non-means-tested benefits

Contributory ESA (but not income-related ESA) is affected by the rules on overlapping benefits (see p1041), which means that you may not be paid it in full if another earnings-replacement benefit is paid to you.

You are not entitled to ESA if you are entitled to statutory sick pay.[77] You can still get contributory ESA if you get statutory maternity pay (SMP), statutory adoption pay (SAP) or ordinary statutory paternity pay (SPP). You can get contributory ESA and additional SPP if the amount is less than the ESA, in which case your ESA is reduced by the amount of the SMP, SAP or additional SPP you get.[78]

You cannot claim ESA and JSA in your own right at the same time. If your partner is entitled to contribution-based JSA, you can claim ESA, although your partner's JSA it is taken into account when assessing your income for income-related ESA.

Passports and other sources of help

If you are entitled to income-related ESA, you also qualify for health benefits such as free prescriptions (see Chapter 13) and education benefits such as free school lunches (see p14). You may also qualify for social fund payments (see Chapters 25 and 26).

If you receive contributory ESA you may also be eligible for a Christmas bonus (see p9).

9. Transfer to employment and support allowance

If you were claiming incapacity benefit (IB), severe disablement allowance (SDA) or income support (IS) on grounds of disability when employment and support allowance (ESA) was introduced on 27 October 2008 and have remained entitled, your claim will continue as an 'existing award'. You cannot currently get ESA. However, most claims will eventually be transferred to claims for ESA and your entitlement will be reassessed under the ESA rules. This process will take place mainly between 2011 and April 2014. At the end of the process, people claiming national insurance (NI) contribution credits only for incapacity for work will also be transferred and reassessed. If you come off your IB/SDA/IS on grounds of disability before your claim is transferred and your entitlement is reassessed, if you then become ill again you will not be able to reclaim these benefits and will instead have to make a new claim for ESA. The main features of the transfer and reassessment rules and process are as follows.[79]

The reassessment process

To have your award converted to an award of ESA, you must satisfy the basic rules for ESA, including having limited capability for work under the work capability assessment (see Chapter 11). You will be sent a questionnaire (ESA50) about limited capability for work, and may be required to attend a medical. If you do not comply without good cause, you may lose your entitlement to benefit (see pp204 and 207).

- All new claims for benefit on the basis of incapacity for work made on or after 31 January 2011 by people not already getting IB, SDA or IS on disability grounds are treated as new ESA claims. There is no linking (including under the 'welfare to work beneficiary' rules) to earlier claims for IB/SDA/IS.[80]
- Claimants who are due to reach pension age (see p531) at any time before 6 April 2014 will not have their claim transferred to ESA.
- The transfer to ESA will usually be triggered by the date you are next due to be assessed for incapacity for work under the personal capability assessment (see p734). If you are exempt from this assessment, you will be allocated a transfer date by the DWP. You will be sent a notice, telling you that you will now be assessed for ESA under the work capability assessment (you will get a telephone call about this first). Your entitlement to your existing award continues and you are not entitled to ESA while you are being assessed.[81] It is not necessary for you to make a claim for ESA.[82]
- Before you are sent the decision on whether your existing award has been transferred to an award of ESA (the 'conversion' decision), you are likely to get a telephone call to advise you of what the decision is likely to be and what your options are.
- If you pass the work capability assessment and satisfy the basic rules of entitlement to ESA on p175 (apart from the rule on IS entitlement), your existing award is converted to an award of ESA. This will take place on a date two to four weeks after the date on which you are notified of the conversion decision on your ESA entitlement. The exact date your award is converted (the 'effective date') depends on the day your IB/SDA/IS is paid. The transfer to ESA will be automatic; you do not need to do anything.
- If you fail the work capability assessment or you do not satisfy the basic ESA rules, including if you do not return the questionnaire or attend the medical without good cause, your IB/SDA/IS on grounds of disability will cease on the effective date (again, this will be from two to four weeks after you are notified). You are not entitled to ESA, but you can appeal in the usual way (see p208) against the conversion decision. **Note:** the time limit for appealing runs from the date you are notified of the conversion decision, not the actual date your benefit award ceases. While appealing against a decision that you have failed the work capability assessment, you are entitled to ESA at the 'assessment phase' rate.[83] You do not need to make a claim to get ESA while appealing. See p208 for more about appeals.
- If you will remain entitled to IS on grounds other than disability (eg, as a carer), you can remain on IS rather than transfer to ESA. Tell the DWP that you wish to remain on IS before your award is due to end. However, if you remain on IS,

you cannot get IB or SDA and your IS will not include the disability premium for incapacity for work.[84]

- Once made, a conversion decision can be altered before the effective date (ie, before the actual date on which the conversion to ESA is made, or IB/SDA/IS otherwise ceases) on a revision, and on or after the effective date on revision or supersession.[85]

Awards of employment and support allowance

Awards of IB and SDA will be converted to awards of contributory ESA (NI contribution condition tests do *not* need to be resatisfied). Awards of IS will be converted to awards of income-related ESA. You can be entitled to both contributory ESA and income-related ESA – eg, if you were previously entitled both to IB and IS. ESA additional components are included straight away. **Note:** the government intends to limit contributory ESA to one year (time in the support group will be ignored). See p181 for more information.

If you are a disabled or deaf student being transferred from IS, the usual requirement not to be in education (see p177) does not apply to you – ie, you can get ESA while in education even if you do not get disability living allowance.[86]

For income-related ESA, any 'transitional addition' (see below) to which you are entitled is not affected by your income.

Transitional addition

If the amount of your ESA is worth less than your IB/SDA/IS on grounds of disability, it is topped up with a 'transitional addition' to make good the shortfall.

The amount of ESA used in this comparison is the amount to which you are entitled on the 'effective date'. The amount of IB/SDA/IS used is the amount to which you were entitled immediately before this date.

The 'effective date' is the actual date on which your IB/SDA/IS is converted to an award of ESA. It will be between two and four weeks after the date you are notified of the conversion decision on your ESA entitlement, depending on the day your IB/SDA/IS is paid.[87]

If your ESA is worth more than your IB/SDA/IS, your ESA is not reduced – ie, you get the rate of ESA to which you are entitled from the effective date.

To work out if you should get a transitional addition with your ESA, the following apply.[88]

- If you are entitled to IB or SDA, the weekly rate of your IB/SDA (including any additions for age and for child or adult dependants) is compared with the amount of contributory ESA you are entitled to on the effective date (including the additional component). If your ESA entitlement is less, you get the difference as a transitional addition of contributory ESA. This counts as contributory ESA.
- If you are entitled to IS, your applicable amount is compared with the applicable amount of your income-related ESA on the effective date. The

applicable amounts used do not include housing costs or amounts for children, but do include the additional ESA component. See Chapter 37 for more information about applicable amounts. If your ESA applicable amount is lower, you get the difference as a transitional addition of income-related ESA. This is added to your ESA applicable amount. When working out your transitional addition, your income is not taken into account – ie, any income you have does not affect your transitional addition. However, your income is taken into account in the normal way when working out how much income-related ESA you are paid overall. So, even if your income increases to the extent that you otherwise lose entitlement to ESA, it does not affect your transitional amount of income-related ESA. In such cases, you still count as having an award of income-related ESA, so that, for example, you can still access payments from the social fund. Other changes that would stop your ESA entitlement altogether (eg, if your partner starts full-time work) mean that all your ESA stops completely, in the normal way.[89]
- In all the comparisons, ESA additional components are included straight away as part of your ESA. Most deductions being made from your IB are ignored.[90]
- Transitional addition is not permanent. It will not be paid after 5 April 2020.
- Your transitional addition is reduced by the amount of the annual increase to your ESA (in income-related ESA, increases in your housing costs are ignored). It is also reduced by other changes in your circumstances which increase the amount of ESA you get – eg, if you become entitled to another premium in your income-related ESA. Transitional addition of contributory ESA is also reduced if you were entitled to an increase:
  - for a child dependant in your IB or SDA and you stop getting child benefit for the child; *or*
  - for an adult dependant in your IB or SDA, and your adult dependant dies or you permanently separate from her/him, or if s/he becomes entitled to a benefit in her/his own right which 'overlaps' (see p1041) with the increase, or either of you stop getting child benefit.

  In these cases, the transitional addition is reduced by the amount the increase was worth before your award was converted to ESA.[91]
- You can appeal about the transitional addition you receive as it is part of the decision that you are given on the transfer to ESA.[92]

After the transfer

If you are transferred to ESA, you will be subject to all the usual ESA rules, such as those on permitted work, work-focused interviews and tax. This applies even if your IB was not taxable because you were transferred to it in 1995 from invalidity benefit.[93]

Any changes of circumstance that occurred before the 'effective date' (ie, before the actual date that your IB/SDA/IS on grounds of disability was converted to an ESA award, or otherwise ceased) and which would have affected your benefit can lead to the conversion decision being revised.[94]

On or after the effective date, a conversion decision can be revised or superseded in the usual way (see Chapter 45).[95]

If you lose entitlement to ESA but reclaim it, the transitional addition can be included again if your new period of limited capability for work is linked to the old one, under the linking rules (see p213). This is also possible if you lost entitlement to income-related ESA because your partner was in full-time work, but s/he has subsequently ceased work, and you reclaim income-related ESA within 12 weeks of your ESA stopping.[96]

Notes

1. **Who can claim employment and support allowance**

1 ss1 and 20(1) WRA 2007
2 s54 WRA 2012
3 Sch 1 paras 1-4 WRA 2007
4 s53 WRA 2012; s1(3A) WRA 2007; DWP, *Proposed Changes to Contribution-based Employment and Support Allowance, Welfare Reform Bill 2011*, September 2011
5 Sch 1 para 4 WRA 2007; reg 12 ESA Regs
6 Reg 11 ESA Regs
7 Reg 12 ESA Regs
8 R(S) 2/87 was not about ESA, but the rule is very similar.
9 Reg 9 ESA Regs
10 Reg 2(1) ESA Regs
11 Sch 1 para 6 WRA 2007
12 Reg 110 ESA Regs
13 Reg 18 ESA Regs
14 Reg 70 and Sch 5 para 11 ESA Regs
15 s115 IAA 1999
16 Regs 41-43 ESA Regs
17 Regs 14 -17 ESA Regs
18 Part 10 ESA Regs
19 s18 WRA 2007; reg 157 ESA Regs
20 Regs 157(3) and 158 ESA Regs
21 Sch 5 para 14 ESA Regs

3. **Claiming for others**

22 s4 WRA 2007; reg 67 and Sch 4 ESA Regs

4. **The amount of benefit**

23 s6 WRA 2007
24 s24(2) WRA 2007; reg 4 ESA Regs
25 Regs 4, 5 and 147A ESA Regs
26 Reg 7(38) SS&CS(DA) Regs
27 Regs 5 and 6 ESA Regs
28 s2(1)(a) WRA 2007; regs 7 and 67(2) and Sch 4 para 1(1)(b) and (c) ESA Regs
29 s2(2) and (3) WRA 2007; reg 67(2) and (3) and Sch 4 paras 1(a), 12 and 13 ESA Regs; Sch 2 para 12 ESA(TP)(EA)(No.2) Regs
30 ss51 and 52 WRA 2012; s1(1A) and (1B) WRA 2007; DWP, *Proposed Changes to Contribution-based Employment and Support Allowance, Welfare Reform Bill 2011*, September 2011
31 s4 WRA 2007
32 s4 WRA 2007; reg 67 and Sch 4 ESA Regs
33 s5 WRA 2007; reg 146 ESA Regs
34 s4(4) and (5) WRA 2007; reg 67 ESA Regs
35 Sch 1 para 6 and Sch 2 paras 4A and 12 ESA(TP)(EA)(No.2) Regs
36 s6 WRA 2007

37 ss2(2) and 4(4) WRA 2007
38 Sch 4 para 13 ESA Regs
39 Regs 47 and 54 ESA Regs
40 House of Commons *Hansard*, Welfare Reform Bill Standing Committee, 19 October 2006, col124; para 42365 DMG
41 Reg 7 ESA Regs
42 *SSWP v PT (ESA)* [2011] UKUT 317 (AAC); Memo DMG 25/11
43 Reg 34 ESA Regs
44 Regs 2 and 35 ESA Regs
45 ss2(3) and 4(5) WRA 2007
46 Sch 4 para 12 ESA Regs
47 Reg 7 ESA Regs
48 *SSWP v PT (ESA)* [2011] UKUT 317 (AAC)
49 Regs 72-79 ESA Regs
50 s3 WRA 2007; regs 72, 72A and 74 ESA Regs
51 Reg 75 ESA Regs
52 R(IB) 1/04 applied this to IB, but guidance at para 44750 DMG on ESA instructs decision makers to take the opposite approach.
53 Sch 1 paras 38 and 54 ESA(TP)(EA)(No.2) Regs

5. **Special benefit rules**
54 Sch 2 paras 5, 6 and 8 WRA 2007; regs 151-155 ESA Regs

6. **Claims and backdating**
55 Reg 3(j) SS(C&P) Regs
56 Reg 2 ESA(TP) Regs
57 Regs 4G and 4H SS(C&P) Regs
58 Reg 4I(1) and (2) SS(C&P) Regs
59 Regs 2 and 5 SS(ME) Regs
60 s19 SSA 1998; reg 23 ESA Regs
61 Reg 6(1F) SS(C&P) Regs
62 Reg 4H(6) and (7) SS(C&P) Regs
63 Reg 10(1A) SS(C&P) Regs
64 Reg 9 and Sch 1 SS(C&P) Regs
65 Reg 13(9) SS(C&P) Regs
66 Reg 19 and Sch 4 para 16 SS(C&P) Regs

7. **Getting paid**
67 Reg 26C(2) SS(C&P) Regs
68 Reg 26C SS(C&P) Regs
69 Reg 7(2)(a) and Sch 3C SS(D&A) Regs
70 Reg 7(2) and (25) and Sch 3C SS(D&A) Regs

8. **Tax, tax credits and other benefits**
71 ss658(4), 661(1) and 677 IT(EP)A 2003
72 Sch 2 para 6A ESA(TP)(EA)(No.2) Regs
73 s1(3)(e) WRA 2007
74 Sch 1 para 6(1)(d) WRA 2007
75 s1(3)(f) and Sch1 para 6(1)(d) WRA 2007
76 Sch 1 para 6(c) and (d) WRA 2007
77 s20 WRA 2007
78 Regs 80-82 ESA Regs

9. **Transfer to employment and support allowance**
79 ESA(TP)(EA)(No.2) Regs
80 Reg 2 ESA(TP) Regs
81 Sch 1 para 10 ESA(TP)(EA)(No.2) Regs
82 Sch 2 para 18 ESA (TP)(EA)(No.2) Regs
83 Regs 7 and 13-15 and Sch 2 paras 5, 10 and 45 ESA(TP)(EA)(No.2) Regs
84 Regs 14(2A) and (2B) and 15(2A) and (2B) ESA(TP)(EA)(No.2) Regs
85 Regs 6 and 16 ESA(TP)(EA)(No.2) Regs
86 Sch 1 para 2 and Sch 2 para 2 ESA(TP)(EA)(No.2) Regs
87 Regs 12 and 13 ESA(TP)(EA)(No.2) Regs; HB/CTB Circular A14/2010 para 14
88 Regs 8-12 ESA(TP)(EA)(No.2) Regs
89 Sch 1 para 6 and Sch 2 para 4A ESA(TP)(EA)(No.2) Regs
90 Reg 8 ESA(TP)(EA)(No.2) Regs
91 Regs 18-20 ESA(TP)(EA)(No.2) Regs
92 Sch 2 paras 5 and 12 ESA(TP)(EA)(No.2) Regs
93 Reg 16 ESA(TP)(EA)(No.2) Regs
94 Reg 17 ESA(TP)(EA)(No.2) Regs
95 Reg 16 ESA(TP)(EA)(No.2) Regs
96 Reg 21 ESA(TP)(EA)(No.2) Regs

11

Chapter 11

Employment and support allowance: limited capability for work

This chapter covers:

Key facts

- If you are too disabled or ill to work and are assessed as having 'limited capability for work', you may be entitled to employment and support allowance (ESA) and/or national insurance credits.
- Having limited capability for work means that, because of your mental or physical condition, it is unreasonable to require you to work. Whether you have limited capability for work is assessed by a test called the 'work capability assessment'.
- The work capability assessment also tests whether you have 'limited capability for work-related activity', which determines whether or not you are placed in the 'support group' for ESA.
- In general, you cannot work and have limited capability for work at the same time, although certain kinds of work are allowed.
- If you disagree with the decision about your limited capability for work, you can apply for a revision or supersession, or appeal against it (see Chapters 45 and 46).

Future changes: April 2013 and after

Major changes are taking place that affect the benefits and tax credits system (see Chapter 2). From October 2013, universal credit (UC) will replace income-related ESA. In the UC rules, whether you have limited capability for work will affect the 'claimant commitment' and the amount of benefit to which you are entitled (see Chapter 4). See CPAG's *Welfare Rights Bulletin* for updates.

1. The work capability assessment

Whether you have 'limited capability for work' is determined by the work capability assessment. If you do not have, or are not treated as having, limited capability for work, you are not entitled to employment and support allowance (ESA) or to national insurance credits (NI) credits (see Chapter 35) on that basis. There are rules about what work you may do while claiming (see p214).

The work capability assessment establishes:[1]

- whether your capability for work is limited by your physical or mental condition; *and if so*
- whether the limitation is such that it is not reasonable to require you to work.

The rules say that this means 'an assessment of the extent to which [a person] who has some specific disease or bodily or mental disablement' is capable of performing specified activities, or is incapable of performing them.[2] If you have certain limitations in performing these activities, you score points in the assessment. The activities, limitations and points are set out in Appendix 10.

There are three main ways of satisfying the work capability assessment:

- you are treated as having limited capability for work (see p201);
- you score sufficient points in the assessment (see p202);
- you do not score sufficient points, but you have 'exceptional circumstances' (see p203).

You may be treated as not having limited capability for work, even if you satisfy the work capability assessment (see below).

Note: the work capability assessment is under review by the government and the activities, descriptors and points are liable to change. See CPAG's *Welfare Rights Bulletin* for updates.

Treated as not having limited capability for work

You are treated as not having limited capability for work (ie, to have failed the work capability assessment), even if you have been assessed as satisfying the assessment, if you:[3]

- are disqualified from receiving contributory ESA for more than six weeks because you are a prisoner. If this applies, but you are entitled to income-related ESA (ie, pending trial or sentence pending conviction), you are only treated as not having limited capability for work after your entitlement has ended; *or*
- attend a training course and receive a training allowance or premium, unless your ESA claim is for a period beginning after you stopped attending the course, or if the training allowance or premium was only for travelling or meal expenses;[4] *or*

- are (or were) a member of the armed forces and the day in question is a day of sickness absence from duty;[5] *or*
- while the work capability assessment is being applied to you, fail to return the ESA50 questionnaire or fail to attend the medical and do not have good cause (see pp204 and 207).

Treated as having limited capability for work

You can be treated as having limited capability for work (ie, without having to score points in the work capability assessment – see p202) if:[6]

- you have applied for ESA but the work capability assessment has not yet been carried out, as long as you provide medical certificates. If your certicate expires, you can be given at least six weeks to supply a new one or to indicate that you wish your limited capability for work to be assessed. However, this rule usually does not apply if, within the last six months, you have failed the assessment or been treated as failing it because you have failed without good cause to return the ESA50 questionnaire (see p204) or attend the medical, or you have been found to be or treated as having been incapable of work – eg, for incapacity benefit or income support. The six months run from the date of the original decision, not from any later decision of the First-tier Tribunal.[7] The rule still applies, however, if you have a new condition, your condition has significantly worsened, or if you failed to return the questionnaire but have now returned it; *or*
- a specific circumstance applies to you – ie, you are:[8]
  - entitled to the support component of ESA on the basis that you meet one of the eating and drinking descriptors in the test of 'limited capability for work-related activity' (see p185);
  - terminally ill (see p184);
  - receiving intravenous, intraperitoneal or intrathecal chemotherapy or recovering from such treatment or are likely to receive such treament within six months from the date the DWP determines whether or not you pass the work capability assessment;
  - given official notice not to work because of being in contact with an infectious disease;
  - pregnant and there is a serious risk to your health or your baby's health if you do not refrain from work;
  - pregnant or have recently given birth, you are not entitled to maternity allowance (MA) or statutory maternity pay, you have a medical certificate giving the expected or actual date of birth, and you are within the period beginning with the first day of the sixth week before the expected week of childbirth (or the actual day of childbirth if earlier) and ending on the 14th day after you have the baby;
  - in the MA period and entitled to MA;

  - an inpatient in hospital or are recovering from treatment as an inpatient, including if you attending a residential programme of rehabilitation for drug or alcohol addiction;
  - receiving plasmapheriesis or radiotherapy, regular weekly treatment for haemodialysis for chronic renal failure, or regular weekly treatment for total parenteral nutrition for gross impairment of enteric function, or are recovering from such treatment. In the first week of such treatment, you must be receiving/recovering from it for a total of at least two days. This continues if your treatment later goes down to one day a week. However, you will not be able to get income-related ESA in any week in which you work (apart from work you can do while claiming – see p214), although you can claim contributory ESA for the days of treatment and recovery.[9]

In addition, you are treated as having limited capability for work:[10]

- on any day on which you are entitled to statutory sick pay, for the purpose of the 196-day qualifying period (see p176) for ESA in youth;
- if you are in education, you are not a 'qualifying young person' (see p94) and you are eligible for income-related ESA because you receive disability living allowance.

Scoring points

The assessment is carried out without referring to any job and does not take into account your education or training, or any language or literacy problems. It is a test of your ability to perform certain activities, taking account of 'specific bodily disease or disablement' and 'specific mental illness or disablement', and the direct results of medical treatment (from a registered doctor) for these.[11] There are two lists of activities: one physical, one mental. Under each activity, there is a further list of statements, called 'descriptors', which describe different levels of difficulty in carrying out the activity. Attached to each descriptor is a points score. You are awarded the highest scoring descriptor in each activity that applies to you, taking into account your ability when wearing or using any aid, appliance or prosthesis that you 'normally use'. That means something which has been prescribed or recommended for you, or that other people in your situation normally use and it is reasonable for you to do so.[12] For the full list of activities, descriptors and points, see Appendix 10.

To satisfy the test by scoring points, you must score a total of 15 points or more. The points can be scored in one or more activities, and scores from the physical and mental activities can be combined. For example, you can score nine points in the physical test and six points in the mental test, which, combined, give a total of 15 and so satisfy the test. To score points in the mental activities, it does not matter if the problem has an underlying physical cause, as long as your mental functioning is affected. But to score points in the physical activities, the underlying cause of the problem must be physical.[13]

Good days and bad days, pain and tiredness

Official guidance to examining healthcare professionals (ie, the people who carry out the medicals) is that they should assess your capability as it is 'most of the time' and that, if you cannot repeat an activity without a reasonable degree of regularity, you should be considered unable to perform it.[14] The following points should apply.

- Your ability to perform an actvity with some degree of repetition should be considered and a 'broad brush' approach applied, rather than just a day-by-day approach.[15]
- A descriptor should apply to you if you cannot perform the activity most of the time. The severity of your condition, the frequency of your good and bad days and the unpredictability of the bad days are all relevant. So, if in a normal week you would have three bad days when a particular descriptor would apply to you, and four good days when it would nearly apply, that descriptor may apply to you, especially if your condition on the bad days is very bad.[16]
- If you have long periods of remission, you may be considered capable of work during these periods. Whether this is the correct approach will depend on the severity of your condition and on the length of your periods of ill health and your periods of remission.[17]
- Pain, fatigue and the increasing difficulty you may have in performing an activity on a repeated basis compared with someone in good health should be taken into account.[18] 'Pain' may include nausea and dizziness.[19] The decision maker (or First-tier Tribunal) should consider whether you can perform the activity without too much discomfort and whether you can repeate the activity within a reasonable time.
- Any risk to your health in peforming an activity should be considered, particularly if carrying it out is against medical advice. If the risk is sufficiently serious, you may be considered incapable of the activity.[20]

Exceptional circumstances

If you do not satisfy the work capability assessment (ie, you are not treated as having limited capability for work and you do not score enough points), you are treated as doing so if:[21]

- you have an uncontrolled or uncontrollable life-threatening disease, and there is medical evidence to show this. There must be reasonable cause for the disease not to be controllable by a recognised therapeutic procedure; *or*
- because of your illness, there would be a substantial risk to the mental or physical health of any person were you to be found not to have limited capability for work. The 'substantial risk' is that which would arise from the sort of work you may be expected to do, or from the journey to or from work, although it is not necessary to go into the detail of individual job descriptions or potential jobseeker's agreements. Arguably, the risk can also arise from

broad factors such as, in mental health cases, apprehension caused by the need to look for work.[22]

The work capability assessment process

Information is sought from your doctor and, unless you are to be treated as having limited capability for work (see p201), you are sent a questionnaire (ESA50) to complete. In most cases, you are required to attend a medical examination with a doctor (or other approved healthcare professional) from the DWP Medical Service (MS). For advice about the questionnaire and medical, see below and p205.

The doctor (or other approved healthcare professional) also carries out as part of the assessment an assessment of whether you have 'limited capability for work-related activity' (see below). This is a test of whether you should be placed in the support group for ESA (see p184). It is carried out at the same time as the assessement of whether you have limited capability for work.[23]

Limited capability for work-related activity assessment

You may automatically count as having limited capability for work-related activity, or you may be required to complete a questionnaire and/or attend a medical (see p185 for details). If you fail to return the questionnaire or take part in the medical and do not have good cause, you are treated as not having limited capability for work-related activity – ie, you are not in the support group. When deciding if you have good cause, the decision maker must take into account:[24]

- whether you were outside Great Britain at the time you were notified;
- your state of health;
- the nature of any disability you have;
- any other matter s/he thinks appropriate.

The questionnaire

Unless it is already accepted that you have limited capability for work, or that you are to be treated as such, you are sent a questionnaire (ESA50) on your limited capability for work for you to complete.

You have four weeks from the date the questionnaire is sent to complete and return it. If you do not return it within this time, a reminder must be sent to you at least three weeks after the questionnaire was sent. You must then be given a further week from the date the reminder was sent to return the questionnaire. If you still do not return it in time, you are treated as capable of work unless that you can show that you had good cause for not returning it.[25]

When deciding whether you had good cause, the decision maker must consider all the circumstances, including:[26]

- whether you were outside Great Britain at the relevant time;
- your state of health;
- the nature of your disability.

If you are late in completing and returning the questionnaire, do so as soon as you can and explain why you were late. If your benefit stops because you are considered not to have had good cause, but you think you did, write to the DWP explaining this. You should also make a fresh claim for benefit. If the decision maker decides that you did not have good cause, you can appeal (see Chapter 46).

Completing the questionnaire

- Read the notes on the form before answering the questions. It may be helpful to draft your answers on a separate sheet of paper first.
- If you have had to get someone else to fill in the questionnaire for you, or you have only be able to do so yourself slowly, or with pain, explain this on the questionnaire.
- If you eventually have to appeal, the First-tier Tribunal may be less likely to believe you have symptoms if you did not mention them on the questionnaire. It may be worth letting someone who knows you well check your answers.
- If you have good and bad days, explain this. Answer the question on the basis of your ability on a bad day, and then give a fuller answer explaining about the good days in the space provided. If necessary, give a rough estimate of how often you could perform the activity and how often you could not.
- Compare the draft of your answers with the list in Appendix 10 and work out your score, so that you have an idea of what your score may be. Your answers should not be exaggerated, but check you have not underestimated any of your problems and that you have given all the detail you can.
- If you have any difficulties with English or with reading and writing, it is vital that you get independent help before you submit the form.
- If someone has helped you fill out the form, put her/his details at the end where the form asks about this.
- Always make a copy of your questionnaire with your answers before returning it to the DWP.

On receiving your completed questionnaire, the decision maker considers whether you should be treated as having limited capability for work or if you clearly score enough points to satisfy the test. If neither of these apply, your case if referred to the MS for a medical examination to be arranged.

Medical examinations

You may be required to attend a medical with an MS examiner as part of the work capability assessment. Bear in mind the following.

- If you fail to attend a medical examination without good cause, you are treated as not having limited capability for work.
- If you cannot attend the medical, contact the MS immediately to explain why and ask for another appointment.
- If you are too ill to travel, ask to be examined at home.

- You can claim your travel expenses for going to the medical. If you have to attend by taxi or minicab, the DWP will not pay your fares unless you get them to agree this before you travel.
- You can take a friend or adviser to the medical with you.

In order to complete the medical report, the MS examiner asks about your condition and assesses whether, in her/his opinion, you have limited capability for work. S/he considers your abilities in each of the specific areas of activity as set out in Appendix 10. The MS examiner is supposed to consider all the information and reach an judgement on the basis of:

- your answers to the questions on the questionnaire;
- what you tell her/him;
- the results of the examination and any tests s/he may carry out;
- your appearance and behaviour during the assessment. This does not just mean during the examination itself. For example, when the MS examiner greets you in the waiting area, s/he may assess your ability to rise from a chair and walk, and whether you have been able to get the medical on your own.

The MS examiner asks about your typical day and uses the information to assess your ability to perform the activities in the work capability assessment. S/he then completes a report (an ESA85) indicating which descriptors s/he thinks apply to you and sends it to the decision maker.

Bear in mind the following.

- Tell the MS examiner in as much detail as possible how your condition affects you.
- Take the medicines and other aids you are taking or using with you. This may lead the examiner to ask you questions s/he would not otherwise have thought to ask.
- If you have taken additional painkillers in order to attend the medical, explain this and what you can and cannot do on your normal dosage.
- The place where the medical takes place is likely to be a very artificial environment and there is only limited time. If this may affect your abilities (eg, you can bend once or twice at the medical, but would not be able to do so on a repeated basis, or would start to experience pain), tell the examiner.
- If you have good and bad days and are seen on a good day, explain to the examiner what it is like on a bad day.
- When asked about the activities you perform on a typical day, explain how your condition affects your ability to do day-to-day activities such as shopping, washing, dressing and watching TV.
- If you are not fluent in English, it is vital that someone who has a good knowledge of English attends with you. Alternatively, the MS should be able to provide (and pay for) an interpreter if you request one.[27]

If you believe you were treated unfairly at the medical, you can make a complaint (ask the MS for its leaflet on this).

Failing to attend a medical examination

If you fail to attend a medical without good cause, you will be treated as not having limited capability for work – ie, you will not be entitled to ESA. You must have been sent notice of the date and time of the medical at least seven days beforehand, unless you agreed to accept less than this.[28]

In deciding whether you have good cause, the decision maker must consider all the circumstances, including those that apply to the questionnaire (see p204). Good cause may also include being too ill or distressed on the day of the medical, or wishing to be examined by someone of the same sex and this was not possible. You may also be able to show that you had good cause if your refusal to attend was based on a firm religious conviction.[29]

If your benefit stops because you are considered not to have good cause for failing to attend the medical, but you think you did, write to the DWP explaining this. You should also make a fresh claim for benefit. If the decision maker does not accept that you had good cause, consider appealing (see Chapter 46).

The decision maker's decision

The decision on whether or not you have limited capability for work (ie, whether you satisfy the work capability assessment and are entitled to ESA) is made by a DWP decision maker. If you have had a medical examination, the MS report (the ESA85) is sent to the decision maker. The decision maker is free to disagree with the MS report, although in practice this is unusual. The MS examiner includes in the medical report a suggested date when the work capability assessment should be applied to you again in order to retest your limited capability for work. You do not have the right of appeal about how often you are retested.

If the decision maker does not consider that you have limited capability for work, you are not entitled to ESA and your claim is refused. If you have been getting ESA, your award is revised or superseded (see Chapter 45) and your benefit is stopped. The decison may include a 'decision maker's justification', which explains why s/he has decided that you do not have limited capability for work. This should not be used to persuade you not to challenge the decision (see p208) if you are unhappy with it.

What to do next

If you are not considered to have limited capability for work and therefore you are not entitled to ESA, but you do not wish to challenge the decision:

- if you do not have a job to return to, you can sign on and claim jobseeker's allowance (JSA – see Chapter 19). Claim as soon as possible, as backdating is possible only in limited circumstances (see p1027);

- remember that if you want to claim ESA again, special rules apply if it is within six months of a decision that you do not have limited capability for work (see p201). However, if you can satisfy these rules and your new period of limited capability for work is not more than 12 weeks after the end of a previous one, the periods are linked so that, for example, you can be entitled to your former rate of ESA straight away (see p212).

If you are not considered to have limited capability for work and therefore not entitled to ESA, but you think you are not well enough to work, you can challenge the decision either by a revision (see Chapter 45), or by appealing to the First-tier Tribunal (see Chapter 46). There are advantages and disadvantages with each option.

- If you ask for a revision, you are only likely to get the decision changed if you provide further evidence to support your argument that you do have limited capability for work, or there has been an obvious mistake. However, this can be a relatively quick way of getting the decision changed.
- If you appeal, the hearing may take some time to be arranged. However, you may be more likely to succeed with an appeal and, under a special rule, you may be able to get ESA while your appeal is pending. Alternatively, you may be able to get JSA.

2. Challenging a decision on limited capability for work

In general, you can challenge a decision by applying for a revision or supersession (see Chapter 45), or by making an appeal (see Chapter 46). Initially, some findings, such as whether you have limited capability for work, are the subject of a 'determination'. It is not until this is included in a decision that you have the right of appeal.[30]

Note: when you appeal against an employment and support allowance (ESA) decision, you enable the whole decision to be looked at again if it is considered right to do so. So you may appeal about a particular part of a decision, but another aspect of it can be looked at if the decision maker or First-tier Tribunal thinks it is right to do so, even if you do not want this to happen. For example, you may be appealing about limited capability for work, but the First-tier Tribunal may go on to look at whether or not you should be in the support group. This could result in your losing some, or even all, of your entitlement.

The decision on your limited capability for work

Initially, the DWP makes a 'determination' on your limited capability for work.[31] The determination should then be incorporated into a decision about your entitlement to benefit or national insurance (NI) credits for limited capability for work. If you appeal against that decision, the First-tier Tribunal reconsiders whether or not you have limited capability for work.

If you appeal

Consider seeking advice (see Appendix 2). Immediately request a copy of the medical evidence that the DWP holds on your file, including a copy of the Medical Service (MS) examiner's report (the ESA85). If you appeal, a copy of the MS report should be included in the appeal papers the DWP sends to you and HM Courts and Tribunals Service.

Discuss your limited capability for work with your own doctor. In practice, it can be very difficult to win an appeal if you cannot get your GP or consultant to support you.

Remember that there are only certain circumstances in which you can work and still be regarded as having limited capability for work (see p200). If you work while you are appealing, you may lose entitlement to benefit, even if you actually win your appeal.

The First-tier Tribunal

The First-tier Tribunal considers your appeal. It must be made up of at least one legally qualified person and one medically qualified person (see p1171).

The following points may be useful.

- Request an oral hearing of your appeal as this will give the First-tier Tribunal the opportunity of hearing from you first-hand about how your condition affects you, and what happened at the medical with the MS examiner.
- Although not formally required, it is often important that you get medical evidence to support your appeal. This could be from your GP or your consultant, if you have one, or from both. It is usually more helpful if such evidence comments on the things at issue in your appeal rather than just sets out your diagnosis and treatment. If your doctor has been treating you on a regular basis for many years, s/he should say so, so that there can be no doubt that s/he is fully aware of your medical history. Check to see if your doctor insists on charging you.
- If you have not been able to obtain a medical report in any other way, you can ask the First-tier Tribunal to obtain one. This is a discretionary decision. There is no charge for this, but you do not have any control over who does the medical, and the report is the First-tier Tribunal's rather than yours.[32] Also consider using previous medical reports if you passed the work capability assessment and if you could get evidence from, for instance, a community nurse or an occupational therapist.
- The First-tier Tribunal cannot carry out its own examination of you.[33] However, it may observe your conduct in the room – eg, how you walk or sit.

- The decision maker or First-tier tribunal should make a reasoned decision based on all the evidence – medical and non-medical. If necessary, point out that the First-tier Tribunal can prefer your own or your doctor's evidence to that of the MS doctor.[34]
- MS medical reports are in electronic form. These can frequently have inconsistencies or errors in them. The First-tier Tribunal must deal with any discrepancies and take these into account when considering the weight to be given to different sources of evidence.[35]
- It is often useful for a person who lives with you or who knows you well to attend the hearing to describe the day-to-day problems you have.
- Take a list of any medication you are taking to the hearing.

For more about First-tier Tribunal hearings, see Chapter 46.

Getting benefit while appealing

While you are appealing against a decision on your limited capability for work, the main benefits you may wish to consider claiming (apart from those to which you are already entitled) are ESA pending the appeal or, usually if you can not get ESA pending the appeal, jobseeker's allowance (JSA). In limited circumstances, it may be possible to claim income support (IS) instead of ESA.

Note: the following rules also apply if you are being transferred from incapacity benefit (IB), severe disablement allowance (SDA) or IS on grounds of disability to ESA, but you have been refused ESA because you have been found not to have limited capability for work (see p193) and have appealed about that. In such cases, if you have been on IB or SDA, you are also treated as satisfying the NI contribution conditions for contributory ESA, so you can get that pending your appeal.[36]

Employment and support allowance

If you appeal against a decision on your limited capability for work (except if the decision was to treat you as not having limited capability because you failed to return the questionnaire or attend the medical – see pp204 and 207), you can be entitled to ESA until the First-tier Tribunal makes its decision. You must submit medical certificates and, although you are treated as having limited capability for work, you must still satisfy most of the other rules for ESA.[37] In this chapter, we refer to this award of ESA as 'ESA pending an appeal', as it is regarded as a separate claim to the original that led to the decision you are appealing against. The following applies.

- ESA pending an appeal is paid at the assessment period rate – ie, it does not include either of the additional components (although it can include any *premiums* and housing costs to which you are entitled).[38] You do not have to reclaim to get ESA pending an appeal.[39]
- Pending the appeal, you are treated as having limited capability for work, so usually the DWP does not assess you in this period. However, if you develop a

new condition or your condition significantly worsens, the DWP can then assess you again. If it determines that you do have limited capability for work, you can get ESA in the normal way (including either of the additional components) from that point on, but the First-tier Tribunal will still consider your appeal for the period up until then. Even if the DWP determines that you do not have limited capability for work, you remain entitled to ESA pending the appeal.[40]

- If your appeal is successful, the original decision about your limited capability for work is changed so that you are entitled to ESA. The DWP usually then applies the First-tier Tribunal's decision to your award of ESA pending an appeal, so that your award of ESA continues in the normal way, and you can qualify for an additional component. **Note**: if you have been transferred from IB/SDA/IS on grounds of disability (see p193), you should still be entitled to ESA, including an additional component and any transitional addition.[41] However, if the DWP considers that your condition improved while the appeal was pending, it could decide that you do not have limited capability for work now.[42] You may appeal against this decision, and should be able to get ESA pending the appeal again.[43]
- If your appeal is unsuccessful, the original decision that you do not have limited capability for work is not changed. Also, from the week after the week in which the First-tier Tribunal notified the DWP of its decision, the DWP treats you as not having limited capability for work during your award of ESA pending an appeal.[44] The effect is that your entitlement to ESA is stopped, although you keep the ESA that was paid to you pending the appeal. Although you can appeal against the decison to treat you as not having limited capability for work, the prospect of success is likely to be limited, as the rules allow the DWP to do this when you have lost your appeal. In order to continue to get ESA in this situation, whether you appeal or not, you need to submit a fresh claim.[45] In the case of a fresh claim, however, note that you cannot usually be treated as having limited capability for work and, therefore, will not be entitled to ESA if you are still within six months of actually failing the work capability assessment – ie, the original decision you appealed against (see p201).

Jobseeker's allowance

Instead of claiming ESA pending an appeal, you may be able to claim JSA, at least until the First-tier Tribunal makes its decision. This may be an attractive option if you cannot get ESA pending an appeal – eg, because you were treated as not having limited capability for work for failing to attend the medical and you have decided not to make a fresh claim for ESA.

To get JSA, however, you have to sign on as available for and actively seeking work (see pp434 and 447), and must be prepared to accept any reasonable work within your limitations, even while the appeal is pending. You can place restrictions on your availability if these are reasonable in light of your condition (see p443). If you win your appeal, you are entitled to ESA, your JSA award is removed and you should get arrears of ESA if they are worth more than the JSA you received.[46]

Income support

Instead of ESA pending an appeal or JSA, in limited circumstances you may be entitled to claim IS – eg, as a lone parent or carer (see p346). You cannot claim IS on grounds of disability, including incapacity for work. Even if you can get IS, you are not entitled to any disability premium on the basis of incapacity for work. You do not have to sign on as available for and actively seeking work in order to get IS. However, unless you win your appeal, you will not be entitled to NI credits for limited capability for work. Therefore, you should check to see how to protect your NI contribution record while on IS (see Chapter 35). Seek advice if necessary. If you win your appeal, you cannot remain entitled to both ESA and to IS at the same time. Normally, your award of IS is removed and you should get arrears of ESA if they are worth more than the IS you received.

If your condition worsens

If your condition has significantly worsened since the decision, or you have a new specific disease or disablement, and you have not already claimed ESA pending the appeal (see p210), you could make a fresh claim for ESA. In this situation, you should be treated as having limited capability for work until a new work capability assessment is carried out, even if is within six months of the decision that you do not have limited capability for work (see p201). If you have already claimed ESA pending the appeal, you could inform the DWP and ask it to make a determination on your limited capability for work (see p208).

3. Periods of limited capability for work, waiting days and linking rules

A **'period of limited capability for work'** generally means a period in which you have, or are treated as having, limited capability for work. Except for employment and support allowance (ESA) in youth, it does not include any period not covered by your claim for ESA.[47] However, see the linking rules below. You are not entitled to ESA for three 'waiting days' at the beginning of your period of limited capability for work.[48] This does not apply if:

- you are transferred from incapacity benefit (IB), severe disablement allowance (SDA) or income support (IS) to an award of ESA (see p193);
- your entitlement to ESA starts within 12 weeks of your entitlement to IS, IB, SDA, pension credit, jobseeker's allowance, carer's allowance, statutory sick pay or maternity allowance coming to an end;

- you are a member of a couple and one of you has already served the waiting days for a claim for income-related ESA, and that person gives up her/his claim so the other member of the couple can claim it instead;
- you are terminally ill, or you have been discharged from Her Majesty's forces and three or more days before the discharge were days of sickness absence.[49]

Linking rules

Different periods of limited capability for work may be joined or 'linked' to form one continuous period. The effect is that you are treated as having had limited capability for work throughout the whole of the linked period. Different periods are linked if they are not more than 12 weeks apart, or not more than 104 weeks apart if you are regarded as a 'work or training beneficiary' (see p214), or satisfy the conditions below.[50] **Note:** at the time of writing, the government intended to abolish the 104 week linking rule for both contributory and income-related ESA from 30 April 2012. It is understood that linked claims under the 104-week linking rule will still be possible up to and including 30 April 2012.

Different periods separated by not more than 104 weeks are linked if:

- your new period of limited capability for work began on the day immediately after the day on which you stopped being in full-time paid work, which is defined in the same way as for working tax credit (WTC – see Chapter 52); *and*
- you had been entitled to ESA within the 104 weeks before your new period of limited capability for work began; *and*
- you were entitled to the disability element of WTC on the day before you stopped work, or you would have been had your income not been too high; *and*
- you were paid either WTC or a child element of child tax credit (CTC) at above the family element for the day before you stopped being in full-time paid work.

Different periods separated by not more than 104 weeks are also linked if:

- you claim ESA after you stop being engaged in 'training' (as defined on p177 or, for occupational or vocational skills, for 16 or more hours a week); *and*
- you were entitled to ESA within the eight weeks immediately before you started the training; *and*
- you had limited capability for work on the day after you stopped training; *and*
- the day after you stopped training is no more than 104 weeks from the end of the last week of your previous entitlement to ESA.

If periods of limited capability for work are linked, it means that:

- the question of whether or not you satisfy the national insurance (NI) contribution conditions for ESA may be decided at the beginning of the first period (see p789);[51]
- you can continue to qualify for ESA in youth (if you still need to qualify via this route because you still do not have enough NI contributions), if this is the basis on which you qualified before;

- you do not have to serve further 'waiting days' (see p212) before becoming entitled to ESA because you have already served them;
- if you had already completed the 'assessment' period in your previous claim, you do not have to complete it again before becoming entitled to one of the additional components. So unless you have been found not to have limited capability for work and are appealing, the work-related activity component is payable straight away. Aternatively, you can get the support component again straight away if you are a 'work or training beneficiary' (see below). If you did not complete the assessment period, you must complete the remaining part of it;[52]
- if you are a 'work or training beneficiary' (see below), you are treated as having limited capability for work throughout the linked period – ie, for up to 104 weeks (if your claim was made before 1 November 2010, you are only treated as having limited capability for work under this rule for 13 weeks);[53] *and*
- if you are a work or training beneficiary (see below) and you were previously in the support group (see p184), you are treated as being in the support group again throughout the linked period – ie, for up to 104 weeks. If your claim was made before 1 November 2010, you are only treated as in support group again under this rule for 13 weeks.[54]

Work or training beneficiary

You count as a work or training beneficiary during a period linking two periods of limited capability for work (ie, up to 104 weeks) if:[55]

- you had limited capability for work for more than 13 weeks in your most recent past period of limited capability for work. If that period started when you were transferred from IB/SDA/IS on grounds of disability to ESA (see p193), it does not matter if it was 13 weeks or less; *and*
- you stopped being entitled to benefit or another advantage (eg, NI credits) for limited capability for work at the end of that period; *and*
- within a month of stopping being entitled to that benefit or advantage, you start work or training.

Even if you satisfy these conditions, you are not a work or training beneficiary if your most recent past period of limited capability for work ended because you were found not to have limited capability for work – ie, you failed the work capability assessment.

4. Work you can do while claiming

The general rule is that you cannot work and be entitled to employment and support allowance (ESA), and therefore be entitled to national insurance (NI) credits for limited capability for work, at the same time.[56] With certain exceptions, in any week (a period of seven days in which you are entitled to ESA) in which you actually do work (paid or unpaid), you are not entitled to ESA and you are treated as not having limited capability for work, even if it has previously been decided that you do.[57]

However, you are only treated as not entitled to ESA on the actual days that you work, rather than the whole week, if you work:

- during the first week of your claim; *or*
- during the last week in which you had limited capability for work or were treated as having limited capability for work.[58]

It is arguable that work which would be disregarded for incapacity for work purposes because it is so minimal that it can be regarded as trivial or negligible[59] should be ignored.

Certain work, however, is allowed. For how earnings from this may affect income-related ESA, see Chapter 40. Note that earnings under the 'permitted work' rules (see p216) that are under the relevant earnings limit are ignored. The following kinds of work are allowed:[60]

- work as a local councillor;
- work (for a maximum of one day or two half days a week) as a member of the First-tier Tribunal if you have been appointed because of your experience of disability issues, or of the Disability Living Allowance Advisory Board;
- domestic work (eg, cooking and cleaning) in your own home;
- the care of a 'relative' (ie, a grandparent, grandchild, uncle, aunt, nephew, niece, and including 'close relatives' – ie, parent, parent-in-law, son, son-in-law, daughter, daughter-in-law, step-parent, stepson, stepdaughter, brother, sister, or the partner of any of these);
- caring for another person living with you under specific legislation relating to accommodating children or temporarily caring for someone else where you are paid for this;
- work you do to protect someone or prevent serious damage to property or livestock during an emergency;
- work done while receiving assistance in pursuing self-employment under s2 of the Employment and Training Act 1973 or s2 of the Enterprise and New Towns (Scotland) Act 1990 (test-trading);
- voluntary work that is not for a relative (any of the people, including 'close relatives', mentioned in the fourth bullet above), the only payment you receive is to cover your reasonable expenses and where it is considered reasonable for you to work free of charge;
- work done in the course of a work placement (unpaid practical work experience with an employer) approved in writing by the DWP before the placement starts;
- for contributory ESA, any work you do in a week in which you are treated as having limited capability for work because you are having certain regular

treatment (eg, haemodialysis for chronic renal failure) or are recovering from that treatment (see p201);[61]
- 'permitted work' (see below).

Permitted work

'Permitted work' (sometimes called 'exempt' work) is work of any kind, which you can do:[62]
- as part of a treatment programme done under medical supervision while you are in hospital or regularly attending hospital as an outpatient, provided you do not earn more than £97.50 a week; *or*
- for an unlimited period, provided do not earn more than £20 a week. This is called the 'permitted work lower limit'; *or*
- for an unlimited period, provided you do not earn more than £97.50 a week and you are in 'supported (sometimes called 'supervised') work' (see below); *or*
- for up to 52 weeks or indefinitely in certain circumstances (see below) provided you work, on average, for less than 16 hours a week and do not earn more than £97.50 a week. This is called the 'permitted work higher limit'. For how your hours are calculated, see p720.

Note: if you have been transferred from incapacity benefit, severe disablement allowance or income support on grounds of disability to ESA (see p193), the permitted work you were doing under the incapacity for work rules (see p736) can continue. However, work of the sort that you have been doing under the incapacity for work rules counts towards the 52-week limit above, and you can only do this work indefinitely if you are in the support group for ESA.[63]

Note: the amounts referred to in the first, third and fourth bullet points above are usually increased in October. See CPAG's *Welfare Rights Bulletin* for updates.

Permitted work higher limit

You can usually undertake work under the permitted work higher limit for up to 52 weeks. If you are treated as having limited capability for work-related activity (ie, you are in the support group – see p184), you can do this work indefinitely. Otherwise, after 52 weeks have passed since you started work (whether or not you actually work for all the 52 weeks), you can do more work which falls under the permitted work higher limit if:
- since the beginning of the last 52-week period of such work, you have ceased to be entitled to ESA or NI credits for limited capability for work for a continuous period lasting more than 12 weeks; *or*
- a further 52 weeks have passed.

Supported work

This means work which is supervised by someone employed by a public or local authority, or by a voluntary organisation or community interest company, whose job it is to find work for people with disabilities. This could include work in a sheltered workshop or with help from social services. The DWP usually says that you need not have the person working alongside you, although the support should be ongoing and regular. Where possible, check in advance that the DWP agrees that the work will count as supported work.

Informing the DWP

Although there are no special rules, you should inform the DWP as soon as possible about any permitted work you do. Under the general benefit rules, you are required to report changes in circumstances that you might reasonably be expected to know might affect your benefit. Also note that if the particular activities you carry out in your work suggest to the DWP that your limited capability might have changed, it might reassess this.

Notes

1. **The work capability assessment**

1 s8(1) WRA 2007
2 Reg 19 ESA Regs
3 Reg 44 ESA Regs
4 Reg 32(2) ESA Regs
5 Reg 32(1) ESA Regs
6 Reg 30 ESA Regs
7 R(IB) 8/04
8 Regs 20, 25 and 26 ESA Regs
9 Regs 44, 46 and 109 ESA Regs; paras 42045-58 DMG
10 Reg 33 ESA Regs
11 Reg 19 ESA Regs
12 *RP v SSWP (ESA)* [2011] UKUT 449 (AAC)
13 *KP v SSWP (ESA)* [2011] UKUT 216 (AAC); [2012] AACR 5
14 *Training and Development ESA Handbook,* Med-ESAHB-001, p53
15 *AF v SSWP (ESA)* [2011] UKUT 61 (AAC); *SAG v Department for Social Development (ESA)* [2011] NICom 171
16 CIB/14534/1996
17 CIB/2620/2000
18 CIB/14587/1996; CIB/14722/1996; CIB/13161/1996; CIB/13508/1996
19 CIB/14722/1996
20 CSIB/12/1996
21 Reg 29 ESA Regs
22 *Charlton v SSWP* [2009] EWCA Civ 42, 6 February 2009; *JW v SSWP* [2011] UKUT 418 (AAC). CSIB/33/2004 is disapproved in *Charlton*, but not on the point it makes about risk arising from apprehension.
23 s9 WRA 2007
24 Regs 36-39 ESA Regs
25 Reg 22 ESA Regs
26 Reg 24 ESA Regs
27 *Training and Development ESA Handbook,* Med-ESAHB-001, p118, and information on the work capability assessment at www.directgov.uk
28 Reg 23 ESA Regs
29 R(IS) 9/51

2. **Challenging a decision on limited capability for work**

30 para 53067 DMG
31 Reg 19 ESA Regs
32 s20 SSA 1998; R(S) 3/84
33 s20(3) SSA 1998
34 CIB/407/1998; CIB/1149/1998; R(M) 1/93; CIB/3074/2003
35 CIB/511/2005
36 Sch 2 para 15 ESA(TP)(EA)(No.2) Regs
37 Reg 30(3) ESA Regs

38 Reg 5(4) ESA Regs provides that the assessment phase applies pending the decision of the First-tier Tribunal.
39 Reg 3(j) SS(C&P) Regs
40 Reg 147A(2) and (4) ESA Regs
41 Reg 21(2)and Sch 2 para 15 ESA(TP)(EA)(No.2) Regs; reg 147A ESA Regs as applied by Sch 2 para 15 ESA(TP)(EA)(No.2) Regs
42 Reg 147A(6) and (7) ESA Regs
43 This is because the DWP will have made a determination that you do not have limited capability for work, and not merely treated you as not having limited capability for work, so reg 30(3) ESA Regs should apply.
44 Reg 147A(5) ESA Regs
45 Reg 3(j) SS(C&P) Regs; Memo DMG 33/10, para 52
46 Memo DMG 51/10; reg 3(5G) and (5H) SS&CS(D&A) Regs

3. **Periods of limited capability for work, waiting days and linking rules**

47 Reg 2 ESA Regs, definition of 'period of limited capability for work'
48 Sch 2 para 2 WRA 2007
49 Reg 144 ESA Regs; Sch 1 para 12 ESA (TP)(EA)(No.2) Regs
50 Regs 2 and 145 ESA Regs
51 Paras 1-3 Sch 1 WRA 2007
52 Regs 5 and 7(1)(b) ESA Regs ; *SSWP v PT (ESA)* [2011] 317 (AAC); Memo DMG 25/11
53 Reg 149 ESA Regs
54 Reg 150 ESA Regs
55 Reg 148 ESA Regs

4. **Work you can do while claiming**

56 Reg 40 ESA Regs
57 Regs 40 and 44 ESA Regs
58 Reg 40(4) ESA Regs
59 CIB/5298/1997; CIB/6777/1999
60 Regs 40 and 45 ESA Regs
61 Reg 46 ESA Regs
62 Reg 45 ESA Regs
63 Sch 2 para 11 ESA(TP)(EA)(No.2) Regs

Chapter 12

Guardian's allowance

This chapter covers:

Key facts

- Guardian's allowance can be paid to you if you are responsible for a child or young person and both of her/his parents have died or, in some circumstances, one of her/his parents has died.
- You do not have to be the child's legal guardian to qualify for guardian's allowance.
- Guardian's allowance is a non-means-tested benefit.
- You do not need to have paid national insurance contributions to qualify.
- You can get guardian's allowance whether or not you are in or out of work.
- Guardian's allowance can be paid in addition to other benefits and tax credits (but the overlapping benefit rules apply if you also get an increase in a non-means-tested benefit for the child).
- Guardian's allowance is ignored when calculating your entitlement to means-tested benefits and tax credits.
- Guardian's allowance is administered and paid by HM Revenue and Customs.
- If you disagree with a guardian's allowance decision, you can apply for a revision or a supersession, or appeal against it (see Chapters 45 and 46).

Future changes: April 2013 and after

Major changes are taking place that affect the benefits and tax credits system (see Chapter 2).

– From April 2013, total benefit payments to many working-age households will be 'capped' (see p25). It is not yet known whether guardian's allowance will be included in this capped amount.

- You will still be able to claim guardian's allowance when universal credit is introduced in October 2013. Guardian's allowance is *not* being abolished.

See CPAG's *Welfare Rights Bulletin* for updates.

1. Who can claim guardian's allowance

You qualify for a guardian's allowance if:[1]

- you are entitled, or treated as entitled, to child benefit for a 'child' or a 'qualifying young person' (see p221). In this chapter the term 'child' is used to refer to both a child and a qualifying young person; *and*
- the child is an 'eligible child' (see p221); *and either*
  - s/he is living with you (see p100). A child who is absent from home may still be treated as living with you in the circumstances described on p100; *or*
  - you or, if you are residing with your spouse or civil partner, you and/or your spouse or civil partner make contributions to the cost of providing for the child at the rate of at least £15.55 a week in addition to any payment you are making to qualify you for child benefit for the child (see below and p101); *and*
- the residence conditions are satisfied (see p1437).

Even if you are not making contributions to the cost of providing for the child, you can be treated as if you are if you give a written undertaking to make the contributions once benefit is paid to you. Any decision to pay you guardian's allowance on this basis may be revised if you do not actually make contributions once benefit is paid to you.[2]

If a child for whom you get guardian's allowance dies, see p226.

Treated as entitled to child benefit

To qualify for guardian's allowance you must either be entitled, or be treated as entitled, to child benefit for the child (see Chapter 7). If you are not actually entitled to child benefit for the child, you are treated as being entitled to it:[3]

- if you are residing with your spouse and s/he is entitled to child benefit for the child; *or*
- for a week in which you are living in Great Britain and would have been entitled to child benefit for the child had you (or your spouse or civil partner, if you reside with her/him) not been getting a family benefit from another country.

You can also be treated as entitled to child benefit for a specific week (normally this is the week before your entitlement to child benefit actually begins, or before your spouse's or civil partner's entitlement begins, if you reside with her/him). This allows your guardian's allowance to start from the date child benefit for the child commences.[4]

A 'child' or 'qualifying young person'

The rules on who counts as a 'child' or a 'qualifying young person' for guardian's allowance are the same as those for child benefit (see p94). In this chapter, the term 'child' is used to refer to both children and qualifying young people.

'Eligible' children

A child is an **'eligible child'** if:[5]

- both the child's parents (or, if the child has been adopted, her/his adoptive parents) have died; *or*
- one of the child's parents (or, if the child has been adopted, one of her/his adoptive parents) has died and:
  - at the time of the death you did not know the whereabouts of the other and you have not been able to trace her/him (see p222); *or*
  - the other is sentenced to a term of imprisonment or is detained in hospital by a court order (but see p222); *or*
- when the child was born her/his parents were unmarried, the mother of the child is dead and the paternity of the child has not been clearly established (but see below if the child has been adopted); *or*
- the child was adopted by only one person and that person has died; *or*
- the child's parents (or, if the child has been adopted, her/his adoptive parents) were divorced or their civil partnership had been dissolved, one parent has died and, at the time of her/his death, the other parent:
  - did not have custody of the child or hold a residence order in respect of the child; *and*
  - was not maintaining the child (and was not liable for maintenance for the child under a court order or under a child support maintenance assessment or calculation).

You cannot qualify for guardian's allowance if you are the surviving parent of a child (but see below if the child has been adopted, or if you are a step-parent).

Parents, adoptive parents and step-parents

A parent of a child may not claim guardian's allowance for that child unless one of the following exceptions apply:[6]

- if a child is adopted, because her/his adoptive parents count as parents, one of her/his biological parents can claim guardian's allowance if the qualifying conditions are met;
- adoptive parents may continue to receive guardian's allowance if they were entitled to it immediately before the adoption;

- a step-parent generally does not count as a parent for guardian's allowance and so may be entitled to guardian's allowance for a stepchild.[7]

Missing parents

If one of the child's parents is dead, you may qualify for guardian's allowance if, at the date of the death, you did not know the whereabouts of the other parent and since then you have failed to discover her/his whereabouts despite making reasonable efforts to do so – eg, asking known relatives and friends and checking old addresses.[8] It may not be necessary to make such efforts if you can show there is a danger that you or the child might experience harm or undue distress if you try to trace the missing parent – eg, if the surviving parent is a threat to the child's physical safety or emotional wellbeing.[9]

If contact has been made with a surviving parent since the death of the other parent (but before the decision on the claim), guardian's allowance cannot be paid, as the whereabouts of the surviving parent was known.[10] This applies even if the contact was only fleeting, such as at the funeral, and even if the surviving parent subsequently disappears.

If such contact has not been made, but you are able to communicate with the surviving parent in some way, this is likely to be sufficient to show that the whereabouts of that parent is known.[11] As 'whereabouts' is not the same as an address, merely showing that you do not know where the surviving parent actually lives may not be sufficient for you to qualify if you know the locality in which s/he is based. However, the locality must be sufficiently defined – if all that is known is that the surviving parent is in a large urban area, you could argue that her/his whereabouts is unknown.

Prison sentences

If one of the child's parents is dead and the other is in prison, you are only entitled to guardian's allowance if the surviving parent is:[12]

- serving a sentence of imprisonment or detention and has at least two years of that sentence remaining from the date of the death; *or*
- detained in hospital by order of a court under particular legislation.

A sentence of imprisonment or detention includes detention in a young offenders' institution and detention and training orders, but does not include any period of imprisonment for contempt of court. There are detailed rules for calculating whether the length of a sentence amounts to two years, so seek advice if you are affected by these rules. Guardian's allowance is reduced if the parent in prison contributes to the cost of providing for the child.[13]

2. **The rules about your age**

There is no upper or lower age limit for entitlement to guardian's allowance.

3. Claiming for others

Guardian's allowance is payable for each eligible child. No additional guardian's allowance is paid for any other dependants you have.

4. The amount of benefit

Guardian's allowance of £15.55 a week is payable for each eligible child.[14]

5. Special benefit rules

Special rules may apply to:

- people going abroad (see p1485) or coming from abroad (see p1437);
- eligible children who are in legal custody (see p693);
- eligible children whose parents were born outside the UK (see p1437).

6. Claims and backdating

The detailed rules about claiming and backdating are in Chapter 42. This section tells you about the specific rules that apply to guardian's allowance.

Making a claim

Claim guardian's allowance in writing on the approved form.[15] Send your claim to the Guardian's Allowance Unit at the Child Benefit Office (see Appendix 1). Keep a copy of your claim in case queries arise.

You must provide any information or evidence required (see p224). HM Customs and Revenue (HMRC) has the discretion to accept claims made in another way. However, as HMRC is unlikely to accept a claim that is not made in writing, it is always best to claim in writing, using the approved form whenever possible. You can amend or withdraw your claim before it is assessed by writing to the Guardian's Allowance Unit.

Forms

The approved form is Form BG1, which you can get from the Guardian's Allowance Unit (telephone: 0845 302 1464; textphone: 0845 302 1474) or from www.direct.gov.uk/en/moneytaxandbenefits.

Who should claim

You must normally claim guardian's allowance yourself. However, if you are unable to manage your own affairs, another person can claim guardian's allowance for you by becoming your 'appointee' (see p1016).

If you are a married woman and you live with your husband, it is you rather than your husband who will be entitled to guardian's allowance.[16]

Information to support your claim

When you claim guardian's allowance, you must:

- satisfy the 'national insurance (NI) number requirement' (see p1023);
- provide proof of your identity, if required (see p1024);
- supply information requested on the claim form. If you do not, your claim might be 'defective' – ie, not valid (but see p1020). If requested, you must provide additional information and evidence relevant to your claim (see p1022). There is a time limit for doing so.

HMRC usually needs to see documents such as an original copy of the child's birth or adoption certificate, and a death certificate if a parent has died.

The date of your claim

The date of your claim is important as it determines the date from which you will be paid guardian's allowance (see p225). The date of your claim is normally the date it is received at the Child Benefit Office (which administers guardian's allowance) or at another office that HMRC has stated, in writing, can receive guardian's allowance claims.[17]

If you submit a claim form that has not been completed correctly, or you make a written claim that is not on the approved form, you may be asked to provide further information or to complete the approved form. If this additional information or form is received by the Child Benefit Office (or by any other office that HMRC has stated in writing can receive it) within one month of it being sent back to you (or longer, if the decision maker thinks the delay is reasonable), your claim is treated as having been made on the date the initial claim was received.[18]

In some circumstances, you can claim before you qualify for guardian's allowance (see p225) or the date of your claim can be backdated (see p225).

If you claim the wrong benefit

The decision maker can treat a claim for child benefit for a child as a claim for guardian's allowance for the same child.[19] If your child benefit claim is accepted as a claim for guardian's allowance, your claim can be backdated for up to three months from the date you claimed child benefit, if you satisfy the qualifying conditions for guardian's allowance over that period (see p1025).

Claiming in advance

You can claim guardian's allowance up to three months in advance. If you qualify for it within the three months after your claim is made, the decision maker has the discretion to treat your date of claim as the date you start to qualify for guardian's allowance.[20]

Backdating claims

Your claim for guardian's allowance can be backdated for up to three months from the date that you make your claim if you satisfy the qualifying conditions over that period.[21] You do not have to show any reasons why your claim was late. The rules on backdating are covered on p1026. There are special rules if you were getting guardian's allowance and move between Great Britain and Northern Ireland or if you have been recognised as a refugee (see p1423).[22]

If you might have qualified for benefit for an even earlier period, but did not claim because you were given the wrong information or were misled by HM Revenue and Customs or the DWP, you could ask for compensation (see p1261) or complain to the Ombudsman through your MP (see p1259). If you claimed child benefit instead of guardian's allowance, see p224.

7. Getting paid

Payment of guardian's allowance is normally made by direct credit transfer into your bank (or similar) account (see p1039). If you are unable to open or manage an account, HM Revenue and Customs (HMRC) may agree to make payment by cheque (see p1040). If you are unable to act for yourself, guardian's allowance can be paid to someone else on your behalf, called your appointee (see p1016). If you also receive child benefit, guardian's allowance is paid at the same time and in the same way as your child benefit (see p110).[23]

When is guardian's allowance paid?	Normally on the same day as child benefit is paid (see p110).
How often is guardian's allowance paid?	Normally four-weekly, three weeks in arrears and one week in advance.

Guardian's allowance is a weekly benefit so cannot be paid for a period of less than a week. Payment starts from the first Monday after the date of your claim (see p224), unless your date of claim is a Monday, when it starts on that day.[24] For details of when your date of claim can be backdated, see above.

If your entitlement to guardian's allowance ends, payment continues up to, but not including, the following payday (which is normally either Monday or Tuesday), unless your entitlement ends on a payday, when your benefit is paid up to, but not including, that day.[25]

Note:
- Even if you have been sanctioned for benefit offences (see p1106), you must be paid your guardian's allowance.
- If you have forgotten your PIN or if a cheque is lost or stolen, see p1043.
- If payment of your guardian's allowance is delayed, you might be able to get an interim payment (see p1046). You may also be eligible for a crisis loan (see p564). If you wish to complain about how your claim has been dealt with, see Chapter 50. You might be able to claim compensation (see p1261).
- If payment of your guardian's allowance is suspended, see p1043.
- If you are overpaid guardian's allowance, you might have to repay it (see Chapter 43). If you have been accused of fraud, see Chapter 44.

Change of circumstances

You must report any change in your circumstances which might affect your benefit (see p1047). Report such changes promptly by writing to the Guardian's Allowance Unit. If you have reported a change verbally or to another office that HMRC has specified in writing can receive such notifications, in some circumstances this may be sufficient.[26] However, in this situation, it is advisable to note the time and date of your conversation, and the name of the person you informed. Confirm your conversation in writing to the Guardian's Allowance Unit promptly, keeping a copy of your letter in case problems arise. The rules about when your benefit will be adjusted following a change in your circumstances are the same as those for child benefit (see p111).

If a child dies

If a child for whom you are receiving child benefit dies, you can qualify for guardian's allowance for the eight-week period that child benefit remains in payment for that child (see p112), if you meet the normal qualifying conditions for guardian's allowance over that time (other than the condition that the child either is living with you, or you are contributing to her/his maintenance).[27]

8. Tax, tax credits and other benefits

Guardian's allowance is not taxable.[28]

Means-tested benefits and tax credits

Guardian's allowance is ignored when calculating your entitlement to means-tested benefits and tax credits.

Non-means-tested benefits

Although increases in non-means-tested benefits for children were abolished on 6 April 2003, some people continue to be entitled to them (see p745). You cannot get such an increase for a child for whom you get guardian's allowance because of the overlapping benefit rules (see p1043).[29] Otherwise, guardian's allowance can be paid in addition to any other non-means-tested benefit.

Entitlement to guardian's allowance does not qualify you for national insurance (NI) credits. However, you (or, in some circumstances your partner) may be able to qualify for NI credits if you receive child benefit for a child aged under 12 (see p781). **Note:** in some circumstances a family member who provides care for the child can get such NI credits (see p783).

Passports and other sources of help

For details of whether you qualify for free school lunches for your children, see p14. Children and young people under 19 may qualify for health benefits (see Chapter 13).

Notes

1. **Who can claim guardian's allowance**

1 ss77 and 122(5) SSCBA 1992
2 Reg 5 SSB(Dep) Regs
3 s122(4) SSCBA 1992; reg 4A SSB(Dep) Regs
4 Reg 4A(1)(b) and (3) SSB(Dep) Regs
5 s77(2) and (8)(a) SSCBA 1992; regs 4-7 GA(Gen) Regs
6 s77(10) and (11) SSCBA 1992; regs 4 and 6(2) GA(Gen) Regs; R(G) 4/83 (appendix)
7 CBTM 12010; but see also R(F)1/08
8 s77(2)(b) SSCBA 1992
9 CBTM 12090
10 CG/60/1992; R(G) 2/83; CSG/8/1992
11 CG/60/1992; CF/2735/2003
12 Reg 7 GA(Gen) Regs
13 s77(8)(c) SSCBA 1992; reg 8 GA(Gen) Regs

4. **The amount of benefit**

14 Sch 4 Part III SSCBA 1992

6. **Claims and backdating**

15 Reg 5(1) CB&GA(Admin) Regs
16 s77(9) SSCBA 1992
17 Reg 5(3) CB&GA(Admin) Regs
18 Reg 10 CB&GA(Admin) Regs
19 Reg 11 CB&GA(Admin) Regs
20 Reg 12 CB&GA(Admin) Regs
21 Reg 6(1) CB&GA(Admin) Regs
22 Reg 6(2) CB&GA(Admin) Regs

7. **Getting paid**

23 Regs 16(3), 17(2) and 18(4) CB&GA(Admin) Regs
24 Reg 13 CB&GA(Admin) Regs
25 Reg 14 CB&GA(Admin) Regs
26 Reg 23 CB&GA(Admin) Regs; for a change notified before 1 January 2010, see *WW v HMRC (CHB)* [2011] UKUT 11 (AAC)
27 s145A(4) SSCBA 1992

8. **Tax, tax credits and other benefits**

28 s677 IT(EP)A 2003
29 Reg 7(4) SS(OB) Regs

Chapter 13

Health benefits

This chapter covers:

Key facts

- Health benefits provide help with the costs of NHS prescriptions, dental treatment, sight tests and glasses, and wigs and fabric supports, as well as fares to receive NHS treatment.
- Health benefits are administered by the NHS Business Services Authority.
- Under the Healthy Start scheme, you can qualify for vouchers for specified types of food and for free vitamins.

Future changes: April 2013 and after

Major changes are taking place that affect the benefits and tax credits system (see Chapter 2). From October 2013, universal credit will replace income support, income-based jobseeker's allowance, income-related employment and support allowance and tax credits, which can be qualifying benefits for health benefits and Healthy Start food and vitamins. It is not yet known what the arrangements will be from October 2013. See CPAG's *Welfare Rights Bulletin* for updates.

1. Health benefits

Although the NHS generally provides free healthcare, there are fixed charges for some items and services such as prescriptions, dental treatment, sight tests and glasses, and wigs and fabric supports. You may also have fares to pay to get to hospital or another establishment for NHS treatment. However, you may qualify for full help with the charges and fares (ie, you may get the items or services free of charge) or you may get partial help.

You qualify for **full help** if you:

- are in an exempt group (see p229); *or*

- satisfy specific conditions; these depend on the item or service. See p230 for prescriptions, p231 for dental treatment and dentures, p232 for sight tests and glasses, p233 for wigs and fabric supports and p233 for fares to receive NHS treatment; *or*
- qualify under the low income scheme (see p234).

Even if you do not qualify for full help with charges, you may still qualify for **partial help** under the low income scheme (see p234). You may qualify for:[1]
- reduced-cost dental treatment (including check-ups) and appliances (including dentures); *and*
- reduced-cost sight tests. There is no set charge for sight tests, so it is worth shopping around if you are not entitled to a free test; *and*
- vouchers towards the cost of glasses and contact lenses; *and*
- in England, reduced-cost wigs and fabric supports (these are free in Wales and Scotland); *and*
- partial help with fares to receive NHS treatment.

In some cases, you must make a claim (see p237). If you pay for an item or service that you could have received free, or at a reduced cost, you can apply for a refund (see p239).

Note: in England, you cannot qualify for reduced-cost prescriptions under the low income scheme, only free prescriptions. If you cannot qualify for free prescriptions, see p231 for information about pre-payment certificates. In Wales and Scotland, prescriptions are always free.

Exempt groups

You qualify for full help with prescriptions, dental treatment and dentures, sight tests and glasses, wigs and fabric supports and fares to receive NHS treatment if you are in an exempt group. You are in an exempt group if:[2]
- you, or a member of your family (see p751 for who counts), are receiving income support (IS), income-based jobseeker's allowance (JSA), income-related employment and support allowance (ESA) or the guarantee credit of pension credit (PC). Members of your family are also exempt;
- you or your partner are receiving:
  - child tax credit (CTC) and are not eligible for working tax credit (WTC) – eg, you do not work sufficient hours to qualify; *or*
  - CTC and WTC; *or*
  - WTC including a disabled worker or severe disability element. Note that, in England, you only qualify for sight tests if your WTC includes a disabled worker element. It is not known if this was an error or the intention.

  In all cases, this only applies if your gross annual income, as calculated by HM Revenue and Customs for tax credit purposes at the time of your tax credit award, does not exceed £15,276.

Your partner and any child(ren) (including qualifying young people) for whom you are responsible are also exempt;
- you, or a member of your family, are an asylum seeker or a dependant of an asylum seeker who is receiving asylum support (see p1421). For these purposes, dependants for whom you are claiming asylum support count as members of your family;
- you are aged 16 or 17 and are receiving support from a local authority after being looked after (in Scotland, receiving support under s29(1) of the Children (Scotland) Act 1995 after leaving care). This does not appear to apply for sight tests in Wales.

Note: even if you are not in one of the exempt groups above, if you are:
- a war disablement pensioner, you may qualify for free prescriptions and wigs and fabric supports. You may also be able to claim money back for dental treatment, fares to hospital, sight tests, glasses or contact lenses. You must have a valid war pension exemption certificate, and you must need the items or treatment, or to travel, because of your war disability. See p237 for information about where to claim;
- a hospital inpatient, all medication and NHS treatment is provided free of charge (including glasses and contact lenses if prescribed through the Hospital Eye Service). If you are an outpatient or are at a walk-in centre, medication taken and treatment given while you are in the hospital or walk-in centre is also provided without charge (but you may be charged for dentures and bridges).

Note: you may also qualify for full help with particular charges if you satisfy conditions – eg, because of your age, health or condition. See the sections on each type of charge below. You may also qualify for full or partial help with charges under the low income scheme (see p234).

Prescriptions

Prescriptions are free in Scotland and Wales. You qualify for free prescriptions in England (and you can get an English prescription filled free in Scotland and Wales) if:[3]
- you are in one of the exempt groups listed on p229; *or*
- you qualify under the low income scheme (see p234); *or*
- you are aged 60 or over; *or*
- you are aged under 16, or you are under 19 and in full-time education; *or*
- you are pregnant or have given birth in the last 12 months; *or*
- you are a permanent resident in a care home and your place is being partly or wholly funded by a local authority; *or*
- you have:

- a continuing physical disability, which prevents you leaving your home except with the help of another person;
- epilepsy requiring continuous anti-convulsive therapy;
- a permanent fistula, including a caecostomy, ileostomy, laryngostomy or colostomy, needing continuous surgical dressing or an appliance;
- diabetes mellitus (except where treatment is by diet alone);
- diabetes insipidus and other forms of hypopituitarism;
- myxoedema;
- hypoparathyroidism;
- forms of hypoadrenalism (including Addison's disease), for which specific substitution therapy is essential; *or*

- myasthenia gravis; *or*
- you are prescribed or given specific medicines in respect of a pandemic disease.

Prescriptions are also free in England if you are undergoing treatment for cancer, the effects of cancer or the effects of cancer treatment. They are also free if you are in prison or a young offenders' institution (or were given the prescription while you were) and if you are detained under the Immigration Act 1971 or s62 of the Nationality, Immigration and Asylum Act 2002.

Pre-payment certificates

In England, if you are not exempt from charges and you need more than three prescription items in three months or 13 items in a year, you can save money by buying a pre-payment certificate.

You apply for a certificate by post or at a registered chemist on Form FP95, which you can get from chemists, some doctors' surgeries and relevant health bodies. You can also apply using a credit or debit card on 0845 850 0030 or at www.nhsbsa.nhs.uk/healthcosts/2131.aspx. You can also pay in monthly instalments by direct debit.

A refund can be claimed in certain circumstances – eg, if you buy a pre-payment certificate and then qualify for free prescriptions.

Dental treatment and dentures

NHS dental check-ups are free in Scotland. In England, Wales and Scotland you qualify for free NHS dental treatment (including check-ups) and appliances (including dentures) if, when your treatment is arranged or charges are made:[4]

- you are in one of the exempt groups listed on p229; *or*
- you qualify under the low income scheme (see p234); *or*
- you are under 18, or you are under 19 and in full-time education; *or*
- in Wales, for free examinations only, you are under 25 or are 60 or over; *or*
- you are pregnant or have given birth within the last 12 months; *or*
- you are a permanent resident in a care home and your place is being partly or wholly funded by a local authority; *or*

- in England and Wales, you are in prison or a young offenders' institution; *or*
- you are a patient of the Community Dental Service (available for people who have difficulty getting treatment because of a disability or for other reasons – contact your health authority for details) or an NHS Hospital Dental Service. Note, however, that there may be a charge for dentures and bridges.

Sight tests and glasses

Free sight tests

NHS sight tests are free in Scotland. In England and Wales you qualify for a free NHS sight test if:[5]

- you are in one of the exempt groups listed on p229; *or*
- you qualify under the low income scheme (see p234); *or*
- you are aged 60 or over; *or*
- you are under 16, or you are under 19 and in full-time education; *or*
- you are registered blind or partially sighted; *or*
- you have been prescribed complex or powerful lenses; *or*
- you have been diagnosed as having diabetes or glaucoma or are at risk of getting glaucoma; *or*
- you are aged 40 or over and are the parent, brother, sister or child of someone with glaucoma; *or*
- you are a patient of the Hospital Eye Service; *or*
- in England, you are on leave from prison or a young offenders' institution.

Vouchers for glasses and contact lenses

If you are given a prescription for glasses following an eye test, you may be entitled to a voucher that you can use to buy glasses or contact lenses if you need these for the first time or because your previous ones have worn out through fair wear and tear, or your new prescription differs from your old one. You qualify if:[6]

- you are in one of the exempt groups listed on p229; *or*
- you qualify under the low income scheme (see p234); *or*
- you are under 16, or under 19 and in full-time education; *or*
- you are a Hospital Eye Service patient needing frequent changes of glasses or contact lenses; *or*
- in England, you are on leave from prison or a young offenders' institution; *or*
- you have been prescribed complex or powerful lenses.

You may be entitled to a voucher if your glasses or lenses need to be replaced or repaired if, because of illness (illness or disability in Scotland), you have lost or damaged them and the cost of repair or replacement is not covered by insurance or warranty. This only applies if:[7]

- you are under 16, or you are under 19 and in full-time education; *or*

- you, or a member of your family, are exempt from charges because you are receiving IS, income-based JSA, income-related ESA, the guarantee credit of PC or tax credits; *or*
- you qualify under the low income scheme (see p234); *or*
- you have been prescribed complex or powerful lenses.

You can redeem the voucher at any supplier when you buy your glasses or contact lenses (or have glasses repaired). Vouchers are, however, only valid for two years.[8] Vouchers might not cover the full cost of the glasses or lenses you choose to buy. Prices vary; you may need to shop around if you do not want to pay the extra cost.

Wigs and fabric supports

Wigs and fabric supports are free in Scotland and Wales. You qualify for free wigs and fabric supports in England if:[9]

- you are in one of the exempt groups listed on p229; *or*
- you qualify under the low income scheme (see p234); *or*
- you are a hospital in-patient; *or*
- you are aged under 16, or you are under 19 and in full-time education; *or*
- you are a permanent resident in a care home and your place is being partly or wholly funded by a local authority; *or*
- you are in prison or a young offenders' institution or are detained under the Immigration Act 1971 or s62 of the Nationality, Immigration and Asylum Act 2002.

Fares to receive NHS treatment

You qualify for full help with your fares to attend a hospital or any other establishment for NHS treatment or services if:[10]

- you are in one of the exempt groups listed on p229; *or*
- you qualify under the low income scheme (see p234); *or*
- you are a permanent resident in a care home and your place is being partly or wholly funded by a local authority; *or*
- you live in the Isles of Scilly or the Scottish Islands or Highlands and have to travel more than a specified distance. Special rules (including maximum costs) apply.[11]

The travel expenses of a companion can also be covered – eg, if your child is attending a hospital and you need to accompany her/him, or if you need to be accompanied for medical reasons. You get help with the cost of travelling by the cheapest means of transport that is reasonable and, in Scotland, if necessary, the cost of overnight accommodation. This usually means standard-class public transport. If you have to travel by car or taxi, you should be paid a mileage allowance, road and toll charges, or taxi fares.

Claim at the place where you receive NHS treatment. You may be able to request payment in advance of travelling if this is necessary or, alternatively, you could apply for a social fund crisis loan from the DWP (see p564).

Travel expenses can be covered if you are travelling abroad to receive NHS treatment if the means and cost of travel, as well as any requirements for a companion, have been agreed in advance with the health service body that has arranged the treatment. In England and Wales, you are entitled to payment for the cost of travel to and from the airport, ferry port or international train station if you are in one of the above groups. You are also entitled to payment or repayment of onward travelling expenses to the treatment centre, whether or not you fall within one of the above groups. In Scotland, the rules do not specify what can be covered.

If you are receiving IS, income-based JSA, income-related ESA or the guarantee or savings credit of PC and are visiting a close relative or partner who is in hospital, you may qualify for a social fund community care grant to help with your fares (see p555).

The low income scheme

You (and members of your family) may be entitled to full or partial help with NHS charges under the low income scheme, even if you do not qualify on other grounds. You must make a claim (see p237). The low income scheme is administered by the NHS Business Services Authority (see Appendix 1).

You (and members of your family) qualify for full help under the low income scheme if:

- you have capital of less than £16,000 (or if you live permanently in a care home, £23,250 in England and Scotland or £22,500 in Wales).[12] Your capital is calculated as for IS (see Chapter 41); *and*
- your income (see p236) does not exceed your 'requirements' (see p235) by more than 50 per cent of the current cost of an English prescription (at the time of writing this was 50 per cent of £7.65 = £3.82).[13] If your income exceeds your requirements by more than this amount, see below to find out if you qualify for partial help with charges.

Partial help with items and services

If you do not qualify for full help with NHS charges, you (and members of your family) may qualify for partial help with these under the low income scheme. You are expected to pay up to a set amount towards the charges. The set amount is:[14]

- for dental charges and charges for wigs and fabric supports, three times the amount by which your income exceeds your requirements (your 'excess income');
- for glasses or lenses, twice the amount of your 'excess income';
- for a sight test or fares to receive NHS treatment, the amount of your 'excess income'.

You cannot get partial help with the cost of prescriptions under the low income scheme (but see p231 for information about pre-payment certificates).

Example

Martin's income exceeds his requirements by £6 so he cannot qualify for full help under the low income scheme. However, he may get partial help. He has to pay the first £18 of dental charges and charges for wigs and fabric supports, the first £6 of the cost of a sight test, the first £12 towards the cost of glasses and lenses and the first £6 of his fares to receive NHS treatment. He has to pay the full cost of prescriptions.

Calculating your requirements

Your 'requirements' are similar to the IS 'applicable amount' (see Chapter 37). The most significant elements and differences are set out below. **Note:** there are no reductions in the applicable amounts of people who are subject to immigration control or not habitually resident in the UK, or for students, people engaged in a trade dispute or people without accommodation.

Your '**requirements**' are made up of the following elements.[15]

- **Personal allowance(s):**

Single person aged under 25	£56.25
Single person aged under 25, entitled to ESA work-related activity or support component, or incapable of work for at least 28 weeks starting on or after 27 October 2008	£71.00
Single person aged 25–59 or lone parent aged under 60	£71.00
Single person or lone parent aged 60 or over	£142.70
Couples, both partners aged under 60	£111.45
Couples, one or both partners aged 60 or over	£217.90

- **Premiums:** the disability, enhanced disability, severe disability and carer premiums are added to your requirements if you would qualify for them under the IS rules (see p820).

  A disability premium can also be included if you or your partner have been incapable of work for 28 weeks. It can also be included if you (or your partner) have been awarded ESA which includes a work-related activity or support component, or if you (or s/he) have been getting ESA for at least 28 weeks. You (and your partner) must be under 60. If you are a single claimant or a lone parent, the amount of the disability premium is increased to £34.05 if you qualify for an ESA support component or if you are getting disability living allowance (DLA) middle or highest rate care component and have been getting ESA, or have been incapable of work, for at least 28 weeks starting on or after 27 October 2008.

An enhanced disability premium can be included if you (or your partner) are getting DLA highest rate care component, or ESA which includes a support component. You (and your partner) must be under 60.

- **Weekly council tax *less* any council tax benefit.**
- **Weekly rent *less* any housing benefit** (HB) and any non-dependant deductions, broadly as they apply under the rules on IS housing costs (see p869). Deductions for fuel and ineligible service charges are made in accordance with HB rules.
- **Weekly mortgage interest and capital payments on loans** secured on a home, to buy a home, or to adapt a home for the special needs of a disabled person, and payments on an endowment policy relating to the purchase of a home. Some other housing costs can be included. Deductions are made for non-dependants.

Note: if you live permanently in a care home, your 'requirements' are your weekly accommodation charge, including meals and services, and a personal expenses allowance. Remember that if your place is being funded by a local authority (fully or in part), you are exempt from some charges.

Calculating your income

Your income is calculated as for IS (see Chapter 40), with modifications. These include the following.[16]

- Your income is normally taken into account in the week in which it is paid. If you are affected by a trade dispute, your normal earnings are taken into account.
- You are entitled to an earnings disregard of £20 if you would qualify for a disability premium (see p824), or you or your partner are aged 60 or over.
- If you (or your partner) are doing permitted work while claiming ESA (see p216), the amount of earnings that can be disregarded is the same as for income-related ESA (see p912). If you and your partner are both doing permitted work, the disregard is applied to your joint income.
- The full amount of your (or your partner's) contributory ESA is taken into account, even if it is paid at a reduced rate because you failed to take part in a work-focused interview.
- Regular liable relative payments (see p804) count as weekly income. Irregular payments are averaged over the 13 weeks prior to your claim. Lump-sum payments are treated as capital.
- Student loans and grants are divided by 52, unless you are in your final year or are doing a one-year course, in which case the loan is divided by the number of weeks you are studying. The £10 disregard from student loans only applies if you are eligible for a premium, you receive an allowance because of deafness, or you are not a student but your partner is. In addition, in England and Wales, sums in excess of a specified amount of a maintenance grant and certain loans

paid to Scottish students studying in England or Wales are disregarded. Also, where a voluntary payment is taken into account, up to £20 of it is disregarded.
- Insurance policy payments for housing costs not met by IS count as income, but payments for unsecured loans for repairs and improvements (including premiums) are ignored.
- If you live permanently in residential or nursing care:
  – in Wales, no tariff income is taken into account;
  – in England and Scotland, the lower threshold for tariff income is £14,250.
  Remember that if your place is being funded by a local authority (fully or in part), you are exempt from some charges.
- The savings credit of PC is ignored as income.

Claims

If you are exempt from charges on the grounds of your **age**, **receipt of a qualifying benefit** or because you are **a full-time student under 19**, complete the back of the prescription form (if required), or complete the appropriate form at your dentist, optician or hospital.

If you are an **asylum seeker** receiving asylum support, a certificate is issued by the UK Border Agency. If you have queries, telephone 0845 602 1739.

In some cases, to qualify for full help with charges, you must have an exemption certificate. If you are:
- exempt because you **receive tax credits**, you should be sent an exemption certificate automatically. This could be up to eight weeks after you are awarded tax credits. If you have not yet been sent your exemption certificate, you can sign the prescription form, or other appropriate form, to say you do not have to pay and use your tax credits award notice as proof of this;
- exempt from charges because you are **pregnant** or have **given birth** in the last 12 months, obtain an exemption certificate by completing a form, which you can get from your doctor, midwife or health visitor;
- entitled to free prescriptions because **you have one of the conditions** listed on p230 or because you are undergoing treatment for cancer, the effects of cancer or the effects of cancer treatment, apply for an exemption certificate on Form FP92A, which you can get from your doctor, hospital or pharmacist.

In other cases, to qualify for help with charges, you must make a claim. If you:
- want to get full or partial help under the **low income scheme**, see below. This includes if you are an asylum seeker, but you are not receiving asylum support. If you *are* receiving asylum support, see above;
- are exempt because you live in a **care home** or you are aged **16 or 17 and were formerly looked after by a local authority**, you must claim under the low income scheme (see p238);
- are a **war disablement pensioner**, contact the Service Personnel and Veterans Agency, Norcross, Thornton Cleveleys, Lancashire FY5 3WP.

Claiming under the low income scheme

To apply for full or partial help with charges under the low income scheme, you must complete Form HC1. You can get this from Jobcentre Plus offices or NHS hospitals, some chemists, GP practices, dentists, opticians or advice centres. You can also request a form online at www.nhsbsa.nhs.uk (for England) or www.scotland.gov.uk/topics/health (for Scotland). You can also get a form by telephoning 0131 275 6386 (in Scotland) or 0845 603 1108 (in Wales). Another person can apply on your behalf if you are unable to act for yourself.

Send the completed form to the NHS Business Services Authority (see Appendix 1). **Note:** if you live in a care home or you are aged 16 or 17 and were formerly looked after by a local authority, you can use a shorter Form HC1(SC).

If you qualify for:

- full help, you are sent an HC2 certificate;
- partial help, you are sent an HC3 certificate which tells you the contribution you must make towards the charges.

When a certificate expires

Certificates are normally valid for 12 months. However, they are normally valid for:[17]

- five years if you are a single person aged 65 or over, or one of a couple, one aged 60 or over and the other aged 65 or over. This only applies if you do not receive earnings, or payments from an occupational pension, a personal pension or an annuity, and you do not have a dependent child or young person as a member of your household; *or*
- six months from the date of claim if you are an asylum seeker receiving asylum support; *or*
- until the end of your course or the start of the next academic year if you are a full-time student.

Make a repeat claim on Form HC1 shortly before the expiry date. If you have a five-year certificate, you must notify the issuing authority of any changes in the composition of your family or household. In other cases, changes of circumstances (eg, starting work and increases in income) do not affect the validity of a certificate. However, if the change could result in increased help (eg, your income has *decreased*), you can reapply for a fresh assessment before the certificate expires.

Proof of entitlement

You are normally asked for proof that you are entitled to full or partial help with charges, although you should not be denied an item or service if you are unable to provide the required evidence. If you have an HC2 or HC3 certificate, show this to the dentist, optician, hospital or pharmacist (you may also have to enter details on the appropriate form). In other cases, you may need to show evidence of your date of birth, student status or exemption certificate.

Overpayments and fraud

If you receive help to which you were not entitled, you can be issued with a penalty notice requiring you to pay the charge you should have paid plus a penalty, unless you can show that you did not act 'wrongfully' or with 'any lack of care'. The penalty can be increased if you do not pay it within 28 days, and court proceedings can be taken to recover the debt. Anyone wrongly claiming help with charges on your behalf can themselves be liable to pay a penalty charge. You can also be prosecuted if you obtain help wrongly, on the basis of a false statement or representation.[18]

Delays and complaints

For general queries, telephone 0845 850 1166 (textphone: 18001 0845 850 1166). You can ask for a formal review of the decision on your claim by writing to the Service Improvement Team, Help with Health Costs, Sandyford House, Newcastle Upon Tyne NE2 1BF. You can also request a review online at www.nhsbsa.nhs.uk.

If there are delays in obtaining a certificate, you can complain to the customer services manager. If necessary, you could pay for the treatment or items you need then try and obtain a refund (see below).

Refunds

If you pay for an item or service that you could have got free, or at reduced cost, you can apply for a refund. Do this within three months of paying the charge, although the time limit can, in some cases, be extended if you can show good cause for applying late – eg, you were ill.[19]

Apply for a refund of a prescription charge on Form FP57, which you must obtain when you pay as one cannot be supplied later. For other items and services, apply for a refund on Form HC5. You can get the forms by telephoning 0845 850 1166, or from a Jobcentre Plus office or NHS hospital. You must submit a receipt or other documents to show that you have paid the charge. If you need an HC2 or HC3 certificate and have not applied for one, send a Form HC1 with your application for a refund.

2. Healthy Start food and vitamins

If you qualify for Healthy Start food and vitamins, you get free vitamins as well as fixed-value vouchers that can be used to buy specified types of food.

Healthy Start food

If you qualify for Healthy Start food, you get fixed-value vouchers (worth £3.10 each) that can be exchanged for 'Healthy Start food' at registered food outlets.[20] If there is no registered food outlet within a reasonable distance of your home, you are paid an amount equal to the value of the vouchers to which you are entitled.[21]

Healthy Start food

'Healthy Start food' means liquid cow's milk and cow's milk-based infant formula, fresh or frozen fruit and vegetables including loose, pre-packed, whole, sliced, chopped or mixed fruit or vegetables (but not fruit or vegetables to which fat, salt, sugar, flavouring or any other ingredients have been added).[22]

Who can claim Healthy Start food

You qualify for Healthy Start food vouchers:[23]

- if you are **pregnant** and have been for more than 10 weeks, and you are:
  - 18 or over and are entitled to (or a member of the family (see p751) of someone who is entitled to) a 'qualifying benefit' (see p241);
  - under 18, whether or not you are entitled to a 'qualifying benefit' (but not if you are excluded from these because you are a 'person subject to immigration control' – see p1410); *or*
- if you are **a mother** who has 'parental responsibility' for a child and:
  - you are 18 or over and either your child is under one or it is less than a year since her/his expected date of birth. This means you can continue to qualify for vouchers for a period after your child is one – ie, if s/he was born prematurely. You must be entitled to (or a member of the family (see p751) of someone who is entitled to) a 'qualifying benefit' (see p241) other than income-related employment and support allowance (ESA); *or*
  - it is less than four months since your baby's expected date of birth and you have not yet notified Healthy Start that s/he was born. You must have been getting a 'qualifying benefit' (see p241) other than income-related ESA before your baby was born. This allows your entitlement to vouchers to continue until you notify the birth. Once you do, you can then qualify under the rule above (if you are 18 or over). Note that, so long as you provided the notification within the four-month period, you can also get extra vouchers for your child from her/his date of birth (see p241).

  Note: although income-related ESA is not a qualifying benefit, see below if you are getting child tax credit (CTC).

  If you qualify for vouchers for more than one child under this rule (eg, you have twins), you get a voucher for each. If you do not have parental responsibility but would otherwise qualify for vouchers, your child qualifies instead of you;
- for **a child under four** who is a member of your family. You or a member of the family must be entitled to a 'qualifying benefit' (see p241) other than

income-related ESA. **Note:** although income-related ESA is not a qualifying benefit, see below if you are getting CTC.

In practice, this means that each week you get one voucher for each of your children aged between one and four, two vouchers for each of your children under one (or within one year of their expected date of birth), plus one voucher if you are pregnant.

Example

Vera is 17 weeks pregnant. She has three children: twin girls aged two and a boy aged seven. She is getting IS. She qualifies for a voucher because she is more than 10 weeks pregnant. Her twins each qualify for a voucher as they are under four. Her son does not qualify for a voucher. Vera gets three vouchers each week totaling £9.30. When the baby is born, Vera will still be entitled to a voucher because she will be a mother of a child under one. The baby will also be entitled to a voucher. She will then get four vouchers each week, totalling £12.40.

Note:

- The **'qualifying benefits'** are income support, income-based jobseeker's allowance, income-related ESA and CTC, provided in the latter case that gross income for CTC purposes does not exceed £16,190 and there is no entitlement to working tax credit (WTC). You are treated as not entitled to WTC during the four-week WTC run-on (see p1304).
- **'Parental responsibility'** means parental responsibility as defined in s3(1) of the Children Act 1989 (in England or Wales) or s1(1) of the Children (Scotland) Act 1995 (in Scotland).[24]
- If you are an asylum seeker receiving asylum support (see p1421), you receive extra asylum support to help you buy healthy food if you are pregnant or have a child under three.

Claims

You must make an initial claim for Healthy Start food vouchers in writing and must provide specified information and evidence.[25] Complete the form in the Healthy Start leaflet (HS01), available from midwives, health visitors, maternity clinics and some doctors' surgeries or from 0845 607 6823. Information about Healthy Start and a claim form are also available at www.healthystart.nhs.uk. You can start to fill in the form online. The form must be countersigned by a health professional (eg, a midwife or health visitor) who certifies when your baby is due (if you are pregnant) and that you have been given appropriate advice about healthy eating and breastfeeding. If you are under 16, your claim must also be signed by your parent or carer. Send the completed form to: Healthy Start Issuing Unit, FREEPOST RRTR-SYAE-JKCR, PO Box 1067, Warrington WA55 1EG.

If you are getting Healthy Start food vouchers while you are pregnant and then inform Healthy Start of your baby's birth by telephone while s/he is under four months old, you can get extra vouchers for her/him from her/his date of birth.[26] You need to make a claim for CTC for her/him (or add her/him to your existing claim) to ensure that you continue to get the vouchers.

If you do not get vouchers to which you think you are entitled, or have any other problems with these, contact the Healthy Start helpline on 0845 607 6823.

Healthy Start vitamins

If you qualify for Healthy Start food vouchers (see p239), you also qualify for Healthy Start vitamins.[27] Mothers and pregnant women are entitled to 56 vitamin tablets and children under four to 10 millilitres of vitamin drops every eight weeks. Your primary care trust, health board or health trust (eg, your NHS maternity or child health clinic or health centre) is responsible for giving you your free vitamins. Ask your local health professional what the local arrangements are.

You do not have to make a separate claim for Healthy Start vitamins. However, you must show evidence to the vitamin supplier that you are entitled (ie, the letter to which your most recent Healthy Start vouchers were attached) and, if requested, proof of your child's age.[28]

3. Free milk for children in daycare

Children under five are entitled to 189–200 millilitres of free milk on each day they are looked after for two hours or more:[29]

- by a registered childminder or daycare provider; *or*
- in a school, playcentre or workplace nursery which is exempt from registration; *or*
- in local authority daycare.

Children under one are allowed fresh or dried milk. This is provided by the welfare food scheme.

Notes

1. **Health benefits**

1 **E** Reg 6 NHS(TERC) Regs; regs 3 and 8 NHS(OCP) Regs
S Reg 5 NHS(TERC)(S) Regs; regs 3 and 8 NHS(OCP)(S) Regs
W Reg 6 NHS(TERC)(W) Regs; regs 3 and 8 NHS(OCP) Regs

2 **E** Regs 3-5 NHS(TERC) Regs; reg 3 POS Regs; reg 8 NHS(OCP) Regs
S Regs 3 and 4 NHS(TERC)(S) Regs; regs 3 and 8 NHS(OCP)(S) Regs
W Regs 3-5 NHS(TERC)(W) Regs; reg 13 NHS(GOS) Regs; regs 3 and 8 NHS(OCP) Regs

3 **E** Regs 7, 7A and 7B NHS(CDA) Regs; regs 4 and 5 NHS(TERC) Regs
S Regs 3 and 4 NHS(FP&CDA)(S) Regs
W Regs 3, 4 and 8 NHS(FP&CDA)(W) Regs; regs 4 and 5 NHS(TERC)(W) Regs

4 **E** s177 NHSA 2006; regs 3 and 7 and Sch 5 NHS(DC) Regs; regs 4 and 5 NHS(TERC) Regs
S Sch 11 NHS(S)A 1978; reg 5 and Sch 2 NHS(DC)(S) Regs; regs 3 and 4 NHS(TERC)(S) Regs
W s126 NHS(W)A 2006; regs 3 and 7 and Sch 5 NHS(DC)(W) Regs; regs 4 and 5 NHS(TERC)(W) Regs

5 **E** Reg 3 POS Regs; regs 3 and 8 NHS(OCP) Regs
W Reg 13 NHS(GOS) Regs; regs 3 and 8 NHS(OCP) Regs

6 **E** Regs 8 and 9 NHS(OCP) Regs
S Regs 8 and 9 NHS(OCP)(S) Regs
W Regs 8 and 9 NHS(OCP) Regs

7 **E** Regs 8 and 15 NHS(OCP) Regs
S Regs 8 and 15 NHS(OCP)(S) Regs
W Regs 8 and 15 NHS(OCP) Regs

8 **E** Reg 12(1) NHS(OCP) Regs
S Reg 12(1) NHS(OCP)(S) Regs

9 **E** Regs 5(3), 7, 7A and 7B NHS(CDA) Regs; regs 4 and 5 NHS(TERC) Regs
S Regs 3 and 4 NHS(FP&CDA)(S) Regs
W Regs 3, 4 and 8 NHS(FP&CDA)(W) Regs

10 **E** s183(a) NHSA 2006; regs 3 and 5 NHS(TERC) Regs
S s75A(1)(b) NHS(S)A 1978; regs 3 and 4 NHS(TERC)(S) Regs
W s131(a) NHS(W)A 2006; regs 3 and 5 NHS(TERC)(W) Regs

11 **E** Reg 9 NHS(TERC) Regs
S Reg 7 NHS(TERC)(S) Regs

12 **E** Sch 1 Table A NHS(TERC) Regs
S Sch Part 1 NHS(TERC)(S) Regs
W Sch 1 Table A NHS(TERC)(W) Regs

13 **E** Reg 5(2)(e) and (f) NHS(TERC) Regs; reg 3(2)(c) and (d) POS Regs; regs 3(2) and 8(3)(e) and (f) NHS(OCP) Regs
S Reg 4(2)(c) and (d) NHS(TERC)(S) Regs; regs 3(2) and 8(3)(e) and (f) NHS(OCP)(S) Regs
W Reg 5(2)(e) NHS(TERC)(W) Regs; reg 13(2)(e) and (f) NHS(GOS) Regs; regs 3(2) and 8(3)(e) and (f) NHS(OCP) Regs

14 **E** Reg 6 NHS(TERC) Regs; regs 7, 14 and 19 NHS(OCP) Regs
S Reg 5 NHS(TERC)(S) Regs; regs 14 and 19 NHS(OCP)(S) Regs
W Reg 6 NHS(TERC)(W) Regs; regs 7, 14 and 19 NHS(OCP) Regs

15 **E** Reg 17 and Sch 1 Table B NHS(TERC) Regs
S Reg 8 and Sch Part 2 NHS(TERC)(S) Regs
W Reg 16 and Sch 1 Table B NHS(TERC)(W) Reg

16 **E** Reg 16 and Sch 1 Table A NHS(TERC) Regs
S Reg 8 and Sch Part 1 NHS(TERC)(S) Regs
W Reg 15 and Sch 1 Table A NHS(TERC)(W) Regs

17 **E** Reg 8 NHS(TERC) Regs
S Reg 10 NHS(TERC)(S) Regs
W Reg 8 NHS(TERC)(W) Regs

18 **E** ss193 and 194 NHSA 2006
S ss99ZA and 99ZB NHS(S)A 1978
W ss141 and 142 NHS(W)A 2006;

19 **E** Reg 11 (NHS)(TERC) Regs; reg 10 (NHS)(CDA) Regs; regs 6 and 20 NHS(OCP) Regs
S Reg 11 NHS(TERC)(S) Regs; regs 10 and 11 (NHS)(CDA)(S) Regs; reg 20 NHS(OCP)(S) Regs
W Reg 10 NHS(TERC)(W) Regs; regs 6 and 20 NHS(OCP) Regs

2. **Healthy Start food and vitamins**

20 Reg 8 HSS&WF(A) Regs
21 Reg 5(2) HSS&WF(A) Regs
22 Regs 2(1) and 5(1) and Sch 3 HSS&WF(A) Regs; HSS(DHSF)(W) Regs
23 Reg 3 HSS&WF(A) Regs
24 Reg 2(1) HSS&WF(A) Regs
25 Reg 4 and Sch 2 HSS&WF(A) Regs
26 Reg 4(2) HSS&WF(A) Regs
27 Reg 3 HSS&WF(A) Regs
28 Reg 8A HSS&WF(A) Regs

3. **Free milk for children in daycare**

29 Reg 18 WF Regs

Chapter 14

Housing benefit and discretionary housing payments

This chapter covers:

Key facts

- Housing benefit (HB) is paid to people with a low income who pay rent.
- The amount of HB you get depends on how much rent you pay. If you are a private tenant and, in exceptional cases, if you are a housing association tenant, the amount of your rent covered by HB might be restricted.
- HB is a means-tested benefit.
- You do not have to have paid national insurance contributions to qualify.
- You can qualify for HB whether you are in or out of work.
- If you need extra financial assistance to meet housing costs (including council tax), you can claim discretionary housing payments to top up your HB.
- HB is administered and paid by local authorities, although it is a national scheme and the rules are mainly determined by DWP regulations.
- If you disagree with an HB decision, you can apply for a revision or a supersession, or appeal against it (see Chapters 45 and 46).

Future changes: April 2013 and after

Major changes are taking place that affect the benefits and tax credits system (see Chapter 2).

- From April 2013, the HB of working-age people in social sector housing (eg, local authority or housing association tenants) will be restricted if they live in a property that is too large for them. The government says HB will be reduced by around 14 per cent of the eligible rent for one extra bedroom and 25 per cent for two or more extra bedrooms.
- From April 2013, total benefit payments to many working-age households will be 'capped' (see p25). There will be limited exceptions, including households in which someone is entitled to working tax credit or receives disability living allowance. HB will be included in the capped amount. At least until universal credit (UC) is introduced, any reduction will be taken from your HB, but you will be left with HB of at least 50 pence.
- From October 2013, when UC is introduced, an amount for help with rent will be included in UC and in pension credit (PC). No new claims for HB will be allowed, probably from April 2014. Those claiming HB will be transferred to UC (or to PC) between April 2014 and October 2017.

See CPAG's *Welfare Rights Bulletin* for updates.

1. Who can claim housing benefit

You qualify for housing benefit (HB) if:[1]

- your income is low enough (see Chapter 40);
- unless you or your partner are getting the guarantee credit of pension credit (PC), your savings and other capital are worth £16,000 or less (see Chapter 41). There is no capital limit if you or your partner are getting the guarantee credit of PC;[2]
- the payments you make can be met by HB (see p247);
- you or your partner count as liable to pay rent (see p248);
- the payments you make are for the home in which you normally live (see p252) or you are only temporarily absent from it;
- you satisfy the 'right to reside test' and the 'habitual residence test' (see Chapter 62); *and*
- you are not a 'person subject to immigration control' (see p1410). There are exceptions to this rule.

If you are at least the qualifying age for pension credit

The HB rules for people who are at least the qualifying age for PC (see p509) who are not (and whose partners are not) on income support (IS), income-based jobseeker's allowance (JSA) or income-related employment and support allowance (ESA) are different (and more generous) than those for other HB claimants. When you reach the qualifying age for PC, check to see if you qualify for HB even if you did not do so before that age. The different rules for income, capital and applicable amounts are covered in other chapters.

Payments that can be met by housing benefit

HB can meet rent that you pay to your landlord. It can also meet other types of payment, such as payments as a licensee, and payments for bed and breakfast and hostel accommodation. In this *Handbook*, we refer to any payments you make as 'rent'. Some types of payment cannot be met by HB (see p248).

HB can meet:[3]

- rent paid in respect of a tenancy. This can include rent or ground rent payable in respect of a lease of 21 years or less.[4] If your lease is for longer than 21 years, the rent or ground rent may be met by IS, income-based JSA, income-related ESA or PC – see p862;
- payments in respect of a licence or other permission to occupy premises;
- 'mesne profits' (in Scotland, 'violent profits'), including payments made if you remain in occupation when a tenancy has been ended;
- other payments for the use and occupation of premises (including boat licence and mooring permit fees if you live in a houseboat[5]);
- payments for eligible service charges (see p263);
- rent, including mooring charges, for a houseboat;
- site rent for a caravan or mobile home (but not a tent, although that might be met through IS, income-based JSA, income-related ESA or PC – see p862);
- rent paid on a garage or land (unless used for business purposes). Either you must be making a reasonable effort to end your liability for it, or you must have been unable to rent your home without it;[6]
- contributions made by a resident of a charity's almshouse;
- payments made under a rental purchase agreement under which the purchase price is paid in more than one instalment and you do not finally own your home until all, or an agreed part of, the purchase price has been paid;
- in Scotland, payments in respect of croft land.

The payment must be in return for your occupation of the home. This usually means that the payments must be made to the person who has the right to let you occupy it, or someone acting on her/his behalf. Payments to someone else might qualify for HB. This depends on, for example, whether you have a valid tenancy agreement with that person.[7]

Payments that cannot be met by housing benefit

HB cannot meet payments:[8]

- by an owner or under a long tenancy (ie, you own your accommodation or have a lease of more than 21 years), unless you have a shared ownership tenancy (ie, you are buying part of your house or flat and renting the rest), in which case you can get HB on the part you rent. You are treated as the owner of the property if you have the right to sell it, even though you may not be able to do so without the consent of other joint owners;[9]
- you make for a dwelling owned (or part-owned) by your partner;
- by a Crown tenant. Some landlords of Crown tenants have rent rebate schemes that are similar to HB;
- under a co-ownership scheme under which you receive a payment related to the value of the accommodation when you leave;
- under a hire purchase (eg, for the purchase of a mobile home), credit sale or a conditional sale agreement except to the extent that it is in respect of land.

In all of the above cases (other than the second), the payments might be met by IS, income-based JSA, income-related ESA or PC instead. In the second case, the payments you make to your partner cannot be met by IS, income-based JSA, income-related ESA or PC, but certain loans and other housing costs you (or your partner) have might be met by those benefits. See Chapter 38 for further information.

In addition, HB cannot meet payments if you are getting IS, income-based JSA or income-related ESA for these.[10] However, if you are now getting your housing costs met through IS, income-based JSA or income-related ESA but were previously getting HB for the same accommodation, your HB continues for your first four weeks on IS, income-based JSA or income-related ESA.[11] Remember that if you buy a home and immediately before that you were renting accommodation and getting HB, your full housing costs might not be met (see p861).

Note: if you live in a care home, you usually cannot get HB for the rent you pay to the home (see p690).

Liability to pay rent

To qualify for HB you must count as liable to pay rent. You count as liable if either you or your partner are liable.[12] You also count as liable if you are treated as liable – ie:[13]

- you have to pay rent in order to continue to live in your home because the liable person is not doing so, and:
  - your former partner is liable to make the payments; *or*
  - you are not the former partner of the liable person and it is reasonable to treat you as liable.[14]

It does not matter whether or not the landlord is prepared to transfer the tenancy to you or wants to evict you. If you are a local authority tenant and the local authority refuses to accept your HB claim, point out that the eligibility rules for HB and for transferring local authority tenancies are quite separate. If the local authority refuses your claim, request a revision or appeal; *or*

- your landlord allows you a rent-free period as compensation for undertaking repairs or redecoration which s/he would otherwise have had to carry out. You must have actually carried out the work. This only applies for a maximum of eight benefit weeks in respect of any one rent-free period. If you expect the work to last longer, arrange with your landlord to schedule the work in periods of eight weeks or less, separated by at least one complete benefit week where you resume paying rent; *or*
- you are the partner of a full-time student who is treated as not liable to pay rent (see p250). This means that you can qualify for HB even if your partner cannot.

Even if you fall into one of these categories, you can still be treated as not being liable to pay rent and so not entitled to HB in certain circumstances (see p250).

If you pay your rent in advance, you are still treated as liable to pay it, even where you paid it before claiming HB.[15]

What 'liable' means

For you to be 'liable' to pay rent, your agreement must be legally enforceable.[16] It is not enough if you only have a moral obligation, such as a promise to pay something whenever you can afford to do so. You can count as liable to pay rent even if someone else has been paying it on your behalf, or if your landlord has failed to provide notice of an address for the purposes of s48 of the Landlord and Tenant Act 1987 so rent is treated as not being due.[17] You can be liable to pay rent by yourself or you can be jointly liable to do so (see p250).

If you have a **written agreement** with your landlord, the local authority uses this to decide if you are liable to pay rent and whether the liability is a genuine part of the agreement. Even if the local authority accepts this, it might still treat you as not liable to pay rent (see p250).[18]

Your agreement can be enforceable even if it is **not in writing**. The fact that you have made a firm promise to pay money to your landlord in return for your occupation of the property should be sufficient to allow you to claim HB. If the local authority refuses to accept that you have a legal liability unless you produce a written agreement, a rent book or some other evidence in writing, argue that this is wrong and seek a revision or appeal.[19]

16/17-year-olds

People under 18 can be liable to pay rent and, therefore, entitled to HB, where there is an intention to create legal relations, regardless of the precise wording of the agreement.

If you are under 16, an adult or social services department is generally responsible for the rent. However, HB departments should not decide HB entitlement based on what they think the social services department ought to provide.

Joint liability

If you are a member of a couple (see p753) and are jointly liable for the rent, only one of you can claim HB.[20]

The way a group of single people living together and paying rent to their landlord is treated depends on how many of you are liable under the agreement. If all, or some of you, have joint liability for the rent, you can each make a separate claim and be paid HB on your share (unless the local authority thinks the joint tenancy has been created to take advantage of the HB scheme – see p252).

People treated as not liable to pay rent

Even if you or your partner are actually liable to pay rent, or you count as liable, you can be treated as though you are not liable to pay rent. In this case, you cannot qualify for HB. This applies if you are in any of the situations below.[21]

- You are a full-time **student** and you are not in one of the categories of student who can qualify for HB (see p647). This does not apply if you are at least the qualifying age for PC (see p509) and neither you nor your partner are getting IS, income-based JSA or income-related ESA.
- You **do not satisfy the habitual residence test** (see p1442).
- You are a member of, and are fully maintained by, a **religious order.**[22]
- You are living in a **care home** or an **independent hospital** (but see p690).[23]
- You **pay rent to someone who also lives in the dwelling and who is a close relative** of yours or your partner (see p251 for who counts).[24] Your landlord might be regarded as living in your dwelling if you share some accommodation with her/him, other than a bathroom, toilet or a hall or passageway.[25] It all depends on the facts. It does not matter if you use the accommodation at different times or if you pay to use it.[26]
- Your **agreement to pay rent is not on a commercial basis.**[27] In deciding whether or not your agreement is commercial, the local authority must look at the whole agreement, taking into account all the circumstances. It must consider, among other things:[28]
  - whether your agreement includes terms that are not legally enforceable. DWP guidance suggests that this might arise, for example, where a tenant does household chores. However, if you do chores in exchange for a lower rent, it could be considered commercial;
  - your agreement to pay rent. The rent does not have to be a market rent. Your agreement can count as commercial even if your landlord is not collecting the full contractual rent from you – eg, if it is not being met by HB because of the rent restriction rules (see Chapter 15);

  - your relationship to your landlord. However, just because you are a relative of, or have a close friendship with, her/him, or s/he provides you with care and support, does not mean that your agreement is non-commercial.
- You are **renting from**:[29]
  - any ex-partner of yours and the home is your former joint home with that ex-partner; *or*
  - any ex-partner of your partner and the home is your partner's former joint home with that ex-partner.
- You or your partner are **responsible for a child of your landlord**.[30] Being responsible for a child means more than caring for her/him. It only applies in situations where the child is included in your HB claim (see p759).[31]
- You, your partner, your ex-partner, your partner's ex-partner or a close relative of yours or your partner who lives with you is either:[32]
  - a **director or employee of a company which is your landlord**; *or*
  - a **trustee or beneficiary of a trust which is your landlord**.

  However, you should be treated as liable if you can show the arrangement was not intended to take advantage of the HB scheme (see p252).
- You are renting accommodation from a trustee of a trust, of which your **child** (or your partner's child) **is a beneficiary.**
- You were **previously the non-dependant** (see p265) of someone who lived, and continues to live, in the accommodation. This should not apply to you if you can show that the agreement was not created to take advantage of the HB scheme (see p252).[33]
- You or your current partner **previously owned or had a long tenancy** in (ie, a lease of more than 21 years) the accommodation and less than five years have passed since you last owned it (or the tenancy ceased).[34]

  This rule does not apply if you can show that you could not have continued to occupy the accommodation without giving up ownership (or the tenancy) – eg, if the lender is seeking possession of your home. Whether you were legally or practically compelled to give up ownership or the tenancy is relevant, but your motivation for doing so is not.[35] You may need to show that you have taken steps to explore alternatives.[36]
- You or your partner are employed by your landlord and are **occupying your accommodation as a condition of employment**. This should not apply if you continue to live in the accommodation after ceasing employment.
- Where none of the above apply, the local authority considers that your **liability to pay rent has been created to take advantage of the HB scheme**.

Close relatives

A 'close relative' is a parent, parent-in-law (including a civil partner's parent), son, son-in-law (including a son's civil partner), daughter, daughter-in-law (including a daughter's civil partner), brother, sister, step-parent (including a parent's civil partner), stepson (including a civil partner's son), stepdaughter (including a civil partner's daughter), or the partners of any of these.[37] It also includes half-brothers and sisters.[38] Relations with in-laws or step-relatives are severed by divorce (or dissolution of a civil partnership) but arguably not by death – eg, a stepchild is still a stepchild after the death of her/his mother.[39]

Agreements taking advantage of the housing benefit scheme

For your agreement to count as 'taking advantage of the HB scheme', it must amount to an abuse of the scheme or to taking improper advantage of it. It must be shown that the main reason you entered into the agreement was to obtain HB.[40] All the circumstances should be taken into account in deciding if this is the case, including what your landlord has to say.[41] An agreement can count as taking advantage of the HB scheme even if it was created from the best of motives.[42] Bear the following in mind.

- Your agreement does not take advantage of the HB scheme just because your landlord is your parent[43] or because you hope to be able to claim HB to help you with your rent – ie, if your main purpose is to get accommodation, not to obtain HB.[44]
- You should not be seen as taking advantage of the HB scheme just because you seek to find out what rent can be covered by HB before moving in.
- Tenants of a landlord who deliberately charges high rents to try and get them paid by HB may be affected by this provision, even if they had no such intention themselves. However, the fact that a landlord sets a high rent does not in itself mean that the liability takes advantage of the HB scheme.[45]
- If your landlord is going to evict you if you cannot get HB, this suggests that the agreement does not take advantage of the HB scheme.[46]

Occupying accommodation as your home

HB is paid for the home in which you normally live.[47] You cannot usually be paid for any other home. However, there are special rules if you:

- have just moved into your home (see p253);
- are temporarily absent from home (see p254);
- are liable to pay rent on more than one home (see p255);
- are in certain other situations (see p256).

Note:

- If you occupy more than one property or room as your home (eg, because you have a large family and rent adjacent flats, or have a live-in carer and rent two adjacent rooms in shared accommodation), you can argue that both properties or rooms count as part of your home – ie, that you only have one home.[48]
- If you have to live in an approved bail or probation hostel or are a prisoner on temporary release, you are not treated as occupying the accommodation in

which you are staying as your home.[49] This means you cannot qualify for HB for any rent you pay there.

Moving home

If you have **just moved into your home** but were liable to pay rent before moving in, you can get HB on your new home for a period of up to four weeks before you moved in.[50] Before moving, you must either have claimed HB or have notified the local authority of the move to the new home. If you have given up your previous home and have no other home, you can argue that the date you move in is the date you move your furniture and belongings in.[51] You can only qualify if your delay in moving was reasonable, *and*:

- you were waiting for a social fund payment for a need connected with the move – eg, removal expenses or to help you set up home. This only applies if:
  - you have a child of five or under living with you; *or*
  - you are at least the qualifying age for PC (see p509) and neither you nor your partner are getting IS, income-based JSA or income-related ESA; *or*
  - you are under the qualifying age for PC (see p509), or you or your partner are getting IS, income-based JSA or income-related ESA, and you qualify for a disability, severe disability or disabled child premium, or a support or work-related activity component; *or*
- you were waiting for adaptations to be finished to meet needs you or a member of your family for benefit purposes have because of a disability. The adaptations must involve a change to the fabric or structure of the dwelling, not just decorating or furnishing it;[52] *or*
- you became liable to make payments on your new home while you were a hospital patient or in 'residential accommodation' (see p255 for the meaning).

Your HB is not actually paid until you move in. If an earlier claim for HB you made before you moved in was turned down, you must claim again within four weeks of moving to qualify.

In addition, if you are **not liable to pay rent in your new accommodation** (including, for example, if you are in prison or hospital), you can get HB for up to four weeks for your former home if you:[53]

- were liable for rent on it immediately before moving into your new accommodation and continue to be liable; *and*
- could not reasonably have avoided liability for rent on your former home.

If you are obliged to pay rent for your old home as well as your new accommodation, you can only get HB for one of these unless you are covered by the rules described on p255.[54]

Temporary absence from home

If you are temporarily absent from your normal home, have not rented it out and intend to return, your HB can continue to be paid for a period. You can argue that you count as temporarily absent from home even if you have not yet stayed there – eg, you move your furniture and belongings in, but then have to go into hospital.[55]

You can get HB for up to **13 weeks** for your normal home while you are away, whatever the reason. You must be unlikely to be away for longer than this.[56]

You can get HB for up to **52 weeks** for your normal home if you are unlikely to be away for longer than this (or in exceptional circumstances, unlikely to be away for substantially longer than this) and:[57]

- you are a remand prisoner held in custody pending trial or sentence. You can argue this applies even if you are simultaneously serving another sentence.[58] Once you are sentenced, you no longer qualify for HB under this rule, but might still qualify under the 13-week rule. The 13 weeks run from the date you were first in prison, so any time you spend in prison awaiting trial or sentence counts towards the 13 weeks. **Note:** you are treated as still in custody if you are a prisoner on temporary release;[59]
- you are required to live in an approved hostel or an address away from your normal home as a condition of bail;
- you are resident in a hospital or similar institution as a patient;
- you, your partner or a dependent child under 16 are undergoing medical treatment or medically approved convalescence in the UK or abroad, other than in 'residential accommodation' (see p255 for the meaning);
- you are providing, or receiving, 'medically approved' care (ie, certified by a medical practitioner) in the UK or abroad. If you are receiving the care, you cannot be in 'residential accommodation' (see p255 for the meaning);
- you are caring for a child under 16 whose parent or guardian is away from home receiving medically approved care or medical treatment;
- you are undertaking a training course (see p255 for the meaning) in the UK or abroad;
- you are a student. For HB (but not council tax benefit), you must not fall into the first category under 'Other situations' on p256, or be entitled to HB on two homes (see p255);
- you are in 'residential accommodation' (see p255 for the meaning) for short-term or respite care;
- you are in 'residential accommodation' (see p255 for the meaning) for a trial period to see if it suits your needs. On the date you enter the accommodation, you must intend to return home if it is not suitable.[60] You can only get HB for up to 13 weeks.[61] If the accommodation does not suit your needs, you can have further trial periods in other accommodation so long as you are not away from home for more than 52 weeks in total;

- you are away from home because of a fear of violence. You need not have experienced actual violence, but you must be in fear of violence in your home or from a former family member. The first category includes violence by neighbours and racial attacks on your home. See below if you need to claim for two homes and p256 if you do not intend to return to your former home.

There must be some causal link between your absence from home and being in one of the situations above.[62]

Unless you are in residential accommodation for a trial period (see p254), your intention to return and whether or not you are unlikely to be away for longer than 13/52 weeks should be considered, initially based on the circumstances on the date you leave your home.[63] If at any time after that date you no longer intend to return or it becomes likely that you will be away from home for more than the 13/52 weeks, your entitlement can be reconsidered.[64]

The 13 and 52 weeks both run from the date you leave home. If, for example, you have been away from home for 10 weeks and then have grounds to continue to get HB for 52 weeks, you only get HB for the balance: 42 weeks. However, a new period of absence starts if you return home for even a short stay. A stay of at least 24 hours may be enough.[65] This does not apply, however, if you are a prisoner on temporary release.[66]

Note: if you have someone living with you who is temporarily absent (eg, s/he is a student who is away during term time), the local authority may use the rules above to decide if s/he is a non-dependant (see p265).[67]

Definitions [68]

For these purposes:

– **'residential accommodation'** means a care home, an independent hospital or an Abbeyfield Home. It includes establishments managed or provided by bodies incorporated by Royal Charter or constituted by an Act of Parliament, other than by local social services;

– a **'training course'** is a course of training or instruction provided by or on behalf of, or approved by, a government department, the Secretary of State, Skills Development Scotland, Scottish Enterprise, or Highlands and Islands Enterprise.

Note: the council tax benefit rules on temporary absence from home are broadly the same as those for HB.

Housing benefit for more than one home

You can usually only get HB for one home. **Note:** if you occupy more than one property as a home (eg, you rent adjacent flats because you have a large family or two adjacent rooms in shared accommodation because you have a live-in carer), you can argue that you only have one home.[69]

If you occupy two homes, you can get HB for both:

- for up to **four weeks** if:[70]
  - you have moved into a new home and you could not reasonably avoid having to pay rent on your old home.[71] The local authority must consider the reasons why you had to move quickly. For example, if you were forced to move quickly to take advantage of better accommodation, you may not have been able to avoid leaving without giving notice; *or*
  - you qualify for HB on a new home because a move was delayed while you were adapting your new home for the disability needs of a member of your family (see p253). You can get HB on both homes for the four weeks prior to the date you move. The adaptations must involve a change to the fabric or structure of the dwelling, not just decorating or furnishing it;[72]
- for up to **52 weeks**, if you have left your home because of a fear of violence (see p254). You must intend to return to your former home, and it must be reasonable for you to receive HB for both homes;[73]
- **indefinitely**, if:[74]
  - you are a member of a couple and you or your partner are a student who is not excluded from HB (see p647) or on a training course (see p255 for the meaning), it is necessary for you to live apart and it is reasonable for you to receive HB for both homes;
  - the local authority has housed you in more than one home because your family is large.

Other situations

If you have left your home because of a **fear of violence** (see p255 for what counts as violence) and cannot be paid HB for two homes (see p255) or while temporarily absent from home (see p254) (eg, you do not intend to return to your former home), you can get HB for four weeks for your former home.[75] This only applies if your liability to pay rent was unavoidable – eg, you should have given your landlord notice, but had to leave in a hurry because of the violence.

If you have **two homes**, and you are only liable to pay for one of them, you are treated as occupying the home for which you pay and therefore get HB for that home, even when you are not there. This applies if:

- you are a single claimant (including a lone parent), and you are either a student eligible for HB (see p647) or on a training course (see p255 for the meaning), and you live in one home during periods of study or training and another home at other times – eg, for vacations;[76] *or*
- you had to move into temporary accommodation because essential repairs are being carried out on your main home.[77] 'Essential repairs' means basic works rather than luxuries, but they need not be crucial to making the house habitable.[78]

Note: you cannot get HB under this rule if you pay rent for both homes, or if you pay rent for one and a mortgage on the other.

2. The rules about your age

There are no lower or upper age limits for claiming housing benefit (HB). However, if you are:

- under 16, there may be a question about whether you have a legally enforceable liability for rent (see p249);
- 16 or 17 and have been looked after by a local authority, you cannot usually claim HB. Instead, your local authority should support and accommodate you. See p673 for further information;
- at least the qualifying age for pension credit (see p509) and neither you nor your partner are getting income support, income-based jobseeker's allowance or income-related employment and support allowance, more generous rules apply.

If you are a single claimant under 35 and are living in private rented accommodation, the amount of your rent that can be met by HB might be restricted to the 'single room rent' or the local housing allowance for one-bedroom shared accommodation (see Chapter 15).

3. Claiming for others

You claim housing benefit for your family (see Chapter 34).

4. The amount of benefit

The amount of housing benefit (HB) you get depends on:

- your 'applicable amount' (see Chapter 37). This is made up of personal allowances, as well as premiums and components for any special needs. It may include a transitional addition if you or your partner were transferred to contributory employment and support allowance (ESA) from income support (IS) 'on the grounds of disability', incapacity benefit (IB) or severe disablement allowance (SDA), or are appealing a decision not to transfer you to ESA (see p840);
- your 'maximum HB' (see p258); *and*
- how much income and capital you have (see Chapters 40 and 41).

Maximum housing benefit

Your '**maximum HB**' is your 'eligible rent' (see p260), calculated on a weekly basis, minus any deductions made for your non-dependants (see p265).[79] The amount depends on whether your 'eligible rent' is restricted (see Chapter 15).

Example

Mr and Mrs Feinstein and their adult son live together in a flat rented from the local authority. Mr Feinstein is the sole tenant. The rent is £75 a week. This does not include any service charges. Their son earns £150 a week gross.

Eligible rent is the contractual rent	£75.00
Minus non-dependant deduction (see p268)	£26.25
Maximum housing benefit	**£48.75**

If you do not qualify for HB currently, you may qualify when:

- the benefit rates go up every April; *or*
- you or your partner reach:
  - the qualifying age for pension credit (PC – see p509). If neither you nor your partner are on IS, income-based jobseeker's allowance (JSA) or income-related ESA, your applicable amount is higher and the income and capital rules are also more generous; *or*
  - 65. Your personal allowance is increased by the equivalent of the amount of the maximum savings credit of PC, whether or not you receive this, if neither you nor your partner are on IS, income-based JSA or income-related ESA.

If your income is too high for you to qualify for HB currently, you might qualify once you, or a family member, become entitled to another benefit (a 'qualifying benefit' – see p277).

If you need extra financial assistance to meet your housing costs, you might be entitled to discretionary housing payments (see p294).

Remember that if you or your partner:

- stop getting IS, income-based JSA, ESA, IB or SDA because of starting work or increasing your hours or your earnings, you may be entitled to extended payments of HB (see p286);
- stop getting IS, income-based JSA or income-related ESA because you are moving onto PC, you may be able to continue to receive HB at the same rate for four weeks (see p285);
- have had limited capability for work (or have been incapable of work) but move into work or training, you might count as a 'work or training beneficiary' (see p214) or a 'welfare to work' beneficiary (see p738). This means you retain

entitlement to the work-related activity or support component or the disability premium if you have limited capability for work (or become incapable of work) again within 104 weeks.

Note: you might get a reduced amount of HB if it is restricted under the 'loss of benefit for benefit offences' rules (see p1106).

If you are on a means-tested benefit

Being on **IS, income-based JSA, income-related ESA or the guarantee credit of PC** is an automatic passport to maximum HB (once you have made a claim for HB). You therefore do not need to work out your applicable amount, income or capital.[80] HB equals 'maximum HB' (see p257).

For these purposes, you are treated as being on:

- income-based JSA:[81]
  - when you satisfy the conditions of entitlement but are not being paid it because of a sanction (see Chapter 20) or because you failed to attend an interview as required (see p422);
  - on your waiting days (see p402); *and*
  - when it is not paid because of the 'loss of benefit' rules (see p1106);
- income-related ESA:[82]
  - when you satisfy the conditions of entitlement but are not being paid it because you are disqualified for the reasons on p178, or during a temporary absence abroad, or because you are a prisoner;
  - on your waiting days (see p212).

Example

Glen and his partner Craig are joint housing association tenants. Glen's aunt lives with them. They pay rent of £100 a week. They receive income-based JSA while they are looking for work. Glen's aunt receives IS. Glen claims HB.

Eligible rent is £100 a week.

Glen's aunt counts as a non-dependant and so £11.45 a week is deducted (see p268).

Therefore, Glen's maximum HB is £88.55 week (£100 – £11.45).

Because they receive income-based JSA, Glen's HB is £88.55 week.

If you are not on a means-tested benefit

If you are **not on IS, income-based JSA, income-related ESA or the guarantee credit of PC**, you need to follow the steps below to calculate your HB.

- **Step one:** check that your capital is not too high (see Chapter 41).
- **Step two:** work out your 'maximum HB' (see p258).
- **Step three:** work out your applicable amount (see Chapter 37).

- **Step four:** work out your income (see Chapter 40, but also p652 if you are a student and p941 if you are getting the savings credit of PC).
- **Step five:** calculate HB.
  - If your **income is less than or equal to your applicable amount**, HB equals 'maximum HB'.
  - If your **income is greater than your applicable amount**, work out the difference. HB equals 'maximum HB' minus 65 per cent of the difference between your income and your applicable amount.

Examples

Mr Jopling is aged 45. He is unemployed and gets contribution-based JSA of £71 a week. Mrs Jopling is aged 46. She works 21 hours a week. She is paid £165 a week after deductions of tax and national insurance contributions. The couple are joint private tenants who pay £120 rent a week. Mrs Jopling claims HB. Her eligible rent is £108 a week because rent restriction rules have been applied.

Mr and Mrs Jopling have no non-dependants. Therefore, her maximum HB is £108 a week.

Mrs Jopling's applicable amount is £111.45 (the standard rate for a couple).

Income to be taken into account is Mr Jopling's JSA and Mrs Jopling's earnings of £155 a week (because £10 of her earnings are disregarded – see p914). £71 + £155 = £226.

The difference between her income and her applicable amount is £114.55 a week.

65% x £114.55 = £74.45 a week.

Mrs Jopling's HB is therefore £108 – £74.45 = £33.55 a week.

Mr Haralambous is 63 years old. He receives contributory ESA including a support component, totalling £105.05 a week. His weekly income from his private pension is £45. His total income is too high to qualify for the guarantee credit of PC. His total weekly income is therefore £150.05 (£105.05 + £45). He is a sole tenant of his council flat. His rent of £100 a week includes his heating and hot water. His eligible rent is £71.55 a week because £25.50 and £2.95 are deducted from his contractual rent for heating and hot water. This is also his maximum HB because he does not have any non-dependants.

His applicable amount is £142.70 (adult personal allowance for a single person at least the qualifying age for PC but under 65).

The difference between his income and his applicable amount is £7.35.

65% x £7.35 = £4.77 a week.

Mr Haralambous's HB is therefore £71.55 – £4.77 = £66.78 a week.

Eligible rent

Your 'eligible rent' is the amount of your rent used to calculate your HB. It can be different from the actual amount of rent you pay. Unless any of the rent restriction rules apply to you, your eligible rent is your contractual rent, minus any ineligible charges (see p262).[83] If any of the rent restriction rules apply to you, your eligible rent is usually your 'maximum rent' as determined under those rules – ie, your contractual rent, minus any amount above the level to which your rent is restricted. See Chapter 15 for details of all the rent restriction schemes and how your 'maximum rent' (and, therefore, your eligible rent) is worked out. **Note:** the rent restriction rules do *not* apply if you are a tenant of the local authority who pays your HB.

If none of the rent restriction rules apply, the local authority has general powers to decrease your eligible rent to an amount it considers appropriate (see p307).

Remember the following.

- If you are in shared accommodation, your eligible rent might be apportioned between you and the people with whom you share (see below).
- If the rent you pay covers both residential and other accommodation (eg, for business use), your HB only covers the rent you pay for the residential accommodation.[84]

If you live in shared accommodation

Unless the 'local housing allowance' rules apply to you (see p309), if you share accommodation with others who are not members of your family for HB purposes and are jointly liable for the rent with them, the local authority apportions the eligible rent between you. It considers:[85]

- the number of jointly liable people in the property (including any students who are treated as not liable to pay rent);[86] *and*
- the proportion of the rent actually paid by each liable person; *and*
- any other relevant circumstances, such as:
  - the number of rooms occupied by each jointly liable person;
  - whether any formal or informal agreement exists between you regarding the use and occupation of the home; *and*
  - if one of the jointly liable people has left the accommodation, the demands being made by the landlord on those who remain, or the possibility of finding other accommodation.

In some circumstances, it could be appropriate to apportion the whole of the rent to you even if you are jointly liable.[87]

If the rent includes any ineligible service charges, these are apportioned between you on the same basis as the rent. If only one of you is liable for the rent, that person is treated as the tenant and the other(s) might count as a non-dependant(s) (see p265).

Example

Sarah and Maude are friends who rent a housing association flat. They are joint tenants and pay rent of £100 a week. Sarah claims HB. The eligible rent is apportioned between them and Sarah's HB is based on £50 (£100 divided by two).

Note: if the 'local housing allowance' rules apply to you, although it is not necessary to apportion the eligible rent if you share accommodation with others who are not members of your family, the local authority *does* apportion your 'cap rent' (see p313).[88]

Ineligible charges

The local authority deducts ineligible charges when it works out your eligible rent. Note, however, that if the 'local reference rent' rules or the 'local housing allowance' rules apply, an adjustment on account of ineligible charges is generally made when the rent officer makes determinations .

Ineligible charges include:

- water charges;[89]
- most fuel charges (see below); *and*
- some service charges (see p264), including charges for meals.

Remember that, in addition, you cannot get HB for:

- payments for any part of your accommodation that is used exclusively for business purposes;[90]
- rent supplements charged to clear your rent arrears.[91]

Fuel charges

Fuel charges are ineligible unless they are for communal areas (see p263).[92] If your fuel charge is:

- specified on your rent book or is **readily identifiable** from your agreement with your landlord, the full amount of the charge is ineligible.[93] If your fuel charge is considered to be unrealistically low in relation to the fuel provided, a flat-rate amount is ineligible instead (see below). This is also the case if your total fuel charge is specified but contains an unknown amount for communal areas. If you are a council tenant, the regulations assume your fuel charges are always specified or readily identifiable, since the local authority is also your landlord.[94]
- **not readily identifiable**, a flat-rate amount is ineligible. The amounts are:[95]

If you and your family occupy more than one room:	
For heating (other than hot water)	£25.50
For hot water	£2.95

For lighting	£2.05
For cooking	£2.95
If you and your family occupy one room only:	
For heating alone, or heating combined with either hot water or lighting or both	£15.25
For cooking	£2.95

These amounts are added together where fuel is supplied for more than one purpose. If you are a joint tenant, all the amounts are apportioned according to your share of the rent (see p261).

If flat-rate fuel amounts have been used in calculating your HB, the local authority must notify you about this and explain that if you can produce evidence from which the actual or approximate amount of your fuel charge can be estimated, the flat-rate amounts may be varied accordingly.[96]

The lower amounts apply if you and your family occupy one room only. The decision maker is likely to say this means that if you occupy one room and share the use of other rooms (such as a communal lounge), the higher amounts apply.[97] You should argue that the lower amounts apply if you are forced to live in one room because the other room(s) in your accommodation are, in practice, unfit to live in – eg, because of severe mould or dampness.

Fuel for communal areas

If you pay a service charge for the use of fuel in communal areas, and that charge is separately identified from any other charge for fuel used within your accommodation, it may be included as part of your eligible rent.[98] Communal areas include access areas like halls and passageways, but not rooms in common use except those in sheltered accommodation – eg, a shared TV lounge or dining room.[99] If you pay a charge for the provision of a heating system (eg, regular boiler maintenance), this is also eligible if the amount is separately identified from any other fuel charge you pay.[100]

Service charges

Many service charges are covered by HB, but only if payment is a condition of occupying the accommodation rather than an optional extra.[101] Eligible and ineligible service charges are listed below. If the local authority regards any of the eligible charges as excessive, it estimates a reasonable amount given the cost of comparable services.[102] If you are in supported accommodation, see p265.

Eligible services

The following services are eligible for HB:

- services for the provision of adequate accommodation including some warden and caretaker services, gardens, children's play areas, lifts, entry phones,

communal telephone costs, portering and rubbish removal.[103] This can include upkeep of a communal garden.[104] TV and radio relay charges are covered – eg, satelite or cable, including free-to-view UK channels;[105]
- laundry facilities (eg, a laundry room in an apartment block), but not charges for the provision of personal laundry;[106]
- furniture and household equipment, but not if there is an agreement that the furniture will eventually become yours;[107]
- cleaning of the outside of windows where neither you nor any member of your household are able to clean them yourself and cleaning of rooms and windows in communal areas, unless payment for these is made by your local authority or the Welsh Ministers.[108]

Ineligible services

The following services are not eligible for HB:[109]
- food, including prepared meals (see below);
- sports facilities;
- TV rental, licence and subscription fees (but see above);
- transport;
- personal laundry service;
- provision of an emergency alarm system;
- medical expenses;
- nursing and personal care;
- counselling and other support services;
- any other charge not connected with the provision of adequate accommodation and not specifically included in the list of eligible charges on p263.

The amount of the charge specified in your rent agreement is not eligible for HB, though local authorities can substitute their own estimate if they consider the amount to be unreasonably low.[110] If the amount is not specified in your rent agreement, the local authority estimates how much is fairly attributable to the service, given the cost of comparable services.[111]

Charges for meals

If your housing costs include an amount for meals, set amounts are ineligible regardless of the actual cost.[112] These are:

If at least three meals a day are provided:	
For the claimant and each additional member of the family aged 16 or over	£25.30
For each additional member of the family aged under 16	£12.80
If breakfast only is provided:	
For the claimant and each additional member of the family, regardless of age	£3.10
In all other cases (part board):	
For the claimant and each additional member of the family aged 16 or over	£16.85

For each additional member of the family aged under 16	£8.45

For these purposes, a person is treated as having reached the age of 16 on the first Monday in September following her/his 16th birthday.
The standard amounts are ineligible for everyone who has meals paid for by you – including meals for someone who is not part of your family, such as a non-dependant.[113]

Service charges in supported accommodation

If you live in supported accommodation, HB can help with your rent. However, HB is not available for the support services provided with your accommodation. Instead, the local authority's Supporting People team funds these – eg, via your landlord or a voluntary organisation.

In some cases, your local authority can charge you for the support services you get. Its means test is used to determine how much you have to pay.

Calculating a weekly amount of housing benefit

HB is always paid for a specific benefit week – a period of seven consecutive days beginning with a Monday and ending on a Sunday.[114] If you pay rent at different intervals (eg, monthly or daily), the amount has to be converted to a weekly figure before HB can be calculated.[115]

Rent-free periods

If you have a regular rent-free period (eg, you pay rent on a 48-week rent year), you get no HB during your rent-free period. Your applicable amount, weekly income, non-dependant deductions, the set deductions for meals and fuel charges and the minimum amount payable (but not your eligible rent) are adjusted.[116]

Note: this does not apply if your landlord has temporarily waived the rent in return for you doing repairs (see p249).

Deductions for non-dependants

If other people normally live with you in your home who are not part of your family for benefit purposes (see p751) (called '**non-dependants**'), a set deduction is usually made from your HB.[117] This is because it is assumed the non-dependant makes a contribution towards your outgoings, whether or not s/he does so. Examples of non-dependants are adult sons or daughters, or elderly relatives who share your home.

Non-dependant deductions: checklist

1. Do you have a non-dependant – ie, someone who normally lives with you?
2. Must a non-dependant deduction be made?
3. What is the correct amount of the non-dependant deduction?

Note: the council tax benefit rules for deductions for non-dependants are broadly the same as those for HB. See pp123-125 for the differences.

Who counts as a non-dependant

A person only counts as your non-dependant if s/he normally lives with you.[118] So, for example, if someone is only staying with you temporarily but has a home elsewhere, or is homeless and is only using your address as a postal address, s/he should not count as a non-dependant. If you think the local authority has wrongly assumed that a person is your non-dependant, ask for a revision or appeal. **Note:** some people do not count as non-dependants even if they normally live with you (see below).

A person is only **living with you** if s/he has her/his home with you and shares some accommodation with you.[119] This includes sharing the kitchen (unless it is only used by someone else to prepare food for her/him[120]), but not a bathroom, lavatory or a communal area such as a hall, passageway or a room in common use in sheltered accommodation. If other areas of the house are shared, the person is treated as living with you. This is the case even if you only use them at different times, so long as you have a shared right to use them and are living in the same household (see p754 for the meaning of 'household').[121] A person who is separately liable to pay rent to your landlord does not count as living with you.

A person should only count as **normally living with you** if s/he has been there long enough to regard your home as her/his normal home.[122] A number of factors should be taken into account to decide whether a person is normally living with you, including:[123]

- the relationship between you;
- how much time s/he spends at your address;
- where s/he has her/his post sent;
- where s/he keeps her/his clothes and personal belongings;
- whether her/his stay or absence from your address is temporary or permanent. The local authority may use the rules on p254 to work this out;[124]
- whether s/he has another place that could be regarded as home and, if for instance, s/he pays rent or water charges there or s/he just travels around.

People who are not non-dependants

The following people do *not* count as non-dependants, and no non-dependant deduction is made for them, even if they normally live with you:[125]

- a member of your family for benefit purposes (see p751);
- a child or qualifying young person living with you who does not count as a member of your household (see p762) – eg, a foster child, or someone placed with you prior to adoption;

- someone who is employed by a charitable or voluntary organisation as a resident carer for you or your partner and who you pay for the service. This can also apply if a public body pays on your behalf;
- any person, or a member of their household, to whom you or your partner are liable to pay rent on a commercial basis;
- someone who jointly occupies your home and is either a co-owner or jointly liable with you or your partner to make payments in respect of occupying it. You do not jointly occupy the home with someone unless you made a joint agreement with your landlord to occupy the home. The fact that you live in the same home does not make you joint occupiers;[126]
- someone who is liable to pay rent on a commercial basis to you or your partner. However, although no non-dependant deduction can be made for her/him, the rent s/he pays can count as your income (see pp924 and 950).

If the person comes within the last three categories above, s/he *does* count as a non-dependant if s/he is treated as not liable for rent under the rules explained on p250 (unless s/he is a student or a 'person subject to immigration control', or s/he has failed the 'habitual residence test').[127]

When no non-dependant deduction is made

Even if you have a non-dependant, no non-dependant deduction is made for her/him if either you or your partner:[128]

- are registered blind or have regained your eyesight within the last 28 weeks; *or*
- receive attendance allowance (AA) (or equivalent benefits paid because of injury at work or a war injury) or the care component of disability living allowance (DLA).

No deduction is made in respect of any non-dependant who is:[129]

- staying with you but whose normal home is elsewhere;
- receiving a training allowance in connection with youth training under specific provisions;[130]
- a full-time student during her/his period of study. This includes those getting JSA who count as full-time students while on training courses under the Employment, Skills and Enterprise scheme. **Note:** unless you or your partner are 65 or over, no deduction is made during the summer vacation only if the student is not in full-time work;
- in hospital for more than 52 weeks. Separate stays in hospital which are not more than 28 days apart are added together when calculating the 52 weeks;
- in prison;
- under 18 years old;[131]

- under 25 and on IS, income-based JSA or income-related ESA which does not include a work-related or support component. S/he can be treated as on income-based JSA or income-related ESA for these purposes (see p259);[132]
- on PC.

The amount of deductions

If you have a non-dependant living with you who is 18 or over, and for whom a deduction must be made, a fixed amount is deducted from your HB, whatever s/he pays you. Unless your non-dependant is in full-time paid work, an £11.45 deduction is made each week. If your non-dependant is in full-time paid work, the amount of the deduction depends on her/his gross weekly income as follows.[133]

Circumstances of the non-dependant	*Deduction*
Aged 18 or over and in full-time paid work with a weekly gross income of:	
£394 or more	£73.85
£316–£393.99	£67.25
£238–£315.99	£59.05
£183–£237.99	£36.10
£124–£182.99	£26.25
All others (for whom a deduction is made)	£11.45

The rules on full-time paid work are in Chapter 31. Remember the following.

- A non-dependant who is not in (or is treated as not in) full-time paid work does not attract the higher levels of deduction even if her/his weekly gross income is £124 or more.
- If someone is on IS, income-based JSA or income-related ESA (see p259) for more than three days in a benefit week, s/he does not count as being in full-time paid work in that week.[134] This means the lower deduction (£11.45) is made (or in some cases no deduction).

Gross income includes wages before tax and national insurance are deducted, plus any other income the non-dependant has (apart from AA, constant attendance allowance, DLA and payments from any of the Macfarlane Trusts, the Eileen Trust, MFET Ltd, the Skipton Fund, the Caxton Foundation, the London Bombings Relief Charitable Fund, the Fund and the Independent Living Fund (2006)[135]).

Try to provide information to show which deduction applies. If you cannot, ask the local authority to consider the circumstances – eg, if your non-dependant is doing a job which is normally very low paid. The local authority should not assume the worst – eg, that your non-dependant is earning the highest amount. It should assess what the likely level of her/his income is on the evidence available.[136]

A deduction is made from your eligible rent for every non-dependant living in your household except in the case of a non-dependant couple (see below).

If you are 65 or over

If you or your partner are 65 or over and a non-dependant moves in with you, so a deduction should be made, or there has been a change of circumstances in respect of a non-dependant, the effect of this can be delayed for 26 weeks (see p293).

Non-dependant couples

Only one deduction is made for a couple (or the members of a polygamous marriage) who are non-dependants. The deduction made is the highest that would have been made if they were treated as individuals.[137] For the purpose of deciding which income band applies (see p268), their joint income counts, even if only one of them is in full-time work.[138]

Non-dependants of joint occupiers

If you share a non-dependant with any other joint occupiers, the deduction is divided between you, taking into account the proportion of housing costs paid by each. No apportionment is made between the members of a couple (or polygamous marriage).[139] If the person is a non-dependant of only one of you, the full deduction is made from that person's benefit.

Income and capital of a non-dependant is greater than yours

Normally, the income and capital of any non-dependant is only relevant when deciding which non-dependant deduction applies. However, unless you are on IS, income-based JSA, income-related ESA or PC guarantee credit, your HB entitlement is assessed on the basis of your non-dependant's income and capital rather than your own if:[140]

- the income and capital of your non-dependant are both greater than yours; *and*
- the local authority is satisfied you have made an arrangement with your non-dependant to take advantage of the HB scheme (see p252).

Any income and capital normally treated as belonging to you is completely ignored, but the rest of the calculation proceeds as normal.

Extra benefit for war pensioners

The local authority has the power to pay extra HB to people getting certain war pensions, by disregarding some or all of the pension as income, rather than just disregarding £10.[141] If the authority uses this power, it must apply the income disregard to all people in receipt of these pensions. See pp920 and 949 for further information. **Note:** the council tax benefit rules for extra benefit for war pensioners are the same as those for HB.

5. Special benefit rules

Special rules may apply to:
- students (see p646);
- people subject to immigration control (see p1410);
- 16/17-year-olds formerly looked after by a local authority (see p673);
- prisoners (see p694);
- people in care homes and other similar accommodation (see p687).

6. Claims and backdating

You should claim housing benefit (HB) as soon as you think you might be entitled to it or you may lose benefit. The rules about backdating are explained on p277.

If you want to claim discretionary housing payments, you must claim separately (see p296).

Note: the council tax benefit (CTB) rules for claims and backdating are broadly the same as those for HB. See pp128-129 for the differences.

Making a claim

A claim for HB must normally be made in writing on a properly completed claim form.[142] You can claim in some other written form (eg, by letter) so long as the written information and evidence you provide is sufficient. See p273 for information about where to claim. Note that if you are making a claim for income support (IS), income-based jobseeker's allowance (JSA), employment and support allowance (ESA), incapacity benefit (IB) or pension credit (PC), you can claim HB and CTB at the same time (see p271).

You may also be able to claim:
- by telephone if:
  - your local authority has published a number for this purpose.[143] The local authority may then provide a written statement of your circumstances. For your claim to be valid, you must approve this statement. Note that even if you cannot claim by telephone, if you telephone to ask to be sent a claim form and you return it within one month, your claim is backdated to the date of your call (see p275); *or*

- you are claiming IS, JSA, ESA, IB or PC by telephone;
- by electronic communication (eg, online or by email), if your local authority has authorised it (by a Chief Executive's Direction).[144]

If you claim in writing, keep a copy in case queries arise. You must provide any information and evidence required (see p275). You can amend or withdraw your claim before a decision is made (see p273).

Forms

Claim forms are available from your local authority or to download at www.direct.gov.uk/en/moneytaxandbenefits.[145]

Note:

- Make your claim as soon as you can so you do not lose benefit. However, ensure your claim is accepted as valid (see p272).
- If you are claiming HB or CTB within a set number of weeks of a previous entitlement ending, you might be given a shortened claim form. This is known as 'rapid reclaim' (see p273).

If you are claiming another benefit

In the following circumstances, you may be able to make your claim for HB with your claim for another benefit.

- If you are claiming IS, JSA, ESA, IB or PC by telephone (see below).
- If you are claiming IS, income-based JSA or PC on a written claim form (see below).
- When you are providing evidence or information or notifying a change of circumstances in connection with your IS, JSA, ESA, IB or PC claim (see p272).

Note: if you are already getting IS, JSA, ESA, IB or PC and want to claim HB or CTB, you must claim directly from your local authority.

If you are **claiming IS, JSA, ESA, IB or PC by telephone**, your HB and CTB claims are usually completed at the same time.[146] The DWP takes your details over the telephone and sends you a statement of your circumstances to check, sign and return to the Jobcentre Plus office, along with evidence to support your claim. Your HB and CTB claims are forwarded to the local authority. You can claim HB and CTB by telephone to the DWP (using the number specified for this purpose) at any time before a decision is made on your claim for IS, JSA, ESA, IB or PC. **Note:** if the local authority or DWP provides a written statement of your circumstances, you must approve this for your claim to be valid.[147]

If you are **claiming IS, income-based JSA or PC on a written claim form**, you are given an HB and CTB claim form with the IS/JSA/PC form. Complete this and return it to the local authority. Unless you are claiming PC, the local authority may ask you to complete its own form. You should do this as soon as possible.

If the DWP agrees, you can claim HB and CTB **when you are providing evidence or information that is required, or notifying a change of circumstances, in connection with your claim for IS, JSA, ESA, IB or PC.**[148] You can do this at any time before a decision is made on the award of benefit to which the evidence, information or change of circumstances relates. Although the rules do not say so, the intention is that you can make your claim for HB and CTB by telephone in this situation.[149] The local authority or DWP might ask you for further information and evidence (see p275).

Making sure your claim is valid

Where possible, your claim for HB should be accompanied by all the information and evidence needed to assess it.[150] Your claim is 'defective' if you:

- do not complete your claim form properly or you claim in writing but not on the claim form (eg, by letter or by electronic communication) and do not provide sufficient information and evidence;
- are allowed to, and claim by, telephone and do not provide all the information required by the local authority or DWP during the telephone call.

It is very important that you provide any information or evidence required. Until you do, you may not count as having made a valid claim. However, you should not delay your claim just because you do not have all the evidence ready to send.

If you have:[151]

- not completed the claim form properly, the local authority can return it to you to do so. However, if you sent or gave your claim form to the DWP, it can ask you to provide the local authority with information needed to complete the form; *or*
- claimed in writing, but not on the claim form (eg, by letter or electronic communication), the local authority can send you a claim form to complete properly; *or*
- claimed HB by telephone to the local authority, the local authority must give you an opportunity to provide the information required; *or*
- claimed HB by telephone to the DWP, the DWP can give you an opportunity to provide the information required. However, if the DWP does not do so, the local authority *must* give you an opportunity to provide the information, unless it thinks it already has sufficient information.

If you return the form completed properly or provide the information or evidence within one month, your claim is treated as though it was received on the date of your original claim.[152] The local authority can allow you longer than one month if it thinks this reasonable. Note that if you claimed HB by telephone to the DWP, and you do not provide the information required within the time limit, the local authority can still treat your claim as though it was received on the date of your original claim if it thinks it already has sufficient information.

Note:

- If your claim is not accepted as valid, you should be given a decision saying so. You can appeal against the decision.
- Even if you provide all the information required with your claim, the local authority (or DWP) might ask you to provide further evidence or information (see p275).

Amending or withdrawing your claim

You may amend or withdraw your claim in writing at any time before a decision is made.[153] If you can claim HB by telephone:

- to the local authority, you can also amend your claim by telephone;
- to the DWP, you can also amend or withdraw your claim by telephone.

Amendments are treated as though they were part of your original claim. A notice to withdraw your claim takes effect from the day it is received. See p1019 for further information about withdrawing claims.

Rapid reclaim

You may be able to complete a shortened HB and CTB claim form (known as 'rapid reclaim') if your circumstances have not changed since the last time you were claiming HB or CTB, and:[154]

- you are reclaiming within 26 weeks, are also reclaiming IS, JSA or IB and are entitled to IS, income-based JSA or IB; *or*
- you are reclaiming within 12 weeks and you are also reclaiming ESA.

You are given the shortened form by the Jobcentre Plus office with the claim form for IS, JSA, ESA or IB. You must send your HB and CTB claim to the local authority, *not* to the DWP. If you fill in the form properly, the local authority should be able to make a decision on your HB or CTB claim without asking you for further information. However, if you do not do so, or any of your details have changed since the last time you claimed HB or CTB, the local authority may send you a full HB or CTB form to complete or ask you for further information.

Where to make your claim

If you claim **in writing**, you must usually send or give your HB claim to the local authority's designated office for the receipt of HB and CTB claims.[155] The address is usually on the claim form or a notice accompanying it. You can also send or give your claim to:[156]

- if you or your partner are also claiming IS, JSA, ESA, IB or PC, either your DWP office or to the local authority's designated office for HB/CTB claims. If you send your HB/CTB claim to the DWP, unless your HB/CTB claim is on the same form as your IS, JSA, ESA, IB or PC claim, the DWP must forward it to the local authority within two working days of the date your HB/CTB claim was received or as soon as practicable after that.[157]

It may be wise to send your HB/CTB form directly to the local authority. If you do this, the local authority verifies your entitlement to IS, JSA, ESA or IB before assessing your HB. This may speed up your HB/CTB claim; *or*

- if you are at least the qualifying age for PC (see p509), any authorised office.

You can also send or give your claim to a county council office if your local authority has arranged for claims to be received there.[158]

Keep a copy of your claim form wherever possible. Ask for confirmation that you have delivered it to the relevant office.

If your local authority has authorised it (by a Chief Executive's Direction) and you are claiming **by electronic communication**, check the correct address for this with your local authority.[159]

If you are allowed to claim **by telephone**, you must make your claim to the telephone number published or specified for this purpose.[160]

Who should claim

If you are a single person or a lone parent, you make a claim for HB on your own behalf. If you are one of a couple, you can decide between you who should claim. The choice of claimant may affect the level of HB you receive – eg, if one of you is a full-time student and not entitled to HB (see p647) or if one of you is getting ESA and the other is getting disability living allowance (DLA). If you are considering changing the claim into your partner's name, check whether this could result in your becoming subject to harsher rent restriction rules (see Chapter 15) or losing entitlement to any premiums or components (see Chapter 37). It is only if you cannot agree who should be the claimant that the local authority can decide for you.[161]

If a person is either temporarily or permanently unable to manage her/his own affairs, the local authority must accept a claim made by someone formally appointed to act legally on her/his behalf – eg, someone appointed with power of attorney, a deputy appointed by the Court of Protection or, in Scotland, a judicial factor or any guardian appointed under the Adults with Incapacity (Scotland) Act 2000 administering the person's estate.[162]

If no one has been formally appointed to look after a claimant's affairs, the local authority can decide to make someone aged over 18 an appointee who can act on her/his behalf.[163] For the purpose of the claim, an appointee has the responsibility of exercising all rights and duties as though s/he were the claimant.[164]

You can write to ask to be an appointee, and can resign after giving four weeks' notice. The local authority may terminate any appointment at any time.[165] If someone is given a formal legal appointment, that person automatically takes over from the person appointed by the local authority.[166]

Information to support your claim

When you claim HB, you must:

- satisfy the national insurance (NI) number requirement (see below and p1023), unless you are living in a hostel;
- provide proof of your identity, if required;
- provide information and evidence required with the claim (see p272) and additional information and evidence relevant to your claim. There is a strict time limit for doing so.

Even if you provide all the information required with your claim (see p272), the local authority (or DWP) might ask you to provide further evidence or information. You must then supply this within one month – or longer if the local authority thinks this is reasonable.[167]

If you or your partner are getting IS or JSA and have notified the DWP that you have started work, the DWP can ask you to provide the local authority with any information or evidence it needs to decide whether you continue to be entitled to HB.[168] This only applies if, as a result of the change, your entitlement to IS or JSA will end or, if you are getting contribution-based JSA, the amount will reduce.

If you have claimed HB in association with a claim for IS, income-based JSA or PC and the DWP has accepted that you satisfy the NI number requirement, the local authority can accept that it is also satisfied for HB purposes.[169] If your claim is for contribution-based JSA or IB, the local authority may still need to verify your partner's NI number and identity.

The local authority may ask you to provide information after you are awarded HB. If you fail to do so, your HB could be suspended or even terminated (see p1045). **Note:** you must actually have been notified; proof of posting to your last known address is not sufficient.[170]

The date of your claim

Your date of claim is important because it affects the date from which your entitlement to HB starts (see p285). Remember: your 'date of claim' is not necessarily the date it is received by the local authority – eg, the date you submit your claim form. It can be an earlier date (see below). In some cases, you can claim in advance (see p276) and in some cases your claim can be backdated (see p277).

Your '**date of claim**' is usually the earliest of:[171]

- the date you first notify a designated office, DWP office or authorised office (see p273) (or county council office, if the local authority has arranged for claims

there) that you want to claim HB (eg, by telephone, in person or where someone does this on your behalf), if a properly completed claim is received in one of those offices within one month. The one-month period can be extended if the local authority thinks it is reasonable; *or*
- the date your valid claim is received by the designated office, DWP office or authorised office (see p273) (or county council office, if the local authority has arranged for claims there).

There are exceptions to the rule if:[172]
- you or your partner have successfully claimed IS, income-based JSA, income-related ESA or the guarantee credit of PC and your HB claim is made within one month of your IS, JSA, ESA or PC claim being received by the DWP. Your claim is treated as having been made on the first day of entitlement to IS, income-based JSA, income-related ESA or PC (including the waiting days for JSA or ESA). For example, if your claim for IS/JSA/ESA/PC is backdated, your date of claim for HB purposes is the date to which that benefit claim is backdated;[173]
- you or your partner are on IS, income-based JSA, income-related ESA or the guarantee credit of PC and have just become liable to pay rent and your HB claim reaches the local authority's designated office or DWP office within one month of your becoming liable. Your claim is treated as having been made on the date that you first became liable;
- you have separated from your partner or s/he has died and s/he was claiming HB for you on the date this happened and you claim within one month of this. Your claim is treated as having been made on the date you separated or your partner died.

Claiming in advance

You can claim HB in advance if:
- you become liable for rent for the first time but cannot move into your accommodation until after your liability begins. You must claim HB as soon as you are liable. Once you have moved in, you may be able to receive HB for up to four weeks prior to moving in (see p253);
- you are not entitled to HB now, but will become entitled within 13 weeks of claiming (17 weeks if you or your partner will be the qualifying age for PC (see p509) within 17 weeks), unless the reason you do not qualify straight away is because you fail the 'habitual residence test' (see p1442). The local authority can treat your claim as having been made in the benefit week immediately before you are first entitled.[174] If this happens, you do not need to make a further claim later.

Housing benefit after an award of a 'qualifying benefit'

You might not be entitled to HB currently, but would be once you or a member of your family become entitled to another 'qualifying benefit' – eg, DLA or carer's allowance. Alternatively, you might be entitled to a higher rate of benefit once the 'qualifying benefit' is awarded. If you are already entitled to HB when the qualifying benefit is awarded, see pp1132, 1139 and 1147.

If you only qualify for HB (or CTB) when the qualifying benefit is awarded, the rules operate in an unfair way. You should, therefore, claim HB (or CTB) while waiting to hear about the claim for a qualifying benefit. Then:

- ask the local authority to check whether you are entitled to HB (or CTB) on the basis of your circumstances, regardless of whether you are entitled to a qualifying benefit. If you are, it should award HB (or CTB). If you later get a qualifying benefit, your award should be revised or superseded (see pp1132 and 1139);
- if you do not qualify for HB (or CTB) until awarded a qualifying benefit, ask the local authority to wait to make a decision on your claim until the award of the qualifying benefit is made. This is what is known as 'stockpiling' your claim.

If the local authority refuses to stockpile your claim, argue that its failure to delay making a decision on your claim was an 'error of law' and, therefore, that there are grounds for an 'any time' revision (see p1129).[175] If you are refused HB (or CTB) but have since been awarded a qualifying benefit, claim again and ask for your claim to be backdated. Argue that you have good cause for your late claim (see below). If you lose benefit because of the way the rules operate, ask your local authority for compensation to cover the period before your fresh HB (or CTB) claim.

Backdating your claim

It is very important to claim in time. Even if your claim is backdated, the arrears of HB you can get are limited. If you are at least the qualifying age for PC and neither you nor your partner are on IS, income-based JSA or income-related ESA, see below. If you have not reached the qualifying age for PC, or you or your partner are on IS, income-based JSA or income-related ESA, see p278.

For backdated HB to be considered, you must ask for HB for a past period. Do this as soon as possible, preferably at the same time as your claim for HB.

Any backdated HB is calculated on the basis of your circumstances and the HB rules as they were over the backdating period.

If you would have been entitled to HB for an earlier period than the backdating rules allow, you could:

- ask for an 'any time' revision if there are grounds (see p1129);

- ask for compensation from the local authority if you were given wrong information or misled by it (see p1261);
- complain to the Ombudsman (see p1261).

If you only qualify for HB when a 'qualifying benefit' is awarded, see p277.

Three months' backdating

If you are at least the qualifying age for PC and neither you nor your partner are on IS, income-based JSA or income-related ESA, your claim for HB can be backdated for up to three months.[176] This applies whatever the reasons were for your delay in claiming and even if you do not ask for HB for a past period until some time after you make your claim for HB. You only need to show that you qualified for HB during that period.

You can get backdated HB for the three months before the date of your HB claim (see p275) – eg, the date your claim was received or the date you notified the local authority that you wanted to claim HB.[177] However, if you or your partner successfully claimed the guarantee credit of PC and your claim for HB is received within one month of your PC claim being received by the DWP, your entitlement to HB cannot begin earlier than three months before your claim for PC was made (or treated as made).

Six months' backdating

Unless you are at least the qualifying age for PC and neither you nor your partner are on IS, income-based JSA or income-related ESA, your claim for HB can be backdated for up to six months.[178] You must show that you qualified for HB during that period *and* prove you had continuous 'good cause' for your failure to claim or to ask for backdated HB (see p279). You can only get backdated HB from the latest of the following:[179]

- the day from when you had continuous 'good cause' for your late claim; *or*
- the day six months before the date of your HB claim (see p275) – eg, six months before the date your claim was received or the date you notified the local authority that you wanted to claim HB; *or*
- the day six months before you asked for backdated HB.

Example

Rose claimed HB on 1 December 2011, within one month of a successful claim for IS (made on 15 November 2011). She asked for backdated HB on 1 December 2011.

The local authority accepts that she had continuous good cause for her late claim from 1 February 2010.

Her claim for HB is treated as made on 15 November 2011 (the first day of entitlement to IS – see p276). Six months before that date is 15 May 2011.

The day six months before she asked for backdated HB is 1 June 2011.
Rose therefore gets backdated HB from 1 June 2011, the latest of the three relevant dates.

Good cause for claiming late

You count as having 'good cause' for your late claim if you can show there is something that would probably have caused a reasonable person of your age and experience to act (or fail to act) as you did, having regard to all the circumstances (including your state of health and the information which you received and which you might have obtained).[180] The more reasonable your behaviour in not claiming earlier given your circumstances, the more likely it will be that you have good cause.[181] It is your mental age, not your chronological age, that is relevant.[182] If you have a mental health problem that makes you act unreasonably, then that must be borne in mind.[183]

The following are examples of situations where you might have good cause for making a late claim.

- You sought advice about your rights but were misled by someone on whom you were entitled to rely. You are entitled to rely on officers from the local authority or the DWP, or independent advisers such as solicitors, Citizens Advice Bureaux, trade union officials or accountants.[184] Relying on the advice of work colleagues, friends, or even a doctor, is not enough.[185] The enquiries that you made need not have been specific, provided the situation is such that you ought to have been told about your possible entitlement.
- You did not seek advice about your rights because you misunderstood them (eg, you reasonably believed you did not need to make a claim), or you mistakenly thought that you understood them, or you mistakenly thought that you had no entitlement and there was nothing for you to enquire about.[186] Generally, you are expected to find out about your rights, but if it was reasonable for you to form one of these views, you can still have good cause.
- The delay was due to some factor beyond your control, such as the failure of the post, or the failure of someone you asked to help with your claim, provided you have checked whether the claim has arrived in good time.[187]
- You are unable to claim because of physical or mental ill health.[188] However, you might reasonably be expected to seek the assistance of friends or relatives if available.
- You have difficulty communicating in English, or understanding documents, or have little knowledge of the benefits system. These matters should be taken into account but are not usually good cause in themselves.[189]
- You only qualify for HB or CTB when a 'qualifying benefit' is awarded (see p277).

Notice of the decision

If you are a person affected by an HB decision, you must be notified of it by the local authority without delay if it is a decision on a claim (within 14 days in other cases) or as soon as 'reasonably practicable'.[190] You can request reasons for a decision. Your request must be in writing and it must be signed by you.[191]

You are a person affected by a decision if you are:[192]

- a claimant;
- someone acting for a claimant who is unable to act for her/himself – eg, an appointee;
- someone from whom the local authority decides to recover an overpayment (including a landlord); *or*
- a landlord or agent, where the decision concerns whether or not to make a direct payment of HB to you.[193]

Information a decision notice should contain

The local authority must include a minimum amount of information in its decision notice and may also include other relevant information.[194] If the decision is one against which you have a right of appeal (see p1158), you must be informed of:[195]

- your right to appeal against the decision; *and*
- your right to a written statement of reasons for the decision (if this is not already included – see p1121).

Other information that must be provided varies with the particular circumstances of your case. In any local authority decision, you should be informed of (where relevant):[196]

- the normal weekly amount of HB to which you are entitled, including the amount and category of any non-dependant deductions and of any notional fuel deductions. You must be told why fuel deductions have been made, and that they can be varied if you provide evidence of the actual amount involved;
- your weekly eligible rent (see p260);
- if you are a private tenant, the day your HB will be paid and whether payment will be made weekly or monthly;
- the date on which your entitlement starts;
- if you are not on IS, income-based JSA, income-related ESA or PC, or you are on PC but are only entitled to the savings credit, how your applicable amount is calculated;
- if you are not on IS, income-based JSA, income-related ESA or PC, how your income has been assessed;
- if you are on PC but are only entitled to the savings credit:
  - the amount of the savings credit taken into account;

  - the amount of income and capital notified to the local authority by the DWP which has been taken into account. The local authority must also tell you about any modifications it makes to your income or capital;
  - the amount of capital the local authority has taken into account, if the DWP notified the local authority that your capital was less than £16,000 but it has increased to more than that figure while an assessed income period was in force (see p520);
- if your level of HB is less than the minimum amount payable, that this is the reason why you have no entitlement;
- if your claim was successful, your duty to notify the local authority of any change in circumstances which might affect your entitlement and what kinds of changes should be reported;
- if your claim was unsuccessful, a statement explaining exactly why you are not entitled;
- if it has been decided to pay your HB directly to your landlord, information saying how much is to be paid to your landlord and when payments will start, and also that where recovery of an overpayment is made from a landlord (see p1089) and recovery is made from a tenant other than the one who was overpaid, that tenant is treated as if the full payment of HB had been made;[197]
- if the income and capital of a non-dependant has been used instead of yours to calculate your HB (see p269), additional information saying that this has happened and why.

7. Getting paid

How payment of housing benefit (HB) is made depends on whether you are the tenant of the housing authority responsible for the payment of HB (a local authority), or you are a private or housing association tenant (see below). If you are unable to act for yourself, payment can be made to someone else on your behalf (see p282). In some circumstances, payment can be made to your landlord (see p283).

How often is HB paid?	Normally in arrears at intervals of a week, two weeks, four weeks or a month, depending on when your rent is normally due. It can also be paid at longer intervals if you agree.[198]

Different rules apply if HB is paid directly to your landlord.[199] If your rent allowance is less than £1 a week, the local authority can choose to pay your benefit up to six months in arrears.[200]

You can insist on two-weekly payments if your rent allowance is more than £2 a week unless HB is paid directly to your landlord.[201]

The local authority can pay your rent allowance weekly either to avoid an overpayment or where you are liable to pay rent weekly and it is in your interests for HB to be paid weekly.[202]

No HB is payable if the amount would be less than 50 pence a week.[203]

Note:

- Your HB might be paid at a reduced rate if you have been sanctioned for benefit offences (see p1106).
- If payment of your HB is delayed, see p289. You might be able to get a payment on account (see p289). If you wish to complain about how your claim has been dealt with, see p1258. You might be able to claim compensation (see p1261).
- If payment of your HB is suspended, see p1043.
- If you are overpaid HB, you might have to repay it (see Chapter 43). If you have been accused of fraud, see Chapter 44.

How your benefit is paid

If **your landlord is the housing authority** responsible for the payment of HB, your HB is paid in the form of a reduction in your rent. This is called a rent rebate.[204] **Note:** if you live in a pilot area, from June 2012, your local authority may decide to pay your HB direct to you. See CPAG's *Welfare Rights Bulletin* for updates.

If **you are a private or housing association tenant**, you receive HB in the form of a rent allowance.[205] If you live in a caravan, mobile home or houseboat, this applies even if you are also liable to make payments to a local authority – eg, for site or mooring fees. HB is normally paid to you in the form of a cheque although, in some cases, it may be paid directly to your landlord or to someone acting on your behalf (see below).

The local authority has the discretion to pay you by whatever method it chooses but, in doing so, it must have regard to your 'reasonable needs and convenience'.[206] It should not insist on payment into a bank account if you do not have one (but it may encourage you to open one), nor should it make you collect it if it is difficult to reach the office by public transport.[207] If it does, you can complain to your local councillor. If that has no effect, ask your MP to take up the matter (see p1259) and also complain to the Ombudsman (see p1261).

If the local authority refuses to replace a payment which has never arrived, you could threaten to sue in the county court (sheriff court in Scotland).

Payment to someone acting on your behalf

If an appointee or some other person legally empowered to act for a claimant has claimed HB on her/his behalf, that person can also receive the payments.[208]

If you are able to claim HB for yourself, you can still nominate an agent to receive or collect it for you. To do this you must make a written request to the local authority. Anyone you nominate must be aged 18 or over.[209]

If a claimant dies, any unpaid HB may be paid to her/his personal representative or, where there is none, to her/his next of kin aged 16 or over.[210] For payment to be made, a written application must be received by the local authority within 12 months of the claimant's death. The local authority may allow longer. If HB was being paid to the landlord prior to the claimant's death, the local authority can pay any outstanding HB to clear remaining rent due.

Payment direct to a landlord

Your HB can be paid directly to your landlord (or the person to whom you pay rent) but only in specific circumstances. Your landlord could contact the local authority about this.[211] The local authority can suspend payment of your HB while it makes enquiries as to who should be paid your HB.[212] If the local authority is suspicious of your landlord, see p284.

If you have just claimed HB or the local authority has done a supersession of your award, and the local authority thinks you have not already paid your rent and that it would be in the interests of the 'efficient administration' of HB, it can make the first payment to your landlord.[213]

Both you and your landlord should be notified if HB is to be paid to your landlord. If it is *not* in your interests to have HB paid directly to your landlord, it is worth trying to persuade the local authority to withhold it rather than paying it to your landlord. *Always* consider seeking advice before you do so.

When payment must be made to your landlord

The local authority *must* pay your HB, including payments on account (see p289),[214] directly to your landlord (or the person to whom you pay rent) if:

- you or your partner are on income support (IS), jobseeker's allowance (JSA), employment and support allowance (ESA) or pension credit (PC) and the DWP has decided to pay part of that benefit to your landlord for arrears (see p1052);[215] *or*
- you have rent arrears equivalent to eight weeks' rent or more, unless the local authority considers it to be in your overriding interest not to make direct payments.[216] Once your arrears have been reduced to less than eight weeks' rent, compulsory direct payments stop. The local authority may then choose to continue direct payments on a discretionary basis (see p284).

Note: if the local housing allowance rules apply to you (see p309), the maximum the local authority can pay to your landlord is the amount of rent and arrears of rent you are liable to pay, even if the amount of HB to which you are entitled is higher than your rent liability.[217]

Payment to your landlord on a discretionary basis

Unless the local housing allowance rules apply to you (see p309), the local authority may pay your HB directly to your landlord (or the person to whom you pay rent):[218]

- if you have requested or agreed to direct payments; *or*
- without your agreement, if it decides that direct payments are in the best interests of you and your family.

If the local housing allowance rules apply to you (see p309), the local authority may pay your HB directly to your landlord (or the person to whom you pay rent) if it:[219]

- thinks you are likely to have difficulty managing your own financial affairs or that it is improbable that you will pay your rent. The local authority can make direct payments (for a maximum of eight weeks) while it considers the situation; *or*
- thinks it will help you to secure or to keep accommodation. **Note:** the government's intention is that this should only apply if the rent is at a level you can afford; *or*
- has already made direct payments during your current award of HB in any of the situations when payments must be made (see above).

If the local housing allowance rules apply to you (see p309), the maximum the local authority can pay to your landlord is the amount of rent and arrears of rent you are liable to pay.[220] This applies even if the amount of HB to which you are entitled is higher than your rent liability.

Whether or not the local housing allowance rules apply to you, the local authority may also pay your HB directly to your landlord (or the person to whom you pay rent) without your agreement if you have left the address for which you were getting HB and there are rent arrears. In this case, direct payments of any unpaid HB due in respect of that accommodation can be made, up to the total of the outstanding arrears.[221]

When the local authority is suspicious about a landlord

If HB is being paid to a landlord, or a request is made for payment to a landlord, and the local authority suspects impropriety on the part of the landlord, it may require the landlord (or her/his agent) to provide information.[222] This must be supplied in typewritten or printed form (or in handwritten or electronic form if the local authority agrees) within four weeks. A further four weeks can be allowed if a written request for an extension of time is made within four weeks of the request for information.[223] The local authority may also refuse to make direct payments where it 'is not satisfied that the landlord is a fit and proper person'.[224]

However, direct payments may be made if:[225]

- the requirements for discretionary direct payments are met; *and*
- the local authority is satisfied that it is in the best interests of you and your family.

If the local authority decides not to make payments to your landlord, it can make payments to you (including sending you a cheque payable to the landlord) or to a trusted third party, such as a social worker or solicitor.[226]

When your entitlement starts

Your entitlement to HB starts:[227]
- if you became liable for rent in the first of the weeks for which you are claiming, from the Monday of that week. This includes where you become liable for daily payments in a hostel or accommodation provided by the local authority on a short-term lease or because you are homeless; *or*
- in all other cases, from the Monday following your date of claim, or following the date from which you are claiming if your claim is backdated (see pp275 and 277).

A benefit week is a period of seven days running from Monday to Sunday.[228] This means that if you claim HB in the same week in which your liability for rent begins or you became liable for rent in the first of the weeks in respect of which you are claiming, your HB starts on the same day your liability actually begins.[229]

Continuing payments

There are two situations when your HB can continue to be paid at the same rate, even though your entitlement might otherwise have changed. If you stop claiming:
- IS, income-based JSA or income-related ESA because you or your partner are moving onto PC, you may be able to continue to receive HB at the same rate for four weeks (see below);
- IS, income-based JSA, income-related or contributory ESA, incapacity benefit (IB) or severe disablement allowance (SDA) because you or your partner start work, or increase your hours or earnings, you may be entitled to extended payments of HB (see p286).

Note: the council tax benefit (CTB) rules for continuing payments are broadly the same as those for HB. See pp130-131 for the differences.

Continuing payments on claiming pension credit

To avoid problems caused by delays in reassessing your HB when you move from IS, income-based JSA or income-related ESA onto PC, providing you otherwise continue to qualify for HB, you continue to receive it at the same rate as before this happened (but see below). You qualify for continuing payments if:[230]

- your partner has claimed PC and the DWP has certified this; *or*
- your IS, income-based JSA or income-related ESA ceased because you reached the qualifying age for PC (see p509) or, if you were getting income-based JSA or income-related ESA beyond that age, this ceased because you turned 65. The DWP must certify this and that you are required to claim or have claimed PC (or are treated as having done so).

You get continuing payments for:[231]

- a period of four weeks from the day after your IS, income-based JSA or income-related ESA ceases; *or*
- if the four-week period ends before the last day of a benefit week, until the end of the benefit week in which the end of the four-week period falls.

Your maximum HB (see p258) is recalculated if your rent increases or there is a change in the non-dependant deductions (see p265) that should be made.[232]

Extended payments of housing benefit

If you (or your partner) are on IS, income-based JSA, income-related or contributory ESA, IB or SDA and your entitlement ends because you (or your partner) start work or increase your hours or pay in your current job, you may be entitled to continue to receive the same amount of HB as you did before your entitlement ended. These extended payments of HB are paid for up to four weeks. You may also be entitled to extended payments of CTB. You do not have to make a fresh claim for HB (but see p288).

Note: you can apply for a revision or supersession of an extended payments decision or appeal against it (see Chapters 45 and 46).

Who can claim extended payments

You qualify for extended payments of HB if you are getting HB and:

- you or your partner:[233]
  - were entitled to IS, income-based JSA or income-related ESA and your entitlement ended because you or your partner started work (including self-employed work) or increased your earnings from, or hours of, work. However, you cannot qualify if, immediately before your entitlement to IS ended, you were getting mortgage interest run-on (see p879); *and*
  - had been continuously entitled to, and in receipt of, either IS, contribution-based or income-based JSA or income-related ESA or a combination of these for at least 26 weeks. This includes periods of less than five weeks when you (or your partner) counted as in full-time paid work (see p718) because you (or s/he) were on an Employment Zone programme; *or*
- unless you are getting PC, you or your partner:[234]

- were *not* entitled to or in receipt of IS, income-based JSA, or income-related ESA; *and*
- were entitled to and in receipt of contributory ESA, IB or SDA and your entitlement ended because you or your partner started work (including self-employed work) or increased your earnings from, or hours of, work; *and*
- had been continuously entitled to, and in receipt of, contributory ESA, IB or SDA or a combination of these for at least 26 weeks.

The rules do not say that the DWP must certify that you satisfy the above conditions. However, the local authority needs to be satisfied that you were entitled to and in receipt of IS, income-based JSA, ESA, IB or SDA.

The end of your entitlement to IS, income-based JSA, ESA, IB or SDA is a change in your circumstances that you must report to the local authority (see p290). Bear the following in mind.

- Although a failure to report this change does not affect your entitlement to extended payments of HB and CTB, this could result in an overpayment of HB and CTB at the end of the extended payment period.
- You could be entitled to a higher rate of HB and CTB than you were before your entitlement to IS, income-based JSA, ESA, IB or SDA ended. Report the change as soon as possible so it can be taken into account.
- If you are claiming IS, JSA, ESA, IB or SDA and you start work or your hours or pay change, you must notify the DWP of the change to avoid an overpayment of those benefits.

If you move home, you can still qualify for extended payments of HB, so long as the day you moved was in the same week, or the week before, you or your partner started work or increased your earnings from, or hours of, work.[235] See below for how the amount of the extended payments can be affected.

Amount of the extended payments and how long they last

Extended payments of HB are paid for four weeks unless:[236]

- any of the weeks count as rent-free periods (see p265); *or*
- your liability to pay rent ceases altogether within the four weeks.

The weekly amount of your extended payments (unless you move into local authority accommodation in a different local authority area – see p288) is the higher of the amount of HB:[237]

- you got in the last (non-rent-free) week before your entitlement to IS, income-based JSA, ESA, IB or SDA ceased; *or*
- to which you would be entitled based on your new circumstances; *or*
- if you are a member of a couple, to which your partner would be entitled if s/he claimed based on her/his circumstances.

Note: report any changes in your circumstances during the four-week period. This is because the weekly amount you get is then the highest of the above amounts.[238]

Example

Jill is a local authority tenant with a non-dependant. Her rent is £97 a week. She was getting HB of £70.75 in the week before her entitlement to IS ceased, because a non-dependant deduction of £26.25 was made. Her weekly HB entitlement based on her circumstances in work is £69.21. Her extended payments are therefore £70.75 a week. In the second week of the four-week period, Jill's non-dependant moves out. Her weekly entitlement based on her circumstances in work is now £95.46 because a non-dependant deduction is no longer made. Her extended payments are now £95.46 for the remainder of the four-week period. This is also Jill's HB entitlement from the end of the period.

You may qualify for extended payments of HB on two homes (see p255). However, if your liability to pay rent for either of these ceases within the four-week period, the amount of your extended payments is reduced by the amount of HB payable for that home.[239]

If you were being paid discretionary housing payments (see p294), ask for these to continue for the extended payment period.

If you **move into local authority accommodation** in a different local authority area, the weekly amount of your extended payments of HB is the amount of HB you got in the last (non-rent-free) week before your entitlement to IS, income-based JSA, ESA, IB or SDA ceased – ie, the amount you got at your old address.[240] The extended payments can be paid to you or to the new local authority landlord. If you or your partner claim HB at your new address, the amount you (or your partner) get is reduced by the weekly amount of the extended payments. The effect of this is that if your new HB entitlement is higher, your extended payments can be 'topped up'.

Note: if you move house in any other circumstances (eg, to private rented or housing association accommodation, or within the same local authority area), your extended payments are worked out under the normal rules (see above). If you also claim HB at your new address, it does not appear that the local authority can reduce the amount of HB you get by the weekly amount of your extended payments.[241] It is not clear if this was the intention.

Claims

You do not have to make a claim for extended payments of HB; they should be made automatically.[242] However, remember to let your local authority know that your (or your partner's) entitlement to IS, income-based JSA, ESA, IB or SDA has ceased.

Ongoing entitlement to housing benefit

Your entitlement to HB continues until at least the end of the extended payment period.[243] Entitlement to HB can continue after that if you qualify under the normal rules, but at the weekly rate based on your new circumstances. You do not have to make a fresh claim. Your HB entitlement will be continuous. This means if you have a form of transitional protection that requires continuous entitlement, your transitional protection continues.

Note:

- Unless you move to local authority accommodation in a different local authority area, if your partner claims HB, this cannot be paid to her/him while you are getting extended payments of HB.[244]
- If you move to local authority accommodation in a different local authority area, and you or your partner claim HB at your new address, the amount you (or your partner) get is reduced by the weekly amount of the extended payments.[245]

Delays and complaints

The local authority must make a decision on your claim, tell you in writing what the decision is, and pay you any HB to which you are entitled within 14 days, or, if that is not reasonably practicable, as soon as possible after that.[246] If you consider a delay is unreasonable, write to the HB manager and threaten to complain to the Ombudsman (see p1261). In serious cases, you may want to seek advice on whether you have grounds for judicial review (see p1202).

Payments on account

If you are a private or housing association tenant and the local authority has not been able to assess your HB within the required period, you should receive a payment on account (sometimes called an interim payment) while your claim is being sorted out.[247] The local authority should automatically do this. You do not have to request a payment on account.[248] Bear the following in mind.

- Payments on account are not discretionary. The local authority *must* pay you an amount which it considers reasonable, given what it knows about your circumstances.
- Payments on account can only be refused if it is clear that you will not be entitled to HB or the reason for the delay is that you have been asked for information or evidence in support of your claim and you have failed, without good cause, to provide it (see p275).[249] If the delay has been caused by a third party (eg, the rent officer, your bank or employer), this does not affect your right to a payment on account.
- The local authority must notify you of the amount of a payment on account and that it can recover any overpayment which occurs if your actual HB entitlement is different from the payment.[250]

- If your payment on account is less than your actual entitlement, your future HB can be adjusted to take account of the underpayment.[251]
- If the local authority has not made a payment on account, complain. You could also complain to the Ombudsman.

Change of circumstances

It is your duty to report any change in your circumstances which you might reasonably be expected to know might affect your right to, the amount of, or payment of, your HB.[252] You should do this promptly to the office handling your claim. You can do this in writing, although in individual cases notification might be accepted in a form other than in writing. In addition, you can report a change by telephone if your local authority has published a telephone number for this purpose or allows you to claim HB by telephone (see p270) (unless it says you must report it in writing). If your local authority authorises it, you can report changes electronically – eg, by email.[253] However, it is always best to report a change in writing and keep a copy in case of a dispute in the future.

There are exceptions to this rule.

- You may report a change in your circumstances to the DWP, instead of the local authority, if the DWP has provided a telephone number for this purpose, and:[254]
  - you or your partner are getting IS or JSA; *and*
  - the change of circumstance is that you or your partner have started work; *and*
  - as a result of the change, entitlement to IS or JSA will end or, if you or your partner are getting contribution-based JSA, the amount will reduce.
- If the change is a birth or a death, there is a special rule (sometimes called 'Tell Us Once'). You can report such a change in person at a local authority (and, in England, a county council) office, if such an office has been specified for reporting these changes.[255] If the change is a death, you can notify it to the DWP by electronic communication, or by telephone if a number has been specified for that purpose. Check with your local authority (eg, at the registrar's office) to see if it provides this service.

If you do not report a change promptly, any resulting overpayment may be recoverable from you (see Chapter 43). If you are considered to have acted knowingly or dishonestly, you may also be guilty of an offence (see Chapter 44). Remember:

- the local authority must tell you in writing about the changes you have to report;[256]
- it is important to report changes to the right department. Your duty to notify changes is to the HB department, not to the local authority as a whole;[257]

- if your benefit is paid to someone else on your behalf, the duty to report any relevant changes also extends to her/him.[258]

If in doubt, always report changes in circumstances. If you think that the local authority might not have taken a change into account, you should check with it.

Note: the CTB rules for change of circumstances are broadly the same as those for HB. See pp131-132 for the differences.

If you do not get pension credit

If you do not get PC, you must report:[259]

- any change to your rent, unless you are a local authority tenant;
- entitlement to IS, income-based JSA or income-related ESA ending. Do not assume that the DWP does this on your behalf;
- any change that results in a child or young person no longer counting as a member of your family for HB purposes (see p759).

You must also report other changes that you 'might reasonably be expected to know' could affect your HB, such as changes to:

- your family income or capital if you do not get IS, income-based JSA or income-related ESA;
- the number of boarders or sub-tenants you have or the payments made by them;
- the number or circumstances of any non-dependants that may affect the level of deductions made to your benefit (see p265);
- any absence from your home which is, or is likely to be, for more than 13 weeks;
- your status – eg, marriage, civil partnership, cohabitation, separation or divorce.

If you get pension credit

If you get PC, you must report:[260]

- any change to your tenancy, apart from changes in your rent if you are a local authority tenant;
- any changes affecting a non-dependant normally living with you or with whom you normally live;
- any absence from your home which is, or is likely to be, for more than 13 weeks.

If you are only getting the savings credit of PC, you must also report:[261]

- changes affecting a child who lives with you that could affect how much HB you get. You need not report changes in the child's age;
- any changes to your capital that do or could take it above £16,000;

- any change in the income or capital of a non-dependant of yours, if your HB has been assessed on the basis of this instead of your own (see p269), and whether s/he has stopped or resumed living with you;
- any change in the income or capital of your partner that has not been taken into account since the determination of your PC award, and whether your partner has stopped or resumed living with you.

If you are on PC, these are the only changes you have to report to the local authority.[262] Other relevant changes in your circumstances should be passed on to the local authority by the DWP.

Other changes

There may be other changes which the local authority requires you to report, depending on the particular circumstances of your case. The need to report these additional changes must be drawn to your attention at the time you claim and also if you are asked for further information.[263] This is important because you only have a duty to report changes that you 'might reasonably be expected to know' could affect your HB.[264]

You do not have to report:[265]

- any changes in your rent if you are a local authority tenant;
- changes in the ages of members of your family, or of non-dependants, unless the change results in a child or young person ceasing to count as a member of your family for benefit purposes.[266]

When changes in circumstances take effect

If you claim HB and then report a change in circumstances before the local authority has assessed your claim, your application is assessed on the basis of the revised information you have provided.

If a change of circumstances takes place once benefit has been awarded, the local authority must establish the date on which that change occurred.[267]

In most cases, a change takes effect from the start of the benefit week after the one in which the change occurred.[268] This applies whether or not a decision is advantageous to you. This means that, on whatever day of the week the change actually occurs, the change is implemented as from the following Monday. However, if you are liable to pay rent on a daily basis (eg, in a hostel), and the change means you are no longer entitled to HB, it takes effect on the day it actually occurs.[269]

Exceptions to the rule

There are a number of exceptions to the general rule described above. These include if:

- the change is one you are required to notify to the local authority (other than one relating to your having to take part in a work-focused interview or, if you are on PC, one of the additional exceptions to the rules described below), it is advantageous to you and you fail to notify the change within the one-month time limit (or any longer period allowed by the local authority – see p1143). In this case, the date of notification is treated as if that is the date the change occurred;

- a payment of income (or arrears of income) for a past period, other than benefit or arrears of benefit, is taken into account from the date it would have been taken into account had it been paid to you on time.[270] Note that arrears of some benefits, working tax credit, child tax credit and discretionary housing payments count as capital and can be disregarded for a period after they are paid (see pp982 and 1001);
- you or your partner are at least 65 and either a non-dependant comes to live with you, or there is a change in respect of a non-dependant so that a higher non-dependant deduction should be made.[271] The effect of this can be delayed for 26 weeks. This does not apply if you or your partner are getting IS, income-based JSA or income-related ESA.

Note: there are other exceptions. These include if there is a change in your rent, if you move to a new home or if you become (or cease to be) entitled to HB for more than one home.[272] In addition, there are exceptions if you or your partner become entitled to ESA which includes a work-related or support component.[273]

There are additional exceptions to the rules described above **if you are on PC** and the amount of this changes because of a change in your circumstances or the correction of an official error (see p1130), and this means there is a change in the amount of HB you can be paid. This includes where you are only getting the savings credit of PC and the change is as a result of a change in the DWP assessment of your income or savings.[274]

Special rules apply if two or more changes occurring in the same benefit week would normally take effect in different benefit weeks.[275]

8. **Tax, tax credits and other benefits**

Housing benefit (HB) is not taxable.

Tax credits

Working tax credit (WTC) counts as income when working out your HB. So does child tax credit, unless you are at least the qualifying age for pension credit (PC – see p509) and neither you nor your partner are on income support (IS), income-based jobseeker's allowance (JSA) or income-related employment and support allowance (ESA).

Means-tested benefits

If you pay council tax, you may be able to claim council tax benefit (CTB) as well as HB. Entitlement to IS, income-based JSA, income-related ESA or the guarantee credit of PC acts as an automatic passport to maximum HB (see p259) because all of your income and capital are ignored.

Non-means-tested benefits

Most non-means-tested benefits are taken into account as income when working out the amount of HB you get. Attendance allowance, disability living allowance, guardian's allowance and child benefit are not taken into account. It can still be worth claiming non-means-tested benefits. If you, your partner or your child(ren) qualify for certain of these, you also qualify for certain premiums and components (see Chapter 37) and potentially a higher rate of HB. If you think you might qualify, seek advice to see if you would be better off.

You may only qualify for HB once you or a member of your family are awarded another benefit (known as a 'qualifying benefit'). You may be entitled to a higher rate of HB once the qualifying benefit is awarded (see p277).

Passports and other sources of help

If you have been awarded HB, you may qualify for a social fund funeral expenses payment (see Chapter 26).

Financial help on starting work

If you stop getting IS, income-based JSA, income-related or contributory ESA, incapacity benefit or severe disablement allowance because you or your partner start work or your hours or earnings in your existing job increase, you may be entitled to extended payments of HB or CTB. You might also be able to get mortgage interest run-on (if you have a home loan – see p879). See p13 for information about other financial help you might get.

9. Discretionary housing payments

Discretionary housing payments are extra payments that can be made by your local authority to help meet your rent or council tax liability. They do not count as housing benefit (HB) or council tax benefit (CTB).

Note:

- You do not have a 'right' to discretionary housing payments. They are paid from a cash-limited budget allocated to your local authority by the government.

- You do not have a right of appeal to the First-tier Tribunal against a discretionary housing payment decision. However, you do have the right to ask the local authority for a review of its decision.[276] You are entitled to written notice and reasons for the review decision as soon as is 'reasonably practicable'.[277] You might be able to challenge a review decision by judicial review (see p1202).

Who can claim discretionary housing payments

A local authority can pay you discretionary housing payments if:[278]

- you are entitled to HB or CTB; *and*
- you appear to require some financial assistance in addition to your HB or CTB to meet your housing costs (including council tax, rent in advance, deposits and removal expenses).

Local authorities have discretion on whether to pay you, the amount to pay you (with certain limits) and over what period to pay you.[279]

Payments not met by discretionary housing payments

Discretionary housing payments cannot be made to you if your need for financial assistance arises as a consequence of:[280]

- ineligible service charges under the HB scheme (see p264);
- water and sewerage charges;
- council tax liability if you are entitled to HB but not CTB, or if you are only entitled to the second adult rebate and are not, or would not otherwise have been, entitled to CTB;
- liabilities that can be met by HB if you are entitled to CTB but not HB;
- your rent payments increasing to cover arrears of rent, service charges or other unpaid charges;
- a reduced benefit decision because you refused to co-operate in pursuing maintenance for your child(ren);
- your benefit being reduced because you refused to attend a work-focused interview;
- your jobseeker's allowance (JSA) stopping or being reduced because you failed to attend an interview as required (see p422), failed to participate in certain training or employment schemes (eg, Mandatory Work Activity or the Work Programme) or you left your work voluntarily or you lost your job because of misconduct (see Chapter 20);
- if you are 16 or 17, your severe hardship payments of JSA (see p408) being reduced because you gave up a place on a training scheme or failed to attend without good cause;
- your benefit being suspended;

- a reduction in the amount of your HB or CTB because an overpayment is being recovered;
- your benefit being restricted under the 'loss of benefit for benefit offences' rules (see p1106).

The amount of discretionary housing payments

Discretionary housing payments are normally paid in weekly amounts. It is up to the local authority to decide for how long you can be paid and how far your payments can be backdated.[281] However, the local authority can only pay discretionary housing payments for periods during which you are (or were) entitled to HB or CTB (or both).

You cannot be paid more than:[282]

- in the case of an amount to assist you to meet your council tax liabilities, your weekly council tax liability;
- in the case of an amount to meet payments in respect of your home, other than council tax, an amount to meet your rent and other amounts listed on p247 (payments that can be met by HB) less any amounts paid for ineligible service charges and rent-free periods.

Claims and getting paid

A claim for discretionary housing payments is separate from your claim for HB or CTB. Ask your local authority how to make a claim. The local authority may accept a claim from you, or from someone acting on your behalf, as long as you are entitled to HB or CTB.[283] Your local authority does not have to insist your claim is made in writing, but it decides what 'form or manner' your claim should take.[284] Note the following.

- You must provide grounds for your claim and provide any other information that the local authority specifies.[285] If you want your claim to be backdated, tell the local authority.
- You must be given written notice of the local authority's decision on your claim and the reasons for its decision as soon as is 'reasonably practicable'.[286]
- The local authority can pay you or, if reasonable, someone else where appropriate.[287]
- It is your duty to report any change in your circumstances that may be relevant to payment of your discretionary housing payments continuing.[288]

Tax, tax credits and other benefits

Discretionary housing payments are not taxable.

Discretionary housing payments are disregarded as income and capital for income support, JSA, income-related employment and support allowance, HB, CTB, working tax credit and child tax credit purposes.[289]

Notes

1. **Who can claim housing benefit**

1 s130 SSCBA 1992; s115 IAA 1999; reg 10 HB Regs; reg 10 HB(SPC) Regs
2 Reg 26 HB(SPC) Regs
3 Regs 11(1) and 12(1) HB Regs; regs 11(1) and 12(1) HB(SPC) Regs
4 CH/3110/2003; R(H) 3/07
5 CH/844/2002; R(H) 9/08
6 Reg 2(4)(a) HB Regs; reg 2(4)(a) HB(SPC) Regs
7 *R v Cambridge CC ex parte Thomas,* 10 February 1995 (QBD); CH/2959/2006
8 Reg 12(2) HB Regs; reg 12(2) HB(SPC) Regs
9 Reg 2(1) HB Regs and reg 2(1) HB(SPC) Regs, definition of 'long tenancy' and 'owner'; CH/2258/2004; *Burton v New Forest District Council* [2004] EWCA Civ 1510, reported as R(H) 7/05; R(H) 3/07; CH/3586/2005; R(H) 8/07; *CR v Wycombe District Council* [2009] UKUT 19 (AAC)
10 Reg 11(2) HB Regs
11 Reg 11(4) HB Regs
12 Reg 8(1)(a) and (b) HB Regs; reg 8(1)(a) and (b) HB(SPC) Regs
13 Reg 8(1)(c)-(e) HB Regs; reg 8(1)(c)-(e) HB(SPC) Regs
14 CSHB/606/2005
15 Reg 8(2) HB Regs; reg 8(2) HB(SPC) Regs
16 *R v Rugby BC HBRB ex parte Harrison* [1994] 28 HLR 36 (QBD); CH/2959/2006
17 CH/3579/2003; CH/257/2005
18 R(H) 3/03
19 *R v Poole BC ex parte Ross* [1995] 28 HLR 351 (QBD); *R v Warrington BC ex parte Williams* [1997] 29 HLR 872 (QBD)
20 s134(2) SSCBA 1992; reg 82(1) HB Regs; reg 63(1) HB(SPC) Regs
21 Regs 9, 10 and 56 HB Regs; regs 9 and 10 HB(SPC) Regs
22 *Scott v SSWP* [2011] EWCA Civ 103
23 Reg 9(4) HB Regs; reg 9(4) HB(SPC) Regs; CH/1326/2004; CH/1328/2004
24 CH/542/2006; R(H) 5/06 decided that the rule did not conflict with the Human Rights Act.
25 Reg 3(4) HB Regs; reg 3(4) HB(SPC) Regs; R(H) 5/06; CPC/1446/2008; *RK v SSWP* [2008] UKUT 34 (AAC)
26 *Thamesdown BC v Goonery* [1995] 1 CLY 2600 (CA)
27 R(H) 1/03; CH/1171/2002; CH/2899/2005
28 Reg 9(2) HB Regs; reg 9(2) HB(SPC) Regs; *R v Poole BC ex parte Ross* [1995] 28 HLR 351 (QBD); CH/1076/2002; CH/296/2004; CH/1097/2004; para A3/3.258-65 GM
29 *DH v Kirklees MBC and SSWP (HB)* [2011] UKUT 301 (AAC)
30 *R (Tucker) v Secretary of State* [2001] EWCA Div 1646, unreported (EWCA). The Court decided that the rule did not conflict with the Human Rights Act.
31 para A3/3.269 GM
32 Reg 9(3) HB Regs; reg 9(3) HB(SPC) Regs; *SD v London Borough of Brent* [2009] UKUT 7 (AAC)
33 Reg 9(3) HB Regs; reg 9(3) HB(SPC) Regs
34 Reg 2(1) HB Regs and reg 2(1) HB(SPC) Regs. Both, definition of 'owner' and 'long tenancy'. CH/1278/2002; CH/0296/2003; *MH v Wirral* MBC [2009] UKUT 60 (AAC); *Bradford MDC v MRC (HB)* [2010] UKUT 315 (AAC); *Nottingham CC v CJ (HB)* [2011] UKUT 392 (AAC)
35 CH/3853/2001; CH/396/2002; R(H) 6/07; *KH v Sheffield City Council* [2008] UKUT 11 (AAC)
36 *CH v Wakefield DC* [2009] UKUT 20 (AAC)
37 **HB** Reg 2(1) HB Regs; reg 2(1) HB(SPC) Regs
CTB Reg 2(1) CTB Regs; reg 2(1) CTB(SPC) Regs
38 R(SB) 27/87
39 paras A3/3.243-45 GM
40 *R v Solihull MBC ex parte Simpson* [1995] 1 FLR 140 (CA); CH/39/2007
41 *R (Mackay) v Barking and Dagenham HBRB* [2001] EWHC Admin 234 (HC)
42 CH/2258/2004

43 *R (Mackay) v Barking and Dagenham HBRB* [2001] EWHC Admin 234 (HC)
44 *R v Sutton LBC HBRB ex parte Keegan* [1992] 27 HLR 92 (QBD)
45 *R v Manchester CC ex parte Baragrove Properties Ltd* [1991] 23 HLR 337 (QBD); *R v Gloucestershire CC ex parte Dadds* [1997] 29 HLR 700 (QBD); CH/39/2007
46 *R v Poole BC ex parte Ross* [1995] 28 HLR 351 (QBD)
47 s130(1) SSCBA 1992; reg 7(1) and (2) HB Regs; reg 7(1) and (2) HB(SPC) Regs
48 R(H) 5/09; *Birmingham City Council v IB* [2009] UKUT 116 (AAC)
49 Reg 7(5), (14) and (15)(c) HB Regs; reg 7(5), (14) and (15)(c) HB(SPC) Regs
50 Reg 7(8) HB Regs; reg 7(8) HB(SPC) Regs
51 R(H) 9/05
52 CH/1363/2006; R(H) 4/07; *Bury MBC v DC (HB)* [2011] UKUT 43 (AAC)
53 Reg 7(7) HB Regs; reg 7(7) HB(SPC) Regs; para A3/3.430 GM
54 CH/2201/2002
55 R(H) 9/05
56 **HB** Reg 7(13) HB Regs; reg 7(13) HB(SPC) Regs
CTB Reg 8(2) and (3)(b) CTB Regs; reg 8(2) and (3)(b) CTB(SPC) Regs
57 **HB** Reg 7(16) HB Regs; reg 7(16) HB(SPC) Regs
CTB Reg 8(2), (3)(c) and (4) CTB Regs; reg 8(2), (3)(c) and (4) CTB(SPC) Regs
58 *MR v Bournmouth BC (HB)* [2011] UKUT 284 (AAC)
59 **HB** Reg 7(14) and (15)(b) HB Regs; reg 7(14) and (15)(b) HB(SPC) Regs
CTB Reg 8(5) and (6)(b) CTB Regs; reg 8(5) and (6)(b) CTB(SPC) Regs
Both CSH/499/2006
60 *SSWP v Selby District Council and Bowman* [2006] EWCA Civ 271, reported as R(H) 4/06
61 **HB** Reg 7(11) HB Regs; reg 7(11) HB(SPC) Regs
CTB Reg 8(3)(a) CTB Regs; reg 8(3)(a) CTB(SPC) Regs
62 *Torbay Borough Council v RF* [2010] UKUT 7 (AAC); [2010] AACR 26
63 CH/1237/2004
64 CH/3893/2004
65 *R v Penwith DC ex parte Burt* [1988] 22 HLR 292 (QBD); para A3/3.460 GM
66 **HB** Reg 7(14) and (15)(a) HB Regs; reg 7(14) and (15)(a) HB(SPC) Regs
CTB Reg 8(5) and (6)(a) CTB Regs; reg 8(5) and (6)(a) CTB(SPC) Regs
67 R(H) 8/09; *SK v South Hams DC (HB)* [2010] UKUT 129 (AAC); [2010] AACR 40
68 Reg 7(18) HB Regs; reg 7(18) HB(SPC) Regs
69 R(H) 5/09; *Birmingham City Council v IB* [2009] UKUT 116 (AAC)
70 Reg 7(6)(d) and (e) HB Regs; reg 7(6)(d) and (e) HB(SPC) Regs
71 CH/1911/2006
72 R(H) 4/07
73 Reg 7(6)(a) HB Regs; reg 7(6)(a) HB(SPC) Regs
74 Reg 7(6)(b) and (c) HB Regs; reg 7(6)(b) and (c) HB(SPC) Regs
75 Reg 7(10) HB Regs; reg 7(10) HB(SPC) Regs
76 Reg 7(3) HB Regs; reg 7(3) HB(SPC) Regs
77 Reg 7(4) HB Regs; reg 7(4) HB(SPC) Regs
78 R(SB) 10/81

4. **The amount of benefit**

79 Reg 70 HB Regs; reg 50 HB(SPC) Regs
80 s130(3) SSCBA 1992; Schs 5 para 4 and 6 para 5 HB Regs; reg 26 HB(SPC) Regs; *R v Penwith DC ex parte Menear* [1991] 24 HLR 120 (QBD); *R v South Ribble DC HBRB ex parte Hamilton* [2000] 33 HLR 104 (CA)
81 Reg 2(3) HB Regs; reg 2(3) HB(SPC) Regs
82 Reg 2(3A) HB Regs; reg 2(3A) HB(SPC) Regs
83 Reg 12B(2) HB Regs; reg 12B(2) HB(SPC) Regs
84 Regs 12B(3) and 12C(2) HB Regs; regs 12B(3) and 12C(2) HB(SPC) Regs; reg 12(4) HB Regs and reg 12(4) HB(SPC) Regs as set out in Sch 3 para 5 HB&CTB(CP) Regs
85 Regs 12B(4) and 12C(2) HB Regs; regs 12B(4) and 12C(2) HB(SPC) Regs; reg 12(5) HB Regs and reg 12(5) HB(SPC) Regs as set out in Sch 3 para 5 HB&CTB(CP) Regs; CH/3376/2002
86 *R (Naghshbandi) v Camden LBC* [2002] EWCA Civ 1038, *The Times,* 5 August 2002, unreported (CA)
87 CH/3376/2002

88 Reg 13D(12) HB Regs; reg 13D(12) HB(SPC) Regs
89 Reg 12B(2) HB Regs; reg 12B(2) HB(SPC) Regs; reg 12(3) HB Regs and reg 12(3) HB(SPC) Regs as set out in Sch 3 para 5 HB&CTB(CP) Regs; *R v Bristol City Council ex parte Jacobs* [1999] 32 HLR 82 (QBD)
90 Regs 12B(3) and 12C(2) HB Regs; regs 12B(3) and 12C(2) HB(SPC) Regs; reg 12(4) HB Regs and reg 12(4) HB(SPC) Regs as set out in Sch 3 para 5 HB&CTB(CP) Regs
91 Reg 11(3) HB Regs; reg 11(2) HB(SPC) Regs
92 Sch 1 para 5 HB Regs; Sch 1 para 5 HB(SPC) Regs
93 Sch 1 para 6(1) HB Regs; Sch 1 para 6(1) HB(SPC) Regs
94 Sch 1 para 6(1)(a) HB Regs; Sch 1 para 6(1)(a) HB(SPC) Regs
95 Sch 1 para 6(2) and (3) HB Regs; Sch 1 para 6(2) and (3) HB(SPC) Regs
96 Schs 1 para 6(4) and 9 para 9(b) HB Regs; Schs 1 para 6(4) and 8 para 9(1)(b) HB(SPC) Regs
97 para A4/4.912-913 GM
98 Sch 1 paras 5 and 6(1)(b) HB Regs; Sch 1 paras 5 and 6(1)(b) HB(SPC) Regs
99 Sch 1 para 8 HB Regs; Sch 1 para 8 HB(SPC) Regs. For the meaning of 'sheltered accommodation, see *Oxford City Council v Basey* [2012] EWCA Civ 115.
100 Sch 1 para 8 HB Regs; Sch 1 para 8 HB(SPC) Regs, definition of 'fuel'
101 Reg 12(1)(e) HB Regs; reg 12(1)(e) HB(SPC) Regs
102 Sch 1 para 4 HB Regs; Sch 1 para 4 HB(SPC) Regs
103 para A4/4.730 GM
104 *CP and others v Aylesbury Vale DC v SSWP (HB)* [2011] UKUT 22 (AAC)
105 Sch 1 para 1(a)(iii) HB Regs; Sch 1 para 1(a)(iii) HB(SPC) Regs
106 Sch 1 para 1(a)(ii) HB Regs; Sch 1 para 1(a)(ii) HB(SPC) Regs
107 Sch 1 para 1(b) HB Regs; Sch 1 para 1(b) HB(SPC) Regs
108 Sch 1 para 1(a)(iv) HB Regs; Sch 1 para 1(a)(iv) HB(SPC) Regs
109 Reg 12B(2)(b) and Sch 1 para 1 HB Regs; reg 12B(2)(b) and Sch 1 para 1 HB(SPC) Regs; reg 12(3)(b) HB Regs and reg 12(3)(b) HB(SPC) Regs as set out in Sch 3 para 5 HB&CTB(CP) Regs
110 Reg 12B(2)(c) and Sch 1 para 3(2) HB Regs; reg 12B(2)(c) and Sch 1 para 3(2) HB(SPC) Regs; reg 12(3)(c) HB Regs and reg 12(3)(c) HB(SPC) Regs as set out in Sch 3 para 5 HB&CTB(CP) Regs
111 Sch 1 para 3 HB Regs; Sch 1 para 3 HB(SPC) Regs
112 Sch 1 paras 1(a)(i) and 2(1) HB Regs; Sch 1 paras 1(a)(i) and 2(1) HB(SPC) Regs
113 Sch 1 para 2(6) and (7) HB Regs; Sch 1 para 2(6) and (7) HB(SPC) Regs
114 Reg 2(1) HB Regs; reg 2(1) HB(SPC) Regs
115 Reg 80 HB Regs; reg 61 HB(SPC) Regs
116 Reg 81(3) and Sch 1 para 7(2) HB Regs; reg 62(3) and Sch 1 para 7(2) HB(SPC) Regs
117 **HB** Reg 70 HB Regs; reg 50 HB(SPC) Regs
CTB Reg 57(1) CTB Regs; reg 40(1) CTB(SPC) Regs
118 **HB** Reg 3(1) HB Regs; reg 3(1) HB(SPC) Regs
CTB Reg 3(1) CTB Regs; reg 3(1) CTB(SPC) Regs
119 Reg 3(4) and Sch 1 para 8 HB Regs; reg 3(4) and Sch 1 para 8 HB(SPC) Regs; CPC/1446/2008; *AM v SSWP (IS)* [2011] UKUT 387 (AAC)
120 CSIS/185/1995
121 *Thamesdown BC v Goonery* [1995] ICLY 2600 (CA); *RK v SSWP* [2008] UKUT 34 (AAC)
122 CIS/14850/1996
123 para A5/5.521 GM
124 R(H) 8/09; *SK v South Hams DC (HB)* [2010] UKUT 129 (AAC); [2010] AACR 40
125 **HB** Reg 3(2) HB Regs; reg 3(2) HB(SPC) Regs
CTB Reg 3(2) CTB Regs; reg 3(2) CTB(SPC) Regs
126 *R v Chesterfield BC ex parte Fullwood* [1993] 26 HLR 126 (CA)
127 Reg 3(3) HB Regs; reg 3(3) HB(SPC) Regs
128 **HB** Regs 2(1), definition of 'attendance allowance', and 74(6) HB Regs; regs 2(1), definition of 'attendance allowance', and 55(6) HB(SPC) Regs
CTB Regs 2(1), definition of 'attendance allowance', and 58(6) CTB Regs; regs 2(1), definition of 'attendance allowance', and 42(6) CTB(SPC) Regs

129 **HB** Reg 74(7) and (10) HB Regs; reg 55(7) and (9) HB(SPC) Regs
CTB Reg 58(7) and (8) CTB Regs; reg 42(7) and (8) CTB(SPC) Regs
130 s2 ETA 1973; s2 Enterprise and New Towns (Scotland) Act 1990
131 **HB** Reg 74(1) HB Regs; reg 55(1) HB(SPC) Regs
CTB Reg 58(1) CTB Regs; reg 42(1) CTB(SPC) Regs
132 Regs 2(3) and 74(8) HB Regs; regs 2(3) and 55(8) HB(SPC) Regs
133 Reg 74(1) and (2) HB Regs; reg 55(1) and (2) HB(SPC) Regs
134 Reg 6(6) HB Regs; reg 6(6) HB(SPC) Regs
135 **HB** Reg 74(9) HB Regs; reg 55(10) HB(SPC) Regs
CTB Reg 58(9) CTB Regs; reg 42(9) CTB(SPC) Regs
136 CH/48/2006
137 **HB** Reg 74(3) HB Regs; reg 55(3) HB(SPC) Regs
CTB Reg 58(3) CTB Regs; reg 42(3) CTB(SPC) Regs
138 **HB** Reg 74(4) HB Regs; reg 55(4) HB(SPC) Regs
CTB Reg 58(4) CTB Regs; reg 42(4) CTB(SPC) Regs
139 Reg 74(5) HB Regs; reg 55(5) HB(SPC) Regs
140 **HB** Reg 26 HB Regs; reg 24 HB(SPC) Regs
CTB Reg 16 CTB Regs; reg 14 CTB(SPC) Regs
141 **HB** s134(8) and (14) SSAA 1992
CTB s139(6) and (11) SSAA 1992
Both Sch Housing Benefit and Council Tax Benefit (War Pension Disregards) Regulations 2007, No.1619

6. **Claims and backdating**

142 **HB** Reg 83(1) and (9) HB Regs; reg 64(2) and (10) HB(SPC) Regs
CTB Reg 69(1) and (9) CTB Regs; reg 53(1) and (9) CTB(SPC) Regs
143 **HB** Reg 83(4A) and (4B) HB Regs; reg 64(5A) and (5C) HB(SPC) Regs
CTB Reg 69(4A) and (4B) CTB Regs; reg 53(4A) and (4C) CTB(SPC) Regs
144 **HB** Reg 83A and Sch 11 HB Regs; reg 64A and Sch 10 HB(SPC) Regs
CTB Reg 69A and Sch 9 CTB Regs; reg 53A and Sch 8 CTB(SPC) Regs
145 **HB** Reg 83(2) HB Regs; reg 64(3) HB(SPC) Regs
CTB Reg 69(2) CTB Regs; reg 53(2) CTB(SPC) Regs
146 **HB** Reg 83(4AA) and (4AB) HB Regs; reg 64(5B) and (5BA) HB(SPC) Regs
CTB Reg 69(4AA) and (4AB) CTB Regs; reg 53(4B) and (4BA) CTB(SPC) Regs
147 **HB** Reg 83(4BA) HB Regs; reg 64(5CA) HB(SPC) Regs
CTB Reg 69(4BA) CTB Regs; reg 53(4CA) CTB(SPC) Regs
148 **HB** Reg 83(4AC)-(4AE) HB Regs; reg 64(5BB)-(5BD) HB(SPC) Regs
CTB Reg 69(4AC)-(4AE) CTB Regs; reg 53(4BB) and (4BD) CTB(SPC) Regs
149 Explanatory memorandum to SI 2008 No.299
150 **HB** Reg 83(1), (4C), (6) and (9) HB Regs; reg 64(2), (5D), (7) and (10) HB(SPC) Regs
CTB Reg 69(1), (4C), (6) and (9) CTB Regs; reg 53(1), (4D), (6) and (9) CTB(SPC) Regs
151 **HB** Reg 83(4D), (4DA), (7) and (7A) HB Regs; reg 64(5E), (5EA), (8) and (8A) HB(SPC) Regs
CTB Reg 69(4D), (4DA), (7) and (7A) CTB Regs; reg 53(4E), (4EA), (7) and (7A) CTB(SPC) Regs
152 **HB** Reg 83(4E), (4F), (8) and (8A) HB Regs; reg 64(5F), (5G), (9) and (9A) HB(SPC) Regs
CTB Reg 69(4E), (4F), (8) and (8A) CTB Regs; reg 53(4F), (4G), (8) and (8A) CTB(SPC) Regs
153 **HB** Reg 87 HB Regs; reg 68 HB(SPC) Regs
CTB Reg 73 CTB Regs; reg 58 CTB(SPC) Regs
154 paras A2/2.560-65 GM; HB/CTB A28/2008; HB/CTB G6/2009
155 **HB** Reg 83(4)(b) HB Regs; reg 64(5)(b) HB(SPC) Regs
CTB Reg 69(4)(b) CTB Regs; reg 53(4)(b) CTB(SPC) Regs
156 **HB** Regs 2, definition of 'appropriate DWP office', and 83(4)(a) and (d)-(f) and (13) HB Regs; regs 2, definition of 'appropriate DWP office', and 64(5)(a) and (d)-(f) and (14) HB(SPC) Regs
CTB Regs 2, definition of 'appropriate DWP office', and 69(4)(a) and (d)-(f) and (15) CTB Regs; regs 2, definition of 'appropriate DWP office', and 53(4)(a) and (d)-(f) and (15) CTB(SPC) Regs

157 **HB** Reg 83(4)(c) HB Regs; reg 64(5)(c) HB(SPC) Regs
CTB Reg 69(4)(c) CTB Regs; reg 53(4)(c) CTB(SPC) Regs
158 **HB** Reg 83(4)(g) HB Regs; reg 64(5)(g) HB(SPC) Regs
CTB Reg 69(4)(g) CTB Regs; reg 53(4)(g) CTB(SPC) Regs
159 **HB** Reg 83A and Sch 11 HB Regs; reg 64A and Sch 10 HB(SPC) Regs
CTB Reg 69A and Sch 9 CTB Regs; reg 53A and Sch 8 CTB(SPC) Regs
160 **HB** Reg 83(4A) and (4AA) HB Regs; reg 64(5A) and (5B) HB(SPC) Regs
CTB Reg 69(4A) and (4AA) CTB Regs; reg 53(4A) and (4B) CTB(SPC) Regs
161 **HB** Reg 82(1) HB Regs; reg 63(1) HB(SPC) Regs
CTB Reg 68(1) CTB Regs; reg 52(1) CTB(SPC) Regs
Both CH/2995/2006
162 **HB** Reg 82(2) HB Regs; reg 63(2) HB(SPC) Regs
CTB Reg 68(2) CTB Regs; reg 52(2) CTB(SPC) Regs
163 **HB** Reg 82(3) and (5) HB Regs; reg 63(3) and (5) HB(SPC) Regs
CTB Reg 68(3) and (5) CTB Regs; reg 52(3) and (5) CTB(SPC) Regs
164 **HB** Reg 82(6) HB Regs; reg 63(6) HB(SPC) Regs
CTB Reg 68(6) CTB Regs; reg 52(6) CTB(SPC) Regs
165 **HB** Reg 82(4) HB Regs; reg 63(4) HB(SPC) Regs
CTB Reg 68(4) CTB Regs; reg 52(4) CTB(SPC) Regs
166 **HB** Reg 82(4)(c) HB Regs; reg 63(4)(c) HB(SPC) Regs
CTB Reg 68(4)(c) CTB Regs; reg 52(4)(c) CTB(SPC) Regs
167 **HB** Reg 86(1) HB Regs; reg 67(1) HB(SPC) Regs
CTB Reg 72(1) CTB Regs; reg 57(1) CTB(SPC) Regs
168 **HB** Reg 86(1A) HB Regs; reg 67(1A) HB(SPC) Regs
CTB Reg 72(1A) CTB Regs; reg 57(1A) CTB(SPC) Regs
169 para A1/1.300 GM
170 *AA v LB Hounslow* [2008] UKUT 13 (AAC)
171 **HB** Regs 83(5)(d) and (e) and 85(1) HB Regs; regs 64(6)(d) and (e) and 66(1) HB(SPC) Regs
CTB Regs 69(5)(d) and (e) and 71(1) CTB Regs; regs 53(5)(d) and (e) and 55(1) CTB(SPC) Regs
172 **HB** Reg 83(5)(a)-(c) HB Regs; reg 64(6)(a)-(c) HB(SPC) Regs
CTB Reg 69(5)(a)-(c) CTB Regs; reg 53(5)(a)-(c) CTB(SPC) Regs
173 *Leicester CC v LG* [2009] UKUT 155 (AAC)
174 **HB** Reg 83(10) and (11) HB Regs; reg 64(11) and (12) HB(SPC) Regs
CTB Reg 69(12) and (13) CTB Regs; reg 53(12) and (12A) CTB(SPC) Regs
175 CG/1479/1999; CIS/217/1999
176 **HB** Reg 64(1) HB(SPC) Regs
CTB Reg 53(1ZA) CTB(SPC) Regs
177 **HB** Regs 57 and 64(1), (1A) and (6) HB(SPC) Regs
CTB Regs 48 and 53(1ZA), (1ZB) and (5) CTB(SPC) Regs
Both *Leicester CC v LG* [2009] UKUT 155 (AAC)
178 **HB** Reg 83(12) HB Regs
CTB Reg 69(14) CTB Regs
179 **HB** Reg 83(12A) HB Regs
CTB Reg 69(14A) CTB Regs
180 R(S) 2/63 (T); CH/2659/2002; CH/474/2002; CH/393/2003; A2/Annex A GM
181 *UH v LB Islington (HB)* [2010] UKUT 64 (AAC)
182 CH/393/2003
183 CH/474/2002
184 R(SB) 6/83; CS/50/1950; R(U) 9/74; CI/146/1991; CI/142/1993; FC/39/1993; *R v Canterbury CC ex parte Goodman*, 11 July 1995, unreported (QBD)
185 R(U) 5/56; R(S) 5/56
186 CI/37/1995
187 R(P) 2/85
188 R(S) 10/59; R(SB) 17/83
189 R(G) 1/75
190 Reg 90 HB Regs; reg 71 HB(SPC) Regs; reg 10 HB&CTB(DA) Regs
191 Reg 90(2) HB Regs; reg 71(2) HB(SPC) Regs; reg 10 HB&CTB(DA) Regs
192 Reg 3 HB&CTB(DA) Regs
193 CH/180/2006
194 **HB** Reg 90 and Sch 9 HB Regs; reg 71 and Sch 8 HB(SPC) Regs
CTB Reg 76 and Sch 8 CTB Regs; reg 61 and Sch 7 CTB(SPC) Regs
195 Reg 10(1) HB&CTB(DA) Regs

196 **HB** Sch 9 paras 9-15 HB Regs; Sch 8 paras 9-15 HB(SPC) Regs
CTB Sch 8 paras 9-16 CTB Regs; Sch 7 paras 9-16 CTB(SPC) Regs
197 Sch 9 paras 11 and 12 HB Regs; Sch 8 paras 11 and 12 HB(SPC) Regs

7. **Getting paid**
198 Reg 92(1) and (6) HB Regs; reg 73(1) and (6) HB(SPC) Regs
199 Reg 92(3) and (4) HB Regs; reg 73(3) and (4) HB(SPC) Regs
200 Reg 91(2) HB Regs; reg 72(2) HB(SPC) Regs
201 Reg 92(5) HB Regs; reg 73(5) HB(SPC) Regs
202 Reg 92(6) HB Regs; reg 73(6) HB(SPC) Regs
203 Reg 75 HB Regs; reg 56 HB(SPC) Regs
204 s134(1A) SSAA 1992
205 s134(1B) SSAA 1992; regs 91A and 94(1) HB Regs; regs 72A and 75(1) HB(SPC) Regs
206 Reg 91(1)(b) HB Regs; reg 72(1)(b) HB(SPC) Regs
207 para A6/6.120 GM
208 **HB** Reg 94(2) HB Regs; reg 75(2) HB(SPC) Regs
CTB Reg 78(2) CTB Regs; reg 63(2) CTB(SPC) Regs
209 Reg 94(3) HB Regs; reg 75(3) HB(SPC) Regs
210 **HB** Reg 97 HB Regs; reg 78 HB(SPC) Regs
CTB Reg 80 CTB Regs; reg 65 CTB(SPC) Regs
211 *R v Haringey LBC ex parte Azad Ayub* [1992] 25 HLR 566 (QBD)
212 R(H) 1/08
213 Reg 96(2) HB Regs; reg 77(2) HB(SPC) Regs
214 *R v Haringey LBC ex parte Azad Ayub* [1992] 25 HLR 566 (QBD)
215 Reg 95(1)(a) HB Regs; reg 76(1)(a) HB(SPC) Regs; Sch 9 SS(C&P) Regs
216 Reg 95(1)(b) HB Regs; reg 76(1)(b) HB(SPC) Regs
217 Reg 95(2A) HB Regs; reg 76(2A) HB(SPC) Regs
218 Reg 96(1)(a) and (b) and (3A)(a) HB Regs; reg 77(1)(a) and (b) and (3A)(a) HB(SPC) Regs
219 Reg 96(3A)(b) HB Regs; reg 77(3A)(b) HB(SPC) Regs
220 Reg 95(2A) HB Regs; reg 76(2A) HB(SPC) Regs
221 Regs 95(2A) and 96(1)(c) HB Regs; regs 76(2A) and 77(1)(c) HB(SPC) Regs
222 s126A SSAA 1992; regs 118 and 119 HB Regs; regs 99 and 100 HB(SPC) Regs
223 Reg 120 HB Regs; reg 101 HB(SPC) Regs
224 Regs 95(3) and 96(3) HB Regs; regs 76(3) and 77(3) HB(SPC) Regs
225 Reg 96(3) HB Regs; reg 77(3) HB(SPC) Regs
226 para A6/6.212 GM
227 Reg 76 HB Regs; reg 57 HB(SPC) Regs; R(H) 7/07
228 **HB** Reg 2(1) HB Regs; reg 2(1) HB(SPC) Regs
CTB Reg 2(1) CTB Regs; reg 2(1) CTB(SPC) Regs
229 Reg 80(2), (3)(a), (4) and (8) HB Regs; reg 61(2), (3)(a), (4) and (8) HB(SPC) Regs
230 **HB** Reg 54(1) and (2) HB(SPC) Regs
CTB Reg 45(1) and (2) CTB(SPC) Regs
231 **HB** Reg 54(3)-(5) HB(SPC) Regs
CTB Reg 45(3)-(5) CTB(SPC) Regs
232 **HB** Reg 54(6) HB(SPC) Regs
CTB Reg 45(6) CTB(SPC) Regs
233 **HB** Reg 72 HB Regs
CTB Reg 60 CTB Regs
234 **HB** Reg 73 HB Regs; reg 53 HB(SPC) Regs
CTB Reg 61 CTB Regs; reg 44 CTB(SPC) Regs
235 **HB** Regs 72(4) and 73(2) HB Regs; reg 53(2) HB(SPC) Regs
CTB Regs 60(4) and 61(2) CTB Regs; reg 44(2) CTB(SPC) Regs
Both CH/1762/2004
236 Regs 72A, 72B(6), 73A and 73B(6) HB Regs; regs 53A and 53B(6) HB(SPC) Regs
237 Regs 72B and 73B HB Regs; regs 52 and 53B HB(SPC) Regs
238 **HB** Regs 72D(2) and 73D(2) HB Regs; regs 52 and 53D(2) HB(SPC) Regs
CTB Regs 60D(2) and 61D(2) CTB Regs; regs 41 and 44D(2) CTB(SPC) Regs
239 Regs 72B(5) and 73B(5) HB Regs; reg 53B(5) HB(SPC) Regs
240 **HB** Regs 72C and 73C HB Regs; regs 52 and 53C HB(SPC) Regs
CTB Regs 60C and 61C CTB Regs; regs 41 and 44C CTB Regs

241 s34(3) WRA 2007; reg 2(1) HB Regs and reg 2(1) HB(SPC) Regs, definitions of 'mover' and 'second authority'
242 s324 WRA 2007
243 **HB** Regs 72D and 73D HB Regs; reg 53D HB(SPC) Regs
CTB Regs 60D and 61D CTB Regs; reg 44D CTB(SPC) Regs
Both s32(1), (2) and (13) WRA 2007
244 **HB** Regs 72B(7) and 73B(7) HB Regs; regs 52(3) and 53B(7) HB(SPC) Regs
CTB Regs 60B(3) and 61B(3) CTB Regs; regs 41(3) and 44B(3) CTB(SPC) Regs
245 **HB** Regs 72C(4) and 73C(4) HB Regs; regs 52(3) and 53C(4) HB(SPC) Regs
CTB Regs 60C(3) and 61C(4) CTB Regs; regs 41(3) and 44C(4) CTB(SPC) Regs
246 **HB** Regs 89(2), 90(1) and 91(3) HB Regs; regs 70(2), 71(1) and 72(3) HB(SPC) Regs
CTB Regs 75(2), 76(1)(a) and 77(3)(b) and (c) CTB Regs; regs 60(2), 61(2)(a) and 62(3)(b) and (c) CTB(SPC) Regs
247 Reg 93(1) HB Regs; reg 74(1) HB(SPC) Regs
248 *R v Haringey LBC ex parte Azad Ayub* [1992] 25 HLR 566 (QBD)
249 Reg 93(1) HB Regs; reg 74(1) HB(SPC) Regs; *R v Haringey LBC ex parte Azad Ayub* [1992] 25 HLR 566 (QBD)
250 Reg 93(2) HB Regs; reg 74(2) HB(SPC) Regs
251 Reg 93(3) HB Regs; reg 74(3) HB(SPC) Regs
252 Reg 88(1) HB Regs; reg 69(1) HB(SPC) Regs; reg 4 SS(NCC) Regs
253 Reg 88A and Sch 11 HB Regs; reg 69A and Sch 10 HB(SPC) Regs
254 **HB** Reg 88(6) HB Regs; reg 69(9) HB(SPC) Regs
CTB Reg 74(7) CTB Regs; reg 59(10) CTB(SPC) Regs
255 Reg 88ZA HB Regs; reg 69ZA HB(SPC) Regs
256 **HB** Sch 9 paras 9(1)(g) and 10(a) HB Regs; Sch 8 paras 9(1)(g) and 10(a) HB(SPC) Regs
CTB Sch 8 paras 9(1)(e), 10(a), 13 (f) and 15 CTB Regs; Sch 7 paras 9(1)(e), 10(a), 13(f) and 15 CTB(SPC) Regs
257 **HB** Regs 2(1), 86(3) and 88(1) HB Regs; regs 2(1), 67(3) and 69(1) HB(SPC) Regs
CTB Regs 2(1), 72(3) and 74(1) CTB Regs; regs 2(1), 57(3) and 59(1) CTB(SPC) Regs
258 **HB** Reg 88(1) HB Regs; reg 69(1) HB(SPC) Regs
CTB Reg 74(1) CTB Regs; reg 59(1) CTB(SPC) Regs
259 **HB** Reg 88(1), (3)(a) and (d) and (4) HB Regs; reg 69(1) and (4)(a) HB(SPC) Regs
CTB Reg 74(1), (3)(d), (4) and (5) CTB Regs; reg 59(1), (4) and (5) CTB(SPC) Regs
260 **HB** Reg 69(6) HB(SPC) Regs
CTB Reg 59(7) CTB(SPC) Regs
261 **HB** Reg 69(7) HB(SPC) Regs
CTB Reg 59(8) CTB(SPC) Regs
262 **HB** Reg 69(8) HB(SPC) Regs
CTB Reg 59(9) CTB(SPC) Regs
263 **HB** Regs 86(3) and 90 and Sch 9 HB Regs; regs 67(3) and 71 and Sch 8 HB(SPC) Regs
CTB Regs 72(3) and 76 and Sch 8 CTB Regs; regs 57(3) and 61 and Sch 7 CTB(SPC) Regs
264 **HB** Reg 88(1) HB Regs; reg 69(1) HB(SPC) Regs
CTB Reg 74(1) CTB Regs; reg 59(1) CTB(SPC) Regs
265 **HB** Reg 88(3) HB Regs; reg 69(3) HB(SPC) Regs
CTB Reg 74(3) CTB Regs; reg 59(3) CTB(SPC) Regs
266 **HB** Reg 88(4) HB Regs; reg 69(4) HB(SPC) Regs
CTB Reg 74(4) CTB Regs; reg 59(4) CTB(SPC) Regs
267 **HB** Reg 79 HB Regs; reg 59 HB(SPC) Regs
CTB Reg 67 CTB Regs; reg 50 CTB(SPC) Regs
Both Reg 8 HB&CTB(DA) Regs
268 **HB** Reg 79(1) HB Regs; reg 59(1) HB(SPC) Regs
CTB Reg 67(1) CTB Regs; reg 50(1) CTB(SPC) Regs
Both Reg 8(2) HB&CTB(DA) Regs
269 Reg 79(8) HB Regs; reg 59(8) HB(SPC) Regs
270 **HB** Reg 79(6) and (7) HB Regs; reg 59 (6) and (7) HB(SPC) Regs
CTB Reg 67(8) and (9) CTB Regs; reg 50(8) and (9) CTB(SPC) Regs
271 **HB** Reg 59(10)-(13) HB(SPC) Regs
CTB Reg 50(10)-(13) CTB(SPC) Regs

272 Reg 79(2), (2A), (2B), (8) and (9) HB Regs; reg 59(2), (2A), (2B), (8) and (9) HB(SPC) Regs
273 Regs 7(2)(o) and 8(14D) HB&CTB(DA) Regs
274 **HB** Reg 60 HB(SPC) Regs
CTB Reg 51 CTB(SPC) Regs
275 Reg 79(4) and (8) HB Regs; reg 59(4) and (8) HB(SPC) Regs

9. **Discretionary housing payments**
276 Reg 8 DFA Regs
277 Reg 6(3) DFA Regs
278 s69 CSPSSA 2000; reg 2(1) DFA Regs
279 Reg 2(2) DFA Regs
280 Reg 3 DFA Regs
281 Reg 5 DFA Regs
282 Reg 4 DFA Regs
283 Reg 6 DFA Regs
284 Reg 6(1)(a) DFA Regs
285 Reg 7 DFA Regs
286 Reg 6(3) DFA Regs
287 Reg 6(2) DFA Regs
288 Reg 7(b) DFA Regs
289 **IS** Schs 9 para 75 and 10 para 7(1)(d) IS Regs
JSA Schs 7 para 71 and 8 para 12(1)(d) JSA Regs
ESA Schs 8 para 62 and 9 para 11(1)(c) ESA Regs
HB Schs 5 para 62 and 6 para 9(1)(d) HB Regs; reg 29 HB(SPC) Regs
CTB Schs 4 para 62 and 5 para 9(1)(d) CTB Regs; reg 19 CTB(SPC) Regs
TC Reg 7 Table 3 para 9 TC(DCI) Regs

Chapter 15

Housing benefit rent restrictions

This chapter covers:

Note: the rules described in this chapter do not apply if you are a local authority tenant.

Key facts

- If you are a private tenant (and in some other exceptional cases), the rent used to calculate your housing benefit (HB) may be restricted – ie, your HB may be based on a rent lower than the rent you pay.
- There are three different sets of rent restriction rules: the **local housing allowance rules**, the **local reference rent rules**, and the **pre-January 1996 rules.**
- If any rent restriction rules apply to you, the local authority uses these to work out the amount of rent that can be covered by HB – your 'maximum rent'. Your HB is calculated using this figure, *not* the rent that you pay, and there could be a shortfall.
- If your rent is restricted, you might be able to get discretionary housing payments to help with any shortfall.

Future changes: April 2013 and after

Major changes are taking place that affect the benefits and tax credits system (see Chapter 2).

- From April 2013, local housing allowance rates will only be increased annually by reference to the Consumer Prices Index (CPI).
- From April 2013, the HB of working-age people in social sector housing (eg, local authority or housing association tenants) will be restricted if they are under-occupying

their homes – ie, if they are living in a property that is too large for them. HB will be reduced by a fixed percentage of the claimant's eligible rent. The government says that this will be around 14 per cent for one extra bedroom and 25 per cent for two or more extra bedrooms.

See CPAG's *Welfare Rights Bulletin* for updates.

1. Which rent restriction rules apply

Rent restriction rules apply if you are not a local authority tenant – eg, you are a private or housing association tenant. However, some tenancies are excluded (see p308). Otherwise, whether rent restriction rules apply, and if so which ones, depends on whether you make a new claim or move on or after 7 April 2008, or whether your rent was already being restricted before that date.

If you are considering a move, or there will be a break in your housing benefit (HB) claim, check whether the rules that will apply to you are more or less favourable than before. In some cases, you can apply to the local authority to find out the rent figure that will be used to calculate your HB (see p332). You can also find out the current rate of the appropriate local housing allowance (see p332).

Claiming or moving on or after 7 April 2008

If you make a new claim for HB on or after 7 April 2008 (or you have a current claim and move on or after that date), work out which rent restriction rules apply as follows.

Step one: do you have an 'excluded tenancy'? If so, the rent restriction rules do *not* apply (see p308).

Step two: do you live in 'exempt accommodation'? If so, the pre-January 1996 rules apply (see p326). In some cases, they also apply if you are an 'exempt claimant' (see p327).

Step three: do you live in a hostel, houseboat, mobile home or caravan or does your rent include board and attendance? If so, the local reference rent rules apply (see p319). They *may* also apply if:

- your landlord is a registered housing association; *or*
- your tenancy is a former local authority or new town letting that has been transferred to a new owner; *or*
- your landlord is a county council and you live in a caravan or mobile home provided on a travellers' site;[1] *or*

- you live in a caravan, mobile home or houseboat, and you are also liable to make payments to a local authority – eg, for site or mooring fees.

Step four: in all other cases, the local housing allowance rules apply (see p309).

Housing benefit was restricted before 7 April 2008

The government intends that, if your HB was being restricted under any of the rules that applied before 7 April 2008, it continues to be restricted under those rules until there is a break in your claim or you move to a new home (see pp318, 319 and 327). If any rent restriction rules still apply to you at that point, your HB will be restricted under the rules that then apply.

Example

Daniel has a private rented flat with his partner and child. He has been getting HB since October 2005. This was being restricted under the local reference rent rules. When his partner has a baby in 2012, they move to a two-bedroom private rented house. The local authority reassesses Daniel's HB claim using the local housing allowance rules.

If you have been getting HB since before 7 April 2008 and you think you may be better off having your HB calculated under the local housing allowance rules, you may be able to surrender your HB claim and make a new claim. The new claim will then be assessed under the local housing allowance rules if they apply to the type of tenancy you have. However, consider the following.

- You need to be sure you *will* be better off if your HB is assessed under the local housing allowance rules; under these:
  - the largest size of property on which your HB can be based is four-bedroom accommodation, even if your accommodation is larger; *and*
  - the published local housing allowances (see p309) are the maximum amounts of rent that can be covered by HB – you may get less HB than this. The income and capital rules apply and HB is calculated in the usual way.[2]
- You may lose entitlement to HB for at least one week because entitlement to HB ends on the Monday following the surrender of your claim, and entitlement under your new claim cannot generally start until the following Monday.[3] If your HB entitlement is high, it could take time to make up the loss.
- You may have some form of transitional protection under previous HB rules that were more favourable to you and could lose this if you break your claim.

Discretion to decrease eligible rent

If none of the rent restriction rules apply to you, the local authority has discretion to decrease your eligible rent to an amount it considers 'appropriate'. The local authority may say that this is also the case if any of the rent restriction schemes apply.[4] However, you can argue that the local authority can only use its discretion to decrease your eligible rent if it has been determined under the normal HB rules.[5] It should have evidence which justifies it doing so and must exercise its discretion properly. All the circumstances should be taken into account, including your health and financial circumstances, the special housing-related needs of anyone occupying your home and whether alternative accommodation is available to HB claimants.[6] Local authorities should rarely use their powers to decrease your HB in this way. If your HB is reduced under this rule, ask for a revision or appeal (see Chapters 45 and 46).

2. **Excluded tenancies**

If you have an 'excluded tenancy', none of the rent restriction rules apply to you. The following are excluded tenancies:[7]

- a regulated or protected tenancy – ie, a tenancy entered into before 15 January 1989 or, in Scotland, 2 January 1989;
- a tenancy in an approved bail or probation hostel. However, if you are required to live in such a hostel, you cannot qualify for housing benefit (HB) towards the rent you pay to the hostel (see p252);
- a housing action trust tenancy;
- a former local authority or new town letting which has been transferred to a new owner, unless there has been a rent increase since the transfer; *and*
  - the local authority considers your rent to be unreasonably high; *or*
  - if the transfer took place before 7 October 2002 only, the local authority considers your accommodation to be unreasonably large.

  If this is the case, the local reference rent rules apply;
- a letting by a registered housing association (in Scotland and Wales) or a registered provider of social housing (in England), a county council letting (if you live in a caravan or mobile home provided on a travellers' site[8]) or a letting in a caravan, mobile home or houseboat (if you are also liable to make payments to a local authority – eg, for site or mooring fees). However, if the local authority considers your accommodation to be unreasonably large or your rent unreasonably high, the local reference rent rules apply;
- a shared ownership tenancy, unless this is with a private landlord, in which case the local housing allowance rules may apply (see p309)

Remember: the rent restriction rules do not apply if you are the tenant of the local authority who pays you HB.

3. The local housing allowance rules

In most cases, if you are a private tenant, the local housing allowance rules determine the amount of rent to be used to calculate your housing benefit (HB). This can include if you have a shared ownership tenancy with a private landlord. If the local housing allowance rules apply, your HB is based on the local housing allowance that is appropriate for you (see below).

The local housing allowance rules apply (unless you have an 'excluded tenancy' or the local reference rent or the pre-January 1996 rules apply) if, on or after 7 April 2008, you:[9]

- claim HB; *or*
- move to a new home while you are entitled to HB; *or*
- live in a former Pathfinder area and the pilot local housing allowance rules applied to you before that date. However, you may have transitional protection (see p318).

Note: if you were claiming HB before 7 April 2008 and your rent was restricted under any of the rules that then applied, these can continue to apply, instead of the local housing allowance rules, until you move to a new home, or there is a break in your HB claim (see pp318, 319 and 327).

Which local housing allowance is appropriate

The local housing allowance that is appropriate for you depends on the area where you live and the category of dwelling that applies to you.

Categories of dwelling

The category of dwelling that applies to you depends on how many bedrooms you are allowed under the size criteria, and whether you are in shared accommodation.

Under the **size criteria**, you are allowed (up to a maximum of four bedrooms):[10]

- one bedroom for each of the following occupiers (each coming only into the first category for which s/he is eligible):
  - a couple (see p753 for who counts);
  - a person who is not a child – ie, someone aged 16 or over;
  - two children of the same sex;
  - two children under 10;
  - a child; *and*
- if you or your partner are a 'person who requires overnight care' (see p310), one additional bedroom for a non-resident carer. Even if both of you require overnight care, only one additional bedroom is allowed.

You cannot be allowed more bedrooms than shown above, even if you need them – eg, if you and your partner or your children need separate bedrooms because of a disability.[11]

Examples

Bill and Sarah have two sons, both under age 10. Sarah's nephew, aged 20, lives with them. They are allowed three bedrooms under the size criteria: one for Bill and Sarah, one for the sons and one for the nephew. Appropriate local housing allowance: dwelling with three bedrooms.

Terry is his father's carer. They live together in the same household and are joint tenants. He is allowed two bedrooms under the size criteria: one for Terry and one for his father. Appropriate local housing allowance: dwelling with two bedrooms.

Michael and Barbara have two daughters, aged 10 and 13 and two sons, aged 15 and 18. Michael's parents live with them. They are allowed five bedrooms under the size criteria: one for Michael and Barbara, one for the daughters, one each for the sons and one for Michael's parents. Appropriate local housing allowance: dwelling with four bedrooms (the maximum allowed).

Occupiers

'Occupiers' means you and anyone else living in the dwelling (other than a joint tenant who is not a member of your household).[12] This therefore includes not only members of your family, but also people who are not part of your family for benefit purposes – eg, a joint tenant who *is* a member of your household, a non-dependant or a live-in carer, but not your foster children.[13] You can argue that it also includes people who normally live with you but who are temporarily away.[14] However, if you share the care of a child, the child is considered to be occupying the home of the parent with whom s/he normally lives.[15]

Person who requires overnight care

You (or your partner) are a 'person who requires overnight care' if you (or s/he):[16]
- are getting attendance allowance or the middle or highest rate of disability living allowance care component; *or*
- have provided the local authority with sufficient certificates, documents, information or evidence to satisfy it that overnight care is required.

In addition, you (or your partner) must satisfy the local authority that you (or s/he) reasonably require, and have arranged for:
- one or more people who do not live with you to provide overnight care and to stay overnight regularly in your home for this purpose; *and*
- a bedroom to be provided for the carer(s) additional to those used by others living in your home.

You can count as a person who requires overnight care even if you are not actually living in your home, provided you can be treated as occupying it – eg, while you are temporarily absent from home.

One-bedroom shared accommodation

The local housing allowance for one-bedroom shared accommodation is appropriate if:[17]

- you are a single claimant under 35 (a 'young individual') and you do not have a non-dependant living with you (see p265). This applies even if you do not live in shared accommodation (but see below for exceptions); *or*
- you (and your partner) live in shared accommodation and are only allowed one bedroom under the size criteria (ie, you are a single claimant (of any age) or a member of a couple without children), neither you nor your partner are a 'person who requires overnight care' (see p310) and you do not have a non-dependant living with you. You count as living in shared accommodation if you do not have the exclusive use of at least two rooms, or the exclusive use of one room as well as the exclusive use of a bathroom, a toilet and a kitchen or facilities for cooking (but see below for exceptions).

There are exceptions to the rule and the local housing allowance for one-bedroom shared accommodation does not apply (even if you live in shared accommodation) if:

- you (or your partner):[18]
  - qualify for a severe disability premium as part of your applicable amount; *or*
  - are under the age of 22 and were looked after (in the care of), or under the supervision of, a local authority under specific legal provisions after you turned 16 or were provided with accommodation by the local authority under s20 of the Children Act 1989; *or*
- if you are a single claimant aged under 35, you are:[19]
  - a 'person who requires overnight care' (see p310); *or*
  - at least 25 and:
    - have been living in a homeless hostel for three months or more (this does not have to be continuous) and while living in such a hostel you have accepted support services to assist you in being rehabilitated or resettled in the community; *or*
    - are an offender subject to specific multi-agency risk management arrangements.

Note: the age threshold for a single claimant was 25 before 1 January 2012. If you were at least 25 but under 35 on that date and getting HB on the basis that the local housing allowance for one-bedroom self-contained accommodation was appropriate for you, see p316 to see if you qualify for transitional protection.

One-bedroom self-contained accommodation

The local housing allowance for one-bedroom self-contained accommodation is appropriate if you are allowed one bedroom under the size criteria – ie, you are a single claimant or are a member of a couple without children, you do not have a non-dependant living with you, and neither you nor your partner are a 'person who requires overnight care' (see p310). You must be renting accommodation where you have:[20]

- the exclusive use of at least two rooms; *or*
- the exclusive use of one room as well as the exclusive use of a bathroom, a toilet and a kitchen or facilities for cooking.

'Room' means a bedroom or a 'room suitable for living in' (other than one you share with someone who is not a member of your household, a non-dependant or someone who pays rent to you or your partner).

Note: if you are a single claimant under 35, the local housing allowance for one-bedroom shared accommodation is appropriate, even if you do not live in shared accommodation, unless any of the exceptions listed on p311 apply.

Dwellings with two or more bedrooms

Unless the local housing allowance for one-bedroom shared or one-bedroom self-contained accommodation is appropriate, the appropriate local housing allowance is the one for the category of dwelling with the number of bedrooms you are allowed under the size criteria (see p309), to a maximum of four bedrooms.[21] So this category applies, for example, if you are a lone parent, you are a member of a couple with children, you have a non-dependant living with you, you are a joint tenant with someone who is a member of your household or you are a 'person who requires overnight care' (see p310). **Note:** if you were getting HB based on the local housing allowance for a dwelling of more than four bedrooms before 1 April 2011, you may qualify for transitional protection (see p317).

Local housing allowance rates

Local housing allowances for each category of dwelling are set by the rent officer and until April 2013 are based on the amount of rent at the 30th percentile point of local market rents for assured tenancies in a 'broad rental market area' as at 2 April 2012.[22] There are upper limits (known as local housing allowance 'caps') that will only affect you if you live in an area where rents are high – eg, in central London.

Broad rental market area[23]

A 'broad rental market area' is an area where you could reasonably be expected to live, taking into account the facilities and services for health, education, recreation, banking and shopping, and the travel distance by public and private transport. It must contain a variety of kinds of residential accommodation and types of lettings, and have sufficient private rented housing to ensure that the local housing allowance for the categories of dwelling in the area is representative of the rents that a landlord might be reasonably expected to obtain in that area.

Local housing allowance 'caps'

The local housing allowance can never be higher than the following:[24]

One-bedroom shared or one-bedroom self-contained accommodation:	£250
Two-bedroom accommodation:	£290
Three-bedroom accommodation:	£340
Four-bedroom accommodation:	£400

Local housing allowances are set by the rent officer annually and are made public.[25] These are available on the Valuation Office Agency website at www.direct.gov.uk/en/diol1/doitonline/DG_196239. From September 2012, they are the lower of the previous year's rate increased by the Consumer Prices Index or the rent at the 30th percentile point of local market rents.

Note: if you were getting HB based on a higher local housing allowance rate than the amounts listed above before 1 April 2011, you may qualify for transitional protection (see p317).

Maximum rent

Your 'maximum rent' for HB purposes is the appropriate local housing allowance for you or, if lower, your 'cap rent'.[26] The local authority might call this your 'maximum rent (LHA)'. The 'eligible rent' used to calculate your HB (see p260) is your 'maximum rent'.[27]

Your **'cap rent'** is the rent you are liable, or treated as liable, to pay for your home.[28] If you share accommodation with others who are not members of your family for HB purposes and you are jointly liable for the rent with them, the local authority apportions the 'cap rent' between you.

Example

Phil, aged 28, shares a private-rented house with four friends. Phil claims HB. The rent is £300 a week. His 'cap rent' is £60 (£300 divided by 5).

The local authority may say it has general discretion to decrease your cap rent to an amount it considers appropriate (but see p307).

Note: if you share accommodation with others who are not members of your family for HB purposes and are jointly liable for the rent with them (eg, you are joint tenants), your maximum rent is based on the local housing allowance that applies to you (and your partner) – see p309 – subject to the cap rent rule.

Examples

Hannah, aged 38, is a joint tenant of a private flat with three friends. The rent for the flat is £200 a week. Hannah works part time and earns £100 a week after deductions of tax and national insurance contributions. Hannah claims HB.

The local housing allowance appropriate for Hannah is that for one-bedroom shared accommodation (£75). Hannah's cap rent is £50 (£200 divided by 4). Her 'maximum rent' (and her 'eligible rent') is, therefore, £50 because this is lower than the local housing allowance.

Hannah has no non-dependants. Therefore, her 'maximum HB' (see p258) is £50.

Her applicable amount is £71 (the standard amount for a single person 25 or over).

Her income to be taken into account is £95 a week (£5 of her earnings are disregarded).

The difference between her income and her applicable amount is, therefore, £24 a week.

65% x £24 = £15.60 a week.

Hannah's HB is therefore £50 – £15.60 = £34.40 a week.

Terry, aged 40, cares for his father. They live together in the same household and are joint tenants. The rent for the flat is £300 a week. Terry is on income support (IS). He claims HB.

The local housing allowance appropriate for Terry is that for two-bedroom accommodation (£250). Terry's cap rent is £150 (£300 divided by 2). His 'maximum rent' (and his 'eligible rent') is therefore £150 as this figure is lower than the local housing allowance.

Terry has no non-dependants. Therefore his 'maximum HB' is £150. Because he is on IS, Terry's HB is £150 a week.

Your 'maximum rent' is based on the local housing allowance that is appropriate when your claim is assessed. Your HB is paid on this basis until the next time the local authority assesses your claim (usually annually), even if the amount of the allowance or your rent changes.[29] When the local authority reassesses your claim it uses the local housing allowance that is then appropriate. Some changes of circumstance can lead to an earlier reassessment – eg, if:[30]

- there is a change in the category of dwelling that applies to you (see p309) – ie, you are allowed more or fewer bedrooms because, for instance, someone has moved in with you or has moved out, or your child has reached aged 16 and is allowed her/his own bedroom; *or*
- a member of your family (or a relative of yours or your partner who lives in the same accommodation as you without a separate right to do so) dies; *or*
- you move to a new home.

Your 'maximum rent' is then based on the local housing allowance that is appropriate for you on the date of the change.[31] However, you may qualify for a protected rate of HB (transitional protection) if you were getting HB on 1 April 2011 (see p317) or if you live in a former Pathfinder area (see p318).

Note: if a member of your family (or a relative) has died, any *decrease* can be delayed for a period (see below).

Example

Cleo rents a three-bedroom house from a private landlord. She pays £170 a week rent. She has one son, aged seven. The appropriate local housing allowance is that for two-bedroom accommodation. When she claims IS and HB, the local housing allowance for two-bedroom accommodation is £105. Cleo's maximum rent (and eligible rent) is £105. Cleo has no non-dependants, so this is also her maximum HB and, therefore, her weekly HB.

Cleo's Aunt Sue comes to live with her. As there has been a change in the category of dwelling that applies to Cleo (this is now for three-bedroom accommodation), the local authority reassesses her claim. The local housing allowance for three-bedroom accommodation is now £158. Cleo's maximum rent (and eligible rent) is £158. Aunt Sue is on incapacity benefit so a non-dependant deduction of £11.45 must be made. Cleo's maximum HB and, therefore, her HB is £146.55 a week (£158 – £11.45).

Delay before a rent restriction is applied

In some situations, a reduction in your HB (a rent restriction) can be delayed. A rent restriction can be delayed:

- in specified circumstances (see below) – ie, if:
  - there has been a death in the household; *or*
  - the costs of the dwelling could be met when they were taken on – eg, you could afford the rent before you became unemployed and had to claim HB;
- if you qualify for 'transitional protection' (see p316).

Specified circumstances

A rent restriction can be delayed if:

- a member of your family (or a relative of yours or your partner who lived in the same accommodation as you without a separate right to do so) dies and you still live there (temporary absences of up to 13 weeks are allowed). In this case, unless your eligible rent for HB purposes under the normal local housing allowance rules is the same or higher:[32]
  - no restriction is made for 12 months from the date of death if no eligible rent applied at the time of death – ie, you were not yet claiming HB. In this case, your eligible rent is your contractual rent, minus any ineligible charges (see p262). If you are in shared accommodation, this can be apportioned between you and the people with whom you share. It only covers the rent you pay for residential accommodation; *or*
  - any eligible rent which applied on the day before the death continues to apply for 12 months from the date of death;
- you, or a member of your family (or a relative of yours or your partner who lives in the same dwelling as you without a separate right to do so) could meet

the costs of the dwelling when you took them on (this could include other bills as well as the rent). No restriction is made for 13 weeks provided neither you nor your partner were entitled to HB in the 52 weeks before your current award of HB.[33] In this case, your eligible rent is your contractual rent, minus ineligible charges (see p262). If you are in shared accommodation, this can be apportioned between you and the people with whom you share. It only covers the rent you pay for residential accommodation.

Your eligible rent can change before the end of the 12-month/13-week period if your eligible rent as calculated under the normal local housing allowance rules is now the same or higher, or you move to a new home or another member of your family (or relative) dies.[34]

Note: if you qualify for transitional protection, different rules may apply after a member of your family or a relative dies.

Relative

For these purposes, 'relative' means a close relative (see p251 for who counts) or a grandparent, grandchild, uncle, aunt, nephew or niece.[35]

Example

Mr and Mrs Connor and their four-year-old son live in a three-bedroom flat. They pay rent of £225 a week. Until her recent death, Mr Connor's mother lived with them. Mr Connor's maximum rent (and hence his eligible rent) was being restricted to the local housing allowance for a three-bedroom property (£190).

When he notifies the local authority of the death of his mother, his new maximum rent (and eligible rent) is the local housing allowance for a two-bedroom property (£150). However, the decrease is delayed for 12 months.

Mr Connor gets IS. Before his mother's death his HB was £178.55 a week (£190 *minus* a non-dependant deduction of £11.45).

For 12 months from his mother's date of death, his HB is £190 a week.

Transitional protection

When HB rules change, you could be entitled to a lower rate of HB than you were before this happened. In some cases, your old (higher) rate of HB can be protected for a period. This is called transitional protection. There are currently three situations when you may qualify for transitional protection. These are if:

- your HB was calculated on the basis of the local housing allowance rules immediately before 1 April 2011; *or*

- you are at least 25 but not yet 35 and your HB was calculated on the basis of the local housing allowance for one-bedroom self-contained accommodation before 1 January 2012; *or*
- you live in a former Pathfinder area.

You were entitled to housing benefit before 1 April 2011

Before 1 April 2011, the local housing allowance rules could be more generous.

- You could be allowed up to five bedrooms under the size criteria (see p309).
- There were no upper limits on the rates of local housing allowances (see p313).
- Your 'maximum rent' (see p313) was the appropriate local housing allowance for you or, if lower, your 'cap rent' plus £15.

If your HB was calculated on the basis of the local housing allowance rules immediately before 1 April 2011, you may qualify for a protected rate of HB when the local authority reassesses your claim for the first time on or after this date. You can only qualify for a protected rate of HB if the reassessment is needed because:[36]

- you are allowed more bedrooms because of a change in the category of dwelling that applies to you (see p309); *or*
- at least a year has passed since the last time your claim was assessed (or reassessed).

Unless your maximum rent for HB purposes under the normal local housing allowance rules (see p313) is the same as or higher, your eligible rent (referred to as your 'protected eligible rent' in this section) is the lower of the following:[37]

- the eligible rent that applied before 1 April 2011 – ie, either the appropriate local housing allowance or your 'cap rent' plus £15; *or*
- your current 'cap rent' (see p313).

Your HB is calculated on the basis of your 'protected eligible rent' for nine months, or until the first of the following occurs, if earlier:[38]

- you are allowed more bedrooms because of a change in the category of dwelling that applies to you and your maximum rent as calculated under the current rules is the same as or higher than your 'protected eligible rent'; *or*
- you are allowed fewer bedrooms because of a change in the category of dwelling that applies to you; *or*
- you move to a new home; *or*
- a member of your family (or a relative of yours or your partner who lives in the same accommodation as you without a separate right to do so) dies. In this case, the rules described on p315 can apply instead.

Example

Mr and Mrs Hussein live in a three-bedroom private flat with their four children. The appropriate local housing allowance for them is that for three-bedroom accommodation.

When they claimed HB in March 2011, their rent was £180 a week and the local housing allowance was £200. Their 'eligible rent' was therefore £195 (their 'cap rent' plus £15), and their HB was calculated on this basis.

In January 2012, Mrs Hussein has a baby, so now the appropriate local housing allowance is that for four-bedroom accommodation. The local housing allowance rates have reduced in the area where they live and the rate for four-bedroom accommodation is £175. Under the normal rules, the maximum rent would therefore be £175 (as this is lower than their 'cap rent'). Their 'protected eligible rent' is therefore the lower of the eligible rent that applied before 1 April 2011 (£195) and the current 'cap rent' (£180). Their HB is calculated on the basis of an eligible rent of £180 for nine months.

You were entitled to HB for one-bedroom self-contained accommodation before 1 January 2012

If you are a single claimant under 35, your HB is based on the local housing allowance for one-bedroom shared accommodation, unless any of the exceptions on p311 apply. However, before 1 January 2012, the age threshold was 25. If you are at least 25 but not yet 35 and your HB was calculated on the basis of the local housing allowance for one-bedroom self-contained accommodation before that date , you may qualify for transitional protection. If you were entitled to HB:[39]

- before 1 April 2011 and you qualify for transitional protection under the rules described above, your HB is not based on the local housing allowance for one-bedroom shared accommodation until that transitional protection ends;
- after 1 April 2011 but before 1 January 2012, your HB is not based on the local housing allowance for one-bedroom shared accommodation until the anniversary of your claim.

Former Pathfinder areas

The local housing allowance rules were piloted in 18 Pathfinder areas from late 2003 until 7 April 2008. The pilot rules were more generous than the current rules. If you live in a former Pathfinder area, you may still have transitional protection. See pp282–83 of the 2011/12 edition of this *Handbook* for further information.

Challenging a rent restriction

You cannot appeal against the amount of the local housing allowance. However, you *can* appeal against local authority decisions about your award of HB which involve the local housing allowance – ie, you can challenge the factual basis on which a particular local housing allowance was used – eg, whether you are a 'young individual' or whether someone occupies accommodation with you.[40]

4. The local reference rent rules

If the local reference rent rules apply, they determine the amount of rent to be used to calculate your housing benefit (HB). Your HB is based on a rent officer's determinations (see p320).

Unless you have an 'excluded tenancy' (see p308) or the pre-January 1996 rules apply (see p326), the local reference rent rules apply to you if, on or after 7 April 2008, you claim HB or move to a new home while you are entitled to HB and:[41]

- you live in a hostel, a houseboat, a mobile home or a caravan; *or*
- your rent includes board and attendance; *or*
- your landlord is a registered housing association, a county council (if you live in a caravan or mobile home provided on a travellers' site[42]) or you are renting a caravan, mobile home or houseboat (where you are also liable to make payments to a local authority – eg, for the site or mooring fees). However, this only applies if the local authority considers your accommodation to be unreasonably large or your rent unreasonably high. Otherwise, you have an 'excluded tenancy' (see p308); *or*
- your tenancy was a local authority or new town letting, but it has been transferred to a new owner. However, this only applies if there has been a rent increase since the transfer; *and*
  - the local authority considers your rent to be unreasonably high; *or*
  - if the transfer took place before 7 October 2002, the local authority considers your accommodation to be unreasonably large.

  Otherwise, you have an 'excluded tenancy' (see p308).

Note: these rules can also apply to other private tenants, but only if you were entitled to HB immediately before 7 April 2008, under the local reference rent rules that then applied. See below for further information.

If you were getting housing benefit before 7 April 2008

Even if you are not someone to whom the current local reference rent rules would apply (eg, you rent a private house or flat), if you were entitled to HB immediately before 7 April 2008 and the local reference rent rules applied to you, they continue to do so until you make a new claim for HB (ie, after a break in your claim) or you move to a new home.[43] If any rent restriction rules still apply to you at that point, your HB is restricted under the rules that are then applicable.

The local reference rent rules continue to apply to you even following any of the changes of circumstance listed below, and then when the local authority has to apply to the rent officer for determinations every 52 weeks thereafter.[44]

Rent officer's determinations

When the local reference rent rules apply, the local authority must apply to the rent officer and ask her/him to make determinations if:[45]

- you make a new claim for HB or move to a new home while you are entitled to HB;
- a previous reference to the rent officer was made in respect of your claim 52 weeks or more ago (but see p319); *or*
- there has been one of the following changes of circumstances since a rent officer's determination:[46]
  - the number of occupiers has changed (except in a hostel). Argue this does not apply if someone who normally lives with you is only away temporarily;[47]
  - there has been a substantial change in the condition of the dwelling or the terms of the tenancy (other than a rent increase);
  - there has been an increase in the rent under a term of the tenancy, unless the previous determination was a significantly high, size-related or exceptionally high rent determination (see p321);[48]
  - a size-related rent determination (see p321) was made and there has since been a change in the composition of the household, or a child living with you has reached the age of 10 or 16; *or*
  - you or your partner become, or cease to be, a 'person who requires overnight care' (see p310) and this affects the size of accommodation you are allowed under the size criteria (see p321); *or*
- your HB was being restricted under the local housing allowance rules, but these no longer apply – eg, if the home you rent was sold to a housing association and the local reference rent rules apply instead.

The local authority *cannot* apply to the rent officer for determinations if:

- a rent officer determination has been made for the same tenancy (or a tenancy in the same dwelling) on substantially the same terms within the last 52 weeks.[49] This means that a determination made for a previous tenant may be valid for your HB claim. A new referral *is* needed if you are a young individual and no single room rent determination has yet been made (see p323);
- you live in a hostel and a rent officer determination has been made for similar accommodation in the hostel, sleeping the same number of people as yours, within the last 12 months and there has been no change of circumstances in respect of that accommodation.[50]

The rent officer makes determinations about the rent for your home, comparing it with the rent for other private sector tenancies in the area. The rent officer also makes determinations that indicate the average rents for specific types of accommodation (see p322).

Determinations about the rent for your home

The rent officer makes significantly high, exceptionally high and size-related rent determinations. S/he uses these to identify the 'claim-related rent' (see p322).

The rent officer makes a **'significantly high rent determination'** if your rent is significantly higher than that paid for similar tenancies and dwellings in the vicinity (ie, the immediate area around your home). This is the amount your landlord might reasonably be paid for your tenancy.[51]

The rent officer makes an **'exceptionally high rent determination'** if s/he considers the 'rent payable' for your home to be exceptionally high. This is the highest amount your landlord might reasonably be paid for an assured tenancy in the neighbourhood that is the same size as your home (or the size you are allowed under the size criteria).[52]

Neighbourhoods and rent payable

A **'neighbourhood'** is:[53]

- if you live in a town or city, the part of the town or city where your home is located that is a distinct area of residential accommodation; *or*
- if you do not live in a town or city, the area surrounding your home that is a distinct area of residential accommodation, which includes homes of the same size as yours (or of a size you are allowed under the size criteria – see below).

'Rent payable' means the size-related rent determination (see below) or, if there is no such determination, the significantly high rent determination (if there is one), or in any other case, the rent you are supposed to pay.

Size-related rent determination

The rent officer makes a **'size-related rent determination'** if your accommodation is larger than you are allowed under the 'size criteria'. This is the amount your landlord might reasonably be paid for a similar tenancy in the vicinity of an appropriate size for you.[54] For these purposes, 'vicinity' means the immediate area around your home, or where there is no dwelling in that area of a size you are allowed under the size criteria, the nearest area where there is one.[55]

Under the **'size criteria'**, the rent officer (ignoring, for example, your kitchen, bathroom and toilet) allows you:[56]

- one bedroom or room 'suitable for living in' for each of the following occupiers (each coming only into the first category for which s/he is eligible):
  - a couple (see p753 for who counts);
  - a person who is not a child – ie, someone aged 16 or over;
  - two children of the same sex;
  - two children under 10;
  - a child;

- if you or your partner are a 'person who requires overnight care' (see p310), one additional bedroom for a non-resident carer. Even if both of you require overnight care, only one additional bedroom is allowed.

Note: unlike with the local housing allowance rules, there is no maximum number of bedrooms.

In addition, you are allowed the following number of rooms 'suitable for living in'.

Number of occupiers	*Number of rooms*
Less than four	One
Four to six	Two
Seven or more	Three

A person counts as an **'occupier'** if the local authority includes her/him on the form used to refer your tenancy to the rent officer.[57] This can include people who are not part of your family for benefit purposes – eg, your non-dependants or a live-in carer, but not your foster children.[58] You can argue that it also includes people who normally live with you but who are temporarily away.[59] However, if you share the care of a child, the child is considered to be occupying the home of only one parent – the parent with whom the child normally lives.[60]

If any of the rooms in your home are not suitable for living in (eg, because of their size or lack of ventilation), argue that they should be ignored.

Example

Alice and Len have three children: two sons, 12 and 14, and a daughter, 17. They are allowed one room for themselves, one for their sons and one for their daughter – three bedrooms (or rooms 'suitable for living in') as well as two other rooms 'suitable for living in'. They are, therefore, allowed five rooms, as well as a kitchen, bathroom and toilet.

Note: if you are a single person under 35, the rent officer must also identify a single room rent. See p323 for further information.

Claim-related rent

The rent officer identifies what is known as the 'claim-related rent'. This is the lowest of the above determinations or, if no such determination was made, the rent you are supposed to pay.[61]

Determinations that indicate average rents

The rent officer determines the local reference rent and a single room rent. These determinations indicate the average rents for specific types of accommodation in a 'broad rental market area'.

Broad rental market area

A 'broad rental market area' (the local authority calls this a 'broad rental market area (local reference rent)') is the area where you could reasonably be expected to live, taking into account the facilities and services for health, education, recreation, banking and shopping, and the travel distance by public and private transport. It must contain a variety of kinds of residential accommodation and types of lettings, and have sufficient private rented housing to ensure that the local reference rents for tenancies in the area are representative of the rents that a landlord might reasonably be expected to obtain in that area.[62]

Local reference rent

The local reference rent is the mid-point of 'reasonable market rents' for assured tenancies in the broad rental market area (see above) appropriate to the size of property in which you live (or the size you are allowed under the size criteria – see p321).[63] It is only provided if the claim-related rent (see p322) exceeds it.[64]

Single room rent

If you are a single claimant under the age of 35 (a 'young individual'), in most cases the rent officer identifies a single room rent.[65] Your 'maximum rent' (see p324) is based on this figure unless you have a non-dependant living with you (see p265) or you:[66]

- qualify for a severe disability premium as part of your applicable amount; *or*
- are a housing association tenant; *or*
- are under the age of 22 and were looked after (in the care of), or under the supervision of a local authority under specific legal provisions after you turned 16 or were provided with accommodation by the local authority under s20 Children Act 1989; *or*
- are a 'person who requires overnight care' (see p310); *or*
- are at least 25 and:
  - have been living in a homeless hostel for three months or more (this does not have to be continuous) and while living in such a hostel have accepted support services to assist you in being rehabilitated or resettled in the community; *or*
  - are an offender subject to specific multi-agency risk management arrangements.

The **single room rent** is the mid-point of 'reasonable market rents' for accommodation in the broad rental market area (see above) in which the tenant has exclusive use of one bedroom only, and other than that only shares a living room, kitchen, a toilet and bathroom, and makes no payment for board and attendance.[67]

Note: the age threshold was 25 before 1 January 2012. If you were at least 25 on that date your HB was not based on the single room rent. However, if the rules above apply, it *will* be based on the single room rent if you are not yet 35 the next time the local authority makes a reference to the rent officer about your claim (see p320).

Service charges in rent officer determinations

The local authority notifies the rent officer of the amount of rent you are supposed to pay, whether this includes service charges and the amount of the charges that can and cannot be met by HB (see p262).[68] The claim-related rent (see p322) does not include ineligible charges unless you live in one-room accommodation and the landlord provides substantial board and attendance. In this case, the claim-related rent and local reference rent (though not the single room rent) include charges for meals.[69]

Notification to the local authority

The rent officer notifies the local authority of the claim-related rent and, if lower, the local reference rent or single room rent.[70] This must be done within five working days of the local authority's request for determinations (25 days if the rent officer intends to visit the property) or as soon as is practicable after that.[71] If the rent officer needs further information, the five (or 25) days run from the date this is received.

Maximum rent

If the 'local reference rent' rules apply, your 'maximum rent' for HB purposes, and therefore your 'eligible rent' (see p260), is usually the lowest of the rent officer's determinations, even if the rent you pay is higher.[72]

Your 'maximum rent' is:[73]

- the lowest of the claim-related rent, the local reference rent or, if you are a single person under 35 and it is relevant, the single room rent; *or*
- if you have been continuously entitled to, and in receipt of, HB for the same property since 5 October 1997, the local reference rent (plus half the difference between the local reference rent and the claim-related rent).[74] If you or your partner are a 'welfare to work' beneficiary (see p738), breaks in your claim of up to 52 weeks are ignored.

Example

Jo and Louis are a couple who rent a three-bedroom mobile home with a living room and separate dining room. They pay rent of £120 a week. The rent officer decides that the accommodation is too big and that the rent is too high so makes significantly high and size-related rent determinations. S/he notifies the local authority of a claim-related rent of £90 and a local reference rent of £80. Jo and Louis's 'maximum rent' is £80 a week.

Once your 'maximum rent' is set, your HB is paid on the basis of this until the next time the local authority makes a reference to the rent officer about your claim (usually annually). However, if you negotiate with your landlord and s/he agrees a new rent which is lower than the maximum rent, your HB is recalculated using your new rent.[75]

Note:

- If you are in shared accommodation, your 'maximum rent' can be apportioned between you and the people with whom you share. It only covers the rent you pay for residential accommodation.[76]
- A rent restriction can be delayed in some circumstances (see below).
- If you are considering renting accommodation to which the local reference rent rules apply and you are likely to claim HB, you can apply to the local authority for a pre-tenancy determination (see p331).

Delay before a rent restriction is applied

A rent restriction can be delayed if:

- a member of your family (or a relative of yours or your partner who lives in the same accommodation as you without a separate right to do so) dies and you still live there (temporary absences of up to 13 weeks are allowed). In this case:[77]
  - no restriction applies for 12 months from the date of death if no 'maximum rent' applied at the time of the death; *or*
  - any 'maximum rent' which applied at the time of death continues to do so for the 12 months from the date of death;
- you, or a member of your family (or a relative of yours or your partner who lives in the same dwelling as you without a separate right to do so), could meet the costs of the dwelling when you took them on (this could include other bills as well as the rent). In this case, no restriction can be made for 13 weeks provided neither you nor your partner were entitled to HB in the 52 weeks before your current award of HB.[78]

For these purposes, **'relative'** means a close relative (see p251 for who counts) or a grandparent, grandchild, uncle, aunt, nephew or niece.[79]

Challenging a rent restriction

You cannot appeal against the rent officer's determinations. However, the local authority *can* ask for them to be redetermined on your behalf.[80] You must apply to the local authority in writing no later than one month after the date you are notified of its decision on your HB claim. The local authority must then apply to the rent officer for a redetermination and pass any representations you make or evidence you supply to her/him within seven days. In practice, if you seek a revision or appeal against an HB decision and this relates in whole, or in part, to the rent officer's determinations, the local authority should apply for a redetermination.[81]

It is not easy to challenge rent officers, but it may still be possible. If, for example, the rent officer has said your rent is significantly high, you may be able to get her/him to reconsider by providing evidence of similar tenancies where tenants who are not on HB are paying the same rent as you. The rent officer must get the advice of one or two other rent officers and notify the local authority of her/his decision within 20 working days.[82]

The rent officer's redetermination might reduce your maximum rent so consider your position carefully before requesting a redetermination (or asking for a revision or an appeal) – you could end up with less HB. However, if the redetermination:[83]

- reduces your maximum rent (see p324), it only applies from the Monday after the date of redetermination, so you have not been overpaid;
- increases your maximum rent, it applies from the date of the original decision and you should be paid any HB arrears.

The local authority can ask for a rent officer redetermination, even if you have not done so.[84] In addition, if it discovers an error in the referral to the rent officer (eg, if it made a mistake about the number of occupiers) or if the rent officer discovers an error (other than in the application of professional judgement), the local authority must apply for a substitute determination.[85] If there has been a property-related error (eg, about the number of rooms or the provision of services or furniture), the rent officer can send a substitute determination automatically.[86] You can seek a redetermination in any of these situations. Otherwise, you are limited to one request for a rent officer determination.[87]

Note: you *can* appeal against local authority decisions about your award of HB which involve rent officer determinations (ie, you can challenge the factual basis on which the rent officer made a determination – eg, whether you are a 'young individual' or or whether someone occupies accommodation with you).[88] If you are in doubt, you may want to appeal *and* ask for a redetermination.

5. The pre-January 1996 rules

Before January 1996, the rent restriction rules were less harsh than the rules that replaced them. These pre-January 1996 rules still apply if you live in 'exempt accommodation' or if you are an 'exempt claimant'.

Exempt accommodation

The pre-January 1996 rules apply to you if you live in 'exempt accommodation' – ie, if it is:[89]

- temporary accommodation for people without a settled way of life, funded by the Resettlement Agency; *or*
- accommodation provided by a housing association, non-metropolitan county council, registered charity or voluntary organisation where that body, or a person acting on its behalf, also provides you with care, support or supervision.[90] You must need the care, support or supervision and it must be more than a token or minimal amount.[91] **Note:** if the person (or body) providing the care, support or supervision has a contract with the local authority Supporting People team to provide these, but is not providing the accommodation, the decision maker is likely to say it is not exempt accommodation.[92]

Exempt claimants

Even if you do not live in 'exempt accommodation', the pre-January 1996 rules apply to you if you are an 'exempt claimant' – ie:[93]
- you have been continuously entitled to and in receipt of housing benefit (HB) since 1 January 1996; *and*
- you continue to occupy the same property as your home (except if you are forced to move because fire, flood or natural catastrophe makes it uninhabitable).

Breaks in your claim of up to four weeks are ignored (52 weeks if you or your partner are a 'welfare to work' beneficiary – see p738), so long as you are someone to whom the local reference rent rules would otherwise apply – eg, you live in a mobile home or caravan (see p319).[94] Otherwise, the local housing allowance rules apply when you make a new claim (see p309).

If you are thinking of making *any* changes to your claim, check whether this would mean you are no longer an 'exempt claimant' and therefore the local reference rent or the local housing allowance rules apply. You are definitely no longer an 'exempt claimant', for example, if you make a new claim for HB separated by more than four weeks (or 52 weeks) from a previous claim or you move (including moving rooms within the same house).[95]

So long as you are someone to whom the local reference rent rules would otherwise apply (eg, you live in a mobile home or caravan – see p319), an exemption can be transferred to you if you claim HB because:[96]
- an exempt claimant dies and you are a member of her/his family, or any relative (see p325 for who counts) occupying the same accommodation without a separate right to do so. You must continue to occupy the same property and claim within four weeks of the death;
- your partner (who was exempt) has been detained in custody and is not entitled to HB under the temporary absence rules (see p254). You must continue to occupy the same property and claim within four weeks of the imprisonment;

- your former partner (who was exempt) has left the dwelling and you are no longer living together as husband and wife. This should also apply if you are no longer living together as civil partners. You must continue to occupy the same property and claim within four weeks of the date s/he left.

The exemption can only be transferred if either the exempt claimant was in receipt of HB at the time s/he died (or left the dwelling), or had become a 'welfare to work' beneficiary (see p738) within the previous 52 weeks.[97] If the exemption cannot be transferred, other rent restriction rules may apply when you make a new claim.

When your rent can be restricted

The local authority must restrict your 'eligible rent' if it decides your accommodation is unreasonably large or your rent is unreasonably high (see below).[98] If you are in a 'protected group' (see p329), this only applies if:[99]

- cheaper suitable alternative accommodation is available to you; *and*
- it is reasonable to expect you to move.

Note: a rent restriction can be delayed in some circumstances (see p331).

Is your accommodation unreasonably large?

Your accommodation counts as unreasonably large if it is larger than is reasonably needed for you and anyone else who occupies the accommodation (including non-dependants and sub-tenants), taking account of suitable alternative accommodation occupied by other households of the same size.[100] The important question is the size of home you need, rather than the size of home you want.[101]

The needs of everyone living in your accommodation, whether or not they are part of your family, must be considered – eg, you might need additional space because someone has a disability, or lives elsewhere but regularly comes to visit you.

Is your rent unreasonably high?

Your rent can count as too high if it is unreasonably high compared with that for suitable alternative accommodation elsewhere.[102] 'Rent' includes, among other things, any service charges or licence fees you have to pay.[103]

When deciding whether your rent is unreasonably high, the local authority may ask a rent officer to assess a reasonable rent for your property, but the figures are not binding. *It* (not the rent officer) must decide whether your rent is unreasonably high, using different criteria from that used by the rent officer.[104]

It is not enough for the local authority to argue that your rent is merely higher than that for suitable alternative accommodation; it must be unreasonably higher.[105] In making this comparison, the local authority must consider the full range of rents that could be paid for such accommodation and not just the cheapest.[106] If your rent is within the range or just above it, the local authority may find it difficult to justify finding your rent to be unreasonably high.[107]

What is suitable alternative accommodation?

It is not sufficient for the local authority to show that cheaper or smaller alternative accommodation exists; it must also be **'suitable'** for the age and health of all the people that the local authority must take into account, having regard to the nature of the accommodation and the facilities available.[108] The local authority must consider these factors, even if you do not raise your housing needs yourself.[109]

The people that the local authority must take into account are:[110]

- you;
- members of your family for HB purposes; *and*
- any relative (see p325 for who counts) of yours or your partner who lives in the same dwelling as you without a separate right to do so.

The local authority must compare your home with **'alternative accommodation'**.

- It cannot just compare homes with the same number of bedrooms; some effort must be made to establish what other facilities are available.[111]
- It must compare your home with other properties offering the same security of tenure. For example, if you have an assured tenancy, the local authority may not rely on comparisons with accommodation that is let on assured shorthold tenancies, or with council or housing association properties.[112]
- It does not have to exclude properties which you cannot take because the landlord wants a deposit that you cannot afford.[113] However, if you are in a 'protected group', you might be able to argue that the accommodation is not available to you (see p330).
- It should not make comparisons with other parts of the country where accommodation costs differ widely from local ones, but it may compare your property with one in a less expensive area within a city.[114]

Are you in a protected group?

If the local authority decides that your rent or the size of your accommodation is unreasonable, it must consider whether you are in a 'protected group'.[115] If you are, it cannot restrict your rent unless cheaper suitable alternative accommodation is available and it is reasonable to expect you to move.

You are in a protected group if any of the people the local authority must take into account:

- are at least the qualifying age for pension credit (see p509); *or*
- satisfy any of the tests for being incapable of work or for having limited capability for work, or can be treated as incapable of or as having limited capability for work (see Chapters 11 and 32);[116] *or*

- have a child (this includes a qualifying young person) living with them for whom they are responsible (see p761).

Is cheaper suitable alternative accommodation available?

The local authority must prove that suitable alternative accommodation (see p329) exists and is actually available to you. It does not need to refer to specific properties, but must have sufficient evidence to demonstrate the existence of an active housing market comprising accommodation of a suitable type, rent and location for you.[117]

In considering whether accommodation is **'available'**, the local authority must take into account personal factors, such as whether you can afford to pay a deposit.[118] If the local authority produces a list of properties that are available to you, try to show that they are not available because of your personal circumstances.[119]

Is it reasonable to expect you to move?

The local authority must show that it is reasonable to expect you to move. It must take into account the adverse effects of a move on:[120]

- your ability to retain your job; *and*
- the education of any child or young person living with you. In considering this, the local authority must justify any decision that it is reasonable to make the child travel to or move school.[121]

The local authority may say that it does not need to consider any other factors, such as your health.[122] However, if there are good reasons why you cannot move other than those listed above, try to argue that alternative accommodation cannot be suitable.[123]

Maximum rent

Your 'maximum rent' for HB purposes (and your 'eligible rent' – see p260) is normally your contractual rent minus ineligible services. If you are in shared accommodation, this can be apportioned between you and the people with whom you share. It only covers the rent you pay for residential accommodation.[124]

However, if the local authority decides your 'eligible rent' should be restricted, it reduces it to the amount it considers appropriate.[125] It must take into account the cost of suitable alternative accommodation and other circumstances that are reasonably relevant to the decision – eg, pregnancy, the difficulty of finding other suitable accommodation and whether the local authority would have to rehouse you if you had to move.[126]

The local authority should not be unduly influenced by the amount of subsidy it is paid by the government, but it can take this into account when deciding on a reasonable level of rent. It cannot be reduced below that payable for suitable alternative accommodation.[127]

Delay before a rent restriction is applied

No restriction can be made for 12 months from the date of the death of a member of your family or a relative (see p325 for who counts) who lives in the same dwelling as you without a separate right to do so.[128] If you or a member of your family for HB purposes (or a relative of yours or your partner who lives in the same dwelling as you without a separate right to do so) could meet the costs of the dwelling when you took them on (this could include other bills as well as the rent), no restriction can be made for 13 weeks provided you were not entitled to HB in the 52 weeks before your current award of HB.[129]

Rent increases

If your landlord increases your rent, the local authority cannot increase your 'eligible rent' by the full amount if it decides that:[130]

- the increase is unreasonably high compared with increases in suitable alternative accommodation. The local authority must consider the amount of the increase, as well as what your rent was and what your rent will be, and compare it with the rent in the suitable alternative accommodation.[131] It should also consider, for example, the quality of the accommodation, your age and state of health, whether you would have to move if the increase is not met and how a move would affect you;[132] *or*
- the increase is unreasonable because a previous increase occurred within the preceding 12 months.

If the local authority considers a rent increase to have been unreasonable, it may refuse to meet all of that increase or meet only so much of it as it considers appropriate. If your rent has been increased for the second time in under 12 months but it is still below the market level for suitable alternative accommodation, or the increase reflects improvements made to your accommodation, argue for the full amount to be allowed.

Challenging a rent restriction

If you disagree with the local authority's decision to apply a rent restriction, or with the amount of the restriction, you can ask for a revision or appeal (see Chapters 45 and 46).

6. If you are considering renting accommodation

If you are considering renting accommodation privately and are likely to claim housing benefit (HB), you might want to find out the rent figure that will be used to calculate it. If you are already claiming HB, you may wish to find out the rent figure that will be used when your claim is reassessed (usually annually).

Local housing allowances

If the local housing allowance rules apply to you, you can check what category of dwelling applies to you (see p309) and then work out the appropriate local housing allowance. You can check the amount of the appropriate local housing allowance on the Valuation Office Agency website at www.direct.gov.uk/en/diol1/doitonline/DG_196239. **Note:** local housing allowances are updated monthly and can go down as well as up.

Pre-tenancy determinations

If the local reference rent rules apply to you, you can apply to the local authority for a pre-tenancy determination.[133] You can also apply if you are already receiving HB and your tenancy is due for renewal. Your current tenancy agreement must have started at least 11 months before your request.[134] The procedure is as follows.

- You must apply in writing on the form approved by your local authority. Both you and your prospective landlord must sign it.[135] The local authority must forward your request to the rent officer within two days of receipt.[136]
- The rent officer must send you, the prospective landlord and the local authority her/his determinations within five working days (unless s/he needs more information from the local authority) or as soon as is practicable after that.[137] If the rent officer needs further information, the five days run from the date this is received.

A pre-tenancy determination is usually valid for a year.[138] So if someone else applied for a pre-tenancy determination for your accommodation in the previous 12 months, it also applies to you.

You cannot appeal against a pre-tenancy determination. However, if you accept the tenancy and claim HB, you can ask for it to be redetermined. If you subsequently negotiate a lower rent with your landlord which is lower than your 'maximum rent', your HB is recalculated using your new rent.[139]

Notes

1. Which rent restriction rules apply

1 The law refers to 'gypsies and travellers' - Sch 2 para 3 HB Regs; Sch 2 para 3 HB(SPC) Regs
2 CH/2986/2005
3 Regs 76(1) and 79(1) HB Regs; regs 57(1) and 59(1) HB(SPC) Regs; reg 8(2) HB&CTB(DA) Regs
4 Regs 12C(2) and (3) and 13D(12) HB Regs; regs 12C(2) and 13D(12) HB(SPC) Regs
5 Reg 12B(6) HB Regs; reg 12B(6) HB(SPC) Regs; *AA v Chesterfield BC* [2011] UKUT 156 (AAC)
6 *R on the application of Laali v Westminster CC* [2002] HLR 179 (HC); *R v Macclesfield BC HBRB ex parte Temsemani* [1999] unreported (QBD); A4 Annex B GM

2. Excluded tenancies

7 Regs 13C(5)(a) and (c) and 14(2)(b) and Sch 2 paras 3-13 HB Regs; regs 13C(5)(a) and (c) and 14(2)(b) and Sch 2 paras 3-13 HB(SPC) Regs
8 The law refers to 'gypsies and travellers' – Sch 2 para 3 HB Regs; Sch 2 para 3 HB(SPC) Regs

3. The local housing allowance rules

9 Reg 13C(1), (2)(a)-(c), (4A)(a) and (5) HB Regs; reg 13C(1), (2)(a)-(c), (4A)(a) and (5) HB(SPC) Regs
10 Reg 13D(2)(c) and (3) HB Regs; reg 13D(2)(c) and (3) HB(SPC) Regs
11 *IB v Birmingham CC v SSWP V EHRC (HB)* [2011] UKUT 23 (AAC); *RG v SSWP and North Wiltshire DC (HB)* [2011] UKUT 198 (AAC); *KM v South Somerset DC (HB)* [2011] UKUT 148 (AAC). Note that leave to appeal to the Court of Appeal has been granted in the first case (*Burnip v Birmingham CC*) and in another case (*Trengrove v Walsall MBC*).
12 Reg 13D(12) HB Regs; reg 13D(12) HB(SPC) Regs. Both, definition of 'occupiers'
13 Reg 21(3) HB Regs; reg 21(3) HB(SPC) Regs; *AA v Chesterfield BC v SSWP (HB)* UKUT 156 (AAC)
14 R(H) 8/09; *SK v South Hams DC (HB)* [2010] UKUT 129 (AAC); [2010] AACR 40
15 *R v Swale BC HBRB ex parte Marchant* [1999] 1 FLR 1087 (QBD); [2000] 1 FLR 246 (CA)
16 Reg 2(1) HB Regs; reg 2(1) HB(SPC) Regs
17 Reg 13D(2)(a) HB Regs; reg 13D(2)(a) HB(SPC) Regs
18 Regs 2(1), definition of 'young individual' sub-paras (b)-(f) and 13D(2)(a) HB Regs; reg 13D(2)(a) and (12) HB(SPC) Regs, definition of 'care leaver'
19 Reg 2(1), (1A)-(1C) HB Regs, definition of 'young individual' sub-paras (g) and (h)
20 Reg 13D(2)(b) HB Regs; reg 13D(2)(b) HB(SPC) Regs
21 Reg 13D(2)(c) HB Regs; reg 13D(2)(c) HB(SPC) Regs
22 Reg 13D(1) HB Regs; reg 13D(1) HB(SPC) Regs; Art 4B(2A) and (4) and Sch 3B RO(HBF)O; Art 4B(2A) and (4) and Sch 3B RO(HBF)(S)O
23 Sch 3B paras 4 and 5 RO(HBF)O; Sch 3B paras 4 and 5 RO(HBF)(S)O
24 Art 4B(12) RO(HBF)O; Art 4B(12) RO(HBF)(S)O
25 Reg 13E HB Regs; reg 13E HB(SPC) Regs; Art 4B(2A) RO(HBF)O; Art 4B(2A) RO(HBF)(S)O
26 Reg 13D(5) HB Regs; reg 13D(5) HB(SPC) Regs
27 Reg 12D(2)(a) HB Regs; reg 12D(2)(a) HB(SPC) Regs
28 Reg 13D(4) and (12) HB Regs; reg 13D(4) and (12) HB(SPC) Regs
29 Regs 12D(2) and 13C(3), (4) and (6) HB Regs; regs 12D(2) and 13C(3), (4) and (6) HB(SPC) Regs
30 Regs 2, definition of 'linked person', 12D(2)(b) and 13C(2)(d) HB Regs; regs 2, definition of 'linked person', 12D(2)(b) and 13C(2)(d) HB(SPC) Regs
31 Reg 13D(1) and (12) HB Regs; reg 13D(1) and (12) HB(SPC) Regs. Both, definition of 'relevant date'

32 Regs 2(1), definition of 'reckonable rent', and 12D(3), (4) and (8) HB Regs; regs 2(1), definition of 'reckonable rent', and 12D(3), (4) and (8) HB(SPC) Regs
33 Reg 12D(5), (6) and (8) HB Regs; reg 12D(5), (6) and (8) HB(SPC) Regs
34 Reg 12D(7) HB Regs; reg 12D(7) HB(SPC) Regs
35 Reg 2(1) HB Regs; reg 2(1) HB(SPC) Regs
36 Reg 12M(1) HB Regs; reg 12M(1) HB(SPC) Regs
37 Reg 12M(2) HB Regs; reg 12M(2) HB(SPC) Regs
38 Reg 12M(3), (4) and (4A) HB Regs; reg 12M(3), (4) and (4A) HB(SPC) Reg
39 Reg 12M(4) and (4A) HB Regs
40 *LB Bexley v LD (HB)* [2010] UKUT 79 (AAC); *SK v South Hams DC (HB)* [2010] UKUT 129 (AAC); [2010] AACR 40

4. **The local reference rent rules**

41 Regs 13(1), 13C(5)(a)-(e) and (6) and 14(1) HB Regs; regs 13(1), 13C(5)(a)-(e) and (6) and 14(1) HB(SPC) Regs
42 The law refers to 'gypsies and travellers' – Sch 2 para 3 HB Regs; Sch 2 para 3 HB(SPC) Regs
43 Reg 13C(2)(a)-(c) HB Regs; reg 13C(2)(a)-(c) HB(SPC) Regs
44 Regs 13(1) and 14(1)(c), (f) and (g) and (8) HB Regs; regs 13(1) and 14(1)(c), (f) and (g) and (8) HB(SPC) Regs
45 Reg 14(1) HB Regs; reg 14(1) HB(SPC) Regs
46 Sch 2 para 2(3)(a)-(d) HB Regs; Sch 2 para 2(3)(a)-(d) HB(SPC) Regs
47 R(H) 8/09; *SK v South Hams DC (HB)* [2010] UKUT 129 (AAC); [2010] AACR 40
48 CH/1556/2006; CH/3590/2007
49 Sch 2 para 2(1) and (2) HB Regs; Sch 2 para 2(1) and (2) HB(SPC) Regs
50 Reg 14(2)(a) and (7) HB Regs; reg 14(2)(a) and (7) HB(SPC) Regs
51 Sch 1 para 1 RO(HBF)O; Sch 1 para 1 RO(HBF)(S)O
52 Sch 1 para 3 RO(HBF)O; Sch 1 para 3 RO(HBF)(S)O
53 Sch 1 para 3(5) RO(HBF)O; Sch 1 para 3(5) RO(HBF)(S)O
54 *Sch 1 para 2 RO(HBF)O*; Sch 1 para 2 RO(HBF)(S)O
55 Sch 1 para 1(4) RO(HBF)O; Sch 1 para 1(4) RO(HBF)(S)O
56 Sch 2 RO(HBF)O; Sch 2 RO(HBF)(S)O
57 Art 2(1) RO(HBF)O; Art 2(1) RO(HBF)(S)O. Both, definition of 'occupier'
58 Reg 21(3) HB Regs; reg 21(3) HB(SPC) Regs
59 R(H) 8/09; *SK v South Hams DC (HB)* [2010] UKUT 129 (AAC); [2010] AACR 40
60 *R v Swale BC HBRB ex parte Marchant* [1999] 1 FLR 1087 (QBD); [2000] 1 FLR 246 (CA)
61 Sch 1 para 6 RO(HBF)O; Sch 1 para 6 RO(HBF)(S)O
62 Sch 1 para 4(6) and (7) RO(HBF)O; Sch 1 para 4(6) and (7) RO(HBF)(S)O
63 Sch 1 para 4 RO(HBF)O; Sch 1 para 4 RO(HBF)(S)O
64 Sch 1 para 9(2) RO(HBF)O; Sch 1 para 9(2) RO(HBF)(S)O
65 Reg 13(5) HB Regs
66 Regs 2(1), definition of 'young individual', and 13(6) HB Regs
67 Sch 1 para 5 RO(HBF)O; Sch 1 para 5 RO(HBF)(S)O
68 Reg 114A(6) and (8)(a) HB Regs
69 Sch 1 paras 5(2)(c) and 7(1) RO(HBF)O; Sch 1 paras 5(2)(c) and 7(1) RO(HBF)(S)O
70 Sch 1 para 9 RO(HBF)O; Sch 1 para 9 RO(HBF)(S)O
71 Art 2(1) RO(HBF)O; Art 2(1) RO(HBF)(S)O. Both, definition of 'relevant period'
72 Reg 12C HB Regs; reg 12C HB(SPC) Regs
73 Reg 13(2), (3) and (5) HB Regs; reg 13(2) and (3) HB(SPC) Regs
74 Reg 13(4) HB Regs; reg 13(4) HB(SPC) Regs; Sch 3 para 8 HB&CTB(CP) Regs
75 Reg 13ZB(1) HB Regs; reg 13ZB(1) HB(SPC) Regs
76 Reg 12C(2) and (3) HB Regs; reg 12C(2) HB (SPC) Regs
77 Regs 2, definition of 'linked person', and 13ZA(1) and (2) HB Regs; regs 2, definition of 'linked person', and 13ZA(1) and (2) HB(SPC) Regs
78 Reg 13ZA(3) and (4) HB Regs; reg 13ZA(3) and (4) HB(SPC) Regs
79 Reg 2(1) HB Regs; reg 2(1) HB(SPC) Regs
80 Reg 16 HB Regs; reg 16 HB(SPC) Regs
81 Reg 16(1)(b) HB Regs; reg 16(1)(b) HB(SPC) Regs
82 Arts 2(1), definition of 'relevant period', and 4 and Sch 3 RO(HBF)O; Arts 2(1), definition of 'relevant period', and 4 and Sch 3 RO(HBF)(S)O

83 Regs 16(5) and 79(1) HB Regs; regs 16(5) and 59(1) HB(SPC) Regs;reg 8(2) and (6) HB&CTB(DA) Regs
84 Reg 15 HB Regs; reg 15 HB(SPC) Regs
85 Reg 17 HB Regs; reg 17 HB(SPC) Regs
86 HB/CTB Circular G5/2005
87 Regs 16(3) and (4) and 18 HB Regs; regs 16(3) and (4) and 18 HB(SPC) Regs
88 *SK v South Hams DC (HB)* [2010] UKUT 129 (AAC); [2010] AACR 40; *LB Bexley v LD (HB)* [2010] UKUT 79 (AAC)

5. **The pre-January 1996 rules**

89 Regs 13C(5)(b) HB Regs; reg 13C(5)(b) HB(SPC) Regs; Sch 3 para 4(1)(b) and (10) HB&CT(CP) Regs; CH/1289/2007
90 R(H) 7/07; R(H) 4/09; CH/3900/2005; CH/2726/2008, *East Hertfordshire DC v KT* [2009] UKUT 12 (AAC); *Bristol CC v AW* [2009] UKUT 109 (AAC)
91 R(H) 7/07; CH/1289/2007; *Salford CC v PF* [2009] UKUT 150 (AAC)
92 R(H) 2/07
93 Reg 13C(2)(a)-(c) HB Regs; reg 13C(2)(a)-(c) HB(SPC) Regs; Sch 3 para 4(1)(a), (2), (3) and (4) HB&CTB(CP) Regs
94 Reg 13C HB Regs; reg 13C HB(SPC) Regs; Sch 3 para 4(2) HB&CTB(CP) Regs
95 Reg 13C(2)(a)-(c) HB Regs; reg 13C(2)(a)-(c) HB(SPC) Regs
96 Reg 13C HB Regs; reg 13C HB(SPC) Regs; Sch 3 para 4(2), (5), (6), (9) and (10) HB&CTB(CP) Regs, definitions of 'relevant date' and 'previous beneficiary'
97 Sch 3 para 4(10) HB&CTB(CP) Regs, definition of 'previous beneficiary'
98 Reg 13(3) HB Regs and reg 13(3) HB(SPC) Regs as set out in Sch 3 para 5(2) HB&CTB(CP) Regs
99 Reg 13(4) HB Regs and reg 13(4) HB(SPC) Regs as set out in Sch 3 para 5(2) HB&CTB(CP) Regs
100 Reg 13(3)(a) HB Regs and reg 13(3)(a) HB(SPC) Regs as set out in Sch 3 para 5(2) HB&CTB(CP) Regs
101 *R v Kensington and Chelsea RBC HBRB ex parte Pirie* [1997] 26 March, unreported (QBD)
102 Reg 13(3)(b) HB Regs and reg 13(3)(b) HB(SPC) Regs as set out in Sch 3 para 5(2) HB&CTB(CP) Regs
103 *R v Beverley DCHBRB ex parte Hare* [1995] 27 HLR 637 (QBD)
104 *R v Kensington and Chelsea RBC HBRB ex parte Sheikh*, 14 January 1997, unreported (QBD)
105 *R v Kensington and Chelsea RBC ex parte Abou-Jaoude*, 10 May 1996, unreported (QBD)
106 *Macleod v Banff and Buchan District HBRB* [1988] SLT 753 (CS); *Malcolm v Tweedale District HBRB* [1994] SLT 1212 (CS); CH/4970/2002
107 *R v Kensington and Chelsea RBC ex parte Abou-Jaoude,* 10 May 1996, ureported (QBD)*; R v Coventry CC ex parte Waite*, 7 July 1995, unreported (QBD)
108 Reg 13(9) HB Regs and reg 13(9) HB(SPC) Regs as set out in Sch 3 para 5(2) HB&CTB(CP) Regs
109 R(H) 2/05
110 Reg 13(10) and (11) HB Regs and reg 13(10) and (11) HB(SPC) Regs as set out in Sch 3 para 5(2) HB&CTB(CP) Regs
111 *R v Lambeth LBC HBRB ex parte Harrington*, 22 November 1996, unreported (QBD)
112 Reg 13(9)(a) HB Regs and reg 13(9)(a) HB(SPC) Regs as set out in Sch 3 para 5(2) HB&CTB(CP) Regs; *R v Kensington and Chelsea RBC ex parte Pirie,* 26 March 1997, unreported (QBD)*; R v Coventry CC ex parte Waite*, 7 July 1995, unreported (QBD)
113 *R v Waltham Forest LBC ex parte Holder* [1996] 29 HLR 71 (QBD); *R v Slough BC ex parte Green*, 15 November 1996, unreported (QBD)
114 *R v Waltham Forest LBC ex parte Holder* [1996] 29 HLR 71 (QBD); *R v Kensington and Chelsea RBC HBRB ex parte Sheikh*, 14 January 1997, unreported (QBD)
115 Reg 13(4) HB Regs and reg 13(4) HB(SPC) Regs as set out in Sch 3 para 5(2) HB&CTB(CP) Regs
116 R(H) 3/06
117 *R v East Devon DC HBRB ex parte Gibson* [1993] 25 HLR 487 (QBD); CH/4306/2003
118 *R v Waltham Forest LBC ex parte Holder* [1996] 29 HLR 71 (QBD)
119 *R v Oadby and Wigston DC ex parte Dickman* [1995] 28 HLR 806 (QBD)
120 Reg 13(9)(b) HB Regs and reg 13(9)(b) HB(SPC) Regs as set out in Sch 3 para 5(2) HB&CT(CP) Regs
121 *R v Kensington and Chelsea RBC HBRB ex parte Sheikh*, 14 January 1997, unreported (QBD)
122 *R v Kensington and Chelsea RBC HBRB ex parte Carney* [1997] Crown Office Digest 124 (QBD)

123 *R v Camden LBC HBRB ex p W* [1999] 21 May, unreported, QBD; *R v Westminster CC HBRB ex p Pallas* [1997] unreported, 23 September, QBD
124 Reg 12(3)-(5) HB Regs and reg 12(3)-(5) HB(SPC) Regs as set out in Sch 3 para 5(1) HB&CTB(CP) Regs
125 Reg 13(3) HB Regs and reg 13(3) HB(SPC) Regs as set out in Sch 3 para 5(1) HB&CTB(CP) Regs
126 *R v City of Westminster HBRB ex parte Mehanne* [1992] 2 All ER 317 (CA)
127 *R v Brent LBC HBRB ex parte Connery* [1989] 22 HLR 40 (QBD)
128 Reg 13(5) HB Regs and reg 13(5) HB(SPC) Regs as set out in Sch 3 para 5(2) HB&CTB(CP) Regs
129 Reg 13(7) and (8) HB Regs and reg 13(7) and (8) HB(SPC) Regs as set out in Sch 3 para 5(2) HB&CTB(CP) Regs
130 Reg 13ZA HB Regs and reg 13ZA HB(SPC) Regs as set out in Sch 3 para 5(3) HB&CTB(CP) Regs
131 *BM v Cheshire West and Cheshire Council* [2009] UKUT 162 (AAC)
132 CH/2214/2003

6. **If you are considering renting accommodation**

133 Reg 14(1)(e) and (2) HB Regs; reg 14(1)(e) and (2) HB(SPC) Regs
134 Reg 14(8) HB Regs; reg 14(8) HB(SPC) Regs. Both, definition of 'prospective occupier'
135 Reg 14(1)(e) and (8) HB Regs; reg 14(1)(e) and (8) HB(SPC) Regs. Both, definition of 'specified matters'
136 Reg 14(5) HB Regs; reg 14(5) HB(SPC) Regs
137 Art 2(1) RO(HBF)O; Art 2(1) RO(HBF)(S)O. Both, definition of 'relevant period'
138 Reg 14(4)(b) and Sch 2 para 2(2)(b) HB Regs; reg 14(4)(b) and Sch 2 para 2(2)(b) HB(SPC) Regs
139 Reg 13ZB(2)-(4) HB Regs; reg 13ZB(2)-(4) HB(SPC) Regs

Chapter 16

Incapacity benefit

This chapter covers:

Key facts

- Incapacity benefit (IB) is a benefit for people who are incapable of work because of sickness or disability.
- In most cases, it is not possible to make a new claim for IB. If you are too ill or disabled to work, you must usually claim employment and support allowance (ESA). If you claim IB, your claim is treated as a claim for ESA.
- Some people who are getting income support on the grounds of disability are still able to make a new claim for IB.
- If you are already entitled to IB, you remain entitled, provided you continue to satisfy the qualifying conditions. Your claim will be transferred to ESA by April 2014 at the latest.
- If you disagree with a decision on your IB, including a decision about being transferred to ESA, you can apply for a revision or supersession, or appeal against it (see Chapters 45 and 46).

Future changes: April 2013 and after

Major changes are taking place that affect the benefit and tax credits system (see Chapter 2). From April 2013, total benefit payments to many working-age households will be 'capped' (see p25). There will be limited exceptions, including households in which someone is entitled to working tax credit or receives disability living allowance. It is not yet known if IB will be included in the capped amount. See CPAG's *Welfare Rights Bulletin* for updates.

1. Who is still entitled

You can only be entitled to incapacity benefit (IB) now if:[1]

- you are already entitled to it (and continue to meet the qualifying conditions on p388); *or*

- you are entitled to income support (IS) on grounds of disability (see p347), claim IB now and meet the qualifying conditions below.

For full details about IB, including special benefit rules, claims and getting paid, see the 2008/09 edition of this *Handbook*.

Transfer to employment and support allowance

People already entitled to IB continue to receive IB until their award is transferred to a claim for employment and support allowance (ESA), and entitlement is reassessed under the work capability assessment. This process is due to be complete by April 2014 (see p193).

The qualifying conditions

You qualify for IB if:

- you are already entitled or are getting IS on grounds of disability; *and*
- you are assessed as, or treated as, incapable of work (see p339 and p734); *and*
- you are within a 'period of incapacity for work' (see p339); *and*
- for short-term IB, you are not more than five years above pension age and, for long-term IB, you are not over pension age (see p339). For the meaning of short-term IB and long-term IB, see p340; *and*
- you are not entitled to statutory sick pay (SSP – see Chapter 28); *and either*
- you have paid (or been credited with) sufficient national insurance (NI) contributions. See p735 of the 2008/09 edition of this *Handbook* for more information. This test applies at the start of your claim; *or*
- you qualify as someone who became incapable of work in youth; *or*
- you are no more than five years over pension age (see p531), your period of incapacity for work began before you reached pension age, and you would qualify for a Category B retirement pension as a widow, widower or surviving civil partner, or a Category A retirement pension had you not deferred claiming it or 'de-retired' (see Chapter 23). (**Note:** this provision only allows you to qualify for short-term IB); *or*
- your spouse died before 9 April 2001 and you qualify as a widow or widower.

There are some groups of claimants to whom special rules apply. These are:

- widows and widowers;
- people who have been incapable of work since 12 April 1995;
- people coming from or going abroad (see Chapter 61);
- people in prison or detention (see Chapter 30).

For full details, including the rules on incapacity for work in youth, widows and widowers and people incapable of work since 12 April 1995, see the 2008/09 edition of this *Handbook*.

Incapable of work

In order to qualify for IB you must be incapable of work or treated as incapable of work. For full details, see Chapters 7 and 28 of the 2010/11 edition of this *Handbook*. This is different from the test of whether you have 'limited capability for work' that applies to ESA (see Chapter 11).

Period of incapacity for work

You are only entitled to IB for any day on which you are incapable of work that forms part of a 'period of incapacity for work'. For full details, see Chapter 12 of the 2010/11 edition of this *Handbook*.

A **'period of incapacity for work'** is either:

- a period of four or more consecutive days when you are incapable of work;[2] *or*
- if you are having plasmapheresis, chemotherapy or radiotherapy, or regular weekly kidney dialysis or total parenteral nutrition, a period of two days when you are incapable of work. These days do not have to be consecutive as long as they are within a period of seven consecutive days.[3] In these circumstances, you are treated as incapable of work on the days that you have this treatment.[4]

The rules about your age

Lower age limit

To qualify for IB on the grounds of being incapable of work in youth, you must be 16 or over.

If you qualify for IB on the basis of your NI contribution record, there is no lower age limit, but you must have paid or been credited with NI contributions over a period of at least two years (see p791). You do not have to start paying NI contributions on earnings until you are 16.

Upper age limit

You are not entitled to long-term IB after you reach pension age (see p531).[5]

If you are not more than five years over pension age, you are entitled to short-term IB if:

- you would have been entitled to a Category A or, on the basis of your late spouse's or late civil partner's NI contributions, a Category B retirement pension had you not deferred claiming it or 'de-retired'; *and*
- your period of incapacity for work began before you reached pension age; *and*
- the period of 364 days during which IB is paid at the short-term rate has not yet run out.[6]

See p341 for the amount of IB paid after you reach pension age and p288 of the 2008/09 edition of this *Handbook* for details of whether you may be better off claiming your retirement pension or remaining on IB after reaching pension age.

2. The amount of benefit

If you are getting incapacity benefit (IB) (either the short-term or long-term rates), you may be entitled to an increase for your adult dependant – ie, your spouse, civil partner or someone who looks after your child (see p740).[7] Your entitlement to an increase may be affected by certain income your adult dependant receives (see p744). This earnings rule is more generous for long-term IB than for short-term IB. This means that if your adult dependant has too much income to entitle you to an increase when you are receiving short-term IB, you may become entitled once you begin to be paid at the long-term rate. If so, you must make a separate claim for this increase within three months of becoming entitled to the long-term rate. If you do not, only three months' arrears are paid.[8]

Increases for dependent children were abolished on 6 April 2003. However, if you were entitled to an increase for a dependent child on 5 April 2003, you may be able to continue to receive it after that date (see p745). If your partner has certain kinds of income, your entitlement to an increase for a child may be affected (see p745).

Rates of incapacity benefit

IB is paid at three rates. The rate you receive depends on the length of time you have either been entitled to IB, or treated as entitled to IB (see below). Days on which you are disqualified from receiving IB (see p271 of the 2008/09 edition of this *Handbook*) are not counted.[9] You receive:

- the lower rate of short-term IB for the first 28 weeks of entitlement;
- the higher rate of short-term IB after 28 weeks of entitlement – ie, from the 197th day of entitlement;
- long-term IB after 52 weeks of entitlement – ie, from the 365th day of entitlement;
- an amount equivalent to the long-term rate after 28 weeks of entitlement if you are terminally ill or receiving the highest rate of disability living allowance (DLA) care component (see Chapter 9). The definition of 'terminally ill' is the same as that for DLA (see p157).[10]

Treated as entitled to incapacity benefit

For the purpose of determining the rate of benefit you receive, you are treated as entitled to IB on:[11]

- the first three days of your 'period of incapacity for work'. You cannot always receive IB for these days, which are called 'waiting days'. See p270 of the 2008/09 edition of this *Handbook*;
- days on which you are entitled to maternity allowance (see Chapter 21);
- days on which you are entitled to statutory maternity pay (SMP) or statutory adoption pay (SAP), but only if:

  - you are incapable of work, and on the day before your SMP or SAP started you were within a period of incapacity for work (see p339) or were receiving statutory sick pay (SSP); *and*
  - the days are not days on which you are treated as capable of work for IB purposes; *and*
  - you satisfy the contribution conditions for IB on the first day in your period of incapacity for work or on a day on which you were receiving SSP;
- days on which you satisfied the contribution conditions for IB and were entitled to SSP, as long as your period of entitlement to SSP ended not more than 57 days before your current period of incapacity for work began;
- certain days of sickness absence from duty if you were a member of the armed forces.

Amount paid

The full weekly rates of IB are as follows, but in certain circumstances your IB may be reduced (see p342).

	Under pension age £pw	*Pension age or over £pw*
Long-term IB		
Claimant	99.15	n/a
Adult dependant	57.60	n/a
Child dependant:		
– eldest eligible child	8.10	n/a
– each other child	11.35	n/a
Short-term IB (higher rate)		
Claimant	88.55	99.15
Adult dependant	44.85	55.45
Child dependant:		
– eldest eligible child	8.10	8.10
– each other child	11.35	11.35
Short-term IB (lower rate)		
Claimant	74.80	95.15
Adult dependant	44.85	55.45
Child dependant:		
– eldest eligible child	n/a	8.10
– each other child	n/a	11.35

If you are terminally ill or you are getting the highest rate of the DLA care component, your IB can be paid at a rate equivalent to the long-term rate of IB after you have been entitled to short-term IB for 196 days.[12]

See Chapter 33 for details of the qualifying conditions for payment of an increase in your IB for dependants.

If IB is payable for a period of less than a week, it is paid at a daily rate of one-seventh of the weekly amount.

If you are entitled to long-term IB, you may also be entitled to:

- an age-related addition (see below); *and*
- a Christmas bonus (see p9).

Your IB is reduced if you:

- receive certain pension payments or certain payments from the Pension Protection Fund (see p343 for details and for details of exceptions);
- are a local councillor and your net councillor's allowances exceed £97.50 (see p887);[13]
- are over pension age (see p531) and are entitled to short-term IB (you cannot qualify for long-term IB if you are over pension age) and your retirement pension, had you claimed it, would have been reduced because your national insurance (NI) contribution record is incomplete. In this situation, your short-term IB will be reduced by the same proportion (see p795). However, as for people under pension age, if you are terminally ill or you are getting the highest rate of the DLA care component, you can receive the equivalent of the long-term rate of IB after the first 196 days of entitlement to short-term IB, if this would be more favourable to you than receiving the higher rate of short-term IB.[14]

The amount of your benefit may also be reduced if you or, in some cases your partner, are required to take part in a work-focused interview and fail to do so (see p1035) or if your partner is required to take part because you get an increase in your IB for her/him (see p1033).

In some circumstances, deductions from your benefit may be made to repay certain loans (see p1054) and, if you get income support (IS) or pension credit (PC) with your IB, deductions may be made from your IB and paid directly to other third parties. This may happen if your IS or PC alone is insufficient to meet those payments (see p1048).

For each week you receive IB you are entitled to NI credits (see p780).

Certain people who are entitled to long-term IB throughout a tax year may also build up entitlement to additional state pension (see p537).[15]

Age-related additions

Once you are entitled to long-term IB, you are paid an age-related addition to your benefit if you were under 45 *either*:[16]

- on the first day of your period of incapacity for work (see p339); *or*
- on the first day of any previous periods of incapacity for work linked to your current one; *or*

- on the first day of your period of entitlement to SSP (see p618), if you were previously on SSP and your current period of incapacity for work started not more than 57 days after your SSP stopped.

Special rules apply to certain widows or if you are a serving member of the armed forces.[17]

This age-related addition is paid at two rates depending on your age on the relevant day.

Age	*£pw*
Under 35	11.70
Under 45	5.90

If you receive a guaranteed minimum pension from a contracted-out occupational pension scheme (which may be from your late spouse's or late civil partner's pension scheme), the amount of your age addition will be reduced by the amount of your guaranteed minimum pension.[18]

Reduction in incapacity benefit for pension payments

If your entitlement to IB started on or after 6 April 2001, your benefit may be reduced if you receive certain kinds of pension payments (but see below if you receive the highest rate of DLA care component).

If the total amount of the gross pension payments you receive is more than £85 a week, your IB is reduced by half the amount of pension payments paid above £85 a week.[19] If the total gross pension payments you receive amount to £85 or less each week, your IB is unaffected. The rules on which pensions are taken into account are similar to those that apply to employment and support allowance (see p186). However, if you are entitled to the highest rate of DLA care component (see Chapter 9), all pension payments you receive are ignored and so do not affect your entitlement to IB.

If you were entitled to incapacity benefit before 6 April 2001

If you were entitled to IB before 6 April 2001 and you have continued to be entitled to IB since that time, any pension payments you receive will not affect your IB.[20] However, see p343 if you get an age addition with your IB and a guaranteed minimum pension from a contracted-out occupational pension scheme.

Notes

1. **Who is still entitled**

1 Reg 2 ESA(TP) Regs
2 s30C(1)(b) SSCBA 1992
3 Reg 6 SS(IB) Regs
4 Reg 13 SS(IFW) Regs
5 s30A(5) SSCBA 1992
6 s30A(2)(b) SSCBA 1992

2. **The amount of benefit**

7 s86A SSCBA 1992; reg 9 SS(IB-ID) Regs
8 Reg 19(2) and (3) SS(C&P) Regs
9 s30D(4) SSCBA 1992
10 s30B(4) SSCBA 1992
11 s30D SSCBA 1992; reg 3 SSCBA(MHMFIB) Regs; regs 7, 7A, 7B and 7C SS(IB) Regs
12 s30B(4) SSCBA 1992
13 s30E SSCBA 1992; regs 8 and 9 SS(IB) Regs
14 s30B(3) and (4) SSCBA 1992
15 s44A SSCBA 1992
16 s30B(7) SSCBA 1992; regs 10 and 11 SS(IB) Regs
17 Regs 12 and 13 SS(IB) Regs
18 s46(3) Pension Schemes Act 1993
19 s30DD SSCBA 1992; R(IB)3/05
20 Reg 6 SS(IB)MA Regs

Chapter 17

Income support

This chapter covers:

Key facts

- Income support (IS) is a benefit for people who are unemployed or working part time who fit into one of the specific groups of people who can claim.
- IS is a means-tested benefit.
- You do not have to have paid national insurance contributions to qualify.
- You cannot qualify for IS if you (or your partner) are in full-time paid work.
- IS is administered and paid by the DWP.
- If you disagree with an IS decision, you can apply for a revision or a supersession, or appeal against it (see Chapters 45 and 46).

Future changes: April 2013 and after

Major changes are taking place that affect the benefits and tax credits system (see Chapter 2).

- From April 2013, total benefit payments to many working-age households will be 'capped' (see p25). There will be limited exceptions, including households where someone is entitled to working tax credit or receives disability living allowance. IS will be included in the capped amount.
- From October 2013, when universal credit (UC) is introduced, no new claims for IS will be allowed. Claimants of IS will be transferred to UC between April 2014 and October 2017.

See CPAG's *Welfare Rights Bulletin* for updates.

1. Who can claim income support

You qualify for income support (IS) if:[1]

- you fit into one of the groups of people who can claim IS (see below to p353);
- neither you nor your partner count as being in full-time paid work (see p353 and Chapter 31);
- you are not studying full time. There are exceptions to this rule (see p640). See p635 if you are at school or college. See p641 if you are studying part time;
- you are not entitled to jobseeker's allowance (JSA), including joint-claim JSA, or employment and support allowance (ESA);
- your partner (if you have one) is not entitled to *income-based* JSA, including joint-claim JSA, *income-related* ESA or pension credit (PC);
- you are at least 16 and are under the qualifying age for PC (see p509);
- your income is less than your applicable amount (see p355);
- your savings and other capital are worth £16,000 or less. Some capital (in particular, your home) is ignored (see Chapter 41);
- you satisfy the 'habitual residence test' and the 'right to reside test', and are present in Great Britain. To find out if you are exempt from the tests, see Chapter 62. To see if you can claim IS during a temporary absence abroad, see p1488; *and*
- you are not a 'person subject to immigration control' (see p1410).[2] There are exceptions to this rule.

In some cases, you (or your partner if you have one) may be required to attend a work-focused interview (see p354).

Note: from some point in the future:

- you will have to accept a 'claimant committment' that records what your responsibilities are in return for getting IS. This could be sometime in 2012. There may be exceptions to this rule;
- the rules may be amended so that even if you satisfy all the rules above, you will only be able to qualify for IS if your partner has limited capability for work.[3] There will be exceptions.

See CPAG's *Welfare Rights Bulletin* for updates.

Groups of people who can claim income support

You can claim IS if you satisfy the other rules for getting IS described above and you fit into one of the groups of people who can claim.[4] If you fit into one of the groups on any day in a benefit week, you count as doing so for the whole week.

Note:

- If you are getting IS on the basis that you fit into one of the groups of people who can claim, but your circumstances change, check to see if you fit into any of the other groups of people who can claim. If you do, your entitlement to IS continues.[5]
- In the past there were additional groups of people who could claim IS. If you are getting IS on the basis that you fit into one of these groups (referred to as 'transitional groups' – see p350), you may continue to qualify on this basis.

Sick and disabled people

You fit into one of the groups of people who can claim IS if any of the following apply to you.[6]

- You are **entitled to statutory sick pay** (SSP).
- You are incapable of work, but are **treated as capable of work because you are disqualified from receiving incapacity benefit** (IB) because of misconduct or failure to accept treatment (see p271 of the 2008/09 edition of this *Handbook*).

You may still fit into one of the groups of people who can claim IS if you are appealing a decision that you are not entitled to IS, IB or national insurance (NI) credits because you are not incapable of work under the own occupation test or thepersonal capability assessment. In this case, your IS might be paid at a reduced rate. See pp311–12 of the 2011/12 edition of this *Handbook*.

Note:

- If you are entitled to IB or severe disablement allowance (SDA), you can claim and qualify for IS in specified circumstances (see p351). You can make a new claim for IS in this situation, even if you have never claimed before.
- The rules changed on 27 October 2008, 30 December 2009 and 25 January 2010. Before these dates, there were additional groups of sick and disabled people who could claim and qualify for IS. You may continue to qualify for IS on this basis. See pp351 and 352 for information about these transitional groups.

Looking after children and other responsibilities

You fit into one of the groups of people who can claim IS if any of the following apply to you.[7]

- You are a **lone parent with a child under seven**; you must be responsible for her/him and s/he must live in your household (see pp761 and 762).[8] You do not have to be the child's parent – eg, you could be her/his grandparent. **Note:** the government intends to reduce the age limit for a child to five (possibly from April 2012) for new IS claims; existing claimants will be transferred to JSA or ESA from some point after that.

Once your only or youngest child turns seven, you cannot qualify for IS unless you fit into one of the other groups of people who can claim – eg, if you have a disabled child, you may be able to qualify for IS as a carer. However, if you were claiming IS as the lone parent of a child of six or over before 25 October 2010, you might be able to continue to receive IS as a lone parent for a period. See p352 for further information about this transitional group.

- You are entitled to and are **on 'parental leave'** from work under specific provisions; *and*
  - during the period for which you are claiming IS, you are not entitled to a payment of any kind from your employer; *and*
  - you and your child(ren) live in the same household (see p 762); *and*
  - you were entitled to working tax credit (WTC), child tax credit (CTC) payable at a higher rate than the family element, housing benefit (HB) or council tax benefit (CTB) on the day before your parental leave began.
- You are entitled to and are **on ordinary paternity leave**;[9] *and*
  - you are not entitled to ordinary statutory paternity pay or to a payment of any kind from your employer during the period for which you are claiming IS; *or*
  - you were entitled to WTC, CTC payable at a higher rate than the family element, HB or CTB on the day before your paternity leave began.
- You are a **lone foster parent** – ie, you are fostering a child under 16 through a local authority or voluntary organisation and are not a member of a couple;
- A **child has been placed with you for adoption** by an adoption agency and you are not a member of a couple.
- You are **pregnant**; *and*
  - incapable of work because of your pregnancy. You only have to show that you are incapable of work, not that there is a serious risk to your health or that of your baby;[10] *or*
  - there are 11 weeks or less before the week your baby is due.
- You **had a baby not more than 15 weeks ago**.

You fit into one of the groups of people who claim IS **while any of the following apply** to you.[11]

- You are looking after a child under 16 because her/his parent or the person who usually looks after her/him is temporarily ill or temporarily away.[12]
- You are responsible for a child under 16 who lives in your household (see pp761 and 762) and your partner is temporarily out of the UK.
- You are looking after your partner, or a child (this includes a 'qualifying young person') for whom you are responsible and who lives in your household (see pp761 and 762), who is temporarily ill.[13]

Carers

You fit into one of the groups of people who can claim IS if you are a carer and any of the following apply to you.[14]

- You receive carer's allowance (CA), or would receive it had it not been restricted under the 'loss of benefit for benefit offences' rules (see p1106).
- The person for whom you care:
  - has claimed attendance allowance (AA) or disability living allowance (DLA). You are entitled to IS for up to 26 weeks from the date of the claim for AA/DLA or until the claim is decided, whichever comes first; *or*
  - receives AA or the highest or middle rate care component of DLA; *or*
  - has been awarded AA or the highest or middle rate care component of DLA on an advance claim but it has not yet gone into payment.

You must be 'regularly and substantially engaged' in providing care. For CA, this means for at least 35 hours a week. However, to qualify for IS if you do not receive CA, the decision maker must look at the quality and quantity of care you provide. This could be less than 35 hours a week.[15]

If you cease meeting these conditions or stop being a carer, you can continue to claim IS for a further eight weeks. After that, you cannot get IS unless you fit into one of the other groups of people who can claim described in this chapter.

Pupils, students and people on training courses

You fit into one of the groups of people who can claim IS if any of the following apply to you.[16]

- You are a person **in 'relevant education' or** are **a full-time student** who can qualify for IS while studying (see pp635 or 640). However, if you are a full-time student who only qualifies because you are a lone parent, see p352.
- You are on a course of **full-time, non-advanced education** (or have been accepted or enrolled on it) and you are under 21 or you turned 21 while on such a course. This only applies if:
  - you are an orphan and have no one acting as your parent; *or*
  - you have to live away from your parents and any person acting in their place because you are estranged from them, are in physical or moral danger or there is a serious risk to your physical or mental health; *or*
  - you live away from your parents and any person acting in their place, they are unable to support you financially and:
    - they are chronically sick, or are mentally or physically disabled (ie, they could get a disability or a higher pensioner premium, are entitled to ESA including a work-related activity or support component or are substantially and permanently disabled); *or*
    - they are detained in custody pending trial or sentence or under a sentence from a court; *or*
    - they are not allowed to come into Great Britain because they do not have leave to enter under UK Immigration Rules.
- You are **aged 16 to 24 and on a training course** provided by Young People's Learning Agency for England (due to be replaced by the Education Funding Agency in April 2012), the Chief Executive of the Skills Funding Agency, the

Welsh Ministers or, in Scotland, by a local enterprise company. This does not apply if you are a child for child benefit purposes (see p94).
Some participants on training schemes have the legal status of employees (and are normally given contracts of employment). You do not qualify for IS if you are in full-time paid work (see p718); you might qualify for WTC instead.
If you receive a training allowance while on a course, your income may be too high for you to qualify for IS. However, you may qualify if, for example, you are on a lower rate of training allowance or you qualify for a disability premium.

Note: the rules changed on 27 October 2008, 30 December 2009 and 25 January 2010. Before these dates, there were additional groups of full-time students and people in 'relevant education' who could claim and qualify for IS. You may continue to qualify for IS on this basis. See p351 for information about these transitional groups.

Others

You fit into one of the groups of people who can claim IS if any of the following apply to you.[17]

- You **have to go to a court or tribunal** as a JP, juror, witness or party to the proceedings.
- You have been **remanded in custody, or committed in custody** but only until your trial or until you have been sentenced. You can only get IS for your housing costs (see Chapter 38).
- You are a **refugee who is learning English** in order to obtain employment. You must be on a course for more than 15 hours a week and, at the time the course started, you must have been in Great Britain for a year or less. You can get IS for up to nine months.
- You are a **'person subject to immigration control'** (see p1410), have limited leave to remain in the UK on the condition that you do not have recourse to public funds, but you are **temporarily without money** because funds from abroad have been disrupted. You must have supported yourself without recourse to public funds during your leave and there must be a reasonable expectation that your supply of funds will be resumed. You can only get IS on this basis for a limited period.[18]
- You are not treated as in full-time work because you **qualify for 'mortgage interest run-on'** (see pp879 and 726).
- You are involved in a **trade dispute** or have been back to work for 15 days or less following a trade dispute (see p701).

Transitional groups

In the past there were additional groups of people who could claim IS. If you fit into one of these groups (referred to as 'transitional groups'), you may continue to qualify for IS on this basis. You may fit into one of these groups if you are claiming IS:

- 'on the grounds of disability' (see below);
- as a disabled worker (see p352);
- as a lone parent of a child aged six or over (see p352).

Claiming income support 'on the grounds of disability'

Before 30 December 2009, you fitted into one of the groups of people who could claim IS if any of the following applied to you.[19]

- You were incapable of work because of illness or disability and you satisfied the 'own occupation test' or the 'personal capability assessment' for IB, or you were treated as incapable of work by a decision maker.
- You were registered blind (certified blind in Scotland). If you regain your sight, you continue to be treated as blind for 28 weeks after you have been taken off the register.
- You were in 'relevant education' (see p634) or were afull-time student (see p637) and you:
  - qualified for a disability premium or a severe disability premium; *or*
  - had been incapable of work (or treated as incapable of work, or treated as capable of work because you were disqualified from receiving IB because of misconduct or a failure to accept treatment) or entitled to SSP for 196 days (28 weeks). Two or more periods of incapacity separated by 56 days (eight weeks) or less were linked together and treated as continuous; *or*
  - were a full-time student and qualified for a disabled students' allowance because you are deaf.

  Note: if you are in relevant education or are a full-time student and do not qualify under these rules, you may qualify for IS in other situations (see pp635 or 640).

If you come within one of the groups above, you count as claiming IS 'on the grounds of disability'.[20] There are two steps involved in working out if you can still qualify for IS 'on the grounds of disability'.

Step one. You must have fitted into one of the groups above before 30 December 2009, and you must continue to do so.

Step two. If you fit into one of the groups above, so long as you continue to do so:[21]

- you can claim and qualify for IS if you are entitled to IB or SDA. You can make a new claim for IS in this situation even if you have never claimed before. **Note:** if you claim ESA, your claim is treated as a claim for IS;[22]
- you can continue to qualify for IS until there is a break in your claim, if you were entitled because you fitted into one of the groups immediately before 30 December 2009. See pp303–04 of the 2010/11 edition of this *Handbook* for further information. You cannot make a new claim for IS in this situation;

- your IS award can be re-instated if it was terminated incorrectly on or after 27 October 2008 as a result of an 'official error'. See p304 of the 2010/11 edition of this *Handbook* for further information. **Note:** if you are now claiming another benefit (eg, JSA or ESA), you may wish to continue claiming that benefit. Seek advice about how you would be better off financially.

If you are getting IS 'on the grounds of disability', you will normally be transferred to ESA some time before April 2014. You should not be worse off; your rate of benefit will be protected until April 2020. See p196 for further information and CPAG's *Welfare Rights Bulletin* for updates.

Disabled workers

Before 25 January 2010, you fitted into one of the groups of people who could claim IS if you were working 16 hours or more a week and did not count as in full-time paid work because:[23]

- you were mentally or physically disabled and because of this your earnings or hours were reduced to 75 per cent or less of those of a person without your disability in the same or a comparable job; *or*
- you were in employment and living in a care home, an Abbeyfield home or an independent hospital.

You can continue to qualify for IS on this basis so long as you continue to fit into this group, until there is a break in your claim. You cannot make a new claim for IS in this situation.

Claiming income support as a lone parent of a child aged six or over

Currently, you fit into one of the groups of people who can claim IS if you are a lone parent and your only or youngest child is under seven (due to be reduced to five). However, the age limit for a child was higher in the past.

- Before 24 November 2008, the age limit for a child was 16. If you were entitled to IS as a lone parent immediately before that date and your only or youngest child was at least 11 but not yet 16, you could continue to receive IS as a lone parent for a period.[24] See p297 of the 2009/10 edition of this *Handbook*.
- Before 26 October 2009, the age limit for a child was 12. If you were entitled to IS as a lone parent immediately before that date and your only or youngest child was at least nine but not yet 12, you could continue to receive IS as a lone parent for a period.[25] See p307 of the 2010/211 edition of this *Handbook*.
- Before 25 October 2010, the age limit for a child was 10. If you were entitled to IS as a lone parent immediately before that date and your only or youngest child was at least six but not yet 10, you could continue to receive IS as a lone parent for a period.[26] See p315 of the 2011/212 edition of this *Handbook*.

Special rules apply if you were claiming IS as a lone parent and you were a **full-time student** or were doing **full-time training on the New Deal for Lone**

Parents immediately before 24 November 2008 (or, from 26 October 2009, immediately before that date or, from 25 October 2010, immediately before that date). Your only or youngest child must have been at least six on the relevant date.[27] In this case, you can continue to receive IS as a lone parent, even if your only or youngest child is older than the rules allow. You can claim as a lone parent until there is a break in your claim for IS, or until:

- you cease to be a full-time student or to attend a full-time course; *or*
- if this is sooner, your only or youngest child reaches the age from when your IS would have stopped under the rules that applied when you started your course.

Example

Joan is a full-time student who can claim IS because she is a lone parent. She has one child who turned seven on 1 May 2011. Joan started her course in October 2010 and it is due to end in June 2012. When she started her course, the rules allowed people to claim IS as lone parents if they were responsible for a child under 10. Under the rules described above, Joan would no longer be able to claim IS as a lone parent from 1 May 2011 (her child's seventh birthday). However, under the special rules, she can continue to claim as a lone parent until her course ends in June 2012.

Note: you cannot challenge the rules that reduced the age limit for a child.[28] If you can no longer claim IS as a lone parent, check to see if you fit into any of the other groups of people who can claim IS described in this chapter. If you do (eg, you are a carer or a lone foster parent of a child under 16), you can continue to qualify for IS on that basis, even if you can no longer qualify as a lone parent.[29]

Remember that if you can no longer qualify for IS:

- you may qualify for JSA or ESA. If you claim JSA there are special rules that help some lone parents satisfy the jobseeking conditions;
- you need to claim CTC for your children if you are not already claiming it. You cannot get allowances and premiums for your children in a new claim for IS or JSA, or with ESA.

Full-time paid work

You cannot usually qualify for IS if you or your partner are in full-time paid work. If you are the IS claimant, this means 16 hours or more each week. For your partner, this means 24 hours or more each week. If you both work less than this, you can get IS. See Chapter 31 for the rules on work.

In some situations you are treated as *not* in full-time work even if you work more than 16/24 hours (see p725). In others, you are treated as in full-time work when you are not (see p723). See p720 for how your hours are calculated and p719 for what counts as paid work.

If you or your partner normally work 16/24 hours or more but are off sick or on maternity, adoption or paternity leave, you do not count as being in full-time paid work.[30] You may, therefore, be able to claim IS if you fit into one of the groups of people who can claim. The rules are different for WTC so you might also qualify for WTC. **Note:** you can claim IS if you are entitled to SSP or are incapable of work because of your pregnancy. Otherwise, you may have to claim ESA rather than IS if you are off work because you are sick.

If you or your partner have just taken up full-time paid work, you may be able to claim IS for help with your housing costs for the first four weeks. This is known as 'mortgage interest run-on' (see p879).

If you work less than 16 hours and your partner works at least 16 hours but less than 24 hours each week, you and your partner might be able to claim WTC. In some cases, you might be able to claim both WTC and IS (see p729). Seek advice to see how you would be better off financially.

If your partner is at least the qualifying age for PC (see p509) and either of you are working 16/24 hours or more each week, your partner might be able to claim PC or WTC (or both if your income is low enough). There is no full-time paid work rule for PC, but earnings are taken into account when working out how much PC you can get.

Note: if you are claiming IS because you are incapable of work (see p347), consult the DWP *before* you do any work. For work you may do while you are claiming, see p735.

Work-focused interviews and work-related activity

In many situations, unless you are a lone parent with a child under one, when you claim IS you must take part in a work-focused interview. If you have a partner, s/he can be required to take part in a work-focused interview. If you or your partner fail to take part in an interview without good cause, your IS might be paid at a reduced rate. Some time during 2012, you may be required to undertake work-related activity. See Chapter 42 for further information.

2. The rules about your age

You must be at least 16 to qualify for income support (IS). If you are 16 or 17, there are some issues to bear in mind (see p357). You may instead qualify for jobseeker's allowance (JSA) or employment and support allowance (ESA). Even if you cannot get IS, JSA or ESA, you may qualify for housing benefit and council tax benefit.

You cannot claim IS if you are at least the qualifying age for pension credit (PC – see p509). Instead, you can claim PC.

3. **Claiming for others**

You claim income support (IS) for yourself and your partner, if you have one. The applicable amount that forms part of the calculation of your benefit includes a personal allowance for a couple. See p753 for who counts as a couple. If you do not fit into one of the groups of people who can claim IS but your partner does, s/he could be the claimant. Whichever one of you claims IS, the other should seek advice about how to protect her/his national insurance (NI) record. See Chapter 35 for more details about NI credits.

In some cases, you need to know who counts as a member of your '**family**' for IS purposes – ie, your partner and any child who is a member of your household and for whom you count as 'responsible' (see below).[31]

Children

There are some situations in which you must show that you are 'responsible' for a child who is living in your household – eg, you may need to show that you are a lone parent in order to fit into one of the groups of people who can claim IS. For when you count as responsible for a child and when s/he counts as living in your household, see p759.

Remember:

- You can count as responsible for any child under 16 and for any qualifying young person – referred to as 'children' in this *Handbook*. You do not have to be the child's parent.[32]
- You can continue to count as responsible for children who have left school or training until the 'terminal date' (see p98) or the end of the child benefit 'extension period' (see p96).
- A young person entitled to IS, jobseeker's allowance or income-related employment and support allowance in her/his own right does not count as your child for IS purposes, nor do certain 16/17-year-olds who are no longer being looked after by a local authority (see p673).
- In some situations, a child does not count as a member of your household even if s/he normally does, or continues to count as a member of your household while s/he is temporarily away from home (see p762).

4. **The amount of benefit**

Income support (IS) tops up your income to a level that is set by the government and which changes every April. The amount you get depends on your needs (your 'applicable amount') and on how much income and capital you have.[33] For the rules on income see Chapter 40, and on capital, Chapter 41. There are three steps involved in working out your IS.

Step one: calculate your applicable amount

Your applicable amount consists of:

- **a personal allowance** (see p815); *plus*
- **premiums** (see p820) for any special needs; *plus*
- **housing costs**, principally for mortgage interest payments (see Chapter 38).

Personal allowances and premiums are increased every April. If you do not qualify for IS currently, you might qualify when the rates go up.

If you have children

IS does not include allowances and premiums for your children. Instead you can claim child tax credit (CTC). However, if you were getting IS on 5 April 2004 and this included allowances and premiums for your children, but you were not yet entitled to CTC, you continue to get allowances and premiums for your children until you claim CTC. See p760 for further information.

Step two: calculate your income

This is the amount you have coming in each week from, for instance, other benefits, part-time earnings, working tax credit and maintenance (see Chapter 40). If you have capital over £6,000 (£10,000 if you live in a care home), it also includes your tariff income (see p926).

Step three: deduct income from applicable amount

Example

Mr and Mrs Hughes, aged 27 and 29, have a daughter aged 10. Mr Hughes has been caring for his daughter who is severely disabled. He gets carer's allowance (CA) of £58.45. Mrs Hughes gets child benefit and CTC, as well as disability living allowance (DLA) for her daughter. The couple have no housing costs to be covered by IS. Their applicable amount is:

Personal allowance	£111.45
Carer premium	£32.60
Total	£144.05

Their income to be taken into account is £58.45 (CA). Child benefit, CTC and DLA are ignored.

Their IS is £144.05 (applicable amount) *minus* £58.45 (income) = £85.60.

If your income is too high for you to qualify for IS currently, you might qualify once you or a member of your family become entitled to another benefit (a 'qualifying benefit'). You should make your claim for IS at the same time as your claim for the qualifying benefit (see p1029).

You might get a reduced amount of IS if:

- you (or, in some cases, your partner) were required to attend a work-focused interview and failed to do so without good cause; *or*
- your IS has been restricted under the 'loss of benefit for benefit offences' rules (see p1106).

Different rules for calculating your benefit can apply if you are in one of the groups to whom special rules apply (see below).

5. Special benefit rules

Special rules may apply to:

- 16/17-year-olds (see below);
- people from abroad (see Chapter 61);
- people who are studying (see Chapter 29);
- people without accommodation, involved in a trade dispute, in hospital or who are prisoners (see Chapter 30);
- people who, or whose partner or children, live in a care home (see p683).

16/17-year-olds

If you are 16 or 17 you are entitled to income support (IS) in your own right if you satisfy the normal rules of entitlement described in this chapter.[34] You must fit within one of the groups of people who can claim IS.[35] You should not have your claim refused or be turned away by the DWP simply because of your age.

However, you should remember the following.

- If you have been looked after by a local authority, you usually cannot claim IS. Instead, your local authority should support and accommodate you. See p674 for exceptions to the rules.
- There are some issues for you to consider (see p671).[36] If you are a 'qualifying young person' for child benefit purposes and are living with someone who counts as responsible for you, s/he might be able to claim child benefit and child tax credit for you (see p673).
- In certain circumstances, you may satisfy the rules for IS *and* income-based jobseeker's allowance (JSA).[37] It is usually better to claim IS because you do not have to be available for and actively seeking work and training and therefore risk benefit sanctions (see Chapter 20). You can still look for work. If you claim IS rather than JSA, however, you might not receive national insurance credits (see Chapter 35).

6. Claims and backdating

The rules about claiming and backdating are in Chapter 42. This section explains the specific rules that apply to income support (IS).

Making a claim

A claim for IS can be made:

- in writing on the form approved by the DWP.[38] Send your completed form to your local Jobcentre Plus office. You may also be able to claim at an alternative office (see p1018). Return the form within one month of your initial contact; *or*
- by telephone on 0800 055 6688 (Welsh 0800 012 1888; textphone 0800 023 4888) Monday to Friday, 8am to 6pm.[39] You are sent a written statement of your circumstances for you to approve and sign.

In practice, the usual way to start your claim is by telephone (see p1018). However, if you claim in writing, keep a copy of your claim form in case queries arise.

You must provide any information or evidence required (see p359). You can amend or withdraw your claim before a decision is made (see p1019).

Forms

Get Form A1 from Jobcentre Plus offices or download it at www.direct.gov.uk/en/moneytaxandbenefits. You may also be able to get the form at your local Citizens Advice Bureau, welfare rights service or advice centre. It is still important to telephone the DWP to let it know you want to claim IS to ensure your date of claim is the earliest possible date (see p360). You are given your date of initial contact to enter on the form.

Note:

- You can make initial contact with the DWP by telephone or letter to say you want to claim. The date of your initial contact is important because it usually determines the date on which your claim is treated as made (see p360).
- If you are claiming IS within 26 weeks of a previous claim, you might be given a shortened claim form. This is known as 'rapid reclaim'.

Housing benefit and council tax benefit

You have to make a separate claim to your local authority for housing benefit (HB) and for council tax benefit (CTB). If you claim IS by telephone, your HB and CTB claims are usually completed at the same time.

If you claim IS on the approved form, you may be given HB and CTB claim forms (these are also available at www.direct.gov.uk/en/moneytaxandbenefits). If you are making a 'rapid reclaim' for IS, you may also be able to make a rapid reclaim for HB and CTB.

Who should claim

If you are a single person or a lone parent, you claim on your own behalf. If you are one of a couple, you must choose which one of you claims for you both. See p753 for who counts as a couple. Where you have a choice about who can claim and you cannot agree, a decision maker decides.[40]

You can change which partner claims, provided the partner previously claiming agrees.[41] It can be worth swapping who claims, for example, if one of you:

- is about to go abroad or otherwise lose entitlement – eg, becomes a student;
- fits into one of the groups of people who can claim IS but the other does not. You should both seek advice about how to protect your national insurance (NI) record;
- is working less than 16 hours a week and the other is working between 16 and 24 hours a week (see p718 for what counts as full-time paid work). In this case, you and your partner might also be able to claim working tax credit (WTC). Seek advice to see how you would be better off financially.

If you cannot make your claim yourself (eg, you are mentally ill or have dementia), an 'appointee' (see p1016) can claim on your behalf.

Information to support your claim

When you claim IS, you must:

- satisfy the NI number requirement (see p1023);
- provide proof of your identity, if required (see p1024);
- supply information and evidence required on the claim form (see p1019) and additional information and evidence relevant to your claim (see p1022). There is a strict time limit for doing so.

It is important that you provide any information or evidence required when you claim – known as the 'evidence requirement'. Until you do, you may not count as having made a valid claim.[42] You should correct any defects in your claim within one month of your initial contact or you might lose benefit.[43] See p1021 for further information about the evidence requirement and to see if you are exempt.

Even if you have provided all that was required when you claimed, you may be asked to provide additional information and evidence. If you do not do so, the decision maker can decide your claim in the way most adverse to you.

If you have a mortgage, you are given an additional form to give to your lender. It provides details about your mortgage and returns the form to the DWP. If it is not possible to assess your housing costs (see Chapter 38) accurately or your entitlement to the severe disability premium, the decision maker can exclude these from your IS until they can be calculated.[44]

The date of your claim

You are usually not entitled to IS for any day before your 'date of claim'.[45] However, in some cases you can claim in advance (see below) and sometimes your date of claim can be backdated (see p361). If you want this to be done, make this clear when you claim or the DWP might not consider it.

Your **'date of claim'** is usually the earliest of:[46]

- the date you first contact a benefit office (eg, you ask to claim IS by telephone or letter or you submit a defective claim) or someone does this on your behalf, so long as a properly completed claim form (if issued) and all the information and evidence required (see p359) are provided within one month; *or*
- the date your properly completed claim form (if issued) and all the information and evidence required are received by the benefit office (or if you may claim at an alternative office (see p1018), that office); *or*
- if you claim by telephone, the date of your call. This includes where you were given time to provide required information or evidence and have done so.[47]

If you claim the wrong benefit

If you claim WTC and you are refused because neither you nor your partner are in full-time paid work for WTC purposes (see Chapter 53), your claim for IS can be backdated to the date you claimed WTC.[48] However, you must claim IS within 14 days of the decision refusing your WTC claim. You can ask for your IS claim to start on a later date instead – eg, if your income is currently too high but is due to decrease.

If you claim IS and you should have claimed carer's allowance (CA) instead of or in addition to IS, a decision maker can treat your IS claim as a claim for CA.[49] This could help you qualify for a backdated carer premium.

Claiming in advance

If you do not qualify for IS from the date of your claim (unless this is because you fail the habitual residence test – see p1442) but will do so within the next three months, you can be awarded IS from the first date on which you qualify.[50] This gives the DWP time to ensure you receive benefit as soon as you are entitled. Let the DWP know you want to claim in advance when you claim. You might have to persuade the DWP that it can accept a claim in advance.

You might not be entitled to IS currently, but would be once you or a member of your family become entitled to another 'qualifying benefit' – eg, disability living allowance or CA. You should make your claim for IS at the same time as the claim for the qualifying benefit. If you are:

- refused IS, claim again when you get a decision about the qualifying benefit and ask for your IS to be backdated to the date of your first IS claim or to the date from which the qualifying benefit is paid, if that is later (see p1029);

- awarded IS, you might be entitled to a higher rate once the outcome of the claim for the qualifying benefit is known. Seek a revision or a supersession if you think this applies to you (see p1147).

Backdating your claim

It is very important to claim in time. A claim for IS can be backdated for a maximum of three months but only in exceptional circumstances. See p1027 for the general rules on backdating. Your claim can be backdated for more than three months if:

- you are claiming backdated IS after being awarded a qualifying benefit and an earlier IS claim had been refused because you did not at that time get a qualifying benefit (see p1029);[51]
- you claimed WTC when you should have claimed IS (see p360).

If you might have qualified for benefit earlier, but did not claim because you were given the wrong information by the DWP or because you were misled by it, you could ask for compensation (see p1261) or complain to the Ombudsman via your MP (see p1260).

7. Getting paid

Income support (IS) is normally made by direct credit transfer into your bank (or similar) account (see p1039).[52] If you are unable to open or manage an account, payment can be made by cheque or by 'simple payment'. If you are unable to act for yourself, payment can be made to someone else on your behalf – called your 'appointee' (see p1016).

When is IS paid?	The day you are paid depends on your national insurance number.[53]
How often is IS paid?	Normally fortnightly in arrears.[54]

You are paid in advance if you are returning to work after a trade dispute.[55]

IS is a weekly benefit. However, if you are only entitled to IS for part of a week, you are only paid for the part-week.[56]

If you are entitled to less than 10 pence a week, you are not paid IS at all, unless you are receiving another social security benefit which can be paid with IS.[57] If you are entitled to less than £1 a week, a decision maker can decide to pay you at 13-week intervals in arrears.[58]

Your entitlement to IS usually starts from the date of your claim (see p360).[59]

Note:

- Deductions can be made from your IS to pay to third parties (see p1048).
- Your IS might be paid at a reduced rate if you have been sanctioned for benefit offences (see p1106).

- If you have forgotten your PIN or if a cheque is lost or stolen, see p1040.
- If payment of your IS is delayed, see p1262. You might be able to get an interim payment (see p1046). You may also be eligible for a crisis loan (see p564). If you wish to complain about how your claim has been dealt with, see p1255. You might be able to claim compensation (see p1261).
- If payment of your IS is suspended, see p1043.
- If you are overpaid IS, you might have to repay it (see Chapter 43). If you have been accused of fraud, see Chapter 44.

Change of circumstances

You must report changes in your circumstances that might affect your benefit (see p1047). You should do this promptly in writing or by telephone (although in individual cases notification might be accepted in a form other than in writing or by telephone. You can also notify changes in your circumstances by electronic communication – eg, online.[60] In some cases, however, the decision maker might say you must report changes in writing. In any case, it is always best to report the change in writing and keep a copy in case of a dispute in the future.

Report changes to the benefit office handling your claim. This could be your Jobcentre Plus office or a benefit delivery centre or regional processing centre. Check with the Jobcentre Plus office if you are in any doubt.

If you have a mortgage, the DWP can ask your lender about any changes in the amount you owe. If you have this information (eg, from an annual statement you receive from your lender), you must also advise the DWP just in case your lender fails to do so. Make sure the DWP takes this information into account so you are not overpaid IS.

When there has been a relevant change of circumstances, a decision maker looks at your claim again and makes a new decision. To see when your IS is then adjusted, see below.

When your income support is adjusted

As a general rule, if you are paid IS in arrears, your IS is adjusted from the beginning of the week in which the change of circumstances takes effect.[61] There are a number of exceptions including the following.[62]

- If a decision is to your advantage, but you failed to notify the DWP of a change within the time limit (normally one month, but this can be extended – see p1142), your IS is adjusted:
  - if you are paid in arrears, from the beginning of the week in which you notified the change; *or*
  - if you are paid in advance, from the day on which you notified the change if this is the day you are paid benefit. If it is not, your IS is adjusted from the next week.
- Your IS is adjusted from the date of the change of circumstances (or the day on which this is expected to take place) if:

- you are paid IS in arrears and the change of circumstances means you no longer qualify for IS, unless this is because your income is too high;
- you live in a care home for part of the week and are entitled to disability living allowance when you are staying elsewhere. This means that you can be paid, for example, the severe disability and enhanced disability premiums when you are staying away from the care home.

8. Tax, tax credits and other benefits

Income support (IS) is not taxable except if you are involved in a trade dispute and you are claiming it for your partner.

Tax credits

If you work less than 16 hours a week and your partner works at least 16 hours but less than 24 hours a week, you and your partner may be able to claim working tax credit (WTC). Before deciding whether to claim, seek advice to see how you would be better off financially.

If you or your partner have just stopped work or reduced your hours, you might get what is known as 'WTC run-on' for a four-week period (see p1304). WTC is taken into account as income when working out your IS, but child tax credit (CTC) is not. IS is an automatic passport to maximum CTC and is usually an automatic passport to maximum WTC.

Means-tested benefits

IS is an automatic passport to maximum housing benefit (HB) and council tax benefit (CTB).

You might be able to choose whether to claim IS, income-based jobseeker's allowance or income-related employment and support allowance. If you have a partner and s/he is at least the qualifying age for pension credit (PC – see p509), s/he may be able to claim PC for you instead of you claiming IS (see p429).

Non-means-tested benefits

In some situations, while you are on IS you get national insurance credits (see Chapter 35).

Most non-means-tested benefits are taken into account as income when working out the amount of IS you get. Attendance allowance, disability living allowance, guardian's allowance and, if you are getting CTC, child benefit are not taken into account. It can be worth claiming non-means-tested benefits. If you or your partner qualify for certain of these, you also qualify for certain premiums (see p820) and, therefore, a higher rate of IS.

You might only qualify for IS once you or a member of your family are awarded another benefit, known as a 'qualifying benefit'. To make sure you do not lose out while awaiting the outcome of a claim for a qualifying benefit, claim IS at the same time. If your IS claim is refused, once the qualifying benefit is awarded claim IS again and ask for it to be backdated to the date of your first claim (see p1029).

Passports and other sources of help

If you are entitled to IS, you also qualify for health benefits such as free prescriptions (see Chapter 13) and education benefits such as free school lunches (see p14). You may also qualify for social fund payments (see Chapters 25 and 26).

Financial help on starting work

If you stop getting IS because you or your partner start work, or your earnings or hours in your existing job increase, you may be able to get mortgage interest run-on (if you have a home loan – see p879) and extended payments of HB or CTB (if you pay rent or council tax – see pp286 and 130). See p13 for information about other financial help you might get.

Notes

1. **Who can claim income support**
 1 s124 SSCBA 1992
 2 s115 IAA 1999
 3 s5 WRA 2009
 4 Reg 4ZA and Sch 1B IS Regs
 5 R(IS) 10/05
 6 Sch 1B para 7(c) and (d) IS Regs
 7 Sch 1B paras 1-2A, 14, 14A and 14B IS Regs
 8 CIS/2260/2002
 9 The rules on paternity leave are in Part 2 PAL Regs
 10 CIS/0542/2001
 11 Sch 1B paras 3 and 23 IS Regs
 12 CIS/866/2004
 13 CIS/4312/2007
 14 Sch 1B paras 4-6 IS Regs
 15 R(IS) 8/02
 16 Sch 1B paras 10-12, 15, 15A and 28 IS Regs
 17 Sch 1B paras 9A and 18-22 IS Regs
 18 Reg 22B IS Regs
 19 Sch 1B paras 7(a) and (b), 10, 12 and 13 IS Regs; reg 2 IS(PCP) Regs
 20 Reg 1(4) ESA(TP) Regs
 21 Reg 2(2)-(5) IS(PCP) Regs; reg 2(2)(d) ESA(TP) Regs
 22 Sch 4 para 11 WRA 2007; reg 3(2) ESA(TP) Regs
 23 Sch 1B paras 8 and 9 IS Regs; reg 4 IS(MA)(No.5) Regs
 24 Sch para 1 SS(LPMA) Regs
 25 Sch para 6 SS(LPMA) Regs
 26 Sch paras 8 and 9 SS(LPMA) Regs
 27 Reg 13 SS(LPMA) Regs
 28 *VL v SSWP (IS)* [2011] UKUT 227 (AAC) decided that the rules did not breach the Human Rights Act 1998 and were not *ultra vires* in respect of s7 Education Act 1996 (parents' duty to ensure their children receive suitable education).
 29 R(IS) 10/05
 30 Reg 5(3A) IS Regs

3. **Claiming for others**
31 s137(1) SSCBA 1992
32 s137(1) SSCBA 1992; reg 14 IS Regs

4. **The amount of benefit**
33 s124(4) SSCBA 1992

5. **Special benefit rules**
34 s124(1)(a) SSCBA 1992
35 s124(1)(e) SSCBA 1992; Sch 1B IS Regs
36 s124(1)(d) SSCBA 1992; reg 13 IS Regs
37 s124(1)(f) and (h) SSCBA 1992; s3(1)(b) JSA 1995; reg 61(1)(c) JSA Regs

6. **Claims and backdating**
38 Reg 4(1A), (5), (6) and (11A) and (11B) SS(C&P) Regs
39 Reg 4(11A) and (11B) SS(C&P) Regs
40 Reg 4(3) SS(C&P) Regs
41 Reg 4(4) SS(C&P) Regs
42 Reg 4(1A), (7A), (9), (12) and (13) SS(C&P) Regs
43 Reg 6(1A) SS(C&P) Regs
44 Reg 13 SS&CS(DA) Regs
45 Reg 19(1) and Sch 4 para 6 SS(C&P) Regs
46 Reg 6(1ZA) and (1A) SS(C&P) Regs; R(IS) 10/06
47 Reg 6(1)(c) and (d) SS(C&P) Regs
48 Reg 6(28) SS(C&P) Regs
49 Reg 9(1) and Sch 1 SS(C&P) Regs; reg 2(3) ESA(TP) Regs
50 Reg 13(1) and (9) SS(C&P) Regs
51 Reg 6(16)-(18) SS(C&P) Regs

7. **Getting paid**
52 Reg 21 SS(C&P) Regs
53 Sch 7 para 3(2) SS(C&P) Regs
54 Sch 7 para 1 SS(C&P) Regs
55 Reg 26(1) and Sch 7 paras 2, 2ZA, 3 and 6(2) SS(C&P) Regs
56 s124(5) and (6) SSCBA 1992; reg 73 IS Regs
57 Reg 26(4) SS(C&P) Regs
58 Sch 7 para 5 SS(C&P) Regs
59 Sch 7 paras 1, 3 and 6(1) SS(C&P) Regs
60 Reg 32ZA SS(C&P) Regs
61 Reg 7 and Sch 3A para 1 SS&CS(DA) Regs
62 Reg 7 and Sch 3A paras 1-6 SS&CS(DA) Regs

Chapter 18

Industrial injuries benefits

This chapter covers:

Key facts

- Industrial injuries benefits are paid if you are disabled as a result of an accident at work or a disease caused by your job (but not if this is self-employment).
- You do not have to show that your employer was at fault.
- The main industrial injuries benefit is **disablement benefit**, but you may also qualify for **reduced earnings allowance** or **retirement allowance**.
- All industrial injuries benefits are non-means-tested benefits.
- You do not have to have paid national insurance contributions to qualify.
- You can qualify for industrial injuries benefits whether you are in or out of work.
- Industrial injuries benefits are administered and paid by the DWP.
- If you disagree with an industrial injuries benefit decision, you can apply for a revision or a supersession, or appeal against it (see Chapters 45 and 46).

Future changes: April 2013 and after

Major changes are taking place that affect the benefits and tax credits system (see Chapter 2).

– From April 2013, total benefit payments to many working-age households will be 'capped' (see p25). There will be limited exceptions, including households in which someone is entitled to working tax credit or receives disability living allowance. Industrial injuries benefits will be included in the capped amount.

– You will still be able to claim industrial injuries benefits when universal credit is introduced in October 2013. Industrial injuries benefits are *not* being abolished.

See CPAG's *Welfare Rights Bulletin* for updates.

1. Who can get industrial injuries benefits

For all industrial injuries benefits in this chapter you must satisfy the **'industrial injury condition'** – ie:[1]

- you have had a 'personal injury' in an 'industrial accident' (see p368) or you have a 'prescribed industrial disease' (see p372); *and*
- at the time of the injury you were an employed earner (see below); *and*
- as a result of that accident or disease you have had a 'loss of faculty' (see p374); *and*
- as a result of that 'loss of faculty' you are 'disabled'.

You are not covered by the scheme if your disability was caused by an industrial accident which happened before, or by a disease the onset of which was before, 5 July 1948. However, you may still be able to claim allowances under either the Workmen's Compensation (Supplementation) Scheme 1982 or the Pneumoconiosis, Byssinosis and Miscellaneous Diseases Benefit Scheme 1983.

You can only qualify for reduced earnings allowance (REA – see p380) and retirement allowance (see p384) if your accident or disease occurred before October 1990.

If you have been injured by your work, you may also have the right to sue your employer. Legal help may be available and you may be able to get a free consultation with a solicitor. Your right to compensation from your employer is separate from your rights to benefit under the industrial injuries scheme (although your compensation may be reduced if you have received benefits from the DWP – see p1058).

Employed earners

You can only claim industrial injuries benefits if you were an 'employed earner' and your accident or disease was caused by your employment.[2] You are an 'employed earner' if you are gainfully employed under a contract of service. This means that there is some obligation by an employer to pay you remuneration for tasks you are bound to perform for the employer under the contract of employment. Some office holders with taxable earnings, such as company directors, are also covered by the scheme.[3] If you are self-employed you are excluded from the scheme, as are most trainees on government training schemes. Trainees are, however, covered by the DWP Analogous Industrial Injuries Scheme, which provides equivalent benefits.

Entitlement to industrial injuries benefits does not depend on your having paid national insurance contributions. However, payment of contributions is a way of deciding whether or not you are an employed earner.

If you pay, or ought to pay, Class 1 contributions (see p773) as an employed earner you can qualify for industrial injuries benefits. This includes those paying Class 1 (and, in the case of volunteer development workers, Class 2 – see p775) contributions while abroad.[4] You can qualify if your earnings are too low to pay contributions – eg, because you work part time or you are too young to pay contributions. You are also treated as an employed earner if you are an apprentice, mine inspector or rescue worker, special constable, taxi driver, office cleaner, agency worker, minister of religion, lecturer, member of an aircrew, mariner or, in some situations, an offshore oil or gas worker.[5]

You are treated as *not* being an employed earner if:[6]

- you are employed by your spouse or civil partner and either your employment is not for the purpose of her/his employment or your earnings are normally below the lower earnings limit (see p773); *or*
- you are employed by a close relative (parent, step-parent, grandparent, son, daughter, stepchild, grandchild, brother, sister, half-brother or half-sister) in a private house where you both live, and your employment is not for your relative's trade or business carried out there; *or*
- you are a member of visiting armed forces, or a civilian employed by them, unless you are normally resident in the UK.

Personal injury

Personal injury includes the obvious, such as broken legs or arms, but also covers the less obvious, such as strains and psychological injury.[7] So an assault at work causing slight physical injury might cause a far greater injury to the mind by resulting in agoraphobia or a breakdown. In difficult cases, the question is whether or not you have experienced a physiological or psychological change for the worse. It is not enough just to be in pain if the pain is merely a symptom of an existing condition and does not make that condition substantially worse.[8] The damage must be to you or part of you. Dislocation of an artificial hip joint counts as a personal injury,[9] but damage to a pair of spectacles[10] does not.

Accident

The term **'accident'** has been defined as an unlooked-for mishap or occurrence.[11] However, an accident need only be unexpected from your point of view.[12] It does not matter if it could have been anticipated by an expert. If you do a heavy or dangerous job where accidents are common, a resulting injury is just as much an accident as if your job is sedentary and comparatively safe. A heart attack can be an injury but there needs to be some external event or series of events causing it, such as heavy lifting or work-related stress.[13] Deliberate acts by third parties can be accidents – eg, assaults on security workers or on staff in shops and hospitals.[14]

An accident is 'industrial' if you can show a connection with your work. This connection is established if the accident arose 'out of and in the course of your employment'.[15] Remember that, despite the name, it is not only industrial workers who can have 'industrial accidents'; all employees can. For example, if you are an office worker and a badly loaded filing cabinet tilts and falls on you, this should count as an 'industrial accident'. There need not be a dramatic event; any accident sustained while you are doing your job can qualify – eg, spilling a hot drink and scalding yourself. An illness brought on by conversation could count as being caused by an industrial accident.[16]

Accident or process?

Benefit is payable for an 'accident', but not for a 'process' (unless it causes a 'prescribed disease' – see p372). To fall from a ladder and break your leg is an 'accident', but to work for many years as a heavy manual worker and have a sore back is a cumulative 'process' as is breathing in dust over many years.[17] However, sometimes a series of events, over a period of time, can be treated as an 'accident' for benefit purposes.[18] The cumulative effect of a series of incidents can also result in an accident.[19] Furthermore, you should not be excluded from entitlement to benefit simply because you cannot identify which incidents caused the injury.[20]

Example

Cyril's job is trimming excess rubber from hot water bottles with a pair of scissors. A particularly hard batch of rubber comes through and each cut requires greater strength. Over two or three days he suffers a strain injury in his hand. The series of cuts constitutes a series of 'accidents' that meets the definition.

It is easier to establish the series of events as an accident if the period of time is fairly short,[21] or if it is noticed at an identifiable moment.[22] An accident is proved if you can establish that an identifiable occurrence must have happened, even if it is impossible to prove when.[23]

In the course of employment

The accident (see p368) must arise 'in the course of employment'. It has been said that:

> 'an accident befalls [a person] in the course of [his or her] employment if it occurs while [he or she] is doing what a person so employed may reasonably do within a time during which he is employed, and at a place where [s/he] may reasonably be during that time to do that thing.'[24]

Difficulties arise when work rules are broken, or when you do something not directly connected with work.

Generally, when you arrive at your employer's workplace and are on her/his private property, you are 'in the course of your employment'. You do not have to have clocked in or have reported to your actual workplace. If you arrive early to get ready for work or to have a meal in the canteen[25] you are covered, although if you arrive early to play a game of pool you are not.[26] You are probably covered during breaks from working if you remain on the employer's property,[27] but probably not if you go elsewhere. So if, during a tea break, you go to a local shop to buy a snack, you are outside the course of your employment.[28] If you are allowed to have a snack either at home or at work while still on duty, you are covered.[29]

While at work most activities are considered to be 'in the course of employment'.[30] Smoking,[31] chatting[32] or sharing sweets[33] are all 'reasonably incidental' to the employment, provided they are not done in breach of instructions.[34] Even if you were doing something in breach of instructions you are still covered if the accident would have been taken as arising out of, and in the course of, your employment if you had not been acting in breach of those orders and what you were doing was done for the purposes of, or in connection with, your employment.[35]

Example

Clara works as a labourer in a paper factory where there is an absolute ban on riding on the load of a forklift truck. She is seen riding on the load, falls off and is injured. Usually she would not be covered, but she saw the load was slipping and rode on the truck in order to hold it on. This was done for the purposes of her employment and so, this time, she is covered.

Even if you are at home, depending on your contract, you may be covered. This may even include a person on sick leave.[36]

In putting forward your claim (see p385) or arguing your case at an appeal (see Chapter 46), you should consider all aspects of your employment, including the wording of your contract and the degree of flexibility in the arrangements between you and your employer.[37]

Accidents while travelling

Accidents while travelling have been a source of much dispute. You are not in the course of your employment (see p369) during ordinary journeys to and from work, unless you are travelling on transport operated by or on behalf of your employer, or arranged by your employer, and not in the ordinary course of public transport service.[38]

Many employees have no set place of work – eg, lorry drivers, local authority home helps, gas and electricity company employees. Obviously a lorry driver is at work when driving her/his lorry, but gas company workers travelling directly from home to their first job of the day are not always in the course of employment (see p369), even if driving a company van. It depends on the circumstances, including the rules for the use of the van.[39] A home help was found to be in the course of her employment travelling between jobs, but not going to the first job or from the last. This is because she became engaged in her employment once she started at the first job and remained engaged until the end of the day.[40]

Some employees with no fixed hours of work may be regarded as covered from the moment of leaving home.[41] Some cases have eased the rules on travelling – eg, to conferences or meetings.[42] You must look at all the factors when deciding whether or not you were in the course of your employment. For example, a police officer who had to travel about 40 miles from home to a training course was in the course of his employment while travelling.[43] Provided you go reasonably directly, with no marked deviation from a proper route, and do not embark on activities unrelated to the journey, you may be covered.

One important factor in deciding whether you are in the course of your employment is whether you receive wages for travelling.[44] However, if you receive a flat-rate travelling allowance as compensation for having to work at a workplace other than your normal base, this may not be enough to make your journey to your alternative workplace part of your work.[45]

Out of employment

As well as arising in the course of your employment (see p369), the accident (see p368) must arise 'out of' your employment, so that in some way the employment contributed to it. The fact that you suffered a displaced retina at work is not sufficient to show it arose 'out of' the employment, but medical evidence which shows that it was caused by sudden head movements while inspecting a production line enables you to establish that an industrial accident (see p369) took place. An unexplained fracture while walking at work is not an industrial accident,[46] but it is if you slip and the fracture occurs while you are falling onto the ground. You are covered even if you are more susceptible to injury because, for example, your bones are brittle[47] or your eyes are weak.

Example

Joe, a farm worker, suffers sudden pain in the groin while doing his normal job of digging. It is found that a previous hernia, which had been surgically repaired, has given way again. The decision maker says that this could have happened at any time and so did not arise 'out of' the employment. Joe's doctor says it could have happened at any time but probably did so at that time because of the heavy digging. The First-tier Tribunal awards him benefit.

An accident also arises out of your employment if it arises in the course of employment (see p369), *and* it is caused by:[48]

- another's misconduct, 'skylarking' or negligence; *or*
- the behaviour or presence of an animal (including a bird, fish or insect); *or*
- your being struck by any object or by lightning.

In all cases, you must not have directly or indirectly contributed to the accident happening by your conduct, either outside your employment or by any act not incidental to the employment.

An accident is deemed to arise out of, and in the course of, your employment if you are helping people in an emergency, or trying to save property at or near where you are employed.[49]

Prescribed industrial disease

It is necessary for the disease to be a **'prescribed industrial disease'**. This means it is on a list[50] set out in regulations of diseases that are known to have a link to a particular occupation, called a 'prescribed occupation' (see below).[51] Each prescribed disease has a statutory definition and you must fit within that definition. It is not sufficient simply to have a medical diagnosis that you have a particular condition.[52] From time to time new diseases are added to the list. However, you cannot claim for a disease for any period before it was added to the list.[53] Each prescribed industrial disease has a letter and number to identify it – eg, prescribed disease A12 is carpal tunnel syndrome and prescribed disease D1 is pneumoconiosis. The complete list is in Appendix 7. Whether or not you have a prescribed industrial disease is known as the 'diagnosis question'.[54]

If the DWP accepts that you have a prescribed industrial disease, other diseases which result from it are included when assessing your 'loss of faculty' and disablement.[55] See p374 for further information on how your disablement is assessed.

Prescribed occupations

Different diseases are 'prescribed' for different types of jobs because different jobs have different health risks. To qualify for benefit on grounds of a prescribed industrial disease it is not enough to have a disease which is on the list. You must also prove:

- that you have worked in one or more of the jobs for which that disease is prescribed ('prescribed occupations'); *and*
- that your job caused the disease.

If the DWP refuses to accept that you have worked in a prescribed occupation, you should obtain advice, preferably from your trade union, or from an advice agency. An expert's report may help to prove your case.

Time limits

For most prescribed diseases you do not have to have worked in a prescribed occupation for any minimum length of time. You can also claim at any time, even if it is many years since you worked in that occupation. However, there are exceptions to these general rules. If you have occupational deafness (prescribed disease A10), you must have worked in a prescribed occupation for 10 years and claim within five years of having done so.[56] If you have occupational asthma (prescribed disease D7), you must claim within 10 years of working in a prescribed occupation.[57] If you have coal miners' chronic bronchitis or emphysema (prescribed disease D12), you must have been working in a prescribed occupation for 20 years.[58] If you have cataract (prescribed disease A2), you must have worked in a prescribed occupation for five years or more in aggregate.[59] If you have osteoarthritis of the knee, you must have worked for a total of 10 years or more, made up of periods underground in a coal mine before 1986 and/or periods from 1986 in certain mining occupations. See Appendix 7 for more examples.

Cause

You must prove that the prescribed disease is caused by your occupation. For some diseases it is assumed that if you have the disease within one month of last working in the prescribed occupation (see p372), the occupation caused the disease.[60] With carpal tunnel syndrome (prescribed disease A12) and dermatitis (prescribed disease D5) this is not assumed and you must establish the link 'on a balance of probabilities'. In other words, it is more likely than not that there is a connection.

There are different time conditions for occupational deafness (prescribed disease A10), tuberculosis (prescribed disease B5), pneumoconiosis (prescribed disease D1), byssinosis (prescribed disease D2), and chronic bronchitis and emphysema (prescribed disease D12). The connection for carpal tunnel syndrome and dermatitis, therefore, has to be proved. The DWP investigates the connection issue, and you may need to ask your GP or consultant for a report linking the disease to your occupation.

Example

Connie, a hospital cleaner, uses a new cleaning material. A rash develops on her hands and she has to give up her job. The medical evidence shows that the cleaning material could have caused the problem but so could several things with which Connie had been in contact outside work. There is a strong argument that the cleaning material caused the rash because the rash developed so soon after using it.

Onset and recrudescence

The **'onset'** (date of starting) of a prescribed disease is taken as the date of the first day you had a relevant 'loss of faculty' (see p374). In deafness cases it is the later of either the date you first experienced the loss of faculty or the date you successfully claimed benefit.[61]

In diseases other than deafness, asthma and respiratory conditions, you can improve and then worsen again. It is important to know whether it is a **'recrudescence'** (fresh outbreak of the existing disease) or a completely new attack. The first is deemed to be a continuation of the existing prescribed disease;[62] with the second, you have to wait 15 weeks before disablement benefit can be claimed. If a further attack starts during a current period of assessment, it is assumed to be a recrudescence unless proved otherwise.

Loss of faculty and disablement

In addition to showing the link between your injury or disease and your occupation, you also need to establish that you have had a 'loss of faculty' and are 'disabled'.

'Loss of faculty' is the damage or impairment of part of the body or mind caused by the industrial accident or disease. **'Disability'** is the inability to do something that is caused by that damage or impairment. **'Disablement'** is the total of all of your disabilities which, taken together, amount to a disablement. This disablement is expressed as a percentage.

In assessing your disablement, the decision maker considers three questions.

- Has the relevant industrial accident (see p369) or prescribed disease (see p372) resulted in a loss of faculty (see below)?
- What is the extent of disablement resulting from a loss of faculty (this is expressed as a percentage – see below)?
- What period is to be taken into account by the assessment (see p377)?

Has the relevant accident or disease resulted in a loss of faculty?

A **'loss of faculty'** is an 'impairment of the proper functioning of part of the body or mind'[63] caused by an accident or disease. A 'loss of faculty' is not the same as disablement. It includes disfigurement even if the disfigurement is not accompanied by a loss of physical faculty.[64] A decision that there has been a personal injury resulting from an industrial accident (see p368) does not itself prevent a decision maker or the First-tier Tribunal from finding that there is no loss of faculty, but this is rare.[65]

What is the extent of disablement?

In order to qualify for disablement benefit (see p378), generally you must reach a threshold of at least 14 per cent disablement. However, a finding of at least 1 per cent may permit a claim for REA (see p380).

The extent of your disablement is assessed on a percentage basis. Any assessment between 14 and 19 per cent is treated as being 20 per cent (except for those entitled to disablement gratuities).[66] If the total disablement from all industrial accidents and diseases is more than 20 per cent, it is rounded to the nearest multiple of 10 per cent with multiples of 5 per cent being rounded upwards.[67]

Some assessments of disablement are set out in regulations.[68] These are known as 'prescribed degrees of disablement' and include various amputations (eg, loss of a hand or a leg) and degrees of hearing loss (see Appendix 6). However, even in these cases, the decision maker must take into account the real disablement resulting from an injury and increase or decrease the figure to arrive at a reasonable assessment[69] – eg, the loss of a right hand is more disabling for a right-handed person than for a left-handed person. The full extent of your disablement caused by the injury must be taken into account. A further disablement or condition which arises at a later date, but which can be shown to be caused by the industrial accident, must be included in the assessment.[70]

Impaired function of the pleura, pericardium or peritoneum caused by diffuse mesothelioma automatically has an assessment of 100 per cent disablement.[71]

Apart from age, sex and physical and mental condition, the personal circumstances of a claimant must be ignored, so that particular problems you may have, like the location of your office, or the distance to the nearest bus stop, are not taken into account.

Your disablement should be assessed by comparing you with a person of the same age and sex whose physical and mental condition is normal.[72]

When there is no prescribed degree of disablement (see above) reference may be made to the prescribed percentages to help with the assessment.[73] Although you may suggest that your assessment should be a particular percentage, the decision maker will come to her/his own judgement.[74] One hundred per cent is often given to people who are not extremely disabled (eg, those with no disabilities other than total deafness) and presumably other assessments should reflect this. It has been held that a percentage disablement awarded by the First-tier Tribunal will only be wrong if it is 'wildly wrong' or if the First-tier Tribunal reached an impossible conclusion on the evidence.[75]

It is important that you are straightforward with the examining healthcare professional. There are checks to establish that your symptoms are consistent with the injury, and that your movements are consistent with the disablement you claim you have. Therefore, how you walk into the room and how you undress are also considered. Make sure that the person examining you is aware of all the things that you now cannot do as a result of your injury or disease.

Offsets if your disability has more than one cause

If a disability has more than one cause, the rules for the assessment are complex. If a disability is congenital or arose before an industrial one, it is deducted from the total disability.[76] The reduction is often called the **'offset'**. The procedure on offsets is complex and frequently leads to disputes. Mistakes are sometimes made because the decision maker incorrectly offsets for medical conditions that have not caused any disability.

Examples

Sam loses a hand, which would normally be 60 per cent, but he had previously lost the index finger. So 14 per cent is deducted, leaving 46 per cent (rounded up to 50 per cent).

Sian has a back injury as a result of an industrial accident. A decision maker has reduced her assessment by 5 per cent on the grounds of a pre-existing disability of which she knew nothing. Many people have spines that are slightly curved due to lifting things. The decision maker may have looked at an X-ray, correctly considered that her curved spine was not due to the relevant accident and then incorrectly reduced her assessment.

In the second example, the decision maker should have considered whether the pre-existing loss of faculty (see p374), the curved spine, really had (or would have) led to disablement that would have occurred even if the industrial accident (see p368) had not happened. S/he should have considered, among other things, whether the loss of faculty led to disablement before the industrial accident occurred. There is no physical disablement if you do not have any pain or restriction of movement and it is, therefore, wrong to reduce your assessment unless there is a good reason for deciding that disablement would have arisen during the period of assessment even if the industrial accident had not occurred.

In the second example, depending on the medical opinion:

- there might be no offset; *or*
- it might be appropriate to make a life award (see p377) with some uniform offset over the whole period in respect of any future back problems Sian is likely to have; *or*
- it might be appropriate to make a stepped assessment, making no offset initially but bringing one in at some future date, or applying different levels of offset for different parts of the period covered by the award.[77]

No reduction is made if 100 per cent is a reasonable assessment for the industrial accident.[78]

The decision maker should also bear in mind that even if you did have a pre-existing problem which caused a disability, the accident may worsen the effects of it, as well as cause a new problem. In such a case, the assessment should reflect the increase in the original problem as well as the new disability.[79]

If another disability arose after an industrial accident, the decision maker first has to assess the disablement arising from the industrial injury. If it is less than 11 per cent, any disability from the other cause is ignored; if it is more than 11 per cent, any extra disablement caused by the effect of the industrial injury on the other disability is added.[80]

Examples

Ali loses a little finger in an industrial accident and is assessed as 7 per cent disabled as a result. He then loses the other fingers of that hand in a non-industrial accident. He continues to be assessed as 7 per cent disabled because of the industrial accident.

Paul loses the middle, ring and little fingers of one hand in an industrial accident and is assessed as 30 per cent disabled as a result. He then loses the index finger of that hand in a non-industrial accident. His total disablement is now 50 per cent. But loss of the index finger only would have been 14 per cent. The disablement resulting from his industrial accident may, therefore, be reassessed at 36 per cent (50 per cent *minus* 14 per cent), which is rounded up to 40 per cent.

Two or more industrial accidents or diseases

If you have more than one industrial accident, the percentages of disablement (see p374 and Appendix 6) can be added together and may entitle you to benefit, even if neither accident would do so on its own. If you have two or more industrial accidents you may end up in a situation where the second or later accident is made worse by the interaction with the effect of the previous accident(s). Your most recent assessment should include an increase for any such interaction.[81] This also applies if an industrial disease (see p372) interacts with the effects of an industrial accident.

Example

Steve has a fall at work and seriously injures his left leg. He receives a life assessment of 10 per cent. Years later, he has a further fall and seriously injures the other leg. He is assessed as 10 per cent disabled for that accident, with a further 5 per cent for the extra disability he has as a result of the interaction between the two injuries. The total of 25 per cent is rounded up, resulting in payment of a 30 per cent pension.

There are special rules if you have pneumoconiosis. The rules allow for certain conditions to be taken into account in order to increase the assessment, even though these conditions did not arise from the pneumoconiosis. Any effect of tuberculosis is assessed with the effects of the pneumoconiosis.[82] If your disability is assessed at 50 per cent because of the pneumoconiosis, any additional disability because of chronic bronchitis or emphysema is added.[83] If you have made such a claim for pneumoconiosis, you cannot then make a separate claim for chronic bronchitis or emphysema.[84]

The period taken into account by the assessment

The decision maker or the First-tier Tribunal makes an assessment (see p374) for a period 'during which the claimant has suffered and may be expected to continue to suffer from the relevant loss of faculty'. Percentage assessments are usually made for six months, or for one or two years, or are given for life,[85] but definite dates must be given.

An assessment is either final or provisional.[86] You get a provisional assessment when there is doubt about what will happen in the future, and you are automatically called for another assessment at the end of the period.[87] Life assessments are final.

If you are given a final assessment for a fixed period this means that the decision maker believes you will no longer be affected by your accident or disease by the end of that period. If you think that the effects of the accident or disease will last for longer, consider an appeal against that assessment (see p1160).

If your condition deteriorates during a period of assessment, or if you still have a disability at the end of a period for which you have been given a final assessment, you should apply for a supersession (see p1135).

An assessment of disablement for occupational deafness is for life.[88]

2. Industrial injuries disablement benefit

The main industrial injuries benefit is industrial injuries disablement benefit (IIDB). There are also a number of benefits which are paid as increases to IIDB. The most important are:

- constant attendance allowance (see p380); *and*
- exceptionally severe disablement allowance (see p380).

Who can claim industrial injuries disablement benefit

You qualify for IIDB if:[89]

- you satisfy the industrial injury condition (see p367) as a result of one or more industrial accidents (see p368) or prescribed diseases (see p372);
- your resulting disablement is assessed as being at least 14 per cent (1 per cent in the case of pneumoconiosis, byssinosis and diffuse mesothelioma) (see p374 and Appendix 6);
- 90 days (excluding Sundays) have elapsed since the date of the accident or of the onset of the prescribed disease or injury (those who have the prescribed disease of mesothelioma can be paid without serving this waiting period).

Disqualification

You may be disqualified for up to six weeks if you do not provide the required information or notify changes in your circumstances, or have a medical examination or treatment. You cannot, however, be disqualified for refusing to have an operation unless it is a minor one.[90]

The rules about your age

There are no specific age rules or requirement to be paying national insurance contributions. You simply must be under a contract of employment. Therefore, a child who is working is covered, as well as a person over pension age. If the contract under which you work is illegal, you must ask the DWP to make a decision that you are covered by the scheme.[91]

If you are aged under 18, you receive a lower rate of benefit.

Claiming for others

There are no increases for adult or child dependents unless you are getting unemployability supplement (abolished for new claims after 5 April 1987).

The amount of benefit

The amount of benefit you get depends on the extent of your disablement. See p374 for how this is assessed.[92]

Extent of disablement	*Benefit per week Claimant aged under 18 without dependants* £	*Benefit per week Any other claimant* £
100%	96.90	158.10
90%	87.21	142.29
80%	77.52	126.48
70%	67.83	110.67
60%	58.14	94.86
50%	48.45	79.05
40%	38.76	63.24
30%	29.07	47.43
11% – 20%	19.38	31.62

Since 1 October 1986, IIDB has been paid only if the assessment of your disablement is at least 14 per cent,[93] except in the cases of pneumoconiosis, byssinosis and diffuse mesothelioma, when it is paid if the assessment is at least 1 per cent.[94]

Before 1 October 1986, IIDB was paid in respect of any assessment of disablement of at least 1 per cent. The old rules are still in force for assessments following claims made before that date.[95] If you are getting a payment as a result of such a small percentage assessment, see p176 of the 17th edition of CPAG's *Rights Guide to Non-Means-Tested Benefits*.

You might be able to get an increase of benefit (see p380).

Increases of industrial injuries disablement benefit

You get increased IIDB if you qualify for constant attendance allowance or exceptionally severe disablement allowance.

Constant attendance allowance

You qualify for constant attendance allowance if:[96]

- you are entitled to industrial injuries disablement pension based on a degree of disablement assessed at 100 per cent; *and*
- you require constant attendance as a result of the relevant loss of faculty (see p374).

Disablement as a result of pre-1948 industrial accidents and diseases, war injuries and injuries incurred while on police or fire duty, may be taken into account in considering the degree of your disablement.[97]

There are two rates.

- The **higher weekly rate** of £126.60 is paid if you are 'so exceptionally severely disabled as to be entirely, or almost entirely, dependent on (constant) attendance for the necessities of life, and [are] likely to remain so dependent for a prolonged period and the attendance so required is whole-time'.[98]
- The **intermediate weekly rate** of £63.30 is paid if you are 'to a substantial extent dependent on (constant) attendance for the necessities of life and [are] likely to remain so dependent for a prolonged period'. This may be increased up to £94.95 a week if 'the extent of such attendance is greater by reason of the beneficiary's exceptionally severe disablement'. If attendance is part time only, the amount payable is 'such sum as may be reasonable in the circumstances' (usually £31.65 a week).[99] Some claimants may be better off claiming the care component of disability living allowance (see p144) or ordinary attendance allowance instead (see p153).

Exceptionally severe disablement allowance

This is paid at the weekly rate of £63.30 if:

- you are entitled to constant attendance allowance (or would be if you were not in hospital) at the higher or intermediate rate; *and*
- you are likely to remain so permanently.[100]

3. Reduced earnings allowance

Reduced earnings allowance (REA) is available if you had an accident or started to have a disease before 1 October 1990. A successful first claim can still be made now if you had an accident or disease before that date.

The amount of REA you get depends on whether your current earnings, or earnings in a job which it is considered you could do, are less than the current earnings in your previous 'regular occupation' (see p383).

Who can claim reduced earnings allowance

You qualify for REA if:[101]

- you satisfy the industrial injury condition (see p367) because of an industrial accident (see p368) before 1 October 1990 or an industrial disease (see p372), the onset of which was before that date (see p373); *and*
- your resulting disablement is assessed as being at least 1 per cent (see p374 and Appendix 6); *and*
- as a result of a relevant loss of faculty *either*:
  - you are incapable and likely to remain permanently incapable of following your regular occupation (see p382) and are incapable of following employment of an equivalent standard (see p383) which is suitable in your case (the 'permanent condition' – see p382); *or*
  - you are, and have been at all times since the end of the 90-day qualifying period for disablement benefit, incapable of following your regular occupation or employment of an equivalent standard (see p383) which is suitable in your case ('the continuing condition' – see p382); *and either*
- you are under pension age (but see below); *or*
- you have not given up regular employment (see p383); *and*
- you have not been in receipt of REA since 1 October 1990 and subsequently ceased to be entitled to it for at least one day (see p383).

If you are claiming on the basis of an industrial disease, that disease (or the extension of an existing category of prescribed diseases) must have been added to the list of prescribed diseases before 10 October 1994.[102]

Some claimants have been successful in claiming REA after pension age and retaining REA rather than moving onto the lower rate of retirement allowance (see p384). This is on the basis that the law allows a person who is over pension age and claiming REA for the first time to be paid REA rather than retirement allowance.[103]

In addition to those rules of entitlement, if you were entitled to REA on either 10 April 1988 or 9 April 1989 and on that date you were over pension age and were retired, or were treated as retired, you remain entitled to the allowance for life. For the meaning of 'retired or treated as retired' in this context, see p69 of the 12th edition of CPAG's *Rights Guide to Non-Means-Tested Benefits*.

Reduced earnings

Although REA compensates for loss of earnings, the fact that you are losing money as a result of an industrial accident or disease is not, in itself, enough. You must meet either the permanent or continuing conditions (see p382).

The permanent condition

Only incapacity at the time of your claim and in the future are relevant. The phrase 'likely to remain permanently incapable' relates only to your 'regular occupation' (see below) and not to 'employment of an equivalent standard' (see p383), so you do not need to prove at the First-tier Tribunal that you are likely to remain incapable of employment of an equivalent standard, just that you are unlikely to be able to perform your normal job.

If you have pneumoconiosis, and you are advised not to work by a decision maker, you are deemed not to be able to work unless the decision maker proves otherwise.[104]

The continuing condition

Only incapacity at the time of your claim and in the past is relevant, so there is less scope for argument than when assessing the future. However, if you returned to work but were 'sheltered' by your colleagues, you can still argue that you were 'incapable' of following your regular occupation (see below).[105] If you have worked since the end of the 90-day period, but the work was for rehabilitation, testing or training, it can be disregarded provided it was for a total period of six months or less, approved by the Secretary of State or done on medical advice. If you have given up work because of your pneumoconiosis on the advice of a decision maker, you are deemed to have been continuously incapable of following that regular occupation.[106]

Regular occupation

Deciding what your 'regular occupation' is involves looking at your work history (part time[107] as well as full time) and the content of the job, as opposed to its title. For example, in one case, a docker still employed to work as a docker but unable to earn as much because he was unable to do the full range of his duties was found incapable of his regular occupation.[108]

If an accident happens when you have just started a new job, that job may well be treated as your regular occupation. Your intentions and prospects need to be considered.[109] But a stop-gap occupation, taken on during poor health, is not treated as your regular occupation.[110] If you are a full-time student, any part-time work counts as your regular occupation.[111] If your earnings come from several jobs, you may face problems. Any employment that is subsidiary to your usual or main job does not count. If you would have been promoted by the time of your claim, but for the accident, the promoted position may count as your regular occupation. It is possible to make a number of separate claims for REA. If you had a number of industrial accidents and had to downgrade your employment each time, you can be compensated for each. The crucial point is whether each accident has led to a change in your regular occupation.[112]

If you have a prescribed disease (see p372) and, because of this, gave up a job before you applied for benefit, it may count as your regular occupation.[113]

Suitable employment of an equivalent standard

Suitability is judged by looking at your education, experience, training, work history and general health.[114] Only employed earner's employment can be treated as suitable, so self-employed work is not considered.[115] The question then is whether the employment is of an equivalent standard. The normal earnings of people employed in what is considered suitable employment are compared with the normal earnings of those employed in the regular occupation.[116] The earnings in both occupations have to be assessed taking into account bonuses, overtime if normally paid[117] and benefits in kind.

If your regular occupation (see p382) was part time, full-time work is not of an equivalent standard even if you are medically fit to do it. Like must be compared with like. However, if there are no jobs of the same number of hours, different work for a similar number of hours may be regarded as equivalent.[118]

Regular employment

When you reach pension age (see p531) you will lose your REA unless you are in 'regular employment'. If you have given up 'regular employment', you receive retirement allowance instead (see p384). This is paid to you at a lower rate.

If you have obtained a full gender recognition certificate, your pension age for this purpose is the relevant age for your acquired gender.[119]

The definition of 'regular employment' was changed from 24 March 1996. **'Regular employment'** since then means working for an average of 10 hours or more a week within a period of five or more weeks of such employment.[120]

The rules about your age

There is no specific age rule for REA but you must have been an employed earner. REA is paid until you reach pension age and it is then replaced with retirement allowance (see p384). If you are now over pension age, but have never claimed REA even though you meet the conditions for entitlement, you are not excluded from claiming REA. The DWP currently makes awards of REA on such claims. If you are considering making a claim for REA and you are about to reach pension age, seek advice before delaying a claim for REA.

Claiming for others

There are no increases for dependants.

The amount of benefit

The amount of REA you get is the amount by which your current earnings, or earnings in a job which it is considered you could do, are less than the current earnings in your previous regular occupation (see p382).[121] Earnings include overtime.

If you are unemployed:

- the DWP's healthcare professional is asked for your limitations;
- a DWP disability employment adviser is asked what job s/he thinks you could do; *and*
- Jobcentre Plus is asked to quote a wage which such a job would pay in your area.

Once the first assessment has been made, the amount is usually increased in line with earnings in that industry or workplace, unless that regular occupation (see p382) has ceased to exist.[122] In that case, it is calculated as rising in line with the nearest 'occupational group' as defined by the DWP. You can ask for a fresh assessment to take into account your normal prospects of advancement, though you have to show that promotion would have happened, say at the end of a period of employment or training, not just that it may have happened if you had been particularly diligent.[123]

The maximum amount of reduced earnings allowance

The maximum amount you may receive for any one award is £63.24 a week.[124] The total you can receive from industrial injuries disablement benefit (IIDB) and REA (whether for one or more awards) is 140 per cent of the standard rate of IIDB.[125]

If you were over pension age and retired before 6 April 1987, your allowance is reduced if it would otherwise mean you would be receiving more than 100 per cent disablement benefit.[126] If you qualified for REA and were retired or treated as retired on either 10 April 1988 or 9 April 1989, you continue to receive the allowance at the same 'frozen' rate. Its value, therefore, erodes over time.

4. Retirement allowance

Retirement allowance is a reduced rate of reduced earnings allowance (REA – see p380) for people over pension age, paid for life.

You qualify for retirement allowance if:[127]

- you are over pension age (see p531);
- you have given up regular employment (see p383);
- you were entitled to REA at a rate of at least £2 a week (in total, if you had more than one award) immediately before you gave up regular employment (see p383);
- you are not entitled to REA.

You must be over pension age to qualify and there are no increases for dependants. You can only get one award of retirement allowance, even if you had more than one award of REA.[128]

The amount of retirement allowance you get is £15.81 a week or 25 per cent of the amount of REA you were receiving, whichever is the lower.

5. **Special benefit rules**

Special rules may apply to:

- prisoners (see p693);
- people going abroad (see Chapter 63).

6. **Claims and backdating**

The rules about claiming and backdating are in Chapter 42. This section tells you about the specific rules that apply to industrial injuries benefits.

Making a claim

Claims for industrial injury benefits must be made in writing.[129] You do this by completing the approved form and sending it to your regional industrial injuries disablement benefit delivery centre (tel: 0800 055 6688). Keep a copy of your claim form in case queries arise.

You must provide any information or evidence required (see below). In certain circumstances, the DWP may accept a written application not on the approved form (see p1019). You can amend or withdraw your claim before a decision is made (see p1019).

Forms

There are different forms depending on the benefit claimed and on the type of accident or disease. Get them from your regional industrial injuries disablement benefit delivery centre or www.direct.gov.uk/en/moneytaxandbenefits.

You can apply for a declaration that you have had an industrial accident, even if you do not wish to claim any benefit. Do this by contacting your local DWP office. This may be wise if you have had an accident, but are not sure whether or not you wish to proceed with a claim for benefit.[130]

Who should claim

You claim for yourself. However, if you are unable to act for yourself, another adult can claim on your behalf – called an 'appointee' (see p1016).

Information to support your claim

When you claim industrial injuries benefits, you must:

- satisfy the national insurance number requirement (see p1023);
- provide proof of your identity, if required (see p1024);

- supply information and evidence required on the claim form (see p1019) and additional information and evidence relevant to your claim (see p1022). There is a strict time limit for doing so.

The date of your claim

The date of your claim is the date it is received at the regional industrial injuries disablement benefit delivery centre.

If you claim the wrong benefit

In some circumstances, it is possible for a claim for one benefit to be treated as a claim for a different benefit (see p1025). However, for industrial injuries benefits it is only possible to 'interchange' constant attendance allowance with disability living allowance and attendance allowance.

Claiming in advance

An advance claim can be made for industial injuries disablement benefit if you have had an accident or have a prescribed disease and you are within the 90-day waiting period. Otherwise it is not possible to claim industrial injuries benefits in advance.

Renewal claims

Assessments can be provisional or final, and for a limited period or for life. A provisional assessment means that the decision maker considers your medical condition has not yet settled down, and might get worse or better. At the end of a provisional assessment you are invited to be re-examined. A final assessment means that the decision maker believes that your condition has settled down and your case is dealt with once and for all. At the end of a period of award, you therefore need to apply for a renewal of benefit.

If you are awarded disablement benefit for a particular disease, you may recover at some point but subsequently have a further attack. If there is a continuation or recrudescence of the old disease, you do not have to wait 15 weeks before gaining entitlement to disablement benefit.

Backdating claims

It is important to claim in time. Your claim can be backdated for up to three months if you satisfy the qualifying conditions over that period. You do not have to show any reasons why your claim was late. The rules on backdating are covered on p1026.

If you might have qualified for benefit earlier but did not claim because you were given the wrong information or were misled by the DWP, ask for a compensation payment (see p1261) or complain to the Ombudsman via your MP (see p1260).

7. Getting paid

Payment of industrial injuries benefits is normally made by direct credit transfer into a bank (or similar) account (see p1039). If you are unable to open or manage an account, payment can be made by cheque (see p1040). If you are unable to act for yourself, benefit can be paid to someone else on your behalf, called your appointee (see p1016).

When are you paid benefit?	On a Wednesday.[131]
How often is benefit paid?	Weekly in advance.[132]

Note:
- You might not be paid your industrial injuries benefit if you have been sanctioned for benefit offences (see p1106).
- If you have forgotten your PIN or if a cheque is lost or stolen, see p1043.
- If payment of your industrial injuries benefit is delayed, see p1262. You might be able to get an interim payment (see p1046). You may also be eligible for a crisis loan (see p564). If you wish to complain about how your claim has been dealt with, see p1255. You might be able to claim compensation (see p1261).
- If payment of your industrial injuries benefit is suspended, see p1043.
- If you are overpaid industrial injuries benefit, you might have to repay it (see Chapter 43). If you have been accused of fraud, see Chapter 44.

Change of circumstances

You must report any change of circumstances that might affect your benefit (see p1047). You should notify changes promptly to the office handling your claim in writing or by telephone (although in individual cases notification might be accepted in a different form). In some cases, however, the decision maker may say you must report changes in writing. In any case, you may want to report the change in writing and keep a copy in case of a dispute in the future.

8. Tax, tax credits and other benefits

Industrial injuries benefits are not taxable.[133]

Tax credits

Industrial injuries benefits are ignored as income for tax credits.

Means-tested benefits

Industrial injuries disablement benefit, reduced earnings allowance and retirement allowance are taken into account in full for all the means-tested benefits.

Non-means-tested benefits

In general, the overlapping benefits rule does not apply to industrial injuries benefits and it is possible for them to overlap – eg, to receive full disablement benefit as well as full incapacity benefit (IB).

Carer's allowance (see Chapter 3) may be paid to someone who is 'regularly and substantially caring' for you while you are receiving constant attendance allowance (see p380).

If you were receiving sickness benefit or IB because of an industrial accident or disease on 12 April 1995, you can continue to qualify for IB, even though you do not satisfy the contribution conditions, provided you remain incapable of work because of the accident or disease.[134]

Passports and other sources of help

You qualify for a Christmas bonus if you receive disablement benefit, but only if it includes unemployability supplement or constant attendance allowance (see p9).

If you have (or you are a dependant of someone who has died and who had) pneumoconiosis (including asbestosis, silicosis and kaolinosis), byssinosis, diffuse mesothelioma, diffuse pleural thickening, or primary carcinoma of the lung if accompanied by asbestosis or diffuse pleural thickening, and you cannot get compensation from your employer (eg, because s/he has ceased trading), or you do not have a realistic chance of obtaining damages from that employer, you may be able to get a one-off lump-sum payment in addition to any industrial injuries benefit.[135] From 1 October 2008 you can be entitled to a one-off lump-sum payment from the DWP for diffuse mesothelioma (including if you are a dependant of someone who had that condition immediately before they died), without the need to have worked.[136] The time limit for claiming is 12 months (from the date of diagnosis or death) and the time limit may be extended if there is good cause. All these lump-sum payments may be recovered (ie, deducted) from compensation (see p1058).

If your spouse or civil partner died as a result of an industrial accident or disease, you may qualify for a bereavement benefit even though the national insurance contribution conditions are not satisfied (see p66).[137]

Notes

1. **Who can get industrial injuries benefits**

1 s94(1) SSCBA 1992
2 ss94(1) and 108(1) SSCBA 1992
3 s2(1) SSCBA 1992; *Vandyk v Minister of Pensions and National Insurance* [1955] QB 29
4 Reg 10C(6) SSB(PA) Regs
5 Regs 2, 4 and 6 SS(EEEIIP) Regs
6 Reg 3 SS(EEEIIP) Regs
7 R(I) 49/52
8 R(I) 1/76
9 R(I) 8/81
10 R(I) 1/82
11 *Fenton v Thorley* [1903] AC 443 (HL)
12 CI/123/1949
13 *Jones v Secretary of State for Social Services* [1972] AC 944 (HL), also reported as an appendix to R(I) 3/69; *SSWP v Scullion* [2010] EWCA Civ 310
14 *Trim Joint District School Board of Management v Kelly* [1914] AC 667 (HL)
15 s94(1) SSCBA 1992
16 CI/105/1998; CI/142/2006
17 *Roberts v Dorothea Slate Quarries Co. Ltd* [1948] 2 All ER 201 (HL)
18 R(I) 24/54; R(I) 43/55
19 CI/3370/1999
20 *Mullen v SSWP* [2002] SC 251; SLT 149; SCLR 475; GWD 3-121, IH (2DIV)
21 R(I) 43/61; R(I) 4/62
22 R(I) 18/54
23 CI/159/1950
24 *Moore v Manchester Liners Ltd* [1910] AC 498 at p500 (HL)
25 *R v National Insurance Commissioner ex parte East* [1976] ICR 206 (DC), also reported as an appendix to R(I) 16/75
26 R(I) 1/59
27 *R v Industrial Injuries Commissioner ex parte AEU* [1966] 2 QB 31 (CA), also reported as an appendix to R(I) 4/66
28 R(I) 10/81
29 *R v National Insurance Commissioner ex parte Reed* (DC), reported as an appendix to R(I) 7/80
30 s94(3) SSCBA 1992
31 *R v Industrial Injuries Commissioner ex parte AEU* [1966] 2 QB 31 (CA), also reported as an appendix to R(I) 4/66
32 R(I) 46/53
33 R(I) 17/63
34 *R v Industrial Injuries Commissioner ex parte AEU* [1966] 2 QB 31 (CA), also reported as an appendix to R(I) 4/66
35 s98 SSCBA 1992; CI/210/1950
36 In CI/14111/96 a Benefits Agency officer, assaulted by a claimant while at home on sick leave, was found to have been injured 'in the course of her employment'. Although this case was subsequently overturned by the Court of Appeal, the Court ruled that a person might be in the course of her/his employment if at the relevant time s/he was carrying out some duty s/he was contracted to do; *CAO v Rhodes* [1999] ICR 178, also reported in R(I)1/99
37 *Nancollas v Insurance Officer* [1985] 1 All ER 833 (CA), also reported as an appendix to R(I) 7/85
38 s99 SSCBA 1992
39 R(I) 1/88
40 R(I) 12/75
41 R(I) 4/70
42 R(I)1/93
43 *Nancollas v Insurance Officer; Ball v Insurance Officer* [1985] 1 All ER 833 (CA), also reported as an appendix to R(I) 7/85
44 *Smith v Stages* [1989] 2 WLR 529 (HL)
45 R(I) 1/91
46 R(I) 6/82
47 R(I) 12/52
48 s101 SSCBA 1992
49 s100 SSCBA 1992
50 Sch 2 SS(IIPD) Regs
51 ss108(1) and 109(1) SSCBA 1992; reg 2 SS(IIPD) Regs
52 R(I) 3/03
53 R(I) 2/03; R(I) 4/96
54 Reg 12 SS&CS(DA) Regs
55 Reg 3 SS(IIPD) Regs
56 Regs 2(c) and 25 SS(IIPD) Regs. Although at one time it was held that the time limit in respect of occupational deafness had been imposed unlawfully, it was made valid retrospectively by Sch 6 para 4(3) SSA 1990.
57 Reg 36 SS(IIPD) Regs

58 Sch 1 SS(IIPD) Regs
59 Reg 2(e) SS(IIPD) Regs
60 There is no such presumption for most diseases falling under the C category of disease. Reg 4(1) SS(IIPD) Regs
61 Reg 6(2)(c) SS(IIPD) Regs
62 Reg 7 SS(IIPD) Regs
63 *Jones v Secretary of State for Social Services* [1972] AC 944 (HL), also reported as an appendix to R(I) 3/69
64 CI/499/2000; s122(1) SSCBA 1992
65 s30 SSA 1998
66 s103(3) SSCBA 1992
67 s103(2) and (3) SSCBA 1992; regs 15A and 15B SS(IIPD) Regs, as amended
68 Sch 2 SS(GB) Regs; Sch 3 SS(IIPD) Regs
69 Reg 11(6) SS(GB) Regs
70 *JI v SSWP (II)* [2011] UKUT 294 (AAC); [2012] AACR 15
71 Reg 20A SS(IIPD) Regs
72 Sch 6 para 1 SSCBA 1992
73 Reg 11(8) SS(GB) Regs; R(I) 5/95; R(I) 1/04
74 CI/636/1993, although the commissioner said that where there are specific submissions backed with expert medical evidence on the percentage assessment, it would be an error of law to arrive at a different figure without giving reasons for this.
75 R(I) 2/06
76 Reg 11(3) SS(GB) Regs
77 CI/34/1993
78 Reg 11(7) SS(GB) Regs
79 R(I) 3/91, which contains a definitive survey of the situations when reg 11 SS(GB) Regs applies
80 Reg 11(4) SS(GB) Regs
81 R(I) 3/91
82 Reg 21 SS(IIPD) Regs
83 Reg 22 SS(IIPD) Regs
84 Reg 2(d) SS(IIPD) Regs
85 Sch 6 para 6 SSCBA 1992
86 Sch 6 para 7 SSCBA 1992
87 Sch 6 para 6(2)(b) SSCBA 1992
88 Reg 29 SS(IIPD) Regs

2. **Industrial injuries disablement benefit**

89 ss103 and 108 SSCBA 1992
90 Reg 40 SS(GB) Regs
91 s97 SSCBA 1992
92 Sch 4 SSCBA 1992
93 s103(1) and Sch 7 para 9(1) SSCBA 1992
94 Reg 20(1) SS(IIPD) Regs
95 Sch 7 para 9(1)(a) SSCBA 1992; reg 14 SS(II&D)MP Regs
96 s104 SSCBA 1992
97 Reg 20 SS(GB) Regs
98 Sch 4 SSCBA 1992; reg 19(b) SS(GB) Regs
99 Sch 4 SSCBA 1992; reg 19(a) SS(GB) Regs
100 s105 SSCBA 1992

3. **Reduced earnings allowance**

101 Sch 7 paras 11 and 12(1), (2) and (7) SSCBA 1992
102 Sch 7 para 11(1)(b) SSCBA 1992
103 Sch 7 paras 11 and 13(1) SSCBA 1992; SS(II)(RE) Regs
104 Reg 23(a) SS(IIPD) Regs
105 R(I) 39/51; R(I) 26/53
106 Reg 23(b) SS(IIPD) Regs
107 *R v National Insurance Commissioner ex parte Mellors* [1971] 2 QB 401 (CA), also reported as an appendix to R(I) 7/69
108 R(I) 28/51
109 R(I) 65/54
110 CI/80/1949
111 Reg 2 SS(II&D)MP Regs
112 *Hagan v Secretary of State for Social Security* [2001] EWCA Civ 1452, reported in R(I) 2/02
113 Reg 17 SS(IIPD) Regs
114 R(I) 22/61
115 Sch 7 para 11(5)(b) SSCBA 1992
116 *R v National Insurance Commissioner ex parte Mellors* [1971] 2 QB 401, [1971] 1 All ER 740
117 R(I) 7/51; R(I) 1/72
118 R(I) 3/83
119 s9 GRA 2004
120 Reg 2 SS(IIRE) Regs; R(I) 3/93; *SSWP v NH (II)* [2010] UKUT 84 (AAC)
121 Sch 7 para 11(10) SSCBA 1992
122 Sch 7 para 11(14) SSCBA 1992
123 Sch 7 para 11(6) SSCBA 1992
124 Regs 2 and 3 and Sch 7 para 11(13) SS(REA) Regs
125 Sch 7 para 11(10) SSCBA 1992
126 Sch 7 para 11(11) SSCBA 1992

4. **Retirement allowance**

127 Sch 7 para 13 SSCBA 1992
128 *TA v SSWP (II)* [2010] UKUT 101 (AAC)

6. **Claims and backdating**

129 Reg 4(1) SS(C&P) Regs
130 s29 SSA 1998

7. **Getting paid**

131 Sch 6 para 3 SS(C&P) Regs
132 Reg 22 SS(C&P) Regs

8. **Tax, tax credits and other benefits**

133 s667 IT(EP)A 2003
134 Regs 14, 17 and 21 SS(IB)(T) Regs
135 The Pneumoconiosis etc (Workers' Compensation) Act 1979
136 Part 4 CMOPA 2008
137 s60(2) and (3) SSCBA 1992

Chapter 19

Jobseeker's allowance: main rules

This chapter covers:

Note: unless otherwise stated, references to income-based jobseeker's allowance (JSA) in this chapter also refer to joint-claim JSA.

Key facts

- Jobseeker's allowance (JSA) is a benefit for people who are looking for work.
- There are three types of JSA: **contribution-based JSA** (a non-means-tested benefit), **income-based JSA** (a means-tested benefit) and **joint-claim JSA** (a means-tested benefit paid if you are a member of a 'joint-claim couple').
- You do not have to have paid national insurance contributions to qualify for income-based JSA or joint-claim JSA.
- You cannot qualify for JSA if you (or your partner) are in full-time paid work.
- You must normally be fit for work, satisfy the 'jobseeking conditions' and sign on every fortnight.
- If you lose your job because of misconduct or if you do not take up a job or a Work Programme or training scheme opportunity and in other situations, you may be 'sanctioned' and your JSA may not be paid.
- JSA is administered and paid by the DWP.
- If you disagree with a JSA decision, you can apply for a revision or a supersession, or appeal against it (see Chapters 45 and 46).

Future changes: April 2013 and after

Major changes are taking place that affect the benefits and tax credits system (see Chapter 2).

- From April 2013, total benefit payments to many working-age households will be 'capped' (see p25). There will be limited exceptions, including households in which someone is entitled to working tax credit or receives disability living allowance. JSA will be included in the capped amount.
- Instead of the requirement to be available for and actively seeking work, there will be new work-related requirements. These are likely to be introduced from October 2013 and will be similar to those for universal credit (UC – see Chapter 4).
- Couples whose youngest child is five or over will have to make a joint claim for JSA. This will not apply if a member of the couple is a carer or is unable to work because of a disability or health condition.
- From October 2013, when UC is introduced, no new claims for *income-based* JSA or *joint-claim* JSA will be allowed. If you are claiming these benefits, you will be transferred to UC between April 2014 and October 2017. You will still be able to claim *contribution-based* JSA.

See CPAG's *Welfare Rights Bulletin* for updates.

1. Who can claim jobseeker's allowance

You qualify for jobseeker's allowance (JSA) if:[1]

- you do not count as being in full-time paid work (see p398) and, if you are claiming income-based JSA, nor does your partner; *and*
- you do not have limited capability for work. However, in certain circumstances, people who are sick or who have gone abroad for NHS hospital treatment can get JSA (see p399); *and*
- you are not in 'relevant education' (see p634). In addition, if you are a full-time student you usually cannot get JSA (see p400); *and*
- you satisfy 'jobseeking conditions' – ie, you must:
  - be available for work (see p434); *and*
  - be actively seeking work (see p447); *and*
  - have a current jobseeker's agreement with the DWP (see p452). **Note:** at some point in future (this is likely to be in 2012), instead of a current jobseeker's agreement, you will have to accept a 'claimant commitment' that records what your responsibilities are in return for getting JSA;

  See Chapter 20 for full details of these conditions; *and*
- you are below pension age (see p531); *and*
- you are not claiming and entitled to income support (IS); *and*

- you are in Great Britain. JSA can continue to be paid in limited circumstances while you are temporarily away (see p1490). Contribution-based JSA can be 'exported' if you are unemployed and looking for work in a European Economic Area country (see p1492).

In addition, you must satisfy extra rules. For contribution-based JSA, see p395. For income-based JSA (or joint-claim JSA), see p396.

You are not usually entitled to JSA for the first three days of your 'jobseeking period' (see below). These are known as 'waiting days' (see p402).

Note: from some point in future, to qualify for JSA you will have to be entitled to be in employment under UK immigration rules. There may be exceptions.

Jobseeking periods

A **'jobseeking period'** is the period during which you either meet the conditions that apply to all types of JSA or do not satisfy the jobseeking conditions but receive hardship payments (see p484).[2] **Note:** if you are a man of at least the qualifying age for pension credit (PC – see p509) but under 65, special rules apply which mean that in some circumstances your jobseeking period continues even though you do not satisfy the jobseeking conditions.[3]

What does not count as part of a jobseeking period

The following do not count as part of a jobseeking period:[4]

- days for which you do not claim (or are not treated as claiming) JSA;
- days for which you lost your entitlement to JSA because you failed to attend the Jobcentre Plus office when required or to 'sign on';
- a period for which you claimed backdated benefit, but which has been refused;
- any week (Sunday to Saturday) for which you are not entitled to JSA because you were involved in a trade dispute for all or part of that week;
- days on which you are not entitled to JSA because you have not provided your or your partner's national insurance (NI) number (see p1023).

Linked jobseeking periods

In some cases, two or more jobseeking periods can be linked together and treated as if they were one jobseeking period. Also, certain periods in which you satisfy other conditions ('linked periods' – see p395) can be linked to a jobseeking period. This means, for example, that:[5]

- the question of whether you satisfy the NI contribution conditions for contribution-based JSA is decided by looking at your situation at the beginning of the first jobseeking period (or a period linked to a jobseeking period if earlier) and not at the beginning of your current claim;[6]
- you do not have to serve another three waiting days (see p402) to get JSA;
- if the jobseeking periods together are longer than 182 days, you cannot get any more contribution-based JSA (see p403);

- if the jobseeking periods together are at least two years, you might be able to get JSA while attending a qualifying course (see p439).

Two jobseeking periods are treated as linked if they are separated by one or any combination of the following:[7]

- any period of no more than 12 weeks; *or*
- a period during which you are doing jury service; *or*
- a 'linked period' (see below); *or*
- any period of no more than 12 weeks which comes between two 'linked periods' or between a jobseeking period and a 'linked period'.

Linked periods

A 'linked period' is any period during which you:[8]

- are entitled to carer's allowance (CA) but only if this allows you to get contribution-based JSA when you would not otherwise satisfy the contribution conditions; *or*
- are incapable of work or treated as incapable of work (see Chapter 32); *or*
- have, or are treated as having, limited capability for work (see Chapter 11); *or*
- are entitled to maternity allowance; *or*
- are undergoing training for which a training allowance is payable (this includes when you were on the New Deal – a scheme no longer offered); *or*
- were on the self-employed employment option of the New Deal (a scheme no longer offered); *or*
- were not entitled to JSA because you counted as being in full-time paid work (see p398) or your earnings or income were too high as a result of your being on the environment task force or voluntary sector option of the New Deal for young people, or the Intensive Activity Period for people aged 25 to 60 or an Employment Zone programme (all schemes no longer offered).

You cannot argue that a period spent taking time out of work to look after children is a 'linked period' for these purposes.[9]

Extra rules for contribution-based jobseeker's allowance

To get contribution-based JSA, in addition to satisfying the rules that apply to all types of JSA (see p393), you must:[10]

- satisfy the contribution conditions (see p789). This depends on your record of NI contributions and credits in the two tax years immediately before the benefit year in which your jobseeking period begins (or in which a period linked to a jobseeking period begins, if earlier). For example, if you claim JSA immediately after a period of limited capability for work, the contribution test is applied using the date on which you first had limited capability for work; *and*
- not have earnings above a 'prescribed amount' (see p897). **Note:** if you have earnings below this amount, your JSA is reduced to take account of them.

Extra rules for income-based jobseeker's allowance

If you do not qualify for contribution-based JSA, or if you do but need additional benefit (for your partner or housing costs), you can qualify for income-based JSA if, in addition to satisfying the rules that apply to all types of JSA (see p393):[11]

- your income is less than your applicable amount (see p404); *and*
- your savings and other capital are worth £16,000 or less. Some capital (in particular your home) is ignored (see Chapter 41); *and*
- you (or if you are a joint-claim couple, at least one of you) are aged 18 or over. If you are a 16/17-year-old (or if you are a joint-claim couple and one of you is 16/17) you might get income-based JSA if you (or the member of the couple who is 16/17) satisfy special rules (see pp405–10); *and*
- neither you nor your partner are claiming and entitled to income-related employment and support allowance (ESA) or PC, your partner is not claiming and entitled to income support (IS), and if you are not a joint-claim couple (see p413), your partner is not claiming and entitled to income-based JSA.
  If you or your partner can qualify for IS, income-related ESA or PC, check whether this would make you better off; *and*
- you are not a member of the family of someone who is claiming and entitled to IS or income-based JSA – ie, you are not her/his child or qualifying young person for these purposes; *and*
- you satisfy the 'habitual residence test' and the 'right to reside test'. To find out if you are exempt from the tests, see Chapter 62; *and*
- you are not a 'person subject to immigration control' (see p1410). There are exceptions to this rule.

When joint-claim couples do not have to satisfy all the conditions

If you are a member of a couple who must make a joint-claim for JSA (see p413), so long as one of you satisfies all the rules for claiming JSA, the two of you can still qualify for joint-claim JSA even if the other does not satisfy the jobseeking conditions or is not in Great Britain. The one who does not satisfy the rules must be below pension age (see p531), not count as being in full-time paid work (see p398) and fit into one of the exempt groups below.[12] You must still make a joint claim for JSA and satisfy all the other requirements.

Exempt groups

You fit into an exempt group if, for at least one day in a benefit week, you:[13]

- are studying full time. You must be:
  - a 'qualifying young person' for child benefit purposes (see p94) or a full-time student (see p637). You must normally be in education at the time you and your partner claim JSA, but there are exceptions; *or*
  - someone who can claim IS while in 'relevant education', other than a refugee learning English (see p635).

You can only fit into this exempt group for one joint claim, unless another one is made because the first ceased when one of you started full-time paid work, or was summoned to do jury service, or was within any of the linked periods on p395;[14] *or*

- are a carer who can claim IS (see p348). If you cease meeting this condition or stop being a carer, you continue to fit into an exempt group for a further eight weeks; *or*
- are entitled to statutory sick pay (SSP); *or*
- are incapable of work but are treated as capable of work because you are disqualified from receiving incapacity benefit (IB) – eg, because of misconduct or failure to accept treatment (see p271 of the 2008/09 edition of this *Handbook*); *or*
- have, or are treated as having, limited capability for work (see p201) or have limited capability for work but are treated as if you do not because you are disqualifed from receiving ESA – eg, because of misconduct or failure to accept treatment (see p178); *or*
- provide medical evidence to show that you have limited capability for work – ie, a self-certificate (for no longer than seven days) or a medical certificate from your doctor (the DWP may accept other evidence if it is unreasonable for you to provide this). You are exempt indefinitely on this basis without having to satisfy the work capability assessment; *or*
- are incapable of work, or have limited capability for work, because of your pregnancy. You only have to show that you are incapable of work, or have limited capability for work, not that there is a serious risk to your health or that of your baby;[15] *or*
- are at least the qualifying age for PC (see p509). In practice, this only applies if you are a man at least that age but under 65. In this situation, you might be better off claiming PC rather than JSA; *or*
- are a refugee learning English in order to obtain employment. You must be on a course for more than 15 hours a week and, at the time the course started, you must have been in Great Britain for a year or less. You can only be exempt for nine months on this ground; *or*
- are required to go to court or tribunal as a justice of the peace, juror, witness or party to the proceedings; *or*
- are not a 'qualifying young person' for child benefit purposes (see p94) and are aged 16–24 and on a training course provided by the Young People's Learning Agency (due to be replaced in April 2012 by the Education Funding Agency) or the Skills Funding Agency in England, the Welsh Ministers or a local enterprise company in Scotland; *or*
- are involved in a trade dispute.

If you fit into some of the exempt groups above, you should also qualify for IS. If you have limited capability for work, you may also qualify for ESA. If you are at least the qualifying age for PC (see p509), you might be able to claim PC. In these cases, you can choose whether to claim IS/ESA/PC or JSA. See p429 for further information before deciding what to do.

Sick and disabled people

The rules changed on 25 January 2010 and again on 1 November 2010. Before these dates, there were other groups of sick and disabled people who were also exempt. You can still fit into one of these groups if:

- immediately before 1 November 2010, you were entitled to JSA and:[16]
  - you were a disabled student – ie, you:
    - would qualify for the disability premium or severe disability premium (see pp824 and 830) were you not a member of a couple; *or*
    - had been incapable of work (or treated as incapable of work, or as capable of work for specified reasons) or entitled to SSP for 196 days (28 weeks). Two or more periods of incapacity separated by 56 days (eight weeks) or less are linked together and are treated as continuous; *or*
    - qualified for a disabled students' allowance because you are deaf; *or*
  - you were incapable of work because of illness or disability – ie, you:
    - satisfied the own occupation test or the personal capability assessment for IB; *or*
    - were treated as incapable of work by a decision maker – eg, you have a severe condition or an infectious disease, or are blind; *or*
  - you were registered blind. If you regain your sight, you continue to be exempt for 28 weeks after being taken off the register.

  You can qualify for joint-claim JSA on this basis until your entitlement to JSA ends;[17] *or*
- immediately before 25 January 2010, you were entitled to JSA and you were working 16 hours or more a week but did not count as in full-time paid work (see below) because:[18]
  - you were in employment and were living in a care home, an Abbeyfield home or an independent hospital; *or*
  - you are mentally or physically disabled and because of this your earnings or hours were reduced to 75 per cent or less of that for a person without your disability in the same or a comparable job.

  This applied even if you claimed on or after 25 January 2010, so long as your claim could be backdated. You can qualify for joint-claim JSA on this basis until your entitlement to JSA ends or, if earlier, until you cease to fit into one of these groups.

Full-time paid work

You cannot usually get JSA if you are in full-time paid work. You cannot get income-based JSA if either you or your partner are in full-time paid work. If you are the JSA claimant, this means 16 hours or more each week.[19] For your partner, this means 24 hours or more each week. All the rules on work are covered in Chapter 31.

If you are a member of a joint-claim couple, you cannot get joint-claim JSA if either one of you is in full-time paid work. If one of you is not working or is working fewer than 16 hours a week, the other can then work up to 24 hours a week. The person working 16 to 24 hours does not have to make a joint claim.[20]

In some situations, you are treated as *not* in full-time work even if you work more than 16/24 hours (see p725). In others, you are treated as in full-time work when you are not (see p723). See p720 for how your hours are calculated and p719 for what counts as paid work.

If your partner normally works 16/24 hours or more but is off sick or on maternity, adoption or paternity leave, s/he does not count as in full-time paid work. You may, therefore, be able to claim income-based JSA. The rules are different for working tax credit (WTC) so you might also qualify for WTC.

If you work less than 16 hours and your partner works at least 16 hours but less than 24 hours each week, you and your partner might be able to claim WTC. In some cases, you might be able to claim both WTC and JSA. Seek advice to see how you would be better off financially.

If you or your partner are at least the qualifying age for PC and either of you is working 16/24 hours or more each week, you might be able to claim PC or WTC (or both if your income is low enough). There is no full-time paid work rule for PC, but earnings are taken into account in working out how much you can get.

Note: if you or your partner have just taken up full-time paid work, you may be able to claim IS for help with your housing costs for the first four weeks. This is known as 'mortgage interest run-on' (see p879).

Limited capability for work

To qualify for JSA you must not have 'limited capability for work'.[21] See Chapter 11 for details about the test that decides this. **Note:** if a decision maker has decided for the purpose of ESA that you have (or do not have) limited capability for work, you are automatically treated as having (or not having) limited capability for work for JSA.[22] You still have to show that you are available for work if you are ill or have a disability, but there are some special rules that allow you to restrict your availability (see p444).

Periods of sickness when you can claim jobseeker's allowance

Even if you have limited capability for work (or are incapable of work), you do not have to stop claiming JSA in some situations. You are treated as not having limited capability for work (or as capable of work), and as available for and actively seeking work, if the only reason why you would not otherwise qualify for JSA is that:

- you are unable to work because you are sick (you can claim for up to two weeks – see below), unless you have stated in writing that you are going to claim or have claimed IB, ESA, severe disablement allowance (SDA) or IS;[23] *or*
- you are unable to work because you are sick and are temporarily absent from Great Britain for the purpose of getting NHS hospital treatment under certain provisions (you can claim for an indefinite period), unless you have stated in writing before the period of temporary absence abroad begins that you have claimed ESA immediately before the beginning of the period.[24]

You have to make a written declaration that you will be unfit for work from a specific date or for a specific period, on a form available at the Jobcentre Plus office.[25]

Two-week periods of sickness

You are allowed up to two two-week periods of sickness in a 'jobseeking period' (see p394) or, if your jobseeking period has lasted more than 12 months, in any successive 12-month period.[26] If you are sick more often than this, or for a longer period, you must claim ESA or PC instead of JSA for the time you are unable to work.

The rules on two-week periods of sickness do not apply to you if you were getting SSP in the eight weeks before you were sick.[27] Instead, you can claim benefit on the basis of having limited capability for work without having to serve any 'waiting days' (see p212).

Full-time training and study

You cannot usually qualify for JSA if you are studying full time (except if you are getting a training allowance) because you are usually treated as unavailable for work (see p441). To find out if you can claim JSA while studying full time, see p641. You might be able to get JSA while studying part time (see p641) or while waiting to go back on your course having taken approved time out because of an illness or caring responsibilities that have now ended (see p661).

Note: you can qualify for JSA in a number of situations when you are studying (see p434) as well as when you are getting a training allowance (see p434) or are on a full-time 'qualifying course' (see p439).

2. The rules about your age

There is no minimum age for entitlement to **contribution-based jobseeker's allowance (JSA)** but, in practice, because you can only qualify if you have paid, or been credited with, sufficient national insurance (NI) contributions in the two tax years before the benefit year in which you claim, you are unlikely to qualify before you are 18.

You cannot usually qualify for:

- **income-based JSA** until you are 18. There are special rules that can help you qualify if you are 16 or 17 (see p405). If you do not qualify, check if you qualify for income support (IS) or employment and support allowance (ESA) instead. Even if you cannot get JSA, IS or ESA, you may qualify for housing benefit;
- **joint-claim JSA** unless you and your partner are both 18. If only one of you is 18 or over, the other must qualify for income-based JSA in her/his own right as a 16/17-year-old (see p405).[28] If both of you are under 18, you do not count as a joint-claim couple and so one of you may be able to claim income-based JSA for the other (see above).

You cannot claim any type of JSA if you are pension age or over (see p531). In practice, there is usually no point in remaining on income-based JSA if you are a man of at least the qualifying age for pension credit (PC – see p509) as you qualify for PC because of your age without having to sign on as unemployed. You may also receive automatic NI credits (see p786). You (and your partner) should be no worse off on PC than on income-based JSA. See p429 for further information.

3. Claiming for others

If you claim **contribution-based jobseeker's allowance** (JSA), you can only claim for yourself. You cannot claim any additions for your partner or children.

You and your partner must usually both claim **joint-claim JSA** if you are a 'joint-claim couple' (see p413).

If you are a member of a couple who does not have to claim joint-claim JSA, you or your partner may claim **income-based JSA** for you both. The applicable amount that forms part of the calculation of your benefit includes a personal allowance for a couple. See p753 for who counts as a couple. Whichever one of you claims, the other can make a claim for national insurance (NI) credits in order to protect her/his NI record (see p780).

In some cases, you need to know who counts as a member of your 'family' for JSA purposes. This is your partner and any child who is a member of your household and for whom you are 'responsible' (see below).[29]

Children

There are some situations in which you must show that you are 'responsible' for a child who is living in your household (see p761). Remember the following.

- You can count as responsible for any child under 16 and for any qualifying young person (referred to as 'children' in this *Handbook*). You do not have to be the child's parent.[30]

- You can continue to count as responsible for children who have left school or training until the 'terminal date' (see p98) or the end of the child benefit 'extension period' (see p96).
- A young person claiming income support, JSA or income-related employment and support allowance in her/his own right does not count as your child for JSA purposes, nor do certain 16/17-year-olds who are no longer being looked after by a local authority (see p673).
- In some situations, a child does not count as a member of your household even if s/he normally does, or continues to count as a member of your household while s/he is temporarily away from home (see p763).[31]

Note: there are different rules about children for the purpose of deciding whether you must claim joint-claim JSA (see p413).

4. The amount of benefit

The amount of jobseeker's allowance (JSA) you get depends on whether you are claiming contribution-based JSA or income-based JSA.

Waiting days

You are not entitled to either income-based or contribution-based JSA for the first three days ('waiting days') of any jobseeking period (see p394) unless:[32]

- your claim is linked to a previous claim for JSA so both are treated as part of the same jobseeking period. For joint-claim couples this includes a previous claim made by either of you separately; *or*
- you (or for joint-claim couples only, either of you) have been entitled to income support (IS), employment and support allowance (ESA), incapacity benefit or carer's allowance within the 12 weeks before you become entitled to JSA; *or*
- you are the member of a joint-claim couple nominated to be paid JSA and are in receipt of a training allowance; *or*
- you are 16 or 17 and getting JSA under the severe hardship rules (see p408).

In addition, you do not have to serve any waiting days if you swap from claiming IS or ESA to claiming JSA, or you and your partner swap which of you claims IS, ESA or JSA for both of you, and the new claim is for JSA.[33]

If you receive income-based JSA, you are entitled to maximum housing benefit and/or council tax benefit during any waiting days.

Amount of contribution-based jobseeker's allowance

Contribution-based JSA is paid at the following weekly rates.[34]

Age of claimant	*£pw*
Under 25	56.25
25 or over	71.00

You are not paid an allowance for your partner or children.

These amounts are reduced penny for penny if you receive certain pension payments of more than £50 in any week.[35] Contribution-based JSA may also be reduced penny for penny by any part-time earnings. For more on how earnings and pension payments affect contribution-based JSA, see p896. Other types of income and any capital, including any earnings and capital of your partner, do not affect your contribution-based JSA.[36]

Contribution-based JSA is paid for a limited period only. You can claim income-based JSA (including joint-claim JSA) to top up your contribution-based JSA if you satisfy the means test.

Duration of contribution-based jobseeker's allowance

You cannot receive more than 182 days of contribution-based JSA in any jobseeking period (see p394) or in two or more jobseeking periods if your entitlement is based on national insurance (NI) contributions in the same two contribution years.[37] However, you can have another 182 days of contribution-based JSA for a later claim if:[38]

- you satisfy the contribution conditions; *and*
- at least one of the two contribution years used to decide whether you satisfy the contribution conditions is later than the second contribution year used to decide your previous entitlement. This can only apply if you are in a later jobseeking period than the one during which you exhausted your entitlement to contribution-based JSA. **Note:** if you are a man aged at least the qualifying age for pension credit (PC – see p509) but under 65, there are special rules that deem your jobseeking period to continue when it would end under the normal rules, so making it difficult for you to requalify for contribution-based JSA.[39]

Each day for which you are entitled to contribution-based JSA, even if you are not paid, counts towards the 182-day total. Because JSA is a weekly benefit, you are entitled on Saturdays and Sundays. Days on which you are entitled to contribution-based JSA but are not paid include days you:[40]

- satisfy the contribution conditions for contribution-based JSA but it is not payable because:
  - you have been sanctioned (see Chapter 20); *or*

  - you failed to attend an interview as required (see p423) or because of the 'loss of benefit for benefit offences' rules (see p1106); *or*
- meet conditions of entitlement but a pension, or a combination of a pension and earnings, means that the amount paid is reduced to nil (see p896); *or*
- are refused contribution-based JSA because you do not meet the jobseeking conditions *and* you are receiving a hardship payment (see p485).

Days on which you are not entitled to JSA, and which do *not* count towards the 182-day total include:
- waiting days (see p402);
- days in any benefit week on which you are not entitled to JSA because you earn more than the prescribed amount (see p897);
- days when you are refused contribution-based JSA because you do not meet the jobseeking conditions and you are *not* getting a hardship payment.

Note: if you are a laid-off or short-time worker (see p483), days you claim contribution-based JSA count towards your 182 days of entitlement, even if your benefit is reduced to take account of your earnings from work. So if you think you are likely to become fully unemployed in the near future and you are not claiming income-based JSA, you might gain more JSA overall by not claiming it until you are fully unemployed. However, if your earnings drop below the lower earnings limit (see p774), you cease to be treated as paying NI contributions. You may then wish to sign on for JSA which entitles you to NI credits.

Amount of income-based jobseeker's allowance

Income-based JSA tops up your income to a level set by the government that changes every April. The amount you get depends on your needs (your 'applicable amount') and on how much income and capital you have.[41] For the rules on income, see Chapter 40 and on capital, Chapter 41.

Your applicable amount consists of:
- a **personal allowance** (see p815); *and*
- **premiums** (see p820) for any special needs; *and*
- **housing costs**, principally for mortgage interest payments (see Chapter 38). **Note:** in some circumstances you can only get help with housing costs for 104 weeks (see p855).

The way income-based JSA is calculated is the same as for IS (see pp355–57).

If you have children

Income-based JSA does not include allowances and premiums for your children. Instead, you can claim child tax credit (CTC). However, if you were getting income-based JSA on 5 April 2004 and this included allowances and premiums for your children, but you were not yet entitled to CTC, you continue to get allowances and premiums for your children until you claim CTC.

You might get a reduced amount of JSA if:

- you are required to make a joint claim for JSA but your partner has not fulfilled all the eligibility conditions (see p414) or has been sanctioned (see Chapter 20); *or*
- you have a partner and s/he has failed to attend a work-focused interview without good cause (see p1033); *or*
- you are receiving a hardship payment of income-based JSA (see Chapter 20); *or*
- your JSA has been restricted under the 'loss of benefit for benefit offences' rules (see p1106).

Different rules for calculating your JSA can sometimes apply if you are in one of the groups to whom special rules apply.

5. Special benefit rules

Special rules may apply to:

- 16/17-olds (see below);
- workers who are laid off or working short time (see p483);
- people from abroad (see Chapter 61);
- people who are studying (see p400 and Chapter 29);
- people without accommodation, involved in a trade dispute or in hospital (see Chapter 30);
- people who, or whose partners or children, live in a care home (see p683).

16/17-year-olds

If you are aged 16 or 17 you can qualify for:

- **contribution-based** JSA if you satisfy the contribution conditions;
- **income-based** JSA if you satisfy the basic rules of entitlement and you are entitled to it under the rules described on p406;
- **joint-claim** JSA if you satisfy the basic rules of entitlement, one of you is 18 or over and the other would qualify for income-based JSA under the rules described below.[42] Usually, you both have to satisfy all the conditions for entitlement to JSA, but see p396 for the exceptions. If both of you are under 18, you do not count as a joint-claim couple and so one of you may be able to claim income-based JSA for the other.

Note: if you are claiming any type of JSA, you can apply for hardship payments if you are sanctioned or there is a doubt about your meeting the jobseeking conditions (see p484).

When you cannot qualify for income-based jobseeker's allowance

You cannot qualify for income-based JSA if you:[43]

- are a member of the family (see p401) of someone who is claiming income support (IS) or income-based JSA; *or*
- qualify for contribution-based JSA; *or*
- were formerly looked after by a local authority in the circumstances described on pp673–74. There are exceptions to those rules.

Remember that, in most cases, you cannot qualify for JSA if you are in 'relevant education' (see p634). Note that you continue to count as in relevant education for a period after it ends (during the child benefit 'extension period') if someone is claiming child benefit for you during that period. If no one is claiming child benefit for you during that period, you can claim JSA if you satisfy the rules on pp407–08.

When you can qualify for income-based jobseeker's allowance

You can qualify for income-based JSA while you are 16 or 17 if you are a person who can claim:

- at any time before age 18 (see below); *or*
- during the child benefit 'extension period' (see p407); *or*
- during other limited periods (see p408); *or*
- on a discretionary basis – ie, you are awarded severe hardship payments (see p408).

You must satisfy all the other rules of entitlement to income-based JSA. You must register for work and training, and must usually show that you are actively seeking both of these. There are special rules for calculating your JSA applicable amount if you are a member of a couple (see p817).

Qualifying at any time before age 18

You can qualify for income-based JSA at any time before you are 18 if you satisfy the normal conditions of entitlement *and:*[44]

- you come within one of the groups of people who can claim IS (see pp346-352). In this case, you can choose whether to claim JSA or IS; *or*
- you have limited capability for work (see Chapter 11). In this case, you can choose whether to claim JSA or employment and support allowance (ESA); *or*
- you are one of a couple and you are responsible for a child under 16 who is a member of your household (see p401).

Qualifying during the child benefit 'extension period'

You qualify for income-based JSA during a period of 20 weeks after leaving education or training (called the child benefit 'extension period' – see p96), if:[45]

- you are married or in a civil partnership and your partner is:
  - 18 or over; *or*
  - under 18, does not qualify for contribution-based JSA, and was not formerly looked after by a local authority in the circumstances described on pp673–74 and:
    - is registered for work and training; *or*
    - is treated as being responsible for a child under 16 who is a member of her/his household (see p401); *or*
    - is laid off or on short-time working and is available for work under the special rules described on p483; *or*
    - is temporarily absent from Great Britain and is taking a child for whom you (or s/he) are responsible and who is a member of your household (see p401) abroad for treatment (for the first eight weeks of the absence); *or*
    - is incapable of work and training because of a physical or mental condition and a doctor confirms s/he is likely to remain incapable for a period of at least 12 months; *or*
    - fits into certain of the groups of people who can claim IS – ie, people with childcare responsibilities and carers (other than those on parental or paternity leave), including those who can claim while pregnant, pupils, students (other than in most cases disabled or deaf students) and people on training courses, refugees learning English, or certain people who are subject to immigration control.

  In many of these cases your partner can claim either JSA or IS (or, if s/he has limited capability for work, s/he may be able to claim ESA), but this allows you to be the claimant instead; *or*
- you are an orphan with no one acting as your parent (including foster carers, a local authority or a voluntary organisation if you are being looked after by them, or any other person with parental responsibility for you); *or*
- you are living away from your parents and any person acting as your parent and:
  - immediately before you were 16 you were in custody, or being looked after by a local authority who placed you with someone other than a close relative (see p437 for who counts); *or*
  - you are living elsewhere:
    - as part of a programme of resettlement or rehabilitation under the supervision of the probation service or a local authority; *or*
    - to avoid physical or sexual abuse; *or*
    - because you need special accommodation because of mental or physical illness or disability; *or*

- your parents are unable to support you financially and they are in custody or unable to enter Great Britain (eg, because of UK immigration rules) or are 'chronically sick or mentally or physically disabled'; *or*
- this is because you are estranged from them (see p635 for the meaning), you are in physical or moral danger, or there is a serious risk to your physical or mental health.

Qualifying during other limited periods

Even if you are not someone who qualifies for income-based JSA at any time before you are 18 (see p406), you may be able to claim it for a limited period.

- You can qualify after the end of the child benefit 'extension period' (see p96) if:[46]
  - you are in one of the groups of people who can claim income-based JSA during that period (see p407) and you are discharged from custody or detention after it ends. You can get income-based JSA for up to eight weeks from the day you were discharged; *or*
  - you have to live away from your parents and anyone acting as your parent following a stay in accommodation provided by a local authority under specified provisions. You can claim for up to eight weeks from the date of leaving the accommodation, whether before or after the end of the child benefit 'extension period'. If you leave less than eight weeks before the end of the 'extension period', you are first entitled to income-based JSA under the rules on p407, and then your benefit can continue under this rule until the end of the eight-week period. Remember that some people cannot claim JSA when they stop being looked after by a local authority (see p673).
- You can claim during any period that you are laid off or are on short-time working and are available for work under the special rules described on p483.[47]
- If you have never been sanctioned (unless this was for failing to carry out a jobseeker's direction) and have accepted an offer to enlist in the armed forces within eight weeks of the offer being made and were not in employment or training when it was made, you can qualify for income-based JSA until you are due to enlist. See Chapter 20 for further information about sanctions.[48]

Qualifying for severe hardship payments

If you do not qualify for income-based JSA under any of the rules for 16/17-year-olds above or for IS, you can still be paid income-based JSA on a discretionary basis if you are in severe hardship or if severe hardship will result if you are not paid.[49] These are referred to as 'severe hardship payments' in this *Handbook*.

You must have a 'severe hardship direction' to get severe hardship payments. Authorised staff in the Jobcentre Plus office can consider whether to issue one but must refer your case to the Under Eighteens Support Team (UEST) for a decision, if their decision is likely to be negative.[50] A decision should be made within 24 hours.

If you are one of a couple and you are only getting income-based JSA at one of the lower couple rates (see p817), you may be eligible for a higher couple rate if a 'severe hardship direction' is made in respect of your partner.

Remember that:

- severe hardship payments are payments of JSA so you are automatically eligible for other benefits (see p428);
- there are special rules about sanctions that only apply to severe hardship payments (see p482).

All your circumstances should be considered when deciding whether you are experiencing severe hardship or it is likely to result if you are not paid. The factors that should be taken into account include:[51]

- your financial circumstances, including your income, capital and outgoings;
- whether the person with whom you live is on a means-tested benefit;
- whether you are homeless or at risk of eviction if severe hardship payments are not paid;
- whether you have any health problems, are pregnant or are vulnerable and at risk for any reason and whether you have access to food and accommodation.

Getting a severe hardship direction

Provide as much evidence as you can to show that you will experience severe hardship without JSA. Explain fully why your parents are not supporting you or why they should not be expected to continue to do so and, if relevant, why it could be damaging if they were to be contacted. The DWP should accept this.

You should not be refused a severe hardship direction just because you are living at home.

If the DWP wants to contact a responsible third party, such as a relative, social worker, youth worker or recognised voluntary worker, to corroborate what you have said it must ask your permission.[52] If you refuse this without good reason, your case is referred directly to the UEST. If you have written evidence from, or are accompanied by, a responsible third party, further enquiries of, or contact with, your parents may not be necessary.

If there is difficulty in obtaining evidence from your parents or a third party, the interviewing officer should consider a short-term severe hardship direction. You can then receive severe hardship payments while further enquiries are made.

Once a severe hardship direction is issued, the normal rules and procedures for claiming income-based JSA apply. Severe hardship payments are paid in arrears, but if payment is due immediately, a 'counter payment' can be made. If you need money urgently, you could apply for a social fund crisis loan (see Chapter 25).

A severe hardship direction normally lasts for eight weeks but it can be longer or shorter than this.[53] For example, a short-term direction should be made if you are starting work or training soon or evidence to support your application is not easily available.[54]

When your severe hardship direction ends, you can apply for it to be renewed. If it is, you can continue to get severe hardship payments. However, if your severe hardship direction is revoked, you can no longer get these payments. A direction can (but does not have to) be revoked if:[55]

- your circumstances have changed and you would no longer experience severe hardship if you did not receive severe hardship payments; *or*
- the direction was given in ignorance of, or because of a mistake about, a material fact and but for this, it would not have been given. This could give rise to a recoverable overpayment (see Chapter 43);[56] *or*
- you failed to follow up an opportunity of a place on a training scheme or rejected an offer of a place and cannot show good cause for having done so. 'Good cause' is not defined in the rules. If your severe hardship direction is revoked on this ground, you can apply for another one straight away but if one is made, your severe hardship payments are reduced for a two-week period. See p480 for further information about severe hardship payment sanctions. **Note:** if you have good cause, you must be given a certificate of good cause if you apply to the DWP for one, so long as it agrees that you have good cause.[57]

Jobseeking conditions

If you are 16 or 17, in general you are subject to the same jobseeking conditions (see p434) as people aged 18 or over.[58] However, there are some important differences (see p479).

Claiming jobseeker's allowance if you are 16 or 17

If you are claiming JSA, the normal rules about claims and payments apply (see p411). However, to claim JSA, including severe hardship payments, you must first register for both work and training at the place specified by the DWP – ie, where the local authority provides careers advice (see below).[59] Ask the Jobcentre Plus office where to register if you are in any doubt. **Note:**

- you do not have to register if you are claiming under the special rules for people laid off or on short-time working (see p483) or if you have accepted an offer to enlist in the armed forces (see p408);[60]
- you must register at the Jobcentre Plus office if you are unable to register at the specified place because there is an emergency affecting it, such as a strike or a fire, or you would experience hardship because of the extra time it would take to register there.[61]

Local authority careers advice

The DWP refers to the places that provide careers advice to young people as 'Local Authorities Youth Services'. Your local authority may call its service Connexions or the Careers Service in England, Careers Wales in Wales and Skills Development Scotland or Careers Scotland in Scotland.

If you are claiming severe hardship payments, remember to state this when you claim JSA. Always insist on your right to make a claim under the severe hardship rules and refuse to be turned away. You must have a severe hardship direction (see p408).

Challenging a jobseeker's allowance decision

You can challenge a decision about whether you satisfy the rules for entitlement to JSA in the usual way. See Chapters 45 and 46 for further information.

For severe hardship payments only, you *cannot* appeal against the decision about whether:[62]

- you would experience severe hardship;
- to issue or revoke a severe hardship direction or how long it should last;
- a certificate of good cause should be issued.

However, you have a right to ask for a revision or seek a supersession of a decision against which you do not have a right of appeal (see pp1133 and 1139). You do not have to show specific grounds in this situation. Any reasons you give for disagreeing with the decision should be considered. You can also ask for a review of a decision not to issue a severe hardship direction.[63]

In addition, you can complain to your MP. You might be able to apply for a judicial review (see p1202). If, for example, you obtain more evidence of your hardship, you could also make a new claim.

Sanctions

See Chapter 20 for the rules on sanctions. **Note:** for certain sanctions, special rules apply if you are 16 or 17 years old or are getting severe hardship payments (see p480).

6. **Claims and backdating**

The rules about claims and backdating are in Chapter 42. This section tells you about the specific rules that apply to jobseeker's allowance (JSA).

While you are getting JSA, you must satisfy jobseeking conditions. For this reason, and as well as giving all the necessary facts about your circumstances, you are expected to attend:[64]

- an interview when you claim (see p415); *and*
- an interview when you sign on (see p419); *and*
- further interviews as required (see p421).

If you fail to sign on or attend an interview, your entitlement to JSA could end (see pp425 and 422). In some cases, if you fail to attend an interview your entitlement to JSA does not end, but you could be sanctioned (see p423).

Two types of officer deal with JSA claims – decision makers and employment officers (EOs – see p1117).

EOs work in Jobcentre Plus offices. They are sometimes called personal advisers. Their job is to agree with you the steps you are willing to take to get back to work, keep a check on those steps, and offer practical help and advice. They are involved in the regular and further interviews you have to attend and the work-focused interviews which your partner may have to attend.

Making a claim

A claim for JSA can be made:

- in writing on the form approved by the DWP;[65] *or*
- by telephone on 0800 055 6688 (Welsh 0800 012 1888; textphone 0800 023 4888) Monday to Friday, 8 am to 8 pm. You are sent a written statement of your circumstances to approve and sign;[66] *or*
- online at www.direct.gov.uk/en/moneytaxandbenefits.[67]

Whichever way you claim, the date of an initial interview (see p415) is set. Your claim is not complete until you attend.

In practice, the usual way to start your claim is by telephone (see p1018), although the government intends to encourage more online claims in future. If you claim in writing, keep a copy of your claim in case queries arise.

You may be sent or given a form to complete about the work for which you are available and how you are actively seeking work. The information you give forms the basis of your jobseeker's agreement.

You must provide information or evidence as required (see p415). You can amend or withdraw your claim before a decision is made (see p1019).

Forms

JSA claim forms are only available from Jobcentre Plus offices. Seek advice if you are unable to use a telephone or claim online and the Jobcentre Plus office tells you that you cannot start your claim in any other way.

Note:

- You can make initial contact with the DWP by telephone or letter to say you want to claim. The date of your initial contact is important because it usually determines the date on which your claim is treated as made (see p416).
- If you are 16 or 17 years old, you normally have to register for work and training (see p410).
- If you are claiming JSA within 26 weeks of a previous claim, you may be able to claim without having to give as much detail of your circumstances as is usually required. This is known as 'rapid reclaim'.

Housing benefit and council tax benefit

You have to make a separate claim to your local authority for housing benefit (HB) and council tax benefit (CTB). If you claim JSA by telephone, your HB and CTB claims are usually completed at the same time.

If you claim JSA on the approved form, you may be given HB and CTB claim forms (or these are available at www.direct.gov.uk/en/moneytaxandbenefits). If you are making a 'rapid reclaim' for JSA, you may also be able to make a 'rapid reclaim' for HB and CTB.

Claiming national insurance credits

If you are claiming national insurance (NI) credits but not JSA (see p780), the normal claim procedures for getting JSA apply to you.

Who should claim

For **contribution-based JSA**, you claim on your own behalf.

For **income-based JSA**, if you are a single person or a lone parent you claim on your own behalf. Unless you must make a joint claim for JSA (see below), if you are a member of a couple you must choose which one of you claims for you both. See p753 for who counts as a couple. If you cannot agree who should claim, a decision maker decides.[68] If you are not the person claiming JSA, you may wish to claim NI credits to protect your NI record (see p780) or to gain help from the Employment, Skills and Enterprise Scheme – eg, via the Work Programme (see p471).

Joint claims for jobseeker's allowance

You must make a joint claim for JSA if you are a member of a couple (see p753) and:[69]

- at least one of you is 18 or over and was born after 28 October 1947. If one of you is 16 or 17, special rules apply (see p405); *and*
- neither of you is responsible for children in the circumstances listed below.

You are known as a **'joint-claim couple'** and both of you must usually:

- claim JSA; *and*
- satisfy all the rules for getting income-based JSA (see pp393 and 396).

There are exceptions. For the rules on when one of you does not have to satisfy all the conditions, see p396 and on what happens if one of you does not claim JSA, see p414.

Responsible for children

You do not have to claim joint-claim JSA if you or your partner are responsible for a child (this includes a 'qualifying young person'). For these purposes, you count as being responsible for a child if:[70]

- you are entitled to child benefit for her/him; *or*
- no one is receiving child benefit for her/him but:
  - you count as responsible because s/he usually lives with you; *or*
  - you are the only person who has claimed child benefit for her/him but your claim has not yet been decided; *or*
- someone else is responsible for her/him but s/he is staying with you so that s/he can attend school; *or*
- you are looking after her/him for the local authority or a voluntary organisation (or in Scotland only, s/he has been boarded out with you) under specific provisions; *or*
- you are looking after her/him with a view to adoption.

Even if you do not get child benefit for your child and none of the other rules above apply, if you share actual responsibility for the child (eg, with your ex-partner) and are a 'substantial minority carer' (ie, you have the child with you for at least 104 nights a year), following a court decision, you may be able to argue that you should still be regarded as responsible for the child.[71] Seek advice and see CPAG's *Welfare Rights Bulletins* 185 pp9–11 and 194 pp5–6.

If you and your partner **become responsible** for a child under 16 while you are claiming joint-claim JSA, you can no longer qualify for joint-claim JSA. However, your JSA can continue without interruption if you provide the DWP with evidence of this if required.[72] You and your partner must notify the DWP which of you is to continue claiming income-based JSA for you both.

If you and your partner **stop being responsible** for any children while you are claiming income-based JSA, or all the children concerned have either died or reached the age of 16 and are not qualifying young people for child benefit purposes (see p94), you and your partner must then claim joint-claim JSA.[73] Your claim for JSA can continue without interruption if the DWP has sufficient information to award you joint-claim JSA and you or your partner have told the DWP which of you has been nominated to receive payment for you both.

If your partner does not claim jobseeker's allowance

If you are a member of a joint-claim couple and you satisfy all the rules for getting income-based JSA (see pp393 and 396), in certain circumstances you can qualify for JSA even if your partner has not made a joint claim with you. This is the case if your partner:[74]

- failed to attend the initial interview (see p415); *or*
- failed to meet the jobseeking conditions (see p434); *or*
- is subject to immigration control (see p1410); *or*
- is temporarily absent from Great Britain; *or*
- does not satisfy the 'habitual residence test' or the 'right to reside test' (see Chapter 62); *or*

- is over pension age (see p531). In this situation, you both might be better off if your partner were to claim pension credit for you rather than JSA; *or*
- works 16 or more but under 24 hours a week; *or*
- has claimed maternity allowance or statutory maternity pay; *or*
- is pregnant and there are 11 weeks or less before the week the baby is due; *or*
- was pregnant and her pregnancy ended not more than 28 weeks ago – ie, when her baby was born, or she had a miscarriage; *or*
- is receiving an unemployment benefit from another country under a reciprocal agreement (see p1480); *or*
- is receiving statutory sick pay and was working 16 hours or more a week immediately before s/he became incapable of work.

In the first four cases, your JSA entitlement is calculated as if you were a single claimant.[75] In the remaining cases, JSA entitlement is calculated for both of you in the normal manner. In all other respects you are treated as a couple and, therefore, your partner's income and capital are taken into account.

Information to support your claim

When you claim JSA you must:

- satisfy the NI number requirement (see p1023);
- provide proof of your identity, if required (see p1024);
- supply information and evidence required on the claim form (see p1019) and additional information and evidence relevant to your claim (see p1022).

It is important that you provide any information or evidence required when you claim. This is known as the 'evidence requirement'. Until you do, you may not count as having made a valid claim.[76] Correct any defects in your claim within one month of your initial contact with Jobcentre Plus or you might lose benefit (see p416). See p1021 for the evidence requirement and to see if you are exempt.

Even if you have provided all that was required when you claimed, you may be asked to provide additional information and evidence. If you do not do so, the decision maker can decide your claim in the way most adverse to you.

If you have a mortgage, you are given an additional form to give to your lender, who provides details about your mortgage and returns the form to the DWP.

The initial interview

You (or, if you are claiming joint-claim JSA, both you and your partner) must usually attend an interview (called the 'initial interview' in this chapter).[77] At the initial interview, you are told what is expected from you in return for receiving JSA. You and your adviser discuss what work you are looking for and what you intend to do to find it. What is discussed at your interview forms the basis of your jobseeker's agreement (see Chapter 20). If attending the Jobcentre Plus office would mean that you would have to be away from home for too long, arrangements can be made for your initial interview to be carried out by a 'visiting EO' and your jobseeker's agreement is treated as existing until that has been done.

If you have been sent a claim form, complete it before your initial interview. If you do not provide all the evidence and information required, your interview might not go ahead unless you are exempt from the evidence requirement (p1021).

You are interviewed by an EO. The initial interview forms the basis of your jobseeker's agreement, which both you and the EO must sign. The EO may refer you to a job vacancy immediately but a jobseeker's agreement should still be completed to establish entitlement in case you do not get the job.

The initial interview also covers what you were doing before you became unemployed and, in particular, why you left your previous job. If the EO thinks that you may have left voluntarilyor been dismissed for misconduct (and therefore might be liable to be sanctioned – see Chapter 20), you are asked to complete a form explaining your side of the story. The form is passed to the decision maker who may need to make further enquiries before reaching a decision on whether you should be sanctioned.

The date of your claim

You are not usually entitled to JSA for any day before your date of claim.[78] However, in some cases you can claim in advance (see p418) and sometimes your claim can be backdated (see p419). If you want this to be done, you should make this clear when you claim or the DWP might not consider it.

Your '**date of claim**' is usually:

- the date you first contact the Jobcentre Plus office if you (and your partner if you are a joint-claim couple) attend your initial interview (see p415) at the time specified by the DWP and a properly completed claim is provided (on a form or by telephone) with all the information and evidence required;[79] *or*
- the date your claim is properly completed if you (and your partner if you are a joint-claim couple) have made your claim by telephone. This is the date of your telephone call if you provide all the information and evidence required during the call;[80] *or*
- if you are not required to attend an initial interview, the earliest of:[81]
  - the date you first contact the Jobcentre Plus office, so long as a properly completed claim (on a form or by telephone) with all the information and evidence required is provided within one month of your first contact; *or*
  - the date on which a properly completed claim (on a form or by telephone) with all the information and evidence required is received at the Jobcentre Plus office;
- if you are a joint-claim couple and only one of you is required to attend an initial interview, the earliest of:[82]

- the date on which a properly completed claim (on a form or by telephone) with all the information and evidence required is received at the Jobcentre Plus office, so long as the person who is required to attend an interview does so; *or*
- the date you or your partner first contact the Jobcentre Plus office, so long as a properly completed claim (on a form or by telephone) with all the information and evidence required is provided within one month of your first contact.

The DWP can extend the time you have to provide or make a properly completed claim up to the date one month after the date you first contacted the Jobcentre Plus office to claim JSA.[83] This is discretionary, so provide your claim as required (see above) wherever possible.

Forms

In this section, the term 'form' refers to a paper form or a claim completed online.

Note: if you are a member of a couple and one of you claims contribution-based JSA but is not entitled to it and a subsequent income-based JSA claim is made by your partner (or you and your partner if you are a joint-claim couple), the date of claim for income-based JSA is the date of the earlier claim for contribution-based JSA.[84] If your partner has been claiming contribution-based JSA, this expires and you claim income-based JSA, the date of claim for your income-based JSA is the day after your partner's entitlement expires.[85]

If you fail to attend the initial interview

If you (or your partner if you are a joint-claim couple) fail to attend an initial interview at the time specified by the DWP or fail to provide a properly completed claim by the date of the interview and cannot show good cause for this, the rules above do not apply. If, without good cause, you fail to attend or attend at the wrong time, so long as a properly completed claim with all the information and evidence required is provided, your date of claim is:

- if you are not a joint-claim couple, the date you eventually go to the Jobcentre Plus office;[86] *or*
- if you are a joint-claim couple and:[87]
  - if you are both required to attend an interview, the date one of you eventually goes to the Jobcentre Plus office. However, in this situation, you can only get the single person's rate of JSA until the other attends an interview;[88] *or*
  - if only one of you is required to attend an interview, the date the person who is required to attend eventually goes to the Jobcentre Plus office.

'Good cause' is not defined. All relevant circumstances must be considered. These may relate to your abilities, or to external factors. The general test is whether there is some factor that would probably cause a reasonable person of your age and experience to act, or fail to act, as you did.[89]

If you claim the wrong benefit

If you claim working tax credit (WTC) and you are refused because neither you nor your partner are in full-time paid work for WTC purposes (see Chapter 53), your claim for JSA can be backdated to the date you claimed WTC.[90] However, you must claim JSA within 14 days of the decision refusing you WTC. You can ask for your JSA claim to start on a later date instead – eg, if your income is currently too high, but is due to decrease.

Claiming in advance

If you do not qualify for JSA from the date of your claim (unless this is because you fail the habitual residence test – see p1442 for who counts), but will do so within the next three months, you can be awarded JSA from the first date on which you will qualify.[91] This gives the DWP time to ensure you receive benefit as soon as you are entitled. Let the DWP know you want to claim in advance when you claim and at your initial interview. You might have to persuade the DWP that it can accept a claim in advance.

You might not currently be entitled to JSA, but would be once you or a member of your family (see p401) become entitled to another 'qualifying benefit' – eg, disability living allowance or carer's allowance. Make your claim for JSA at the same time as the claim for the qualifying benefit. If you are:

- refused JSA, claim again when you get a decision about the qualifying benefit and ask for your JSA to be backdated to the date of your first JSA claim or to the date from which the qualifying benefit is paid, if that is later. See p1029 for further information;
- awarded JSA, you might be entitled to a higher rate once the outcome of the claim for the qualifying benefit is known. Seek a revision or a supersession if you think this applies to you. See p1147 for further information.

How your claim is dealt with

It is unlikely that you will get an immediate decision on your claim. For contribution-based JSA, your NI contribution record needs to be checked. For income-based JSA, your benefit needs to be calculated. If the delay is caused by doubt as to whether you meet the jobseeking conditions, you may be able to receive hardship payments (see p484).

Backdating your claim

It is very important to claim in time. A claim for JSA can be backdated for a maximum of three months, but only in exceptional circumstances. The general rules on backdating are covered on p1027. There are special backdating rules if you make a new claim for JSA after you failed to sign on or attend an interview (see p425).

Your claim can be backdated more than three months if:
- you claim JSA after being awarded a qualifying benefit and an earlier JSA claim was refused because you did not get a qualifying benefit at that time (see p1029); *or*
- you claimed WTC when you should have claimed JSA (see p418).

If you might have qualified for JSA earlier but did not claim because you were given the wrong information or were misled by the DWP, you could ask for compensation (see p1261) or complain to the Ombudsman via your MP (see p1260).

If you want to get your jobseeker's agreement backdated, see p455.

After you have been awarded jobseeker's allowance

Once you have been awarded JSA, in order to continue to receive it you (and if you are a joint-claim couple, you and your partner) have to:
- sign on regularly at the Jobcentre Plus office and attend regular interviews; *and*
- attend further interviews as required (see p421).

Note:
- If you have a partner (and you are not getting joint-claim JSA), s/he might be required to attend a work-focused interview (see p1033). If s/he fails to do so without good cause, your income-based JSA might be paid at a reduced rate.
- In some cases, if you fail to provide information when required to do so, your JSA could be suspended or even terminated (see p1043).

Signing on and regular interviews

Unless you are allowed to sign on by post (see p420), while you are getting JSA you (and if you are a joint-claim couple, both of you) must normally attend the Jobcentre Plus office in order to sign a declaration that:[92]
- you have been available for and actively seeking work or could be treated as if you were (see pp434 and 447) and, for most 16/17-year-olds, that you have been actively seeking suitable training (see p480). See p449 for information about proving you are actively seeking work; *and*
- there has been no change in your circumstances that might affect the amount of or your right to JSA (other than those you may have already notified to the DWP).

Generally, you must sign on every fortnight. This is the case even if you are paid weekly. You are told your regular signing day and time at the start of your claim. You can be notified of the time and place you should attend by phone, post or electronic means.[93] You can also be instructed to attend at other times in order to sign on more frequently (see below) or for special interviews.

If you are told you are not entitled to JSA, you can argue that you no longer have to sign on – eg, while you are appealing against the decision.[94] However, if your appeal is successful, in order to be paid arrears you need to show that you have satisfied the jobseeking conditions since the last time that you signed on, which can often be difficult. So it is always best to continue to sign on to protect your position.

Each time you sign on, you are interviewed. The aims of the interview are to:

- keep a regular check on what you are doing to find work and make sure that your jobseeker's agreement remains up to date and relevant. Take your records of your attempts to find work with you;
- discuss any difficulties you are experiencing and identify any help and support that the DWP can give you;
- check whether there have been any relevant changes in your circumstances;
- refer you to job, training or employment scheme vacancies – eg, Work Experience or the Work Programme (see p421).

You may be referred to an EO for a more in-depth interview if what you say raises a doubt about whether you remain entitled to JSA.

Note: your entitlement to JSA can end if you fail to sign on or to attend an interview (see pp425 and 422).

Signing on by post

The DWP might allow you to sign on by post – eg, if you live a long way from the Jobcentre Plus office, or you have a mental or physical disability which restricts your mobility. Even so:

- you must attend your initial interview (see p415) and further interviews as required (see p421). You could try to get an interview arranged with a visiting EO nearer your home, if attending at the Jobcentre Plus office would result in your being away from home for a long time;
- you must send a signed declaration and show that you are available for and actively seeking work (see pp434 and 447). If this is not received at the time specified by the DWP, your entitlement to JSA ends unless you can show 'good cause' for the delay (see p425). If you cannot show this, you must make a fresh claim for JSA and attend a new initial interview (see p415).

More frequent signing on

You may be required to sign on and attend interviews more frequently than once every two weeks if the Jobcentre Plus office thinks you need more help to find work, if you are suspected of fraud or if you have no fixed abode.

Because decisions about how often you have to sign on and attend interviews are made by EOs, you do not have a right of appeal. However, you can ask for the frequency to be altered – eg, if your circumstances change or the cost of travel causes hardship. If you are suspected of fraud, see Chapter 44.

Referral to job, training or employment scheme vacancies

While you are claiming JSA, you may be referred to job vacancies. Bear in mind that the law now gives some workers minimum rights on the rate of pay, hours, rest breaks and holidays (see p491) and you should not be expected to accept jobs that do not meet these standards.

If you are not considered ready for a job, you are likely to be referred to a place on a training or employment scheme – eg, Work Experience or the Work Programme. Some of these are compulsory and you can be sanctioned for failing to attend, or for leaving early (see p471). A scheme or programme that is not compulsory may become so if you are issued with a jobseeker's direction (see p469).

You risk being sanctioned if, without good cause, you refuse to apply for a notified job vacancy (see p462). Alternatively, you could be issued with a jobseeker's direction (eg, to take some action to improve your job prospects) and risk being sanctioned if you refuse or fail to carry it out (see p469). A refusal to apply for a job or vacancy on a scheme or programme may also raise doubts about whether you are available for work (see p434).

Referral to a disability employment adviser

If you have a disability that affects your search for work, you may be eligible for specialist help from the DWP, including being referred to a disability employment adviser. Every Jobcentre Plus office has a disability adviser who is responsible for good practice relating to disabled people.

You may want to ask to be referred to an adviser if, for example:

- you think the service from the Jobcentre Plus office is not meeting your needs; *or*
- your health problem or disability has worsened significantly, or you have a new disability or health problem and need specialist help; *or*
- you need new skills in order to do a job; *or*
- you need practical help with looking for a job – eg, help in getting to interviews or identifying specialist equipment; *or*
- you are not clear about the effect your disability has on the job options open to you.

Further interviews

If you remain unemployed for a period of time, you must attend a number of other interviews. If you fail to do so, your entitlement to JSA can end or you can be sanctioned (see p422).

You are asked to attend interviews at **regular intervals**, linked to the length of time you have to be unemployed to qualify for various schemes and programmes to help you get back into work (eg, when you have been unemployed for six months in some cases and in others a year).

At the interview, an EO reviews your situation, the type of work you are looking for and the steps you are taking to find it. You may be asked to agree to a change of your jobseeker's agreement (see p455) to record any change in the type of work for which you are looking or steps you will take to find it.

You can be called for an interview **at any time** – eg, if the DWP thinks you need more help with your search for work or there is a question about whether you fulfil the jobseeking conditions.

Travel expenses

Your travel expenses to and from the Jobcentre Plus office to **sign on** are *not* reimbursed. If this causes you hardship, ask if you can sign on by post (see p420).

You *can* have your travel costs reimbursed if you are given an appointment for an **interview** on a day other than the day you normally attend to sign on, or if you have to attend a different office on your normal signing-on day and you incur additional costs. If you are signing on by post but are required to visit the Jobcentre Plus office for an interview, you are also entitled to a refund of travel costs.

Failure to attend an interview

Your entitlement to JSA can end if you fail to attend an interview when required to do so (see p424). However, in some cases, if you fail to attend an interview when required, your entitlement to JSA does not end – instead, you are sanctioned (see below). You may be able to get hardship payments (see p484).

Notification of your regular interviews (see p419) is given when you first claim JSA. Notification of other interviews can be in writing, by telephone or email. If you can show you did not receive the notification, this means that you have not failed to attend and therefore your entitlement to JSA should not end, nor should your JSA cease to be paid. The law normally assumes that when a letter has been sent correctly addressed and with the full postage paid, it will be received. So if notification was sent to you, you need to put forward a good case to show why this assumption should not be made – eg, you have always responded properly to other notifications when these were received from the Jobcentre Plus office or there are problems with your postal address.[95]

Note:

- If you fail to attend your initial interview (ie, when you claim JSA – see p415), you might not be awarded JSA or your date of claim might be affected.
- If the requirement to attend is for a training or employment scheme or programme, your entitlement does not end, but you can be sanctioned under other rules (see pp433 and 473).

When you are sanctioned

Your entitlement to JSA does not end if you fail to attend an interview when required, but you contact the EO within five working days of the date you failed to attend. However, unless you can show 'good cause' for your failure (see below) you are sanctioned.

If you are 18 or over:[96]

- your JSA is not paid for a fixed period of one week. However, if you are a member of a joint-claim couple this only applies if both of you failed to attend;
- your JSA is paid at a reduced rate for a fixed period of one week if you are a member of a joint-claim couple and only one of you failed to attend. The person who did not fail to attend is paid at the rate of:[97]
  - contribution-based JSA, if s/he satisfies the rules for claiming it; *or*
  - hardship payments, if you and your partner qualify (see p484); *or*
  - in any other case, income-based JSA calculated as if s/he were a single person. However, any income or capital you or your partner have is taken into account in the calculation.

If you fail to attend on a second or subsequent occasion during the same jobseeking period, you are not paid JSA (or JSA is paid at a reduced rate) for two weeks.[98]

If you are 16 or 17, special rules apply; your income-based JSA is paid at a reduced rate.[99] The rules are the same as for other sanctions for 16/17-year-olds (see p483).

'Good cause'

You can avoid a sanction if you make contact with an EO within five working days of your failure to attend. You must show that you had 'good cause' for the failure. A decision maker decides whether you have good cause and you have the right to appeal against her/his decision. You have **automatic good cause** for a failure to attend if:[100]

- you are someone who does not have to be available for work immediately (see p436) and you were given less than:
  - 48 hours' notice, if you have caring responsibilities or are engaged in voluntary work; *or*
  - 24 hours' notice, if you are providing a service; *or*
  - seven days' notice, if you have caring responsibilities for a child under 16; *or*
- on the day you failed to attend you were someone who was treated as being available for employment in the circumstances listed on pp437–41, although there are limited exceptions to this rule;[101] *or*
- the day you failed to attend was in a week during which you were treated as actively seeking work because of an absence from home (see p451).

If you do not have automatic good cause, you may still have good cause for other reasons. When deciding good cause, the decision maker must take into account all the circumstances of your case, including:[102]

- whether you misunderstood what you had to do because of language, learning or literacy difficulties, or because you were misled by an EO;
- whether you (or someone for whom you care) were attending a medical or dental appointment which it would have been unreasonable to expect you to rearrange;
- any transport difficulties;
- any religious reasons why you could not attend;
- whether you were attending a job interview.

When your entitlement to jobseeker's allowance ends

Unless you contact an EO within five working days of the date you failed to attend, your entitlement to JSA ends if you fail to attend at a place specified by an EO in a notification:[103]

- at the right time – eg, you attend late. This only applies if, on a previous occasion, you failed to attend at the right time but attended some time on the right day and the DWP gave or sent you a written notice warning you that, if you failed to attend your next appointment at the right time, your entitlement to JSA could cease or you could be sanctioned; *or*
- on the right day. The rules do not make any provision for you to be given a warning in the way that they do for the situation where you fail to attend at the right time.

You lose JSA for the whole period between the date on which your entitlement ends and the date on which you are treated as having claimed again. The date on which your entitlement to JSA ends is the *earliest* of the following days:[104]

- the day after the last day for which you have provided information that shows you continue to be entitled to JSA – eg, at your regular fortnightly interview. In many cases, this means the day after the last day on which you signed on;
- the day on which you should have attended.

The date on which you are treated as having claimed JSA again is normally the first day on which you contact the Jobcentre Plus office again. However, if this was the same day as the failure to attend (eg, you came on the right day but were late for the appointment) you are treated as having made your fresh claim on the *following* day.[105] See below to see if your new claim can be backdated.

Note: your entitlement to JSA does not end if you fail to attend, but you contact the EO within five working days. However, you may be sanctioned instead (see p423).

Backdating your new claim

If your entitlement to JSA has ceased because you failed to attend an interview and you have to make a new claim, it may be possible to get your new claim backdated and so avoid some, or all, of the loss of JSA. Your claim can be backdated:

- under any of the normal rules (see p1027); *or*
- under the special rules described below.

Your claim can be backdated to the day after your entitlement to JSA ended if:[106]

- you failed to attend because of one of the circumstances listed on pp437–441 that allow you to be treated as being available for employment and you make a new claim for JSA no later than the day after those circumstances cease to apply. There are limited exceptions to this rule;[107] *or*
- you failed to attend because you were away from home while eligible to be treated as actively seeking work because of an absence from home (see p451) and you make a new claim for JSA no later than the day after you returned home; *or*
- you are normally allowed to sign on by post, you did not receive the instruction to attend the Jobcentre Plus office and you made a new claim for JSA immediately after you were informed that you had failed to attend the appointment.

Note: the rules for backdating are the same if your entitlement to JSA ends when you fail to sign on (see below). Your claim can be backdated under the rules described above.

Failure to sign on

Your entitlement to JSA ends if you fail to sign a declaration on the day you were notified to do so, unless you can show 'good cause' within five working days of your failure to sign on.[108]

Note: if you fail to sign on because you did not show up at the Jobcentre Plus office, you may instead lose your entitlement (or be sanctioned) under the rules about failure to attend an interview (see p422).

When deciding whether you have good cause, the decision maker must take into account all the circumstances of your case, including whether there were adverse postal conditions and whether you misunderstood what you had to do because of language, learning or literacy difficulties or because you were misled by an EO.[109]

You lose JSA for the whole period between the date on which your entitlement ends and the date on which you are treated as having claimed again. The date on which your entitlement to JSA ends is the *earliest* of the following days:[110]

- the day after the last day for which you have provided information that shows you continue to be entitled to JSA (eg, at your regular fortnightly interview). In many cases, this means the day after the last day on which you signed on;
- the day on which you should have signed on.

The date on which you are treated as having claimed JSA again is normally the first day on which you contact the Jobcentre Plus office again. See p425 to see if your new claim can be backdated. The rules are the same as for failure to attend an interview.

The effect of this is that if you fail to sign on you may lose JSA for the full period for which you would have been paid if you had signed on at the right time. In addition, you lose JSA for the days between the day you missed signing on and the day you next contact the Jobcentre Plus office. If you have missed signing on, it is possible to provide the necessary information at a later date.[111] As soon as you contact the Jobcentre Plus office again, ask it to accept the information you would have provided on the signing on day. If this is accepted, the decision maker should revise the decision that stopped your benefit so that you are paid up to the date you failed to sign on.

7. Getting paid

Jobseeker's allowance (JSA) is normally paid by direct credit transfer into your bank (or similar) account (see p1039). If you are unable to open or manage an account, payment can be made by cheque or by 'simple payment' (see p1040). If you are unable to act for yourself, payment can be made to someone else on your behalf – called your 'appointee' (see p1016).

When is JSA paid?	The day you are paid depends on your national insurance number.
How often is JSA paid?	Normally, fornightly in arrears.[112]

JSA is a weekly benefit, although in some cases it can be paid for part weeks.[113] Most questions about entitlement are decided in relation to a particular **'benefit week'** – ie, the period of seven days ending on the day of the week allocated to you according to your national insurance (NI) number; this is usually the day on which you are paid.[114]

If you are entitled to less than 10p a week, you are not paid JSA at all,[115] but you are still eligible for NI credits (see p780). If you are entitled to less than £1 a week, a decision maker can decide to pay you every 13 weeks in arrears.[116]

If you and your partner are a joint-claim couple, you must nominate which one of you receives payment for you both. If you cannot agree, a decision maker decides.[117] Note that if your JSA is being paid at a reduced rate because one of you has been sanctioned, it is paid to the other member of the couple.[118] Even if you are not the person nominated to receive the JSA, if you separate from your partner and s/he cannot be traced, you can be paid any arrears of JSA that are due.[119]

Note:

- Deductions can be made from your JSA to pay to third parties (see p1048).
- You might not be paid JSA, or it might be paid at a reduced rate, if you have been sanctioned for benefit offences (see p1106). **Note:** you may also be sanctioned for other reasons (see Chapter 20).
- If you have forgotten your PIN or if a cheque is lost or stolen, see p1040.
- If payment of your JSA is delayed, see p1262. You might be able to get an interim payment (see p1046). You may also be eligible for a crisis loan (see p564). If you wish to complain about how your claim has been dealt with, see p1255. You might be able to claim compensation (see p1261).
- If payment of your JSA is suspended, see p1043.
- If you are overpaid JSA, you might have to repay it (see Chapter 43). If you have been accused of fraud, see Chapter 44.

Change of circumstances

You must report changes in your circumstances that might affect your benefit, including any that are likely to occur (see p1047).[120] You should do this promptly in writing or by telephone (although in individual cases notification might be accepted in a form other than in writing or by telephone). You can also notify changes in your circumstances by electronic communication – eg online (see p1047).[121] In some cases, however, the decision maker might say that you must report changes in writing. In any case, it is always best to report the change in writing and keep a copy in case of a dispute in the future.

If you have a mortgage, the DWP can ask your lender about any changes in the amount you owe during your JSA claim. If you have this information (eg, from an annual statement you receive from your lender), you must also advise the DWP in case your lender fails to do so. Make sure the DWP takes this information into account so you are not overpaid JSA.

When there has been a relevant change of circumstances, a decision maker looks at your claim again and makes a new decision. To see when your JSA is then adjusted, see below.

When your jobseeker's allowance is adjusted

As a general rule, your JSA is adjusted from the first day of the benefit week in which the change occurs or is expected to do so.[122] There are a number of exceptions to this rule, including the following.[123]

- If a decision is to your advantage, but you failed to notify the DWP of a change within the time limit (normally one month, but this can be extended – see p1142), your JSA is adjusted:
  - if you are paid in arrears, from the first day of the benefit week in which you notified the change; *or*

- if you are paid in advance, from the day on which you notified the change, if this is the first day of the benefit week. If it is not, your JSA is adjusted from the next week.
- Your JSA is adjusted from the date of the change of circumstances (or the day on which this is expected to take place) if the change of circumstances means you no longer qualify for JSA, unless this is because your income is too high.

8. Tax, tax credits and other benefits

Jobseeker's allowance (JSA) is taxable.[124] The maximum amount of JSA that is taxable is:

- if you are claiming for yourself, an amount equal to the appropriate personal allowance for a person of your age (see p815); *or*
- if you are a member of a couple, an amount equal to the income-based JSA personal allowance for an adult couple (half this amount if your partner is unable to claim JSA because s/he is involved in a trade dispute).

The tax is not deducted while JSA is being paid but reduces the refund you would otherwise receive through Pay As You Earn (PAYE) when you return to work.

Any tax refunds of PAYE payments are paid to you at the end of the tax year to which they relate. Any other tax refund is paid only when you stop getting JSA.

Tax credits

If you work less than 16 hours each week and your partner works at least 16 hours but less than 24 hours each week, you and your partner might be able to claim working tax credit (WTC). However, before deciding whether to claim, seek advice to see how you would be better off financially.

If you or your partner have just stopped work or reduced your hours, you might get what is known as 'WTC run-on' for a four-week period (see p1304).

WTC is taken into account as income when working out your income-based JSA, but child tax credit (CTC) is not. Income-based JSA is an automatic passport to maximum CTC and is usually an automatic passport to maximum WTC.

Means-tested benefits

Income-based JSA is an automatic passport to maximum housing benefit (HB) and council tax benefit (CTB). Your contribution-based JSA counts as income for the purposes of these benefits if you do not get income-based JSA.

If you are getting contribution-based JSA, you may also be entitled to income-based JSA to top this up.

You cannot claim JSA and income support (IS) at the same time. You cannot claim income-based JSA at the same time as pension credit (PC) or income-related employment and support allowance (ESA). If you have a partner, s/he can claim IS, income-related ESA or PC and you can claim contribution-based JSA (but not income-based JSA).

Income support, income-related employment and support allowance and pension credit

In some situations you need to choose whether to claim income-based JSA or IS (or income-related ESA or PC). You should consider the following.

- The rates of IS, the guarantee credit of PC and income-based JSA are usually the same. The rate of income-related ESA can be higher or lower than the rate of IS, income-based JSA or PC.
- If you need help with housing costs (see Chapter 38):
  - the upper limit for loans can be higher for IS, income-based JSA and income-related ESA than for PC (see p867);
  - you might only get help with your housing costs for 104 weeks if you claim income-based JSA (see p855). You can get help indefinitely if you claim IS, income-related ESA or PC.
- You do not have to sign on, look for work or risk being sanctioned if you are claiming IS, ESA or PC (nor does your partner).
- You may want to claim JSA or ESA instead of IS in order to receive national insurance (NI) credits (see p780). You might not be entitled to NI credits if you claim IS.
- If you are sanctioned, you or your partner should claim IS, ESA or PC if eligible. You cannot get hardship payments (see p484) if you or your partner are in one of the groups of people who can claim IS.
- If you claim PC:
  - there is no capital limit and the tariff income rules are more generous;
  - you can qualify for the savings credit of PC if your partner is 65 or over;
  - there is no rule preventing you or your partner from doing full-time paid work (known as 'remunerative work'), although any earnings are taken into account when working out how much PC you can get.

Non-means-tested benefits

While you are on JSA you are entitled to NI credits (see p780).

Most non-means-tested benefits are taken into account when working out the amount of income-based JSA you can get. Attendance allowance (AA), disability living allowance (DLA), guardian's allowance and, if you are getting CTC, child benefit, are not taken into account. It can be worth claiming non-means-tested benefits. If you or your partner qualify for certain of these, you also qualify for certain premiums (see p820) and, therefore, a higher rate of income-based JSA.

You might only qualify for income-based JSA once you or a member of your family are awarded another benefit – known as a 'qualifying benefit'. To make sure you do not lose out while awaiting the outcome of a claim for a qualifying benefit, claim JSA at the same time. If your claim for income-based JSA is refused, once the qualifying benefit is awarded, claim JSA again and ask for it to be backdated to the date of your first claim (see p1029).

Contribution-based JSA is affected by the overlapping benefit rules (see p1041).

Passports and other sources of help

If you are entitled to income-based JSA, you also qualify for health benefits such as free prescriptions (see Chapter 13) and education benefits such as free school lunches (see p14). You may also qualify for social fund payments (see Chapters 25 and 26).

Financial help on starting work

If you stop getting JSA because you or your partner start work, or your earnings or your hours in your existing job increase, you might be able to get mortgage interest run-on (if you have a home loan – see p879), extended payments of HB or CTB (if you pay rent or council tax – see pp286 and 130). See p13 for information about other financial help you might get.

Notes

1. Who can claim jobseeker's allowance

1 ss1-3 and 3A JSA 1995
2 Reg 47(1) and (2) JSA Regs
3 Reg 49 JSA Regs
4 Reg 47(3) JSA Regs
5 Sch 1 para 3 JSA 1995
6 s2(1) and (4) JSA 1995
7 Reg 48 JSA Regs
8 Reg 48(2) and (3) JSA Regs
9 *LE v SSWP* [2009] UKUT 166 (AAC). The judge decided that the rule indirectly discriminated against women but that the discrimination was justified.
10 s2 JSA 1995
11 ss3, 3A and 13 JSA 1995
12 Reg 3D JSA Regs; Sch 1 para 8A JSA 1995
13 Sch A1 JSA Regs
14 Reg 3D(3) and (4) JSA Regs
15 *CIS/0542/2001*
16 Sch A1 paras 6(a) and (b), 9, 10, and 11 JSA Regs; reg 4(3) SS(MA)(No.5) Regs 2010
17 Reg 4(4) SS(MA)(No.5) Regs 2010
18 Sch A1 paras 7 and 8 JSA Regs; reg 4(3), (5), (7) and (8) SS(MA)(No.5) Regs 2009
19 Reg 51 JSA Regs
20 Reg 3E(2)(g) JSA Regs
21 s1(2)(f) JSA 1995
22 Sch 1 para 2 JSA 1995; reg 10 SS&CS(DA) Regs
23 Regs 14(1)(l), 19(1)(l) and 55(1) JSA Regs
24 Regs 14(1)(ll), 19(1)(ll) and 55A(1) JSA Regs
25 Regs 55(2) and 55A(2) JSA Regs
26 Reg 55(3) JSA Regs
27 Reg 55(4) JSA Regs

2. The rules about your age

28 s3A(1)(e) JSA 1995; reg 58 JSA Regs

3. Claiming for others

29 s35(1) JSA 1995
30 s35 JSA 1995; reg 77 JSA Regs
31 Reg 78 JSA Regs

4. **The amount of benefit**
32 Sch 1 para 4 JSA 1995; reg 46 JSA Regs
33 Reg 14A SS&CS(DA) Regs
34 s4(1) and (2) JSA 1995; reg 79 JSA Regs
35 ss4(1) and 35(1) JSA 1995; reg 81(1) JSA Regs
36 Reg 80(2) JSA Regs
37 s5(1) JSA 1995
38 s5(2) JSA 1995
39 Reg 49 JSA Regs
40 Reg 47(2) and (4) JSA Regs
41 ss4(3) and (3A) and 13 JSA 1995

5. **Special benefit rules**
42 s3A(d) and (e) JSA 1995
43 ss3(1)(c) and (d) and 3A(1)(b) and (c) JSA 1995; reg 57(1), definition of 'young person', JSA Regs
44 ss3(1)(f)(iii) and 3A(1)(e)(ii) JSA 1995; reg 61(1)(b), (c) and (g) and (2)(b) JSA Regs
45 ss3(1)(f)(iii) and 3A(1)(e)(ii) JSA 1995; regs 57 and 59 JSA Regs
46 ss3(1)(f)(iii) and 3A(1)(e)(ii) JSA 1995; reg 60 JSA Regs
47 Reg 61(1)(a) and (2)(a) JSA Regs
48 Reg 61(1)(f) and (2)(e) JSA Regs
49 ss3(1)(f)(ii), 3A(1)(e)(i) and 16 JSA 1995
50 DWP guidance, *Making a Severe Hardship Decision*, para 121 (www.dwp.gov.uk/docs/jsa-16-17-severe-hardship.pdf)
51 DWP guidance, *Making a Severe Hardship Decision*, paras 42-68, 106-120 and 209-12 (www.dwp.gov.uk/docs/jsa-16-17-severe-hardship.pdf)
52 DWP guidance, *Making a Severe Hardship Decision*, paras 5-41 (www.dwp.gov.uk/docs/jsa-16-17-severe-hardship.pdf)
53 s16(2) and (4) JSA 1995
54 DWP guidance, *Making a Severe Hardship Decision*, para 137 (www.dwp.gov.uk/docs/jsa-16-17-severe-hardship.pdf)
55 s16(3) JSA 1995
56 s71A SSAA 1992
57 s17(4) JSA 1995
58 Regs 64-66 JSA Regs
59 Reg 62 JSA Regs
60 Reg 62(1) JSA Regs
61 Reg 62(2) and (3) JSA Regs
62 Sch 2 para 1(a) SSA 1998
63 DWP guidance, *Making a Severe Hardship Decision*, paras 124-5 (www.dwp.gov.uk/docs/jsa-16-17-severe-hardship.pdf)

6. **Claims and backdating**
64 s8(1) JSA 1995
65 Reg 4(1A), (6), (11A) and (11B) SS(C&P) Regs
66 Reg 4(11A) and (11B) SS(C&P) Regs
67 Reg 4ZC SS(C&P) Regs
68 Reg 4(3B)(a) SS(C&P) Regs
69 s1(2B) and (4) JSA 1995; reg 3A(1) JSA Regs; CJSA/2633/2004
70 s1(4) JSA 1995; reg 3A(1) JSA Regs
71 *Hockenjos v Secretary of State for Social Security* [2004] EWCA Civ 1749, reported as R(JSA) 1/05 and R(JSA) 2/05
72 Sch 1 para 9A JSA 1995; reg 3B JSA Regs
73 Sch 1 paras 9B and 9C JSA 1995; reg 3C JSA Regs
74 s1(2C) JSA 1995; reg 3E JSA Regs
75 Sch 5 paras 10, 13A and 17A JSA Regs
76 Reg 4(1A), (7B), (9), (12) and (13) SS(C&P) Regs
77 Reg 4(6)(a) SS(C&P) Regs
78 Reg 19(1) and Sch 4 para 1 SS(C&P) Regs
79 Reg 6(4ZA), (4ZB)(a) and (4A)(a)(i) SS(C&P) Regs
80 Reg 6(1)(c) and (d) SS(C&P) Regs
81 Reg 6(4A)(b) SS(C&P) Regs
82 Reg 6(4ZC)(a) and (b) SS(C&P) Regs
83 Reg 6(4AB) SS(C&P) Regs
84 Reg 4(3B)(b) SS(C&P) Regs
85 Reg 4(3B)(c) SS(C&P) Regs
86 Reg 6(4A)(a)(ii) SS(C&P) Regs
87 Reg 6(4ZB)(b) and (4ZC)(c) SS(C&P) Regs
88 Sch 5 para 17A JSA Regs
89 CS/371/1949
90 Reg 6(28) SS(C&P) Regs
91 Reg 13(1) and (9) SS(C&P) Regs
92 s8 JSA 1995; regs 24(6) and 65A JSA Regs
93 Regs 23 and 23A JSA Regs
94 CJSA/1080/2002
95 Regs 23 and 23A JSA Regs; s7 Interpretation Act 1978; R(JSA) 1/04
96 s8(2) and (2A) JSA 1995; regs 27A and 27B(1)(a) JSA Regs
97 Reg 74B JSA Regs
98 Regs 27A, 27B(1)(b) and 74B JSA Regs
99 Reg 68 JSA Regs
100 Reg 30 JSA Regs
101 The exceptions are those treated as available under reg 14(1)(h)-(j) and (nn)-(q) JSA Regs
102 Reg 28 JSA Regs
103 s8(2)(c) JSA 1995; reg 25(1)(a) and (b) and (1A) JSA Regs

104 Reg 26 JSA Regs; *SSWP v Michael Ferguson* [2003] EWCA Civ 536, reported as R(JSA) 6/03; R(JSA) 2/04
105 Reg 6(4C) SS(C&P) Regs
106 Reg 6(4B) SS(C&P) Regs
107 The exceptions are those treated as available under reg 14(1)(h)-(j) and (nn)-(q) JSA Regs
108 Regs 25(1)(c) and (1A) and 27 JSA Regs; *SSWP v Michael Ferguson* [2003] EWCA Civ 536, reported as R(JSA) 6/03
109 Reg 29 JSA Regs
110 Reg 26 JSA Regs; *SSWP v Michael Ferguson* [2003] EWCA Civ 536, reported as R(JSA) 6/03; R(JSA) 2/04
111 R(JSA) 2/04

7. **Getting paid**
112 Reg 26A SS(C&P) Regs
113 s1(3) JSA 1995; reg 150 JSA Regs
114 Reg 1(3) JSA Regs
115 Reg 87A JSA Regs
116 Reg 26A(3) SS(C&P) Regs
117 s3B JSA 1995
118 s20A(7) JSA 1995
119 Reg 30A SS(C&P) Regs
120 Reg 24(7) JSA Regs; reg 3 SS(NCC) Regs
121 Reg 24B JSA Regs; reg 32ZA(2) SS(C&P) Regs
122 Reg 7 and Sch 3A para 7 SS&CS(DA) Regs
123 Reg 7 and Sch 3A paras 8-13 SS&CS(DA) Regs

8. **Tax, tax credits and other benefits**
124 ss671-75 IT(EP)A 2003

Chapter 20

Jobseeking conditions, sanctions and hardship payments

This chapter covers:

Key facts

- To qualify for jobseeker's allowance (JSA), you must usually satisfy the jobseeking conditions – ie, you must be available for work, you must actively seek work and you must have a current jobseeker's agreement.
- If a decision maker decides you should be sanctioned (eg, because you lose your job or a place on an employment scheme through misconduct or you fail to apply for a job), your JSA might not be paid or you might be paid at a reduced rate for a certain period.
- You may qualify for hardship payments in a number of situations, including if you do not satisfy the jobseeking conditions and if you are sanctioned.

Future changes: April 2013 and after

Major changes are taking place that affect the benefits and tax credits system (see Chapter 2). From October 2013 when universal credit is introduced, the 'claimant commitment' will include a record of the work-related requirements that claimants must undertake. These will be work-focused interviews, work preparation, work search and being available for work, and will replace the current jobseeking conditions. See CPAG's *Welfare Rights Bulletin* for updates.

1. Jobseeking conditions

To qualify for jobseeker's allowance (JSA), you must usually satisfy three jobseeking conditions. You must be available for work, actively seeking work and have a current jobseeker's agreement with the DWP. **Note:**

- In some cases, you can place restrictions on the work you are available to do (see p443).
- If you are a member of a joint-claim couple, you may be able to qualify for joint-claim JSA even if one of you does not satisfy the jobseeking conditions (see p396).
- If you do not satisfy the jobseeking conditions, or there is doubt about whether you do, you may be able to get hardship payments (see p484).

Full-time training and study

You cannot usually qualify for JSA if you are studying full time because you are usually treated as unavailable for work (see p441). However, you *can* qualify for JSA if you:

- count as a full-time student while you are participating in the Employment, Skills and Enterprise Scheme (see p471) – eg, if you are studying more than 16 hours a week;
- are getting a training allowance (see below);
- are on certain short-term courses or Venture Trust training programmes or a full-time 'qualifying course' (see p438).

Note: even if none of the above apply, you might be able to get JSA while studying full or part time, or while waiting to go back on your course having taken approved time out because of an illness or caring responsibilities that have now ended (see Chapter 29).

Getting a training allowance

Provided you are not a child or qualifying young person for child benefit purposes (see p94), if you are receiving training and getting a specified type of training allowance you can get income-based JSA without having to satisfy the jobseeking conditions.[1] For these purposes, 'training' does not include training for people aged 16–24 provided by the Young People's Learning Agency (due to be replaced by the Education Funding Agency from April 2012), the Skills Funding Agency, the Welsh Ministers or by Skills Development Scotland, Scottish Enterprise or the Highlands and Islands Enterprise. However, if you are receiving this type of training, you might qualify for income support (IS – see p349).

Available for work

To qualify for JSA, you must be available for work. The general rule is that to be available for work you must be:[2]

- 'willing and able' to take up work 'immediately' (see p436); *and*
- available at any time of the day and on any day of the week; *and*
- prepared to take a job that would involve working for *at least* 40 hours a week; *and*
- prepared to work for *less than* 40 hours a week if required to do so. In practice, this means that you must be prepared to work part time.

However, you may be able to place restrictions on your availability for work (see p443) such as the number of hours, days and times you are available.

You do not have to be available for work if you are participating in the Employment, Skills and Enterprise Scheme and either you count as a full-time student or it is the first week after you are released from detention in prison, a remand centre or youth custody.[3] However, you are likely to be required to take specific steps while participating. Some people getting a training allowance do not have to be available for work (see p434).

Remember that in some circumstances you can be treated as being available for work even if you are not (see p437). In some cases, you can qualify for joint-claim JSA even if you or your partner (but not both of you) are not available for work (see p396). Special rules allow you to count as available for work for the first 13 weeks of a period when you are laid off or on short-time working (see p483). If you are not available or treated as available for work, you cannot get JSA under the normal rules, but you may be able to get hardship payments (see p484).

Your availability for work is considered at an initial interview when you first claim JSA. Your jobseeker's agreement (see p452) contains details of your 'pattern of availability' as well as any other restrictions you may place on your availability.

Note: the DWP can decide that you are not available for work without having to show that you have turned down a job.[4] However, the fact that you turn down a job does not necessarily mean that you are not available.

If you are a lone parent

Even if you are a lone parent and so have childcare responsibilities, you must be available for work to qualify for JSA. However, some special rules can apply.

- You only need to be able to take up a job on one week's (or in some cases 28 days') notice (see p436).
- If you are looking after a child under 16, you can be treated as available for work:
  - when your child is sick;
  - during the school holidays and at times when s/he is excluded from school and not receiving education provided by the local authority (see p438).
- You may be able to restrict your availability for work in any way if you are the subject of a parenting order or have entered into a parenting contract in respect of a child under 16 (see p443).
- You may be able to restrict your hours to less than 40 a week (see p445).

- If you have a child under 13, you only need to be available for work during your child's normal school hours (see p446).

Willing and able to take up work immediately

Being **willing** to work is essentially a test of your attitude – your desire and willingness to work. What you do in practice to display this willingness is usually dealt with under the rules for actively seeking work (see p447).

You must be prepared to take up work as an employed person – being only available for self-employment is not sufficient.[5] However, this means that you do not count as being unavailable for work if you refuse to work as a self-employed person.

In order to be **able** to work it must be lawful for you to work in Great Britain.[6] Your immigration status may affect this – eg, if a condition of your entry is that you do not work. In addition, there must be nothing to prevent you from receiving job offers (eg, because you are away from home for more than a short time) and nothing to prevent you from acting on them straight away – eg, because you have other commitments that you cannot abandon easily.

Being able to take up work **immediately** means that you must usually be able to start work without any delay, with little more than the time needed to get washed and dressed and have breakfast.[7] You can be allowed more time than this in the following situations. You only need to be available for work:

- on **one week's notice** if you are doing voluntary work or have caring responsibilities (see p437 for what counts).[8] You must be willing and able to attend an interview in connection with opportunities for work on 48 hours' notice. However, if you have caring responsibilities for a child under 16 and you can show these make it unreasonable for you to take up a job or attend an interview within these periods, you only have to be available on **28 days' notice** and be willing and able to attend an interview on seven days' notice;
- on **24 hours' notice** if you are providing a paid or unpaid service, but do not qualify as a carer or a volunteer.[9] This includes services you provide for family or friends on a non-commercial basis, such as giving someone a regular lift to work in your car.[10] It could also include activities that are of service to the community in general – eg, offenders working in the community as part of their punishment (see p437) and tribunal members – eg, of the First-tier Tribunal and employment tribunals;
- **after your notice period** has passed if you are working part time. This applies if you have a duty to give your employer notice that you are leaving work under employment law.[11] If you must, under the terms of your contract, give longer notice, argue that a longer notice period should apply.

Note: if it has been recorded in your jobseeker's agreement that you are only available to work at certain times, you are *not* required to be able to take up employment at times that you are not available.[12] However, you must be willing and able to take up the offer as soon as you reach the next period in your **pattern of availability** (the days and times you are available).

Definitions[13]

'Voluntary work' is work which is done for a charity or other not-for-profit organisation or for anyone other than a member of your family (see p401 for who counts), for which you receive no payment other than for your reasonable expenses.

'Caring responsibilities' means responsibility for looking after a member of your household (see p754 on the meaning of household) or a close relative who is a child under 16, someone over pension age or someone who needs care because of her/his mental or physical condition.

'Close relative' means partner, parent, step-parent, parent-in-law, parent of a civil partner, grandparent, son, stepson, son-in-law, son of a civil partner, daughter, stepdaughter, daughter-in-law, daughter of a civil partner, brother, sister, grandchild or the partner of any of these.

If you are an **offender** you may be required, as part of your punishment, to do unpaid work in the community. You count as being available for work if arrangements are made so that you can be notified of a vacancy or interview and you can leave the unpaid work in order to take up a job within 24 hours.[14] If you are required to attend a course, you have to be available for work immediately because this is unlikely to count as providing a service. To be considered available for work, make sure that you can be contacted at short notice and are allowed to leave the course to attend an interview if required. If you are released early from prison under the Home Detention Curfew scheme, you can be available for work during daytime hours.

Treated as being available for work

Even if you are not actually available for work, you can be treated as if you are for periods during your claim.[15] You must still satisfy the other conditions of entitlement to JSA. Remember that special rules allow you to count as available for work for up to 13 weeks of being laid off or on short-time working (see p483).

General rules

You are treated as available for work:[16]

- during any part week at the **beginning of your claim** if, in respect of all the days concerned, you satisfy the rules for being available for work and:[17]
  - you have an agreed 'pattern of availability' (ie, the particular days and times you are available for work) or are allowed to place restrictions on the number of hours you are prepared to work under the rules described on p445;[18] *or*
  - you do not have an agreed 'pattern of availability' and are available for work for eight hours each day;

- during any part week at the **end of your claim**;
- if you are **sick** for a two-week period or are temporarily absent from Great Britain for the purpose of getting NHS hospital treatment (see p399);
- if you were **recently found not to have limited capability for work**, but only if your time limit for claiming JSA is extended because you were not told promptly enough that your entitlement to IS, employment and support allowance (ESA) or incapacity benefit (IB) had ended so you could not claim JSA in time. You are treated as available for work during the period for which the time limit is extended.

Note: the government says that from 23 April 2012, you will also be treated as available for work for four weeks if you notify the DWP that you have experienced, or been threatened with, domestic violence from your partner, your former partner or a family member.[19] This period will be extended to 13 weeks if you provide relevant evidence during the four-week period. You will only be treated as available for work under this rule once in any 12-month period. The four and 13 weeks run on whether or not you are entitled to JSA for the whole period. However, you will be able to ask for the 13-week period to be suspended.

Looking after a child under 16

You are treated as available for work if you are looking after a child under 16 and:[20]

- you are a member of a couple and looking after the child while your partner is temporarily absent from the UK (for a maximum of eight weeks). You must be responsible for the child (see p761) and s/he must be a member of your household; *or*
- the person who normally looks after the child is ill, temporarily away from home or looking after a member of the family who is ill (for a maximum of eight weeks). You must be looking after the child full time;
- you have caring responsibilities for the child (see p437 for what counts) and you are looking after her/him:
  - during the school holidays or other similar vacation. This only applies if it would be unreasonable to make other arrangements; *or*
  - at a time when s/he is excluded from school and is not receiving education provided by the local authority. This only applies if there are no other arrangements it would be reasonable for you to make.

Studying and training

In some cases, you can study or take part in training courses while on JSA so long as you satisfy the rules of entitlement. See p400 for further information about studying and claiming JSA. Some people getting training allowances do not have to satisfy the jobseeking conditions (see p434). **Note:** if you are participating in the Employment, Skills and Enterprise Scheme (see p471) and count as a full-time student, you do not have to be available for work.[21] However, you are likely to be required to take specific steps while participating.

In some situations in which you would not normally count as being available for work while studying, special rules apply. You count as available:[22]

- for one period of up to two weeks in any 12 months when you are a full-time student (see p637) on an **employment-related course** which has been approved in advance by your employment officer (EO). See below for more generous rules if you are on a 'qualifying course';
- if you are attending a compulsory residential course as part of an **Open University course** (for up to one week for each course);
- if you are attending a residential training programme run by **the Venture Trust** (for one programme only for a maximum of four weeks in any 12-month period).

Special rules apply if you are attending a **'qualifying course'** with the approval of an EO. You can get JSA while attending a 'qualifying course' if:[23]

- you are aged 25 or over; *and*
- you had been 'receiving benefit' (see below) during a jobseeking period (see p394) for at least two years at the time the course starts. When working out whether you have been 'receiving benefit' for two years, the rules for linking jobseeking periods apply (see p394); *and*
- an EO approves your attendance; *and*
- you satisfy the special conditions for being treated as available for and actively seeking work (see below and p450).

Once you have started the course, the course becomes compulsory. This means that if you abandon it without good cause or are dismissed because of misconduct, you could be sanctioned (see p471).

Qualifying courses and receiving benefit[24]

A **'qualifying course'** is a course of further or higher education which is employment-related and lasts no more than 12 consecutive months. A course of a higher standard than this can also be a qualifying course if your EO agrees.

'Receiving benefit' means getting benefit as an unemployed person (eg, JSA) or national insurance (NI) credits for unemployment, or because you are a man born before 6 October 1954 who has not yet reached 65 (see p786). There are also rules for those who were getting IS as an asylum seeker. See p367 of the 2011/12 edition of this *Handbook* for details.

If you are on a 'qualifying course', you are treated as being available for work in any week:[25]

- which falls entirely or partly in term time, so long as you provide written evidence within five days of its being requested, confirming that you are attending and making satisfactory progress on the course. This must be signed by you and by the college or educational establishment;
- in which you are taking exams relating to the course; *or*
- which falls entirely in a vacation, if you are willing and able to take up any 'casual employment' immediately. '**Casual employment**' means employment that you can leave without giving notice or, if you must give notice, that you can leave before the end of the vacation.

Temporary absence from Great Britain

You are treated as available for work when you are temporarily absent from Great Britain and you are:[26]

- taking a child or qualifying young person who is a member of your household (see p762) and for whom you are responsible (see p761) abroad temporarily for medical treatment (for a maximum of eight weeks). The treatment must be under the supervision of a person qualified in medical, physiotherapeutic or similar practices;[27] *or*
- attending a job interview. You must tell your EO in advance and confirm it in writing if required to do so (for a maximum of seven days); *or*
- a member of a couple and the pensioner, enhanced pensioner, higher pensioner, disability or severe disability premium is being paid for your partner (see Chapter 34) and you are both away from Great Britain (for a maximum of four weeks); *or*
- abroad for the purpose of getting NHS hospital treatment (see p399); *or*
- a member of a joint-claim couple (see p413) on the date of your claim and on the day your partner makes the claim for JSA, you are:
  - in Northern Ireland (for a maximum of four weeks) but only if you are unlikely to be away for more than 52 weeks; *or*
  - attending a job interview (for a maximum of seven days).

If you are looking after a child because your partner is temporarily absent from the UK, see p438.

Other

You are treated as available for work:[28]

- if you have been **discharged from detention** in prison, a remand centre or a youth custody institution, but only if you have not been required to participate in the Employment, Skills and Enterprise Scheme – see p471 (for one week from the date of discharge);[29]
- during **temporary police detention** (legal custody in Scotland) of up to 96 hours, but not if you come within the definition of 'prisoner' (see p694);

- if you are required to **attend a court or tribunal** as a justice of the peace, juror, witness or party to any proceedings (but not if you come within the definition of 'prisoner' – see p694) (for a maximum of eight weeks). You must have notified your EO beforehand;[30]
- if you are engaged in crewing or launching a lifeboat, are carrying out duties as a part-time firefighter or are engaged during an emergency as a member of an organised group which is helping to save lives, prevent injury or a serious threat to the health of others, or protect property;[31]
- for one period of up to two weeks in any 12 months when you are **attending a residential work camp** in Great Britain, organised by a charity, local authority or voluntary organisation for the benefit of the community or the environment;[32]
- if you are dealing with circumstances arising from:
  - a domestic emergency affecting you or a close friend or close relative (see p437 for who counts); *or*
  - the death or serious illness of a close friend or close relative; *or*
  - the death of someone for whom you had caring responsibilities (see p437 for what counts); *or*
  - the funeral of a close friend or close relative.

  You are only treated as available during the time it takes to deal with the matter and only for up to a week at a time and on no more than four occasions in any 12-month period. However, if you have caring responsibilities for a child under 16, you can be treated as available for up to eight weeks in either of the first two situations (or a combination of these), on one occasion in any 12-month period. If this applies, you can then only be treated as being available for up to a week on three more occasions in the 12-month period.[33]

If you are selected as a **juror**, you must attend court when asked to do so. However, if this is for more than eight weeks and you lose JSA, this is not necessarily made up by the court. You may be able to claim IS instead of JSA.

Treated as being unavailable for work

Even if you are (or can be treated as) available for employment, you are nevertheless treated as unavailable for work if:[34]

- you are a full-time student (see p637 for who counts), *unless* you are:[35]
  - on a 'qualifying course' (see p439); *or*
  - on an employment-related course or a residential training programme run by the Venture Trust (see p439); *or*
  - a lone parent, or a member of a couple who are both students, you (or your partner) are responsible for a child (see p761) and it is the summer vacation. You must satisfy all the normal rules on being available for work or be treated as being available for work because you are on an employment-related

course or a residential training programme run by the Venture Trust (see p439);

Note: you do not have to be available for work if you are participating in the Employment, Skills and Enterprise Scheme, but you are likely to be required to take specific steps while participating;[36]

- you are on temporary release from prison;
- you are receiving maternity allowance or statutory maternity pay;
- you are on paternity or adoption leave;
- it is during any part week at the beginning of your claim. You are treated as unavailable for work unless you come under the rule for being treated as available for that period (see the general rules on p437).

Unavailable for part of a week

On occasion, you might be **unavailable for work for a short period** during a benefit week – eg, because you are away from home. If this happens and you have put restrictions on the times that you are available (see p445):[37]

- your JSA is not affected if the period during which you are *not* available comes entirely outside your 'pattern of availability' – ie, the particular days and times that you are available for work; *or*
- you lose JSA for the whole of that benefit week if all or part of the period during which you are not available comes within your 'pattern of availability'.

If this happens and you have *not* put any restrictions on the times you are available, you may lose benefit for that week because you are not available to take up work immediately.[38] For this reason, it is best to avoid signing a jobseeker's agreement with totally unrestricted times as your availability.

If you are arrested and held by the police for a short time but then released, you can be treated as available for work for up to 96 hours while you are detained (see p440).

If you are doing **voluntary work** and have placed restrictions on the total number of hours you are available to work (see p445), any voluntary work you do (see p437 for what counts) within your 'pattern of availability' (see above) must be ignored for the purpose of deciding if you are available, so long as you are willing and able to rearrange the voluntary work within:[39]

- one week's notice, in order to take up any job whose hours fall within your pattern of availability;
- 48 hours' notice, to attend an interview in connection with an opportunity for work at a time that falls within your pattern of availability.

There is a similar rule if you are a part-time student (see p643).

Restrictions on availability for work

You can restrict your availability for work **in any way** if the restrictions are reasonable in light of your physical or mental condition, and in some cases if you have specified caring responsibilities for a child under 16. See below for further information.

If you can prove that you still have a reasonable prospect of securing employment (see below), you can place some restrictions on the work you are available to do. These are:[40]

- the **type of work** for which you are available (see p444);
- the **number of hours, days and times you are available** (see p445);
- the **terms and conditions** of employment for which you are available, including the rate of pay (see p446);
- the **location** of the job (see p447).

Any restrictions are entered in your jobseeker's agreement. If you and the DWP have not agreed in advance that there are certain types of work which you cannot or are unwilling to do, it may prove difficult to justify turning down such a job if it is offered to you later.

A 'reasonable prospect' of securing employment

You must show that you have a reasonable prospect of securing employment despite any restrictions you are allowed to place on your availability, unless you can restrict your availability in any way (see below).[41] If you impose more than one type of restriction, the cumulative effect on your job prospects is considered. The DWP must consider all the evidence and in particular:[42]

- your skills, qualifications and experience; *and*
- the type and number of job vacancies within daily travelling distance of your home; *and*
- the length of time you have been unemployed; *and*
- the job applications which you have made and their outcome; *and*
- whether you are willing to move home to take up a job, but only where you are placing restrictions on the type of job you are prepared to do.

Your job prospects may be poor. However, if you do not put any restrictions on the work you will take, you are accepted as being available for work. Therefore, think carefully about whether it is sensible to apply restrictions.

Restricting your availability in any way

You can restrict your availability for work in any way if:[43]

- the restrictions are reasonable in light of your physical or mental condition (see p444); *or*
- you have caring responsibilities (see p437 for what counts) for a child under 16 and you are the subject of a parenting order or have entered into a parenting

contract in respect of the child under specific provisions. The restrictions must be reasonable in light of the terms of the order or contract.

This means that you can restrict the type of work for which you are available, as well as the number of hours, the days and times, the terms and conditions of employment, the location of the job, and any other matter whatsoever. If the restrictions you impose are reasonable ones in light of your physical or mental condition, or the terms of the order or contract, you do not have to show that you have reasonable prospects of securing employment (see p443).

Physical or mental condition

If you want to restrict your availability for work because of your physical or mental condition, you are normally expected to provide medical evidence. However, if you have no prospects of work at all, you should consider whether you are capable of work. If not, it may be in your interest to claim ESA or pension credit (PC) instead of JSA. If you have been found not to have limited capability for work following a work capability assessment, and are appealing against the decision, see p210 if you need to claim JSA during this period.

If you also place restrictions on your availability for work that are *not* connected with your physical or mental condition, you must show that you have a reasonable prospect of securing employment (see p443) with all your restrictions. Therefore, think carefully before placing additional restrictions on your availability.

The type of work

The general rule is that you have to be available for any type of employment, but you are allowed to place restrictions on the sort of jobs for which you are available provided you have a reasonable prospect of securing employment (see p443).[44] In addition, special rules allow you to make restrictions:

- during your 'permitted period' if you have one (see below);
- if you are a laid-off or short-time worker (see p483);
- because of a sincerely held religious belief or conscientious objection (see p445).

Permitted periods

A **'permitted period'** is a period of one to 13 weeks from the date you claim JSA during which you are allowed to be available only for vacancies in your 'usual occupation' and which pay at least what you would normally receive.[45] Any other restrictions you place on your availability must be consistent with the conditions of work that are normal in your usual occupation.

Usual occupation

The term 'usual occupation' is not defined in the rules. The DWP says that if you have followed an occupation for a long time, this can count as your usual occupation, and also that a new occupation may count as your usual occupation if you intend to follow that type of work in future.[46]

Not everyone is allowed a permitted period. Whether or not you are allowed one and, if so, how long it lasts, are matters that you and the EO need to discuss when arriving at your jobseeker's agreement.[47] The DWP must consider:[48]

- your 'usual occupation' and any relevant skills or qualifications you may have; *and*
- the length of time you have spent training for or have worked in that occupation, and the length of time since you have worked in the occupation; *and*
- the availability and location of jobs in that area of work.

Religious or conscientious objection

You do not have to be available for work that offends a sincerely held religious belief or a sincere conscientious objection – eg, a job in a company associated with live animal exports if you have a conscientious objection to these.[49] You must still have reasonable prospects of securing employment despite those restrictions (see p443).[50]

The number of hours, days and times

You are allowed to restrict the total number of hours you are available, so long as you are available for at least 40 hours a week and:[51]

- you have agreed with the DWP a 'pattern of availability' (ie, the particular days and times that you are available for work) and this has been recorded in your jobseeker's agreement;[52] *and*
- you still have reasonable prospects of securing employment despite the restrictions (see p443) and they do not *considerably* reduce your prospects of securing employment.

You must be prepared to work for the maximum number of hours for which you are available, or for a lower number. However if your EO notifies you of a vacancy, you are allowed to refuse it if it would be for less than 24 hours a week (16 hours a week if it is agreed you need only be available for less than 24 hours a week – eg, because you have caring responsibilities – see below).[53] This is because you can show 'good cause' for refusing to apply and cannot be sanctioned (see p466).

Note: you are allowed to restrict the total number of hours you are available to *less* than 40 in some situations if you have caring responsibilities or if you are a lone parent (see p446). If you are a short-time or laid-off worker, see p483.

Caring responsibilities

If you have caring responsibilities (see p437 for what counts), you can restrict the total hours you are available to less than 40 hours a week if:[54]

- you are available for employment for at least 16 hours a week and for as many hours as your caring responsibilities permit; *and*
- you have a reasonable chance of securing employment (see p443) despite the restricted hours you are available. You do not have to show this if you have caring responsibilities for a child under 16 and an EO decides that you would not satisfy this condition because of the type and number of job vacancies within daily travelling distance of your home.

When deciding whether you are available for employment for as many hours as your caring responsibilities permit, the DWP must consider relevant factors. These include the particular hours and days you spend caring, whether your caring responsibilities are shared with someone else, and the age and physical and mental condition of the person for whom you care.[55]

If you are a carer and you cannot make yourself available for work at least 16 hours a week, you might be able to claim IS or, if you are at least the qualifying age (see p509), PC rather than JSA.

If you are a lone parent

If you are a lone parent and a child for whom you are responsible and who lives in your household is under 13, you only need to be available for work during your child's normal school hours.[56] This means that you can restrict the total number of hours, days and times you are available. You also count as a person with caring responsibilities, so you may be able to restrict the total number of hours further (see above).

The terms and conditions of employment

You can make restrictions on the terms and conditions of employment for which you are available (including the rate of pay – but see below) provided you can show you still have reasonable prospects of securing employment despite those restrictions (see p443).[57]

The rate of pay

You can restrict the rate of pay:

- during your 'permitted period' (see p444), if you have one, to the rate you are accustomed to receiving in your usual occupation;[58]
- for six months from the date you claimed JSA, so long as you still have reasonable prospects of securing employment (see p443).[59]

Any restrictions you may place on the rate of pay should be recorded in your jobseeker's agreement. It is *vital* that the wage or salary you say you are willing to accept should not be higher than the going rate for the jobs you have said you are looking for. Remember that you should not be expected to work for a rate of pay below the national minimum wage (see p491).

The location of the job

You can make restrictions on the localities within which you are available for work, so long as you can show you still have reasonable prospects of securing employment in the selected areas (see p443).[60]

Actively seeking work

To qualify for JSA, you must be actively seeking work. Special rules apply if you have been allowed a 'permitted period' (see p450).

You do not have to actively seek work if you are participating in:

- New Enterprise Allowance (see p471);[61] *or*
- the Employment, Skills and Enterprise Scheme (see p471) and either you count as a full-time student or it is the first week after you are released from detention in prison, a remand centre or youth custody.[62]

However, you are likely to be required to take specific steps while participating. Some people getting a training allowance (see p434) do not have to actively seek work.

In some cases you can be treated as if you are actively seeking work even if you are not (see p450).[63] In some cases you can qualify for joint-claim JSA even if you or your partner (but not both of you) are not actively seeking work (see p396).

What you must do

To be actively seeking work:

- you must take, in each benefit week, such 'steps' as you can reasonably be expected to have to take in order to have the best prospects of securing employment;[64]
- you are expected to take more than two steps during a week unless taking less steps is all that it is reasonable for you to do.[65] **Note:** it is possible that in some weeks there may be no steps that you could reasonably be expected to take.[66]

Note: the government says that from spring 2012, you will be expected to spend several hours a day seeking work and that you will have to look for any suitable job within 90 minutes of home. See CPAG's *Welfare Rights Bulletin* for updates.

The normal actively seeking work rule is adapted to cover any part-week at the beginning of your claim. You satisfy the test so long as you take reasonable steps in the part-week to ensure you have the best chance of getting a job.[67]

Your jobseeker's agreement says what steps you have agreed to take to find work, but you do not necessarily have to take all the steps each week to prove you are actively seeking work.[68] The test for whether you have been actively seeking work is what you *did*, not what you did not do.

To prove that you are actively seeking work, you must give details of the steps you have taken when you sign on. It is, therefore, extremely important that you keep records of your attempts to get a job.

You might not count as actively seeking work if it is considered that you should be taking more steps or ones that give you a better chance of finding work. You may be asked at an interview to change the steps and the EO may propose a change in your jobseeker's agreement (see p455).

What counts as a 'step'

Steps are not limited to actually applying for job vacancies. Anything you do that might lead to your applying for or being offered employment should count as a step. Steps include:[69]

- applying for jobs in writing, personally or by phone;
- seeking information from advertisements, advertisers, agencies or employers;
- registering with an agency or appointing someone else to help you find work – eg, an agent if you are looking for work in the entertainment field;
- preparing a CV;
- asking a previous employer for a reference;
- preparing a list of, or looking for information about, employers who may be able to offer you a job;
- looking for information about an occupation with a view to finding a job in that occupation;
- getting specialist advice following referral by an EO on how to improve your chances of finding a job – eg, from a disability employment adviser.

There are many other things that could count as steps – eg, searching for jobs on the Jobcentre Plus website and making enquiries about jobs via the internet or by email. Remember to keep a record as proof.

When the DWP decides whether you have been actively seeking work, it must disregard a step if (unless there are reasons beyond your control) you:[70]

- act in a violent or abusive manner; *or*
- spoil an application if the step is completing a job application; *or*
- undermine your prospects of getting a job by your behaviour or appearance.

In these circumstances, the DWP might issue a jobseeker's direction (see p469) and sanction you if you fail to comply with it.

Deciding what steps are reasonable

When the DWP decides whether the steps you took in a particular week were reasonable, all the circumstances in your individual case must be considered, including:[71]

- your skills, qualifications and abilities;
- any physical or mental limitations you may have;
- how long you have been unemployed, and your work experience;
- the steps you have taken in previous weeks and how those steps have improved your chances of finding a job;

- the availability and location of job vacancies;
- any time you have spent:
  - launching or crewing a lifeboat or acting as a part-time firefighter, undertaking duties as a member of the Territorial Army or reserve force, attending an Outward Bound course or taking part in an organised group helping in an emergency;
  - undertaking voluntary work and the extent to which it may have improved your chances of finding a paid job;
  - improving your chances of finding a job by training to use aids to overcome any physical or mental disabilities you may have or, if you are blind, training to use a guide dog;
  - as a part-time student on an employment-related course or time you have spent on a government-sponsored employment or training programme for which no training allowance is paid, if this is for less than three days a week;
- any circumstances that have resulted in your being treated as being available for work (see p437);
- whether you have applied for, taken part in or accepted a place on a course funded by the government or European Union, which is designed to help you select, train for, obtain or retain employment or self-employment;
- if you are homeless, the steps which you needed to take and did take to find a home. It should be accepted that being homeless may limit the steps you can take to look for work and that you need time to look for somewhere to live.

If your chances of getting work are poor, there may only be a limited number of steps you can take each week, but it may be reasonable for the DWP to expect you to pursue all of them every week. If your chances of getting work are good, there may be many steps you could take each week but it would not be reasonable for the DWP to expect you to take all of them.[72]

Proving you are actively seeking work

It is important to keep careful records of the steps you take to get a job.

- Make a note every time you do anything that might count as a 'step' towards actively seeking work (see p448). Include the dates and times, who you spoke to and what was said.
- Keep copies of any letters or emails you send, and of any advertisements to which you reply.
- Tell the EO if you have difficulty reading or writing, or with the English language. You can get a friend or relative to help you compile your record (and to help you look for jobs). The DWP may be prepared to accept an oral report. You could keep a written record in your first language and take an interpreter or ask for an interpreter to be provided by the DWP.

Actively seeking work during your 'permitted period'

If you have been allowed a 'permitted period' (see p444), you count as actively seeking work during that period even if you are only looking for jobs in your normal line of work or at your normal level of pay, or both.[73] If you have been self-employed in your usual occupation at any time within the 12 months before you claim JSA, you count as actively seeking work if you are seeking self-employment in that occupation.

Treated as actively seeking work

Even if you are not actively seeking work, you can be treated as if you are.

- You can count as actively seeking work while you are laid off or on short-time working (see p484).[74]
- You are allowed two weeks (longer in some circumstances) during which you are regarded as actively seeking work while away from home (see p451).
- Other situations in which you can be treated as actively seeking work generally mirror those where you are treated as 'available for work' and have the same maximum lengths (see p437).[75] However, in most cases you are only considered to be actively seeking work if the situation affects you for at least three days in the 'benefit week' (see p426 for the definition). There are differences.
  - You are treated as actively seeking work in any week which is part of a period in which you are taking active steps to set yourself up as self-employed under a scheme to assist people to do so.[76] This only applies during a single period lasting no more than eight weeks in any period of entitlement to JSA, starting with the week in which you are accepted on a place under the scheme. The scheme must be provided or funded by a specified government agency. **Note:** if you are participating in New Enterprise Allowance (see p471), you do not have to actively seek work.[77]
  - You are not treated as actively seeking work just because you have caring responsibilities for a child under 16 in the situations when you can be treated as available for work described on p438.
  - You are treated as actively seeking work for any week in which you spend at least three days on a government-sponsored employment or training course or programme for which you are not paid a training allowance.[78] This does not apply if you are on Work Experience (see p474). **Note:** if you are participating in the Employment, Skills and Enterprise Scheme and either count as a full-time student or it is the first week after you are released from detention in prison, a remand centre or youth custody, you do not have to actively seek work, but you are likely to be required to take specific steps while participating.[79]
- If you are attending a **'qualifying course'** with the approval of an EO (see p439) and are treated as being available for work, you are also treated as actively seeking work.[80] If this is in any week that falls entirely in a vacation,

you must take such steps as can reasonably be expected in order to have the best prospects of securing 'casual employment' (see p440 for the meaning).

Note: the government says that from 23 April 2012, you will also be treated as actively seeking work for four weeks if you notify the DWP that you have experienced, or been threatened with, domestic violence from your partner, your former partner or a family member.[81] This period will be extended to 13 weeks if you provide relevant evidence during the four-week period. You will only be treated as available for work under this rule once in any 12-month period. The four and 13 weeks run on whether or not you are entitled to JSA for the whole period. However, you will be able to ask for the 13-week period to be suspended.

Absence from home

While you are on JSA, you can be treated as actively seeking work while away from home – eg, on holiday.[82] You still have to be available for work, so you are expected to give an assurance that you are willing and able to cut your absence short if notified of a job. In any 12-month period, you can be away from home for up to:[83]

- three weeks, if during each week you spend at least three days on an Outward Bound course; *or*
- if you are blind, two weeks, plus up to four other weeks spent attending training in the use of guide dogs for at least three days a week; *or*
- two weeks, in any other case.

If you are away for longer than this and so cannot be treated as actively seeking work, you must show that you are looking for work while you are away.

If you are considering going away from home, remember the following.

- You must inform the DWP before you go away. Your EO can require you to give notice in writing.
- You must be available for work and able to receive information about job offers. You must, therefore, provide details of how you can be contacted or how you plan to contact the DWP while you are away.[84]
- You must usually be in Great Britain to qualify for JSA. To see if you can get JSA while temporarily away see p1490, and to see if you can be treated as available for work, see p440. If you are unemployed and want to look for work in a European Economic Area country, see p1492 to see if you can export your contribution-based JSA. See p399 if you are going to be temporarily away for the purpose of getting NHS hospital treatment. Even if you cannot get JSA while you are away, you might be able to get NI credits (see p780).
- Before you leave, check with your Jobcentre Plus office when you must sign on when you return home (see p419). This could be a day that is not your usual signing day. If you do not sign on when you are supposed to, you may lose

benefit for the whole of the period you were away unless you can show you had 'good cause' for failing to sign on (see p425).

The jobseeker's agreement

To qualify for JSA you must agree and sign a 'jobseeker's agreement'. It enables the DWP to monitor and direct your search for a job and gives you a chance to put any restrictions on your availability for work that are agreed on record. It is discussed with you during your initial interview (see p415).

Some people getting a training allowance do not have to have a current jobseeker's agreement (see p438). In some cases you can qualify for joint-claim JSA even if you or your partner (but not both of you) do not have a current jobseeker's agreement (see p396).

Until you have agreed the contents of the jobseeker's agreement with your EO, your claim for JSA is not passed to a decision maker to decide whether you are entitled to JSA. However, see below for situations when you can be treated as having signed an agreement. If a decision on your claim is delayed or JSA is refused because you have not entered into a jobseeker's agreement, you may be able to get hardship payments (see p484).

The agreement is not valid until it has been signed by you and the EO.[85] It can be in electronic form and can be signed by an electronic signature.[86] You must be given a copy.[87] To find out when your agreement can be backdated, see p455. For what happens if you cannot agree, see p454.

Future changes

From some point in future (probably in 2012), instead of having a current jobseeker's agreement, you will have to accept a 'claimant commitment', which will set out the responsibilities you must meet to qualify for JSA. See CPAG's *Welfare Rights Bulletin* for updates.

What is in the jobseeker's agreement

A jobseeker's agreement must contain specific information such as your name and the date of the agreement. It must also include:[88]

- the type of job you are looking for – ie, the type of work you are going to actively seek. If you are allowed to place restrictions on the type of work for which you are available, these are entered in a separate box;[89]
- unless you say that you are prepared to work at any time, the total number of hours that you are available for work each week, with a breakdown of what hours you are available on each day. This is known as your 'pattern of availability'. For information on restricting the number of hours and the times for which you are available, see p445;

- how quickly you must be available for work (see p436) and other restrictions you are placing on the work for which you are available – eg, the level of pay or the distance you are prepared to travel;
- the steps you are to take to seek work or to improve your chances of work – eg, attending relevant courses;
- if you have been allowed a 'permitted period' (see p444), the dates on which it starts and ends;
- a statement of your rights if you and the EO cannot agree on what should be in the agreement.

The agreement also advises you to keep a record of what you do to find work and that if you do not do enough, your JSA might be affected.

Your jobseeker's agreement is not binding on you or the DWP; there is no penalty if you fail to keep it.[90] However, the contents of the agreement and whether you have abided by it are very important evidence if there is ever a dispute about whether you are available for, or actively seeking, work. If you have done everything in your jobseeker's agreement, argue that you should not be accused of not actively seeking work.[91]

Treated as signing a jobseeker's agreement

There are rules that treat you as signing a jobseeker's agreement. These are mainly to deal with situations where there is an unavoidable delay between the date you claim JSA and the date of your initial interview with an EO (see p415), and so enable JSA to be put into payment prior to the interview. You can be treated as signing a jobseeker's agreement:[92]

- for the period from your date of claim until the date of your interview with a visiting EO, if relevant;
- if you stop claiming JSA before your interview;
- for as long as you are treated as being available for work because of circumstances that arose between the date of your claim and your interview;
- if there are circumstances affecting the normal procedures for claiming, awarding or paying JSA (eg, a computer failure at the DWP, a strike by staff or severe weather), which make it impracticable or difficult for you to comply with them;[93]
- if you sign on after a period of claiming JSA while getting a training allowance (and not having to have a current jobseeker's agreement), from the date your training course ends until your interview;
- for the period of your temporary absence from Great Britain if you are a member of a joint-claim couple and on the date the other member of the couple makes a claim for JSA you are:
  - in Northern Ireland (for a maximum of four weeks) but only if you are unlikely to be away for more than 52 weeks; *or*
  - attending a job interview (for a maximum of seven days).

Note: the government says that from 23 April 2012, if you have not yet signed a jobseeker's agreement, you will be treated as doing so for four weeks if you notify the DWP that you have experienced, or been threatened with, domestic violence from your partner, your former partner or a family member.[94] This period will be extended to 13 weeks if you provide relevant evidence during the four-week period. You will only be treated as available for work under this rule once in any 12-month period. The four and 13 weeks run on whether or not you are entitled to JSA for the whole period. However, you will be able to ask for the 13-week period to be suspended.

Disputes about a jobseeker's agreement

Your EO is not allowed to sign your jobseeker's agreement unless s/he is satisfied that you will qualify as being available for and actively seeking work if you comply with its terms.[95] If s/he thinks you are placing unreasonable restrictions on your availability for work or that the steps you propose to take to actively seek work are not sufficient, s/he will not sign an agreement based on your proposals.

If this situation arises, the EO may refer a proposed jobseeker's agreement (including one proposed by you) to a decision maker. If you ask your EO to do so, s/he must refer the proposed agreement to a decision maker immediately.[96] You should immediately apply for hardship payments (see p484).

The decision maker decides:[97]

- whether it is reasonable to expect you to comply with the jobseeker's agreement; *and*
- whether you would qualify as being available for and actively seeking work if you were to comply with it.

The decision maker may also direct the EO to enter into a jobseeker's agreement on whatever terms the decision maker considers appropriate and may also order that, if the agreement is entered into, it should be backdated.[98]

The decision maker must make a decision within 14 days of the agreement being referred, unless to do so would be impracticable, and must notify you of the decision.[99] If you are happy with the decision, you must see your EO and sign the agreement. If you are unhappy with it, you can ask for the decision to be revised or superseded, or appeal to the First-tier Tribunal (see Chapters 45 and 46).

If the decision maker decides in your favour, your jobseeker's agreement is normally backdated and you are paid arrears of JSA from the date of your claim. However, if the decision maker decides against you, you are unlikely to get any backdating. You therefore risk losing benefit if you refuse to sign the jobseeker's agreement and insist on it being referred to a decision maker.

Rather than refusing to sign the jobseeker's agreement proposed by your EO, it may be better to sign it and then write to the DWP saying that you would like to change it (see p455). You should not lose JSA so long as you comply with the original agreement while the variation is being considered. It is important you make it clear that you intend to do so. If there is a doubt about whether you are available for or actively seeking work, payment of your JSA could be suspended (see p1043).

Backdating the jobseeker's agreement

A jobseeker's agreement is automatically backdated to the first day from which you claimed JSA, so long as you and your EO can agree about what it should contain and it is not referred to a decision maker.[100] This includes any date to which your claim has been backdated (see p1027).

If the agreement is referred to a decision maker, it is only backdated if s/he makes a direction ordering this.[101] S/he must consider all the relevant circumstances including:[102]

- whether it was reasonable for you to refuse to accept the agreement proposed by the EO; *and*
- whether the terms of any alternative agreement that you may have proposed are reasonable; *and*
- whether you have subsequently said that you would be prepared to accept the agreement proposed by the EO; *and*
- the date on which you were first prepared to enter into an agreement that the decision maker considers to be reasonable; *and*
- the fact that the first opportunity you had to sign a jobseeker's agreement was later than the date of your claim for JSA.

Changing your jobseeker's agreement

The terms of your jobseeker's agreement can be changed by agreement between you and your EO. Any change must be in writing and signed by you and the EO.[103] This can be in electronic form and can be signed by an electronic signature.[104]

Both you and the EO can propose changes at any time. Put your proposals in writing, giving full details of the changes you want to make and your reasons. Explain how your proposals give you a reasonable chance of finding a job.

An EO cannot agree to a change unless s/he considers that the terms mean that you satisfy the jobseeking conditions.[105] If you and the EO:

- agree the proposed changes, you must be given a copy of the new jobseeker's agreement;[106]
- do not agree the proposed changes, these can be referred to a decision maker.[107] They *must* be referred to a decision maker if you request this.

When a referral to a decision maker is made

When a proposed change to a jobseeker's agreement is referred to a decision maker, your existing agreement remains in force until a decision is made. Payment of your JSA might be suspended if you do not stick to the terms of the agreement if this causes a doubt about whether you are available for or actively seeking work.

If the decision maker believes that both your and the EO's proposals are reasonable and you would qualify as being available for and actively seeking work, the DWP says s/he should change the agreement along the lines you propose.[108]

The decision maker can direct a change of the jobseeker's agreement and the terms on which you and the EO must agree to change it. S/he can also say when the new agreement takes effect.[109] If a change you proposed is accepted and it makes the terms of the agreement less restrictive, argue that the new agreement should take effect from the date on which you proposed the change.[110]

If you fail to sign the new agreement within 21 days of the date a change in your jobseeker's agreement is directed, the decision maker can bring the agreement to an end.[111] If this happens, you no longer get JSA, including during any revision or appeal period, unless you qualify for hardship payments (see p484).

If you are unhappy with the decision maker's decision, you can request a revision or appeal to the First-tier Tribunal (see Chapters 45 and 46). If your appeal is eventually allowed, the original jobseeker's agreement revives and you are owed arrears even if the First-tier or Upper Tribunal directs another change in the agreement.[112]

2. Sanctions

Even if you are entitled to jobseeker's allowance (JSA), you may find that you are sanctioned for a period. This may happen, for example, if you are dismissed from a job for misconduct or leave a job without just cause, or if you fail to attend a training or employment scheme. There are employment-related sanctions (see p458), jobseeker's direction sanctions (see p469) and training and employment scheme sanctions (see p471).

If you are sanctioned, JSA is not paid or is paid at a reduced rate during a fixed or variable 'sanction period'. For information about the amount of JSA payable if you are sanctioned, see p477. If your JSA is not paid or is paid at a reduced rate, you might be able to get hardship payments (see p484).

Some special rules apply if you are 16 or 17 (see p480).

Sanction	*Period*
Losing a job because of misconduct	Variable: 1–26 weeks
Leaving a job voluntarily	Variable: 1–26 weeks
Failing to apply for or accept a job	Variable: 1–26 weeks
'Neglecting to avail' yourself of a job opportunity	Variable: 1–26 weeks
Failing to carry out a jobseeker's direction	Fixed: 1, 2 or 4 weeks

Employment, Skills and Enterprise Scheme sanctions	Fixed: 2, 4 or 26 weeks
Mandatory Work Activity sanctions	Fixed: 13 or 26 weeks
Other training scheme/employment programme sanctions	Fixed: 2 or 4 weeks

Once a sanction period has begun, it continues unbroken until the sanction period comes to an end.[113] If you take a job or training for a short period but then claim again during the period of the sanction, you are still caught by the sanction.

Bear the following in mind.

- The days in your sanction period count towards your 182 days of entitlement to contribution-based JSA even though you are not actually paid any benefit.
- You are treated as being on income-based JSA if you are not being paid it because of a sanction, so you remain entitled to maximum housing benefit and council tax benefit.[114]
- If you are sanctioned, check whether you (or if you are a member of a 'joint-claim couple', your partner) can claim income support (IS), income-related employment and support allowance (ESA) or pension credit (PC) instead of JSA. If you are not a member of a joint-claim couple and you have a partner, s/he may qualify for JSA, IS, income-related ESA or PC instead.
- If you disagree that you should be sanctioned or disagree with the sanction period, you can challenge the decision (see p478).

Additional rules apply if you have been sanctioned because of benefit offences (see p1106) or because you failed to attend an interview as required (see p422).

Future changes

From some point in future (probably in 2012), tougher sanctions will be introduced. JSA may be paid at a reduced rate:

- for up to three years – ie, if a claimant loses a job through misconduct or without a good reason voluntarily leaves a job, fails to apply for or accept a notified job vacancy, neglects to avail her/himself of a reasonable opportunity of employment or fails to participate in specified training schemes or employment programmes;
- for up to 26 weeks – eg, if a claimant loses a place on a training scheme or employment programme through misconduct or fails without a good reason to participate in certain interviews, fails to apply for or accept a place on a training scheme or employment programme, gives up or fails to attend such a scheme or programme or fails to carry out a jobseeker's direction;
- if a claimant's entitlement to JSA ended because s/he was not available for or actively seeking work, during the period of up to 13 weeks from entitlement ending.

Hardship payments will be available, but will be recoverable. See CPAG's *Welfare Rights Bulletin* for updates.

Employment-related sanctions

You can be sanctioned if you:[115]

- lose a job because of 'misconduct' (see below); *or*
- leave a job voluntarily (see p459); *or*
- refuse or fail to apply for or accept a job (see p462); *or*
- 'neglect to avail' yourself of a job (see p463).

Employment for these purposes does not include self-employment.[116] When considering whether you should be sanctioned, the decision maker should only look at your last employment preceding your claim and your subsequent actions.[117]

Losing a job because of misconduct

You can be sanctioned if you lose your job because of misconduct.[118] This includes if you are suspended from work for misconduct or if you resigned rather than be dismissed.[119] You cannot be sanctioned for misconduct in self-employment.

The sanction period is variable (see p468).

What is misconduct?

'Misconduct' is not defined in the rules. However, bear the following in mind.

- You are guilty of misconduct only if your actions or omissions are 'blameworthy'. This does not mean that it has to be established that you did anything dishonest or that you deliberately did something wrong; serious carelessness or negligence may be enough.[120]
- Everyone makes mistakes or is inefficient from time to time. So, for example, if you are a naturally slow worker who, despite making every effort, cannot produce the output required by your employer, you are not guilty of misconduct even if the poor performance may justify your dismissal.[121]
- The misconduct has to have some connection with your employment. It does not have to take place during working hours to count as misconduct. However, a sanction cannot be imposed if the actions or omissions took place before your employment began – eg, you gave inaccurate information about yourself when applying for the job.[122]
- Some behaviour is clearly misconduct – eg, dishonesty (whether or not connected with your work) if it causes your employer to dismiss you because s/he no longer trusts you.[123]
- Some behaviour is not necessarily misconduct.
  - Bad timekeeping and failing to report in time that you are sick might amount to misconduct – eg, if you were persistently late or failed to report that you were sick on a number of occasions.
  - A refusal to carry out a reasonable instruction by an employer is not misconduct if you had a good reason for refusing or your refusal was due to a genuine misunderstanding.[124]

- Breaking rules covering personal conduct might be misconduct, depending on the seriousness of the breach. A breach of a trivial rule might not be misconduct.[125]
- A refusal to work overtime is misconduct if you were under a duty to work overtime when required and the request to do it was reasonable.

Although evidence from your employer is taken into account, the fact that s/he did not describe your actions as 'misconduct' does not guarantee that you can escape a sanction. However, this should go heavily in your favour.

Whether misconduct caused the loss of employment

Your misconduct need not be the only cause of the loss of your employment, but it must be an immediate and substantial reason for your losing your job.[126] If your misconduct was not the real reason for your dismissal (eg, your employer used this as an excuse to dismiss you, but really only wanted to reduce numbers of staff), you should not be sanctioned.

It is not relevant that your dismissal was unreasonable or an overreaction on your employer's part. However, seek advice to see whether you might have a case for unfair dismissal at an employment tribunal.

If there was misconduct, the exact way in which you lost your employment is not important. You may be summarily dismissed, be dismissed with notice or resign as an alternative to possible dismissal.[127]

Leaving your job voluntarily

You can be sanctioned if you leave your job 'voluntarily' without 'just cause' (see p460).[128] A sanction can only be imposed if:

- you were in employment (not self-employment); *and*
- you were not in a 'trial period' (see p464).

The decision maker has to show that you left your employment voluntarily. You must then show that you had 'just cause' for leaving if you want to avoid a sanction.

The sanction period is variable (see p468).

Whether you left voluntarily

'Voluntarily' is not defined in the rules, but the DWP says it means that you have *brought your employment* to an end by your own acts and of your own free will.[129] You have not left your employment voluntarily if you had no choice in the matter or there is convincing evidence (eg, medical evidence from your GP) that you were not responsible for your actions.

If you resign because you genuinely believe that your employer is about to end your employment or because you were given the 'choice' of resignation or dismissal, you have not left your job voluntarily. However, the DWP may then consider whether you lost your job through misconduct (see p458).

You are likely to be treated as leaving your job voluntarily if you resign giving notice. However, when deciding the length of the sanction period, the decision maker should take into account whether you:[130]

- were willing to work your notice (but your employer would not let you) and you might have had a better chance of finding other work while you were still in the job;
- tried to withdraw your notice, even if this was not accepted.

Your employer may have given you notice to end your employment but then cancelled or suspended it, allowing you to continue in the same employment. If you decide not to continue in the employment and it is clear that you have a genuine choice to remain, you are likely to be treated as leaving voluntarily.[131] However, the circumstances may be such as to amount to 'just cause' (see below) or to justify a reduction in the sanction period (see p468).

You have *not* left your job voluntarily if:

- you **volunteer, or accept your employer's proposal, for redundancy.**[132] This only applies where there is a redundancy situation at your workplace – eg, if a whole factory or department is closing down or if there is a cut in the number of people needed to carry out certain tasks.[133] This is the case even if you were offered, or you could have applied for, alternative jobs with the same employer. However, if you refuse other work, you might be sanctioned for another reason – eg, refusing employment or 'neglecting to avail' yourself of an opportunity of employment (see pp462 and 463). **Note:** there is no special rule to help you if you take early retirement (see p462);
- your **employer ends your contract of employment.**[134] A change in your terms or conditions by your employer can mean that s/he has ended your existing contract of employment – eg, if a change is imposed without your agreement and the new terms are less favourable than before. If you leave your employment as a result, try to argue that you have not left your job voluntarily but have been dismissed, or that you had 'just cause' for leaving.

'Just cause' for leaving your job

If the decision maker says that you left your job voluntarily, it is up to you to show that you had 'just cause' for doing so. 'Just cause' is not defined in the rules. It is not the same as 'good cause', which applies to other sanctions. The decision maker must take all the circumstances into account when deciding if you have just cause. This must include:[135]

- any caring responsibilities you have (see p437 for what counts) for a child under 16, which made it unreasonable for you to stay in your job. In deciding whether it was unreasonable, the decision maker must look at whether childcare was (or could have been) reasonably available to you and, if so, if it was (or would have been) unsuitable because of your, or the child's, needs; *and*

- any childcare expenses you had to pay as a result of being in the job, if they amounted to an unreasonably high proportion of the income you received. The proportion that is considered reasonable increases the more you are paid.

To have 'just cause' for leaving your job, you must show that you acted reasonably in leaving and also that the circumstances of your case make it proper that public funds should support you.[136] You cannot argue you had 'just cause' simply because the conditions of your employment were poor, but see p491 if there was a breach in the law on minimum working conditions. You are expected if possible to take steps through the proper channels to sort out any problems – eg, by raising them with your employer or using any grievance procedure, rather than leaving immediately,[137] and to look for another job seriously before giving one up. Even if you could have declined to take up the job without being sanctioned (eg, because you were in a 'permitted period' – see p444), this does not necessarily give you 'just cause' for voluntarily leaving the job later. However, this could be relevant to the length of any sanction period (see p468).[138]

You might have 'just cause' for leaving a job in the following situations.

- Your **chances of getting other employment**, including self-employment, **were good** and, in addition, there were strong reasons for leaving your job and you acted reasonably in doing so.[139]
- You genuinely did not know or were mistaken about the **conditions of the job** (eg, it was beyond your physical or mental capacity, or was harmful to your health), you gave it a fair trial before leaving and it was reasonable for you to have left when you did.[140]
- You left your job for **personal or domestic reasons** – eg, you gave up work to look after a sick relative.[141] You have to justify leaving your job before looking for alternative employment. It could be helpful to show that you tried to negotiate an arrangement with your employer to resolve the problem – eg, for a reduction in your hours or time off work.
- If you leave your job to **move with your partner** who has taken a job elsewhere, you can try to argue that you have 'just cause' or that the length of the sanction period should be limited.[142] Relevant factors may include how important it was to your partner's career to make the move and how good your chances are of finding work in the new area.
- Your employer made a **change in the terms and conditions of your employment** that does not amount to your contract of employment ending. You are expected to use any grievance procedure first.

  Decision makers are not allowed to take 'any matter relating to the level of remuneration' into account when deciding whether or not you have 'just cause' for leaving your job (but see p491 if your employer is paying below the national minimum wage).[143] This appears to mean that if you leave your job because your employer cuts your wages unilaterally, you are not able to show 'just cause'. However, a cut in pay can mean your existing contract of employment has ended and, therefore, you have been dismissed rather than having left your job.

- You left your job because of a **firm offer of alternative employment**, but claimed JSA because the offer fell through. You should be treated as having 'just cause' for leaving, unless the offer was cancelled before you left your previous employment or you changed your mind and did not take the new job and you could have stayed in the existing employment, or did not ask your employer if you could stay.[144]

Even if it is decided that you do not have 'just cause' for leaving your job, these factors may work in your favour in reducing the sanction period.

Taking retirement

If you take retirement before pension age, you might be regarded as having left your job voluntarily.[145] Under employment law, your employer cannot, except in special situations, make you retire at any particular age, so taking retirement is something you do of your own choice. However, you might be able to show 'just cause' if, for example, you can show that the work was getting too much for you because of your age or your health.

Employers sometimes institute special early retirement schemes (ie, allowing you to take your occupational pension at an earlier age than normal) which run for a limited period, often in order to deal with a redundancy situation. In that case, you come under the special rules about redundancy (see p460). Employers often try to avoid using the word 'redundancy' and you may have to prove to the decision maker that a redundancy situation existed.

If you take early retirement under some other special scheme, you cannot show 'just cause' merely because your action was in your employer's interest.[146] However, this might be an argument for reducing the length of the sanction period, particularly if you worked in the public sector and could say that your action was in the public interest.[147]

Refusing or failing to apply for or to accept a job

You can be sanctioned if you are notified by the DWP of a job vacancy and you do not apply for it or refuse to accept it when offered to you.[148] This does not apply if you can show 'good cause' (see p465). **Note:** the decision maker cannot apply this sanction if the job was vacant because of a stoppage of work caused by a trade dispute.[149]

If you repeatedly fail to take jobs that are offered to you, a decision maker may also decide you are not available for or actively seeking work and refuse you JSA altogether.

The sanction period is variable (see p468).

Notification of a job vacancy

To be sanctioned, you must have been notified of a job vacancy by the DWP orally, in writing or by other means. No sanction should be imposed if you did not receive the notification. A job advert that is simply displayed in a Jobcentre Plus office or on the Jobcentre Plus website does not by itself amount to a notification by the DWP. However, if you identify a vacancy yourself and then discuss it with a DWP adviser, the DWP may say you have been 'notified'.[150] You must be given sufficient information to enable you to pursue the vacancy or to make an informed decision about whether to pursue it.[151]

If you are notified of a vacancy and are unsure about what your financial situation would be, check the amount of benefits and tax credits for which you would qualify if you took the job – eg, working tax credit, council tax benefit and housing benefit. If you need help with the calculations, seek advice. Remember that you may not be able to show 'good cause' for refusing a job because of your income or the rate of pay (see p467).

Treated as refusing to apply for or accept a job

The DWP might treat you as having refused to apply for or accept a job if:[152]

- you fail to complete the job application form properly or give inappropriate answers to questions on the form. However, if you submit your application to the DWP and it does not pass this on to a potential employer, you can argue that you did not fail to apply for the job; *or*
- you fail to attend or are late for a job interview, or you go to the wrong place through your own negligence; *or*
- you behave in such a way that you lose the chance of getting the job. This should only apply to things you actually said or did (or refused to do) and should not apply just because a prospective employer disliked your appearance or manner; *or*
- you accept a job but fail to start it or impose unreasonable conditions so that the offer is withdrawn.

You can be expected to apply for and accept temporary work. You cannot escape a sanction on the grounds that a job is temporary, but the decision maker should take the date the job would have ended into account when deciding the period of any sanction (see p468).

'Neglecting to avail' yourself of a job

You can be sanctioned if you fail to take up ('neglect to avail' yourself of) a reasonable opportunity of employment without 'good cause' (see p465).[153] You do not have to be notified of a vacancy by the DWP for this sanction to apply.

The sanction period is variable (see p468).

When this sanction applies

In practice, this sanction usually applies in situations where you do not return to work with a former employer after what was originally intended to be a temporary break – eg, if you decide not to resume work after maternity leave or you refuse an offer of alternative employment in a redundancy situation. A sanction should only be imposed if you 'neglect to avail' yourself of an opportunity of employment that was in a 'qualifying former employment' (see below). This is because you automatically have good cause for 'neglecting to avail' yourself of the job if it is *not* a qualifying former employment (see p466).

The DWP is likely to apply a sanction if, for example, you knew you had a reasonable chance of getting the job and did not take the necessary steps to get it. However, it cannot apply the sanction if:

- the job was vacant because of a stoppage of work caused by a trade dispute;[154] *or*
- the 'opportunity' is for further work with an employer you have been working for during a 'trial period' (see below).

'Qualifying former employment'

A job counts as a 'qualifying former employment' if:[155]

- it is with an employer you previously worked for or an employer who took over the business from your former employer; *and*
- it is not more than a year between the date you last worked for the employer and the date the question of a sanction arises; *and*
- the terms and conditions are not less favourable than those of the job you had when you last worked for the employer.

The date on which you last worked for the employer is the date you last attended work, not the last date for which you were paid.

Trial periods

In certain circumstances, you may take a job for a trial period and leave it without the risk of being sanctioned for leaving voluntarily or for 'neglecting to avail' yourself of a reasonable opportunity of employment (see pp459 and 463).[156] The rules lay down both a minimum and a maximum length for the trial period. You *must* leave the employment within the specified times to avoid being sanctioned. You do not have to have agreed with the DWP that you were taking up the employment on a trial basis. If you leave shortly before or after the trial period and are sanctioned, you can try to argue for a shorter sanction period (see p468).[157]

Trial period

A *'trial period'* is the period of eight weeks starting with the beginning of your fifth week and ending at the end of your 12th week in a job. For this purpose, weeks in which you work for fewer than 16 hours are ignored.[158] The DWP includes periods when you are not actually working but you are required by contract to be in a certain place in order to carry out a job.[159] Periods when you are off work sick or on holiday, even if you are paid, do not count when calculating the number of hours.

To be sure you are covered by this rule, you must work at least some of the fifth week and leave before you have worked all of the 12th. In calculating the fifth and the 12th weeks, the 'week' starts on the day you begin work and ends at midnight seven days later.[160]

The **trial period rule applies** if, for at least 13 weeks before the day you begin employment, you have not:[161]

- worked (including as a self-employed person); *or*
- been a full-time student (see p637) or in 'relevant education' (see p634). You do not count as a full-time student if you were in receipt of a training allowance.[162]

Even if you cannot satisfy this 13-week rule, if all the other trial period rules are met, you can argue for the minimum sanction.[163]

If you are dismissed or you leave the job as an alternative to being dismissed, you might still be sanctioned if this was because of misconduct.

Note: if you do not claim JSA for more than 12 consecutive weeks (ie, until after the trial period), a new 'jobseeking period' (see p394) begins when you next claim. This means:

- you have to serve a further three waiting days (see p402) before getting JSA; *and*
- you may not qualify for contribution-based JSA if you no longer satisfy the contribution conditions.

Employment-related sanctions and 'good cause'

A sanction cannot be imposed if you have 'good cause' for:

- refusing or failing to apply for, or refusing to accept, a job (see p462);
- 'neglecting to avail' yourself of a job opportunity (see p463).

A sanction also cannot be imposed if you have good cause for failing or refusing to carry out a reasonable jobseeker's direction (see p469). The 'good cause' rules in this section apply.

The factors which may mean you have 'good cause' depend on the sanction. The decision maker must take all the circumstances into account. Some circumstances:

- automatically count as 'good cause' (see p466);
- must be taken into account when deciding whether you have 'good cause' (see p467);
- do not count as 'good cause' (see p467).

There are some special rules for 16/17-year-olds (see p481).

Different 'good cause' rules apply when a sanction is connected with a training or employment scheme. Remember that you can be sanctioned for leaving a job voluntarily without 'just cause' rather than 'good cause'.

Circumstances that count as good cause

You have 'good cause' if:[164]

- you refuse to apply for or accept a job involving fewer than 24 hours' work a week (16 hours if you have been allowed to restrict your availability for work to less than 24 hours a week – see p445). This ground does not apply if you refuse or fail to carry out a jobseeker's direction. However, you may be able to challenge the direction as unreasonable (see p470);
- you do not accept a job that is vacant because of a trade dispute – ie, you are not required to be a strike-breaker;[165]
- you are within your 'permitted period' (see p444) and have restricted the type of work for which you are available to your usual occupation or to at least your usual rate of pay, and you refuse a job that does not meet these conditions;
- you have trained for a particular type of work for at least two calendar months. You do not have to accept work in any other kind of employment for four weeks after your training ends. A 'week' for these purposes means any period of seven consecutive days.[166] 'Training' for these purposes is not defined and should be given its ordinary everyday meaning;
- you have 'neglected to avail' yourself of an opportunity of employment, unless it is a 'qualifying former employment' (see p463);
- you have been laid off or are on short-time working, have been accepted as available only for casual employment (see p483), and you refuse to take some other type of work;
- you come under the rules that exempt you from having to be able to start work immediately or you have said that you are only available to work at certain times and you are not required to take up employment at times when you are not available, and you refuse to take a job where you would have to start work immediately or during times when you are not required to be available (see p436);
- you fail or refuse to apply for or accept a notified job vacancy, or 'neglect to avail' yourself of an opportunity of employment in a 'qualifying former employment' (see p463) while on a 'qualifying course' as a full-time student (see p439) and:
  - this happens in the four weeks before the end of the course or your examinations; *or*
  - it is other than casual employment during your vacation, unless it is permanent full-time paid work (16 hours or more a week).

Circumstances that must be taken into account

If you do not have automatic good cause, the decision maker must take certain circumstances into account when deciding whether you have 'good cause'.[167] These must include:

- any restrictions you have been allowed to place on your availability for work, having regard to any discrepancy between these and the requirements of the job, although minor differences might not count. Although you do not necessarily have good cause for refusing to apply for a job covered by your restrictions, it is a very significant factor to take into account;[168]
- any condition of yours or personal circumstances that suggest that a particular job, or carrying out a jobseeker's direction, would be likely to cause you excessive physical or mental stress or significant harm to your health;
- any sincerely held religious or conscientious objection;
- any caring responsibilities (see p437 for what counts) that make it unreasonable for you to do the job or carry out a jobseeker's direction. If you have caring responsibilities for a child under 16, the decision maker must look at whether childcare would have been (or was) reasonably available and, if so, whether it was unsuitable for your, or the child's, needs;
- the travelling time involved between your home and the place of work (or a place mentioned in a jobseeker's direction), but see p468 for when this does not count as good cause;
- expenses unavoidably incurred (eg, childcare and travelling expenses), or that you had to (or would have had to) incur if you had taken the job or carried out the jobseeker's direction, if they amounted (or would have amounted) to an unreasonably high proportion of the income you would have received. The proportion that is considered reasonable increases the more you are paid.

Account should also be taken of any other factor that appears relevant. See, in particular, p491 for when the terms of a job on offer break the laws on minimum working conditions.

Circumstances that do not count as good cause

You cannot refuse to apply for a job simply because of the rate of pay offered.[169] However, see p491 if the rate of pay is below the minimum wage.

In addition, you cannot show good cause if you refuse or fail to apply for a job or to carry out a jobseeker's direction because of:[170]

- your income or outgoings or those of any member of your household (see p754), either as they are now or as they would be if you took the job or carried out the direction. For these purposes, 'outgoings' do not include any expenses (including for childcare) taken into account that would be an unreasonably high proportion of your income (see above).

You cannot, for example, argue that you need a high wage because you have a large mortgage or an expensive lifestyle. You might be able to show good cause if:[171]
- you have been allowed to place restrictions on the rate of pay you will accept because of your physical or mental condition (see p444), or under the rules about a 'permitted period' (see p444); *or*
- the job you have refused to accept would have been paid on a commission-only basis; *or*
- unless it is unreasonable because of your health or caring responsibilities (see p437 for what counts), the travelling time between your home and the place of work (or a place mentioned in a jobseeker's direction) if this is less than:[172]
  - one hour either way, during the first 13 weeks you are entitled to JSA; *or*
  - one and a half hours either way, in all other cases.

Length of the sanction period

Unless you are 16 or 17 (see p482), the sanction period for all the employment related sanctions is variable. A variable sanction can be any length from one week to 26 weeks.[173] Sanction periods are usually complete weeks, but there is nothing in the rules to prevent them including part-weeks. However, a sanction of at least one week must be imposed, even if the decision maker thinks that the appropriate sanction period is less than one week.

Deciding the length of the sanction period

In deciding the length of the sanction period, the decision maker can take into account anything that provides some reason for your conduct. You should be given a chance to provide information and evidence.[174] The rationale behind sanctions is that your conduct should not result in unnecessary expenditure of public funds. However, bear the following in mind.
- A 26-week sanction period should only be imposed in the most serious cases. In other cases, the correct length of the sanction period should be determined by referring to any aggravating or mitigating factors.[175]
- A lot of caselaw on variable sanction periods was decided when the minimum period of a sanction was one day and the maximum six weeks, and when payment of benefit was reduced rather than stopped altogether. Although the principles still apply, they should be applied less harshly.
- If you would have been allowed to give up a job during a 'trial period' (see p464) but for the fact that you left the job too soon, you can argue that the appropriate sanction is one that reflects the balance of the minimum trial period, plus a further period to reflect the possibility that if you had given the job a longer trial, you might have decided to stay.[176]
- There should be a difference in the sanction imposed if you have simply failed to apply for a job vacancy, as opposed to refusing to accept an offer of

employment or losing your job through misconduct, particularly if you were unlikely to get the job.[177]

Decision makers must consider:[178]

- how long the employment you left or failed to take up was likely to have lasted, if this would have been less than 26 weeks. The decision maker should not impose a sanction for a period longer than the job would have lasted;
- if you left a job:
  - because of misconduct but your employer is prepared to take you back, the date you are to resume work. The decision maker should end the sanction period by at least that date;
  - voluntarily and the job was for 16 hours or less a week, the rate of pay and hours of work in that job. If the job did not provide an adequate income, this is a mitigating factor;
  - voluntarily or you 'neglected to avail' yourself of a reasonable opportunity of employment, any physical or mental stress connected with the job.

The decision maker should also take account of any time during which you were not receiving JSA since the date you, for example, stopped work. The DWP says that having calculated the length of the sanction period that is appropriate in your case, the decision maker subtracts days you were not receiving JSA.[179] The result of this deduction may be that the sanction period is reduced to nothing, so you are not sanctioned if more than 26 weeks have passed between your leaving your last job and claiming JSA.

Jobseeker's direction sanctions

You can be sanctioned if you refuse or fail to carry out a reasonable jobseeker's direction, without 'good cause' (see p465).[180] The 'good cause' rules are the same as for employment-related sanctions.

The sanction period is fixed at one, two or four weeks (see p470).

A jobseeker's direction

A **'jobseeker's direction'** is a written notice from your employment officer (EO) telling you to take specific action to assist you to find a job or increase your chances of employment.[181] For example, you might be directed to take part in a 'back to work session' (see p470) or to apply for a specific job vacancy, to attend a training or employment scheme, or to improve your appearance or behaviour in order to present yourself better to potential employers. You can be given an opportunity to take the action voluntarily before any direction is given. It must be clear that you are being given a jobseeker's direction.

A jobseeker's direction can be given at any time and more than once. It states the time within which you are expected to comply with it and checks are made to ensure that you have done so. Each refusal to carry out a direction could result in you being sanctioned.

Is a jobseeker's direction 'reasonable'?

A jobseeker's direction must be reasonable. It would not be reasonable, for example, if it would not help you find a job or increase your chances of being employed, was at odds with your sincere conscientious or religious beliefs or might unlawfully discriminate on grounds such as gender, disability, religion or nationality.

Any jobseeker's direction must be relevant to *your* needs and to the circumstances of the local labour market. If the EO accepts that a jobseeker's direction was unreasonable, or could not be carried out in the time required, s/he cancels the direction.

If a jobseeker's direction requires you to apply for a job that is for less than 24 hours a week (16 hours a week if you have been allowed to restrict your availabilty for work to less than 24 hours a week), you can argue that you have good cause for refusing or failing to carry it out, or that the direction is unreasonable. This is because you should not be sanctioned for refusing to apply for, or accept, a notified job vacancy for less than 24/16 hours a week (see p466).

Length of the sanction period

If you are sanctioned because you refused to carry out a jobseeker's direction, the sanction period is fixed at one, two or four weeks.[182] If the sanction relates to a 'back to work session', a sanction is imposed for one week.[183] A 'back to work session' is a seminar or appointment which provides you with information, support and advice with a view to assisting you to find, or improve your chances of finding, employment.[184]

Unless a one-week sanction applies (see above), a sanction is imposed for:[185]

- two weeks; *or*
- four weeks, if you are sanctioned within 12 months of a previous fixed-period sanction (including where the previous sanction was a training scheme or employment programme sanction under the rules described on pp474–476). The 12 months run from the date the previous sanction took effect to the date of the decision imposing the current sanction.[186]

The sanction period usually starts on the first day of the benefit week after the date of the decision to sanction you.[187]

If you are given a four-week sanction but later the first (two-week) sanction is removed (eg, by the First-tier Tribunal), ask a decision maker to reduce the four-week sanction period.[188] If s/he fails to do so, appeal. If you have already appealed against the second sanction, the Tribunal should take the removal of the first sanction into account.[189]

Training and employment scheme sanctions

If participation or attendance on a training or employment scheme is compulsory, you can be sanctioned if you fail to participate or attend. When a sanction can be imposed and how long it lasts depends on the scheme. For:

- the Employment, Skills and Enterprise Scheme (including the Work Programme), see below;
- Mandatory Work Activity, see p473; *and*
- other training schemes and employment programmes (including Work Experience), see p474.

The sanction period is fixed at two, four, 13 or 26 weeks, depending on the scheme and the number of times you have been sanctioned. See pp472, 473 and 476 for further information. **Note:**

- Although other training schemes and initiatives to help you find work are not compulsory, your EO can compel you to attend one by issuing a jobseeker's direction (see p469).
- Seek advice if you are unsure whether a scheme or programme is compulsory.
- Some training schemes and employment programmes are no longer offered – eg, the Flexible New Deal, the Community Task Force and the Intensive Activity Period. However, if you had a sanction relating to one of these, it could affect the length of some further fixed-period sanctions (see p476).

The Employment, Skills and Enterprise Scheme

The Employment, Skills and Enterprise Scheme (the Scheme) is aimed at helping people claiming JSA to find employment or self-employment and to obtain the necessary skills to do so. It currently includes:

- the Work Programme (back-to-work and in-work support);
- Skills Conditionality (skills training);
- sector-based work academies (pre-employment training, work experience and a guaranteed job interview). **Note:** it is voluntary to agree to participate, in sector-based work academies, but if you agree it becomes compulsory and you can be sanctioned. However, the government says that sanctions should not be applied other than in cases of misconduct;
- New Enterprise Allowance (self-employment support); *and*
- Community Action Programme (26 weeks of community work for 30 hours a week – in pilot areas only).

Schemes can be added to or removed from the Scheme.

You can be required to participate in the Scheme; it is then compulsory.[190] You must be given notice in writing.[191] The notice must give you specified information, including the day on which your participation will begin and what you must do to participate. The requirement to participate:[192]

- is suspended if you are no longer required to meet the jobseeking conditions; *or*
- ceases if your award of JSA ends or you are given written notice that you are no longer required to participate.

Note: if you are participating in New Enterprise Allowance, you do not have to actively seek work.[193] If you are participating in any part of the Scheme and count as a full-time student (eg, you are doing full-time training), you do not have to be available for work or to actively seek work.[194] If you are required to participate in any part of the Scheme and it is the first week after you are released from detention in prison, a remand centre or youth custody, you do not have to be available for work or to actively seek work.[195] However, you may be required to take specifed steps while participating.

The sanction period is fixed at two, four or 26 weeks (see below).

When you can be sanctioned

If you fail to participate in the Scheme (ie, you fail to comply with any requirements in the notice), you are notified by the DWP. You are sanctioned unless you show 'good cause' for your failure within five working days of the date you are notified of the failure.[196]

'Good cause' is not defined in the rules but in deciding whether you have good cause, the DWP must take all your circumstances into account, and in particular your physical and mental health or condition.[197] The DWP says that the circumstances that count as good cause for the other training scheme and employment programmes (see p475) should be considered.[198]

Fixed sanction periods

If you are sanctioned because you fail to participate in the Scheme without 'good cause', a sanction is imposed for:[199]

- two weeks; *or*
- four weeks, if you are given a sanction within 12 months of a previous Scheme sanction; *or*
- 26 weeks, if you are given a Scheme sanction on three or more occasions and it is no more than 12 months since the previous one. See p473 for when a sanction period can end early.

The 12 months run from the date the previous sanction took effect to the date of the decision imposing the current sanction.[200]

If you are given a four- or 26-week sanction but later the first (two-week or four-week) sanction is removed (eg, by the First-tier Tribunal), ask a decision maker to reduce the sanction period.[201] If s/he fails to do so, appeal. If you have already appealed against the second sanction, the Tribunal should take the removal of the first sanction into account.[202]

Instead of lasting 26 weeks, a **sanction can end early** if:

- you begin to participate in the Scheme again. In this case, the sanction period lasts four weeks or until the end of the benefit week in which you begin to participate again, if this is longer;[203]
- the DWP notifies you that you no longer have to participate in the Scheme. In this case, the sanction period ends one week after the date of the notice or at the end of the benefit week in which you are no longer required to participate, if this is longer.[204]

Mandatory Work Activity

Mandatory Work Activity is a scheme that provides four weeks of work (or work-related activity) of up to 30 hours a week. If you are 18 or over you can be required to participate in Mandatory Work Activity; it is then compulsory.[205] You must be given notice in writing.[206] The notice must give you specified information, including the day on which your participation will begin and what you must do to participate. The requirement to participate ceases if your award of JSA ends or you are given written notice that you are no longer required to participate.[207]

The sanction period is fixed at 13 or 26 weeks (see below).

When you can be sanctioned

If you fail to participate in Mandatory Work Activity (ie, you fail to comply with any requirements in the notice), you are notified by the DWP. You are sanctioned unless you show 'good cause' for your failure within five working days of the date you are notified of the failure.[208]

'Good cause' is not defined in the rules but in deciding whether you have good cause, the DWP must take all your circumstances into account and, in particular, your physical or mental health or condition.[209] The DWP says that the circumstances that count as good cause for the other training scheme and employment programmes (see p475) should be considered.[210]

Fixed sanction periods

If you are sanctioned because you fail to participate in Mandatory Work Activity without 'good cause', a sanction is imposed for:[211]

- 13 weeks; *or*
- 26 weeks if you have already had a sanction imposed for failing to participate in Mandatory Work Activity within the last 12 months. The 12 months run from the date the previous sanction took effect to the date of the decision imposing the current sanction.[212]

If you are given a 26-week sanction but later a 13-week sanction is removed (eg, by the First-tier Tribunal), ask a decision maker to reduce the 26-week sanction period.[213] If s/he fails to do so, appeal. If you have already appealed against the second sanction, the First-tier Tribunal should take the removal of the earlier sanction into account.[214]

Note: once you have been sanctioned, the 13- or 26-week sanction period continues even if you start to participate in Mandatory Work Activity again – ie, the sanction period *cannot* end early.

Other training schemes and employment programmes

There are other compulsory training schemes and employment programmes. At the time of writing, the following schemes/programmes for young people aged 16 to 24 are included:[215]

- training schemes provided by specified bodies; *and*
- Work Experience (work placements of two to eight weeks – 12 weeks if you are offered an apprenticeship) if you have been unemployed at least 13 weeks. **Note:** it is voluntary to agree to join Work Experience, but if you agree it becomes compulsory and you can be sanctioned. The government says that sanctions should not be applied other than in cases of misconduct. See p476 for special rules about good cause.

In addition, if you are on a 'qualifying course' and are, therefore, treated as available for work (see p439), your course counts as compulsory and you can be sanctioned under the rules described in this section if you give up your place or fail to attend the course without good cause, or you lose your place through misconduct.[216]

Note: schemes can be added to or removed from the list of those that are compulsory. See CPAG's *Welfare Rights Bulletin* for updates.

When you can be sanctioned

If attendance on a training scheme or employment programme listed above is compulsory, you can be sanctioned if you:[217]

- lose your place because of **'misconduct'**. (See the information on p458. References to an employer should be read as references to your scheme or programme provider); *or*
- **give up or fail to attend without 'good cause'**. You are treated as failing to attend if you have been absent without authorisation, even if the absence is only for one day.[218] You might be treated as failing to attend if you arrive late and are not allowed to attend;[219] *or*
- are **notified of a place and refuse or fail to apply for or accept it** without 'good cause'. See the information in the section about refusing or failing to apply for or accept a job on p462. References to an employer should be read as references to your scheme or programme provider; *or*
- **'neglect to avail'** yourself of a reasonable opportunity of a place without 'good cause'. You do not have to be notified by the DWP for this sanction to apply.

If you refuse to start a compulsory scheme or programme once you have received your official referral letter, or if you leave a scheme or programme without good cause or before receiving your official referral letter, you might be sanctioned instead under the rules about failing to attend interviews (see p422).

The sanction period is fixed at two or four weeks, depending on the number of times you have been sanctioned. See p476 for further information.

Other scheme and programme-related sanctions and 'good cause'

A training scheme or employment programme sanction cannot be imposed if you have 'good cause' for:

- giving up or failing to attend; *or*
- refusing or failing to apply for or accept a place; *or*
- 'neglecting to avail' yourself of a place.

There are some special rules for 16/17-year-olds (see p481).

When deciding whether you have 'good cause', the decision maker must consider all the circumstances of your case, but certain circumstances always count as good cause. You may also have good cause in other situations.[220] The decision maker should consider all the reasons you put forward. The rules do not specify any particular factors to be taken into account.

Note: these good cause rules do *not* apply to Employment, Skills and Enterprise Scheme or Mandatory Work Activity sanctions.

Circumstances that count as good cause

You have 'good cause' if:[221]

- you had a disease or physical/mental disability that meant you were unable to attend, or your health (or that of others) would have been at risk if you had done so;
- you gave up a place and your continued participation would have put your health and safety at risk;
- your failure to participate resulted from a sincerely held religious or conscientious objection;[222]
- the travelling time to and from the scheme or programme would have exceeded one hour in each direction. If there are no appropriate schemes within an hour's travelling distance, you may be expected to travel for over one hour. You may have good cause if travel is difficult – eg, because of a disability or poor health, or if the distance involved is very long;
- you are on a full-time 'qualifying course' (see p439) and you:[223]
  - failed to attend or you abandoned the course because it was unsuitable for you or you lacked the ability to do it, or it is less than four weeks since you started it; *or*
  - failed to apply for or attend an employment programme, if this was at a time that would have prevented you from attending the qualifying course;

- you had caring responsibilities (see p437 for what counts) and no close relative (see p437 for who counts) of the person cared for or member of that person's household was available to provide the care, and it was not practical to make other arrangements;
- you were attending court as a party to the proceedings, a witness or a juror;
- you were arranging or attending the funeral of a close relative or a close friend;
- you had to deal with a domestic emergency;
- you were crewing or launching a lifeboat, working as a part-time firefighter or doing work as part of an organised group for the benefit of others in an emergency.

For sanctions in respect of **Work Experience** only:
- if you fail to start or you leave early, you have good cause if you were not given a written notification by the DWP that warned you beforehand about when you could be sanctioned and that payment of your JSA could cease or be reduced;[224] *and*
- you have good cause if:[225]
  - you were aged 16 or 17 on the first day of Work Experience; *or*
  - you give up your place no later than one week after you start and you at least attended the first day of Work Experience, provided you did not lose your place through misconduct.

Note: the government says that for Work Experience sanctions should not be applied other than in cases of misconduct.

Fixed sanction periods

If you are sanctioned under the rules described in this section, a sanction is imposed for:[226]
- two weeks; *or*
- four weeks, if you are sanctioned within 12 months of a previous sanction under these rules (or a previous jobseeker's direction sanction – see p469). The 12 months run from the date the previous sanction took effect to the date of the decision imposing the current sanction.[227]

The sanction period usually starts on the first day of the benefit week after the date of the decision to sanction you.[228]

If you are given a four-week sanction but later the first (two-week) sanction is removed (eg, by the First-tier Tribunal), ask a decision maker to reduce the four-week sanction period.[229] If s/he fails to do so, appeal. If you have already appealed against the second sanction, the Tribunal should take the removal of the first sanction into account.[230]

Note: special rules can apply if you are 16 or 17 (see p482).

Deciding whether you should be sanctioned

A decision maker decides whether you should be sanctioned, often some time after the incident occurred. Do not presume that because you have not yet been informed of any sanction that your previous failure has been excused.

If there is a possibility that you will be sanctioned, make sure you give full details of your side of the story. If you:

- **left or were dismissed** from a job and it appears there may have been misconduct or you may have left your job voluntarily without just cause, your former employer is asked for a statement. You should be given an adequate chance to comment on what s/he says.[231] Your remarks may be passed to her/him for further comments. Make sure you explain why you disagree with the allegation of misconduct or why you had 'just cause' for leaving your job. If you are going to an employment tribunal (eg, to claim unfair dismissal), you should say so. Discuss your reply with whomever is advising you on this, as you may be asked questions at the employment tribunal hearing by your former employer about what you have said;
- **refused to apply for or accept a job**, what the potential employer says might be taken into account. Make sure you explain what enquiries you made about the nature of the job, and your reasons for not applying for or accepting it;
- **refuse or fail to carry out a jobseeker's direction**, you are asked for your reasons. If the direction is not cancelled, your case is referred to a decision maker to decide whether you should be sanctioned.

For **training and employment scheme and employment programme-related sanctions**, your scheme or programme provider refers your case to a decision maker. Before a sanction is imposed, you should be given an adequate chance to comment on any statements made against you.[232]

Amount of jobseeker's allowance payable

JSA is **not paid** during the sanction period if you are sanctioned and you are a single person or a member of a couple (other than a joint-claim couple), or if you are a member of a joint-claim couple and both of you are sanctioned.[233]

JSA is **paid at a reduced rate** during the sanction period if you are a member of a joint-claim couple and only one of you is sanctioned. In this situation, the JSA is paid to the person who has not been sanctioned.[234] The person who has not been sanctioned is paid at the rate of:[235]

- contribution-based JSA, if s/he satisfies the rules for claiming it; *or*
- hardship payments, if you and your partner qualify (see p489); *or*
- in any other case, income-based JSA calculated as if s/he is a single person. However, any income or capital either of you have is taken into account in the calculation.

JSA is **paid at the full rate** that applies to you if you (or if you are a member of a joint-claim couple, the one who was sanctioned) are getting a training allowance, unless you are getting specified training for young people.[236] If you are getting this type of training, check to see whether you can claim IS instead.

If your JSA is not paid or is paid at a reduced rate, you might be able to get hardship payments (see p484).

Check to see whether you (or your partner) qualify for IS, income-related ESA or PC instead of JSA. If you are a member of a couple (other than a joint-claim couple), your partner might be able to claim JSA instead of you.

Note: special rules can apply if you are 16 or 17 (see p482).

Specified training for young people[237]

Specified training for young people is training secured by the Young People's Learning Agency for England (due to be replaced by the Education Funding Agency from April 2012), the Chief Executive of Skills Funding Agency or the Welsh Ministers or in Scotland, provided by a local enterprise company pursuant to arrangements with Skills Development Scotland, Scottish Enterprise or Highlands and Islands Enterprise.

Challenging a sanction decision

If you disagree with a sanction decision, you can apply for a revision or supersession, or appeal against it in the usual way.[238] You can challenge:

- the decision to give you a sanction – eg, whether you have been properly notified of any requirements or whether you have 'good cause'; *and*
- the length of the sanction period.

If you are sanctioned for failing to comply with a jobseeker's direction (see p469), you can challenge this on the basis that the direction that led to the sanction was not reasonable or that you have 'good cause' for not complying with it (see p465).

Appeals

It is often worth appealing to the First-tier Tribunal. Even if it agrees that a sanction should be applied, it can reduce the length of a variable sanction period. However, the Tribunal could decide to extend your sanction period or decide that the circumstances justify a different sanction. Seek advice if you are worried this might happen in your case. Take the following into account.

- An appeal gives you a chance to challenge your former employer's (or the scheme or programme provider's) version of events. Note that employers can be invited to attend appeal hearings, but rarely do so.
- Attend the appeal hearing if you can. However, if you do not attend and fresh allegations are made against you, an adjournment should be considered to allow you to attend or to answer the allegations in writing.

Relationship with unfair dismissal and other proceedings

Sometimes the same facts have to be considered by other bodies – eg, employment tribunals and the criminal courts. The questions and legal tests that other bodies use may not be the same as those which apply to JSA.

DWP decision makers, the First-tier Tribunal and employment tribunals are entirely independent of each other; decisions by one are not binding on the other. This means:

- a finding by an employment tribunal that a dismissal was fair does not prevent a decision maker or the First-tier Tribunal from concluding that you did not lose your job through misconduct;[239]
- although the First-tier Tribunal normally accepts a criminal conviction as proof that you have done what is alleged, it must go on to consider whether this was connected with your employment, whether it amounts to misconduct and whether the misconduct was the reason you lost your employment;
- the decision maker or the First-tier Tribunal does not have to wait for the outcome of other proceedings before making a decision, but they are more likely to do so if there is a conflict of evidence.[240]

3. Special rules for 16/17-year-olds

If you are 16 or 17, there are some special rules on jobseeking conditions (see below) and on sanctions (see p480).

Jobseeking conditions

If you are 16 or 17, in general you are subject to the same jobseeking conditions as people aged 18 or over. However, there are some important differences.

Availability for work

Usually you can restrict your availability to jobs where the employer provides 'suitable training'.[241] You do not have to show that you have a reasonable prospect of securing employment (see p443) despite this restriction.

You *cannot* restrict your availability to jobs offering suitable training if:

- you have been sanctioned either under the normal rules or under the special rules for severe hardship payments, unless the sanction was for failing to carry out a jobseeker's direction or was an Employment, Skills and Enterprise Scheme sanction;
- you are claiming jobseeker's allowance (JSA) under the special rules for people laid off or on short-time working (see p483); *or*
- you are claiming under the special rules for people waiting to enlist in the armed forces (see p408).

Suitable training

Deciding whether training is 'suitable training'[242] involves considering factors such as your personal abilities and skills, your preference and the preference of your training provider, the level of qualification you are aiming for, the length of the training, how easily you can travel to the training and how soon the training will begin.

If you have only worked for a short time but you received training for that type of work or obtained relevant qualifications, you could argue that you have a usual occupation and so should be given a 'permitted period' (see p444).

Actively seeking work and training

If you are 16 or 17:[243]

- you are required to actively seek both work *and* training;
- you are expected to take more than one step during a week (at least one to find work and one to find training) unless taking one step is all that it is reasonable for you to do;
- in addition to the normal list of activities that count as a step (see p448), the activities of seeking training and seeking full-time education also count.

For this purpose, training means 'suitable training' (see above).

These exceptions do not apply if you are claiming under the special rules for people laid off or on short-time working or for people waiting to enlist in the armed forces (see pp483 and 408). The first two exceptions do not apply if your JSA is not payable because you failed to attend an interview as required (see p422) or you have been sanctioned either under the normal JSA rules or under the additional rules for severe hardship payments, unless the sanction was for failing to carry out a jobseeker's direction or was an Employment, Skills and Enterprise Scheme sanction.

Jobseeker's agreement

If you are 16 or 17, in general, your jobseeker's agreement is the same as those for people aged 18 or over, although it places emphasis on training. However, it must explain the rules about sanctions for claimants under 18 and about when JSA is not payable or is payable at a reduced rate because you failed to attend an interview as required (see p422), unless you are claiming JSA because you are laid off or are on short-time working (see p483) or you have accepted an offer to enlist in the armed forces.[244]

Sanctions

If you are aged 16 or 17, you can be sanctioned in the same way as claimants aged 18 and over if:

- you are receiving contribution-based JSA;[245] *or*

- you are receiving income-based JSA, including under the severe hardship rules; *and*
  - have left a job voluntarily without 'just cause' (see p459); *or*
  - have lost a job because of misconduct (see p458); *or*
- the sanction is an Employment, Skills and Enterprise Scheme sanction.

If the sanctions are for other reasons, including where they are training related, special rules apply to 16/17-year-olds for good cause (see below) and for sanction periods (see p482). If you are 16 or 17, you may apply for hardship payments (see p484) in the same way as people aged 18 and over.

Good cause

Certain sanctions do not apply if you can show 'good cause' for acting or failing to act as you did. When deciding whether you have good cause, the decision maker should consider the factors that apply to sanctions for people aged 18 and over (see pp465 and 475). You might also have good cause under additional rules applying to training-related sanctions and to employment-related sanctions for 16/17-year-olds.

Training-related sanctions

If you give up or fail to attend a compulsory training scheme or employment programme listed on p474 or fail to accept or 'neglect to avail' yourself of a place on one, you cannot be sanctioned if you can show 'good cause'. In addition to any other ground on which you can argue 'good cause' (see p475), you have this automatically if:[246]

- it is the first time that you have acted or failed to act in a way that could lead to this type of training-related sanction (under the normal or severe hardship payment rules); *and*
- you were a 'new jobseeker':
  - when you first started the scheme or programme, if a sanction is being considered because you gave up a place; *or*
  - at the time of the act or omission, if the sanction is for another reason.

New jobseeker[247]

You are a '**new jobseeker**' for these purposes if, since you left full-time education, you have *never:*

- worked for 16 hours or more a week or done a complete training course; *or*
- lost a place on a training scheme or employment programme because of misconduct, or (unless you had good cause) failed to complete a training course or given up a place on a scheme or programme.

A different system of training-related sanctions applies if you are getting **severe hardship payments** (see p408).[248] In practice, this system adopts the same approach as above – ie, you are only sanctioned if it is the second time you have done something connected with a training scheme or employment programme that deserves a sanction, unless you lost a place on a course because of misconduct or you were not a 'new jobseeker' at the relevant time.

Employment-related sanctions

If you have neglected to avail yourself of a reasonable opportunity of a job (see p463), or refused or failed to apply for a notified job vacancy (see p462), in addition to any other ground on which you can argue good cause (see p465), you have automatic good cause if your employer did not offer you suitable training (see p480 for what counts).[249] This rule does not apply if:

- your JSA has been reduced in the past for the same reasons or because of a training scheme or employment programme-related sanction under the rules described on pp474–76 or under the special system for severe hardship payments (see p481); *or*
- your JSA has been stopped in the past because you lost a job because of misconduct or left a job voluntarily without 'just cause' (see pp458 and 459); *or*
- you are claiming under the special rules for 16/17-year-olds who are on short-time working, have been laid off or have accepted a firm offer to join the armed forces (see p408).

Sanction periods and amount of jobseeker's allowance payable

A fixed sanction period of two weeks applies if:[250]

- a fixed-period sanction (of whatever length) would be applied to you if you were 18 or over (see p476), unless this is under the rules for the Employment, Skills and Enterprise Scheme; *or*
- a sanction would be applied to you if you were 18 or over because you failed to attend an interview as required (see p422); *or*
- you refuse or fail to apply for or to accept a job (see p462), or 'neglect to avail' yourself of a job opportunity (see p463).

During the sanction period you continue to be paid benefit, but at a reduced rate (see p483). If you stop claiming JSA before the two weeks is over and then claim again, you are paid JSA at the reduced rate for the remainder of the two-week period. If you reach the age of 18 before the end of your two-week sanction, the sanction ends and you are paid the full rate of JSA for an 18-year-old.

If you are getting a training scheme sanction under the special system for **severe hardship payments** (see p481), your JSA is paid at a reduced rate for two weeks.[251] If your severe hardship direction is revoked, you can apply for severe hardship payments again immediately, but they are paid at a reduced rate for two weeks.

Note: if you are being sanctioned for any other reason, the ordinary sanction periods and amounts of JSA apply. You might qualify for hardship payments (see p484).

Reduced rates of jobseeker's allowance

Your JSA is reduced by 40 per cent of the single person's (or lone parent's) personal allowance, even if you are a member of a couple, or by 20 per cent if you or any member of your family (see p401 for who counts) are pregnant or seriously ill.[252] 'Seriously ill' is not defined.

4. Special rules for laid-off and short-time workers

If, because of 'temporary adverse industrial conditions', you have a job but:[253]

- your work and wages have been suspended, you count as being **laid off** – eg, you are a farm worker whose work is suspended because of a food safety scare;
- your hours of work have been reduced, you count as being on **short-time working** – eg, you are a secretary in a solicitor's office whose hours are reduced because the property market is flat and there is no conveyancing to be done.

You must be available for and actively seeking work to qualify for jobseeker's allowance (JSA). Special rules allow you to be treated as available for and actively seeking work for up to 13 weeks if you have been laid off or put on short-time working, even though you are still subject to your normal employment contract and so have a duty to return to work or to working full time as soon as your employer wants you to do so.

Availability for work

You are treated as available for work for the first 13 weeks of a period of being laid off or of short-time working, provided:[254]

- you are willing and able to:
  - return immediately to the job from which you were laid off or to full-time working in the job in which you are being kept on short time; *and*
  - take up immediately (subject to the rules on p436) any 'casual employment' that is within daily travelling distance of your home. If you are a short-time worker, this only has to be during the hours when you are not working in your normal job; *and*
- in the case of short-time working only, the weekly total of the number of hours during which you are working and the number of hours during which you are available for 'casual employment' is at least 40 hours (unless you are restricting your hours of availability to less than 40 because of a physical or mental condition or because of caring responsibilities – see pp444 and 445).

A **'week'** for this purpose means any period of seven consecutive days.[255] **'Casual employment'** is work that the employer is prepared for you to leave without giving any notice.[256]

You are not entitled to a 'permitted period' (see p444) unless you lose your job completely during the first 13 weeks of being laid off or being on short time.[257] In this case, you are allowed a permitted period, but it must end by a date no more than 13 weeks after the start of your JSA claim.

Actively seeking work

You are treated as actively seeking work during any benefit week (see p426 for the meaning) in which you are subject to the special rules on availability described above for at least three days. You must take all the steps that you can reasonably be expected to take which give you the best prospects of finding 'casual employment'.[258]

5. Hardship payments

Hardship payments are reduced-rate payments of income-based jobseeker's allowance (JSA) that are made in limited circumstances. You can get hardship payments if you have been sanctioned, and also in other specified situations. In addition:

- you must be in a 'vulnerable group' (see p487); *or*
- if you are not in a vulnerable group, a decision maker must be satisfied that you or your partner would experience hardship if you are not paid (see p488).

Future changes

From some point in the future (probably in 2012) when tougher sanctions are introduced, hardship payments will still be available, but will be recoverable. See CPAG's *Welfare Rights Bulletin* for updates.

When you can get hardship payments

You can qualify for hardship payments in a number of situations. You cannot qualify for hardship payments if you or your partner are entitled to income support (IS) or income-related employment and support allowance (ESA), or come within one of the groups of people who can claim IS (see Chapter 17).[259] In this case, you or your partner can claim IS or income-related ESA instead of hardship payments. If you or your partner are at least the qualifying age for pension credit (PC – see p509), you (or your partner) might qualify for PC instead of hardship payments.

If you do not qualify for hardship payments, you may be able to claim an interim payment of JSA (see p1046).

If, after receiving hardship payments, you are awarded full income-based JSA, IS, income-related ESA or PC for the same period, the income-based JSA, IS, income-related ESA or PC is reduced by the amount of hardship payments you were paid.[260]

At the beginning of a claim

You qualify for hardship payments at the beginning of a claim for JSA if you are waiting for a decision about whether you (or if you are a member of a joint-claim couple, you or your partner) satisfy the 'jobseeking conditions' (see p434).[261] If there is any other reason for the delay in deciding your claim, you are not eligible under this rule.

If you are **in a vulnerable group** (see p487), you get hardship payments from the later of:

- the fourth day of your jobseeking period (ie, after the three waiting days) or the date of your claim if the waiting days rule does not apply (see p402); *or*
- the date from which a decision maker decides that you count as being in a vulnerable group.

Normally you can only get hardship payments from the day that you make a 'hardship statement', but a payment can be made for a period before the date of the statement if the decision maker is satisfied that you have experienced hardship because of a lack of resources during that period.[262] You cannot, however, get hardship payments for any period before your claim for JSA is made, unless it is a period for which a backdated claim is accepted.

If you are **not in a vulnerable group** (see p487), you get hardship payments from the later of:[263]

- the 18th day after your claim for JSA or the 15th day after your claim if the waiting days rule does not apply (see p402); *or*
- the date you submitted your hardship statement (see p489).

You get hardship payments until the decision maker makes a decision on your claim, so long as you continue to satisfy the other conditions for getting income-based JSA.

If you cannot qualify for hardship payments, you might be able to get a crisis loan (see p564).

The jobseeking conditions are not satisfied

If a decision maker decides that you (or if you are a member of a joint-claim couple, you or your partner) do not satisfy the 'jobseeking conditions' (see p434), you can qualify for hardship payments, but only if you are **in a vulnerable group** (see p487).[264] This does not apply if you (or if you are a joint-claim couple, either of you) are treated as unavailable for work for one of the reasons listed on p441.

You get hardship payments indefinitely from the day the decision maker decides that you do not satisfy the jobseeking conditions. You must continue to satisfy the other conditions for getting income-based JSA.

Jobseeker's allowance is suspended

You can qualify for hardship payments if your JSA is suspended because there is doubt about whether you (or if you are a member of a joint-claim couple, you or your partner) are meeting the 'jobseeking conditions' (see p434).[265]

If you are **in a vulnerable group** (see p487), you get hardship payments from the date that the suspension begins.

If you are **not in a vulnerable group**, you cannot get hardship payments until the 15th day of the suspension.[266] If you are subject to successive 14-day suspensions (eg, at each signing day the employment officer doubts that you took sufficient steps to find work) and so never reach the 15th day of any suspension period and receive payment, seek advice as this may be unlawful.

You get hardship payments until the decision maker makes a decision, so long as you satisfy the other conditions for getting income-based JSA. If you are a member of a joint-claim couple, both of you must satisfy these conditions (or one of you if the other is in an exempt group – see p396). If the decision maker eventually decides that you do not satisfy the jobseeking conditions, you can only continue to get hardship payments if you are in a vulnerable group.

Jobseeker's allowance is not paid because of a sanction or a failure to attend an interview

If you are sanctioned or your JSA is not being paid because you failed to attend an interview as required (see p422), you can qualify for hardship payments.[267] However, unless you are in a vulnerable group, you cannot qualify for hardship payments under this rule, no matter how long the sanction lasts, if you (or if you are a joint-claim couple, you or your partner) are:[268]

- sanctioned for refusing to carry out a jobseeker's direction relating to a 'back-to-work session' (see p470); *or*
- required to participate in the Employment, Skills and Enterprise Scheme (see p471).

If you are **in a vulnerable group** (see p487), you get hardship payments from the first day of the period when JSA is not paid. If you are **not in a vulnerable group**, you cannot get hardship payments until the 15th day of the period. This means that if the period is for two weeks or less, you do not get benefit at all unless you are in a vulnerable group. The DWP says that if during a sanction period another sanction is imposed for a different reason, you cannot get hardship payments for the first 14 days of the period of the new sanction.[269]

Hardship payments continue until the end of the period so long as:

- if you are a single person or a member of a couple (but not a joint-claim couple), you satisfy the other conditions for getting income-based JSA; *or*
- if you are a member of a joint-claim couple, you both satisfy the other conditions for getting income-based JSA, or one of you does and the other is in an exempt group (see p396).

Hardship and vulnerable groups

Even if you come within one of the situations when hardship payments can be made, you cannot get them unless the decision maker is satisfied that you are in a vulnerable group or that you or your partner would experience hardship if payments were not made.[270] Hardship payments can be made sooner if you are in a vulnerable group. In some situations, you can only get hardship payments if you are in a vulnerable group.

Vulnerable groups

You are in a vulnerable group if:[271]

- you or your partner are **pregnant** and would experience hardship if no payment were made;
- you or your partner are **responsible for a child under 16 or a qualifying young person** who would experience hardship if no payment were made. See p761 for when you count as responsible for a child or young person. **Note:** if you are a lone parent and are responsible for a child under seven (five from some time in 2012), you can claim IS and cannot claim hardship payments;
- your income-based JSA includes a **disability premium** or would include one if your claim were to succeed and the person for whom the premium is paid would experience hardship if no payment were made;
- you or your partner have a **chronic medical condition** and as a result your (or your partner's) functional capacity is 'limited or restricted by physical impairment', and the decision maker is satisfied that:
  - it has lasted or is likely to last for at least 26 weeks; *and*
  - the health of the person with the condition will decline further than that of a 'normal healthy adult' within the next two weeks and that person would experience hardship if no payment were made;
- you and/or your partner:
  - are **caring for someone** who:
    - is getting attendance allowance (AA) or the highest or middle rate of the care component of disability living allowance (DLA). If the person has claimed one of these benefits, you count as being in a vulnerable group for up to 26 weeks from the date of the claim or until the claim is decided, whichever is first; *or*
    - has been awarded AA or the highest or middle rate of DLA care component but it is not yet in payment; *and*
  - would not be able to continue caring if no hardship payment were made. You do not have to show that the person you are caring for would experience hardship.

  The care must be provided for a considerable portion of each week.

  This rule does not apply if the person who is being cared for is in a care home, an Abbeyfield Home or an independent hospital;[272]

- you or your partner are a **16/17-year-old** who can claim income-based JSA (see p405) and would experience hardship if no payment were made (or if you are a joint-claim couple, the couple would experience hardship);
- you or your partner are claiming JSA on the basis of a **severe hardship direction** (see p408). You do not have to show that you would experience hardship. However, you do not count as being in a vulnerable group if the person subject to the direction does not satisfy the jobseeking conditions; *or*
- you (or if you are a joint-claim couple, at least one of you) are under 21 at the date of your hardship statement and within the last three years were **being looked after by the local authority** under the Children Act 1989, were someone the local authority had a duty to keep in touch with under that Act, or you qualified for advice and assistance from the local authority under that Act. Remember that if you are 16 or 17 and were being looked after by a local authority when you reached 16, you usually cannot claim income-based JSA. Instead, your local authority should support and accommodate you. See p673 for further information and exceptions to the rule.

Deciding hardship

'Hardship' is not defined in the rules. The DWP says that it means 'severe suffering or privation' (meaning 'a lack of the necessities of life').[273] When deciding whether or not someone would experience hardship, the decision maker must consider:[274]

- whether you or a member of your family (see p401 for who counts) qualify for a disability premium or the disabled child or severely disabled child element of child tax credit (CTC);
- the resources likely to be available to you or a member of your family (see p401 for who counts) if no hardship payments are made, how far these fall short of the amount of hardship payments to which you would be entitled (see p489) and the length of time this is likely to be the case. Also included are any resources that may be available from someone in your household who is not a member of your family for benefit purposes (eg, your parents);
- whether there is a 'substantial risk' that you or a member of your family (see p401 for who counts) would be without essential items (eg, food, clothes, heating and accommodation) or whether they would be available at considerably reduced levels and, if so, for how long.

If your claim is refused, consider applying for a revision or appealing (see Chapters 45 and 46).

Available resources

When deciding whether you have resources available to you, the decision maker normally takes into account income and capital that is disregarded when calculating income-based JSA – eg, DLA or savings below £6,000 (see p971). You should only be treated as having resources that are likely to be actually available to you. For example, you may have savings in a bank account but they are subject to a notice period for withdrawal and so you may face hardship until you get access to your capital.

The rules about your age

You cannot usually qualify for hardship payments until you are 18. However, if you are aged 16 or 17, you can claim if you come into any of the categories of 16/17-year-olds who qualify for income-based JSA (see p405). If you are 16 or 17 and have been sanctioned, in many situations you do not need to claim hardship payments because you continue to get income-based JSA but at a reduced rate (see p482).

The amount of hardship payments

The weekly amount of hardship payments you get depends on your needs. Your personal allowance, premiums and housing costs are calculated as for income-based JSA. The normal disregards for capital and income are applied when calculating your hardship payments. However, your applicable amount is normally reduced by 40 per cent of:[275]

- if you are not a member of a couple, the appropriate personal allowance for a single person of your age;
- if you are a member of a couple (other than a joint-claim couple), the appropriate personal allowance for a single person:
  - aged under 25, if both of you are aged 16 or 17, or if one of you is between 18 and 25 years old and the other is a 16/17-year-old who would not be eligible for income-based JSA in her/his own right;
  - aged 25 or over, in all other cases, so long as one of you is 18 or over;
- if you are a joint-claim couple, the appropriate personal allowance for a single person aged 25 or over.

The reduction is only 20 per cent if you or a member of your family (see p401 for who counts) is pregnant or seriously ill. 'Seriously ill' is not defined in the rules.

As hardship payments are paid at a reduced rate, consider whether there are other benefits or tax credits you (or your partner) can claim. Also check whether you qualify for any passported benefits (see p430).

Claiming hardship payments and getting paid

Because hardship payments are a type of income-based JSA, you do not have to make a claim for them but you must satisfy the decision maker that you are in hardship. You cannot get hardship payments until you (or if you are a joint-claim couple, either of you) have made and signed a **'hardship statement'**.[276]

You are asked about your personal circumstances and medical conditions, what savings you have, what other benefits you are getting, what other money you have coming in and how much you owe. You are asked to give permission for the DWP to contact your GP if further medical evidence is required.

Although you cannot receive hardship payments until you have made your hardship statement, there is no general rule to prevent you from receiving these for a period before the date on which you made the statement. A special rule applies where you qualify for hardship payments because you are waiting for a decision at the beginning of your JSA claim (see p485).

The likelihood of being able to convince the decision maker that you are experiencing hardship increases over time. You should make a fresh hardship claim at any time you are without the normal payment of JSA.

While you are receiving hardship payments, you (or if you are a joint-claim couple, one of you) normally have to make a 'hardship declaration' at the Jobcentre Plus office each time you sign on, to confirm that you are still in hardship.[277] If it seems that you are no longer in hardship, the decision maker can revise or supersede the decision to award you hardship payments.

Challenging a hardship payment decision

If you are refused hardship payments, you have a right of appeal to the First-tier Tribunal (see Chapter 46) but this takes time and you may be able to get matters resolved more quickly if you ask first for the decision to be revised (see p1126). To help you do this, you can ask for a written statement of reasons for the decision if this has not already been provided (see p1121).

Remember to tell the DWP if your circumstances worsen while you are seeking a revision or appealing. Ask it to consider whether hardship payments can now be paid based on your new circumstances.

Tax, tax credits and other benefits

Hardship payments are taxable in the same way as any other type of JSA (see p428).

Claiming other benefits or tax credits

As hardship payments are paid at a reduced rate, if you have a partner consider whether s/he could claim JSA (or IS, ESA or PC) instead of you. If so, you should continue to claim hardship payments until her/his claim has been decided (to cover the period while the claim is being processed). However, let the DWP know that this is what you are doing so that there is no overpayment. If your partner's claim for benefit is accepted, your entitlement to hardship payments ends. You may wish to continue to sign on to protect your national insurance (NI) record (see p780), although you cannot be awarded NI credits in respect of a sanction period.[278]

If your partner counts as being in full-time paid work for working tax credit (WTC) purposes (see Chapter 53), check to see if you might be better off claiming WTC.

Passported benefits

Hardship payments are a type of income-based JSA and you are still entitled to full housing benefit and council tax benefit, payments from the social fund[279] and other passported benefits in the usual way (see p430).

6. Laws about minimum working conditions

Employers are required to provide certain minimum working conditions. These rules are relevant to the jobseeker's allowance (JSA) rules about sanctions and being available for work. A brief summary of the rules follows.

The Working Time Regulations

These regulations are designed to protect the health and safety of workers. The main rules are:

- a limit on the hours in the average working week;
- minimum annual holiday entitlement;
- entitlement to breaks from work (both daily breaks and a longer break once a week) and to rest periods while at work;
- special protection for night workers.

This *Handbook* cannot cover the detailed rules nor the complicated system of exceptions to them. Seek specialist advice if you think your employer is breaking these rules.

The National Minimum Wage Act

This Act provides that the minimum hourly rate of pay in any job should be:

- if you are aged 21 or over, £6.08;
- if you are aged 18–20, £4.98;
- if you are under age 18 and not of compulsory school age, £3.68;
- if you are in the first year of employment or are under 19, and you are employed under a contract of apprenticeship (or treated as if you are), £2.60.

The effect on jobseeker's allowance

The rules about minimum working conditions can affect your claim for JSA if you leave a job and also if you are looking for work.

Leaving a job voluntarily

If you give up a job because you believe that your employer is not complying with the legal requirements described on p491, you cannot necessarily argue 'just cause' (see p460). This is because of the principle that leaving a job must always be seen as the last resort and you should first do everything else possible to resolve problems before giving up your job.

If all else fails or if you think that the hours you are being expected to work or the amount of pay you are receiving is intolerable, you might decide to give up work. In that case, the laws about minimum working conditions could help you to show 'just cause'. You should point out that the intention of the Working Time Regulations is to protect the health and safety of workers, so conditions that do not comply with them should be regarded as unacceptable.

In considering 'just cause', no account should be taken of the 'level of remuneration' of the job in question. However, the DWP says this does not apply if you left your job because you tried to get your employer to pay the national minimum wage and your employer was not doing so.[280]

Placing restrictions on your availability

It should be possible for you to place a restriction on your availability for work – ie, that you will not accept a job if terms do not comply with the legal requirements – eg, if an employer is offering a job at less than the minimum wage. You can try to argue that the rule that says you must still have reasonable prospects of finding work despite the restriction (see p443) should not apply as the DWP ought to assume that all employers will obey the law.

Refusing to apply for a job

Try to argue that you have 'good cause' (see p465) for not applying for any job where the terms do not comply with the legal requirements. You need to be careful to make sure that this is so, particularly where the Working Time Regulations are concerned, in view of the many exceptions and opt-outs that might apply. If the terms offered break the rules about the hour limit on the average working week, it is possible that the DWP might suggest that you should agree to an 'individual opt-out'. Argue that this would be unreasonable, as the working time rules are intended to protect the health and safety of workers. The DWP says you *do* have good cause for refusing a job if you do so because it does not pay at least the national minimum wage that applies to you.[281]

Notes

1. **Jobseeking conditions**
1 Regs 1(3) and 170 JSA Regs
2 s6(1) JSA 1995; regs 6, 7(1) and (2) and 10 JSA Regs
3 Regs 2(1) and 5A JSA(ES&ES) Regs
4 R(U) 44/53
5 s6(1) JSA 1995
6 *Shaukat Ali v CAO,* appendix to R(U) 1/85
7 *Secretary of State for Social Security v David,* 15 December 2000 (CA), reported as R(JSA) 3/01
8 Regs 4 and 5(1)-(1B) and (6) JSA Regs
9 Reg 5(2) JSA Regs
10 C(U) 96/1994
11 Reg 5(3) JSA Regs
12 Reg 5(4) JSA Regs
13 Reg 4 JSA Regs
14 paras 21287-93 DMG
15 Reg 14 JSA Regs
16 Reg 14(1)(i), (j), (l), (ll) and (o) JSA Regs
17 Reg 14(2A) JSA Regs
18 R(JSA) 2/07
19 Reg 14A JSA Regs, to be inserted by reg 2(2) JSA(DV)(A) Regs, draft
20 Reg 14(1)(e), (g), (t) or (u) JSA Regs
21 Regs 2(1) and 5A(2) JSA(ES&ES) Regs
22 Reg 14(1)(a), (f) and (k) JSA Regs
23 Reg 17A(2), (3) and (5) JSA Regs
24 Reg 17A(7)-(8) JSA Regs
25 Reg 17A(3) and (7) JSA Regs
26 Reg 14(1)(c), (m), (n), (nn), (p) and (q) JSA Regs
27 Reg 14(4) JSA Regs
28 Reg 14(1)(b), (d), (h), (r) and (s) and (2) JSA Regs
29 CJSA/5944/1999
30 Reg 14(2B) JSA Regs
31 Reg 14(5) JSA Regs
32 Reg 4 JSA Regs
33 Reg 14(2ZA) and (2ZB) JSA Regs
34 Reg 15 JSA Regs
35 Regs 14(1)(a) and (k) and 15(1)(a), (2) and (3) JSA Regs
36 Regs 2(1) and 5A(2) JSA(ES&ES) Regs
37 Reg 7(3) JSA Regs
38 *Secretary of State for Social Security v David,* 15 December 2000 (CA), reported as R(JSA) 3/01
39 Reg 12 JSA Regs
40 s6(3) JSA 1995; regs 6, 7 and 8 JSA Regs
41 Reg 10 JSA Regs
42 Reg 10(1) JSA Regs
43 Reg 13(3) and (3A) JSA Regs
44 Reg 8 JSA Regs
45 s6(5), (7) and (8) JSA 1995; reg 16 JSA Regs
46 paras 21399 and 21403-04 DMG
47 Reg 31(f) JSA Regs
48 Reg 16(2) JSA Regs
49 para 21451 DMG
50 Reg 13(2) JSA Regs
51 Reg 7(2) JSA Regs
52 R(JSA) 2/07
53 Reg 72(5A)(b) JSA Regs
54 Regs 4 and 13(4), (6) and (7) JSA Regs
55 Reg 13(5) JSA Regs
56 Reg 13A JSA Regs
57 Reg 8 JSA Regs
58 Reg 16(1) JSA Regs
59 Regs 8 and 9 JSA Regs
60 Reg 8 JSA Regs
61 Reg 5A(1) JSA(ES&ES) Regs
62 Regs 2(1) and 5A(2) and (3) JSA(ES&ES) Regs
63 ss1(2)(c) and 7 JSA 1995
64 s7(1) JSA 1995
65 Reg 18(1) JSA Regs
66 CJSA/2162/2001
67 Reg 18A JSA Regs
68 CJSA/1814/2007
69 Reg 18(2) JSA Regs
70 Reg 18(4) JSA Regs
71 Reg 18(3) JSA Regs
72 paras 21616-20 DMG
73 Reg 20 JSA Regs
74 Reg 21 JSA Regs
75 Reg 19 JSA Regs
76 Reg 19(1)(r) and (3) JSA Regs
77 Reg 5A(1) JSA(ES&ES) Regs
78 Reg 19(1)(q) JSA Regs
79 Regs 2(1) and 5A(2) and (3) JSA(ES&ES) Regs
80 Reg 21A JSA Regs
81 Reg 19(1)(x) JSA Regs, to be inserted by reg 2(3) JSA(DV)(A) Regs, draft
82 Reg 19(1)(p) JSA Regs
83 Reg 19(2) JSA Regs
84 R(U) 4/66
85 s9(3) JSA 1995

86 s9(3A) JSA 1995
87 s9(4) JSA 1995
88 s9(1) JSA 1995; reg 31 JSA Regs
89 *HS v SSWP* [2009] UKUT 177 (AAC); [2010] AACR 10
90 CJSA/1814/2007
91 CJSA/2162/2001
92 Reg 34 JSA Regs
93 CJSA/935/1999
94 Reg 34(g) JSA Regs, to be inserted by reg 2(4) JSA(DV)(A) Regs, draft
95 s9(5) JSA 1995
96 s9(6) JSA 1995
97 s9(6)(a) and (b) JSA 1995
98 s9(7)(b) and (c) JSA 1995
99 s9(7)(a) and (8)(b) JSA 1995; reg 33 JSA Regs
100 Reg 35 JSA Regs
101 s9(7)(c) JSA 1995
102 s9(8)(a) JSA 1995; reg 32 JSA Regs
103 s10(1) and (2) JSA 1995
104 s10(2A) JSA 1995
105 s10(4) JSA 1995
106 s10(3) JSA 1995
107 s10(5) JSA 1995
108 s10(7)(a) JSA 1995; reg 39 JSA Regs; para 21951 DMG
109 s10(6)(b) and (d) JSA 1995
110 R(JSA) 2/07
111 s10(6)(c) JSA 1995; reg 38 JSA Regs
112 CJSA/4435/1998

2. **Sanctions**
113 R(U) 24/56
114 Reg 2(3)(a) HB Regs; reg 2(3)(a) HB(SPC) Regs
115 ss19(6) and 20A(2)(d)-(g) JSA 1995
116 Reg 75(4) JSA Regs
117 CJSA/3304/1999
118 ss19(6)(a) and 20A(2)(d) JSA 1995
119 R(U) 10/71; R(U) 2/76
120 R(U) 8/57, para 6
121 para 34106 DMG
122 R(U) 26/56; R(U) 1/58; para 34194 DMG
123 R(U) 10/53
124 R(U) 14/56
125 R(U) 24/56
126 R(U) 1/57; R(U) 14/57; CU/34/1992
127 R(U) 2/76
128 ss19(6)(b) and 20A(2)(e) JSA 1995
129 para 34241 DMG
130 R(U) 1/96; R(U) 27/59
131 para 34256 DMG
132 ss19(7) and 20A(9) JSA 1995; reg 71 JSA Regs; R(U) 3/91
133 Reg 71(2) JSA Regs
134 R(U) 25/52
135 Reg 73A JSA Regs
136 *Crewe v Social Security Commissioner* [1982] 1 WLR 1209 (CA), also reported as R(U) 3/81; R(U) 20/64(T); R(U) 4/87
137 R(U) 20/64(T)
138 R(JSA) 1/08
139 paras 34379-83 DMG; R(U) 4/73
140 R(U) 3/73
141 R(U) 14/52
142 R(U) 19/52; R(U) 4/87; CJSA/2507/2005
143 ss19(9) and 20A(9) JSA 1995
144 paras 34384-86 DMG
145 R(U) 26/51; R(U) 20/64; R(U) 4/70; R(U) 1/81
146 R(U) 3/81
147 R(U) 4/87
148 ss19(6)(c) and 20A(2)(f) JSA 1995
149 s20(1) JSA 1995
150 para 34399 DMG
151 R(U) 32/52
152 para 34400 DMG; CJSA/2082/2002; CJSA/2692/1999
153 ss19(6)(d) and 20A(2)(g) JSA 1995
154 ss20(1) and 20B(1) JSA 1995
155 Reg 72(9) JSA Regs
156 ss20(3)and 20B(3) JSA 1995
157 R(U) 13/52; CJSA/1703/2006; R(JSA) 1/08
158 Reg 74(4) JSA Regs
159 para 34237 DMG
160 Reg 75(2) JSA Regs
161 Reg 74 JSA Regs
162 Reg 1(3) JSA Regs, definition of 'full-time student'
163 R(JSA) 1/08
164 Reg 72(3A)-(5A), (8) and (9) JSA Regs
165 ss20(1) and 20B(1) JSA 1995
166 Reg 75(2) JSA Regs
167 Reg 72(2)-(3) JSA Regs
168 *HS v SSWP* [2009] UKUT 177 (AAC); [2010] AACR 10
169 ss19(9) and 20A(9) JSA 1995
170 Reg 72(6) JSA Regs
171 Reg 72(7) JSA Regs
172 Reg 72(6)(b) JSA Regs
173 ss19(3) and 20A(4) JSA 1995
174 R(U) 8/74(T)
175 CJSA/1703/2006
176 R(JSA) 1/08
177 CJSA/3875/2002
178 Reg 70 JSA Regs
179 paras 34051-53 DMG
180 ss19(5)(a) and 20A(2)(a) JSA 1995
181 ss19(10)(b) and 20A(9) JSA 1995
182 ss19(2) and (5)(a) and 20A(2)(a) and (3) JSA 1995; reg 69(1) JSA Regs
183 Reg 69(1)(f) JSA Regs

184 Reg 1(3) JSA Regs
185 Reg 69(1)(a) and (b) JSA Regs
186 *SSWP v JB (JSA)* [2010] UKUT 4 (AAC); [2010] AACR 25
187 Reg 69(2) JSA Regs
188 Reg 3(6) SS&CS(DA) Regs
189 CJSA/2375/2000
190 s17A(4) JSA 1995; reg 3 JSA(ES&ES) Regs
191 Reg 4 JSA(ES&ES) Regs
192 Reg 5 JSA(ES&ES) Regs
193 Reg 5A(1) JSA(ES&ES) Regs
194 Reg 5A(2) JSA(ES&ES) Regs
195 Reg 5A(3) JSA(ES&ES) Regs
196 Regs 2(2), 6 and 7 JSA(ES&ES) Regs
197 Reg 7(3) JSA(ES&ES) Regs
198 para 34796 DMG
199 Reg 8(4)-(6) JSA(ES&ES) Regs
200 *SSWP v JB (JSA)* [2010] UKUT 4 (AAC); [2010] AACR 25
201 Reg 3(6) SS&CS(DA) Regs
202 CJSA/2375/2000
203 Reg 8(7) and (8) JSA(ES&ES) Regs
204 Reg 8(11) JSA(ES&ES) Regs
205 s17A(4) JSA 1995; reg 3 JSA(MWAS) Regs
206 Reg 4 JSA(MWAS) Regs
207 Reg 5 JSA(MWAS) Regs
208 Regs 2(2), 6 and 7 JSA(MWAS) Regs
209 Reg 7(3) JSA(MWAS) Regs
210 para 34796 DMG
211 Reg 8 JSA(MWAS) Regs
212 *SSWP v JB (JSA)* [2010] UKUT 4 (AAC); [2010] AACR 25
213 Reg 3(6) SS&CS(DA) Regs
214 CJSA/2375/2000
215 ss19(2) and (5)(b) and (c) and 20A(2)(b) and (c) and (3) JSA 1995; reg 75(1)(a) and (b) JSA Regs
216 Reg 75(1)(b)(iii) JSA Regs
217 ss19(5)(b) and (c) and 20A(2)(b) and (c) JSA 1995
218 para 34688 DMG
219 R(JSA) 2/06
220 The list in reg 73(2) JSA Regs is without prejudice to any other circumstances in which someone might be regarded as having good cause. R(JSA) 2/06 suggests otherwise, but it is suggested that in this respect the decision is wrong.
221 Reg 73(2) JSA Regs
222 R(JSA) 7/03 discusses the meaning of 'conscientious objection' in this context.
223 Reg 73(2B) and (4) JSA Regs
224 Reg 73(2A) JSA Regs
225 Reg 73(2C) JSA Regs
226 Reg 69(1)(a) and (b) JSA Regs
227 *SSWP v JB (JSA)* [2010] UKUT 4 (AAC); [2010] AACR 25
228 Reg 69(2) JSA Regs
229 Reg 3(6) SS&CS(DA) Regs
230 CJSA/2375/2000
231 paras 34077-82 and 34228-31 DMG
232 para 34685 DMG
233 ss17A(6) and (7), 19(1) and 20A(5)(a) JSA 1995; reg 8(1)-(3) JSA(ES&ES) Regs; reg 8(1)-(3) JSA(MWAS) Regs
234 ss17A(6) and (7) and 20A(5)(b) and (7) JSA 1995; reg 8(1) and (3) JSA(ES&ES) Regs; reg 8(1) and (3) JSA(MWAS) Regs
235 s20A(6) JSA 1995; reg 74B JSA Regs; reg 8(1) and (3) JSA(ES&ES) Regs; reg 8(1) and (3) JSA(MWAS) Regs
236 Reg 74A JSA Regs
237 Regs 74A and 170(2) JSA Regs
238 Sch 3 para 3(d) and (da) SSA 1998
239 R(U) 2/74
240 R(U) 10/54

3. **Special rules for 16/17-year-olds**
241 Reg 64(2) and (3) JSA Regs
242 Reg 57(1) JSA Regs
243 Regs 65 and 65A JSA Regs
244 Reg 66 JSA Regs
245 Reg 57 JSA Regs, definition of 'young person'
246 Reg 67(1) JSA Regs
247 Reg 67(3) JSA Regs
248 ss16(3)(b), 17(1), (1A) and (3) and 20(2)(b) JSA 1995; reg 63 JSA Regs
249 Reg 67(2) JSA Regs
250 Reg 68 JSA Regs
251 ss16(3)(b), 17(3) and 20(2)(b) JSA 1995; reg 63 JSA Regs
252 Regs 63(1) and (3) and 68(1) and (2) JSA Regs

4. **Special rules for laid-off and short-time workers**
253 Reg 4 JSA Regs
254 Reg 17(1)-(3) JSA Regs
255 Reg 17(5) JSA Regs
256 Reg 4 JSA Regs
257 Reg 17(4) JSA Regs
258 Reg 21 JSA Regs

5. **Hardship payments**
259 Regs 140(3) and 146A(3) JSA Regs
260 Regs 146 and 146H JSA Regs; reg 5 SS(PAOR) Regs
261 Regs 141(2), 142(2), 146C(2) and 146D(2) JSA Regs
262 Regs 141(3) and 146C(3) JSA Regs
263 Regs 142(2) and 146D(2) JSA Regs
264 Regs 141(4) and 146C(4) JSA Regs

265 Regs 141(5), 142(3), 146C(5) and 146D(3) JSA Regs
266 Regs 142(4) and 146D(4) JSA Regs
267 Regs 141(6), 142(5), 146C(6) and 146D(5) JSA Regs
268 Regs 140(4A)-(4C), 140A, 146A(5), (5A) and (5B) and 146B JSA Regs
269 para 35304 DMG
270 Regs 140(1) and (2) and 146A(1) and (2) JSA Regs
271 Regs 140(1) and 146A(1) JSA Regs
272 Regs 140(4) and 146A(4) JSA Regs
273 para 35155 DMG
274 Regs 140(5) and 146A(6) JSA Regs
275 Regs 145 and 146G JSA Regs
276 Regs 143 and 146E JSA Regs
277 Regs 144 and 146F JSA Regs
278 Reg 8A(5) SS(CR) Regs
279 SF Dirs 8 and 25

6. **Laws about minimum working conditions**

280 para 34284 DMG
281 para 34437 DMG

Chapter 21

Maternity allowance

This chapter covers:

Key facts

- You can qualify for maternity allowance (MA) if you are pregnant or have recently given birth and you are not entitled to statutory maternity pay.
- MA is paid for a maximum of 39 weeks.
- MA is a non-means-tested benefit, although you must satisfy an employment and an earnings condition to qualify.
- You do not need to have paid national insurance contributions to qualify.
- You may qualify for MA on the basis of past as well as present employment or self-employment.
- You may not be able to get MA and another earnings replacement benefit at the same time because of the overlapping benefit rules.
- If you return to work before the end of your MA period, your partner may be entitled to additional statutory paternity pay from her/his employer for the remainder of the MA period.
- MA is administered and paid by the DWP.
- If you disagree with a decision on MA, you can apply for a revision or supersession, or appeal against it (see Chapters 45 and 46).

Future changes: April 2013 and after

Major changes are taking place that affect the benefits and tax credits system (see Chapter 2).

- From April 2013, total benefit payments to many working-age households will be 'capped' (see p25). There will be limited exceptions, including households in which

someone is entitled to working tax credit or receiving disability living allowance. It is not yet known whether MA will be included in the capped amount.
- You will still be able to claim MA when universal credit is introduced in October 2013. MA is *not* being abolished.
- A new rule is to be introduced, which means you will have to be entitled to work in order to qualify for MA (see p23).
- The government is proposing to introduce a new system of parental leave and pay, possibly from 2015. Under the scheme proposed the MA period would be reduced to 18 weeks and 21 weeks of parental pay would be introduced, which could be shared between parents. The right to up to two weeks' paternity pay near the birth would be retained.[1]

See CPAG's *Welfare Rights Bulletin* for updates.

1. Who can claim maternity allowance

You qualify for maternity allowance (MA) if you:[2]

- are pregnant or have recently given birth, and you are within your 'maternity allowance period'; *and*
- satisfy the employment condition (see p499); *and*
- satisfy the earnings condition (see p499); *and*
- are not entitled to statutory maternity pay (SMP).

In certain circumstances you may be disqualified from receiving MA – eg, if you work during your MA period. See p500 for details.

Maternity allowance period

MA can only be paid during the **'maternity allowance period'**.[3] This is a period of 39 consecutive weeks which starts from, at the earliest, the beginning of the 11th week before your expected week of childbirth (EWC), unless your baby is born before this, and, at the latest, the day after your baby is born. Within these limits, the rules for when your MA period starts are normally the same as those for statutory maternity pay (SMP – see p597), but note that:[4]

- if you are not working at the beginning of the 11th week before your EWC, your MA period will start from the beginning of that week (but if your baby was born before this, it will start from the day after the birth); *and*
- if you are not entitled to MA during the 11th week before your EWC, but you *become entitled* to it before your baby is born (perhaps because you then meet the earnings or employment condition), as long as you have stopped work, the earliest day on which your MA period can start is the day you become entitled to MA and the latest it can start is the day after the birth.

Employment condition

To qualify for MA, you must have been an employed earner or self-employed earner for at least 26 weeks in the 66 weeks immediately before your EWC. This 66-week period is known as the **'test period'**.[5] If you are an employed or self-employed earner for just part of a week, the whole of that week counts. The 26 weeks do not need to be consecutive and you do not need to have worked in the same job for the whole period. You need only show that you have been an employed and/or self-employed earner for any part of each of the 26 weeks. For the meaning of employed and self-employed earner, see p769.

See p501 if you have worked abroad.

Earnings condition

To qualify for MA, your average weekly earnings (or, if you are self-employed, the average weekly earnings you are treated as having) must be at least equal to the MA threshold of £30 a week (for how earnings are averaged, see below).[6]

Earnings from employment

If you are employed, your gross earnings are used to calculate your average weekly earnings. What counts as earnings for MA purposes is the same as for SMP (see p593).[7] If you get a backdated pay rise for the period over which your earnings are averaged, the pay rise is included in the calculation (see below).[8]

Earnings from self-employment

If you are self-employed you are treated as earning a certain amount and this figure is used to calculate your average weekly earnings, irrespective of the amount you actually earn. For each week for which you have:[9]

- a national insurance (NI) small earnings exception certificate (see p775), you are treated as having earnings equal to the MA threshold (£30 a week);
- paid a Class 2 NI contribution, you are treated as having earnings of an amount 90 per cent of which is equal to the maximum amount of MA that can be paid for that week. From 9 April 2012, as the maximum amount of MA is £135.45, you are treated as having earnings of £150.50 a week. (Between 11 April 2011 and 8 April 2012 you would have been treated as having weekly earnings of £143.03.) If you have paid a Class 2 contribution for at least 13 weeks in your 66-week test period, you will qualify for MA of £135.45 a week.[10]

Calculating average earnings

Your average weekly earnings are calculated as follows.

- If you have paid Class 2 contributions as a self-employed person for at least 13 of the weeks in your 66-week test period, no calculation is needed – you automatically qualify for MA of £135.45 a week.
- If you have not paid Class 2 contributions in at least 13 weeks in your 66-week test period (eg, because you were not self-employed or your earnings from self-

employment were not high enough), add together your earnings in the 13 weeks in your 66-week test period when your earnings are highest and divide the total by 13.[11]

In both cases, the 13 weeks do not need to be consecutive and if you have more than one job, the earnings from all your jobs, including earnings you are treated as having from self-employment, are counted.[12] If you are not paid weekly, work out your weekly earnings by dividing the payments you receive by the nearest number of weeks in the period for which they are paid.[13]

More than one job

If you get SMP, you cannot receive MA for the same week for the same baby, even if you have more than one job or have been self-employed as well as employed.

Disqualification from benefit

You will be disqualified from receiving MA for a period if:[14]

- you work for more than 10 days during your MA period. Both employed and self-employed work counts and the 10 days do not need to be consecutive. If you work for part of a day it counts as a full day. (Any payment you receive for the 10 days' work does not affect your MA.) Inform the DWP if you work during your MA period (see p504);
- without good cause, you fail to take 'due care of your health' or to answer 'reasonable enquiries' from the DWP about whether you are doing so. The enquiries should not relate to any medical examination, treatment or advice you have or have not been given;
- before the birth of your baby you fail to attend a medical examination without good cause. You must have been given written notice of the examination at least three days beforehand by the DWP or someone acting on its behalf.

The question of whether or not you have good cause for your behaviour depends on your circumstances.

The DWP can disqualify you for as long as is reasonable given the circumstances. However, if you are disqualified because:

- you have worked for more than 10 days, the disqualification must be for at least the number of days that you worked in excess of those 10 days;
- you have not attended a medical examination, the disqualification cannot continue once you have given birth.

You can challenge the DWP's decision on whether you have good cause or on the length of the disqualification period (see Chapters 45 and 46).

Note: if you are employed and on maternity leave, working for more than 10 days may affect your continued entitlement to leave. If you do not want your maternity leave to end, seek employment advice before agreeing to such work.

2. **The rules about your age**

There are no upper or lower age limits for receiving maternity allowance.

3. **Claiming for others**

You claim maternity allowance for yourself. You cannot claim any additions for your partner or children.

4. **The amount of benefit**

Claimant	The lesser of £135.45 or 90% of earnings
Maternity allowance threshold	£30

You only qualify for maternity allowance (MA) if your average weekly earnings are at least equal to the MA threshold.[15] See p499 for how your average earnings are calculated. The amount of MA you receive is either 90 per cent of your average weekly earnings or £135.45 a week, whichever is less.[16] MA is only payable during your 'maternity allowance period' (see p498).

5. **Special benefit rules**

Special rules may apply if:
- you are in prison or legal custody (see p692);
- you go abroad (see Chapter 63).

There are also special rules if you have been employed abroad.
- If, following a period of employment abroad, you have returned to Great Britain and you remained ordinarily resident in Great Britain while you were away, you may be able to rely on periods of employment abroad to satisfy the employment and earnings condition for maternity allowance (MA).[17]
- In some circumstances, you may be able to rely on periods you have worked in other European Economic Area countries to qualify for MA (see p1439).

6. **Claims and backdating**

The rules about claiming and backdating are in Chapter 42. This section tells you about the specific rules that apply to maternity allowance (MA).

If you are (or have recently been) employed, you may be entitled to statutory maternity pay (SMP – see Chapter 27) from your employer (or ex-employer) instead of MA. If you were employed in the 15th week before your expected week of childbirth (EWC), the DWP expects you to have applied for SMP from your employer. If your employer (or ex-employer) has decided you are not entitled to SMP, it should give you Form SMP1 explaining why and you should send this to the DWP to support your claim for MA. If you disagree with your employer's decision, ask HM Revenue and Customs (HMRC) to make a decision on your entitlement to SMP (see Chapter 47). If you are challenging the SMP decision, make a copy of the SMP1 for HMRC. The DWP normally asks HMRC to decide your entitlement to SMP before it makes a decision on your MA claim.

Making a claim

A claim for MA must be made in writing, normally on the approved form. Send it to the DWP office which covers your area. The relevant address is included on the form or you can get it by telephoning Jobcentre Plus, or from your local Jobcentre Plus office. Keep a copy of your claim form in case queries arise.

You must complete the form in accordance with the instructions on it. See p502 for the information and evidence you can be expected to provide in connection with your claim. Your claim will not be accepted unless it is received after the 15th week before your EWC.[18] The decision maker at the DWP may accept a written application not on the approved form (see p1019).[19] You can amend or withdraw your claim before a decision is made (see p1019).

Forms

The appropriate form is Form MA1, which you can get from your local antenatal clinic, by telephoning the Jobcentre Plus national contact centre number (see p1018) or from www.direct.gov.uk/en/moneytaxandbenefits.

Who should claim

If you are unable to manage your own affairs, another person can claim MA for you as your 'appointee' (see p1016).

Information to support your claim

When you claim MA, you must:

- satisfy the national insurance number requirement (see p1023);
- provide proof of your identity, if required (see p1024);
- supply the information requested on the claim form. If you do not, your claim might be 'defective' – ie, not valid (see p1019). You must also provide additional information and evidence relevant to your claim if requested (see p1022). There is a time limit for doing so.

You must provide medical evidence, normally a certificate from your doctor or a registered midwife, giving the expected date of birth of your child and, if you are claiming MA after your baby is born, giving the date of the baby's birth (Form MAT B1).[20] This certificate will not be accepted as evidence of your EWC if it is issued before the 20th week before your EWC. If you cannot obtain a MAT B1, the DWP can accept other medical evidence of the expected or actual date of birth, if this is sufficient – eg, a birth certificate.

If you have been employed, the DWP also expects you to provide pay slips or some other written proof of your earnings and an SMP1 form from any employer for whom you worked during the 15th week before your EWC (see p505).

Do not delay sending in your claim for MA because you are waiting for your SMP1 or evidence of your earnings. You can send these in later.

The date of your claim

The date of your claim is normally the date it is received at a DWP office.[21]

If the claim form you submit is 'defective' because it has not been completed correctly, or you make a written claim which is not on the approved form, you may be asked to provide further information or to complete the approved form. As long as the additional information or form is received by the DWP within a month of the DWP first telling you of the defect or supplying you with the correct form (or longer if the decision maker thinks that the delay is reasonable), your claim is treated as made on the date the initial claim was received (see p1019).[22] In some circumstances you can claim before you qualify for MA, or the date of your claim can be backdated (see p504).

If you claim the wrong benefit

A claim for employment and support allowance may be treated as a claim for MA and *vice versa* (see p1025).[23] This may allow you to get your claim for MA backdated for more than the normal three months.

If your employer (or former employer) has decided that you are not entitled to SMP and you claim MA within three months of being notified of your employer's decision in writing, your claim for MA is treated as having been made either on the date on which you gave your employer notice of when you wanted the maternity pay period to start or at the beginning of the 14th week before your EWC, whichever is later.[24]

Claiming in advance

You cannot make a claim for MA until after the 15th week before your EWC (ie, until week 26 of pregnancy) but you should claim as soon as possible after that.[25] However, it may be worth waiting a few weeks before claiming if this means you will have higher average earnings, which would increase the amount of your MA. If you plan to stop work after the 11th week before the EWC and you claim while you are still working, the DWP will send you Form BM25A, notifying you of your entitlement and asking to be informed of the actual date that you stop work.

Backdating your claim

A claim for MA can be backdated for up to three months if you satisfy the qualifying conditions over that period. You do not have to show any reasons why your claim was late.[26]

If you might have qualified for benefit earlier but did not claim because you were given the wrong information or misled by the DWP, you could ask for compensation (see p1261) or complain to the Independent Case Examiner or to the Ombudsman through your MP (see pp1256 and 1259).

If you claimed ESA instead of MA, or if you have been refused SMP, see p503.

7. Getting paid

Payment of maternity allowance (MA) is normally made by direct credit transfer into your bank (or similar) account (see p1039). If you are unable to open or manage an account, the DWP may agree to pay you another way (see p1040). MA can be paid to someone else on your behalf, called your appointee (see p1016).

When is MA paid?	The day you are paid depends on your national insurance number.
How often is MA paid?	Normally fortnightly in arrears.[27]

MA is a daily benefit, which means that it can be paid for periods of less than a week. The daily rate is one-seventh of the weekly amount.[28]

Note:

- MA can only be paid during the maternity allowance period (see p498).
- Even if you have been sanctioned for benefit offences (see p1106), you must be paid your MA.
- If you have forgotten your PIN or if a cheque is lost or stolen, see p1043.
- If payment of your MA is delayed, see p1262. You might be able to get an interim payment (see p1046). You may also be eligible for a crisis loan (see p564). If you wish to complain about how your claim has been dealt with, see Chapter 50. You might be able to claim compensation (see p1261).
- If payment of your MA is suspended, see p1043.
- If you are overpaid MA, you might have to repay it (see Chapter 43). If you have been accused of fraud, see Chapter 44.

Change of circumstances

You must report any change in your circumstances that might affect your benefit (see p1047). Report such changes promptly either by writing to or telephoning the office handling your claim, unless the DWP has decided you can tell it about the change another way. In some cases, the decision maker might say you must report changes in writing.[29] In practice, it is *always* advisable to report the change in writing or to confirm a telephone conversation in writing and keep a copy of your letter in case of a future dispute. If the change of circumstances is a birth or death, you may be able to report the change in other ways (see p1047).

If the change affects your entitlement to MA, a decision maker looks at your claim again and makes a new decision (see p1135). The date from which the new decision takes effect depends on whether or not it is advantageous to you and whether you reported the change in time (see p1141).

8. Definitions of terms

- The **'expected week of childbirth'** is the week, starting on a Sunday, in which your baby is due to be born.
- The **'maternity allowance period'** is the 39-week period during which maternity allowance (MA) can be paid. See p498 for when it can start.
- The **'test period'** is the period of 66 weeks immediately before the week in which your baby is due, which is used to calculate entitlement to MA.
- The **'maternity allowance threshold'** is the minimum level of average earnings you need to qualify for MA.

Example

Rita's baby is due on Saturday 14 July 2012. The dates given in the example on p609 apply.

Rita's 66-week 'test period' runs from Sunday 3 April 2011 to Saturday 7 July 2012.

Appendix 4 contains a table of relevant dates for all the weeks in 2012/13.

9. Tax, tax credits and other benefits

Maternity allowance (MA) is not taxable.[30]

Tax credits

You may qualify for working tax credit (WTC – see Chapter 52) as well as MA because sometimes you can be treated as in full-time work for WTC purposes while getting MA (or for some periods when you are on maternity, paternity or adoption leave see p1302).

If you are entitled to WTC, you may be able to get help with the cost of childcare for your new baby, as well as for any other children for whom you are responsible, before you return to work (see p1314).

MA is ignored when calculating your entitlement to WTC and child tax credit.

Means-tested benefits

In some circumstances, being pregnant or on maternity leave may allow you to qualify for income support (IS – see p347). Alternatively, you may qualify for income-related employment and support allowance (ESA – see Chapter 10) as you are treated as having limited capability for work during the MA period or, in certain circumstances, if you are pregnant (see p201). It is not possible to qualify for both IS and ESA at the same time, so if you are unsure which you would be better off claiming, seek advice.

You cannot claim jobseeker's allowance (JSA) if you are getting MA because you are treated as unavailable for work, but your partner may qualify.[31] If you are a member of a couple who would normally have to make a joint claim for JSA (see p413) and you get MA, you may not need to make a joint claim for your partner to qualify (see p414).

The MA you get is taken into account in full when calculating your entitlement to IS, income-based JSA, income-related ESA, housing benefit and council tax benefit.

For pension credit (PC – see Chapter 22), any MA you receive counts as benefit income but is ignored when calculating your qualifying income for the savings credit of PC.[32]

Non-means-tested benefits

MA is affected by the overlapping benefit rules (see p1041).

You cannot get contribution-based JSA (see Chapter 19) or statutory sick pay (SSP) if you are receiving MA. If the father of your baby (or your partner, if your partner is not the father) would be entitled to additional statutory paternity pay (SPP), you may choose to return to work before the end of your maternity allowance period, in order to let her/him get additional statutory paternity leave and pay (see p588).

You can get national insurance credits for each week you receive MA (because you are normally treated as having limited capability for work in those weeks – see p780).

You may qualify for both MA and contributory ESA (because you can be treated as having limited capability for work if you are entitled to MA, see p201) but you cannot receive both benefits in full because of the overlapping benefit rules (see p1041). A claim for MA may be treated as a claim for ESA (see p1025).

Passports and other sources of help

For details of whether you may qualify for:

- a Sure Start maternity grant from the social fund, see p573;

- other help from the discretionary social fund, see Chapter 25;
- certain health service benefits and Healthy Start food vouchers and vitamins, see Chapter 13.

Notes

1 HM Government, *Consultation on Modern Workplaces*, May 2011

1. **Who can claim maternity allowance**

2 s35 SSCBA 1992
3 ss35(2) and 165 SSCBA 1992; reg 2(2) SMP Regs
4 ss35(2) and 165 SSCBA 1992; reg 2 SMP Regs; reg 3 SS(MatA) Regs
5 s35(1)(b) SSCBA 1992
6 ss35(1)(c) and (6A) and 35A(4) SSCBA 1992
7 s35A(4)(a) SSCBA 1992; reg 2 SS(MatA)(E) Regs
8 Reg 6(2) SS(MatA)(E) Regs
9 Reg 3 SS(MatA)(E) Regs
10 s35A(5)(c), (5A) and (5B) SSCBA 1992; reg 5 SS(MatA)(E) Regs
11 Reg 6(1) SS(MatA)(E) Regs
12 Reg 4(1) SS(MatA)(E) Regs
13 Reg 6(3) SS(MatA)(E) Regs
14 Reg 2 SS(MatA) Regs

4. **The amount of benefit**

15 s35(1)(c) SSCBA 1992
16 ss35(1) and 35A SSCBA 1992

5. **Special benefit rules**

17 SS(MatA)(WA) Regs

6. **Claims and backdating**

18 Reg 14(1) SS(C&P) Regs
19 Reg 4(1) SS(C&P) Regs
20 Reg 2(3) SS(ME) Regs
21 Reg 6(1) SS(C&P) Regs
22 Regs 4(7), (7ZA) and (8) and 6(1) SS(C&P) Regs
23 Reg 9 and Sch 1 Part I SS(C&P) Regs
24 Reg 10(3) and (4) SS(C&P) Regs
25 Reg 14 SS(C&P) Regs
26 Reg 19(2) SS(C&P) Regs

7. **Getting paid**

27 Reg 24 SS(C&P) Regs
28 s35(5) SSCBA 1992
29 Reg 32(1)-(1B) SS(C&P) Regs

9. **Tax, tax credits and other benefits**

30 s677 IT(EP)A 2003
31 Reg 15(1)(c) JSA Regs
32 Regs 9 and 15(1) SPC Regs

22

Chapter 22

Pension credit

This chapter covers:

Key facts

- Pension credit (PC) is a benefit for people on a low income who are at least the qualifying age.
- Women can claim PC when they reach pension age. Men can claim when they reach what would be the pension age for a woman with the same date of birth.
- There are two types of pension credit: **guarantee credit** ensures a minimum level of income and **savings credit** rewards you for making provision for your retirement, such as savings or occupational pensions. You can be entitled to either guarantee credit, savings credit or both.
- PC is a means-tested benefit.
- You can qualify for PC whether or not you are in or out of work.
- PC is administered and paid by the Pension Service, which is part of the DWP.
- If you disagree with a PC decision, you can apply for a revision or supersession, or appeal against it (see Chapters 45 and 46).

Future changes: April 2013 and after

Major changes are taking place that affect the benefits and tax credits system (see Chapter 2). These changes affect working-age benefits and so do not affect PC directly, and PC will not be included in the 'capped' amount on total benefit payments. However, some adjustments will be made to PC because of the impact of the changes.

- A housing element will be introduced in PC to cover rental costs. This is needed because of the planned abolition of housing benefit.
- An element to provide income-related help for dependent children will be introduced. This is needed because of the planned abolition of child tax credit.

These changes are expected to be phased in from 2013. See CPAG's *Welfare Rights Bulletin* for updates.

1. Who can claim pension credit

Guarantee credit

You are entitled to guarantee credit if:[1]

- you have reached the qualifying age (see below);[2]
- you are in Great Britain (with exceptions for periods of temporary absence) and satisfy the 'habitual residence' test and the 'right to reside' test (see Chapter 62);[3]
- you have no income or your income is below the appropriate minimum guarantee (see p510);[4]
- you are not a 'person subject to immigration control', although there are exceptions to this rule (see p1414).[5]

Savings credit

You are entitled to savings credit if:[6]

- you or your partner are 65 or over;[7]
- you are in Great Britain (with exceptions for periods of temporary absence) and satisfy the 'habitual residence' test and the 'right to reside' test (see Chapter 62);[8]
- you are not a 'person subject to immigration control', although there are exceptions to this rule (see p1414);[9]
- you have 'qualifying income' that exceeds the 'savings credit threshold' but is not so high that it produces a nil award (see p513).[10]

2. The rules about your age

Entitlement to pension credit for both men and women is linked to the minimum qualifying age at which a woman can receive state retirement pension.[11] The qualifying age will rise steadily to 66 by 2020 and will eventually go up to 68.[12] When you reach the qualifying age depends on your date of birth. **Note:** this applies to both men and women.

- If your date of birth is before 6 April 1950, your qualifying age is 60.
- If your date of birth is between 6 April 1950 and 5 December 1953 inclusive, see Appendix 5 to find your qualifying age.

- If your date of birth is after 5 December 1953, your qualifying age is 65 or over. To check your your pension age, see http://pensions-service.direct.gov.uk/en/state-pension-age-calculator/home.asp.

In addition, you or your partner must be 65 or over in order to qualify for the savings credit element.[13]

3. Claiming for others

You claim pension credit for yourself and your partner (if you have one) and for each additional spouse in a polygamous marriage. The standard minimum guarantee that forms part of the calculation of your benefit includes an allowance for a couple (see p753 for when you count as a couple). It does not include amounts for children.

4. The amount of pension credit

The amount of pension credit (PC) you receive depends on whether you are single or a member of a couple, or have any disabilities, any caring responsibilities or any eligible housing costs. The maximum amount of guarantee credit you could receive is reduced by your income (subject to any applicable disregards). For savings credit, the rules are slightly more complicated (see p513). For information on income and capital, see Chapters 40 and 41. However, for information on qualifying income for savings credit, see p513.

Guarantee credit

Your maximum guarantee credit is known as the 'appropriate minimum guarantee'[14] and is made up of:
- standard minimum guarantee; *and*
- where applicable, additional amounts.

Standard minimum guarantee

If you do not have any additional needs, you receive an award of PC which ensures that your weekly income is brought up to one of the following standard minimum guarantee levels.

Single person[15]	£142.70
Couple[16]	£217.90
Each additional spouse in a polygamous marriage[17]	£75.20

Additional amounts

If you have additional needs, such as a disability, caring responsibilities or housing costs, your award brings income to the level of the standard minimum guarantee plus additional amounts. These broadly correspond to the premiums and housing costs payable with income support (IS), with an additional transitional amount to ensure that those in receipt of IS, income-based jobseeker's allowance (JSA) or income-related employment and support allowance (ESA) at the time they first become entitled to PC are not worse off as a result of the change.

Additional amounts

Severe disability[18] The qualifying rules are broadly the same as for the IS severe disability premium (see p830).	£58.20	£116.40 (if both partners qualify)
Carer[19] The rules are the same as those for the IS carer premium (see p834).	£32.60	£32.60 (for each partner who qualifies)
Housing costs[20] These provisions are covered in Chapter 38 and broadly mirror those for IS, but with some exceptions.	See Chapter 38	
Transitional[21]	See below	

Transitional amount

If you are in receipt of IS, income-based JSA or income-related ESA immediately before you first become entitled to PC, in order to ensure you are not worse off by moving onto PC, your appropriate minimum guarantee may include a transitional amount.[22] You are eligible for this extra amount if, on the day you first become entitled to PC, your IS, income-based JSA or income-related ESA applicable amount (less any amounts for dependent children) exceeds your appropriate minimum guarantee.

The transitional amount reduces over time by any increase in your appropriate minimum guarantee and ceases when you or your partner stop being entitled to PC (disregarding any break in entitlement of less than eight weeks).[23]

The guarantee credit calculation

Step one: calculate your appropriate minimum guarantee

This consists of:

- standard minimum guarantee for you and your partner, if you have one; *plus*
- additional amounts for any special needs and/or housing costs.

Step two: calculate your income

This is the amount you have coming in each week from, for example, some benefits, private pensions and earnings.[24] Not all income counts (eg, disability living allowance (DLA), attendance allowance (AA), child tax credit and child benefit) and some income is subject to disregards (see Chapter 40) but also see p520 for assessed income periods. If you have capital over £10,000, you are treated as having £1 for every £500 (or part of £500) capital that exceeds £10,000.[25]

Step three: deduct income from appropriate minimum guarantee

The amount of your guarantee credit is your appropriate minimum guarantee less any relevant income you have.[26] If your income is above the appropriate minimum guarantee, you do not qualify for any guarantee credit, but you might qualify for some savings credit. Additionally, you may qualify for guarantee credit if you or your partner become entitled to a qualifying benefit, like AA, which would increase the amount of your appropriate minimum guarantee.

Examples

Barbara is single and aged 68. She is in receipt of AA. She lives alone and no one gets carer's allowance for looking after her. She lives in rented accommodation.

Her appropriate minimum guarantee is:

Standard minimum guarantee (single person rate)	£142.70
Severe disability additional amount	£58.20
Total	£200.90

Her weekly income is her basic state pension of £107.45. AA is ignored as income.

She is therefore entitled to £93.45 guarantee credit to bring her total income up to £200.90.

She is not entitled to any savings credit as she does not have any qualifying income above the savings credit threshold (see p513).

She is also entitled to maximum housing benefit (HB) and council tax benefit (CTB) and any other passports that may apply.

Maria and Geoff are a couple. Maria is 62 and Geoff is 67. Their 24-year-old daughter lives with them and she is in receipt of income-based JSA. They have eligible weekly housing costs of £40. Maria receives the middle rate care component of DLA and Geoff gets AA.

Their appropriate minimum guarantee is:

Standard minimum guarantee (couple rate)	£217.90
Eligible housing costs	£40.00
Total	£257.90

Their joint weekly income for calculating PC is £264.85, made up of basic state pension of £171.85 (Maria £64.40, Geoff £107.45), occupational pension of £90 and £3 deemed income from £11,500 savings. DLA and AA are ignored as income.

They are not entitled to any guarantee credit because their income exceeds their appropriate minimum guarantee of £257.90. Their appropriate minimum guarantee does not include a severe disability addition because their 24-year-old daughter lives with them. However, they are entitled to some savings credit as they have qualifying income above the savings credit threshold (see below).

Savings credit

In order to qualify for this element of PC you must have qualifying income above the '**savings credit threshold**' of:[27]

Single person	£111.80
Couple	£178.35

'**Qualifying income**' for the purposes of entitlement to savings credit is all income that counts for guarantee credit (see Chapters 40) except:[28]

- working tax credit;
- incapacity benefit (IB);
- contributory ESA;
- contribution-based JSA;
- severe disablement allowance;
- maternity allowance;
- maintenance payments for you, or your partner, from a spouse or former spouse.

The amount of savings credit to which you are entitled is subject to a maximum figure, known as the '**maximum savings credit**'.[29]

Single person	£18.54
Couple	£23.73

The savings credit calculation

To calculate savings credit, follow the steps below.[30] If you have already calculated whether you are entitled to the guarantee credit, you have already worked out the amounts in Steps one and two. If you are entitled to the guarantee credit, you only need to follow Steps one to four below.

Step one: calculate your total income figure

This is any income that counts for PC purposes and includes qualifying income.

Step two: calculate your appropriate minimum guarantee

This is the standard minimum guarantee plus any additional amounts.

Step three: calculate 60 per cent of any qualifying income above the savings credit threshold

This is 60 per cent of all your income that counts for guarantee credit, other than non-qualifying income listed on p513, above the savings credit threshold of £111.80 (if you are single) or £178.35 (if you are a couple). The figure you calculate is the maximum savings credit you can receive, but it is subject to a cap: you cannot get more than £18.54 if you are single, or £23.73 if you are a couple.

Step four: compare total income with appropriate minimum guarantee

If your total income (Step one) is less than your appropriate minimum guarantee (Step two) **the amount at Step three is your savings credit**. If your total income is more than your appropriate minimum guarantee, go to Step five.

Step five: calculate 40 per cent of total income exceeding your appropriate minimum guarantee

This is 40 per cent of your total income, not just qualifying income, above your appropriate minimum guarantee.

Step six: deduct amount at Step five from amount at Step three

This is your savings credit.

If you cannot deduct it because it is more than the amount at Step three, you do not get any savings credit.

Examples

Terry and Julie are a couple over 65. They have a total weekly income of £201.85 made up of £171.85 basic state pension and £30 personal pension – all of this is qualifying income.
Step one: their total income is £201.85.
Step two: their appropriate minimum guarantee is £217.90 (standard minimum guarantee with no additional amounts).
Step three: their total qualifying income of £201.85 exceeds the savings credit threshold of £178.35 by £23.50.
£23.50 x 60% = £14.10.
Step four: their total income (Step one) is less than their appropriate minimum guarantee (Step two) so the amount in Step three (£14.10) is their savings credit.
They also qualify for guarantee credit of £16.05 to bring their income to the standard minimum guarantee (£217.90) for a couple. Their total income is £232 (£201.85 + £16.05 guarantee credit + £14.10 savings credit).
They may also be entitled to maximum HB and CTB and other passports (see p523).

Angelina and Michael are a couple. Michael is 67 and Angelina is 58. They have a total weekly income of £290.60, made up of £107.45 state pension, £80 private pension, £99.15 IB for Angelina, and £4 deemed income from £12,000 savings. They have eligible housing costs of £15 a week.

Step one: their total income is £290.60.

Step two: their appropriate minimum guarantee is £232.90 (£217.90 standard minimum guarantee + housing costs of £15).

Step three: their total qualifying income of £191.45 (state pension, private pension and deemed income from savings – IB is not qualifying income) exceeds the savings credit threshold of £178.35 by £13.10. 60 per cent of £13.10 is £7.86.

Step four: their total income (Step one) is more than their appropriate minimum guarantee (Step two) so proceed to Step five.

Step five: their total income of £290.60 exceeds their appropriate minimum guarantee of £232.90 by £57.70.

£57.70 x 40% = £23.08.

Step six: the amount at Step five (£23.08) cannot be deducted from the amount of Step three (£7.86) so they are not entitled to savings credit.

They are also not entitled to guarantee credit as their income is greater than their appropriate minimum guarantee.

5. Special benefit rules

Special rules may apply to:

- 'people subject to immigration control' (see p1410);
- people in hospital (see p675);
- people in care homes and other special accommodation (see p683);
- prisoners (see p691).

You are not entitled to any pension credit if you are a member of, and are fully maintained by, a religious order.[31]

6. Claims and backdating

The rules about claiming and backdating are covered in Chapter 42. This section explains specific rules that apply to pension credit (PC).

Making a claim

A claim can be made:[32]

- by telephone. Call the Pension Service on 0800 99 1234 (textphone 0800 169 0133) from 8am to 8pm, Monday to Friday. If you choose not to claim by telephone, you are sent a claim form (PC1) to complete. If English is not your first language, someone can telephone on your behalf and say you want to apply using another language and a member of staff and an interpreter will call you back at an agreed time to help you claim;

- in writing on the approved form (PC1). This can be obtained by phoning (see p515) or can be downloaded from www.direct.gov.uk. To find out where to send the completed form, call the Pension Service on 0845 606 0265 (0845 606 0275 in Welsh), or check on http://pensions-service.direct.gov.uk/en/find-pension-centre/home.asp. You may be able to take or send the form to a local authority housing benefit (HB) or council tax benefit (CTB) office or, in England, a county council or 'alternative office' (see p1018);
- in person at a DWP office.

If you apply in writing, keep a copy of your claim form in case queries arise.

You must provide any information or evidence required (see below). In certain circumstances, the DWP may accept a written application not on the approved form (see p1019). You can amend or withdraw your claim before a decision is made (see p1019).

If you are under 65 and have been awarded the guarantee credit, when you turn 65 you are contacted to assess whether you are entitled to any savings credit and whether you should be given an assessed income period (see p520). The Pension Service either telephones you and completes the form over the telephone or sends you the form to complete. You must provide the information requested as part of this review within one month of being asked to do so.[33]

If you claim PC by telephone, you can also claim HB and/or CTB at the same time. The telephone call constitutes the claim and the Pension Service sends the information direct to the relevant local authority. You are sent a 'statement of details', which is a record of the HB/CTB telephone claim. You are not required to sign and return an HB/CTB claim form when you claim in this way.[34]

Who should claim

If you are a single person, you must claim on your own behalf. If you are one of a couple, you must choose which one of you claims for you both (see p753). If you have a choice about who can claim but you cannot agree, a decision maker decides.[35]

You can swap who claims as long as the partner previously claiming agrees. It may be worthwhile doing so, for example, if one of you is about to go abroad.

An 'appointee' can claim on your behalf if you cannot claim for yourself – eg, if you have a mental health condition (see p1016).

Information to support your claim

When you claim PC, you must:

- satisfy the national insurance number requirement (see p1023);
- provide proof of your identity, if required (see p1024);

- supply information and evidence required on the claim form and additional information and evidence relevant to your claim (see p1022). There is a strict time limit for doing so.

Information and evidence relevant to your claim includes specific details of any personal pension scheme to which you belong.[36] Additionally, you may be required to provide, within one month of being notified of the requirement, information and evidence of any likely future changes in circumstances that are needed to enable the decision maker to decide whether to apply an assessed income period and, if so, the length of that period.[37]

When you claim you are asked about your circumstances, including information about any income or savings and any housing costs you or your partner have. Where further information or verification is needed, a letter is sent for you to complete, sign and return with any requested verification.

If the claim was made in writing to the local authority or, in England, to the county council, the local authority or county council can accept and obtain information and evidence, and give advice about the PC claim.

For claims made in the advance period (the four months before you reach the qualifying age) the one-month time limit starts from the day after the advance period ends.[38]

Once your claim has been decided, you are sent a statement of details, setting out the information on which the award is based. You are asked to check this and report any omissions or changes.

The date of your claim

You are normally not entitled to PC on any day before your 'date of claim'. However, you can claim PC in advance before you qualify (see p518) and your date of claim can be backdated (see p518).

Your '**date of your claim**' (unless the backdating rules apply) is:[39]

- the date your written or telephone claim, properly completed with all the required information and evidence, is received at the appropriate office (the DWP, local authority HB/CTB office or county council); *or*
- the date your 'defective claim' (ie, not properly completed with all the required information and evidence) is received at the appropriate office and you correct the defect within one month (or a longer period that the DWP considers reasonable) of being notified of the defect; *or*
- the date you contact the appropriate office of your intention to claim, and you submit a properly completed claim with all the required information and evidence within one month of this date.

If you are making an advance claim for PC before you have reached the qualifying age and your claim is defective, you may correct it at any time before the end of the advance period.[40]

Claiming in advance

You can make an advance claim for PC to give the DWP time to ensure you receive your benefit as soon as you become entitled. However, you cannot make an advance claim if the reason you do not qualify straight away is because you fail the habitual residence test (see p1442). PC can be claimed up to four months before you qualify, whether this is before you reach the qualifying age and know you will be entitled when you reach that age *or* after you reach the qualifying age when you know you will have a future entitlement – eg, because of a drop in income.[41] The date of claim is the date you qualify.[42]

Backdating your claim

It is important that you claim in time because PC can only be backdated for up to three months. Your claim can be backdated if you satisfy the qualifying conditions over the period for which you require backdating – you do not have to show why your claim was late.[43] If you want your claim to be backdated, it is important that you request this as claims are not automatically backdated. You can do so on Part 10 of the claim form. If you make a telephone claim, you should be asked about the date from which you want your claim to start.

If you claim backdated PC within three months of being awarded a qualifying benefit and an earlier PC claim was refused because you did not get a qualifying benefit at that time, your PC can be backdated to the date of your earlier PC claim or the date when the qualifying benefit was first payable, whichever is later (see p1029 for more information on qualifying benefits).[44]

For general rules on backdating, see Chapter 42.

7. Getting paid

Payment of pension credit (PC) is normally made by direct credit transfer into a bank (or similar) account (see p1039). If you are unable to open or manage an account, payment can be made by cheque or by 'simple payment' (see p1040). If you are unable to act for yourself, PC can be paid to someone else on your behalf, called your appointee (see p1016).

	Qualifying age on or after 6 April 2010	*Qualifying age before 6 April 2010*
When is PC paid?	The day you are paid depends on your national insurance number.[45]	Monday, or the same day as your retirement pension is paid.[46]
How often is PC paid?	Weekly, fortnightly or four-weekly in arrears.	Weekly in advance. If you were entitled to income support (IS) immediately before 6 October 2003 paid in arrears, PC is also paid in arrears.[47]

If you are entitled to less than 10 pence a week, you are not paid PC, unless you are receiving another social security benefit that can be paid with PC,[48] although you will still have an underlying entitlement. If your entitlement is less than £1 a week, a decision maker can decide to pay you quarterly in arrears.

There may be a delay between the date of your claim and the date PC becomes payable. This is because payment does not normally start until the first payday following the claim.[49] There are exceptions to this rule.[50]

Note:

- Deductions can be made from your PC to pay to third parties (see p1048).
- Your PC might be paid at a reduced rate if you have been sanctioned for benefit offences (see p1106).
- If you have forgotten your PIN or if a cheque is lost or stolen, see p1043.
- If payment of your PC is delayed, see p1262. You might be able to get an interim payment (see p1046). You may also be eligible for a crisis loan (see p564). If you wish to complain about how your claim has been dealt with, see p1255. You might be able to claim compensation (see p1261).
- If payment of your PC is suspended, see p1043.
- If you are overpaid PC, you might have to repay it (see Chapter 43). If you have been accused of fraud, see Chapter 44

Change of circumstances

The DWP should inform you of the main kinds of changes in your circumstances that you need to report, but might not actually list them all. In any case, it is your duty to report *any* change in your circumstances which you might reasonably be expected to know could affect your right to, the amount of, or the payment of your benefit (see p1047). Notify changes promptly to the office handling your claim.[51]

In some cases, the decision maker may say you must report changes in writing. In any case, you may want to report the change in writing and keep a copy in case of a dispute in the future. If your circumstances change you may be entitled to more or less PC or even none at all. See p520 for the circumstances that do not need to be reported during the assessed income period.

If there are any changes to the amount of housing costs you owe or the interest payable, your lender is required to report these to the DWP.[52] If you have this information, you must also inform the DWP in case your lender fails to do so. To avoid an overpayment, make sure that the DWP takes this information into account.

If there has been a relevant change of circumstances, a decision maker looks at your claim again and makes a new decision. To find out when the new decision takes effect, see p1141.

When your pension credit is adjusted

Generally, your PC is adjusted from the day the change occurs or is expected to occur, if this is the day you are paid benefit. If it is not, your PC is adjusted from the start of the next benefit week.[53]

However, there are a few exceptions to this general rule.[54]

Assessed income period

An assessed income period is a set period during which you are not required to report any changes in certain types of your income, known as 'retirement provision'.[55]

'**Retirement provision**' means income from:[56]

- retirement pension (other than one payable under the Social Security Contributions and Benefits Act 1992);
- an annuity (other than retirement pension income);
- capital.

The effect of this is that if you have an increase in, or subsequently start to receive, your 'retirement provision' during your assessed income period, you do not have to report this to the DWP. All other income changes that affect your PC entitlement must be reported to the DWP as soon as they occur. During the assessed income period your PC entitlement may change as a result of 'deemed increases in retirement provision' (see p521).

An assessed income period is only set if you or your partner are 65 or over. Also, an assessed income period is not made if:[57]

- you are a member of a couple and one of you is under 60; *or*
- you have been awarded PC or your PC has been increased because an element of your 'retirement provision' that is due to be paid has temporarily stopped; *or*
- you have failed to provide sufficient information, as requested by the DWP at the end of the assessed income period, to enable the DWP to determine whether your 'retirement provision' will vary throughout the 12 months that follow the day the previous assessed income period ends. If the assessed income period has expired and the DWP already has enough information to set a new period, it may do so automatically. You are sent notification of the income and circumstances on which the new assessed income period has been based and are asked to inform the DWP if these have changed.[58]

An assessed income period can be set for five years or for an indefinite period if you are aged 75 or over.[59] If the amount assessed as your 'retirement provision' seems unlikely to represent your typical 'retirement provision' throughout the following 12 months, an assessed income period is made for less than five years or not at all.[60] If you have asked for your claim to be backdated (see p518), when deciding whether your retirement provision is likely to be typical throughout the

12 months, the decision maker looks at the 12 months starting with the date from when your claim is backdated, as opposed to the date you make your claim.[61]

Deemed increases in retirement provision

During an assessed income period your PC entitlement may change as a result of a deemed increase in retirement provision. If the terms of your retirement provision provide for periodic increases and the date and amount of such increases, and the DWP is informed of these, the increase will be in line with these terms.[62] Otherwise, the increase will be in line with the social security uprating for additional pensions.[63] There is no deemed increase if your retirement provision arrangements do not provide for periodic increases in the amount payable.[64] If your retirement provision includes income from capital, it is deemed not to change unless it is capital that counts as having a tariff income.[65] In that case, it may be deemed to increase or decrease in line with any changes made to the tariff income rules – currently £1 for every £500 (or part of £500) over £10,000.

If the adjustment to your retirement provision results in a change in the amount of PC to which you are entitled, the DWP amends your PC payment automatically.[66] This takes effect from the start of the benefit week if the increase or uprating date also falls on that day. In all other cases, it takes effect from the start of the next benefit week.[67] However, if the period for which the first increase in retirement provision is paid is not the same length as the period of the last regular payment, the adjustment takes effect from the date of the second payment of the increased amount if that falls on the same day as the start of the benefit week; otherwise, from the start of the next benefit week.

Example

Ruth's occupational pension is paid at the end of each month. Her last payment was made on 31 March 2012. An annual increase of 1.8 per cent takes effect on 16 April 2012 and is first included in the payment on 30 April 2012. The period from 16 April to 30 April (15 days) is not the same length as the last regular payment (one month), so any resulting adjustment to Ruth's PC is not applied until the start of the benefit week following the second payment of the increased amount.

Decreases in retirement provision

If your retirement provision decreases during an assessed income period, you can report this and your PC is adjusted. This does not end the period, but instead your PC award is adjusted via a supersession.[68] It is in your interests to report decreases in order to gain from any increased PC during a current assessed income period, otherwise you have to wait until the reassessment at the end of the period and any PC adjustment only applies from the start of your next assessed income period.

When an assessed income period ends

Certain circumstances bring your assessed income period to an end. These are where:[69]

- you become a member of a couple;
- you cease to be a member of a couple;
- you reach (or, if you are a couple, the other member of the couple reaches) the age of 65;
- you are no longer entitled to PC;
- you are single and enter a care home on a permanent basis;
- payments of retirement provision due to you stop temporarily or are less than the amount due and your PC award is superseded as a result.

8. Tax, tax credits and other benefits

Pension credit (PC) is not taxable.

Tax credits

PC acts as a passport to maximum tax credits, although you need to make a separate claim.[70] Child tax credit (CTC) does not count as income when calculating PC, but working tax credit (WTC) does.[71]

Means-tested benefits

If you receive the guarantee credit, you automatically qualify for maximum housing benefit (HB) and/or council tax benefit (CTB) but you still have to make a separate claim (but see p515 for claiming HB/CTB at the same time as claiming PC). If you are only entitled to the savings credit, your HB/CTB claim is subject to a standard calculation. The Pension Service provides the local authority with the assessed income figure (the figure the DWP used to work out your PC entitlement). The local authority modifies this to take certain income into account – eg, savings credit.[72] Although savings credit counts as income for HB and CTB, the HB/CTB applicable amount for people aged 65 or over is increased by an amount equal to the maximum savings credit (see p513) to minimise any loss in HB/CTB as a result of having more qualifying income (see Chapter 37).

The £16,000 capital limit for HB/CTB does not apply if you receive the guarantee credit (with or without the savings credit). In all other cases it continues to apply, including if you receive just the savings credit.

If you are a man aged between the qualifying age for PC (see p509) and 65, you can choose between claiming income-based jobseeker's allowance (JSA) or PC. When deciding which benefit to claim, you should be aware of the different rules for these two benefits to ensure you will be better off. For example, there is no capital limit or 16-hour work rule for PC, but there is for income-based JSA.

Similarly, if you are a man aged between the qualifying age for PC (see p509) and 65, you can choose between claiming employment and support allowance (ESA) and PC, or, in some situations, claim contributory ESA and PC. However, regardless of age, no one can get income-related ESA and PC at the same time. Also, if you are a member of a couple and you claim PC, your partner cannot be entitled to income-related ESA. You may want to seek advice about any 'better-off' considerations.

Non-means-tested benefits

Some non-means-tested benefits are taken into account as income when calculating entitlement to PC, others have a £10 disregard and some are disregarded entirely. See Chapter 40 for details.

Qualifying for certain non-means-tested benefits can help you qualify for more PC. For example, if you get carer's allowance, you may be entitled to a carer addition with your appropriate minimum guarantee.

Passports and other sources of help

If you are entitled to PC, you may also be eligible for:

- a Christmas bonus (see p9);
- health benefits if you are getting the guarantee credit of PC (see Chapter 13);
- free school lunches if you are getting the guarantee credit of PC. This only applies in England and Wales – claimants in Scotland can qualify via CTC (see p14);
- social fund payments (both discretionary and regulated) if you receive either or both elements of PC (see Chapters 25 and 26);
- home insulation grants and discretionary grants from the local authority towards the cost of home improvements (see p16).

Notes

1. Who can claim pension credit
1 s2 SPCA 2002
2 s1(6) SPCA 2002
3 s1(2)(a) SPCA 2002; regs 2-4 SPC Regs
4 s2(2) SPCA 2002; reg 6 SPC Regs
5 s4(2) SPCA 2002
6 s3 SPCA 2002
7 s3(1) SPCA 2002
8 s1(2)(a) SPCA 2002; regs 2-4 SPC Regs
9 s4(2) SPCA 2002
10 s3(2)-(4) SPCA 2002

2. The rules about your age
11 s1(6) SPCA 2002
12 s126 and Sch 4 PA 1995
13 s3(1) SPCA 2002

4. The amount of pension credit
14 s2(3) SPCA 2002
15 Reg 6(1)(b) SPC Regs
16 Reg 6(1)(a) SPC Regs
17 Reg 6 and Sch 3 para 1(5) SPC Regs
18 Reg 6(4) and (5) SPC Regs
19 Reg 6(6)(a) SPC Regs
20 Reg 6(6)(c) SPC Regs
21 Reg 6(6)(b) SPC Regs
22 Reg 6(6)(b) and Sch 1 para 6 SPC Regs
23 Sch 1 para 6(8)-(9) SPC Regs
24 s15 SPCA 2002; regs 14-24 SPC Regs
25 Reg 15(6) SPC Regs
26 s2(2) SPCA 2002
27 Reg 7(2) SPC Regs
28 Reg 9 SPC Regs
29 s3(7) SPCA 2002; reg 7(1)(a) SPC Regs
30 s3(3) SPCA 2002; reg 7(1)(b)-(c) SPC Regs

5. Special benefit rules
31 ss2(9) and 3(8) SPCA 2002; regs 6(2)(b) and 7(3)(b) SPC Regs

6. Claims and backdating
32 Reg 4D SS(C&P) Regs
33 Reg 7(1B) SS(C&P) Regs
34 HB/CTB Bulletin G20/2008
35 Reg 4D(7) SS(C&P) Regs
36 Reg 7(4) SS(C&P) Regs
37 Reg 7(1A) and (1B) SS(C&P) Regs
38 Reg 7(1C) SS(C&P) Regs
39 Reg 4F SS(C&P) Regs
40 Regs 4D(12) and 4E(3) SS(C&P) Regs
41 Regs 4E and 13D(4) SS(C&P) Regs
42 Reg 13D SS(C&P) Regs
43 Reg 19(2) and (3) SS(C&P) Regs
44 Reg 6(16) SS(C&P) Regs

7. Getting paid
45 Reg 26BA SS(C&P) Regs
46 Reg 26B SS(C&P) Regs
47 Reg 36(6) SPC(CTMP) Regs
48 Reg 13 SPC Regs
49 Reg 16A(1) and (4) SS(C&P) Regs
50 Reg 16A(2) SS(C&P) Regs
51 Reg 32(1A) and (1B) SS(C&P) Regs
52 Sch 9A para 10 SS(C&P) Regs
53 Reg 7 and Sch 3B para 1(b) SS&CS(DA) Regs
54 Reg 7 and Sch 3B SS&CS(DA) Regs
55 ss6-10 SPCA 2002; regs 10-12 SPC Regs
56 s7(6) SPCA 2002
57 Reg 10(1) SPC Regs
58 Reg 32(6) SS(C&P) Regs; Memo DMG 23/08
59 s9(1)(b) SPCA 2002
60 s9(2) SPCA 2002
61 para 83045 DMG
62 Reg 10(4) SPC Regs
63 Reg 10(6) SPC Regs
64 Reg 10(2)(a) SPC Regs
65 Reg 10(2)(b) and (7) SPC Regs
66 s10 SPCA 2002
67 Reg 10(5)-(7) SPC Regs
68 s8 SPCA 2002
69 s9(4) SPCA 2002; reg 12 SPC Regs

8. Tax, tax credits and other benefits
70 s7(2) TCA 2002; reg 4(d) TC(ITDR) Regs
71 s15(1)(b) SPCA 2002
72 **HB** Reg 27 HB(SPC) Regs
CTB Reg 17 CTB(SPC) Regs

Chapter 23

Retirement pensions

This chapter covers:

Significant changes have been made to the rules on state retirement pensions. These include changes to the age at which you become eligible for a pension, the amount of contributions required to be paid in order to qualify and changes to the way credits for gaps in your contribution record are treated. The new rules apply to people who become eligible for state retirement pensions on or after 6 April 2010. This chapter sets out the rules from April 2010. For details of the rules for people claiming pensions before this date, see the 2009/10 edition of this *Handbook*. For details of the changes to the contribution conditions, see Chapter 35.

Key facts

- State retirement pension is a non-means-tested, contributory benefit, paid to people who have reached pension age.
- There are different categories of state retirement pension: **Category A**, based on your national insurance (NI) contribution record, **Category B**, based on your spouse's or civil partner's NI contribution record, and **Category D**, which is non-contributory.
- You can qualify for retirement pension whether or not you are in or out of work.
- Retirement pension is affected by the overlapping benefit rules.
- Retirement pension is administered and paid by the Pension Service, which is part of the DWP.

- If you disagree with a decision on your state retirement pension, you can apply for a revision or a supersession, or appeal against it (see Chapters 45 and 46).

Future changes: April 2013 and after

Major changes are taking place that affect the benefits and tax credits system (see Chapter 2). These changes affect working-age benefits, so do not affect state retirement pension, and state retirement pension will not be included in the 'capped' amount on total benefit payments.

1. Who can claim a retirement pension

There are three main categories of retirement pension:

- Category A retirement pension, based on your own national insurance (NI) contribution record;
- Category B retirement pension, based on your spouse's or civil partner's (or late spouse's or civil partner's) NI record;
- Category D retirement pension, a non-contributory pension payable to those over 80.

The type of pension you receive largely depends on your contribution record. See Chapter 35 for full details of the contribution conditions for pensions.

You can get a retirement pension when you reach pension age (see p531).

You do not automatically become entitled to your retirement pension just by reaching pension age. You must claim, unless you fall within the exceptions on p536. If you do not claim, you are treated as having deferred your retirement (see p529).

You do not have to retire from work. If you decide to carry on working, your earnings do not reduce the pension you receive.

There are some groups of claimants to whom special rules apply (see p533).

Following the introduction of the Gender Recognition Act in April 2005, if you are a transgender person and have been granted a full gender recognition certificate, your retirement pension is paid on the basis of your acquired gender. For periods before 6 April 2005 your retirement pension is also based on your acquired gender where you have undergone gender reassignment surgery, on the basis that, under the equal treatment directive (Directive 79/9), it would be discriminatory not to do so.[1] Therefore, if your acquired gender is female, you qualify for a pension at the pension age for a woman and if your acquired gender is male, you qualify for a pension at 65, until the pension ages for men and women are equalised (see p531).

Category A retirement pension

You qualify for a Category A pension if:[2]

- you satisfy the contribution conditions (see p793) on the basis of your own contribution record. If you do not satisfy the contribution conditions, you may qualify based on the contributions of your late or former spouse or civil partner; *and*
- you are over pension age.

Category B retirement pension

You qualify for a Category B pension if:[3]

- you were married or had a civil partner when you reached pension age (or married or formed a civil partnership after that age); *or*
- you are a widow, widower or surviving civil partner; *or*
- you were entitled to widowed parent's allowance immediately before reaching pension age and have not remarried or formed a new civil partnership;[4] *or*
- in certain circumstances (see p528) you were entitled to widowed parent's allowance or bereavement allowance before reaching pension age.[5]

Married people and civil partners

If you are married (except if you are a man and your wife was born before 6 April 1950) or you have a civil partner (except if your partner was born before 6 April 1950), you are entitled to a Category B retirement pension if:

- you and your spouse or civil partner have both reached pension age; *and*
- your spouse or civil partner satisfies the relevant contribution conditions.

Widows, widowers and surviving civil partners

If you are a widow, widower or surviving civil partner, your entitlement depends on:

- whether you became a widow, widower or surviving civil partner before or after reaching pension age; *and*
- the date on which you became a widow, widower or surviving civil partner.

Women widowed after pension age

You are entitled to a Category B retirement pension based on your late husband's contributions if:[6]

- you were married to him when he died; *and*
- he satisfied the relevant contribution conditions.

Men widowed after pension age

If you are a man widowed after reaching pension age before 6 April 2010, you are entitled to a Category B retirement pension based on your late wife's contributions if:[7]

- she died on or after 6 April 1979 and you were married to her when she died; *and*
- both of you had reached pension age when she died; *and*
- she satisfied the relevant contribution conditions.

If you are a man widowed after reaching pension age on or after 6 April 2010, you are entitled to a Category B retirement pension based on your late wife's contributions if:[8]

- you were married to her when she died; *and*
- she satisfied the relevant contribution conditions.

Surviving civil partners after pension age

If you reached pension age before 6 April 2010 and your civil partner dies, you are entitled to a Category B retirement pension based on your late civil partner's contributions if:[9]

- you were civil partners; *and*
- you had both reached pension age when your civil partner died; *and*
- your civil partner satisfied the relevant contribution conditions.

If you reached pension age on or after 6 April 2010 and your civil partner dies, you are entitled to a Category B retirement pension on your late civil partner's contributions if:[10]

- you were civil partners; *and*
- your civil partner satisfied the relevant contribution conditions.

Widowed people and surviving civil partners before pension age

If you were widowed on or after 9 April 2001, or you are a person who becomes a surviving civil partner on or after 5 December 2005, and you have now reached pension age, you are entitled to a Category B retirement pension based on the contributions of your late spouse or civil partner if:[11]

- because of the death of your late spouse or civil partner, you were entitled to bereavement allowance at any time before reaching pension age, or widowed parent's allowance at any time when you are over age 45 but not immediately before reaching pension age; *and*
- following the death of your spouse or civil partner, you have not remarried or formed a new civil partnership.

When Category B retirement pension can be paid

Once you qualify for a Category B retirement pension, it is paid for life. It does not cease if you live with a new partner, remarry or form a civil partnership.[12] If you are approaching pension age and considering remarriage, assess your position and, if necessary, take advice. There may be financial benefits in postponing any wedding or civil partnership so that you are still a widow, widower or surviving civil partner immediately before attaining pension age. Seek financial advice before deciding what to do.

Category D retirement pension

You qualify for a Category D pension if:[13]

- you are aged 80 or over;
- you were ordinarily resident in Great Britain (see p1430) on the day you reached the age of 80;
- you have been resident in Great Britain for a period of at least 10 years in any continuous period of 20 years immediately before you reached the age of 80; *and*
- you are entitled either to no other retirement pension or to an amount of retirement pension less than the current rate of a Category D retirement pension.

Graduated retirement benefit

'**Graduated retirement benefit**' is an increase in the weekly rate of retirement pension. However, although described as an increase in pension rate, graduated retirement benefit can be paid to a person over pension age who is not entitled to a retirement pension because s/he does not satisfy the NI contribution conditions.[14] Between 1961 and 6 April 1975, those paying flat-rate Class 1 contributions also paid graduated contributions. Payment of graduated contributions ceased on 5 April 1975.

You are also entitled to an age addition of 25p a week if you are over 80 and receiving graduated retirement benefit even if you are not receiving any other retirement pension.[15]

If you are a widow, you may add half of your husband's entitlement to your own. Similarly, a widower entitled to a Category B retirement pension (or who would be if he did not have a Category A retirement pension) may also add half his wife's entitlement to his own.[16] From 5 December 2005, this rule also applies to surviving civil partners.

If you are entitled to only a very small amount, however, you receive a lump-sum payment instead of weekly payments. Graduated retirement pension is increased if you defer entitlement to a retirement pension (see below).[17]

Deferring your retirement pension

Once you have reached pension age, you are allowed to defer your entitlement to a Category A or Category B retirement pension. In return for doing so, you later become entitled to a higher rate of pension or a lump sum.[18]

The same applies to graduated retirement benefit (see above).[19] You can choose to defer your pension before you claim it or, if you are already claiming your pension, you can choose to stop getting it in order to get more later on – but you can only do this once.[20] To stop claiming, you must notify the Pension Service by telephone or in writing.[21] The rules were changed in April 2005 to encourage more people to defer their pensions. Before this date, you could only defer your pension for a maximum period of five years. There is no longer a five-year limit for deferral. You can choose to have a higher rate of pension or the same rate of pension paid with a one-off lump sum. To get a lump sum you have to defer your pension for 12 months or more. For periods you defer your pension after 6 April 2005, your pension is increased by one-fifth of 1 per cent for each week of deferment (10.4 per cent for each year). For example, if you defer your pension for 12 months it would increase by 10.4 per cent, which would be approximately £1 for every £10 of state pension. For periods before 6 April 2005, the increase in pension is one-seventh of 1 per cent. You will not be entitled to any increase unless you defer your pension for long enough to earn an increase of at least 1 per cent.[22] A one-off lump sum is based on the amount of pension that you would have received had you not deferred your claim, plus interest.[23] The DWP publishes a guide, *State Pension Deferral: your guide* (SPD1), available from www.direct.gov.uk.

The benefits that are increased in this way include any additional pension under the additional state pension scheme (see p538), an incapacity increase and any increase resulting from your late spouse's or civil partner's deferment, but not increases for dependants or age additions.[24]

You may be entitled to claim the extra pension accrued from your late spouse's or late civil partner's deferment when you claim your own pension, as long as you were still married or in the civil partnership at the time s/he died and you have not remarried or formed a new civil partnership before you reach pension age.[25] If you are a man or in a civil partnership, there is an additional condition that you must be over pension age at the time your wife or civil partner dies. However, this condition does not apply to widowers and civil partners who reached pension age on or after 6 April 2010. If you were under pension age when your wife or civil partner died and you reached pension age before 6 April 2010, you can claim up to three months of your late wife's or civil partner's deferred pension, but not a lump sum.[26]

You do not receive an increase in pension for any period that you receive any other contributory benefit, severe disablement allowance, carer's allowance or maternity allowance,[27] nor for any day when you would have been disqualified from receiving a Category A or B retirement pension because you were in prison.

If you are receiving a means-tested benefit, deferring your retirement pension may lead to a problem under the notional income rules. These sometimes entitle the DWP to treat you as if you were claiming your pension when your entitlement to benefit is calculated, even if you are not. For further details of the notional income rules, see p932. In addition, for periods on or after 6 April 2011, you cannot gain an increase in pension for any period in which you are in receipt of pension credit (PC) or your partner is in receipt of PC, income support, income-based jobseeker's allowance or income-related employment and support allowance.

2. The rules about your age

Category A or B pension can be claimed when you reach pension age. Category D pension can be claimed if you are over 80.

For many years, pension age has been 60 for women and 65 for men. Pension age for both men and women is being equalised between April 2016 and November 2018. Women born on after 6 November 1953 will reach pension age at 65 and those born between 6 April 1950 and 5 November 1953 will reach it at an age between 60 and 65. From December 2018, the pension age for men and women will increase to 66 by October 2020. Between 2024 and 2046, the pension age for men and women will increase gradually to 68.[28] The current rules provide for the increase to 67 to occur between 2034 and 2036 but the government has announced plans to bring forward the increase in pension age to 67 so that it is completed by 2028. The precise date on which you will reach pension age depends on your date of birth. Appendix 5 contains further details.

If you are a married man born after 5 April 1945 or a widower whose late wife was born after 5 April 1950, the rules for Category B retirement pension are the same as those that currently apply to women.[29]

3. Claiming for others

You claim retirement pension for yourself. You cannot normally claim any additions for your partner or children.

If you were entitled to an increase in your retirement pension for a dependent child on 5 April 2003, or for an increase in your retirement pension for your spouse or partner or someone who cares for your child on 5 April 2010, you may be able to continue to receive it (see pp745 and 740).

4. The amount of benefit

Category A retirement pension

Category A retirement pension is paid at a weekly rate of £107.45.[30] In addition, you may receive:

- an age addition of 25p a week if you are over 80;
- graduated retirement benefit based on earnings between 1961 and 1975 (see p529);

- an additional state pension if you reached pension age after 5 April 1979 (see p538);
- a higher pension if you deferred entitlement to pension (see p529);
- an amount equal to the age-related addition to long-term incapacity benefit if you were receiving this within eight weeks (104 weeks if you are a 'welfare to work beneficiary' – see p738) of reaching pension age (see p526).[31] If you have an additional state pension, this amount is offset against it.[32]

Note: if you are still entitled to an increase in your retirement pension for an adult or child dependant, see pxviii for the amounts.

Category B retirement pension for a spouse or civil partner

Category B retirement pension is paid at the weekly rate of £64.40.[33] In addition, you may receive:
- an age addition of 25p a week if you are over 80;
- a higher pension from deferring entitlement to pension (see p529).

Note: if you are still entitled to an increase in your retirement pension for a child dependant, see pxviii for the amount.

Category B retirement pension for a widow, widower or civil partner

Category B retirement pension is paid at the weekly rate of £107.45.[34] In addition, you may receive:
- an age addition of 25p a week if you are over 80;
- graduated retirement benefit based on your late spouse's/civil partner's graduated contributions between 1961 and 1975 (see below);
- a higher pension if your late spouse/civil partner deferred entitlement to pension (see p529);
- an additional state pension based on earnings after 5 April 1979 (see p537).

Note: if you are still entitled to an increase in your retirement pension for a child dependant, see pxviii for the amount.

Category D retirement pension

Category D retirement pension is paid at a weekly rate of £64.40.[35] In addition, you receive an age addition of 25p a week because you are over 80.

Graduated retirement benefit

The amount of graduated retirement benefit you can receive depends on the amount of graduated contributions paid on earnings between 1961 and 1975.

5. Special benefit rules

Special rules may apply to:

- people coming from or going abroad (see below);
- divorced people and former civil partners (see below);
- prisoners (see p691).

People coming from or going abroad

If you have lived elsewhere than the UK during your working life, your pension may be affected – eg, it may be paid at a reduced rate. However, there are reciprocal arrangements with many countries that may help you qualify for a full pension. If you have worked in another European Economic Area (EEA) state, you may benefit from European Union law (see p1499). Your employment in another EEA state counts towards your national insurance contribution record to entitle you to retirement pension. If you are not an EEA national, you may still be able to benefit from a reciprocal agreement or an association or co-operation agreement (see p1429).

If you are going to live abroad, you can take your pension with you to any other country. However, unless you are moving to live in another EEA state or a country with which the UK has a reciprocal agreement for pensions, the amount of state retirement pension you receive is frozen at the rate at which it was paid when you went abroad.

Divorced people and former civil partners

If you are divorced or have ended a civil partnership and you cannot qualify for a Category A pension on the basis of your own contributions, you may qualify by using the contributions of your former spouse or civil partner. You can replace them with your own, either for all the years in your working life up to and including the one in which your marriage or civil partnership ended or for all the years during which you were married or in a civil partnership.

If your former spouse's or civil partner's contribution record was incomplete, you may not be able to receive a full pension, but you may still receive a higher amount than you would have qualified for on your own contributions.

You may qualify if:[36]

- you have been divorced or your civil partnership has ended; *or*
- your marriage was not void (see p70) and has been annulled by a court; *and either*
  - your decree absolute of divorce, civil partnership dissolution or nullity is dated after you reach pension age; *or*
  - your decree absolute of divorce, civil partnership dissolution or nullity is dated before you reach pension age and you do not remarry or form a new civil partnership before you reach that age.

6. Claims and backdating

The general rules about claiming and backdating are in Chapter 42. This section tells you about the specific rules that apply to retirement pension.

You can request a forecast of the amount of pension that you will receive by post, by calling 0845 300 0168 or online at www.direct.gov.uk/en/pensionsandretirementplanning/statepension/statepensionforecast.

Note: you can defer claiming your retirement pension. In return for doing so, you later become entitled to a higher rate of pension or a lump sum. See p529 for further details. You can also stop claiming your retirement pension.

Making a claim

You must usually make a claim for retirement pension (unless you come within the exceptions on p536). A claim for retirement pension can be made:[37]

- in writing by completing the approved form. Send it to the Pension Service. You may also be able to make your claim by taking or sending it to an alternative office (see p1018); *or*
- by telephone on 0800 731 7898 (textphone 0800 731 7339); *or*
- online at www.direct.gov.uk/en/pensionsandretirementplanning.

If you claim in writing, keep a copy of your claim form in case queries arise.

You must provide any information or evidence required (see p535). In certain circumstances, the DWP may accept a written application not on the approved form (see p1019). You can amend or withdraw your claim before a decision is made (see p1019).

Note: you do not have to make a claim for a Category A or B pension if you have received written notification from the DWP that you do not need to claim (see p536). However, if you defer your claim, or stop claiming, you do need to make a claim (see p529). There are other exceptions to the rule on claiming (see p536).

Forms

The retirement pension form (BR1) is normally sent to you by the DWP about four months before you reach pension age. Otherwise, get it from the state pension claim line on 0800 731 7898 (textphone 0800 731 7339) *or* at www.direct.gov.uk/en/pensionsandretirementplanning.

Who should claim

You must normally claim retirement pension on your own behalf. However, retirement pension can be claimed by another adult on your behalf if you are unable to act for yourself. This person is called your 'appointee' (see p1016).

Information to support your claim

When you claim retirement pension, you must prove you have reached pension age (see below). You must also:

- satisfy the national insurance (NI) number requirement (see p1023);
- provide proof of your identity, if required (see p1024);
- supply all the information and evidence required relevant to your claim (see p1022). There is a strict time limit for doing so.

Proving your age

It is up to you to prove you have reached pension age. For most claimants, it is sufficient to produce your birth certificate, but problems can occur if you were born in a country which did not have a formal system of registering births. Other evidence which can prove your birth date includes:

- passport or identity card;
- school or health records;
- army records;
- statements from people who know you.

The date of your claim

The date of your claim is:[38]

- the date your written or telephone claim, properly completed with all the required evidence and information, is received at the appropriate office (the DWP, local authority housing benefit/council tax benefit office or other designated office). In this case, a claim made by telephone will be the date of the telephone call. **Note:** telephone claims cannot be made at designated offices; *or*
- the date your 'defective claim' (ie, not properly completed with all the required information and evidence) is received at the appropriate office and you correct the defect within one month (or a longer period that the DWP considers reasonable) of being notified of the defect.

If you claim the wrong benefit

In certain circumstances, if you have claimed the wrong benefit, it is possible for your claim to be interchanged with another benefit.[39] For retirement pensions, this interchange is only possible with widows' benefits or bereavement benefits.

Claiming in advance

Claims for retirement pensions may be made up to, but no more than, four months in advance.[40] You should take advantage of this, as it can take a long time to sort out your contribution record.

Exceptions to the rule on claiming

- You do not need to make a claim for a Category A or B retirement pension if eight weeks before you reach pension age you were in receipt of income support, jobseeker's allowance, employment and support allowance, incapacity benefit (IB) or pension credit and you were not entitled to or waiting for a decision on a claim for carer's allowance, short-term IB, severe disablement allowance, widowed mother's allowance or widow's pension. You also must have received notification from the DWP (by two weeks before you reach pension age), stating that you need not make a claim.[41] If this applies but you defer your entitlement to a Category A or B retirement pension, you will, however, need to make a claim.[42]
- If you are a widow, you do not need to make a claim for Category A or B retirement pension if *either*:
  - you are over 65 when you stop getting widowed mother's allowance or widowed parent's allowance; *or*
  - you are getting a widow's pension or bereavement allowance immediately before your 65th birthday.
- You do not need to make a claim for Category A retirement pension if you are entitled to another retirement pension and you get divorced or your civil partnership is dissolved.[43] You need not claim your Category B retirement pension if you are entitled to either or both a Category A retirement pension or graduated retirement benefit, and you marry or enter into a civil partnership, or your spouse or civil partner becomes entitled to a Category A retirement pension or (from 13 July 2009) s/he dies while entitled to such a pension.[44]
- You do not need to make a claim for Category D retirement pension if you were 'ordinarily resident' in Great Britain (see p1430) on your 80th birthday and you are already receiving another retirement pension.[45]

Backdating your claim

It is very important to claim in time because the maximum period for backdating is 12 months. You cannot backdate your claim for any period before the date you would have first become entitled to your pension.[46] You do not have to show any reasons why your claim is late. The rules on backdating are covered on p1026. In some limited circumstances, if you were not notified that your contribution record was insufficient for the years 1996 to 2002, it is possible for the claim to be backdated beyond the 12-month period to 1 October 1998.[47] If you claim more than 12 months after you became entitled to your pension, you are treated as having deferred your retirement.[48]

If you might have qualified for benefit earlier but did not claim because you were given the wrong information or were misled by the DWP, you could ask for a compensation payment (see p1261) or complain to the Ombudsman via your MP (see p1259).

7. Getting paid

Payment of retirement pension is normally made by direct credit transfer into a bank (or similar) account (see p1039). If you are unable to open or manage an account, payment can be made by cheque or by 'simple payment' (see p1040).

Payment can also be made to someone else on your behalf – called your appointee (see p1016).

When are retirement pensions paid?	The day you are paid depends on your national insurance number.[49]
How often are retirement pensions paid?	Weekly, fortnightly or four-weekly in arrears.

If you reached pension age before 6 April 2010, you are paid in advance on a Monday or a Thursday, depending on your circumstances.[50]

Note:

- Deductions can be made from your retirement pension to repay certain loans (see p1048).
- Even if you have been sanctioned for benefit offences (see p1106), you must be paid your retirement pension.
- If you have forgotten your PIN or if a cheque is lost or stolen, see p1040.
- If payment of your retirement pension is delayed, see p1262. You might be able to get an interim payment (see p1046). You may also be eligible for a crisis loan (see p564). If you wish to complain about how your claim has been dealt with, see p1255. You might be able to claim compensation (see p1261).
- If payment of your retirement pension is suspended, see p1043.
- If you are overpaid retirement pension, you might have to repay it (see Chapter 43). If you have been accused of fraud, see Chapter 44.

Change of circumstances

You must report changes in your circumstances that might affect your benefit. See Chapter 42 for more information.

You should notify changes promptly in writing or by telephone to the office handling your claim (although in individual cases, notification might be accepted in another form). In some cases, however, the decision maker might say you must report changes in writing. In any case, you might want to report the change in writing and keep a copy in case of a dispute in the future.

8. The additional state pension scheme

Most employees pay national insurance (NI) contributions that give entitlement to the basic state retirement pension. Those employees, but not the self-employed, can also earn additional pension. The additional state pension provides for earnings-related pensions to be paid to people who have paid (or whose late spouses/civil partners have paid) Class 1 contributions in excess of the minimum required for entitlement to basic state retirement pension. For earnings-related additions to invalidity benefit and incapacity benefit, see CPAG's *Welfare Benefits and Tax Credits Handbook* 2006/07 edition, p284.

The rules for the additional state pension were subject to major changes in April 2002. Before this date, the additional state pension was calculated under the state earnings-related pension scheme (SERPS). The rules since April 2002 are based on the state second pension – a simplified and more generous version of SERPS. In particular, under the new scheme, certain low-paid employees are deemed to have a minimum level of earnings.

If a couple divorces, it is possible to apply for a share of any additional pension.[51]

You are not in the additional state pension scheme if you are either contracted out by your employer or covered by an appropriate personal or stakeholder pension scheme. If you are contracted out by your employer, you and your employer pay NI contributions at a lower rate (see p773).[52] From 6 April 2012 you cannot contract out of the additional state pension scheme on a defined contribution (or money purchase) basis. You can only contract out through a defined benefit (or salary-related) pension scheme.[53] If you are in a personal, stakeholder or occupational scheme that contracts out on a defined contribution basis, you will automatically be brought back into the additional state pension scheme. You can continue to pay into your personal and stakeholder pension but you will no longer receive a rebate on your NI contributions. You need to contact your employer for details of how this may affect your occupational pension.

For more information on contracting out, see the DWP's *Abolition of Contracting Out* factsheet, available at www.direct.gov.uk.

Calculating the additional state pension

The additional pension is calculated by adding together:

- the amount of additional pension accrued under the rules up to 6 April 2002 (under the previous scheme of SERPS); *and*
- the amount of additional pension accrued under the additional state pension (the state second pension).

The additional state pension depends on your earnings factor in each relevant year in which you have paid contributions (or for Category B retirement pensions, your spouse's or civil partner's earnings factor in each relevant year in which s/he has paid contributions). The additional state pension is calculated on the basis of 'accrual bands' related to surpluses in your earnings factor (see p788). The calculation of the additional state pension is being changed to enable it to become a flat-rate top-up to the basic state pension. From 2010/11, there were two accrual bands, a lower one (for earnings below the lower earnings threshold – see p773) and an upper one (for earnings above the lower earnings threshold).[54] From 6 April 2012, earnings in the lower accrual band will be treated as producing a flat-rate amount (currently £88.40, equivalent to £1.70 a week), which will be increased annually.[55] The upper accrual band will continue but will not be increased. Therefore, eventually the two accrual bands will have the same value, leaving a flat-rate amount with the additional earnings-related element of the additional state pension ceasing to accrue from around 2030.

A pension forecast gives you a calculation of the amount of additional pension to which you are entitled at current values and an estimate of the additional pension you will receive should you continue working.

Claimants who reached pension age before 6 April 1999

If you reached pension age before 6 April 1999 (ie, if you are a man who was born before 6 April 1934 or a woman who was born before 6 April 1939), the rules were generally more favourable. For an example of how this worked in practice, see the 21st edition of CPAG's *Rights Guide to Non-Means-Tested Benefits*, p244.

Payment to widows, widowers and surviving civil partners

At present, a widow, widower or surviving civil partner who is eligible for a basic state retirement pension based on her/his spouse's/civil partner's contributions can, in certain circumstances, also receive any additional state pension based on her/his spouse's/civil partner's contributions.

It was originally intended that people whose spouses/civil partners died after 5 April 2000 would only inherit a maximum of 50 per cent of that spouse's additional state pension entitlement. However, because of a failure by the (then) Department of Social Security to advise people about the change, the government decided not to implement the change to inherited additional state pensions from SERPS until 6 October 2002 and to phase the reduction over a period of 10 years rather than introduce an immediate 50 per cent cut. This phased reduction only applies to the additional pension inherited under the SERPS scheme. Any additional pension derived from the state second pension scheme is only inheritable at 50 per cent. The percentage of the deceased person's additional state pension entitlement from SERPS which can be inherited by her/his surviving spouse/civil partner is reduced if the deceased person reached pensionable age from 5 October 2002 as follows.[56]

Date when deceased person reached pensionable age	*Maximum % of additional pension passing to surviving spouse or civil partner*
6.10.02 to 5.10.04	90
6.10.04 to 5.10.06	80
6.10.06 to 5.10.08	70

6.10.08 to 5.10.10	60
6.10.10 onwards	50

Note: it is the date on which the deceased person reached pension age which is important for this purpose, not the date on which s/he died.

People who are able to prove that they were given incorrect or incomplete information about the reduction in inherited SERPS additional pension and who have experienced financial loss as a result may also be able to claim compensation for maladministration (see p1261).

The maximum amount of inherited additional pension from state second pension is 50 per cent.

In certain circumstances, a widow, widower or surviving civil partner may be entitled to an additional pension based on both her/his own contributions and those of her/his spouse.[57]

9. Tax, tax credits and other benefits

Retirement pensions are taxable.[58]

Tax credits

Retirement pensions are partially taken into account as income for tax credits (see Chapter 55).

Means-tested benefits

Retirement pensions are taken fully into account for the purposes of means-tested benefits, but pensioners receive a higher rate of some means-tested benefits.

Non-means-tested benefits

Retirement pensions are affected by the overlapping benefit rules (see p1041).

Retirement pensions overlap with contribution-based jobseeker's allowance, incapacity benefit, contributory employment and support allowance, severe disablement allowance, carer's allowance, maternity allowance, widowed parent's allowance and bereavement allowance.

There are special rules if you are entitled to both a Category A and Category B retirement pension.

Passports and other sources of help

You qualify for a Christmas bonus if you receive retirement pension (see p9). People aged 60 or over qualify for free prescriptions and eye tests regardless of their income.

Notes

1. **Who can claim a retirement pension**
 1 *Timbrell v SSWP* [2010] EWCA Civ 701; [2011] AACR 13; R(P) 1/09; R(P) 2/09; *MP v SSWP (RP)* [2009] UKUT 205(AAC); [2010] AACR 13
 2 ss44(1) and 48 SSCBA 1992
 3 ss48A, 48B and 48BB and Sch 3 Part I para 5 SSCBA 1992
 4 s48BB(1) and (2) SSCBA 1992
 5 s48BB(3) and (4) SSCBA 1992
 6 s48B(1) SSCBA 1992
 7 s51(1)(a) SSCBA 1992
 8 s48B(1) SSCBA 1992
 9 s51(1A)(b) SSCBA 1992
 10 s48B(1A) SSCBA 1992
 11 s48BB SSCBA 1992
 12 ss48C(1) and 51(4) SSCBA 1992
 13 s78(3) SSCBA 1992; reg 10 SS(WB&RP) Regs
 14 s36(7) NIA 1965, as kept in force by Sch 1 SS(GRB) No.2 Regs
 15 Reg 17(1)(h) and (3) SS(WB&RP) Regs
 16 s37 NIA 1965, as kept in force by Sch 1 SS(GRB) No.2 Regs
 17 s36(4) NIA 1965, as kept in force by Sch 1 SS(GRB) No.2 Regs
 18 s55 and Sch 5 SSCBA 1992
 19 Sch 2 SS(GRB) No.2 Regs
 20 s54 SSCBA 1992 and reg 2(2) SS(WB&RP) Regs
 21 Reg 2(3) SS(WB&RP) Regs
 22 Sch 5 para 1(2) SSCBA 1992
 23 Sch 5 para A1 SSCBA 1992; SS(DRPSAPGRB)(MP)Regs
 24 Sch 5 para 2(5) SSCBA 1992
 25 Sch 5 para 4 SSCBA 1992
 26 Reg 30(5B)-(5G) SS(C&P) Regs
 27 Reg 4(1)(b)(i) SS(WB&RP) Regs

2. **The rules about your age**
 28 s126 and Sch 4 PA 1995
 29 ss48A-48C SSCBA 1992, as inserted by Sch 4 para 3 PA 1995

4. **The amount of benefit**
 30 ss44(4) and 45 SSCBA 1992
 31 ss30B(7) and 47(1) SSCBA 1992; reg 3A SS(WB&RP) Regs
 32 s47(2) SSCBA 1992
 33 s48A and Sch 4 SSCBA 1992
 34 s48B SSCBA 1992
 35 s78(6) and Sch 4 para 7 SSCBA 1992

5. **Special benefit rules**
 36 s48 SSCBA 1992; regs 1(3) and (3A), 8 and 8A SS(WB&RP) Regs

6. **Claims and backdating**
 37 Reg 4 SS(C&P) Regs
 38 Reg 6 SS(C&P) Regs
 39 Reg 9(1) and Sch 1 SS(C&P) Regs
 40 Reg 15 SS(C&P) Regs
 41 Reg 3(za) SS(C&P) Regs
 42 Reg 3A(4) SS(C&P) Regs
 43 Reg 3(ca) SS(C&P) Regs
 44 Reg 3(cb) SS(C&P) Regs
 45 Reg 3(b) SS(C&P) Regs
 46 Reg 19 and Sch 4 para 13 SS(C&P) Regs
 47 Reg 6(31) and (32) SS(C&P) Regs
 48 s55(3)(a) SSCBA 1992

7. **Getting paid**
 49 Reg 22C SS(C&P) Regs
 50 Reg 22 and Sch 6 para 5 SS(C&P) Regs

8. **The additional state pension scheme**
 51 s47 WRPA 1999
 52 s41 PSA 1993
 53 s15 PA 2007; reg 2 Pensions Act 2007 (Commencement No.4) Order 2011, No.1267
 54 s45(2)(c) and Sch 4A SSCBA 1992
 55 s45(2)(d) and Sch 4B SSCBA 1992
 56 The Social Security (Inherited SERPS) Regulations 2001, No.1085
 57 s52(3) SSCBA 1992

9. **Tax, tax credits and other benefits**
 58 s677 Income Tax (Earnings and Pensions) Act 2003

24

Chapter 24

Severe disablement allowance

This chapter covers:

Key facts

- Severe disablement allowance (SDA) is a benefit for people who are incapable of work.
- SDA was abolished on 6 April 2001, but certain people entitled to it before that date can continue to receive it.
- SDA is a non-means-tested benefit.
- SDA is administered and paid by the DWP.
- If you disagree with an SDA decision, you can apply for a revision or a supersession, or appeal against it (see Chapters 45 and 46).

Future changes: April 2013 and after

Major changes are taking place that affect the benefit and tax credits system (see Chapter 2). From April 2013, total benefit payments to many working-age households will be 'capped' (see p25). It is not yet known if SDA will be in the capped amount. See CPAG's *Welfare Rights Bulletin* for updates.

1. Who is still entitled

You can only get severe disablement allowance (SDA) now if:[1]

- you were getting SDA before 31 January 2011 and there has been no break in your entitlement since that date; *and*
- you continue to meet the qualifying conditions for SDA (see p543); *and either*
- you will reach pension age before 6 April 2014; *or*
- no decision has yet been made on converting your SDA to employment and support allowance (ESA) (see p543).

Until 31 January 2011, in some circumstances, you could requalify for SDA following a break in your entitlement. This is now not possible as, from 31 January 2011, a claim for SDA is treated as a claim for ESA.

Qualifying conditions

To be entitled to SDA now, you must continue to satisfy the usual qualifying conditions for it, including being incapable of work or treated as incapable of work (see p339 and Chapter 32).[2]

See p735 for the very limited circumstances when you may work and still be treated as incapable of work.

You and, in some circumstances, your partner may be required to attend work-focused interviews (see pp1031 and 1033).

See Chapter 4 of the 2000/01 edition of the *Welfare Benefits Handbook* for further details of the qualifying conditions for SDA.

Transfer to employment and support allowance

If you are entitled to SDA and will reach pension age on or after 6 April 2014, at some time before 31 March 2014 the decision maker will carry out a 'work capability assessment' (see Chapter 11).[3] If the decision maker determines that:

- you have limited capability for work and you meet the basic rules of entitlement to ESA (see below and p175), you will be transferred to contributory ESA and your SDA will stop. You will not need to satisfy the national insurance contribution conditions for contributory ESA. If the amount of SDA you receive (including any additions for your dependants) is more than the amount of contributory ESA to which you are entitled, you will qualify for a transitional addition to ensure your income does not fall (see p195);
- you do not have limited for capability for work or you do not meet the basic rules of entitlement to ESA, your entitlement to SDA will stop and you will not be awarded ESA, although you will be able to challenge this decision.

In deciding whether you meet the basic rules of entitlement to ESA described on p175, the rule on entitlement to IS is ignored.

Note:

- If you also get IS on the grounds of disability (see p351), the decision on whether to transfer you to ESA applies to both your IS and SDA claim. If you qualify for IS on a ground other than disability (see p346) and want to continue to get IS rather than transfer to ESA, your entitlement to SDA will stop.
- If you are transferred to contributory ESA you may also qualify for income-related ESA.
- From 1 May 2012, you can only get contributory ESA for a maximum of 365 days. However, days you are either in the 'support group' or in the assessment phase immediately before being in the support group are not counted.

If your SDA is converted into contributory ESA this is likely to affect you, but at the time of writing full details of the new rules were unavailable. See CPAG's *Welfare Rights Bulletin* for updates.

If you reach pension age before 6 April 2014 and continue to satisfy the qualifying conditions you can remain on SDA. When you reach the age of 65 you no longer have to show you are incapable of work or sufficiently disabled to qualify but, as SDA is affected by the overlapping benefit rules, you will not qualify for both retirement pension and SDA in full (see p1041).

2. The amount of benefit

The current basic rate of severe disablement allowance (SDA) is £69 a week. You may also be entitled to an age addition (see pxviii for amounts).

You may be entitled to an increase in your SDA for an adult dependant (see Chapter 33). Increases for dependent children and young people were abolished on 6 April 2003, but some people can continue to qualify for them (see p745).

Note:

- You must report any change of circumstances that might affect your entitlement to SDA (see p1047).
- If you have been overpaid SDA, see Chapter 43.
- If you have been sanctioned for benefit offences, see p1106.

3. Tax, tax credits and other benefits

- Severe disablement allowance (SDA) is not taxable.
- SDA is disregarded when calculating entitlement to tax credits.
- SDA counts in full as income for means-tested benefits.
- SDA is subject to the overlapping benefit rules (see p1041).
- You can qualify for national insurance credits while incapable of work (see p780).

Notes

1. **Who is still entitled**
   1 Art 4 WRPA(No.9)O; reg 2 ESA(TP)Regs; reg 24 ESA(TP)(EA)(No.2) Regs
   2 s68 SSCBA 1992; reg 4 WRPA(No.9)O
   3 ESA(TP)(EA)(No.2) Regs

25

Chapter 25

Social fund: discretionary payments

This chapter covers:

Key facts

- The discretionary social fund includes **community care grants**, **budgeting loans** and **crisis loans**.
- These are one-off payments to cover the cost of items for which it is difficult to budget, as well as travel expenses and living expenses in an emergency.
- You are eligible if you satisfy the qualifying rules, but payments are discretionary and budget-limited.
- Discretionary social fund payments are administered and paid by the DWP.
- If you disagree with a discretionary social fund decision, you can seek a review (see Chapter 48).

Future changes: April 2013 and after

Major changes are taking place that affect the benefits and tax credits system (see Chapter 2).

- From April 2013, the discretionary social fund will be abolished.
- Budgeting loans and 'alignment' crisis loans (paid while waiting for benefit claims to be processed) will be replaced by 'short-term advances'.
- Community care grants and all other crisis loans will be replaced by 'locally administrated assistance' provided by the local authority.

See CPAG's *Welfare Rights Bulletin* for updates.

1. General matters

The discretionary social fund (SF) is different from most other social security provision because:

- it is strictly budget-limited and there is no legal entitlement to a payment;
- most payments are in the form of loans, recoverable by deductions from weekly benefit; *and*
- there is no right of appeal to an independent tribunal, although there is an internal review system and the right to request a further review by a social fund inspector (see p1236).

Legal framework

Payments can be made from the discretionary SF in the form of:

- community care grants (CCGs) to meet needs relating to community care;
- budgeting loans (BLs) to meet intermittent expenses;
- crisis loans (CLs) to meet immediate, short-term needs.[1]

Decisions are made on behalf of the Secretary of State by 'appropriate officers', more commonly referred to as decision makers.[2]

Legally binding 'directions' set out the eligibility conditions for each type of payment, the procedure for reviews and the criteria for managing district budgets.[3]

The rules on the procedural aspects of applying for a grant, loan or review, and the acceptance and recovery of loans, are set out in regulations.[4]

Court decisions create binding caselaw, although they are sometimes only relevant to the particular case in question. Social fund inspector (SFI) decisions do not create binding caselaw but can be useful guidance (see p1237).

Legislation on the SF, together with commentary, can be found in *Social Security Legislation, Volume II* (see Appendix 3). The SF Directions can be found in the *Social Fund Guide* (see p548).

Budgetary control

The government sets the national budget for the SF, and can allocate additional funds to a district – eg, where there has been severe flooding.[5]

An area decision maker is responsible for issuing guidance to decision makers on what needs the budget can afford to meet each month (see p548). However, there is no monthly limit on expenditure since the directions only prohibit exceeding the annual district budget.[6]

Decision makers must consider the budget, but it is only one of the factors they must take into account. It is unlawful to refuse an application solely on budgetary grounds, without considering its urgency and priority, unless the district budget is exhausted.

Guidance

In addition to the legal framework there are several forms of guidance available. These are not legally binding, but decision makers must take them into account.

The *Social Fund Guide* (see Appendix 3) contains national guidance from the Secretary of State on how to interpret the law and directions and on administering the SF.[7] Each district also has local guidance.

Decisions of the SFIs (see p1236) are a useful guide to interpretation and decision making. The SF Independent Review Service (IRS – see Appendix 1) produces an electronic *Journal* which includes a digest of decisions (available on the IRS website).

Advice by the SF Commissioner, who is responsible for the IRS, contains guidance to SFIs on specific areas of the law, which they are expected to follow. The guidance is published on the IRS website and in the *Journal*.

Applications

Where and how to apply

An application for a payment from the discretionary SF should normally be made to your local Jobcentre Plus office. If you are moving out of care and claiming a CCG, apply to the office covering the area to which you are moving, unless you are only claiming removal expenses and/or fares. If you are applying for a CL, you can apply to the office nearest to where your need arises.

Applications for CCGs and BLs must be made in writing, either on an approved form (SF300 for CCGs and SF500 for BLs), or in some other written form, accepted as sufficient by the Secretary of State. An application for a CL is usually made by telephone but can be made in writing on form SF401R for rent in advance, board and lodging costs, and hostel charges, and form SF300 for items and services following a disaster. In practice, the DWP strongly encourages telephone claims. If a CL is awarded following a verbal application, you can confirm your identity and your agreement to the terms of the loan on the telephone. If a CL is refused following a verbal application, you should still receive a written decision together with notification of your right to request a review. If you have difficulty making yourself understood on the telephone, you should be offered an immediate office interview instead.[8]

You can get the application forms from your local DWP office, or download them from www.direct.gov.uk.

Always apply for a CCG rather than a loan if you may be eligible. However, the decision maker has discretion to decide that an application for a CL should be treated as an application for a CCG and vice versa, if information in the application warrants it.[9] If information in a BL application indicates that an application for a CCG or CL might succeed, you should be invited to apply on the appropriate form.[10]

An application can be made on your behalf by another person, so long as you give your written consent (this is not necessary, however, if an appointee is acting for you). Consent can be verbal for a CL claim made by telephone.[11]

Your application is treated as made on the day it is received by the DWP.[12] If your application was incomplete and you comply with a request for additional information, your application is treated as made on the day it was originally received.[13] You are not normally required to produce corroborating evidence and should not be asked for evidence for which you have to pay.[14] It is sometimes helpful, however, to submit supporting evidence that confirms the existence and urgency of your need. If you have someone who knows about your needs (eg, a support or social worker), it is helpful to include her/his details on the form.

Repeat applications

If you have been awarded or refused a CCG or CL for an item or service, you cannot get a CCG or CL for the same item or service if you reapply for it within 12 months of a previous application, unless there has been a relevant change of circumstances. In addition, if you have been awarded a CL for living expenses, a repeat application for living expenses will not be considered if it is for the same period as your earlier award, unless the need arises because of disaster, emergency or other circumstance beyond your control.[15] The rule does not apply to BLs. A relevant change in circumstances could be a change in your personal circumstances or, for example, an increase in the amount available from the district budget.[16]

Decisions

Although awards are discretionary, decision makers must act in accordance with the SF directions and take account of the national and local guidance (see p548).[17] They are also told to 'take particular care that their decisions are not in any way affected by bias or prejudice on such grounds as colour, ethnic or national origin, sexual orientation, sex or religion'.[18]

You should receive a written decision on your application, with an explanation for a refusal or part refusal, together with a notification of your right to request a review (see p1232).

There are no legal time limits in which the DWP must make decisions, but the *Social Fund Guide* instructs decision makers to decide applications 'without delay' once they have all the necessary information and never to delay a decision until the need has passed.[19] Applications for a CL should, where possible, be dealt with on the day the need arises.[20] If there are unreasonable delays, complain to the district manager and, if necessary, ask your MP to take up your case with the manager or the Ombudsman (see p1259).

Payments and overpayments

Payment should normally be made to you, but the DWP can decide to pay a supplier directly[21] and, where appropriate, pay you in the form of food vouchers, travel warrants, cash or instalments. You can request a review of a decision to pay a supplier directly.

If you misrepresent or fail to disclose any material fact, any payment you receive in consequence is recoverable from you.[22] See Chapter 43 for details about overpayments and recovery. You must be notified in writing of any overpayment decision and you have the right to request a review (see Chapter 48).[23]

Tax

Social fund loans and grants are not taxable.

Other benefits and tax credits

Payments from the discretionary SF are disregarded as income and capital for the purposes of means-tested benefits and tax credits, and do not affect entitlement to any non-means-tested benefits.

2. Community care grants

Community care grants (CCGs) are non-repayable grants to help people live independently in the community. There is no legal entitlement to a CCG, but you can request a review if you are not satisfied with a decision (see Chapter 48). You must meet both the eligibility conditions and the qualifying conditions.

Eligibility conditions

To be eligible for a CCG, you must satisfy all of the following conditions, which are laid down in legally binding directions.

- **You must be in receipt of a 'qualifying benefit'** when your application for a CCG is treated as made (see p549).[24] Qualifying benefits are: income support (IS), income-based jobseeker's allowance (JSA) (including payments on account and hardship payments), income-related employment and support allowance (ESA) and pension credit (PC) (guarantee or savings credit). The only exception to this rule is if you are due to leave institutional or residential care (see p552) within six weeks of the date your application for a CCG is made and you are likely to get a qualifying benefit when you leave. If you receive a backdated award of a qualifying benefit which covers the date you applied for a CCG, you are eligible for a CCG. You are not eligible, however, if you apply for a CCG on one of the three 'waiting days' for JSA (see p402) or ESA (see p212) unless you are moving out of institutional or residential care (see p552). You are treated as being 'in receipt of' a qualifying benefit if it is being paid to you, or to an appointee on your behalf.[25] The High Court has held that you are not 'in receipt of' a qualifying benefit if your partner or another member of your family is the claimant.[26] If you are a member of a 'joint-claim couple' (see p413), you are only eligible for a CCG if you are the partner being paid JSA.[27]

- **You must not have too much capital.**[28] Any CCG awarded is reduced by the amount of capital you have in excess of £500 (£1,000 if you or your partner are 60 or over). Capital is calculated as for the qualifying benefit which you are receiving (see Chapter 38). Payments made from the Family Fund to you, your partner or child, and refugee integration loans are ignored. Capital held by your children should be disregarded. Capital below the above limits should not be taken into account as a resource from which a need could be met (see p558).
- **You or your partner must not be involved in a trade dispute,**[29] unless your claim is for travel expenses to visit a sick person (see p555).
- **You must not be a 'person subject to immigration control'** (there are exceptions to this rule) – see p1410.
- **The CCG must not be for an excluded item** (see p555).[30]
- **You must be awarded a CCG of at least £30,**[31] unless your award is for daily living expenses or travel expenses.

Qualifying conditions

As well as meeting the eligibility conditions, you must also show that you need a CCG for one of the following qualifying conditions:[32]

- to help you, or a member of your family, or other person for whom you or a member of your family will be providing care, to establish yourself (or her/himself) in the community following a stay in institutional or residential accommodation in which you (or s/he) received care (see p552); *or*
- to help you, or a member of your family, or other person for whom you or a member of your family will be providing care, to remain in the community rather than enter institutional or residential accommodation in which you (or s/he) will receive care (see p552); *or*
- to help you to set up home in the community as part of a planned resettlement programme following a period during which you have been without a settled way of life (see p553); *or*
- to ease exceptional pressures on you and your family (see p553); *or*
- to allow you, or your partner, to care for a prisoner or young offender on temporary release (see p554); *or*
- to help you, or one or more members of your family, with travel expenses within the UK in certain circumstances (see p555).

Moving out of institutional or residential accommodation

A CCG can be paid to help you, or a member of your family, or other person for whom you or a member of your family will be providing care, to establish yourself (or her/himself) in the community, following a stay in institutional or residential accommodation in which you (or s/he) received care.[33]

Interpretation

- See p554 for the meaning of 'family'.
- 'Institutional or residential accommodation' means accommodation in which residents receive a significant and substantial amount of care, supervision or protection because they are unable to live independently in the community or might be a danger to others in the community.[34] Examples of accommodation given are hospitals, care homes, foster care, hostels, prisons and youth centres.[35] Decision makers are told to treat applications from discharged prisoners with particular urgency and sensitivity, bearing in mind the pressures they face and the risk of reoffending.[36] If you cannot establish that you lived in institutional or residential accommodation, you may still be eligible for a CCG to help you remain in the community, or for planned resettlement (see below and p553).
- You should be eligible if you are establishing yourself in the community for the first time because, for example, you have always lived in care, or you have recently arrived in the UK and have been in a refugee camp overseas or a refugee hostel in the UK (the High Court has ruled that 'the community' is restricted to the UK).[37] The High Court has said that you must be actually or imminently in the community to qualify.[38]
- A 'stay in' institutional or residential accommodation normally means at least three months, or a pattern of frequent or regular admission.[39] The High Court has ruled, however, that undue importance should not be attached to the reference to three months[40] and the SF Commissioner advises that a stay of less than three months can satisfy the direction.[41]

Staying out of institutional or residential accommodation

A CCG can be paid to help you, or a member of your family, or other person for whom you or a member of your family will be providing care, to remain in the community, rather than enter institutional or residential accommodation in which you (or s/he) will receive care.[42]

Interpretation

- See above for the meaning of 'institutional or residential accommodation'.
- See p554 for the meaning of 'family'.
- There is no requirement that a CCG must be able to 'prevent' you going into institutional or residential accommodation. The legal test is whether a CCG will 'help' you remain in the community. Decision makers should consider

whether a CCG would improve your independent life in the community and, therefore, reduce the risk of or delay your admission into care. Going into hospital, even for a short admission, should count as entering care in this context.[43] The risk of care does not have to be immediate, but should be more than a remote possibility (if it is immediate, the application should be given higher priority).[44] If your condition makes you liable to repeated stays in care, you could still get a CCG if it could reduce the frequency or length of stays.

- Actual or potential risk to physical or mental health because of a lack of items such as basic furniture, cooking facilities, clothes, bedding and heaters can be used to argue that a CCG for such items will lessen the risk of entry into hospital or other types of institutional or residential accommodation.

Planned resettlement

A CCG can be paid to help you set up home in the community as part of a planned resettlement programme.[45]

Interpretation

- A programme of resettlement involves help to set up home and help with matters such as budgeting, literacy, careers guidance and benefits advice. 'Setting up home' involves more than just moving into a new property and may still be in process (or even begin) some time after a move has occurred.[46]
- People without a settled way of life might have been in a night shelter, hostel, emergency shelter, temporary supported lodging scheme, or temporary accommodation provided for asylum seekers, or sleeping rough, but this is not an exhaustive list.[47] It could also, for example, cover people moving between the houses of friends or relatives.[48]
- Planned resettlement programmes may be run by local authorities, voluntary organisations, housing associations and registered charities.[49] Again, this is not an exhaustive list and you can argue you are part of a programme planned by any other organisation or person (including yourself), even if they are unconnected to your accommodation.[50] Decision makers are told they may need to check that a resettlement programme exists at the accommodation you are moving from and that you are on such a programme.[51]
- If you cannot qualify for a CCG under this section, you may still be eligible for a CCG to help you move out of, or stay out of, institutional or residential accommodation (see p552).

Easing exceptional pressures on families

A CCG can be paid to ease exceptional pressures on you and your family.[52] The scope for applications on this basis is very wide.

When making your application, always fully explain all the pressures your family is experiencing and how a CCG will ease those pressures and help you to continue living independently in the community.

Exceptional pressures

The following points may be relevant.[53]

- 'Exceptional' means something greater than the normal range of pressures experienced by most families.
- The overall effect of the different pressures on a family should be assessed, including their cumulative impact. Therefore, always list all the pressures affecting your family and explain their overall effect.
- Whether the pressures were foreseeable or are common is irrelevant, although higher priority should be given to a new, unforeseeable need.
- The breakdown of a relationship, particularly involving domestic violence, is a common source of exceptional stress, as is disability.
- Low income, lone parenthood and poor or overcrowded living conditions can be the source of exceptional pressures.
- Pressures that arise from a sudden event (eg, a disaster or fire) can be exceptional and traumatic. Pressures which have existed for a long time do not necessarily become easier to handle.
- There does not have to be any risk of a person going into care for exceptional pressures to exist.
- Mental stress, anxiety, depression, disability and illness are all sources and symptoms of exceptional pressures.
- Exceptional pressures experienced by children are valid – eg, health risk or discomfort arising from lack of clothes or facilities in the home.
- Refugees moving into the community from temporary accommodation provided by the UK Border Agency may face exceptional family pressures.
- Letters of support from professionals can help your case.

Family

The law refers to 'easing exceptional pressures on a person and his family'. This implies that people not living in a family are excluded. This interpretation was endorsed in a High Court case.[54] But it could include, for example, a parent whose child stays with her/him only part of the time.

The SF Commissioner advises that a family could include:[55]

- couples (with or without children);
- 'nuclear' and extended families;
- relationships of long-term interdependence, even where there are no blood or marriage ties;
- a woman who has been pregnant for 24 weeks or more.

Prisoners on temporary release

A CCG can be paid to allow you or your partner to care for a prisoner or young offender on temporary release.[56]

Amount

You will normally be awarded one-seventh of your IS, income-based JSA, income-related ESA, or PC personal allowance for each day you are caring for a prisoner or young offender. If the prisoner is your partner, the suggested amount is one-seventh of the difference between your personal allowance and the couple rate.[57] The £30 minimum rule (see p551) does not apply.[58]

Travel expenses

A CCG can be paid to assist you and/or a member of your family with travel expenses in the UK (including overnight accommodation charges) to:[59]

- visit someone who is ill (in hospital or elsewhere); *or*
- attend a relative's funeral; *or*
- ease a domestic crisis (not defined); *or*
- visit a child who is with the other parent pending a court decision; *or*
- move to suitable accommodation.

Amount

A CCG for travel expenses should be calculated as follows:[60]

- the cost of standard rate public transport (excluding air fares); *or*
- the cost of petrol, either up to the cost of public transport if available or in full if public transport is not available or you are unable to use it; *or*
- taxi fares, if public transport is unavailable or you or your partner cannot use public transport and have no access to private transport; *plus*
- the cost of an escort's fare if you cannot travel alone; *plus*
- the reasonable cost of necessary overnight accommodation.

The £30 minimum rule (see p551) does not apply to a CCG for travel expenses.[61]

Excluded items

The SF directions exclude payment for the items listed below.[62]

Items excluded from community care grants and crisis loans

- A need which occurs outside the UK. This rule may constitute unlawful discrimination in the case of European Economic Area nationals (see p1480).
- An educational or training need, including clothing and tools.
- 'Distinctive' school uniform, or any equipment or sports clothes for school use. You may, however, be eligible for a budgeting loan (BL) (see p560). You may also be eligible for a grant for school uniform from your local authority.
- Travel expenses to and from school. You may, however, be eligible for a BL (see p560). You may also be eligible for help from your local authority.
- School meals taken during school holidays by children who are entitled to free school meals.

- Expenses in connection with court proceedings (including a community service order) – eg, legal fees, court fees, fines, costs, damages and travel expenses. You can, however, get a crisis loan (CL) for emergency travel expenses (see p569).
- Removal charges where you are permanently rehoused following a compulsory purchase order, a redevelopment or closing order, or where there is a compulsory exchange of tenancies or you are permanently rehoused as homeless under the Housing Acts. In all these circumstances, your local authority may help you. Alternatively, you may be eligible for a BL (see p560).
- The cost of domestic assistance or respite care. This would include the cost of home care or short breaks in residential care.
- Repairs to property owned by public sector housing bodies including local authorities, most housing associations, housing co-operatives and housing trusts.
- Medical, surgical, optical, aural or dental items or services. A medical item does not include an everyday item needed because of a medical condition – eg, cotton sheets and non-allergic bedding (when a person is allergic to synthetic), built-up shoes, special beds and incontinence pads. If an item is not in ordinary, everyday use, it should only be treated as a medical item if its sole purpose is to cure, alleviate, treat, diagnose or prevent a medical condition. Wheelchairs (or parts for them) and stairlifts should not be excluded under this test, but you can be refused a payment if help is available from the NHS, social services or elsewhere.[63]
- Work-related expenses. This includes fares when seeking work and the cost of work clothes.[64] You may be able to get help with fares to interviews from Jobcentre Plus. Alternatively you may be eligible for a BL (see p560).
- Debts to government departments – eg, national insurance arrears.
- Investments.
- Council tax and council water charges.
- Housing costs (other than those listed on p557), including:
  - repairs and improvements to your home, including garage, garden and outbuildings (but see below for minor repairs and improvements);
  - deposits to secure accommodation;
  - mortgage payments, rent, service charges, water and sewerage charges and any other accommodation charges.

  Note: repairs and improvements are only excluded if they relate to the structure or permanent fixtures of your home (eg, windows) as opposed to movable items – eg, stairlifts.[65]

Housing costs that are not excluded

You can be awarded:[66]

- a CCG or CL for minor repairs and improvements ('minor' is not defined but relevant factors include the nature and extent of the work, the time needed to complete it and the cost of materials and labour[67]);
- a CCG for overnight accommodation as part of a travel expenses payment (see p555);
- a CL for rent in advance for fresh accommodation where the landlord is not a local authority;
- a CL for housing costs not met by housing benefit, IS, income-based JSA, income-related ESA or PC, and not eligible for direct deductions (see p1048) – eg, emptying cesspits or septic tanks;
- a CL for board and lodging or hostel charges.

A BL is also payable for rent in advance, removal expenses, and the improvement, maintenance and security of the home (see p560).

Additional items excluded from community care grants

- The cost of purchasing, renting or installing a telephone and of any call charges. You may, however, be eligible for help from your local authority social services department if you are chronically sick or disabled.
- Any expenses which the local authority has a statutory duty to meet (discretionary powers do not trigger the exclusion, nor should statutory duties not undertaken by the local authority).
- The cost of any fuel and standing charges.
- Any daily living expenses, such as food and groceries, except where incurred in caring for a prisoner on temporary release or where the maximum amount for a CL has already been awarded (see p569).
- Any item worth less than £30, or several items which together are worth less than £30 (unless the award is for daily living expenses or travel expenses).[68]

Maternity and funeral expenses

Community care grants cannot meet maternity and funeral expenses as these are provided for by the regulated SF (see Chapter 26).[69] Although maternity and funeral expenses are not defined, they do not include items such as clothing for a pregnant woman or a growing (as opposed to newborn) baby, suitable clothes for a funeral, fares to attend a funeral (if not met by a funeral payment) and headstones.[70] The SF Commissioner's Advice states that only maternity expenses to meet the immediate needs of a recently born baby (and not the mother) are excluded from the discretionary SF.[71] A CCG could, therefore, be paid for items such as highchairs, stair gates, prams and even a cot or carrycot if the baby used something else to sleep in immediately after birth.

What to claim for

You can claim for help with any expenses which are not excluded (see p555). Examples include:

- furniture, cookers, beds, bedding and household equipment, floor covering, curtains and heaters;
- moving expenses, including removal costs, fares and storage charges;
- connection charges when setting up or moving home;
- reconnecton charges for fuel where you have been disconnected – though the DWP might only accept this where you are also having direct deductions from your benefit to pay off your debt;
- items which will improve your living conditions, such as minor repairs, redecoration, installation of a pre-payment meter, or a washing machine;
- clothing and footwear;
- maternity and funeral expenses that are arguably not covered by the regulated SF (see p557);
- items needed because of disability (including wheelchairs, stair lifts, special clothing, an orthopaedic mattress or an upright armchair).

Decision making and priorities

When deciding an application for a CCG, the law requires decision makers to have regard to all the circumstances of each case and, in particular:[72]

- the nature, extent and urgency of the need;
- the existence of resources which could meet the need;
- whether any other person or body could wholly or partly meet the need;
- the district budget (see p547);
- the SF directions (see p547);
- national and local guidance (see p548).

The High Court has ruled that need and the priority of an application (see below) should be assessed before budgetary considerations are taken into account.[73] Decision makers must have regard to the district grants budget, however, when they decide whether to award a CCG and how much to pay.

Decision makers should exercise their discretion sensitively and with imagination and avoid a rigid interpretation of the guidance.[74]

The *Social Fund Guide* suggests that applications for CCGs are prioritised according to how effective a payment is likely to be in improving your circumstances in the immediately foreseeable future and in meeting one of the purposes for which a CCG can be awarded (see p551).[75]

Circumstances which may affect priority include:[76]

- mental or physical disability and illness and general frailty;
- physical or social abuse or neglect;
- a long period of residential or institutional care or sleeping rough;

- unstable family circumstances;
- behavioural problems – eg, because of drug or alcohol misuse.

Examples where higher priority should be given include where an award of an item would significantly reduce the risk of your going into care, or would immediately alleviate exceptional pressure on your family in a substantial and noticeable way, or where the lack of an item would seriously undermine your becoming established in the community.[77]

Local guidance specifies which level of priority can be met by the budget, but invariably this tends to be high priority only.

When deciding whether there are other resources which could meet your need, decision makers should not take into account any capital you have below £500 (£1,000 if you or your partner are 60 or over), or your IS, income-based JSA, income-related ESA or PC. Any other income you have should only be taken into account if it is available to meet your needs and is not required to meet other expenses. Attendance allowance and the care component of disability living allowance (DLA) should be treated as required to meet disability-related expenses, unless there is evidence to the contrary (the mobility component of DLA must always be disregarded).[78]

Amount and payment

The amount allowed is likely to be the lowest price that meets the need, taking into account prices charged in national catalogue outlets and high street chain retailers.[79] A higher amount can be considered if there are special needs – eg, disability or the size of your family.[80] Make these needs clear on your claim form. It is not normally necessary to submit written estimates from a supplier, although you may be asked for one if you are asking for removal expenses.[81] You may be offered less than the appropriate amount if the budget is under exceptional pressure but the amount must still be sufficient to cover the cost of the item or service needed.[82] There is no legal maximum award but the minimum in most cases is £30 (see p551). If you are dissatisfied with the amount you have been awarded, consider requesting a review (see p1232).

An award should normally be paid to you but can also be paid directly to a supplier on your behalf. This should only happen in exceptional circumstances – eg, where there is firm evidence that the grant will not be used for its intended purpose.[83]

Tactics

- When completing the application form (SF300), give specific details of each item you need and its cost (or an estimate of the cost).
- Your application must establish that you need a CCG for one of the purposes set out on p551. Explain how the payment you are requesting will help the

relevant person to become established or remain in the community, or will help ease exceptional pressures on you and your family.

- Submit supporting evidence if you have it – eg, from a doctor or social worker.
- If you are dissatisfied with a decision, consider asking for a review (see p1232).

3. Budgeting loans

Budgeting loans (BLs) are interest-free loans intended to help people with intermittent expenses which are difficult to budget for after a period on a qualifying benefit (see below). There is no legal entitlement to a BL, but unlike community care grants (CCGs) and crisis loans (CLs) (see pp550 and 564), decision making is based on legally binding rules about who is in your household, rather than on discretion.

Although you can request a review (see p549), if you are refused a BL or are given less than you asked for, a decision is only likely to be changed if it was based on incorrect information about your circumstances, or if the amount you are allowed to borrow has increased (see p1234).

Eligibility

To be eligible for a BL, you must satisfy all of the following conditions, which are laid down in legally binding directions.

- **You must be in receipt of a 'qualifying benefit'** when your BL application is determined. Qualifying benefits are: income support (IS), income-based jobseeker's allowance (JSA) (including payments on account and hardship payments), income-related employment and support allowance (ESA) and pension credit (PC) (guarantee or savings credit).[84] You are treated as being in receipt of a qualifying benefit if it is being paid to you, or to an appointee on your behalf.[85] You are eligible if you receive a backdated award of a qualifying benefit, covering the date your application is determined.[86] The High Court has held that you are not 'in receipt of' a qualifying benefit if your partner or another member of your family is the claimant.[87] If you are a member of a 'joint-claim couple' (see p413), you are only eligible for a BL if you are the partner being paid JSA.[88]
- **You and/or your partner, between you, must have been receiving a qualifying benefit throughout the 26 weeks before the date on which your application is determined**, disregarding any number of breaks of 28 days or less.[89] A period covered by a payment of arrears should count, as should any benefit received while in Northern Ireland.[90] The three waiting days at the start of a claim for JSA or ESA (see pp402 and 212) do not count.[91] More than one partner could help you satisfy the qualifying period.

- **You must not have too much capital.**[92] Any BL award is reduced by the amount of capital you have in excess of £1,000 (£2,000 if you or your partner are 60 or over). Capital is calculated as for the qualifying benefit that you are receiving (see Chapter 38). Payments made from the Family Fund to you, your partner or child, and **refugee integration loans** are ignored.[93] Capital held by your child(ren) should be disregarded.
- **You, or your partner, must not be involved in a trade dispute** (see p700).[94]
- **You must not be a 'person subject to immigration control'** (there are exceptions to this rule) – see p1410.
- **The loan must be for one or more of the following categories of allowable expenses:**[95]
  - furniture and household equipment;
  - clothing and footwear;
  - rent in advance and/or removal expenses to secure fresh accommodation;
  - improvement, maintenance and security of the home;
  - travelling expenses;
  - expenses associated with seeking or re-entering work;
  - hire purchase (HP) and other debts for any of the above items.

  You are required to tick the category of expense for which you need the loan on the application form. You are not required to specify the particular items you need – eg, bed, winter coat. The exclusions which apply to CCGs and CLs (see p555) do not apply to BLs. **Note:** maternity and funeral expenses are due to be added to this list in 2012. See CPAG's *Welfare Rights Bulletin* for updates.
- **The loan must be a minimum of £100 and a maximum of £1,500** (less any outstanding social fund (SF) loans you and your partner have).[96] You must state how much you are asking for on your application.
- **You must be likely to be able to repay the loan** (see p562).[97]

Decision making and priorities

When deciding a BL application, the law requires decision makers to consider:[98]

- the prescribed factual criteria relating to your personal circumstances (see p657);
- the existence of resources which could meet the need;
- the district budget (see p547);
- the SF directions;
- national and local guidance (see p548);
- the likelihood of repayment and the time it would take.

In practice, decisions are determined by two factors.

- **The 'weighting' of your application.** This depends on who is in your household. See p562 for more details.
- **The baseline figure.** This is the amount determined by the Secretary of State that a single person should receive. The maximum payable for applications

with a higher weighting is calculated by multiplying this baseline figure by the weighting of the application. If, for example, the baseline figure is £300, the maximum payable for an application with a weighting of one and one-third will be £400. The baseline figure may vary over the course of the year.

The actual amount you can borrow also depends on the amount you can repay within 104 weeks and whether you already have any outstanding BLs (see below).

Although decisions are legally made by decision makers, decision making is largely an automated process, with weightings and awards automatically calculated by computer.

The weighting of applications

The weighting of your application is as follows:[99]

- single people have a weighting of one;
- couples without children have a weighting of one and one-third;
- families (including lone parents) with children have a weighting of two and one-third.

Amount

The actual amount of BL you will be offered depends on the following factors.[100]

- **The amount you request.** You will not be offered more than you ask for, but you may be offered less because of the factors below.
- **The legal minimum and maximum amounts and the capital rules.** You cannot be offered a loan of less than £100 or more than £1,500 (less any outstanding SF loans). The amount of your award will also be reduced if you have too much capital (see p551).
- **The weighting of your application** and the baseline figure (see above).
- **The amount of any outstanding BL debt you or your partner have.**
  - If you have no outstanding BLs, you will be offered the maximum amount appropriate to the weighting of your application, or the amount you have requested, if this is lower.
  - If you do have an outstanding BL debt, the maximum amount you can borrow is reduced by the amount of your outstanding BL debt.
- **The amount you are likely to be able to repay.** Generally, this is the amount you can repay within 104 weeks (see below).[101]

Repayments

All loans must be repaid to the DWP.[102]

The decision maker may give you more than one option for repaying a loan, depending on whether you have any other SF loans outstanding and your other financial commitments. S/he may offer an option of a higher loan with an increased repayment rate, but you cannot be asked to repay at a rate higher than 20 per cent of your IS/income-based JSA/income-related ESA applicable amount or PC appropriate minimum guarantee plus any child tax credit or child benefit you receive. The loan must be repaid within 104 weeks.[103]

You will receive a written decision on your application for a BL with details of any loan offers and repayment terms. You have 14 days from the date the decision was sent to return the declaration agreeing to one of the offers made to you (the time limit can be extended for 'special reasons').[104]

Methods of repayment

Both BLs and CLs are nearly always recovered by direct deductions from benefit, although you can make a payment at any time to pay off, partially or wholly, the debt. Deductions can only be made from the following benefits:[105]

- IS;
- PC;
- JSA (contribution-based or income-based);
- ESA (contributory or income-related);
- incapacity benefit;
- severe disablement allowance;
- carer's allowance;
- disablement benefit, reduced earnings allowance and industrial death benefit;
- bereavement benefits (excluding the lump-sum bereavement payment) and widows' benefits;
- retirement pensions;
- maternity allowance.

Increases of benefit for age and dependants, and additional benefit under the additional state pension scheme, are also subject to deduction. Deductions from benefit cannot be made where you are subject to a debt relief order (DRO). Formerly, deductions could be made where there was an order for bankruptcy, but this has now been held not to be permissible. The loan is also not recoverable by deduction from benefit at the end of the DRO/bankruptcy. It is now unclear whether deductions can still be made where there has been a sequestration order under Scottish bankruptcy law.[106] However, from 19 March 2012 social fund loans can no longer be included in DROs or bankruptcy proceedings.

A loan can be legally recovered from:[107]

- you (the applicant) or the person who the loan was for;
- your partner, if you are living together as a couple as defined for IS purposes (see p753);
- a 'liable relative' (see p804) or a person who has given a sponsorship undertaking.

Rescheduling repayment terms

You cannot request a review of a decision relating to repayment terms or recovery. If you have accepted a loan, however, and the repayment terms are causing hardship (eg, because your financial situation has deteriorated), you can ask the DWP to reschedule the loan by lowering the weekly repayment rate.

Tactics

- Always apply for a CCG, if you are eligible (see p550), rather than a BL. **Note:** your application for a BL will *not* normally be considered for a CCG (see p548).
- When completing the BL application form (SF500), give details requested about your debts and commitments, as these will affect the standard repayment rate of any loan offer (see p562).
- State how much you are applying for. Bear in mind the minimum and maximum amounts (see p561) and the capital rules (see p551). The local guidance, obtainable from your local DWP office (see p548), should indicate the maximum BL applicable to your situation (see p561). You can use this figure to work out roughly how much you are likely to be offered, depending on your circumstances (see p562).
- Consider the repayment terms carefully before accepting a BL. Deductions of significant amounts from your weekly benefit may leave you seriously short of money. However, BLs are at least interest free. If you accept a BL but later find that the repayments are causing you hardship, ask for the loan to be rescheduled – ie, for repayments to be reduced.

4. **Crisis loans**

Crisis loans (CLs) are interest-free loans that are intended to help people with their immediate short-term needs in a crisis. Unlike budgeting loans (BLs), you do not have to be in receipt of benefit to qualify. There is no legal entitlement to a CL, but you can request a review if you are refused a payment or get less than you asked for (see p1232).

Eligibility

To be eligible for a CL, you must satisfy all of the following conditions, which are laid down in legally binding directions.

- **You must be aged 16 or over.**
- **You must be without sufficient resources to meet the immediate short-term needs of yourself and/or your family** (see p565).[108]
- **You must not be an excluded person** (see p566).[109]
- **You must not be a 'person subject to immigration control'** (there are exceptions to this rule) – see p1410.
- **The CL must not be for an excluded item** (see p567).[110]
- **The CL must be to help you meet:**[111]
  - expenses in an emergency, or as a consequence of a disaster, where a CL is the only means by which serious damage or serious risk to the health and

safety of yourself or a member of your family may be prevented (see p567); *or*

- rent in advance payable to a landlord who is not a local authority and where a community care grant (CCG) is being awarded following a stay in institutional or residential accommodation (see p569).

- **The loan cannot exceed £1,500** (less any outstanding social fund (SF) loans you and your partner have).[112] There are also more specific maximum amounts relating to items, services and living expenses (see p569). There is no legal minimum amount of CL.
- **You must be likely to be able to repay the loan** (see p569).[113]
- **You must not have had more than two previous CLs for living expenses within the previous 12 months.**[114] This does not apply if it is an alignment payment (loan made while waiting for a benefit claim to be processed) or there is a disaster or emergency which you could not have avoided.

Resources

You must be without sufficient resources to meet the immediate short-term needs of yourself and/or your family. All resources that are actually available to you, or could be obtained in time to meet the need, should be taken into account.[115] Resources available on credit should only be taken into account if you are not on income support (IS), income-based jobseeker's allowance (JSA), income-related employment and support allowance (ESA) or pension credit (PC) and can afford the required repayments.[116]

The following resources should be disregarded:[117]

- other SF payments, housing benefit (HB) and the mobility component of disability living allowance;
- any run-on payments of HB, council tax benefit or mortgage interest;
- refugee integration loans;
- the value of your home, premises acquired for occupation within the next six months, and premises occupied by a relative or your ex-partner;
- the value of any reversionary interest – ie, an interest in property or capital which you will only be able to enjoy in the future when a specified event occurs;
- your business assets;
- any sum paid to you because of damage to, or loss of, your home or personal possessions and intended for their repair or replacement;
- any sum acquired on the express condition that it is used for essential repairs or improvements to your home;
- any compensation award set aside for the replacement of lost livelihood;
- personal possessions, except those acquired for the purpose of qualifying for a CL;

- any payments from the Independent Living Funds, the Macfarlane Trust, the Variant Creutzfeldt-Jakob Disease Trusts and the Skipton Fund;
- payments made under s17 of the Children Act (s22 of the Children (Scotland) Act), unless they are for the same need as the CL.

Decision makers are also advised to disregard other resources if it is reasonable to do so.[118] You could argue that money set aside to meet forthcoming bills (eg, council tax and fuel) is not available and should be disregarded. The SF Commissioner advises social fund inspectors (SFIs) to start from the premise that IS premiums, other benefits and capital are not available to meet the need, unless there is clear evidence to the contrary.[119]

Decision makers are told not to refer applicants to employers, relatives or close friends routinely, unless there is reason to believe their help will be forthcoming.[120] They are also reminded that social services do not normally meet financial needs.[121] The possibility of getting a BL should not be used as a reason for refusing a CL.[122]

Excluded people

People excluded in all circumstances

The following people are excluded from getting a CL in all circumstances:[123]

- people in hospital and care homes (independent or local authority), *unless* their discharge is planned to take place within the next two weeks. (**Note:** people in care homes in Scotland are only excluded if they are receiving nursing or personal care);
- prisoners and people lawfully detained, including those released on temporary licence (but not those released on parole or on bail pending a court hearing);[124]
- members of religious orders who are fully maintained by the order;
- people in 'relevant education' (see p634) who are not entitled to IS, income-based JSA or income-related ESA.

People excluded in some circumstances

The following people are excluded from getting a CL except in very limited circumstances:[125]

- full-time students not on IS, income-based JSA, income-related ESA or PC (including payments on account) – they can only get a CL for expenses arising out of a disaster;
- someone who is a 'person from abroad' (ie, who fails or would fail the habitual residence test for the purposes of IS, PC, income-based JSA or income-related ESA – see p1443) – s/he can only get a CL for expenses arising out of a disaster;
- people involved in a trade dispute (see p700);
- people subject to certain disallowances or sanctions to their JSA, ESA, IS or PC (see p567).

People subject to disallowances or sanctions

Generally you cannot get a CL if you are in a trade dispute or subject to disallowances or sanctions unless the CL is for expenses arising from a disaster, or the application is not as a result of the disallowance or sanction.

However, the restriction does not apply to some lone parents (see p1035), or if you are receiving a JSA hardship payment as a vulnerable person (although in the latter case, the amount payable for living expenses is restricted – see p569), or if your fraud sanction is limited to 20 per cent. Your partner can apply for a CL if you are subject to a disallowance or sanction, but the amount payable for living expenses is restricted (see p569).[126]

Excluded items

You cannot get a CL for any of the items listed on p555.

In addition, you cannot get a CL for the following:[127]

- telephone purchase, installation, call and rental charges;
- mobility needs (this does not include travel expenses);
- holidays;
- television or radio, TV licence, aerial or TV rental;
- garaging, parking, purchase and running costs of any motor vehicle except where payment is being considered for emergency travel expenses.

Since 4 April 2011, you can no longer get a CL for items such as cookers and beds except if there has been a disaster.

Emergencies and disasters

Most CLs can only be awarded in an emergency or following a disaster. The SF Commissioner's Advice defines an emergency as 'an unforeseen circumstance or pressing need, either of which requires immediate remedy or action' and a disaster as 'an event that causes great distress or destruction'.[128] Both the risk of an emergency, as well as an emergency or disaster that has already occurred, could trigger a payment. Always explain why a particular situation constitutes an emergency or disaster for you or your family. The consequences, rather than the causes, of the crisis should be the key issue.[129] Self-inflicted crises are not excluded and decision makers should not deny you a CL based on their judgements about your behaviour. Loss of money in the past should not prejudice the payment of a CL needed because of a further loss.

A CL has to be the only means of preventing serious damage or serious risk to health or safety. If a decision maker suggests there are 'other means', which you believe are impractical or unavailable, ask for a review. The burden of proof is on the decision maker (or SFI) to show that there are other means which are actually available to you.[130] 'Health' and 'safety' are not defined, but health includes both physical and mental health, while safety relates to actual or potential danger.[131] Lack of adequate cooking, heating or sleeping facilities could seriously undermine your health, particularly if you already have health problems.[132] Any supporting evidence from a doctor or social worker will help your case. Survival for a period without money or a CL does not mean that a CL is not the only means of preventing serious damage or risk to your health or safety.

Decision making and priorities

When deciding an application for a CL, the law requires decision makers to have regard to all the circumstances of each case and, in particular:[133]

- the nature, extent and urgency of the need;
- the existence of resources which could meet the need;
- whether any other person or body could wholly or partly meet the need;
- the district budget (see p547);
- the SF directions (see p547);
- national and local guidance (see p548);
- the likelihood of repayment and the time it would take.

The High Court has ruled that need and the priority of an application should be assessed before budgetary considerations are taken into account.[134] The *Social Fund Guide* states that an application for a CL to prevent serious damage or risk to health or safety will by its nature be high priority.[135]

Decision makers should exercise their discretion flexibly and avoid a rigid interpretation of the guidance.

Living expenses for a short period

A CL could be awarded to meet day-to-day living expenses if:

- you are waiting for your first benefit payment or wages;[136]
- you are facing hardship because your employer has imposed a compulsory unpaid holiday;[137]
- you have lost money or you have lost a cheque and replacement is delayed or not made (see p1043 on lost payments);[138]
- you cannot get IS, income-based JSA or income-related ESA because your capital is over the prescribed limit (see p971) but you cannot realise your assets immediately;[139]
- you are homeless and need living expenses (the *Social Fund Guide* stresses the risk to physical and mental health brought about by sleeping rough and prolonged homelessness);[140]
- you have been discharged from prison and have insufficient money to meet your needs until your first payment of benefit (this can apply even if you have been paid a discharge grant).[141]

A CL should only cover living expenses for more than 14 days in exceptional circumstances – eg, a continuing crisis, loss of money which would normally cover you until your next income is due, or no money because of misfortune or mismanagement.[142]

Other needs

A CL could also be awarded to meet:

- emergency travel expenses if you are stranded away from home, or emergency fares to hospital;[143]
- fuel reconnection charges or enough to charge a fuel card or buy a token for a prepayment meter sufficient to restore supply but not future consumption;[144]
- up to four weeks' rent (up to the level of your likely HB) payable in advance to a landlord other than a local authority, where a CCG is also awarded to help you return to the community;[145]
- the effects of disasters – eg, fire or flood (see p567).[146]

Amount

There is no legal minimum. There is a general legal maximum of £1,500 less any outstanding SF loan(s) you have. You also cannot be awarded more than you can afford to repay,[147] usually calculated by multiplying your weekly repayment rate by 104. If you already have one or more loans, you may find you are offered less than you asked for. There are also more specific legal maximums for items, services and living expenses.

Items and services. The maximum you can get is the reasonable cost of purchase (including delivery and installation) or the cost of repair, if cheaper.[148] You should not normally be required to provide estimates and decision makers are not expected to check the amount requested against a price list.[149]

Living expenses.[150]

- The normal maximum you can get is 60 per cent of the appropriate IS or income-based JSA personal allowance for you *and* any partner (see pp753 and 816) plus £64.99 for each child.
- If you have been disallowed JSA because you have been sanctioned (see Chapter 20) or have failed to satisfy the jobseeking conditions, the maximum CL payable to your partner for living expenses is restricted to 60 per cent of her/his JSA personal allowance (see p816) plus £64.99 for each child.
- If you are getting a hardship payment of JSA (see p484), the maximum CL you can get for living expenses is the lesser of:
  - 60 per cent of the normal income-based JSA personal allowance for you and any partner (see pp753 and 816) plus £64.99 for each child;
  - the hardship rate of income-based JSA payable for you and any family.

Repayments

The guidance says that a CL must be repaid to the DWP within 104 weeks and the total debt must not exceet £1,500. When considering your ability to repay, the decision maker will take into account any existing debts you have. CLs can be recovered by weekly deductions from most benefits. The rules are the same as for BLs (see p563).

Rescheduling repayment terms

You cannot request a review of a decision relating to the rate of repayment or the recovery of loans. You can request a change in your repayment terms, however, by writing to the DWP, either before accepting a loan, or at any time after accepting a loan (rescheduling), explaining why the repayment terms are unacceptable – eg, because they will cause you more hardship. Give details of your financial commitments and any relevant changes in your financial circumstances.

Tactics

- Make sure you explain all your needs and circumstances and that a CL is the only way you can avoid a serious risk to your health (see p569). Bear in mind the rules on repeat applications on p549.
- If you claim on the telephone you will normally receive a decision in the same call. If not, you should insist on, and normally receive, a decision on the day your need arises. If there are unreasonable delays, complain to the district manager and, if necessary, ask your MP or an advice agency to intervene. Decisions should be based on your circumstances when you apply and a decision should never be delayed on the basis that the need will pass.
- If you are dissatisfied with the decision, consider requesting a review (see p1232). Insist on the review being carried out speedily. You can reschedule the repayment terms of a loan if they are causing you hardship (see above).
- If you are refused a CL on the grounds that another section should pay an interim payment, ask the member of staff to check that the payment is being made. If it is not, ask for a review.

Notes

1. **General matters**

1 s138 SSCBA 1992
2 s139(1) SSCBA 1992
3 ss138 and 140 SSCBA 1992; s66 SSAA 1992; SF Dirs
4 SF(AM) Regs; SF(AR) Regs; SF(RDB) Regs; SF(Misc) Regs
5 s168 SSAA 1992
6 SF Dir 40 and 42; part 5 paras 44-49 SFG
7 s140(2) SSCBA 1992
8 part 3 para 25 SFG
9 s140(4)(aa) SSCBA 1992; SF Dir 49; part 3 para 20 SFG
10 part 2 para 407 SFG
11 Reg 5 SF(AM) Regs
12 Reg 6(2) SF(AM) Regs
13 Reg 6(3) and (4) SF(AM) Regs
14 part 2 paras 30-31 and part 3 paras 33-34 SFG
15 s140(4)(a) SSCBA 1992; SF Dir 7; part 2 paras 56-57 and part 3 paras 181-84 SFG
16 part 2 para 57 and part 3 para 198 SFG
17 s140 SSCBA 1992
18 part 1 para 14 SFG
19 part 2 para 18 and part 3 para 15 SFG
20 part 3 para 19 SFG
21 s138(3) SSCBA 1992
22 s71ZA SSAA 1992; SF Dir 43
23 SF Dir 44

2. **Community care grants**

24 SF Dir 25
25 SF Dir (General)
26 *R v SFI ex parte Davey,* 19 October 1998, unreported (HC)
27 part 2 para 44-45 SFG
28 SF Dir 27
29 SF Dir 26
30 SF Dir 29
31 SF Dir 28
32 SF Dir 4
33 SF Dir 4(a)(i)
34 part 2 para 100 SFG
35 part 2 para 107 SFG
36 part 2 para 141 SFG
37 *R v SFI ex parte Mohammed* [1993] COD 263 (HC)
38 *R v Secretary of State for Social Security ex parte Healey* [1991] COD 68 (HC)
39 part 2 para 102 SFG
40 *R v SFI ex parte Sherwin* [1991] COD 68 (HC)
41 SF Commissioner's Advice on 'Direction 4(a)(i)', 1 May 2001
42 SF Dir 4(a)(ii)
43 SF Commissioner's Advice on 'Direction 4(a)(ii)', 1 October 2003
44 part 2 para 168 SFG
45 SF Dir 4(a)(v)
46 SF Commissioner's Advice on 'Direction 4(a)(v)', 1 May 2003
47 part 2 para 308 SFG
48 SF Commissioner's Advice to SFIs, IRS, *The Journal*, Winter 2001/02
49 part 2 para 311 SFG
50 SF Commissioner's Advice on 'Direction 4(a)(v)', 1 May 2003
51 part 2 para 313 SFG
52 SF Dir 4(a)(iii)
53 part 2 paras 227-230 SFG
54 *R v Secretary of State for Social Security ex parte Healey* [1991] COD 68 (HC)
55 SF Commissioner's Advice on 'Direction 4(a)(iii)', 4 February 2002
56 SF Dir 4(a)(iv)
57 part 2 para 303 SFG
58 SF Dir 28(b)
59 SF Dir 4(b)
60 part 2 paras 339-41 SFG
61 SF Dir 28(b)
62 SF Dirs 23 and 29
63 CSB/1482/1985; *R v SFI ex parte Connick* 8 June 1993, unreported (HC); part 3 paras 222-27 SFG; SF Commissioner's Advice on 'Excluded Items', 18 June 2001
64 part 3 paras 228 SFG
65 SF Commissioner's Advice on 'Housing Costs (General)', 1 March 2003
66 SF Dirs 23(2f) and 29(d)
67 part 2 para 84 and part 3 paras 218 SFG
68 SF Dir 28
69 s138(1)(b) SSCBA 1992; *R v SFI ex parte Harper* [1998] COD 221 (HC)
70 part 2 paras 68-76 and part 3 paras 239-47 SFG
71 SF Commissioner's Advice on 'Maternity Expenses', 2 January 2002
72 s140 SSCBA 1992

73 *R v SFI ex parte Taylor* [1998] COD 152 (HC)
74 part 2 para 13 SFG
75 part 2 paras 348-50 SFG
76 part 2 para 352 SFG
77 part 2 para 353 SFG
78 SF Commissioner's Advice on 'Capital Resources', 18 June 2003 and 'Income Resources', 14 October 2003
79 part 2 para 368 SFG
80 part 2 para 369 SFG
81 part 2 para 125 SFG
82 part 2 paras 374-75 SFG
83 part 2 paras 318-19 and part 3 paras 310-11 SFG

3. **Budgeting loans**
84 SF Dir 8(1)(a)
85 SF Dir (General)
86 part 4 para 28 SFG
87 *R v SFI ex parte Davey*, 19 October 1998, unreported (HC)
88 part 4 para 32 SFG
89 SF Dir 8(1)(c) and 8(2)
90 part 4 paras 28-29 SFG
91 SF Dir 8(3); part 4 para 30 SFG
92 SF Dir 9
93 SF Dir 9(3)
94 SF Dir 8(1)(b)
95 SF Dir 2
96 SF Dir 53(3) and (4)
97 SF Dir 11
98 s140(1A) SSCBA 1992
99 SF Dir 52
100 SF Dir 53
101 part 4 para 74 SFG
102 s78(1) SSAA 1992
103 part 4 paras 71-79 SFG
104 Reg 7(5) and 7(6) SF(AM) Regs
105 Reg 3 SF(RDB) Regs
106 *SSWP v Payne & Anor* [2011] UKSC 60
107 s78(3) SSAA 1992

4. **Crisis loans**
108 SF Dir 14
109 SF Dirs 15-16
110 SF Dir 23
111 SF Dir 3
112 SF Dir 21
113 SF Dir 22
114 SF Dir 14C
115 part 3 para 53 SFG
116 part 3 para 54 SFG
117 part 3 paras 55-65 SFG
118 part 3 paras 55 and 66 SFG
119 SF Commissioner's Advice on 'Crisis Loans and Resources', 18 June 2001, part 3 para 55 SFG
120 part 3 para 69 SFG
121 part 3 para 70 SFG
122 SF Commissioner's Advice on 'Direction 3 – Only Means', 29 April 2001
123 SF Dir 15
124 part 3 para 69 SFG
125 SF Dirs 16 and 17
126 SF Dirs 17 and 18
127 SF Dir 23(2)
128 SF Commissioner's Advice on 'Direction 3 – Emergency/Disaster', 11 August 2003
129 SF Commissioner's Advice on 'Direction 3 – Emergency/Disaster', 11 August 2003
130 SF Commissioner's Advice on 'Direction 3 – Only Means', 29 April 2002
131 SF Commissioner's Advice on 'Direction 3 – Serious Risk', 11 August 2003
132 SF Commissioner's Advice on 'Direction 3 – Serious Risk', 11 August 2003
133 s140 SSCBA 1992
134 *R v SFI ex parte Taylor* [1998] COD 152 (HC)
135 part 3 para 315 SFG
136 part 3 para 283 SFG
137 part 3 para 284 SFG
138 part 3 paras 277-78 SFG
139 part 3 paras 285-86 SFG
140 part 3 paras 290-94 SFG
141 part 3 paras 298-301 SFG
142 part 3 paras 279-80 SFG
143 part 3 paras 276 SFG
144 part 3 paras 287-89 SFG
145 part 3 paras 295-96 SFG
146 part 3 paras 253-59 SFG
147 SF Dir 22
148 SF Dir 21
149 part 3 para 339 SFG
150 SF Dirs 18 and 20

Chapter 26

Social fund: regulated payments

This chapter covers:

Key facts

- The regulated social fund covers one-off payments for specific circumstances. These are Sure Start maternity grants, funeral expenses payments, cold weather payments and winter fuel payments.
- Conditions of entitlement are laid down in regulations.
- Regulated social fund payments are administered and paid by the DWP.
- If you disagree with a decision, you can apply for a revision or appeal against it (see Chapters 45 and 46).

Future changes: April 2013 and after

Major changes are taking place that affect the benefits and tax credits system (see Chapter 2). However, there are no plans to change the regulated social fund. It is not yet clear what levels of universal credit will count as qualifying benefits for regulated payments. See CPAG's *Welfare Rights Bulletin* for updates.

1. Sure Start maternity grants

You are entitled to a Sure Start maternity grant if you satisfy all of the following rules.

- You or your partner have been awarded one of the following qualifying benefits in respect of the day you claim a maternity grant:[1]
  - income support;
  - income-based jobseeker's allowance (including hardship payments);

- income-related employment and support allowance;
- child tax credit paid at a rate exceeding the family element (see p1309);
- working tax credit including the disabled worker or severe disability element (see p1311);
- pension credit (guarantee or savings credit).

You are eligible if you receive a backdated award of a qualifying benefit covering the date you claim a maternity grant. If you are waiting for a decision on a claim for a qualifying benefit, the DWP may defer making a decision on your maternity grant claim until the qualifying benefit claim has been decided. If your claim for a maternity grant is refused while you are waiting for a decision on a claim for a qualifying benefit, you should reclaim a maternity grant within three months of being awarded the qualifying benefit (see p1029). **Note:** if you do not claim a maternity grant within the time limits (see p575), a backdated award of a qualifying benefit will not qualify you for a grant. If you are not entitled to a qualifying benefit in your own right because you are under 16 (or under 19 and in 'relevant education' – see p634), a member of your family can claim a maternity grant for you if s/he is getting a qualifying benefit in respect of you.

- One of the following applies:[2]
  - you or a member of your family are pregnant or have given birth in the last three months (including stillbirth after 24 weeks of pregnancy[3]);
  - you are the parent (but not the mother) of a child who is less than 12 months old, you are responsible for the child and are not the mother's partner;
  - you are the guardian of a child who is less than 12 months old;
  - you or your partner have a child who is less than 12 months old placed with you for adoption and you are responsible for the child;
  - you have adopted a child who is less than 12 months old under a recognised adoption which takes place outside the UK;
  - you or your partner have been granted a residence order or adoption order for a child who is less than 12 months old;
  - you and your spouse have been granted a parental order allowing you to have a child by a surrogate mother.

  In the last six cases, you are entitled to a payment even if one has already been made to the birth mother or a member of her family.[4]
- There is no other member of your family who is under 16 at the time of claim. However, a grant can be awarded for each child of a multiple birth provided there is no other child under 16. If you are under 20 and another member of your family claims for you, the grant is payable, provided you do not have other children under 16.[5]
- You or your partner are not involved in a trade dispute (see p700), unless specified circumstances apply.[6]
- You claim within the time limits (see p575).

- You have received health and welfare advice from a health professional (see p575).[7]
- You are not a 'person subject to immigration control' (there are exceptions to this rule) – see p1410.

The terms 'partner' and 'family' in the above rules have almost the same meanings as they do for IS purposes (see p751).[8]

Note: maternity expenses will be included as one of the allowable expenses for budgeting loans in 2012. See CPAG's *Welfare Rights Bulletin* for updates.

The rules about your age

There are no special rules on age.

Amount

You are entitled to a grant of £500 for each child or expected child.[9] The payment is not affected by any capital you have.

Claiming and getting paid

Claim on Form SF100, which you can get from your local Jobcentre Plus office or from www.direct.gov.uk. There are strict time limits for claiming (see below). The back of your claim form must be signed by a health professional (ie, midwife, health visitor or doctor) to confirm that you have received health and welfare advice on your baby or your maternal health.

Your date of claim is normally the date your form is received by the DWP.[10] If you make a written claim in some other way, you should be sent the appropriate form to complete. If you return it within one month, or such longer period as the Secretary of State considers reasonable, your date of claim is the date the DWP received your initial application.[11] See p573 for when your claim can be backdated if you are subsequently awarded a qualifying benefit.

If you claim before the birth, you need to submit a maternity certificate (MAT B1), a note from your doctor or midwife or an ante-natal clinic appointment card showing your expected date of childbirth. If you claim after your child is born, you are usually asked for a maternity, birth or adoption certificate.

The rules on getting paid and the recovery of overpayments are as for most other benefits (see pp1038 and 1079).

Time limits

You can claim a maternity grant at any time from 11 weeks before the first day of your expected week of childbirth until three months after the actual date of the birth. If you adopt a child, have a residence order for a child, or have a child by a surrogate mother, you can claim up to three months following the date of the adoption, residence order or parental order subject to the child being under 12 months when the claim is made. There is no provision for claiming outside the time limits.[12]

2. Funeral expenses payments

You qualify for a funeral expenses payment if you satisfy all of the following rules.

- You or your partner (see p579) have been awarded one of the following qualifying benefits in respect of the day you claim a funeral payment:[13]
  - income support (IS);
  - income-based jobseeker's allowance (including hardship payments);
  - income-related employment and support allowance;
  - housing benefit (HB);
  - council tax benefit (including second adult rebate where you are the 'second adult' – see p117);
  - child tax credit paid at a rate which exceeds the family element (see p1309);
  - working tax credit which includes the disabled worker or severe disability element (see p1310);
  - pension credit (guarantee or savings credit – see Chapter 22).

  You are eligible if you receive a backdated award of a qualifying benefit which covers the date you claim a funeral payment. If you are waiting for a decision on a claim for a qualifying benefit, the DWP may defer making a decision on a claim for a funeral payment until the qualifying benefit claim has been decided. If your claim for a funeral payment is refused while you are waiting for a decision on a claim for a qualifying benefit, reclaim within three months of being awarded the qualifying benefit (see p1029). **Note:** if you do not claim a funeral payment within the time limit (see p582), a backdated award of a qualifying benefit will not qualify you for a grant.
- You or your partner are in one of the categories of eligible people listed on p577 who can be treated as responsible for the funeral expenses.
- You or your partner accept responsibility for funeral expenses (see p579).[14] If you are claiming as a close relative or close friend (see p579), it must also be reasonable for you to accept responsibility (see p579).
- The funeral (ie, burial or cremation) takes place in the UK,[15] unless you or your partner are covered by specified European Union legislation, in which case the funeral can take place in any European Economic Area (EEA) state or Switzerland (see p579).[16]
- A social fund funeral payment has not already been made in respect of the deceased (but the amount of a previous award can be revised up to the maximum allowed under the rules).[17]
- The deceased was 'ordinarily resident' in the UK when s/he died (see p1430).[18]

- You are not a 'person subject to immigration control' (there are exceptions to this rule) – see p1410.
- You claim within the time limits (see p582).

Note: funeral expenses will be included as one of the allowable expenses for budgeting loans in 2012. See CPAG's *Welfare Rights Bulletin* for updates.

Eligible people

You are only eligible for a funeral payment if you or your partner fall into one of the following categories of people who can be treated as responsible for the funeral costs.[19] See p577 for definitions of the terms used.

- You were the 'partner' of the deceased when s/he died.
- The deceased was a 'child' for whom you were responsible when s/he died and there is no 'absent parent', or there is an absent parent but s/he (or her/his partner) was getting a qualifying benefit (see p576) when the child died. If there is an absent parent who was not getting a qualifying benefit when the child died, you may qualify for a payment as a close relative of the deceased under the rules below. If the deceased was a stillborn child, you are eligible for a funeral payment if you were the parent or the parent's partner, and it does not matter whether there is an absent parent.
- You were a parent, son or daughter of the deceased and it is reasonable for you to accept responsibility for the funeral expenses (see p579).
- You were another 'close relative' or a 'close friend' of the deceased and it is reasonable for you to accept responsibility for the funeral expenses (see p579), and you are not excluded by the rules below.

Exclusion of certain close relatives and friends

If you claim as a 'close relative' or 'close friend' of the deceased (see p579), you cannot get a payment if:

- the deceased had a partner (unless that partner died before the funeral without making a claim for a funeral payment);[20]
- the deceased was a child or stillborn child and a responsible person or parent is able to claim a funeral payment under the rules set out above;[21]
- there is a parent, son or daughter of the deceased, apart from:[22]
  - anyone under the age of 18;
  - anyone aged 18 or 19 who counts as a qualifying young person for child benefit purposes (see p93);
  - anyone who (or whose partner) has been awarded a qualifying benefit (see p576);
  - anyone estranged from the deceased when s/he died (estranged is not defined but has connotations of emotional disharmony);[23]
  - students aged 18 on a full-time course of advanced education (see p637), or aged 19 to pension age on any full-time course (see Chapter 29);

  - members of a religious order which fully maintains them;
  - prisoners (including those in youth custody or a remand centre) who (or whose partners) were getting a qualifying benefit immediately before being detained;
  - inpatients receiving free treatment in a hospital or similar institution, who (or whose partners) were getting a qualifying benefit immediately before becoming a patient;
  - asylum seekers receiving asylum support from the UK Border Agency or a local authority (see p1421);
  - anyone who is ordinarily resident (see p1430) outside the UK;
- there is a close relative of the deceased who was in *closer contact* with the deceased than you were, taking into account the nature and extent of such contact;[24]
- there is a close relative of the deceased who was in *equally close contact* with the deceased as you were and who (or whose partner) is not getting a qualifying benefit (see p576).[25]

Note: the last two bullet points do not apply if the close relative was under the age of 18 when the deceased died, or was a student, member of a religious order, prisoner, inpatient or asylum seeker as set out above, or was ordinarily resident outside the UK.[26]

If you are refused a payment on this ground, the DWP (not you) must establish there is another close relative who is not getting a qualifying benefit.[27]

Examples

Jane is not entitled to a funeral payment because, although she looked after her brother for many years before he died, he had a son who is not getting a qualifying benefit (see p576). Although the son rarely saw his father, they were not estranged.

Yuri is entitled to a funeral payment when his close friend Robert dies because although Robert had two surviving close relatives, a son and a sister-in-law, the son is getting HB and Yuri was in closer contact with Robert than either of them were.

Definitions[28]

'Child' is defined as for IS purposes (see p759). You are 'responsible' for a child if you get, or could get, child benefit for her/him (see p761).

'Stillborn child' means a child born dead after 24 weeks of pregnancy.

'Absent parent' means a parent of a deceased child, where the child:
- was not living in that parent's household at the date of death; *and*
- was living with another person who was responsible for her/him.

'Close relative' means parent, parent-in-law, son, son-in-law, daughter, daughter-in-law, step-parent, stepson, stepson-in-law, stepdaughter, stepdaughter-in-law, brother, brother-in-law, sister, sister-in-law.

'Close friend' is not defined in the law. It can include a relative who is not a close relative – eg, a grandparent or grandchild.[29]
'Partner' has the same meaning as for IS (see p753). You also count as a partner, however, if you were living in a care home (see p683) when the deceased died, *and*:
– you and your spouse or civil partner were living in the same home; *or*
– you were a member of a couple before one or both of you moved into such a home.[30]
This rule is designed to enable a surviving partner to claim a funeral payment where one or both partners were in a home at the date of death.

Accepting responsibility for funeral costs

To qualify for a funeral payment, you or your partner must 'accept responsibility' for funeral expenses.[31] The key factor is whether you are liable to pay the costs of a funeral, rather than whether you have made the arrangements.[32]

If the funeral director's account or contract is in your name, you should normally be treated as having accepted responsibility. If the account or contract is in someone else's name (or another person has paid the bill), you can still be 'responsible' if:

- s/he is acting as your agent – eg, because you are too distressed to act on your own behalf;[33] *or*
- s/he transfers liability to you, prior to full payment, with the consent of the funeral director.[34]

If you are a close relative (see p578) or close friend of the deceased, it must also be 'reasonable' for you to accept responsibility for the funeral expenses, in the light of the nature and extent of your contact with the deceased.[35] In one case, it was held reasonable for a person to have accepted responsibility for his father's funeral even though he had not seen him for 24 years. This did not erase the contact they had had in the previous 30 years.[36]

European Economic Area nationals

You can get a funeral payment for a funeral that takes place in any member state of the EEA or Switzerland (see p1500) if:[37]

- you are a 'worker' or self-employed, or retain that status; *or*
- you are a member of the family of a 'worker' – ie:
  - the worker's spouse or civil partner;
  - the worker's/spouse's/civil partner's child, grandchild or other descendant who is either under 21 or dependent;
  - a dependent relative of the worker, spouse or civil partner in the ascending line – eg, a parent or grandparent; *or*
- you have the right to reside in the UK .

For more details on the benefit rights of EEA nationals, see Chapter 64.

If you have ever been refused a payment for a funeral that took place in an EEA state and you satisfied the above rules, you should ask for a revision (see p1129).

The rules about your age

There are no special rules on age.

Amount of the payment

You are entitled to a payment that is sufficient to cover:[38]

- the necessary costs of purchasing a new burial plot with the exclusive right of burial in it and necessary burial fees. The burial of ashes following cremation is not, however, covered;
- the necessary cremation fees, including medical references, certificates and removing a pacemaker (restricted to £20 if not carried out by a doctor);
- the costs of documentation necessary for the release of the deceased's assets;
- the reasonable cost of transport for the portion of journeys in excess of 80 kilometres (50 miles), undertaken to:
  - transport the body within the UK to a funeral director's premises or to a place of rest;
  - transport the coffin and bearers in a hearse and the mourners in another vehicle from the funeral director's premises or place of rest to the funeral. The cost of this plus burial in an existing plot cannot exceed the cost of such transport plus the purchase and burial costs of a new plot;[39]
- the necessary expenses of one return journey for the responsible person to arrange or attend the funeral. The maximum allowed is the cost of a return journey from home to the place where the burial or cremation costs are incurred;
- up to £700 for any other funeral expenses – eg, funeral director's fees, religious costs, flowers, other transport costs.

Note:

- The cost of any items or services provided under a pre-paid funeral plan or equivalent arrangement cannot be met. Expenses not covered by the plan can be met if they fall into the above categories, but the maximum allowed under the last category is restricted to £120.[40]
- Costs relating to religious requirements cannot be included in the amount allowed for burial and transport.[41]
- If the amount awarded does not cover your funeral expenses, try making an application for a community care grant (eg, for the cost of a headstone), but see p557.

Deductions from awards

The following are deducted from an award of a funeral payment:[42]

- the deceased's assets available to you or a member of your family (defined as for IS purposes – see p970) without probate or letters of administration. However, if you have a joint account with the deceased, those assets become yours at the point of death and cannot be deducted.[43] Assets at the date of death count, even if you have spent or distributed them prior to your claim for a funeral payment.[44] Arrears of the deceased's attendance allowance (and probably other benefits) paid to you as next of kin also count;[45]
- a lump sum legally due to you or a member of your family from an insurance policy, occupational pension scheme, burial club or equivalent source on the death of the deceased;
- any contribution towards funeral expenses made to you or a member of your family by a charity, or a relative of yours or of the deceased;
- a funeral grant paid by the government for a war disablement pensioner;
- an amount paid or payable under a pre-paid funeral plan or equivalent arrangement (whether or not the plan was fully paid).

Any capital you have apart from the above has no effect on the amount of the funeral payment. Any payments from the Macfarlane Trust, the Macfarlane (Special Payments) Trusts, MFET Ltd, the Fund, the Eileen Trust, the CJD Trusts, the Skipton Fund, the Caxton Foundation or the London Bombings Relief Charitable Fund are not deducted from an award of a funeral payment.[46]

Claiming and getting paid

Claim on Form SF200, which you can get from your local Jobcentre Plus office or from www.direct.gov.uk or by telephone (via the Bereavement Service on 0845 606 0265, textphone 0845 606 0285). There are strict time limits for claiming (see p582). When completing the form, bear in mind the rules about accepting responsibility for the funeral expenses and your contact with the deceased.

Your date of claim is normally the date the form is received by the DWP or the date you make your phone claim.[47] If you do not complete the SF200 properly or apply in writing but not on the form, you should be sent the form to complete or correct. If you submit it within one month, or such longer period as the Secretary of State considers reasonable, your claim is treated as being made on the date you originally applied.[48] See p576 for when your claim can be backdated if you are subsequently awarded a qualifying benefit.

Payment is normally made directly to the funeral director, unless you have already paid the bill.[49]

The rules relating to the recovery of overpayments are as for other benefits (see p1067), but see p582 for recovery from the deceased's estate.

Time limits

You can claim at any time from the date of death up to three months after the date of the funeral.[50] There is no provision for late claims. See p581 for details of the date your claim is treated as made.

Recovery from the deceased's estate

The Secretary of State is entitled to recover funeral expenses payments from the deceased's estate and normally seeks to do so.[51] Funeral expenses are a first charge on the estate and have priority over anything else (although there may be insufficient assets for full repayment).[52]

3. Cold weather payments

You qualify for a cold weather payment if:

- a period of cold weather has been forecast or recorded for the area in which your normal home is situated (see below);[53] *and*
- you have been awarded pension credit (guarantee or savings credit) for at least one day during the period of cold weather. You also qualify if you have been awarded income support (IS), income-based jobseeker's allowance (JSA) or income-related employment and support allowance (ESA) for at least one day during the period of cold weather and:
  - your IS or income-based JSA includes a disability, severe disability, enhanced disability, disabled child, pensioner or higher pensioner premium (see p820); *or*
  - your income-related ESA applicable amount includes the pensioner premium, severe disability premium, enhanced disability premium, or the work-related activity or support component; *or*
  - you are responsible for a child under five; *or*
  - you are getting child tax credit which includes a disability or severe disability element (see p1309);[54] *and*
- you are not living in a care home;[55] *and*
- you are not a 'person subject to immigration control' (there are exceptions to this rule) – see p1410.

A period of cold weather

This is a period of seven consecutive days during which the average of the mean daily temperature, as forecast or recorded for that period at your designated local weather station, is equal to or below zero degrees celsius.[56]

The rules about your age

There are no special rules about your age.

Amount of the payment

The sum of £25 is paid for each week of cold weather.[57]

Claiming and getting paid

You do not need to make a claim for a cold weather payment. The DWP should automatically pay you if you qualify. Your district DWP should publicise when there are periods of cold weather in your area. If you do not receive payment and you think you are entitled, submit a written claim and ask for a written decision. The rules relating to the recovery of overpayments are as for other benefits (see p1066).

Time limits

A payment cannot be made more than 26 weeks from the last day of the winter period (1 November to 31 March) in which the cold weather period fell.[58]

4. Winter fuel payments

You qualify for a winter fuel payment if:[59]

- you are at least the qualifying age for pension credit (PC – see p509) in the week beginning on the third Monday in September (the 'qualifying week'); *and*
- you are ordinarily resident in Great Britain (see p1430);
  Note: you may be entitled to a payment if you are currently residing in another European Economic Area country or in Switzerland (see p1500); *and*
- if a claim is required, you claim in time (see p584); *and*
- you are not excluded from a payment under the rules below.

Exclusions

You are excluded from entitlement to a payment if, during the qualifying week (see above):[60]

- you are serving a custodial sentence;
- you have been receiving free inpatient treatment for more than 52 weeks in a hospital or similar institution (see p675);
- you are receiving PC, income-based jobseeker's allowance (JSA) or income-related employment and support allowance (ESA) and you are living in residential care. You count as 'living in residential care' if you are living in a care home (ie, an independent home which is registered or exempt from registration, or a local authority home which provides board) throughout the qualifying week and the 12 preceding weeks, disregarding temporary absences;[61]

- you are a 'person subject to immigration control', although there are exceptions to this rule (see p1410).

The rules about your age

You must be at least the qualifying age for PC (see p509) in the qualifying week (see p583).

Amount

Subject to the rules below, you are entitled to a winter fuel payment of:

- £200 if you are aged between the qualifying age for PC and 79 (inclusive) in the qualifying week (see p583); *or*
- £300 if you are aged 80 or over in the qualifying week.[62]

If you do not get PC, income-based JSA or income-related ESA and you share your accommodation with another qualifying person (whether as a partner or friend), you will get £100 if you are both aged between the qualifying age for PC and 79 or £150 if you are both aged 80 or over. If only one of you is aged 80 or over, that person will get £200 and the other person £100. If you do get PC, income-based JSA or income-related ESA, you (and your partner if you have one) will get £200 if one or both of you is aged between the qualifying age for PC and 79, or £300 if one or both of you is aged 80 or over, regardless of whether there is anyone else in your household who qualifies.[63]

If you are living in residential care (see p583) in the qualifying week and are not getting PC, income-based JSA or income-related ESA, you are entitled to a payment of £100 if you are aged between the qualifying age for PC and 79, or £150 if you are aged 80 or over.[64]

Claiming and getting paid

You should automatically receive a payment without having to make a claim if you received a payment the previous year, or you are getting a state retirement pension or any other social security benefit (apart from child benefit, housing benefit or council tax benefit) in the qualifying week.[65]

Otherwise, you must claim a winter fuel payment before 31 March following the qualifying week.[66] To ensure you receive your payment before Christmas, you should submit your claim before the qualifying week. A claim can be accepted in any written format but it is best to use the designated form, which you can get from the winter fuel payments helpline on 0845 915 1515 (local rate) (textphone: 0845 601 5613) or from www.direct.gov.uk. You should get a written decision.

If you are a member of a couple and your partner is receiving IS, the payment can be made to either of you (even though your partner is under the qualifying age for PC – see p531).[67]

The government aims to make payments between mid-November and Christmas.

Notes

1. **Sure Start maternity grants**
1 Reg 5(2) SFM&FE Regs
2 Reg 5(3) SFM&FE Regs
3 Reg 3(1) SFM&FE Regs
4 Reg 3(A) SFM&FE Regs
5 Reg 5A SFM&FE Regs
6 Reg 6 SFM&FE Regs
7 Reg 5(4) SFM&FE Regs
8 Reg 3(1) and (2) SFM&FE Regs
9 Reg 5(1) SFM&FE Regs
10 Reg 6(1)(a) SS(C&P) Regs
11 Regs 4(7) and 6(1)(b) SS(C&P) Regs
12 Reg 19 and Sch 4 para 8 SS(C&P) Regs

2. **Funeral expenses payments**
13 Reg 7(3) and (4) SFM&FE Regs
14 Reg 7(7) SFM&FE Regs
15 Reg 7(9)(b) SFM&FE Regs
16 Reg 7(9)(a) SFM&FE Regs
17 Reg 4(1) and (2) SFM&FE Regs
18 Reg 7(5) SFM&FE Regs
19 Reg 7(8)(a)-(e) SFM&FE Regs
20 Regs 7(8)(e) and 8(4) SFM&FE Regs
21 Reg 7(8)(e) SFM&FE Regs; R(IS) 7/04
22 Reg 8(1) and (2) SFM&FE Regs
23 R(SB) 2/87
24 Reg 8(7)(a) SFM&FE Regs
25 Reg 8(7)(b) SFM&FE Regs
26 Reg 8(8) SFM&FE Regs
27 *Kerr v Department for Social Development (NI)* [2004] All ER(D) 65; [2004] UKHL 23
28 Reg 3(1) SFM&FE Regs
29 CIS/788/2003
30 Reg 3(2) SFM&FE Regs
31 Reg 7(7) SFM&FE Regs
32 CSB/488/1982
33 CIS/12344/1996; R(IS) 6/98
34 CIS/85/1991
35 Reg 7(8)(e) SFM&FE Regs
36 CIS/12783/1996
37 Reg 7(10) SFM&FE Regs
38 Reg 9(1), (2) and (3) SFM&FE Regs
39 Reg 9(8) SFM&FE Regs
40 Reg 9(10) SFM&FE Regs
41 Reg 9(7) SFM&FE Regs
42 Reg 10(1) SFM&FE Regs
43 para 39404 DMG
44 R(IS) 14/91
45 R(IS) 12/93
46 Reg 10(2) SFM&FE Regs
47 Reg 6(1)(a) SS(C&P) Regs
48 Regs 4(7) and 6(1)(b) SS(C&P) Regs
49 Reg 35(2) SS(C&P) Regs
50 Sch 4 para 9 SS(C&P) Regs
51 s78(4) SSAA 1992; CIS/616/1990
52 R(SB) 18/84

3. **Cold weather payments**
53 Reg 2(1) and (2) SFCWP Regs
54 Reg 1A(2) and (3) SFCWP Regs
55 Reg 1A(4) SFCWP Regs
56 Reg 1(2) SFCWP Regs
57 Reg 3 SFCWP Regs
58 Reg 2(6) SFCWP Regs

4. **Winter fuel payments**
59 Reg 2 SFWFP Regs
60 Reg 3 SFWFP Regs
61 Reg 1(2) and (3) SFWFP Regs
62 Reg 2 SFWFP Regs
63 Reg 2(1)(ii)(aa), (2) and (3) SFWFP Regs
64 Reg 2(2)(b) SFWFP Regs
65 Reg 4 SFWFP Regs
66 Reg 3(1)(b) and (2) SFWFP Regs
67 Reg 36(2) SS(C&P) Regs

27

Chapter 27

Statutory maternity, paternity and adoption pay

This chapter covers:

Note: there are two types of statutory paternity pay (SPP): ordinary SPP and additional SPP. In this chapter, when the term 'SPP' is used, the rules described apply to both ordinary and additional SPP. If this is not the case, the type of SPP to which they apply is stated. Similarly, when rules apply differently to SPP paid for a birth (SPP (birth)) and SPP paid for an adoption (SPP (adoption)), this is specified. Otherwise, the rules apply to both SPP (birth) and SPP (adoption).

Key facts

- Statutory maternity pay (SMP), statutory paternity pay (SPP) and statutory adoption pay (SAP) are payments made to certain employees by their employers.
- You may be entitled to **statutory maternity pay (SMP)** if you are pregnant or have recently given birth. You may be entitled to **statutory paternity pay (SPP)** if you are the father of a baby, if your partner has recently given birth, if s/he is adopting a child, or if you are jointly adopting a child with her/him. You may be entitled to **statutory adoption pay (SAP)** if you are adopting or jointly adopting a child.
- SMP, SPP and SAP are non-means-tested benefits, although each has an employment and an earnings condition.
- You do not have to have paid national insurance contributions to qualify.

- You do not need to intend to return to work to qualify for SMP, SPP or SAP (although for additional SPP, the person getting maternity allowance (MA), SMP or SAP must have done so). You do not have to repay SMP, SPP or SAP, even if you do not return to work.
- You may be entitled to more maternity, paternity or adoption pay under your employment contract.
- SMP, SPP and SAP are normally administered and paid by your employer.
- If you disagree with your employer's decision on your entitlement, or if your employer has failed to make a decision, see Chapter 47.

Future changes: April 2013 and after

Major changes are taking place that will affect the benefits and tax credits system (see Chapter 2).

- From April 2013, total benefit payments to many working-age households will be 'capped' (see p25). There will be limited exceptions, including households in which someone is entitled to working tax credit or receiving disability living allowance. It is not yet known whether SMP, SPP or SAP will be included in the capped amount.
- You will still be able to claim SMP, SPP and SAP when universal credit is introduced in October 2013. SMP, SPP and SAP are *not* being abolished.
- A new rule will be introduced, probably in October 2013, limiting payment of SMP, SPP or SAP to people entitled to be in employment (see p23).
- The government has announced proposals to introduce a new system of parental leave and pay, possibly from 2015. These propose to reduce the MA period to 18 weeks and introduce 21 weeks of parental pay, which could be shared between parents. A further four weeks' 'reserved parental pay' would be paid to ensure each parent takes at least four weeks' parental pay. The right to up to two weeks' paternity pay near the birth would be retained.[1]

See CPAG's *Welfare Rights Bulletin* for updates.

1. Who is entitled

The table below details which statutory payment you may qualify for, given your circumstances.

Only women can qualify for statutory maternity pay (SMP), men or women can qualify for statutory adoption pay (SAP) or statutory paternity pay (SPP).

Event	*Circumstances*	*Benefit you may qualify for*
Adoption	You are the sole adopter	SAP
	You and your partner are jointly adopting a child	SAP or SPP (adoption)
	Your partner is the adopter	Ordinary SPP (adoption)

Birth	You are the mother of the baby	SMP or MA
	You are the father of the baby or the partner of the mother	SPP (birth)

If you are jointly adopting a child with your partner (see p590 for the meaning of partner), you can choose whether to request SPP or SAP from your employer (you cannot get both for the same adoption). In this situation, your partner may be able to qualify for ordinary SPP while you get SAP or *vice versa*. However, you cannot both qualify for SAP for the same adoption and you can only receive additional SPP (adoption) if your partner was getting SAP.[2]

There are some groups of people to whom special rules apply (see p599).

Statutory maternity pay

You qualify for SMP if you:[3]

- are pregnant and within the 11 weeks before your 'expected week of childbirth' (EWC – see p608), or you have recently given birth; *and*
- satisfy the continuous employment rule (see p591); *and*
- satisfy the earnings condition (see p593); *and*
- have given the appropriate notice and information (see p603); *and*
- are not carrying out work for the employer paying you SMP (but see p594); *and*
- do not work for other employers after the birth (but see p595 for an exception).

Statutory paternity pay

Ordinary and additional statutory paternity pay

'Ordinary SPP', which is paid for one or two weeks usually at some time in the eight weeks after the birth or adoption, can be paid whether or not your partner is entitled to maternity allowance (MA), SMP or SAP. However, your entitlement to 'additional SPP' is dependent on the other parent of the child giving up her/his MA, SMP or SAP and is intended to allow you to swap the role of main carer of a child within the maternity allowance, maternity pay or adoption pay period (see pp498 and 608). It can usually only be paid from 20 weeks after the birth or adoption (see p598). You may qualify for both ordinary SPP and additional SPP for the same birth or adoption.

See p587 for the relationship between SPP and SAP. See p610 if you are entitled to statutory sick pay (SSP).

You qualify for SPP if:[4]

- you satisfy the continuous employment rule (see p591); *and*
- you satisfy the earnings condition (see p593); *and*
- you satisfy the particular conditions for either SPP (birth) or SPP (adoption) (see pp589 and 590); *and*

- you have given your employer the required notice and information including, for additional SPP, a declaration from the mother or other adopter of the child (see p604); *and*
- you are not carrying out work for the employer paying you SPP (but see p594); *and*
- you do not do any work for other employers (but see p595 for an exception); *and*
- for additional SPP:[5]
  - the EWC (see p608) started on or after 3 April 2011 or notification of the adoption match was received on or after that date; *and*
  - the baby's mother has been entitled to MA (see Chapter 21) or SMP or your partner has been entitled to SAP; *and*
  - at least two weeks before the MA period, maternity pay period or adoption pay period is due to end, payment of MA, SMP or SAP stops as a result of her/him returning to work (see pp500 and 594). This can be as a result of returning to work for the same employer or for another employer and, for MA, it also can be as a result of self-employment. The return to work must occur at least two weeks after the birth or adoption placement (but see p598 for the earliest date on which your additional SPP can start).

HM Revenue and Customs (HMRC) considers that you only qualify for additional SPP if the baby's mother (for additional SPP (birth)) or your partner (for additional SPP (adoption)) has stopped getting MA, SMP or SAP and has actually returned to work. It considers that if s/he does not return to work immediately (eg, because she takes sick leave or annual leave directly after ending her/his period of maternity leave or adoption leave), you will not qualify for additional SPP until s/he does return to work. However, once s/he has returned to work, if s/he takes any subsequent period of leave your additional SPP is unaffected.

Note: if the child's mother or adopter dies, the qualifying conditions for additional SPP are modified (see p601).

Statutory paternity pay (birth)

You qualify for SPP (birth) if, as well as satisfying the general conditions for SPP outlined above, you satisfy the following particular conditions:

- while receiving SPP you intend to care for the child or, for ordinary SPP, to support the child's mother; *and either*
- you are the child's father and you have, or you expect to have, responsibility for her/his upbringing (for additional SPP this must be, apart from the mother's responsibility, the main responsibility); *or*
- you are the partner of the child's mother and you have, or you expect to have (apart from the mother's responsibility), the main responsibility for the child's upbringing (see below for the meaning of partner).

Statutory paternity pay (adoption)

You qualify for SPP(adoption) if, as well as satisfying the general conditions for SPP outlined above, you satisfy the following particular conditions:

- your partner is adopting a child or you and your partner are jointly adopting a child. For additional SPP both you and your partner must have been matched with the child for adoption. See below for the meaning of partner; *and*
- while receiving SPP you intend to care for the child or, for ordinary SPP, to support the person adopting the child; *and*
- for ordinary SPP only, you have, or you expect to have (along with the adopter or the other adopter), the main responsibility for the upbringing of the child; *and*
- the adoption is under UK law (if the child is adopted from abroad, see p602); *and*
- you have not elected to receive SAP.

Who counts as a partner

For the purpose of SPP you count as the partner of the adopter or of the child's mother if *either*:[6]

- you are her/his spouse or civil partner; *or*
- you live with her/him and the child in an 'enduring family relationship'. In this situation, however, a parent, grandparent, sister, brother, aunt, uncle, half-sister or half-brother cannot count as your partner and, if you are adopted, neither can your adoptive parents.

Statutory adoption pay

See p588 for the relationship between SPP and SAP. See p610 if you are entitled to statutory sick pay.

You qualify for SAP if:[7]

- a child has been, or is expected to be, placed with you for adoption under UK law (but see p602 if the child is adopted from abroad); *and*
- you satisfy the continuous employment rule (see p591); *and*
- you satisfy the earnings condition (see p593); *and*
- you have given the required notice and information (see p606); *and*
- you have not elected to receive ordinary SPP. (**Note:** you cannot get ordinary or additional SPP if you have elected to receive SAP); *and*
- your co-adopter is not claiming SAP, if you have jointly adopted the child; *and*
- you are not carrying out work for the employer paying you SAP (but see p594); *and*
- you do not do any work for other employers (but see p595 for an exception).

Continuous employment rule

To satisfy the continuous employment rule:[8]

- you must have been employed by your employer (see below) for a continuous period of at least 26 weeks ending with:
  - for **SMP** and **SPP** (birth), the 15th week before the EWC (see p608); *or*
  - for **SPP** (adoption) and **SAP**, the week in which you are notified that you have (or, for ordinary SPP, the adopter has) been matched with a child for adoption (see p609); *and either*
- for **ordinary SPP**, you must also have been continuously employed by that same employer from the end of:
  - the 15th week before the EWC until the day that the child is born (for ordinary SPP (birth)); *or*
  - the week in which the adopter was notified of being matched with a child until the day of the adoption placement (for ordinary SPP (adoption)); *or*
- for **additional SPP**, you must also have been continuously employed by that same employer over the period from:
  - the 15th week before the EWC (for additional SPP (birth)); *or*
  - the week in which you were notified of being matched with a child (for additional SPP (adoption)),

  until the week before your additional paternity pay period begins (see p598).

For adoptions, the date you are notified of a match is the date you receive the adoption agency's notification rather than the date it is sent.[9]

See p600 if your employer has dismissed you 'solely or mainly' to avoid paying you SMP, SPP or SAP.

See p592 if there have been breaks in your employment.

Note:

- For a birth, if the baby is born in or before the 15th week before the EWC, you satisfy the continuous employment rule for both SMP and ordinary SPP (birth) if you would have done so had the baby been born on the expected date or, for additional SPP (birth), had the baby been born after the 15th week before the EWC. In this situation, to qualify for additional SPP, you must also be continuously employed by the same employer from the date of the baby's birth until the week before your additional paternity pay period begins.[10]
- For SMP, if you are employed for only part of the 15th week before your EWC, the whole week still counts towards your period of continuous employment.
- For SAP, if you are employed for only part of the week in which you receive the notification of a match, the whole week still counts.[11]

Employed by an employer

To satisfy the continuous employment rule, you must have been continuously employed by an employer who was liable to pay secondary Class 1 national insurance (NI) contributions for you, or who would have been liable to pay them had your earnings been high enough (see p773).[12] If you are under 16, you count as employed if your employer would have been liable to pay secondary Class 1 NI contributions on your earnings had you been older.

If you count as an 'employed earner' for NI purposes (see p769), or if you would but for being under the age of 16, you normally count as an employee for SMP, SPP and SAP purposes – eg, if you are an agency worker you may count as employee.[13]

You do not need to have a written contract of employment to count as an employee. Your employer cannot restrict your right to SMP, SPP or SAP by its own rules or contract with you and cannot require you to contribute towards the cost of SMP, SPP or SAP.[14] Periods of employment for the same employer in another European Economic Area state may count towards your period of continuous employment.[15] However, even if you are an employee you may not be entitled to SMP, SPP or SAP if your employer is based outside Great Britain (see p1495).[16] See p1494 if you are employed abroad.

Breaks in employment

For **SMP**, **SPP** and **SAP**, if you return to work for the same employer following a break in your employment, certain weeks when you were not employed can still count towards your 26 weeks of continuous employment. These include weeks in which, for all or part of the week, you were:[17]

- incapable of work because of sickness or injury, unless your incapacity lasted for more than 26 consecutive weeks;
- absent because your employer temporarily had no work to offer you – eg, you are an agency worker and the agency is unable to find you work in any particular week;
- absent from work, but because of an arrangement or custom, you are regarded as continuing in employment – eg, on public holidays or an annual shutdown, or if you are a teacher employed on a term-by-term contract;
- for SMP only, absent from work wholly or partly because of pregnancy or childbirth if there were no more than 26 weeks between your contracts with your employer, and you were employed by your employer both before and after you had your baby but not during the period of your absence;
- for SMP only, absent from work while on paternity, adoption or parental leave.

If it is your employer's practice to offer work for separate periods of six months or less, at least twice a year, to people who have worked for them before (eg, if you are a supply teacher or agency worker), then in some circumstances you do not have to have returned to work in order to benefit from the above rules.[18]

Note: the above rules are only relevant when there is a *break* in your employment with your employer. So, for example, more than 26 weeks' sickness absence should count towards your continuous employment if you remain employed by your employer while off sick.

If your employment is legally transferred from one employer to another, your employment is unbroken.[19] If you have been reinstated or re-engaged following an unfair dismissal claim any period between your dismissal and reinstatement or re-engagement counts towards your 26 weeks' continuous employment.[20]

See p705 if your continuity of employment is affected by a strike and p600 if you have been dismissed by your employer.

The earnings condition

To qualify for SMP, SPP or SAP your average gross weekly earnings during the 'relevant period' (see p594) must be at least equal to the lower earnings limit for NI contributions.[21] The lower earnings limit used is the one in force at the end of:

- the 15th week before the EWC (see p608) (unless your baby is born prior to or during the 15th week before the EWC), for **SMP** or **SPP** (birth);[22]
- the week in which you or the adopter are notified by the adoption agency of being matched with the child (see p609), for **SAP** and **SPP** (adoption).

For the tax year 2012/13 the lower earnings limit is £107 a week (see Appendix 8 for the amounts for other years). If your average weekly earnings during the relevant period fall below the lower earnings limit (eg, because you are sick and receiving just SSP), you will not qualify for SMP, SPP or SAP.

See p600 if you have been dismissed.

What counts as earnings

As well as your gross wages, bonuses and any overtime pay you receive during the relevant period, your earnings include payments such as:[23]

- SSP, SMP, SAP and SPP;
- arrears of pay following reinstatement or re-engagement in your job or a continuation of your contract of employment under the Employment Rights Act 1996.

Certain payments (eg, return-to-work credit) are ignored.[24]

Pay rises

For **SMP**, if you are awarded a pay rise that affects your wages for any part of the period running from the first day of your relevant period (see p594) until the last day of your statutory maternity leave, your employer should reassess your average earnings over the relevant period to take account of this increase (even if the pay rise did not actually increase your wages for any week in the relevant period). If you would have been awarded a pay rise but for being on maternity leave, you are still treated as receiving it. For these purposes 'statutory maternity leave' includes both ordinary and additional maternity leave under the Employment Rights Act 1996. Your employer should recalculate your average weekly earnings as if your earnings in each of the weeks of your relevant period included the increase, and pay any arrears of SMP due to you.[25] If you become entitled to SMP as a result of the pay rise, your employer should deduct any payments of MA that you have received for the same period from the SMP you are owed.[26]

For **SPP** and **SAP**, only a backdated pay rise that is paid in respect of the relevant period is included in the calculation of your average earnings. Your employer should recalculate your average weekly earnings following the rise and pay any arrears of SPP or SAP due to you.[27]

Meaning of the 'relevant period'

For **SMP** and **SPP** (birth) the **'relevant period'** for calculating your average earnings is the period between:[28]

- your last normal payday that falls either:
  - in or before the 15th week before the EWC (see p608); *or*
  - before the week in which the baby is born,

  whichever is earlier; *and*
- the day after your last normal payday falling at least eight weeks before that.

For **SAP** and **SPP** (adoption), the relevant period is the period between:

- your last normal payday that falls in or before the week in which you or the adopter are notified of being matched with a child for adoption (see p609); *and*
- the day after your last normal payday falling at least eight weeks before that.

For this purpose, a week runs from Sunday to Saturday. If you are paid at intervals of one or more calendar months, your average earnings are calculated by dividing your earnings by the number of calendar months in the relevant period (to the nearest whole number), multiplying by 12 and dividing by 52.[29]

Working during your statutory maternity, paternity or adoption pay period

Your entitlement to SMP, SPP or SAP is not affected by work you do on a self-employed basis during your maternity, paternity or adoption pay period (as long as no Class 1 NI contributions are payable on your earnings from that work), but your entitlement might be affected if you work for an employer.

Working for the employer who is paying you

You can do up to 10 days' work for the employer who pays you **SMP**, **additional SPP** or **SAP** during your maternity, additional paternity or adoption pay period (see p608) without your entitlement to those payments being affected. These 10 days (called 'keeping in touch days') do not have to be consecutive, but if you work for only part of a day it will still count as a full day of work.

However:[30]

- you lose a week's SMP or SAP for every week in which you do any work for that employer in excess of those 10 days. This applies even if you only work for part of the week;
- if you do any work for the employer who is liable to pay you additional SPP in excess of the 10 'keeping in touch days', your additional paternity pay period will end and so your additional SPP will stop.

If you do *any* work for the employer who is paying you **ordinary SPP** during the ordinary paternity pay period, your employer is not liable to pay you ordinary SPP for the week in which you work.[31]

The above rules apply even if you are working for the employer under a different contract than the one you had before your maternity, paternity or adoption pay period began.

Note:

- If you intend to work for more than 10 days for the employer who is paying you SMP or SAP, this may affect your continued entitlement to maternity or adoption leave (and so may also affect your entitlement to SMP or SAP for the remainder of the maternity or adoption pay period). If you do not want to bring your period of leave to an end, seek employment advice before agreeing to such work. For additional SPP, such work would bring your period of additional paternity leave to an end.
- For SMP, if you return to work for your employer but you are subsequently off work sick during the maternity pay period, you are not entitled to SSP. Instead, you can get SMP for each week in which you are off work for a whole week. If your partner or the father of your child gets additional SPP (birth) in respect of the child for whom you receive SMP, s/he should inform her/his employer, in writing, of a change of circumstances such as reinstatement of your SMP. If you are in this situation, and her/his additional SPP is affected, seek advice.

Working for another employer

The general rule is that if you work for another employer (who is not liable to pay you SMP, SPP or SAP) while on maternity, paternity or adoption leave you cannot get SMP, SPP or SAP for the week in which you work and for the remainder of your maternity, paternity or adoption pay period.[32]

However, this is subject to two exceptions.

- For SMP, if the work is done while you are on maternity leave but before your baby is born, your entitlement to SMP is unaffected.[33]
- Your SMP, SPP or SAP is not affected by any work that you do for an employer who is not liable to pay you SMP, SPP or SAP if you also worked for that employer in the:
  - 15th week before the EWC, for SMP and SPP (birth); *or*
  - week in which you or the adopter were notified that you had been matched with a child for adoption, for ordinary SPP (adoption) and SAP; *or*

- 15th week before the expected week of the child's placement for adoption, for additional SPP (adoption).[34]

Notify the employer paying you SMP, SPP or SAP of any work that you do for another employer within seven days of the first day in your maternity, paternity or adoption pay period on which you do such work. For SPP and SAP, your employer has the right to request this information in writing.[35]

2. The rules about your age

There are no upper or lower age limits for statutory maternity pay, statutory paternity pay or statutory adoption pay.

3. Claiming for others

You are not entitled to an increase in statutory maternity pay, statutory paternity pay or statutory adoption pay for any dependants that you have.

4. The amount of benefit

	Period of payment	*Gross amount*
Statutory maternity pay (SMP)	First six weeks	90% of average weekly earnings
	Remaining 33 weeks (see below)	Lesser of £135.45 or 90% of average weekly earnings
Statutory paternity pay (SPP)	Two weeks for 'ordinary SPP' normally up to 19 weeks for additional SPP (see p598)	Lesser of £135.45 or 90% of average weekly earnings
Statutory adoption pay (SAP)	39 weeks	Lesser of £135.45 or 90% of average weekly earnings

Statutory maternity pay

SMP lasts for up to 39 weeks. For the first six weeks it is paid at the 'earnings-related' rate of 90 per cent of your average weekly earnings in the relevant period (see p594), and for the remaining 33 weeks either £135.45 a week or the earnings-related rate, whichever is lower.[36]

Statutory paternity pay and statutory adoption pay

SPP and SAP are paid at the same rate. You receive either 90 per cent of your average weekly earnings calculated over the relevant period (see p594) or £135.45 a week, whichever is less.[37]

Period of payment

Statutory maternity pay

SMP can only be paid during the **'maternity pay period'**.[38] This is a period of 39 consecutive weeks which starts from, at the earliest, the beginning of the 11th week before the expected week of childbirth (EWC), unless your baby is born before this, and at the latest, the day after your baby is born. Within these limits, you can normally choose when your maternity pay period begins by notifying your employer of when you want your SMP to start. However, if you have to stop work earlier than planned, your maternity pay period may begin earlier. If:

- your baby is born before the 11th week before the EWC, or before the date you had arranged to start your SMP, your maternity pay period will begin on the day after the birth;
- you are off work because of your pregnancy on or after the start of the fourth week before your EWC (but not later than the day after you have your baby), your SMP will start on the day after the first day of such absence in that period. This does not apply if your absence is not related to your pregnancy;
- you leave your job, see p600.

If your baby is born earlier or later than expected but after your maternity pay period has begun, your maternity pay period is not affected. If your maternity pay period starts earlier than you intended because your baby is born early, it does not entitle you to more than the 39 weeks' maximum SMP – the maternity pay period simply starts and ends sooner than you originally planned.

Statutory paternity pay

Ordinary statutory paternity pay

Ordinary SPP can be paid for a maximum of two consecutive weeks – called the **'ordinary paternity pay period'** – although you can choose to receive it for just one week.[39] The earliest ordinary SPP can be paid is from the child's date of birth or the date of the child's placement for adoption, and the latest is eight weeks after those dates. If the child is born before the EWC (see p608), the latest ordinary SPP (birth) can be paid is eight weeks after the first day of the EWC.[40]

As long as you request that your ordinary SPP be paid within this period and you give your employer sufficient notice of when you want it to be paid (see p604), you can choose to start your ordinary paternity pay period either on:[41]

- a particular date; *or*
- the day of the baby's birth, or the day of the child's placement for adoption (without specifying an actual date). If you are at work on that day, your ordinary paternity pay period will begin on the next day; *or*
- a day falling a certain number of days after that (without specifying an actual date).

See p594 if you work during your paternity pay period. See p600 if you give up or lose your job.

Additional statutory paternity pay

Additional SPP can only be paid during the **'additional paternity pay period'**. Usually, the earliest your additional paternity pay period can start (and so the earliest you can get additional SPP) is from:[42]

- 20 weeks after the birth (or from the date the mother's maternity allowance (MA) or SMP stopped as a result of her return to work, if this is later), for additional SPP (birth); *or*
- 20 weeks after the adoption placement (or from the date your partner's SAP stopped as a result of her/his return to work, if this is later), for additional SPP (adoption).

The latest the additional paternity pay period can end is the date the mother's or adopter's maternity allowance period, maternity pay period or adoption pay period ends (see pp498, 597 and below). You can choose the number of weeks for which you want to be paid additional SPP within this period. Although the rules state that your additional paternity pay period cannot last for more than 26 weeks, in practice, the dates when your additional paternity pay period can start and end generally mean that the maximum period for which you can get additional SPP is 19 weeks.[43] When the mother or adopter has died, in some circumstances the additional paternity pay period can start earlier, and additional SPP can therefore be paid for longer (see p601).

See p594 if you work during your paternity pay period. See p600 if you give up or lose your job.

Statutory adoption pay

SAP can only be paid during the **'adoption pay period'**.[44] This is a period of 39 consecutive weeks which normally begins, at the earliest, 14 days before the day you expect the child to be placed with you and at the latest on the date of placement. As long as you request that your SAP starts within these time limits and give your employer the required period of notice (see p606), you can choose whether you want your adoption pay period to begin either:[45]

- on a particular date (but if the child is placed with you before that date, then the adoption pay period will begin on the date of placement); *or*

- on the day of placement (without specifying an actual date). If you are working on that day, your adoption pay period will begin on the next day.

Your adoption pay period may end early if the child either:[46]
- is returned to the adoption agency (in Scotland, to the adoption agency or society) after being placed with you; *or*
- dies, if this happens after being placed with you for adoption; *or*
- is not actually placed with you but your adoption pay period has already begun.

In these circumstances, your adoption pay period will end eight weeks after the end of the week the child is returned, or dies, or that you are notified that the placement is not to take place, if this is earlier than it would have otherwise ended. In this situation a week runs from Sunday to Saturday.

See p594 if you work during your adoption pay period. See p600 if you give up or lose your job.

More than one job

If you satisfy the conditions of entitlement to SMP, SPP or SAP with more than one employer (or under two or more contracts with the same employer), you can get SMP, SPP or SAP from each job (although if your earnings from any of your jobs are aggregated when calculating your liability to pay NI contributions, those jobs are counted as one and the amount of SMP, SPP or SAP your employers have to pay is apportioned between them).[47]

If you are both employed and self-employed you may get SMP from your employer even if you are still working on a self-employed basis, but if you are entitled to SMP you cannot also get MA for the same period in respect of the same pregnancy.[48]

5. Special benefit rules

Special rules may apply to you if:
- you are in prison or detention (see p691);
- you are abroad (see p1494);
- you give up your job or have been dismissed (see p600);
- you have been involved in a trade dispute (see p705);
- your baby is stillborn, you have had a multiple birth or adopted more than one child (see p601);
- you have adopted a child from abroad (see p602).

If you give up your job or are dismissed

Special rules may apply to you if you give up your job or are dismissed. Your employer is still liable to pay you statutory maternity pay (SMP), statutory paternity pay (SPP) or statutory adoption pay (SAP) if:

- after your maternity, paternity or adoption pay period (see p608) has started, you give up your job, are dismissed or your job ends. Your employer should pay you SMP, SPP or SAP until your maternity, paternity or adoption pay period finishes (but see p1230 if your employer is insolvent);[49] *or*
- your employer dismisses you at any time provided the dismissal was 'solely or mainly' to avoid paying SMP, SPP or SAP and you had been employed by that employer for at least eight continuous weeks. This also applies to additional SPP if the employer is solely or mainly trying to avoid paying you ordinary SPP and *vice versa*. The amount of your SMP, SPP or SAP is calculated using your average earnings for the eight-week period ending with the last day for which you were paid;[50] *or*
- you satisfy the qualifying conditions for SMP, SPP or SAP and your job ends for any reason at any time after:[51]
  - the beginning of the 15th week before your expected week of childbirth (EWC), for SMP; *or*
  - the day on which the child is born, for ordinary SPP (birth); *or*
  - the day on which the child is placed for adoption, for ordinary SPP (adoption); *or*
  - the beginning of the week before your additional paternity pay period begins, for additional SPP; *or*
  - the beginning of the week in which you were notified of being matched with a child for adoption, for SAP.

For SMP, if your job ends at any time after the start of the 15th week before your EWC or, for SAP, if it ends before the adoption pay period is due to start, you are not required to have given your employer notice of your intention to take maternity or adoption leave, although you still need to give your employer information to support your entitlement to SMP or SAP as detailed on pp603 and 606 – eg, evidence of the expected date of birth for SMP.[52]

If you qualify for SMP but your job ends before your maternity pay period was due to start, your SMP will start at the beginning of the 11th week before your EWC or, if your job ends after this, on the day after you finish work, unless your baby is born before these dates.[53] If you qualify for SAP but your job ends before your adoption pay period was due to start, it will start 14 days before the expected date of placement or, if your job ends after this, on the day after you finish work, unless your child is placed with you before this.[54]

If you are dismissed while pregnant or on maternity, paternity or adoption leave, seek advice about your right to claim unfair dismissal.

If you start work for another employer after giving up your job or being dismissed, see p595.

Stillbirths, multiple births and adoptions

If your baby is stillborn after 24 weeks of pregnancy, SMP and ordinary SPP (birth) are payable in the same way as for a live birth.[55] (HM Revenue and Customs (HMRC) interprets this as birth after the start of the 24th week of pregnancy – therefore if you have a stillbirth certificate you can qualify.) If the baby is stillborn earlier, this is treated as a miscarriage and SMP and SPP (birth) are not payable. You may qualify for statutory sick pay (SSP – see Chapter 28) or employment and support allowance (ESA – see Chapter 10) if you are unfit for work. If the baby is born alive but then dies (even after only a moment), this is a live birth and you can get SMP or ordinary SPP (birth) even if it happens before the 24th week of pregnancy. Additional SPP (birth) is not payable if your baby has died in any of these circumstances.

No extra SMP, SPP or SAP is payable if you or your partner give birth to more than one baby, or have more than one child placed with you for adoption, unless this happens as part of a different adoption arrangement.[56]

Additional statutory paternity pay following death of mother or adopter

If the mother of the child (for additional SPP (birth)) or your partner (for additional SPP (adoption)) dies before the end of her/his maternity allowance period, maternity pay period or adoption pay period, you may still qualify for additional SPP. In this situation the normal rules for additional SPP apply with the following modifications.

If the death occurs:

- after your additional paternity pay period has begun, and you inform your employer of this in writing as soon as reasonably practicable, you can amend the date on which you want your additional paternity pay period to end, although the latest it can end is the date the maternity allowance period, maternity pay period or adoption pay period would have ended;[57]
- before your additional paternity pay period has begun, the earliest your additional paternity pay period can begin is the date of death, and the latest it can end is the date that, had s/he not died, the mother's maternity allowance period or maternity pay period or your partner's adoption pay period would have ended. Within these limits, the maximum period for which you can receive additional SPP is 39 weeks.[58] It is not necessary for the mother or your partner to have returned to work, or even have started getting maternity allowance (MA), SMP or SAP, for you to qualify, provided that had s/he lived, you both would have met the qualifying conditions.[59]

If the death occurred before your additional paternity pay period had begun, the rules regarding the notice and information you must give your employer (see p604) and the time limits for providing this are modified. Use Form SC10, available from www.hmrc.gov.uk, to give your employer the necessary information. The notice and information must be given as soon as reasonably practicable after the death, but no longer than eight weeks after. (It is sufficient to inform your employer of the date you want to start your additional paternity pay period within this time, as long as you then provide the remaining information as soon as reasonably practicable after that.) If you do so you can qualify from the date the mother or your partner died. If you do not apply within this time, you can still qualify but you must give at least six weeks' notice of the date you want your additional SPP to start.[60]

If you are adopting a child from abroad

If you are adopting a child from abroad you may be entitled to SPP (adoption) or SAP. To qualify you must satisfy the normal rules of entitlement for SPP (adoption) or SAP described in this chapter but with certain modifications. Although you must have official notification that you have been approved for adoption from UK authorities (see p609), you will not have been matched with a child for adoption by UK authorities under UK law, and it is primarily the rules that refer to the date of placement and the date of notification of being matched for adoption (both of which do not apply to overseas adoptions) that are modified.[61] See *Employer Helpbook for Statutory Adoption Pay* (E16) or *Employer Helpbook for Ordinary and Additional Statutory Paternity Pay* (E19), available at www.hmrc.gov.uk, for further details. Use Form SC5 (for ordinary SPP), Form SC9 (for additional SPP) or Form SC6 (for SAP), available from HMRC's website, to apply for SPP or SAP from your employer for an overseas adoption. If a placement is made under UK law, the normal rules of entitlement to SPP and SAP apply.

6. Claims and backdating

Making a claim

It is not necessary for you to complete a claim form to qualify for statutory maternity pay (SMP), statutory paternity pay (SPP) or statutory adoption pay (SAP). Instead, you must just give your employer certain notice and information.

Notification sent to your employer in a properly addressed and pre-paid letter is treated as having been given on the day it is put in the post.[62]

It is important to remember that there are different notice requirements for entitlement to statutory maternity, paternity and adoption leave. If your employer offers its own maternity, paternity or adoption pay scheme as well as SMP, SPP or SAP, the notice requirements for this scheme may also be different. Check this with your employer.

Notice and information for statutory maternity pay

To qualify for SMP you must give your employer:

- notice (in writing if your employer requests this) of the date from which you want to get SMP. This notice must be given at least 28 days before you expect payment to start or, if that is not practicable, as soon as reasonably practicable after that.[63] See p597 for when it is possible for your SMP to start; *and*
- evidence of the expected date of birth (normally a MAT B1 form issued by your doctor or registered midwife – see below). You must provide this evidence no more than three weeks after the start of your maternity pay period. This time limit can be extended to the end of the 13th week of the maternity pay period if you have good cause for the delay.[64]

The terms 'as soon as reasonably practicable' and 'good cause' are not defined in the regulations – you must show that any delay was reasonable, given your circumstances.

If you give your employer less notice than this or you do not provide the above evidence within the time limit, your employer may not pay you SMP. If you think your employer's decision is wrong, you can challenge it (see Chapter 47).

The earliest you can be issued with a MAT B1 form is the start of the 20th week before your expected week of childbirth (EWC). If you do not have a MAT B1, your employer can accept other medical evidence, but it must be substantially like Form MAT B1.[65]

If your employment ends in or after the 15th week before your baby is due, see p600.

If your baby is born early

If your baby is born early, before the date you planned to start your maternity pay period, even if you did not give your employer the correct notice, your maternity pay period will normally begin on the day after you had your baby rather than the day that you planned.

To qualify for SMP you must inform your employer (in writing if your employer requests this) of the date on which your baby was born if either:

- your baby is born during or before the 15th week before your EWC; *or*
- you had informed your employer of the date from which you wanted your SMP to start, but the baby was born before that date.

You must do this within four weeks of the birth or, if that is not practicable, as soon as reasonably practicable after that.[66]

In addition, if your baby is born before you intended to start your maternity pay period, you must give your employer evidence of the week in which you had the baby (eg, a birth certificate, or a MATB1 form if the child's date of birth is given on this) and of the expected date of birth, within three weeks of the start of your maternity pay period. This time limit can be extended to the end of the 13th week of the maternity pay period if you have good cause for the delay.[67]

Notice and information for statutory paternity pay

To qualify for SPP you must give your employer certain notice and information.

Ordinary statutory paternity pay

To qualify for ordinary SPP you must give your employer, in writing:[68]

- notice of when you want your ordinary SPP to start (see p597 for when it can start) and whether you want to get it for one or two weeks; *and*
- the particular information required for either SPP (birth) (see p605) or SPP (adoption) (see p605).

You must give your employer this notice and information at least 28 days before you want your ordinary SPP to start or, if this is not practicable, as soon as is reasonably practicable after that date. If you do not, your ordinary SPP can start later, once the necessary notice has been given, as long as payment would still fall within the period for which ordinary SPP can be paid (see p597).

To provide the above notice and information to your employer you may use Form SC3 for ordinary SPP (birth) or Form SC4 for ordinary SPP (adoption), available on HM Revenue and Customs' (HMRC's) website (www.hmrc.gov.uk).

In addition, for ordinary SPP, if you notified your employer that you want to start your paternity pay period:[69]

- on the day the child is born or is placed with you for adoption, or on a day falling a certain number of days after that, you must tell your employer the actual date of birth or placement, as soon as is reasonably practicable after that date;
- on a specific date, but the child is not born or placed with you until after that date, you must give your employer notice of the new date on which you want your paternity pay period to start, as soon as is reasonably practicable.

Additional statutory paternity pay

To qualify for additional SPP you must give your employer, in writing:[70]

- notice of when you want your additional SPP to start and end (see p598 for when it can start and the latest it can end); *and*
- the particular information required for either SPP (birth) (see p605) or SPP (adoption) (see p605); *and*
- a signed declaration from the child's mother (for additional SPP (birth)) or from your partner (for additional SPP (adoption)) giving her/his name, address and national insurance number, which confirms:

- the date s/he intends to return to work and that s/he has informed her/his employer of this; *and*
- s/he has been getting maternity allowance (MA), SMP or SAP, and the start date of her/his maternity allowance, maternity or adoption pay period; *and*
- to her/his knowledge, you are the only person applying for additional SPP in respect of the child; *and*
- she consents to your employer processing this information.

You must give your employer this notice and information at least eight weeks before your additional paternity pay period is to start. If you do not, your additional SPP can start later, once the necessary notice has been given, as long as payment would still fall within the additional paternity pay period (see p598).

To provide the above notice and information to your employer you may use Form SC7 for additional SPP (birth) or Form SC8 for additional SPP (adoption), available on HMRC's website (www.hmrc.gov.uk). These forms include a declaration for the child's mother or your partner to complete and sign.

If, within 28 days of receiving the above information, your employer requests the following information from you, you must provide it within 28 days of the request. Your employer can request:[71]

- the name and address of the employer of the child's mother (for additional SPP (birth)) or of your partner (for additional SPP (adoption)) or, if s/he is self-employed, her/his business address; *and*
- a copy of the child's birth certificate (for additional SPP (birth)); *or*
- a document from the adoption agency (such as a matching certificate) giving the details of the agency, the date you were notified of the adoption match and the expected date of placement (for additional SPP (adoption)).

Note: these rules are modified if the child's mother or adopter dies.

Statutory paternity pay (birth)

The particular information that you must also give your employer, in writing, in order to qualify for ordinary or additional SPP (birth) is:

- the EWC (and, if the child has already been born or for additional SPP, the date of birth); *and*
- a declaration stating that you meet the conditions specific to SPP (birth) described on p589 – eg, that you are the partner of the child's mother and will have main responsibility for her/his upbringing.

Statutory paternity pay (adoption)

The particular information that you must also give your employer, in writing, in order to qualify for ordinary and additional SPP (adoption) is:

- the date you expect the child to be placed for adoption or the date s/he was placed if the placement has already happened (for additional SPP (adoption) you only need to provide the latter date); *and*

- the date on which the adopter (or you, for additional SPP) was notified of the adoption match (see p609); *and*
- a declaration stating that, for ordinary SPP, you meet the first three of the particular conditions specific to SPP (adoption) described on p590 or, for additional SPP, that you meet the first two of those conditions.

Notice and information for statutory adoption pay

To qualify for SAP you must give your employer:[72]

- notice (in writing if your employer requests this) of:
  - when you want your SAP to start (see p598 for when it can start); *and*
  - the date on which you expect the child to be placed with you for adoption;
- a written declaration that you want to receive SAP rather than SPP; *and*
- documents from the adoption agency giving:
  - its name and address and your name and address; *and*
  - the date on which the child is expected to be (or was) placed with you; *and*
  - the date on which it informed you that the child would be placed with you for adoption.

  The 'matching certificate', provided by the adoption agency or adoption society, will give this information.

This notice and information must be given at least 28 days before your adoption pay period is due to start or, if this is not practicable, as soon as is reasonably practicable after that date, otherwise your employer may not pay you SAP. In this situation, it may be possible to argue that your SAP should start later, once the necessary time limit for providing the notice or information has passed, as long as payment would still fall within the adoption pay period (see p598). This may mean, however, that you might not be entitled to SAP for a full 39 weeks. If you are in this position, seek advice. If you think your employer's decision is wrong, you can challenge it (see Chapter 47).

In addition to the above notice, if you choose to start your adoption pay period on the day the child is placed with you, you must give your employer further notice of the date on which the placement occurs as soon as is reasonably practicable.[73]

If your employment ends before your adoption pay period begins, see p600.

Who should claim

If you are entitled to SMP, SPP or SAP but are not well enough to deal with your own affairs, HMRC can appoint someone else to act for you.[74] This person is your 'appointee' (see p1016). An application for someone to be your appointee can be made to your local HMRC enquiry centre.

If you claim the wrong benefit

If you are sick with a pregnancy-related illness in the four weeks before the week your baby is due, your employer can start your maternity leave (even if it is sooner than you had planned) and pay you SMP rather than SSP. It cannot do this if your illness is *not* pregnancy-related.[75]

See p503 for when you can get a claim for MA backdated if your employer has informed you that you are not entitled to SMP.

Backdating your entitlement

To qualify for additional SPP, you must give your employer eight weeks' notice of when you want payment to start (but see p601 if the baby's mother or your partner has died).

For SMP, ordinary SPP or SAP, you must normally give your employer at least 28 days' notice or your notice must be given as soon as is reasonably practicable after that date. Provided you gave notice as soon as was reasonably practicable, your SMP, ordinary SPP or SAP should be paid from the day you have chosen to start your maternity, ordinary paternity or adoption pay period. To qualify you must also give your employer the information and evidence detailed on pp603–604 within the time limits outlined on those pages.

What amounts to '**as soon as is reasonably practicable**' is not defined in the regulations – you have to show that your delay was reasonable given your circumstances. If you disagree with your employer's decision, you can ask HMRC to make a decision on your entitlement (see Chapter 47).

7. Getting paid

Statutory maternity pay (SMP), statutory paternity pay (SPP) and statutory adoption pay (SAP) are usually paid in the same way and at the same intervals as your normal wages or salary.[76] See p597 for the period over which you can be paid.

Note:

- If you are also entitled to contractual maternity, paternity or adoption pay from your employer, SMP, SPP or SAP will form part of your payments. Any payment of SMP, SPP or SAP you receive will go towards discharging your employer's contractual liability for the same period.[77]
- Your employer cannot pay you SMP, SPP or SAP by making a payment in kind, or by providing board and lodging, a service or some other facility.[78]
- If you become entitled to SMP because of a pay rise or because payments you received were retrospectively treated as earnings under backdated tax

legislation, your employer can deduct any maternity allowance (MA) that you received for the same period from the SMP you are owed.[79]

- If your entitlement has been decided by a decision maker from HM Revenue and Customs (HMRC) or by the First-tier Tribunal or Upper Tribunal, your employer may be required to pay you within a certain time limit (see p1230). If your employer cannot or will not pay you, see p1230 for details of when payment can be made by HMRC.
- The rules on overpayments described in Chapter 43 do not apply to SMP, SPP or SAP. If your employer pays you SMP, SPP or SAP and later decides that you were not entitled to it, it may attempt to recover the sum considered overpaid by making a deduction from your wages. If this happens, seek advice. If your employer decides that you have been paid SMP in error, consider claiming MA. You may be able to get this backdated (see p503).
- If your employer becomes insolvent, see p1230.
- For additional SPP and SAP, HMRC, not your employer, pays you if you are entitled for a period after you were imprisoned or detained (see p691), or while you were in detention if you were subsequently released without charge, found not guilty or given a non-custodial sentence.[80]

Change of circumstances

You must keep your employer informed of any change of circumstances that may affect your entitlement, such as starting work for someone else during the maternity, paternity or adoption pay period.[81] It is advisable to do this in writing, but for additional SPP, you *must* write to your employer to inform it of certain changes – eg, if the mother of the child (for additional SPP (birth)) or your partner (for additional SPP (adoption)) no longer intends to return to work.[82]

8. Definitions of terms

- The **'expected week of childbirth'** (EWC) is the week, starting on a Sunday, in which your baby is due to be born.
- The **'relevant period'** is the period which is used to calculate your average earnings for statutory maternity pay (SMP), statutory paternity pay (SPP) and statutory adoption pay (SAP). See p594 for how the period is worked out.
- **'SPP (birth)'** is SPP that you qualify for on the basis of either your partner giving birth to a child, or you being the father of a child.
- **'SPP (adoption)'** is SPP that you qualify for on the basis that a child has been, or is to be, placed with your partner for adoption, or with you and your partner for joint adoption.
- **'Maternity pay period'** is the period of up to 39 weeks during which SMP can be paid. See p597 for when it can start.

- The **'adoption pay period'** is the period of up to 39 weeks when statutory adoption pay can be paid. See p598 for when it can start.
- The **'additional paternity pay period'** is the period when additional SPP can be paid. See p598 for when it can start.
- The **'ordinary paternity pay period'** is the period when ordinary SPP can be paid. See p597 for when it can start.
- You are **'matched for adoption'** when an adoption agency or society decides that you would be a suitable adoptive parent for a particular child. It should be able to provide you with a **matching certificate** to verify this.
- **'Official notification'** regarding an overseas adoption is a written notification issued by or on behalf of a relevant UK authority stating that it has issued, or is going to issue, a certificate to the overseas authority confirming that you are approved for adoption (sometimes called a Certificate of Eligibility and Suitability to Adopt).

Example of relevant dates for a birth

Rita's baby is due on Saturday 14 July 2012. The following dates apply.

– The EWC begins on the Sunday before – ie, Sunday 8 July 2012.

– The first week before the EWC begins on Sunday 1 July 2012.

– The 11th week before the EWC begins on Sunday 22 April 2012. This is normally the earliest date from which Rita can be paid SMP (or maternity allowance).

– The 15th week before the EWC runs from Sunday 25 March to Saturday 31 March 2012.

Appendix 4 contains a table of relevant dates for all the weeks in 2012/13.

9. Tax, tax credits and other benefits

Statutory maternity pay (SMP), statutory paternity pay (SPP) and statutory adoption pay (SAP) are treated as earnings and you pay tax and national insurance (NI) contributions as appropriate.[83]

Tax credits

If you get SMP, SPP or SAP you may be entitled to working tax credit (WTC – see Chapter 52) because you can sometimes be treated as in full-time work for WTC purposes when getting one of these payments (or for some periods when you are on maternity, paternity or adoption leave – see p1302).

If you are entitled to WTC, you may be able to get help with the cost of childcare for your new baby or the child placed with you for adoption, as well as for any other children for whom you are responsible, before you return to work (see p1314).

You may also qualify for child tax credit (CTC – see Chapter 51).

The first £100 of your weekly SMP, SPP or SAP is ignored when calculating your entitlement to WTC and CTC, and any SMP, SPP or SAP you receive over £100 is counted as employment income.

Means-tested benefits

In some circumstances being pregnant or on maternity, paternity or adoption leave may allow you to qualify for income support (IS – see p347 for details). If you are getting SMP, SPP or SAP you may be able to get an allowance for childcare costs deducted from your earnings when calculating your entitlement to housing benefit (HB) and council tax benefit (CTB) (see p915).

In certain circumstances, you can be treated as having limited capability for work while you are pregnant (see p201), and so may qualify for income-related employment and support allowance (ESA).

You cannot claim jobseeker's allowance (JSA) if you are getting SMP or if you are on ordinary or additional paternity leave, or ordinary or additional adoption leave, because you are treated as unavailable for work, but your partner may qualify.[84] If you are a member of a couple who would normally have to make a joint claim for JSA (see p413) and you are pregnant or have recently given birth, in some circumstances you do not need to meet the jobseeking conditions or to make a joint claim to qualify (see pp397 and 414).

Your net SMP, SPP or SAP (after deductions for Class 1 NI, tax and half of any occupational or personal pension payments) is taken into account in full for IS, income-related ESA and income-based JSA.

SMP, SPP and SAP are treated as earnings for pension credit, HB and CTB. This means that when calculating your entitlement, it may be possible to deduct certain work-related expenses from your SMP, SPP or SAP (see pp904 and 942) as well as any tax, NI and half of any occupational or personal pension payments you pay. You may also be entitled to an earnings disregard (see pp913 and 945).

Non-means-tested benefits

You cannot get contribution-based JSA if you are receiving SMP (see Chapter 19) or if you are on ordinary or additional paternity leave, or ordinary or additional adoption leave as you are treated as unavailable for work. You cannot get statutory sick pay (SSP) when you are receiving SMP. See p623 for how your SSP entitlement is affected if you are pregnant. You cannot receive SPP or SAP for any week in which you are entitled to SSP.[85]

If you are getting SMP, additional SPP or SAP, you can get NI credits for any week in which your pay falls below the lower earnings limit (see p785) by writing to the NI Contributions Office (see Appendix 1). It is important to claim credits in order to protect your future entitlement to contributory benefits.

Employment and support allowance

You can qualify for contributory ESA as well as ordinary SPP if you satisfy the conditions for contributory ESA during your ordinary paternity pay period.

You can only qualify for contributory ESA while you are getting SMP, additional SPP or SAP if you have limited capability for work (or you can be treated as having limited capability for work – see p201) and if, on the day before your maternity, additional paternity or adoption pay period began:[86]

- you had (or could be treated as having) limited capability for work; *and*
- you satisfied the NI contribution conditions for contributory ESA or the conditions for ESA in youth. **Note:** from 1 May 2012 it is not possible to make a new claim for ESA under the ESA in youth provisions (see p176). At the time of writing it was unclear how this will affect the relationship between contributory ESA and SMP, additional SPP or SAP. See CPAG's *Welfare Rights Bulletin* for updates.

However, if you are entitled to contributory ESA and either SMP, additional SPP or SAP, your contributory ESA is reduced by the amount of SMP, additional SPP or SAP you receive for the same week.

If you are pregnant or have recently given birth, in some circumstances you can be treated as having limited capability for work (see p201).

Passports and other sources of help

For details of :

- Sure Start maternity grants from the social fund, see p573. In some circumstances you may qualify for a maternity grant even if you are not the mother of the child;
- other help from the discretionary social fund, see Chapter 25;
- free prescriptions, free NHS dental treatment and Healthy Start food vouchers and vitamins, see Chapter 13.

Notes

1 HM Government, *Consultation on Modern Workplaces*, May 2011

1. Who is entitled

2 ss171ZB(4), 171ZL(4) and (4A) and 171ZEB(2)(e) and (4) SSCBA 1992
3 ss164 and 165 SSCBA 1992
4 ss171ZA(2) and (3), 171ZB(2) and (3), 171ZC ,171ZE(4)-(7), 171ZEA(2) and (3) and 171ZEB(2)-(4) SSCBA 1992; regs 4 and 11 SPPSAP(G) Regs; regs 4 and 12 ASPP(G) Regs; reg 4(2)(b) and (c) PAL Regs
5 Regs 3, 4(1)(b), 6, 12(1)(b), 13 and 19 ASPP(G) Regs
6 Regs 4 and 11 SPPSAP(G) Regs; regs 2, 4(2)(a) and 12(2)(a) ASPP(G) Regs; reg 2 PAL Regs
7 s171ZL(2)-(4) SSCBA 1992; reg 3(2) SPPSAP(G) Regs
8 **SMP** s164(2)(a) SSCBA 1992
SPP ss171ZA(2)(b) and (d) and (3), 171ZB(2)(b) and (d) and (3), 171ZEA(2)(b) and 171ZEB(2)(b) SSCBA 1992; regs 4(3) and (4) and 12(3) and (4) ASPP(G) Regs
SAP s171ZL(2)(b) and (3) SSCBA 1992
9 ss171ZB(2) and (3) and 171ZL(2) and (3) SSCBA 1992; reg 2(2) SPPSAP(G) Regs; reg 2(5)(b) ASPP(G) Regs
10 Reg 4(2)(a) SMP Regs; reg 5 SPPSAP(G) Regs; reg 5 ASPP(G) Regs
11 Reg 11(4) SMP Regs; reg 33(4) SPPSAP(G) Regs
12 ss171(1), 171ZJ(1) and (2) and 171ZS(1) and (2) SSCBA 1992; reg 17 SMP Regs; reg 32 SPPSAP(G) Regs; reg 24 ASPP(G) Regs
13 Reg 17 SMP Regs; reg 32 SPPSAP(G) Regs; reg 24 ASPP(G) Regs
14 ss164(6) and (7), 171ZF and 171ZO SSCBA 1992
15 Regs 2 and 5 SMP(PAM) Regs; regs 3, 5 and 6 SPPSAP(PAM) Regs; reg 4 OSPP(A)ASPP(A)&SAP(AO)(PAM) Regs
16 Reg 17(3) SMP Regs; reg 32(3) SPPSAP(G) Regs; reg 24(4) ASPP(G) Regs
17 Reg 11(1) SMP Regs; reg 33 SPPSAP(G) Regs; reg 25 ASPP(G) Regs
18 Reg 11(3A) SMP Regs; reg 33(3) SPPSAP(G) Regs; reg 25(3) ASPP(G) Regs
19 Reg 14 SMP Regs; reg 36 SPPSAP(G) Regs; reg 28 ASPP(G) Regs
20 Reg 12 SMP Regs; reg 34 SPPSAP(G) Regs; reg 26 ASPP(G) Regs
21 ss164(2)(b), 171(4), 171ZA(2)(c), 171ZB(2)(c),171ZEA(2)(c), 171ZEB(2)(c), 171ZJ(6)-(8), 171ZL(2)(d) and 171ZS(6)-(8) SSCBA 1992; regs 4(3)(b) and (4) and 12(3)(b) and (4) ASPP(G) Regs
22 ss164(2)(b) and 171ZA(2)(c) and (3) SSCBA 1992; reg 4(2)(b) SMP Regs; reg 5(b) SPPSAP(G) Regs; reg 5(1)(b) ASPP(G) Regs
23 Reg 20 SMP Regs; reg 39 SPPSAP(G) Regs; reg 31 ASPP(G) Regs
24 Reg 20(2)(a) SMP Regs; reg 39(2)(a) SPPSAP(G) Regs; reg 31(2)(a) ASPP(G) Regs
25 Reg 21(7) SMP Regs
26 Reg 21B SMP Regs
27 Reg 40(7) SPPSAP(G) Regs; reg 32(7) ASPP(G) Regs
28 Reg 21 SMP Regs; reg 40 SPPSAP(G) Regs; reg 32 ASPP(G) Regs
29 Reg 21(5) and (6) SMP Regs; reg 40(5) and (6) SPPSAP(G) Regs; reg 32(5) and (6) ASPP(G) Regs
30 ss165(4) and (5), 171ZEE(7) and (8) and 171ZN(3) and (4) SSCBA 1992; reg 9A SMP Regs; reg 27A SPPSAP(G) Regs; reg 20(4) ASPP(G) Regs
31 s171ZE(5) and (6) SSCBA 1992;
32 ss165(6), 171ZE(7), 171ZEE(7) and (8) and 171ZN(5) SSCBA 1992; reg 8(2) SMP Regs; regs 17(1) and 26(1) SPPSAP(G) Regs; reg 20(1) ASPP(G) Regs
33 s165(6) SSCBA 1992
34 Reg 8(1) SMP Regs; regs 10, 16 and 25 SPPSAP(G) Regs; regs 11 and 18 ASPP(G) Regs
35 Reg 24 SMP Regs; regs 17(2) and (3) and 26(2) and (3) SPPSAP(G) Regs; reg 20(2) and (3) ASPP(G) Regs

4. **The amount of benefit**
36 s166 SSCBA 1992
37 Regs 2 and 3 SPPSAP(WR) Regs; reg 2 ASPP(WR) Regs
38 s165 SSCBA 1992; reg 2 SMP Regs; reg 1(2) SMPSS(MA) Regs
39 s171ZE(2) SSCBA 1992; regs 6(3) and 12(3) SPPSAP(G) Regs
40 s171ZE(3) SSCBA 1992; regs 8 and 14 SPPSAP(G) Regs
41 Regs 6 and 12 SPPSAP(G) Regs
42 s171ZEE(2)-(5) SSCBA 1992; regs 7 and 14 ASPP(G) Regs
43 s171ZEE(4) SSCBA 1992; regs 7(3) and 14(3) ASPP(G) Regs
44 Reg 21 SPPSAP(G) Regs; reg 2 SPPSAP(G)(A) Regs
45 s171ZN(2) SSCBA 1992; reg 21 SPPSAP(G) Regs
46 Reg 22 SPPSAP(G) Regs
47 ss164(3), 171ZD(1), 171ZED(1) and 171ZM(1) SSCBA 1992; reg 18 SMP Regs; reg 38 SPPSAP(G) Regs; reg 30 ASPP(G) Regs
48 s35(1)(d) SSCBA 1992

5. **Special benefit rules**
49 ss164(2)(a) and (3), 171ZD, 171ZED and 171ZM SSCBA 1992
50 ss164(8), 171ZD(2), 171ZED(2) and 171ZM(2) SSCBA 1992; reg 3(1) SMP Regs; regs 20 and 30 SPPSAP(G) Regs; reg 23 ASPP(G) Regs
51 ss164(2)(a), 171ZA(2)(b) and (d), 171ZB(2)(b) and (d), 171ZEA(2)(b) and (d), 171ZEB(2)(b) and (d) and 171ZL(2)(b) and (3) SSCBA 1992; reg 4(3) and 12(3) ASPP(G) Regs
52 Regs 22 and 23(4) and (5) SMP Regs; regs 24 and 29 SPPSAP(G) Regs
53 s165(2) SSCBA 1992; reg 2(5) SMP Regs
54 s165(2) SSCBA, 1992; reg 29 SPPSAP(G) Regs
55 ss171(1) and 171ZA(5) SSCBA 1992
56 ss171(1), 171ZA(4), 171ZB(6), 171ZEA(4), 171ZEB(5) and 171ZL(5) SSCBA 1992
57 Regs 7(4) and (5) and 14(4) and (5) ASPP(G) Regs
58 Regs 9(1)(b)-(e), (2) and (3) and 16(1)(b)-(e), (2) and (3) ASPP(G) Regs
59 Regs 9 and 16 ASPP(G) Regs
60 Regs 9(1)(a)(ii), 10, 16(1)(a)(ii) and 17 ASPP(G) Regs
61 SSCBA(AAO) Regs; SPP(A)&SAP(AO)(No.2) Regs; ASPP(AO) Regs; Statutory Paternity Pay (Adoption) and Statutory Adoption Pay (Adoptions from Overseas) (Administration) Regulations 2003, No.1192

6. **Claims and backdating**
62 Regs 22(4) and 23(3) SMP Regs; reg 47 SPPSAP(G) Regs; reg 39 ASPP(G) Regs
63 s164(4) and (5) SSCBA 1992
64 Reg 22 SMP Regs
65 Reg 2 SMP(ME) Regs
66 Reg 23 SMP Regs
67 Reg 22(1) and (2) SMP Regs
68 s171ZC(1) and (3)(c) SSCBA 1992; regs 9 and 15 SPPSAP(G) Regs
69 Regs 7 and 13 SPPSAP(G) Regs
70 s171ZEC(1) and (3)(c) SSCBA 1992; regs 8 and 15 ASPP(G) Regs
71 Regs 8(3) and (5) and 15(3) and (5) ASPP(G) Regs
72 s171ZL(6) and (7) SSCBA 1992; regs 23 and 24 SPPSAP(G) Regs
73 Reg 23 SPPSAP(G) Regs
74 Reg 31 SMP Regs; reg 46 SPPSAP(G) Regs; reg 38 ASPP(G) Regs
75 Sch 11 para 2(h) SSCBA 1992; reg 2(4) SMP Regs

7. **Getting paid**
76 Reg 27 SMP Regs; reg 41 SPPSAP(G) Regs; reg 33 ASPP(G) Regs
77 ss171ZG(2)and 171ZP(5) and Sch 13 para 3 SSCBA 1992; reg 22 ASPP(G) Regs
78 Reg 27 SMP Regs; reg 41 SPPSAP(G) Regs; reg 33 ASPP(G) Regs
79 Reg 21B SMP Regs
80 Reg 44 SPPSAP(G) Regs; reg 36 ASPP(G) Regs
81 Reg 24 SMP Regs; regs 17(2) and 26(2) SPPSAP(G) Regs
82 Regs 8(7)and 15(7) ASPP(G) Regs

9. **Tax, tax credits and other benefits**
83 s4(1)(a)(ii)-(v) SSCBA 1992
84 Reg 15(bc) and (c) JSA Regs
85 Regs 18(a) and 27(1)(a) SPPSAP(G) Regs; reg 21(1)(a) ASPP(G) Regs
86 s20(2)-(5), (6) and (7) WRA 2007; regs 80-82 ESA Regs

28

Chapter 28

Statutory sick pay

This chapter covers:

Key facts

- Statutory sick pay (SSP) is paid by employers to certain employees who are unfit for work.
- SSP can be paid for up to 28 weeks.
- SSP is a non-means-tested benefit.
- You may qualify for certain means-tested benefits or tax credits as well as your SSP.
- Your entitlement to SSP is not based on your national insurance contribution record, but your normal earnings must be above a certain amount to qualify.
- If you qualify, SSP is the minimum amount your employer should pay while you are sick. You may be entitled to more under your contract.
- In some circumstances, you may qualify for SSP even if you have been dismissed by your employer.
- If you do not qualify for SSP, you may qualify for employment and support allowance instead.
- SSP is normally administered and paid by your employer.
- If you disagree with your employer's decision on your entitlement to SSP, or if your employer has failed to make a decision, you can ask HM Revenue and Customs to decide if you are entitled (see Chapter 47).

Future changes: April 2013 and after

Major changes are taking place that affect the benefits and tax credits system (see Chapter 2).

- From April 2013, total benefit payments to many working-age households will be 'capped' (see p25). There will be limited exceptions, including households in which someone is entitled to working tax credit or receiving disability living allowance. It is not yet known whether SSP will be included in the capped amount.
- You will still be able to claim SSP when universal credit is introduced in October 2013. SSP is *not* being abolished.
- A new rule will be introduced, probably in October 2013, limiting payment of SSP to people who are entitled to be in employment (see p23).

See CPAG's *Welfare Rights Bulletin* for updates.

1. Who is entitled to statutory sick pay

You qualify for statutory sick pay (SSP) if:[1]

- you are an employee (see below); *and*
- you are incapable of work (see p616); *and*
- you are within a period of incapacity for work (see p617); *and*
- you are within your period of entitlement to SSP (see p618); *and*
- the day is a qualifying day (see p620); *and*
- your normal earnings are equal to or more than the lower earnings limit for national insurance (NI) contributions (see p619).

There are some groups of people to whom special rules apply (see p623). Certain people do not qualify for SSP (see p618). See below if your employer has dismissed you solely or mainly to avoid paying SSP.

Employees

To be entitled to SSP you must be an employee. If you count as an 'employed earner' for NI purposes (see p769), or if you would but for being under the age of 16, then you normally count as an employee for SSP purposes (so, for example, you may count as an employee if you are an agency worker).

You do not have to have a written contract of employment; it is the fact that you are employed that matters. Your right to SSP cannot be taken away by any document, whether you sign it or not and, if your employer dismisses you to avoid paying SSP, see p616.[2]

However, even if you are an employee, you are treated as if you are not (and so your employer does not have to pay you SSP) if your employer is:

- not resident and not present in Great Britain, and does not have a place of business in Great Britain (and is not treated as having one); *or*
- exempt from the social security legislation because of an international treaty.[3]

See p618 for details of employees who are not entitled to SSP.

Dismissal from work

If your employer dismisses you during your period of entitlement to SSP solely or mainly to avoid paying you SSP, it is still liable to pay you SSP. In these circumstances, your employer should continue to pay you SSP until either your period of entitlement to SSP ends or until your contract would have ended had you not been dismissed, whichever occurs first.[4] If your employer dismisses you for another reason (ie, not solely or mainly to avoid paying you SSP), normally you will not be entitled to SSP from that employer once your contract ends.

Incapable of work

To qualify for SSP, you must be 'incapable of work'. However, the tests of limited capability for work described in Chapter 11 and of incapacity for work described in Chapter 32 do not apply to SSP.[5]

To be **'incapable of work'** for SSP purposes, you must be:[6]

- incapable of doing work that you could reasonably be expected to do under the terms of your contract because you have a specific disease , or a physical or mental disablement; *or*
- treated as incapable of such work (see p617).

HM Revenue and Customs (HMRC) relies on employers to administer SSP and, normally, after seven days of absence your employer will expect you to provide a medical certificate from a doctor (see p625 and below) as evidence of your incapacity for work.

Medical certificates

On a medical certificate, also called a 'statement of fitness to work' or 'fit note', your doctor can state either that you are not fit for work, or that you 'may be fit for work taking account of the following advice'. S/he can specify whether s/he thinks you may benefit from a phased return to work, altered hours, amended duties or workplace adaptations to facilitate your return to work if such altered arrangements are available and your employer agrees.[7] However, it is for your employer to decide whether you are incapable of work with or without any altered arrangements suggested by a doctor. If your employer considers you are capable of work, it will not pay you SSP. If you disagree, you can challenge your employer's decision (see Chapter 47). If you are only fit for work if your duties are changed to such an extent that it would not be reasonable to expect you to do them, given the terms of your contract (whether these are written down or not), you may be able to argue that you still qualify for SSP. However, seek independent advice on your employment situation before refusing to accept a change in your duties.

If your employer doubts your incapacity for work, HMRC suggests that your employer may seek medical advice from its own medical officer, your doctor (with your permission) or from the HMRC's Medical Service (MS).

If your employer requests HMRC's help in deciding whether you are capable of work, the MS will normally contact your doctor and you may be asked to attend a medical examination with the MS. This can only be done with your consent but, since your employer could simply refuse payment, you are unlikely to gain much by not consenting.

Your employer is then given the MS's view on whether you are capable of work, but is not given any medical report or other explanation. It is still up to your employer to decide whether to pay SSP.

Treated as incapable of work

Even if you are not actually incapable of work, your employer (or HMRC – see Chapter 47) has the discretion to treat you as incapable of work if:[8]

- you have been officially excluded or prevented from working because you have an infection, disease or contamination detailed under public health legislation (or it is suspected that you have), or you have been in contact with a case of such an infection, disease or contamination; *or*
- you are under medical care in connection with a specific disease or physical or mental disablement; *and*
  - a doctor has stated that you should not work as a precautionary measure or in order to convalesce; *and*
  - you do not go in to work for your employer.

If you are incapable of work for just part of a day, you must be treated as incapable of work for the whole day provided you do not do any work on that day. If you are a shift worker and you are incapable of work for part of a day but you do some work on that day, you should still be treated as incapable of work for the whole day if you only finish a shift that began the day before and you do not do any work on a shift that starts on that day and ends the next.

Period of incapacity for work

For SSP to be paid to you, you must also be within a 'period of incapacity for work'. This is defined as four or more consecutive days of incapacity for work (see p616).[9] This means that you can only qualify for SSP if you are incapable of work for at least four days in a row. Every day of the week (including Sunday[10]) counts for this purpose even if it is not a day on which you would normally work. Days of incapacity for work which fall before or after the period covered by your contract can still be included in your period of incapacity for work (but see p620 if you have not yet started work).[11]

Two or more periods of incapacity for work can be 'linked' and treated as a single period if they are separated by eight weeks or less.[12]

Period of entitlement to statutory sick pay

You only qualify for SSP if you are within 'a period of entitlement'. In certain circumstances, a period of entitlement cannot arise and so you will not qualify for SSP (see below).

When entitlement to statutory sick pay starts

A period of entitlement normally starts on the first day of your period of incapacity for work, unless your contract of employment starts either during your period of incapacity for work or between two linked periods of incapacity for work.[13]

When entitlement to statutory sick pay ends

A period of entitlement to SSP ends (and so your SSP will stop) if:[14]

- your period of incapacity for work ends (see p617); *or*
- you reach your maximum 28 weeks' entitlement to SSP from a particular employer (see p622);[15] *or*
- your contract of employment ends (unless it has been brought to an end by your employer solely or mainly to avoid paying SSP – see p616); *or*
- in certain circumstances, you are pregnant or have just had a baby (see p623); *or*
- you reach the third anniversary of the start of the period of entitlement; *or*
- you are imprisoned or detained in legal custody (see p691).

Two or more periods of incapacity for work that are separated by eight weeks or less are linked and treated as a single period.[16] This is why it may be possible for you to have a period of entitlement which lasts for three years and not to have exhausted your 28 weeks' entitlement to SSP over that period.

If you have received your maximum 28 weeks' entitlement to SSP from a particular employer and you are still incapable of work, see p622.

If your employer stops paying you SSP because it decides your period of entitlement has ended, you should be given a statement explaining why and you can challenge the decision, see p626.

When statutory sick pay is not paid

In certain circumstances a period of entitlement to SSP cannot arise. As a result, you will not qualify for any SSP during your period of incapacity for work.

A period of entitlement cannot arise if:[17]

- your normal weekly earnings are below the lower earnings limit (see p619); *or*
- at some time in the 85 days before the date on which your period of entitlement would have begun you were entitled to employment and support allowance (ESA) or, in some circumstances, you would have been entitled. For this to apply, you must have made a claim for ESA or for another benefit that was treated as a claim for ESA; *or*

- at some time during the 57 days before the date on which your period of entitlement would have started, you qualified for either:
  - incapacity benefit (IB), or you would have done had you satisfied the contribution conditions; *or*
  - severe disablement allowance (SDA).

  In order to have qualified for these benefits you must have claimed them. In these circumstances, if you do not qualify for SSP, you may qualify for ESA if you have limited capability for work (see Chapter 10). **Note:** you will not be disentitled to SSP on the grounds that you previously qualified for IB, if you are now not entitled to IB and you are pension age or over (see p531); *or*
- you are a 'work or training beneficiary' (see p214) who was previously getting ESA, you are within a period of limited capability for work (see p212), and your period of entitlement would have started within your 104-week linking period. In this situation, you may be able to qualify for ESA again while you are unable to work, but note that the government plans to abolish this 104-week linking period for some, if not all, claimants from 1 May 2012 (at the time of writing further details were not available, see CPAG's *Welfare Rights Bulletin* for updates); *or*
- you are a 'welfare to work beneficiary' (see p738) who was previously getting IB or SDA, and your period of entitlement would have started within your 104-week linking period (see p739). This does not apply if you are pension age or over and not entitled to IB. Otherwise, in these circumstances you may qualify for ESA if you have limited capability for work (see Chapter 10); *or*
- at the time when your period of entitlement would have begun there is a strike at your workplace (but see p705); *or*
- you have not yet started work under your contract of employment (but see p620 if you had an earlier contract with the same employer); *or*
- at the time when your period of entitlement would have begun you were entitled to statutory maternity pay (SMP) or maternity allowance (MA) (see p623); *or*
- you are within the period immediately before or after you give birth (see p623); *or*
- you are in prison or legal custody (see p691).

If your employer decides not to pay you SSP on any of the above grounds, you should be given a statement and you can challenge the decision (see p626).

People with low earnings

You cannot get SSP if your 'normal weekly earnings' are less than the lower earnings limit for NI contributions, currently £107 a week (see p773).

Your **'normal weekly earnings'** are calculated by averaging your gross earnings from your employer (ie, before tax and NI contributions are deducted) over the period between:[18]

- your last normal payday before your period of entitlement to SSP began (see below); *and*
- the day after the last normal payday that falls at least eight weeks before this.

Only payments actually made in this period count, even if in theory you should have been paid more.[19] However, if your employer has unlawfully withheld *all* of your wages for the period over which your earnings are averaged, you should not be excluded from entitlement to SSP on the basis you have low earnings, if you otherwise would have qualified.[20]

If you are paid every one or more calendar months, your average earnings are calculated by dividing your earnings over the above period by the number of calendar months in the period (to the nearest whole number), multiplying by 12 and dividing by 52. If you are paid at other intervals and the period is not an exact number of weeks, the average is calculated by dividing your earnings by the number of days in the above period and multiplying by seven.

As well as your wages, your gross earnings include certain other payments, such as:[21]
- SSP, SMP, statutory paternity pay and statutory adoption pay;
- maternity pay;
- arrears of pay following reinstatement or re-engagement in your job or a continuation of a contract of employment under the Employment Rights Act 1996.

Certain payments (eg, return-to-work credit) are ignored.[22]

There are special rules if you have not been employed sufficiently long to have been paid wages over this eight-week period.[23]

See p622 if you have more than one job.

People who have not yet started work

If you have agreed to work for an employer but have not started work when your period of incapacity for work begins, you are not entitled to SSP from that employer for any day during the same period of incapacity for work, unless your current contract of employment can be linked to a previous one with the same employer in which you did some work. Your employment is linked if there are eight weeks or less between the date your new contract starts and the date your last contract with the employer ended.[24] You do not have to have written contracts for this to apply.

Qualifying days

You can only be entitled to SSP for 'qualifying days', although SSP is not paid for your first three qualifying days. These are known as 'waiting days' (see p621).[25]

Qualifying days are usually those days of the week on which you would normally work if you were not sick. However, other days may be selected as qualifying days by agreement between you and your employer if they would better reflect your contract of employment – eg, if you work a complicated shift pattern.

For this purpose, a week begins on Sunday and there must be a minimum of one qualifying day in each week.[26]

If there is no agreement between you and your employer about which days are qualifying days, or if the only agreement is to treat days of incapacity or days that fall in a period of incapacity for work or a period of entitlement as qualifying days, such an agreement is ignored and the qualifying days are presumed to be:

- the days on which it is agreed that you are required to work; *or*
- Wednesday, if it is agreed that you are not required to work on any day in that week – eg, offshore oil workers, who may work two weeks 'on' and then two weeks 'off'; *or*
- if you cannot agree about which days you are or are not required to work, every day in the week, except days on which you and your employer agree that no employee works (if you can agree at least to that extent).[27]

'**Required to work**' means required by the terms of your contract of employment.[28] Days when you can choose whether or not to work do not count – eg, voluntary overtime shifts.

Waiting days

SSP is not paid for the first three qualifying days (see p620) in a period of entitlement.[29] These are called **'waiting days'** and as they must be qualifying days, they will not necessarily be the first three days of your sickness.

If your period of incapacity for work can be linked to an earlier one in your period of entitlement with the same employer (see p618), any waiting days you served in the earlier linked period(s) do not have to be served again. So, for example, you can get SSP from your first qualifying day if your present period of incapacity for work is linked to an earlier one in which you served three waiting days. Two or more periods of incapacity for work are linked and treated as one if they are separated by eight weeks or less.

2. The rules about your age

There are no lower or upper age limits for entitlement to statutory sick pay.

3. Claiming for others

You cannot receive an increase in statutory sick pay for any dependants you have.

4. The amount of benefit

Statutory sick pay (SSP) is not paid for the first three qualifying days in a period of entitlement (see p621).[30] After that, it is payable at a rate of £85.85 a week.[31]

SSP is a daily benefit so it can be paid for periods of less than a week. The daily rate is calculated by dividing the weekly amount of SSP by the number of qualifying days you have in that week (a week for these purposes runs from Sunday to Saturday).[32]

The weekly rate of SSP is below the lower earnings limit for national insurance so, unless you have other earnings such as occupational sick pay, you do not have to pay NI contributions while on SSP (but you can qualify for credited national insurance (NI) contributions – see p780).

People with more than one job

If you cannot work, you are entitled to SSP from any job for which you fulfil the qualifying conditions. So, you could get payments of SSP for each of two contracts with the same employer (eg, if you are both a daytime teacher and an evening tutor with a local authority) or payments from two separate employers. However, if the earnings from any of your different jobs are added together when calculating your liability to pay Class 1 NI contributions (which usually means you contribute less than if they had been treated separately – see p774) you can only receive a total of £85.85 from those jobs and your employer's liability to pay you SSP is apportioned accordingly.[33]

It is possible for you to be unable to work on one contract and be entitled to SSP, but at the same time be able to work on a different contract – eg, if you perform different tasks for each.

Maximum entitlement to statutory sick pay

You are entitled to a maximum of 28 weeks' SSP from a particular employer in any one period of entitlement (see p618). Twenty-eight weeks' entitlement is equal to 28 times the weekly rate of SSP (adjusted for the annual increase in the weekly amount).[34]

SSP you received from your employer in any previous linked periods of incapacity for work in the same period of entitlement counts in calculating the 28-week maximum. Previous periods of incapacity for work are linked to your current one if they are separated by eight weeks or less.[35] Once you have reached your maximum 28 weeks' entitlement to SSP with a particular employer, you cannot qualify for SSP again from that employer in respect of the same contract, until your current period of incapacity for work ends and a new one arises. This normally means more than eight weeks must separate the end of your last period of incapacity for work and the start of your present one (but see p618 if you got employment and support allowance (ESA), severe disablement allowance or incapacity benefit in the intervening period).

If you are still incapable of work after you have received your 28-week entitlement to SSP, consider claiming ESA (see Chapter 10).

5. Special benefit rules

Special rules may apply to you if you are:

- abroad (see p1494);
- a woman who is pregnant or who has recently given birth (see below);
- involved in a trade dispute (see p705);
- in prison or detention (see p691).

Women who are pregnant or who have recently given birth

If you are entitled to statutory maternity pay (SMP – see p588) or maternity allowance (MA – see p498), you cannot get statutory sick pay (SSP) during the maternity pay period or the MA period.[36] Within the limits set out on pp498 and 597 (and unless your baby is born early), you have a right to choose when your maternity pay or MA period begins. So, for example, your employer cannot insist that you claim SMP or MA at the earliest possible date in order to limit the period for which it has to pay SSP.

Even if you are not entitled to SMP or MA:

- you cannot get SSP (because a period of entitlement cannot arise) if your period of incapacity for work started at some time during the 18 weeks which run from the first of the following dates:
  - the beginning of the week in which you had your baby (but see below); *or*
  - if you are incapable of work either wholly or partly because of your pregnancy on a day that falls in the four weeks before your 'expected week of childbirth' (see p505), the beginning of the week that contains the first such day;[37]
- if SSP is already being paid to you (because your period of entitlement started before the above period, or because your incapacity for work was not initially linked to your pregnancy), your SSP will stop from the first of the following dates:[38]
  - the first day falling on or after the beginning of the fourth week before your 'expected week of childbirth' when you are incapable of work wholly or partly because of your pregnancy; *or*
  - the date on which you have your baby.

In this situation a week begins on a Sunday. If your baby is stillborn before the 24th week of pregnancy, you qualify for SSP if you satisfy the other conditions of entitlement.

6. Claims and backdating

To qualify for statutory sick pay (SSP), you must notify your employer of your incapacity for work, rather than notifying the DWP or HM Revenue and Customs (HMRC). The rules are described below. It may be possible to get your entitlement backdated (see p626).

Making a claim

You do not need to complete a claim form to qualify for SSP, you just must inform your employer that you are sick (see below). Your employer should then decide whether you are entitled to SSP. Employers are given guidance on the SSP scheme in E14 *Employer Helpbookfor Statutory Sick Pay,* available on online at www.hmrc.gov.uk.

Telling your employer that you are sick

Your employer can decide both the time within which it wants to be notified of your sickness absence and the way that it should be told. Your employer must take reasonable steps to inform you of how and when it wants to be notified of your absence.[39] However, your employer cannot insist that you notify it of your sickness:[40]

- earlier than the first qualifying day (which is not necessarily your first day of sickness – see p620), or by a specific time on the first qualifying day;
- personally;
- by providing medical evidence;
- more than once a week;
- on a printed form or other document it provides.

Time limits

The following time limits apply for notifying your employer of your absence.[41]

- You must notify your employer of your absence within the time limit set by your employer, if your employer has taken reasonable steps to inform you of this time limit (unless it requires you to give notice earlier than the first qualifying day).
- If your employer has not taken reasonable steps to inform you, or if it has made no arrangements about the notification it requires, you must notify your employer of your incapacity for work in writing on or before the seventh day after your first qualifying day (see p620).
- This seven-day time limit, or your employer's time limit, can be extended by one month if you have good cause for the delay in informing your employer. What amounts to 'good cause' is not defined in the regulations, but you must show that your delay was reasonable given the circumstances.

- If it is not practical for you to inform your employer within that time, the time limit can be extended further, as long as you have notified it as soon as is reasonably practicable and you have notified it on or before the 91st day after your first qualifying day.

Notice sent in a properly addressed pre-paid letter is treated as having been given on the day the letter was posted. If you do not notify your employer of your absence within the above time limits, you can still be entitled to SSP, but your entitlement will start from a later date.

Information to support your claim

Your employer can require you to provide 'such information as may reasonably be required' for the determination of your claim for SSP.[42]

Medical evidence

For the first seven days of your incapacity for work, your employer cannot insist that you obtain a medical certificate, as you are only required to provide a self-certificate as evidence of your incapacity for work.[43] After the first seven days, an employer would normally expect you to provide a medical certificate from a doctor. If you provide a certificate from someone else, such as an osteopath or chiropractor, this can be accepted if your employer considers it sufficient to show that you are incapable of work. Whatever type of medical evidence you provide, it is up to your employer to decide whether or not to accept it. See Chapter 47 if you want to challenge your employer's decision. See p616 for further details of medical certificates.

Who should claim

As your employer cannot insist that you personally notify it of your incapacity for work, someone else can notify your employer on your behalf.

If you are not well enough to be able to deal with your own affairs, HMRC can appoint someone else to act for you. This person is your 'appointee' (see p1016). An application for someone to act as your appointee should be made to your local HMRC enquiry centre. You can obtain the address from www.hmrc.gov.uk.

If you claim the wrong benefit

A claim for another benefit cannot be treated as a request for SSP. However, if you have notified your employer of your sickness, but you are not entitled to SSP, you may be able to get a claim for employment and support allowance (ESA) backdated more than the normal three months (see p190).[44]

Backdating your entitlement

To qualify for SSP, you must notify your employer of your sickness (see p624). Even if you have not notified your employer promptly, your entitlement can still be backdated if you have notified your employer within the time limits explained on p624 – ie, within the time arranged by your employer, or within seven days if no time limit has been arranged or, in the circumstances described, within either one month or 91 days.

If your entitlement is backdated in this way, your SSP should be paid from your fourth qualifying day (see p620). (It is not paid for the first three qualifying days in a period of entitlement, called waiting days, unless your period of incapacity for work is linked to an earlier one in the same period of entitlement – see p621.)

If you notify your employer of your sickness late but your entitlement cannot be backdated, your entitlement is just delayed. You can still qualify for a total of 28 weeks' payment of SSP from the date your entitlement begins if you are off work for that long.[45]

If statutory sick pay ends or is refused

If your employer decides that you are not entitled to SSP or stops paying you, it should provide you with a statement (normally on Form SSP1) within certain time limits, giving you the reasons for its decision.[46] If you do not agree with your employer's decision, see Chapter 47 for how to challenge it.

Whether or not you agree with your employer's decision, you should consider claiming other benefits. If you are not well enough to work, consider claiming ESA (see Chapter 10). The DWP will normally ask HMRC to make a decision on your entitlement to SSP before it makes a decision on your claim for ESA. Even if you do not qualify for ESA, you should normally still send medical certificates to the Jobcentre Plus or DWP office that covers your local area in order to claim national insurance credits (see p780).

7. Getting paid

Statutory sick pay (SSP) is usually paid in the same way and at the same intervals as your normal wages or salary.

SSP is a daily benefit, which means that if you qualify for it, it can be paid for a period of less than a week. See p622 for the way the daily rate is calculated.

Note:

- If you are entitled to contractual sick pay from your employer, SSP forms part of your weekly pay. Any payment of SSP goes towards discharging your employer's liability to pay you contractual sick pay for the same period.[47]
- Your employer cannot pay you SSP by making a payment in kind or by providing board and lodging, a service or some other facilities.[48]

- Deductions that can be made from your wages (eg, union subscriptions) can also be made from your SSP.[49]
- If your entitlement to SSP has been decided by an HM Revenue and Customs (HMRC) decision maker or by the First-tier Tribunal or Upper Tribunal, your employer may be required to pay your SSP within a certain time limit (see p1230).
- If your employer cannot or will not pay you, see p1230 for details of when payment of SSP can be made by HMRC.
- The rules on overpayments and recovery of overpaid benefit described in Chapter 43 do not apply to SSP. If your employer pays you SSP and later decides that you were not entitled to it, it may attempt to recover the sum it considers overpaid by making a deduction from your wages. If this happens, seek advice. If your employer decides that you have been overpaid SSP in error, consider claiming employment and support allowance (ESA). If you claim ESA within three months of your employer's decision, you can be treated as having made your ESA claim on the first day of your sickness (see p190).

Change of circumstances

Notify your employer of any change in your circumstances that might affect your entitlement to SSP.

8. Tax, tax credits and other benefits

Statutory sick pay (SSP) is treated like any other earnings and you pay tax and, if you also receive earnings and/or occupational sick pay in the same week, national insurance (NI) contributions by Pay As You Earn in the normal way.[50]

Tax credits

In some circumstances, you can be treated as being in full-time work for working tax credit (WTC – see Chapter 52) while you are getting SSP (see p1302). It is not necessary for you to have claimed WTC before you became ill, so if you are not getting WTC, perhaps because your income was too high before you went on SSP, check whether you can qualify for it now. Also, in some circumstances, entitlement to SSP can help you to qualify for the disabled worker element and/or a childcare element within your WTC (see pp1311 and 1314).[51]

For WTC and child tax credit, any SSP that you receive during the course of the tax year is taken into account as employment income (see Chapter 55).

Means-tested benefits

You cannot qualify for income-related employment and support allowance (ESA) (or contributory ESA – see p628) for days when you are incapable of work during your period of entitlement to SSP.[52] However, for the linking rules relating to payment of housing costs within means-tested benefits, in some circumstances you can be *treated* as getting income-related ESA, or income support (IS) or income-based jobseeker's allowance (JSA), while you get SSP (see p876).

Entitlement to SSP may allow you to qualify for IS (see p347). If your partner is not in full-time paid work, s/he may qualify for JSA. If you are a 'joint-claim couple' for JSA (see p413), you do not need to meet the jobseeking conditions if you get SSP (see p396) and, in some circumstances, your partner may qualify for JSA for you both even if you do not make a joint claim (see p414).

Your net SSP payment (ie, your SSP minus any deductions made for tax, Class 1 NI contributions and half of any contribution you make towards a personal or occupational pension scheme) counts in full as your income when calculating your entitlement to IS and income-based JSA.[53]

SSP is treated as earnings for pension credit (PC – see Chapter 22), housing benefit (HB – see Chapter 14) and council tax benefit (CTB – see Chapter 8) and when calculating your entitlement to PC, HB and CTB, it may be possible to deduct certain work-related expenses from your SSP (see pp904 and 942) as well as any tax, NI and half of any occupational or personal pension payments you pay. You may also be entitled to an earnings disregard (see pp912 and 945).

If you pay for childcare and you were working for at least 16 hours a week immediately before your SSP started, you may also qualify for a deduction from your earnings for certain childcare charges when calculating your entitlement to HB and CTB (see p915). In some circumstances, your earnings and any WTC and CTC you receive can be added together before applying this deduction.

Non-means-tested benefits

You cannot get ESA, statutory paternity pay (SPP) or statutory adoption pay (SAP) while you are getting SSP.[54]

You cannot qualify for SSP while you are getting maternity allowance (MA) or statutory maternity pay (SMP).[55]

SSP counts towards the earnings condition for MA, SMP, SPP and SAP, and counts as earnings for carer's allowance (see Chapter 6), increases in non-means-tested benefits for dependants (see Chapter 33) and reduced earnings allowance (see p380) and so may affect your entitlement to these benefits.

Payment of SSP does not affect your entitlement to other non-means-tested benefits.

Unless you have other earnings such as occupational sick pay, you do not have to pay NI contributions while on SSP as the weekly rate of SSP is below the NI lower earnings limit. Instead, you are entitled to Class 1 NI credits (see p780).[56] You claim them by writing to the NI Contributions Office (see Appendix 1).

Passports and other sources of help

If you are on a low income, you might be entitled to certain health benefits (see Chapter 13).

Notes

1. **Who is entitled to statutory sick pay**
   1 ss151, 152, 153, 154 and 155 and Schs 11 and 12 SSCBA 1992
   2 ss151 and 163(1) SSCBA 1992; regs 4 and 16 SSP Regs
   3 Reg 16(2) SSP Regs
   4 Reg 4 SSP Regs
   5 s171G(1)(b) SSCBA 1992
   6 s151(4) SSCBA 1992
   7 Sch 1 SSP(ME) Regs
   8 Reg 2 SSP Regs
   9 s152(2) SSCBA 1992
   10 s152(5) SSCBA 1992
   11 s152(6) SSCBA 1992
   12 s152(3) SSCBA 1992
   13 s153(2), (7) and (8) SSCBA 1992
   14 s153(2) and (12) SSCBA 1992; reg 3(1), (3) and (4) SSP Regs
   15 ss153(2)(b) and 155 SSCBA 1992
   16 s152(3) SSCBA 1992
   17 s153(3) and Sch 11 SSCBA 1992; reg 3 SSP Regs
   18 s163(2) SSCBA 1992; regs 17 and 19 SSP Regs
   19 CSSP/2/1984; CSSP/3/1984
   20 *Seaton v HMRC* [2011] UKUT 297 (TCC)
   21 Reg 17 SSP Regs
   22 Reg 17(2) SSP Regs
   23 Reg 19(7) and (8) SSP Regs
   24 Sch 11 para 6 SSCBA 1992
   25 ss154 and 155(1) SSCBA 1992
   26 s154(3) SSCBA 1992
   27 Reg 5(2) and (3) SSP Regs
   28 R(SSP) 1/85
   29 s155(1) SSCBA 1992

4. **The amount of benefit**
   30 s155(1) SSCBA 1992
   31 s157 SSCBA 1992
   32 s157(3) SSCBA 1992
   33 Regs 20 and 21 SSP Regs
   34 s155(2)-(4) SSCBA 1992; reg 6 SSP Regs
   35 s152(3) SSCBA 1992

5. **Special benefit rules**
   36 s153(2)(d) and (12) SSCBA 1992
   37 Reg 3(5) SSP Regs
   38 Reg 3(4) SSP Regs

6. **Claims and backdating**
   39 Reg 7(1) and (4) SSP Regs
   40 Reg 7(1), (4) and (5) SSP Regs
   41 Reg 7(1)-(3) SSP Regs
   42 s14(1) SSAA 1992
   43 Reg 2(2) SSP(ME) Regs
   44 Reg 10(1A) and (2) SS(C&P) Regs
   45 s156(3) SSCBA 1992
   46 Reg 15 SSP Regs

7. **Getting paid**
   47 Sch 12 para 2 SSCBA 1992
   48 Reg 8 SSP Regs
   49 s151(3) SSCBA 1992

8. **Tax, tax credits and other benefits**
   50 s4(1) SSCBA 1992
   51 Regs 6, 9 and 13 WTC(EMR) Regs
   52 s20(1) WRA 2007
   53 Regs 35(2)(b) and 40(4) and Sch 9 paras 1 and 4 IS Regs; regs 98(2)(c) and 103(6) and Sch 7 paras 1 and 4 JSA regs
   54 s20(1) WRA 2007; regs 18 and 27 SPPSAP(G) Regs; reg 21(1)(a) ASPP(G) Regs
   55 s153(2)(d) SSCBA 1992; regs 18 and 27 SPPSAP(G) Regs; reg 21(1)(a) ASPP(G) Regs
   56 Reg 8B(2)(iii) SS(Cr) Regs

Part 4

Special benefit rules

Chapter 29

Studying and benefits

This chapter covers:

Note: Scotland has a different education system from England and Wales. The same terms are often used within the education systems of all three countries, but they can have different technical meanings – eg, further, higher and advanced education. Within benefit rules, terms are used to define different levels of education (eg, relevant, non-advanced and advanced) for benefit purposes. However, these are terms that are not generally used by education institutions.

Note: only the benefits covered in this chapter are potentially affected if you are studying.

Key facts

- If you are a part-time student, your benefits are usually not affected by your studying, although there are extra conditions to meet for jobseeker's allowance.
- Most full-time students are excluded from claiming means-tested benefits, but there are some exceptions for parents, disabled students, some young people on further education courses and some other groups. Full-time students can claim pension credit.
- Even if you are a student who can claim means-tested benefits, most student funding counts as income and will reduce or stop your benefit.
- If you are a full-time student and are taking time off your course but have not abandoned it completely, you still count as a student and cannot claim benefits unless you are in one of the groups of full-time students who are eligible to claim.
- Full-time and part-time students can claim tax credits.
- Full-time students cannot claim carer's allowance.

- Some benefits (eg, maternity allowance, statutory sick pay, child benefit and disability living allowance) have no special rules for full-time students, so full-time students can claim these in the same way as anyone else.
- If you or your partner are a 'person subject to immigration control', you should get advice before making a claim as your right to remain in the UK may be affected.

Future changes: April 2013 and after

Major changes are taking place that affect the benefits and tax credits system (see Chapter 2). From October 2013, a new benefit, universal credit (UC), will be introduced (see Chapter 4). In general, students will not be eligible for UC, but there are likely to be exceptions along the same lines as currently – eg, student parents may be able to get amounts for children and housing costs. See CPAG's *Welfare Rights Bulletin* for updates.

1. Income support and jobseeker's allowance

If you are studying, you may count as being in 'relevant education' (see below), or as a 'full-time student' (see p637). You cannot usually qualify for income support (IS) or jobseeker's allowance (JSA) (either contribution-based or income-based). There are some exceptions, however, which are outlined in this section. You may also be able to qualify if you are studying part time (see p641).

Relevant education

If you are in relevant education you can only qualify for IS in some circumstances and you cannot usually qualify for JSA (see pp635 and 636).[1]

You count as in **'relevant education'** if you are a 'qualifying young person' for child benefit purposes (see p94) – ie, you are under 20 and in full-time, non-advanced education or approved training which you were accepted on, enrolled on or started on when you were under 19.[2] For these purposes, 'full-time' means more than 12 hours a week in term time, not including meal breaks and unsupervised study. 'Non-advanced' means anything below degree, HNC or HND level.

Note: you can continue to count as in relevant education for a period after your education or training ends – eg, if you have enrolled on another course or during what is known as the child benefit 'extension period' (see p94).

When you turn 20 you are no longer treated as in relevant education even if you are still studying. However, you may then count as a 'full-time student' (see p637). You can qualify for IS or JSA if you are in one of the categories of full-time students who can claim (see pp640 and 641).

Entitlement to income support while in relevant education

You can qualify for IS while in relevant education (see p634) if:[3]

- you are the parent of a child for whom you are treated as responsible and who is a member of your household (see p761); *or*
- you are a student from abroad with limited leave to remain in the UK without recourse to public funds and your funds from abroad are temporarily disrupted but are likely to resume. You can get IS for a maximum of six weeks; *or*
- you are a refugee who is learning English to obtain employment (see p350); *or*
- you are an orphan and have no one acting in place of your parents; *or*
- you have left local authority care and you have to live away from your parents and any person acting in their place (see below). **Note:** if you are a care leaver aged 16 or 17 (see p671), you can only qualify for IS while you are in relevant education if you are a lone parent and treated as responsible for a child;[4] *or*
- you have to live away from your parents and any person acting in their place (see below) because:
  - you are estranged from them; *or*
  - you are in physical or moral danger; *or*
  - there is a serious risk to your physical or mental health.

  The physical or moral danger does not have to be caused by your parents. Therefore, a young person who is a refugee and cannot rejoin her/his parents can claim IS while at school;[5] *or*
- you live apart from your parents and any person acting in their place, they are unable to support you *and*:
  - they are in prison; *or*
  - they are unable to come to Britain because they do not have leave to enter under the UK Immigration Rules;[6] *or*
  - they are chronically sick, or are mentally or physically disabled. This covers people who could get a disability premium or higher pensioner premium, get employment and support allowance (ESA) including a work-related or support component, have an armed forces grant for car costs because of disability, or who are substantially and permanently disabled.

You may be able to claim IS under some of the above rules beyond age 20 if you are in one of the groups of full-time students who can claim (see p640).

A **'person acting in place of your parents'** can include a local authority or voluntary organisation if you are being cared for by them, or foster carers, but only until you leave care.[7] It does not include a person who is your sponsor under the Immigration Rules.[8] In the last bullet point above, however, a person acting in place of your parents includes the person with whom you are placed, but does not expressly include the local authority.[9]

'Estrangement' implies emotional disharmony,[10] where you have no desire to have any prolonged contact with your parents or they feel similarly towards you. It is possible to be estranged even though your parents are providing some financial support or you still have some contact with them. If you are being cared for by a local authority, it is also possible to be estranged from the local authority. If you are, you could qualify for IS if you have to live away from accommodation provided by a local authority.[11]

Note: until recently you could claim IS if you were in relevant education and had a disability. In some circumstances you can still qualify on this basis (see p351), but most people with a disability have to claim employment and support allowance (ESA–see p644).

Entitlement to jobseeker's allowance while in relevant education

You cannot qualify for JSA while in relevant education unless you are someone who can qualify for IS while in relevant education (see p635),[12] or you are treated as not being in relevant education. If you *can* qualify for IS while in relevant education (see p635), it may be better for you to claim IS.

So long as you do not count as a full-time student (see p637), you do not count as in relevant education for JSA and may therefore qualify for benefit if you are on a non-advanced course, or one that does not count as a full-time course under the rules for full-time students and:[13]

- you previously ceased relevant education and it is after your 'terminal date' for child benefit purposes (see p98); *and*
- you got JSA, incapacity benefit (IB), ESA or IS on the grounds that you were incapable of work, or were on a course of 'training' (see p643):
  - for at least three months immediately before the date you started the course; *or*
  - for at least three out of the last six months immediately before you started the course and for any remaining part of the six months you were working full time or earning too much to qualify for benefit.

All of the three- or six-month period must fall after your 'terminal date'. You do not count as in relevant education either during your course or after you have left it.[14]

When someone else is entitled to benefits for you

If you cannot qualify for IS or JSA because you are in relevant education, someone else may be able to get child benefit, child tax credit (CTC) and working tax credit (WTC) if they are treated as 'responsible' for you. In some circumstances you may count as both a person who can qualify for IS while in relevant education and as a person for whom someone else can qualify for child benefit and CTC. Seek advice on how you would be better off financially.

When you leave relevant education

Once you have left relevant education, you may be able to qualify for IS or JSA if you satisfy the rules for getting those benefits (see Chapters 17 and 19). Remember you can continue to count as in relevant education for a period after your education or training ends – eg, if you have enrolled on another course or during the child benefit 'extension period' (see p96). While you continue to be treated as in relevant education, you are only entitled to IS in the circumstances outlined on p635.

Full-time students

If you are a full-time student, you cannot usually qualify for IS or JSA for the duration of your course, including vacations.[15] See p640 for exceptions to this rule. See p661 if you give up, change or take time out of your course and p641 if you are studying part time.

You count as a full-time student if you are not in relevant education (p634), you are not getting a training allowance and:[16]

- you are under 19 and attending or undertaking a full-time course of 'advanced education'. **'Advanced education'** means degree or postgraduate-level qualifications, teaching courses, diplomas of higher education, HND or HNC of the Business Technology Education Council or the Scottish Qualifications Authority and all other courses above advanced GNVQ or equivalent, OND, A levels, a Scottish national qualification (higher or advanced level). See below for what counts as a full-time course; *or*
- you are 19 or over but under pension age (see p531) and attending or undertaking a full-time course of study. If your course is full time you are treated as a full-time student regardless of the level of the course, unless you are aged under 20 and can still be treated as in 'relevant education' (see p634). See below for what counts as a full-time course; *or*
- you are on a sandwich course (see p638).

You are treated as a student until either the last day of your course or until you abandon or are dismissed from it.[17] The **'last day of the course'** is the date on which the last day of the final academic year is officially scheduled to fall.[18]

For JSA, the period of study includes periods during which you are doing work connected to the course, even if this is after the normal end of your study.[19]

Full-time courses

If your course is funded by the Young People's Learning Agency for England (due to be replaced by the Education Funding Agency from 1 April 2012) or the Chief Executive of Skills Funding Agency, the Welsh government or Scottish Ministers, the definition of 'full time' depends on your personal pattern of attendance on the course. For all other courses, the term 'full time' applies to the course as a whole, not your personal pattern of attendance. However, for such courses the rules contain no definition of when it is classed as a full-time course.

In **England and Wales** your course counts as full time and you are treated as a full-time student if:[20]

- it is totally or partly funded by the Young People's Learning Agency for England (due to be replaced by the Education Funding Agency from 1 April 2012) or the Chief Executive of Skills Funding Agency or the Welsh government and your personal 'learning agreement' involves more than 16 hours of 'guided learning' each week. Courses include academic or vocational courses leading to a recognised qualification. The Young People's Learning Agency/Chief Executive of Skills Funding Agency and the Welsh government also fund basic literacy and numeracy courses, English as a Second Language programmes, Access and similar courses that prepare you to move on to qualification-bearing courses, and courses developing independent living skills for people with learning difficulties. The number of guided learning hours you do each week is set out in your learning agreement. This is signed by you and the college. The DWP uses this agreement to decide whether or not you are on a full-time course;[21] *or*
- it is not funded by the Young People's Learning Agency/Chief Executive of Skills Funding Agency or the Welsh government and is a 'full-time course of study'.

In **Scotland** your course counts as full time and you are treated as a full-time student if:[22]

- it is totally or partly funded by Scottish Ministers at a college of further education, is not higher education *and* your personal learning document states that your course:
  - involves more than 16 hours a week of classroom-based or workshop-based programmed learning under the guidance of a teacher; *or*
  - involves more than 21 hours' study a week, 16 hours or less of which involve classroom-based or workshop-based programmed learning and the rest of which involve using structured learning packages with the help of a teacher.

  The number of hours of 'learning' you do each week is set out in your learning document. This is signed by you and the college. The DWP uses this document to decide whether or not you are on a full-time course; *or*
- it is a course of higher education which is funded in whole or in part by Scottish Ministers and is a full-time course of study; *or*
- it is not funded by Scottish Ministers and is a full-time course of study.

Sandwich courses

A course is a 'sandwich course' if it consists of alternate periods of full-time study at your education institution and periods of industrial, professional or work experience organised so that, taking the course as a whole, you attend the periods of full-time study for an average of at least 18 weeks in each year.[23] This does not apply if it is a course of initial teacher training. If your periods of full-time study and work experience alternate within any week of your course, the days of full-time study are aggregated with each other and with any weeks of full-time study to determine the number of weeks of full-time study in each year.

Work experience includes periods of employment abroad for modern language students whose course is at least half composed of modern language study.

Health-related courses

If you attend a health-related course for which you are entitled to receive an NHS bursary, you are treated as a full-time or part-time student as appropriate, and not an employee.[24]

Modular courses

A modular course is one that consists of two or more modules and your college or university requires you to complete successfully a specific number of modules before it considers you to have completed the course.[25] You are treated as a full-time student if you are currently attending part of a modular course that would be classed as a full-time course.[26] You are treated as a full-time student for the period beginning on the day your course is defined as a full-time course and ending on the last day on which you are registered with your college or university as attending or undertaking that part of your course. This includes any vacations in that period, or the vacation immediately following that part of your course, unless that vacation follows the last day on which you are required to attend or undertake your course, or on such earlier date that you finally abandon or are dismissed from that part of the course.[27]

If you have failed examinations or failed to complete successfully a module relating to a period when the course was classed as a full-time course, any period in which you attend or undertake the course in order to re-take those examinations or modules is classed as part of the full-time course and you are treated as a full-time student (even if your college or university registers you as a part-time student during your re-sit period).[28]

Because the rules provide no definition of what is a full-time course, unless funded by the Young People's Learning Agency for England (due to be replaced by the Education Funding Agency from 1 April 2012) or the Chief Executive of Skills Funding Agency, or Scottish Ministers (see p638), you may be able to argue that you are not attending a full-time course, even if:[29]

- you are currently attending or undertaking a modular course on a full-time basis;[30]
- you have transferred to part-time attendance because of exam or module failure; *or*
- you are taking time out of the course (see p661).

If you are in one of these situations, seek advice.

Other courses

If your course does not automatically count as full time under the rules above, whether it counts as a 'full-time course of study' depends on the college or university. Definitions are often based on local custom and practice within education institutions. The college or university's definition is not absolutely final, but if you want to challenge it you will have to produce a good argument showing why it should not be accepted.[31] If your course is only for a few hours each week, argue that it is not full time. However, a course could be full time even though you only have to attend a few lectures a week.[32]

Full-time students entitled to income support

Even if you are a full-time student, you can qualify for IS (although most student funding will count as income) if you are:[33]

- a lone parent of a child under seven. **Note:** it is proposed that you will only be able to claim IS as a lone parent if your youngest child is under five from sometime in 2012 (see CPAG's *Welfare Rights Bulletin* for updates). If the rule goes ahead, there may be transitional protection for full-time students. There was transitional protection for full-time students when the age changed previously (see the 2011/12 edition of this *Handbook*; *or*
- a lone foster carer of a child under 16; *or*
- a student from abroad with limited leave to remain in the UK without recourse to public funds and your funds from abroad are temporarily disrupted but are likely to resume. You can get IS for a maximum of six weeks; *or*
- single, or are one of a couple and both of you are full-time students, *and*:
  - you fit into one of the groups of people who can claim IS (see Chapter 17); *and*
  - you, or if you are one of a couple, either one or both of you are responsible for a child or young person (see p100); *and*
  - it is the summer vacation;
- a refugee who is learning English to obtain employment (see p350); *or*
- in, enrolled in or accepted for full-time non-advanced education, and aged under 21, or you are 21 and you reached that age while in such education. In addition, you must:
  - have no parents (or anyone acting in their place); *or*
  - have to live away from your parents (or anyone acting in their place) because you are estranged from them, or are in physical or moral danger or there is a serious risk to your physical or mental health; *or*
  - be living away from your parents (or anyone acting in their place) and they cannot support you financially and they are:
    - chronically sick or mentally or physically disabled; *or*
    - detained in custody pending trial or sentence or having been sentenced; *or*
    - prohibited from entering or re-entering Great Britain.

Full-time students entitled to jobseeker's allowance

Even if you are a full-time student you can qualify for JSA (although most student funding will count as income) if you are:

- single and responsible for a child, or if you are one of a couple, both of you are full-time students and either one or both of you is responsible for a child (see p100). This exception only applies during the summer vacation and if you are actually available for work, or treated as available because you are on either of the courses in the next bullet point;[34] *or*
- on an employment-related course of up to two weeks that has been approved in advance by the DWP,[35] or a Venture Trust training programme of up to four weeks.[36] In either case, only one course is allowed in any 12-month period; *or*
- participating in the Employment, Skills and Enterprise Scheme (p471) – ie, you have been required to attend full-time training under the Scheme;[37] *or*
- aged 25 or over and on an approved employment-related course (see p400);[38]
- waiting to go back to your course, having taken approved time out because of an illness or caring responsibility and that has now come to an end (see p661).

Maintaining two homes

In some cases, if you qualify for IS, income-based JSA or housing benefit, you may be entitled to help with the costs of more than one home if you have to live away from your normal home in order to attend a course. For further details, see pp255 and 852.

Part-time students

If you are studying but are not in relevant education (see p634) or attending a full-time course (see p637), you are treated as attending a part-time course and classed as a part-time student.

Entitlement to income support while studying part time

You can get IS while studying part time if you are not on a full-time course and you satisfy the other rules for getting IS (see Chapter 17).

If you are currently studying part time on a course you previously attended full time, or if you are attending a modular or similar course (see p639) on a part-time basis, the DWP may argue that you are attending a full-time course and should, therefore, be treated as a full-time student. It may be possible to challenge this interpretation.[39] Seek specialist advice if you are in this situation.

Entitlement to jobseeker's allowance while studying part time

You count as a part-time student if your course is not full time.[40] You can qualify for JSA while studying part time if you meet the jobseeking conditions – ie, you are available for work, actively seeking work and you have a valid jobseeker's agreement (see Chapter 20). If you have agreed restrictions with the DWP on the hours that you are available for work, there are special rules that can help you claim JSA and study part time (see p643).

When you claim JSA you may be asked to fill in a 'student questionnaire'. Your answers are taken into account when deciding whether you are available for and actively seeking work. The DWP needs to be satisfied that you are genuinely available for and actively seeking work while you are studying part time.

Availability for work and part-time study

Your availability for work should not be affected by your part-time course if your hours of study or training are at times outside your agreed pattern of availability (see p445) – ie, they do not clash with the times you are willing and able to work. If the hours of your course *do* clash with the times you say you are available for work (as set out in your jobseeker's agreement – see p452), you are only accepted as available for work if either:[41]

- you are able to rearrange the hours of the course or study to fit around your job; *or*
- you are willing and able to give up the course should a job become available.

Deciding whether you are available for work

A number of factors should be considered when deciding whether you are available for work while you are studying part time. If, for example, it appears you are not willing or able to give up your course or that you cannot confine your study to times that would fit in with employment, you are treated as not being available for work. The factors that may be relevant include:[42]

- where you are studying or training and, if it is away from home, whether you can be contacted if a job becomes available;
- the extent of your efforts to find employment;
- how important the successful completion of the course is to your future career, including whether it will enhance your chances of finding employment;
- whether you gave up a job or training to do the course;
- the days and hours you are required to attend the course;
- whether the times of attendance could be altered to fit in with any job you might obtain or whether successful completion of the course is possible if you miss some of the scheduled attendances;
- the duration of the study or training;
- whether a fee was paid and, if so, the amount and whether any of the fee could be refunded or transferred if you abandoned or interrupted your studies. If you have paid a fee, it may be more difficult (depending on the amount) to convince the DWP that you are prepared to abandon the course;
- whether you received a grant and, if so, the source, the amount and whether you would have to repay any or all of it if you interrupted or abandoned the course.

The guidance for decision makers states that where a number of claimants are following the same course, some may be able to show that they are available, but others may not.[43] The DWP should not operate a blanket policy of treating all students on the same course as not being available. Equally, you cannot assume that you will be treated as available if other people on your course are getting JSA. Each claim should be considered individually. The DWP assumes that you may be less willing to leave a course if you are near its end or as the chance of obtaining a qualification approaches.[44]

Restricted availability for work and part-time study

There are special rules that can help you qualify for JSA if you are a part-time student. These say that in certain circumstances the fact that you are on your course will be ignored when deciding whether you are available for work if the hours of your course fall wholly or partly within the times you say you are available for work. However, you still have to be available for and actively seeking work during the rest of the week when you are not on your course.

These rules apply to you if you are a part-time student, and you are willing and able to rearrange the hours of your course to take up a job and the restrictions on your hours of availability have been agreed with the DWP because:[45]

- of your physical or mental condition (see p444); *or*
- of your caring responsibilities (see p445); *or*
- you are working 'short time' (see p483); *or*
- they leave you available for work for at least 40 hours a week (see p445).

You must also satisfy one of two conditions.

- For the three months immediately before the date you started the course you were unemployed and getting JSA, or incapable of work and getting IS, IB or ESA, or you were on a course of 'training'.
- In the six months immediately before you started the course, you were unemployed and getting JSA, or incapable of work and getting IS, IB or ESA, or you were on a course of 'training' for a total of at least three months and, for any remaining part of the six months, you were working full time or earning too much to qualify for benefit.

The three-month and six-month periods can only begin after you have reached your terminal date (see p98) and are treated as having ceased to be in relevant education (see p98).

'Training' means training for which young people aged under 18 are eligible, or for which a person aged 18–24 may be eligible, provided or arranged by the Young People's Learning Agency for England (due to be replaced by the Education Funding Agency from 1 April 2012) or the Chief Executive of Skills Funding Agency, the Welsh government or Skills Development Scotland.[46]

Calculating income and capital

The normal rules for assessing your income and capital apply if you are a student (see Chapters 40 and 41). However, there are special rules for assessing the amount of money available from grants, loans and other types of financial support that apply to students (see p652), including people claiming IS while in 'relevant education'.[47] These rules do not apply if you are receiving a training allowance. For which student grants or loans do not count as income, see pp655 and 657.

2. Employment and support allowance

Whether you can qualify for employment and support allowance (ESA) while studying depends on your age and the type of ESA you want to claim. You can qualify for contributory ESA (see p175) unless it is contributory ESA in youth (see p176) and you are 'receiving full-time education' (see below). You cannot qualify for income-related ESA if you are 'receiving education' unless you are getting disability living allowance (DLA – see p645). There are some exceptions to the rules (see below). You may be able to qualify if you are studying part time (see p646).

Note: in certain circumstances if you are attending a training course and are paid a training allowance you cannot qualify for ESA because you do not count as having limited capability for work (see p200).[48]

Contributory employment and support allowance in youth

Note: contributory ESA in youth will be abolished for new claims from 1 May 2012.

You cannot qualify for contributory ESA in youth (see p176) if you are 'receiving full-time education'.[49] You count as receiving 'full-time education' if:[50]

- you are at least 16 but under 19; *and*
- you attend a course of education for 21 hours or more a week. 'Course of education' is not defined in the rules, so can include both non-advanced and advanced courses. When calculating the 21 hours, any instruction or tuition that is not suitable for people of the same age as you who do not have a disability is ignored. Both the course content and the method of teaching must be taken into account in deciding this.[51]

Temporary interruptions of education are disregarded.

You *can* claim contributory ESA in youth even if you are studying, so long as you meet the other conditions of entitlement, if you are:

- under 19 and attending a course of education for less than 21 hours a week; *or*

- 19 or over. In this case, it does not matter how many hours you study. However, the rules are different for income-related ESA. If you want to claim income-related ESA as well as, or instead of, contributory ESA in youth, see below.

Note: if you are under 25, there are special rules that may help you qualify for contributory ESA in youth if you have completed a course of 'full-time advanced or secondary education' or 'training' which you started at least three months before your 20th birthday (see p176).

Income-related employment and support allowance

Unless you are getting DLA, you cannot qualify for income-related ESA if you are 'receiving education'.[52] You cannot usually qualify for the duration of your course, including vacations. See p646 if you have finished studying and p661 if you give up, change or take time out from your course.

For income-related ESA purposes, you count as 'receiving education' if you are:

- a 'qualifying young person' for child benefit purposes (see p94);[53] *or*
- undertaking a 'course of study'.[54] The DWP may refer to you as a 'full-time student'. The definition is the same as the definition of full-time student for income support (IS) and jobseekers's allowance (JSA) (see p637). A 'course of study' is the same as a 'full-time course' for IS and JSA, and, for ESA, also includes a sandwich course (see p637).

Note: the term **'full-time student'** is used in the rest of this chapter to refer to someone who is 'receiving education' for income-related ESA purposes.

Note that unless you are a 'qualifying young person' for child benefit purposes, if you qualify for income-related ESA as a full-time student because you are getting DLA, you automatically count as having limited capability for work (see p201).[55]

Unless it is a modular course (the definition is the same as for IS/JSA – see p639) or you are a qualifying young person for child benefit purposes (see p94) you are treated as a full-time student from the date you start to undertake your course until the last day of the course, or until you abandon it or are dismissed from it.[56] The last day of the course is the last day of the final academic term.[57]

Note: the rules described in this section are used to determine whether or not you can qualify for income-related ESA while you are studying. See p652 for the rules about how student support is taken into account for income-related ESA.

Maintaining two homes

In some cases, if you are a 'full-time student' and you qualify for income-related ESA or housing benefit, you may be entitled to help with the costs of more than one home if you have to live away from your normal home in order to attend a course. For further details, see pp255 and 852.

When you stop being a full-time student

Once you stop being a full-time student (see p645), you may be able to claim income-related ESA (see Chapter 10). However, bear the following in mind.

- If you were a 'qualifying young person' for child benefit purposes (eg, you were under 20 and on a full-time course of non-advanced education – see p94), you continue to count as a qualifying young person for a period after your education or training ends (eg, if you have enrolled on another course or during the child benefit 'extension period' – see p96). While you continue to be treated as a qualifying young person, you can only qualify for income-related ESA if you are receiving DLA. If you cannot qualify for ESA in your own right, your parents may be able to continue to claim child benefit and tax credits for you.
- If you counted as a full-time student other than where this is because you were a 'qualifying young person' for child benefit purposes (see p94), you continue to be treated as a full-time student until the last day of your course, or until you abandon the course or are dismissed from it (see p661).

Studying part time

You can qualify for ESA if you are studying part time. This can mean different things for contributory ESA and for income-related ESA.

You can qualify for **contributory ESA in youth** if you are under 19 and attending a course of education for less than 21 hours a week. Remember that if you are 19 or over, it does not matter how many hours you study; you can qualify for contributory ESA if you are studying part time *or* full time.

You can qualify for income-related ESA if you do not count as a full-time student under the rules described on p645.

When someone else is entitled to benefits for you

If you are under 20, a 'qualifying young person' for child benefit purposes (see p94) and cannot qualify for ESA because you are 'receiving full-time education' (see p644) or are a full-time student (see p645), someone else may be able to qualify for child benefit, child tax credit (CTC) and working tax credit if they are treated as 'responsible' for you. In some circumstances you may count as both a person who can qualify for ESA and a person for whom someone else can qualify for child benefit and CTC. Seek advice on how you would be better off financially.

3. Housing benefit and council tax benefit

Note: if you have reached the qualifying age for pension credit (PC – see p509) and neither you nor your partner are in receipt of income support (IS), income-based jobseeker's allowance (JSA) or income-related employment and support allowance (ESA), the student rules for housing benefit (HB) and council tax benefit (CTB) do not apply and there are no restrictions on you studying and qualifying for HB/CTB.[58]

Whether you can claim HB (see Chapter 14) or CTB (see Chapter 8) depends on whether you are classed as a full-time or a part-time student.

Full-time students

If you are a full-time student (see p637), you cannot usually qualify for HB or CTB, but there are some exceptions (see below).

The rules for deciding if you are a full-time student are similar to the rules for IS and JSA (see p637), except that there is no separate rule in HB/CTB if you are in 'relevant education' (see p634). Students who are qualifying young persons (see p94) and some other full-time students can qualify for HB/CTB.

Part-time students

You may be able to qualify for HB or CTB if you are studying part time. The rules for deciding if you are a part-time student are similar to the rules for IS and JSA (see p641), except that there is no separate rule in HB/CTB if you are in 'relevant education' (see p634).

Partners of students

If your partner is not a student, s/he can qualify for HB/CTB if s/he meets the qualifying conditions.[59] The claim is assessed in the normal way, except that (for HB) the rules about being away from term-time accommodation (see p648) apply to the partner's claim.[60] Additionally, the special rules for assessing any income you receive from grants, loans and other types of financial support for students apply (see p652).

Council tax and council tax benefit

Most full-time students are exempt from council tax and are not liable to pay. In a small number of exceptional cases (eg, some full-time students who live with non-student adults), the student may be liable to pay council tax. In this case, check if the student can claim CTB (see below) or, alternatively, council tax second adult rebate. If you are living in halls of residence predominantly provided to accommodate students, or in a dwelling wholly occupied by students or certain other persons, the dwelling is exempt from council tax. See CPAG's *Council Tax Handbook* for more details.

Full-time students entitled to housing benefit and council tax benefit

You can qualify for HB and CTB (although most student funding will count as income) if:[61]

- you are on IS, income-based JSA or income-related ESA; *or*
- you are under 21, not following a course of higher education (higher education includes degree courses, teacher training, HND, HNC and postgraduate courses), or are aged 21 and you reached that age while on such a course and are still on it, or you are a child or a 'qualifying young person' for child benefit purposes (see p94); *or*
- you and your partner are both full-time students and either or both of you are responsible for a child or qualifying young person (see p94). Note that, unlike for IS and JSA, this provision applies throughout the year; *or*
- you are a lone parent with a dependent child or qualifying young person aged under 20 (see p94); *or*
- you are a lone foster carer and the child has been formally placed with you by a local authority or voluntary agency; *or*
- you meet the conditions for the disability premium (see p824). **Note:** you cannot qualify for a disability premium if you have limited capability for work; *or*
- you have been (or have been treated as) incapable of work (see p339) for 196 days (28 weeks); *or*
- you have had (or have been treated as having) limited capability for work (see p199) for 196 days (28 weeks). Two or more periods are joined to form a single period if they are separated by 12 weeks or less. **Note:** claims from 27 October 2008 are assessed under these rules rather than the incapacity for work rules in the bullet point above, unless, broadly, you already get incapacity benefit or IS because of incapacity for work; *or*
- you meet the conditions for the severe disability premium (see p830); *or*
- you qualify for a disabled students' allowance because you are deaf; *or*
- you are waiting to go back to your course, having taken approved time out because of an illness or caring responsibility and this has now come to an end (see p662).

Note: even if you are a full-time student who fits one of the exception categories listed above, you still cannot qualify for HB if the circumstances under the two headings below apply to you.

Being away from your term-time accommodation

Even if you are a full-time student who can qualify for HB (see p647), if your main reason for occupying your home is to enable you to attend your course, you cannot qualify for HB on that home for any full week when you are absent from it outside your period of study (see p653).[62]

This rule does not apply if:

- you are away from home because you are in hospital;[63]
- the main reason for occupying your home is *not* to enable you to attend your course but for some other purpose – eg, to provide a home for your children or

for yourself because you do not have a home elsewhere where you normally live when you are not attending your course. If this applies, any absences outside your period of study are dealt with under the temporary absence rules (see p254).

Accommodation rented from an educational establishment

If you are a full-time student who can qualify for HB (see p647), you can usually get HB even if you rent your accommodation from your educational establishment.[64] If you are a part-time student, this rule applies if you would be able to qualify for HB if you were treated as a full-time student.

You cannot, however, get HB if you are a:

- full-time student waiting to go back to your course having taken approved time out because of illness or caring responsibilities (see p662) and your illness or caring responsibilities have not yet ended; *or*
- part-time student whose only basis of entitlement to HB if you were a full-time student would be that you are receiving IS, income-based JSA or income-related ESA.

The above two exceptions do not apply if:

- your educational establishment itself rents the accommodation from a third party other than on a long lease or where the third party is an education authority providing the accommodation as part of its functions; *or*
- the accommodation is owned by a separate legal body – eg, a company established under the Business Expansion Scheme to build halls of residence.

You cannot get HB if the local authority decides that your educational establishment has arranged for your accommodation to be provided by a person or body other than itself in order to take advantage of the HB scheme.

Living in different accommodation during term time

The rules about claiming HB for two homes are explained on p255.

If you are one of a couple and receive HB for two homes, the assessment of HB for each home is based on your joint income and your applicable amount as a couple.

Calculating housing benefit

If you or your partner are on IS, income-based JSA, income-related ESA or the guarantee credit of PC, you are entitled to maximum HB or CTB (see Chapter 14).

If you are not on IS, income-based JSA, income-related ESA or the guarantee credit of PC but you or your partner are eligible for HB/CTB, your entitlement is calculated in the same way as for other claimants (see Chapters 39, 40 and 47), except that there are special rules for assessing the amount of money available from grants, loans and other types of financial support for students (see p652).

Note that, for courses lasting more than one year, in many cases loans and grants are not counted as income over the summer vacation. You may find, therefore, that your HB entitlement is higher over this period, or that you are only entitled to HB during the summer vacation, and that you need to make a new claim or check that your entitlement is reviewed at that time (see p653 for grant income and p656 for loans).

Payments

Students are covered by all the normal rules on the administration and payment of HB (see Chapter 14). However, there is a provision that can apply specifically to students. The local authority may decide to pay a rent allowance once each term, although students have the same right as other claimants to insist on fortnightly payments if their entitlement is more than £2 a week (see p281).[65]

4. **Other benefits and tax credits**

Carer's allowance

You cannot qualify for carer's allowance (CA – see Chapter 6) if you are in full-time education.[66] Usually, if the course you are attending is described by the university, college or school as full time then you will be regarded as being in full-time education, although there may be exceptions – eg, if you have been exempted from parts of the course.[67] So the actual hours you attend may not be crucial; but if you are attending for 21 hours a week or more (as specified by the institution) you are treated as being in full-time education. When calculating the 21 hours you include only hours spent in 'supervised study'. You ignore any time spent on meal breaks or unsupervised study undertaken on or off the premises of the educational establishment.[68]

'Supervised study' does not depend on whether your supervisor (ie, teacher, tutor, lecturer) is present with you.[69] If your study is directed to your course of education and the curriculum of your course and it is undertaken to meet the reasonable requirements of your course, it normally counts as supervised study. It counts regardless of whether that study is undertaken on or off the premises of the education institution you attend.

'Unsupervised study' means work beyond the reasonable requirements of your course. In assessing your hours of attendance, evidence from your education institution about the amount of time you are expected to study to complete your course is important.

You are treated as still in full-time education during vacations and any temporary interruption of the course, but not if you have abandoned the course or been dismissed from it.

Child benefit

You can qualify for child benefit (see Chapter 7) for a 'qualifying young person' – eg, someone who is under 19 (or under 20 in certain circumstances) and in full-time, non-advanced education or training, including for a period after the young person leaves education or training (see p94).

Incapacity benefit

If you are claiming for a period which starts on or after 27 October 2008, you can only qualify in limited circumstances and you may have to claim employment and support allowance (ESA) instead of incapacity benefit (IB) (see p337). See previous versions of this *Handbook* for the rules about IB and full-time study.

Pension credit

If you are a student who has reached the qualifying age for pension credit (PC) (or you are a student who has not reached this age but you have a partner who has), you (or your partner) may be eligible for PC (see Chapter 22). Unlike income support (IS), jobseeker's allowance (JSA) and ESA, students are not excluded from PC.

In addition, the more generous income and capital rules for PC benefit men and women who have reached the qualifying age for PC who are students or whose partners are students (regardless of their partner's age) as student grants and loans are not taken into account as income.[70] Check to see if you would be better off if you (or your partner) were to claim PC rather than IS, income-based JSA or income-related ESA. If you, or your partner, receive PC the more generous rules for calculating housing benefit and council tax benefit may also apply (see p649).

Social fund payments

You are not excluded from access to a social fund payment simply because you are studying (but see p566 for crisis loans). However, to claim a payment from the social fund (except a crisis loan) you must be in receipt of an appropriate 'qualifying benefit' (see Chapters 25 and 26).

Working tax credit and child tax credit

You are not excluded from qualifying for tax credits simply because you are a student. However, special rules apply to calculating your income from a grant, loan or other financial support for students (see p1336).

Health benefits

Students are not excluded from qualifying for NHS benefits (see Chapter 13).

National insurance credits

You may be able to receive NI credits (see Chapter 35) for a tax year in which you were on a full-time course.

5. Calculating income from grants and loans

The rules in this section only apply to the calculation of income support (IS), income-based jobseeker's allowance (JSA), income-related employment and support allowance (ESA), housing benefit (HB) and council tax benefit (CTB). They apply if you are a part-time or a full-time student. For the rules on *entitlement* to these benefits if you are studying, see the relevant section in this chapter.

If you (or your partner) are a student, some of your (or your partner's) income from a grant, a loan and certain other forms of financial support for students is taken into account when calculating the amount of your benefit under the special rules set out below.[71] Your other income and capital are dealt with under the normal rules (see Chapter 40 and 41).

The DWP has issued guidance to decision makers concerning the treatment of various types of financial support to students. Often this guidance only covers some of the benefits to which this section refers. For example, guidance may have been issued for HB/CTB purposes but no equivalent guidance has been issued for IS/JSA/ESA. Additionally, the legislation and guidance may not cover all sources of student support across the UK, particularly as new sources of support are introduced. You should, therefore, check the current position.

Note:

- The information in this section applies to support available to new students for the academic year 2011/12. For the treatment of grant and loan income for students who started their course in previous academic years, see the relevant edition of this *Handbook*.
- Grant and loan income does not affect your contribution-based JSA or contributory ESA.
- Any student income you have from a grant or loan is not taken into account as income if you are claiming HB or CTB and you:
  - are getting IS, income-based JSA, income-related ESA or the guarantee credit of pension credit (PC); *or*
  - have reached the qualifying age for PC (see p509) and you (or your partner) are not getting IS, income-based JSA or income-related ESA.[72]

Student support

There are many types of financial support available to students attending a course at school, sixth-form or further education college, or who are undergraduates (including certain courses below degree level) or postgraduates. These are paid in the form of either a grant or a loan. Some types of grant or loan are available to all students who meet the conditions of entitlement; others are available on a discretionary basis. The support available to students varies, depending on whether you live in England, Wales, Scotland or Northern Ireland. For more information, see CPAG's *Student Support and Benefits Handbook* (England, Wales and Northern Ireland) and *Benefits for Students in Scotland Handbook*.

Grants

The term **'grant'**[73] includes any kind of educational grant or award, bursary (such as those paid by the NHS for certain health-related courses), scholarship, studentship, exhibition or supplementary allowance. It does not include payments from access funds (see p659), education maintenance allowances or similar payments (or the equivalent in Scotland, Wales and Northern Ireland).

Some grants are ignored as income (see p655) and others are taken into account. When calculating income from a grant, special rules and disregards apply.

If you are assessed as entitled to a parental (or partner's of a parent) or partner's contribution to your grant it counts as income whether or not it has been paid to you.[74] However, only the amount of contribution you actually receive counts if:

- for IS, you are a lone parent, a lone foster carer or a disabled student (see p640); *or*
- for JSA, you qualify for a disability premium (see p824); *or*
- for ESA, you are a lone parent or a full-time student who gets disability living allowance (DLA) (see p645).

General rule on calculating grant income

Your grant income is apportioned:[75]

- if it is payable for your period of study (unless you are attending a sandwich course), over the number of benefit weeks in your period of study;
- if it is payable for a period other than your period of study, over the number of benefit weeks in the period for which the grant is payable.

In most cases, the former applies and your grant income is assessed over a period starting from the 'benefit week' which coincides with (or immediately follows) the first day of your 'period of study' (see p654) and ending with the benefit week, the last day of which coincides with (or immediately precedes) the last day of your period of study. In this context, **'benefit week'** means the week for which benefit is paid.[76]

This means your grant income is apportioned over the number of complete benefit weeks in your period of study. Any part-weeks at the beginning or end of that period are ignored. **Note:** this rule does not apply to an NHS bursary (see p654).

'Period of study' means:[77]

- for a course of one year or less, from the start of the course to the last day of the course;
- for a course of more than one year, in the first and subsequent years (but not the final year), from the start of the course, or the start of the year of the course to:
  - where the grant is payable for a period of 12 months, the day before the start of the next year of the course; *or*
  - in any other case, the day before the start of your normal summer vacation;
- in the final year of a course lasting more than one year, from the start of the final year of the course and ending with the last day of the course.

Specific types of grant income

If you are attending a **sandwich course** (see p638) your grant income is taken into account over a different period. Any periods spent on placement or work experience in your period of study are excluded and your grant is apportioned over the remaining 'benefit weeks' in your period of study.[78] **Note:** this only applies if your grant is payable for your period of study. If your grant is payable for a different period, it is taken into account over the number of benefit weeks in the period for which it is payable.

Postgraduate awards made by research councils and the British Academy are apportioned over the number of benefit weeks in the period for which they are payable (usually a calendar year).

NHS bursaries paid to students in England, Wales and Scotland are paid in monthly instalments. They should be taken into account over 52 or 53 weeks (if there are 53 benefit weeks, including part-weeks, in the year).[79]

If you are studying for an undergraduate diploma or degree or postgraduate qualification in **social work,** you may be eligible for a non-means-tested bursary administered by the NHS in England, the Care Council for Wales or the Scottish Social Services Council. The bursary or grant counts in full as grant income and is apportioned according to the rules above.

If you receive a **supplementary allowance** for an adult dependant as part of a student loan (or you could have received one had you taken reasonable steps to apply for one), the allowance is apportioned over the same period as a student loan (see p656).

If you receive a supplementary allowance from any other source, but you do not receive a student loan (or could not have received one even if you had taken reasonable steps to apply for one) it is apportioned over the same period as 'basic' grant income (see p653).[80] If you receive a supplementary allowance for an adult dependant as part of an NHS bursary, this is apportioned over 52 or 53 weeks.[81]

Note: students on health-related courses, except nursing and midwifery diploma courses, may be eligible for supplementary allowances for an adult dependant under both an NHS bursary and (reduced-rate) student loan. These separate allowances for an adult dependant are, therefore, taken into account over different periods.

In Scotland, a **care leavers' grant** of up to £105 a week towards accommodation, which is paid during the long vacation only, is taken fully into account as income for each week in which it is paid.

The **Scottish young person's bursary** is apportioned in the same way as the student loan (see p656).

Grant income that is ignored

The following grant income is ignored:[82]

- any allowance for tuition and examination fees;
- disabled students' allowance;
- any allowance to meet the cost of residential study away from your normal educational establishment during term time;
- any allowance for the cost of your normal home (away from college) but, for IS, JSA and ESA, only to the extent that your rent is not met by HB;
- any amount for a partner or child living abroad;
- for IS/JSA/ESA only, any amount intended to maintain a dependent child (unless you still have amounts for children included in your IS/JSA and do not get child tax credit);
- any amount intended for the childcare costs of a dependent child;
- parents' learning allowance;
- higher education grant;[83]
- special support grant;[84]
- if you have been required to make a contribution to your own grant (eg, because you have other income, such as maintenance), an amount equivalent to that contribution is disregarded.[85] In the case of a couple, the amount of any contribution that one member has been assessed to pay to her/his partner who is a student is disregarded from the non-student's income;[86]
- an education maintenance allowance, 16-19 bursary or similar payments, including a Care to Learn payment, a further education Welsh Assembly learning grant or Passport to Study grant;[87]
- higher education bursary for care leavers.

In addition to the amounts ignored under the rules above, the following fixed sums are ignored.[88] These disregards apply only to the grant you receive for your period of study and not to any supplementary allowances you may be paid during the long vacation.[89]

- A fixed amount of £390 for books and equipment (2011/12 academic year – see p656). If your grant includes a specific amount to cover the cost of books and equipment, that amount is ignored in addition to this fixed amount.
- A fixed amount of £303 for the cost of travel (2011/12 academic year – see p656). If your grant includes a specific amount to cover the cost of travel

expenses for attendance on your course, that amount is ignored in addition to this fixed amount. If your actual travel costs are higher than any sum specified in your grant for travel (which is ignored under the rules above) plus this fixed amount, the additional costs are not ignored and are taken into account.[90]

Note: if you also receive a student loan, the above two fixed sums are not disregarded when calculating your grant income, but are disregarded from your loan income instead (see p657).

Note: for the purpose of these fixed amounts, the 2011/12 academic year began on 1 August 2011 if your period of study (see p653) began in August 2011. If your period of study began on or after 1 September 2011, the fixed sums apply from that date.

At the time of writing, the amounts for 2012/13 were not available. See CPAG's *Welfare Rights Bulletin* for updates.

Loans

A loan is treated as income but is subject to special rules and disregards. Note that some supplementary allowances paid under the student loan provisions are paid as non-repayable grants and are treated as grant income (see p653).

Calculating income from a student loan

How your, or your partner's, student loan is treated depends on whether your course lasts for one year or less, or for a longer period.[91] The maximum amount of available loan is taken into account even if you do not apply for a loan or for the maximum amount,[92] unless, for ESA only, you are taking time out for ill health and are not receiving a student loan.[93]

You are treated as having a parental or partner's contribution to your loan whether or not it has been paid to you. However, only the amount of contribution you actually receive counts if:[94]

- for IS, you are a lone parent, a lone foster carer or a disabled student (see p640); *or*
- for JSA, you qualify for a disability premium (see p824); *or*
- for ESA, you are a full-time student who gets DLA (see p645).

A student loan paid to a student on a Postgraduate Certificate in Education course is treated in the same way as student loans and supplementary allowances for undergraduate students.

Dependants' grants are taken into account over the same period as the student loan if you have a student loan or you are eligible for one.[95]

If you attend a nursing or midwifery diploma course, no loan income should be taken into account as a student loan is not available for these courses. If you are on another health-related course, only the lower maximum loan rate should be taken into account.

Your loan (including any additional weeks' allowance) is treated as explained below.

Loan income that is ignored

- Loans paid for tuition fees (known as a 'fee loan' or a 'fee contribution loan').[96]
- If you have been required to make a contribution to your own loan (eg, because you have other income, such as maintenance), an amount equivalent to that contribution is disregarded as income.[97] In the case of a couple, the amount of any contribution that one member has been assessed to pay to her/his partner who is a student is disregarded from the non-student's income.[98]

Once any of the above income has been deducted from your loan income, also ignored is a fixed amount of:[99]

- £390 for the cost of books and equipment (2011/12 academic year – see below); *and*
- £303 for the cost of travel (2011/12 academic year – see below).

If your actual costs are higher than the amounts for books and equipment and travel, any additional costs cannot be ignored.[100]

Note:

- If you also receive a grant, the two fixed sums above are ignored from your loan income rather than your grant income (see p655).
- For the purpose of the above fixed amounts, the 2011/12 academic year began on 1 August 2011 if your period of study (see p653) began in August 2011. If your period of study began on or after 1 September 2011, the fixed sums apply from that date.

At the time of writing, the amounts for 2012/13 were not available. See CPAG's *Welfare Rights Bulletin* for updates.

Ten pounds a week is ignored for each week in the period over which your loan income is taken into account (see below). This amount may overlap with other disregards applied to certain war pensions (see p920) and access funds (see p659). A combined maximum sum of £20 a week can be ignored.

The period over which loan income is taken into account

Academic year

The rules give a definition of an 'academic year' for the purposes of calculating student loan income. This definition may be different from the actual academic year of the education institution you attend.

'Academic year' means a period of 12 months beginning on 1 January, 1 April, 1 July or 1 September according to whether your course begins in the winter, the spring, the summer or the autumn respectively. If you are required to begin attending your course during August or September and to continue attending through the autumn, the 'academic year' of your course is treated as beginning in the autumn rather than summer – ie, from 1 September.[101]

Benefit weeks

Loan income is apportioned over a period of 'benefit weeks'.

The first benefit week may fall before the start of your actual academic year and the last benefit week may fall either before or after the last day of your academic year (academic years vary between education institutions). This may mean your benefit is recalculated several times depending on when your actual academic year falls in relation to the relevant benefit weeks. You need to make a new claim or check that your entitlement is revised at these times.

If you are required to start attending your course in August, or your course is for less than one academic year, the period begins with the benefit week, the first day of which coincides with, or immediately follows, the first day of the course.[102]

If your academic year starts other than on 1 September, your loan payable for that academic year is apportioned equally between the benefit weeks in the period beginning with the benefit week, the first day of which coincides with, or immediately follows, the first day of that academic year and ending with the benefit week, the last day of which coincides with, or immediately precedes, the last day of that academic year. Excluded from that are any benefit weeks falling entirely within the quarter during which, in the opinion of the decision maker, your longest vacation falls.[103]

'Quarter' means one of the periods from 1 January to 31 March, 1 April to 30 June, 1 July to 31 August, or 1 September to 31 December.[104]

In the first, or only, year of your course your loan income (calculated under the rules below) is ignored for each benefit week that falls before the start of your 'period of study' (the first day of the first term). This is because you cannot be treated as a student until you actually start your course.[105]

A course lasting for one academic year or less

Your loan is apportioned over the benefit weeks beginning with the benefit week, the first day of which coincides with, or immediately follows, the first day of the 'academic year' (or, if a course begins in August, from the first day of the first benefit week on or after the first day of the course) and ending with the benefit week, the last day of which coincides with, or immediately follows, the last day of the course.

A course lasting for more than one academic year

Unless it is your final year (see p659), your loan is apportioned over the period from the earlier of:

- the first day of the first benefit week in September; *or*
- the first benefit week, the first day of which coincides with, or immediately follows, the first day of the autumn term.

It is taken into account until the last day of the benefit week that coincides with, or immediately precedes, the last day of June.

Final year of a course

Your loan is taken into account over the period beginning with either:

- if the final academic year starts on 1 September, the benefit week, the first day of which coincides with, or immediately follows, the earlier of 1 September or the first day of the autumn term; *or*
- the benefit week, the first day of which coincides with, or immediately follows, the first day of the academic year.

It is taken into account until the benefit week, the last day of which coincides with, or immediately precedes, the last day of the course.

Calculating income from other types of loan

Professional and career development loans paid under s2 of the Employment and Training Act 1973 are treated as income.[106] However, this income is ignored except where it is intended to meet 'daily living expenses' and your course or education has not been completed.[107]

Any financial support you receive that is paid in the form of a loan (other than a student loan or a professional and career development loan), including a loan received from an overseas source, does not count as a student loan or a grant.[108] It is taken into account as 'other income' (see p918).

Payments from access funds

Access funds (which include the Learner Support Fund available to some students in further education, the Financial Contingency Fund in Wales, the Access to Learning Fund offered by higher education institutions in England, the 16-19 bursary in England and discretionary funds in Scotland) are administered by colleges and universities.[109] Individual education institutions may call all or part of these funds by other names – ie, access bursary, mature students' bursary and childcare support. Payments from access funds should be distinguished from payments with similar names from other sources – ie, hardship loans.

How a payment from access funds is treated depends on whether it is paid as a single lump-sum payment, in instalments or to bridge the period before you start your course or receive a student loan payment.

A single lump-sum payment

A single lump-sum payment is treated as capital but is disregarded for 52 weeks if the payment is intended for and used for any items, expenses or charges which you or your partner may incur (other than 'daily living expenses').[110] However, if the payment is intended for but not used for these items, expenses or charges it is taken into account as capital immediately. A single lump-sum payment made for 'daily living expenses' counts as capital immediately.

'Daily living expenses' are:

- food;
- ordinary clothing or footwear – ie, for normal daily use, but not including school uniforms or that used solely for sporting activities;
- household fuel;
- for IS/JSA/ESA only, rent for which HB is payable;
- for HB/CTB, your 'eligible rent', minus any non-dependant deductions (see Chapter 14);
- for IS/JSA/ESA only, housing costs met by IS, income-based JSA or income-related ESA (see Chapter 38);
- council tax;
- water charges.

Payments made in instalments

Payments made in instalments are treated as income, but are disregarded in full.[111] However, if the payment is intended and used for 'daily living expenses' (see above), it is taken into account as income for each week it is intended to cover, except for the first £20 a week, which is disregarded. This amount may overlap with other disregards applied to certain war pensions (see p920) and student loans (see p657). A combined maximum sum of £20 a week can be ignored.

Payments before course starts or student loan received

A payment (whether paid as a single payment or in instalments) is ignored, even if it is for 'daily living expenses', if it is made:[112]

- on or after whichever is the earlier of 1 September or the first day of your course, if it is intended to bridge the period before you receive your student loan; *or*
- before the first day of your course, if it is made in anticipation of your becoming a student.

Other sources of income intended to cover study costs

If you receive a payment from any source other than a grant or student loan, which is intended to cover items or expenses that would be ignored when calculating grant income, the payment made from that other source for those items or expenses is also ignored.[113] You must show that the payment is necessary for you to be able to attend the course. Any sum paid, which is not necessary (or is likely to exceed the sum necessary) for you to attend the course, counts as income. For example, if your grant or student loan does not cover all your tuition fees, any money received from another source, such as a parent, intended to make up the difference is ignored as income. However, if the amount you receive is greater than is likely to be necessary to pay the difference, the amount above that sum counts as income.

Student support once you have completed your course

For IS/JSA/ESA only, any grant income, student loan, assessed contribution made by a parent or spouse/civil partner as part of the loan or grant, or a professional and career development loan that you received no longer counts as income once you have completed the course.[114] However, as most (but not all) types of student support are not taken into account for a period after your course is due to end, it should also be ignored as income for HB/CTB once you have completed the course.

Presumably, any student financial support you have left once you have completed your course counts as capital (see Chapter 41) as there are no provisions to disregard it under the rules about capital.

6. Giving up, changing or taking time out from your course

This section only applies to income support (IS), jobseeker's allowance (JSA), income-related employment and support allowance (ESA), housing benefit (HB) and council tax benefit (CTB).
However, this section does *not* apply if (for IS and JSA) you are (or were) in 'relevant education (see p634), or (for ESA) you are (or were) a 'qualifying young person' for child benefit purposes (see p645). See p636 for information about qualifying for IS or JSA when you leave relevant education. See p646 for information about qualifying for income-related ESA when you are no longer a qualifying young person for child benefit purposes.
Note: there is no equivalent rule for HB and CTB.

If you abandon your course or are dismissed from it, you can qualify for IS, JSA or income-related ESA from the day after that date so long as you satisfy the other rules for getting these benefits (see Chapters 10, 17 and 19). If you are on a sandwich course (see p638), or your course includes a compulsory or optional period on placement, you count as a full-time student during the sandwich or placement period even if you have been unable to find a placement or your placement comes to an end prematurely.[115]

If you attend a course at an education institution that provides training or instruction to enable you to take examinations set and marked by an entirely different and unconnected body (ie, a professional institution) and you abandon or take time out from it because you fail the examinations set by the other body (or you finish the course at the education institution but fail the exams), you may be able to argue that you are not a student from the date you left the course at your education institution even if you intend to re-sit the examinations set by the other body at a later date.[116]

If you are taking time out of your course for any other reason and for however long a period, you cannot qualify for IS, JSA or income-related ESA during your period of absence,[117] except in the limited circumstances set out below (but if you are taking time out from a modular or similar course, see also p639).

You may retain entitlement to some student support on a statutory or discretionary basis – eg, through student loans or hardship funds. You should seek specialist advice.

If you complete one course and start a different course you are not treated as a student in any period between the courses.[118]

Changing from full-time to part-time attendance

If, for personal reasons, you have to change from full-time to part-time attendance on a 'traditional' full-time course, you may be able to argue that you have abandoned your full-time course and are registered on a part-time course and, therefore, that you are not a full-time student.[119]

If, because of exam failure or any other reason, you change to a different course, or your college requires you to change the level of course (eg, from A level to GCSE) and this involves a change from full-time to part-time study, argue that you are a part-time student.[120]

However, changing your attendance may affect your entitlement to any student support you may be receiving. Seek advice on this before acting.

Time out to be a carer

If you are a full-time student and you have taken time out from your course to care for someone, you cannot qualify for IS, JSA or income-related ESA unless you are someone who can qualify while studying (see pp640, 641 and 645). However, you can qualify for JSA, HB and CTB, but not IS or income-related ESA, when your caring responsibilities have come to an end.[121] **Note:** the rules do not provide a definition of caring responsibilities or when they come to an end. You can then qualify for a maximum period of one year, provided you are not eligible for a student grant or loan during the period, until whichever is the earlier of:

- the day you rejoin your course; *or*
- the first day from which your education institution has agreed you can rejoin your course.

This means that you may not qualify for benefit for the whole of the period after your caring responsibilities end until the date you actually rejoin your course.

Time out because of illness

If you are a full-time student and you have taken time out from your course because you are ill, you cannot qualify for income-based ESA unless you get disability living allowance.

Once your illness has ended, you can qualify for JSA, HB and CTB. The rules are the same as for when caring responsibilities have ended (see p662).

Time out because you are pregnant

If you are a full-time student and you have taken time out from your course because you are pregnant, you cannot qualify for IS, JSA or income-based ESA, unless you are someone who can qualify while studying (see pp640, 641 and 645). It has been decided that, for JSA, this provision does not *directly* discriminate against women under European Union (EU) law.[122] It was also subsequently decided that it does not *indirectly* discriminate against women under EU law, and that it is not incompatible with the Human Rights Act.[123] **Note:**

- Check to see whether you qualify for statutory maternity pay or maternity allowance.
- Once your baby is born, you may then qualify for IS, HB or CTB – eg, you may qualify for IS if you are a lone parent or for HB if you and your partner are both full-time students.

Calculating income from grants and loans

Grants

For IS, income-based JSA and income-related ESA, if you cease to be a full-time student before your course finishes, any grant you have received is taken into account as if you were still a student (see p653) until the earliest of the following:[124]

- the date you repay the grant; *or*
- the last date of the academic term or vacation in which you ceased to be a full-time student; *or*
- if the grant is paid in instalments, the day before the next instalment would have been paid had you still been a full-time student.

For HB/CTB it is not taken into account as if you were still a student.[125] Instead, it is taken into account until the grant provider asks you to repay it, and until then should be calculated over an appropriate period.[126] It could be argued that your grant should be taken into account as income only to the end of the period which your last instalment was meant to cover.

Loans

For income-related ESA, if you suspend attendance at your course because of illness or disability and that is confirmed in writing by the educational institution, you are not treated as having any part of a student loan which has not been paid to you.

If you abandon or are dismissed from your course before it finishes, there are special rules on how your student loan is treated for IS, income-based JSA, income-related ESA, HB and CTB.

If you abandon your course before you have received the final instalment of your student loan, it is taken into account using the formula:[127]

$$\frac{A - (B \times C)}{D}$$

A = the maximum amount of student loan available to you (see p656) – including any amount, paid as a grant, intended for the maintenance of your dependants – that you would have received had you remained a student until *the last day of the academic term* in which you abandoned or were dismissed from your course, less any disregards that apply (see p657). This amount is the 'relevant payment'. If, however, you were paid in two or more instalments in a quarter (eg, monthly, as is currently the case for Scottish students studying in Scotland), A = the relevant payment that you would have received calculated in the same way, except that it is the amount that you would have received had you remained a student up until *the day you abandoned or were dismissed from your course.*

B = the number of benefit weeks immediately following the benefit week which includes the first day of your 'academic year' to the benefit week immediately before that which includes the day on which you abandoned or were dismissed from your course (for HB/CTB, calculate up until the week that includes the one in which you left the course).

C = the weekly amount of student loan for the 'academic year' which would have been taken into account to calculate your benefit under the normal rules (see p656) but without applying the £10 a week disregard (see p657). This applies regardless of whether you were actually entitled to benefit before you abandoned or were dismissed from your course.

D = the number of benefit weeks beginning with the benefit week which includes the day on which you abandoned or were dismissed from your course and ending with the benefit week which includes the last day of the last 'quarter' (see p659) for which your 'relevant payment' (see A) would have been payable to you had you remained on your course, or to the day before you would have been due your next loan payment, if earlier.

Example

Bhavna abandons her three-year degree course at a university outside London on 2 November 2012 during the first term of her second year. Her benefit week starts on a Tuesday. Her assumed maximum loan income would have been taken into account for 42 weeks (first complete benefit week in September to last complete benefit week in June).

Note: the following figures are from 2011/12, because at the time of writing the 2012/13 figures were not finalised. However, the dates are for the 2012/13 academic year.

Step A: calculate the relevant payment

Loan instalment paid for first term	£1,650
less deduction for books and travel	£693
Total taken into account	**£957**

Step B: calculate the benefit weeks prior to leaving the course

4.9.12 to 29.10.12	**= 8 weeks**

Step C: calculate maximum loan for the academic year

Maximum loan	£4,950
less deduction for books and travel	£693
Total loan	£4,257
Weekly amount (£4,257 divided by 42 weeks)	**= £101.36 a week**

Step D: calculate complete benefit weeks from the benefit week including the date of abandonment to the end of the benefit week including the end of the quarter

30.10.12 to 31.12.12	**= 9 weeks**

$$\frac{957 - (8 \times 101.36)}{9}$$ **= £16.24 a week**

Therefore, £16.24 a week is taken into account for the period from 30.10.12 to 31.12.12 (9 weeks) and nothing thereafter.

Note: this formula can result in a nil loan income figure depending on the exact date in your term that you abandon, or are dismissed from, your course.

If you voluntarily repay your student loan, for IS, income-based JSA and income-related ESA you are treated as still having that loan income calculated under the above rules.[128] However, for all the benefits, guidance to decision makers says you should not be treated as having any loan income if the Student Loans Company demands you repay the loan instalment immediately.[129]

Notes

1. **Income support and jobseeker's allowance**
   1 s124(1)(d) SSCBA 1992; s1(2)(g) JSA 1995
   2 **IS** Reg 12 IS Regs
   JSA Reg 54 JSA Regs
   3 Regs 4ZA and 13(2)(a)-(e) IS Regs
   4 Reg 2(1)(b)(i)&(ii) C(LC)SSB Regs; reg 13(2)(a) and (b) IS Regs; para 30524 DMG
   5 R(IS) 9/94
   6 R(IS) 9/94
   7 CIS/11766/1996
   8 R(IS) 9/94
   9 Reg 13(3)(a)(ii) IS Regs
   10 R(SB) 2/87
   11 CIS/11441/1995
   12 s1(2)(g) JSA 1995; regs 54, 57(2) and (4)(a) and 61(1)(c) JSA Regs
   13 Reg 54(3)-(5) JSA Regs
   14 Reg 54(3) and (4) JSA Regs
   15 **IS** Reg 4ZA(2) IS Regs
   JSA Reg 15(a) JSA Regs
   16 **IS** Reg 61(1) IS Regs
   JSA Reg 1(3) JSA Regs
   Both Definition of 'full-time student'
   17 **IS** Reg 2(1) IS Regs, definition of 'period of study'
   JSA Reg 1(3A) JSA Regs
   HB Reg 53(2)(b) HB Regs
   CTB Reg 43(2)(b) CTB Regs
   18 **IS** Reg 61(1) IS Regs, definition of 'last day of the course'
   JSA Regs 130 JSA Regs, definition of 'last day of the course'
   HB Reg 53(1) HB Regs, definition of 'last day of the course'
   CTB Reg 43(1) CTB Regs, definition of 'last day of the course'
   19 Reg 4 JSA Regs, definition of 'period of study'
   20 **IS** Reg 61(1) IS Regs, definitions of 'full-time course of advanced education' and 'full-time course of study'; para 30148 DMG
   JSA Reg 1(3) JSA Regs, definition of 'full-time student' – the definition of 'full-time course' is found within that definition
   HB Reg 53(1) HB Regs, definition of 'full-time course of study'
   CTB Reg 43(1) CTB Regs, definition of 'full-time course of study'
   21 paras 30197-98 DMG
   22 **IS** Reg 61 IS Regs definitions of 'full-time course of advanced education' and 'full-time course of study'; paras 30149 DMG
   JSA Reg 1(3) JSA Regs, definition of 'full-time student' – the definition of 'full-time course' is found within that definition
   HB Reg 53(1) HB Regs, definitions of 'full-time course of study' and 'higher education'
   CTB Reg 43(1) CTB Regs, definitions of 'full-time course of study' and 'higher education'
   23 **IS** Reg 61(1) IS Regs
   JSA Reg 1(3) JSA Regs
   HB Reg 53(1) HB Regs
   CTB Reg 43(1) CTB Regs
   All definition of 'sandwich course'
   24 R(IS) 19/98
   25 **IS** Reg 61(4) IS Regs
   JSA Reg 1(3C) JSA Regs
   HB Reg 53(4) HB Regs
   CTB Reg 43(4) CTB Regs
   26 **IS** Reg 61(2)(a) IS Regs
   JSA Reg 1(3A)(a) JSA Regs
   HB Reg 53(2)(a) HB Regs
   CTB Reg 43(2)(a) CTB Regs
   27 **IS** Reg 61(3)(b) IS Regs
   JSA Reg 1(3B)(b) JSA Regs
   HB Reg 53(3)(b) HB Regs
   CTB Reg 43(3)(b) CTB Regs
   28 **IS** Reg 61(3)(a) IS Regs
   JSA Reg 1(3B)(a) JSA Regs
   HB Reg 53(3)(a) HB Regs
   CTB Reg 43(3)(a) CTB Regs
   29 R(IS) 15/98; R(IS) 7/99; CJSA/836/1998; R(IS) 1/00

30 *Chief Adjudication Officer v Webber* [1997] 4 All ER 274
31 R(SB) 40/83; R(SB) 41/83
32 **IS** Reg 61 IS Regs, definitions of 'full-time course of advanced education' and 'full-time course of study'
JSA Reg 1(3) JSA Regs, definition of 'full-time student' – the definition of 'full-time course' is found within that definition
33 Reg 4ZA and Sch 1B IS Regs
34 Reg 15(2) and (3) JSA Regs
35 Reg 14(1)(a) JSA Regs
36 Reg 14(1)(k) JSA Regs
37 Reg 5A(2) JSA(ES&ES) Regs
38 Regs 17A and 21A JSA Regs
39 CIS/152/1994; R(IS) 15/98; CJSA/836/1998; R(IS) 1/00
40 Reg 1(3) JSA Regs, definition of 'part-time student'
41 para 21241 DMG
42 para 21242 DMG
43 para 21243 DMG
44 para 21244 DMG
45 Reg 11 JSA Regs
46 Reg 11(3) JSA Regs
47 Regs 2(1)and 61(1) IS Regs, definitions of 'student' and 'course of study'

2. **Employment and support allowance**
48 Reg 32(2) and (3) ESA Regs
49 Sch 1 para 4(1)(b) WRA 2007
50 Reg 12 ESA Regs
51 R(S) 2/87 was not about ESA, but the rule is very similar.
52 Sch 1 para 6(1)(g) WRA 2007; reg 18 ESA Regs
53 Reg 15 ESA Regs
54 Reg 14 ESA Regs
55 Regs 14 and 33(2) ESA Regs
56 Reg 17(1)(b) ESA Regs
57 Reg 2(1) ESA Regs

3. **Housing benefit and council tax benefit**
58 There are no student rules in the HB(SPC) Regs and the CTB(SPC) Regs.
59 **HB** Reg 8(1)(e) HB Regs
CTB Reg 57(3) and (4) CTB Regs
60 Reg 58 HB Regs
61 **HB** Reg 56(2) HB Regs
CTB Reg 45(3) CTB Regs
62 Reg 55(1) HB Regs
63 Reg 55(2) HB Regs
64 Reg 57 HB Regs
65 Reg 92(7) HB Regs

4. **Other benefits and tax credits**
66 Reg 5 SS(ICA) Regs
67 *SSWP v Deane* [2010] EWCA Civ 699
68 Reg 5(2) SS(ICA) Regs
69 R(G) 2/02
70 s15 SPCA 2002; reg 15 SPC Regs

5. **Calculating income from grants and loans**
71 **IS** Regs 2(1) and 61(1) IS Regs
JSA Regs 1(3) and 130 JSA Regs
ESA Reg 131 ESA Regs
HB Reg 53(1) HB Regs
CTB Reg 43(1) CTB Regs
IS/HB/CTB definition of 'student'
JSA/ESA definition of 'full-time student'
IS/JSA/HB/CTB definition of 'course of study'
72 **HB** Reg 29 HB(SPC) Regs
CTB Reg 19 CTB(SPC) Regs
73 **IS** Reg 61(1) IS Regs
JSA Reg 130 JSA Regs
ESA Reg 131(1) ESA Regs
HB Reg 53(1) HB Regs
CTB Reg 43(1) CTB Regs
All definition of 'grant'
74 **IS** Reg 61(1) IS Regs
JSA Reg 130 JSA Regs
ESA Reg 131(1) ESA Regs
HB Reg 53(1) HB Regs
CTB Reg 43(1) CTB Regs
All definition of 'grant income'
75 **IS** Reg 62(3) IS Regs
JSA Reg 131(4) JSA Regs
ESA Reg 132(4) ESA Regs
HB Reg 59(5) HB Regs
CTB Reg 46(5) CTB Regs
76 Sch 7 para 4 SS(C&P)Regs
77 **IS** Reg 61(1) IS Regs
JSA Reg 1(3) JSA Regs
ESA Reg 131(1) ESA Regs
HB Reg 53 HB Regs
CTB Reg 43 CTB Regs
All definition of 'period of study'
78 **IS** Reg 62(4) IS Regs
JSA Reg 131(6) JSA Regs
ESA Reg 132(7) ESA Regs
HB Reg 59(8) HB Regs
CTB Reg 46(8) CTB Regs
79 **IS** Reg 62(3A) IS Regs
JSA Reg 131(5) JSA Regs
ESA Reg 132(5) ESA Regs
HB Reg 59(6) HB Regs
CTB Reg 46(6) CTB Regs
80 **IS** Reg 62(3) IS Regs
JSA Reg 131(4) JSA Regs
ESA Reg 132(4) ESA Regs
HB Reg 59(5) HB Regs
CTB Reg 46(5) CTB Regs

81 **IS** Reg 62(3A) IS Regs; R(IS)15/95
JSA Reg 131(5) JSA Regs
ESA Reg 132(5) ESA Regs
HB Reg 59(6) HB Regs
CTB Reg 46(6) CTB Regs
82 **IS** Reg 62(2) and (2A) IS Regs
JSA Reg 131(2) and (3) JSA Regs
ESA Reg 132(2) and (3) ESA Regs
HB Reg 59(2) and (3) HB Regs
CTB Reg 46(2) and (3) CTB Regs
83 **IS/JSA** para 30328 DMG
ESA para 51918 DMG
HB/CTB paras C2.165-66 GM
84 **IS/JSA** paras 30329-30 DMG
ESA paras 51919-20 DMG
HB/CTB paras C2.170-73 GM
85 **IS** Reg 67A IS Regs
JSA Reg 137A JSA Regs
ESA Reg 141 ESA Regs
HB Reg 67 HB Regs
CTB Reg 54 CTB Regs
86 **IS** Reg 67 IS Regs
JSA Reg 137 JSA Regs
ESA Reg 140 ESA Regs
HB Reg 66 HB Regs
CTB Reg 53 CTB Regs
87 **IS** Sch 9 para 11 and Sch 10 para 63 IS Regs
JSA Sch 7 para 12 and Sch 8 para 52 JSA Regs
ESA Sch 8 para 13 and Sch 9 para 52 ESA Regs
HB Sch 5 para 11 and Sch 6 para 51 HB Regs
CTB Sch 4 para 12 and Sch 5 para 53 CTB Regs
88 **IS** Reg 62(2A) IS Regs
JSA Reg 131(3) JSA Regs
ESA Reg 132(3) ESA Regs
HB Reg 59(3) HB Regs
CTB Reg 46(3) CTB Regs
89 CIS/91/1994
90 R(IS) 7/95
91 **IS** Reg 61(1) IS Regs
JSA Reg 130 JSA Regs
ESA Reg 131(1) ESA Regs
HB Reg 53(1) HB Regs
CTB Reg 43(1) CTB Regs
All definition of 'student loan'
92 **IS** Reg 66A(3) and (4) IS Regs
JSA Reg 136(3) and (4) JSA Regs
ESA Reg 137(4) and (5) ESA Regs
HB Reg 64(3) and (4) HB Regs
CTB Reg 51(3) and (4) CTB Regs
93 Reg 137(4A) ESA Regs
94 **IS** Reg 66A(4) IS Regs
ESA Reg 137(5) ESA Regs
JSA Reg 136(4) JSA Regs
95 **IS** Reg 62(3B) IS Regs
ESA Reg 132(6) ESA Regs
HB Reg 59(7) HB Regs
96 **IS** Reg 66C IS Regs
JSA Reg 136B JSA Regs
ESA Reg 139 ESA Regs
HB Reg 64A HB Regs
CTB Reg 51A CTB Regs
97 **IS** Reg 67A IS Regs
JSA Reg 137A JSA Regs
ESA Reg 141 ESA Regs
HB Reg 67 HB Regs
CTB Reg 54 CTB Regs
98 **IS** Reg 67 IS Regs
JSA Reg 137 JSA Regs
ESA Reg 140 ESA Regs
HB Reg 66 HB Regs
CTB Reg 53 CTB Regs
99 **IS** Reg 66A(2) and (5) IS Regs
JSA Reg 136(2) and (5) JSA Regs
ESA Reg 137(3) and (6) ESA Regs
HB Reg 64(2) and (5) HB Regs
CTB Reg 51(2) and (5) CTB Regs
100 R(IS) 7/95
101 **IS** Reg 61(1) IS Regs
JSA Reg 130 JSA Regs
ESA Reg 131(1) ESA Regs
HB Reg 53(1) HB Regs
CTB Reg 43(1) CTB Regs
All definition of 'academic year'
102 **IS** Reg 66A(2)(a) IS Regs
JSA Reg 136(2)(a) JSA Regs
ESA Reg 137(3)(a) ESA Regs
HB Reg 64(2)(a) HB Regs
CTB Reg 51(2)(a) CTB Regs
103 **IS** Reg 66A(2)(aa) IS Regs
JSA Reg 136(2)(aa) JSA Regs
ESA Reg 137(3)(b) ESA Regs
HB Reg 64(2)(b) HB Regs
CTB Reg 51(2)(b) CTB Regs
104 **IS** Reg 66A(2)(aa) IS Regs
JSA Reg 136(2)(aa) JSA Regs
ESA Regs 104(6) and 137(3)(c) ESA Regs
HB Reg 64(2)(b) HB Regs
CTB Reg 51(2)(b) CTB Regs
All The Education (Student Support)(No.2) Regulations 2008, No.1582
105 CIS/3734/2004
106 **IS** Reg 41(6) IS Regs
JSA Reg 104(5) JSA Regs
ESA Reg 105(4) ESA Regs
HB Reg 41(4) HB Regs
CTB Reg 31(4) CTB Regs

107 **IS** Sch 9 para 13 IS Regs
JSA Sch 7 para 14 JSA Regs
ESA Sch 8 para 15 ESA Regs
HB Sch 5 para 13 HB Regs
CTB Sch 4 para 14 CTB Regs
108 R(IS) 16/95
109 **IS** Reg 61(1) IS Regs
JSA Reg 130 JSA Regs
ESA Reg 131(1) ESA Regs
HB Reg 53(1) HB Regs
CTB Reg 43(1) CTB Regs
All definition of 'access funds'
110 **IS** Reg 68(3) and (4) IS Regs
JSA Reg 138(3) and (4) JSA Regs
ESA Regs 2(1) and 142(3) ESA Regs
HB Regs 2(1) and 68(3) and (4) HB Regs
CTB Regs 2(1) and 55(3) CTB Regs
111 **IS** Reg 66B IS Regs
JSA Reg 136A JSA Regs
ESA Regs 2(1) and 138 ESA Regs
HB Regs 2(1) and 65 HB Regs
CTB Regs 2(1) and 52 CTB Regs
112 **IS** Reg 66B(4) IS Regs
JSA Reg 136A(4) JSA Regs
ESA Reg 138(4) ESA Regs
HB Reg 65(5) HB Regs
CTB Reg 52(4) CTB Regs
113 **IS** Reg 66(1) IS Regs
JSA Reg 135(1) JSA Regs
ESA Reg 136(1) ESA Regs
HB Reg 63 HB Regs
CTB Reg 50 CTB Regs
114 **IS** Sch 9 paras 13 and 61 IS Regs
JSA Sch 7 paras 14 and 59 JSA Regs
ESA Sch 8 paras 15 and 54 ESA Regs

6. **Giving up, changing or taking time out from your course**

115 CIS/368/1992; R(IS) 6/97
116 R(JSA) 2/02; CJSA/1965/2008
117 R(IS) 7/99
118 R(IS) 1/96
119 paras 30230-33 DMG; paras C2.41-42 GM
120 CIS/152/1994; R(IS) 15/98
121 **JSA** Reg 1(3D) and (3E) JSA Regs
HB Reg 56(6) and (7) HB Regs
CTB Reg 46(6) and (7) CTB Regs
122 R(JSA) 3/02
123 *CM v SSWP* [2009] UKUT 43 (AAC); R(IS) 7/09
124 **IS** Regs 29(2B) and 32(6A) IS Regs
JSA Regs 94(2B) and 97(7) JSA Regs
ESA Regs 91(4) and 94(7) ESA Regs
125 para C2.425 GM
126 *Leeves v Chief Adjudication Officer*, reported as R(IS)5/99; reg 31(1) HB Regs
127 **IS** Reg 40(3A), (3AAA), (3AA) and (3AB) IS Regs
JSA Reg 103(5), (5ZA), (5AZA) and (5ZB) JSA Regs
ESA Reg 104(4)-(6) ESA Regs
HB Reg 40(7)-(9) HB Regs
CTB Reg 30(8)-(10) CTB Regs
128 Reg 6(6)(a) SS&CS(DA) Regs; CJSA/549/03
129 para 30470 DMG; para C2.421 GM

Chapter 30

Benefits in hospital, prison and other special circumstances

This chapter covers:

People coming from or going abroad are covered in Chapters 61, 62 and 63. People who are studying are covered in Chapter 29.

There are some special rules if you are a **foster carer**. See the chapters in this *Handbook* about the benefits you want to claim. To find out whether:

- you are treated as in full-time work, see pp725 and 1301;
- you can claim income support (IS), see Chapter 17. You may fit into one of the groups of people who can claim IS if you are a foster carer and are not a member of a couple;
- fostering allowances are taken into account as income or can be disregarded, see pp894, 922 and 955;
- you can be credited with Class 3 national insurance contributions for the purpose of satisfying the qualifying conditions for Category A and B retirement pensions, widowed parent's allowance and bereavement allowance, see p781.

Key facts

- Being 16 or 17 does not, in itself, prevent you from qualifying for most of the benefits in this *Handbook*. However, you might not be able to qualify for income support (IS), income-based jobseeker's allowance (JSA) or housing benefit if you were formerly looked after by a local authority.
- Many benefits are affected if you (or your partner or children) are away from your normal home for a period because you are in hospital (or a similar

institution), a care home (or similar accommodation) or in prison. They are also affected if you (or your partner) are involved in a trade dispute. In some cases, benefit is no longer paid; in others, it is paid at a reduced rate.

- IS, income-based JSA and income-related employment and support allowance (ESA) are paid at a reduced rate if you do not have accommodation.

Future changes: April 2013 and after

Major changes are taking place that affect the benefits and tax credits system (see Chapter 2).

- From April 2012, ESA in youth will be abolished for new claimants. If you are already entitled when this happens, your entitlement will end once you have been receiving ESA in youth for one year. **Note:** you may then qualify for income-related ESA.
- From April 2013, a new benefit, personal independence payment (PIP), will replace disability living allowance (DLA) for adults. It is likely that PIP will be affected in the same way as DLA if you are in a care home or similar accommodation.

It is not yet known how the changes will affect hospital patients, those without accommodation, prisoners, and people involved in a trade dispute. See CPAG's *Welfare Rights Bulletin* for updates.

1. 16/17-year-olds

If you are 16 or 17, you can qualify for any of the benefits for people of working age or the tax credits in this *Handbook*, other than bereavement allowance, council tax benefit (CTB) and statutory adoption pay. You are not liable for council tax, so you do not need to claim CTB. However, you might not be able to qualify for income support (IS), income-based jobseeker's allowance (JSA) and housing benefit (HB) if you were formerly looked after by a local authority.

What you need to consider

If you are 16 or 17 and want to claim benefit, you should consider the following.

- You can only qualify for **JSA** in specified circumstances. If you cannot qualify under the ordinary rules, you may qualify on a discretionary basis if you would otherwise experience severe hardship ('severe hardship payments') – see pp405–11. There are also special rules about JSA sanctions (see Chapter 20).
- You may qualify for **contributory employment and support allowance** (ESA) if you first had limited capability for work before you were 20 (or in some cases 25), even if you do not have sufficient national insurance contributions or credits. For information about ESA, see Chapter 10.
- The **rate of some benefits** (IS, JSA ESA, HB and industrial injuries disablement benefit) you get can be lower than for older claimants. See Chapter 37 and the chapter about the benefit you are claiming for more information.

- You may qualify for **health benefits** (eg, free prescriptions, dental treatment and sight tests) in your own right. Otherwise, you may qualify for these if a member of your family is getting a qualifying benefit or tax credit, or her/his income is low. See Chapter 13 for further information.
- If you are pregnant, you can qualify for **Healthy Start food and vitamins**, even if you are not entitled to a qualifying benefit or tax credit (see Chapter 13). Check to see if you and your baby can continue to qualify once the baby is born. **Note:** you and your baby may continue to qualify if a member of your family is entitled to a qualifying benefit or tax credit, even if you are not.

If you are studying or on training, see below. To find out about paying for housing, see below.

Studying and training

If you are studying full time, your entitlement to carer's allowance (CA), IS, ESA, HB and JSA might be affected. See Chapter 29 for the special rules if you are studying full or part time.

To find out what help is available to finance your studies, contact your local authority or college. Also see CPAG's *Student Support and Benefits Handbook* (for England and Wales) and *Benefits for Students in Scotland Handbook*. **Note:** even if you can qualify for benefit while studying full time, student support (eg, grants and loans) can be taken into account as income when working out the amount of your means-tested benefits (see Chapter 29). However, education maintenance allowance (if you are still getting this) and payments from the 16–19 Bursary Fund are paid in addition to your benefits.

If you are receiving IS, income-based JSA, income-related ESA or child tax credit (CTC), you may qualify for free school lunches. See p14 for further information.

If you are getting training, in most cases, you can get income-based JSA without having to satisfy the jobseeking conditions (see p434). You may fit into one of the groups of people who can claim IS if you are on a specified training course (see p349). However, if you qualify for a means-tested benefit while you are getting training, some payments you receive (eg, a training allowance) can be taken into account when working out the amount you get (see p928). In addition, if you receive a training allowance:

- you might be treated as not having limited capability for work – see p200. If this happens, you cannot qualify for ESA;
- in some cases, if you are also getting a non-means-tested benefit (eg, contributory ESA or CA), this is reduced by the amount of the training allowance. See p1042 for information about the overlapping benefit rules.

Paying for housing

If you qualify for HB and are living in private rented accommodation, the amount you get might be restricted, based on the rent for one-bedroom shared accommodation, even if you are living in larger accommodation (see pp311 and 323). If you are living with someone else who is claiming HB or CTB, or help with her/his housing costs paid with IS, income-based JSA, income-related ESA or pension credit (PC), no non-dependant deduction can be made for you (see pp124, 267 and 871).

Someone else claims benefit for you

If you cannot qualify for benefits and tax credits in your own right, someone else may be able to include you in her/his claim.

- S/he can qualify for **child benefit** and **CTC** for you if you count as a 'qualifying young person' (eg, you are in or are enrolled to undertake full-time non-advanced education or approved training) and s/he is treated as 'responsible' for you (see pp94 and 1269). S/he may also qualify for working tax credit.
- Her/his **HB** and **CTB** can include an allowance and premiums for you if you count as a qualifying young person and s/he is responsible for you and you live in the same household (see p761). In some cases, allowances and premiums for you can continue to be included in IS and income-based JSA (see p760).
- S/he may be able to continue to receive an **increase in non-means-tested benefit** for you (see p745).
- If you are pregnant, s/he can claim a **Sure Start maternity grant** for you if s/he has been awarded a qualifying benefit (see p573), even if s/he still has dependent children of her/his own.
- You may qualify for **free school lunches** if the person claiming for you receives a qualifying benefit or tax credit (see p14).

16/17-year-olds formerly looked after by a local authority

Special rules affect your entitlement to IS, income-based JSA and HB if you are aged 16 or 17 and were formerly looked after by a local authority. You cannot get IS, income-based JSA or HB if you are 16 or 17 and:[1]

- you were looked after (see p674) by a local authority (and in Scotland, were provided with accommodation) for at least 13 weeks. The 13-week period must start after your 14th birthday and end after you turn 16 (in England or Wales) or school-leaving age (in Scotland). The local authority must be obliged to provide you with after-care services;[2] *or*
- in England or Wales, you are not subject to a care order, but you were in hospital, or detained in a remand centre or a young offenders' or similar institution when you became 16 and, immediately before you were in hospital or detained, you were looked after by a local authority for at least 13 weeks since your 14th birthday.[3]

The 13 weeks do not have to be continuous. Some pre-planned short-term placements, after which you return to the care of your parent, or person acting as your parent, do not count towards the 13 weeks.[4]

There are exceptions to the rules (see below).

Being 'looked after'

Being 'looked after' means, for example, you were subject to a care, supervision or permanence order or, in England and Wales, provided with accommodation by the local authority under specified functions.

If these rules apply to you:

- your local authority must assess and meet your needs for maintenance, accommodation and support; *and*
- you cannot be treated as a member of the family of a person claiming IS, income-based JSA, income-related ESA, HB or CTB, so for example s/he cannot get allowances and premiums for you with her/his HB and CTB.[5]

Local DWP and social services offices should liaise to ensure any disputes about who is responsible for supporting you are quickly resolved. If you are refused both benefit and social services support, seek specialist advice.

Note: if you were formerly looked after by a local authority, you *can* qualify for ESA.[6]

Exceptions

You *can* get IS or income-based JSA (but not HB) if you are in one of the following groups of people who can claim IS (see p346) – ie, you are:[7]

- a lone parent of a child under seven. **Note:** the government intends to reduce the age to five;
- a lone foster parent;
- getting statutory sick pay, incapable of work but treated as capable or appealing against an incapacity for work decision;
- a lone parent in 'relevant education'.

In England and Wales, you are not excluded from IS, income-based JSA or HB if you have been in a family placement for at least six months and you have left local authority care (unless the placement has broken down).[8] In Scotland, you are not excluded if you are living with your family or another person who has parental responsibility for you (unless you are receiving regular financial assistance from the local authority under s29(1) of the Children (Scotland) Act 1995).[9]

Note: in the past, you could also claim IS on the grounds of being blind, incapable of work, a disabled or deaf student or a disabled worker. You may be able to continue to do so in limited circumstances. See pp351, 352 and 351 for further information.

2. **Hospital patients**

Many benefits are affected after you, your partner or child have been in hospital as a patient for a period. In some cases, benefit is no longer paid. In other cases, it is paid at a reduced rate. Until the period has passed, your benefits are paid as normal. You can arrange for someone else to collect your benefit while you are in hospital and if you are unable to manage your affairs, someone else can act as your appointee.

Always inform the DWP (and local authority) promptly if your benefits may be affected by the rules described below to avoid being overpaid or underpaid.

Who counts as a patient

You count as a '**patient**' for benefit purposes if you are being maintained free of charge while undergoing medical or other treatment as an inpatient in a hospital or 'similar institution' and:[10]

- the treatment is funded by the NHS; *or*
- the hospital (or similar institution) is maintained and administered by the Defence Council.

You should *not* count as a patient if you are getting treatment as a private patient, or if you are meeting the cost of your treatment in a private hospital, or if your placement is funded by a local authority.[11]

Hospitals and similar institutions[12]

'Hospitals' include all NHS hospitals, armed forces hospitals and special hospitals such as Broadmoor and Rampton. Prison hospital wings, however, do not count as hospitals.
A 'similar institution' is not defined in the rules, but could include some care homes, hospices and rehabilitation units that provide medical or nursing care.[13]

Medical or other treatment[14]

'Medical or other treatment' is treatment is by a doctor, dentist or professionally qualifed or trained nurse, or by someone under the supervision of such a person.

If you are in a care home, you do not count as a patient merely because the NHS is contributing to the cost of your nursing care. However, if your nursing needs are more than merely incidental and ancillary to any other care needs you may have, the NHS may decide to meet the care home costs in full. In this case, you may count as a patient. The primary care trust should make an assessment to see if you come under this rule. If it decides that you do, you are only treated as a patient from the day of the decision.[15] If the primary care trust has never considered the matter, the DWP might decide itself that you should be treated as a patient. However, if you are *not* getting medical or other treatment at the care home, but get this elsewhere (eg, at an out-patient clinic), you do not count as a patient.[16]

When you count as a patient

You count as a patient from the day after the day you enter hospital (or a similar institution). You do not count as a patient:

- for attendance allowance (AA) and disability living allowance (DLA) only, on the day you leave;[17] *or*
- for all other benefits, on the day after the day you leave.[18]

Example

Hilda is claiming DLA and income support (IS). She is taken ill and admitted to hospital on 1 January. After successful treatment, she is discharged on 21 January.

For DLA purposes, she counts as a patient from 2 January up to and including 20 January = 19 days.

For IS purposes, she counts as a patient from 2 January up to and including 21 January = 20 days.

Social fund payments

Some social fund payments are affected if you are a patient.

- You cannot get a **crisis loan** if you are a hospital inpatient, unless your discharge is planned to take place in the next two weeks.[19] You do not have to be receiving free treatment or treatment provided by the NHS.
- You cannot get a **winter fuel payment** if you have been a patient for more than 52 weeks.[20] The definition of 'patient' is the same as for other benefits (see above).

Jobseeker's allowance

To qualify for jobseeker's allowance (JSA), you must be available for work and actively seeking work (see Chapter 20). You cannot qualify for JSA if you have limited capability for work. So if you are in hospital for a period, you may have to claim employment and support allowance (ESA) or pension credit (PC) instead of JSA or, if you are a member of a couple, your partner may have to claim IS, JSA, ESA or PC instead of you. However if you are unable to work because you are sick, you can be treated as not having limited capability for work and as available for and actively seeking work:

- for two weeks;

- indefinitely, if you are absent from Great Briain for NHS hospital treatment.

See p399 for further information.

Your income-based JSA can be affected if you or your partner or child are a patient for a period. See p679 for how means-tested benefits are affected after 28 (or 84 days) and pp680–82 for how means-tested benefits are affected after 52 days. **Note:** if *you* are the patient, the rules are only relevant in the limited cirumstances in which you can qualify for JSA while you are in hospital – eg when you are abroad for NHS hospital treatment.

Benefits affected after 28 or 84 days

Payment of AA and DLA can be affected after you have been a patient for 28 (or 84 days). Entitlement to child benefit can be affected after your child has been a patient for 84 days. For information on how carer's allowance and means-tested benefits might then be affected, see pp678 and 679.

Attendance allowance and disability living allowance

AA and DLA are paid as normal until you have been a patient for 28 days. After 28 days, you cannot be paid AA (including constant attendance allowance – see p380) or DLA.[21] However, if you are being paid DLA for a child under 16, this continues until s/he has been a patient for 84 days.[22]

Entitlement to AA or DLA continues even though payment ends. Therefore, payment can begin again following discharge from hospital. If you expect to be re-admitted within 28 days, you can be paid at a daily rate from the day of your discharge.[23]

There is a 28-day 'linking rule'. This means that:[24]

- different periods spent as a patient separated by 28 days or less are linked together and treated as one period; *and*
- periods spent as a resident in a care home link with periods spent as a patient if they are 28 days or less apart.

Example

Horace is claiming AA. He goes into hospital for an operation on 16 July and is discharged on 30 July. He counts as a patient from 17 July up to and including 29 July = 13 days. His AA is not affected by his stay in hospital.

Horace has to go back into hospital for further treatment on 10 August. He counts as a patient again, from 11 August. As there are 28 days or less between his discharge and re-admission, the two spells in hospital are linked. When he has been a patient for a further 15 days, he cannot be paid AA.

Note:

- If you are awarded AA or DLA while you are a patient, payment cannot begin until you are discharged.[25]
- You can continue to be paid the mobility component of DLA while you are a patient if:[26]
  - you had a Motability agreement (see p170) when you became a patient, but only until the agreement ends (unless you immediately renew an agreement under the Wheelchair Scheme). You are paid the amount payable under the agreement; *or*
  - you have been a patient since 31 July 1995 (other than under 'section' under the Mental Health Acts). You are paid at the lower rate (even if you would otherwise qualify for the higher rate). This transitional protection ends if you cease to be a patient for more than 28 consecutive days.
- If you are terminally ill, you can be paid AA or DLA while you are in a hospice which is not an NHS or Defence Council hospital or similar institution, so long as the DWP has been informed that you are terminally ill.[27] In most cases, the DWP must be informed in writing.

Child benefit

Your entitlement to child benefit can be affected if your child is absent from home for a period. However, certain absences from home can be ignored, including periods of up to 84 days when your child is receiving inpatient treatment in a hospital or similar institution. There are rules that can help you retain your entitlement to child benefit when your child has been absent from home in hospital for 84 days or more. See p100 for further information. If your child benefit entitlement *does* end, you can reclaim when s/he is discharged and returns home.

Carer's allowance

To qualify for carer's allowance (CA) the person you care for must be receiving AA or the highest or middle rate of DLA care component. So your entitlement to CA ends when the person you care for no longer receives AA or DLA – ie, after s/he has been a patient for 28 (or 84) days. If the person you care for is discharged and receives AA or the DLA care component, you can reclaim CA if you again satisfy the rules for entitlement. Your claim can be backdated to the date from when the AA or DLA is payable (see the 'qualifying benefit' rules on p1029).

Remember that once you have been caring for a disabled person for a period, a temporary break in caring does not affect your CA (see p85). This includes if you (or the person you care for) are a patient. You can remain entitled to CA for up to 12 weeks in any period of 26 weeks. This can be useful if you (or the person you care for) are in and out of hospital. However, if the person you care for has been a patient for a total of 28 (or 84) days, s/he can no longer be paid AA or DLA (see p677). Your entitlement to CA then ends, even if you have not yet had a break of 12 weeks.

Means-tested benefits

If payment of your (or your partner's) AA or DLA, or your (or your partner's) entitlement to CA, stops, the rate of IS, income-based JSA, income-related ESA or PC to which you are entitled may be lower because you are no longer entitled to certain premiums (additional amounts for PC). Housing benefit (HB) and council tax benefit (CTB) are likewise affected, but only if you are not (or are no longer) entitled to IS, income-based JSA, income-related ESA or the guarantee credit of PC. If your child's DLA has stopped, see below.

- When payment of AA or DLA stops:[28]
  - if you are a single claimant, you are no longer entitled to the severe disability premium (severe disability additional amount for PC) (see p830);
  - if you are a member of a couple and you are getting the severe disability premium (additional amount), you (or your partner) are treated as getting AA or DLA if the only reason you (or s/he) do not get it is that you (or s/he) are a patient. Your carer is treated as getting CA if s/he would be entitled to and receiving it, but for the fact that you have been a patient for longer than 28 days.[29] In this situation you can therefore continue to qualify for the premium/additional amount. In all cases, it is paid at the single person's rate.
- Entitlement to the disability premium (for IS, JSA, HB and CTB), the enhanced disability premium (for IS, JSA, ESA, HB and CTB) and the higher pensioner premium (for IS and JSA) are not affected by the payment of AA or DLA stopping.[30] However, these premiums can be affected once you (or your partner) have been a patient for 52 weeks (see p680).
- If you or your partner are claiming CA, the carer premium (carer additional amount for PC) can continue to be paid for up to eight weeks after CA entitlement stops (see p834). After that, you are no longer entitled to a carer premium. If you lose your CA because *you* are a patient, the person you were caring for may become entitled to the severe disability premium (additional amount) (see p830).

Children

If amounts of benefit are included in your HB or CTB for a child getting DLA (or in your IS or income-based JSA if still included), entitlement to the disabled child and enhanced disability premium is not affected by payment of her/his DLA stopping, so long as s/he continues to count as a member of your family for benefit purposes (see p751).[31] However, for IS and income-based JSA, these premiums (if still included) *are* affected once your child has been a patient for 52 weeks (see p680). If you are claiming CA, the carer premium (carer additional amount for PC) can continue to be paid for up to eight weeks after CA stops (see p834).

If your child ceases to be regarded as a member of your family or child benefit stops because your child is no longer treated as living with you, this may affect whether you can get personal allowances and premiums for your child in your HB or CTB (or IS or income-based JSA if still included). See Chapter 34 for further information.

Benefits affected after 52 weeks

Some benefits are affected after you or your partner or child (or an adult dependant or a non-dependant) have been a patient for more than 52 weeks. See below for means-tested benefits. See p682 for non-means-tested benefits.

Means-tested benefits

You still count as a couple while you and your partner are only temporarily apart. However, for IS, JSA, ESA, PC and HB only, you no longer count as a couple if you are likely to be separated for more than 52 weeks or, in exceptional circumstances, such as a stay in hospital, substantially more than 52 weeks.[32] If you no longer count as a couple, your means-tested benefits are assessed as if you are a single claimant (or lone parent).

The rate of IS, income-based JSA or income-related ESA may be lower if you (or your partner or child) have been a patient for a continuous period of more than 52 weeks, because you are no longer entitled to certain premiums. You may have already lost premiums after 28 (or 84) days – ie, the severe disability and carer premiums (see p679). HB and CTB are likewise affected, but only if you are not (or are no longer) entitled to IS, income-based JSA or income-related ESA. HB, CTB and help with your housing costs with IS, income-based JSA, income-related ESA and PC may no longer be payable once you have been away from home for more than 52 weeks (see p682).

There are no 'linking rules' with these provisions. This means that if you are discharged from hospital and then are re-admitted, a new period as a patient starts and you can again be entitled to IS, income-based JSA, income-related ESA, HB or CTB premiums at the rate you were getting before admission to hospital.

Note:

- If you have a non-dependant living with you and s/he has been a patient for 52 weeks, non-dependant deductions made for her/him (from your IS, income-based JSA, income-related ESA or PC housing costs, HB or CTB) stop. See p682 for further information.
- For HB and CTB, if you are a member of a couple, a deduction for childcare charges can be made from earnings if one of you is in full-time paid work and the other is in hospital (see pp915 and 947).

Premiums and components: single claimants and lone parents

If you are a single claimant or a lone parent and you have been a patient for more than 52 weeks:[33]

- the disability and enhanced disability premiums are not included in your IS, income-based JSA or income-related ESA applicable amount. The work-related activity component and the support component are not included in your income-related ESA applicable amount. **Note:** if you qualify, the pensioner premium *is* included in your income-based JSA applicable amount;
- HB and CTB may be paid at a reduced rate. The enhanced disability premium is not included in your applicable amount.[34] However, the disability premium can still be included.

Premiums and components: couples

If you are a member of a couple and:

- both you and your partner have been a patient for more than 52 weeks, the higher pensioner, the disability and the enhanced disability premiums are not included in your IS, income-based JSA or income-related ESA applicable amount. The work-related component and the support component are not included in your income-related ESA applicable amount. **Note:** if your partner qualifies, the pensioner premium *is* included in your IS or income-based JSA applicable amount;[35]
- only one of you has been a patient for more than 52 weeks:
  - for IS and income-based JSA, you are paid the normal rate, but without any of the premiums that are only included in your applicable amount for the one who is the patient, other than the pensioner premium;[36]
  - for income-related ESA, you are paid the normal rate if you are the patient. However, if your partner is the patient, you are paid the normal rate less any premiums and any work-related activity or support component.[37] In the latter case, you are better off if you can be assessed as a single claimant or lone parent (see above);
- both you and your partner have been a patient for more than 52 weeks, HB and CTB may be paid at a reduced rate. The enhanced disability premium is not included in your applicable amount.[38] However, the disability premium can still be included.

Premiums: children

If you have a child and you (or s/he) are a patient, s/he may no longer count as a member of your family once you (or s/he) have been away from home for a period (see p762). If this happens, you can no longer get allowances and premiums for your child with HB and CTB (and IS or income-based JSA, if still included). However, if s/he still counts as a member of your family:

- you are paid the normal rate of HB and CTB; your entitlement to the disabled child and enhanced disability premium is not affected if you or your child has been a patient for more than 52 weeks;[39]
- if your child is the patient and your IS or income-based JSA still includes amounts and premiums for your children (see p760), you are paid the normal rate less any disabled child premium and enhanced disability premium included in your applicable amount for your child.[40]

Paying for your normal home while you are a patient

If you are getting HB, CTB, or help with your housing costs with your IS, income-based JSA, income-related ESA or PC, these might no longer be payable once you have been absent from home for more than 52 weeks – eg, because you are in hospital, either as an NHS or a private patient (see pp254, 119 and 850). Another person (eg, your partner) might be able to get these instead if s/he is (or can be treated as) liable (see pp248 and 848).

Note:

- There are no 'linking rules' with these provisions. This means that if you are discharged from hospital and then are re-admitted, a new period as a patient starts and you can again be entitled to HB or CTB and to help with housing costs (paid with IS, income-based JSA, income-related ESA or PC).
- You can be treated as occupying, but temporarily absent from, a new dwelling, even if you have not yet stayed there, if you move your furniture and belongings in but cannot move in yourself because you have to go into hospital.[41]

Non-dependants

If you have a non-dependant living with you, non-dependant deductions made for her/him (from your IS, income-based JSA, income-related ESA or PC housing costs, HB or CTB) stop once s/he has been a patient for 52 weeks.[42] Your non-dependant counts as a 'patient':

- for IS, JSA, ESA, HB and CTB, if s/he is getting medical or other treatment as an inpatient in a hospital or similar institution;
- for PC, if s/he is an inpatient residing in a hospital or similar institution.

The treatment does not have to be free or provided by the NHS. Separate periods spent as a patient which are not more than 28 days apart are added together when calculating the 52 weeks. See Chapters 8, 14 and 38 for further information about non-dependant deductions.

Non-means-tested benefits

Contributory ESA may be paid at a reduced rate if you have been a patient for a continuous period of more than 52 weeks. You are paid the normal rate, less any work-related activity or support component.[43] **Note:** the government intends to limit entitlement to contributory ESA to one year for those in the work-related activity group from 1 May 2012. In practical terms, unless you are in the support group, once you have been receiving it for a year, you will not be paid any contributory ESA.

Increases for dependants

If you are entitled to an increase in a non-means-tested benefit for an adult or child dependant (see Chapter 33), this is no longer payable once you (or both you and your dependant) have been a patient for 52 weeks or more, unless you apply to the DWP to pay the increase on your behalf to:[44]

- the dependant for whom the increase is paid; *or*
- someone else approved by the DWP. The DWP must be satisfied that the payment will be used for the benefit of:
  - the dependant for whom the increase is paid, if you are a patient; *or*
  - at least one of your children, if both you and your dependant are patients.

There are no 'linking rules' with this provision. This means that if you (or your dependant) are discharged from hospital and are then re-admitted, a new period as a patient starts and you can be paid the increase again. Remember that if an increase for a child stops being paid for more than 58 days, you might lose your entitlement to it (see p745).

3. People in care homes and similar accommodation

Most benefits are paid as normal if you (or a member of your family) live in a care home or similar type of accommodation. However, some benefits are no longer payable and some might be paid at a reduced rate. **Note:** if your place in a care home is funded by the NHS, you may count as a 'patient'. In this case, your benefits are affected by the rules for patients instead.

Always inform the DWP (and local authority) promptly if your benefits may be affected by the rules described below, to avoid being overpaid or underpaid.

Care homes and similar accommodation

There is not sufficient space in this *Handbook* to cover the different kinds of care homes and similar accommodation, and the funding arrangements for people living in them. Some homes are run by local authorities and some are independent. You may be able to get help from the local authority with your care home fees, or you may have to pay these yourself. What help you can get to pay for your place depends on whether it is funded by the NHS or by the local authority. Local authority help is means tested, so you may have to contribute part of the cost.

Attendance allowance and disability living allowance care component

You cannot be paid attendance allowance (AA) and disability living allowance (DLA) care component once you have been a resident in a care home for a period of 28 days if the 'costs of any qualifying services' provided for you are borne out of public funds under specified provisions (see below).[45] Until then, AA and DLA care component are paid as normal. You count as in a care home if it is an establishment that provides you with accommodation as well as nursing or personal care.[46] **Note:**

- DLA *mobility* component is paid as normal however long you are a resident in a care home.
- If you are awarded AA or the care component of DLA while you are resident in a care home in the circumstances described above, you cannot be paid for the time you stay in the accommodation.[47]

Entitlement to AA or DLA continues even though payment ends. Therefore, payment can begin again when you are no longer resident in a care home. If you expect to return within 28 days, you can be paid at a daily rate from when you leave.[48]

Specified provisions

The specified provisions are:[49]

- Part III of the National Assistance Act 1948, Part IV of the Social Work (Scotland) Act 1968, the Mental Health (Care and Treatment) (Scotland) Act 2003, the Community Care and Health (Scotland) Act 2002 and the Mental Health Act 1983; *or*
- any other Acts relating to people with disabilities or (in the case of DLA only) young people, or education or training – eg, in some special residential schools.

In most cases, a local authority pays for the services in a care home under one of these provisions, but it is always worth checking. Local authorities also have powers to provide accommodation under housing legislation and the Local Government Act 1972, in which case AA and DLA are not affected.[50] **Note:** the First-tier Tribunal is entitled to decide that your placement is being funded under a different legal power than the one the local authority has stated.[51]

'Qualifying services' means the costs of accommodation, board and personal care. The 'costs of any qualifying services' does *not* include the cost of:[52]

- domiciliary services (including personal care) provided to people in a private dwelling;

- improvements to, or furniture or equipment provided for:
  - a private dwelling because of the needs of a disabled person;
  - a care home, for which a grant or payment was made out of public funds, except where the grant or payment is of a regular or repeated nature;
- social and recreational activities outside the care home;
- buying or running a motor vehicle used in connection with any qualifying service provided in the care home; *and*
- NHS services.

Bear in mind that:
- if the NHS provides nursing services in a care home and your nursing needs are more than merely incidental and ancillary to other care needs, you are treated as a 'patient' for DLA and AA purposes[53] (see p675);
- if the local authority pays for the services, it assesses what you must pay towards the costs, using a means test that takes account of your income and capital. You may lose AA or DLA even though you are meeting some of the costs yourself. There are exceptions to the rules (see below). If you are self-funding, see below;
- if you think the DWP has refused payment of AA or DLA wrongly, you can seek a revision or appeal against the refusal.

Exceptions to the rules

There are exceptions to the rules. You can continue to be paid AA and the care component of DLA, even *after* 28 days, if:
- you are terminally ill and are in a hospice, that is not an NHS or Defence Council hospital or similar institution, so long as the DWP has been informed that you are terminally ill. In most cases, the DWP must be informed in writing;[54] *or*
- for DLA only, you are a student and the cost of your accommodation is wholly or partly met from a student grant or loan, or from a grant made to education institutions under specific legislation;[55] *or*
- you are under 16 and being looked after by a local authority or under 18 and receiving services because of your disability or health, but only if you have been placed by the local authority in a private dwelling with a family, a relative or some other suitable person;[56] *or*
- your accommodation is outside the UK and the costs of any qualifying services are being borne by a local authority under specified legislation relating to education – eg, at the Peto Institute in Hungary or the Higashi School.[57]

If you are self-funding

You can continue to be paid AA and the care component of DLA, even *after* 28 days, if you are meeting the whole costs of all the 'qualifying services' from your own resources, or with the help of another person or a charity – known as 'self-funding'.[58] This applies whether you are in an independent or local authority home. You count as self-funding *even if*:

- you are claiming benefits such as income support (IS), employment and support allowance (ESA), pension credit (PC), AA or DLA;
- a local authority has arranged and contracted to pay for your placement, so long as you are paying the whole costs of all the 'qualifying services'.

This also applies if a local authority is temporarily funding your placement while you sell a property – eg, your former home. You must be liable and able to repay the local authority in full when the property is sold (known as 'retrospective self-funding').[59] This includes where you have entered into what is known as a 'deferred payment agreement' with the local authority. The local authority disregards the value of your home for the first 12 weeks that you are permanently in a care home, so you are not liable to repay local authority funding provided, and are not retrospectively self-funding, during this period.

If you move into a care home and are initially receiving help with the fees from the local authority, the DWP may terminate payment of your AA or DLA. However, if you are likely to become self-funding in the future (eg, if you are only getting local authority help while you sell your former home, or your capital is likely to increase above the limit of the local authority's means test), the DWP should simply *suspend* payment of your AA or DLA. Then when you repay the local authority and become self-funding, payment can resume and any arrears can be paid to you. However, if the DWP terminated payment of your AA or DLA and refuses to pay you arrears when you become self-funding, you can argue that the decision to terminate payment should be revised on the grounds of 'official error'.[60]

When you count as being a resident in a care home

The general rule is that you do not count as a resident in a care home on the day you enter and the day you leave.[61] Note that if you are a patient in a hospital or similar institution and enter a care home, you count as a resident in the care home from the day you enter. If you leave a care home and enter a hospital or similar institution as a patient, you cease to count as a resident in the care home on the day after you leave.[62]

There is a 28-day 'linking rule'. This means that different periods as a resident in a care home separated by 28 days or less link together for the purpose of calculating the 28 days for which you can continue to be paid AA or the care component of DLA. Periods spent as a patient in a hospital or similar institution also count towards the 28-day limit on payment if they are separated by 28 days or less from periods when you are resident in a care home in the circumstances described above.[63]

It can be important to plan periods of respite care in the light of the linking rules so that you can continue to be paid AA and the DLA care component for as long as possible. This also enables your carer to keep her/his carer's allowance (CA).

How other benefits are affected

If your payments of AA or DLA care component stop, CA is affected in the same way as for hospital patients (see p678). Remember that the carer premium (carer's additional amount for PC) can continue to be paid for up to eight weeks after CA stops (see p834).

Once payment of AA or DLA care component stops because you have been resident in a care home for 28 days, if you are claiming any of the means-tested benefits, you are no longer entitled to the severe disability premium (severe disability additional amount for PC). In addition, you may no longer be entitled to the disability premium, the enhanced disability premium or the higher pensioner premium if the only reason you qualified was because you were receiving AA or DLA care component.

Note: if you are still being paid AA or DLA care component (eg, because you have not yet been in a care home for 28 days), you may be entitled to a severe disability premium, even if you were not before – eg, if you are no longer treated as living with a non-dependant or a partner.

If your partner or child is living in a care home, see p689 for how your means-tested benefits are affected.

Means-tested benefits

Whether or not your means-tested benefits are affected depends on whether you (or your partner or child) are temporarily or permanently living in a care home. However, if you are in a care home (on either basis), your means-tested benefits are generally calculated in the usual way, but if payment of your AA or DLA care component stops, you may no longer be entitled to certain premiums.

Care homes

For means-tested benefits, when the term 'care home' is used, it means:[64]

- a care home (a care home service in Scotland) as defined in s3 of the Care Standards Act 2000 and paragraph 2 of Schedule 12 to the Public Services Reform (Scotland) Act 2010. So long as the home comes within the definition, it counts as a care home even if it also has some other function, such as an educational institution;[65]
- an Abbeyfield Home run by the Abbeyfield Society or affiliates of that society;
- an independent hospital (an independent healthcare service in Scotland) as defined in s275 of the National Health Service Act 2006 (in England) other than a health service hospital, s2 of the Care Standards Act 2000 (in Wales) and s10F(1)(a) and (b) of the National Health Service (Scotland) Act 1978 (in Scotland).

If you are not sure if you live in a relevant home, seek advice.

Note:

- If you have a partner, you may no longer count as a couple if you (or your partner) are resident in a care home. If your child is resident in a care home, s/he may no longer count as a member of your family for benefit purposes. See p689 for further information.
- For IS and JSA, in limited cases, you or your partner do not (or for income-related ESA, your partner does not) count as in full-time paid work if you (or s/he) are in employment while living in a care home (see p726).
- For PC, if you have an 'assessed income period' (see p520), it comes to an end if you do not have a partner and are provided with accommodation in a care home (other than in an Abbeyfield Home) on a permanent basis.[66]

Permanent residence in a care home

For IS, income-based JSA, income-related ESA and, if you and your partner are under the qualifying age for PC (see p509), HB, if you are permanently resident in a care home the threshold for calculating your **tariff income** is increased to £10,000 (see p971). This also applies if you live in Polish resettlement accommodation (certain care homes for Polish people who came to the UK as refugees after the Second World War). Some temporary absences from the care home or resettlement accommodation are ignored.[67] For HB, the £10,000 threshold is only relevant (and only applies) in the limited situations in which you can get HB while living in a care home (see p690). For PC and, if you or your partner are at least the qualifying age for PC, HB, the threshold is always £10,000 (see p995). The £10,000 threshold is not needed for CTB; if you are a permanent resident in a care home, you are not liable for council tax there.

HB, CTB and help with your housing costs (paid with IS, income-based JSA, income-related ESA or PC) are no longer payable for your former home once you are a permanent resident in a care home. Another person (eg, your partner) might be able to get these instead, if s/he is (or can be treated as) liable (see pp848 and 248).

For CTB, if you become a permanent resident in a care home and your previous home is unoccupied, you can apply for it to be exempt from council tax. See CPAG's *Council Tax Handbook* for details.

If payment of your **AA or DLA care component** stops because you are in a care home, you are no longer entitled to premiums (additional amounts in PC) that depend on receipt of AA or DLA care component (see p687). However, for IS only, if you only live in a care home part of the week and are entitled to DLA when you are staying elsewhere, you can be paid, for example, the severe disability and enhanced disability premiums when you are staying away from the care home from the date the change occurs (or is expected to occur).[68] **Note:** there is no equivalent rule for ESA. It is not clear if this was an error or the intention. However, you qualify for the enhanced disability premium if you are getting the ESA support component, even if you are not receiving DLA care component.

Temporary residence in a care home

If you are a temporary resident in a care home (eg, for respite care or for a trial period), you can continue to get HB, CTB and help with your housing costs (paid with IS, income-based JSA, income-related ESA or PC) for your normal home. If you intend to return home, you can get these for:[69]

- up to 13 weeks, if you are in a care home for a trial period. On the date you enter the accommodation, you must intend to return home if the accommodation is not suitable.[70] You can get HB, CTB and help with your housing costs for the full 13 weeks, even if you have made a definite decision to stay long term in the care home. If the home does not suit your needs you can have further trial periods in other homes, provided you are not away from home for more than 52 weeks; *or*
- up to 13 weeks, for any reason if you are unlikely to be away from home for longer than this, or for up to 52 weeks, if you are unlikely to be away for longer than this (or in exceptional circumstances, substantially longer than this) and satisfy other conditions – eg, if you are in a care home for temporary respite care.

For these purposes, for HB and CTB, a care home includes those managed or provided by bodies incorporated by Royal Charter or constituted by an Act of Parliament, other than by local social services; for PC, a care home does *not* include an Abbeyfield Home.

There are no linking rules with these provisions. This means that if you go home, a new period of temporary absence can begin when you go back into the care home.

Partners and children

If **you or your partner** move into a care home:

- **permanently** (for PC only, other than to an Abbeyfield Home), you no longer count as a couple.[71] This also applies if you and your partner are both in care homes permanently, even if you are in the same home and the same room.[72] If you do not count as a couple, your benefit, and that of your partner, is calculated as if you are a single claimant;
- **temporarily**, you still count as a couple if you intend to live together again. For IS, JSA, ESA, PC and HB only, this only applies if you are unlikely to be apart for more than 52 weeks, or in exceptional circumstances, substantially longer than 52 weeks.[73] If you still count as a couple:
  - for PC, HB and CTB, your benefit continues to be assessed under the normal rules. This means that once the person in the care home stops getting AA or DLA care component, no severe disability premium (additional amount) can be included in your applicable amount for either of you;
  - for IS, income-based JSA and income-related ESA, your applicable amount is calculated in a special way. You receive the amount for two single claimants

if this is higher than the amount you receive as a couple. This can include the severe disability premium in respect of either or both of you, as if you were single claimants, even if you are not normally entitled to it at home.[74]

If **your child** lives in a care home or is being looked after by a local authority in residential accommodation, entitlement to a personal allowance and premiums for her/him within your HB and CTB (or your IS or income-based JSA, if included – see p760) may be affected if you no longer get child benefit for her/him or if s/he no longer counts as a member of your family. Remember that, in some cases, you can receive benefit for her/him on the days when s/he comes home. See p762 for further information. Entitlement to premiums for your child is also affected if s/he is no longer paid DLA.

Housing benefit for your care home

You cannot usually get HB for the rent you pay to your care home.[75] For these purposes, a care home does *not* include an Abbeyfield Home. There are very limited exceptions to the rules – ie, if you were entitled to HB for your care home when the rules changed at various times in the past and you have transitional protection. Broadly speaking, you can get HB for the rent you pay if you were entitled to it for residential accommodation under the HB rules before 30 October 1990 or before 1 April 1993.[76] In some cases, this only applies if you do not break your claim and continue to live in the same home, disregarding certain temporary absences.

Note: if you are on a placement under the Adult Placement Scheme (a scheme similar to fostering, but for adults) living with an approved carer, the normal conditions of entitlement to HB apply.[77] You can get HB for the rent you pay.

Social fund payments

Some social fund payments are affected if you are in a care home. You cannot get:

- a crisis loan if you are in a care home unless your discharge is planned to take place in the next two weeks (see p566). In Scotland, you are only excluded if you are getting nursing or personal care;
- a cold weather payment if you are in a care home (see p687 – the meaning is the same as for means-tested benefits) or Polish resettlement accommodation, unless you are responsible for a child under five or you are getting child tax credit which includes a disabled child or severely disabled child element;[78]
- a winter fuel payment if you are getting income-based JSA, income-related ESA or PC and are (and for a period have been) in a care home or Polish resettlement accommodation (see p583).[79]

4. Prisoners

Most benefits are affected if you are a prisoner. Some are not payable, some are suspended and some are only payable for a temporary period. There are issues to consider if you are given an alternative sentence to prison.

Always inform the DWP (and local authority) as soon as you, or a member of your family, enter or leave prison to avoid any underpayment or overpayment of benefit. If you are being held on remand and are then sentenced, notifiy the benefit authorities as soon as this happens. You should not assume that the prison will do this for you.

Non-means-tested benefits

You are disqualified from getting most non-means-tested benefits while you are a prisoner. For statutory sick pay (SSP), statutory maternity pay (SMP), statutory adoption pay (SAP) or ordinary or additional statutory paternity pay (SPP), see below. For other non-means-tested benefits, see p692. In some cases, payment of your benefit is only suspended pending the outcome of your trial or sentence (see p693). For benefits that are payable, see p693.

Note: non-means-tested benefits (other than SSP, SMP, SAP and SPP) are not affected if you are detained as a result of a criminal conviction in a hospital or similar institution as a person with a mental disorder, unless this is under specified provisions (see p692).[80] However, check whether your benefit is affected under the special rules for hospital patients instead.

Statutory sick, maternity, adoption and paternity pay

If you are detained in legal custody or sentenced to a term of imprisonment (except if the sentence is suspended) you:[81]

- are not entitled to SSP. In addition, you are not entitled during any subsequent period during the same period of incapacity for work;
- cannot be paid SMP or ordinary SPP for the whole of your maternity or paternity pay period (see p608), even if you are released from prison during it. If you cannot be paid SMP, check to see if you be paid maternity allowance instead.

However, you are paid SAP or additional SPP for any period during which you are detained in custody if you are subsequently released without charge or after being found not guilty, or you are convicted but do not receive a custodial sentence. Payment of SAP or additional SPP should also resume for any period of entitlement subsequent to your release.

Note: you do not count as in legal custody if you are on bail, or living in approved premises – eg, a bail or probation hostel, or are simply helping the police with their enquiries.

Other non-means-tested benefits

If you count as a prisoner you cannot be paid attendance allowance (AA), bereavement benefits, disability living allowance (DLA), carer's allowance (CA), contributory employment and support allowance (ESA), incapacity benefit (IB), maternity allowance (MA), reduced earnings allowance (REA), retirement allowance, retirement pension or severe disablement allowance (SDA).[82] However, see below to check if your benefit is only suspended pending trial or sentence.

You cannot be paid an increase in CA, IB, MA, retirement pension or SDA for your spouse or civil partner if s/he is a prisoner.[83] You cannot qualify for an increase in these benefits for an adult looking after a child (see p742) if the adult is a prisoner.[84] This rule is not relevant for the other benefits listed above as there are no increases for a spouse/civil partner/adult caring for a child.

When you count as a prisoner

You count as a 'prisoner' if you are imprisoned or detained in legal custody (in Great Britain or abroad) in connection with criminal proceedings – ie, not for civil offences.[85] You therefore do *not* count as a prisoner and benefits are payable, provided you satisfy the normal rules of entitlement, if you are:

- on bail, or living in approved premises – eg, a bail or probation hostel;
- released on parole, temporary licence or under a home detention curfew (electronic tagging).

You count as a prisoner even if, although you received a prison sentence as a result of a criminal conviction, you are currently detained in a hospital or similar institution (eg, if you are transferred from prison) as a person with a mental disorder under ss45A or 47 of the Mental Health Act 1983, s59A of the Criminal Procedure (Scotland) Act 1995 or s136 of the Mental Health (Care and Treatment)(Scotland) Act 2003. However, this only applies until you would have been expected to be released under your original sentence or, if you are held under an indeterminate sentence (eg, you are a life prisoner), until you are released.[86] After that, if you are still in hospital, your benefit might be affected under the rules that apply to hospital patients (see p675).

Note:

- It appears that this rule applies to contributory ESA, but the rules are contradictory.[87]
- If you are detained in a hospital or similar institution under provisions other than those listed above, you might be paid non-means-tested benefits. However, check to see if your benefit is affected under the rules that apply to patients.

For non-means-tested benefits that are payable, see p693.

You cannot qualify for (and therefore cannot be paid) contribution-based jobseeker's allowance (JSA) while you are in prison as you are unable to satisfy the jobseeking conditions. Note, however, that unless you count as a prisoner, you are treated as available for and actively seeking work during temporary police detention (legal custody in Scotland) of up to 96 days (see Chapter 20).

Benefits suspended

If you are a remand prisoner awaiting trial or sentence, payment of contributory ESA, IB, SDA, AA, DLA, CA, MA, REA, retirement pension, retirement allowance and bereavement benefits is suspended pending the outcome. An increase of CA, IB, retirement pension or SDA for your spouse or civil partner is likewise suspended if s/he is a remand prisoner. If you (or s/he) subsequently receive a sentence of imprisonment or detention (including a suspended sentence), you are not paid the benefits for the whole period you are in prison (see p692).[88]

If you (or your spouse or civil partner) do not receive a sentence of imprisonment or detention or your conviction is quashed, full arrears of any benefit that have been withheld are payable when you are released.[89] Arrears are only payable if the normal conditions of entitlement for benefit were met while you (or your spouse/civil partner) were a remand prisoner. For the purpose of entitlement to an increase in your benefit for a spouse or civil partner, you should be treated as still 'residing with' her/him while s/he is in prison, unless your marriage/partnership has broken down and your separation is likely to be permanent.[90]

Benefits payable

You are entitled to **disablement benefit** (but not any of the increases discussed on p380) for periods when you are a prisoner. However, you are not paid until you are released and you can only get a maximum of 12 months' arrears.[91] If you are in prison for more than a year, you should be paid for the 12-month period which gives you the most benefit.[92] You are entitled to full arrears for any period you were on remand, if you are not subsequently sentenced to imprisonment or detention.[93]

You are entitled to **child benefit**[94] and **guardian's allowance**[95] while you are a prisoner. You must continue to be 'responsible' for the child (see p100). If you are in prison for some time, you may want to arrange for child benefit to be paid to the person looking after your child. If *your child* is a prisoner, entitlement to child benefit usually ends after eight weeks.[96] There are exceptions to the rules (see p106). However, full arrears are payable at the end of any period of remand if your child is not sentenced to imprisonment or detention. Once entitlement to child benefit ends, entitlement to guardian's allowance in respect of the child also ends.

Note: if child benefit stops because your child is a prisoner, this may affect whether you can get an increase for her/him with your non-means-tested benefits, and personal allowances and premiums for her/him with your housing benefit (HB) and council tax benefit (CTB) (and income support (IS) or income-based JSA if still included). If you lose the increase in your non-means-tested benefits (or the allowance and premiums included in your IS or income-based JSA), you may no longer qualify for these (see pp745 and 760).

Means-tested benefits

For means-tested benefits, you count as a prisoner if you are:[97]

- detained in custody (eg, in prison or a young offenders' institution) awaiting trial or sentence (on remand) or following a sentence of imprisonment; *or*
- on temporary release under specific provisions (this does not include parole licence).

You do not count as a prisoner if you are detained in hospital under specific mental health provisions (but see below if you received a prison sentence as a result of a criminal conviction). Check to see if your benefit is affected by the special rules for hospital patients instead. In addition, you do not count as a prisoner if you are:

- released on licence or parole; *or*
- on bail or living in approved premises – eg, a bail or probation hostel; *or*
- released under a home detention curfew (electronic tagging).

For **IS, income-based JSA, income-related ESA and pension credit (PC)**, if you count as a prisoner:

- you cannot qualify for JSA as you are unable to satisfy the jobseeking conditions. If you need help with your housing costs for your home, you must claim IS, income-related ESA or PC for this (see p695);
- you can qualify for IS, income-related ESA and PC guarantee credit for up to 52 weeks while you are detained in custody awaiting trial or sentence. However, you only get the amount for help with your housing costs. Once you have been sentenced, you are no longer entitled to any IS, income-related ESA or PC;[98]
- you cannot get any PC savings credit;[99]
- you may be entitled to the PC severe disability additional amount if you do not receive a sentence of imprisonment and you are given arrears of AA or DLA on your release.[100]

Note that if, although you received a prison sentence as a result of a criminal conviction, you are currently detained in a hospital or similar institution (eg, you are transferred from prison) as a person with a mental disorder under ss45A or 47 of the Mental Health Act 1983, s59A of the Criminal Procedure (Scotland) Act 1995 or s136 of the Mental Health (Care and Treatment) (Scotland) Act 2003 special rules apply. Although you are a patient, you are treated in a similar way to prisoners. You are not entitled to any IS, income-related ESA or PC, but only until you would have been expected to be released under your original sentence or, if you are held under an indeterminate sentence (eg, you are a life prisoner), until you are released.[101] After that, if you are still in hospital, your benefit might be affected under the rules that apply to hospital patients (see p675). Although there is no specific rule for JSA, you cannot qualify for JSA in this situation as you are not able to satisfy the jobseeking conditions. **Note:** if you are detained in a hospital or similar institution under provisions other than those listed p694, you may qualify for IS, JSA or ESA. However, check to see if your benefit is affected under the rules that apply to patients (see p675).

If you are a prisoner and have a partner or children, or if your partner (or child) is a prisoner, see p696.

Paying for your normal home while you are a prisoner

While you are detained in custody **awaiting trial or sentence**, you can get HB and CTB and help with your housing costs (paid with IS, income-related ESA or PC) for your normal home. These are paid for up to 52 weeks, so long as you intend to return home and you are unlikely to be away for longer than this (or, in exceptional circumstances, substantially longer than this).[102] You cannot get help with your housing costs with income-based JSA and must claim IS, income-related ESA or PC for this. Note that you fit into one of the groups of people who can claim IS in this situation (see p350).

If you are serving a **custodial sentence**, you may be able to get HB and CTB for up to 13 weeks, so long as you are unlikely to be away from your normal home for longer than this – ie, you are serving a short sentence.[103] The 13 weeks run from the date you were first in prison.[104] So any time you spend in prison awaiting trial or sentence counts towards the 13 weeks. If you are serving a sentence of more than 13 weeks, you may still be entitled to HB and CTB, as prisoners serving short sentences are often released early under a home detention curfew (electronic tagging). If you are serving a sentence of up to a year, it is possible to be released within 13 weeks.

You are treated as a prisoner during periods of **temporary release** under specific provisions. This means that, even if you return home, you are not entitled to IS, income-based JSA, income-related ESA or PC and cannot get help with your housing costs.[105] For HB and CTB, you are still treated as if you are away from home and these periods count towards the 13/52 weeks for which HB and CTB may be payable.[106] **Note:**

- You should report the change in your circumstances as soon as possible – ie, when you are remanded in custody, are serving a custodial sentence or are being released from custody.
- If you do not qualify for HB for 52 or 13 weeks under the rules described above, you can continue to get HB for a former home for up to four weeks if you are

still liable to pay rent for it, and you could not reasonably have avoided this liability – eg, because your tenancy agreement required you to give notice.[107]

- Housing costs (paid with IS, income-based JSA, income-related ESA or PC) and HB can be paid to another person (eg, your partner), if s/he is (or can be treated as) liable (see pp848 and 248).
- If your home is unoccupied while you are a prisoner, you can apply for it to be exempt from council tax, provided you are not in prison for non-payment of a fine or council tax. See CPAG'S *Council Tax Handbook* for details.

If you are not already getting HB and CTB (or IS, income-related ESA or PC) when you go into prison, you should make a claim to protect your position. These benefits can only be backdated for a limited period. See the chapter in this *Handbook* about the benefit you want to claim for details.

If you have a **non-dependant** who is a prisoner, no non-dependant deduction is made for her/him.[108] See pp265 and 869 for further information about non-dependant deductions.

Partners and children

If you have a **partner** and one of you is a prisoner:

- you no longer count as a couple for IS, income-based JSA, income-related ESA or PC purposes;[109]
- you continue to count as a couple:
  - for HB purposes, so long as you intend to live together again and the prisoner is unlikely to be away for substantially longer than 52 weeks;[110]
  - for CTB purposes so long as you are only temporarily apart.[111] Unlike for HB, this is not defined in the rules.

  If the one who is not a prisoner is working, s/he may be able to have childcare costs deducted from her/his earnings (see pp915 and 947).[112]

Once you no longer count as a couple, the one who is *not* a prisoner can claim benefit as a single person (or lone parent).

If your **child** is a prisoner, entitlement to a personal allowance and premiums for her/him with your HB and CTB (and with your IS or income-based JSA if they are still included – see p760) might be affected if you no longer get child benefit for her/him or if s/he no longer counts as a member of your family – eg, because s/he is in custody. See p762 for further information.

Social fund payments

Most prisoners are excluded from getting a crisis loan (see p566). You cannot get a winter fuel payment if you are serving a custodial sentence (see p583). You cannot get other social fund payments if you are not getting a qualifying benefit (see Chapters 25 and 26).[113] If you are released on temporary licence, a person caring for you may be able to claim a community care grant to help with living expenses (see p554).

Benefits and alternatives to prison

There are a number of alternatives to prison. While awaiting trial or sentence, you might be on bail, including on the condition that you live in approved premises (eg, a bail hostel) or elsewhere away from home. See below for how this affects your benefits.

You might be given a **community sentence** that involves punishment or supervision in the community. Although you do not count as a prisoner, you should bear the following in mind.

- There might be a question as to whether you satisfy the jobseeking conditions for JSA (but see p437). Seek advice if you think you have been wrongly refused.
- If you undertake basic skills education and are treated as a full-time student, this may affect your entitlement to benefits (see Chapter 29).
- Argue that the notional income rules for means-tested benefits should not apply where you participate in unpaid work as part of your sentence (see p935).

If you are on bail or living in approved premises

Your non-means-tested benefits are paid as normal if you are on bail or living in approved premises (eg, a bail or probation hostel) or other accommodation as a condition of bail. However, special rules can apply for means-tested benefits.

If you have a partner and you are temporarily separated because one of you is living away from home, you still count as a couple for means-tested benefit purposes if you intend to live together again. For IS, JSA, income-related ESA, PC and HB, this only applies if you are unlikely to be apart for more than 52 weeks or, in exceptional circumstances, substantially longer than 52 weeks.[114] For CTB purposes, this applies if you are temporarily apart; this is not defined in the rules.[115] For IS, income-based JSA and income-related ESA only, if one of you is living in an approved bail or probation hostel, your applicable amount is calculated in a special way – at either the single rate for each of you added together, or the couple rate, whichever is the greater.[116]

Paying for your normal home

If you are required to live away from home in an approved bail or probation hostel, you cannot get HB for the rent you pay for that accommodation.[117] However, you can continue to get HB, CTB and help with your housing costs paid with IS, income-based JSA, income-related ESA or PC for your normal home. If you are required to live in the approved hostel or an address away from home as a condition of bail, these are paid for up to 52 weeks (so long as you intend to return home and you are unlikely to be away for longer than this or, in exceptional circumstances, substantially longer than this).[118] Otherwise, these are paid for up to 13 weeks (so long as you are unlikely to be away for longer than this) – see pp254 and 850.

If you are no longer entitled to help with housing costs paid with IS, income-based JSA, income-related ESA or PC, or HB these can be paid to another person if s/he is (or can be treated as) liable (see pp848 and 248).

Benefits on release

If you are **temporarily released** (on temporary licence), you no longer count as a prisoner for non-means-tested benefits. You still count as a prisoner for means-tested benefits. However, someone caring for you might qualify for a community care grant (CCG) for her/his expenses for looking after you (see p554).

When you are **permanently released** from prison, you should claim any benefits to which you are entitled as soon as possible. The prison gives you a discharge form that can help you prove your identity. You may also be interviewed by a DWP liaison officer before you leave prison, who should point out which benefits you might be able to claim.

- As IS, income-based JSA and income-related ESA are generally paid in arrears, you may need to apply for an interim payment (see p1046) or a social fund crisis loan to meet your initial expenses.
- You may qualify for a CCG to help you settle back into the community – eg, for clothes, furniture and household equipment. You can apply up to six weeks before you are released if you are, or expect to be, in receipt of IS, income-based JSA, income-related ESA or PC (see p550).
- For JSA, you are treated as satisfying the jobseeking conditions for the first seven days after your release.[119]
- If you are at least 25 and are an offender who is subject to multi-agency risk management arrangements, you are exempt from the HB rent restriction rules for single claimants under 35 (see pp311 and 323).
- You may receive a discharge grant from the Prison Service, which counts as capital for IS, income-based JSA and income-related ESA purposes.[120] The rules do not say how it should be treated for HB, CTB or PC.
- If you are released without being sentenced to imprisonment or detention, you should receive any arrears of your non-means-tested benefits that were suspended (see p693).
- See p779 for information about national insurance contributions and credits. If you are released following the quashing of a conviction, you are entitled to credits for the period you were imprisoned or detained (see p787).

Help with travelling expenses

The Prison Service can help you with travelling expenses when you are temporarily or permanently released from prison.

The Assisted Prison Visits Unit can help a partner or close relative (or another person if s/he is your only visitor) with the cost of visiting you in prison, or a friend with the cost of bringing your children to visit you. S/he must be on a low income – eg, on IS, income-based JSA, income-related ESA or PC. S/he may also qualify if s/he is getting child tax credit or working tax credit, or health benefits on low-income grounds.

Application forms are available from the establishment being visited and from the Assisted Prison Visits Unit, PO Box 2152, Birmingham B15 1SD (telephone 0845 300 1423 or textphone 0845 304 0800, Monday to Friday, 10.15–11.45 am and 2.15–3.45 pm). You can also email assisted.prison.visits@noms.gsi.gov.uk.

5. People without accommodation

Entitlement to non-means-tested benefits and pension credit (PC) is unaffected if you do not have accommodation, but income support (IS), income-based jobseeker's allowance (JSA) and income-related employment and support allowance (ESA) are paid at a reduced rate.

If you become homeless and have no money, you can apply for a social fund crisis loan or an interim payment. It is possible to get help at any time in an emergency.

If you are homeless, the local authority may have a duty to assist you with accommodation or advice. A child or young person may be entitled to help from social services.

Note: if you set up home as part of a resettlement programme after you have beeen homeless, you may be entitled to a community care grant. If you are at least 25 and have been living in a homeless hostel for at least three months and have accepted rehabilitation or resettlement support, you are exempt from the housing benefit (HB) rent restriction rules for single people under 35.

Income support, income-based jobseeker's allowance and income-related employment and support allowance

Your IS, income-based JSA and income-related ESA are paid at a reduced rate if you are a person 'without accommodation'.[121] You get the normal rate, but without any premiums.[122] In addition, for income-related ESA, you do not get either the work-related activity or support component.

Having no fixed address is *not* the same as having no accommodation. If you have accommodation, but are staying in different places on different nights (eg, with different friends or relatives), your IS, income-based JSA or income-related ESA should be paid as normal.[123]

The meaning of 'accommodation'

'Accommodation' is not defined in the rules and should be interpreted widely and flexibly. The DWP says that to count as having accommodation, you must have:[124]

'an effective shelter from the elements which is capable of being heated; and in which occupants can sit, lie down, cook and eat; and which is reasonably suited for continuous occupation. The site of the accommodation may alter from day to day, but it is still accommodation if the structure is habitable.'

Examples include tents, caravans and other substantial shelters. However, the DWP is likely to say that cardboard boxes, bus shelters, sleeping bags and cars do not qualify as accommodation.[125]

Note: if you are temporarily absent from the accommodation you normally occupy as your home, even if you are living a lifestyle as though you have no accommodation (eg, you are sleeping rough), you should be treated as having accommodation.[126]

Available for and actively seeking work

You must satisfy the jobseeking conditions to get JSA (see Chapter 20). Being homeless may, of course, reduce your prospects of finding work, but personal circumstances that reduce your chances of being employed should not prevent you getting JSA.

You can be available for work if you do not have accommodation, but it must be possible for you to be contacted at short notice if you are to satisfy the requirement that you are willing and able to take up any job immediately, or at 24 hours' or one week's (or 28 days') notice (see p436). You may satisfy this requirement by daily visits to the Jobcentre Plus office, or a drop-in centre or support group where a message can be left for you – eg, to notify you of vacancies.

The fact that you are homeless should be taken into account when deciding whether you are actively seeking work. In deciding what steps it is reasonable for you to take to find work, the DWP must take into account the fact that you have no accommodation and the steps you need to take (and took) to find a home.[127]

6. People involved in a trade dispute

If you (or your partner) are involved in a trade dispute, income support (IS) and jobseeker's allowance (JSA) are affected, as well as benefits paid by your employer, increases for dependants paid with non-means-tested benefits and some social fund payments. You can still qualify for housing benefit (HB), council tax benefit (CTB), income-related employment and support allowance (ESA) and pension credit (PC), but there are issues to consider.

Whether or not you are involved in a trade dispute is a complex area of law. If there is any doubt, seek specialist advice from your trade union or an advice or law centre.

If you need financial help when you return to work after a trade dispute, you may qualify for an IS loan for the first 15 days.

Income support and jobseeker's allowance

IS and JSA are both affected if you (or your partner) are involved in a trade dispute. You are treated as being in full-time paid work for the first seven days you are involved in one. You (and your partner) cannot qualify for IS or income-based JSA for that period.[128] This does not apply if your partner was already entitled to IS or income-based JSA, or you were already entitled to IS, when you became involved in the dispute. If the dispute causes a series of stoppages, this only applies for seven days from the start of the first stoppage.[129] After the seven-day period, you are not treated as being in full-time paid work, but your IS or your partner's IS or income-based JSA is calculated under special rules (see p703).[130] Bear the following in mind.

- You fit into one of the groups of people who can claim IS while you are involved in a trade dispute and for the first 15 days after you return to work (see p350) so you can qualify for IS during this period.[131] Note that if you are not involved in a trade dispute but your partner is, you can claim IS instead of her/him if you fit into one of the groups of people who can claim IS, but you should seek advice about whether it is in your interests to swap which one of you claims.
- You are not entitled to JSA (including hardship payments) for the whole of any week (seven days from Sunday) if you (or if you are a joint-claim couple, both of you) are involved in a trade dispute for one or more days during that week.[132] Weeks when you are not entitled to JSA do not count as part of your 'jobseeking period' (see p394).[133] This means, for instance, that they do not count towards your 26 weeks' entitlement to contribution-based JSA.
- If you have a partner and only one of you is involved in a trade dispute, unless you are a joint-claim couple (see p413), the one who is not involved can claim income-based JSA. If you are a joint-claim couple, you can both claim income-based JSA;[134] the one involved in the trade dispute does not have to satisfy the jobseeking conditions (see p396).

Trade disputes

A '**trade dispute**' is any dispute between employers and employees or between employees and employees connected with terms or conditions of employment, or the employment or non-employment of anyone.[135] Note that what counts as a trade dispute for benefit purposes goes beyond what counts as lawful industrial action for employment law purposes.

You count as **involved in a trade dispute** if:[136]

- you are not working because of a 'stoppage of work' caused by a trade dispute at your 'place of work' (see below). You are treated as involved in the trade dispute until the stoppage ends, even if you are not a party to the dispute or your contract has been terminated as part of the dispute (but see below);[137] *or*
- you withdraw your labour to further a trade dispute, whether or not there is a stoppage of work at your place of work.

For IS and income-based JSA, a decision can be made on your claim as if you are involved in a trade dispute, and an award of benefit can be made at a reduced rate, pending a decision on whether you are actually involved.[138] You cannot appeal to the First-tier Tribunal against this decision.[139] The decision maker should then carry out a revision of the decision once full information and evidence is available and you can appeal to the First-tier Tribunal against this.

Stoppage of work and place of work

A **'stoppage of work'** could be due to a strike, lock-out or any other stoppage caused by a trade dispute. The stoppage does not have to involve everybody, or stop all work.[140] The DWP says that there is no 'stoppage' if normal work continues through the employment of replacement workers or reorganisation.[141]

'Place of work' means the place or premises where you are employed, but it does not include a separate department carrying out a different branch of work, which is commonly undertaken as a separate business elsewhere – eg, a colliery canteen worker laid off during a miners' strike was not 'involved in a trade dispute at her place of work'.[142] It can be difficult to establish that separate branches are commonly separate businesses and not part of integrated activities.[143]

You **do *not* count as being involved in a trade dispute**:
- if you can prove you are not directly interested in the dispute – ie, you will not be affected by its outcome.[144] This could apply if your terms and conditions will not be affected by the outcome of the dispute or your employment has permanently ended and you will not gain anything from the dispute. However, it may be difficult to convince the DWP that your employment has permanently ended. When a dispute is settled, it is common for the employer to agree to re-employ those who were dismissed during its course;[145] *or*
- if you can prove that during a stoppage of work:[146]
  - you have been made redundant; *or*
  - you have become genuinely employed elsewhere – ie, not just to avoid the trade dispute rules;[147] *or*
  - if you genuinely resume employment with your employer and then leave for a reason other than the trade dispute (but note that if you are claiming JSA you may be sanctioned if you leave – see p459).

For income-based JSA (if your partner is claiming) and IS, even if you are (or count as) involved in a trade dispute, the special rules for those involved in a trade dispute do not apply during a period:[148]

- when you have limited capability for work (see Chapter 11) (or are incapable of work – see Chapter 32); *or*
- from the sixth week before the week you are due to have a baby to the end of the seventh week after the week the baby is born; *or*
- from the day you return to work with the same employer, even if the dispute is continuing or you are doing a different job.

The amount of income support or income-based jobseeker's allowance

Special rules reduce the amount of IS or income-based JSA that is payable if you or your partner are involved in a trade dispute. Your applicable amount is calculated in a special way and it is assumed that you have a set level of strike pay. Certain income is taken into account even if it would be disregarded were you (or your partner) not involved in a trade dispute. **Note:** if you are entitled to IS of less than £5 a week, you are only paid if you are receiving another benefit that can be paid together with IS as a single payment.[149]

Applicable amount

Your IS or income-based JSA applicable amount is calculated as follows.

If you are a **single claimant, or a member of a couple (without children)** both involved in a trade dispute:

- your applicable amount for IS is reduced to nil;[150]
- you are not entitled to any JSA.

If you are a **lone parent, or a member of a couple (with children)** both involved in a trade dispute:

- you are not entitled to a personal allowance or any premiums in IS payable in respect of yourself (or of either of you if you are a member of a couple). Your applicable amount only includes:[151]
  - personal allowances, the family premium and any premiums for your children (if still included); *and*
  - housing costs;
- you are not entitled to any JSA.

If you are a **member of a couple (with or without children)** and only one of you is involved in a trade dispute, for both IS and JSA, you are not entitled to any premiums payable solely for the person involved in the trade dispute. Your applicable amount only includes:[152]

- half the normal personal allowance for a couple and half of any premiums paid at the couple rate;

- any premiums payable solely in respect of the person not involved in the trade dispute;
- personal allowances, the family premium and premiums for any children (if still included); *and*
- housing costs.

Actual and assumed strike pay

If you (or your partner) are involved in a trade dispute, £38 a week is deducted from your IS or income-based JSA as 'assumed strike pay', whether or not you or your partner actually receive any payments.[153] Any payments you or your partner actually receive from a trade union in excess of £38 a week count as income; payments of up to £38 are ignored. If you and your partner are both involved in a trade dispute, only £38 in total is ignored.[154]

Example

Cliff is on strike. His partner is not involved in the dispute. Their only income is £45 a week strike pay.

Applicable amount	£55.70 (half normal amount)
less income	£7.00 (strike pay over £38)
	= £48.70
less	£38.00 (assumed strike pay)
= IS payable	£10.70

Other income and capital

Other income and capital are treated as normal except that the following payments are taken into account in full as income:

- any refunds of income tax paid or due under the PAYE rules;[155]
- any payment received or due because you are not working – eg, a loan or grant from social services;[156]
- if you still get allowances and premiums for your children in your IS or JSA, payments made under the Children Act 1989 or Children (Scotland) Act 1995 to promote the welfare of children. Otherwise they count in full as capital;[157]
- charitable or voluntary payments and certain personal injury payments (see p924), except any payments from the Macfarlane Trusts, the Eileen Trust, MFET Ltd, the Skipton Fund, the Caxton Foundation, the Fund or the Independent Living Fund (2006);[158]
- payments in kind (except payments from the above trusts or funds) paid to the person involved in the trade dispute or to a third party (unless for items allowable under the notional income and capital rules – see pp934 and 990);[159]
- holiday pay payable more than four weeks after your employment is terminated or interrupted (subject to any earnings disregard);[160]

- an advance of earnings or a loan from an employer (subject to any earnings disregard).[161]

Benefits paid by your employer

Statutory sick pay (SSP), statutory maternity pay (SMP), statutory paternity pay (SPP) and statutory adoption pay (SAP) are all affected if you are involved in a trade dispute.

Statutory sick pay

You cannot qualify for SSP if you are not within a 'period of entitlement'. A period of entitlement cannot arise if, on the date it would begin, there is a stoppage of work because of a trade dispute at your place of work (ie, you became incapable of work during the trade dispute), unless you can prove that you did not have a direct interest in the dispute on or before that date.[162] You are not entitled to SSP throughout your period of sickness, even if the trade dispute ends. You might, however, qualify for ESA. **Note:** you can continue to qualify for SSP if you were already entitled to SSP when the trade dispute began.

'Stoppage of work' and 'trade dispute' are not defined in the SSP rules. However, an overtime ban or working to grade does not count as a stoppage of work.[163] For information about what might count as a 'stoppage of work' and 'place of work', see p702.

Statutory maternity, paternity and adoption pay

To qualify for SMP, SPP or SAP, you must have been employed for a continuous period of at least 26 weeks ending on a specified date (the 'continuous employment rule' – see p591). For the purpose of this rule, any week in which you are not working because of a stoppage of work because of a trade dispute at your place of work does not break your continuity of employment.[164] However, unless you can prove that you at no time had a direct interest in the trade dispute:

- any such week does *not* count towards the total of 26 weeks' employment you need to qualify for SMP, SPP or SAP; *and*
- if you are dismissed during the stoppage of work, your continuity of employment ends on the day you stopped work.

This could mean that you cannot qualify for SMP, SPP or SAP.

For information about the meaning of 'trade dispute', 'stoppage of work' and 'place of work', see p701. The rules are the same as for JSA.[165]

Increases for dependants

You are not entitled to an increase of incapacity benefit (IB), severe disablement allowance (SDA), carer's allowance (CA) or Category A retirement pension for an adult dependant who is involved in a trade dispute.[166] For information about what counts as being involved in a trade dispute, see p701. The rules are the same as for JSA. If the adult dependant returns to work, you can only reclaim an increase for her/him with IB. **Note:** you cannot make a new claim for an increase for an adult dependant with SDA, CA or Category A retirement pension. If you are getting an increase in one of those benefits and lose your entitlement to it, you cannot claim it again.

Social fund payments

Involvement in a trade dispute has no effect on entitlement to a funeral expenses, cold weather or winter fuel payment. However, other social fund payments are affected. For information about when you count as involved in a trade dispute, see p701. The rules are the same as for JSA.

You do not count as being involved in a trade dispute during a period when you are incapable of work or from the sixth week before the week you are due to have a baby to the end of the seventh week after the week the baby is born.[167] **Note:** the rules were not amended when employment and support allowance (ESA) was introduced.

Sure Start maternity grant

If you or your partner are involved in a trade dispute, your entitlement to a Sure Start maternity grant is not affected if your qualifying benefit is income-related ESA or pension credit (PC). However, you can only qualify for a Sure Start maternity grant if your qualifying benefit is:[168]

- IS or income-based JSA, if the trade dispute has been going on for at least six weeks when you claim a maternity grant; *or*
- child tax credit or working tax credit, if you claimed the relevant tax credit before the trade dispute began.

Social fund discretionary payments

If you or your partner are involved in a trade dispute, you cannot qualify for a **community care grant** (CCG) unless it is for travel expenses to visit somebody who is ill, and only in the following situations.[169]

- You are involved in a trade dispute and are visiting:
  - your partner in a hospital or similar institution; *or*
  - a dependant in a hospital or similar institution (but only if you have no partner living with you who could get a CCG under these provisions or if s/he is also in hospital); *or*
  - a close relative (not defined) or a member of your household who is critically ill (whether or not s/he is in a hospital or similar institution).
- You (or a dependant) are not involved in a trade dispute, but your partner is, and you (or your dependant) are visiting:
  - a close relative who is in a hospital or similar institution or who is critically ill; *or*

- someone else who was a member of your household before going into a hospital or similar institution or who is critically ill and was a member of your household before getting ill.

You cannot qualify for a **budgeting loan** if you or your partner are involved in a trade dispute.[170]

If you or your partner are involved in a trade dispute, you can only qualify for a **crisis loan** for:[171]

- expenses arising from a disaster; *or*
- the cost of items needed for cooking (including cooking utensils) or space heating (including fireguards).

Housing benefit, council tax benefit, employment and support allowance and pension credit

Your entitlement to HB, CTB, ESA and PC is not affected if you or your partner are involved in a trade dispute. However, bear the following in mind.

- For income-related ESA, your partner is treated as not in full-time paid work if s/he is involved in a trade dispute, and for the first 15 days following her/his return to work after having been involved in a trade dispute.[172]
- For HB, CTB and PC, it does not matter if you or your partner are treated as in full-time paid work. See Chapter 31 for further information.
- You may become entitled to HB, CTB, income-related ESA or PC (or an increased amount of these) if your (or your partner's) income drops because of a trade dispute.
- If your earnings are reduced due to a trade dispute, the DWP or local authority should take this into account and not just consider your pre-strike earnings.[173] Your earnings can be averaged over a different period than normal if this results in a more accurate estimate (see pp936 and 955).

Non-dependants

Non-dependant deductions can be made from your IS, JSA, ESA or PC housing costs and from HB and CTB. These deductions are usually higher if your non-dependant is in full-time paid work. However, if your non-dependant is involved in a trade dispute, this may mean that the non-dependant deduction should be reduced. See pp125, 268 and 871 for further information.

Income support loans on return to work

If you return to work with the same employer, whether or not the trade dispute has ended, you can qualify for IS for the first 15 days back at work, in the form of a loan.[174] You fit into one of the groups of people who can claim IS and are not treated as being in full-time paid work for this period.[175] However, if you are a member of a couple you are not entitled to IS if your partner is in full-time paid work.[176] See Chapter 31 for what counts as full-time paid work.

Your income and capital are calculated as if you were still involved in the trade dispute, except that the rules about actual and assumed strike pay do not apply, nor do those on the treatment of payments you get because the person involved in the trade dispute was not working.[177]

Repayment of the loan

Any IS paid during your first 15 days back at work can be recovered by deductions from your earnings.[178] If this is not practical (eg, because you are currently unemployed), it can be recovered directly from you.[179] The rules specify the amount of earnings you must be left with after deductions are made to repay your IS loan.[180] They also specify the calculations that your employer must make if your earnings come above that level on a particular payday.[181] If your loan is recovered by deductions from your earnings, your employer is required to make monthly payments to the DWP of all the amounts deducted.[182]

Your employer can begin making deductions from your earnings from the first payday after receiving a deduction notice from the DWP. If one month has passed since getting the notice, s/he *must* start making deductions on the next payday.[183] Your employer cannot make a deduction if you satisfy her/him that you did not receive the IS loan. The deduction notice expires automatically after 26 weeks.

You must tell the DWP within 10 working days if you leave a job or start another while part of your IS loan remains unpaid.[184] It is a criminal offence to fail to do so.[185] It is also a criminal offence for your employer to fail to keep records of deductions and supply the DWP with these.[186] If your employer fails to make a deduction (or makes too low a deduction) which should have been made from your pay, the DWP can recover the amount from your employer instead.[187]

Notes

1. **16/17-year-olds**

1 **IS** Reg 4ZA(3A) IS Regs
JSA Reg 57 JSA Regs, definition of 'young person'
Both ss6 and 8(6) C(LC)A 2000; C(LC)SSB(S) Regs

2 s6 C(LC)A 2000; reg 3 CL(E) Regs; reg 40(1) CPP&CR(E) Regs; regs 3 and 4 C(LC)(W) Regs; C(LC)SSB(S) Regs

3 Reg 3 CL(E) Regs; reg 4(1) and (2) C(LC)(W) Regs

4 ss6 and 8(6) C(LC)A 2000; regs 40(2) and 48 CPP&CR(E) Regs; reg 3(3) CL(E) Regs; reg 3(2) and (2A) C(LC)(W) Regs; reg 2(4)(a) C(LC)SSB(S) Regs

5 **IS** Reg 14(2)(c) IS Regs
JSA Reg 76(2)(d) JSA Regs
ESA Reg 2(1) ESA Regs, definition of 'young person'
HB Reg 19(2)(c) HB Regs; reg 19(2)(c) HB(SPC) Regs
CTB Reg 9(2)(c) CTB Regs; reg 9(2)(c) CTB(SPC) Regs

6 The C(LC)A 2000 was not amended to exclude formerly looked-after young people from entitlement to ESA.

7 Reg 2 C(LC)SSB Regs; reg 2(3) C(LC)SSB(S) Regs. Note that the C(LC)SSB Regs have been amended to include entitlement to income-related ESA, but this is not needed because the C(LC)A 2000 was not amended (see the note above).

8 Reg 3(5) and (6) CL(E) Regs; reg 4(4)-(6) C(LC)(W) Regs

9 Reg 2(2) C(LC)(SSB(S) Regs

9 Reg 2(2) C(LC)(SSB(S) Regs

2. **Hospital patients**

10 Reg 2(4) SS(HIP) Regs; reg 6 SS(AA) Regs; regs 8 and 12A SS(DLA) Regs; NHSA 2006; NHS(W)A 2006; NHS(S)A 1978; NHSCCA 1990

11 para 18059 DMG

12 paras 18028-33 DMG

13 *White v CAO, The Times,* 2 August 1993 (CA); *Botchett v CAO, The Times,* 8 May 1996, 2 CCLR 121 (CA); *R v North and East Devon Health Authority ex parte Coughlan* [1999] 2 CCLR 285 (CA)

14 *SSWP v Slavin* [2011] EWCA Civ 1515, 9 December 2011

15 para 18067 DMG

16 R(DLA) 2/06; *SSWP v Slavin* [2011] EWCA Civ 1515, 9 December 2011

17 Reg 6(2A) SS(AA) Regs; regs 8(2A) and 12A(2A) SS(DLA) Regs

18 Reg 2(5) SS(HIP) Regs

19 SF Dir 15

20 Regs 1(2), definition of 'free in-patient treatment', and 3 SFWFP Regs

21 Regs 6 and 8(1) SS(AA) Regs; regs 8, 10(1), 12A and 12B(1)(a) SS(DLA) Regs; reg 21 SS(GB) Regs

22 Regs 8, 10(2), 12A and 12B(1)(b) SS(DLA) Regs

23 Reg 25 SS(C&P) Regs

24 Reg 8(2) SS(AA) Regs; regs 10(5) and 12B(3) SS(DLA) Regs

25 Reg 8(3) SS(AA) Regs; regs 10(3) and 12B(2) SS(DLA) Regs

26 Regs 12B(3)-(9) and 12C(1) and (2) SS(DLA) Regs

27 Reg 8(4)-(5) SS(AA) Regs; regs 10(6)-(7) and 12B(9A) and (12) SS(DLA) Regs

28 **IS** Sch 2 paras 13(3A) and 15(5)(b)(i) IS Regs
JSA Sch 1 paras 15(5) and 20(6)(b)(i) JSA Regs
ESA Sch 4 paras 6(5) and 11(2)(b)(i) ESA Regs
PC Reg 6(5) and Sch 1 para 1(2)(b) SPC Regs
HB Sch 3 paras 14(5) and 20(6)(b)(i) HB Regs; Sch 3 paras 6(7) and 12(1)(b)(i) HB(SPC) Regs
CTB Sch 1 paras 14(5) and 20(6)(b)(i) CTB Regs; Sch 1 paras 6(7) and 12(1)(b)(i) CTB(SPC) Regs

29 Note that there is no such deeming rule in the PC Regs. It is not needed because the PC Regs set out the beneft rates in a different way than for other benefits.

30 **IS** Sch 2 paras 12(1)(d) and 13A(1) IS Regs
JSA Sch 1 paras 14(1)(g)(ii) and 15A(1) JSA Regs
ESA Sch 4 para 7 ESA Regs
HB Sch 3 paras 13(1)(a)(iii) and 15(1) HB Regs; Sch 3 para 7 HB(SPC) Regs
CTB Sch 1 paras 13(1)(a)(iii) and 15(1) CTB Regs; Sch 1 para 7 CTB(SPC) Regs
31 **IS** Sch 2 paras 13A(1) and 14(1)(a) IS Regs
JSA Sch 1 paras 15A(1) and 16(1)(a) JSA Regs
HB Sch 3 paras 15(1) and 16(a) HB Regs; Sch 3 paras 7 and 8(a) HB(SPC) Regs
CTB Sch 1 paras 15(1) and 16(a) CTB Regs; Sch 1 paras 7 and 8(a) CTB(SPC) Regs
32 **IS** Reg 16(1) and (2) IS Regs
JSA Reg 78(1)-(2) JSA Regs
ESA Reg 156(1)-(3) ESA Regs
PC Reg 5(1)(a) SPC Regs
HB Reg 21(1) and (2) HB Regs; reg 21(1) and (2) HB(SPC) Regs
CTB Reg 11(1) CTB Regs; reg 11(1) CTB(SPC) Regs
33 **IS** Reg 2(1), definition of 'long-term patient', and Sch 2 paras 11(2)(a) and 13A(2)(b) IS Regs
JSA Reg 1(3), definition of 'long-term patient', and Sch 1 paras 12(5)(a) and 15A(2)(b) JSA Regs
ESA Schs 4 para 7(2)(a) and 5 para 13 ESA Regs
HB Sch 3 para 15(2) HB Regs
CTB Sch 3 para 15(2) CTB Regs
34 **HB** Sch 3 para 15(2) HB Regs
CTB Sch 3 para 15(2) CTB Regs
35 **IS** Reg 2(1), definition of 'long-term patient', and Sch 2 paras 10(6), 11(2)(b) and 13A(2)(c) IS Regs
JSA Reg 1(3), definition of 'long-term patient', and Sch 1 paras 12(5)(b), 13(2)(b), 15A(2)(c), 20F(5), 20G(2)(b) and 20IA(2)(b) JSA Regs
ESA Schs 4 para 7(2)(b) and 5 para 13 ESA Regs
36 **IS** Reg 2(1), definition of long-term patient', and Sch 2 paras 10(6), 11(2)(c) and 13A(2)(d) IS Regs
JSA Reg 1(3), definition of 'long-term patient', and Sch 1 paras 12(5)(c), 13(2)(c), 15A(2)(c), 20F(5), 20(G)(a) and 20IA(2)(a) JSA Regs
37 Sch 5 para 13 ESA Regs
38 **HB** Sch 3 para 15(2) HB Regs
CTB Sch 3 para 15(2) CTB Regs
39 **HB** Sch 3 paras 15(1) and 16(a) HB Regs; Sch 3 paras 7 and 8(a) HB(SPC) Regs
CTB Sch 1 paras 15(1) and 16(a) CTB Regs; Sch 1 paras 7 and 8(a) CTB(SPC) Regs
40 **IS** Reg 2(1), definition of 'long-term patient', and Sch 2 paras 13A(2)(a) and 14(2) IS Regs
JSA Reg 1(3), definition of 'long-term patient', and Sch 1 paras 15A(2)(a) and 16(2) JSA Regs
41 R(H) 9/05
42 **IS** Sch 3 para 18(7)(g) IS Regs
JSA Sch 2 para 17(7)(g) JSA Regs
ESA Sch 6 para 19(7)(g) ESA Regs
PC Sch 2 para 14(7)(e) SPC Regs
HB Reg 74(7)(f) HB Regs; reg 55(7)(f) HB(SPC) Regs
CTB Reg 58(7)(d) CTB Regs; reg 42(7)(d) CTB(SPC) Regs
43 Sch 5 para 13 ESA Regs
44 Reg 2(2) and (3) SS(HIP) Regs

3. **People in care homes and similar accommodation**

45 ss67(2) and 72(8) SSCBA 1992; regs 7 and 8(1) SS(AA) Regs; regs 9 and 10(1) SS(DLA) Regs
46 ss67(3) and 72(9) SSCBA 1992
47 Reg 8(3) SS(AA) Regs; reg 10(3) SS(DLA) Regs
48 Reg 25 SS(C&P) Regs
49 Reg 7(2) SS(AA) Regs; reg 9(2) SS(DLA) Regs
50 CDLA/1465/1998; CDLA/2127/2000
51 CA/2985/1997
52 ss67(4) and 72(10) SSCBA 1992; reg 7(3) SS(AA) Regs; reg 9(6) SS(DLA) Regs
53 R(DLA) 2/06
54 Reg 8(4) and (5) SS(AA) Regs; reg 10(6) and (7) SS(DLA) Regs
55 Reg 9(3) SS(DLA) Regs
56 Reg 9(4)(a) and (b) and (5) SS(DLA) Regs
57 Reg 9(4)(c) SS(DLA) Regs
58 Reg 8(6) SS(AA) Regs; reg 10(8) SS(DLA) Regs; *Steane v CAO and Secretary of State*, 24 July 1996 (CA), reported as R(A) 3/96
59 R(A) 1/02; CA/3800/2006; *CAO v Creighton and others*, 15 December 1999 (NICA), reported as R 1/00 (AA); *SSWP v DA* [2009] UKUT 214 (AAC)
60 *SSWP v JL (DLA)* [2011] UKUT 293 (AAC)
61 Reg 7(4) SS(AA) Regs; reg 9(7) SS(DLA) Regs

62 Reg 7(5) and (6) SS(AA) Regs; reg 9(8) and (9) SS(DLA) Regs
63 Reg 8(2) SS(AA) Regs; reg 10(5) SS(DLA) Regs
64 **IS** Reg 2(1) IS Regs
JSA Reg 1(3) JSA Regs
ESA Reg 2(1) ESA Regs
PC Reg 1(2) SPC Regs
HB Reg 2(1) HB Regs; reg 2(1) HB(SPC) Regs
CTB Reg 2(1) CTB Regs; reg 2(1) CTB(SPC) Regs
65 *SA v SSWP (IS)* [2010] UKUT 345 (AAC)
66 Reg 12(c) SPC Regs
67 **IS** Reg 53(1A), (1B) and (1C) IS Regs
JSA Reg 116(1A), (1B) and (1C) JSA Regs
ESA Reg 118(2), (3) and (4) ESA Regs
HB Reg 52(3)-(5), (8) and (9) HB Regs
68 Sch 3A para 3(h) SS&CS(DA) Regs
69 **IS** Sch 3 para 3(8)-(12) IS Regs
JSA Sch 2 para 3(8)-(12) JSA Regs
ESA Sch 6 para 5(8)-(12) ESA Regs
PC Sch 2 para 4(8)-(12) SPC Regs
HB Reg 7(11)-(13), (16) and (17) HB Regs; reg 7(11)-(13), (16) and (17) HB(SPC) Regs
CTB Reg 8(2)-(4) CTB Regs; reg 8(2)-(4) CTB(SPC) Regs
70 *SSWP v Selby District Council and Bowman* [2006] EWCA Civ 271, 13 February 2006, reported as R(H) 4/06
71 **IS** Reg 16(3)(e) IS Regs
JSA Reg 78(3)(d) JSA Regs
ESA Reg 156(4)(d) ESA Regs
PC Reg 5(1)(b) SPC Regs
HB Reg 21(2) HB Regs; reg 21(2) HB(SPC) Regs
CTB Reg 11(1) CTB Regs; reg 11(1) CTB(SPC) Regs
72 Appendix to CIS/4934/1997; CIS/4965/1997; CIS/5232/1997; CIS/3767/1997
73 **IS** Reg 16(1) and (2) IS Regs
JSA Reg 78(1)-(2) JSA Regs
ESA Reg 156(1)-(3) ESA Regs
PC Reg 5(1)(a) SPC Regs
HB Reg 21(1) and (2) HB Regs; reg 21(1) and (2) HB(SPC) Regs
CTB Reg 11(1) CTB Regs; reg 11(1) CTB(SPC) Regs
74 CIS/1544/2001
75 Reg 9(1)(k) HB Regs; reg 9(1)(k) HB(SPC) Regs
76 Sch 3 para 9 HB&CTB(CP) Regs
77 HB/CTB Circular A20/05
78 Reg 1A(4) and (5) SFCWP Regs
79 Regs 1 and 2 SFWFP Regs

4. **Prisoners**

80 **ESA** Reg 160(3) ESA Regs
Other benefits Reg 2(3) SS(GB) Regs
81 Reg 3(1) and (2) SSP Regs; reg 9 SMP Regs; regs 18(c) and 27(1)(c) SPP&SAP(G) Regs; reg 21(1)(c) ASPP(G) Regs
82 **ESA** s18(4)(b) WRA 2007; reg 160 ESA Regs
Other benefits s113(1)(b) SSCBA 1992; reg 2 SS(GB) Regs
83 s113(1)(b) SSCBA 1992
84 Regs 10(2)(d) and 12 and Sch 2 para 7(b)(ii) SSB(Dep) Regs; reg 14 SS(IB-ID) Regs
85 **ESA** s18(4)(b) WRA 2007; reg 160(6) ESA Regs
Other benefits s113(1)(b) and Sch 9 para 1 SSCBA 1992; reg 2(9) and (10) SS(GB) Regs; reg 10(2)(d) and Sch 2 para 7(b)(ii) SSB(Dep) Regs; R(S) 8/79
86 **ESA** Reg 160(3), (4) and (4A) ESA Regs
Other benefits Reg 2(3), (4) and (4A) SS(GB) Regs
All CSS/239/2007
87 Sch 5 para 12 ESA Regs suggests the rule does not apply, but this may be a drafting error.
88 **ESA** Reg 160(1), (2) and (5)(c) ESA Regs
Other benefits Reg 2(2) and (8)(c) SS(GB) Regs
All R(S) 1/71
89 **ESA** Reg 161 ESA Regs
Other benefits Reg 3 SS(GB) Regs
90 CS/541/1950
91 Regs 2(6) and (7) and 3(1) SS(GB) Regs
92 Reg 2(7) SS(GB) Regs; para 12091 DMG
93 Reg 2(2) and (7) SS(GB) Regs
94 s113(1)(b) SSCBA 1992. Child benefit is not in Parts 2-5 of that Act.
95 Reg 2(5) SS(GB) Regs
96 Sch 9 para 1(a) SSCBA 1992; regs 16 and 17 CB Regs
97 **IS** Reg 21(3) IS Regs
JSA Reg 85(4) JSA Regs
ESA Reg 69(2) ESA Regs
PC Reg 1(2) SPC Regs
HB Reg 7(14) and (16)(c)(i) HB Regs; reg 7(14) and (16)(c)(i) HB(SPC) Regs
CTB Reg 8(4)(a) and (5) CTB Regs; reg 8(4)(a) and (5) CTB(SPC) Regs
98 **IS** Schs 1B para 22, 3 para 3(11) and (12) and 7 para 8 IS Regs
ESA Schs 5 para 3 and 6 para 5(11) and (12) ESA Regs
PC Reg 6(2)(a), (3), (6)(c), (7), (9) and (10) SPC Regs
99 Reg 7(3) SPC Regs

100 Reg 6(3)(b) and (4) SPC Regs
101 **IS** Reg 21(3ZA)-(3ZC) and Sch 7 para 2A IS Regs
ESA Reg 69(3)-(5) and Sch 5 para 12 ESA Regs
PC Reg 8 and Sch 3 para 2 SPC Regs
All *JB v SSWP (IS)* [2010] UKUT 263 (AAC)
102 **IS** Sch 3 para 3(11)(c)(i) and (12) IS Regs
ESA Sch 6 para 5(11)c)(i) and (12) ESA Regs
PC Sch 2 para 4(11)(c)(i) and (12) SPC Regs
HB Reg 7(16)(c)(i) and (17) HB Regs; reg 7(16)(c)(i) and (17) HB(SPC) Regs
CTB Reg 8(3)(c) and (4)(a) CTB Regs; reg 8(3)(c) and (4)(a) CTB(SPC) Regs
103 **HB** Reg 7(13) HB Regs; reg 7(13) HB(SPC) Regs
CTB Reg 8(3)(b) CTB Regs; reg 8(3)(b) CTB(SPC) Regs
104 CSH/499/2006
105 **IS** Reg 21(3) and Sch 7 para 8(a) IS Regs
JSA Reg 85(4) JSA Regs
ESA Reg 69(2) and Sch 5 para 3(a) ESA Regs
PC Regs 1(2) and 6 SPC Regs
106 **HB** Reg 7(14) and (15) HB Regs; reg 7(14) and (15) HB(SPC) Regs; R(IS) 17/93
CTB Reg 8(5) and (6) CTB Regs; reg 8(5) and (6) CTB(SPC) Regs
107 Reg 7(7) HB Regs; reg 7(7) HB(SPC) Regs; paras A3/3.430-32 GM
108 **IS** Sch 3 para 18(7)(g) IS Regs
JSA Sch 2 para 17(7)(g) JSA Regs
ESA Sch 6 para 19(7)(g) ESA Regs
PC Sch 2 para 14(7)(e) SPC Regs
HB Reg 74(7)(f) HB Regs; reg 55(7)(f) HB(SPC) Regs
CTB Reg 58(8)(b) CTB Regs; reg 42(8)(b) CTB(SPC) Regs
109 **IS** Reg 16(3)(b) IS Regs
JSA Reg 78(3)(b) JSA Regs
ESA Reg 156(4) ESA Regs
PC Reg 5(1)(c)(ii) and (iii) SPC Regs
110 Reg 21(2) HB Regs; reg 21(2) HB(SPC) Regs
111 Reg 11(1) CTB Regs; reg 11(1) CTB(SPC) Regs
112 **HB** Reg 28 HB Regs; reg 31 HB(SPC) Regs
CTB Reg 18 CTB Regs; reg 21 CTB(SPC) Regs
113 Note that *Stewart v SSAP* [2011] EWCA Civ 907, 29 July 2011, decided that exclusion of prisoners from entitlement to a funeral expenses payment did not breach the Human Rights Act 1998.
114 **IS** Reg 16(2) IS Regs
JSA Reg 78(2) JSA Regs
ESA Reg 156(3) ESA Regs
PC Reg 5(1)(a) SPC Regs
HB Reg 21(1) and (2) HB Regs; reg 21(1) and (2) HB(SPC) Regs
CTB Reg 11(1) CTB Regs; reg 11(1) CTB(SPC) Regs
115 Reg 11(1) CTB Regs; reg 11(1) CTB(SPC) Regs
116 **IS** Sch 7 para 9(a)(v) IS Regs
JSA Schs 5 para 5(a)(vi) and 5A para 4(a)(vi) JSA Regs
ESA Sch 5 para 4(a)(v) ESA Regs
117 Reg 7(5) HB Regs; reg 7(5) HB(SPC) Regs
118 **IS** Sch 3 para 3(11)(c)(i) and (12) IS Regs
JSA Sch 2 para 2(11)(c)(i) and (12) JSA Regs
ESA Sch 6 para 5(11)(c)(i) and (12) ESA Regs
PC Sch 2 para 4(11)(c)(i) and (12) SPC Regs
HB Reg 7(16)(c)(i) and (17) HB Regs; reg 7(16)(c)(i) and (17) HB(SPC) Regs
CTB Reg 8(3)(c) and (4)(a) CTB Regs; reg 8(3)(c) and (4)(a) CTB(SPC) Regs
119 Regs 14(1)(h) and 19(1)(h) JSA Regs
120 **IS** Reg 48(7) IS Regs
JSA Reg 110(7) JSA Regs
ESA Reg 112(6) ESA Regs

5. **People without accommodation**

121 This rule was challenged under the Human Rights Act, but the Court decided the rules did not conflict with it: *R(RJM) v SSWP* [2008] UKHL 63
122 **IS** Sch 7 para 6 IS Regs
JSA Schs 5 para 3 and 5A para 2 JSA Regs
ESA Sch 5 para 1 ESA Regs
123 paras 24157 and 54157 DMG
124 paras 24158-59 and 54158-59 DMG
125 paras 24159-60 and 54159-60 DMG; R(IS) 23/98
126 paras 24162 and 54162 DMG
127 Reg 18(3)(j) JSA Regs

6. **People involved in a trade dispute**

128 **IS** Reg 5(4) IS Regs
JSA Reg 52(2) and (2A) JSA Regs
129 paras 32678-79 DMG

130 **IS** Reg 6(4)(b) IS Regs
JSA Reg 53(g) and (gg) JSA Regs
131 Sch 1B para 20 IS Regs
132 ss14, 15A and 35(1), definition of 'week', JSA 1995
133 Reg 47(3)(e) JSA Regs
134 ss15 and 15A JSA 1995; reg 3D and Sch A1 para 17 JSA Regs
135 s126 SSCBA 1992; ss14 and 35(1), definition of 'trade dispute', JSA 1995
136 s14(1) and (2) JSA 1995
137 R(U) 1/65; paras 32121-25 and 32160-61 DMG
138 Regs 13(2)(a)(i) and 15(a)(i) SS&CS(DA) Regs
139 Sch 2 paras 13 and 19 SS&CS(DA) Regs
140 R(U) 7/58; R(U) 1/87
141 para 32107 DMG
142 s14(4) and (5) JSA 1995; CU/66/1986(T)
143 R(U) 4/62; R(U) 1/70
144 s14(1)(b) JSA 1995
145 *Presho v Insurance Officer* [1984] (HL) (see R(U) 1/84); *Cartlidge v CAO* [1986] 2 All ER 1 (CA); R(U) 1/87
146 s14(3) JSA 1995
147 R(U) 6/74
148 **IS** ss126(1) and (2) and 127(a) SSCBA 1992
JSA s15(4) JSA 1995; reg 171 JSA Regs
149 Reg 26(4) SS(C&P) Regs
150 s126(3)(a) and (d)(i) SSCBA 1992
151 s126(3)(b) and (d)(ii) SSCBA 1992
152 **IS** s126(3)(c) SSCBA 1992
JSA ss15(2)(a) and (b) and 15A(4) and (5) JSA 1995
153 **IS** s126(5)(b) and (7) SSCBA 1992
JSA ss15(2)(d) and 15A(5) JSA 1995; reg 172 JSA Regs
154 **IS** Sch 9 para 34 IS Regs
JSA Sch 7 para 36 JSA Regs
155 **IS** s126(5)(a)(ii) SSCBA 1992; reg 48(2) IS Regs
JSA ss15(2)(c)(i) and 15A(5) JSA 1995; reg 110(2) JSA Regs
156 **IS** s126(5)(a)(i) SSCBA 1992
JSA ss15(2)(c)(ii) and 15A(5) JSA 1995
157 **IS** Reg 41(3) and Schs 9 para 28 and 10 para 17 IS Regs
JSA Reg 104(3) and Schs 7 para 29 and 8 para 22 JSA Regs
158 **IS** Reg 48(9), (10)(a) and (c) and Schs 9 paras 15(3)(b) and 39, and 10 para 22 IS Regs
JSA Reg 110(9) and (10)(a) and (c) and Schs 7 paras 15(3)(b) and 41, and 8 para 27 JSA Regs
159 **IS** Reg 42(4) and Sch 9 para 21 IS Regs
JSA Reg 105(10) and Sch 7 para 22 JSA Regs
160 **IS** Reg 35(1)(d) IS Regs
JSA Reg 98(1)(c) JSA Regs
161 **IS** Reg 48(5) and (6) IS Regs
JSA Reg 110(5) and (6) JSA Regs
162 Sch 11 paras 2(g) and 7 SSCBA 1992
163 R(SSP) 1/86
164 **SMP** Reg 13 SMP Regs
SPP/SAP Reg 35 SPP&SAP(G) Regs; reg 27 ASPP(G) Regs; s35 JSA 1995
165 Note, however, that reg 13 SMP Regs was not amended when the JSA 1995 came into force.
166 s91 SSCBA 1992; s14 JSA 1995
167 s126(1) and (2) SSCBA 1992; s14 JSA 1995; reg 171 JSA Regs; reg 3 SFM&FE Regs; SF Dirs 8, 17 and 26
168 Regs 3(1) and 6 SFM&FE Regs; s126 SSCBA 1992; s14 JSA 1995
169 SF Dir 26; s14 JSA 1995
170 SF Dir 8(1)(b); s14 JSA 1995
171 SF Dir 17(1) and (2)(a); s14 JSA 1995
172 Reg 43(2)(b)and Sch 6 para 2(8) ESA Regs
173 *R v HBRB London Borough of Ealing ex parte Saville* [1986] HLR 349
174 s127 SSCBA 1992
175 Reg 6(4)(b)and Sch 1B para 20 IS Regs
176 s127(b) SSCBA 1992
177 s127(a) SSCBA 1992; regs 35(1)(d), 41(3) and (4), 42(4) and 48(6) and (10) and Schs 9 paras 15, 21, 28 and 39, and 10 para 17 IS Regs
178 s127(c) SSCBA 1992; reg 18 SS(PAOR) Regs
179 Reg 26 SS(PAOR) Regs
180 Reg 19(3)-(5) SS(PAOR) Regs
181 Reg 22(2)-(4) SS(PAOR) Regs
182 Reg 27(2) SS(PAOR) Regs
183 Regs 20, 21 and 22(5)-(6) SS(PAOR) Regs
184 Reg 28 SS(PAOR) Regs
185 Reg 29 SS(PAOR) Regs
186 Regs 27 and 29 SS(PAOR) Regs
187 Reg 27(5) SS(PAOR) Regs

Part 5

Common benefit rules

Chapter 31

Work and benefits

This chapter covers:

Key facts

- You cannot usually qualify for income support (IS) or income-based jobseeker's allowance (JSA) if you (or your partner) are in full-time paid work.
- You cannot qualify for contribution-based JSA if *you* are in full-time paid work.
- You cannot qualify for employment and support allowance (ESA) or IS if you are claiming on the basis that you are incapable of work if you do *any* work, unless this is work you may do while claiming (called 'permitted work') . You cannot qualify for income-related ESA if your partner is in full-time paid work.
- Your eligibility for housing benefit, council tax benefit and pension credit is not affected if you or your partner are in full-time paid work.
- Earnings affect the amount of all of your means-tested benefits.
- Entitlement to non-means-tested benefits and tax credits is affected by issues to do with work and employment.

Future changes: April 2013 and after

Major changes are taking place that affect the benefits and tax credits system (see Chapter 2).

- From April 2013, total benefit payments to households will be 'capped' (see p25). There will be limited exceptions, including households in which someone is entitled to working tax credit – ie, s/he is in full-time paid work.
- From October 2013, you will be able to qualify for universal credit if you are working full or part time and also if you are out of work.

See CPAG's *Welfare Rights Bulletin* for updates.

1. The full-time paid work rule

Work affects income support (IS), jobseeker's allowance (JSA), employment and support allowance (ESA), housing benefit (HB), council tax benefit (CTB) and pension credit (PC) in different ways. If you or your partner (or a non-dependant) work full time and are paid for the work, you count as being in what the DWP calls 'remunerative work'. This is called 'full-time paid work' in this *Handbook*.

- If you are in full-time paid work, you cannot usually qualify for IS or JSA.[1] **Note:** you cannot qualify for IS based on your incapacity for work in any week in which you do *any* work (even if it is part time), unless it is work you may do while claiming (see p735).
- Unless it is work that you may do while claiming (see p214), you cannot qualify for ESA in any week in which you do *any* work and are paid (or expect to be paid) for the work. You count as being in what the DWP calls 'remunerative work'. This is called 'paid work' in this *Handbook* (see p719).[2]
- If your partner is in full-time paid work, you cannot usually qualify for IS, *income-based* JSA or *income-related* ESA.[3] Your partner's working hours do not affect your entitlement to *contribution-based* JSA or *contributory ESA*.
- Your eligibility for HB, CTB and PC is not affected if you or your partner are in full-time paid work. For HB and CTB, however, this can affect the way your income is calculated – eg, whether you can get an additional earnings disregard (see pp915 and 947) or a childcare costs disregard (see pp915 and 947).
- If you have a non-dependant living with you, the amount of the non-dependant deduction made from your IS, income-based JSA, income-related ESA or PC housing costs, and from your HB and CTB, can be higher if your non-dependant is in full-time paid work (see pp869, 123 and 265).

See p719 for what counts as paid work and p720 for how your hours are calculated. 'Work' includes self-employment and work which is done from home. In some circumstances you may be treated as not in full-time paid work even if you are (see p725). In others, you may be treated as if you are in full-time paid work when you are not (see p723).

Note: income from work affects your entitlement to IS, income-based JSA, income-related ESA, PC, HB and CTB and you might not satisfy the means test.

Example

Della works 15 hours a week and so can qualify for IS unless her income is too high. For HB or CTB, it does not matter how many hours she works. However, if she is not getting IS, her income may affect the amount she can get.

If you or your partner are in full-time paid work you might be able to claim working tax credit (WTC). The rules on what counts as full-time paid work for

WTC are different from those for IS/JSA/income-related ESA. So you may be able to choose whether to claim IS/JSA/income-related ESA or WTC. You may be able to claim both IS/JSA/ESA/PC and WTC. For IS and JSA, if you are a single claimant, this only applies in limited situations – eg, if you are a 'term-time only' worker or you are off sick and getting statutory sick pay. For ESA, this only applies if your partner counts as in full-time paid work for WTC purposes; you cannot qualify for ESA if *you* work, unless it is work you may do while claiming (see p214). See p729 for factors to consider.

What counts as full-time work

For IS, JSA, HB and CTB, **you** count as in 'full-time work' if you work 16 hours or more a week.[4] **Your partner** counts as in 'full-time work':

- for IS, income-based JSA (but not joint-claim JSA) and income-related ESA, if s/he works 24 hours or more a week;[5]
- for HB and CTB, if s/he works 16 hours or more a week.[6]

For all the means-tested benefits, **your non-dependant** counts as in full-time paid work if s/he works 16 hours or more a week.[7] See p720 for how the hours are calculated.

Note:

- For ESA, there is no rule for when *you* count as in full-time work because you cannot qualify for ESA if you do any number of hours of work, unless it is 'permitted work' (see p214).
- For PC, there is no rule for when you or your partner count as in full-time work because it does not matter how many hours you (or s/he) work.
- For joint-claim JSA, you do not have to make a joint claim with your partner if s/he works 16 or more but less than 24 hours a week.[8]
- For HB and CTB, you and your partner may have to work more than 16 hours to benefit from an additional earnings disregard (see pp915 and 947).

What counts as paid work

'Paid work' includes work for which you are paid or expect to be paid – ie, you expect to get payment for the work you are doing, now or at some date in the future, even if no payment is finally made.[9] The question of whether or not you are paid or are working in expectation of payment has to be decided at the time the work is done, not, for example, at the end of the year or accounting period.[10] Note the following.

- You must have a real likelihood of getting payment, not just a hope or desire to make money – eg, a self-employed writer who has never sold a manuscript and has no publication agreement may be working without real expectation of payment and so is not in full-time paid work even if s/he spends a lot of time writing.[11]

- Some of the initial work necessary to set up a business may not count as paid work if it is unpaid preparatory work done in the hope of further work that will be paid.[12]
- If you have a business but it is not yet making money or has ceased to make a profit, you may count as working in expectation of payment if you are making drawings against future profit or if the business is likely to yield profit in the future. Ultimately, it depends on how viable your business is. If there is no realistic possibility of it yielding a profit, the decision maker is likely to want to know why you are working for nothing.[13]
- Paid work includes work for which you receive payment in kind (such as free meals or accommodation or free produce for farmworkers).[14]

How your hours are calculated

When calculating your (or your partner's or non-dependant's) hours, include all the hours you (or they) actually work for which payment is made or which are worked in expectation of payment. If you (or they) do more than one job, add the total hours from each together. If routine paid overtime is done, include those hours. If work is casual or intermittent – eg, you are a seasonal worker who works in the summer but you are unemployed the rest of the year, you can argue that it is only the hours worked that are relevant (but see p722 for 'term-time only' workers).[15] Bear in mind that:

- if your hours fluctuate, the rules specify how your hours are averaged (see p721);
- for IS, JSA and income-related ESA only, paid lunch hours and breaks count towards the total hours;[16]
- for PC, HB and CTB, the rules do not say how to calculate the hours of work unless these fluctuate. However, for PC, the DWP says you should only count the hours for which payment is made or which are worked in expectation of payment, including overtime, but not including paid breaks – eg, lunch or tea breaks. Your word should be accepted unless there is reason for doubt;[17]
- for JSA only, the hours that you (or your partner or non-dependant) spend caring for someone in the circumstances that would allow you to claim IS as a carer (see p348) are ignored unless you are employed and are being paid to act as a carer.[18] For IS and ESA, although hours are not ignored, you and your partner (for IS), and your partner (for ESA) are treated as not in full-time paid work in this situation (see p725).

If you are unsure if you (or your partner) are in full-time paid work, see p723. Appeal if you think the average hours have been calculated unfairly if this means you cannot claim the benefit or tax credit you want. Work out first whether you are better off claiming IS/JSA/income-related ESA or WTC (see p729). Likewise, appeal if your non-dependant's hours have been calculated unfairly and the DWP or local authority is making a non-dependant deduction that is too high.

If your hours fluctuate

If your (or your partner's or your non-dependant's) hours fluctuate, an average of the weekly hours is calculated as follows.

Regular pattern of work

If there is a regular pattern of work (a 'work cycle'), the average hours worked throughout each cycle is used – eg, if you regularly work three weeks on and one week off, your hours are the average over the four-week period.[19] Weeks when you are on paid holiday, or are absent from work without 'good cause' (see p724) or because you are off sick or on maternity, paternity or adoption leave, are disregarded.[20] **Note:**

- If you work casually or intermittently (eg, you are a seasonal worker who works in the summer but you are unemployed the rest of the year), you can argue that your 'work cycle' is that part of the year in which you are working and that you do not count as in full-time work when you are unemployed.[21]
- If you (or your partner or non-dependant) have a 'work cycle' that lasts a year with periods in which you do not work (eg, in an educational establishment):
  - for JSA and ESA, this rule applies. In practice, if the average hours of work you (or your partner) do over the whole cycle means you (or your partner) are not in full-time paid work, you can claim JSA or income-related ESA. However, you may only qualify during periods when your income is sufficiently low – eg, during unpaid summer holidays. You could also claim WTC if you (or your partner) work sufficient hours each week during term-time;
  - for IS, PC, HB and CTB, the 'term-time only' worker rule applies (see p722).

Example

Sheila is a school meals worker. She works 20 hours a week, 38 weeks of the year. She gets four weeks' paid holiday, but otherwise is not paid when she is not working at the school. Her average hours are calculated as follows:

20 hours x 38 weeks = 760 hours. 52 weeks – 4 weeks' paid holiday = 48 weeks.

760 hours divided by 48 weeks = 15.84 average hours a week.

Sheila can claim JSA if her income is low enough as she is not in full-time paid work for JSA purposes. She might also qualify for WTC. She cannot qualify for IS as the 'term-time only' worker rule applies and her hours during term time are too high.

No regular pattern of work

If there is no regular pattern of work (no recognisable 'work cycle'), an average of your hours is used. This is the average over the five weeks immediately before the date of your claim (or of a supersession decision for IS, JSA and, in respect of your partner's hours only, income-related ESA), or the average over a longer or a shorter period if this would give a fairer average.[22] The five-week period may not be appropriate if the average is distorted because, for example, you have done a short period of overtime that is not typical, or you have been off sick.[23]

No work pattern yet established

If you (or your partner or non-dependant) have not yet established a pattern of work (a 'work cycle'), the number of hours or average number of hours you are expected to work each week is used.[24] This may apply, for example, if you have just started work or your working arrangements have changed and your previous work cycle no longer applies. Once there is sufficient evidence to calculate your average hours, the decision can be revised or superseded.

'Term-time only' workers

For IS, PC, HB and CTB, if you have a regular pattern of work (a recognisable 'work cycle') that lasts for a year (eg, in a school or an educational establishment where you have periods of school holidays or similar vacations when you do not work), the 'term-time only' worker rule applies. The average number of hours in the periods when you are actually working (eg, during term time) determines whether you are in full-time paid work throughout the year.[25] People who work in schools, colleges or similar institutions and have long periods in which they do not work are affected by this rule.

In practice, if your average hours of work during term time mean you are in full-time paid work during term time, you also count as being in full-time paid work over the school holidays, even if you do no work and are not paid. This means:

- if you or your partner count as in full-time paid work, you cannot claim IS during the school holidays.
  You might be able to claim JSA or ESA. You can claim WTC if you normally work sufficient hours each week (see Chapter 53);[26]
- if your non-dependant counts as in full-time paid work, higher rate non-dependant deductions may apply.

Note that this rule can also apply to other seasonal workers. However, if you work casually or intermittently and are unemployed the rest of the year, you can argue that this rule does not apply to you.[27] If your contract comes to an end before a period of absence from work, you should not count as a term-time only worker, unless you are expected to start work again and there is some commitment by you and your employer that this will happen.[28]

Sometimes it might not be clear whether you have a 'work cycle' that lasts a year – eg, if you have only started your job recently or have a fixed-term contract that finishes at the end of the school term, or you are employed on a casual or relief basis.[29] It takes time before it can be said that you have a yearly work cycle.[30] However, if you have an indefinite contract to work in term-time only, the decision maker is likely to say that you have a yearly work cycle from the start.[31]

If you are unsure whether you are in full-time paid work

If you are unsure whether you or your partner (for IS and JSA) or your partner (for ESA) are working for 16/24 hours or more a week, you should make a claim in any event. If your situation then changes or it becomes clearer that the hours are low enough, provide details of the hours you have worked since you claimed. Provided you do this before the decision maker makes a decision, s/he should take the new information into account. If you are refused benefit but later your circumstances change, make a fresh claim.

Alternatively, if you are refused WTC because you or your partner do not count as in full-time paid work for WTC purposes and within 14 days of that decision you claim IS or JSA, your claim for IS or JSA can be backdated to the date you claimed WTC.[32] This rule does not apply to ESA. However, your ESA claim can be backdated for up to three months (see p190).

If your (or your partner's) circumstances change while you are claiming:

- IS, JSA or ESA, you may be uncertain about whether you (or your partner) now count as in full-time paid work – eg, if your average weekly hours change or you are now getting regular overtime. If it appears that you (or your partner) are now working 16/24 hours or more a week, report this to the DWP to avoid an overpayment. Also check to see if you qualify for WTC. Remember, you cannot qualify for ESA if *you* do *any* paid work, unless it is work you may do while claiming (see p214);
- HB or CTB, report this to the local authority. A change in your hours of work might affect your entitlement to an additional earnings, or a childcare costs disregard.

If your non-dependant's circumstances change while you are claiming HB or CTB (or help with housing costs in IS, income-based JSA, income-related ESA or PC), report this to the local authority (or DWP) to enable your non-dependant deduction to be adjusted.

2. People treated as in full-time paid work

You or your partner can be treated as being in full-time paid work, even if you are not, if:

- for income support (IS), jobseeker's allowance (JSA), housing benefit (HB) and council tax benefit (CTB), you or your partner (or for employment and support allowance (ESA), your partner) normally work full time, but are off work because of a **recognised, customary or other holiday** and there is a common

intention that the employment will be resumed once the holiday is over.[33] Whether you count as on holiday depends on your contractual or legal entitlement to holiday. You can argue that you only count as on holiday if you are paid for it.[34] However, for JSA, even if you do not count as in full-time paid work because you are on unpaid leave, you are likely to have difficulty persuading the DWP that you are available for and actively seeking work (see Chapter 20). Remember that in some cases, if you are a full-time 'term-time only' worker and your cycle of work lasts a year, you are treated as in full-time work during the school holidays (see p722);
- for IS, JSA, HB and CTB, you or your partner (or, for ESA, your partner) are **absent from full-time paid work without 'good cause'**.[35] What constitutes 'good cause' for these purposes is not defined in the rules but all of your circumstances should be taken into account. Whether or not your employer has authorised the absence is not conclusive, although if it is authorised it is likely that you have good cause;
- for IS and JSA, you or your partner stopped full-time paid work, but you are still **within the period covered by payment in lieu of earnings or wages, or certain holiday pay** (unless they can be disregarded). For ESA, this rule applies if you stopped paid work or if your partner stopped full-time paid work.[36]
  Note: most earnings and payments *are* disregarded if the employment ends before entitlement to IS, JSA or ESA starts; you (or your partner) are *not* treated as in full-time paid work and you can claim IS, JSA or ESA as soon as the work finishes. See p907 for details on payments when you stop work.

For IS, JSA, PC, HB and CTB, **your non-dependant** can also be treated as in full-time paid work under the rules above. For ESA, your non-dependant can also be treated as in full-time paid work if s/he normally works full-time but is off work because of a recognised, customary or other holiday, or s/he is away from work 'without good cause'.

If you or your partner are **involved in a trade dispute**:
- for IS, you are treated as being in full-time paid work for the first seven days;[37]
- for JSA, if you are the one involved in the dispute, you cannot qualify for JSA at all (see p701);
- for income-based JSA (not including joint-claim JSA), if your partner is the one involved in the trade dispute, s/he is treated as being in full-time paid work for the first seven days if s/he would not be entitled to JSA in her/his own right because of this. This does not apply if you were receiving income-based JSA when s/he became involved;[38]
- for joint-claim JSA, you (or s/he) are treated as being in full-time paid work for the first seven days. This does not apply if you were receiving joint-claim JSA when you or your partner became involved.[39]

See Chapter 30 for further information about entitlement to, and the amount of, IS or JSA during a trade dispute.

3. People treated as not in full-time paid work

There are situations when you (or your partner or non-dependant) are treated as not in full-time paid work, even if you actually are. For income support (IS), jobseeker's allowance (JSA) and employment and support allowance (ESA), see below. For housing benefit (HB), council tax benefit (CTB) and pension credit (PC), see p726.

Income support, jobseeker's allowance and employment and support allowance

For IS and JSA, you (and for IS, JSA and income-related ESA, your partner and your non-dependant) are treated as *not* being in full-time paid work if you (or s/he):[40]

- are on **maternity, adoption or paternity leave or are absent from work because you are sick,**[41] even if when you are not on leave or off sick you normally work 16/24 hours or more each week. You might also be able to claim working tax credit (WTC);
- are working on a training scheme and are **being paid a training allowance** under specific provisions;
- for JSA only, are **on Work Experience** (see p474) or are participating in **Mandatory Work Activity** (see p473) or a training or employment scheme under the **Employment, Skills and Enterprise Scheme** (see p471);
- are **a volunteer** (other than for a relative) or are working for a charity or voluntary organisation and are giving your services free (except for your expenses);
- are **providing care** for someone:
  - who is staying with you but who is not normally a member of your household and you receive payments from a health authority, local authority or voluntary organisation for caring for her/him;
  - for IS and ESA, in the circumstances described on p348. This means that any hours of work you do are ignored, not just the hours you spend caring. For JSA, although you are not treated as not being in full-time paid work, the hours you spend caring are ignored in this situation (see p720);
- are a **foster carer** (or in Scotland **a kinship carer**) receiving a payment for a child you are looking after from a local authority or voluntary organisation. Note that for WTC purposes, you can count as being in full-time paid work (see p1301). You may wish to consider how you would be better off financially;
- work as a **part-time firefighter, auxiliary coastguard, member of the Territorial Army or reserve forces, or member of a lifeboat crew;**

- are performing duties as a **local authority councillor**;
- for IS and ESA only, are working as a **childminder** in your (or her/his) home;
- are engaged in an activity for which you (or s/he) receive, or expect to receive, a **sports award** from the Sports Council and no other payment is made (or is expected to be made);
- are **receiving assistance in pursuing self-employment** while on a programme under s2 of the Employment and Training Act 1973 or s2 of the Enterprise and New Towns (Scotland) Act 1990 (or an Employment Zone programme – no longer offered);[42]
- for IS only, **qualify for mortgage interest run-on** (see p879);
- are doing **work** which is study **in connection with your course of education as a student**.[43]

Note: for ESA, *you* do not count as in paid work if you are doing work you may do while claiming (see p214).[44]

You, your partner or your non-dependant (for IS), and you or your partner (for JSA) and your partner or your non-dependant (for income-related ESA) can also be treated as not in full-time paid work if you (or s/he) are **involved in a trade dispute** (see p701).[45] For JSA (other than joint-claim JSA), if you are the one involved in the dispute, this rule does not apply; you cannot qualify for JSA if *you* are a person involved in a trade dispute. For IS and JSA, this rules only applies if you or your partner have been involved in the trade dispute for more than seven days. **Note:** for IS, you, your partner or non-dependant (and for ESA, your partner or non-dependant) are also treated as not in full-time paid work for the first 15 days following a return to work after having been involved in a trade dispute.

Rules before 25 January 2010

Before 25 January 2010, there were two other situations when, for IS and JSA, you (and for IS, JSA and ESA, your partner and your non-dependant) were treated as *not* being in full-time paid work. These were if you (or s/he) were in employment while living in a care home, an Abbeyfield home or an independent hospital, or if you (or s/he) were disabled and because of this your earnings or hours were 75 per cent lower than than would be expected for a person without a disability in a comparable job.[46] You can continue to count as not in full-time paid work if you were entitled to IS, JSA or ESA on this basis before 25 January 2010, even if you claimed it on or after that date.[47] See pp694–95 of the 2011/12 edition of this *Handbook* for further information. Note that you might also qualify for WTC. Check to see how you would be better off financially.

Housing benefit, council tax benefit and pension credit

You (or your partner or non-dependant) are treated as *not* being in full-time paid work if:[48]

- you (or your partner or non-dependant) are **on maternity, adoption or paternity leave or are absent from work because you are sick**, even if when you are not on leave or off sick you normally work 16 hours or more each week. However, for HB and CTB, you and your partner *can* count as in full-time paid work on such leave to enable you to get an earnings disregard for childcare costs (see pp915 and 947);
- the only payment you (or your partner or non-dependant) receive is a **sports award** from the Sports Council.

In addition, you (or your partner or non-dependant) are treated as *not* being in full-time paid work in a benefit week, if in that week you (or s/he) are on IS or income-based JSA (or for HB and CTB only, income-related ESA) for more than three days.[49] **Note:** the PC rule was not amended when ESA was introduced. It is not clear if this was intentional.

4. Self-employed people

Some self-employed people may work long hours for little financial reward, sometimes even making a loss. Nevertheless, if you are in full-time work and the work is done in expectation of payment, it counts as full-time paid work. The DWP counts payments from your business to meet living expenses, whether in cash or in kind, as payment for work unless the drawings are from the business capital.[50] If you simply invest in a business and do not help to run it you are not treated as self-employed.[51] Note the following.

- It is sometimes difficult to establish whether or not you are in full-time paid work – eg, if there is a lull in your business and there are periods when you have no work, or if you only work part of the year (eg, seasonally) on a regular basis. Whether or not you are in full-time paid work depends on if you are carrying out activities in connection with self-employment and, if so, how many hours you are doing in expectation of payment (using the rules described earlier in this chapter). If you have ceased trading, you should not count as in full-time paid work.[52]
- When calculating the number of hours you work each week, the decision maker counts all those necessary to run your business, including time you spend visiting potential customers, providing estimates, advertising or canvassing, bookkeeping and making trips to wholesalers and retailers, cleaning the business premises and doing research work – eg, if you are a writer.[53] The hours spent on services for which you are paid count, as well as other time which is essential for your business – eg, preparation time or unsuccessfully soliciting new customers.[54] The decision maker should accept your statement about the hours you work unless there is a reason for doubt.[55]

- The hours your partner spends helping you in your business do not affect your entitlement to *contribution-based* jobseeker's allowance (JSA) or *contributory* employment and support allowance (ESA), but if your partner works 24 hours a week or more you are not entitled to income support, *income-based* JSA or *income-related* ESA.

5. Non-means-tested benefits

Entitlement to non-means-tested benefits is affected by issues to do with work and employment. For the rules for a specific benefit, see the relevant chapter in this *Handbook*, but a summary of these is as follows.

- You cannot qualify for **carer's allowance** if you are 'gainfully employed' – ie, you earn more than a set amount each week.
- You cannot qualify for **benefits based on your incapacity for work or limited capability for work** (eg, incapacity benefit or contributory employment and support allowance) in any week you actually do any work unless this is work you may do while claiming – called 'permitted work'.
- To qualify for **industrial injuries benefits**, you must have been an employed earner when you had an accident or contracted a disease.
- You cannot qualify for **contribution-based jobseeker's allowance** (JSA) if you are in full-time paid work. The rules described in this chapter apply.
- To qualify for **maternity allowance** you must satisfy an employment condition.
- **Statutory sick pay, statutory maternity pay, statutory paternity pay and statutory adoption pay** are linked to you being employed (not self-employed) and in some cases you can get them even if your employment ends.
- You might not qualify for **benefits for your children** (ie, child benefit or guardian's allowance), or for an allowance in your housing benefit or council tax benefit (or, if still included, in your income support or income-based JSA) for a child who is aged 16 or over who does paid work for 24 hours a week or more.
- **Adult dependants' additions** are affected by the adult dependant's earnings.

Deciding whether you are an employed earner or self-employed also affects both your national insurance contributions (see Chapter 35) and the way your income from earnings is assessed (see Chapter 39).

6. Working tax credit and out-of-work benefits

Full-time paid work affects working tax credit (WTC). The rules for WTC are in Chapter 53. Because of differences in the rules for WTC and income support (IS), jobseeker's allowance (JSA) and employment and support allowance (ESA) or because decision makers at the DWP and HM Revenue and Customs interpret the rules differently, you may be refused WTC *and* IS, JSA or ESA. If this happens, appeal against both decisions and ask for the appeals to be heard together so the First-tier Tribunal can decide which benefit or tax credit is appropriate.

You might be able to claim WTC *or* IS/JSA/ESA if you have a partner and s/he works 16 hours or more a week. This is because your partner can work up to 24 hours a week if you are getting IS, income-based JSA or income-related ESA.[56] There is no limit on the number of hours your partner can work if you are getting contribution-based JSA or contributory ESA.

If you or your partner are (for IS), or your partner is (for ESA) a **childminder** working from home, you (or s/he) are treated as not in full-time paid work (see p725). This also applies if you or your partner are (for IS and JSA) or your partner is (for ESA) a **foster carer** or **kinship carer**. You may, therefore, be able to claim either IS/JSA/ESA or WTC if you (or your partner) work 16 hours or more a week. There are also generous rules on the calculation of income (see Chapter 40).

In some situations you might be able to claim both IS/income-based JSA/income-related ESA and WTC. For example, if you are a single claimant, you might be able to claim IS or income-based JSA and WTC if you are a 'term-time only' worker or are off sick and getting statutory sick pay. If you are a member of a couple, you might be able to claim income-related ESA and WTC if your partner is working 16 or more, but less than 24, hours a week. However, whether you can be paid IS, income-based JSA or income-related ESA with WTC depends on your income.

Note:

- WTC counts in full as income for IS, income-based JSA and income-related ESA.
- Only taxable JSA and contributory ESA count as income for WTC. Otherwise, IS, JSA and income-related ESA are disregarded.[57]

Choosing which benefit or tax credit to claim

If you can choose whether to claim IS, JSA, income-related ESA or WTC, check which passported benefits you lose or gain (see p5). Also consider the following.

- You get free school lunches if you are getting IS, income-based JSA or income-related ESA, but (generally) not if you are getting WTC (see p14).

- If you claim IS, income-based JSA or income-related ESA, you can get help with your housing costs (see Chapter 38). You cannot get help with housing costs with WTC .
- There is a capital limit for IS, income-based JSA and income-related ESA, but not for WTC.
- You can get help with your childcare costs if you claim WTC, but not if you claim IS, JSA or ESA.
- If you and your partner are responsible for any children and one of you works at least 16 hours a week, your hours are added together to work out if you can get a 30-hour element in your WTC (see p1311).

Notes

1. **The full-time paid work rule**

1 s124(1)(c) SSCBA 1992; s1(2)(e) JSA 1995
2 Sch 1 para 6(1)(e) WRA 2007; regs 40 and 41 ESA Regs
3 s124(1)(c) SSCBA 1992; s3(1)(e) JSA 1995; Sch 1 para 6(1)(f) WRA 2007
4 **IS** Reg 5 IS Regs
JSA Reg 51 JSA Regs
HB Reg 6(1) HB Regs; reg 6(1) HB(SPC) Regs
CTB Reg 6(1) CTB Regs; reg 6(1) CTB(SPC) Regs
5 **IS** Reg 5(1A) IS Regs
JSA Reg 51(1)(b) JSA Regs
ESA Reg 42(1) ESA Regs
6 **HB** Reg 6(1) HB Regs; reg 6(1) HB(SPC) Regs
CTB Reg 6(1) CTB Regs; reg 6(1) CTB(SPC) Regs
7 **IS** Regs 2(1) and 5 IS Regs
JSA Reg 51(1)(c) JSA Regs
ESA Sch 6 para 2(1) ESA Regs
HB Reg 6(1) HB Regs; reg 6(1) HB(SPC) Regs
CTB Reg 6(1) CTB Regs; reg 6(1) CTB(SPC) Regs
PC Sch 2 para 2(1) SPC Regs
8 Reg 3E(2)(g) JSA Regs
9 R(IS) 5/95; *Fiore v CAO*, 20 June 1995
10 *CAO v Ellis*, 15 February 1995 (CA), reported as R(IS) 22/95; CTC/626/2001
11 R(IS) 1/93
12 *Kevin Smith v CAO*, 11 October 1994 (CA), reported as R(IS) 21/95
13 *CAO v Ellis*, 15 February 1995 (CA), reported as R(IS) 22/95; CIS/434/1994
14 CFC/33/1993; R(FIS) 1/83
15 R(JSA) 1/07
16 **IS** Reg 5(7) IS Regs
JSA Reg 51(3)(a) JSA Regs
ESA Regs 42(2) and 45(9) and Sch 6 para 2(7) ESA Regs
17 Ch78 App5 paras 21, 23, 30 and 47 DMG
18 Reg 51(3)(c) JSA Regs
19 **IS** Reg 5(2)(b)(i) IS Regs
JSA Reg 51(2)(b)(i) JSA Regs
ESA Regs 42(2) and 45(8)(b)(i) and Sch 6 para 2(2)(a) ESA Regs
PC Sch 2 para 2(4) SPC Regs
HB Reg 6(2)(a) HB Regs; reg 6(2)(a) HB(SPC) Regs
CTB Reg 6(2)(a) CTB Regs; reg 6(2)(a) CTB(SPC) Regs
20 R(JSA) 5/03
21 R(JSA) 1/07

22 para 20322 DMG
IS Reg 5(2)(b)(ii) IS Regs
JSA Reg 51(2)(b)(ii) JSA Regs
ESA Regs 42(2) and 45(8)(b)(ii) and Sch 6 para 2(2)(b) ESA Regs
PC Sch 2 para 2(2)(b) SPC Regs
HB Reg 6(2)(b) HB Regs; reg 6(2)(b) HB(SPC) Regs
CTB Reg 6(2)(b) CTB Regs; reg 6(2)(b) CTB(SPC) Regs
23 CFC/2963/2001
24 **IS** Reg 5(2)(a) IS Regs
JSA Reg 51(2)(a) JSA Regs
ESA Regs 42(2) and 45(8)(a) and Sch 6 para 2(3) ESA Regs
PC Sch 2 para 2(4) SPC Regs
HB Reg 6(4) HB Regs; reg 6(4) HB(SPC) Regs
CTB Reg 6(4) CTB Regs; reg 6(4) CTB(SPC) Regs
All R(IS) 8/95
25 **IS** Regs 2(2)(b)(i) and 5(3B) IS Regs
PC Sch 2 para 2(3) SPC Regs
HB Reg 6(3) HB Regs; reg 6(3) HB(SPC) Regs
CTB Reg 6(3) CTB Regs; reg 6(3) CTB(SPC) Regs
All *Stafford and Banks v CAO* [2001] UKHL 33 (HL), reported as R(IS) 15/01
26 Reg 7 WTC(EMR) Regs
27 R(JSA) 1/07
28 CJSA/3832/2006
29 R(JSA) 8/03
30 CIS/914/1997; CJSA/2759/1998
31 R(JSA) 5/02
32 Reg 6(28) SS(C&P) Regs

2. People treated as in full-time paid work

33 **IS** Reg 5(3) IS Regs
JSA Reg 52(1) JSA Regs
ESA Reg 42(3) and Sch 6 para 2(4) ESA Regs
PC Sch 2 para 2(5) SPC Regs
HB Reg 6(5) HB Regs; reg 6(5) HB(SPC) Regs
CTB Reg 6(5) CTB Regs; reg 6(5) CTB(SPC) Regs
All R(U) 1/62
34 R(JSA) 5/03; para 20309 and Ch78 App 5 paras 73 and 74 DMG
35 **IS** Reg 5(3) IS Regs
JSA Reg 52(1) JSA Regs
ESA Reg 42(3) and Sch 6 para 2(4) ESA Regs
PC Sch 2 para 2(5) SPC Regs
HB Reg 6(5) HB Regs; reg 6(5) HB(SPC) Regs
CTB Reg 6(5) CTB Regs; reg 6(5) CTB(SPC) Regs
36 **IS** Reg 5(5) and (5A) IS Regs
JSA Reg 52(3) and (3A) JSA Regs
ESA Regs 41(2) and (3) and 42(4) and (5) ESA Regs
37 Reg 5(4) IS Regs
38 Reg 52(2) JSA Regs
39 Reg 52(2A) JSA Regs

3. People treated as not in full-time paid work

40 **IS** Regs 5(3A) and 6(1) and (5) IS Regs
JSA Regs 52(1) and 53(a)-(f) and (h)-(m) JSA Regs
ESA Reg 43 and Sch 6 para 2(5), (6) and (8) ESA Regs
41 CIS/621/2004
42 **IS** Reg 2(1) IS Regs
JSA Reg 1(3) JSA Regs
ESA Reg 2(1) ESA Regs
All definition of 'self-employment route'
43 R(FIS) 1/86; CDWA/1/1992
44 Reg 41(1) ESA Regs
45 **IS** s127(b) SSCBA 1992; reg 6(4)(b) IS Regs
JSA Reg 53(g) and (gg) JSA Regs
ESA Reg 43(2) and Sch 2 para 2(8) ESA Regs
46 **IS** Reg 6(4)(a) and (d) IS Regs
JSA Reg 53(c) and (h) JSA Regs
ESA Reg 43(2)(a) and (d) and Sch 6 para 2(8) ESA Regs
47 Reg 4(3)-(8) SS(MA)(No.5) Regs
48 **PC** Sch 2 para 2(7) and (8) SPC Regs
HB Reg 6(7) and (8) HB Regs; reg 6(7) and (8) HB(SPC) Regs
CTB Reg 6(7) and (8) CTB Regs; reg 6(7) and (8) CTB(SPC) Regs
49 **PC** Sch 2 para 2(6) SPC Regs
HB Reg 6(6) HB Regs; reg 6(6) HB(SPC) Regs
CTB Reg 6(6) CTB Regs; reg 6(6) CTB(SPC) Regs

4. Self-employed people

50 para 20238 DMG
51 CIS/649/1992
52 R(JSA) 1/09; *GM v SSWP (JSA)* [2010] UKUT 221 (AAC)
53 para 20265 DMG

54 R(FIS) 6/85; *Kazantzis v CAO* [1999], reported as R(IS) 13/99
55 para 20267 DMG

6. **Working tax credit and out-of-work benefits**

56 **IS** Reg 5(1A) IS Regs
JSA Reg 51(1)(b) JSA Regs
ESA Reg 42(1) ESA Regs
57 Reg 7(3) Table 3 paras 13, 16, 17 and 26 TC(DCI) Regs

Chapter 32

Incapacity for work

This chapter covers:

If you are too ill or disabled to work and are making a new claim for benefit, in most cases the benefit you claim is employment and support allowance. This chapter does not apply to you as you must show that you have 'limited capability for work', rather than incapacity for work. See Chapter 11 for more information. Also, this chapter does not apply to the assessment of your incapacity for work for the purpose of statutory sick pay (see Chapter 28) or industrial injuries benefits (see Chapter 18).

Key facts

- If you are too ill or disabled to work and are assessed as having 'incapacity for work', you may receive incapacity benefit, income support on the grounds of disability or severe disablement allowance and/or national insurance credits.
- Having incapacity for work means that, because of your mental or physical condition, it is unreasonable to require you to work. Whether you have incapacity for work is assessed by a test called the 'personal capability assessment'.
- Existing awards of benefit on the basis of incapacity for work are being transferred to claims for employment and support allowance, and your entitlement will be reassessed under the test of 'limited capability for work', not incapacity for work. This process is due to be complete by 2014.
- In general, you cannot work and have limited capacity for work at the same time, although certain kinds of work are allowed.
- If you stop receiving a benefit for incapacity for work because you start work or training, you may count as a 'welfare to work beneficiary' and benefit from special rules in other benefits.
- If you disagree with the decision about your limited capacity for work, you can apply for a revision or supersession, or appeal against it (see Chapters 45 and 46).

1. Incapacity for work

If you are too ill to work, you may still receive one of the following on the basis of being 'incapable of work':[1]

- incapacity benefit (IB);
- severe disablement allowance (SDA);
- income support (IS);
- the disability premium within IS, housing benefit (HB) and council tax benefit (CTB), if your entitlement to the premium depends on your showing that you have been incapable of work;
- national insurance (NI) credits for incapacity.

If you are found capable or incapable of work for one of the above, this also applies to claims for all the others,[2] and also to a claim for jobseeker's allowance (see Chapter 19).[3]

Who still receives benefit for incapacity for work

On 27 October 2008, benefits paid for incapacity for work (IB, SDA and IS) were replaced, for most new claimants, with employment and support allowance (ESA). However, you still receive IB, SDA and IS on the basis of incapacity for work if:

- you have an existing award of IB, SDA or IS for incapacity for work and you have not yet had your claim transferred to ESA; *or*
- you have an existing award of IB or SDA, in which case you can still make a claim for IS for incapacity work (and other 'grounds of disability' – see p351) before your claim is transferred to ESA;[4] *or*
- you have an existing award of IS on the grounds of disability, in which case you can still make a claim for IB before your claim is transferred to ESA.[5]

Note: if you stop being entitled to benefit on the basis of incapacity for work, you cannot return to it if you claim benefit again on the basis of being too ill to work.[6] Instead, you must make a new claim for ESA.

While you remain entitled to benefit for incapacity for work, you should be entitled to the disability premium and NI credits on the basis of incapacity for work.

If you are entitled to IB or SDA, also consider applying for IS, HB and CTB. These benefits may be paid in addition to your IB or SDA, although any IB you receive is treated as income when calculating your entitlement to IS, HB and CTB.

Assessing incapacity for work

New assessments of incapacity for work are no longer carried out. Instead, when your incapacity for work is due to be reassessed by the DWP (or your circumstances change so that it needs to be reassessed), this will trigger a transfer of your claim to one for ESA (see p193), and you will then be subject to the test of limited capability for work (see Chapter 11). If you have an appeal against a decision about whether you are incapable of work that has not yet been decided, the First-tier Tribunal will still assess you for incapacity for work, but you are not entitled to benefit on the basis of incapacity for work while the appeal is pending. For details about the benefits you may be able to get while the appeal is pending, see Chapter 29 of the 2011/12 edition of this *Handbook*.

For full details of the test of incapacity for work and appeals concerning incapacity for work, see Chapter 28 of the 2010/11 edition of this *Handbook*. Note, however, that you are now given four, rather than six, weeks to return the questionnaire, with the further reminder sent when three weeks have passed.

Work you may do while claiming

The general rule is that you cannot work and be incapable of work at the same time. With certain exceptions, even if it has been determined that you are incapable of work, you are treated as capable of work for any week (starting on a Sunday) in which you actually *do* work. **Note:** this also applies if you work while appealing against a decision on your incapacity. You are treated as capable of work for the whole week, even if you do not work for the whole week. This applies whether or not you are paid for the work.[7]

However, you will only be treated as capable of work on the actual days that you work, rather than for the whole week, if you work:

- during the first week of your claim; *or*
- during the last week that you were incapable of work; *or*
- during any week when you are undergoing plasmapheresis, parenteral chemotherapy, radiotherapy treatment, regular weekly renal dialysis or total parenteral nutrition treatment.[8]

If the amount of work you do is so minimal that it can be regarded as trivial or negligible, you should not be treated as capable of work.[9]

In addition, the following kinds of work are allowed:[10]

- 'approved work' (ie, work on a trial basis for which you are not paid) that has been arranged in writing by the DWP and you are getting IB, IS, SDA, or any other benefit or increase (including a disability premium) or NI credits, on the basis of incapacity for work;
- the care of a spouse or partner, a grandparent, grandchild, uncle, aunt, nephew, niece or a 'close relative' (parent, parent-in-law, son, son-in-law, daughter, daughter-in-law, step-parent, stepson, stepdaughter, brother, sister, or the spouse, civil partner or partner of any of the preceding people[11]);
- domestic work (ie, cooking and cleaning) in your own home;
- work which you do only to protect someone or prevent serious damage to property or livestock during an emergency;

- work as a local councillor;
- work (for a maximum of one day a week, although this can be two half days) as a member of the First-tier Tribunal, if you have been appointed because of your experience of disability issues, or work as a member of the Disability Living Allowance Advisory Board;
- voluntary work if the work is not for a 'close relative' (see p735) and if the only payment you receive for the work is to cover your reasonable expenses (note, however, that the fact that you do not accept a wage will not necessarily mean that you are a volunteer);[12]
- work done while receiving assistance in pursuing self-employment under s2 of the Employment and Training Act 1973 or s2 of the Enterprise and New Towns (Scotland) Act 1990 (test-trading);
- 'permitted work' (see below).

Note: if you are treated as capable of work, you will not qualify for IB, SDA or IS on the basis of your incapacity for work. If you disagree with the decision that you do not qualify, you can challenge it either by asking for a revision (see Chapter 45), or by appealing (see Chapter 46).

Permitted work

'Permitted work' is work of any kind, which you can do:[13]

- as part of a **treatment programme** under medical supervision while you are in hospital or regularly attending hospital as an outpatient, as long as you do not earn more than £97.50 a week; *or*
- for an unlimited period, as long as you do not earn more than £20 a week. This is called the **permitted work lower limit**; *or*
- for an unlimited period, as long as you do not earn more than £97.50 a week and you are in 'supported work' (see p737). This is called **supported permitted work**; *or*
- for up to 52 weeks (or indefinitely in certain circumstances – see below), as long as you work on average for less than 16 hours a week and do not earn more than £97.50 a week. This is called the **permitted work higher limit**.

Note: the earnings limits referred to in the first, third and fourth bullet points above are usually increased each October – see CPAG's *Welfare Rights Bulletin* for updates.

For the 16-hour rule, see p737. For how your earnings are assessed, see Chapter 39 (for contributory ESA) and Chapter 40 (other benefits).

Note: if you work for 16 hours a week or more for payment or in expectation of payment, unless that work can be ignored (see p725), you will not be entitled to IS. Also, earnings from 'permitted work' are treated as income for the purpose of calculating your entitlement to means-tested benefits and tax credits.

Permitted work higher limit

You can usually do this work for up to 52 weeks. However, if you are exempt from the personal capability assessment under transitional rules or because you have a severe condition, you can do this work indefinitely. Otherwise, after 52 weeks have passed since you started (whether or not you actually work for all of the 52 weeks or not), you can do more work which falls under the permitted work higher limit if:

- since the beginning of the last 52-week period of such work, you have ceased to be entitled to IB or SDA, or (on the basis of incapacity for work) IS, HB, CTB or NI credits for a continuous period lasting more than eight weeks. However, in practice, you are likely to have to claim ESA and meet the limited capability for work test if you claim again on the basis of being too ill to work (see p193); *or*
- a further 52 weeks have passed.

Informing the DWP

There are no special rules about informing the DWP about doing permitted work, but you should inform the DWP as soon as possible. This is because, under the general benefit rules, you are required to report changes in your circumstances that you might reasonably be expected to know could affect your benefit (see p1047).

Note: if the particular activities you carry out in your work suggest that you might be capable of work, the DWP may reassess this and it would probably trigger the transfer of your claim to one for ESA.

Supported work

The definition of 'supported work' is the same as in the permitted work rules for limited capability for work (see p216).

16-hour rule

Permitted work (see p736) may sometimes only be disregarded if you do such work for less than 16 hours a week.[14]

It is the average number of hours that you work which is important. Even if you work more than 16 hours in a week, you are not treated as capable of work in that week if the average number of hours you normally work is less than 16. If you work for 16 hours or more in a week, the decision maker should consider your average hours:

- if you have a normal work cycle, over the period of that cycle;
- otherwise, over the week in question and the four weeks before it.[15]

Only the hours you actually work (not the hours you are contracted to work) and weeks in which you actually do any work (not weeks of sickness or holiday) count.[16]

Although you will not be considered to be capable of work simply because you are doing any of the above types of work, if you are claiming IS, the type of work that you do and any earnings you receive may still affect your entitlement. If the work is done for payment or in expectation of payment and you work for 16 hours or more a week, you will not qualify for IS (see p719) unless you can be treated as not being in full-time work (see p719). See p904 for how earnings may affect your entitlement to IS.

'Welfare to work beneficiary'

If you stop receiving a benefit for incapacity for work because you start work or training, you may count as a 'welfare to work beneficiary' and you may benefit from special rules – eg, you can remain entitled to the disability premium in a means-tested benefit, or linking rules in the housing costs rules may apply to you. Note, however, that these rules do not mean that you can return to receiving benefit for incapacity for work.

You are a welfare to work beneficiary if:[17]

- you have stopped receiving a benefit (see below) to which you were entitled on the basis of being incapable of work after being incapable of work for a period of more than 196 days. The 196 days can include days of incapacity for statutory sick pay – known as your 'last period of incapacity for work' (you do not have to have been receiving benefit for all of the 196 days). The 196 days do not need to fall consecutively, as two or more periods of incapacity for work can be linked if they are separated by eight weeks or less. The days within each period of incapacity count towards the 196-day total; *and*
- you are within the 104-week period which runs from the first day after the end of that period of incapacity for work (called the 104-week linking period); *and*
- within a month of your entitlement to benefit ceasing, you start a training course for which you receive a training allowance, or you start work and you are paid for that work or you expect to be paid.

Even if you satisfy these conditions, you are not a welfare to work beneficiary if:

- your 'last period of incapacity for work' (see p339) ended because you were found to be capable of work and either you did not appeal against this or you appealed but did not win your appeal; *or*
- the work that you have started within a month of your benefit stopping is work that you can do while still being considered incapable of work (see p736).

You will have been receiving benefit based on your incapacity for work if you were receiving IB, SDA, IS on the basis of your incapacity for work, NI credits for incapacity for work (see p780) or a disability premium in your IS, HB or CTB paid on the grounds that you are incapable of work.[18]

The 104-week linking period

You are only a welfare to work beneficiary for a fixed 104-week period running from the day after the end of your last 'period of incapacity for work' (see p339). This 104-week period is not affected by whether or not you have periods of incapacity for work within it.

Once your 104-week linking period ends, you are no longer considered to be a welfare to work beneficiary. In order to qualify again, you need to satisfy all the rules (see p738).

Notes

1. **Incapacity for work**

1 ss171A(1) and 171(G) SSCBA 1992
2 s17 SSA 1998; reg 10 SS&CS(DA) Regs
3 Sch 1 para 2 JSA 1995
4 Reg 2(2)(d) ESA(TP) Regs
5 Reg 2(2)(e) ESA(TP) Regs
6 Reg 24 ESA(TP)(EA)(No.2) Regs
7 s171D SSCBA 1992; reg 16 SS(IFW) Regs
8 Regs 13(2) and 16(3) SS(IFW) Regs
9 CIB/5298/1997
10 ss171D and 171F SSCBA 1992; regs 10A, 16 and 17 SS(IFW) Regs
11 Reg 2(1) SS(IFW) Regs
12 Reg 2(1) SS(IFW) Regs
13 Reg 17 SS(IFW) Regs
14 Reg 17(4) and (8) SS(IFW) Regs
15 Reg 17(8) SS(IFW) Regs
16 CIB/1723/2000
17 Reg 13A SS(IFW) Regs
18 Reg 13A(4) SS(IFW) Regs

33

Chapter 33

Claiming for others: non-means-tested benefits

This chapter covers:

Key facts

- Increases for adult and child dependants can sometimes be included in existing claims for non-mean-tested benefits.
- Increases must be claimed before you can become entitled to them.
- Increases cannot usually be included in new claims.
- Earnings rules and rules about getting other benefits may apply, which may mean that the increase is reduced or you are not entitled to it at all.

1. Increases for your adult dependant

If you are receiving a non-means-tested benefit, it may be possible to claim an increase either for your **'spouse'** or **'civil partner'**, or for an **adult who looks after your child**, but not for both. See p741 for what these terms mean.

If you are already entitled to an increase in your carer's allowance (CA) or category A retirement pension, this can continue for the time being. Otherwise, new claims for increases for adult dependants can only be made for incapacity benefit (IB) and severe disablement allowance (SDA) and, in most cases, only if you are already entitled to the benefit.

Increases can be included in the following benefits:

- IB paid at the long-term or short-term rate (see Chapter 16). However, although you can still claim an increase if you are already entitled to IB, new claims for IB are possible only in limited circumstances (see p337);
- SDA (see Chapter 24). You can still claim an increase if you are already entitled to SDA;

- CA (see Chapter 6), but only if you claimed and were entitled to it before 6 April 2010. Inclusion of the increase stops (and you cannot then reclaim it) if you stop satisfying the rules below and, in any case, on 6 April 2020;[1]
- Category A retirement pension (see Chapter 23), but only if you claimed and were entitled to it before 6 April 2010. Note that increases were only included for dependent spouses. Inclusion of the increase stops (and you cannot then reclaim it) if you stop satisying the rules below and, in any case, on 6 April 2020. You also lose entitlement (and cannot reclaim) if you are a man and your wife reaches pension age (see p531).[2]

Note:
- If you are transferred from IB or SDA to employment and support allowance (ESA), your ESA does not include an increase for an adult dependant. If this means you lose out, you are paid a transitional addition (see p193).
- If you make a claim for an adult dependant who is your partner and your benefit would be increased because of this, your partner may be required to attend a work-focused interview as a condition of your getting the full amount of benefit (see p1033).

You can choose not to claim an increase in your non-means-tested benefit for a dependant, but if you are entitled to an increase and are also receiving a means-tested benefit, see p748.

Increase for your spouse or civil partner

Your '**spouse**' is your husband or wife. See p68 for who can be recognised as married (p69, if your marriage is polygamous). Your '**civil partner**' is someone of the same sex with whom you are registered as civil partners.[3] You may be entitled to an increase for your spouse or civil partner if her/his earnings are not too high (see p744). An increase *can* be paid even if your spouse or civil partner is not living with you, provided you are contributing to her/his maintenance.

You *cannot* qualify for an increase for your spouse or civil partner if you are receiving an increase for an adult who cares for your child (see p742).

See p745 for the amount of the increase you receive.

Who can claim

You qualify for an increase for your spouse or civil partner if:[4]
- you make a separate claim for the increase (see p746);[5] *and*
- your spouse or civil partner's earnings, or the payments s/he receives from an occupational or personal pension, are not too high (see p744); *and*
- you are not getting an increase for a dependent adult who is looking after your child (see p742); *and either*
  - you are residing with your spouse or civil partner; *or*

– in some retirement pension cases only, you are 'contributing to the maintenance' of your spouse at a weekly rate of at least the amount of the increase (see p745).

Additional conditions for specific benefits

You only qualify for an increase for your spouse or civil partner if, in addition to the above conditions, you satisfy the following.

For **IB** or **SDA**, *either*:[6]

- your spouse or civil partner is at least the qualifying age for pension credit (see p509) or over; *or*
- your spouse or civil partner is under the qualifying age for pension credit (see p509), you are 'residing with' (and not merely 'contributing to the maintenance' of) her/him and entitled to child benefit.

For **CA**, you must reside with your spouse or civil partner to get the increase. You cannot qualify just by contributing to her/his maintenance.[7]

For **Category A retirement pension**, you may be residing with your spouse, or contributing to her/his maintenance at a weekly rate of at least the amount of the increase.[8] However, if you are a woman, you can only get an increase for your husband in your **Category A retirement pension** if:

- immediately before you became entitled to the Category A retirement pension, you were entitled to IB, including an increase for an adult dependant; *and*
- since then, you have not stopped residing with your husband or stopped contributing to his maintenance at a rate at least equal to the rate of the increase and your husband's earnings have not been higher than the rate of the increase.[9]

If your spouse or civil partner receives benefit

You may not be entitled to an increase for your spouse or civil partner if s/he is claiming an earnings-replacement benefit (see p1041) in her/his own right. This is a frequent source of overpayment and it is very important that when you complete the claim form you give full details of any benefits your spouse or civil partner is receiving.

Increase for someone who looks after a child

If you are not claiming an increase in your benefit for your spouse or civil partner, you may get an increase for an adult dependant who is looking after a child for whom you are responsible. 'Child' is defined in the same way as for child benefit and includes a 'qualifying young person' (see p94). You may benefit under these rules if, for example, you live with someone to whom you are not married or with whom you are not in a civil partnership and one of you stays at home to look after the child. You may also get an increase for someone you employ to care for your child.

Who can claim

You qualify for an increase for an adult dependant (who is not your spouse or civil partner) if:[10]

- you make a separate claim for the increase (see p746);[11] *and*
- your dependant's earnings, or any payments s/he receives from an occupational or personal pension, are not too high (see p744); *and*
- your dependant looks after a child;

and either:

- if you are claiming an increase to CA , or Category A retirement pension , you are entitled to child benefit for that child. In some circumstances, even if you are receiving child benefit, you will be treated as if you are not; *or*
- if you get IB or SDA, you are entitled to child benefit for the child (or you are treated as entitled to child benefit). However, see p193 for the effect of the introduction of ESA on entitlement to IB and SDA;

and either:

- you reside with your dependant; *or*
- you contribute to the maintenance of your dependant at a rate equal to at least the rate of the increase; *or*
- you employ your dependant at a cost to you of at least the standard rate of the increase and the employment started before you became unemployed, incapable of work or retired (whichever applies to you) unless the need for you to employ your dependant arose afterwards;

and:

- you do not also get an increase for your spouse or civil partner; *and*
- your dependant is not absent from Great Britain, unless s/he is residing with you outside Great Britain and you still qualify for benefit.

Note: for the definitions of 'who counts as a child', 'treated as' entitled or not entitled to child benefit, 'residing with', 'contributing to the maintenance' and 'living with', see p707 of the 2009/10 edition of this *Handbook*.

Additional conditions for specific benefits

For **CA**, you must reside with your dependant to get the increase. You cannot qualify just by contributing to her/his maintenance or employing her/him.[12] If your spouse or civil partner is entitled to a **Category B retirement pension** on the basis of your national insurance (NI) contribution record, you are not entitled to an increase in your Category A retirement pension for an adult dependant who is caring for a child.[13]

If your dependant receives benefit

You may not be entitled to the increase if your dependant is claiming an earnings-replacement benefit (see p1041) in her/his own right. This is a frequent source of overpayment and it is important that you give full details of any benefits received by your dependant when you complete the claim form.

The earnings rules

You are not entitled to an increase in your benefit for a spouse/civil partner or for a dependent adult who cares for your child if her/his earnings are too high (but see below if you employ your dependant).

Earnings

Earnings include any payments received from an occupational or personal pension scheme or periodic payments from the Pension Protection Fund (see p888).[14] If your dependant's earnings fluctuate, you do not automatically lose your entitlement to the increase every time s/he earns too much in a particular week (although you have no right to be paid the increase during the following week if that happens).[15] This means that you do not have to make a fresh claim every time your dependant's earnings exceed the limit (although you must inform the DWP of any such changes). For full details of how earnings are calculated, see p890.

When the increase is not paid

If you are residing with an adult dependant and are claiming an increase in **long-term IB**, **SDA** or **Category A retirement pension**, your increase is not paid if, in the previous week, your dependant earned more than £71.[16]

If you are claiming an increase in your **IB** for your spouse/civil partner or adult dependant and s/he is treated as incapable of work while doing 'approved work' (see p735), any payment for this is ignored.[17]

In any other case (eg, if you are not residing with your dependant or if you are claiming an increase in any other non-means-tested benefit), your increase is not paid if your dependant's earnings in the previous week were more than the standard rate of the increase which you have claimed.[18]

This means that the earnings rule is more generous for long-term than for short-term IB, so you may not be entitled to an increase during the first year of your entitlement to IB but qualify after you transfer to long-term IB. You must then make a separate claim for the increase.

If you employ your dependant

If you are claiming an increase for an adult dependant who is not your spouse or civil partner but is looking after a child (see p742), her/his earnings do not affect your entitlement to an increase if s/he is employed by you but is not residing with you. If s/he is residing with you and you are employing her/him to care for a child, the wages you pay to her/him for this work are ignored.[19]

Amount of increase for an adult dependant

Increases for spouses/civil partners and adult dependants who are caring for a child are paid as follows.[20]

	£pw
Short-term IB (claimant not over pension age)	44.85
Short-term IB (claimant over pension age)	55.70
Long-term IB	57.60
SDA	34.60
CA	34.40
Category A retirement pension	61.85

If you are over pension age, an increase in your retirement pension or short-term IB may be reduced if your contribution record is incomplete (see p795).[21]

2. Increases for child dependants

You cannot make a new claim for an increase for a child dependant. These increases have been replaced by child tax credit. However, you remain entitled to an increase for a child dependant if you were entitled to one on 5 April 2003 , or your entitlement was backdated to include 5 April 2003.

You lose this transitional protection if:

- your entitlement to an increase for a child dependant ceases; *or*
- your increase stops being paid for more than 58 days. If the benefit with which you are paid the increase is terminated, your increase also stops. However, you keep your transitional protection as long as the benefit is awarded to you again and you reclaim the increase within three months of the date the benefit is re-awarded on revision, supersession or appeal.[22]

Earnings limit

If you live together with someone as a couple, your partner's earnings affect your entitlement to an increase for a child. You count as a couple if you live with your spouse or civil partner, or with someone as if you were married or were registered as civil partners. You do not get an increase for your first child for any week if, in the previous week, your partner earned £215 or more. After that, you lose entitlement for another child for each complete £28 a week your partner earns in addition to £215.

Amount of increase for a child dependant

The basic rate of the increase is £11.35 for each child.[23] However, if you are in receipt of child benefit at the only or eldest child rate for the same child, the £11.35 is reduced to £8.10.[24]

For all other rules on increases for child dependants, see pp746–48 of CPAG's *Welfare Benefits Handbook* 2002/03.

3. Special benefit rules

There are some groups of claimants to whom special rules apply. These are covered below and in Chapters 29 and 30. Special rules apply to:

- claimants or their dependants who are in hospital (see p675);
- claimants or their dependants who are in prison or detention (see p691);
- adult dependants involved in trade disputes (see p700);
- people whose marriage is polygamous (see below).

Note: your increase may not be affected in the same way as your basic benefit.

Polygamous marriages

You only qualify for an increase in your non-means-tested benefit for your spouse if you are recognised as having a valid marriage under UK law (see p68). You are not normally treated as having a valid marriage unless your marriage is a monogamous one.[25] This means if your marriage is polygamous, you are not generally entitled to an increase in your benefit for your spouse.[26] Seek further advice if necessary.

Even if you do not qualify for an increase in your non-means-tested benefit for your spouse because your marriage is polygamous, you may still qualify for an increase for her/him if s/he is caring for a child (see p742).

4. Claims, backdating and getting paid

You must make a claim for an increase for a dependant.[27] The rules are described in brief below, but see also Chapter 42, which explains the rules in more detail.

Making a claim

In general, a claim for an increase should be made on the appropriate claim form (this might be a written statement sent to you after a telephone call to the DWP). However, the DWP may accept a written application which is not on the appropriate form if it is sufficient in the circumstances (see p1019).[28]

Claims for dependants' increases can be backdated for up to three months from the date you make your claim if you satisfy the conditions of entitlement to the benefit and to the dependant's increase over that period.[29] You do not have to show reasons why your claim was late to qualify for backdated benefit.

See p1022 for details of evidence that may be required to support your claim.

Who should claim

You must normally claim benefit (including increases for dependants) on your own behalf. However, if your benefit is being claimed by another adult on your behalf because you are not able to act for yourself (called your 'appointee'), the increase in that benefit should also be claimed by your appointee (see p1016).

The date of your claim

The date of your claim for an increase for a dependant is normally the date it is received at the DWP office.[30]

If the claim you submit is incomplete or not on the correct form, you may be asked to provide further information or to complete the correct form. As long as this additional information or form is returned within a month of its being sent back to you (or longer if the decision maker thinks the delay is reasonable), your claim is treated as being made on the date the initial claim was received at the DWP office.[31]

It may be possible to claim in advance or your date of claim may be backdated.

If you claim the wrong benefit

If someone has claimed benefit for her/himself (other than a claim for child benefit) and is not entitled to it, but you are entitled to an increase in your non-means-tested benefit for that person, her/his claim can be treated as a claim for an increase in your benefit.[32]

When someone else has claimed an increase in a benefit for an adult dependant but is not entitled to it, that claim may be treated as a claim for an increase in your non-means-tested benefit for the same adult.[33]

If a claim for another benefit is treated as a claim for an increase in your benefit for an adult dependant, this may allow you to backdate your claim for the increase for more than the usual three months. If you satisfy the qualifying conditions for the increase and for the benefit to which the increase applies, you can get the increase backdated for up to three months before the date of the claim for the other benefit.

See p1025 for more details on interchanging claims in this way.

Getting paid

If you are claiming an increase for your dependants, the increase is included in the payments of the benefit concerned, and is paid in the same way and on the same day as that benefit. See the relevant benefit chapter for details.

Change of circumstances

The DWP should inform you of the main kinds of changes in your circumstances that you need to report, but might not list them all. In any case, it is your duty to report *any* change in your circumstances that you might reasonably be expected to know might affect your right to, the amount of, or the payment of your benefit (see p1047).[34] You should, for example, inform the DWP of a change in your adult dependant's earnings.

Do this promptly in writing or by telephone to the office handling your claim (although in individual cases notification might be accepted in a form other than in writing or by telephone). In some cases, however, the decision maker might say that you must report changes in writing. In any case, you might want to report the change in writing and keep a copy in case of a dispute in the future.

5. Tax, tax credits and other benefits

Increases of retirement pensions, carer's allowance and incapacity benefit (IB), apart from the lower rate of short-term IB and transitional IB (see p264 of the 2008/09 edition of this *Handbook*) for adult dependants, are taxable.[35] Other increases are not. Increases are generally taken into account, along with the benefit itself, as income for tax credits (see p1332). As with means-tested benefits (see below) this may mean that your income becomes too high to qualify and may also affect your entitlement to payments from the social fund, free school lunches and health benefits.

Means-tested benefits

Means-tested benefits include an amount for your partner and, for housing benefit (HB) and council tax benefit (CTB) (and in some cases income support (IS) and income-based jobseeker's allowance (JSA)), an amount for children who are members of your household (see Chapter 34). This is your 'family' for the purpose of means-tested benefits.

Any increase in your non-means-tested benefit for your partner is treated as income for means-tested benefits. Any increase in your non-means-tested benefit for a child who is a member of your family is treated as income for HB and CTB (and, if a child is included in your claim, for IS and income-based JSA). It may be ignored when calculating your entitlement to IS or income-based JSA if a child is not included in your claim and when calculating your entitlement to income-related employment and support allowance (ESA).

If you are receiving a means-tested benefit, you may not be better off claiming an increase in your non-means-tested benefit for an adult dependant. If the increase is for your partner, it affects the amount of means-tested benefit you receive and may mean your income is too high for you to qualify for that means-tested benefit.

However, if you fail to claim an increase in your non-means-tested benefit for an adult or child dependant to which you are entitled, you may still be treated as receiving the increase for the purpose of calculating your entitlement to IS, income-based JSA, income-related ESA

and, if you are under the qualifying age for PC (see p509), HB or CTB. This is because you can be treated as if you are receiving income for which you fail to apply (called 'notional income'). See p933 for more information. You should only be treated as having notional income if your entitlement to an increase is straightforward. If you would have to satisfy further conditions to qualify for the increase, you should not be treated as receiving it.

Non-means-tested benefits

The overlapping benefit rules (see p1041) apply to increases in non-means-tested benefits for dependants. These rules mean you may not be entitled to an increase in more than one benefit for the same child or adult and that you may not qualify for an increase if someone else is receiving an increase for your dependants. You also may not be entitled to an increase for an adult dependant if s/he is claiming an earnings replacement benefit in her/his own right.

Notes

1. **Increases for your adult dependant**
 1 s15 WRA 2009
 2 s4 PA 2007
 3 s1 CPA 2004
 4 ss83-85, 86A and 90 SSCBA 1992; regs 8 and 12 and Sch 2 SSB(Dep) Regs; regs 9 and 10 SS(IB-ID) Regs
 5 Reg 2(3) SS(C&P) Regs
 6 s86A SSCBA 1992; reg 9(1) SS(IB-ID) Regs
 7 Sch 2 para 7 SSB(Dep) Regs; s90 SSCBA 1992
 8 ss83 and 84 SSCBA
 9 s84 SSCBA 1992
 10 ss85 and 90 SSCBA 1992; regs 10 and 12 and Sch 2 SSB(Dep) Regs; regs 9, 10 and 14 SS(IB-ID) Regs
 11 Reg 2(3) SS(C&P) Regs
 12 Sch 2 para 7 SSB(Dep) Regs
 13 s85(3) SSCBA 1992
 14 s89 SSCBA 1992; Sch 2 para 9 SSB(Dep) Regs
 15 Reg 10 and Sch 2 para 7 SSB(Dep) Regs; reg 10 SS(IB-ID) Regs
 16 Regs 8(2) and (3) and 12 SSB(Dep) Regs; reg 10 SS(IB-ID) Regs
 17 Reg 9(2A) SS(IB-ID) Regs
 18 ss82 and 83(2)(b) SSCBA 1992; reg 12 and Sch 2 para 7 SSB(Dep) Regs; reg 10(1) SS(IB-ID) Regs
 19 Reg 10 and Sch 2 para 7 SSB(Dep) Regs; reg 10 SS(IB-ID) Regs
 20 Sch 4 SSCBA 1992
 21 Reg 6(3) SS(WB&RP) Regs; reg 13 SS(IB-ID) Regs

2. **Increases for child dependants**
 22 Art 3 TCA(No.3)O
 23 Sch 4 SSCBA 1992
 24 Reg 8(2) SS(OB) Regs

3. **Special benefit rules**
 25 *Hyde v Hyde* [1866]
 26 Reg 2 SSFA(PM) Regs

4. **Claims, backdating and getting paid**
 27 s1 SSAA 1992
 28 Reg 4(1) SS(C&P) Regs
 29 Reg 19(2) and (3) SS(C&P) Regs
 30 Reg 6(1) SS(C&P) Regs
 31 Regs 4(7) and 6(1) SS(C&P) Regs
 32 Reg 9(4) SS(C&P) Regs
 33 Reg 9(5) SS(C&P) Regs
 34 Reg 32(1A) and (1B) SS(C&P) Regs

5. **Tax, tax credits and other benefits**
 35 s617 ICTA 1988

Chapter 34

Claiming for others: means-tested benefits

This chapter covers:

For information on claiming for others in non-means tested benefits, see Chapter 33. For child tax credit and working tax credit, see Chapters 51 and 52.

Note: unless otherwise stated, references to income-based jobseeker's allowance (JSA) in this chapter also refer to joint-claim JSA.

Key facts

- Amounts can be included in means-tested benefits for couples and, in some cases, for dependent children.
- Pension credit and income-related employment and support allowance do not include amounts for children.
- New claims for income support and income-based jobseeker's allowance do not include amounts for children.

Future changes: April 2013 and after

Major changes are taking place that affect the benefits and tax credits system (see Chapter 2). From October 2013, universal credit will replace means-tested benefits and will include amounts for couples and for dependent children (see Chapter 4). See CPAG's *Welfare Rights Bulletin* for updates.

1. **Who is included in your claim**

The definition of **'family'** for the purposes of income support (IS), income-based jobseeker's allowance (JSA), income-related employment and support allowance (ESA), housing benefit (HB) and council tax benefit (CTB) includes your partner and your dependent children. However, although your partner is always included in the assessment of your applicable amount for means-tested benefits, amounts of benefit for your dependent children can only be included in HB and CTB and, in some circumstances, IS and income-based JSA (see p760). Amounts for dependent children are not included in ESA or pension credit (PC). Instead, claim child tax credit (CTC – see Chapter 51).

Note:

- Even if your applicable amount for HB or CTB includes amounts for your child(ren), provided the child is not included in your claim for IS or income-based JSA, you can claim CTC in addition to HB and CTB.
- In this chapter the terms 'child' and 'children' include some qualifying young people (see p761).

When your benefit is worked out, the needs of your partner and her/his income and capital are usually added to yours. For HB and CTB and, in some cases, IS and income-based JSA, the needs of your dependent child(ren) are added to yours. If your child's needs are included in your IS or income-based JSA, there are special rules for the treatment of her/his income and capital (see pp902 and 972).

Couples

If you are a member of a couple, your 'family' for benefit purposes includes your partner. See p753 for full details.

Children

You can get amounts (called allowances and premiums) for your child(ren) in your applicable amount for some benefits (see Chapter 37). However, for other benefits, although amounts for a child cannot be included in your claim, s/he can still count as part of your family for the purpose of that benefit. Even when amounts of benefit for your child cannot be included in your claim, there are other circumstances in which it may still be important that you are regarded as having a child as part of your 'family'. This applies particularly to IS (see p355), income-based JSA (see p401), income-related ESA (see Chapter 10) and, in some cases, for the calculation of housing costs (see Chapter 38).

For IS, income-based JSA, income-related ESA, HB and CTB, for amounts for a child to be included in your claim and for your child(ren) to count as part of your 'family', you must be responsible for the child(ren) and s/he must be living in your household. Certain 16/17-year-olds formerly looked after by a local authority are, however, excluded (see p671).[1]

See p759 for full details.

2. **Couples**

You and your partner are considered to be a 'couple' for mean-tested benefit purposes if you are both 16[2] or over and you are:[3]

- married and living in the same household; *or*
- not married but 'living together as husband and wife'; *or*
- of the same sex, registered as civil partners and living in the same household; *or*
- of the same sex, not registered as civil partners but living together as if you were civil partners.

In these circumstances, you must claim as a couple. Your partner's income and capital are counted when assessing your entitlement and you receive the amount of benefit for couples. If one member of a couple is claiming a means-tested benefit, the other member cannot claim the same benefit for the same period.[4] For income support (IS), income-based jobseeker's allowance (JSA), income-related employment and support allowance (ESA), housing benefit (HB) and council tax benefit (CTB), partners can choose who should be the claimant.[5] The same rule applies to pension credit (PC), but the claimant must be aged 60 or over to qualify.[6]

Note:

- If you are a 'joint-claim couple' for JSA, both you and your partner need to be available for and actively seeking work.
- Special rules apply if either you or your partner are under 18 (see pp671 and 817).
- For PC only, if your partner is a 'person subject to immigration control' (see p1410), you are treated as not being members of the same household and so cannot count as a couple.[7]

Spouse or civil partner

Being **married** to someone does not necessarily mean that you cannot be treated as part of a couple with someone else instead.[8]

You count as **'polygamously married'** if you are married to more than one person and your marriages took place in a country that permits polygamy.[9] For ESA only, you and all your partners must also be living in the same household (see p754). There are special rules if you are polygamously married (see p69).[10] These specify that any income and capital of any polygamous partners is taken into account, but an increased amount of benefit is allowed to take into account their needs.

You count as someone's **civil partner** if you are both of the same sex and have been registered as her/his civil partner.[11]

Living in the same household

The term **'household'** is not defined. Whether two people should be treated as members of the same household is a question of fact. A house can contain a number of separate households and if one person has exclusive occupation of separate accommodation from another, s/he is not considered to be living in the same household. Physical presence together is not, in itself, conclusive. There must be a 'particular kind of tie' binding two people together in a domestic establishment. This could include a household in, for example, a hotel or boarding house.[12] However, it must also involve two or more people living together as a unit and, as such a unit, enjoying a reasonable level of independence and self-sufficiency. In one case, it was held that a married couple sharing a room in a residential home because they needed help with organising their personal care and domestic activities were not self-sufficient and did not live in a domestic establishment, and therefore did not share a household.[13]

You and another person may be regarded as members of the same household when you think you should not be. If this occurs, it is important to show that, although you both live in the same house, you maintain separate households.

A separate household might exist if there are:

- independent arrangements for storing and cooking food;
- independent financial arrangements;
- separate eating arrangements;
- no evidence of family life;
- separate commitments for housing costs, even if the liability is to another person in the same premises.

You cannot be a member of more than one household at the same time.[14] If two people can be shown to be maintaining separate homes, they cannot be said to be sharing the same household.[15] Even if you have the right to occupy only part of a room, you may have your own household.[16]

Living together as husband and wife or civil partners

If you are **'living together as'** husband and wife or civil partners (ie, cohabiting), you must claim means-tested benefits as a couple.

If you are in a same-sex relationship, for benefit purposes you may be regarded as living together as civil partners or as if you were civil partners. You only count as living together as if you were civil partners if, were you in a relationship with someone of the opposite sex, you would count as living together as husband and wife.[17] This means that the test described below is the same for same-sex couples as it is for different-sex couples.

If you are awarded IS/income-based JSA/income-related ESA (and, arguably, PC), the local authority should not make a separate decision about whether you are cohabiting when considering your claim for HB and CTB.[18] However, the local authority can find that the benefit claim on which your HB/CTB claim is based is fraudulent. If so, it can decide that you are therefore not entitled to HB/CTB.[19] Also, if you have not been awarded IS, income-based JSA, income-related ESA or PC, the local authority has a duty to consider whether you are cohabiting and may reach a different conclusion from that of the DWP.

The factors below are used as 'signposts' to determine whether or not you are cohabiting.[20] No one factor, in itself, is conclusive, as it is your 'general relationship' as a whole that is important.[21] Each case depends on its own particular facts and circumstances. Official guidance advises decision makers also to consider things like 'mutual love', 'faithfulness', 'devotion' and 'interdependence'.[22] These do not necessarily conflict with the factors below, but like other individual factors should not be regarded as conclusive. For example, there is no rule to say that if your partner stays with you for three nights or more a week, you are automatically treated as a couple who are living together.

Cohabitation signposts

Do you live in the same household?

Do you have a sexual relationship?

What are your financial arrangements?

Is your relationship stable?

Do you have children?

How do you appear in public?

Living in the same household

In all cases, you must spend the major part of your time in the same household (see p754). If one of you has a separate address where you usually live, you should not be considered to be cohabiting. You cannot be a member of more than one household at the same time, so if you are a member of one couple, you cannot also be treated as part of another.

Even if you *do* share a 'household', you may not be cohabiting. It is essential to look at *why* two people are in the same household.[23] For example, in one case, a couple who were living in the same household for reasons of 'care, companionship and mutual convenience' were found not to be 'living together as husband and wife'.[24]

A separated couple living under the same roof should not be treated as a couple if they are maintaining separate households.[25] If a relationship has only recently broken down, continuing financial support and shared responsibilities and liabilities may be particularly inconclusive, especially if there is evidence of active steps being taken to live apart. The way people live and their attitudes may be more significant. Any 'mere hope' of a reconciliation is not a 'reasonable expectation' if at least one partner has accepted that the relationship is at an end.[26]

Note: for couples who are still married the only issue is whether they are living in the same 'household' and, in this case, a shared attitude that the relationship is at an end may not be enough to show there is no shared household.[27]

Being in a sexual relationship

In practice, a decision maker may not ask you about the existence of a sexual relationship, in which case s/he only has the information if you volunteer it. If you do not have a sexual relationship, you should make this known (and perhaps offer to show your separate sleeping arrangements).

Having a sexual relationship is not sufficient, by itself, to prove you are cohabiting. If you have never had a sexual relationship there is a strong (but not necessarily conclusive) presumption that you are not cohabiting.[28] A couple who abstain from a sexual relationship before marriage on grounds of principle or for religious reasons should not be counted as cohabiting until they are formally married.[29] Even if the initial decision maker does not go into the question of whether or not there is a sexual relationship, if you appeal, the First-tier Tribunal may ask such questions in order to determine whether or not you are cohabiting.[30]

Your financial arrangements

If one partner is supported by the other, or household expenses are shared, this may be treated as evidence of cohabitation. However, it is important to consider how they are shared. There is a difference between, on the one hand, paying a fixed weekly contribution or rigidly sharing bills 50/50 and, on the other hand, a free common fund attributable to income and expenditure. The former does not imply cohabitation, the latter might.

The financial relationship between lodger and landlord often comes under scrutiny. Decision makers sometimes claim that the payments are too high or too low and so indicate that the relationship is not purely financial. It is important to explain how the payments came to be as they are. However low or high the charge may appear, it is the reasoning which led to it at the time which is important. There may be many motives for having a lodger apart from purely commercial ones or cohabitation – eg, for company or security. Friendship between a lodger and landlord does not mean they are cohabiting.

A stable relationship

Marriage and civil partnership are expected to be stable and lasting. It follows that an occasional or brief association should not be regarded as cohabiting. However, the fact that a relationship is stable does not make it cohabitation – eg, you can have a stable landlord/lodger relationship, but not be cohabiting.

The way you spend your time together, the activities you do together and the things you do for each other are relevant, so questions such as how you spend your holidays and how you organise the shopping, the laundry and cleaning may be important.

Children

If you have had a child together and live in the same household as the other parent, there is a strong (but not conclusive) presumption of cohabitation.

Your appearance in public

Decision makers may check the electoral roll and claims for national insurance benefits to see if you present yourselves as a couple. Many couples retain their separate single identities publicly. They should, however, be aware that they may be regarded as cohabiting.

Challenging a 'living together' decision

Sometimes benefit is stopped or adjusted because someone regularly stays overnight, even though you might have none of the long-term commitments generally associated with marriage or a civil partnership. However, couples with no sexual relationship who live together (eg, as landlord/lodger or as flat-sharers) also sometimes fall foul of the rule. People who provide mutual support and share household expenses are not necessarily cohabiting.[31]

If you disagree with a decision that you are cohabiting, you should challenge the decision, either by asking the decision maker to look at it again (see Chapter 45) or by appealing to the First-tier Tribunal (see Chapter 46), and consider carefully what evidence to submit in relation to each of the six questions on p754 and any other matters you consider relevant. Possibilities include evidence of the other person having another address[32] (eg, a rent book and other household bills), receipts for board and lodging, statements from friends and relatives, or evidence of a formal separation, divorce proceedings or a dissolution application or order.

You do not have to prove that you are not cohabiting when you first apply for benefit,[33] though you are required to provide any information reasonably required to decide your claim.[34] Neither party has the burden of proof in this situation – a decision should simply be made on all the evidence available.[35] In contrast, if your benefit as a single person is stopped because it is alleged that you are cohabiting, the burden of proof is on the decision maker to prove you are.[36]

If your benefit is stopped because you are cohabiting, challenge the decision and/or re-apply immediately if your circumstances change. Also apply immediately for any other benefits for which you might qualify – eg, HB/CTB, as the local authority may reach a different decision to the DWP.[37] You should apply for other benefits for which you previously automatically qualified – eg, health benefits (see Chapter 13).

If you are still entitled to a means-tested benefit, even though it is decided that you are cohabiting, you should be paid as a couple.

If you have no money at all, you may be able to get a social fund crisis loan (see p564).

Couples living apart

If you separate permanently you can claim as a single person immediately. However, you continue to be treated as a couple while you and your partner are temporarily apart.[38] Your former household need not have been in this country.[39] The following rules apply in determining whether you still count as a couple.

- For **IS, income-based JSA, income-related ESA, PC** and **HB**, you count as a couple, even if you or your partner are temporarily living away from your family, unless you:[40]
  - have no intention of resuming living together; *or*
  - are likely to be separated for more than 52 weeks. However, you can still be treated as a couple if you are likely to be separated for more than 52 weeks provided it is not 'substantially' longer and there are exceptional circumstances, such as a stay in hospital, or if there is no control over the length of the absence.
- For **CTB**, you count as a couple, even if you or your partner are temporarily living away from your family. Unlike for HB, this is not defined in the rules.[41]
- For **IS, income-based JSA, income-related ESA** and **PC**, you no longer count as a couple if:[42]
  - either of you are in custody;
  - either of you are released on temporary licence from prison;
  - either of you are a compulsory patient detained in hospital under the mental health provisions;
  - either of you are staying permanently in a care home, an Abbeyfield Home or an independent hospital;
  - you are abroad and do not qualify for IS, income-based JSA, income-related ESA or PC (see Chapter 63). Your partner might be able to qualify for one of those benefits in her/his own right. However, if your partner is temporarily abroad you continue to be treated as a couple (but if you are likely to be separated for more than 52 weeks, see above). However, after four weeks, or eight (26 for ESA) if s/he has taken a child abroad for medical treatment, the amount of IS, income-based JSA, income-related ESA or PC you receive is that for a single claimant.[43] You can qualify for IS as a lone parent if you have children under 16 and you do not have to claim JSA and show that you are available for and actively seeking work.[44] **Note:** your partner's income and capital continue to be treated as yours for as long as you continue to be treated as a couple.

Even if you are no longer treated as a couple for the purposes of calculating your benefit, you may still be liable to maintain your partner (see p799).

- For **IS, income-based JSA** and **income-related ESA** only, you are still treated as a couple if you are temporarily living apart (but if you are likely to be separated for more than 52 weeks, see p758) and one of you is at home or in hospital, or in local authority residential accommodation or in a care home, and the other is:[45]
  - resident in a care home, independent hospital or Abbeyfield Home, but not counted as a patient; *or*
  - in a home for the rehabilitation of alcoholics or drug addicts; *or*
  - in Polish resettlement accommodation; *or*
  - on a government training course and has to live away from home; *or*
  - in an approved probation or bail hostel.

  Although your income and capital are calculated in the normal way for a couple, your applicable amount is calculated as if each of you were single claimants if this comes to more than your usual couple rate. If you have housing costs (see Chapter 38), your applicable amount includes these and also, in some circumstances, the costs of the temporary accommodation of the partner away from home.[46] If both homes are rented, see p255 for when HB can be paid for more than one home. If you own your home and your partner is staying in rented accommodation, you may get your housing costs met by IS, income-based JSA or income-related ESA and your partner may qualify for HB.

Where questions of 'intention' are involved (eg, in deciding whether you or your partner intend to resume living with your family), the intention must be 'unqualified' – ie, it must not depend on a factor over which you have no control, such as the right of entry to the UK being granted by the Home Office[47] or the offer of a suitable job.[48]

3. Claiming for children

A child counts as a member of your family for means-tested benefits. In some cases, amounts can be included for her/him in your benefit if you or your partner are 'responsible' for her/him (see p761)and s/he is living in your 'household' (see p762). You do not have to be a parent.[49]

Note:

- As you cannot claim joint-claim jobseeker's allowance (JSA) if you are responsible for children (see p413), references to income-based JSA in this section do not include joint-claim JSA.
- The law refers to someone aged under 16 as a 'child' and to someone aged 16–20 as a 'qualifying young person'. In this chapter, the term 'child' is used to refer to both.

- Even where amounts of benefit for your child cannot be included in your claim, there are circumstances in which it may be important that a child is still considered to be part of your family. This applies particularly to income support (IS), income-based JSA, income-related employment and support allowance (ESA) and, in some cases, when calculating housing costs.
- The rules do not say when a child counts as a member of your family for pension credit (PC) purposes.

Amounts of benefit (allowances and premiums in your applicable amount) for a child (including a new child) can only be included in your claim for:[50]
- **housing benefit** (HB) or **council tax benefit** (CTB) if the child is a member of your family; *or*
- **IS** or **income-based JSA** if the child is a member of your family and:
  - your current claim for IS or income-based JSA began before 6 April 2004; *and*
  - you had a dependent child(ren) included in that claim before 6 April 2004 but you have not yet been awarded child tax credit (CTC).

Otherwise, amounts of benefit for a child cannot be included in your IS, income-based JSA, income-related ESA or PC. Instead, claim CTC for the child (see p1269).

Income support and income-based jobseeker's allowance

Any new claim for IS or income-based JSA does not include amounts of benefit for a child (see p759).

If you were on IS or income-based JSA before 6 April 2004 and your claim included a dependent child before that date, it may continue to include amounts of benefit for all the children in your family, even those who become part of your family after that date. However, your claim will cease to include amounts for children at some point. While you remain on IS or income-based JSA, this will depend on when you become entitled to CTC.[51]

Your IS/income-based JSA claim ceases to include amounts for children at the earliest of:
- the point you make a claim for and are awarded CTC; *or*
- the point the claim for your child is automatically transferred to a CTC claim.

The DWP and HM Revenue and Customs refer to this transfer process as 'migration'. When this process will begin is yet to be announced. It now seems possible that the DWP will wait until the introduction of universal credit (UC) in October 2013, when IS claims will be transferred to UC, which will include amounts for children (see Chapter 4). See CPAG's *Welfare Rights Bulletin* for updates.

If you were awarded CTC before 6 April 2004, your IS/income-based JSA award ceased to have amounts included for children from that date.[52]

Who counts as a child

A person usually counts as a child (but see below) if:[53]

- s/he is aged under 16; *or*
- s/he is aged 16 or over but under 20 and counts as a 'qualifying young person' for child benefit purposes. This includes, for example, most young people who are at school or college full time studying for GCSEs or A levels (or equivalent), or who are doing approved training (but see p94).

Who does not count as a child

The DWP does *not* count someone as a child for means-tested benefits if:[54]

- s/he is entitled to IS, income-based JSA or income-related ESA in her/his own right; *or*
- s/he is excluded from entitlement to IS, income-based JSA and HB because s/he is aged 16 or 17, left local authority care on or after 1 October 2001 and certain other conditions apply (see p671).

Responsibility for a child

For IS, income-based JSA, income-related ESA, HB and CTB, a child counts as a member of your family if you are 'responsible' for her/him and s/he is living in your 'household'. Amounts of benefit for a child who is part of your family can be included in your claim for HB or CTB and, in some cases, in certain claims for IS or income-based JSA made before 6 April 2004 (see p760).

The rules are different for different benefits. You are treated as 'responsible' for a child if:

- for **income-based JSA**, either you get child benefit for the child or, if no one gets child benefit for the child, the child 'usually lives' with you or you are the only person who has applied for child benefit.[55] However, if you share actual responsibility for the child (eg, with your ex-partner), a court decision means that even if you do not get child benefit for the child, you might be regarded as responsible for the child if you are the 'substantial minority carer' – ie, you have the child with you for at least 104 nights a year.[56] However, this depends on the child benefit rules unlawfully discriminating against you. Arguably, that may be difficult to show in some cases. If, for example, you are a woman who has separated from a male partner, showing discrimination may be difficult because child benefit is usually awarded to the mother when a couple separate.[57] Seek advice if necessary (see Appendix 2). If a child for whom you are responsible gets child benefit for another child, you are also responsible for that child;[58]
- for **income-related ESA**, the child 'usually lives' with you. This is not defined in the rules;[59]
- for **HB** and **CTB**, the child is 'normally living' with you.[60] This means that s/he spends more time with you than with anyone else.[61] If it is unclear in whose

household the child lives, or if s/he spends an equal amount of time with two parents in different homes (this may not mean literally three and a half days with each parent[62]), you are treated as having responsibility if:[63]
- you get child benefit for the child (see Chapter 7);
- no one gets child benefit, but you have applied for it;
- no one has applied for child benefit, or both of you have applied, but you appear to have the most responsibility.

However, if you are a 'substantial minority carer' (see p761), you may be able to argue that you should be regarded as responsible for the child even if you do not get child benefit;[64]

- for **IS**, you get child benefit for the child (see Chapter 7).[65] If no one gets child benefit, you are responsible if you are the only one who has applied for it. In all other cases, the person responsible is the person with whom the child usually lives.[66] However, if you are a 'substantial minority carer' (see p761), you may be able to argue that you should be regarded as responsible for the child even if you do not get child benefit.[67] If a child for whom you are responsible gets child benefit for another child, you are also responsible for that child.[68]

For **HB** and **CTB**, it is important to look at who gets child benefit only when it is unclear in whose household the child *normally* lives. For **IS**, it is essential to look first at who gets child benefit and only if this is not decisive is it relevant to look at where the child *usually* lives. This difference may, for example, mean that in some situations one parent may be able to claim IS for a child while the other parent can claim income-based JSA, HB or CTB for the same child at the same time.

For IS, income-based JSA, HB and CTB, a child can only be the responsibility of one person in any week for the purpose of that benefit.[69] For ESA, the rules do not expressly say this but, in any case, a person can only be responsible for a child if the child usually lives with her/him. If benefit is paid for a child, there is no provision that allows benefit to be split between parents if a child divides her/his time equally between the homes of two parents.

Benefit payable to one person for her/his dependant can be paid to someone else instead,[70] but this is an exceptional measure that only applies if the person paid the benefit is not using it for the child or dependant, or is otherwise squandering it.[71] For HB, rent restrictions apply, limiting the amount of HB you can claim for the size of the accommodation you may need for a child if someone else is considered to be responsible for her/him (see p321).[72]

Living in the same household

If you count as responsible for a child, that child is usually treated as a member of your household despite any temporary absence. For what 'household' means, see p754. However, s/he does *not* count as a member of your household if s/he:[73]

- for **IS, income-based JSA, income-related** ESA and **HB**:

  - has no intention of resuming living with you; *or*
  - is likely to be absent for more than 52 weeks, unless there are exceptional circumstances, such as being in hospital, or if you have no control over the length of absence and the absence is unlikely to be substantially longer than 52 weeks;
- for **CTB**, is temporarily living away from your family. Unlike for HB, this is not defined in the rules;[74]
- for **IS, income-based JSA, income-related ESA, HB** and **CTB**:
  - is being fostered by you or your partner following a formal placement with you by social services. However, you can claim benefit for a child you are fostering privately or if social services have made a less formal arrangement for the child to live with you;
  - is living with you or your partner prior to adoption and has been placed by social services or an adoption agency;
  - is boarded out with you or your partner, whether or not with a view to adoption (for income-based JSA, income-related ESA, HB and CTB only);
  - has been placed with someone else prior to adoption;
  - is in the care of, or being looked after by, the local authority and not living with you. You should receive IS or income-based JSA for her/him for the days when s/he comes home – eg, for the weekend or a holiday.[75] Make sure you tell the decision maker in good time. The local authority can also increase your applicable amount to include the child for HB and CTB for all that week whether the child returns for all or only part of it;[76]
- for **IS, income-based JSA** and **income-related ESA** is not living with you and:
  - has been in hospital or in a local authority home (for non-temporary accommodation) for more than 12 weeks and has not been in regular contact with you or other members of your household. The 12 weeks run from the date s/he went into hospital or the home, or from the date you claim IS/ income-based JSA/income-related ESA, if later.[77] However, the 12 weeks run from the date s/he went into the hospital or home if:[78]
    - you were getting income-based JSA immediately before your claim for IS; *or*
    - you were getting IS or income-related ESA immediately before your claim for income-based JSA; *or*
    - you were getting IS or income-based JSA immediately before your claim for ESA;
  - is in custody. Note that if children can still be included in your claim, you should receive IS or income-based JSA for any periods your child spends at home;[79]
  - has been abroad for more than four weeks, or for more than eight weeks (26 weeks for income-related ESA) to get medical treatment.[80] The four-/eight-/ 26-week period runs from the day s/he went abroad or from the day you claim IS/income-based JSA/income-related ESA, if later. However, the four-/

eight-/26-week period is calculated from the day after the child went abroad if:[81]
  - you were getting income-based JSA immediately before your claim for IS; *or*
  - you were getting IS or income-related ESA immediately before your claim for income-based JSA; *or*
  - you were getting IS or income-based JSA immediately before your claim for ESA;
- for **IS** and **income-based JSA**, is living with you and away from her/his parental or usual home in order to attend school. The child is not treated as a member of your family, but remains a member of her/his parent's household.[82]

To be considered part of your family for IS, income-based JSA, ESA, HB and CTB, a child must be a member of the same household as you. If your family includes a child, you can receive an amount of benefit for that child in your HB and CTB and, in some circumstances, your IS or income-based JSA (see p759).

When to stop claiming for a child

If you still have amounts of benefit for a child included in your claim for IS or income-based JSA, this will cease at the point you become entitled to CTC.

Otherwise, a child stops counting as a member of your family (and you can no longer claim amounts of benefit for her/him in your IS, income-based JSA, HB or CTB) when you no longer fulfil the conditions described above – ie:
- you are no longer responsible for her/him (see p761); *or*
- s/he is no longer a member of your household (see p762); *or*
- s/he no longer counts as a child (see p761).

For example:
- for **all benefits**, you no longer count as responsible for a child as soon as s/he starts normally/usually living elsewhere;
- for **IS**, you stop claiming for a child as soon as someone else starts receiving child benefit for her/him;[83]
- for **IS, income-based JSA, HB** and **CTB**, you stop claiming if the child becomes entitled to IS, income-based JSA or income-related ESA in her/his own right;[84]
- for **all benefits**, a young person counts as a child until s/he is 16, or 20 if s/he counts as a 'qualifying young person' – eg, because s/he is in full-time non-advanced education or approved training (see p634). After leaving such education or training a young person can continue to count as a child until the end of the week which includes the 'terminal date' (see p98), or until s/he reaches 20 or gets a full-time job if that is earlier. 'Full-time' work for dependent children means at least 24 hours a week.[85]

Notes

1. **Who is included in your claim**

1 s137(1) SSCBA 1992; s35(1) JSA 1995
IS Reg 14(2)(c) IS Regs
JSA Reg 76(2)(d) JSA Regs
ESA Reg 2(1) ESA Regs, definitions of 'family' and 'young person'
HB Reg 19(2)(c) HB Regs; reg 19(2)(c) HB(SPC) Regs
CTB Reg 9(2)(c) CTB Regs; reg 9(2)(c) CTB(SPC) Regs

2. **Couples**

2 CFC/7/1992
3 s137(1) SSCBA 1992
IS Reg 2(1) IS Regs
JSA s35(1) JSA 1995; reg 1(3) JSA Regs
ESA Sch 1 para 6(5) and (6) WRA 2007; reg 2(1) ESA Regs
PC s17(1) SPCA 2002; reg 1(2) SPC Regs
HB Reg 2(1) HB Regs; reg 2(1) HB(SPC) Regs
CTB Reg 2(1) CTB Regs; reg 2(1) CTB(SPC) Regs
4 ss124(1)(f)-(h) and 134(2) SSCBA 1992; s3(1)(c)-(de) JSA 1995; Sch 1 para 6(1)(d) WRA 2007; s4(1) SPCA 2002
5 **IS** Reg 4(3) SS(C&P) Regs
JSA Reg 4(3B) SS(C&P) Regs
ESA Reg 4I SS(C&P) Regs
HB Reg 82(1) HB Regs; reg 63(1) HB(SPC) Regs
CTB Reg 68(1) CTB Regs; reg 52(1) CTB(SPC) Regs
6 s1(2)(b) and (6) SPCA 2002
7 Reg 5(1)(h) SPC Regs
8 R(SB) 8/85
9 **IS** Reg 2(1) IS Regs
JSA Reg 1(3) JSA Regs
ESA Reg 2(1) ESA Regs
PC s12 SPCA 2002
HB Reg 2(1) HB Regs; reg 2(1) HB(SPC) Regs
CTB Reg 2(1) CTB Regs; reg 2(1) CTB(SPC) Regs
10 **IS** Regs 18 and 23 IS Regs
JSA Regs 84 and 88(4) and (5) JSA Regs
ESA Regs 68 and 83 ESA Regs
PC Reg 8 and Sch 3 SPC Regs
HB Regs 23 and 25 HB Regs; regs 22 and 23 HB(SPC) Regs
CTB Regs 13 and 15 CTB Regs; regs 12 and 13 CTB(SPC) Regs
11 s1 CPA 2004
12 *Santos v Santos* [1972] 2 All ER 246; CIS/671/1992; CIS/81/1993
13 CIS/4935/1997
14 R(SB) 8/85
15 R(SB) 4/83
16 CSB/463/1986
17 **IS** Reg 2(1) IS Regs
JSA s35(1A) JSA 1995; reg 1(3) JSA Regs
ESA Sch 1 para 6(6) WRA 2007; reg 2(1) ESA Regs
PC s17(1A) SPCA 2002; reg 1(2) SPC Regs
HB Reg 2(1) HB Regs; reg 2(1) HB(SPC) Regs
CTB Reg 2(1) CTB Regs; reg 2(1) CTB(SPC) Regs
IS/HB/CTB s137(1A) SSCBA 1992
18 *R v Penwith DC HBRB ex parte Menear* 24 HLR 120, 11 October 1991
19 *R v South Ribble BC HBRB ex parte Hamilton*, 24 January 2000 (CA)
20 *Crake and Butterworth v SBC* [1982] 1 All ER 498
21 R(SB) 17/81; R(G) 3/71; CIS/87/1993
22 Ch 11 DMG
23 *Crake and Butterworth v SBC,* quoted in R(SB) 35/85
24 R(SB) 35/85
25 para 11018 DMG
26 CIS/72/1994
27 CIS/2900/1998
28 CIS/87/1993
29 CSB/150/1985
30 CIS/87/1993; CIS/2559/2002
31 CSSB/145/1983
32 R(SB) 13/82
33 CIS/317/1994

34 **IS/ESA/PC** Reg 7(1) SS(C&P) Regs
JSA Reg 24 JSA Regs
HB Reg 86 HB Regs; reg 67 HB(SPC) Regs
CTB Reg 72 CTB Regs; reg 57 CTB(SPC) Regs
35 CIS/317/1994
36 R(I) 1/71
37 R(H) 9/04
38 **IS** Reg 16(1) IS Regs
JSA Reg 78(1) JSA Regs
ESA Reg 156(1) and (2) ESA Regs
PC Reg 5(2) SPC Regs
HB Reg 21(1) HB Regs; reg 21(1) HB(SPC) Regs
CTB Reg 11(1) CTB Regs; reg 11(1) CTB(SPC) Regs
39 CIS/508/1992
40 **IS** Reg 16(1) and (2) IS Regs
JSA Reg 78(2) JSA Regs
ESA Reg 156(1)-(3) ESA Regs
PC Reg 5(1)(a) SPC Regs
HB Reg 21(1) and (2) HB Regs; reg 21(1) and (2) HB(SPC) Regs
41 Reg 11(1) CTB Regs; reg 11(1) CTB(SPC) Regs
42 **IS** Reg 16(3) IS Regs
JSA Reg 78(3) JSA Regs
ESA Reg 156(4) ESA Regs. This wrongly refers to Chapter 4, but correctly refers to the rules on temporary absence from Great Britain.
PC Reg 5(1)(b)-(d) and (f) SPC Regs
43 **IS** Sch 7 paras 11 and 11A IS Regs
JSA Sch 5 paras 10 and 11 JSA Regs
ESA Sch 5 paras 6 and 7 ESA Regs
PC Regs 3 and 5(1)(d) SPC Regs
44 Sch 1B para 23 IS Regs
45 **IS** Sch 7 para 9 IS Regs
JSA Reg 85 and Sch 5 para 5 JSA Regs
ESA Sch 5 para 4 ESA Regs
46 **IS** Sch 7 para 9 col (2) IS Regs
JSA Reg 85 and Sch 5 para 5 col (2) JSA Regs
ESA Sch 5 para 4 col 2 ESA Regs
47 CIS/508/1992; CIS/13805/1996
48 CIS/484/1993

3. **Claiming for children**

49 s137 SSCBA 1992; s35 JSA 1995; reg 77 JSA Regs; reg 2(1), definition of 'family', ESA Regs
50 Reg 1 SS(WTCCTC)(CA) Regs
51 Reg 1(3) and (7) SS(WTCCTC)(CA) Regs
52 Reg 1(2) and (6) SS(WTCCTC)(CA) Regs
53 **IS/HB/CTB** s137 SSCBA 1992
IS Reg 14 IS Regs
JSA s35 JSA 1995; regs 1(3) and 76 JSA Regs
ESA Reg 2(1) ESA Regs
HB Reg 19 HB Regs; reg 19 HB(SPC) Regs
CTB Reg 9 CTB Regs; reg 9 CTB(SPC) Regs
54 **IS** Reg 14(2) IS Regs
JSA Reg 76(2) JSA Regs
ESA Reg 2(1) ESA Regs, definition of 'young person'
HB Reg 19(2) HB Regs; reg 19(2) HB(SPC) Regs
CTB Reg 9(2) CTB Regs; reg 9(2) CTB(SPC) Regs
All para 2208 DMG. This does not refer to IB, contributory ESA or tax credits, which arguably should also be included in the list.
55 Reg 77(1)-(3) JSA Regs
56 Reg 77 JSA Regs, as applied in *Hockenjos v Secretary of State for Social Security* [2004] EWCA Civ 1749, reported as R(JSA) 2/05
57 CJSA/2507/2002
58 Reg 77(2) JSA Regs
59 Reg 156(10) ESA Regs
60 **HB** Reg 20(1) HB Regs; reg 20(1) HB(SPC) Regs
CTB Reg 10(1) CTB Regs; reg 10(1) CTB(SPC) Regs
61 CFC/1537/1995
62 CFC/1537/1995
63 **HB** Reg 20(2) HB Regs; reg 20(2) HB(SPC) Regs
CTB Reg 10(2) CTB Regs; reg 10(2) CTB(SPC) Regs
64 *Hockenjos v Secretary of State for Social Security* [2004] EWCA Civ 1749, reported as R(JSA) 1/05, applies only to JSA. However, it may support arguments concerning HB/CTB based on the HRA 1998. Note that, in the context of CTC, the argument has been rejected by *Humphreys v HMRC* [2010] EWCA Civ 56
65 Reg 15(1) IS Regs
66 Reg 15(2) IS Regs

67 *Hockenjos v Secretary of State for Social Security* [2004] EWCA Civ 1749, reported as R(JSA) 2/05, applies only to JSA. However, it may support arguments concerning IS based on the HRA 1998. Note that, in the context of CTC, the argument has been rejected by *Humphreys v HMRC* [2010] EWCA Civ 56
68 Reg 15(1A) IS Regs
69 **IS** Reg 15(4) IS Regs
JSA s3(1)(d) JSA 1995; reg 77(5) JSA Regs
HB Reg 20(3) HB Regs; reg 20(3) HB(SPC) Regs
CTB Reg 10(3) CTB Regs; reg 10(3) CTB(SPC) Regs
70 Reg 34 SS(C&P) Regs
71 *Barber v SSWP* [2002] EWHC Admin 1915, 17 July, unreported
72 *R v Swale BC, ex parte Marchant, The Times*, 17 November 1999 (CA)
73 **IS** Reg 16 IS Regs
JSA Reg 78 JSA Regs
ESA Reg 156 ESA Regs
HB Reg 21 HB Regs; reg 21 HB(SPC) Regs
CTB Reg 11 CTB Regs; reg 11 CTB(SPC) Regs
74 Reg 11(1) CTB Regs; reg 11(1) CTB(SPC) Regs
75 **IS** Regs 15(3) and 16(6) IS Regs
JSA Regs 77(4) and 78(7) JSA Regs
ESA Reg 156(8) ESA Regs
76 **HB** Reg 21(5) HB Regs; reg 21(5) HB(SPC) Regs
CTB Reg 11(4) CTB Regs; reg 11(4) CTB(SPC) Regs
77 **IS** Reg 16(5)(b) IS Regs
JSA Reg 78(5)(c) JSA Regs
ESA Reg 156(6)(c) ESA Regs
78 **IS** Reg 16(5A) IS Regs
JSA Reg 78(6) JSA Regs
ESA Reg 156(7) ESA Regs
79 **IS** Regs 15(3) and 16(6) IS Regs
JSA Regs 77(4) and 78(5)(i) and (7) JSA Regs
ESA Reg 156(6)(h) and (8) ESA Regs
80 **IS** Reg 16(5)(a) and (aa) IS Regs
JSA Reg 78(5)(a) and (b) JSA Regs
ESA Reg 156(6)(a) and (b) ESA Regs
81 **IS** Reg 16(5A) IS Regs
JSA Reg 78(6) JSA Regs
ESA Reg 156(7) ESA Regs
82 **IS** Reg 16(7) IS Regs
JSA Reg 78(8) JSA Regs
83 Reg 15 IS Regs
84 **IS** Reg 14(2)(b) and (d) IS Regs
JSA Reg 76(2)(b), (c) and (e) JSA Regs
HB Reg 19(2) HB Regs; reg 19(2) HB(SPC) Regs
CTB Reg 9(2) CTB Regs; reg 9(2) CTB(SPC) Regs
85 Regs 1(3), definition of 'remunerative work', and 7 CB Regs

35

Chapter 35

National insurance contributions

This chapter covers:

Key facts

- Entitlement to contributory benefits and sometimes the amount that is paid depends on your national insurance (NI) contribution record. In the case of Category B retirement pension and bereavement benefits, it depends on the NI contribution record of your spouse or civil partner, or your late spouse or civil partner.
- Depending on your circumstances, you may be liable to pay NI contributions from the age of 16 until you reach pension age.
- If you are not liable to pay NI contributions, in some circumstances you can be credited with them or you may be able to make voluntary payments.
- There are different types of NI contributions (called 'classes') and not all classes of NI contributions or all types of credited NI contributions count for all contributory benefits.
- NI contributions are collected by HM Revenue and Customs.

Future changes: April 2013 and after

The pension age of women is being gradually raised, so that by November 2018 the pension age of both men and women will be 65. After that, the pension age of both men and women will rise. See p531 for details and CPAG's *Welfare Rights Bulletin* for updates.

1. How decisions are made

Most decisions on national insurance (NI) contributions are made by an officer of HM Revenue and Customs (HMRC). Appeals against such decisions can be decided by an HMRC review or by the First-tier Tribunal (Tax).[1] The process is similar to appealing against an HMRC decision on your entitlement to a statutory payment (see p1225).

Decisions relating to entitlement to NI credits are made either by HMRC or the DWP, depending on the type of NI credit under consideration.

If you disagree with a decision on your entitlement to NI credits, you can apply for a revision or supersession of the decision (see Chapter 45), or you can appeal. Your appeal will be decided by the First-tier Tribunal (Social Security and Child Support).[2] See Chapter 46.

2. **Contributions: liability and payment**

Classes of contribution

There are six different classes of national insurance (NI) contribution.[3] The class you pay depends on whether you are an employed or self-employed earner, or a voluntary contributor. Not all classes of contribution count for all benefits.[4] In some circumstances you may qualify for credited NI contributions (see p779). Contributions are paid for a tax year – ie, 6 April to 5 April.

Class of contribution	*Payable by*	*Giving entitlement to*
Class 1	Employed earners and their employers	All benefits with contribution conditions
Class 1A and 1B	Employers of employed earners	No benefits
Class 2	Self-employed earners	All benefits with contribution conditions except contribution-based jobseeker's allowance
Class 3	Voluntary contributors	Bereavement benefits and retirement pensions
Class 4	Self-employed earners	No benefits

The amount of Class 1 or 4 contributions you pay depends on your earnings. You do not necessarily gain more benefit by paying higher contributions.

Employed earners and self-employed earners

An '**employed earner**' is 'a person who is gainfully employed in Great Britain either under a contract of service, or in an office (including an elective office) with general earnings'.[5] This means you are an 'employed earner' if income tax is, or should be, deducted from your earnings under the Pay As You Earn scheme.

Office holders include judges, company directors and registrars of births, deaths and marriages.

A **'self-employed earner'** is anyone 'gainfully employed in Great Britain otherwise than in employed earner's employment'.[6]

It is normally clear whether you are employed or self-employed. If there is a dispute, it usually concerns whether you are employed under a *contract of service* (in which case you are an employee) or a *contract for services* (in which case you are self-employed). When considering this, the decision maker must take into account factors such as how closely your work is supervised, whether you can employ a substitute to do your job for you, the method of payment, whether the contract is for a fixed period, and whether you have to provide your own equipment. No one criterion is conclusive and different weight is attached to each in different cases.[7]

Note:

- Certain people are deemed to be employed earners.[8] These are office cleaners, many agency workers, people employed by their spouse or civil partner for the purposes of their spouse's or civil partner's employment, some entertainers and most ministers of religion. Before 6 April 2012, lecturers, teachers and instructors were also deemed to be employed earners.
- Examiners, moderators and invigilators are deemed to be self-employed.[9]
- If you have two or more jobs, it is possible to be both employed and self-employed.

Employment for which contributions not payable

You do not have to pay NI contributions on earnings from certain kinds of employment – eg, if you are employed:[10]

- in your home by a close relative as long as you both live in the home and the job is not for the purposes of any trade or business carried out there. **'Close relative'** is a parent, grandparent, step-parent, son, daughter, grandson, granddaughter, stepson, stepdaughter, sibling, half-sibling (step-parents and stepchildren include those relationships formed by civil partnerships);
- by your spouse or civil partner if it is not for the purposes of your spouse's or civil partner's employment;
- as a self-employed earner if you are not ordinarily self-employed.

Age limits

Contributions are intended to be paid during a normal working life, and so are not payable if you are under 16[11] or over pension age (see p531).[12] HM Revenue and Customs (HMRC) should send you a certificate of age exemption when you reach pension age. Ask at your local HMRC enquiry centre if it does not, or contact the National Insurance Contributions Office (see Appendix 1). Employers of people over pension age still have to pay the employer's NI contributions at the full (contracted-in) rate. See p786 for details of credited contributions for men approaching pension age.

These age rules currently discriminate against men (and, in some circumstances, also against women) on the grounds of gender, but see p1243.

If you have obtained a full gender recognition certificate, your pension age and therefore the age limit for payment of your contributions will change to that of your recognised gender. In some circumstances, your pension age can be changed in this way without a full certificate (see p1247).[13]

Residence and presence in Great Britain

European Union co-ordination rules and reciprocal agreements

The rules on liability for NI contributions when you have come to the UK from abroad or if you go abroad are complex. In particular, the rules described below may not apply if you are covered by the European Union co-ordination rules (see p1503) or if you move from or to a country which has a reciprocal agreement with the UK (see p1429). The international caseworker at the HMRC's Contributions Office deals with enquiries about liability for NI contributions if you are going abroad (tel: 0845 915 4811, or for address see Appendix 1).

Class 1 contributions must usually be paid by employees who are employed in Great Britain[14] and who are resident, present (except for temporary absences) or ordinarily resident in Britain at the time.[15]

If you are employed by an overseas employer and are not ordinarily resident or employed in the UK, you are not liable for Class 1 contributions until you have been resident in Britain for a year.[16]

If you are working abroad, you must still pay Class 1 contributions for the first year if your employer has a place of business in Britain, you were resident in Britain before your employment started and you are still ordinarily resident in Britain.[17] After that year you are entitled, but not obliged, to pay Class 3 contributions.[18]

Class 2 contributions must be paid if you are self-employed in Great Britain and are either ordinarily resident in Britain, or have been resident here for at least 26 weeks during the last year.[19] If you are present in Britain, and self-employed, they may be paid voluntarily if you are not required to pay them.[20] If you are self-employed outside Great Britain, you may pay Class 2 contributions if you wish, provided you were employed or self-employed immediately before you left Britain and, *either*:

- you have been resident in Great Britain for a continuous period of at least three years at some time in the past; *or*

- you have paid contributions producing an earnings factor of at least 52 times the lower earnings limit in each of three years in the past (see pp788 and 774 for the meaning of these terms). Each set of 52 flat-rate contributions paid before April 1975 counts as satisfying that condition in respect of one year.[21]

Certain volunteer development workers who are employed abroad may be allowed to pay Class 2 contributions. These are paid at a special rate and give entitlement to contribution-based jobseeker's allowance (JSA).[22]

Class 3 contributions are always voluntary. They may be paid if you are resident in Great Britain throughout the course of the year in respect of which you wish to pay the contributions or if:

- you arrived in Britain in the year for which you want to pay contributions and either you were liable to pay Class 1 or 2 contributions earlier that year or you have been ordinarily resident for at least part of the year; *or*
- you arrived in Britain in the year for which you want to pay contributions, or in the previous year, and you have been in Britain for a continuous period of 26 weeks.

Normally, they may be paid while you are abroad if you satisfy either of the conditions which would allow you to pay Class 2 contributions, but you do not need to have been employed or self-employed before you left Britain. You may also pay them if you paid Class 1 contributions for the first year you were employed abroad.[23]

Class 4 contributions are payable only if you are resident in the UK for income tax purposes.[24]

If you wish to pay Class 2 or 3 contributions while abroad, leaflet NI38 contains an application form.

The meaning of the terms 'resident' and 'present' are explained on p1429. Members of the armed forces are deemed always to be present in Great Britain and there are special rules for aircrew, mariners, share fishermen and offshore workers on the continental shelf.

For the factors which are taken into account in deciding where you are 'ordinarily resident', see p1430.

Northern Ireland and Isle of Man contributions count towards British benefits, as do contributions paid in other countries in some circumstances. In particular, this may apply if you have paid contributions in the European Economic Area (see p1500). You may also be entitled to benefits from other countries while you are in this country (see Chapter 61).

Reduced liability for married women and widows

Women who were married or widowed on 6 April 1977 could choose to pay reduced Class 1 or no Class 2 contributions, provided they applied to do so before 12 May 1977.[25]

If you 'elected' to pay at this reduced rate, you can continue to do so until you either apply to pay the full rate again (called 'revoking an election') or until the right to pay reduced contributions is automatically lost. Situations in which the right is automatically lost include on divorce or when you have two consecutive tax years either with no earnings from self-employment or on which you have had to pay Class 1 contributions.[26]

There are disadvantages to reduced liability, but it is worth thinking carefully about your position if you are considering giving it up. Once lost, the right cannot be reclaimed. The following considerations are relevant.

- Reduced contributions do not entitle you to contributory benefits and, in some circumstances, revoking your election may mean that you can build up your pension entitlement (see p793). However, even with reduced liability you may still qualify for bereavement benefits and Category B retirement pension, non-contributory benefits and means-tested benefits.
- Although you may also gain an additional pension under the additional state pension scheme if you start to pay full Class 1 contributions, it might be better to continue to pay reduced contributions and put the money into a private scheme instead. An independent financial adviser should be able to advise you on this.
- If you are employed with earnings below the primary threshold but above the lower earnings limit (see p774), you are normally treated as having paid Class 1 contributions on those earnings for the purpose of entitlement to contributory benefits. If you have elected to pay reduced contributions, you are only treated as having paid a reduced rate of contribution on those earnings and so will not build up entitlement to contributory benefits.[27]
- You cannot qualify for most types of NI credits unless you revoke the election (see p779).

If you are thinking of giving up your reduced liability seek independent advice (see Appendix 2).

To revoke your election, complete the form in HMRC leaflet CF9 for married women or CF9A for widows.

Class 1 contributions

Class 1 contributions are paid by both employed earners (see p769 – known as primary contributors) and their employers (secondary contributors).[28]

The amount of the Class 1 contributions you pay depends on the amount you earn in relation to the upper and lower earnings limit set for the tax year, and to the amount of that year's 'primary threshold'. If your earnings are equal to or below the primary threshold you do not have to pay NI contributions on them (but if they are between the lower earnings limit and the primary threshold, you are treated as if you had paid Class 1 NI contributions on those earnings).

If you earn more than the primary threshold, you are liable to pay Class 1 contributions of 12 per cent of your earnings between the primary threshold and upper earnings limit, plus 2 per cent of the earnings you have above the upper earnings limit. If you are contracted out of the additional state pension scheme (see p537), the amount you pay on your earnings between the primary threshold and the upper accrual point is reduced to 10.6 per cent.[29]

Year	*Lower earnings limit*	*Primary threshold*	*Upper accrual point*	*Upper earnings limit*
2011/12	£102	£139	£770	£817
2012/13	£107	£146	£770	£817

See Appendix 8 for the earnings limits and primary threshold for earlier years.

If you are paid monthly, the lower earnings limit and upper accrual point are multiplied by four-and-one-third to give monthly equivalents. In 2012/13, the monthly equivalent of the primary threshold is £634 and the upper earnings limit is £3,540.[30]

Example

If your weekly earnings in the tax year 2012/13 are £190, your Class 1 contribution is:

£190 – £146 = £44

12% x £44 = £5.28

If you are a married woman or widow with reduced liability for contributions (see p772), in 2012/13 you pay 5.85 per cent of your earnings between the primary threshold and the upper earnings limit plus 2 per cent of your earnings above the upper earnings limit.[31]

Note: the percentage rates of Class 1 contributions changed on 6 April 2011. For the rates for earlier tax years, see previous editions of CPAG's *Welfare Benefits and Tax Credits Handbook*.

Payment

It is your employer's responsibility to deduct Class 1 contributions from your earnings and pay them with its own contributions to HMRC.[32] If your employer has deducted Class 1 contributions from your earnings, but has failed to pay them to HMRC, you are treated as though they had been paid unless you have been negligent, or consented to or connived in that arrangement.[33]

More than one job

If you have more than one job, the basic rule is that your liability to pay Class 1 contributions is calculated for each job as if the other(s) did not exist.[34]

Example

Mary earns £60 a week working part time in a school and £90 a week working in a pub in the evenings. Neither she nor her employers pay any Class 1 contributions because her earnings in each job are below the lower earnings limit. As a result, unless she is entitled to NI credits (see p779), Mary is not earning any entitlement to contributory benefits.

There are some exceptions to this rule – eg, if you have:[35]

- more than one job, you can claim a refund if, during a tax year, you pay more than the annual maximum;
- two different jobs for the same employer or employers who carry on business in association with each other, earnings from these jobs are normally added together and your NI contributions are based on your total earnings. This is to stop employers avoiding the liability to pay contributions.

Class 2 contributions

You must pay Class 2 contributions if you are a self-employed earner (see p769) unless you are exempt from liability. The main ground for being exempt is that you have obtained a certificate of exception because your earnings are below a certain level (£5,595 a year in 2012/13). This is also known as a '**small earnings exception**' (see p776).[36] Certain expenses are deducted when calculating your earnings.[37]

Even if you have a small earnings exception, you may still choose to pay Class 2 contributions to protect your NI contribution record for contributory ESA, retirement pension and bereavement benefits.[38]

Class 2 contributions are payable at a flat rate.[39] The current and recent rates are:

2011/12	£2.50 a week
2012/13	£2.65 a week

Married women and widows with reduced liability for contributions (see p772) are not liable for Class 2 contributions.[40] Volunteer development workers employed abroad and share fishermen pay Class 2 contributions at special rates which count towards contribution-based JSA, unlike other Class 2 contributions.[41]

If you are self-employed and also have a job as an employed earner, you pay both Class 1 and Class 2 contributions, subject to a maximum.[42]

From April 2011, Class 2 contributions are due on 31 January and 31 July each year or can be paid by monthly or six-monthly direct debit.[43]

Applying for a small earnings exception

To apply for a certificate of exception, complete Form CF10, available from local offices of the HMRC and on HMRC's website. A certificate can only be backdated for up to 13 weeks before the date of application, at HMRC's discretion.[44] Usually your earnings are estimated as below the minimum level if they were below that level in the previous year and there has been 'no material change of circumstances'.

You can apply for a refund of any Class 2 contributions you have paid if your earnings in that year were, in fact, sufficiently low to entitle you to an exemption from liability. The application must be made in writing after the end of the relevant tax year (ie, on or after 6 April) and must be made no later than the 31 January following the end of the relevant tax year.[45]

Class 3 contributions

Payments of Class 3 contributions are voluntary.[46] They give entitlement only to bereavement benefits and retirement pension and are not payable if your earnings factor is otherwise sufficient in that tax year to meet the contribution condition for those benefits (see pp793, 792 and 793).[47]

If there are years for which you do not have a full contribution record, perhaps because you did not qualify for credited NI contributions and have been abroad or in prison, or you were employed but your earnings were below the lower earnings limit, it may be beneficial to pay Class 3 contributions in some circumstances, but there are often time limits for doing so (see p778).

Class 3 contributions are paid at a flat rate. The current and recent rates are:[48]

2011/12	£12.60 a week
2012/13	£13.25 a week

You can normally request a state pension forecast to help you decide whether to pay Class 3 contributions. At the time of writing, pension forecasts were temporarily unavailable for women born after 5 April 1953 or men born after 5 April 1951; instead, less detailed state pension statements are provided. To obtain a forecast or statement either telephone the Future Pension Centre (tel: 0845 3000 168 or textphone: 0845 3000 169) or apply by post using Form BR19, which you can obtain from www.direct.gov.uk or from your local Jobcentre Plus or DWP office. Alternatively, you may be able to apply for a forecast online at www.direct.gov.uk.

Any accidental overpayment of Class 3 contributions for a particular year should be refunded if you make a written application.[49] In addition, if changes to the retirement pension contribution conditions in 2010 mean you have paid Class 3 contributions for no gain in pension entitlement, you may qualify for a refund. If you reach pension age on or after 6 April 2010 and:

- you were not aware of the changes to the contribution conditions for retirement pension (see p793) and, as a result, you paid Class 3 (or voluntary Class 2) contributions on or after 25 May 2006 (when these plans were announced) but before 26 July 2007, you can request a refund of those contributions; *or*
- despite already having at least 30 qualifying years for your retirement pension, you paid Class 3 (or voluntary Class 2) contributions on or after 26 July 2007 in the mistaken belief that this would increase the rate of your retirement pension, you can request a refund of those contributions. Arguably, this can apply even if HMRC sent you notification of the retirement pension changes before you paid the contributions.[50]

Class 4 contributions

Class 4 contributions are paid by self-employed earners (see p769) when their profits in a tax year are above a certain level (in 2012/13, above £7,605). They are paid in addition to Class 2 contributions, but give no extra entitlement to benefit.[51] The amount paid is 9 per cent of profits between £7,605 and £42,475, plus 2 per cent of profits above £42,475. The current and recent rates are:

Year	*9% on profits between*	*2% on profits above*
2011/12	£7,225 and £42,475	£42,475
2012/13	£7,605 and £42,475	£42,475

Your Class 4 contributions are calculated on your taxable profits using the income tax self-assessment procedure and are usually collected with your income tax by HMRC. You may apply for permission to defer payment for a specified period if the amount to be paid has not yet been established.[52]

If you are liable to pay Class 1 and/or Class 2 and Class 4 contributions, the total payable is subject to a maximum.[53]

Note: the percentage rates of Class 4 contributions changed on 6 April 2011. For earlier rates see previous editions of CPAG's *Welfare Benefits and Tax Credits Handbook*.

Pre-1975 contributions

The present contribution system was introduced on 6 April 1975. Between 5 July 1948 and 5 April 1975, Class 1 contributions were paid by a 'flat-rate stamp' in the same way as Class 2 and Class 3 contributions. Graduated contributions giving entitlement to graduated retirement benefit (see p529) were introduced in 1961, but were collected separately.

Before 6 April 1975, contribution years were not the same as tax years, as they are now. Instead, the month in which they began depended on the last letter of the contributor's NI number. There were complicated transitional arrangements in both 1948 and 1975 so that you may have had a contribution year that was not 12 months long. That may explain what would otherwise be anomalies in your contribution record.

Late payment of contributions

Contributions can still count for benefit purposes if they are paid late, but normally only if they are paid within the two years (Class 1) or six years (Class 2 or Class 3) after the end of the tax year in which they were due (but see below for exceptions and note that different time limits apply for voluntary Class 2 contributions).[54] Students, apprentices, trainees and prisoners may pay Class 3 contributions to cover their period of education, apprenticeship or imprisonment at any time before the end of the sixth complete tax year after that period finished.[55]

However, even if paid within these time limits, contributions paid late normally cannot count for benefit entitlement for a period before the date on which they were actually paid. In the case of the second contribution condition for contribution-based JSA and contributory ESA, contributions paid late also cannot count for benefit entitlement unless they were either paid before the start of the relevant benefit year (see p789) or, if they were paid after this, until six weeks after they have been paid.[56] Only in limited circumstances can contributions which are paid after the above time limits count for benefit purposes.[57] For example:

- If you reach pension age between 6 April 2008 and 5 April 2015 and you have paid sufficient NI contributions and/or received sufficient NI credits for at least 20 years to count as qualifying years for retirement pension, you can pay additional Class 3 contributions for six tax years falling at any time from the start of the 1975/76 tax year and they will count for benefit purposes. If you reached pension age before 6 April 2010, years of home responsibilities protection can count towards the 20 years (see p795) but at least one of those 20 years must consist of paid (not just credited) contributions. You must pay these contributions within six years of reaching pension age. If you pay these contributions on or after 6 April 2011 they will count for benefit purposes from the date that you pay them and therefore may help to increase your retirement pension entitlement from that date. If you paid them before 6 April 2011 your retirement pension could be increased for an earlier period too, if you had already reached pension age.[58]
- If credits which were awarded to you as a result of a particular official error were removed from your contribution record on or after 1 July 2007 you can pay voluntary Class 2 and Class 3 contributions for the tax years 1993/94 to 2007/08 at any time up to 5 April 2014 and they will count for benefit purposes

from the date that you pay them. Class 2 contributions are voluntary if you are entitled, but not liable to pay them. The official error is defined on p787.[59]

See p776 for advice on whether you should pay Class 3 contributions.

Voluntary contributions may be paid on behalf of a contributor after her/his death, provided they are paid no later than s/he would have been allowed to pay them.[60] This may be useful to gain entitlement to, or increase the rate of, widowed parent's allowance or bereavement allowance (see pp66 and 67).

3. **National insurance credits**

In some circumstances, you can be 'credited' with earnings or with Class 3 contributions. Such 'credits' can help you satisfy:

- the second contribution condition for benefits with two contribution conditions – ie, contribution-based jobseeker's allowance (JSA), contributory employment and support allowance (ESA), widowed parent's allowance, bereavement allowance and, when entitlement is based on the 'old contribution conditions', Category A and B retirement pensions (see p793);
- the single contribution condition for Category A and B retirement pensions if this applies to you (see p793).

Most kinds of credits count for all these benefits; the following credits do not:

- credits for certain parents and carers (see p781), starting credits (see p784) and some credits for some tax credits (see p786) which only count for Category A and B retirement pensions, widowed parent's allowance and bereavement allowance; *and*
- credits for bereavement (see p786) and some education and training credits (see p784) which only count for contribution-based JSA and contributory ESA.

Note:

- You can only receive sufficient credits in any tax year to meet the minimum contribution condition for that year.[61]
- Credits cannot help you to satisfy the first contribution condition for benefits with two contribution conditions or to qualify for a bereavement payment, which has a single contribution condition.
- Married women currently opting for reduced liability for contributions (see p772) can only qualify for credits for certain parents and carers (see p781), for family members providing childcare (see p783), and for official error (see p787), starting credits (but see p784) and credits following bereavement (see p786). They are not entitled to other types of credits.[62]

Certain kinds of credits are usually awarded automatically – eg, if you qualify on the basis of getting JSA or ESA. For others, you must apply. Enquiries about credits can be made to the National Insurance (NI) Contributions Office (see Appendix 1).

Credits for unemployment, incapacity for work or limited capability for work

You can be credited with earnings equal to the lower earnings limit for *either:*[63]

- each complete week (ie, the seven days from Sunday to Saturday) for which you receive JSA (or for which you would have received JSA but for the loss of benefit for benefit offences rules – see p1106); *or*
- each complete week for which you satisfy or can be treated as satisfying the following qualifying conditions for JSA (see Chapter 19) – ie, that you :
  - are available for work; *and*
  - are actively seeking work; *and*
  - are not engaged in full-time paid work (see p718); *and*
  - are not in relevant education; *and*
  - do not have limited capability for work (see Chapter 11); *and*
  - are under pension age;

  or you would have satisfied these conditions in that week but for having limited capability for work or being incapable of work (see p399) for part of the week. You must make a written claim for these credits, either on the first day for which you are claiming them or within a reasonable period of time after that, and you must provide the DWP with the evidence it requires to show that you satisfy the conditions; *or*
- each complete week in which you would have satisfied the above conditions for JSA except that you are being treated as in full-time paid work because you received a compensation payment – eg, pay in lieu of notice (see p723); *or*
- each complete week during which you:
  - were entitled to statutory sick pay (SSP); *or*
  - had limited capability for work (or during which you would have had limited capability for work if you had been entitled to contributory ESA or if you had claimed ESA or maternity allowance – MA); *or*
  - were incapable of work or could be treated as incapable of work (see Chapter 32) or you would have been had you made a claim for incapacity benefit (IB) or MA.

  However, you cannot qualify for credits for days on which you were treated as not having limited capability for work or not being incapable of work for ESA or IB purposes (or on which you would have been, had you otherwise been entitled to ESA or IB).

Credits for SSP, limited capability for work or incapacity for work must be claimed before the end of the benefit year (ie, by the first Saturday in January – see p789) following the tax year in which you are entitled to the credit. This time limit can be extended if it is considered reasonable to do so, given your circumstances.[64]

Entitlement to credits for unemployment is one reason why you might continue to 'sign on' at the Jobcentre Plus office, even if you do not qualify for JSA, as this will protect your right to contributory benefits.

However, you will not get credits for unemployment for weeks in which:[65]

- you would not have been entitled to JSA (whether or not you actually claimed it) because you are involved in a trade dispute; *or*
- you are not being paid JSA (or if you are a member of a joint-claim couple, you are not being paid JSA or your JSA is reduced) because of an employment-related sanction, jobseeker's direction sanction, training scheme or employment scheme sanction (see p456) because you failed to attend an interview as required (see p422) or you are receiving hardship payments (see Chapter 20); *or*
- you are a 16/17-year-old receiving JSA severe hardship payments (see p408).

Credits for certain parents and carers

These credits count for Category A and B retirement pensions, widowed parent's allowance and bereavement allowance. They replace **home responsibilities protection** for the tax years from 6 April 2010. For how previous years' home responsibilities protection are treated, see pp782 and 795. You can be credited with Class 3 contributions for each week which falls after 6 April 2010 if:

- for any part of the week, you get child benefit for a child under the age of 12;[66] *or*
- you reside with someone who, for any part of the week, gets child benefit for a child aged under 12 and:
  - you share responsibility with that person for a child under 12; *and*
  - in the tax year to which the credit relates, the earnings factor of the person receiving child benefit is higher than 52 times that year's lower earnings limit (see p788). In calculating this, any credits s/he receives for getting child benefit for a child under 12 are ignored;[67]

  In this situation you must apply to HM Revenue and Customs (HMRC) for the credits; *or*
- in that week you are caring for someone for at least 20 hours, or for more than one person for a total of at least 20 hours; *and*:[68]
  - the person(s) for whom you care is entitled to a qualifying benefit (see p782); *or*
  - the decision maker considers that the level of care provided is appropriate.

  Unless you are a woman who has elected to pay reduced rate NI contributions (see p772) and are getting carer's allowance (CA), you must apply to the DWP for these credits. You can continue to qualify for these credits for the 12 weeks after the week in which you stop satisfying this condition – this allows you to have breaks in caring of up to 12 weeks without losing credits; *or*

- in that week you satisfy the conditions for carers who may qualify for income support (IS) described on p348 (the rules do not state that you must get IS to qualify for credits in this situation);[69] *or*
- for any part of the week you are an approved foster carer (including a kinship carer in Scotland). To qualify for credits on this ground you must make an application to HMRC;[70] *or*
- the week falls in the 12 weeks:[71]
  - before the date you become entitled to CA; *or*
  - following the week you stop being entitled to CA (unless you already qualify for credits for CA for that week – see p784).

For these purposes, a **'qualifying benefit'** includes attendance allowance, the middle or highest rate of disability living allowance care component, constant attendance allowance in respect of an industrial or war disablement, and certain payments under the Pneumoconiosis, Byssinosis and Miscellaneous Diseases Benefits scheme or Workmen's Compensation (supplementation) scheme.[72]

Unless you are entitled on the basis that you get child benefit for a child under 12, you will only qualify for these credits if you are ordinarily resident in Great Britain and not in prison or in legal custody.[73]

If you have to apply to the DWP or HMRC for these credits, your application must be received before the end of the tax year following the tax year to which the credits relate. This time limit can be extended if the DWP or HMRC consider it reasonable in the circumstances. Applications to HMRC can be made on Form CF411A, available from www.hmrc.gov.uk. Applications to the DWP can be made on Form CC1, available from www.direct.gov.uk.

Credits for home responsibilities protection

Changes from 6 April 2010

Home responsibilities protection, which helped you satisfy the second contribution condition for retirement pension, bereavement allowance and widowed parent's allowance, was abolished on 6 April 2010 and was replaced with NI credits for certain parents and carers (see p781). Years of home responsibilities protection which were awarded for tax years up to and including 2009/10 either still help you meet the second contribution condition for the above benefits (see p795) or are converted to NI credits, as described below. Home responsibilities protection was not awarded for years before 6 April 1978.

Any year of home responsibilities protection which you received for the tax years up to and including 2009/10 is converted into 52 Class 3 NI contributions:

- for Category A and Category B retirement pensions, if the 'single contribution condition' is used to determine your entitlement (see p793);
- for widowed parent's allowance and bereavement allowance, if the contributor died on or after 6 April 2010.

However:

- for Category A and B retirement pensions, this conversion can only be done for a maximum of 22 tax years;
- for widowed parent's allowance and bereavement allowance, it can only be done for half the requisite number of years needed to qualify for a full basic widowed parent's allowance and bereavement allowance (see p794).[74]

Credits for family members providing childcare

These credits count for:

- Category A retirement pension and Category B retirement pension for spouses and civil partners, if the contributor (see p788) reaches pension age on or after 6 April 2012;
- Category B retirement pension for widows, widowers and surviving civil partners, widowed parent's allowance and bereavement allowance if the contributor died on or after 6 April 2012 (and, for Category B pension, did not reach pension age before that date).

From 6 April 2011, you can be credited with a Class 3 contribution for each week during which you provide childcare for a child aged under 12, if:[75]

- you are a specified family member of the child (you do not need to be a blood relative and many ex-family members count – see p784); *and*
- someone is getting child benefit for the child for that week and s/he has paid, or is treated as having paid, sufficient Class 1 NI contributions in respect of the tax year in which the week falls for the year to count as a qualifying year for her/his retirement pension (see p793); *and*
- you are not entitled to credits on the basis of being a parent or carer (see p781); *and*
- you are ordinarily resident in Great Britain.

You must apply for these credits after the end of the tax year in question and must include the name and date of birth of the child, details of the weeks in which you provided care and, if requested by the DWP or HMRC, a declaration from the person getting child benefit for the child. There is no set number of hours for which you must care for the child to qualify and no time limit for claiming, but you can only get these credits for weeks falling after 6 April 2011. Only one person can qualify for these credits for a particular week for the same child. However, if childcare is shared it may be possible for someone else to get credits for different weeks in a tax year or, if you look after more than one child, for you each to get credits for the same week in respect of one of the children.

Family member

You count as a specified 'family member' if you are:[76]

– the child's parent, grandparent, great or great-great-grandparent, sibling, aunt, or uncle (including if you are an adopted, step- or half-sibling of the child or of the child's parent);
– a spouse or civil partner, or former spouse or civil partner, of any of the above relatives;
– a partner or former partner of any of the above (including, for instance, a former partner of a former spouse of one of the above relatives);
– a son or daughter of any of the above;
– a spouse, civil partner or partner (or former spouse, civil partner or partner) of the child's first cousin.

A 'partner' is someone with whom the relative lives as if they are husband and wife or civil partners.

Credits for carer's allowance

You can be credited with earnings equal to the lower earnings limit for each week in which you receive CA (see Chapter 6), or would receive it but for the loss of benefit for benefit offences rules (see p1106).[77] You also receive credits if the only reason that you do not receive CA is because you are receiving a bereavement benefit or widow's benefit instead.

If you are looking after a disabled person but are not entitled to credits under these provisions, you may qualify for credits for certain carers (see p781).

Starting credits

You can receive Class 3 credits for the tax years in which you reach the age of 16, 17 and 18 if you would otherwise have had an insufficient contribution record for those years to count towards the contribution conditions for Category A and B retirement pensions, widowed parent's allowance and bereavement allowance.[78]

However, for Category A and B retirement pensions, you can only qualify for these credits:

- for tax years falling before 6 April 2010; *and*
- if you have to make an application for an NI number to be allocated to you, if your application for an NI number was made before 6 April 2010.

No credits were made under this provision for years before 6 April 1975.

Education and training credits

For the purpose of qualifying for contribution-based JSA and contributory ESA, you can be credited with earnings equal to the lower earnings limit for either one of the two complete tax years that fall before the relevant benefit year (see p789), if:

- for any part of those tax years you were on:[79]
  - a course of full-time training, including training to acquire occupational or vocational skills (or, if you are disabled, a part-time course of at least 15 hours a week); *or*
  - a course of full-time education; *or*
  - an apprenticeship; *and*
- in the other tax year in which you must satisfy the second contribution condition for the benefit (see p791) you have an earnings factor of 50 times the lower earnings limit without recourse to this provision; *and*
- you are at least 18 or will become 18 during the tax year in question; *and*
- you were under 21 when the course or apprenticeship started; *and*
- your course of education, training or apprenticeship has finished.

You can also receive credits which count for all benefits for each week in which you are undertaking a training course approved by a DWP decision maker if:[80]

- the training is full time, unless either you are disabled, when it must be for at least 15 hours a week, or it is an introductory course; *and*
- the training is not part of your job; *and*
- the training is intended to last for one year or less (except in certain circumstances if it is a course for disabled people); *and*
- you were 18 or over at the beginning of the tax year in which the week falls.

Credits for statutory maternity, additional paternity and adoption pay

You can be credited with earnings equal to the lower earnings limit for each week for which you receive statutory maternity pay, additional statutory paternity pay or statutory adoption pay.[81] This will be important only if you are receiving an amount that is less than the lower earnings limit (currently £107 a week). You must claim these credits by writing to the NI Contributions Office (see Appendix 1). Your claim must be received before the end of the benefit year (see p789) following the tax year in which the week falls, but this time limit may be extended if it is reasonable to do so.

Credits for jury service

You are entitled to be credited with earnings equal to the lower earnings limit for each week after 6 April 1988 during which you spend at least part of the week on jury service, unless you are self-employed in that week.[82] You must claim these credits by writing to the NI Contributions Office (see Appendix 1). Your claim must be received before the end of the benefit year (see p789) following the tax year in which the week falls (or such further period as is reasonable).

Credits following bereavement

If your entitlement to a bereavement benefit has ended, you can be credited with sufficient earnings for each year up to and including the one in which your bereavement benefit stopped to enable you to satisfy the second contribution condition for contribution-based JSA or contributory ESA (but see note below).[83]

For the purpose of satisfying the second contribution condition for contributory ESA, you are also entitled to credits for each year up to and including the one in which your entitlement to widow's allowance (abolished in April 1988) or widowed mother's allowance ceased (but see note below).[84]

Note: you cannot qualify for credits following bereavement if your entitlement to widows' or bereavement benefits stopped because you married or entered into a civil partnership, or if payment stopped because you started cohabiting (see p71).[85]

Credits for men born before 6 October 1954

If you are a man who was born before 6 April 1954, you can be credited with earnings (known as 'autocredits') from the tax year in which you would have reached pension age had you been a woman (see Appendix 6) up to, but not including, the tax year in which you reach the age of 65.[86] You cannot qualify for these credits for any year in which you were abroad for more than 182 days. Also, if you are self-employed, you must *either*:

- be liable for at least one Class 2 contribution in any of the above tax years; *or*
- have a small earnings exception (see p775) for at least one week in any of the above tax years,

to qualify for credits for the other weeks in that year.

Credits for tax credits

You are entitled to be credited with earnings equal to the lower earnings limit for each week for any part of which you receive the disabled worker element or severe disability element of working tax credit (WTC).

Alternatively, for Category A or B retirement pension, widowed parent's allowance, or bereavement allowance purposes, a credit is given for each week for which WTC is paid to you. In this case, if WTC was paid to you as a member of a couple but only one of you has earnings, the credits will be awarded to that person; otherwise they are awarded to the person to whom WTC is paid.

In both cases, you only qualify for these credits during any week in which you were *either*:[87]

- employed and earning less than the lower earnings limit for that year; *or*
- self-employed but not liable to pay Class 2 contributions because you have a small earnings exception (see p775).

This provision also existed for working families' tax credit and disabled person's tax credit, and for family credit and disability working allowance, all of which have been abolished (see CPAG's *Welfare Benefits Handbook* 1999/00 and 2002/03 for details).

Credits for a quashed conviction

If you were imprisoned or detained in legal custody after being convicted of an offence, and that conviction has subsequently been quashed by the courts, you can be credited with earnings for each week during at least part of which you were imprisoned or detained.[88] Your application for these credits should be sent in writing, by post or email, to the NI Contributions Office (see Appendix 1).

Credits for official error

Some people were wrongly awarded credits for incapacity for work or approved training in the tax years from 1993/94 to 2007/08 as a result of an official error arising from discrepancies between the DWP and HMRC computer systems. If this applied to you (or, in some cases, your spouse or civil partner), you (or your spouse or civil partner) may, in very limited circumstances, be credited with earnings to satisfy the second contribution condition for Category A or B retirement pensions and JSA.[89]

Effectively, this means that the official mistake is rectified by ensuring you are awarded the credits which were previously given erroneously.

There were similar rules to enable you to satisfy the second contribution condition for incapacity benefit (but you can now only claim this in limited circumstances – see p337).[90] See CPAG's *Welfare Benefits and Tax Credits Handbook* 2009/10 edition for details.

Credits for service families

From 6 April 2010, you can be credited with earnings equal to that year's lower earnings limit for each week during any part of which you were:[91]

- the spouse or civil partner of a member of the armed forces (or someone treated as such for the purpose of occupying accommodation); *and*
- accompanying, or were treated as accompanying, her/him on an assignment outside the UK.

To qualify for these credits, you must make a claim for them (normally on Form MODCA1) once you have a confirmed date for the end of the overseas posting. Send your application to the NI Contributions Office (see Appendix 1). Your application should be made before the end of the tax year following the tax year in which the overseas assignment ended. This time limit can be extended if it is reasonable given your circumstances. The decision maker has discretion to accept an application made before you receive confirmation of the end date of the overseas assignment. If your application is accepted, you can be awarded credits for the period before your application, but you have to make a further application under these rules for credits for any subsequent period.

4. Contribution conditions for benefits

Entitlement to contributory benefits normally depends on the national insurance (NI) contribution conditions being met. For contribution-based jobseeker's allowance (JSA) and contributory employment and support allowance (ESA) (unless you can qualify for contributory ESA without satisfying the contribution conditions), your entitlement is based on your own NI contribution record. For other contributory benefits, the relevant '**contributor**' is:

- for Category A retirement pension, you or your late spouse or civil partner, or your former spouse or civil partner (see p527);
- for Category B retirement pension, your spouse or civil partner, or your late spouse or civil partner;
- for bereavement payment, widowed parent's allowance or bereavement allowance, your late spouse or late civil partner.

You may be credited with earnings or contributions to fill gaps in your contribution record (see p779). These credits can only count towards the second contribution condition (but not the first contribution condition) for benefits which have two contribution conditions, or towards the single contribution condition for Category A or B retirement pension (see p793).

If you are a widow, widower or surviving civil partner, you may be able to combine your own contribution record with that of your late spouse or civil partner in order to claim a Category A retirement pension (see p527). You may also be able to combine your own contribution record with that of your former spouse or civil partner to qualify for a Category A retirement pension if you have been divorced or your civil partnership has been dissolved.

It may be possible for you to rely on the contributions you have paid in other European Economic Area states to qualify for contributory benefits (see p1500).

For the contribution conditions for incapacity benefit (IB), see CPAG's *Welfare Benefits and Tax Credit Handbook* 2008/09 edition.

Earnings factors

Payment of Class 1, 2 and 3 contributions gives rise to an 'earnings factor', which is used to calculate your entitlement to contributory benefits (including the additional pension payable under the additional state pension scheme – see p537).

For Class 1 contributions, the earnings factor is the amount of earnings, excluding those earnings above the upper earnings limit (or above the upper accrual point for additional state pension – see p774), on which those contributions have been paid. Each Class 2 and Class 3 contribution gives rise to an earnings factor equal to that year's lower earnings limit.[92]

From 6 April 2002, certain people may be deemed to have an earnings factor equal to the lower earnings threshold to build up their entitlement to additional state pension.

Jobseeker's allowance and employment and support allowance

Contributory employment and support allowance from 1 May 2012

Under new rules, which are likely to be introduced on 1 May 2012, you will only be able to get contributory ESA for a maximum of 365 days. However, as days you are in the support group or the assessment phase (if this is immediately followed by you being in the support group) are not counted, your contributory ESA will only stop after 365 days if you are not in the support group. If your entitlement ends because you have reached the 365-day maximum, you will only be able to qualify for contributory ESA again if:[93]

- you satisfy the NI contribution conditions for contributory ESA, but one of the tax years in which you satisfy the second contribution condition falls after the last tax year you relied on to meet this condition in your earlier claim; *or*
- you have continued to have limited capability for work since your contributory ESA entitlement ended and you now have, or are treated as having, limited capability for work-related activity (see p185). In this situation, you will not have to satisfy the contribution conditions again.

Contribution-based JSA and contributory ESA have two contribution conditions.

However, you can qualify for contributory ESA without having to satisfy the contribution conditions if:

- you are entitled to ESA in youth (see p176), as this has no contribution conditions (but note that ESA in youth is likely to be abolished for new claimants from 1 May 2012); *or*
- you are transferred to contributory ESA, having previously received IB or severe disablement allowance (SDA) (see p193). In this situation, the contribution conditions for contributory ESA are waived; *or*
- you were getting IB or SDA but, following a determination that you do not have limited capability for work, your IB or SDA is not converted into contributory ESA and you have appealed against the decision. In this situation, you are treated as satisfying the contribution conditions for contributory ESA while you are pursuing your appeal (see p210).

Definition of terms

A '**benefit year**' is almost the same as a calendar year and runs from the first Sunday in January.[94]

The **'relevant benefit year'** for **contribution-based JSA** is the benefit year in which the jobseeking period began or, if earlier, the benefit year in which a period that is linked to the jobseeking period began (see p394).[95]

The **'relevant benefit year'** for **contributory ESA** is the benefit year in which your current period of limited capability for work started. However, if you otherwise would not meet the contribution conditions for contributory ESA, your relevant benefit year can instead be any benefit year which includes any part of your period of limited capability for work (or any part of any period(s) of limited capability for work that can be linked to your current period – see p212). **Note:** a period of limited capability for work cannot include a period which falls before the three-month time limit for backdating an ESA claim.[96]

The first condition

To qualify for contribution-based JSA and contributory ESA (unless you can qualify for contributory ESA without satisfying the contribution conditions – see above), you must have paid sufficient contributions of the appropriate class in one of the last two complete tax years before the relevant benefit year (see p789).

The contributions must be:[97]

- for contribution-based JSA, Class 1 (unless you are a share fisherman or volunteer development worker, when special Class 2 contributions can count);
- for contributory ESA, Class 1 or 2.

The earnings on which you paid (or were treated as having paid) Class 1 contributions and, for contributory ESA, the earnings factor (see p788) from your Class 2 contributions must be at least equal to 26 times that year's lower earnings limit (eg, £2,782 in 2012/13 – 26 x £107). In calculating the earnings on which you paid Class 1 contributions, you cannot include any earnings above the lower earnings limit, so you must have worked for at least 26 weeks in one of the last two tax years before your relevant benefit year to meet this condition. The 26 weeks do not need to be consecutive but must fall in a single tax year.[98]

Note:

- The first contribution condition can be relaxed in some circumstances (see p791).
- The contributions must be paid before the week for which contribution-based JSA or contributory ESA is claimed.
- A widow can be treated as satisfying the first NI contribution condition for contributory ESA if she was entitled to widowed mother's allowance but her entitlement has ended (this does not apply if her entitlement ended because she married or entered into a civil partnership, or if payment stopped because she started cohabiting).[99] She may also be credited with contributions to satisfy the second condition (see p786). This help with the first contribution condition for contributory ESA does not extend to widows, widowers or surviving civil partners who lose entitlement to bereavement benefits.

When the first condition is relaxed

In some situations, the first contribution condition is relaxed, so that sufficient contributions paid in *any* one tax year are enough to satisfy the condition, as long as they were paid before the week for which you are claiming the benefit.

For contribution-based JSA and contributory ESA, this applies if you were entitled to credits for service families (see p787) in at least one week in the tax year before the relevant benefit year (see p789).[100]

For contributory ESA it also applies if you:[101]

- were entitled to carer's allowance (CA) (even if it was not paid because of the overlapping benefit rules – see p1041) in the last complete tax year before the relevant benefit year;
- were entitled to NI credits at some time in any tax year before the relevant benefit year because you had been in prison or a detention centre and your conviction was subsequently quashed by the courts (or you would have been entitled to such credits had you claimed them);
- were in full-time paid work (see p1296) for more than two years immediately before your period of limited capability for work began and you were entitled to working tax credit which included a disabled worker or severe disability element (see p1311).

Note: some people may have been wrongly refused contributory ESA between 1 November 2010 and 30 October 2011. This may apply to you if you fall into one of the groups in the above bullet points but, despite the rules being relaxed, you did not meet the first contribution condition, although you had paid in any one tax year before your relevant benefit year Class 1 or 2 contributions producing an earnings factor of at least 25 times the lower earnings limit for that year. The DWP should contact you if this applies to you. If not, seek advice.[102]

The second condition

To qualify for contribution-based JSA and contributory ESA, you must have also either paid the appropriate class of contributions, or received NI credits, producing an earnings factor (see p788) at least equal to 50 times the lower earnings limit in each of the last two complete tax years ending before the relevant benefit year.[103] Class 1 contributions (or special Class 2 contributions – see p790) count for contribution-based JSA; Class 1 and 2 contributions count for contributory ESA. Not all types of NI credits count for JSA and ESA (see p779).

The timing of your claim

In rare cases, it may be beneficial for you to delay a claim for contribution-based JSA so that you can draw on a different year's contribution record. This is because the years in which you must meet the contribution conditions depend on the benefit year in which your jobseeking period starts. So, for example, if your current jobseeking period is not linked to an earlier one (see p394) and you claim before Sunday 1 January 2012, you must meet the second contribution condition in the tax years 2008/09 and 2009/10, whereas if you claim on 1 January 2012, you must meet it in 2009/10 and 2010/11.

Any day for which you do not claim does not count as part of your jobseeking period (see p394),[104] so it is easy to postpone when that period begins. However, if you claim and are refused benefit because the contribution conditions are not satisfied, your jobseeking period will have started. You would then normally have to wait for more than 12 weeks to make a fresh claim. The 12-week gap would break the jobseeking period.

The situation is different for contributory ESA. If your claim for contributory ESA is refused on the grounds that you do not meet the contribution conditions, in some cases it can be worth putting in a later claim that falls in a different benefit year (see p789).

Example

Shanti lives with her partner who works full time. Shanti was self-employed and paid Class 2 NI contributions throughout the tax years 2009/10 and 2010/11 (in the tax year 2008/09 she did not pay NI contributions or get NI credits). In December 2011 she became ill and claimed contributory ESA. The relevant benefit year (see p789) was 2011 and the two complete tax years falling before that are 2008/09 and 2009/10. Having no contributions or credits for 2008/09, Shanti was refused contributory ESA. If she claims again in the 2012 benefit year (which started on 1 January 2012) the contributions she paid in 2009/10 and 2011/12 are counted and she may qualify for contributory ESA. The rules allow 2012 to count as her relevant benefit year as part of her period of limited capability for work falls in that year.

Bereavement payment

The only contribution condition for a bereavement payment is that your spouse or civil partner must actually have paid in any one tax year before s/he reached pension age (or before her/his death, if s/he died before reaching pension age) contributions of Classes 1, 2 or 3, producing an earnings factor (see p788) of at least 25 times the lower earnings limit – eg, £2,675 in 2012/13 (25 x £107).[105]

The sum of any contributions paid in any year may be counted if s/he only became liable to pay contributions in either the last complete tax year before the benefit year in which s/he reached pension age or in which s/he died (if s/he died before reaching pension age), or in the tax year before that.

In certain circumstances, the contribution condition for bereavement payment is treated as satisfied if your late spouse or civil partner had previously successfully claimed and met the first contribution condition for maternity allowance (MA) or IB. (MA no longer has contribution conditions, although it did for women whose expected week of childbirth fell before 20 August 2000.[106])

The payment of 25 flat-rate contributions in a contribution year before 6 April 1975 also satisfies this condition.[107]

Category A and B retirement pensions from 6 April 2010

A single contribution condition for Category A and B retirement pensions was introduced on 6 April 2010. The 'single contribution condition' applies if:[108]

- for Category A retirement pension, and for Category B pension for spouses and civil partners (see p527), the contributor reaches pension age on or after 6 April 2010; *or*
- for Category B retirement pension for widows, widowers and surviving civil partners (see p527), the contributor (ie, your late spouse or civil partner) had not reached pension age before 6 April 2010 and died on or after that date.

Otherwise the 'old contribution conditions' for Category A and B retirement pensions still apply (see below).

If the single contribution condition applies, to qualify for a full basic Category A or B retirement pension, the contributor must have paid Class 1, 2, or 3 NI contributions, or received NI credits, with an earnings factor of at least 52 times that year's lower earnings limit for each of at least 30 years of her/his working life – eg, £5,564 in 2012/13 (52 x £107).[109] Contributions paid before 6 April 1975 also count towards satisfying this condition, but not all credits count (see p779).

If this condition is met for less than 30 years, as long as the condition is met in at least one year, a reduced rate of the basic pension can be awarded. You qualify for one-thirtieth of the basic weekly pension for each year in which the contribution condition is satisfied. Any additional pension to which you are entitled is also paid.[110]

Category A and B retirement pensions before 6 April 2010, widowed parent's allowance and bereavement allowance

The single contribution condition for Category A and B retirement pensions, described above, was introduced on 6 April 2010. However, entitlement to Category A or B retirement pension will still be assessed on the basis of the 'old contribution conditions' if the contributor reached pension age before 6 April 2010 or, when entitlement to Category B retirement pension is based on the contribution record of a late spouse or civil partner, if s/he reached pension age or died before 6 April 2010.

There are two contribution conditions for widowed parent's allowance and bereavement allowance, and, if the old contribution conditions apply, for Category A or B retirement pension.

The first condition

The contributor (see p788) must have paid in any one tax year before s/he died or reached pension age Class 1, 2 or 3 contributions with an earnings factor of 52 times that year's lower earnings limit – eg, £5,564 in 2012/13 (52 x £107).[111] The payment of 50 flat-rate contributions for any time before 6 April 1975 also satisfies this condition.[112]

The first condition is deemed to be satisfied if the contributor was receiving the support or work-related activity component of ESA (see p184) or long-term IB either:

- in the year in which s/he died (if s/he died before reaching pension age) or in which s/he reached pension age; *or*
- in the preceding year.[113]

The second condition

To satisfy the second contribution condition, the contributor must have paid or been credited with contributions with an earnings factor of at least 52 times that year's lower earnings limit for each of the requisite number of years.[114] Class 1, 2 and 3 contributions and contributions paid before 6 April 1975 count towards satisfying this condition, but not all NI credits count (see p779).

The requisite number of years needed to satisfy this condition depends on the length of the contributor's 'working life'. Your 'working life' is the period inclusive of the tax year in which you reach the age of 16 up to but excluding the year in which you reach pension age or in which you die (if earlier).[115]

If you were over 16 on 5 July 1948, your working life is taken as having started either on 6 April 1948 or on 6 April of the year between 1936 and 1948 that you first started paying contributions, if you paid contributions before 5 July 1948.[116]

The requisite number of years is then calculated as follows.[117]

Length of 'working life'	*Requisite number of years*
1–10 years	Length of working life minus 1
11–20 years	Length of working life minus 2
21–30 years	Length of working life minus 3
31–40 years	Length of working life minus 4
41–50 years	Length of working life minus 5

To calculate the number of years before 6 April 1975 in which you satisfied the contribution condition, add together all the contributions paid or credited before 6 April 1975, and divide the answer by 50. If that does not produce a whole number, round the result up, as long as that does not produce a number greater than the number of years of your working life before 6 April 1975.

A reduced rate of benefit may be paid if you have not met the second contribution condition for the requisite number of years (see p795) and, in some circumstances, past years of home responsibilities protection may reduce the number of years over which you must meet the second contribution condition (see below).

Home responsibilities protection

Home responsibilities protection was abolished on 6 April 2010. However, you can still rely on years of home responsibilities protection which were awarded for the tax years up to and including the 2009/10 tax year to meet the second contribution condition for:

- widowed parent's allowance and bereavement allowance if your late spouse or civil partner died before 6 April 2010; *or*
- Category A and B retirement pensions if the old contribution conditions apply (see p793).

See CPAG's *Welfare Benefits and Tax Credits Handbook* 2009/10 edition for further details of home responsibities protection if this applies. If the conditions in the bullet points above do not apply, past years of home responsibilities protection are converted into NI credits (see p782).

Reduced benefit because of insufficient contributions

Benefit can be paid at a reduced rate if the second contribution condition is not satisfied for the requisite number of years, provided it is satisfied in at least 25 per cent of the requisite number. The benefit is paid at a percentage of the amount which would otherwise be paid. The percentage is calculated by expressing the number of years in which the condition is satisfied as a percentage of the requisite number of years and rounding it up to the nearest whole number.[118] Thus, if you are a widow and your husband's working life was 12 years, so that the requisite number of years is 10, if he only satisfied the condition in eight years, you receive 80 per cent of the standard rate of widowed parent's allowance or bereavement allowance.

If you still qualify for them, increases for adult dependants are reduced in the same proportion, but increases for children are paid in full (see Chapter 33).[119]

It may be possible for you to pay Class 3 contributions (see pp776 and 778) to increase the number of years in which the second contribution condition is satisfied. Whether this is worthwhile will depend on the length of time for which benefit will be paid (remember, for example, that you can only be entitled to bereavement allowance for a maximum of 52 weeks), the amount of the Class 3 contributions you will need to pay, and the amount of benefit to which such payment will entitle you. If in doubt, seek advice.

Notes

1. **How decisions are made**
 1 s11 SSC(TF)A 1999; Part III SSC(DA) Regs; arts 6 (c)(i) and 7 First-tier Tribunal and Upper Tribunal (Chambers) Order 2010, No.2655
 2 Sch 3 para 17 SSA 1998; s17 SSC(TF)A 1999; arts 2-4 National Insurance Contribution Credits (Transfer of Functions) Order 2009, No.1377

2. **Contributions: liability and payment**
 3 s1(2) SSCBA 1992
 4 s21(1) and (2) SSCBA 1992; s2 JSA 1995; Sch 1 paras 1 and 2 WRA 2007
 5 s2(1)(a) SSCBA 1992
 6 s2(1)(b) SSCBA 1992
 7 *Ready Mix Concrete South East Ltd v Ministry of Pensions and National Insurance* [1968] 2 QB 497 (QBD); *Global Plant v Secretary of State for Health and Social Security* [1971] 3 All ER 385 (QBD)
 8 Sch 1 paras 1-5A SS(CatE) Regs
 9 Sch 1 paras 6 SS(CatE) Regs
 10 Sch 1 paras 7-12 SS(CatE) Regs
 11 ss6(1), 11(1) and 13(1) SSCBA 1992; reg 93 SS(Con) Regs
 12 ss6(3) and 11(2) SSCBA 1992; regs 49(2A) and 91 SS(Con) Regs
 13 *Richards v SSWP*, C-423/04 [2006] ECR, unreported; R(P) 1/07; *Grant v United Kingdom*, No.32570/03, 23 May 2006, unreported (ECtHR); CP/3485/2003; R(P) 1/09; R(P) 2/09; CSP/503/2007; *CT v SSWP* [2009] UKUT 49 (AAC); *Timbrell v SSWP* [2010] EWCA Civ 701; see also paras 75024-52 DMG
 14 ss2(1)(a) and 6 SSCBA 1992
 15 Reg 145(1)(a) SS(Con) Regs
 16 Reg 145(2) SS(Con) Regs
 17 Reg 146 SS(Con) Regs
 18 Reg 146(2)(b) SS(Con) Regs
 19 ss2(1)(b)and 11 SSCBA 1992; reg 145(1)(d) SS(Con) Regs
 20 Reg 145(1)(c) SS(Con) Regs
 21 Regs 147 and 148 SS(Con) Regs
 22 Regs 149 and 151 SS(Con) Regs
 23 Regs 49A, 145(1)(e), 146(2)(b), 147, 148 and 148A SS(Con) Regs
 24 Reg 91(b) SS(Con) Regs
 25 Reg 127 SS(Con) Regs
 26 Regs 128(1) and 130 SS(Con) Regs
 27 Reg 6 SSC(NPPC1C) Regs
 28 ss6 and 7 SSCBA 1992
 29 ss6, 6A and 8 SSCBA 1992; ss8 and 41 PSA 1993
 30 Reg 11(2)(b), (2A)(a) and (3)(a) SS(Con) Regs
 31 s19(4) SSCBA 1992; reg 131 SS(Con) Regs
 32 Sch 1 para 3 SSCBA 1992
 33 Reg 60 SS(Con) Regs
 34 Regs 13, 14, 15 and 21 SS(Con) Regs
 35 Sch 1 para 1 SSCBA 1992; regs 13, 14, 15 and 21 SS(Con) Regs
 36 s11 SSCBA 1992; regs 43 and 46 SS(Con) Regs
 37 Reg 45 SS(Con) Regs
 38 Reg 46 SS(Con) Regs
 39 s11(1) SSCBA 1992
 40 Reg 127(1) SS(Con) Regs
 41 Regs 125, 149, 151 and 152 SS(Con) Regs
 42 Reg 21 SS(Con) Regs
 43 Regs 89 and 90 SS(Con) Regs
 44 s11(5) SSCBA 1992; reg 44 SS(Con) Regs
 45 Reg 47 SS(Con) Regs
 46 s13 SSCBA 1992
 47 s14 SSCBA 1992
 48 s13(1) SSCBA 1992
 49 Reg 56 SS(Con) Regs
 50 *Clifford Bonner and Others v HMRC* [2010] UKUT 450 (TCC)
 51 s15(1) and (3) SSCBA 1992
 52 Regs 95-99 SS(Con) Regs
 53 Reg 100 SS(Con) Regs
 54 Reg 4 SS(CTCNIN) Regs
 55 Reg 48(3)(b) SS(Con) Regs
 56 Reg 4(7) and (8) SS(CTCNIN) Regs
 57 Regs 50 and 61 SS(Con) Regs; regs 4(11), 5A, 6, 6A and 6B SS(CTCNIN) Regs
 58 s13A SSCBA 1992; reg 3(8D) SS&CS(DA) Regs; reg 6C SS(CTCNIN) Regs

59 Regs 50(B) and 61A SS(Con) Regs, but see also regs 4(1A) and 6B SS(CTCNIN) Regs
60 Reg 62 SS(Con) Regs

3. **National insurance credits**
61 Reg 3 SS(Cr) Regs
62 Regs 7(3), 7A(2)(b), 7B(3), 7C(4), 8(2)(b), 8A(5)(e), 8B(3), 9B(3), 9C(4), 9D(4) and 9E(8) SS(Cr) Regs
63 Regs 8A and 8B SS(Cr) Regs
64 Reg 8B(4) SS(Cr) Regs
65 Reg 8A(5) SS(Cr) Regs
66 s23A(2) and (3)(a) SSCBA 1992
67 s23A(2) and (3)(c) SSCBA 1992; regs 2, 5(1)(a), 6 and 9 SS(CCPC) Regs
68 s23A(2) and (3)(c) SSCBA 1992; regs 5(1)(b), 7(1)(c), 10 and 11 SS(CCPC) Regs
69 s23A(2) and (3)(c) SSCBA 1992; reg 5(1)(c) SS(CCPC) Regs
70 s23A(2) and (3)(b) SSCBA 1992; regs 4 and 9 SS(CCPC) Regs
71 Reg 7 SS(CCPC) Regs
72 Reg 2 SS(CCPC) Regs
73 Reg 8 SS(CCPC) Regs
74 s23A(5)-(7) SSCBA 1992
75 Reg 9F SS(Cr) Regs
76 Sch SS(Cr) Regs
77 Reg 7A SS(Cr) Regs
78 Reg 4 SS(Cr) Regs
79 Reg 8 SS(Cr) Regs
80 Reg 7 SS(Cr) Regs
81 Reg 9C SS(Cr) Regs
82 Reg 9B SS(Cr) Regs
83 Reg 8C SS(Cr) Regs
84 Reg 3(1)(b) SSB(MW&WSP) Regs
85 HMRC includes same-sex partners in this exclusion because cohabitation stops payment not entitlement to the benefit.
86 Reg 9A SS(Cr) Regs
87 Regs 7B and 7C SS(Cr) Regs
88 Reg 9D SS(Cr) Regs
89 Regs 8E and 8F SS(Cr) Regs
90 Reg 8D SS(Cr) Regs
91 Reg 9E SS(Cr) Regs

4. **Contribution conditions for benefits**
92 Sch 1 SS(EF) Regs
93 ss51 and 52 WRA 2012
94 s21(6) SSCBA 1992; s2(4) JSA 1995; Sch 1 para 3 WRA 2007
95 s2(4) JSA 1995
96 Sch 1 para 3(1)(f) WRA 2007; regs 2(1) and 13 ESA Regs
97 **JSA** s2 JSA 1995; regs 158 and 167 JSA Regs
ESA Sch 1 para 1 WRA 2007
98 **JSA** ss1(2)(d) and 2 JSA 1995; reg 45A JSA Regs
ESA Sch 1 para 1 WRA 2007; reg 7A ESA Regs
99 Reg 3(1) SSB(MW&WSP) Regs
100 Reg 45B JSA Regs; reg 8(2)(ca) ESA Regs
101 Reg 8 ESA Regs
102 Regs 23(3) and 28 Social Security (Miscellaneous Amendments) (No.3) Regulations 2011, No.2425
103 s2 JSA 1995; Sch 1 para 2 WRA 2007
104 Reg 47(3)(a) JSA Regs
105 s21and Sch 3 para 4 SSCBA 1992
106 Sch 3 paras 7 and 9 SSCBA 1992
107 Reg 13(1) SS(STB)(T) Regs
108 Sch 3 para 5A(1) SSCBA 1992
109 s122(1), definition of 'qualifying earnings factor', and Sch 3 para 5A SSCBA 1992
110 Reg 6A SS(WB&RP) Regs
111 Sch 3 para 5 SSCBA 1992
112 Reg 6 SS(WBRP&OB)(T) Regs
113 Sch 3 para 5(6) and (6A) SSCBA 1992
114 Sch 3 para 5(3) SSCBA 1992
115 Sch 3 para 5(8) SSCBA 1992
116 Reg 7(7) SS(WBRP&OB)(T) Regs; s20 and Sch 3 para 5(5) SSCBA 1992
117 Sch 3 para 5(5) SSCBA 1992
118 Reg 6 SS(WB&RP) Regs
119 s60(4)-(6) SSCBA 1992; reg 6(3) SS(WB&RP) Regs

Chapter 36

Maintenance

This chapter covers:

This chapter explains how maintenance affects your entitlement to benefits. How to claim maintenance for yourself or your children, and how maintenance is calculated and enforced, is beyond the scope of this *Handbook*. You may be able to claim maintenance through the courts or, if it is for children, via the Child Support Agency (part of the Child Maintenance and Enforcement Commission). However, it is advisable to consult a solicitor if you need to claim maintenance or if maintenance is being sought from you. If you are on a low income, you may qualify for help with the costs of legal advice.

Key facts

- Maintenance is money you receive from someone who has a duty to support you or children who live with you.
- If you receive child maintenance, it does not affect your means-tested benefits or tax credits.
- Other types of maintenance may be treated as income and could reduce your benefits.
- If you have to pay maintenance, this does not entitle you to additional amounts in means-tested benefits and tax credits.
- If you receive benefits and have to pay child support, you may be liable to pay a minimum amount which can be deducted from your benefits.
- If you receive benefits and you are in arrears with child support, a deduction may be made from them towards the arrears.

1. What is maintenance

Maintenance is financial support paid for another person. In some cases, there is a legal liability to maintain (or to pay towards the maintenance of) another person. If you are, or have been, married or in a civil partnership, you may be able to get maintenance for yourself ('spousal maintenance') on a voluntary basis or under a court order. You should seek legal advice about this.

You may be able to get child maintenance for a child who lives with you if one or both of the child's parents do not live with her/him on a full-time basis. Child maintenance may be paid voluntarily, following a court order (or, in Scotland, a registered agreement) or following an application to the Child Support Agency (CSA) ('child support maintenance'). For further information about the child support scheme, see CPAG's *Child Support Handbook*.

Maintenance may also be legally required if you have come to the UK following a formal sponsorship undertaking. Your sponsor is liable to maintain you if you are not able to support yourself.

Who is liable to maintain you if you are on means-tested benefits

If someone is 'liable to maintain' you, it means that s/he must pay maintenance for you to live on. If you are claiming income support (IS), income-based jobseeker's allowance (JSA) or income-related employment and support allowance (ESA), the Secretary of State for Work and Pensions can take proceedings against anyone who is legally supposed to maintain you. If that person fails to maintain you, s/he can be prosecuted (see p800). In practice, it is very rare for the Secretary of State to take this action. You should not be refused benefit solely because someone is liable to support you and is not doing so. However, if the Secretary of State does pursue the liable person for maintenance, any money that is recovered may affect your benefit.

These rules only apply to maintenance for an adult, and do not apply if you are claiming pension credit (PC). For child support maintenance, see p800.

While you are on IS, income-based JSA or income-related ESA, the law states that you must be maintained by your spouse or civil partner if you are married, in a civil partnership or separated. Liability ceases (for social security purposes) on divorce or dissolution of a civil partnership.[1] If you have to live apart from your spouse or civil partner because you need care or treatment (eg, in hospital or in a care home), you may be assessed and paid as separate individuals for benefit purposes (see p758). However, your spouse or civil partner is still liable to maintain you and may be asked to make a financial contribution towards your care.

While you are on IS, if you are the subject of a formal sponsorship/undertaking you must be maintained by a sponsor who has undertaken to support you.[2]

In practice, however, if you have come to the UK as the result of a maintenance undertaking, you may not be able to claim IS (see p1413).

Proceedings against people who are liable to maintain you

If the DWP takes proceedings to pursue someone who is liable to maintain you for maintenance, the magistrates' court (sheriff court in Scotland) can make an order telling the liable person what s/he has to pay.[3] The fact that you may have agreed not to ask for maintenance does not prevent an order being made,[4] although the court must take all the circumstances of the liable person into account.[5]

Prosecution

A person who is liable to maintain you (see p799) can be prosecuted if IS, income-based JSA or income-related ESA is paid as a result of her/his persistently refusing or neglecting to pay money for you to live on. The maximum penalty is three months' imprisonment or a fine of £2,500, or both.[6] If you are charged with such an offence, see a solicitor.

Collection of maintenance by the DWP

If the DWP obtains an order for maintenance for your support from a magistrates' court, including via orders made in the county court or High Court but registered in the magistrates' court (sheriff court in Scotland), the court order may be payable directly to you, to the DWP (through the court), or, in Scotland, via your solicitor. If the order requires the liable person to make payments to the DWP, the DWP can give notice in writing that payments be made direct to you.[7] The DWP will ask you to agree to this by signing a form.

Payments that the liable person has agreed to pay without a court order are only likely to be collected by the DWP if, for example, maintenance is in arrears or you ask for this arrangement because you do not want any contact with the liable person.

2. Child maintenance

This section applies if a child lives with you, but one or both of her/his parents do not live with her/him full time. You can apply to the Child Support Agency (CSA) for child maintenance, but you do not have to do so, even if you are on benefits. You may be referred to the Child Maintenance Options service, an impartial service provided by the Child Maintenance and Enforcement Commission. This provides information about the choices available for arranging child maintenance. You can use the Child Maintenance Options service whether or not you claim benefits. If you prefer not to consult the service, your benefits are unaffected.

What is child maintenance

'**Child maintenance**' means any payment directly or indirectly made by a liable relative (but not you or your partner, or a sponsor) towards the living costs of a child or young person who lives with you.[8] The liable relative (see p804) will usually be your ex-partner and/or the parent of the child(ren) who lives with you. Child maintenance payments include:

- any payment made voluntarily;
- child support maintenance (maintenance assessed by the CSA);
- payments under a court order or consent order;
- in Scotland, payments under a registered maintenance agreement.

CPAG's *Child Support Handbook* has more information about how and when you can apply to the CSA. All the payments in the above list are treated in the same way for the purposes of means-tested benefits and tax credits (see p802).

Child support maintenance

Maintenance assessed by the CSA is called 'child support maintenance'. It is a type of child maintenance and treated in the same way for benefit purposes.

Definitions

'**Non-resident parent**' is the parent who the CSA has decided does not provide the main day-to-day care of the child.

The parent who has the main day-to-day care of the child is the '**parent with care**'.

Sometimes the person who has principal care of the child will not be the child's parent and is called the '**person with care**'.

A '**qualifying child**' is a child for whom child support can be paid. This includes under-16-year-olds, 16–18-year-olds in full-time non-advanced education and, for a short time after leaving education, young people aged 16 or 17 who are registered for training and for whom child benefit is payable. Those 16–18-year-olds who are no longer in full-time non-advanced education also continue to be qualifying young people while child benefit is payable for them.

Note: the definition of a 'qualifying child' for child support is *not* the same as the definition of a child or young person for whom child benefit can be paid (see Chapter 7). This is because, under the 'old' and 'new' child support schemes (see below), a young person cannot be a qualifying child once s/he is 19 or over. However, the age limit is expected to be aligned with that for child benefit for new applicants when a new 'gross income' scheme for calculating child support begins in 2012 (see p802).

More information about who is a 'qualifying child' for child support purposes is in CPAG's *Child Support Handbook*. If you want to claim maintenance for a young person who is not a qualifying child, you cannot do this via the CSA. Seek advice from a solicitor.

The CSA currently operates two child support schemes, in which child support is calculated in different ways and some other rules also apply differently. Some parents are covered by the new scheme (the 'new rules') and others continue to be dealt with under the old scheme (the 'old rules').

A third child support scheme (the 'gross income' scheme) is expected to be available for new applicants at some point in 2012. This will base the maintenance calculation on gross income, using the latest tax year information from HM Revenue and Customs. Over the next few years, existing applicants will be able to choose between applying to the new scheme or making their own arrangements. All parents will go through a 'gateway' system, signposting them to advice and support, and will be encouraged to make their own arrangements if they can. Some parents may be required to take steps to look into making their own arrangements. In the future, fees may apply for using the CSA. If you need more information about child support and about dealing with the CSA, see CPAG's *Child Support Handbook*. If you need support on whether to use the CSA, you can get advice and information from Child Maintenance Options.

When the 'old rules' apply and when the 'new rules' apply

The child support scheme that applies to you depends, in most cases, on when your child support maintenance calculation ('new rules') or assessment ('old rules') was due to take effect (this date is called the 'effective date'), as follows:[9]

- effective date before 3 March 2003: old rules apply;
- effective date on or after 3 March 2003: new rules apply.

The effective date is usually the date on which the non-resident parent is contacted by the CSA to notify her/him of the child support application and gather information. See CPAG's *Child Support Handbook* for full details. A new 'gross income' scheme for calculating child support is expected to start in 2012 (see above). Initially this will be for new applicants.

How child support maintenance is paid

If you use the CSA to apply for child maintenance, the payments may be made to you directly by the non-resident parent, or via the CSA's collection service.

3. How maintenance affects means-tested benefits and tax credits

Maintenance of any kind is not taken into account for tax credits (see p1341).

Child maintenance (see p803) is completely ignored for all means-tested benefits. However:

- other maintenance payments made by 'liable relatives' may affect income support (IS), income-based jobseeker's allowance (JSA) and income-related employment and support allowance (ESA) (see below);
- for housing benefit (HB) and council tax benefit (CTB), other maintenance may be partly disregarded or taken into account in full (see below);
- for pension credit (PC), other maintenance may or may not be taken into account as income (see p804).

Child maintenance

Child maintenance is fully disregarded as income for the following benefits and tax credits:[10]

- IS;
- income-based JSA;
- income-related ESA;
- PC;
- HB;
- CTB;
- child tax credit (CTC);
- working tax credit (WTC).

Child maintenance includes all payments for children and young people for whom child benefit can be claimed (see p94). You may receive maintenance payments for a young person for whom child support maintenance (see p801) would currently not be payable – eg, because s/he is 19.[11] This is still treated as child maintenance and is disregarded in the normal way. However, if the payment is for a young person for whom child benefit cannot be claimed, it is not child maintenance. It may be a liable relative payment (see p804) or it may be treated under the normal income rules – eg, as a voluntary payment (see Chapter 40).

It is your responsibility to tell the DWP that you are receiving child maintenance and the amount you receive. It should not affect your benefit, but it may be important to report it so that the DWP can verify that it is child maintenance and not some other payment which must be taken into account. If you have problems getting the DWP to assess your benefit correctly, seek advice.

Other maintenance payments

Other maintenance may be payments to a child or young person in your family that do not count as child maintenance, or payments to support you or your partner – eg, spousal maintenance.

For **HB and CTB**, maintenance other than child maintenance is taken into account as income. However, £15 a week is disregarded if:[12]

- your applicable amount includes the family premium; *and*

- the maintenance payments are made by your former partner or your partner's former partner.

If you receive maintenance from more than one person, only £15 of the total is disregarded.[13]

If you are claiming HB or CTB and you are receiving regular payments of maintenance, they are taken into account as income. If you are paid irregularly or in lump sums, these are taken into account as capital. See Chapters 40 and 41 for information about the income and capital rules.

You are usually better off if maintenance can be treated as capital, as it does not affect your benefit unless it takes your total capital over £6,000, or £10,000 if you have reached the qualifying age for PC (see p509) or you live in a care home.

For **PC**, spousal maintenance is taken into account as income for the guarantee credit only.[14] Spousal maintenance means maintenance from your spouse/civil partner, former spouse/civil partner, or from your partner's spouse/civil partner or former spouse/civil partner.

For **IS, income-based JSA or income-related ESA**, the treatment of maintenance other than child maintenance depends on whether or not it is a 'liable relative payment' (see below).

For **tax credits**, any maintenance you receive from an ex-partner, or your partner receives from her/his ex-partner, is not taken into account as income (see p1341). Payments of maintenance made by the parent of a child or a qualifying young person (if the parent is not currently your partner) are also ignored.[15]

Liable relative payments for income support, income-based jobseeker's allowance and income-related employment and support allowance

Most payments from the following people (known as **'liable relatives'**) count as liable relative payments:[16]

- a spouse or civil partner. This includes one from whom you are separated or divorced, or where your civil partnership has been dissolved;
- a parent of a child or young person under 20 who counts as a member of your family for benefit purposes. However, a child maintenance payment is not a liable relative payment;
- a parent of a young person under 20 who is claiming IS, income-based JSA or income-related ESA in her/his own right;
- a person who is maintaining a child or young person under 20 who is a member of your family for benefit purposes, or who is maintaining a young person who claims IS, income-based JSA or income-related ESA in her/his own right. This applies if there is no legal decision that the person making the payments is the child's or young person's father, but he may reasonably be treated as the father because of contributing to maintenance. Child maintenance payments are not liable relative payments;

- if you are the subject of a formal sponsorship/undertaking, a sponsor who has given an undertaking to support you financially (see p1413), or a sponsor who has given an undertaking to maintain someone who is a member of your family for benefit purposes.

The definition of parent for the liable relative rules covers any situation in which a child or young person is treated as her/his child or as a member of her/his family and so includes step-parents.

Note: despite the term 'liable relative', not all these people are legally liable to maintain you (see p799). The DWP can only pursue those who are legally liable to maintain you or your child (see p799). In addition, some payments you receivve from a liable relative may not count as liable relative payments (see p806).

Periodical payments

'Periodical payments' are any regular payments made by a liable relative (see p804), unless they do not count as liable relative payments (see p806). Periodical payments include small payments which are less than the weekly amount of your IS, income-based JSA or income-related ESA and payments made instead of regular payments – ie, in advance or in arrears.[17] However, arrears of payments which were due before the period of your benefit claim should not be taken into account.[18]

Periodical payments that are received on time are treated as covering a period equal to the interval between them – eg, monthly payments are spread over a month. Payments are converted to a weekly amount – eg, monthly payments are multiplied by 12 and divided by 52 to produce a weekly income figure.[19]

Arrears of periodical payments due during your claim

If you receive a payment that includes a lump sum for arrears (or an advance payment) during your claim and it is not specified which period it covers, the payment is spread over a period calculated by dividing it by the weekly amount of maintenance you should (or would) have received.[20]

Example

Tia should receive maintenance of £80 a month. It is not paid for three months and she then receives £200.

£80 a month is treated as producing a weekly income of:

$$\frac{£80 \times 12}{52} = £18.46$$

The £200 is taken into account for:

$$\frac{£200}{£18.46} = 10.83 \text{ weeks}$$

Tia is assumed to have an income of £18.46 for the next 10 weeks and six days. The maintenance payments due are still two weeks and one day in arrears (3 x £80 is £240, so she is still owed £40).

If a payment is specifically identified as being arrears of maintenance for a particular period, the DWP can attribute it to the past period which it was intended to cover, unless it is 'more practicable' to choose a later week.[21] In this case, the DWP can recover the full amount of extra benefit paid to you while maintenance was not being received.[22] This can still be done if, after your claim ends, you receive a payment for arrears of maintenance that should have been paid while you were claiming. If you disagree with the way a payment has affected your benefits, seek advice about appealing.

Lump-sum payments

Lump-sum liable relative payments are treated as income.[23] They cannot be treated as capital. They are spread over a period so as to disqualify you from IS, income-based JSA or income-related ESA for as long as possible.

A lump sum is treated as income and divided by the total of:[24]

- the weekly IS, income-based JSA or income-related ESA you would otherwise receive; *plus*
- £2.

However, if you receive periodical payments at the same time as the lump sum and they are less than the total of weekly IS/JSA/ESA plus £2, the lump sum is divided by the difference between that amount and the amount of the periodical payment. If you have not yet been awarded CTC for your children, the IS or income-based JSA amounts used will include amounts for your children (see p815). See Chapter 37 for further information about how your IS, income-based JSA or income-related ESA is calculated. If you receive a lump sum that is treated as income and are disqualified from receiving IS, income-based JSA or income-related ESA under the rules described above, ask the DWP to recalculate the period of your disqualification when:

- your circumstances change so that your entitlement to IS, income-based JSA or income-related ESA would be higher; *or*
- benefit rates increase (in April).

Payments that do not count as liable relative payments

Certain types of payment from 'liable relatives' (see p804) do not count as liable relative payments.[25] They are, therefore, dealt with under the normal income and capital rules (see Chapters 40 and 41) and you are usually better off. You should ensure that your solicitor takes account of this when negotiating payments with your former partner. For example:

- some payments can be disregarded as income or capital (see pp901 and 977);
- some payments made to someone else for the benefit of you or a member of your family (or paid to you or a member of the family to pay to someone else) do not count as your income or capital (see pp902 and 977 for more information about this).

If you receive a payment that does not count as a liable relative payment, it is usually better if it can be treated as capital (see p804). If the payment is more than the upper capital limit (see p971), whether it is capital or a lump sum treated as income (see p926), you will not receive any means-tested benefit, but you might be able to reclaim sooner if the payment is capital.

The following payments from liable relatives (see p804) do not count as liable relative payments:[26]

- any payment from a 'disposition of property' (see below) as a consequence of divorce, nullity, separation or dissolution of a civil partnership;
- any gifts not exceeding £250 in any period of 52 weeks;
- payments made after the liable relative has died;
- any payment in kind;
- any payment made to someone else (such as mortgage capital payments), or paid to you or a member of your family to pay to someone else, unless:
  - it is made for the benefit of you or your partner, or made directly or indirectly by a person liable to maintain you or a member of your family because s/he is a sponsor; *and*
  - the payment is for food, ordinary clothing or footwear, fuel, rent, housing costs, council tax or water charges;
- any payment to, or for, a child or young person who does not count as a member of your household for benefit purposes;
- money that is not a periodical payment because at least part of it has:
  - been taken into account under a previous claim; *or*
  - already been recovered from overpaid IS, income-based JSA or income-related ESA; *or*
- been used by you before the DWP makes its decision, provided you did not use it for the purpose of gaining entitlement to IS, income-based JSA or income-related ESA – eg, it should not be taken into account if you have used it to clear debts, such as your solicitor's bill;
- child maintenance payments (see p801). These are fully disregarded for IS, income-based JSA and income-related ESA.

Disposition of property

Any payment arising from a 'disposition of property' does not count as a liable relative payment (see p806). A **'disposition'** means that property is rearranged to give each partner in a marriage or civil partnership a share of the assets, as part of a separation agreement, divorce, nullity proceedings, judicial separation or the dissolution of a civil partnership. **'Property'** is not confined to houses and land, but includes any asset, such as the contents of the home or money in accounts. There is a disposition when those contents are divided up or your former partner buys out your interest.[27] Any lump sum paid in settlement of a claim to a share in any property does not count as a liable relative payment. Only lump sums that are paid instead of income should be treated as income.[28] It is important to take this into account in any negotiations with your former partner. You should make sure your solicitor knows about this rule.

If possible, you should ensure that a court order makes it clear that any lump sum is in settlement of a claim to an interest in property. However, this is not essential and the DWP should accept a letter from your solicitor explaining why a lump sum was asked for and agreed.

Note: the proceeds of the sale of your former home may be disregarded altogether for a period of time (see p977). Other capital, such as the home you live in and its contents, is disregarded indefinitely. If you are claiming or may need to claim benefit, you should consider asking for a greater share of the home and accepting less income or capital, which would be taken into account to reduce your benefit.

4. How contributing to maintenance affects your benefit entitlement

If you contribute to the maintenance of an adult or child, this may affect your own benefit entitlement. You may be entitled to an increase in certain benefits, although this is rare. If you are liable to pay child support maintenance, deductions can be made from certain benefits paid to you. If you are liable to maintain someone who is claiming income support (IS), income-based jobseeker's allowance (JSA) or income-related employment and support allowance (ESA) and you fail to do so, the DWP may decide to pursue you for maintenance (see p799).

Non-means-tested benefits if you pay maintenance

If you are contributing to the maintenance of your spouse, civil partner or an adult who cares for a child, you may receive an increase in certain non-means-tested benefits in respect of her/him, even if you do not live together. However, you cannot make a new claim for these increases. See Chapter 33 for details of the rules. If you receive unemployability supplement, see p379.

It is no longer possible to qualify for an increase in a non-means-tested benefit for a child you maintain, but if you were receiving one on 5 April 2003 you may continue to get it (see p745). These increases have been replaced by child tax credit.

If you contribute to the maintenance of a child, including paying child support, you may qualify for child benefit (see p101) and/or guardian's allowance (see p219). However, if you are not the person with whom the child lives, another claimant of child benefit may have priority over you (see p102).

If you receive a non-means-tested benefit on the basis that you are contributing to the maintenance of a dependant and fail to do so, and that person is claiming IS, income-based JSA or income-related ESA, part of your non-means-tested benefit may be recovered. This applies if, as a result of your failure to pay, the dependant's IS, income-based JSA or income-related ESA is increased. The extra IS, income-based JSA or income-related ESA that would not have been paid if you had paid the maintenance can be recovered from your child benefit or guardian's allowance, or from the dependant's increase in incapacity benefit (IB), severe disablement allowance (SDA), carer's allowance (CA), maternity allowance (MA) or Category A or C retirement pension.[29]

Non-resident parents on benefit

If you are a child's non-resident parent in the child support system (see p801), a deduction for child support can be made from certain benefits. The deductions are different depending on whether you are covered by the 'old' or 'new' rules (see p802). If you are in arrears with child support payments, deductions can also be made from certain benefits towards the arrears (see p1054). The deduction from benefits is expected to be at least £7 a week for all non-resident parents under the new simplified calculation (see p801).

'Old rules'

If you are a non-resident parent on IS, income-based JSA, income-related ESA or pension credit (PC), a deduction of £7.10 a week can be made from your benefit as a contribution towards child support maintenance for your child(ren) (see p1048 for how this fits in with other deductions that can be made from your benefit).[30] If you have children from two or more different relationships, only one deduction can be made and the £7.10 is apportioned between the people who care for them.[31]

The deduction does not apply if you:[32]

- are aged under 18;
- would qualify for a family premium (see p822) or have 'day-to-day care' of any child (see CPAG's *Child Support Handbook* for details of 'day-to-day care');
- receive:
  - IB, contributory ESA or SDA;
  - MA;
  - statutory sick pay or statutory maternity pay;
  - attendance allowance or disability living allowance;

- CA;
- industrial injuries disablement benefit or a war disablement pension;
- an Armed Forces Compensation Scheme payment or a payment from the Independent Living Funds.

If one of the above benefits is not paid solely because of overlapping benefit rules or an inadequate contribution record, you are still exempt from deductions.

'New rules'

If you are a non-resident parent and you are liable to pay the flat rate of maintenance (currently £5), a deduction of £5 can be made from certain benefits (see p1054). If your current partner is also a non-resident parent with a child support maintenance application in force and either you or your partner get IS, income-based JSA, income-related ESA or PC, you pay half the flat rate.[33] If you are a non-resident parent, you or your partner are on one of the benefits prescribed for the flat rate and you are regarded as having 'shared care' of your child(ren), a nil rate calculation will apply and your benefit will not be reduced.[34] For what counts as 'shared care', and more details about who is liable to pay the flat rate, see CPAG's *Child Support Handbook*.

No deduction will be made, as you will be liable to pay the nil rate, if you:[35]

- are a student, child or prisoner;
- are a 16/17-year-old and receive (or your partner receives) IS, income-based JSA or income-related ESA;
- receive an allowance for Work-based Training for Young People (Skillseekers in Scotland);
- are in a care home and receive one of the prescribed benefits for the flat rate of child support or have the whole or part of the cost of your accommodation met by the local authority;
- have a net income of less than £5 a week.

Transitional amount

You may have deductions made at a lower rate than described above for a transitional period if your old maintenance assessment converts to a new maintenance calculation. This applies if you had nothing to pay under the 'old rules', but under the 'new rules' you are liable to pay the flat rate. At the time of writing, it is not clear what the deduction will be under the new 'gross income' scheme (see p802), or whether there will be a transitional period for non-resident parents on benefit who move onto that scheme. For more information on conversion and transitional amounts, see CPAG's *Child Support Handbook*.

Challenging a decision to make deductions

If you think that a decision to make deductions for child support from your benefits is wrong, you can apply in writing to the DWP for a revision or a supersession (see p1116), or you can appeal (see p1155). See p1048 for more information about the rules on deductions. However, you cannot do this if you disagree with a decision on your child support liability, as this is a Child Support Agency (CSA) decision and you will need to challenge the CSA. If you disagree with the rate of child support applied to you, see CPAG's *Child Support Handbook*.

Notes

1. **What is maintenance**

1 s105(3) SSAA 1992
2 s78(6)(c) and (9) and s105(3) and (4) SSAA 1992
3 **IS** s106 SSAA 1992
JSA s23 JSA 1995
ESA s23 WRA 2007
4 *National Assistance Board v Parkes* [1955] 2 QBD 506 (QBD)
5 **IS** s106(2) SSAA 1992
JSA s23 JSA 1995; reg 169 JSA Regs
ESA s23 WRA 2007; reg 147 ESA Regs
6 s105(1) SSAA 1992
7 **IS** s106(4)(a) SSAA 1992
JSA s23 JSA 1995; reg 169 JSA Regs
ESA s23 WRA 2007; reg 147 ESA Regs

2. **Child maintenance**

8 **IS** Reg 54 IS Regs
JSA Reg 117 JSA Regs
ESA Reg 119 ESA Regs
HB Sch 5 para 47A HB Regs
CTB Sch 4 para 48A CTB Regs
9 CSPSSA 2000

3. **How maintenance affects means-tested benefits and tax credits**

10 **IS** Sch 9 para 73 IS Regs
JSA Sch 7 para 70 JSA Regs
ESA Sch 8 para 60 ESA Regs
PC Reg 5 SPC Regs
HB Sch 5 para 47A HB Regs; reg 29 HB(SPC) Regs
CTB Sch 4 para 48A CTB Regs; reg 19 CTB(SPC) Regs
CTC/WTC Reg 19 Table 6 para 10 TC(DCI) Regs
11 **IS** Reg 14 IS Regs
JSA Reg 76 JSA Regs
12 **HB** Sch 5 para 47(1) HB Regs; Sch 5 para 20(1) HB(SPC) Regs
CTB Sch 4 para 48(1) CTB Regs; Sch 3 para 20(1) CTB(SPC) Regs
13 **HB** Sch 5 para 47(2) HB Regs; Sch 5 para 20(2) HB(SPC) Regs
CTB Sch 4 para 48(2) CTB Regs; Sch 3 para 20(2) CTB(SPC) Regs
14 Reg 15(5)(d) SPC Regs
15 Reg 19 Table 6 para 10 TC(DCI) Regs
16 **IS** Reg 54 IS Regs
JSA Reg 117 JSA Regs
ESA Reg 119 ESA Regs
17 **IS** Reg 54 IS Regs
JSA Reg 117 JSA Regs
ESA Reg 119 ESA Regs
All definition of 'periodical payment'
18 **IS** Reg 54 IS Regs
JSA Reg 117 JSA Regs
ESA Reg 119 ESA Regs
All definition of 'periodical payment'
19 **IS** Reg 58 IS Regs
JSA Reg 122 JSA Regs
ESA Reg 124 ESA Regs
20 **IS** Reg 58(4) IS Regs
JSA Reg 122(4) JSA Regs
21 **IS** Reg 59(1) IS Regs
JSA Reg 123(1) JSA Regs
ESA Reg 125(1) ESA Regs
22 s74(1) SSAA 1992; reg 7(1) SS(PAOR) Regs
23 **IS** Regs 54, definition of 'payment', and 55 IS Regs
JSA Regs 117, definition of 'payment', and 118 JSA Regs
ESA Regs 119, definition of 'payment', and 120 ESA Regs

24 **IS** Reg 57 IS Regs
JSA Reg 121 JSA Regs
ESA Reg 123 ESA Regs
25 **IS** Reg 54 IS Regs
JSA Reg 117 JSA Regs
Both definition of 'payment'
26 **IS** Reg 54 IS Regs
JSA Reg 117 JSA Regs
ESA Reg 119 ESA Regs
All definition of 'payment'
27 CSB/1160/1986; R(SB)1/89
28 R(SB) 1/89

4. **How contributing to maintenance affects your benefit entitlement**

29 s74(3) SSAA 1992; reg 9 SS(PAOR) Regs
30 s43 CSA 1991; regs 13 and 28 CS(MASC) Regs; Sch 9 para 7A SS(C&P) Regs
31 Reg 28(3) CS(MASC) Regs
32 Reg 28(1) and Sch 4 CS(MASC) Regs
33 Reg 4(3) CS(MCSC) Regs
34 Sch 1 Part 1 para 8 CSA 1991
35 Sch 1 para 5 CSA 1991; reg 5 CS(MCSC) Regs

Chapter 37

Applicable amounts

This chapter covers:

This chapter explains the amounts allowed for meeting your needs when calcualting your entitlement to income support, income-based jobseeker's allowance (JSA), income-related employment and support allowance, housing benefit and council tax benefit. The rules for pension credit (PC) are mainly dealt with in Chapter 22. However, the additional amounts in the guarantee credit of PC for claimants who are severely disabled or who are carers have rules which are similar to those for the severe disability premium and carer premium, and are dealt with in this chapter (see pp830 and 834).

Note: unless otherwise stated, references to income-based jobseeker's allowance (JSA) in this chapter also refer to joint-claim JSA.

Key facts

- Applicable amounts are used in means-tested benefits to help calculate the amount of benefit to which you are entitled.
- Applicable amounts differ according to the benefit you are claiming. In general, they comprise personal allowances, premiums, housing costs and, in some cases, components. You may have one or more of these included.
- In some cases, if you were on a benefit for incapacity for work and have been transferred to employment and support allowance (ESA), your applicable amount for income-related ESA, housing benefit and council tax benefit can also include a transitional addition.

Future changes: April 2013 and after

Major changes are taking place that affect the benefits and tax credits system (see Chapter 2).

From October 2013, a new benefit, universal credit (UC), will be introduced which will replace most means-tested benefits. This will include allowances for single claimants, couples and children, as well as additions for disabled children and adults, carers, housing costs and childcare costs (see Chapter 4). These allowances and additions will be similar to the applicable amounts that apply to means-tested benefits at the moment, but there will be a number of important differences. See CPAG's *Welfare Rights Bulletin* for updates.

1. What is the applicable amount

For income support (IS), income-based jobseeker's allowance (JSA) and income-related employment and support allowance (ESA), your applicable amount is the amount you are expected to live on each week. For housing benefit (HB) and council tax benefit (CTB), it is the amount used to see how much help you need with your rent or council tax. This chapter explains how you work out your applicable amount for these benefits. For the way benefit payable is calculated, see p355 for IS, p402 for income-based JSA, p182 for income-related ESA, p257 for HB and p120 for CTB.

What is included in your applicable amount

For IS, income-based JSA, income-related ESA, HB and CTB, your applicable amount is made up of:

- **personal allowances**: the amount the law says you need for living expenses (see p815);
- **premiums**: the amount given for certain extra needs you or your family may have (see p820);
- for income-related ESA and, in some circumstances, for HB and CTB, **a support or work-related activity component** (see p837);
- for IS, income-based JSA and income-related ESA only, **housing costs** (see Chapter 38); *and*
- for income-related ESA, HB and CTB only, any **transitional addition** following the transfer of your incapacity benefit (IB), severe disablement allowance (SDA) or IS on grounds of disability claim to ESA (see p174).

When your applicable amount is reduced

Your applicable amount for IS, income-based JSA, income-related ESA, HB and CTB is reduced in certain circumstances. The most important of these are if:

- for IS and income-based JSA only, you are involved in a trade dispute (see p700);
- you are a couple and one of you is a 'person subject to immigration control' (see p1410);

- you are without accommodation (see p699);
- you are a prisoner (see p691);
- for IS, income-based JSA and income-related ESA only, you are a patient in hospital for 52 weeks or more (see p675).

2. **Personal allowances**

The amount of your personal allowance for income support (IS), income-based jobseeker's allowance (JSA), income-related employment and support allowance (ESA), housing benefit (HB) and council tax benefit (CTB) depends on your age and whether you are claiming as a single person or a couple. For HB and CTB and, in some circumstances, for IS and income-based JSA, you also get an allowance for each dependent child (but see p816 if your child has capital).

If you are polygamously married (see p753), you receive an extra amount for each additional spouse in your household. However, unless you are entitled to joint-claim JSA, if any additional spouse is under the age of 18, you only receive an extra amount for her/him if:[1]

- for IS, income-based JSA and income-related ESA, s/he is either responsible for a child (see p761) or would otherwise meet the special conditions for qualifying for JSA as a 16/17-year-old (see p405); *or*
- for IS and income-related ESA, s/he would qualify for that benefit in her/his own right were s/he not a member of a polygamous marriage.

Personal allowances for children

For when children can be included in your claim, see p759. See p761 for who counts as a child.

HB and **CTB** include personal allowances and premiums for dependent children. Since 6 April 2004, new claims for **IS** and **income-based JSA** have *not* included such allowances or premiums.

However, you may be entitled to continue having them included in your claim for IS or income-based JSA for a time in certain circumstances. This applies if you:

- have a claim which began before 6 April 2004; *and*
- had a dependent child(ren) included in the claim before 6 April 2004; *and*
- have not yet been awarded child tax credit (CTC).

In these circumstances, if you are entitled to them, the personal allowance and premiums continue to be included in your claim (and amounts for a new child can be added) until you are awarded CTC.

Income-related ESA does not include any allowances or premiums for children.

If your child has capital

If you are still entitled to amounts for children in your IS/income-based JSA, you do not get any allowance or premium for a child if s/he has over £3,000 capital, except a family premium. See p902 for how a child's income affects benefit. For HB and CTB, your child's income and capital do not affect your benefit.

Rates of personal allowances (aged 18 or over)

Note: some **16/17-year-olds** may also be entitled to these rates (see p817). Some allowances refer to the qualifying age for pension credit (PC).[2] For this, see p509.

	IS/JSA/ESA/HB/CTB	*HB/CTB only – claimant or partner is qualifying age for PC or over and not claiming IS, income-based JSA or income-related ESA*
Single claimant:		
Aged 18–24	£56.25	
Aged 25 or over	£71.00	
Aged 18 or over and ESA does or (national insurance (NI) credits only) would include a support or work-related activity component (see p837) (ESA/HB/CTB only)	£71.00	
Aged between qualifying age for PC and 64 inclusive		£142.70
Aged 65 or over		£161.25
Lone parent:		
Aged 18 or over	£71.00	
Couple:		
Both aged 18 or over	£111.45	
One or both aged between qualifying age for PC and 64 inclusive		£217.90
One or both aged 65 or over		£241.65
One aged under 18 (some IS/JSA/ESA cases only – see p817 – and all HB/CTB cases)	£111.45	
One aged under 18 (other IS/JSA/ESA cases – see p817):		
either	£71.00	
or	£56.25	

Polygamous marriages, each additional qualifying partner living in the same household:[3]		
Partner aged 18 or over, or under 18 in certain circumstances (see p815)	£40.45	
Claimant and all partners aged under 65		£75.20
One or more aged 65 or over		£80.40

Rates of personal allowances (16/17-year-olds)

For **IS** and **income-based JSA**, if you are single and aged 16 or 17 (including if you are a lone parent), you get the same rate as single 18–24-year-olds – ie, £56.25. If you are in a couple (unless one of the special circumstances below applies) and your partner is also aged under 18, you get £56.25. If your partner is aged 18 or over, see the table below. For **income-related ESA**, you get £56.25 or, if your ESA includes the support or work-related activity component, £71. If you are in a couple (unless one of the special circumstances below applies) and your partner is also under 18, the same applies.

For **HB**, if you are single (including if you are a lone parent), you get the same rate as 18–24-year-olds (ie, £56.25), unless you are entitled to ESA and you qualify for either a support or work-related activity component (see p837), in which case you get £71. If you are in a couple and your partner is also aged under 18, you get £84.95. If your partner is aged 18 or over, or if you are entitled to ESA including a component, you get £111.45. For this purpose, you can count as qualifying for an ESA component even if your actual award of ESA is nil – eg, because you are only entitled to NI contribution credits.

CTB is not payable to single people under 18 or to couples if both of you are under 18 because you are not liable to pay council tax at that age (see p120). If one of you is 18 or over, you get the same personal allowance as couples who are 18 or over (see p816).

Note: most 16/17-year-olds who have previously been looked after by a local authority cannot claim IS/JSA or HB (see p671).

Couples in special circumstances

Special rules apply if one of you is a 'person subject to immigration control' (see p1410).

Note: the following rules apply to IS, income-based JSA and income-related ESA only.[4]

The amount paid to couples depends on your ages and whether one or both of you are, or would be, eligible for IS, income-based JSA (including JSA discretionary severe hardship payments – see p408) or income-related ESA, if you were a single person. For income-related ESA, the amount of your allowance can also depend on whether you qualify for a support or work-related activity component (see p837). For some couples, the amount may be no more than that for a single person.

Age	*£pw*
Both aged 16–17, higher rate	
ESA assessment phase	84.95
ESA main phase	111.45
Other benefits	84.95
Both aged 16–17, not eligible for higher rate	
ESA assessment phase	56.25
ESA main phase	71.00
Other benefits	56.25
One aged 16–17, one 18 or over, higher rate	
ESA assessment phase	
ESA main phase	111.45
Other benefits	111.45
	111.45
One aged 16–17, one 25 or over, not eligible for higher rate	
ESA assessment phase	
ESA main phase	71.00
Other benefits	71.00
	71.00
One aged 16–17, one 18–24, not eligible for higher rate	56.25
ESA assessment phase	71.00
ESA main phase	56.25
Other benefits	

If both members of the couple are aged 16 or 17, they get the higher rate if:

- for **IS:**
  - one is responsible for a child; *or*
  - *both* would qualify for IS or income-related ESA were they not a couple; *or*
  - the claimant's partner would qualify for income-based/discretionary JSA (see p819);
- for **JSA:**
  - one is responsible for a child; *or*
  - both would qualify for income-based JSA; *or*

  - the claimant would qualify for income-based JSA and the partner would qualify for IS or income-related ESA were s/he not a member of a couple, or both qualify for discretionary JSA; *or*
  - one would qualify for discretionary JSA and the other for income-based JSA, IS or income-related ESA were s/he to make a claim; *or*
  - they are married or civil partners and both qualify for income-based JSA or one does and the other is registered for work or training;
- for **ESA:**
  - one is responsible for a child; *or*
  - both would qualify for income-related ESA were they not a couple; *or*
  - the claimant's partner would qualify for IS; *or*
  - the claimant's partner qualifies for income-based/discretionary JSA.

  The higher rate is paid at the main phase rate if the claimant qualifies for a support or work-related activity component (see pp184 and 185). Otherwise, it is paid at the assessment phase rate.

If one member of the couple is aged 16–17 and one is 18 or over, they get the higher rate if:
- for **IS**, the younger partner qualifies for IS or income-related ESA (or would do so were s/he not a member of a couple) *or* income-based/discretionary JSA (see below);
- for **JSA**, the younger partner is treated as responsible for a child, or qualifies for income-based/discretionary JSA or either IS (including where s/he would do so were s/he not a member of a couple) or income-related ESA (were s/he to make a claim);
- for **ESA**, the younger partner would either qualify for IS or income-related ESA (were s/he not a member of a couple), or for income-based/discretionary JSA. It is paid at the same rate in the assessment phase and main phase.

Entitlement to a particular rate of personal allowance may depend on whether a person aged under 18 qualifies for income-based or discretionary JSA. In this context, someone who is under 18 qualifies for:
- income-based JSA, if s/he is aged 16 or 17 and would qualify under the rules for income-based JSA described on p406;
- discretionary JSA, if s/he is subject to a severe hardship direction (see p408).

Children

HB and **CTB** include personal allowances for children. For **IS** and **income-based JSA**, you are only entitled to personal allowances for children in limited circumstances (see p815). **Income-related ESA** does not include personal allowances for children.

The rate for your dependent children is the same for IS, income-based JSA, HB and CTB, and is not affected by your (or your partner's) age.

Note, however, that this rate does not apply to joint-claim JSA, as you cannot claim this type of JSA if you have children.

Under 20	£64.99

3. Premiums

Premiums are added to your personal allowances and are intended to help with extra expenses caused by age, disability or, in some circumstances, children.

- **Family premium:** for housing benefit (HB) and council tax benefit (CTB), but only for some income support (IS) and income-based jobseeker's allowance (JSA) claims (see p822). Not for income-related employment and support allowance (ESA).
- **Disabled child premium:** for HB and CTB, but only for some IS and income-based JSA claims (see p823). Not for income-related ESA.
- **Disability premium:** for IS, income-based JSA, HB and CTB (see p824). Not for income-related ESA.
- **Enhanced disability premium:** for IS, income-based JSA, income-related ESA, HB and CTB (see p827).
- **Pensioner premium:** for IS, income-based JSA and income-related ESA (see p828). Not for HB or CTB.
- **Higher pensioner premium:** for IS and income-based JSA (see p828). Not for income-related ESA, HB or CTB.
- **Severe disability premium:** for IS, income-based JSA, income-related ESA, HB and CTB. A similar allowance applies to the guarantee credit of pension credit (PC – see p830).
- **Carer premium:** for IS, income-based JSA, income-related ESA, HB and CTB. A similar allowance applies to the guarantee credit of PC (see p834).

See p835 for information about backdating premiums. See the table on p821 for the premium rates.

Premiums for families with children

For when children can be included in your claim for IS, income-based JSA, HB and CTB, see p759. **HB** and **CTB** include premiums for families with dependent children. These are the family premium, disabled child premium and the child rate of the enhanced disability premium. Since 6 April 2004, new claims for **IS** and **income-based JSA** have not included these premiums.

However, in certain circumstances, you can continue having them included in your claim for IS or income-based JSA for a time. This will apply if you:

- have a claim which began before 6 April 2004; *and*
- had a dependent child(ren) included in the claim before 6 April 2004; *and*
- have not yet been awarded child tax credit (CTC).

In these circumstances, if you are entitled to them, the premiums will continue to be included in your claim (and amounts for a new child added) until you are awarded CTC.

Income-related ESA does not include the family premium or premiums for dependent children.

If your child has capital

Even if you are still entitled to amounts for children in your IS/income-based JSA, if a child has over £3,000 capital, you do not get any allowance or premium for that child, except for a family premium. See p902 for how a child's income affects benefit. For HB and CTB, your child's income and capital do not affect your benefit.

Premium rates

The rates of premiums are the same for all claimants, except that the rates of the pensioner premium for IS and income-based JSA may be different from those for income-related ESA.

If you have reached the qualifying age for pension credit

If you or your partner have reached the qualifying age for PC (see p509) and are not getting IS, income-based JSA or income-related ESA, your HB or CTB can only include the family, disabled child, enhanced disability for a child, severe disability and carer premiums.[5] In these circumstances, your HB or CTB cannot include a disability premium and no lone parent increase to the family premium is payable.

Premium rates

Where payable, the following premiums can be paid on top of any other premiums, except that the enhanced disability premium cannot be paid on top of the pensioner premium or higher pensioner premium.[6]

Family premium	
Ordinary rate	£17.40
Disabled child premium	£56.63
(for each qualifying child)	
Severe disability premium	
Single (or one partner qualifies)	£58.20
Couple (both partners qualify)	£116.40

Carer premium	
Single (or one partner qualifies)	£32.60
Couple (both partners qualify)	£65.20
Enhanced disability premium	
Child rate (for each qualifying child)	£22.89
Single	£14.80
Couple (one or both partner(s) qualify)	£21.30

Only one of the following premiums can be paid. If you qualify for more than one, you get whichever is highest:[7]

Family premium for HB/CTB (lone parent increase)	
HB/CTB	£4.80
Disability premium	
Single	£30.35
Couple	£43.25
Pensioner and higher pensioner premiumfor IS/income-based JSA	
Single (income-based JSA only; not payable in IS)	£71.70
Couple	£106.45
Pensioner premium for income-related ESA	
Claimant entitled to support component:	
Single	£37.65
Couple	£72.40
Claimant entitled to work-related activity component:	
Single	£43.55
Couple	£78.30
Claimant not entitled to either component:	
Single	£71.70
Couple	£106.45

Entitlement to some premiums depends on receipt of other 'qualifying' benefits. Once you have qualified for a premium, if you or your partner cease to receive a qualifying benefit because you are receiving another benefit at the same or a higher rate (see p1041), or because you or your partner are on an employment training course or getting a training allowance, you continue to receive the relevant premium.[8] In addition, you or your partner must be getting the benefit for yourself (or for your partner) and not on behalf of someone else – eg, as an appointee (see p1016).[9]

Family premium

For **HB**, **CTB** and, if applicable, **IS** and **income-based JSA**, you are entitled to a family premium if your family includes a child (see p759).[10] For **IS** and **income-based JSA**, you are only entitled to a family premium for a time and in certain circumstances (see p820). The premium is paid, even if you are not the parent of the child and even if you do not receive a personal allowance in your IS/income-based JSA for any child because s/he has capital over £3,000. **Income-related ESA** does not include a family premium.

Only one family premium is payable regardless of the number of children you have.

If a child who is being looked after by a local authority or who is in custody comes home for part of a week, your IS or income-based JSA includes a proportion of the premium, according to the number of days the child is with you.[11] For HB and CTB, you may be paid the full premium if your child who is being looked after by a local authority is part of the household for any part of the week, provided the local authority thinks it is reasonable, given how often and for how long the child is at home with you.[12]

Lone parents

The lone parent rate of the family premium is only payable in **HB** and **CTB**, and only if you were entitled to it on 5 April 1998 and certain changes in your circumstances do not occur. For more information, see p793 of the 2011/12 edition of this *Handbook*.[13]

Disabled child premium

For **HB**, **CTB** and, if applicable, **IS** and **income-based JSA**, you are entitled to a disabled child premium for each child in your family who gets disability living allowance (DLA) (or extra-statutory payments to compensate for non-payment of DLA) or who is blind. For **IS** and **income-based JSA,** you are only entitled to the premium in certain circumstances (see p820).[14] **Income-related ESA** does not include the disabled child premium.

A child is treated as blind if s/he is registered as blind and for the first 28 weeks after s/he has been taken off the register on regaining her/his sight.[15] If DLA stops because the child has gone into hospital, see p679.

If your child is looked after by the local authority or in custody for part of the week, this premium is affected in the same way as the family premium.

For how to qualify for DLA, see Chapter 9.

For IS and income-based JSA, if your child has over £3,000 capital or has been in hospital for more than 52 weeks, you do not get this premium.[16] Your child's capital does not affect your HB or CTB.[17]

If your child dies

If your child dies, you may be able to continue receiving the disabled child premium for eight weeks.[18] This applies if:

- you get child benefit for the child following her/his death (see p112); *and*
- you were getting the disabled child premium included in your applicable amount for that child immediately before her/his death.

Disability premium

You can qualify for a disability premium in your applicable amount for **IS, income-based JSA, HB** and **CTB** if you satisfy the conditions below. **Income-related ESA** does not include the disability premium. You qualify if:[19]

- you get a qualifying benefit or are registered blind; *or*
- you satisfy the incapacity for work condition – in most cases this will only be if your incapacity began before 27 October 2008 (see p826); *or*
- for joint-claim JSA only, you satisfy the limited capability for work condition; *and*
- the circumstances in which the disability premium cannot apply (see below) do not apply to you.

You cannot qualify for a disability premium on any grounds within your **HB** or **CTB** if:

- you have, or are treated as having, limited capability for work (see below);[20] *or*
- you have reached the qualifying age for PC (see p509) and neither you nor your partner are getting IS, income-based JSA, or income-related ESA.

For **IS** and **income-based JSA**, you may not be entitled to the disability premium once you or your partner have been receiving free treatment as a hospital inpatient for more than 52 weeks (see p680).

For **IS**, you cannot, in general, get the disability premium on the basis of incapacity for work that starts on or after 27 October 2008. However, if you already qualify on this basis, it can continue for the time being (see p826). **Note:** see also the rules for transferring claims to ESA on p193.

The way in which you can get a disability premium differs depending on whether or not you have a partner (see p753). In either case, the person who satisfies the qualifying conditions set out below has to be aged under the qualifying age for PC (see p509). There is a single rate and a couple rate that applies whether one or both of the couple satisfy any of the conditions on p825. For **IS** and **income-based JSA**, if you or your partner have reached the qualifying age for PC, you may get the higher pensioner premium instead.

Housing benefit and council tax benefit and limited capability for work

You cannot qualify for a disability premium within *your* HB and CTB if you have (or are treated as having) limited capability for work (see Chapter 11). This applies even if you would otherwise qualify for the premium – eg, if you (or your partner) get DLA or are registered blind. However, if your *partner* is the HB/CTB claimant and s/he does not have (and is not treated as having) limited capability for work, the disability premium can be included.[21]

If you claim ESA or NI credits on the basis of limited capability for work and you are a member of a couple, it may be beneficial for your partner to become the HB and CTB claimant instead of you if this would mean the disability premium could still be included (local authorities are advised to tell you if this is the case[22]). Remember that:

- if you have (or are treated as having) limited capability for work, although you cannot qualify for a disability premium within your HB/CTB, you may qualify for either the support or work-related activity component in your applicable amount for HB/CTB, although this is not normally until after the 'assessment phase' has ended (see p838);
- if your partner has limited capability for work, but you do not, you can still qualify for the disability premium within your HB/CTB (eg, because you or your partner get DLA) which would be paid at the higher, couple rate. However, if the disability premium is awarded, you cannot qualify for a support or work-related activity component in your applicable amount for HB/CTB.

You qualify for a disability premium if any of the following apply:

- you (or your partner) are getting a **qualifying benefit**. These are:[23]
  - DLA (see Chapter 9), or an equivalent benefit paid to meet attendance needs because of an injury at work (see Chapter 18) or a war injury;[24]
  - attendance allowance (AA) or DLA if you (or your partner) were getting either benefit, but payment was suspended when one of you became a hospital inpatient.[25] In the case of IS and income-based JSA only, you or your partner must have previously qualified for a disability premium;
  - incapacity benefit (IB) paid at the long-term rate (see Chapter 16);
  - for IS and income-based JSA, your partner or for 'joint-claim JSA', you or your partner, IB paid at the long-term rate which stopped at pension age for income-based JSA (including joint-claim JSA)[26] or when retirement pension became payable for IS. For IS, you must have been continuously entitled to IS or income-based JSA since that time.[27] If it is your partner who has reached pension age or who began receiving a retirement pension, s/he must still be alive.[28] You or your partner must have previously qualified for a disability premium;[29]
  - war pensioner's mobility supplement;
  - the disabled worker element or severe disability element of working tax credit (WTC);
  - severe disablement allowance (SDA – see Chapter 24);
  - an NHS invalid trike or private care allowance (for you or your partner) because of a disability.[30] Extra-statutory payments to compensate you or your partner for not getting these benefits also count.[31]

You must be getting the qualifying benefit for yourself, not on behalf of someone else – eg, as an appointee (see p1016). The same applies if it is your partner who gets the benefit.[32] If you qualify because of entitlement to SDA or IB, for IS/HB/CTB *you* must be getting the benefit, for income-based JSA your partner must be getting it or, for joint claim JSA, you or your partner can be getting it.

Once you qualify for the premium, you or your partner are treated as still getting a qualifying benefit you no longer receive because of the overlapping benefit rules (see p1041);[33]

- you (or your partner) are **registered as blind** with a local authority. If you (or your partner) regain your sight, you still qualify for 28 weeks after being taken off the register;
- you are **'incapable of work'** or you are treated as incapable or (for IS and joint-claim JSA only) you are entitled to statutory sick pay (SSP), and you have been incapable of work or treated as incapable of work (or for IS and joint-claim JSA, entitled to SSP) for a continuous qualifying period of:[34]
  - 196 days if you have been certified as 'terminally ill' – ie, it can reasonably be expected that you will die within six months as a consequence of a progressive disease;[35]
  - 364 days in all other cases.

  This applies to IS/HB/CTB and joint-claim JSA. For IS, it only applies if you are entitled to IS on the basis of incapacity for work. For HB/CTB and joint-claim JSA, breaks in entitlement/incapacity of up to 56 days (or 104 weeks if you are a 'welfare to work beneficiary' – see p738) are ignored. For IS, however, a break in your incapacity will result in your losing the disability premium on incapacity grounds;[36]
- for IS only, you have been entitled to SSP for a continuous period of 196 days and are terminally ill (breaks in entitlement of up to 56 days are ignored);[37]
- for joint-claim JSA only, either you or your partner have (or are treated as having) limited capability for work (see Chapter 11) for a continuous qualifying period of:
  - 196 days if you or s/he are 'terminally ill'; *or*
  - 364 days in all other cases.

  For this purpose, gaps in your periods of limited capability for work which last no more than 12 weeks are ignored.[38]

Incapacity for work

For **IS**, **HB** and **CTB**, if you are *already getting* the disability premium on the grounds of incapacity for work, it can continue. However, remember that for HB and CTB, if you claim benefit on the basis of limited capability for work, the premium will stop (see p824).

You can only still make a new claim for **IS** on the basis of incapacity for work if you are entitled to IB or SDA (see p351).

If you have been receiving IS on the grounds of incapacity for work since before 27 October 2008, you continue to qualify for the disability premium for incapacity for work, including if you did not qualify for the premium (ie, you had not been incapable of work for long enough) on this date. If you have a break in your incapacity, you will lose entitlement to the disability premium on that basis.

For new claimants of **HB** and **CTB**, it is understood that the disability premium can still be included on the basis of incapacity for work in the normal way if your incapacity for work began before 27 October 2008. If your health condition or disability began on or after that date, you are likely to be assessed under the limited capability for work test (in which case, see p824).[39]

Training

If you go on a government training course or you receive a training allowance for any period, you keep the disability premium even though you may cease to receive one of the qualifying benefits, or cease to be entitled to SSP or, for HB/CTB, be incapable of work during the course, as long as you continue to be entitled to IS, income-based JSA, HB or CTB. After the course, the premium continues if you are getting a qualifying benefit, remain entitled to SSP (for IS only), or remain incapable of work.[40]

Enhanced disability premium

This premium can be paid in respect of disabled children and disabled adults. For **HB**, **CTB** and, if applicable, **IS** and **income-based JSA**, you qualify for one enhanced disability premium for each child who receives DLA highest rate care component (or extra-statutory payments to compensate for non-payment of this) and who is a member of your family (see p751 for the meaning of 'family'). For **IS** and **income-based JSA**, you are only entitled to the child rate of this premium in certain circumstances (see p820). If your child dies, the premium continues for eight weeks if you or your partner continue to get child benefit for her/him (see p112).[41] **Income-related ESA** does not include the child rate of this premium (although you can qualify for the adult rate).

For **IS, income-based JSA, income-related ESA, HB and CTB**, you are entitled to an enhanced disability premium for an adult (at the single or couple rate) if *either:*

- you or your partner receive DLA highest rate care component and have not reached the qualifying age for PC (see p509); *or*
- for income-related ESA, you qualify for the support component (see p184); *or*
- for HB and CTB, the decision maker has determined that you have, or can be treated as having, limited capability for work-related activity (see p185).

This premium can be paid in addition to either or both the disability and severe disability premiums (see p821). For more details of the premiums with which the enhanced disability premium can be paid, see p821.

Once you or your partner reach the qualifying age for PC, you are paid the pensioner premium (or, for HB/CTB, the higher personal allowance) instead.

In most cases, you (or the family member) are treated as receiving the highest rate of DLA care component during any period when DLA is suspended while you are in hospital. The exception is if you are in one of the groups of people listed below who cannot qualify for the premium.

The following people cannot qualify:

- for the child rate, for **IS and income-based JSA only**, children who have been in hospital for more than 52 weeks, or with more than £3,000 in capital;[42]
- some people who have been in hospital for more than 52 weeks or, in some cases, if their partner has (see p680).

Pensioner premiums

These premiums are the pensioner premium and the higher pensioner premium. Both are paid at the same rate.[43]

You qualify for a pensioner premium if:

- your partner has reached the qualifying age for PC (see p509). This applies to IS, income-based JSA and income-related ESA; *or*
- you have reached the qualifying age for PC. This applies to men claiming income-based JSA and income-related ESA. Women of the same age must claim PC instead of income-based JSA or income-related ESA.

You qualify for a higher pensioner premium instead of a pensioner premium in IS or income-based JSA if:

- your partner is aged 80 or over; *or*
- you or your partner are sick or disabled and certain conditions are satisfied (see below).

There are no pensioner premiums in HB or CTB (you get a higher personal allowance instead).

Although paid at the same rate as the pensioner premium, qualifying for the higher pensioner premium may be important – eg, because it qualifies you for a £20 earnings disregard (see p913) or because it meets one of the qualifying conditions for the disabled worker element of WTC (see p1311). For joint-claim JSA, there is no pensioner premium or higher pensioner premium on age grounds if your partner is aged 75 or over.

These premiums are paid at a single or couple rate. The couple rate of the premium is included in your applicable amount even if only one partner fulfils the condition. The pensioner premium rate for income-related ESA depends on whether or not you are entitled to a work-related activity or support component (see p838) and whether you are a member of a couple.

Higher pensioner premium

Note: these rules refer to the **'qualifying age for PC'**. For this, see p509.

You qualify for the higher pensioner premium for **IS** or **income-based JSA** if:[44]

- for IS and income-based JSA (but not joint-claim JSA), your partner is aged 80 or over. If you are a joint-claim couple and one of you is aged 80 or over, see p414;
- for IS, your partner has or, for income-based JSA, you or your partner have reached the qualifying age for PC and receive a qualifying benefit (see p825, but also including AA), are registered blind, or have an NHS trike or a private car allowance.

  If your AA or DLA stops because you go into hospital, see p677. If you stop getting IB, or if you are getting SDA, see below;
- for income-based JSA, you (or, for joint-claim JSA, you or your partner) were getting a disability premium as part of your IS or income-based JSA before you reached the qualifying age for PC and you have continued to claim income-based JSA since then. You must have been getting a disability premium at some time during the eight weeks (104 weeks if you are a 'welfare to work beneficiary'[45] – see p738) before you reached the qualifying age for PC and have received that benefit continuously since then.[46] You are treated as being continuously entitled to benefit if there is a break in your entitlement to IS or income-based JSA of eight (or 104) weeks or less, which includes the day you reached the qualifying age for PC;
- for IS, you were getting a disability premium as part of your IS or income-based JSA at some time in the eight weeks (104 weeks if you are a 'welfare to work beneficiary') before your partner reached the qualifying age for PC and have continued to get IS since then. You are treated as being continuously entitled to IS or income-based JSA if there is a break in your entitlement to benefit of eight (or 104) weeks or less, which includes the day your partner reached the qualifying age for PC.[47]

Note: you may not be entitled to the higher pensioner premium once you or your partner have been receiving free treatment as a hospital inpatient for more than 52 weeks (see p680).

Previous entitlement while on IS helps you qualify when you claim income-based JSA and *vice versa*.[48]

In the case of couples, the person who was the benefit claimant before s/he reached the qualifying age for PC must continue to claim after that, but it is not necessary for the claimant to have been the person who qualified for the disability premium.

If you stop getting incapacity benefit

If your partner (or, for joint-claim JSA, you or your partner) stops getting IB because s/he has reached pension age (see p531)[49] or, for IS, because s/he gets retirement pension instead, you still get a higher pensioner premium if you remain continuously entitled to IS or income-based JSA. Once you qualify for a higher pensioner premium, breaks of eight weeks (104 weeks if you are a 'welfare to work beneficiary') or less in your entitlement to IS or income-based JSA are ignored.[50] Previous entitlement to IS counts for income-based JSA and *vice versa*.[51] If it is your partner who who has reached pension age or has changed to retirement pension, s/he must still be alive.[52] The higher pensioner premium or a disability premium must also have been applicable to you for IS, or applicable to you or your partner for income-based JSA.[53]

If you get severe disablement allowance

If you get SDA by the time you reach 65, you are awarded it for life.[54] This also applies even if it ceases to be paid because you get retirement pension at a higher rate.[55]

Severe disability premium and pension credit additional amount

You qualify for a severe disability premium or for the additional amount for severe disability in the guarantee credit of PC if all the following apply to you.[56]

- You receive a **qualifying benefit** (see p831).
- If you are a **couple**, for **IS, income-based JSA, income-related ESA, HB** and **CTB**, your partner must also be getting a qualifying benefit, or be registered blind or treated as blind because it is no more than 28 weeks since s/he stopped being registered.[57] For PC, both partners must be getting a qualifying benefit or one must be getting a qualifying benefit and the other registered blind or treated as blind. For PC only, either partner can be the claimant.[58] If you are a member of a couple, you and your partner are treated as getting any of these benefits while either or both of you are in hospital, but only if you are not claiming the amount for severe disability on the basis that your partner (or you, for PC) is blind or treated as blind.[59] For IS, income-based JSA, income-related ESA, HB and CTB, the benefit must be paid for yourself/selves; receipt of benefit for someone else (eg, a child) does not count.[60] It is probably intended that the same rule should apply to PC.
- **No non-dependant aged 18 or over is 'normally residing with you'** (see p832) – eg, a grown-up son or daughter or your parents. It does not matter whose house it is.[61] For IS, income-based JSA, income-related ESA, PC and HB, someone is only counted as residing with you if you share accommodation apart from a bathroom, lavatory or a communal area such as a hall, passageway or a room in common use in sheltered accommodation. If s/he is separately liable to make payments for the accommodation to the landlord, s/he does not count as residing with you.[62] This is not explicitly stated in the rules for CTB, although the same test may, in practice, be applied.
- **No one gets carer's allowance (CA) for looking after you** or, if you are a couple, no one gets CA for both of you (but see p831 for an exception when you and/or your partner go into hospital). For couples, if a person is getting CA for one (but not both) of you, you can get the amount for severe disability, but

only at the single person's rate. Only actual receipt of CA counts (except when it is not paid because of the loss of benefit rules – see p1106),[63] so no account is taken of any underlying entitlement to CA if it is awarded but not paid because of the overlapping benefit rules, or of any extra-statutory payments to compensate for it not being paid. Similarly, no account is taken of any backdated payments or arrears of CA.[64] You should also argue that no account should be taken of any CA which has been overpaid and that, if you have been denied the premium because of a CA overpayment, it should be repaid to you (see p835).

A '**qualifying benefit**' is either AA, the middle or highest rate care component of DLA, constant attendance allowance, or exceptionally severe disablement allowance (or the equivalent war pension).[65]

You are **treated as receiving** the middle or highest rate care component of DLA, or you or your partner are treated as receiving a qualifying benefit, if you receive an extra-statutory payment to compensate you for not receiving that benefit.[66]

Couples

Couples get the couple rate only if both of you are getting a qualifying benefit and no one gets CA for either of you. However, if CA is paid for one of you or if your partner does not get a qualifying benefit but is registered blind (or treated as blind), you still get the single rate. (In polygamous marriages the single rate is awarded for each eligible wife who gets a qualifying benefit while CA is not paid.)

Note: you and/or your partner are treated as getting a qualifying benefit, even though it has stopped because you/your partner have been in hospital for more than four weeks, but the severe disability premium is paid at the single rate only. Similarly, for couples only, for IS, income-based JSA, income-related ESA, HB or CTB, a person is treated as receiving CA even if s/he is no longer getting it because the person for whom s/he is caring has been in hospital for more than four weeks.[67]

Note also: for couples on **IS, JSA and income-related ESA** only, if you (or your partner) temporarily move into a care home (see p683), although you remain members of the same household,[68] your applicable amount is the greater of:

- the normal amount for you as a couple; *or*
- the total of the applicable amounts for each of you as if you and your partner were single claimants (or lone parents) living in your present accommodation.[69] This means that, if the person who stays at home gets a qualifying benefit (or, for income-related ESA, the highest or middle rate care component of DLA), a severe disability premium is included in the applicable amount of that person.

For PC, if you (or your partner) temporarily move into a care home, you still count as a couple if you have not been apart for substantially more than 52 weeks (see p687). So for PC, once the person in the care home loses her/his AA or DLA care component, no severe disability premium can be paid for either member of the couple even if the person at home gets a qualifying benefit.

Non-dependants

The following people who live with you do *not* count as non-dependants.[70]

For IS, income-based JSA, income-related ESA, PC, HB and CTB:

- anyone aged under 18;
- anyone else who receives a qualifying benefit;[71]
- anyone who is registered blind (or treated as blind);[72]
- anyone staying in your home who normally lives elsewhere. In deciding whether someone normally lives with you or elsewhere, it may be relevant to consider: why the residence started; the relationship and its history, if any, between those concerned; the motivations involved; the purpose for which residence has been taken up; its duration; and whether there is any other home in which residence is, or could be, taken up;[73]
- any person (and, for IS, income-based JSA, income-related ESA and PC only, her/his partner) employed by a charitable or voluntary body as a resident carer for you or your partner if you pay a charge for that service (even if the charge is only nominal).[74] **Note:** these rules do not apply to a live-in carer employed directly by you (even if, for example, you are paying her/him from direct payments made to you by social services for that purpose under the Health and Social Care Act 2001.

For IS, income-based JSA, income-related ESA, HB and CTB:

- any member of your family (see p751 for who counts as part of your family). This may include any child under the age of 20 (see p759) as well as your partner, although your partner must be getting a qualifying benefit (or would be if s/he were not in hospital), or be registered or treated as blind (see p347) if you are to be paid the severe disability premium (see p830);
- any child or qualifying young person who is living with you but who is not a member of your household (see p762).[75]

For IS, income-based JSA, income-related ESA and PC:

- any person (or her/his partner) who jointly occupies (see p834) your home and is either the co-owner with you or your partner or jointly liable with you or your partner to make payments to a landlord for occupying it. If this person is a close relative (see p834), however, s/he *will* count as a non-dependant *unless* the co-ownership or joint liability to make payments to a landlord existed either before 11 April 1988 or by the time you or your partner first moved in;
- any person (or any member of her/his household) who is liable to pay you or your partner on a commercial basis (see p834) for occupying the dwelling (eg, tenants or licensees), unless s/he is a close relative of you or your partner;

- any person (or any member of her/his household) to whom you or your partner are liable to make such payments on a commercial basis, unless s/he is a close relative of you or your partner.

For PC:

- any child or qualifying young person.[76]

Note: for IS, income-based JSA, income-related ESA and PC, if someone comes to live with you in order to look after you (or your partner) and has not lived with you before, your severe disability premium or amount for severe disability remains in payment for the first 12 weeks after the carer moves in, even if s/he would otherwise count as a non-dependant.[77] After that, you lose the premium or the amount for severe disability. The carer should then consider claiming CA (see Chapter 6).

For HB only:[78]

- any person who jointly occupies your home and is either the co-owner with you or your partner, or liable with you or your partner to make payments for occupying it. A joint occupier who was a non-dependant at any time within the previous eight weeks counts as a non-dependant if the local authority thinks that the change of arrangements was created to take advantage of the HB scheme;
- any person who is liable to pay you or your partner on a commercial basis for occupying the dwelling unless s/he is a close relative of you or your partner, or if the local authority thinks that the rent or other agreement has been created to take advantage of the HB scheme (but this cannot apply if the person was otherwise liable to pay rent for the accommodation at any time during the eight weeks before the agreement was made);
- any person, or any member of her/his household, to whom you or your partner are liable to make payments for your accommodation on a commercial basis unless s/he is a close relative of you or your partner.

For CTB only:[79]

- any person who is jointly and severally liable (see p834) with you to pay council tax. If s/he was a non-dependant at any time within the eight weeks before s/he became liable for council tax, s/he counts as a non-dependant if the local authority thinks that the change of arrangements was created to take advantage of the CTB scheme;
- any person who is liable to pay you or your partner on a commercial basis for occupying the dwelling unless s/he is a close relative (see p834) of you or your partner, or if the local authority thinks that the liability to make payments has been created to take advantage of the CTB scheme (but this cannot apply if the

person was otherwise liable to pay rent for the accommodation at any time during the eight weeks before that liability arose).

Definitions

'Close relative' is a parent, parent-in-law (including a civil partner's parent), son, son-in-law (including a son's civil partner), daughter, daughter-in-law (including a daughter's civil partner), brother, sister, step-parent (including a parent's civil partner), stepson (including a civil partner's son), stepdaughter (including a civil partner's daughter), or the partners of any of these.[80]

'Jointly occupies' has a technical meaning. It is a legal relationship involving occupation by two or more persons (whether as owner-occupiers or as tenants or licensees), with one and the same legal right.[81] It does not exist if people merely have equal access to different parts of the premises.

'Commercial basis' has no technical meaning, and there is no requirement that there need be any intention to make a profit.[82] It may be sufficient if a 'reasonable' charge is made, even if this does not fully cover the cost of the accommodation and meals being provided.[83] The reasonableness of the charge made should be judged solely against the cost of occupying the dwelling, disregarding the additional costs of providing food, clothing and care for the claimant.[84] A useful, but not conclusive, test to apply is to consider whether the same arrangement *might* have been entered into with a lodger rather than with the claimant.[85] It is not relevant whether the non-dependant depends financially on the charge being paid or if s/he would take action against the claimant if s/he did not pay.[86] These last two matters are relevant to whether there is a *liability* (see below).

'Liability' means a legal or contractual liability (as distinct from a moral or ethical obligation), although there is no requirement that any arrangements need be in writing.[87] However, even though a landlord may have expected relatives of a liable person to share her/his home in order to provide care, it cannot be inferred that they are also liable. Nor can it be assumed that someone is owed a liability in recompense merely for allowing another person to occupy her/his home.[88] Any liability must arise from the costs of occupying the home. People with no contractual capacity (eg, people with very severe learning disabilities) cannot establish liability under English law. Consistency of approach has been urged for England and Scotland, where the law is different in that a liability can exist even where there is no contractual capacity.[89]

Carer premium and pension credit additional amount

You qualify for this if you or your partner are entitled to CA (see Chapter 6).[90]

You are entitled to CA even if you do not receive it because of the overlapping benefit rules (see p1041) – eg, you get long-term IB or retirement pension instead.

If the person you or your partner are getting CA for dies, or you or your partner stop being entitled to CA for another reason, your entitlement to a carer premium continues for a further eight weeks. The eight-week period runs from the Sunday after the death (or from the date of the death, if the death occurs on a Sunday). In other cases, it runs from the date entitlement to CA stops. If you first claim IS, income-based JSA, income-related ESA or (if you or your partner are below the qualifying age for PC) HB or CTB after the CA stops, you continue to qualify for a carer premium for the eight weeks after the death or, if it stops for another reason, after entitlement to CA stops.[91]

A double rate premium is awarded if both you and your partner satisfy the conditions for it.

Carers and severe disability

Before claiming CA, you should consider how your claim may affect the entitlement to the severe disability premium or the amount for severe disability in the guarantee credit of PC (see p830) of the disabled person for whom you care – particularly if the only financial advantage to you as the carer is the amount of the carer premium, which may be worth considerably less than the severe disability premium (but see p830 for the rules on notional income).

Any backdated award of CA does not affect a disabled person's entitlement to the severe disability premium or the amount for severe disability in the guarantee credit of PC.[92] There may, therefore, be scope for careful planning to take advantage of this rule so that carers can be paid CA or the carer premium for the same period that the disabled person has already received the severe disability premium or the amount for severe disability in PC.

Although the severe disability premium or amount for severe disability is not payable throughout any period during which a carer is receiving CA, if it is later decided that CA has been overpaid (ie, that the carer was not in fact entitled to receive CA), you should ask for any decision denying you entitlement to the severe disability premium or the amount for severe disability to be revised. The carer must be both entitled to *and* in receipt of CA for the severe disability premium not to be payable.[93]

Other than for HB/CTB, if payment of CA stops, the severe disability premium can be backdated to the date the CA stopped.[94]

4. Backdating premiums

To qualify for the disability premium, enhanced disability premium, higher pensioner premium, severe disability premium, disabled child premium or carer premium, you and/or a member of your family usually must have been awarded the qualifying benefit that applies to each premium. The date you can begin to get your premium may therefore depend on the date from when your qualifying benefit is awarded. However, because of the time it may take to deal with your claim for the qualifying benefit, or if your claim is backdated (see p1026) or initially refused but awarded some time later after a revision (see p1126), supersession (see p1135) or appeal (see p1155), you may not get your premium straight away and you may have to apply for it to be backdated.

If you are already getting benefit

If you are already getting income support (IS), jobseeker's allowance (JSA), employment and support allowance (ESA), housing benefit (HB) or council tax benefit (CTB), you should ask for your award of this benefit either to be revised or superseded and for your premium to be backdated either to the same date from when your qualifying benefit is awarded, or to when you first got (or claimed) IS, JSA, ESA, HB or CTB, if that is later. In such circumstances, there is no limit to the period for which arrears can be paid to you.[95]

If you were refused benefit

If you have previously claimed **IS** or **income-based JSA**, but your claim was refused because you or a member of your family did not at that time get the qualifying benefit for the premium, you should make another IS or income-based JSA claim once the qualifying benefit is awarded. To get full backdating you should have claimed the qualifying benefit before, or no later than 10 days after, the first IS or income-based JSA claim. You must then make your second claim for IS or income-based JSA within three months of the decision awarding the qualifying benefit. The second claim is backdated, including the premium, to the date of the first IS or income-based JSA claim or to the date from when the qualifying benefit was awarded, if that is later.[96] If the qualifying benefit is initially refused, or awarded at a lower rate than you need for the premium, but is later decided in your favour, to get full backdating you must make your second IS or income-based JSA claim within three months of the date the qualifying benefit is decided in your favour on revision, supersession or appeal.[97]

For **income-related ESA, HB** and **CTB**, the rules are different. For **income-related ESA,** a new claim can be backdated for a maximum of three months; you do not need to establish a reason for the backdating. For **HB** and **CTB,** you may be limited to a maximum of six months or three months, depending on your age (see p277).

If you lose entitlement to benefit

If you lose your existing **IS** or **income-based JSA** as a result of having your (or a member of your family's) qualifying benefit stopped or reduced, or while you are waiting for a claim for a qualifying benefit to be decided, and that qualifying benefit is then awarded, or reinstated on a revision, supersession or appeal (or you make a later claim for the qualifying benefit), you should make a new claim for IS or income-based JSA. Provided you claim within three months of the favourable decision on the qualifying benefit, your IS or income-based JSA is fully backdated to the date entitlement had previously ended, or to the date from when the qualifying benefit is payable if that is later.[98]

If you lose your **HB** or **CTB** because you lose entitlement to a qualifying benefit, the decision ending your HB/CTB can be revised if the qualifying benefit is reinstated. Your HB/CTB can be fully backdated in this situation. You need to tell the local authority that you have had your qualifying benefit reinstated, but you do not need to make a fresh claim for HB/CTB.[99]

Backdating of pension credit

For backdating of pension credit, see p518.

5. Components

Your applicable amount for **income-related employment and support allowance** (ESA) and, in certain circumstances, **housing benefit** (HB) and **council tax benefit** (CTB) may also include either:[100]

- a support component (see p838); *or*
- a work-related activity component (see p838).

You cannot be awarded both these components at the same time.

For **HB** and **CTB**, you can qualify for one of these components if either you *or* your partner meet the conditions for it (it does not matter if the claim for ESA is refused). For **income-related ESA**, it must be you who meets the conditions. **Note:**

- These components cannot be included in your applicable amount for **income support** (IS), **income-based jobseeker's allowance** (JSA) or **pension credit** (PC).
- You cannot qualify for a component in your **HB** or **CTB** applicable amount if you have reached the qualifying age for PC (see p509).
- For **income-related ESA,** if you or (if you are a member of a couple) your partner have been receiving free treatment as a hospital inpatient for a continuous period of more than 52 weeks, you cannot qualify for either component.[101]

Rates of components

You can only be entitled to one component and there is no higher rate of the support or work-related component paid for couples.

For **income-related ESA**, your applicable amount includes either the support or work-related activity component if you are the claimant and you meet the conditions for that component (see p838). If you have a partner and both you and your partner have limited capability for work, you can choose which of you becomes the claimant for income-related ESA. If only one of you would qualify for a component, or only one of you would qualify for a support component, it may be beneficial for that person to be the claimant. If in doubt, seek advice.

For **HB** and **CTB**, you qualify for either a support or work-related activity component if either you or your partner satisfy the conditions for the component (see below). If you qualify for one component and your partner qualifies for the other, the component that *you* qualify for is awarded.[102]

Rates of components[103]

Support component	£34.05
Work-related activity component	£28.15

In some cases, if you are aged under 18 or under 25 you may also be entitled to a higher personal allowance once you become entitled to a support component or a work-related activity component (see pp816 and 817).

For **ESA**, your work-related activity component may be reduced or stopped altogether if you are required to take part in a work-focused health-related assessment or a work-focused interview and you do not do so (see p185).

Support component

In order to qualify for a support component with your **income-related ESA**, you must meet the conditions for the component described on p184.

For **HB** and **CTB**, you can qualify for a support component if:[104]

- you or your partner have claimed ESA and, unless you are terminally ill in the circumstances detailed below, the ESA assessment phase has ended (see p180); *and*
- you are not entitled to a disability premium (p824); *and*
- the decision maker has determined that either you or your partner have limited capability for work-related activity (see p185).

Work-related activity component

In order to qualify for a work-related activity component with your **income-related ESA**, you must meet the conditions for the component described on p185.

For **HB** and **CTB**, you can qualify for a work-related activity component if:[105]

- you or your partner have claimed ESA and, unless you are terminally ill in the circumstances detailed below, the ESA assessment phase has ended (see p180); *and*
- you are not entitled to a disability premium (p824); *and*
- the decision maker has determined that you or your partner have or can be treated as having limited capability for work (see p199).

If you are **terminally ill** (ie, you are suffering from a progressive disease because of which your death can reasonably be expected within six months) and you have either claimed ESA expressly on that ground, or have asked for a revision or supersession and have said expressly that you are terminally ill), it is not necessary for the assessment phase to have ended for you to qualify for either the support or work-related activity component.

You keep the maximum work-related activity component in HB/CTB even if you lose it in ESA because of a sanction.[106] The full, unsanctioned amount of ESA continues to be taken into account as your income.

Backdating components

For **income-related ESA**, your entitlement to either the support or work-related activity component normally starts once the 'assessment phase' has ended (see p180). The assessment phase is usually expected to last for the first 13 weeks of your claim. Earlier periods on ESA may be linked to your current one when calculating the length of your claim (see p213). However, if your assessment phase ends later than this, your entitlement to a component can be backdated to the beginning of the 14th week of your claim.[107] If you make a claim or request a revision or supersession of your entitlement expressly on the grounds of being terminally ill (see p184), you do not have to wait for the assessment phase to end to qualify for the support component, but can qualify either from the date of your claim or from the date on which you became terminally ill, if that is later.[108]

If you are getting **HB** and/or **CTB** and you become entitled to a support or work-related activity component, you qualify for that component within your applicable amount for HB or CTB from the Monday on or after your entitlement to the component began. However, if your HB or CTB entitlement starts after the date your entitlement to the component began, you can qualify for the component in your HB and CTB applicable amount from the date your entitlement to HB or CTB began.[109]

If you only become entitled to HB or CTB once a component is awarded to you, you should claim (or reclaim) HB and CTB as promptly as you can since you can only get a maximum of six months' backdating, depending on the circumstances (see p277).

6. Transitional addition

If you are claiming incapacity benefit (IB), severe disablement allowance (SDA) or income support (IS) on grounds of disability, your claim will be transferred to employment and support allowance (ESA) and you entitlement will be reassessed. This will happen between 2011 and 2014 (see p193 for details). When this happens, you may have a transitional addition included in your applicable amount for income-related ESA, housing benefit (HB) or council tax benefit (CTB).

Income-related employment and support allowance

If your claim for IS on grounds of disability is transferred to an award of income-related ESA and your ESA is worth less than your IS, you will be entitled to a transitional addition of ESA. This transitional addition is calculated by comparing your IS applicable amount with your applicable amount for ESA. If you are entitled to a transitional addition, it is included as part of your ESA applicable amount. See p195 for details.

Housing benefit and council tax benefit

If your claim for IB or SDA has been transferred to contributory ESA (see p193):

- you may no longer be entitled to the disability premium in your HB/CTB applicable amount, as this is not paid in HB/CTB if you are the claimant and have limited capability for work;
- if your HB/CTB applicable amount would be reduced because of the transfer of your (or your partner's) IB or SDA claim to contributory ESA, it will include a transitional addition to make up the difference and ensure that you do not immediately lose out.[110]

A transitional addition is not necessary if:[111]

- you (or your partner) are transferred to income-related ESA. In this case, you are entitled to maximum HB/CTB; *or*
- you (or your partner) are over the qualifying age for pension credit (p509). In this case, your applicable amount is not affected by the transfer to ESA.

You are entitled to a transitional addition in your HB/CTB if:[112]

- you (or your partner) have been transferred to contributory (but not income-related) ESA and on the date of the transfer your HB/CTB applicable amount is reduced as a result; *or*
- on transfer to ESA, you (or your partner) are found not to have limited capability for work, you have appealed against this and you are entitled to contributory (but not income-related) ESA pending the appeal (see p210), and your applicable amount for HB/CTB would be reduced as a result. If you win your appeal, the transitional addition is recalculated (because your contributory ESA applicable amount may now include a component).[113]

The amount of the transitional addition is the amount by which your old HB/CTB applicable amount exceeds your new HB/CTB applicable amount, following the transfer from IB or SDA to contributory ESA. All the parts of the applicable amount that apply to your claim, including personal allowances, premiums and the support or work-related activity component, are taken into account.[114]

The transitional addition is not permanent. It is reduced by annual increases to your HB and CTB and any other changes of circumstances that increase your applicable amount – eg, the birth of a child, or becoming a member of a couple. The transitional addition is reduced by the amount of the increase.[115] It is not affected by changes in your income or the number of non-dependants.

Your transitional addition ends on 5 April 2020, or earlier if any of the following apply:[116]

- the transitional addition ends because it is reduced to nil by annual increases or other changes in your circumstances;
- you (or your partner) stop being entitled to ESA;
- your award of HB/CTB is terminated;
- you (or your partner) become entitled to income-related ESA, or to income-based jobseeker's allowance or IS.

However, once ended, your transitional addition can be included again if:[117]

- it was ended because you (or your partner) stopped being entitled to contributory ESA or because your HB/CTB award was terminated; *and*
- before 5 April 2020, you (or your partner) become entitled to contributory ESA or to HB/CTB again; *and*
- in the case of a new award of HB/CTB, this is within 12 weeks of the transitional addition ending (or 104 weeks if you or your partner are a 'work or training beneficiary' – see p214); *or*
- in the case of a new contributory ESA award, this is within 12 weeks of the transitional addition ending (or 104 weeks if you or your partner are a 'work or training beneficiary' – see p214).

If your transitional addition is included again, the amount of it is the amount if would have been had it not ended, allowing for reductions as a result of increases to your applicable amount that have occured in the meantime.

Notes

2. **Personal allowances**

1 **IS** Reg 18(2) IS Regs
JSA Reg 84(2) JSA Regs
ESA Reg 68(2) ESA Regs

2 **IS** Sch 2 Part 1 IS Regs
JSA Sch 1 Part 1 JSA Regs
ESA Sch 4 Part 1 ESA Regs
HB Sch 3 Part 1 HB Regs; Sch 3 Part 1 HB(SPC) Regs
CTB Sch 1 Part I CTB Regs; Sch 1 Part 1 CTB(SPC) Regs

3 **IS** Reg 18(1)(b) IS Regs
JSA Regs 84(1)(b) and 86B(b) JSA Regs
ESA Reg 68(1)(b) ESA Regs
HB Reg 23(b) HB Regs; Sch 3 para 1 HB(SPC) Regs
CTB Reg 13(b) CTB Regs; Sch 1 para 1 CTB(SPC) Regs

4 **IS** Sch 2 para 1(3) IS Regs
JSA Sch 1 para 1(3) JSA Regs
ESA Sch 4 para 1(3) ESA Regs

3. **Premiums**

5 **HB** Sch 3 paras 3 and 6-9 HB(SPC) Regs
CTB Sch 1 paras 3 and 6-9 CTB(SPC) Regs

6 **IS** Sch 2 para 6(2) IS Regs
JSA Sch 1 paras 7(2) and 20C(2) JSA Regs
ESA Sch 4 para 3 ESA Regs
HB Sch 3 para 6 HB Regs
CTB Sch 1 para 6 CTB Regs

7 **IS** Sch 2 para 5 IS Regs
JSA Sch 1 paras 6 and 20B JSA Regs
HB Sch 3 para 5 HB Regs
CTB Sch 1 para 5 CTB Regs

8 **IS** Sch 2 para 7 IS Regs
JSA Sch 1 paras 8 and 20D JSA Regs
ESA Sch 4 para 4 ESA Regs
HB Sch 3 para 7 HB Regs; Sch 3 para 5 HB(SPC) Regs
CTB Sch 1 para 7 CTB Regs; Sch 3 para 5 CTB(SPC) Regs

9 **IS** Sch 2 para 14B IS Regs
JSA Sch 1 paras 19 and 20L JSA Regs
ESA Sch 4 para 10 ESA Regs
HB Sch 3 para 19 HB Regs; Sch 3 para 11 HB(SPC) Regs
CTB Sch 1 para 19 CTB Regs; Sch 1 para 3 CTB(SPC) Regs
See also R(IS) 10/94

10 **IS** Sch 2 para 3 IS Regs
JSA Sch 1 para 4 JSA Regs
HB Sch 3 para 3 HB Regs; Sch 3 para 3 HB(SPC) Regs
CTB Sch 1 para 3 CTB Regs; Sch 1 para 3 CTB(SPC) Regs

11 **IS** Regs 15(3) and 16(6) IS Regs
JSA Regs 74(4) and 78(7) JSA Regs

12 **HB** Reg 21(4)-(5) HB Regs; reg 21(4)-(5) HB(SPC) Regs
CTB Reg 11(3)-(4) CTB Regs; reg 11(3)-(4) CTB(SPC) Regs

13 **HB** Sch 3 para 3 HB Regs
CTB Sch 1 para 3 CTB Regs

14 **IS** Sch 2 paras 14 and 15(6) IS Regs
JSA Sch 1 para 16 JSA Regs
HB Sch 3 paras 16 and 20(7) HB Regs; Sch 3 paras 8 and 12(3) HB(SPC) Regs
CTB Sch 1 paras 16 and 20(7) CTB Regs; Sch 1 paras 8 and 12(3) CTB(SPC) Regs

15 **IS** Sch 2 paras 12(1)(a)(iii) and (2) and 14(c) IS Regs
JSA Sch 1 para 14(1)(h) and (2) JSA Regs
HB Sch 3 paras 13(1)(a)(v) and (2) and 16(c) HB Regs; Sch 3 para 8(b) HB(SPC) Regs
CTB Sch 1 paras 13(1)(a)(v) and (2) and 16(c) CTB Regs; Sch 1 para 8(b) CTB(SPC) Regs

16 **IS** Sch 2 para 14(2)(a) IS Regs
JSA Sch 1 para 16(2)(a) JSA Regs

17 **HB** Reg 25(3) HB Regs; reg 23(3) HB(SPC) Regs
CTB Reg 15(3) CTB Regs; reg 13(3) CTB(SPC) Regs

18 **IS** Sch 2 para 14 IS Regs
JSA Sch 1 para 16 JSA Regs
HB Sch 3 para 16 HB Regs; Sch 3 para 8 HB(SPC) Regs
CTB Sch 1 para 16 CTB Regs; Sch 1 para 8 CTB(SPC) Regs

19 **IS** Sch 2 para 11 IS Regs
JSA Sch 1 paras 13, 14, 20G and 20H JSA Regs
HB Sch 3 para 12 HB Regs
CTB Sch 1 para 12 CTB Regs
20 **HB** Sch 3 para 13(9) HB Regs
CTB Sch 1 para 13(10) CTB Regs
21 The relevant rules on limited capability for work and the disability premium refer only to the claimant. See also HB/CTB Circular A11/2008, paras 56-58.
22 HB/CTB Circular A11/2008, para 57
23 **IS** Sch 2 para 12(1)(a)(i) IS Regs
JSA Sch 1 paras 14(1)(a)-(d) and 20H(1)(a)-(d) JSA Regs
HB Sch 3 para 13(1)(a)(i) HB Regs
CTB Sch 1 para 13(1)(a)(i) CTB Regs
24 **IS** Reg 2(1) IS Regs
JSA Reg 1(3) JSA Regs
HB Reg 2(1) HB Regs
CTB Reg 2(1) CTB Regs
All Definition of 'attendance allowance'
25 **IS** Sch 2 para 12(1)(d) IS Regs
JSA Sch 1 paras 14(1)(g)(ii) and 20H(1)(h)(ii) JSA Regs
HB Sch 3 para 13(1)(a)(iii) HB Regs
CTB Sch 1 para 13(1)(a)(iii) CTB Regs
26 R(IS) 7/02
27 **IS** Sch 2 para 12(1)(c)(i) IS Regs
JSA Sch 1 paras 14(1)(g)(i) and 20H(1)(h)(i) JSA Regs
HB Sch 3 para 13(1)(a)(ii) HB Regs
CTB Sch 1 para 13(1)(a)(ii) CTB Regs
28 **IS** Sch 2 para 12(1)(c)(i) IS Regs
JSA Sch 1 paras 14(1)(g)(i) and 20H(1)(h)(i) JSA Regs
29 **IS** Sch 2 para 12(1)(c) IS Regs
JSA Sch 1 paras 14(1)(g) and 20H(1)(h) JSA Regs
30 **IS** Sch 2 para 12(1)(a)(ii) IS Regs
JSA Sch 1 paras 14(1)(e) and (f) and 20H(1)(f) and (g) JSA Regs
HB Sch 3 para 13(1)(a)(iv) HB Regs
CTB Sch 1 para 13(1)(a)(iv) CTB Regs
31 **IS** Sch 2 para 14A IS Regs
JSA Sch 1 paras 18 and 20K JSA Regs
HB Sch 3 para 18 HB Regs
CTB Sch 1 para 18 CTB Regs
32 **IS** Sch 2 para 14B IS Regs
JSA Sch 1 paras 19 and 20L JSA Regs
HB Sch 3 para 19 HB Regs
CTB Sch 1 para 19 CTB Regs
See also R(IS) 10/94
33 **IS** Sch 2 para 7(1)(a) IS Regs
JSA Sch 1 paras 8(1)(a) and 20D(1)(a) JSA Regs
HB Sch 3 para 7(1)(a) HB Regs
CTB Sch 1 para 7(1)(a) CTB Regs
34 **IS** Sch 2 para 12(1)(b) IS Regs, as applied to incapacity for work cases by reg 23A ESA(TP)(EA)(No.2) Regs
JSA Sch 1 para 20H(1)(e) JSA Regs
HB Sch 3 para 13(1)(b) HB Regs
CTB Sch 1 para 13(1)(b) CTB Regs
35 s30B(4) SSCBA 1992
36 Under reg 2 ESA(TP) Regs, linking periods of incapacity for IS is no longer possible.
37 Sch 2 para 12(1)(b) IS Regs, as substituted by reg 23A ESA(TP)(EA)(No.2) Regs
38 Sch 1 para 20H(1)(ee) JSA Regs
39 Email from DWP to Simon Osborne, CPAG, 15 December 2008
40 **IS** Sch 2 paras 7(1)(b) and 12(5) IS Regs
JSA Sch 1 paras 8(1)(b) and 20D(b) JSA Regs
HB Sch 3 paras 7(1)(b) and 13(5) HB Regs
CTB Sch 1 paras 7(1)(b) and 13(5) CTB Regs
41 **IS** Sch 2 para 13A IS Regs
JSA Sch 1 paras 15A and 20IA JSA Regs
ESA Sch 4 para 7 ESA Regs
HB Sch 3 para 15 HB Regs; Sch 3 para 7 HB(SPC) Regs
CTB Sch 1 para 15 CTB Regs; Sch 1 para 7 CTB(SPC) Regs
42 **IS** Sch 2 para 13A IS Regs
JSA Sch 1 para 15A JSA Regs
43 **IS** Sch 2 paras 9 and 9A IS Regs
JSA Sch 1 paras 10, 11, 20E and 20F JSA Regs
ESA Sch 4 para 5 ESA Regs
44 **IS** Sch 2 para 10 IS Regs
JSA Sch 1 paras 12 and 20F JSA Regs
45 Sch 1 paras 12(3) and 20F(3) JSA Regs
46 Sch 1 paras 12(1)(a)(ii) and (c)(ii) and (2) and 20F(1)(b) and (2) JSA Regs
47 Sch 2 para 10(1)(b)(ii), (3) and (4) IS Regs; reg 32 IS(JSACA) Regs
48 Sch 1 para 12(1)(a)(ii) and (c)(ii) and 20F(1)(b) JSA Regs; reg 32 IS(JSACA) Regs
49 R(IS) 7/02
50 **IS** Sch 2 para 12(1)(c)(i) and (1A) IS Regs
JSA Sch 1 paras 12(2)(a) and (3), 14(1)(g)(i), 20F(2)(a) and (3) and 20H(1)(h)(i) JSA Regs
51 Sch 1 para 12(2) JSA Regs; reg 32 IS(JSACA) Regs
52 **IS** Sch 2 para 12(1)(c)(i) IS Regs
JSA Sch 1 paras 14(1)(g)(i) and 20H(1)(h)(i) JSA Regs

53 **IS** Sch 2 para 12(1)(c) IS Regs
JSA Sch 1 para 14(1)(g) and 20H(1)(h) JSA Regs
54 CIS/458/1992
55 **IS** Sch 2 para 7(1)(a) IS Regs
JSA Sch 1 paras 8(1)(a) and 20D(1)(a) JSA Regs
56 **IS** Sch 2 para 13 IS Regs
JSA Sch 1 paras 15 and 20I JSA Regs
ESA Sch 4 para 6 ESA Regs
PC Reg 6(4) and Sch 1 paras 1-2 SPC Regs
HB Sch 3 para 14 HB Regs; Sch 3 para 6 HB(SPC) Regs
CTB Sch 1 para 14 CTB Regs; Sch 1 para 6 CTB(SPC) Regs
57 **IS** Sch 2 para 13(2A) IS Regs
JSA Sch 1 para 15(3) and 20I(2) JSA Regs
ESA Sch 4 para 6(3) and (9) ESA Regs
HB Sch 3 para 14(3) HB Regs; Sch 3 para 6(3) HB(SPC) Regs
CTB Sch 1 para 14(3) CTB Regs; Sch 1 para 6(3) CTB(SPC) Regs
58 Sch 1 para 11(b) and (c) SPC Regs
59 **IS** Sch 2 para 13(3A)(a) IS Regs
JSA Sch 1 paras 15(5)(a) and 20I(4)(a) JSA Regs
PC Sch 1 para 1(2)(b) SPC Regs
ESA Sch 4 para 6(5)(a) ESA Regs
HB Sch 3 para 14(5) HB Regs; Sch 3 para 6(7) HB(SPC) Regs
CTB Sch 1 para 14(5) CTB Regs; Sch 1 para 6(7) CTB(SPC) Regs
60 **IS** Sch 2 para 14B IS Regs
JSA Sch 1 paras 19 and 20L JSA Regs
ESA Sch 4 para 10 ESA Regs
HB Sch 3 para 19 HB Regs; Sch 3 para 11 HB(SPC) Regs
CTB Sch 1 para 19 CTB Regs; Sch 1 para 11 CTB(SPC) Regs
See also R(IS) 10/94, upheld in *Rider v CAO, The Times*, 30 January 1996 (CA)
61 *Bate v CAO* [1996] 2 All ER 790 (HL), reported as R(IS) 12/96
62 **IS** Reg 3(4) and (5) IS Regs
JSA Reg 2(6) and (7) JSA Regs
ESA Reg 71(6) ESA Regs
HB Reg 3(4) HB Regs; Sch 3 para 6(7) HB(SPC) Regs
CTB Sch 1 para 14(2)(b) CTB Regs; Sch 1 para 6(7) CTB(SPC) Regs
63 **IS** Sch 2 para 13(2)(a)(iii) and (b) IS Regs
JSA Sch 1 paras 15(1)(c) and (2)(d) and 20I(1)(d) JSA Regs
ESA Sch 4 para 6(2)(a)(iii) and (b) ESA Regs
PC Sch 1 para 1(1)(a)(iii) SPC Regs
HB Sch 3 para 14(2)(a)(iii) and (b) HB Regs; Sch 3 para 6(2)(a)(iii) and (b) HB(SPC) Regs
CTB Sch 1 para 14(2)(a)(iii) and (b) CTB Regs; Sch 1 para 6(2)(a)(iii) and (b) CTB(SPC) Regs
64 **IS** Sch 2 para 13(3ZA) IS Regs
JSA Sch 1 paras 15(7) and 20I(6) JSA Regs
ESA Sch 4 para 6(6) ESA Regs
PC Sch 1 para 2(c) SPC Regs
HB Sch 3 para 13(6) HB Regs; Sch 3 para 6(8) HB(SPC) Regs
CTB Sch 1 para 14(6) CTB Regs; Sch 1 para 6(8) CTB(SPC) Regs
65 **IS** Reg 2(1) IS Regs
JSA Reg 1(3) JSA Regs
ESA Reg 2(1) ESA Regs
PC Reg 1(2) SPC Regs
HB Reg 2(1) HB Regs; reg 2(1) HB(SPC) Regs
CTB Reg 2(1) CTB Regs; reg 2(1) CTB(SPC) Regs
All Definition of 'attendance allowance'
66 **IS** Sch 2 para 14A IS Regs
JSA Sch 1 paras 18 and 20K JSA Regs
PC Sch 1 para 1(2)(a)(ii) SPC Regs
ESA Sch 4 para 9 ESA Regs
HB Sch 3 para 18 HB Regs; Sch 3 para 10 HB(SPC) Regs
CTB Sch 1 para 18 CTB Regs; Sch 1 para 10 CTB(SPC) Regs
67 **IS** Sch 2 para 13(3A) IS Regs
JSA Sch 1 paras 15(5) and 20I(4) JSA Regs
ESA Sch 4 para 6(5) ESA Regs
PC Reg 6(5) and Sch 1 para 1(2)(b) SPC Regs
HB Sch 3 para 14(5) HB Regs; Sch 3 para 6(7) HB(SPC) Regs
CTB Sch 1 para 14(5) CTB Regs; Sch 1 para 6(7) CTB(SPC) Regs
68 **IS** Reg 16(1) IS Regs
JSA Reg 78(1) JSA Regs
ESA Reg 156 ESA Regs
69 **IS** Sch 7 para 9 IS Regs
JSA Schs 5 para 5 and 5A para 4 JSA Regs
ESA Sch 5 para 4 ESA Regs
All R(IS) 9/02

70 **IS** Reg 3 and Sch 2 para 13 IS Regs
JSA Reg 2 and Sch 1 paras 15 and 20I JSA Regs
ESA Reg 71 and Sch 4 para 6 ESA Regs
PC Sch 1 para 2 SPC Regs
HB Reg 3 HB Regs; reg 3 HB(SPC) Regs
CTB Reg 3 CTB Regs; reg 3 CTB(SPC) Regs
71 **IS** Sch 2 para 13(3)(a) IS Regs
JSA Sch 1 paras 15(4)(a) and 20I(3)(a) JSA Regs
ESA Sch 4 para 6(4)(a) ESA Regs
PC Sch 1 para 2(2)(a) SPC Regs
HB Sch 3 para 13(4) HB Regs; Sch 3 para 6(6) HB(SPC) Regs
CTB Sch 1 para 14(4) CTB Regs; Sch 1 para 6(6) CTB(SPC) Regs
72 **IS** Sch 2 para 13(3)(d) IS Regs
JSA Sch 1 paras 14(1)(h) and (2), 15(4)(c), 20H(1)(i) and (3) and 20I(3)(c) JSA Regs
ESA Sch 4 para 6(4)(c) and (9) ESA Regs
PC Sch 1 para 2(2)(b) and (c) SPC Regs
HB Sch 3 para 14(4)(b) HB Regs; Sch 3 para 6(6)(b) HB(SPC) Regs
CTB Sch 1 para 14(4)(b) CTB Regs; Sch 1 para 6(6)(b) CTB(SPC) Regs
73 CIS/14850/1996 para 10
74 **IS** Reg 3(2)(c) and (d) IS Regs
JSA Reg 2(2)(c) and (d) JSA Regs
ESA Reg 71(2)(c) and (d) ESA Regs
PC Sch 1 para 2(d) and (e) SPC Regs
HB Reg 3(2)(f) HB Regs; reg 3(2)(f) HB(SPC) Regs
CTB Reg 3(2)(f) CTB Regs; reg 3(2)(f) CTB(SPC) Regs
75 **IS** Reg 3(2)(b) IS Regs
JSA Reg 2(2)(b) JSA Regs
ESA Reg 71(2)(b) ESA Regs
HB Reg 3(2)(c) HB Regs; reg 3(2)(c) HB(SPC) Regs
CTB Reg 3(2)(c) CTB Regs; reg 3(2)(c) CTB(SPC) Regs
76 **PC** Sch 1 para 2(2)(f) SPC Regs
77 **IS** Sch 2 para 13(3)(c) and (4) IS Regs
JSA Sch 1 paras 15(4)(b) and (6) and 20I(3)(b) and (5) JSA Regs
ESA Sch 4 para 6(4)(b) and (7) ESA Regs
PC Sch 1 para 2(3)-(4) SPC Regs
78 Regs 3 and 9(1) HB Regs; regs 3 and 9(1) HB(SPC) Regs
79 Reg 3 CTB Regs; reg 3 CTB(SPC) Regs
80 **IS** Reg 2(1) IS Regs
JSA Reg 1(3) JSA Regs
ESA Reg 2(1) ESA Regs
HB Reg 2(1) HB Regs; reg 2(1) HB(SPC) Regs
CTB Reg 2(1) CTB Regs; reg 2(1) CTB(SPC) Regs
All definition of 'close relative'
81 *Bate v CAO* [1996] 2 All ER 790 (HL)
82 R(IS) 11/98, tribunal of commissioners
83 CSIS/43/1989
84 CIS/754/1991 and R(IS) 11/98 para 12
85 R(IS) 11/98, para 8
86 R(IS) 11/98, paras 10 and 11
87 CIS/754/1991
88 CSIS/641/1995
89 CIS/754/1991, referring to CSIS/28/1992 and CSIS/40/1992
90 **IS** Sch 2 para 14ZA IS Regs
JSA Sch 1 paras 17 and 20J JSA Regs
ESA Sch 4 para 8 ESA Regs
PC Reg 6(6)(a) and Sch 1 para 4 SPC Regs
HB Sch 3 para 17 HB Regs; Sch 3 para 9 HB(SPC) Regs
CTB Sch 1 para 17 CTB Regs; Sch 1 para 9 CTB(SPC) Regs
91 **IS** Sch 2 paras 7 and 14ZA(3) and (4) IS Regs
JSA Sch 1 paras 8, 17(3) and (4) and 20J(3) and (3A) JSA Regs
ESA Sch 4 para 8(2)-(4) ESA Regs
PC Sch 1 para 4(2) and (3) SPC Regs
HB Sch 3 paras 7 and 17(3) and (4) HB Regs; Sch 3 paras 5 and 9(3) HB(SPC) Regs
CTB Sch 1 paras 7 and 17(3) and (4) CTB Regs; Sch 1 paras 5 and 9(3) CTB(SPC) Regs
92 **IS** Sch 2 para 13(3ZA) IS Regs
JSA Sch 1 paras 15(7) and 201(6) JSA Regs
ESA Sch 4 para 6(6) ESA Regs
PC Sch 1 para 1(2)(c) SPC Regs
HB Sch 3 para 14(6) HB Regs; Sch 3 para 6(8) HB(SPC) Regs
CTB Sch 1 para 14(6) CTB Regs; Sch 1 para 6(8) CTB(SPC) Regs

93 **IS** Sch 2 para 13(2)(a)(iii) and (b) IS Regs
JSA Sch 1 paras 15(1)(c) and (2)(d) and 20I(1)(d) JSA Regs
ESA Sch 4 para 6(2)(a)(iii) and (b) ESA Regs
PC Sch 1 para 1(1)(ii), (b) and (c)(iv) SPC Regs
HB Sch 3 para 14(2)(a)(iii) and (b) HB Regs; Sch 3 para 6(2)(a)(iii) and (b) HB(SPC) Regs
CTB Sch 1 para 14(2)(a)(iii) and (b) CTB Regs; Sch 3 para 6(2)(a)(iii) and (b) CTB(SPC) Regs
94 Reg 7(2)(bc) SS&CS(DA) Regs

4. **Backdating premiums**
95 **IS/JSA/ESA** Regs 3(7) and 6(2)(e) SS&CS(DA) Regs
HB/CTB Regs 4(7B) and 7(2)(i) HB&CTB(DA) Regs
96 Reg 6(16)-(18) SS(C&P) Regs
97 Reg 6(26) SS(C&P) Regs
98 Reg 6(19), (20) and (30) SS(C&P) Regs
99 Reg 4(7C) HB&CTB(DA) Regs

5. **Components**
100 **ESA** s4(2), (4) and (5) WRA 2007
HB Reg 22 and Sch 3 paras 21-24 HB Regs
CTB Reg 12 and Sch 1 paras 21-24 CTB Regs
101 Reg 69(2)and Sch 5 para 13 ESA Regs
102 **HB** Sch 3 para 22(2) HB Regs
CTB Sch 1 para 22(2) CTB Regs
103 **ESA** Sch 4 paras 12 and 13 ESA Regs
HB Sch 3 paras 25 and 26 HB Regs
CTB Sch 1 paras 25 and 26 CTB Regs
104 **HB** Sch 3 paras 22 and 24 HB Regs
CTB Sch 1 paras 22 and 24 CTB Regs
105 **HB** Sch 3 para 23 HB Regs
CTB Sch 1 para 23 CTB Regs
106 Because there is no provision to remove it in these circumstances.
107 Regs 6(2)(r) and 7(38) SS&CS(DA) Regs
108 Reg 7(1)(a) ESA Regs; regs 3(9)(c), 6(2)(a) and 7(2)(be) SS&CS(DA) Regs
109 Regs 4(7B), 7(2)(o) and 8(14D) HB&CTB(DA) Regs

6. **Transitional addition**
110 Sch 3 paras 27 and 30 HB Regs; Sch 1 paras 27 and 30 CTB Regs
111 HB/CTB Circular A14/2010, paras 21-3
112 Sch 3 para 27(1) HB Regs; Sch 1 para 27(1) CTB Regs
113 HB/CTB Circular A14/2010, para 28 and Annex C
114 Sch 3 para 30 HB Regs; Sch 1 para 30 CTB Regs
115 Sch 3 para 31 HB Regs; Sch 1 para 31 CTB Regs; HB/CTB Circular A14/2010, paras 32-3
116 Sch 3 para 27(2) HB Regs; Sch 1 para 27(2) CTB Regs
117 Sch 3 paras 28 and 29 HB Regs; Sch 1 paras 28 and 29 CTB Regs

Chapter 38

Housing costs

This chapter covers :

Note: in this chapter, unless otherwise stated, references to income-based jobseeker's allowance (JSA) also refer to joint-claim JSA.

Key facts

- If you own or are buying your home, income support (IS), income-based jobseeker's allowance (JSA), income-related employment and support allowance (ESA) and pension credit can include help with a variety of housing payments, including mortgages and loans for repairs and improvements.
- The amount of help you get is not based on what you pay your lender. It is calculated in a special way using a standard rate of interest.
- Housing costs are usually paid directly to your lender.
- You might not get your full housing costs with IS, JSA and ESA met during an initial 'waiting period'.
- In some cases, if you are claiming JSA, you can only get help with your housing costs for 104 weeks.

Future changes: April 2013 and after

Major changes are taking place that affect the benefits and tax credits system (see Chapter 2).

– From October 2013, universal credit will include help with housing costs for those who are not working full time, but only for 104 weeks (although there may be exceptions). The rules will be broadly the same as currently for IS, JSA and ESA.

- The government may decide to put a charge on property in return for long-term help with housing costs – ie, after a claimant has been getting help with housing costs for a certain period.

See CPAG's *Welfare Rights Bulletin* for updates.

1. When you can get help with housing costs

You can get help with your housing costs if:[1]

- you or someone in your family (for income support (IS) and income-based jobseeker's allowance (JSA)), or you or your partner (for pension credit (PC) and income-related employment and support allowance (ESA)) are liable to pay the housing costs (see below). See p849 for who counts as your 'family';
- the housing costs are for the home in which you normally live (see p849);
- they are a type of housing cost that can be met (see p856).

Liable to pay housing costs

You count as liable to pay housing costs if:[2]

- **you, or your partner, are liable** to pay them. You do not have to be legally liable.[3] However, you do not count as liable to pay housing costs if you pay these to someone who is a member of your household (see p754 for the meaning of 'household'). If you or your partner share liability with someone, you might only get help with your share of the housing costs. However, if the other person is not paying her/his share, you can argue that you should get help with the full amount;[4]
- **you are treated as liable** to pay them. You are treated as liable if:
  - you share the costs with other members of your household; *and*
  - at least one of those with whom you share is liable.

  You can be paid for your share,[5] as long as the people with whom you share are not 'close relatives' (see p849 for who counts) of yours or your partner and it is reasonable to treat you as sharing responsibility for the costs;
- **someone else is liable to pay them but is not paying** so you have to meet the cost yourself in order to continue to live in your home. You must show that it is reasonable for you to pay instead of her/him – eg, if you have given up your home to live with and care for someone and s/he has now gone into a care home, or if you have separated from your partner (even if you have not lived in the home continuously since your partner left[6]).

If you are not required to pay any housing costs currently (eg, if under the terms of your mortgage you do not have to pay) you cannot receive IS, income-based JSA, income-related ESA or PC for housing costs. This applies to special mortgage schemes for pensioners where the mortgage is repaid from your estate when you die rather than by your making regular monthly payments.[7]

For IS and JSA only, if you are on strike, a member of your family (see below for who counts) who is not affected by the strike is treated as liable for your housing costs.[8]

Definitions

'Close relative' means a parent, parent-in-law (including a civil partner's parent), son, son-in-law (including a son's civil partner), daughter, daughter-in-law (including a daughter's civil partner), brother, sister, step-parent (including a parent's civil partner), stepson (including a civil partner's son), stepdaughter (including a civil partner's daughter), or the partners of any of these. 'Sister' or 'brother' includes a half-sister or half-brother. An adopted child ceases to be related to her/his birth family on adoption and becomes the relative of her/his adoptive family.[9]

For IS, JSA and ESA purposes, **'member of the family'** means your partner and any child (this includes some qualifying young people) who lives in your household and for whom you or your partner count as 'responsible' (see p759).[10]

Costs for the home in which you normally live

Housing costs are paid for the home in which:[11]

- for IS, JSA and ESA, you and your 'family' (see above) normally live;
- for PC, you and your partner normally live.

You cannot usually be paid for any other home. If you are liable to pay the mortgage on a property but have no immediate intention of living there, you cannot get help with the cost.[12]

If you live permanently in a care home, an independent hospital or, for IS, JSA and ESA only, an Abbeyfield Home, you cannot get help with housing costs for your former home.[13] If you are only staying in the accommodation temporarily, you might get help with the housing costs on your normal home (see p850).

Your home

Your **'home'** is defined as the building, or part of the building, in which you live. This includes any garage, garden, outbuildings and other premises and land which it is not reasonable or practicable to sell separately.[14] You can argue that a home can consist of more than one building if you occupy more than one dwelling – eg, because your family is too large for one.[15]

There are special rules if you:

- have just moved into your home (see below);
- are temporarily absent from home (see below);
- are liable to pay housing costs on more than one home (see p852).

Moving home

If you have just moved into your home but were liable to pay housing costs before moving in, your IS, income-based JSA, income-related ESA or PC can include these costs for a period of up to four weeks before you moved in if your delay in moving was reasonable, you claimed IS, JSA, income-related ESA or PC before moving in, *and*:[16]

- you were waiting for adaptations to be finished to meet the disability needs of:
  - for IS, JSA and ESA, you or a member of your family (see p849 for who counts); *or*
  - for PC, you, your partner or someone under 20 for whom you or your partner are responsible ('responsible' is not defined in the rules).

  The adaptations must involve a change to the fabric or structure of the dwelling, not just decorating or furnishing it;[17]
- you became responsible for the housing costs while you were in hospital, or were in a care home or an independent hospital (or for IS, JSA and ESA only, in an Abbeyfield Home); *or*
- you were waiting for a social fund payment for a need connected with the move – eg, for removal expenses or items to help you set up home (see Chapter 25). In addition:
  - for IS, JSA and ESA only, you must have a child of five or under living with you, or be getting child tax credit for a child of any age which includes a disability or severe disability element; *or*
  - for IS and JSA only, you must qualify for a disability, severe disability or disabled child or pensioner premium; *or*
  - for ESA only, you must be getting ESA including a work-related or support component, or qualify for a severe disability or pensioner premium.

The amount for housing costs is not actually included until you move in. If the earlier IS, JSA, ESA or PC claim you made before you moved was turned down, you must claim again within four weeks of moving in to qualify.

Temporary absence from home

If you are temporarily absent from home but are still entitled to IS, income-based JSA, income-related ESA or PC, have not rented out your home and intend to return, your housing costs continue to be paid for a period. You can argue that you count as temporarily absent from home even if you have not yet stayed there – eg, you move your furniture and belongings in but then have to go into hospital.[18]

You can get housing costs for up to **13 weeks** while you are away, whatever the reason. You must be unlikely to be away for longer than this.[19]

You can get housing costs for up to **52 weeks** if you are unlikely to be away for longer than this (or in exceptional circumstances, unlikely to be away for substantially longer than this) and you are:[20]

- in hospital. If you are claiming JSA, you must be treated as capable of work during a two-week period of sickness (see p400). If you are sick for longer than this you should claim IS, income-related ESA or PC;
- as long as it is not in a care home or an independent hospital (or for IS, JSA and ESA only, an Abbeyfield Home):
  - receiving care (approved by a doctor) in the UK or abroad;
  - receiving medical treatment or convalescing in the UK or abroad (approved by a doctor) or your partner or a dependent child (or for PC only, a dependant under 20) is;
- attending a 'training course' away from home in the UK or abroad (see below for the meaning);
- required to live in an approved hostel or an address away from your normal home as a condition of bail;
- for IS, ESA and PC only, in prison on remand pending trial or sentence. You can argue that this applies even if you are simultaneously serving another sentence.[21]

  If you were claiming JSA before going into prison, you must instead claim IS, income-related ESA or PC to cover your housing costs. Once you are sentenced, you are no longer entitled to IS, ESA or PC;
- in a care home or an independent hospital (or for IS, JSA and ESA only, an Abbeyfield Home) for short-term or respite care;
- in a care home or an independent hospital (or for IS, JSA and ESA only, an Abbeyfield Home) for a trial period to see if it suits your needs. On the date you enter the accommodation, you must intend to return home if it is not suitable.[22] You can only get your housing costs met for up to 13 weeks.[23] If the accommodation does not suit your needs, you can have further trial periods in other homes, so long as you are not away from home for more than 52 weeks in total;
- providing care for someone living in the UK or abroad (approved by a doctor);
- caring for a child under 16 (or for PC only, someone under 20) whose parent or guardian is receiving medical treatment or care (approved by a doctor) away from home;
- away from home because of a fear of violence (see p852 if you need to claim for two homes and for what counts as violence);
- a full-time student (see p637); *and*
  - living apart from your partner but cannot get housing costs for two homes (see p853); *or*

– a single claimant or a lone parent who is liable to pay housing costs on both a term-time and a home address.

There must be some causal link between your absence from home and being in one of the situations above.[24] Unless you are in a care home, independent hospital (or for IS, JSA or ESA, an Abbeyfield Home) for a trial period, your intention to return and whether or not you are unlikely to be away for longer than 13/52 weeks should be considered initially based on the circumstances on the date you leave your home.[25] If at any time after that date you no longer intend to return or it becomes likely that you will be away from home for more than the 13/52 weeks, your entitlement can be reconsidered.[26]

The 13 and 52 weeks both run from the date you leave home. If, for example, you have been away from home for 10 weeks and then have grounds to continue to get housing costs for 52 weeks, you only get these for the balance: 42 weeks. However, a new period of absence starts if you return home even for a short stay – eg, a day or a weekend.[27]

Note: if you have someone living with you who is temporarily absent (eg, a student who is away during term time), the DWP may use the rules above to decide if s/he is a non-dependant (see p869).[28]

If you have to live in temporary accommodation while essential repairs are done to your normal home and you only have to pay for housing costs for one of the homes, your IS, income-based JSA, income-related ESA or PC covers these costs.[29] This is not subject to the normal limits on temporary absence from home.[30] If you have to pay housing costs for both homes, you may be able to claim IS, income-based JSA, income-related ESA or PC for both for up to four weeks (see below). After that you are only paid for one home. This could be your normal home if you are unlikely to be away for more than 13/52 weeks or your temporary home if you will be away for longer.

Training course[31]

A training course is a course of training or instruction provided by or approved by, or on behalf of, or by arrangement with a government department, the Secretary of State, Skills Development Scotland, Scottish Enterprise or Highlands and Islands Enterprise.

Housing costs for more than one home

In most cases, you can only be paid housing costs for one home. If you occupy more than one dwelling as a home (eg, because you have a large family), you can argue that you only have one home.[32]

If you have to pay housing costs for two homes, you *can* get IS, income-based JSA, income-related ESA or PC for both:[33]

- for up to **four weeks** if you have moved into a new home and cannot avoid having to pay for the other one as well;[34]

- **indefinitely** if you left your home because of a fear of violence. Provided you left home because of this and are still away from home because of this, it does not matter if you were away from home for some other reason during this period – eg, because you were in prison.[35] You have to show that it is reasonable for you to get payment for two homes. Thus, if you do not intend to return home or someone else is paying the mortgage, you might not get IS, income-based JSA, income-related ESA or PC for both homes.
  'Violence' means violence against you and not caused by you.[36] For the purpose of these rules, it must be fear of violence:[37]
  - in your home. Fear of a racial attack should be covered provided the attack would take place in your home. Remember that your garden and garage, for example, count (see p849); *or*
  - for IS, JSA and ESA, from a former member of your family (see p849); *or*
  - for PC, from a close relative (see p849) or former partner;
- **indefinitely** if you are one of a couple and you or your partner are a full-time student or on a training course and living away from your home (see below).

If you have to live in temporary accommodation while essential repairs are done to your normal home and you only have to pay for housing costs for one of the homes, see p852.

If you have to live away from your normal home because you or your partner are a **full-time student** (see p637) or on a **training course** (see p852 for what counts):

- if you are one of a couple and have to live apart, you can get IS, income-based JSA, income-related ESA or PC for both of your homes if it is reasonable for you to get help with both;[38]
- if you are a single person or lone parent and are having to pay housing costs for *either* your normal home *or* your term-time accommodation but not both, you can get IS, income-based JSA, income-related ESA or PC, for the home for which you pay.[39]

If neither of the above applies, you may only get help with your usual home for up to 52 weeks during a temporary absence (see p850).[40]

If you are getting IS, income-based JSA, income-related ESA or PC for your term-time accommodation and you stop living there during a vacation, you cannot get housing costs unless you are away because you are in hospital.[41]

2. Modified rules

Modified rules were introduced on 5 January 2009 as a means of helping those affected by the recession and to assist them in retaining their homes. If the modified rules apply to you:

- the upper limit for your loans is £200,000 (see p867); *and*
- if you have to serve a waiting period before housing costs can be met, a 13-week waiting period applies (see p874); *and*
- if you are claiming jobseeker's allowance (JSA), you may only be able to get help with housing costs for your mortgage or loan for repairs and improvements for a maximum of 104 weeks (see p855).

The modified rules apply if your claim for income support (IS), contribution-based or income-based JSA or contributory or income-related employment and support allowance (ESA) is (or was) made after 4 January 2009. They can apply even if your income is too high for you to qualify for IS, income-based JSA or income-related ESA until housing costs are included – ie, if you have to serve a waiting period, you do not have to be receiving IS, JSA or ESA during that period.

You must meet *at least one* of the following conditions.[42]

- Neither you nor your partner have ever been awarded IS, ESA or JSA in the past, nor have either of you received pension credit (PC) at any time before your claim was made (or treated as made) – eg, this is your first claim. However, you cannot meet this condition if you are treated as being in continuous receipt of the benefit you are now claiming under the linking rules on pp875–79, for a period beginning on or before 4 January 2009 and ending immediately before the date your claim is made (or treated as made).
- You or your partner have been awarded IS, JSA or ESA in the past, but you did not receive IS, JSA, ESA or PC, and your partner did not receive PC, immediately before your current claim was made (or treated as made) – ie, there was a gap between your previous and current claims. However, you cannot meet this condition if you are treated as being in continuous receipt of IS, JSA or ESA under the linking rules on pp875–79 during the gap between your previous and current claim – ie, during the period beginning when you were last receiving IS, ESA or JSA (whether on your own or as a member of a couple) and ending immediately before the date your current claim is made (or treated as made).
- You (or your partner) were receiving PC before your (or her/his) claim for IS, ESA or JSA was made or treated as made. However, you cannot meet this condition if you or your partner were getting PC which included help with housing costs in the 12 weeks or less (26 weeks or less in some cases) before becoming entitled to IS, income-based JSA or income-related ESA in the circumstances described on p866.
- The modified rules have applied to you before – ie, on a previous claim.

The modified rules also apply if you were entitled to IS, contribution-based or income-based JSA or contributory or income-related ESA on 4 January 2009 but were still in a 26- or 39-week waiting period (see p874).

Examples

Martin claims IS on 1 April 2012 when he has to give up work to care for his disabled son. He has never claimed or been entitled to IS, JSA or ESA before. The modified rules apply. Full housing costs are included after a 13-week waiting period and his upper limit is £200,000. He can get help with his housing costs indefinitely.

Julia was claiming and entitled to IS until she returned to work in December 2008. She was made redundant in March 2012 and claimed JSA. The modified rules apply. Full housing costs are included after a 13-week waiting period and her upper limit is £200,000, but she can only get help with housing costs for 104 weeks. She was entitled to IS in the past and she is not treated as receiving IS, JSA or ESA between the end of her IS claim and her claim for JSA.

Ruth receives IS as a lone parent until her youngest child turns 10 on 1 July 2010. She then claims JSA. When she was claiming IS, the 39-week waiting period applied to her. The modified rules do not apply when she claims JSA because she was receiving IS immediately before her claim for JSA was made. Housing costs are included straight away; weeks when she was receiving IS count towards her 39-week waiting period and she had received IS for more than 39 weeks. She can get help with her housing costs indefinitely, but her upper limit for loans is £100,000.

Edwina is a lone parent. She claimed IS on 10 February 2012 when she and her partner separated. She had never claimed or been entitled to IS, JSA or ESA before. However, her former partner had claimed IS for her for a few years until they separated.
The modified rules do not apply because she is treated as receiving IS immediately before her entitlement began (see p877). Although her mortgage was taken out in 2005, because she was abandoned by her partner, the 26-week waiting period applies (see p874) and her upper limit for loans is £100,000. The weeks when her partner was receiving IS for her count towards the 26 weeks so she can get help with her housing costs straight away.

Note:

- It is not clear how long the modified rules will continue to apply, but they will apply until at least January 2013. See CPAG's *Welfare Rights Bulletin* for updates.
- Different rules applied between 5 January 2009 and 5 January 2010. For full details of the rules, see pp833–34 of CPAG's *Welfare Benefits and Tax Credits Handbook* 2009/10 edition.

Limit on the time you can get help with housing costs

If you are claiming JSA and the modified rules apply to you (see p853), you can no longer get help with mortgages, other home loans or loans for repairs and improvements (see pp857 and 861) once you have been getting help with either or both of these types of housing costs for 104 weeks.[43]

The earliest the 104 weeks can start is 4 January 2009. The DWP only counts the weeks when housing costs are included in your applicable amount. The following are ignored:

- weeks in your 13-week waiting period;
- weeks in which your housing costs are based on an upper limit of £100,000 (see p867);
- if you have claimed JSA before, weeks when housing costs were included in your applicable amount in your previous claim. This only applies if you are not treated as receiving JSA continuously during the period between your previous and current claims, under the linking rules described on pp875–79.

Example

Jim claims JSA. After he serves his 13-week waiting period, he gets help with his housing costs for 26 weeks. His JSA stops when he takes a temporary job for 10 weeks. When he claims JSA again, housing costs can only be included in his applicable amount for a further 78 weeks (104 – 26). This is because he is treated as receiving JSA during the 10-week gap between claims.

Note: this rule does not apply and you can get help with your housing costs indefinitely if:

- you are claiming JSA and the modified rules do not apply to you – eg, you qualify for a £100,000 upper limit on loans or a 26- or 39-week waiting period; *or*
- you or your partner were claiming and entitled to IS or ESA and this was no more than 12 weeks before your entitlement to JSA started. However, any entitlement to IS which is 'mortgage interest run-on' (see p879) is ignored if you or your partner were getting JSA immediately before this;[44] *or*
- you are claiming IS, ESA or PC.

3. The types of housing costs that can be met

Your income support (IS), income-based jobseeker's allowance (JSA), income-related employment and support allowance (ESA) and pension credit (PC) can include help with:

- mortgages and other loans for house purchase (see p857);
- loans used to pay for certain repairs and improvements or to meet a service charge for these (see p861);
- 'other housing costs' – eg, ground rent, payments under co-ownership schemes and service charges (see p862).

Note: if you are a tenant, you cannot get IS, income-based JSA, income-related ESA or PC for your rent.[45] Rent is covered by housing benefit (HB).

Mortgages and loans

An amount for qualifying home loan payments can be included in your IS, income-based JSA or income-related ESA applicable amount and in your PC appropriate minimum guarantee (see Chapter 37). However, restrictions might be made if you took out or increased the loan while entitled to IS, JSA, income-related ESA or PC (see p858).

You must have a home loan.[46] The term **'home loan'** refers to, for example, a mortgage, a hire purchase agreement or other loan to help you buy your home.

Note: payment of your IS, income-based JSA, income-related ESA or PC housing costs is usually made directly to the lender.

Loans that qualify

Your loan qualifies if it was:[47]

- **taken out to buy the home in which you normally live.** Loans taken out to buy an existing property as well as those to pay for materials and labour to build your own home are covered. If all or part of your loan was not taken out with the immediate intention of paying for your home (eg, it was to buy a car or set up a business), or is for deferred interest, you cannot get help with the loan (or part of the loan) even if it is secured on your home (but see p863);[48]
- **taken out to buy an additional interest in the home in which you normally live,** for example:[49]
  - by buying out your ex-partner's share in your home after you separate. However, if your ex-partner has registered a right to occupy your home (a 'Class F land charge') you cannot get help with a loan to pay her/him to remove it;[50]
  - by purchasing the freehold on a leasehold property;[51]
  - by buying your partner's share from a trustee if s/he is bankrupt;[52]
  - by buying out sitting tenants;[53]
- **taken out to repay a loan which itself would have qualified.** However, if the second loan is also for things that do not qualify for help (eg, to pay debts or for a holiday) you only get help with the amount of the original loan.

Example

Mr Clay took out a mortgage of £60,000. £45,000 was to pay off a mortgage to buy his home and £15,000 was to pay off business debts. He gets help with the loan of £45,000.

Note: loans for costs necessary to help you buy the home or the additional interest (eg, search, valuation or legal fees and stamp duty) are covered.[54] If your home is used for both business and domestic purposes, you can only get help with the loan for the part where you live.[55]

The rules for help with mortgages and loans changed on 2 October 1995. If you took out your loan before that date, you might still be able to get help under the old, more favourable rules (see p863).

Taking out or increasing loans while entitled to benefit

Even if your loan qualifies (see above), you cannot usually get IS, income-based JSA, income-related ESA or PC to help you pay the cost if the loan was incurred (eg, it was taken out or increased) during a 'relevant period' (see below) and this was after 1 October 1995 (for IS and PC), 7 October 1996 (for JSA) or 27 October 2008 (for ESA).[56] **Note:** the rule can also apply if the loan was incurred before these dates (see below).

The DWP is likely to say that this rule even applies if you are awarded backdated IS, income-based JSA, income-related ESA or PC for the day on which you became liable for or increased your loan.[57]

Other dates

You cannot get IS, income-based JSA, income-related ESA or PC to help with a loan incurred during a 'relevant period':[58]

- after 2 May 1994, if you did not qualify for IS for the loan in the 26 weeks before 2 October 1995 (for IS, ESA and PC) or in the 26 weeks before 7 October 1996 (for JSA) or you did not qualify for IS or PC for the loan after 1 October 1995 or JSA for the loan after 7 October 1996 (for ESA);
- for IS and PC only, in the 26 weeks before 2 October 1995 when you were not entitled to IS, but you or your partner became entitled to IS or income-based JSA after 1 October 1995 and within 26 weeks of your or your partner's IS ceasing. This does not apply to loans for which you were getting IS housing costs without restriction before 2 October 1995;
- for JSA only, in the 26 weeks before 7 October 1996 when you were not entitled to IS, but you or your partner became entitled to JSA after 6 October 1996 and within 26 weeks of your or your partner's IS ceasing. This does not apply to loans for which you were getting IS housing costs without restriction before 7 October 1996;
- for ESA only, in the 26 weeks before 27 October 2008 when you were not entitled to IS, income-based JSA or PC, but you or your partner became entitled to income-related ESA after 27 October 2008 and within 26 weeks of your or your partner's IS, income-based JSA or PC ceasing. This does not apply to loans for which you were getting IS housing costs without restriction before 27 October 2008.

Relevant periods

A **'relevant period'** is a period:

- for IS and JSA:[59]

  - when you were entitled to IS, income-based JSA or income-related ESA (for IS) or IS, JSA or income-related ESA (for JSA); *or*
  - when you were living as a member of the family (see p849 for who counts) of someone who was entitled to IS, income-based JSA or income-related ESA (for IS) or IS, JSA or income-related ESA (for JSA); *or*
  - of up to 26 weeks between two of either of the types of period above.

  Note: official guidance suggests that for JSA, the DWP might only apply this rule if you (or the family member with whom you were living) were entitled to IS, *income-based* JSA or income-related ESA;[60]
- for ESA and PC:[61]
  - when you were entitled to IS, income-based JSA, income-related ESA or PC; *or*
  - when your partner was entitled to IS, income-based JSA, income-related ESA or PC; *or*
  - of up to 26 weeks between two of either of the types of period above.

For these purposes, you and your partner are:
- treated as entitled to IS, JSA, income-related ESA or PC during periods when you were on a specified New Deal programme or scheme, even if as a result you counted as being in full-time paid work (see p718) or had too much income to qualify for IS, JSA, income-related ESA or PC;[62]
- *not* treated as entitled to IS, JSA or income-related ESA under the linking rules described on pp875–79.[63]

Note: if you become liable for the loan during a period of 26 weeks or more between two relevant periods, you *can* get help with the cost.

Full help with a new or increased loan

You *can* get IS, income-based JSA, income-related ESA or PC for housing costs even if you took out your loan during a 'relevant period' (see p858), if you:
- have taken out or increased your loan to buy a home which is better suited than your former home to the **special needs of a 'disabled person'** (see p860 for who counts).[64] There is no rule that says you must buy the home or take out the loan within a certain time before or after the disabled person moves in.[65] However, there does need to be a link between the purchase of the home, the loan and the move.[66] The person has to qualify as disabled at the time the loan is taken out.[67] S/he does not have to be a member of your family or to have previously lived with you;
- increased your loan and moved to a new home because you needed to provide separate sleeping accommodation for a **boy and a girl aged 10 or over but under 20** and for IS, ESA or JSA, for whom you or your partner are responsible and who live with you or, for PC, who live with you and who you or

your partner are looking after.[68] You can argue that this should apply if both children will be 10 or over in the reasonably near future.[69]

Disabled person

For these purposes, a disabled person is:[70]

- someone who is getting ESA that includes a work-related activity or support component;
- for IS, JSA and ESA, a child or young person who counts as disabled or severely disabled for the purpose of the child tax credit, disabled child or severely disabled child element;
- for IS and JSA, someone for whom you or someone living with you are getting a disabled child, disability, enhanced pensioner or higher pensioner premium (or who would get one of these premiums if s/he were on IS or JSA);
- for ESA and PC, someone who would qualify for a disability premium if s/he were on IS and someone who is 75 or over;
- for PC, anyone under 20 for whom you or your partner are responsible ('responsible' is not defined in the rules) who gets disability living allowance or who is registered blind (in Scotland, certified blind), or anyone who would qualify for a higher pensioner premium if s/he were on IS.

A person continues to count as a disabled person even if, under the incapacity or capability for work rules, s/he is either disqualified from receiving benefit or is treated as capable of work or as not having limited capability for work. For IS, JSA and PC, this includes if s/he is disqualified from receiving ESA while a prisoner or because of her/his absence abroad.

Restricted help with a new or increased loan

You *can* get IS, income-based JSA, income-related ESA or PC for your housing costs even if you took out your loan during a 'relevant period' (see p858), but the amount you get might be restricted to your former housing costs if:

- you took out a loan:[71]
  - to pay off an original home loan – eg, you have remortgaged your home; *or*
  - paid off an original loan and have now taken out a new loan for a new property, even if this is some time later – eg, you have moved home.

  The original loan must have qualified (see pp857 and 861) and be one for which you can get IS, income-based JSA, income-related ESA or PC even when taken out during a 'relevant period'. Unless the loan was to buy a home for a disabled person or to provide separate sleeping accommodation for a boy and girl aged 10 or over but under 20 (see p859), you cannot get help with any increase in your housing costs. Thus, if your original mortgage was £30,000 and you took out a new loan for £35,000, you can only get housing costs on £30,000 of the second loan.

  If, following divorce or separation, you buy your former partner's share of your home, you cannot get help with the mortgage for that share. Similarly, if you take out a loan or increase an existing loan to buy a home after separation, the restriction, in principle, applies. However, you can argue that each of you should be entitled to housing costs up to the amount of the loan you were liable to pay when you were together – eg, if you were liable to pay £50,000 when you were together, you should each be entitled to housing costs on a mortgage of up to £50,000 when you separate;[72]

- you buy a home and the week before:
  - you **were in rented accommodation and getting housing benefit** (HB). To begin with you only get the amount of HB you were entitled to plus any 'other housing costs' (see p862) you were already getting;[73]
  - you **were only getting 'other housing costs'** (see p862) paid with your IS, income-based JSA, income-related ESA or PC – eg, as ground rent.[74] To begin with, you only get the amount you had been getting for those other costs.

In both cases, you get any subsequent increases in the standard rate of interest (see p865) or the 'other housing costs' and do not lose these if the interest rate or costs go down again.[75]

Loans for repairs and improvements

IS, income-based JSA, income-related ESA and PC do not meet the cost of repairs and improvements to your home or the cost of service charges for these (although service charges for *minor* repairs and maintenance *can* be covered as 'other housing costs' – see p863). However, if you take out a loan to pay for specified types of repairs and improvements (see below) or a service charge (or to pay off an earlier loan taken out for this purpose), you can get help with this.[76]

You must use the loan for the repairs and improvements or service charge within six months (longer if this is reasonable). A bank overdraft that is taken out to pay for the repairs or improvements counts as a loan.[77]

Repairs and improvements that qualify

You can only get help with loans for repairs or improvements undertaken to maintain the fitness of your current home,[78] or any part of the building in which it is contained, for human habitation. This includes loans towards the cost of necessary survey work.[79] In addition, the loan must be for:[80]

- providing a bath, shower, toilet, wash basin and the necessary plumbing and hot water;
- repairs to your heating system;
- damp-proof measures (you can argue this includes repairs to a roof[81]);
- providing:
  - ventilation and natural lighting;
  - drainage facilities;
  - facilities for preparing and cooking food (but not for storing it);[82]
  - home insulation;
  - electric lighting and sockets;

- storage facilities for fuel or refuse;
- repairing unsafe structural defects;
- adaptations for a disabled person (see p860 for who counts);
- providing separate sleeping accommodation for children of different sexes aged 10 or over but under 20 for whom you or your partner are responsible and who live with you. For PC, 'responsible' is not defined in the rules. For IS, JSA and ESA, see p761.

  You can argue that this should apply if both children will be 10 or over in the reasonably near future.[83]

If your loan is also for other repairs and improvements, you are only paid housing costs for the proportion which relates to any of the items listed above.

Note:

- The rules for help with loans for repairs and improvements changed on 2 October 1995. If you took out your loan before that date, you might still be able to get help under the old, more favourable, rules (see p863).
- Payment of your IS, income-based JSA, income-related ESA or PC housing costs is usually made directly to the lender.

Help with 'other housing costs'

You are paid the normal weekly charge for all 'other housing costs' covered by IS, income-based JSA, income-related ESA and PC.[84] These are:

- service charges (see p863). Note that some service charges are excluded;
- rent or ground rent if you have a lease of more than 21 years. If your lease is of 21 years or less, the rent or ground rent might be met by HB instead (see p247);[85]
- rentcharge payments;
- payments under a co-ownership scheme;
- rent if you are a Crown tenant (minus any water charges[86]);
- payments for a tent and its pitch if that is your home.

If you pay your other housing costs annually or irregularly, the weekly amount is worked out by dividing what is payable for the year by 52.[87]

If your other housing costs have been waived because you or your partner (or for IS, JSA or ESA only, a member of your family – see p849 for who counts) have paid for repairs or redecoration that are not your responsibility, you can still get IS, income-based JSA, income-related ESA or PC for them for up to eight weeks.[88]

Charges that cannot be met

The following charges cannot be met:[89]

- fuel, where this is included in your 'other housing costs'. If there is no specific charge for fuel, set deductions are made;

Heating	£25.50	Lighting	£2.05
Hot water	£2.95	Cooking	£2.95

- amounts for repairs and improvements listed on p861. You are expected to take out a loan to pay for these and can claim help with this;[90]
- ineligible services listed on p264. These are the same as for HB.[91]

Service charges

A **'service'** is something that is agreed and arranged on your behalf and for which you are required to pay. So, for example, if you own a flat and the freeholder arranges for the exterior of the building to be painted, for which you have to pay a share of the cost, your IS, income-based JSA, income-related ESA or PC includes this as a service charge. Some service charges are ineligible (see p264). Some service charges can only be met if they relate to the provision of 'adequate accommodation'.[92]

Bear the following in mind.

- Service charges to cover minor repairs and maintenance are eligible. However, those to cover any of the repairs and improvements listed on p861 are not.[93]
- Payments for support services are not eligible. Instead, you can get help with these via your local authority's Supporting People team (see p265).
- House insurance paid under the terms of your lease can be a service charge, but insurance required by a bank as a condition of your mortgage is not.[94]
- Services provided by an authority that you arrange yourself are not covered. Thus, charges for water and sewerage paid to a water company are not met.[95]

Old rules: housing costs that are no longer paid

You can continue to get help with certain types of housing costs that could be paid with IS before 2 October 1995, but which can no longer be paid with IS, income-based JSA or income-related ESA. These are:[96]

- accumulated arrears of interest;
- interest on a secured loan that was not for house purchase, taken out when you were one of a couple, where your partner had left and could not (or would not) pay the cost, or had died;
- interest on a loan for repairs and improvements under the pre-2 October 1995 rules.

You can continue to get help with these if they were included in your housing costs before 2 October 1995, you fulfil the qualifying conditions *and* you remain in receipt of (or are treated as in receipt of) IS or income-based JSA. You are treated as receiving IS or income-based JSA during the linking periods described on pp875–79. You are treated as receiving IS when you are receiving income-related ESA. See CPAG's *National Welfare Benefits Handbook* 1995/96 edition, pp30–32 for more details on how these costs were assessed.

Note: if you are claiming PC, you should not be worse off than you were on IS, income-based JSA or income-related ESA. See p511 to see if you qualify for a transitional amount as part of your appropriate minimum guarantee.

4. The amount of housing costs you get

Once you have worked out which housing costs can be met by income support (IS), income-based jobseeker's allowance (JSA), income-related employment and support allowance (ESA) or pension credit (PC) you can calculate the amount you get.

- **Step one:** calculate the weekly amount of:
  - housing costs for home loans. **Note:** these might be restricted if you took out or increased your loan while entitled to IS, JSA, income-related ESA or PC (see p858);
  - housing costs for loans for repairs and improvements;
  - 'other housing costs'.
- **Step two:** add these amounts together.
- **Step three:** deduct any restrictions being made because your housing costs are too high (see p867).
- **Step four:** deduct any amounts for other people living in your home (known as non-dependants – see p869).

For IS, JSA and ESA only, a reduced amount might also be paid during a 'waiting period' in the early weeks of your claim (see p873).

Note:

- In some cases, if you are claiming JSA, you can only get help with your housing costs for 104 weeks (see p855).
- You might only get your share of the housing costs if you share liability or are treated as liable because you share the costs with someone (see p848).

How your housing costs for loans are calculated

Your IS, income-based JSA, income-related ESA or PC housing costs for loans for house purchase and repairs and improvements are calculated using a standard rate of interest (see below). They do not always cover the whole of your loan payments. You cannot get help with associated insurance premiums – eg, if you have an endowment mortgage, you do not get the insurance element paid.

There can be a limit on the amount of housing costs that can be paid. If the total of your loans is more than an upper limit (usually £100,000 or £200,000) your housing costs might only be calculated using this figure (see p867). Whether or not your loans are lower than the upper limit, if your housing costs are still thought to be excessive, your housing costs might be restricted (see p868).

Remember that your housing costs may also be restricted if you took out or increased your loan for house purchase while on IS, income-based JSA, income-related ESA or PC (or in a period between claims) – see p858.

Note:

- If your housing costs as calculated below mean that they are actually more than the interest you have to pay, your lender must first apply the excess to any arrears you have, then to repaying the loan itelf.[97]
- There is often a shortfall between the IS, income-based JSA, income-related ESA or PC you get for your housing costs and what you have to pay your lender. See p866 for ideas about what to do if your housing costs are not met in full.

The formula

The weekly amount of housing costs for loans is worked out using a special formula.[98] A standard rate of interest is used, not what you actually have to pay, even if this is higher or lower. At the time of writing the **standard rate of interest** was 3.63 per cent.[99]

The amount of your loans that qualify (see pp857 and 861) less any restrictions that have been made (see pp860 and 867) is multiplied by the standard rate of interest. This figure is divided by 52 to reach a weekly amount.

Example

Mr and Mrs Khan have a repayment mortgage and a loan for repairs and improvements. The outstanding loans of £30,000 and £5,000 qualify. They also have a loan for a conservatory. This does not qualify. They pay interest at the rate of 6.1%.

£30,000 x 3.63% (standard interest rate) = £1,089.

£5,000 x 3.63% = £181.50.

Their weekly IS housing costs are (£1,089 ÷ 52) + (£181.50 ÷ 52) = £24.43.

Note: the standard rate of interest is set by the DWP and can be varied. You can find out the current rate at www.direct.gov.uk/en/moneytaxandbenefits or see CPAG's *Welfare Rights Bulletin* for updates.

Transitional rules

The rules for calculating housing costs changed on 2 October 1995. If you were on IS both on and after 1 October 1995 and the amount of IS, income-based JSA or income-related ESA housing costs to which you are now entitled is less because of the rules since 2 October 1995, you can get an extra payment to make up the loss.[100]

See CPAG's *Welfare Benefits and Tax Credits Handbook* 2008/09 edition, pp810–11 for more details.

Note: if you are claiming PC, you should not be worse off than you were on IS, income-based JSA or income-related ESA. See p511 to see if you qualify for a transitional amount as part of your appropriate minimum guarantee.

When housing costs are recalculated

Even if there is a reduction in the amount of your outstanding loan, your IS, income-based JSA, income-related ESA or PC housing costs are usually only recalculated annually, on the anniversary of the date these housing costs were first met by your benefit.[101] If there are other changes, your housing costs are recalculated on the date of the change. However, if you are getting PC, you or your partner are at least 65, and a non-dependant has come to live with you or your non-dependant's circumstances have changed and this means the amount of housing costs to which you are entitled reduces, your housing costs are recalculated 26 weeks after the date of the change (or if there is more than one change in respect of the same non-dependant, the first of these changes).[102]

If you or your partner were getting (or treated as getting) IS, income-based JSA, income-related ESA or PC which included help with housing costs in the 12 weeks or less before becoming entitled to another of those benefits, the same amount of housing costs are met as were met when you were getting the other benefit, unless there has been a change of circumstances affecting the calculation of the housing costs, other than a reduction in the amount of your outstanding loan.[103] For IS, JSA and ESA, the 12 weeks is extended to 26 weeks if you or your partner reclaimed IS, income-based JSA, income-related ESA or PC within 26 weeks of a previous claim during which you were getting housing costs and you have been receiving payments under an employment insurance policy which has since run out.

If your housing costs are not met in full

If you do not have enough money to pay your housing costs, you may be in danger of losing your home, particularly if you are on IS, JSA, ESA or PC for a long time. You should inform your lender and discuss how to resolve the situation. Your lender may be prepared to accept interest-only payments for a while. It is important to discuss this in order to avoid falling into arrears and risk losing your home. Seek independent debt advice.

If you have to make payments towards the shortfall:

- you may be able to increase your income by taking in lodgers (but see pp924 and 950);
- some payments made direct to the lender by relatives, friends or a charity towards housing costs not being met can be ignored in calculating your entitlement to IS, income-based JSA or income-related ESA;[104]
- if you get charitable or voluntary payments, these are ignored as income (see pp924 and 955).

Ultimately, you may have to sell your home and buy somewhere cheaper. If you move out and put your house up for sale, the capital value of your property can be disregarded for a period while you take reasonable steps to sell it (see pp977 and 998).[105] If you rent it while trying to sell, see pp925 and 950 for how the income is treated.

Restrictions if your housing costs are too high

Your housing costs can be restricted if your:

- loans exceed an upper limit (see below); *or*
- total housing costs are considered excessive (see p868).

Your housing costs can also be restricted if you take out or increase a loan while entitled to IS, JSA, income-related ESA or PC or in a period between claims (see p858).

The upper limit

If the total of your loans is more than an upper limit, your housing costs might not be met in full.[106] This includes all mortgages taken out to buy your home and also any loans for repairs and improvements. The restriction is applied proportionately to each loan. If a loan was taken out to adapt your home for a disabled person (see p860 for who counts), it is ignored when working out if your loans exceed the upper limit. If you are getting housing costs on more than one home (see p852), you can be paid up to the limit for each.[107]

Your upper limit is:

- £200,000 if you are claiming IS, JSA or ESA and the modified rules described on p853 apply to you. See below if you become entitled to PC ; *or*
- £100,000 in most other cases.

If you are entitled to IS, JSA or ESA with an upper limit of £200,000, but you then claim PC, this upper limit continues to apply if:[108]

- the modified rules described on p853 applied to you (or your partner) ; *and*
- you (or your partner) were entitled to IS, JSA or ESA no more than 12 weeks before you became entitled to PC (or where your claim for PC is backdated, before the date you claimed PC); *and*
- immediately before your (or your partner's) entitlement to IS, JSA or ESA ended, your (or her/his) applicable amount included an amount of housing costs for a mortgage (or other house purchase loan) or a loan for repairs and improvements.

Note: there is no upper limit if you have been entitled to IS, income-based JSA or income-related ESA since before 2 August 1993, unless you take out or increase a loan after that date.[109] Between 2 August 1993 and 12 April 199 the limit was £150,000 and between 11 April 1994 and 10 April 1995 the limit was £125,000.

See pp838–39 of CPAG's *Welfare Benefits and Tax Credits Handbook* 2011/12 edition for details of the old limits.

Excessive housing costs

Whether or not an upper limit applies to you (see p867), your housing costs can be restricted if:[110]

- your home (excluding any part which you let) is too big for:
  - for IS and JSA, you and your family (see p849 for who counts) and any of your non-dependants (see p869) (including foster children);
  - for ESA and PC, you and your partner, anyone under 20 living with you and any other non-dependants (see p869).

  When deciding if your home is too big, a comparison is made with other suitable accommodation given the size of your household. Everyone's needs must be considered – eg, if a member of your family needs extra space because of a disability or you have a child or relative in a care home who regularly comes to stay with you, your need for a large home may be justified; *or*
- the area in which you live is more expensive than other areas where there is suitable accommodation. The area should not be chosen on too wide a basis. 'Area' means something more confined, restricted and compact than a locality or district. It might be a neighbourhood or even a large block of flats;[111] *or*
- the outgoings on your home which are met by IS, income-based JSA, income-related ESA or PC housing costs are higher than those in other suitable accommodation in the area.

The capital value of your home cannot be taken into account.[112]

When no restriction should be made

No restriction can be made, even if suitable accommodation is available, if it is not reasonable for you and your family (for IS and JSA) or you and your partner (for ESA and PC) to look for cheaper accommodation. Account should be taken of:[113]

- the general level of housing costs in the area and whether suitable accommodation is available. This means that property must be generally available, not necessarily available to you personally;[114]
- your family circumstances (for IS and JSA) or your circumstances and those of the people who live with you (for ESA and PC) – eg, your employment prospects, the age and health of your family members and whether the move would have a detrimental effect on a child's or young person's education if s/he were to change schools.

These are not the only situations which count.[115] A move may not be reasonable if:

- the size of your family would make it difficult to find accommodation;

- you need to be near relatives or friends to provide (or receive) care or support;
- you have moved a number of times recently;
- it would be difficult to sell your property,[116] you have negative equity, or selling would cause you financial hardship;[117]
- you have lived in your home for many years and it is now too large because you are separated or divorced, your children have left home, or your partner has died;
- before your claim you were advised by the DWP that your housing costs would not be restricted;[118]
- you could not get another mortgage on a property.[119]

Even if it is reasonable for you to move, a restriction can be delayed in certain circumstances (see below). If it *is* appropriate to restrict your housing costs, these are limited to help with the amount of loan you would need in order to get suitable alternative accommodation.[120] This must be assessed in practical and realistic terms. Any loans that are repayable on the sale of your home which would leave you with less money to purchase another home should be taken into account.[121] However, if the equity in your property was sufficient to buy a new home outright, without a loan, your housing costs could be nil.[122]

Delaying a restriction

Your housing costs cannot be restricted for 26 weeks if you or a member of your family (for IS and JSA – see p849 for who counts), or you and your partner (for ESA and PC), were able to meet these costs when they were first taken on, and for a further 26 weeks if you are trying to find cheaper accommodation.[123] If your housing costs are restricted following a supersession (eg, full housing costs are included, but the decision maker later decides these should be restricted), the 26-week periods begin when the supersession takes effect.[124]

Periods of 12 weeks or less when you stop getting IS, income-based JSA, income-related ESA or PC can be included when calculating the 26 weeks.[125] In addition, the rules specify other periods that count towards the 26-week periods.[126]

Deductions for non-dependants

If other people normally live with you in your home who are not part of your family (see p849) for benefit purposes (called **non-dependants**), a set deduction is usually made from your housing costs.[127] This is because it is assumed the non-dependant makes a contribution towards your outgoings, whether or not s/he does so. Examples of non-dependants are adult sons or daughters, or elderly relatives who share your home.

For information about whether someone may count as normally living with you, see pp265–67. What needs to be considered is the same as for housing benefit.

The DWP may use the rules on p850 to work out if someone is only temporarily absent from your home.[128] If you think the DWP has wrongly assumed that a person is normally living with you, ask for a revision or appeal (see Chapters 45 and 46).

People who are not non-dependants

No deduction is made from your housing costs if the person living with you is not treated as a non-dependant (though any rent or lodging charges s/he pays to you affect the amount of your IS, income-based JSA, income-related ESA or PC – see pp924 and 950). The following people do not count as non-dependants even if they normally live with you:[129]

- for IS, JSA and ESA only, a member of your family for benefit purposes (see p849 for who counts);
- for IS, JSA and ESA only, a child or qualifying young person living with you who does not count as a member of your household (see p762) – eg, a foster child or a child placed with you prior to adoption;
- for PC only, your partner and anyone under 20 for whom you or your partner are responsible ('responsible' is not defined in the rules);
- someone who is liable to pay you, or your partner, in order to live in your home – eg, a sub-tenant, licensee or boarder along with other members of her/his household. This does not apply if the person is a close relative of yours or your partner (see p849 for who counts).
  The payment must be on a commercial basis. A low charge does not necessarily mean that the arrangement is not commercial. You do not have to make a profit. An arrangement between friends can be commercial;[130]
- for IS, JSA and ESA only, someone other than a close relative (see p849 for who counts) to whom you, or your partner, are liable to make payments on a commercial basis (ie, as a sub-tenant, licensee or boarder) in order to live in her/his property. Other members of her/his household also do not count as non-dependants;
- someone who jointly occupies your home and is a co-owner or joint tenant with you or your partner. Your joint occupier's partner is also not a non-dependant. For IS, JSA and ESA only, close relatives (see p849 for who counts) who jointly occupy your home are treated as non-dependants unless they had joint liability prior to 11 April 1988 or joint liability existed on or before the date you first lived in the property (or your partner did if s/he is the joint owner/tenant). However, no non-dependant deduction is made for them even though they are non-dependants (see p871);
- someone who is employed by a charitable or voluntary organisation as a resident carer for you, or your partner, and who you pay for that service (even if the charge is nominal). If the carer's partner lives in your home s/he also does not count as a non-dependant.

When no deduction is made

Even if you have a non-dependant in your home, no deduction is made for her/him if you (or your partner):[131]

- are registered blind (certified blind in Scotland). If you regain your sight, you continue to be treated as blind for 28 weeks after you have been taken off the register;
- get attendance allowance (AA) (or equivalent benefits paid because of injury at work or a war injury) or the care component of disability living allowance (DLA).

In addition, no deduction is made for a non-dependant:[132]

- who is staying with you but whose normal home is elsewhere;
- who is 16 or 17 years old;
- for whom a deduction is already being made from your housing benefit (HB);
- who is under 25 years old and getting IS or income-based JSA;
- for IS, JSA and PC only, who is under 25 and getting contributory or income-related ESA. If the non-dependant is getting income-related ESA, this only applies if it does *not* include a work-related activity or support component (see Chapter 10);
- for ESA only, who is under 25 and getting income-related ESA which does *not* include a work-related activity or support component (see Chapter 10);
- who is getting PC;
- who gets a training allowance in connection with youth training under specific provisions;[133]
- who is a full-time student during her/his period of study (see p637). This includes those getting JSA who count as full-time students while on training courses under the Employment, Skills and Enterprise Scheme. **Note:** unless you are getting PC and you or your partner are 65 or over, no deduction is made during the summer vacation only if the student is not in full-time paid work (see p718);
- who is not living with you at present because s/he:
  - has been in hospital for more than 52 weeks. Separate stays in hospital which are not more than 28 days apart are added together when calculating the 52 weeks;
  - is a prisoner (see p694);
- for IS, JSA and ESA only, who is a close relative (see p849 for who counts) and a co-owner or joint tenant with you, or your partner. For PC, no deduction is made because co-owners and joint tenants do not count as non-dependants, even if they are close relatives.

The amount of the deduction

If you have a non-dependant living with you who is 18 or over and for whom a deduction must be made, a fixed amount is deducted from your housing costs, whatever s/he pays you. Unless your non-dependant is in full-time paid work, an £11.45 deduction is made each week. If your non-dependant is in full-time paid work, the amount of the deduction depends on her/his weekly gross income.[134]

Gross weekly income	*Weekly non-dependant deduction*
£394 or more	£73.85
£316–£393.99	£67.25
£238–£315.99	£59.05
£183–£237.99	£36.10
£124–£182.99	£26.25
Less than £124	£11.45

The rules on full-time paid work are covered in Chapter 31. **Note:**
- A non-dependant who is not in (or is treated as not in) full-time paid work does not attract the higher level of deduction even if her/his weekly gross income is £124 or more.
- For PC, if someone is getting IS or income-based JSA for more than three days in a benefit week, s/he does not count as in full-time paid work in that week.[135] This means the lower deduction (£11.45) is made (or, in some cases, no deduction is made).

Gross income includes wages before tax and national insurance are deducted plus any other income the non-dependant has (but not AA, DLA or certain payments from the Macfarlane Trusts, the Eileen Trust, MFET Ltd, the Fund or the Independent Living Fund (2006), the London Bombings Relief Charitable Fund, the Skipton Fund and the Caxton Foundation, or for PC only, payments in kind).[136]

You should try to provide information to show which deduction applies. If you cannot, ask the DWP to consider the circumstances – eg, if your non-dependant is doing a job which is normally very low paid. The DWP should not assume the worst – eg, that your non-dependant is earning the highest amount. It should assess the likely level of your non-dependant's earnings on the evidence available.[137]

A deduction is made for each non-dependant in your home. However, if you have a non-dependant couple and a non-dependant deduction applies to both members, only one deduction is made – the highest applicable. The couple's joint income counts.

If you are a joint owner with someone other than your partner, any deductions are shared proportionally between you and the other owner(s).

5. Waiting periods

Even if you qualify for help with your housing costs, these are not usually met until you have been entitled to (or treated as entitled to) income support (IS), jobseeker's allowance (JSA) or employment and support allowance (ESA) for a number of weeks. This is known as a 'waiting period'.[138] If you claim pension credit (PC), there is no waiting period and you get help with your housing costs straight away.

While in your waiting period, you may be entitled to some IS, JSA or ESA even though housing costs are not included in your applicable amount – ie, if your income is lower than your personal allowance(s) plus your premiums and components. In this case, the decision maker should do a supersession when your waiting period ends, and your housing costs are then included. However, even if you are *not* entitled to some IS, JSA or ESA during your waiting period, your housing costs can still be included when it ends if you are *treated* as entitled to IS, JSA or ESA during the period. In some cases, you have to make a fresh claim for IS, income-based JSA or income-related ESA (when sufficient weeks have passed).

Note: for information about when you can be treated as entitled to IS, JSA or income-related ESA, see the linking rules on pp875–79.

Your housing costs can be included straight away (without a waiting period) if:[139]

- you can be treated as entitled to IS, JSA or ESA for sufficient weeks during the period before your claim;
- you have already been entitled to IS, JSA or ESA for sufficient weeks when you agree to pay your loan or other housing costs (but see p858 for the rules restricting housing costs if you take out or increase a loan while entitled to IS, JSA or income-related ESA or in a period between claims);
- you were getting help with your housing costs when your IS, JSA or ESA ceased because you:
  - became a 'welfare to work beneficiary' or a 'work or training beneficiary' (see pp738 and 214); *or*
  - started full-time paid work or training for work or self-employment, or increased your hours or your pay (so long as you qualify for a longer linking period – see p879).

  This only applies if you claim IS, income-based JSA or income-related ESA again within 104 weeks (if you are a 'welfare to work beneficiary or a 'work or training beneficiary') or 52 weeks (if you qualify for a longer linking period);
- your partner is at least the qualifying age for PC (see p509) or for JSA only, you are over that age. **Note:** if *you* are at least the qualifying age for PC, you can claim PC;
- you are claiming for payments as a Crown tenant, under a co-ownership scheme or for a tent.

In addition, if you (or your partner) reclaim IS, income-based JSA or income-related ESA within 26 weeks of a previous award of benefit which included housing costs and you (or s/he) have been receiving payments under an employment insurance policy which has since run out, periods between those claims are ignored when calculating the waiting periods.[140] Because the number of weeks in the previous claim can be added to the number of weeks in your current claim for that benefit, this means that you can requalify for housing costs sooner.

All other claimants get a reduced amount of help initially. You are expected to use mortgage payment protection policy payments, savings or income to meet any shortfall. If you do not have enough to pay the shortfall, approach your lender to discuss how you can protect your home.

The 13-week waiting period

If the modified rules described on p853 apply to you, your waiting period is 13 weeks.[141] You get nothing for the first 13 weeks, then full housing costs after you have been entitled (or treated as entitled) to IS, JSA or ESA for 13 weeks.

Note: if the 13-week waiting period applies:

- the upper limit for your loans is £200,000 (see p867); *and*
- if you are claiming JSA, you may only be able to get help with housing costs for your mortgage (or other loan for house purchase) or loan for repairs and improvements for a maximum of 104 weeks (see p855).

The 26- and 39-week waiting periods

If the modified rules described on p853 do *not* apply to you, a 26- or 39-week waiting period applies. **Note:** if one of these waiting periods applies:

- the upper limit for your loans is usually £100,000 (see p867); *and*
- if you are claiming JSA, you can get help with housing costs for your mortgage (or other loan for house purchase) or loan for repairs and improvements indefinitely.

The **26-week waiting period** applies if you:[142]

- agreed to pay your loan or other housing costs before 2 October 1995 (the DWP calls these 'existing housing costs');
- agreed to pay your loan after 1 October 1995, provided it replaced a loan you agreed to pay before that date. You must have been liable for the housing costs under both the old and the new agreements and the new loan must be for the same (or lower) amount as the earlier loan;
- are exempt from the 39-week waiting period – eg, because you are a lone parent whose partner abandoned you or died, a carer, in prison awaiting trial or sentence (for IS or income-related ESA only) or you have been refused payments under a mortgage payment protection policy because of a pre-

existing medical condition or because you are HIV positive.[143] For full details of who is exempt from the 39-week waiting period, see p846 of the 2011/12 edition of this *Handbook*.

No housing costs are included in your applicable amount until you have been entitled (or treated as entitled) to IS, JSA or ESA for eight weeks, 50 per cent are included for the next 18 weeks and full housing costs are included after you have been entitled (or treated as entitled) to IS, JSA or ESA for 26 weeks.

Unless the 26-week waiting period applies, the **39-week waiting period** applies if you agreed to pay your loan or other housing costs after 1 October 1995 (the DWP calls these 'new housing costs').[144] No housing costs are included in your applicable amount until you have been entitled (or treated as entitled) to IS, JSA or ESA for 39 weeks.

If you have two loans or agreements to pay other housing costs and one was agreed before and one after 1 October 1995, the relevant waiting periods apply to each.[145]

Note: in practical terms, if you make a new claim for IS, JSA or ESA and the modified rules described on p853 do not apply, in most cases, you will have already served your 26- or 39-week waiting period so housing cost should be included in your applicable amount straight away. See the examples on p855.

6. Linking rules

You are treated as entitled to or receiving income support (IS), jobseeker's allowance (JSA) or income-related employment and support allowance (ESA) for certain periods, even though you were not actually entitled to or receiving it. These are known as 'linking rules'. They can:

- help you get full housing costs earlier. Periods when you are treated as *entitled to* IS, JSA or income-related ESA can count towards your waiting period (see p873);
- prevent the £200,000 upper limit for loans and the 13-week waiting period from applying if you are treated as *receiving* IS, income-based JSA or income-related ESA during specified periods;
- link periods that count towards the 104-week time limit for help with housing costs with JSA if you are treated as *receiving* JSA continuously between them (see p855);
- allow you to continue to get help with certain types of housing costs that are no longer met (see p863) if there is a break in your claim.

General rules

You are treated as entitled to and receiving:[146]

- IS for any period when you were entitled to or receiving income-based JSA or income-related ESA;
- JSA for any period when you were entitled to or receiving IS or income-related ESA;
- income-related ESA for any period when you were entitled to or receiving IS, income-based JSA or pension credit (PC);
- IS or JSA for any period when you were receiving JSA as a 'joint-claim couple' (see p413);
- IS, JSA or income-related ESA during a period of no more than 12 weeks (104 weeks if you or your partner are a 'welfare to work beneficiary' or a 'work or training beneficiary' (see pp738 and 214), or 52 weeks if you qualify for a longer linking period – see p879) between two periods when:
  - for IS and JSA, you were entitled to, receiving, or treated as receiving, IS, JSA or income-related ESA, or were treated as entitled to one of these while your income or capital was too high in the circumstances described below; *or*
  - for ESA, you were entitled to, receiving, or treated as receiving, IS, income-based JSA, income-related ESA or PC, or were treated as entitled to one of these while your income or capital was too high in the circumstances described below;
- IS or JSA during any period for which you are awarded IS, JSA or income-related ESA after a revision, supersession or an appeal;
- income-related ESA during any period for which you are awarded IS, income-based JSA, income-related ESA or PC after a revision, supersession or an appeal.

Income or capital is too high

You can be treated as entitled to IS, income-based JSA or income-related ESA (for a period of no more than 39 weeks) if you were not entitled to one of these benefits (or for ESA only, to PC) only because your income was too high or your capital was over £16,000, including if your contribution-based JSA was the same as or higher than your income-based JSA applicable amount (or your contributory ESA was the same as or higher than your income-related ESA).

This applies if:[147]

- on all the days in the period, you have been entitled to contribution-based JSA, statutory sick pay, incapacity benefit or contributory ESA (or national insurance credits for unemployment, incapacity or limited capability). A claim for IS, *income-based* JSA or *income-related* ESA is not required;[148] *or*
- for IS only, you are treated as receiving IS or income-based JSA.[149]

This also applies if you are a lone parent or a carer (see p877).[150] In this case, you or someone claiming on your behalf must have previously claimed and been refused IS or income-based JSA or, for IS and JSA only, contribution-based JSA or, for JSA and ESA only, income-related ESA or, for ESA only, PC. However, this rule does not apply if, during the 39-week period:

- for IS and JSA, you or your partner count as being in full-time paid work (see Chapter 31), or you are a full-time student who cannot claim IS or JSA (see p637); *or*
- for ESA, you count as being in paid work or your partner counts as being in full-time paid work (see Chapter 31), or you are in full-time education and are getting disability living allowance; *or*
- you are temporarily absent from Great Britain other than:
  - for IS and ESA, during the first four weeks of absence in specified circumstances or if you are away solely because you are accompanying a dependent child for medical treatment; *or*
  - for JSA, in circumstances in which you would normally continue to qualify for JSA (see p1490).

Carer

For these purposes, you count as a carer if:

– for IS and ESA, you are someone who would qualify for IS as a carer (see p348); *or*

– for JSA, you are a carer who is allowed to restrict the hours you are available for work (see p445).

If the rules above apply and you were not entitled to IS, income-based JSA or income-related ESA only because your *income* was too high and you were getting payments under a mortgage payment protection policy, you are treated as entitled to IS, income-based JSA or income-related ESA for *any* period for which the payments were made.[151] This could be longer than 39 weeks.

Couples and former couples

You are treated as entitled to and receiving IS, income-based JSA or income-related ESA during the time when:[152]

- your former partner was receiving or was treated as receiving IS, income-based JSA (but for IS and JSA, not joint-claim JSA), income-related ESA or PC for you both, provided you claim IS, income-based JSA or income-related ESA within 12 weeks of separating (104 weeks if you are a 'welfare to work beneficiary' or a 'work or training beneficiary' (see pp738 and 214) or 52 weeks if you qualify for a longer linking period – see p879);
- your partner was receiving or was treated as receiving IS, income-based JSA or income-related ESA (or for ESA only, PC) on her/his own, provided you make a claim for IS, income-based JSA or income-related ESA within 12 weeks of becoming a couple (or a 'joint-claim couple' – see p413). Unless you are a joint-claim couple, the time limit is 104 weeks if you or your partner are a

'welfare to work beneficiary' or a 'work or training beneficiary' (see p738 and 214), or 52 weeks if you qualify for a longer linking period (see p879);
- your partner was receiving or treated as receiving IS, income-based JSA (but for IS and JSA, not joint-claim JSA) or income-related ESA (or for ESA only, PC) for you both, if you take over the claiming role.

Employment and training schemes

You are treated as entitled to and receiving IS, income-based JSA or income-related ESA during:[153]
- the time when you or your partner were on a specified New Deal programme or scheme, provided your partner was claiming IS or income-based JSA (but for IS and JSA, not joint-claim JSA) or income-related ESA (or for ESA only, PC) for you immediately before this and you claim IS, income-based JSA (but not joint-claim JSA) or income-related ESA immediately after;
- periods when you stop receiving IS, income-based JSA or income-related ESA (or for ESA only, PC) because you or your partner are on:
  - training under specific provisions or an employment training rehabilitation course;
  - a specified New Deal programme or scheme and, as a result, count as being in full-time paid work (see Chapter 31) or have too much income (see Chapter 40);
- any period when you were receiving contribution-based JSA immediately before starting on a specified New Deal programme or scheme.

Other

You are treated as entitled to and receiving IS, income-based JSA or income-related ESA during the time when someone who was not your partner (the 'former claimant' – eg, your parent or an adult acting as your parent) was entitled to:[154]
- IS or income-based JSA;
- for JSA only, income-related ESA;
- for ESA only, income-related ESA or PC.

In all cases, you and a child or young person must have counted as a member of the former claimant's family and the child or young person must now count as a member of *your* family (see p849 for who counts). You must make a claim for IS, income-based JSA or income-related ESA within 12 weeks of the former claimant's entitlement ceasing (104 weeks if you are a 'welfare to work beneficiary' or a 'work or training beneficiary' – see pp738 and 214 – or 52 weeks if you qualify for a longer linking period – see p879). So, for example, this applies if your mother or father was claiming benefit for you and your child, but you are now claiming IS, income-based JSA or income-related ESA.

Longer linking periods

Some of the 12-week periods and time limits above are extended to 52 weeks – referred to in this *Handbook* as 'longer linking periods'. You qualify for a longer linking period if you stop getting IS, JSA or income-related ESA because:[155]

- you or your partner:
  - start work or increase your hours; *or*
  - are taking steps to get work under certain training schemes; *or*
  - are getting assistance in pursuing self-employment while on a training course funded under specific provisions;[156] *and*
- as a result, your earnings or your income are too high, or (for IS and JSA) you or your partner count as being in full-time paid work, or (for ESA) you count as being in paid work or your partner counts as in full-time paid work (see Chapter 31).

You only qualify for a longer linking period if, immediately before the day your entitlement to IS, income-based JSA or income-related ESA ceased, you had served enough of your waiting period (see p873) so that housing costs:[157]

- were included in your IS, income-based JSA or income-related ESA (in full or in part); *or*
- would have been included but for a non-dependant deduction (see p869).

7. Mortgage interest run-on

When you (or your partner) return to work or increase your hours and so count as being in full-time paid work, you no longer qualify for income support (IS), income-based jobseeker's allowance (JSA) or income-related employment and support allowance (ESA). However, you might qualify for mortgage interest run-on. If you do, you are paid IS for your housing costs for the first four weeks after you go into full-time paid work, even if the benefit you were claiming was income-based JSA or income-related ESA.

Who can claim mortgage interest run-on

You qualify for mortgage interest run-on if:[158]

- you or your partner take up a new job or increase your weekly hours of work and so count as being in full-time paid work (see p718). You must expect the work to last for at least five weeks; *and*
- throughout the 26 weeks before the day you count as being in full-time paid work, you or your partner were receiving IS, income-based JSA or income-related ESA. Periods when you were receiving mortgage interest run-on do not count towards the 26 weeks;[159] *and*

- on the day before you or your partner commenced the work, your IS, income-based JSA or income-related ESA applicable amount included any of the following housing costs:
  - mortgages and other home purchase loans (see p857); *or*
  - loans for repairs and improvements (see p861); *or*
  - 'other housing costs' (see p862); *and*
- you or your partner are still liable to pay the housing costs.

If you qualify, you are paid IS for the housing costs for the first four weeks of full-time paid work.[160] Mortgage interest run-on is paid to you, *not* directly to your lender.[161]

The amount of mortgage interest run-on

You are paid the lowest of:[162]
- the weekly amount of IS, income-based JSA or income-related ESA housing costs that you were getting immediately before you or your partner took up full-time paid work. See p864 for how these costs are calculated; *or*
- your or your partner's IS, income-based JSA or income-related ESA entitlement in the week before you took up full-time paid work (or the amount to which you would have been entitled had you not been getting a training allowance).

Your mortgage interest run-on can be adjusted if there are changes in the:[163]
- IS applicable amount (see Chapter 37);
- amount of housing costs you can get because:
  - the standard rate of interest used to calculate housing costs (see p865) or your non-dependant deductions (see p869) have changed; *or*
  - you have been entitled to IS for 26 weeks.

Your earnings from the full-time paid work and any other income you get are disregarded.[164] All of your capital is also disregarded.[165]

Claims

Although you do not have to make a claim to qualify for mortgage interest run-on,[166] you must let your local DWP (or Jobcentre Plus) office know you are starting full-time paid work. Mortgage interest run-on should then be paid automatically.

Tax, tax credits and other benefits

Mortgage interest run-on is not taxable.

Mortgage interest run-on is a payment of IS. You might, therefore, get health benefits and education benefits (see p14) and qualify for social fund payments.

Notes

1. **When you can get help with housing costs**

1 **IS** Sch 3 para 1 IS Regs
JSA Sch 2 para 1 JSA Regs
ESA Sch 6 para 1 ESA Regs
PC Sch 2 para 1 SPC Regs
2 **IS** Sch 3 paras 2 and 5(5) IS Regs
JSA Sch 2 paras 2 and 5(5) JSA Regs
ESA Sch 6 paras 4 and 7(5) ESA Regs
PC Sch 2 paras 3 and 6(5) SPC Regs
3 CSB/213/1987
4 R(IS) 4/00
5 R(IS) 4/95
6 *Ewens v Secretary of State for Social Security*, reported as R(IS) 8/01
7 CIS/636/1992, confirmed by the Court of Appeal in *Brain v CAO*, 2 December 1993
8 **IS** Sch 3 para 2(2) IS Regs
JSA Sch 2 para 2(2) JSA Regs
9 **IS** Reg 2(1) IS Regs
JSA Reg 1(3) JSA Regs
ESA Reg 2(1) ESA Regs
PC Reg 1(2) SPC Regs
All R(SB) 22/87
10 **IS** s137(1) SSCBA 1992
JSA s35(1) JSA 1995
ESA Reg 2(1) ESA Regs
11 **IS** Sch 3 para 3(1) IS Regs
JSA Sch 2 para 3(1) JSA Regs
ESA Sch 6 para 5(1) ESA Regs
PC Sch 2 para 4(1) SPC Regs
12 CIS/297/1994
13 **IS** Sch 3 para 4(1)(b) IS Regs
JSA Sch 2 para 4(1)(b) JSA Regs
ESA Sch 6 para 6(1)(b) ESA Regs
PC Sch 2 para 5(1)(b) SPC Regs
14 **IS** Reg 2(1) IS Regs
JSA Reg 1(3) JSA Regs
ESA Reg 2(1) ESA Regs
PC Reg 1(2) SPC Regs
All definition of 'dwelling occupied as the home'; s137(1) SSCBA 1992 and reg 2(1) ESA Regs, definition of 'dwelling'
15 *SSWP v Mohamed Miah*, reported as R(JSA) 9/03; R(H) 5/09
16 **IS** Sch 3 para 3(7) and (13) IS Regs
JSA Sch 2 para 3(7) and (13) JSA Regs
ESA Sch 6 para 5(7) and (13) ESA Regs
PC Sch 2 para 4(7) SPC Regs
17 CH/1363/2006; R(H) 4/07
18 R(H) 9/05
19 **IS** Sch 3 para 3(10) IS Regs
JSA Sch 2 para 3(10) JSA Regs
ESA Sch 6 para 5(10) ESA Regs
PC Sch 2 para 4(10) SPC Regs
20 **IS** Sch 3 para 3(11)-(13) IS Regs
JSA Sch 2 para 3(11)-(13) JSA Regs
ESA Sch 6 para 5(11)-(13) ESA Regs
PC Sch 2 para 4(11)-(13) SPC Regs
21 *MR v Bournemouth BC (HB)* [2011] UKUT 284 (AAC)
22 *SSWP v Selby District Council and Bowman* [2006] EWCA Civ 271, 13 February 2006, reported as R(H) 4/06
23 **IS** Sch 3 para 3(8) and (9) IS Regs
JSA Sch 2 para 3(8) and (9) JSA Regs
ESA Sch 6 para 5(8) and (9) ESA Regs
PC Sch 2 para 4(8) and (9) SPC Regs
24 *Torbay Borough Council v RF* [2010] UKUT 7 (AAC); [2010] AACR 26
25 CH/1237/2004
26 CH/3893/2004
27 *R v Penwith District Council ex parte Burt* [1990] 22HLR 292 (QBD)
28 R(H) 8/09; *SK v South Hams DC (HB)* [2010] UKUT 129 (AAC); [2010] AACR 40
29 **IS** Sch 3 para 3(5) IS Regs
JSA Sch 2 para 3(5) JSA Regs
ESA Sch 6 para 5(5) ESA Regs
PC Sch 2 para 4(5) SPC Regs
30 CIS/719/1994
31 **IS** Sch 3 para 3(13) IS Regs
JSA Sch 2 para 3(13) JSA Regs
ESA Sch 6 para 5 (13) ESA Regs
PC Sch 2 para 4(13) SPC Regs
32 R(H) 5/09
33 **IS** Sch 3 para 3(6) IS Regs
JSA Sch 2 para 3(6) JSA Regs
ESA Sch 6 para 5(6) ESA Regs
PC Sch 2 para 4(6) SPC Regs
34 CH/1911/2006
35 CIS/543/1993
36 CIS/339/1993
37 **IS** Sch 3 para 3(6)(a) IS Regs
JSA Sch 2 para 3(6)(a) JSA Regs
ESA Sch 6 para 5(6)(a) ESA Regs
PC Sch 2 para 4(6)(a) SPC Regs

38 **IS** Sch 3 para 3(6)(b) IS Regs
JSA Sch 2 para 3(6)(b) JSA Regs
ESA Sch 6 para 5(6)(b) ESA Regs
PC Sch 2 para 4(6)(b) SPC Regs
39 **IS** Sch 3 para 3(3) IS Regs
JSA Sch 2 para 3(3) JSA Regs
ESA Sch 6 para 5(3) ESA Regs
PC Sch 2 para 4(3) SPC Regs
40 **IS** Sch 3 para 3(11)(c)(viii) IS Regs
JSA Sch 2 para 3(11)(c)(viii) JSA Regs
ESA Sch 6 para 5(11)(c)(viii) ESA Regs
PC Sch 2 para 4(11)(c)(viii) SPC Regs
41 **IS** Sch 3 para 3(4) IS Regs
JSA Sch 2 para 3(4) JSA Regs
ESA Sch 6 para 5(4) ESA Regs
PC Sch 2 para 4(4) SPC Regs

2. **Modified rules**

42 Regs 1, definition of 'relevant benefit', and 8 SS(HCSA)(A&M) Regs
43 Regs 3, 6(a), 7, 8 and 11(b) SS(HCSA)(A&M) Regs; Sch 2 para 4A JSA Regs
44 Sch 2 para 4A(3) and (4) JSA Regs, as inserted by reg 6 SS(HCSA)(A&M) Regs; Sch 2 para 4A(6) and (7) JSA Regs, as inserted by reg 11 SS(HCSA)(A&M) Regs

3. **The types of housing costs that can be met**

45 **IS** Sch 3 para 4(1)(a) IS Regs
JSA Sch 2 para 4(1)(a) JSA Regs
ESA Sch 6 para 6(1)(a) ESA Regs
PC Sch 2 para 5(1)(a) SPC Regs
46 CIS/14483/1996
47 **IS** Sch 3 para 15 IS Regs
JSA Sch 2 para 14 JSA Regs
ESA Sch 6 para 16 ESA Regs
PC Sch 2 para 11 SPC Regs
48 R(IS) 14/01; CPC/3322/2007
49 R(IS) 11/94
50 R(IS) 4/95
51 R(IS) 7/93
52 R(IS) 6/94
53 R(IS) 24/95
54 R(IS) 11/94
55 **IS** Sch 3 para 5 IS Regs
JSA Sch 2 para 5 JSA Regs
ESA Sch 6 para 7 ESA Regs
PC Sch 2 para 6 SPC Regs
56 **IS** Sch 3 para 4(2)-(4) IS Regs
JSA Sch 2 para 4(2)-(4) JSA Regs
ESA Sch 6 para 6(2)-(4) ESA Regs
PC Sch 2 para 5(2)-(4) SPC Regs
All *Saleem v Secretary of State for Social Security*, reported as R(IS) 5/01; *SSWP v Mohammed* [2011] EWCA Civ 1358, 23 November 2011
57 CPC/3226/2005; CPC/3992/2007; CIS/88/2008
58 **IS** Sch 3 para 4(2) and (3) IS Regs
JSA Sch 2 para 4(2) and (3) JSA Regs
ESA Sch 6 para 6(2) and (3) ESA Regs
PC Sch 2 para 5(2) and (3) SPC Regs
59 **IS** Sch 3 para 4(4) IS Regs; reg 32 IS(JSACA) Regs
JSA Sch 2 paras 4(4) and 18(1)(c) JSA Regs
60 para 23466 DMG
61 **ESA** Sch 6 para 6(4) ESA Regs
PC Sch 2 para 5(2) and (4) SPC Regs
62 **IS** Sch 3 para 4(4A) IS Regs
JSA Sch 2 para 4(4A) JSA Regs
ESA Sch 6 para 6(5) ESA Regs
PC Sch 2 para 5(5) SPC Regs
63 **IS** Sch 3 para 4(4B) IS Regs
JSA Sch 2 para 4(4B) JSA Regs
ESA Sch 6 para 6(6) ESA Regs
64 **IS** Sch 3 paras 1(3) and (4) and 4(9) IS Regs
JSA Sch 2 paras 1(3) and (4) and 4(9) JSA Regs
ESA Sch 6 paras 1(3) and (4) and 6(11) ESA Regs
PC Sch 2 paras 1(2)(a) and (3) and 5(10) SPC Regs
All R(IS)12/08
65 CIS/3295/2003
66 *Ahmed v SSWP* [2011] EWCA Civ 1186, 21 October 2011, reported as [2012] AACR 23
67 R(IS) 20/98
68 **IS** Sch 3 para 4(10) IS Regs
JSA Sch 2 para 4(10) JSA Regs
ESA Sch 6 para 6(12) ESA Regs
PC Sch 2 para 5(11) SPC Regs
All *Saleem v Secretary of State for Social Security*, reported as R(IS) 5/01; CIS/1068/2003
69 CIS/14657/1996; *SSWP v CA* [2009] UKUT 13 (AAC)
70 **IS** Sch 3 para 1(3) and (4) IS Regs
JSA Sch 2 para 1(3) and (4) JSA Regs
ESA Sch 6 para 1(3) and (4) ESA Regs
PC Sch 2 para 1(2)(a) and (3) SPC Regs
71 **IS** Sch 3 para 4(6) IS Regs
JSA Sch 2 para 4(6) JSA Regs
ESA Sch 6 para 6(8) ESA Regs
PC Sch 2 para 5(7) SPC Regs
All *AH v SSWP (IS)* [2010] UKUT 353 (AAC)
72 CIS/11293/1995

73 **IS** Sch 3 para 4(8) IS Regs
JSA Sch 2 para 4(8) JSA Regs
ESA Sch 6 para 6(10) ESA Regs
PC Sch 2 para 5(9) SPC Regs
All CIS/4712/2002
74 **IS** Sch 3 para 4(11) IS Regs
JSA Sch 2 para 4(11) JSA Regs
ESA Sch 6 para 6(13) ESA Regs
PC Sch 2 para 5(12) SPC Regs
75 R(IS) 8/94
76 **IS** Sch 3 para 16 IS Regs
JSA Sch 2 para 15 JSA Regs
ESA Sch 6 para 17 ESA Regs
PC Sch 2 para 12 SPC Regs
All CIS/1480/2005
77 R(IS) 22/98
78 R(IS) 5/96
79 CIS/14657/1996
80 **IS** Sch 3 para 16(2) IS Regs
JSA Sch 2 para 15(2) JSA Regs
ESA Sch 6 para 17(2) ESA Regs
PC Sch 2 para 12(2) SPC Regs
81 CIS/2132/1998
82 R(IS) 16/98; *DC v SSWP (JSA)* [2010] UKUT 459 (AAC)
83 CIS/14657/1996; *SSWP v CA* [2009] UKUT 13 (AAC)
84 **IS** Sch 3 para 17(1) IS Regs
JSA Sch 2 para 16(1) JSA Regs
ESA Sch 6 para 18(1) ESA Regs
PC Sch 2 para 13(1) SPC Regs
85 CH/3110/2003; R(H) 3/07
86 **IS** Sch 3 para 17(5) IS Regs
JSA Sch 2 para 16(5) JSA Regs
ESA Sch 6 para 18(5) ESA Regs
PC Sch 2 para 13(5) SPC Regs
87 **IS** Sch 3 para 17(3) IS Regs
JSA Sch 2 para 16(3) JSA Regs
ESA Sch 6 para 18(3) ESA Regs
PC Sch 2 para 13(3) SPC Regs
88 **IS** Sch 3 para 17(4) IS Regs
JSA Sch 2 para 16(4) JSA Regs
ESA Sch 6 para 18(4) ESA Regs
PC Sch 2 para 13(4) SPC Regs
89 **IS** Sch 3 para 17(2) IS Regs
JSA Sch 2 para 16(2) JSA Regs
ESA Sch 6 para 18(2) ESA Regs
PC Sch 2 para 13(2) SPC Regs
90 CIS/15036/1996; CIS/488/2008
91 **IS** Sch 3 para 17(2)(b) IS Regs
JSA Sch 2 para 16(2)(b) JSA Regs
ESA Sch 6 para 18(2)(b) ESA Regs
PC Sch 2 para 13(2)(b) SPC Regs
92 R(IS) 4/91; CIS/1460/1995; CIS/15036/1996
93 **IS** Sch 3 para 17(2)(c) IS Regs
JSA Sch 2 para 16(2)(c) JSA Regs
ESA Sch 6 para 18(2)(c) ESA Regs
PC Sch 2 para 13(2)(c) SPC Regs
94 R(IS) 4/92; R(IS) 19/93
95 CIS/4/1988
96 Reg 3 IS(AT) Regs; Sch 6 para 20(2) ESA Regs

4. **The amount of housing costs you get**

97 Regs 34A and 34B and Sch 9A para 4A SS(C&P) Regs
98 **IS** Sch 3 para 10 IS Regs
JSA Sch 2 para 9 JSA Regs
ESA Sch 6 para 11 ESA Regs
PC Sch 2 para 7(1) SPC Regs
99 **IS** Sch 3 para 12 IS Regs
JSA Sch 2 para 11 JSA Regs
ESA Sch 6 para 13 ESA Regs
PC Sch 2 para 9 SPC Regs
100 **IS** Sch 3 para 7 IS Regs
JSA Sch 2 para 18 JSA Regs
ESA Sch 6 para 20(1)(b) ESA Regs
101 **IS** Sch 3 paras 6(1A) and (1B) and 8(1A) and (1B) IS Regs; reg 7(14) and (23) and Sch 3A paras 12 and 13 SS&CS(DA) Regs
JSA Sch 2 paras 6(2) and 7(2)-(2B) JSA Regs; reg 7(18) and (23) and Sch 3A paras 12 and 13 SS&CS(DA) Regs
ESA Sch 6 paras 8(2) and (3) and 9(2) and (3) ESA Regs; reg 7(17D) and (23) and Sch 3C paras 9 and 10 SS&CS(DA) Regs
PC Sch 2 para 7(2) and (4C) SPC Regs; reg 7(17A) SS&CS(DA) Regs
102 Reg 7(17B) and (17C) SS&CS(DA) Regs
103 **IS** Sch 3 para 1A IS Regs
JSA Sch 2 para 1A JSA Regs
ESA Sch 6 para 3 ESA Regs
PC Sch 2 para 7(4A)-(5) SPC Regs
104 **IS** Reg 42(4)(a)(ii) IS Regs
JSA Reg 105(10)(a)(ii) JSA Regs
ESA Reg 107(3)(c) ESA Regs
105 **IS** Sch 10 para 26 IS Regs
JSA Sch 8 para 6 JSA Regs
ESA Sch 9 para 6 ESA Regs
PC Sch 5 para 7 SPC Regs
106 **IS** Sch 3 para 11(4) and (5) IS Regs
JSA Sch 2 para 10(3) and (4) JSA Regs
ESA Sch 6 para 12(3) and (4) ESA Regs
PC Sch 2 para 8(1) and (2) SPC Regs
All Regs 3-6 and 8-11 SS(HCSA)(A&M) Regs
107 **IS** Sch 3 para 11(6) IS Regs
JSA Sch 2 para 10(5) JSA Regs
ESA Sch 6 para 12(5) ESA Regs
PC Sch 2 para 8(3) SPC Regs

108 Reg 12 SS(HCSA)(A&M) Regs
109 **IS** Sch 3 para 14(3AA) IS Regs
JSA Sch 2 para 13(4A) JSA Regs
ESA Schs 6 paras 12(11) and (12) and 15(6) ESA Regs
All Reg 4 IS(G)A No.3 Regs; reg 28 IBS(MA) Regs
110 **IS** Sch 3 para 13 IS Regs
JSA Sch 2 para 12 JSA Regs
ESA Sch 6 para 14 ESA Regs
PC Sch 2 para 10 SPC Regs
111 R(IS) 12/91
112 **IS** Sch 3 para 13(2) IS Regs
JSA Sch 2 para 12(2) JSA Regs
ESA Sch 6 para 14(2) ESA Regs
PC Sch 2 para 10(2) SPC Regs
113 **IS** Sch 3 para 13(4) and (5) IS Regs
JSA Sch 2 para 12(4) and (5) JSA Regs
ESA Sch 6 para 14(4) and (5) ESA Regs
PC Sch 2 para 10(4) and (5) SPC Regs
114 R(SB) 7/89
115 R(SB) 6/89; R(SB) 7/89
116 R(IS) 10/93
117 CIS/347/1992
118 CSB/617/1988. This case has been reported as R(SB) 4/89, but the reported version omits the relevant paragraphs.
119 R(SB) 7/89
120 **IS** Sch 3 para 13(3) IS Regs
JSA Sch 2 para 12(3) JSA Regs
ESA Sch 6 para 14(3) ESA Regs
PC Sch 2 para 10(3) SPC Regs
121 CJSA/2683/2002
122 R(IS) 9/91; CJSA/2536/2000
123 **IS** Sch 3 para 13(6) IS Regs
JSA Sch 2 para 12(6) JSA Regs
ESA Sch 6 para 14(6) and (10) ESA Regs
PC Sch 2 para 10(6) SPC Regs
All *Secretary of State for Social Security v Julien*, reported as R(IS) 13/92; R(SB) 7/89; CIS/104/1991
124 CJSA/2536/2000
125 **IS** Sch 3 para 13(7) IS Regs
JSA Sch 2 para 12(7) JSA Regs
ESA Sch 6 paras 14(7) and (10) and 20(1)(c) ESA Regs
PC Sch 2 para 10(7) and (10) SPC Regs
126 **IS** Sch 3 paras 13(9) and 14(15) IS Regs
JSA Sch 2 paras 12(9) and 18(1)(c) JSA Regs
ESA Sch 6 paras 14(9) and (10) and 20(1)(c) ESA Regs
PC Sch 2 para 10(7), (9) and (10) SPC Regs
127 **IS** Reg 3 and Sch 3 para 18 IS Regs
JSA Reg 2 and Sch 2 para 17 JSA Regs
ESA Reg 71 and Sch 6 para 19 ESA Regs
PC Sch 2 paras 1(4)-(9) and 14 SPC Regs
128 R(H) 8/09; *SK v South Hams DC (HB)* [2010] UKUT 129 (AAC); [2010] AACR 40
129 **IS** Reg 3 IS Regs
JSA Reg 2 JSA Regs
ESA Reg 71 ESA Regs
PC Sch 2 para 1(4)-(7) SPC Regs
130 CSB/1163/1988
131 **IS** Sch 3 para 18(6) IS Regs
JSA Sch 2 para 17(6) JSA Regs
ESA Sch 6 para 19(6) ESA Regs
PC Sch 2 para 14(6) SPC Regs
132 **IS** Sch 3 para 18(7) IS Regs
JSA Sch 2 para 17(7) JSA Regs
ESA Sch 6 para 19(7) ESA Regs
PC Sch 2 para 14(7) SPC Regs
133 Made under s2 ETA 1973 and s2 Enterprise and New Towns (Scotland) Act 1990 or by the Secretary of State for people enlisted in HM Forces for any special term of service specified in regulations made under s2 Armed Forces Act 1966.
134 **IS** Sch 3 para 18(1) and (2) IS Regs
JSA Sch 2 para 17(1) and (2) JSA Regs
ESA Sch 6 para 19(1) and (2) ESA Regs
PC Sch 2 para 14(1) and (2) SPC Regs
135 Sch 2 para 2(6) SPC Regs
136 **IS** Sch 3 para 18(8) IS Regs
JSA Sch 2 para 17(8) JSA Regs
ESA Sch 6 para 19(8) ESA Regs
PC Sch 2 para 14(8) SPC Regs
137 CH/48/2006

5. **Waiting periods**

138 **IS** Sch 3 paras 6 and 8 IS Regs
JSA Sch 2 paras 6 and 7 JSA Regs
ESA Sch 6 paras 8 and 9 ESA Regs
All SS(HCSA)(A&M) Regs
139 **IS** Sch 3 para 9 IS Regs
JSA Sch 2 para 8 JSA Regs
ESA Sch 6 para 10 ESA Regs
All SS(HCSA)(A&M) Regs
140 **IS** Sch 3 para 14(8) and (9) IS Regs; regs 5(d) and 10(h) SS(HCSA)(A&M) Regs
JSA Sch 2 para 13(10) and (11) JSA Regs; regs 6(e) and 11(i) SS(HCSA)(A&M) Regs
ESA Sch 6 para 15(13) and (14) ESA Regs; regs 4(d) and 9(h) SS(HCSA)(A&M) Regs
All Regs 3 and 8 SS(HCSA)(A&M) Regs
141 Regs 3-6 and 9-11 SS(HCSA)(A&M) Regs

142 **IS** Sch 3 paras 1(2), 6 and 8(2)-(5) IS Regs
JSA Sch 2 paras 1(2), 6 and 7(3)-(6) JSA Regs
ESA Sch 6 paras 1(2), 8 and 9(4)-(7) ESA Regs
All CJSA/2028/2000
143 **IS** Sch 3 para 8(2)-(5) IS Regs
JSA Sch 2 para 7(3)-(6) JSA Regs
ESA Sch 6 para 9(4)-(7) ESA Regs
144 **IS** Sch 3 paras 1(2) and 8 IS Regs
JSA Sch 2 paras 1(2) and 7 JSA Regs
ESA Sch 6 paras 1(2) and 9 ESA Regs
All CJSA/2028/2000
145 **IS** Sch 3 para 11(2) IS Regs
JSA Sch 2 para 10(1) JSA Regs
ESA Sch 6 para 12(1) ESA Regs

6. **Linking rules**

146 **IS** Sch 3 para 14(1)(a), (3A) and (15) IS Regs; reg 32 IS(JSACA) Regs
JSA Sch 2 paras 13(1)(a), (2A) and (4) and 18(1)(c) JSA Regs
ESA Sch 6 paras 15 (1)(a), (5), (15) and (16) and 20(1)(c) ESA Regs
147 **IS** Sch 3 para 14(4) and (5) IS Regs; reg 32 IS(JSACA) Regs
JSA Sch 2 paras 13(5) and (6) and 18(1)(c) JSA Regs; reg 32 IS(JSACA) Regs
ESA Sch 6 paras 2(9), 15(8) and (9) and 20(1)(c) ESA Regs
All CIS/621/2004
148 CJSA/4613/2001
149 Sch 3 para 14(5)(c) IS Regs; reg 32 IS(JSACA) Regs
150 **IS** Sch 3 para 14(4), (5A) and (5B) IS Regs; reg 32 IS(JSACA) Regs
JSA Sch 2 paras 13(7) and (8) and 18(1)(c) JSA Regs; reg 32 IS(JSACA) Regs
ESA Sch 6 paras 2(9), 15(8), (10) and (11) and 20(1)(c) ESA Regs
All CIS/621/2004
151 **IS** Sch 3 para 14(6) IS Regs
JSA Sch 2 para 13(9) JSA Regs
ESA Sch 6 para 15(12) ESA Regs
152 **IS** Sch 3 para 14(1)(c), (d) and (e), (3A), (14) and (15) IS Regs
JSA Sch 2 paras 13(1)(c), (d), (dd) and (e), (4) and (16) and 18(1)(c) JSA Regs
ESA Sch 6 paras 15(1)(c), (d) and (e), (15) and (19) and 20(1)(c) ESA Regs
153 **IS** Sch 3 para 14(1)(ee), (3), (3ZA), (3A), (3B) and (15) IS Regs
JSA Sch 2 paras 13(1)(ee), (3), (3A) and (4) and 18(1)(c) JSA Regs
ESA Sch 6 paras 15(1)(f), (3), (4), (5) and (7) and 20(1)(c) ESA Regs
154 **IS** Sch 3 para 14(1)(f) and (3A) IS Regs
JSA Sch 2 para 13(1)(f) and (4) JSA Regs
ESA Sch 6 paras 15(1)(g) and (5) and 20(1)(c) ESA Regs
155 **IS** Sch 3 para 14(11) and (12) IS Regs
JSA Sch 2 para 13(13) and (14) JSA Regs
ESA Sch 6 paras 2(9) and 15(16) and (17) ESA Regs
156 Schemes mentioned in reg 19(1)(r)(i)-(iii) JSA Regs
157 **IS** Sch 3 para 14(13) IS Regs
JSA Sch 2 para 13(15) JSA Regs
ESA Sch 6 para 15(18) ESA Regs

7. **Mortgage interest run-on**

158 Reg 6(5) and (8) IS Regs
159 Reg 6(7) IS Regs
160 Reg 6(6) IS Regs
161 Sch 9A para 3(9) SS(C&P) Regs
162 Sch 7 para 19A(1) IS Regs
163 Sch 7 para 19A(2) and (3) IS Regs
164 Schs 8 para 15C and 9 para 74 IS Regs
165 Sch 10 para 62 IS Regs
166 Reg 3(h) SS(C&P) Regs

Chapter 39

Income: non-means-tested benefits

This chapter covers:

Key facts

- Your own earnings from employment or self-employment may affect your entitlement to carer's allowance, contribution-based jobseeker's allowance (JSA), contributory employment and support allowance (ESA), incapacity benefit (IB) and severe disablement allowance (SDA).
- Your own occupational or personal pension may reduce the amount of contribution-based JSA, contributory ESA or IB you can receive. Your partner's or adult dependant's earnings and pension may affect an increase in non-means-tested benefits for a child or adult dependant.
- Contributory ESA, IB and SDA may be paid at a reduced rate if you are a local councillor with allowances above a set limit.

Future changes: April 2013 and after

Major changes are taking place that affect the benefits and tax credits system (see Chapter 2). When universal credit (UC) is introduced in October 2013, the government proposes aligning the earnings rules for contribution-based JSA and contributory ESA with those for UC. See CPAG's *Welfare Rights Bulletin* for updates.

1. Income for non-means-tested benefits

The rules in this section apply to all non-means-tested benefits except contribution-based jobseeker's allowance (JSA – see p896) and contributory employment and support allowance (ESA – see p898).

Some non-means-tested benefits may be affected by:

- your own earnings and occupational or personal pension (see below);
- your partner's or adult dependant's earnings and occupational or personal pension, but this can only affect an increase in your benefit for a child or adult dependant (see p888);
- other benefits you get ('overlapping benefits') – see p1041.

No other kind of income affects entitlement.

Benefits affected by earnings or pensions

You are not entitled to any of the following benefits if you earn more than a certain amount:

- carer's allowance (CA);
- incapacity benefit (IB);
- severe disablement allowance (SDA).

Your occupational or personal pension may affect your IB or SDA.

Payment of an increase for an adult dependant may be affected by the earnings or pensions of your dependant, and payment for a child dependant may be affected by the earnings or pensions of your partner.

Carer's allowance

You are not entitled to CA if your earnings are above £100 a week.[1] Earnings of £100 a week or less do not affect the amount of CA. Only your own earnings count, not those of a partner. Any pension payments you get do not affect your benefit. See p890 for how earnings are worked out. For more about the earnings limit and when all your earnings can be ignored, see p85. If you stop work and then claim CA, final earnings generally do not affect your entitlement (see p890).

Incapacity benefit and severe disablement allowance

Your entitlement to IB or SDA can be affected by the following income.

- **Earnings from permitted work**. Normally you are not entitled to IB or SDA for any week in which you work. However, certain types of work can be ignored, including 'permitted work'. Whether the work you do counts as permitted work depends, in part, on whether your earnings are below certain limits (see pp736 and 216). If your earnings in any week are higher than these limits, you are not entitled to IB or SDA for that week.
  - The **lower limit** is £20 a week.
  - The **higher limit** is £97.50 a week (this usually increases in October).

  Only your earnings count towards these limits, not your partner's. Any pension payments you get do not count towards these limits.
- **Councillors' allowances**. IB or SDA is paid at a reduced rate if you are a local councillor and your net allowances are more than £97.50 in a week. Your IB

or SDA in that week is reduced by the amount by which the net allowances exceed £97.50 (the limit usually increases in October).[2] See p899 for the way the net weekly allowance is worked out (the same way as for ESA).

- **Pensions.** If you get certain kinds of pension payments, these can affect the amount of IB. See p343 for which pensions count and how they reduce your IB. Any pension payments you get do not affect the amount of SDA. If you claim an increase in your IB or SDA for a dependant, her/his pension payments can affect this entitlement.

See p890 for how earnings are worked out.

Increases for dependants

Your partner's or adult dependant's earnings (see p889), including most pension payments s/he gets (see below), count towards the earnings limit for increases for dependants.

- **Increases for adult dependants** in CA, maternity allowance (MA) and retirement pension were abolished from 6 April 2010. However, you can continue to get an increase if you were already entitled (see p740). The increase stops if your adult dependant has earnings or pensions income above the earnings limit, but starts again if her/his income drops below the limit. You may not be paid an increase in IB or SDA for an adult dependant if her/his earnings or pensions income is over the relevant earnings limit. For the amount of the earnings limits for adult dependants and how entitlement is affected, see p744.
- **Increases for child dependants** in non-means-tested benefits were abolished from 6 April 2003. If already entitled, you can continue to get the increase. Payment stops if your partner's earnings or pensions income is over the earnings limit. See p745 for more details.
- If your IB or SDA is converted to contributory employment and support allowance (ESA) which includes a transitional addition for an increase for a dependant, you will not lose this if your dependant later has earnings above the IB/SDA limit.[3]

Pension payments that count as earnings are occupational or personal pensions (including from the Pension Protection Fund) in connection with the end of employment. They must be arranged by an employer or out of money some or all of which is from an employer, or under an approved personal pension scheme, including if you are self-employed, or under a statutory scheme.[4] This includes schemes for early retirement on health or other grounds[5] or, in some cases, voluntary redundancy.[6] The payments must be periodical so it does not include lump sum or redundancy payments not related to a specific period even if you choose a lump sum instead of a periodical payment.[7] It is the gross amount of pension paid that counts, less any deductions for income tax, less any compulsory reductions made by the pension scheme to acquire additional pension rights.[8] A payment is converted into weekly amounts[9] and counted from the first day of the benefit week in which it is actually made.

Earnings from employment

To work out how earnings from employment affect entitlement:

- check whether the payment counts as earnings (see below) and whether it can be disregarded (see p893);
- work out weekly net earnings (see p890);
- work out the date from when earnings count and the period they cover (see p891);
- apply the earnings rule for the benefit you are claiming (see p887).

If you are employed by someone else (including employment by a limited company in which you have shares), 'earnings' means 'any remuneration or profit derived from ... employment'. The main type of **income which counts as earnings** is, therefore, your wages. The following are also included:[10]

- any bonus or commission (including tips);
- holiday pay (but not if it is payable more than four weeks after your job ends or is interrupted);
- compensation for unfair dismissal and certain other types of compensation under the Employment Rights Act 1996 or under trade union legislation;[11]
- an equal pay settlement;[12]
- any payments made by your employer for expenses not 'wholly, exclusively and necessarily' incurred in carrying out your job, including any travel expenses to and from work, and any payments made to you for the cost of arranging care for members of your family;
- a retainer (eg, you may be paid during the school holidays if you work for the school meals service) or a guarantee payment – ie, payment for a workless period under the Employment Rights Act 1996;[13]
- statutory or occupational maternity pay, paternity pay (during ordinary paternity leave), adoption pay and sick pay;[14]
- certain payments at the end of a job (see p890).

This list is not exhaustive, and other payments derived from your employment may also count as earnings.[15]

Note: it is the pay you actually receive which should be taken into account rather than what you may be legally entitled to,[16] so if you receive less than the national minimum wage, it is that lesser amount that counts as your 'earnings'.

The following are examples of payments that do not count as earnings:

- periodic payments made as part of a redundancy scheme;[17]
- except in respect of increases for dependants, occupational pension payments;[18]

- payments towards expenses that are 'wholly, exclusively and necessarily' incurred in the performance of your employment, such as travelling expenses during the course of your work.[19] See p906 for other examples.

Payments at the end of a job

If you stop work and claim CA, final earnings generally do not affect your benefit. The same applies if your partner stops work and you claim an increase to a non-means-tested benefit for her/him. As long as your entitlement begins after the employment ends, earnings disregarded are:[20]

- final wages, paid or due, including bonus, commission, tips and expenses that count as earnings;
- holiday pay;
- pay in lieu of notice;
- pay in lieu of remuneration – eg, loss of earnings payment to a councillor;
- statutory or contractual redundancy pay and other compensation payments (other than from an employment tribunal complaint).

Certain final payments are taken into account (unless you are retiring over pension age):

- maternity pay, paternity pay (during ordinary paternity leave), adoption pay and sick pay;
- employment tribunal award or settlement of a complaint to a tribunal or court – ie, compensation for unfair dismissal and certain other types of compensation under the Employment Rights Act 1996 or under trade union legislation;[21]
- a retainer.

Your partner's occupational or personal pension counts if you are claiming an increase for her/him.

If you are already entitled to CA or a dependency increase while working, final earnings when you stop work are not disregarded.

For IB and SDA, if you stop permitted work, final earnings do count towards the earnings limit but not after your final working week (see pp735 and 200).

Calculating net earnings from employment

For the earnings rules for the non-means-tested benefits in this *Handbook* (other than contribution-based JSA – see p896 – or contributory ESA – see p898), your 'earnings' are your net earnings. **'Net' earnings** are your 'gross' earnings less any deductions made for income tax, Class 1 national insurance (NI) contributions (but not Class 3 voluntary contributions[22]) and half of any contribution you make towards a personal or occupational pension scheme.[23] It is the amount of your earnings calculated on a weekly basis which is important. So, for example, if you are paid monthly, this figure is multiplied by 12 and divided by 52 to arrive at a weekly figure.[24] If you are paid for a period of less than a week, this payment is treated as a payment for a week.[25]

If your earnings fluctuate and have changed more than once, or your employment is such that you do not work every week, your weekly earnings may be averaged as follows:[26]

- if you have a regular pattern of work, over one complete 'cycle' of work. This includes periods where you do no work if this forms part of your regular pattern of work – eg, if you regularly work three weeks on and one week off, your earnings will be averaged over four weeks; *or*
- in any other case, over five weeks, or whatever other period will enable your average weekly earnings to be assessed more accurately.[27]

The date from when earnings from employment are counted

You are usually treated as having received earnings on the first day of the benefit week in which they are due to be paid (or the following week for an increase for an adult dependant in CA, or in retirement pension if s/he does not live with you).[28]

The **'benefit week'** is the seven days corresponding to the week for which the particular benefit you are claiming is paid (see the relevant chapter for the benefit you are claiming).[29]

The date that a payment is due may well be different from the date of actual payment. Earnings are due on the employee's normal payday. If your contract of employment does not reveal the date when the payment is due and there is no evidence to suggest differently, the date the payment was received should be taken as the date it was due.[30]

If your contract of employment is terminated without proper notice, outstanding wages, wages in hand, holiday pay and any pay in lieu of notice are due on the last day of employment and are treated as paid on that day, even if this does not happen.[31] (See p890 for when these final payments are disregarded.) If an employment tribunal awards you compensation for loss of earnings (eg, for being dismissed in circumstances constituting sex discrimination or an equal pay settlement), there is disagreement whether the relevant date is the date when the earnings were due to be paid, or when the compensation was awarded.[32]

The period covered by earnings from employment

Your earnings count for a future period starting from the date worked out above. The length of that period is worked out as follows.[33]

- Where a payment of income is made in respect of an identifiable period, it is taken into account for the number of benefit weeks corresponding to that period. For example, a week's part-time earnings are taken into account for a week, and if you are paid monthly, your earnings are taken into account for the number of weeks between the date you are treated as paid and the date your next monthly earnings are treated as paid – eg, for CA with a benefit week that starts on a Monday, if monthly earnings are paid on 20 July 2012 and due again on 20 August, they are taken into account for five weeks from Monday 16 July to Sunday 19 August. If a payment is for an identifiable period but is a one-off (eg, holiday pay when you leave a job if your final payments count – see p890), it is taken into account for the number of weeks from the date it is due to the date the next normal monthly earnings would be treated as paid.[34]

- If the payment does not relate to a particular period, it is divided by the amount of the weekly earnings limit (see pp744 and 887) plus one penny, and then rounded down to the nearest whole number. If part of the payment should be disregarded (see p893), the weekly earnings limit is increased (for the purpose of this calculation only) by the amount of the appropriate disregard (see p893). The result of this calculation is the number of full weeks for which you will not get benefit (see the example below).
- If you get two payments of different types of earnings (eg, wages and holiday pay), and the periods worked out as above overlap, they are taken into account consecutively.[35]

Example

Bob receives a Category A retirement pension with an increase for his wife, who lives with him. She receives £700 net earnings for work which cannot be attributed to any specific period of time. The £700 figure includes a tax refund of £150 paid through the PAYE system.

The earnings limit for the dependant's increase is £71.

The £150 tax refund is disregarded.

The period over which the income is taken into account is:

£700 ÷ (£71 + £0.01 + £150) =

£700 ÷ 221.01 = 3.17 weeks

This means that Bob is not entitled to the dependant's increase for three weeks.

Earnings from self-employment

If you are self-employed, your weekly earnings (including any allowance from a DWP scheme to assist you with your business[36]) are averaged over a period of a year unless:[37]

- you have recently become self-employed; *or*
- there has been a change which is likely to affect the normal pattern of your business,

in which case your earnings are averaged over whatever other period the decision maker considers will give the most accurate figure. This means that when you first claim, you must provide an up-to-date set of accounts. If you receive royalties or similar payments (eg, from copyrights), the period for which these payments count is calculated in a similar way to that for payments made for unspecified periods to employees.[38]

The figure used for your earnings is your 'net profit' from self-employment or, if you are a member of a partnership or a share fisherman, your share of the net profit. Unless you are a childminder, a member of a partnership or a share fisherman (in which case, see below) your 'net profit' is calculated taking your earnings over the period and deducting:[39]

- expenses incurred during the period wholly and exclusively for the purposes of the business. Where a car or telephone, for example, is used partly for business and partly for private purposes, the costs of it can be apportioned and the amount attributable to business use can be deducted.[40] Certain expenses cannot be deducted, including business entertainment, repayment of capital on a business loan, capital expenditure and depreciation, or providing board and lodging or renting a room in your home;
- income tax and NI contributions;[41] *and*
- half of any contributions you have made during the period towards a personal pension scheme or retirement annuity contract.

Childminders are always treated as self-employed. If you are a childminder, your net profit is deemed to be one-third of your earnings less income tax, your NI contributions and half of certain pension contributions (see p890).[42] The rest of your earnings are completely ignored.

If you are a member of a partnership or a share fisherman, the expenses incurred wholly and exclusively for the purposes of the business are deducted before calculating your share of the profits. After that, income tax, NI contributions and half of any premiums paid in respect of a personal pension or under a retirement annuity contract are deducted from your share.[43]

Disregarded earnings

Some of your income, which might otherwise be classed as earnings, is specifically disregarded and does not affect your benefit. Some care and childcare costs can also be disregarded. The same earnings disregards apply whether you are an employee or self-employed (and, if you are a childminder, they apply in addition to the other disregards explained above).

Earnings which can be disregarded are:[44]

- any payment made to you by someone who normally lives with you on an informal or non-contractual basis as part of her/his contribution towards shared living expenses;
- the first £20 a week of any income for renting out room(s) in your home;
- the first £20 of any income you receive each week for providing board and lodging in your home. If you get more than £20 a week, 50 per cent of the excess is also disregarded. This disregard applies to each person who lodges

with you – eg, if you are providing bed and breakfast accommodation and in one week five different people each stay for one night and pay £20 each, the full £100 is disregarded;
- payments from a local authority or voluntary organisation for fostering or accommodating a child under formal arrangements;
- payments from a health authority, local authority or voluntary organisation for providing temporary care. There is no set time after which care is no longer temporary. In one case, a carer could not have payments disregarded for a placement that had lasted five years;[45]
- income tax refunds;
- if you are an employee, any loan or advance of earnings from your employer;
- certain bounty payments made to part-time firefighters, auxiliary coastguards, members of the territorial or reserve armed forces and part-time lifeboat crews;
- unless you are abroad yourself, earnings payable abroad which cannot be brought into Great Britain – eg, because of exchange control regulations;
- unless you are abroad yourself, any bank charges for converting earnings paid in another currency into sterling.

Childcare costs

In addition to the earnings disregards, certain childcare costs may also be deducted from earnings.[46] The following rules apply to IB and SDA and to dependency increases. Different rules (see p895) apply to the treatment of childcare costs if you are claiming CA (although the following rules do apply to CA dependency increases).

An allowance of up to £60 a week may be deducted from your earnings if:
- you are a lone parent; *or*
- you are a member of a couple and both you and your partner are working (full or part time); *or*
- you are a member of a couple and your partner is incapacitated (see below).

This only applies if you have any child(ren) in your family under the age of 11 for whom you are paying charges for childcare (not counting charges paid by you to your partner or by your partner to you, or charges in respect of compulsory education) which is provided:
- by a registered childminder or other registered childcare provider (such as a nursery or after-school club for the under-eights); *or*
- for children aged eight or over but under 11, by a school on school premises or by a local authority – eg, an out-of-hours or holiday play scheme; *or*
- by a childcare scheme operating on Crown property; *or*
- in schools or establishments exempt from registration.[47]

Your partner counts as **'incapacitated'** if:[48]

- s/he is getting long-term IB, SDA, attendance allowance, disability living allowance (or an equivalent award under the war pensions or industrial injuries schemes), or would do were s/he not a hospital inpatient; *or*
- s/he is provided with an invalid carriage or other vehicle by the NHS; *or*
- you or your partner are getting housing benefit (HB) or council tax benefit (CTB) and either childcare costs have been allowed for under the rules applying to claims for these benefits (see p915) or a disability premium for your partner has been awarded.

Note: these rules have not been amended to allow your partner to count as 'incapacitated' if s/he receives ESA.

To calculate childcare costs:[49]

- monthly charges are added over the previous year and divided by 52;
- weekly (or other non-monthly) charges are averaged over the last four weeks if the child is not yet school age, otherwise a formula is used to average costs over term time and holidays;
- if you have just started to use childcare, the DWP uses an estimate from the childcare provider or from you.

Care costs and carer's allowance

If you are getting CA and because of your work, you have to pay for someone (other than a 'close relative') to look after the severely disabled person you care for or to look after a child(ren) under 16 for whom you or your partner are getting child benefit, those care costs can be deducted when your earnings are calculated (in addition to any disregarded earnings).[50] The maximum deduction is 50 per cent of the figure which would otherwise be your net earnings. Any disregarded income is deducted from your net earnings before calculating the 50 per cent figure. **'Close relative'** means a parent, son, daughter, brother, sister or partner (see p753) of you or the severely disabled person for whom you care. There is, therefore, no restriction on charges paid to someone who is only a close relative of the child being looked after – eg, the parent of the child if you are not married and s/he is not also your partner.

Notional earnings

You are deemed to have notional earnings only if it is not possible to work out your earnings when your claim is decided.[51] This may apply if, for example, you have just started employment and your pay depends on your performance, or you have just started a business and there is no way of calculating what profits you will make. If so, you are treated as earning such amount as is considered reasonable taking into account the number of hours you work and the earnings paid for comparable work in the area.

Estimates of the appropriate deductions for income tax and NI contributions and half of any occupational or personal pension contributions are deducted from your notional earnings, as are any earnings disregards or, where relevant, allowances for childcare or care costs.

2. Income for contribution-based jobseeker's allowance

Any earnings and pension payments you receive can affect your entitlement to contribution-based jobseeker's allowance (JSA).[52] Any other income you (or your partner) receive does not affect your contribution-based JSA (although claiming certain other benefits could affect JSA entitlement – see p428). Similarly, any savings you have and any income (including earnings and pension payments) or savings of any member of your family do not affect your entitlement to contribution-based JSA. For the rules on the treatment of your (or a family member's) income or savings for income-based JSA, see Chapters 40 and 41.

Earnings

Contribution-based JSA can be affected by your earnings and your pension payments. It is not affected by any other income you have, nor by your partner's earnings or income.

The rules on the following are the same as for income-based JSA (see Chapter 40):[53]

- what counts as earnings (p905);
- calculating net earnings from employment (p904);
- payments at the end of a job (p907);
- calculating net earnings from self-employment (p910);
- working out average earnings from self-employment (p911);
- childminders (p912);
- how earnings are assessed (p936);
- converting income into a weekly amount (p937);
- the period covered by income (p938); *and*
- the date from when a payment is counted (p939).

Different rules apply to disregarded earnings and how earnings affect your contribution-based JSA.

Disregarded earnings

For contribution-based JSA, £5 a week of your earnings is disregarded. If you are an auxiliary coastguard, a part-time firefighter, a part-time lifeboat crewmember or a member of the territorial or reserve forces, £20 a week is disregarded.[54]

How earnings affect your benefit

Your benefit is reduced by the full amount of any earnings you receive over the amount of disregarded earnings.[55] You are not entitled to contribution-based JSA for any week in which your earnings exceed a prescribed amount (see below).[56] The days in any week when your earnings exceed the prescribed amount do not count towards your maximum 182 days of contribution-based JSA (see p403).

Calculating the 'prescribed amount'

The 'prescribed amount' is not the same for everyone. It is calculated by adding together the amount of the relevant earnings disregard and the rate of contribution-based JSA paid to someone your age (see p403), and then deducting one penny.

Example

Maggie, aged 35, is entitled to contribution-based JSA of £71 a week. She works part time. Her earnings disregard is £5 a week. Applying the formula: (£71 + £5) – £0.01 = £75.99. If Maggie earns more than £75.99 a week, she is not entitled to contribution-based JSA.

Pension payments

Certain pension payments you receive may also affect your contribution-based JSA.[57] Your contribution-based JSA is reduced by the amount of weekly pension *above* £50 a week, regardless of your age. A pension of £50 or less a week is ignored for contribution-based JSA.[58] In this context, **'pension payments'** means periodical payments made under:[59]

- a personal pension scheme; *or*
- a pension connected with the ending of your employment as an earner under an occupational pension scheme or a public service pension scheme; *or*
- Pension Protection Fund and Financial Assistance Scheme payments (paid when occupational schemes close because of employer insolvency).

Although the meaning of pension payments is slightly different from that which applies to other non-means-tested benefits, it should still cover most periodical pension payments (including contractual redundancy/early retirement payments[60]). The amount of pension taken into account is the gross amount before tax is deducted, converted into a weekly amount.[61] **Note:** lump-sum payments may still count as pension payments for the purposes of JSA if they are calculated on the basis of a weekly or monthly entitlement.[62]

The amount of your pension payments may mean that you are not paid any JSA. However, unless your earnings also exceed the prescribed amount (see above), you remain *entitled* to contribution-based JSA even though it is not paid because your pension payments are too high (so long as you also satisfy the other conditions for getting JSA – see p393). Any day on which you are entitled to JSA (even if it is not paid) counts towards your 182 days' entitlement to contribution-based JSA (see p403). A combination of earnings and pension payments may also mean that you are not paid any JSA, even though you may remain entitled to it.

Any pension payments you receive because of the death of the person who was a member of the pension scheme are ignored when calculating your contribution-based JSA.[63] For example, if your late partner was a member of a scheme, any payment made to you following her/his death does not affect your contribution-based JSA.

Any pension payment you receive is counted from the first day of the benefit week in which the payment is actually made to you.[64]

Example

Brian claims JSA and is entitled to contribution-based JSA from Wednesday 2 May 2012. His benefit week begins on a Friday. He starts receiving a personal pension of £68 a week from Monday 7 May 2012. £18 a week is deducted from his contribution-based JSA (£68 – £50) from the benefit week starting Friday 4 May 2012.

If your pension is increased when you are on contribution-based JSA, the change should be taken into account from the first day of the benefit week in which the increase is paid.[65]

3. Income for contributory employment and support allowance

Your entitlement to contributory employment and support allowance (ESA) can be affected by the following income.

- **Earnings from permitted work.** Normally you are not entitled to ESA for any week in which you work. However, there are some kinds of work that you can do while claiming, including 'permitted work' (see p216). There are limits to the amount you can earn in permitted work.
  - The lower limit is £20.
  - The higher limit is £97.50 (this usually increases in October).

  If your earnings in any week are higher than the relevant limit, you are not entitled to ESA for that week.[66] Earnings are worked out for contributory ESA permitted work limits under the same rules that apply to earnings for income-related ESA, except that only your own earnings count, not your partner's. Only your earnings count, not any other kind of income. The following rules in Chapter 40 apply to permitted work for contributory ESA:
  - earnings of employed earners (p904);

  - earnings from self-employment (p910);
  - notional income – but only the rules on cheap or unpaid labour (p935);
  - working out weekly income, where these rules apply to earnings rather than other types of income (p936).
- **Councillors' allowances.** Contributory ESA is paid at a reduced rate if you are a local councillor and your net allowances are more than £97.50 in a week (the limit usually increases in October).[67] A basic allowance or special responsibilities allowance is converted into a weekly amount in a set way – eg, if paid monthly, multiply by 12 and divide by 52. Ignore any payments for expenses and, from the allowances, deduct any other expenses incurred in the relevant week in connection with your council duties, but do not deduct any tax or national insurance.[68] Your contributory ESA is reduced by the amount by which the net allowances exceed £97.50.
- **Pensions.** Certain kinds of pension payments you get can reduce the amount of contributory ESA to which you are entitled (see p186).

Notes

1. **Income for non-means-tested benefits**

1 Reg 8 SS(ICA) Regs
2 s30E(1) SSCBA 1992; reg 8 SS(IB) Regs
3 Regs 19 and 20 ESA(TP)(EA)(No.2) Regs
4 s89 SSCBA 1992; Sch 2 para 9 SSB(Dep) Regs
5 CP/7/1987
6 CP 7/1987
7 R(U) 5/85
8 Reg 10(4)(a) SSB(CE) Regs; R(U) 4/83; para 15286 DMG
9 Reg 9A SSB(Dep) Regs; para 15290 DMG
10 Reg 9 SSB(CE) Regs
11 Reg 9(1)(g) and (h) SSB(CE) Regs
12 *Minter v Kingston Upon Hull CC and Potter v SSWP* [2011] EWCA Civ 1155
13 Reg 9(1)(e) SSB(CE) Regs; CIS/743/1992
14 Reg 9(1)(j) SSB(CE) Regs
15 R(IS) 9/95; CIS/743/1992
16 R(IB) 7/03
17 Reg 9(1)(b) SSB(CE) Regs
18 Reg 2(1) SSB(CE) Regs
19 Reg 9(3) SSB(CE) Regs; *Parsons v Hogg* [1985] 2 All ER 897 (CA), appendix to R(FIS) 4/85
20 Sch 1 para 12 SSB(CE) Regs
21 Reg 9(1)(g) and (h) SSB(CE) Regs
22 CIS/521/1990
23 Reg 10(4) SSB(CE) Regs
24 Regs 6(1) and 8(1)(b)(i) SSB(CE) Regs
25 Reg 8(1)(a) SSB(CE) Regs
26 Reg 8(3) SSB(CE) Regs
27 CG/4941/2003
28 Reg 7(b) SSB(CE) Regs
29 Reg 2(1) SSB(CE) Regs
30 R(SB) 33/83
31 R(SB) 22/84; R(SB) 11/85
32 CIS/590/1993; *SSWP v JP (JSA)* [2010] UKUT 90 (AAC)
33 Reg 6(2) SSB(CE) Regs
34 *Cotton v SSWP* [2009] EWCA Civ 1333; [2010] AACR 17
35 Reg 6(3) SSB(CE) Regs; *Cotton v SSWP* [2009] EWCA Civ 1333; [2010] AACR 17
36 Reg 12(1) SSB(CE) Regs
37 Reg 11(1) SSB(CE) Regs
38 Reg 11(2) SSB(CE) Regs

39 Reg 13(1)(a) and (b), (4) and (5) SSB(CE) Regs
40 R(IS) 13/91; R(FC) 1/91; CTC/26/1989
41 See also reg 14 SSB(CE) Regs
42 Reg 13(10) SSB(CE) Regs
43 Reg 13(5) SSB(CE) Regs
44 Sch 1 SSB(CE) Regs
45 CG/1752/2006
46 Regs 10(2) and 13(2) and Sch 2 SSB(CE) Regs
47 Sch 2 para 2 SSB(CE) Regs
48 Sch 2 para 8 SSB(CE) Regs
49 Sch 2 paras 4-7 SSB(CE) Regs
50 Regs 10(3) and 13(3) and Sch 3 SSB(CE) Regs
51 Reg 4(1) and (3) SSB(CE) Regs and CIB/1650/2002, disapplying reg 4(2) of these Regs

2. Income for contribution-based jobseeker's allowance

52 s4(1) JSA 1995
53 Reg 80 JSA Regs
54 Regs 99(3) and 101(3) and Sch 6 JSA Regs
55 Reg 80 JSA Regs
56 s2(1)(c) JSA 1995; reg 56(1) and (2) JSA Regs
57 s4(1) JSA 1995
58 Reg 81(1) JSA Regs
59 s35(1) JSA 1995
60 R(JSA) 1/01
61 Reg 81 JSA Regs; paras 23921 and 23931 DMG; R(U) 8/83
62 R(JSA) 6/02
63 Reg 81(2)(c) JSA Regs
64 Reg 81(1A) JSA Regs
65 Reg 81(1B) JSA Regs

3. Income for contributory employment and support allowance

66 Regs 40(1) and (2)(f) and 45 ESA Regs
67 Regs 76(1), 79 and 94(1) ESA Regs
68 R(IB) 3/01

Chapter 40

Income: means-tested benefits

This chapter covers:

This chapter explains the rules for working out your weekly income for income support, income-based jobseeker's allowance (JSA), income-related employment and support allowance, pension credit, housing benefit and council tax benefit. For the rules on non-means-tested benefits, see Chapter 39, for tax credits, see Chapter 55 and for health benefits, see Chapter 13.

Note: unless otherwise stated, references to income-based JSA in the chapter also to refer to joint-claim JSA.

Key facts

- Your entitlement to income support (IS), income-based jobseeker's allowance (JSA), income-related employment and support allowance (ESA), pension credit (PC), housing benefit (HB) and council tax benefit (CTB) and the amount you get depends on how much income you have.
- Your own income counts and, if you are a member of a couple, your partner's income also counts. The income of your child is ignored for new claims and for most existing claims.
- Some income may be completely or partly ignored, or it may count in full.
- Some income may be treated as capital and some capital may be treated as income.
- If you get IS, income-based JSA, income-related ESA or the guarantee credit of PC, you are entitled to the maximum HB and CTB, so you do not need to work out your income again for HB and CTB.

Future changes: April 2013 and after

Major changes are taking place that affect the benefits and tax credits system (see Chapter 2). From October 2013, a new benefit, universal credit (UC), will be introduced which will replace most means-tested benefts. UC will be means tested. Income will be taken into account, but there will be important differences particularly in the way that earnings are treated. See CPAG's *Welfare Rights Bulletin* for updates.

1. People under pension credit age

This part applies to:

- income support (IS), including if your partner is claiming IS and you are over the qualifying age for pension credit (PC – see p509);
- income-based jobseeker's allowance (JSA), including for men over the qualifying age for PC but under 65;
- income-related employment and support allowance (ESA), including for men over the qualifying age for PC but under 65;
- housing benefit (HB) and council tax benefit (CTB) if you and your partner (if you have one) are under the qualifying age for PC.

The rules for IS, ESA, JSA, HB and CTB are very similar. Where there are differences, these are indicated.

Note: in this part, whenever HB or CTB is referred to, this only applies to the rules for people under the qualifying age for PC.

Whose income counts

Income of a partner

If you are a member of a couple (see p753), your partner's income is added to yours.[1]

Note: for HB and CTB, if you or your partner (if you have one) are getting IS, income-based JSA or income-related ESA, all of your (and your partner's) income is ignored.[2]

If, for IS, income-based JSA or income-related ESA, the rate of the normal personal allowance for a couple of £111.45 is reduced to £71 or £56.25 because you or your partner are under 18 (see p817), an amount of income equivalent to the reduction is ignored.[3]

Income of a dependent child

The income of a dependent child does *not* affect:

- IS or income-based JSA,[4] unless you have been getting benefit since before 6 April 2004 with a child included in your claim and you do not yet have a child tax credit (CTC) award (see p903);
- income-related ESA, HB and CTB.[5]

Maintenance paid to or for a child is usually disregarded (see p922).

The income of a dependent child may affect IS and income-based JSA if you have been getting benefit since before 6 April 2004 with a child included in your claim and you do not yet have an award of CTC. Once CTC is awarded, amounts for children are no longer included in your IS or income-based JSA and any income of a dependent child is ignored.

Even when you can still have a child included in your IS or JSA claim, if s/he has capital of over £3,000, you do not get benefit for her/him[6] (although you can still get a family premium) and her/his income is not counted as yours.[7] If your child has capital of £3,000 or less, any income is treated as yours but may be disregarded as follows.[8]

- Earnings of a dependent child at school/college are ignored.
- Earnings from a dependent child's part-time work (less than 16 hours a week) are ignored even if s/he has left school.
- If a child has left school/college and is working 24 hours or more a week, you usually do not get benefit for her/him and her/his earnings do not count with yours. If s/he is working 16 hours or more but less than 24 hours a week, her/his earnings are treated as your income while you are still entitled to claim for that child – eg, during the summer holidays. Ignore £5 a week and any earnings above the child's personal allowance.
- If you get a disabled child premium for your child, her/his earnings are still treated as your income as described above, but you ignore £20 a week and any earnings above the child's personal allowance, disabled child premium and any enhanced disability premium. All your disabled child's earnings are ignored if her/his earning capacity is less than 75 per cent of what it would be were s/he not disabled.[9]
- Income other than earnings and maintenance is taken into account up to the level of the child's personal allowance, and any disabled child premium and enhanced disability premium. Income above that level is ignored.[10]

What counts as income

All income is taken into account for IS, income-based JSA and income-related ESA unless it is specifically disregarded.

If you get IS, income-based JSA or income-related ESA, all your income is ignored for HB and CTB. Otherwise, all income is taken into account for HB and CTB other than income that is specifically disregarded.

The way income from employment and self-employment is treated is explained below and on p910. Some of your earnings are disregarded (see p912). Most other types of income are taken into account, less any tax due on them.[11] For HB and CTB, changes in tax and national insurance (NI) rates and in the maximum rate of CTC or working tax credit (WTC) may be ignored for up to 30 weeks (for earnings, see p904).[12]

Income only counts if it is paid to you for your own use, and does not count if you cannot prevent it being paid to a third party (eg, under an attachment of earnings order), although other payments for you made to a third party might count (see p934).[13]

Income is converted into a weekly amount (see p937).

Income or capital?

The difference between income and capital is not defined. Payments of income are normally made in respect of a specified period or periods and form, or are intended to form, part of a regular series of payments.[14] In this way, payments of income can usually be distinguished from payments of capital. However, sometimes a one-off payment can be income depending on what it is paid for – eg, a settlement for underpaid wages under equal pay legislation.[15] Some income is treated as capital (see p976) and some capital is treated as income (see p926).

Earnings of employed earners

This section explains how any earnings received by you or your partner and, in some cases, a dependent child (see p902) are treated. The same rules apply to your (but not your partner's or child's) earnings if you are claiming contribution-based JSA (see p896). For the rules on earnings for non-means-tested benefits, see Chapter 39.

To work out how earnings are taken into account:

- check whether the payments count as earnings (see p905). In some cases, payments are treated as capital, as income other than earnings, or ignored altogether;
- calculate net earnings (see below);
- work out weekly net earnings (see p936);
- deduct the appropriate weekly earnings disregard (usually £5, £10, £20 or £25 – see p912) and, for HB and CTB (if you qualify), the additional earnings disregard (see p915) and disregard for childcare costs (see p915);
- for HB and CTB, the amount worked out as above is your weekly income from earnings in the benefit assessment. For IS, income-based JSA and income-related ESA, work out the period covered by payments of earnings (see p938). Normally a payment counts from the date it is due to be paid and for the length of time it has been paid – eg, a month's wages count for a month, starting from the day they are due, at the weekly rate as calculated (see p936).

There are special rules for how payments affect benefit when you leave a job (see p907).

Note: the rules about earnings and about cheap or unpaid labour (see p935) are also relevant for 'permitted work' you can undertake while claiming either contributory or income-related ESA (see p200). There are some special rules for disregarded earnings (see p912).

Calculating net earnings from employment

Both your 'gross' earnings and 'net' earnings must be calculated so that a proper assessment can be made of your income from employment.

'Gross' earnings means the amount of earnings received from your employer less deductions for any expenses wholly, necessarily and exclusively incurred by you in order to carry out the duties of your employment.[16] See below for what counts as earnings and for examples of expenses that can be deducted.

'Net' earnings means your gross earnings less any deductions made for:[17]

- income tax;
- Class 1 NI contributions (but not Class 3 voluntary contributions[18]);
- half of any contribution you make towards a personal or occupational pension scheme.

For HB and CTB, if your earnings are estimated, the amount of tax and NI you would expect to pay on those earnings is estimated. This amount, plus half of any pension contribution you are paying, is then deducted.[19]

For HB and CTB, the local authority has the discretion to ignore changes in tax or NI contributions and the maximum rate of WTC or CTC for up to 30 benefit weeks. This can be used, for example, if Budget changes are not reflected in your actual income until several months later. When the changes are eventually taken into account and your benefit entitlement is either increased or reduced accordingly, you are not treated as having been underpaid or overpaid benefit during the period of the delay.[20]

What counts as earnings

'Earnings' means 'any remuneration or profit derived from ... employment'.

As well as your wages, this includes:[21]

- any bonus or commission (including tips);
- holiday pay (but see p907 if your job ends or you are off work);
- for HB and CTB, any statutory sick pay (SSP) or contractual sick pay.[22] For IS, income-based JSA and income-related ESA, all sick pay is treated as income other than earnings and, therefore, does not attract an earnings disregard and is counted in full less any tax, Class 1 NI contributions and half of any pension contributions;[23]
- for HB and CTB, any statutory maternity pay (SMP), statutory paternity pay (SPP) or statutory adoption pay (SAP), or any other payment made to you by your employer while you are on maternity, paternity or adoption leave.[24] For IS, income-based JSA and income-related ESA, all maternity, ordinary paternity or adoption pay is treated as income other than earnings and therefore does not attract an earnings disregard and is counted in full less any tax that is payable, Class 1 NI contributions and half of any pension contributions;[25]
- any payments made by your employer for expenses not 'wholly, exclusively and necessarily' incurred in carrying out your job, including any travel expenses to and from work, and any payments made to you for looking after members of your family. The latter can apply if you are looking after your child, even if they cannot be included in your claim for IS, income-based JSA or income-related ESA;

- a retainer (eg, payments during the school holidays if you work for the school meals service[26]) or a guarantee payment – eg, if you are working short time or laid off;[27]
- certain compensation payments in respect of the termination of your employment, including employment tribunal awards and pay in lieu of notice (see p907 for the way these are treated when you stop work). For IS/JSA/ income-related ESA, compensatory refunds of contributions to an occupational scheme[28] are not treated as earnings;
- an equal pay settlement – eg, through a 'single status agreement';[29]
- any payment of a non-cash voucher which is liable for Class 1 NI contributions.[30] Non-cash vouchers that are *not* liable for contributions are classed as payments in kind (see below).[31]

Examples of payments not counted as earnings include the following.

- Payments in kind (eg, petrol) are ignored[32] unless you are on IS or income-based JSA and involved in a trade dispute (see p700), although the notional income rules may be applied instead (see p932).[33] Although non-cash vouchers which are liable for Class 1 NI contributions are not treated as payments in kind, vouchers which are not liable for contributions (eg, certain childcare and charitable vouchers) are treated as payments in kind and these are disregarded.[34]
- The value of any free accommodation provided as part of your job should be ignored.[35]
- An advance of earnings or a loan from your employer is treated as capital[36] (although it is still treated as earnings for IS or income-based JSA if you or your partner are involved in a trade dispute, or have been back at work after a dispute for no longer than 15 days).[37]
- Payments towards expenses that are 'wholly, exclusively and necessarily' incurred during the course of your work, such as travelling expenses, are ignored.[38] For example, deductions could be made for:
  - tools or work equipment;
  - special clothing or uniform;[39]
  - telephone costs (including rental);[40]
  - postage;
  - fuel costs (including standing charges);
  - secretarial expenses;[41]
  - running a car (including petrol, tax, insurance, repairs and maintenance and rental on a leased car);[42]
  - armed forces local overseas allowance (for extra overseas living expenses),[43] but not lodgings allowances if you are stationed in the UK,[44] and probably not rent allowances for police officers;[45]
  - professional expenses for membership fees to an approved body if also deducted for income tax.[46]

If any expenditure serves a dual purpose for both business and private use, it should be apportioned as appropriate to the circumstances (and any determination by HM Revenue and Customs (HMRC) normally followed).[47]

- If you are a local councillor, travelling expenses and subsistence payments are (and basic allowances may be[48]) ignored as expenses 'wholly, exclusively and necessarily' incurred in your work.
- Earnings payable abroad which cannot be brought into Britain (eg, because of exchange control regulations) are ignored.[49] **Note:** if your earnings are paid in another currency, any bank charges for converting them into sterling are deducted before taking them into account.[50]
- Any occupational pension[51] counts as income other than earnings and the net amount is taken into account in full.[52] See p897 (and p186) for the occupational pension rules for contribution-based JSA (and contributory ESA).

Payments when you stop work

When you stop work and claim benefit, your final earnings are usually ignored with some exceptions. If you were claiming benefit while working, final earnings are generally taken into account, as explained below.

Your job ends before benefit starts

If your employment ends before your entitlement to benefit begins, any payments that count as earnings (see p905), including wages, holiday pay (but see below) and pay in lieu of notice, are ignored for that benefit, except for the following payments, which are taken into account.[53]

- A retainer counts as earnings.
- If you were in full-time work, certain employment tribunal awards (and 'out-of-court' settlements) count as earnings, including:
  - compensation because of unfair dismissal;[54]
  - a 'protective' award when an employer fails to comply with redundancy procedures and, for JSA, a compensatory award in respect of trade union activity;[55]
  - for IS, income-related ESA, HB and CTB, pay under a continuation of contract award or for arrears of pay in respect of a reinstatement or re-engagement order.[56]

  If you were in part-time work, these are all ignored for IS, income-related ESA, HB and CTB but count for JSA.
- Guarantee payments for workless days or while suspended on medical or maternity grounds count as earnings, including when awarded by an employment tribunal.[57]
- Arrears of sick pay, maternity, paternity and adoption pay (statutory or contractual) or lump sum advance payments are taken into account for IS, JSA and income-related ESA as income, without any earnings disregard, from

when they are paid for the same length of time covered by the arrears. For HB and CTB, they are ignored.[58]

- Statutory redundancy pay counts as capital.[59]
- Contractual redundancy pay (deducting an amount for statutory entitlement) is ignored completely for JSA.[60] For IS, income-related ESA, HB and CTB, it counts as capital unless, for IS and income-related ESA, you work part time and have not been paid all pay in lieu of notice due, in which case it is ignored.[61]
- Some redundancy schemes make periodic payments after leaving work. These are treated as income other than earnings.[62]
- *Ex gratia* payments and other kinds of compensation (other than employment tribunal awards) are treated in the same way as contractual redundancy pay.
- Holiday pay is usually ignored. However, if your job ends, it counts as capital if your contract provides for it to be payable more than four weeks after termination of employment – eg, in some cases if you leave without giving notice.[63]

For what counts as 'full time', see p718. For this rule, the IS definition also applies to income-related ESA (except for term-time workers whose hours are assessed under the JSA rule).[64]

Note: these rules only apply to benefits you claim after employment ends. So, for example, if you are already getting HB/CTB when you leave your job, but not IS, JSA or income-related ESA, your final earnings are disregarded for IS/JSA/income-related ESA in this way, but not for HB/CTB. See p909 for how final payments are treated when you are already getting benefit.

Example

Gina is made redundant from a full-time job on 31 May and leaves with one month's wages, her full four weeks' pay in lieu of notice, contractual redundancy pay of £5,000 and three days' holiday pay. All are due to be paid on 31 May. She claims IS, HB and CTB after her job ends. Final wages, pay in lieu of notice and holiday pay are ignored. Redundancy pay is treated as capital. Her capital is below the limit and she is entitled to benefit from 1 June.

You stop work but your job has not ended

If you stop work before your benefit begins but your employment has not ended (eg, you go on sick leave or maternity leave), statutory and contractual sick pay, maternity, paternity and adoption pay are taken into account as income without any earnings disregard for IS, JSA and income-related ESA.[65] For HB and CTB, they count as earnings with the usual disregard.[66] If holiday pay is due to be paid more than four weeks after you stopped work, it is treated as capital (unless, for IS/JSA, you are involved in a trade dispute). If it is paid less than four weeks after you stopped work, it is ignored.[67] All other payments that count as earnings are ignored, except for a retainer or guarantee payments for workless days or for medical or maternity suspension.[68]

Note: these rules only apply to benefits you claim after you stop work. If, for example, you are already getting HB/CTB when you stop work, but not IS/JSA/income-related ESA, your final earnings are ignored in this way for IS/JSA/income-related ESA, but not for HB/CTB.

If you are suspended from work, any earnings are taken into account as normal.

You were working while claiming benefit

If your job ends or you stop work before your entitlement to benefit begins, any payments that count as earnings are ignored with some exceptions, as described on p907. If, however, you were claiming benefit while you were in work, any payments made to you when that job ends are taken into account as earnings as follows.[69] For IS, JSA and income-related ESA, some different kinds of payments count consecutively in the order below,[70] but for HB and CTB final earnings are averaged as normal.

- Final earnings are taken into account as normal (including wages, bonuses and expenses that count as earnings).
- For IS, income-related ESA, HB and CTB, pay in lieu of notice is taken into account; for IS and income-related ESA, final earnings are taken into account first followed by pay in lieu of notice.
- Contractual redundancy pay, *ex gratia* payments and other types of compensation (other than employment tribunal awards) above the level of entitlement to statutory redundancy pay:
  - for IS and income-related ESA, are treated as capital if you work out your notice or get full pay in lieu of notice. Otherwise, they are taken into account as earnings for one week only;
  - for JSA, are treated as earnings, together with pay in lieu of notice, up until the end of the fixed-term contract, if you had one, or until the end of the notice period (sometimes longer if the employer says it covers a longer period). For JSA, if none of the payment covers pay in lieu of notice or early termination of a fixed-term contract, the total of these payments covers a standard number of weeks arrived at by dividing the payment by the weekly maximum statutory redundancy (£430) if this is shorter than the notice period;
  - for HB and CTB, are treated as capital except for any amount representing loss of income which is taken into account as earnings.
- Holiday pay normally counts as earnings. However, it counts as capital if it is payable more than four weeks after employment ends or is interrupted – eg, if you are off sick before your employment ends. For IS, JSA and income-related ESA, it counts for the number of weeks covered by the holiday pay (not the

number of working weeks[71]) starting after the period covered by other payments listed in the above three bullet points.

- An employment tribunal award (eg, for unfair dismissal) is taken into account as earnings.
- Arrears of sick pay, maternity, paternity and adoption pay count as earnings for HB and CTB, and as income other than earnings for IS, JSA and income-related ESA.[72]
- Statutory redundancy payments are treated as capital.

Example

Neelam has been getting HB and CTB while working part time. She earned £50 a week. She finishes work on 16 July and on that day is given £60, made up of £30 final wages and £30 holiday pay. For HB/CTB, the £60 wages and holiday pay are taken into account as normal, deducting the earnings disregard. She claims JSA on 17 July. For JSA, her final wages and holiday pay are ignored so none of the £60 is taken into account. Her JSA starts on 20 July after the three waiting days.

Earnings from self-employment

Calculating net earnings

Your '**net profit**' over the period before your claim must be worked out. This consists of your self-employed earnings *minus*:[73]

- reasonable expenses (see below); *and*
- income tax and NI contributions; *and*
- half of any premium paid in respect of a personal pension scheme contract which is eligible for tax relief.[74]

Drawings from capital do not count as income whether the business is in profit or not.[75] If you receive payments for board and lodging charges, these do not count as earnings[76] but as other income (less any disregards, see p925).

If you are getting help under a DWP scheme to assist you with your business and this is classed as the 'self-employment route' (eg, the New Enterprise Allowance), income and expenses are treated differently (see p928).

Reasonable expenses

Expenses must be reasonable and 'wholly and exclusively' incurred for the purposes of your business.[77] This involves similar considerations to those that apply in the allowances permitted in the assessment of 'gross' earnings of employed earners. If a car or telephone, for example, is used partly for business and partly for private purposes, the costs of it can be apportioned and the amount attributable to business use can be deducted.[78]

Reasonable expenses include:[79]

- repayments of capital on loans for replacing equipment and machinery;
- repayment of capital on loans for, and income spent on, the repair of a business asset except where this is covered by insurance;
- interest on a loan taken out for the purposes of the business;
- excess of VAT paid over VAT received.

Reasonable expenses do not include:[80]
- any capital expenditure;
- depreciation, although the normal accountancy practice in valuing stock should be applied so that the 'cost of sales' (the cost of any opening stock plus purchases less any closing stock) should be set against actual sales;[81]
- money for setting up or expanding the business – eg, the cost of adapting the business premises;
- any loss incurred before the beginning of the current assessment period. If the business makes a loss, the net profit is nil. The losses of one business cannot be offset against the profit of any other business in which you are engaged, or against your earnings as an employee[82] (although where two businesses or employments share expenses, these may be apportioned and offset);[83]
- capital repayments on loans taken out for business purposes;
- business entertainment expenses;
- for HB and CTB, debts (other than proven bad debts) – but the expenses of recovering a debt can be deducted.

Working out average earnings from self-employment

For **IS**, **income-based JSA** and **income-related ESA**, the weekly amount is the average of earnings:[84]
- over a period of any one year (normally the last year for which accounts are available);
- over a more appropriate period where you have recently taken up self-employment or there has been a change which will affect your business or for any other reason if a different period may enable any part or all of your income and expenditure to be calculated more accurately.

For **HB/CTB**, the amount of your weekly earnings is averaged out over an 'appropriate' period (usually based on your last year's trading accounts), which must not be longer than a year.[85]

For **all benefits**, if your earnings are royalties, copyright payments or payments under the Public Lending Right Scheme, the amount of earnings is divided by the weekly amount of benefit that would be payable if you had not received this income plus the amount that would be disregarded from those earnings (for income-related ESA, any contributory ESA that would be payable without this income is also taken into account).[86] For IS, income-based JSA and income-related

ESA, you are not entitled to benefit for the resulting number of weeks. For HB and CTB, earnings are taken into account for the resulting number of weeks.

If you stop doing self-employed work, any earnings from that work are disregarded except for royalties and copyright and Public Lending Right Scheme payments.[87]

Childminders

Childminders, in practice, are always treated as self-employed. Your net profit is deemed to be one-third of your earnings less income tax, your NI contributions and half of personal pension scheme contributions (see p910).[88] The rest of your earnings are completely ignored.

Disregarded earnings

Some of your earnings from employment or self-employment are disregarded and do not affect your benefit. The amount of the 'disregard' depends on your circumstances. For IS, income-based JSA, HB and CTB, the three main levels of disregard are £25, £20 or £5/£10. For HB and CTB, there is an additional disregard depending on the hours you work, a childcare costs disregard (see p915) and a permitted work disregard.

For income-related ESA, the main level of disregard is £20. However, different rules apply if you are doing 'permitted work' (see p913).

For the amount of disregarded earnings for contribution-based JSA, see p896.

Disregards for income-related employment and support allowance

For income-related ESA, the main level of disregard is £20. However, if you are doing 'permitted work', more earnings can be disregarded (see p913).

Twenty pounds of your earnings (including those of your partner) is disregarded if:[89]

- you are doing work you may do while claiming ESA (see p200), but only if it is:
  - as a councillor; *or*
  - as a member of a Disability Living Allowance Advisory Board or as a disability member of the First-tier Tribunal. However, if you are also doing 'permitted work', see p913; *or*
  - during an emergency to protect someone or to prevent serious damage to property or livestock; *or*
  - it is done while receiving assistance in pursuing self-employment under s2 of the Employment and Training Act 1973 or s2 of the Enterprise and New Towns (Scotland) Act 1990; *or*
- *your partner* is in part-time employment of under 24 hours a week[90] or s/he would be treated as not in full-time paid work for IS purposes (other than if this is because of qualifying for mortgage interest run-on). See the list on pp725–26). However, if you are doing 'permitted work', see p913; *or*

- your partner is working but does not count as in full-time paid work because s/he:
  - is childminding in her/his home; *or*
  - is a carer (under the rules for who can claim IS, see p348); *or*
  - is receiving assistance under the 'self-employment route' – eg, for JSA, HB and CTB, New Enterprise Allowance; *or*
  - is an auxiliary coastguard, part-time firefighter, part-time member of a lifeboat crew or member of the Territorial Army; *or*
  - is working as a councillor; *or*
  - would not qualify for JSA on the grounds that s/he has been involved in a trade dispute (see p701), or it is the first 15 days following her/his return to work after having been involved in a trade dispute.

If you are doing **'permitted work'** (see p216) for which you are allowed to earn £20 or £97.50, any earnings that do not exceed the relevant limit are disregarded (except where you are self-employed and your earnings are royalties, copyright payments or Public Lending Right Scheme payments, in which case the disregard is £20).[91] In addition, if your earnings from 'permitted work' are less than the relevant limit, the remainder of the disregard can be used – up to a maximum of £20:[92]
- on your earnings from work undertaken as a member of a disability living allowance advisory board or as a disability member of the First-tier Tribunal; *or*
- on your partner's earnings.

Note: earnings for permitted work (for both contributory and income-related ESA) are assessed in the same way as earnings are generally for income-related ESA described in this chapter except the rules that treat you as having income even when you do not have it ('notional income') only apply where you are doing cheap or unpaid labour (see p935).[93]

Disregards for other means-tested benefits

£25 disregard

Lone parents on HB or CTB have £25 of their earnings ignored.[94] This does not apply to anyone claiming IS, income-based JSA or income-related ESA.

£20 disregard

For IS, income-based JSA, HB and CTB, £20 of your earnings (including those of your partner) is disregarded if:
- for IS or income-based JSA, you are a lone parent;[95]
- you or your partner qualify for a disability premium (see p824).[96] For IS and income-based JSA, you are treated as qualifying for the premium if you would do so but for the fact that you are in hospital;

- for HB and CTB, you or your partner qualify for a severe disability premium, or the work-related activity or support component (see pp830 and 838);[97]
- you or your partner qualify for a carer premium (see p834). The disregard applies to the carer's earnings. For a couple, if both partners get the carer premium, £20 is disregarded from their combined earnings. If you are the carer and the claimant and your earnings are less than £20, up to £5 (£10 for HB/CTB) of the disregard can be used on your partner's earnings (or all of what is left of it if your partner's earnings are from one of the services in the bullet point below) – but the total disregard cannot be more than £20;[98]
- you or your partner are an auxiliary coastguard, part-time firefighter, part-time member of a lifeboat crew or member of the Territorial Army.[99] If you earn less than £20 for doing any of these services, you can use up to £5 (for HB and CTB up to £10, if you have a partner) of the disregard on another job[100] or on a partner's earnings from another job;[101]
- for IS and income-based JSA only, you are a member of a couple, your benefit would include a disability premium but for the fact that one of you qualifies for the higher pensioner premium (see p828), and one of you is under the qualifying age for PC (see p509) and either of you are in employment. You are treated as qualifying for the higher pensioner premium if you would do so but for the fact that you are in hospital;[102]
- for IS and income-based JSA only, you or your partner qualify for the higher pensioner premium (see p828) and, immediately before reaching the qualifying age for PC (see p509), you or your partner were in part-time employment and you were entitled to a £20 disregard because of qualifying for a disability premium. Since reaching the qualifying age for PC, you or your partner must have continued in part-time employment, although breaks of up to eight weeks when you were not getting IS, income-based JSA or income-related ESA are ignored. You are treated as qualifying for the higher pensioner premium even if you are in hospital.[103]

If you qualify under more than one category, you still have a maximum of only £20 of your earnings disregarded.

Basic £5 or £10 disregard

For IS, income-based JSA, HB and CTB, if you do not qualify for a £25 or £20 disregard (or, for HB and CTB, the permitted work disregard), £5 of your earnings is disregarded if you are single. If you claim as a member of a couple, £10 of your total earnings is disregarded – whether or not you are both working.[104]

Permitted work disregard for housing benefit and council tax benefit

If you or your partner are doing 'permitted work' (see pp216 and 736) and getting contributory ESA, incapacity benefit (IB), severe disablement allowance

(SDA) or NI credits for limited capability for work or incapacity, the permitted work earnings limit for that benefit or credit (either £20 or £97.50) is also disregarded from earnings for HB and CTB.[105] This is instead of the usual disregard of £5, £10, £20 or £25.

For couples, this permitted work disregard applies if either you or your partner are doing permitted work. If earnings from permitted work are less than the limit, you can use up the rest:

- on your partner's earnings, up to a maximum of £20 or up to the limit if s/he is also doing permitted work, but there is only one disregard between you; *or*
- on your own earnings from other work (see p735 for other work you may do while claiming one of these benefits). If you are a lone parent, the £25 disregard applies instead of the £20 permitted work disregard.

Note: there is also an earnings disregard for permitted work for income-related ESA but not for IS.

Additional disregard for housing benefit and council tax benefit

For **HB/CTB only**, whichever earnings disregard applies is increased by £17.10 if:[106]

- you or your partner receive the 30-hour element as part of your (or your partner's) WTC (see p1311); *or*
- you or your partner are aged 25 or over and work 30 hours a week or more on average; *or*
- you or your partner work 16 hours or more a week on average and your HB/CTB includes the family premium (see p822); *or*
- you are a lone parent and work 16 hours or more a week on average; *or*
- you or your partner work 16 hours or more a week on average and your HB/CTB includes the disability premium (see p824), or the work-related activity component or the support component (see pp185 and 184). For couples, the partner for whom the premium/component is awarded must be working 16 hours a week or more on average.

The additional earnings disregard does not apply if your total earnings are less than the total of £17.10 plus any earnings disregard and childcare costs disregard (see p915). In this case, £17.10 is disregarded from any WTC which is awarded to you or your partner, but the earnings disregard is not increased.

Note: as with the ordinary earnings disregards, only one additional disregard can be allowed from your (or your partner's) earnings.

Childcare costs for housing benefit and council tax benefit

Note: for **IS**, **income-based JSA** and **income-related ESA**, no allowance is made for any childcare charges you may have to pay.

For **HB/CTB**, an allowance of up to £175 a week for one child, or up to £300 a week for two or more children, can be deducted from your (or your partner's) earnings (from employment or self-employment) for childcare costs if you are:[107]

- a lone parent working 16 hours a week or more; *or*
- a couple and both of you work 16 hours a week or more, or one of you works 16 hours a week or more and the other is 'incapacitated' (see p917), or is in hospital or prison.

Lone parents and couples can still make this deduction for childcare costs if they are off work sick, although for lone parents it stops after 28 weeks (see p917).

If you or your partner (if you have one) also get WTC or CTC, in some circumstances your earnings (and, if applicable, those of your partner) and the WTC/CTC are added together before the deduction for childcare costs is made. This applies if your earnings, once other HB/CTB deductions have been taken off, are less than the deduction for childcare costs.[108]

The childcare allowance only applies to charges you pay for certain types of childcare provided for any child(ren) in your family under the age of 15 (or 16 if s/he is disabled). A child is not treated as having reached the age of 15/16 until the day before the first Monday in September following her/his 15th/16th birthday.[109] A child is defined as disabled if s/he is:[110]

- in receipt of disability living allowance (DLA), or payment has been suspended because s/he is a hospital inpatient; *or*
- registered as blind, or was taken off the register before the first Monday in September following her/his 16th birthday, but no more than one year and 28 weeks before then.

The childcare must be provided:[111]

- by a registered childminder or other registered childcare provider (such as a nursery or local authority daycare service); *or*
- out of school hours for children between the ages of eight and 15/16, by a school on school premises or a local authority – eg, an out-of-hours or holiday play scheme; *or*
- by another relevant childcare provider (see p1315 – these are the same as for WTC).

You cannot include charges for care provided by a relative of the child in the child's own home even if s/he is a registered childminder, nor charges paid by you to your partner or by your partner to you for a child in your family. Charges for compulsory education do not count.

If you or your partner are on maternity, paternity or adoption leave, you will be treated as working, and so be able to deduct childcare charges if you (or your partner):[112]

- were working in the week immediately before the maternity, paternity or adoption leave began; *and*
- are entitled to SMP, SPP, SAP or maternity allowance (MA) (see Chapters 27 and 21), or are getting IS because you are on paternity leave.

You are no longer treated as working and thus cannot get childcare charges deducted when:

- the maternity, paternity or adoption leave comes to an end; *or*
- if you are not receiving the childcare element of WTC, you or your partner stop getting SMP, SPP, SAP or MA, or IS because you are on paternity leave; *or*
- if you are receiving the childcare element of WTC when you stop getting SMP, SPP, SAP or MA or IS because you are on paternity leave, you stop getting the childcare element of WTC.

You can deduct charges for childcare for the new child in your family while you are still on maternity, paternity or adoption leave.

Childcare costs and ill health or disability

Provided you were working at least 16 hours a week immediately before you started getting one of the following benefits, you can still deduct charges for childcare while off work sick for the first 28 weeks while you are getting:[113]

- SSP;
- ESA;
- short-term lower rate IB;
- IS on incapacity grounds;
- NI credits for incapacity or limited capability for work.

After 28 weeks, lone parents who are off work sick can no longer deduct childcare charges, but couples can do so (before or after 28 weeks) if one of them works 16 hours or more a week and the other is treated as 'incapacitated'.

You (or your partner) are treated as **'incapacitated'** if:[114]

- you get ESA which includes a support or work-related activity component; *or*
- you get short-term higher rate or long-term IB; *or*
- you get SDA; *or*
- you get attendance allowance (AA), DLA or constant attendance allowance (or an equivalent award under the war pensions or industrial injuries schemes) or you would receive one of these benefits but for the fact that you (or your partner) are in hospital; *or*
- you have an invalid carriage or similar vehicle; *or*
- your HB and CTB includes a disability premium, support component or work-related activity component for the incapacitated person's incapacity or limited capability for work; *or*

- you (but not your partner) have been treated either as having limited capability for work or as incapable of work for a continuous period of 196 days or more (disregarding any break of up to 84 or 56 days respectively).

Calculating childcare costs

The costs to be taken into account are estimated over whatever period, not exceeding a year, that will give the best estimate of the average weekly charge based on information to be provided by the childminder or care provider.

Points to note

- These rules do *not* apply to IS, JSA or income-related ESA and *only* apply to HB and CTB. There are also separate childcare costs rules for non-means-tested benefits (see p894).
- The maximum amount that can be deducted for one child is £175, even if the actual cost of your childcare is more. Even if you have to pay for childcare for more than two children or the actual cost is more, £300 is the maximum.
- The costs of any childcare outside the child's home provided by a relative (other than your partner – but a former partner, who may even be the child's parent, is not excluded) may be allowed provided s/he is a registered childminder.
- It is not necessary for the childcare to be provided only while you are at work, nor for it to be work-related, and there is no requirement for the charges to be reasonable (so the £175/£300 charge could be incurred for only one hour of childcare).

Income other than earnings

As well as income from earnings, most other forms of income are taken into account in full less any tax due. To work out the weekly income to take into account, check whether the payment can be disregarded in part or in full, deduct any tax due and work out the weekly amount (see p936). Where a taxable benefit or other unearned income is not taxed at source and you have not yet had a tax assessment, ask HMRC for a forecast of tax due on that income; otherwise the DWP itself needs to calculate how much tax to deduct.[115]

Benefits and tax credits

Benefits and tax credits that count in full:

- carer's allowance (CA);
- CTC counts in full for HB and CTB, but is disregarded for IS, income-based JSA and income-related ESA. See p921 if your CTC is reduced to recover a tax credit overpayment;
- child's payment under the Armed Forces and Reserved Forces Compensation Scheme (but if it is paid for a dependent child it is usually ignored – see p902);

- contribution-based JSA;
- contributory ESA. If ESA is paid at a reduced rate because of a sanction, it is still the full rate that counts;[116]
- IB and SDA;
- industrial injuries benefits, except constant attendance allowance and exceptionally severe disablement allowance which are disregarded;
- MA;
- retirement pensions;
- SSP, SMP, SPP and SAP count for IS, income-based JSA and income-related ESA only, less any Class 1 NI contributions and half of any pension contributions and any tax.[117] These are treated as earnings for HB and CTB and, therefore, may benefit from an earnings disregard (see p912);[118]
- widow's pension, bereavement allowance and industrial death benefit;
- WTC is taken into account (but see p921 if a tax credit overpayment is being deducted):
  - for IS, income-based JSA and income-related ESA;
  - for HB and CTB, except for those whose earnings are too low to use the whole £17.10 additional full-time earnings disregard (see p915). In this case, £17.10 is disregarded from your WTC instead of your earnings. You must satisfy the conditions for the additional earnings disregard and have earnings of less than £17.10 plus whichever other earnings disregard applies plus any childcare costs disregard.[119]

Benefits that are ignored completely:

- AA;[120]
- child benefit.[121]However, for IS and income-based JSA, it is taken into account if you have been getting IS or income-based JSA since before 6 April 2004 with a child already included in your claim (ie, you still have amounts for children in your claim) and you do not yet have an award of CTC. In this case, child benefit continues to be taken into account until your CTC award begins;[122]
- CTC is ignored completely for IS, income-based JSA and income-related ESA.[123] CTC is taken into account in full for HB and CTB;
- constant attendance allowance, exceptionally severe disablement allowance or severe disablement occupational allowance paid because of an injury at work or a war injury;[124]
- DLA care component and mobility component;[125]
- guardian's allowance;[126]
- mobility supplement under the War Pensions Scheme;[127]
- Christmas bonus (see p9);[128]
- any extra-statutory payment made to you to compensate for non-payment of IS, income-based JSA, income-related ESA, mobility supplement, AA or DLA;[129]
- social fund payments.[130] They are also disregarded as capital indefinitely;[131]

- HB and CTB;[132]
- any supplementary payments to war widows, widowers or surviving civil partners for pre-1973 service;[133]
- any increase for a child dependant is ignored for IS or income-based JSA if you get CTC and for income-related ESA. For all benefits, any increase for adult or child dependants who are not members of your family (see p751) paid with a benefit (eg, IB or retirement pension) or a service pension is ignored;[134]
- IS, income-based JSA and income-related ESA are ignored for HB and CTB.[135] There are special HB and CTB rules for these claimants (see pp120 and 259);
- any payment made by the DWP to compensate for the loss of HB;[136]
- any payment in consequence of a reduction in liability for council tax.[137]

Benefits that have £15 ignored:
- for HB/CTB only, widowed mother's allowance and widowed parent's allowance.[138]

Benefits that have £10 ignored:[139]
- for IS, income-based JSA and income-related ESA only, widowed mother's allowance and widowed parent's allowance;
- war disablement pension;
- guaranteed income payment and survivor's guaranteed income payment under the Armed Forces and Reserve Forces Compensation Scheme (or if another pension reduces the payment to below £10, ignore the remainder from the pension);
- war widow's, widower's or surviving civil partner's pension;
- an extra-statutory payment made instead of the above pensions;
- similar payments made by another country;
- a pension from Germany or Austria paid to the victims of Nazi persecution.

Even if you have more than two payments which attract a £10 disregard, only £20 in all can be ignored.[140] However, the £10 disregard allowed on the payments above is in addition to the total disregard of any mobility supplement or AA (ie, constant attendance allowance, exceptionally severe disablement allowance and severe disablement occupational allowance) paid as part of a war disablement pension.

The £10 disregard may overlap with other disregards such as on student loans and access funds (see pp657 and 660) when a combined maximum of £20 is allowed.

Local authorities are given a limited discretion to increase the £10 disregard on war disablement, war widows' or widowers' pensions and the guaranteed income payment and survivor's guaranteed income payment, when assessing income for HB and CTB.[141] Some local authorities disregard the full amount of these pensions, and some do not increase the disregard at all, so you should check your own local authority's policy. It has been held that a local authority must at least consider the nature and purpose of such pensions when deciding whether or not to disregard them, and the courts have indicated that it may be appropriate to apply a disregard to retrospective awards.[142]

Benefit delays

Problems can arise where a decision maker tries to take into account a benefit you are not receiving (such as child benefit) because it has been delayed. In such a case, the benefit should not be treated as income possessed by you. For IS, income-based JSA and income-related ESA, you should get your full benefit and leave the DWP to deduct the difference from arrears of the delayed benefit when it is eventually awarded.[143]

For the treatment of payments of arrears of certain benefits and tax credits, see p982.

Tax credit payments and overpayments

For **HB/CTB**, if a tax credit overpayment from a previous year is being recovered from the current year's tax credit award, it is the amount of your tax credit award less any reduction to recover the overpayment that is taken into account.[144] Because HB/CTB entitlement is based on the amount of tax credits you are actually paid at the time, local authorities do not treat you as having been underpaid HB or CTB for the earlier period when tax credits were being overpaid, so your HB/CTB award is not revised for that period.[145]

The situation where you have been overpaid in the same year as your tax credit award and your tax credits are reduced accordingly is similar – ie, it is the reduced amount that is taken into account. This is because it is the actual amount of the tax credit award still due to be paid to you that is taken into account, instalment by instalment.[146]

For **IS, income-based JSA** and **income-related ESA**, the rules are less clear, but the intention seems to be to take into account the actual award paid – eg, after any overpayment has been deducted.[147]

If you stop work, WTC entitlement continues for four weeks and is treated as income if you claim IS, JSA or income-related ESA (or HB/CTB). It sometimes happens that WTC payments wrongly continue beyond this even when you have told HMRC that you have stopped work, and HMRC treats this as an overpayment. If you are prevented from getting full benefit because WTC is taken into account as income after the date you informed HMRC of your change of circumstances, you should consider appealing. Arguably, WTC should be ignored in these circumstances.[148]

Maintenance payments

If you get child maintenance (see p800) for a child who is a member of your family, it is all ignored if it is made by the child's parent (who is not your partner), a former spouse or civil partner or by someone who can reasonably be treated as the child's father because of the financial support he makes.[149]

If you get another kind of maintenance from a former partner:[150]

- £15 is ignored for HB and CTB if you have a family premium included in your HB or CTB;
- it counts in full for other benefits (although if you live in a care home, some may be ignored).

There are special rules about the treatment of maintenance that you receive for yourself (see Chapter 36).

If you get payments towards maintenance from someone who is neither a former partner nor parent of your child (eg, a grandparent), this normally counts as a voluntary payment and is ignored (see p924).[151]

If you pay maintenance

If you *pay* maintenance to a former partner or a child not living with you, your payments are not disregarded for the purpose of calculating your income for any benefits.[152] Even if you are on IS, income-based JSA or income-related ESA, you may still have to pay child support maintenance (see p809).

Student loans and grants

For the special rules on the treatment of student grants and loans and other payments made to students, see Chapter 29.

Adoption, fostering, guardianship and residence order payments

Adoption allowance

An adoption allowance is disregarded in full except in the two cases below.[153]

- If the adoption allowance is paid for a child who is not a member of your family (eg, because the adoption order has not yet been granted), it is fully disregarded in England.[154] In Scotland and Wales, any amount you spend on the child is disregarded and any you keep or use for yourself is taken into account.[155]
- For IS and income-based JSA, if you have been getting benefit since before 6 April 2004 with a child included in your claim and do not yet have an award of CTC, the adoption allowance is taken into account in full up to the level of the adopted child's personal allowance and any disabled child premium.[156] Above that level it is ignored. If the child has capital over £3,000, you get no benefit

for that child and all the adoption allowance is disregarded.[157] Seek advice to check if you would be better off claiming CTC instead.

Fostering allowance

The way a fostering allowance is treated depends on whether the arrangement is official or private. If a child is placed or boarded out with you by the local authority or a voluntary organisation under specific legal provisions,[158] the child is not counted as a member of your family (see p762) and any fostering allowances you receive while the child is placed with you should be ignored altogether.[159] If the fostering arrangement is a private one, any money you receive from the child's parent(s) is counted as maintenance (see p799). If the money you receive is not from the child's parent(s), you should probably be treated as a childminder (see p912).

Residence order allowance and similar payments

If you are paid a residence order allowance by the local authority (in England and Wales), this is treated in the same way as an adoption allowance (see p922).[160] Any payments made by the biological parents count as maintenance (see p799). In Scotland, kinship care payments can be made under different legal provisions. If made under s22 of the Children (Scotland) Act 1995 or reg 33 of the Looked After Children (Scotland) Regulations 2009, they are ignored altogether but if made under s50 of the Children Act 1975, they are treated in the same way as an adoption allowance.[161]

Special guardianship allowance

The law treats a special guardianship allowance, payable in England and Wales for a child who is a member of your family, in the same way as an adoption allowance (see p922), but official guidance advises that it should be fully disregarded for IS and income-based JSA.[162]

Charitable, voluntary and personal injury payments

Payments from the Macfarlane Trust and similar funds

Any payments from the following funds, including payments in kind, are disregarded in full:[163]

- the Macfarlane Trusts, the Fund, the Eileen Trust, the Skipton Fund, the Caxton Foundation or MEFT Ltd (for people infected with HIV or hepatitis C through blood products and NHS treatment);
- the Independent Living Funds.

Payments can still be disregarded if you give them to certain relatives or they inherit them from you after your death. Also disregarded are payments from the

London Bombings Relief Fund, although these are generally made as lump-sum capital payments.

Any income or capital that derives from any such payments is also disregarded.

Other payments

Most other charitable or voluntary payments that are made irregularly and are intended to be made irregularly are treated as capital and are unlikely to affect your claim unless they take your capital above the limit.[164] However, if you are on IS or income-based JSA, they count as income if you are involved in a trade dispute and, for IS only, for the first 15 days following your return to work after a dispute (see p700).[165]

Payments made on a regular basis

Charitable and voluntary payments and certain personal injury payments (see below) are ignored if they are made, or are due to be made, regularly.[166]

A **'voluntary payment'** is one given without getting anything back in return.[167]

For IS and income-based JSA, these payments are not disregarded where you are involved in a trade dispute and, for IS only, for the first 15 days following your return to work after a trade dispute.

Payments from a former partner, or the parent of your child, are dealt with as maintenance (see p804).

The **personal injury payments** that qualify under the above rules are:[168]

- payments from a trust fund set up out of money paid because of any personal injury to you; *or*
- payments under an annuity purchased either under an agreement or court order set up because of any personal injury to you, or from money paid because of any personal injury to you; *or*
- payments you get under an agreement or court order because of any personal injury to you. This does not include an occupational pension – eg, where you have retired early because of personal injury.[169]

See also p934 for payments made to someone else on your behalf and p931 for payments disregarded under miscellaneous income.

Concessionary coal to former British Coal workers and their surviving partners is ignored (except to strikers). Cash in lieu of coal counts in full.[170]

Income from tenants and lodgers

Lettings without board

If you let out a room(s) in your home to tenants, sub-tenants or licensees under a formal contractual arrangement, £20 of your weekly charge for each tenant, sub-tenant or licensee (and her/his family) is ignored.[171] The balance counts as income.

If someone shares your home under an informal arrangement, any payment s/he makes to you for living and accommodation costs is ignored,[172] but a non-dependant deduction may be made from any HB/CTB or housing costs paid with IS/income-based JSA/income-related ESA (see pp266, 123 and 869).

Boarders

If you have a boarder(s) on a commercial basis in your own home, and the boarder or any member of her/his family is not a close relative of yours, the first £20 of the weekly charge is ignored and half of any balance remaining is then taken into account as your income.[173] For HB and CTB, this applies even if the boarder is a close relative and it is not a commercial arrangement. However, there might still be a non-dependant deduction for them (see p265). This disregard applies for each boarder you have. The charge must normally include at least some meals.[174] If you have a business partner, even though your gross income includes just your share of the weekly charge to boarders, you still get the full disregard of £20 plus half the excess for each boarder.[175]

Note: if you let part of your home, any income left after applying the above disregards may be considered to be intended to be used to meet any housing costs of your own which are not met by IS, income-based JSA, income-related ESA or HB, and may, therefore, be offset accordingly (see p929).[176]

Tenants in other properties

If you have a freehold interest in a property other than your home and you let it out, the rent is normally treated as capital.[177] This rule also applies if you have a leasehold interest in another property which you are sub-letting. The full rent would count initially (as well as the capital value of the property itself) but if you spend some on a debt that is immediately repayable (eg, a mortgage) after a period (eg, a month for monthly-paid rent) only what remains continues to count as capital. If you spend it on something else, the notional capital rules could treat you as still having the money – see p985. [178]

The rent is treated as income if the property you let is in one of the categories where the capital value is disregarded (see p977) and, in this case, the expenses listed on p926 are deducted from the income.

Income from capital

In general, actual income generated from capital (eg, interest on savings) is ignored as income[179] but counts as *capital*[180] from the date you are due to receive it. However, income derived from the following categories of disregarded capital (see p977) is treated as income:[181]

- your home;
- your former home, if you are estranged, divorced or your civil partnership has ended;

- property which you have acquired for occupation as your home but into which you have not yet been able to move;
- property which you intend to occupy as your home but which needs essential repairs or alterations;
- property occupied wholly or partly by a partner or relative of any member of your family who has reached the qualifying age for PC (see p509) or is incapacitated;
- property occupied by your former partner, but not if you are estranged, divorced or your civil partnership has ended;
- property for sale;
- property which you are taking legal steps to obtain to occupy as your home;
- your business assets;
- a trust of personal injury compensation.

Some expenses are deducted from this income. Income from any of the above categories (other than your current home, business assets or a personal injuries trust) is ignored up to the amount of the total mortgage repayments (ie, capital and interest, and any payments that are a condition of the mortgage such as insurance or an endowment policy),[182] council tax and water charges paid in respect of the property for the same period over which the income is received.[183]

Tariff income from capital

If your capital is over a certain level, you are treated as having an assumed income from it, called your '**tariff income**'. You are assumed to have an income of £1 for every £250, or part of £250, by which your capital exceeds £6,000 but does not exceed £16,000.[184]

For IS, income-based JSA, income-related ESA and HB, if you are in a care home or similar accommodation (see p971), tariff income applies between £10,000 and £16,000.

If you are underpaid because of a reduction in your capital affecting your tariff income, ask for a revision or supersession (see p1135). Report any increase in your capital to the DWP for IS, income-based JSA and income-related ESA[185] and, except if the increase does not stop you getting some IS/income-based JSA, to the local authority for HB/CTB.[186] If there is a change in your capital which increases the amount of your tariff income and, as a result of which, you are overpaid, see p1079 for IS, income-based JSA and income-related ESA, and pp1082 and 1094 for HB and CTB on recovery of overpayments.

Capital that counts as income

Sometimes the rules treat capital as though it is income.

The following count as income:

- instalments of capital outstanding when you claim benefit, if they would bring you over the capital limit. For IS, income-based JSA and income-related ESA, the instalments to be counted are any outstanding either when your benefit claim is decided, or when you are first due to be paid benefit, whichever is earlier, or at the date of any subsequent supersession.[187] For HB and CTB, it is any instalments outstanding when your claim is made or treated as made, or when your benefit is revised or superseded.[188] The outstanding instalments-count as income by spreading them over the number of weeks between each instalment.[189]

If instalments are outstanding in this way on your child's capital, a similar rule applies for IS or income-based JSA, but only if you have been getting benefit since before 6 April 2004 with a child included in your claim and do not yet have an award of CTC. If the total of these instalments and your child's existing savings come to more than £3,000, the outstanding instalments should count as your child's income[190] and be spread over the period between each instalment;[191]

- any payment from an annuity[192] (see p981 for when this is disregarded);
- any professional and career development loan paid under s2 of the Employment and Training Act 1973[193] (see p659);
- for IS only, a tax refund if you or your partner have returned to work after a trade dispute (see p700);[194]
- for IS and income-based JSA, if you have been getting benefit since before 6 April 2004 with a child included in your claim and do not yet have an award of CTC, certain social services payments for strikers if you or your partner are involved in (or, for IS only, have returned to work after) a trade dispute. These are payments from social services to assist children in need or young people who have previously been looked after by them;[195]
- periodic payments made under an agreement or court order for any personal injury to you (see p923 for when these are disregarded);[196]
- some lump sums from liable relatives (see p803).

Capital which is counted as income cannot also be treated as producing a tariff income (see p926).[197]

Sometimes you may find that withdrawals from a capital sum are treated as income.[198] This is most likely if the sum was intended to help cover living expenses over a particular period – eg, a bank loan taken out by a mature student. If this is not the intended use of any capital sum, dispute the decision. Even if the sum is intended for living expenses, argue that, unless it is actually paid in instalments, it should be treated as capital.[199] A loan that you have an obligation to repay immediately should not be treated as your income (or capital), however it is paid.[200]

Income tax refunds

PAYE refunds (employed earners) and tax refunds under Schedule D (self-employed) are treated as capital.[201]

For IS and JSA, tax refunds paid during a trade dispute are treated as income and taken into account.[202] For IS only, if you or your partner have returned to work after a trade dispute (see p700), tax refunds are treated as income and are taken into account in full.[203]

Income from employment and training programmes

Payments from employment or training programmes under s2 of the Employment and Training Act 1973 or s2 of the Enterprise and New Towns (Scotland) Act 1990 are treated as follows.[204]

Payments taken into account:

- for ESA, payments made as a substitute for ESA or JSA; for other benefits, payments made as a substitute for IS, JSA, ESA, IB or SDA – eg, a training allowance;
- payments intended for certain living costs while you are participating in a scheme to enhance your employment prospects. Payments for food, ordinary clothing or footwear, fuel, rent met by HB, housing costs met by IS, JSA or income-related ESA, council tax or water charges are all taken into account.

All other payments are disregarded – eg:

- travel expenses;
- training premium;
- childcare expenses;
- special needs payments;
- Employment, Skills and Enterprise Scheme and Mandatory Work Activity expenses;[205]
- New Enterprise Allowance weekly allowance;
- return-to-work credit (paid to sick or disabled people returning to work);
- in-work credit (paid to lone parents starting work).

For ESA, any payment for expenses incurred in complying with a requirement to undertake work-related activity (see p1031) are ignored.[206]

If you have been getting help under the 'self-employment route' (eg, for JSA, HB and CTB, the New Enterprise Allowance), any payments to meet expenses 'wholly and necessarily' incurred while trading, or used for the repayment of a loan necessary for the business, are also disregarded if they are from a special account set up for this programme).[207] Income built up in your special account while you are getting this help, for HB/CTB, is treated as capital.[208] For IS/JSA/ESA, at the end of the programme, this is treated as income and spread over the same number of weeks in the future for which you have been receiving assistance, less any income tax due on the profits and an earnings disregard appropriate to your circumstances (see p912).[209]

Occupational pensions and annuities

The following income is **taken into account in full:**

- an occupational pension (except for any discretionary payment from a hardship fund) or income from a personal pension;[210]
- payments from an annuity, except (for IS, income-based JSA and income-related ESA only) payments under an annuity purchased either under an agreement or court order set up because of any personal injury to you, or from money paid because of any personal injury to you (see p924). However, in the case of home income plans, income from the annuity equal to the interest payable on the loan with which the annuity was bought is ignored if:[211]
  - you used at least 90 per cent of the loan made to you to buy the annuity; *and*
  - the annuity will end when you and your partner die; *and*
  - you or your partner are responsible for paying the interest on the loan; *and*
  - you (if you took out the loan), or your partner (if s/he did), were at least 65 at the time the loan was made; *and*
  - the loan is secured on a property which you or your partner own or in which you have an interest, and the property on which the loan is secured is your home, or that of your partner.

  If the interest on the loan is payable after income tax has been deducted, it is an amount equal to the net interest payment that is disregarded; otherwise it is the gross amount of the interest payment.

Mortgage and insurance payments

The following income is ignored:

- for IS, income-based JSA and income-related ESA only, payments you receive under a mortgage protection policy on your home count as income up to the level of the housing costs included in your 'applicable amount'. If the payments are higher than this, disregarded from the excess is whatever you use to pay: [212]
  - the interest on a qualifying loan which is not met by the DWP – eg, if the interest on the loan is higher than the DWP's standard interest rate;
  - capital repayments on a qualifying loan; *and*
  - any premiums you pay on the policy and any buildings insurance policy on your home.

  Any amount of the mortgage protection policy payments left over counts as your income;
- for IS, income-based JSA and income-related ESA only, and as long as you have not already used insurance payments for the same purpose, any money you receive which is given, and which you use, to make:[213]
  - payments under a secured loan which do not qualify under the housing costs rules (see Chapter 38);

- interest payments which are not met under the housing costs rules, even though some interest payments under the loan may be met;
- capital repayments on a qualifying loan;
- payments of premiums on an insurance policy which you took out to insure against the risk of not being able to make the payments in the above three categories, and premiums on a building insurance policy;
- payment of any rent that is not covered by HB (see Chapter 14);
- payment of the part of your accommodation charge in a care home that exceeds that payable by a local authority;

If you are using maintenance from a former partner or parent of your child (but not child maintenance which is disregarded whatever you use it for) to pay these costs, it may be taken into account as a 'liable relative payment' (see p803) unless paid direct to someone else (eg, a lender – see p806), except maintenance for rent which counts even if paid direct to a landlord;

- for HB and CTB only, payments you receive under an insurance policy to insure against the risk of being unable to maintain payments on a loan secured on your home. However, anything you get above the total of the following counts as your income:[214]
  - the amount you use to maintain your payments; *and*
  - any premium you pay for the policy; *and*
  - any premium for an insurance policy to insure against loss or damage to your home;
- payments you receive under an insurance policy to insure against the risk of being unable to maintain hire purchase or similar payments or other loan payments – eg, credit card debts. However, anything you get above the amount you use to make your payments and the premium for the policy counts as your income.[215]

Social services, community care and other payments

The following payments are ignored:

- a payment from a social services department under ss17, 23B, 23C or 24A of the Children Act 1989, or, in Scotland, a payment from a social work department under s12 of the Social Work (Scotland) Act 1968 or under ss22, 29 or 30 of the Children (Scotland) Act 1995 – ie, payments from social services to assist children in need or young people who have been in care or who have been looked after.[216] For IS and income-based JSA, such payments are not ignored if you or your partner are involved in or, for IS only, have returned to work after a trade dispute (see p700);
- a payment from a social services department under s23C of the Children Act 1989 or ss22 or 29 of the Children (Scotland) Act 1995 to someone formerly in your care as a child or young person who has passed it on to you, and who is now aged 18 or over but continues to live with you. For IS and income-based

JSA, such payments are not ignored if you or your partner are involved in or, for IS only, have returned to work after a trade dispute (see p700);[217]
- any community care or healthcare direct payments. Local authorities or the NHS pay these to disabled people or carers to buy their own services instead of providing services directly. A direct payment is not ignored as income of the person you pay for services even if this is your partner;[218]
- any payment you or your partner receive for looking after a person temporarily in your care if it is paid under community care arrangements by a health authority, primary care trust, local health board, local authority, voluntary organisation or by the person being looked after.[219] Any HB paid to you by a local authority for that person is not ignored, although see p924 for other possible disregards;
- payments under the Supporting People programme for support services to help you live independently are ignored indefinitely.[220] Landlords receiving such payments for providing the services do not benefit from this disregard, although other disregards may apply (see p924);
- if you live in a care home and the local authority arranged your place, local authority payments towards your fees are ignored for IS, JSA and income-related ESA. If the local authority did not arrange your place, any payment intended and used for your maintenance is fully disregarded if it is a voluntary or charitable payment, and partly disregarded if not – up to the difference between the care home fees and your applicable amount;[221]
- a lump-sum payment from the local authority to enable you to make adaptations to your home for a disabled child. This is treated as capital and ignored.[222]

Miscellaneous income

The following income is ignored:
- education maintenance allowances and 16–19 Bursary Fund payments (paid in England).[223] These are paid to some young people staying on at school or other non-advanced education;
- any payment to cover your expenses if you are working as an unpaid volunteer, or working unpaid for a charity or voluntary organisation;[224]
- payments in kind (unless, for IS or income-based JSA, you or your partner are involved in a trade dispute, see p700).[225] These may include food, fuel, cigarettes,[226] clothing, holidays, gifts, accommodation, transport, or nursery education vouchers (but see p932 for the rules on notional income and p906 for the rules on non-cash vouchers paid as earnings). Items for essential living needs provided from the UK Border Agency to an asylum-seeking partner are ignored for IS, income-based JSA and income-related ESA;

- a payment (other than a training allowance) to a disabled person under the Disabled Persons (Employment) Act 1944 to assist her/him to obtain or retain employment;[227]
- any payments, other than for loss of earnings or a benefit, made to jurors or witnesses for attending at court;[228]
- Victoria Cross or George Cross payments or similar awards;[229]
- income paid outside the UK which cannot be transferred here;[230]
- if income is paid in another currency, any bank charges for converting the payment into sterling;[231]
- fares to hospital and refunds for prescription or dental charges;[232]
- payments instead of milk tokens and vitamins, or Healthy Start food vouchers;[233]
- payments to assist prison visits;[234]
- for HB and CTB, if you make a parental contribution to a student's grant or loan, an equal amount of any 'unearned' income you have for the period the grant or loan is paid. If your 'unearned' income does not cover the contribution, the balance can be disregarded from your earnings. If you are a parent of a student under 25 in advanced education who does not get a grant or loan (or who only gets a smaller discretionary award) and you contribute to her/his living expenses, the amount of your 'unearned' income that is ignored is the amount equal to your contribution up to a maximum of £56.25 (less the weekly amount of any discretionary award the student has). This is only ignored during the student's term. Again, any balance can be disregarded from your earnings;[235]
- any payment of a sports award made by the Sports Council out of National Lottery funds *except* for any part of any award which is made for 'ordinary living expenses' – ie, food, ordinary clothing or footwear, household fuel, council tax, water charges and rent (less any non-dependant deductions) for which HB could be payable or housing costs that could be met by IS, income-based JSA or income-related ESA. Payments for clothes and shoes used just for sport, and payments for vitamins, minerals or other special dietary supplements intended to enhance performance are ignored;[236]
- any discretionary housing payments paid by a local authority;[237]
- any payment for expenses if you are part of a service-user group being consulted by a public, local or health authority or registered social landlord (expenses do not count as earnings either).[238]

Notional income

You may, in certain circumstances, be treated as having income even if you do *not possess it, or have used it up.*

Deprivation of income to claim or increase benefit

If you deliberately get rid of income in order to claim or increase your benefit, you are treated as though you are still in receipt of the income.[239] The basic issues involved are the same as those for the deprivation of capital (see p985). **Note:** the rule can only apply if the purpose of the deprivation is to gain benefit for *yourself* (or your family). It should not apply if, for example, you stop claiming CA solely so that another person (who is not a member of your family) can become entitled to the severe disability premium (see p830).[240] However, if you do not claim a benefit which would clearly be paid if you did, it may be argued that you have failed to apply for income (see below). The rule still applies if you move from one benefit to another in the case of IS, JSA and ESA. For example, if you got rid of income to increase your ESA then claim JSA instead, you are still treated as having the income in your JSA claim. If you get CTB but not HB, this deprivation rule may not apply to you.[241]

Failing to apply for income

If you fail to apply for income to which you are entitled without having to fulfil further conditions, you are deemed to have received it from the date you could have obtained it.[242]

This does not include, for example, income from:

- a discretionary trust; *or*
- a trust set up from money paid as a result of a personal injury; *or*
- funds administered by a court as a result of a personal injury; *or*
- a rehabilitation allowance made under the Employment and Training Act 1973; *or*
- JSA (for IS, JSA and ESA) or ESA (for ESA only); *or*
- if you are under the qualifying age for PC (see p509), a personal or occupational pension scheme or payments from the Pension Protection Fund. However, for IS, income-based JSA and income-related ESA, if you or your partner have reached that age, you are treated as receiving income in certain circumstances if you defer or fail to claim your pension or purchase an annuity;[243] *or*
- WTC and CTC.[244]

For other income or benefits, it must still be certain that it would be paid upon application (and the rule ceases to apply as soon as a claim is made[245]). It may, therefore, be difficult to establish that there is 'no doubt' that CA, for example, would be paid to a carer who does not wish to claim it because of the effect on another person's severe disability premium (see p830).[246]

Income due to you that has not been paid

This applies to IS, income-based JSA and income-related ESA only.[247] You are treated as possessing any income owing to you. Examples of when this rule may apply could include:

- when wages are legally due to you but are not paid; *or*
- an occupational pension payment that is due but has not been received, unless the pension scheme has insufficient funds.[248]

This rule should not apply if:
- any social security benefit has been delayed; *or*
- you are waiting for a late payment of a government training allowance or a benefit from a European Economic Area country; *or*
- money is due to you from a discretionary trust, or a trust set up from money paid as a result of a personal injury; *or*
- you are owed earnings when your job has ended because of redundancy but these have not been paid to you.[249]

The income must be due to *you* (or your family) and for your own benefit.[250]

Unpaid wages

This applies to IS, income-based JSA and income-related ESA only. If you have wages due to you, but you do not yet know the exact amount or you have no proof of what they will be, you are treated as having a wage similar to that normally paid for that type of work in that area.[251] If your wages cannot be estimated, you might qualify for an interim payment (see p1046).[252]

Income paid to someone else on your behalf

If money is paid to someone on your behalf (eg, a landlord for your rent), this can count as notional income.[253] Even if it does count as notional income, it is still subject to the usual disregards that would apply if it were actual income – eg, a voluntary or charitable payment of income is ignored whether it is paid directly to you or to someone else on your behalf. See p990 for a description of these third-party rules – the notional income rules are the same as those for notional capital.

Income in kind given to a third party for you is ignored (eg, a food parcel used to prepare meals for you), unless, for IS or income-based JSA, you or your partner are involved in a trade dispute. However, money given to someone who uses it to buy you goods or services counts as notional income under the usual rules.

Income paid to you for someone else

If you or your partner get a payment for somebody not in the 'family' (see p751) (eg, a relative living with you), it counts as your income if you keep any of it yourself or spend it on yourself or your partner unless it is – eg:[254]
- from the Macfarlane Trusts or one of the similar funds listed on p923;
- concessionary coal under the Coal Industry Act 1994;
- a payment for an approved employment-related course of education, the Employment, Skills and Enterprise Scheme or Mandatory Work Activity scheme;

- income in kind (eg, a food parcel given to you to make meals for someone else), although it does count for IS or income-based JSA if you or your partner are involved in a trade dispute.

If you have been on IS or income-based JSA since before 6 April 2004 with a dependent child included in your claim and you do not yet have a CTC award, income paid to your dependent child for someone not in the family also counts as yours in the same way as it would if it were paid to you or your partner.

Cheap or unpaid labour

If you are helping another person or an organisation by doing work of a kind which would normally command a wage, or a higher wage, you are deemed to receive a wage similar to that normally paid for that kind of job in that area.[255]

The burden of proving that the kind of work you do is something for which an employer would pay, and what the comparable wages are, lies with the decision maker.[256]

The rule does not apply if:[257]

- you are on an unpaid approved work placement or work experience; *or*
- you are on a government employment or training programme with no training allowance or only travel or meals expenses; *or*
- you can show that the person (including a limited company[258]) cannot, in fact, afford to pay, or pay more; *or*
- you work for a charitable or voluntary organisation or as a volunteer, and it is accepted that it is reasonable for you to give your services free of charge.[259] A 'volunteer' is someone who, without any legal obligation, performs a service for another person without expecting payment.

Sometimes it may also be reasonable to do a job free of charge from a sense of community duty, particularly if the job would otherwise remain undone, and there would be no financial profit to an employer.[260]

If you are caring for a sick or disabled relative, it is usually accepted that it is reasonable to do this free of charge rather than expecting her/him to pay you from benefits. However, if you need to show that it is reasonable, you should take into account:[261]

- how much care you give;
- the expectations you both have;
- your housing arrangements;
- whether you gave up work to care;
- the risk of your losing entitlement to carer's allowance if you were paid, or to a social services assessment of your needs;
- whether your relative would actually pay you.

It may also be reasonable to provide such support out of family duty.[262]

Working out weekly income

For HB and CTB, to assess your current normal weekly income:

- average your earnings over a past period (see below for earnings from employment and p911 for self-employed earnings);
- estimate income other than earnings (see p918 for what income counts) by looking at an appropriate period of up to 52 weeks. The period chosen must give an accurate assessment of your income.[263] CTC and WTC are taken into account instalment by instalment – eg, if paid weekly or four-weekly, each instalment counts for the seven or 28 days ending on the day it is due to be paid;
- for earnings from employment and income other than earnings, convert income into a weekly amount if necessary (see p937);
- deduct appropriate earnings disregard/s (see p912).

For IS, income-based JSA and income-related ESA, as well as working out weekly income, you also need to know the period that payments cover. These rules apply to earnings from employment and income other than earnings (see p911 for how self-employed earnings are assessed):

- work out the period covered by the income (see p938);
- work out the date from which to start taking the income into account (see p939);
- convert income into a weekly amount if necessary (see p937). There are special rules covering variable income (see p937), payments for less than a week (see p937) and overlapping payments (see p938).

Averaging earnings for housing benefit and council tax benefit

For HB and CTB, earnings as an employee are usually averaged out over:

- the previous five weeks if you are paid weekly; *or*
- two months if you are paid monthly.[264]

If your earnings vary, or if there is likely to be, or has recently been, a change (eg, you usually do overtime but have not done so recently, or you are about to get a pay rise), the local authority may average them over a different period if this is likely to give a more accurate picture of what you are going to earn.[265]

If you are on strike, the local authority should not take into account your pre-strike earnings and average them out over the strike period.[266]

If you have only just started work and your earnings cannot be averaged over the normal period (ie, five weeks or two months) an estimate is made, based on any earnings you have been paid so far if these are likely to reflect your future average wage. If you have not yet been paid or your initial earnings do not represent what you will normally earn, your employer must provide an estimate of your average weekly earnings.[267] Remember that if you start work after having been on certain benefits, you may get four weeks extended payments of HB at the same amount (see p286).If your earnings change during your award, your new weekly average figure is estimated on the basis of what you are likely to earn over whatever period (up to 52 weeks) best allows an accurate estimate.[268] If averaging does not result in a weekly figure, the amount is converted (see below).

Converting income into a weekly amount

IS, income-based JSA, income-related ESA, HB and CTB are all calculated on a weekly basis, so your earnings and other income have to be converted into a weekly amount if necessary.

The following rules apply to income from employment and income other than earnings.[269] For income from self-employment, see p910.

To convert income to a weekly amount:

- if the payment is for less than a week, it is treated as the weekly amount;
- if the payment is for a month, multiply by 12 and divide by 52;
- for IS, income-based JSA and income-related ESA, multiply a payment for three months by four and divide by 52;
- for IS, income-based JSA and income-related ESA, divide a payment for a year by 52 (unless it is a WTC payment in which case divide by 365 and multiply by seven);
- for all five benefits, for any other period, divide the payment by the number of days in the period then multiply by seven.

If you work on certain days but are paid monthly, it is necessary to decide whether the payment is for the days worked or for the whole month. This generally depends on the terms of your contract of employment,[270] but may depend on how your employer has arranged to make payments to you.[271]

Variable income

For IS, income-based JSA and income-related ESA, if your income fluctuates or your earnings vary because you do not work every week, your weekly income may be averaged over the cycle, if there is an identifiable one, or, if there is not, over five weeks, or over another period if this would be more accurate.[272] If the cycle involves periods when you do no work, those periods are included in the cycle, but not other absences – eg, holidays, sickness.

Part-weeks

For IS, income-based JSA and income-related ESA, there are rules about the calculation of income for part-weeks.

- If income covering a period up to a week is paid before your first benefit week and part of it is counted for that week, or if, in any case, you are paid for a period of a week or more and only part of it is counted in a particular benefit week, multiply the whole payment by the number of days it covers in the benefit week, then divide the result by the total number of days covered by the payment.[273]

- If any payment of MA, IB or SDA falls partly into the benefit week, only the amount paid for those days is taken into account. For any payment of IS, JSA or ESA, that amount is the weekly amount multiplied by the number of days in the part-week and divided by seven.[274]

Overlapping payments

For IS, income-based JSA or income-related ESA, if you have regularly received a certain kind of payment of income from one source and in a particular benefit week you receive that payment and another of the same kind from the same source (eg, if your employer first pays you sick pay in arrears and this then overlaps with a payment in advance), the maximum amount to be taken into account is the one paid first.[275]

This does not apply if the second payment was due to be taken into account in another week, but the overlapping week is the first in which it could practically be counted (see p939).

The period covered for income support, jobseeker's allowance and employment and support allowance

For IS, income-based JSA and income-related ESA, there are special rules for deciding the length of the period for which, and the date from which, payments of earnings and other income count. These rules are designed to give a clearer indication of how you are expected to make use of any earnings or other income you receive for each week of your claim for IS, income-based JSA or income-related ESA. These rules, however, do not apply to self-employed earnings (see p910).

- If a payment of income is made for an identifiable period, it is taken into account for a period of equal length.[276] For example, a week's part-time earnings are taken into account for a week. If you are paid monthly, the payments are taken into account for the number of weeks between the date you are treated as paid and the date you are next due to be paid.
- If the payment does not relate to a particular period, the amount of the payment is divided by the amount of the weekly IS, income-based JSA or ESA to which you would otherwise be entitled. If part of the payment should be disregarded, the amount of IS, income-based JSA or income-related ESA is increased by the appropriate disregard. The result of this calculation is the number of weeks that you are not entitled to IS, income-based JSA or income-related ESA.[277]

Example

Conor receives £750 net earnings for work which cannot be attributed to any specific period of time. He and his partner are both aged 28. Their rent and council tax are met by

HB and CTB. Conor's income-based JSA is £111.45. As a couple they are entitled to a £10 earnings disregard.

Divide £750 by the weekly JSA (£111.45) plus the disregard (£10)

750 ÷ 121.45 = 6.1753

This is six weeks, with 0.1753 x £121.45 left over = £21.29

This means that Conor is not entitled to income-based JSA for six weeks and the remaining £21.29 (less a £10 earnings disregard, leaving £11.29) is taken into account in calculating his benefit for the following week.

Payments made on leaving a job, if not ignored, are taken into account for a forward period (see p907).

The date from which a payment is counted

For IS, income-based JSA and income-related ESA, the date from which a payment of earnings and/or other income counts depends on when it was due to be paid. If it was due to be paid before you claimed IS, income-based JSA or income-related ESA, it counts from the date on which it was due to be paid.[278] Otherwise it is treated as paid on the first day of the benefit week in which it is due, or on the first day of the first benefit week after that in which it is practicable to take it into account.[279]

Payments of IS, JSA, MA, IB, SDA and ESA are treated as paid on the day they are officially due.[280]

The **'benefit week'** for JSA, and usually also for IS and ESA although this may vary, is normally the seven days ending with the day allocated to you according to your national insurance number (also your payday).[281]

The date that a payment is due may well be different from the date of actual payment. Earnings are due on the employee's normal payday. If the contract of employment does not reveal the date of due payment, and there is no evidence to indicate otherwise, the date the payment was received should be taken as the date it was due.[282] If your contract of employment is terminated without proper notice, outstanding wages, wages in hand, holiday pay and any pay in lieu of notice are due on the last day of employment and are treated as paid on that day, even if this does not happen (although these are usually disregarded).[283]

If you receive compensation (eg, in a sex discrimination equal pay case), there is disagreement as to whether the relevant date is the date when the earnings in question were due to be paid[284] or when the compensation was awarded.[285]

If income due to you has not been paid, you may be able to get a crisis loan from the social fund (see p564).

For the treatment of payments at the end of a job, see p907.

2. People over pension credit age

This part applies to:
- pension credit (PC);
- housing benefit (HB) and council tax benefit (CTB) if you or your partner are over the qualifying age for PC (see p509) and not on income support (IS), income-based jobseeker's allowance (JSA) or income-related employment and support allowance (ESA). If you do get IS, income-based JSA or income-related ESA, all your income is ignored for HB and CTB.

If you are under the qualifying age for PC or you have a partner and both of you are under that age, this part does not apply – see p902 instead. **Note:** if you or your partner get IS, income-based JSA or income-related ESA, pp902–39 explains how your income is treated.

The rules for PC and, if you or your partner (if you have one) are over the qualifying age for PC, for HB and CTB, are very similar. Where there are differences, they are indicated.

Note: in this part, whenever HB or CTB are referred to, this only applies to the rules for people over the qualifying age for PC.

Whose income counts

If you are a member of a couple (see p753), your partner's income is added to yours.[286]

The income of a dependent child does *not* affect:
- PC;
- HB or CTB.[287]

What counts as income

Pension credit

For PC, **'income'** means:[288]
- earnings (see pp942 and 944);
- certain benefits and tax credits, including state retirement pensions and war pensions (see p947);
- maintenance (see p949);
- income from tenants and lodgers (see p950);
- income from capital (see p950);
- other specified miscellaneous income, including occupational and personal pensions (see p951);
- notional income (see p953);
- any income paid in lieu of the above.

For each type of income, some income is taken into account and some is ignored in the assessment of PC. If the rules do not specify a type of income as being included in the assessment, it is ignored and does not affect your benefit.

For the rules on 'qualifying income' for the savings credit and the 'assessed income period', both of which only apply to PC, see Chapter 22.

Housing benefit and council tax benefit

How your income affects your entitlement to HB and CTB depends on whether you are getting PC and, if you are, which type of PC.

If you get pension credit guarantee credit

If you (or your partner) are getting the guarantee credit of PC, all of your (and your partner's) income is ignored.[289] This is because entitlement to PC guarantee credit acts as a passport to maximum HB and CTB.

If you get pension credit savings credit

If you (or your partner) are only getting the savings credit of PC, your income for HB and CTB purposes is the income (and capital) figure used by the DWP to work out your PC, *plus*:[290]

- the amount of savings credit of PC;
- any income (and capital) of your partner which was not taken into account in the PC calculation – eg, if a partner abroad is no longer included for PC but is for HB/CTB; *and*
- any income of a non-dependant, but only in the very limited circumstances where her/his income can be treated as yours under the HB rules (see p269);[291]

minus:[292]

- any childcare charges earnings disregard;
- the higher amount disregarded, where applicable, for:
  - lone parent earnings;
  - payments of maintenance made by your former partner (or your partner's former partner), or payments of maintenance made by the parent of a child or young person who is a member of your family, as long as that parent is neither yourself nor your partner;
- any additional full-time earnings disregard (see p947);
- any earnings disregarded from permitted work (see p946);
- any discretionary increase to the £10 disregard for war pensions, and war widows' and widowers' pensions.

If you do not get pension credit

If you or your partner are over the qualifying age for PC (see p509) and are not getting the guarantee or savings credit of PC (or IS, income-based JSA or income-related ESA), income is defined in the same way as for PC (see p940).[293] As for PC, some income is taken into account and some disregarded but the rules on this are not always the same as for PC. Any differences are explained in each relevant section.

Net weekly income

The income that is taken into account is the amount after deducting any tax or national insurance (NI) contributions.[294]

For HB and CTB, the local authority may ignore changes (eg, Budget changes) in tax or NI contributions and the maximum rate of tax credits for up to 30 benefit weeks. When the changes are eventually taken into account, you are not treated as having been underpaid or overpaid benefit during the period of the delay.[295]

Once you have worked out what income should be taken into account, this is converted into a weekly amount (see p955) and the total taken into account in the benefit assessment (see p956 for the date from which a payment is counted). Chapters 8, 14 and 22 explain how income affects the amount of CTB, HB or PC you get.

Earnings of employed earners

This section explains how any earnings received by you or your partner (see p751) are treated for PC and for HB and CTB.

Calculating net earnings from employment

It is your net earnings that are taken into account in the assessment. See p955 for how earnings are converted into a weekly amount. **'Net earnings'** means your 'gross earnings' (see below) *minus*:[296]

- any deductions made for income tax; *and*
- Class 1 NI contributions; *and*
- half of any contribution you make towards a personal or occupational pension scheme.

If your earnings are estimated for HB or CTB, the amount of tax and NI you would expect to pay on those earnings are estimated and deducted, together with half of any pension contributions you are paying.[297]

For HB and CTB, the local authority has the discretion to ignore changes in tax or NI contributions for up to 30 benefit weeks. When the changes are eventually taken into account, you are not treated as having been underpaid or overpaid benefit during the period of the delay.[298]

'Gross earnings' means the amount of earnings received from your employer less deductions for any expenses 'wholly, necessarily and exclusively incurred' by you in order to carry out the duties of your employment.[299] A range of deductions may be made (see p904).

What counts as earnings

'**Earnings**' means 'any remuneration or profit derived from ... employment'.

As well as your wages, this includes:[300]

- any bonus or commission (including tips);
- holiday pay – but this is ignored if your employment ends before your PC entitlement starts;
- statutory sick pay (SSP) and contractual sick pay,[301] statutory maternity pay (SMP), statutory paternity pay (SPP) or statutory adoption pay (SAP) or any other payment made to you by your employer while you are on maternity leave;[302]
- any payments made by your employer for expenses not 'wholly, exclusively and necessarily' incurred in carrying out your job, including any travel expenses to and from work, and any payments made to you for looking after members of your family;
- pay in lieu of notice, or pay in lieu of remuneration except for periodic payments following redundancy. However, all earnings, including pay in lieu, are ignored if your employment ends before your PC entitlement starts;
- a retainer fee (eg, payment during the school holidays if you work for the school meals service[303]) or a guarantee payment;[304]
- an equal pay settlement – eg, through a 'single status agreement';[305]
- any payment of a non-cash voucher which is liable for Class 1 NI contributions.[306] Non-cash vouchers that are *not* liable for contributions (eg, certain childcare and charitable vouchers) are classed as payments in kind and ignored.[307]

Examples of payments not counted as earnings:

- If you become entitled to HB, CTB or PC after your employment ends, all earnings are disregarded except certain royalties.[308]
- Payments in kind (eg, petrol) are ignored.[309]
- An advance of earnings or a loan from your employer is treated as capital, according to PC guidance.[310]
- The value of free accommodation provided as part of your job is ignored, according to PC guidance.[311]
- Payments towards expenses that are 'wholly, exclusively and necessarily' incurred, such as travelling expenses during the course of your work, are ignored.[312]
- If you are a local councillor, travelling expenses and subsistence payments are (and basic allowances may be[313]) ignored as expenses 'wholly, exclusively and necessarily' incurred in your work.
- If your earnings are paid in another currency, any bank charges for converting them into sterling are deducted before taking them into account.[314]

- The net amount of any occupational pension,[315] although not counted as earnings (and therefore having no earnings disregard), is still taken into account in full.[316]
- Any compensation payments made by an employment tribunal for unfair dismissal or unlawful discrimination do not count as earnings.[317]
- Any lump-sum payments made under the Iron and Steel Employees Re-adaptation Benefits Scheme are not treated as earnings.[318]

Payments at the end of a job

Redundancy payments are treated as capital.[319]

If you leave a job, any earnings should be disregarded except certain copyright royalties, payments for patents, trademarks or under the Public Lending Rights Scheme.[320]

However, these rules only apply if you leave your job before you claim benefit. If you are already getting HB/CTB or PC when you leave your job, your earnings are not disregarded for that benefit. If you are already getting HB/CTB but not PC, your earnings are disregarded for PC.

For PC, any final payment is treated as paid on the date your next regular payment of earnings would have been paid and taken into account for the same period unless the final payment is higher than the normal amount. If it is higher, the final payment is taken into account over the corresponding multiple of the regular payment period with any remainder counting for a further payment period.[321]

Example

Sandra has been getting PC and working part time. She earns £25 a week, paid on a Friday. She finishes work on Wednesday 4 August and on that day is given £35 made up of £15 final wages and £20 holiday pay. This £35 is treated as paid on Friday 6 August and taken into account for two benefit weeks – £25 in the first week and the remaining £10 in the second week.

Earnings from self-employment

Even if you are an employee, any other earnings from work you do as a self-employed person are assessed under the following rules for PC and, if you or your partner are over the qualifying age for PC (see p509), for HB and CTB.

Calculating net earnings

Your **'net profit'** over the period before your claim must be worked out. This consists of your self-employed earnings *minus*:[322]

- reasonable expenses (see p910 – the rules are the same as those for people under the qualifying age for PC except that expenses relating to debts are not excluded); *and*

- income tax and NI contributions; *and*
- half of any premium paid in respect of a personal pension scheme which is eligible for tax relief.[323] For PC, you must supply certain information about the scheme or annuity contract to the relevant authority if requested.[324]

If you receive payments for board and lodging charges, these do not count as earnings[325] but as other income (less any disregards – see p950).

Working out average earnings from self-employment

The weekly amount is the average of earnings:[326]

- over a period of one year (normally the last year for which accounts are available);
- over a more appropriate period where you have recently taken up self-employment or there has been a change which will affect your business.

Childminders

Childminders, in practice, are always treated as self-employed. Your net profit is deemed to be one-third of your earnings less income tax, your NI contributions and half of certain pension contributions.[327] The rest of your earnings are completely ignored.

Disregarded earnings

Some of your earnings from employment or self-employment are disregarded and do not affect your PC, HB or CTB. The amount of the 'disregard' depends on your circumstances. The three main levels of disregard are £25, £20 or £5/£10, but additional disregards may apply in special circumstances.

For the treatment of childcare costs for claims for HB/CTB, see p947.

£25 disregard

Lone parents on HB or CTB have £25 of their earnings ignored.[328] This does not apply to anyone claiming PC.

£20 disregard

Twenty pounds of your earnings (including those of your partner, if any) is disregarded if:

- for PC, you are a lone parent;[329]
- you or your partner are in receipt of long-term incapacity benefit (IB), severe disablement allowance (SDA), attendance allowance (AA), disability living allowance (DLA), any mobility supplement or the disability or severe disability element of working tax credit (WTC) or, for PC only, ESA or, for HB and CTB only, ESA including a work-related activity or support component;[330]
- you or your partner are registered or certified as blind;[331]

- for HB and CTB only, you or your partner are, or are treated as, incapable of work and have been, or have been treated as, incapable of work for a continuous period of 196 days if you are terminally ill, or 364 days in any other case;[332]
- for HB and CTB only, you or your partner have (or are treated as having) limited capability for work and the assessment phase has ended;[333]
- you or your partner qualify for a carer premium (see p834). For a couple, if both partners get the carer premium, £20 is disregarded from their combined earnings;[334]
- you or your partner previously had an earnings disregard of £20 in (for PC) your IS, income-based JSA or income-related ESA or (for HB/CTB) in your HB or CTB, *and* that previous award was not more than eight weeks before, for PC, the date you or your partner first became entitled to PC or, for HB/CTB, you or your partner reached the qualifying age for PC (see p509).[335] This £20 disregard continues, provided there is no break of more than eight weeks in either your claim for PC or HB/CTB or in employment;
- for PC only, you or your partner, immediately before reaching pension age, had a £20 disregard in an award of PC because you or your partner were in receipt of long-term IB or SDA.[336] This £20 disregard continues so long as there is no break of more than eight weeks in your claim for PC. **Note:** the rules were not amended to include situations where you or your partner were previously in receipt of ESA;
- you or your partner are an auxiliary coastguard, part-time firefighter, part-time member of a lifeboat crew or member of the Territorial Army.[337] If your, or your partner's, earnings from any of these jobs come to less than £20 a week, what is left over of the £20 disregard can be used against your, or your partner's, earnings from any other employment.

If you qualify under more than one category, you still have a maximum of only £20 of your earnings disregarded.

Permitted work disregard for housing benefit and council tax benefit

For HB and CTB only, £20 or £97.50 is disregarded from earnings if you or your partner are doing 'permitted work' in the circumstances described on p914.[338]

Basic £5 or £10 disregard

If you do not qualify for a £25 or £20 disregard (or, for HB and CTB, a permitted work disregard), £5 of your earnings is disregarded if you are single. If you claim as a member of a couple, £10 of your total income is disregarded, whether or not you are both working.[339]

Additional disregard for housing benefit and council tax benefit

For **HB/CTB only**, whichever earnings disregard applies is increased by £17.10 if:[340]

- you or your partner receive the 30-hour element as part of your (or your partner's) WTC (see p1311); *or*
- you or your partner work 30 hours a week or more on average; *or*
- you or your partner work 16 hours or more a week on average and your HB/CTB includes the family premium (see p822); *or*
- you are a lone parent and work 16 hours or more a week on average; *or*
- you or your partner work 16 hours or more a week on average and one or both of you get long-term IB, ESA which includes a support or work-related activity component, SDA, AA, DLA, mobility supplement, WTC disabled worker or severe disability element, are registered blind or have been incapable of work for 364 days (196 days if terminally ill). For couples, the partner who is disabled is the one who must be working 16 hours a week or more on average.

The only exception is where your total earnings are less than the total of £17.10, plus any earnings disregard and childcare costs disregard (see below). In this case, £17.10 is disregarded from any WTC awarded to you or your partner, but the earnings disregard is not increased.

Note: as with the ordinary earnings disregards, only one additional disregard can be allowed from your (or your partner's) earnings.

Childcare costs for housing benefit and council tax benefit

For **HB/CTB**, an allowance of up to £175 a week for one child, or up to £300 a week for two or more children, can be deducted from your (or your partner's) earnings (from employment or self-employment) for childcare costs in certain circumstances.[341] The rules are the same as those for people under the qualifying age for PC (see p915), except you can also have an allowance deducted if you are a couple and one of you works 16 hours or more a week and the other is aged 80 or over. There is no allowance for childcare costs for PC.

Benefits and tax credits

Some benefits and tax credits are taken into account as income and others are disregarded wholly or partly.

Benefits and tax credits that count in full:

- carer's allowance (CA);
- a war orphan's pension, dependant's allowance or payment under the Armed Forces and Reserve Forces Compensation Scheme for someone whose parent died and who is still eligible as an adult because of disability;[342]
- contribution-based JSA;
- IB and SDA;

- contributory ESA. If ESA is paid at a reduced rate because of a sanction, it is still the full rate that counts;[343]
- industrial injuries benefits, except constant attendance allowance and exceptionally severe disablement allowance, which are disregarded;
- maternity allowance (MA);
- retirement pensions;
- SSP, SMP, SPP and SAP (these are treated as earnings and therefore may benefit from an earnings disregard – see p912);[344]
- widow's pension, bereavement allowance and industrial death benefit;
- WTC generally counts in full. However, for HB and CTB, if your earnings are too low to use the whole £17.10 additional full-time earnings disregard (see p947), £17.10 is disregarded from your WTC instead of your earnings.[345] If a tax credit overpayment is being recovered from your WTC award, it is the amount of the WTC award less the overpayment that is taken into account for PC, HB and CTB;
- foreign social security benefits which are similar to the benefits listed above.[346]

Benefits and tax credits that are ignored completely:[347]
- AA;[348]
- bereavement payments (these are taken into account as capital);[349]
- child benefit;[350]
- child tax credit (CTC);[351]
- constant attendance allowance, exceptionally severe disablement allowance or severe disablement occupational allowance paid because of an injury at work or a war injury;[352]
- DLA care component and mobility component;[353]
- guardian's allowance;[354]
- mobility supplement under the War Pensions Scheme;[355]
- Christmas bonus (see p9);[356]
- social fund payments;[357]
- HB and CTB;[358]
- supplementary payments to pre-1973 war widows or widowers;[359]
- increases for child dependants. Increases for adult dependants are only ignored if the dependant is not your partner.[360]

Benefits that have £15 ignored:
- for HB/CTB only, widowed mother's allowance and widowed parent's allowance.[361]

Benefits that have £10 ignored:
- for PC only, widowed mother's allowance and widowed parent's allowance;[362]
- war disablement pension;[363]

- guaranteed income payment and survivor's guaranteed income payment under the Armed Forces and Reserve Forces Compensation Scheme (if reduced to under £10 by another pension, the remainder is disregarded from the pension);[364]
- war widow's, widower's or surviving civil partner's pension;[365]
- an extra-statutory payment made instead of the above pensions;[366]
- similar payments made by another country;[367]
- a pension from Germany or Austria paid to the victims of Nazi persecution.[368]

The £10 disregard allowed on these war pensions is additional to the total disregard of any mobility supplement or AA (ie, constant attendance allowance, exceptionally severe disablement allowance and severe disablement occupational allowance) paid as part of a war disablement pension.

Local authorities have discretion to increase the £10 disregard on war disablement, war widows' or widowers' pensions and on the guaranteed income payment and survivor's guaranteed income payment, when assessing income for HB and CTB.[369] Some local authorities disregard the full amount of these pensions, and some do not increase the disregard at all, so you should check your own local authority's policy. It has been held that a local authority must at least consider the nature and purpose of such pensions when deciding whether or not to disregard them, and the courts have indicated that it may be appropriate to apply a disregard to retrospective awards.[370]

Benefit delays

If you have made a claim for benefit but have not yet been paid, the benefit should not be treated as income possessed by you. For PC, you should get your full benefit and leave the DWP to deduct the difference from arrears of the delayed benefit when it is eventually awarded.[371]

For the treatment of payments of arrears of certain benefits and CTC and WTC, see p1001.

Maintenance payments

For **HB/CTB**, if you have a family premium included in your HB/CTB, £15 of any maintenance payments for you or your partner made by your (or your partner's) spouse/civil partner or former spouse/civil partner is disregarded.[372] If you receive maintenance from more than one person, only £15 of the total is disregarded. Other kinds of maintenance (eg, for a child) do not count as income and are ignored completely.[373]

For **PC**, any maintenance payments for you or your partner made by your (or your partner's) spouse/civil partner or former spouse/civil partner count in full as income. Maintenance for a child is ignored completely.[374]

If you *pay* maintenance to a former partner or a child not living with you, your payments are not disregarded for the purpose of calculating your income for PC,

HB or CTB.[375] Even if you are on PC, you may still have to pay child support maintenance (see p809).

Income from tenants and lodgers

How income from tenants is treated depends on whether or not you live in the same property.

Lettings without board

If you own or are the tenant of your home, and you rent out a room(s) under an agreement, £20 of your weekly charge for each person is ignored. The balance is taken into account.[376]

If someone shares your home under an informal arrangement and is not paying rent under an agreement, any money s/he does pay is ignored,[377] but a non-dependant deduction may be made from any HB/CTB or housing costs paid with PC.

Boarders

If you have a boarder(s) on a commercial basis in your own home who is not a close relative (see p849), the first £20 of the weekly charge is ignored. Half of any balance remaining is taken into account as your income.[378]

For HB and CTB, this applies even if the boarder is a close relative or it is not a commercial arrangement (and there could be a non-dependant deduction). For PC in these circumstances, all the payment the boarder gives you is ignored, although there could be a non-dependant deduction from any housing costs paid with PC.[379]

This disregard applies for each boarder you have. The charge must normally include at least some meals.[380] If you have a business partner, even though your gross income includes just your share of the weekly charge to boarders, you still get the full disregard of £20 plus half the excess for each boarder.[381]

Tenants in other properties

Rent from a property other than your home is not taken into account as income.[382] Instead, the value of the property counts as capital and therefore is treated as producing a 'deemed income' (see p951). If the value of the property can be disregarded (see p997), both the rent and the capital value are ignored (there is no deemed income).[383]

Income from capital

The general rule is that capital (unless disregarded) is assumed to provide a set rate of income called 'deemed income' (see p951). Actual income generated from capital is ignored as income with the exception of the following types of capital.[384] In these cases, any actual income (but no deemed income) is taken into account.[385] **Note:** for HB and CTB, it is only taken into account in these cases if the total capital listed below is worth more than £10,000.[386]

Actual income from the following capital is taken into account:

- the value of the right to receive a payment in the future of:
  - income under a life interest or life rent;
  - rent, unless you only have a reversionary (ie, future) interest in the property (for the way actual rent is treated, see p950);
  - the surrender value or income under an annuity;
- property held in a trust, including a discretionary trust, but not charitable trusts or, for PC, trusts set up out of payments from personal injury to you or your partner or, for HB/CTB, from the Independent Living Funds, Macfarlane Trusts, the Fund, the Eileen Trust, MFET Ltd, the Skipton Fund, the Caxton Foundation or the London Bombings Relief Charitable Fund.

If deemed income is taken into account, actual income from the same capital is ignored.

There are no rules that treat capital of any kind as though it were income.

Deemed income

There is no upper capital limit for PC. If you have capital above £10,000, you are treated as having an assumed income of £1 for every £500, or part of £500, by which your capital exceeds £10,000.[387]

For HB and CTB, the following apply.

- If you or your partner are getting the guarantee credit of PC, all of your (and your partner's) capital is ignored.[388]
- In any other case, there is a capital limit of £16,000.[389] If you have capital above £10,000, you will be treated as having an assumed income of £1 for every £500, or part of £500, of capital between £10,000.01 and £16,000.[390]

For PC, HB and CTB, you are not treated as having deemed income on capital that is disregarded (see p997).

Example

Frank, aged 72, has savings of £12,000. Deemed income is taken into account for PC (he gets savings credit only), HB and CTB of £4 a week for each benefit. Any interest from the savings is ignored as income.

Occupational and personal pensions

The following income is taken into account:[391]

- an occupational pension;
- income from a personal pension;

- income from a retirement annuity contract (including an annuity purchased for you or transferred to you on divorce);
- payments from a former employer for early retirement on the grounds of ill health or disability, unless this was under a court order or settlement of a claim;[392]
- overseas pension;
- Civil List Act pension;[393]
- payment under an equity release scheme.[394] This provides regular payments from a loan secured on your home. For some home income plans, interest on the loan can be disregarded (see p929);
- payments from the Financial Assistance Scheme and periodic payments from the Pension Protection Fund (these help some people with underfunded occupational schemes whose employer has gone out of business).

Some charitable trusts provide discretionary income to people retired from specific occupations. This is ignored for PC, HB and CTB.[395]

Specified miscellaneous income

The following rules apply.

Income counted in full:

- copyright royalties, payments for patents, trademarks or under the Public Lending Rights Scheme – add these payments to your earnings (if any) if you are the first owner of the copyright or patent or author of the book and deduct the appropriate earnings disregards on p945.[396]

Income that is ignored:

- income paid outside the UK which cannot be transferred here;[397]
- if income is paid in another currency, any bank charges for converting the payment into sterling;[398]
- income from an annuity is normally taken into account. However, an amount equal to the interest payable on the loan with which the annuity was bought is ignored if:[399]
  - you used at least 90 per cent of the loan made to you to buy the annuity; *and*
  - the annuity will end when you and your partner die; *and*
  - you or your partner are responsible for paying the interest on the loan; *and*
  - you (if you took out the loan) or your partner (if s/he did) were at least 65 at the time the loan was made; *and*
  - the loan is secured on a property which you or your partner own or have an interest in, and the property on which the loan is secured is your home or your partner's home.

  If the interest on the loan is payable after income tax has been deducted, it is an amount equal to the net interest payment that is disregarded, otherwise it is the gross amount of the interest payment;

- any discretionary payment made to you by trustees is ignored altogether, *except* where the payment is for the purpose of:
  - obtaining food, ordinary clothing or footwear, or household fuel; *or*
  - paying rent, council tax or water charges for which you or your partner (if any) are liable. **'Rent'** means eligible rent under the HB rules, less any non-dependant deductions; *or*
  - meeting housing costs which could be met by the PC rules,

  in which case £20 of the payment is disregarded, or if the payment is less than £20, the whole of the payment is disregarded.[400] If this disregard overlaps with certain other disregards (eg, certain war pensions), a combined maximum of £20 is allowed.[401] **Note:** this is a weekly disregard so payments spread over different or successive benefit weeks attract a £20 disregard for each.

  School uniforms and sportswear are examples of clothing and footwear that are not ordinary;
- periodic payments made to you or your partner under an agreement entered into in settlement of a claim for any injury to you or your partner;[402] any payment ordered by a court to be made to you or your partner because of an accident, injury or disease you or your partner (or, for HB and CTB only, your child) have.[403]

Notional income

You may, in certain circumstances, be treated as having income although you do not possess it or have used it up in the PC assessment and in HB and CTB.

If you are working, but earning less than the going rate, there are no rules to treat you as though your wages were higher than those you actually get, as there are for IS.

Deprivation of income to claim or increase benefit

If you deliberately get rid of income in order to claim or increase your benefit, you are treated as though you are still in receipt of the income.[404] The basic issues involved are the same as those for the deprivation of capital (see p1003). If you deferred your retirement pension to get extra increments, then take a lump sum instead, you are not treated as still having the increments (see below for what happens if you fail to apply for or defer your pension). **Note:** the rule can only apply if the purpose of the deprivation is to gain benefit for *yourself* (or your partner). It should not apply if, for example, you stop claiming CA solely so that another person (who is not your partner) can become entitled to the severe disability premium (see p830).[405] However, if you do not claim a benefit which would clearly be paid if you did, it may be argued that you have failed to apply for income (see p954).

Failing to apply for income

Sometimes you can be treated as having pension income even though you have not applied for it.[406] There are no rules to treat you as having any other income, such as another benefit, that you could have applied for but did not.

If you defer your Category A or B pension, graduated retirement benefit or any shared additional pension paid on divorce, you are *not* treated as having that income for HB and CTB before you actually claim it. However, for PC, you *are* treated as having that income. The amount that counts for PC is the pension to which you would expect to be entitled were you to claim, less any overlapping benefit you get – eg, SDA or CA. If you have deferred claiming your pension for at least 12 months, the amount is based on your taking the lump-sum option (there is a choice when claiming a deferred pension to take a lump sum or to take extra pension income). To take account of the time it can take to process claims, you are only treated as having this income from the date you could expect to get it were you to make a claim.

For PC, HB and CTB, you are treated as having any amount of Category C or D pension and age addition to which you might expect to be entitled if you were to claim (for PC, deducting any overlapping benefit you get).

You are treated as having any income from an occupational pension you have elected to defer beyond the scheme's retirement age,[407] as though you had claimed it (for PC, taking account of the time it might take to process and deducting any overlapping benefit). If you have reached the qualifying age for PC (see p509) and are entitled to money-purchase benefits under an occupational or personal pension scheme and you fail to purchase an annuity (because you defer or do not apply), you are treated as having the amount of income you have foregone. If your scheme does not allow income withdrawal, you are treated as having income you could have received if you had chosen a different kind of scheme. However, if you give up a small occupational or personal pension in favour of a lump sum within the 'trivial commutation' limit (your pension provider can advise on this), you are not treated as having that income.[408]

Income paid to someone else on your behalf

Any money that counts as income (see p940) and is paid to someone on your behalf is normally treated as being yours and is then either taken into account or ignored as income under the rules described in this chapter. The exception is for payments of income made under an occupational or personal pension scheme (or, for HB and CTB only, from the Pension Protection Fund) if you or your partner (if any) are bankrupt (or the subject of a sequestration order). In this case, if the payment is made to the trustee or other person acting on your creditors' behalf and you (and your partner) have no income other than the payment made, it is not treated as being yours.[409]

Other income

Only income that is specified in the rules can affect your benefit. That income is listed on p940 and described above. Any other kind of income is ignored. The following are some examples of income that is ignored and does not affect your benefit.

- **Student loans and grants** are disregarded.[410]
- For HB and CTB only, there is a specific disregard if you make a **parental contribution** to a student's grant or loan. An equal amount of income you have for the period the grant or loan is paid is ignored.[411] If you are a parent of a student under 25 in advanced education who does not get a grant or loan (or who only gets a smaller discretionary award) and you contribute to her/his living expenses, your contribution up to a maximum of £56.25 (less the weekly amount of any discretionary award the student has) is ignored from your income during term time.[412] In either case, it is deducted from earnings if you do not have enough other income to use the full disregard.
- **Adoption allowances, fostering allowances, residence order payments** and **kinship care payments** are disregarded in full.[413]
- **Charitable and voluntary payments** are not taken into account as income, so if a charity or a person gives you voluntary payments, these do not reduce your benefit. Note that maintenance payments can affect your benefit (see p949).
- Payments for expenses if you are part of a **service user group** are ignored. Other payments count as earnings but if you choose not to take them or have them paid to someone else on your behalf, they will not count as your notional income.[414]

Working out weekly income

To assess your weekly income:

- work out whether income is taken into account, or fully or partly disregarded (see p940);
- if income varies, work out average income (see below);
- convert into a weekly amount if necessary (see p956);
- add any deemed weekly income from capital (see p951);
- for HB and CTB, if you are working and eligible for a childcare cost disregard, deduct the eligible childcare charges (see p947).

Variable income

If your earnings vary because you do not work the same hours every week, your weekly income may be averaged over the cycle, if there is an identifiable one.[415] If you do not work a recognisable cycle or your income fluctuates, your income is worked out on the basis of:

- the last two payments before your claim was made or treated as made (or, where applicable, before your claim was superseded) if those payments are at least one month apart; *or*
- the last four payments before your claim was made or treated as made (or, where applicable, before your claim was superseded) if the last two payments are less than a month apart; *or*
- calculating (or estimating for HB or CTB) any other payments that would give a more accurate figure for your average weekly income.[416]

In all cases, if the cycle involves periods when you do no work, those periods are included in the cycle, but not other absences – eg, holidays, sickness.

The payment is treated as if made for a period of a year if you are entitled to:[417]

- royalties or other sums for the use of any copyright, patent or trademark; *or*
- payments for any book registered under the Public Lending Rights Scheme 1982; *or*
- payments made on an occasional basis.

Converting income into a weekly amount

PC, HB and CTB are calculated on a weekly basis so your earnings and other income have to be converted into a weekly amount if necessary.

The following rules apply to income from employment and other income.[418] For income from self-employment, see p944.

- If the payment is for less than a week, it is treated as the weekly amount.
- If the payment is for a month, multiply by 12 and divide by 52.
- Multiply a payment for three months by four and divide by 52.
- Divide a payment for a year by 52.
- Multiply payments for any other periods by seven and divide by the number of days in the period.

The date from which a payment is counted

For PC, at the start of a claim or a new 'assessed income period' (see p520), the total weekly income is taken into account from the first day of the first 'benefit week' or new assessed income period.[419] A **'benefit week'** is the seven days ending on the day PC is payable if paid in arrears, or starting on that day if paid in advance.[420]

The general rule is that social security benefits are treated as paid on the last day of the PC benefit week in which the benefit is payable, but on the first day if the benefit is paid in advance.[421] Some benefits are treated slightly differently. Contribution-based JSA, IB, contributory ESA, SDA and MA are treated as paid on the day that benefit is payable.

For other types of income, the general rule is that changes to income take effect from the first day of the benefit week in which the change takes place.[422] If that is not practicable, the change is put into effect from the start of the next benefit week. However, if there is a change to the amount of deemed income from capital or an increase in WTC, the change is put into effect from the benefit week that starts on or after the change takes place.[423]

Notes

1. **People under pension credit age**

1 **IS/HB/CTB** s136(1) SSCBA 1992
JSA s13(2) JSA 1995
ESA Sch 1 para 6(2) WRA 2007; reg 83 ESA Regs

2 **HB** Schs 4 para 12 and 5 para 4 HB Regs
CTB Schs 3 para 12 and 4 para 4 CTB Regs

3 **IS** Reg 23(4) IS Regs
JSA Reg 88(3) JSA Regs
ESA Reg 83(4) ESA Regs

4 **IS** Reg 23(2) IS Regs
JSA Reg 88(2) JSA Regs

5 **ESA** Reg 83(2) ESA Regs
HB Reg 25(3) HB Regs
CTB Reg 15(3) CTB Regs

6 **IS** Reg 17(b) IS Regs
JSA Reg 83(b) JSA Regs

7 **IS** Reg 44(5) IS Regs
JSA Reg 106(5) JSA Regs

8 **IS** Reg 44(4) and Sch 8 para 15 IS Regs
JSA Reg 106(4) and Sch 6 para 18 JSA Regs
Both Reg 1 SS(WTCCTC)(CA) Regs

9 **IS** Sch 8 paras 14 and 15 IS Regs
JSA Sch 6 paras 17 and 18 JSA Regs

10 **IS** Reg 44(4) IS Regs
JSA Reg 106(4) JSA Regs

11 **IS** Reg 40 and Sch 9 para 1 IS Regs
JSA Reg 103(1) and (2) and Sch 7 para 1 JSA Regs
ESA Reg 104 and Sch 8 para 1 ESA Regs
HB Reg 40 and Sch 5 para 1 HB Regs
CTB Reg 30 and Sch 4 para 1 CTB Regs

12 **HB** Reg 34 HB Regs
CTB Reg 24 CTB Regs

13 R(IS) 4/01

14 *R v SBC ex parte Singer* [1973] 1 WLR 713

15 *Minter v Kingston Upon Hull City Council and Potter v SSWP* [2011] EWCA Civ 1155

16 *Parsons v Hogg* [1985] 2 All ER 897 (CA), appendix to R(FIS) 4/85

17 **IS** Reg 36(3) IS Regs
JSA Reg 99(1) and (4) JSA Regs
ESA Reg 96(3) ESA Regs
HB Reg 36(3) HB Regs
CTB Reg 26(3) CTB Regs

18 CIS/521/1990

19 **HB** Regs 29(2) and 36(6) HB Regs
CTB Regs 19(2) and 26(6) CTB Regs

20 **HB** Reg 34 HB Regs
CTB Reg 24 CTB Regs
Both para BW2.34 GM

21 **IS** Reg 35(1) IS Regs
JSA Reg 98(1) JSA Regs
ESA Reg 95(1) ESA Regs
HB Reg 35(1) HB Regs
CTB Reg 25(1) CTB Regs
All R(SB) 21/86

22 **HB** Reg 35(1)(i)-(j) HB Regs
CTB Reg 25(1)(i)-(j) CTB Regs

23 **IS** Regs 35(2)(b) and 40(4) and Sch 9 paras 1, 4 and 4A IS Regs
JSA Regs 98(2)(c) and 103(6) and Sch 7 paras 1, 4 and 5 JSA Regs
ESA Regs 95(2)(b) and 104(8) and Sch 8 paras 1, 4 and 5 ESA Regs

24 **HB** Reg 35(1)(i)-(j) HB Regs
CTB Reg 25(1)(i)-(j) CTB Regs

25 **IS** Regs 35(2)(b) and 40(4) and Sch 9 paras 1 and 4 IS Regs
JSA Regs 98(2)(c) and 103(6) and Sch 7 paras 1 and 4 JSA Regs
ESA Regs 95(2)(b) and 104(8) and Sch 8 paras 1 and 4 ESA Regs

26 **IS** Reg 35(1)(e) IS Regs
JSA Reg 98(1)(d) JSA Regs
ESA Reg 95(1)(e) ESA Regs
HB Reg 35(1)(e) HB Regs
CTB Reg 25(1)(e) CTB Regs

27 R(IS) 9/95

28 **IS** Reg 35(3)(a)(iv) IS Regs
JSA Reg 98(3)(d) JSA Regs
ESA Reg 95(4) ESA Regs, definition of 'compensation'
29 *Minter v Kingston Upon Hull City Council and Potter v SSWP* [2011] EWCA Civ 1155
30 **IS** Reg 35(1)(j) IS Regs
JSA Reg 98(1)(h) JSA Regs
ESA Reg 95(1)(k) ESA Regs
HB Reg 35(1)(k) HB Regs
CTB Reg 25(1)(k) CTB Regs
31 **IS** Reg 35(2A) IS Regs
JSA Reg 98(2A) JSA Regs
ESA Reg 95(3) ESA Regs
HB Reg 35(3) HB Regs
CTB Reg 25(3) CTB Regs
32 **IS** Reg 35(2)(a) and Sch 9 para 21 IS Regs
JSA Reg 98(2)(a) and Sch 7 para 22 JSA Regs
ESA Reg 95(2)(a) and Sch 8 para 22 ESA Regs
HB Reg 35(2)(a) and Sch 5 para 23 HB Regs
CTB Reg 25(2)(a) and Sch 4 para 24 CTB Regs
33 CIS/11482/1995
34 para 26096 DMG
35 **IS** Reg 35(2)(a) IS Regs
JSA Reg 98(2)(a) JSA Regs
ESA Reg 95(2)(a) ESA Regs
HB Reg 35(2)(a) HB Regs
CTB Reg 25(2)(a) CTB Regs
All para 26040 DMG
36 **IS** Reg 48(5) IS Regs
JSA Reg 110(5) JSA Regs
ESA Reg 112(5) ESA Regs
HB Reg 46(5) HB Regs
CTB Reg 36(5) CTB Regs
37 **IS** Reg 48(6) IS Regs
JSA Reg 110(6) JSA Regs
38 **IS** Reg 35(2)(c) IS Regs
JSA Reg 98(2)(d) JSA Regs
ESA Reg 95(2)(c) ESA Regs
HB Reg 35(2)(b) HB Regs
CTB Reg 25(2)(b) CTB Regs
39 R(FC) 1/90
40 CFC/26/1989
41 R(FIS) 4/85
42 R(IS) 13/91; R(IS) 16/93; CFC/26/1989
43 CCS/318/1995 (applying the identical provisions in child support law)
44 CCS/5352/1995
45 R(CS) 2/99, following CCS/10/1994 and R(CS) 10/98, and CCS/2561/1998, but see CCS/12769/1996 for a contrary view
46 CCS/3882/1997
47 R(FIS) 4/85; R(FC) 1/91; R(IS) 13/91
48 CIS/77/1993; CIS/89/1989
49 **IS** Sch 8 para 11 IS Regs
JSA Sch 6 para 14 JSA Regs
ESA Sch 7 para 9 ESA Regs
HB Sch 4 para 13 HB Regs
CTB Sch 3 para 13 CTB Regs
50 **IS** Sch 8 para 12 IS Regs
JSA Sch 6 para 15 JSA Regs
ESA Sch 7 para 10 ESA Regs
HB Sch 4 para 14 HB Regs
CTB Sch 3 para 14 CTB Regs
51 **IS** Reg 35(2)(d) IS Regs
JSA Reg 98(2)(e) JSA Regs
ESA Reg 95(2)(d) ESA Regs
HB Reg 35(2)(c) HB Regs
CTB Reg 25(2)(c) CTB Regs
52 **IS** Reg 40(4) and Sch 9 para 1 IS Regs
JSA Reg 103(6) and Sch 7 para 1 JSA Regs
ESA Reg 104(8) and Sch 8 para 1 ESA Regs
HB Reg 40(10) and Sch 5 para 1 HB Regs
CTB Reg 30(11) and Sch 4 para 1 CTB Regs
53 **IS** Sch 8 paras 1(1)(a) and (2) and 2 IS Regs
JSA Sch 6 paras 1(1)(a) and (2) and 2 JSA Regs
ESA Sch 7 paras 1(1)(a) and (2) and 2 ESA Regs
HB Sch 4 paras 1(b) and 2(b)(i) HB Regs
CTB Sch 3 paras 1(b)and 2(b)(i) CTB Regs
54 **IS** Reg 35(1)(g) IS Regs
JSA Reg 98(1)(f) JSA Regs
ESA Reg 95(1)(g) ESA Regs
HB Reg 35(1)(g) HB Regs
CTB Reg 25(1)(g) CTB Regs
55 **IS** Reg 35(1)(h) IS Regs
JSA Reg 98(1)(g) JSA Regs
ESA Reg 95(1)(i) ESA Regs
HB Reg 35(1)(h) HB Regs
CTB Reg 25(1)(h) CTB Regs
56 **IS** Reg 35(1)(h) IS Regs
HB Reg 35(1)(h) HB Regs
ESA Reg 95(1)(i) ESA Regs
CTB Reg 25(1)(h) CTB Regs

57 **IS** Sch 8 paras 1(1)(a), (2)(a)(ii), (2)(b)(ii) and 2 IS Regs
JSA Sch 6 paras 1(1)(a), (2)(a)(ii), (2)(b)(ii) and 2 JSA Regs
ESA Sch 7 paras 1(1)(a), (2)(a)(ii), (2)(b)(ii) and 2 ESA Regs
HB Sch 4 paras 1(b)(i)(bb), (b)(ii)(bb) and 2 HB Regs
CTB Sch 3 paras 1(b)(i)(bb), (b)(ii)(bb) and 2 CTB Regs
58 **IS** Regs 35(2)(b) and 40(4) and Sch 9 paras 4 and 4A IS Regs; R(IS) 8/99
JSA Regs 98(2)(c) and 103(6) and Sch 7 paras 4 and 5 JSA Regs
ESA Regs 95(2)(b) and 104(8) and Sch 8 paras 4 and 5 ESA Regs
HB Reg 35(1)(i) to (j) and Sch 4 paras 1(b) and 2(b)(i) HB Regs
CTB Reg 25(1)(i)-(j) and Sch 3 paras 1(b) and 2(b)(i) CTB Regs
59 **IS** Reg 35(3)(a)(iii) IS Regs
JSA Reg 98(2)(f) JSA Regs
ESA Reg 95(4) ESA Regs, definition of 'compensation'
HB because not listed as earnings in reg 35 HB Regs
CTB Reg 25 CTB Regs
60 Regs 98(1)(b), (3)and 104(4) and Sch 6 para 1(1) JSA Regs
61 **IS** Reg 35(1)(i) and (3) and Sch 8 paras 1(1)(a) and 2 IS Regs
JSA Reg 98(1)(b) and Sch 6 paras 1(1)(a) and 2 JSA Regs
ESA Reg 95(1)(j) and (4) and Sch 7 paras 1(1)(a) and 2 ESA Regs
HB Reg 35 HB Regs
CTB Reg 25 CTB Regs
All CJSA/82/98
62 **IS** Reg 35(1)(b) IS Regs
JSA Regs 98(2)(b) and 103(6)(a) JSA Regs
ESA Reg 95(1)(b) ESA Regs
HB Reg 35(1)(b) HB Regs
CTB Reg 25(1)(b) CTB Regs
63 **IS** Regs 35(1)(d) and 48(3) IS Regs
JSA Regs 98(1)(c) and 110(3) JSA Regs
ESA Regs 95(1)(d) and 112(3) ESA Regs
HB Regs 35(1)(d) and 46(3) HB Regs
CTB Regs 25(1)(d) and 36(3) CTB Regs
64 Sch 7 para 14 ESA Regs
65 **IS** Regs 35(2)(b) and 40(4) IS Regs
JSA Regs 98(2)(c) and 103(6) JSA Regs
ESA Regs 95(2)(b) and 104(8) ESA Regs
66 **HB** Reg 35(1)(i) to (j) and Sch 4 paras 1(c) and 2(b)(ii) HB Regs
CTB Reg 25(1)(i) to (j) and Sch 3 paras 1(c) and 2(b)(ii) CTB Regs
67 **IS** Regs 35(1)(d) and 48(3) and Sch 8 paras 1(1)(b) and 2 IS Regs
JSA Regs 98(1)(c) and 110(3) and Sch 6 paras 1(1)(b) and 2 JSA Regs
ESA Regs 95(1)(d) and 112(3) and Sch 7 paras 1(1)(b) and 2 ESA Regs
HB Regs 35(1)(d) and 46(3) and Sch 4 paras 1(c) and 2(b)(ii) HB Regs
CTB Regs 25(1)(d) and 36(3) and Sch 3 paras 1(c) and 2(b)(ii) CTB Regs
68 **IS** Sch 8 paras 1(1)(b) and 2 IS Regs
JSA Sch 6 paras 1(1)(b) and 2 JSA Regs
ESA Sch 8 paras 1(1)(b) and 2 ESA Regs
HB Sch 4 paras 1(c) and 2(b)(ii) HB Regs
CTB Sch 3 paras 1(c) and 2(b)(ii) CTB Regs
69 **IS** Reg 35 IS Regs
JSA Reg 98 JSA Regs
ESA Reg 95 ESA Regs
HB Reg 35 HB Regs
CTB Reg 25 CTB Regs
70 **IS** Reg 29(4) and (4C) IS Regs
JSA Reg 94(4) JSA Regs
ESA Reg 91(6) and (8) ESA Regs
71 R(JSA) 1/06
72 **IS** Regs 35(2)(b) and 40(4) IS Regs
JSA Regs 98(2)(c) and 103(6) JSA Regs
ESA Regs 95(2)(b) and 104(8) ESA Regs
73 **IS** Regs 37(1) and 38(3) IS Regs
JSA Regs 100(1) and 101(4) JSA Regs
ESA Regs 97(1) and 98(3) ESA Regs
HB Regs 37 and 38(3) HB Regs
CTB Regs 27 and 28(3) CTB Regs
74 **IS** Reg 2(1) IS Regs
JSA s35(1) JSA 1995
ESA Reg 2(1) ESA Regs
HB Regs 2(1) and 38(11) and (12) HB Regs
CTB Regs 2(1) and 28(11) and (12) CTB Regs
75 *AR v Bradford Metropolitan District Council* [2008] UKUT 30 (AAC), reported as R(H) 6/09
76 **IS** Reg 37(2)(a) IS Regs
JSA Reg 100(2)(a) JSA Regs
ESA Reg 97(2)(a) ESA Regs
HB Sch 5 para 42 HB Regs
CTB Sch 4 para 23 CTB Regs
77 **IS** Reg 38(3)(a), (4), (7) and (8)(a) IS Regs
JSA Reg 101(4) and (8) JSA Regs
ESA Reg 98(3)(a), (4), (7) and (8)(a) ESA Regs
HB Reg 38(3)(a), (4), (7) and (8)(a) HB Regs
CTB Reg 28(3)(a), (4), (7) and (8)(a) CTB Regs
78 R(IS) 13/91; R(FC) 1/91; CFC/26/1989

79 **IS** Reg 38(6) and (8)(b) IS Regs
JSA Reg 101(7) and (9) JSA Regs
ESA Reg 98(6) and (8)(b) ESA Regs
HB Reg 38(6) and (8)(b) HB Regs
CTB Reg 28(6) and (8)(b) CTB Regs
80 **IS** Reg 38(5) IS Regs
JSA Reg 101(6) and (8) JSA Regs
ESA Reg 98(5) ESA Regs
HB Reg 38(5) HB Regs
CTB Reg 28(5) CTB Regs
81 R(FC) 1/96
82 **IS** Reg 38(11) IS Regs
JSA Reg 101(12) JSA Regs
ESA Reg 98(11) ESA Regs
HB Reg 38(10) HB Regs
CTB Reg 28(10) CTB Regs
All R(FC) 1/93
83 CFC/836/1995
84 **IS** Regs 30 and 38(10) IS Regs; R(JSA) 1/09; *GM v SSWP (JSA)* [2010] UKUT 221 (AAC); [2011] AACR 9
JSA Regs 95 and 101(11) JSA Regs
ESA Regs 92 and 98(1) ESA Regs
85 **HB** Regs 30(1) and 33(2) HB Regs
CTB Regs 20(1) and 23(2) CTB Regs
86 **IS** Reg 30(2) IS Regs
JSA Reg 95(2) JSA Regs
ESA Reg 92(2) ESA Regs
HB Reg 37(3) and (4) HB Regs
CTB Reg 27(3) and (4) CTB Regs
87 **IS** Sch 8 para 3 IS Regs
JSA Sch 6 para 4 JSA Regs
ESA Sch 7 para 4 ESA Regs
HB Sch 4 para 2A HB Regs
CTB Sch 3 para 2A CTB Regs
88 **IS** Reg 38(9) IS Regs
JSA Reg 101(10) JSA Regs
ESA Reg 98(9) ESA Regs
HB Reg 38(9) HB Regs
CTB Reg 28(9) CTB Regs
89 Sch 7 para 7 ESA Regs
90 Sch 7 para 14 ESA Regs; para 49158 DMG
91 Sch 7 paras 5 and 5A ESA Regs
92 Sch 7 paras 6 and 7(3) ESA Regs
93 Reg 88 ESA Regs
94 **HB** Sch 4 para 4 HB Regs
CTB Sch 3 para 4 CTB Regs
95 **IS** Sch 8 para 5 IS Regs
JSA Sch 6 para 6 JSA Regs
96 **IS** Sch 8 para 4(2) IS Regs
JSA Schs 6 para 5(1) and (2) and 6A para 1(1) and (2) JSA Regs
HB Sch 4 para 3(2) HB Regs
CTB Sch 3 para 3(2) CTB Regs
97 **HB** Sch 4 para 3(2) HB Regs
CTB Sch 3 para 3(2) CTB Regs
98 **IS** Sch 8 paras 6A and 6B IS Regs
JSA Schs 6 paras 7 and 8, and 6A para 2 JSA Regs
HB Sch 4 paras 5 and 6 HB Regs
CTB Sch 3 paras 5 and 6 CTB Regs
99 **IS** Sch 8 para 7(1) IS Regs
JSA Schs 6 para 9(1) and 6A para 3 JSA Regs
HB Sch 4 para 8(1) HB Regs
CTB Sch 3 para 8(1) CTB Regs
100 **IS** Sch 8 para 8 IS Regs
JSA Schs 6 para 10 and 6A para 4 JSA Regs
HB Sch 4 para 9 HB Regs
CTB Sch 3 para 9 CTB Regs
101 **IS** Sch 8 para 7(2) IS Regs
JSA Schs 6 paras 9-10 and 6A paras 3 and 4 JSA Regs
HB Sch 4 para 8(2)(b) HB Regs
CTB Sch 3 para 8(2)(b) CTB Regs
102 **IS** Sch 8 para 4(3) IS Regs
JSA Schs 6 para 5(3) and 6A para 1(3) JSA Regs
103 **IS** Sch 8 para 4(4) and (7) IS Regs
JSA Schs 6 para 5(4) and (7) and 6A para 1(4) and (5) JSA Regs
104 **IS** Sch 8 paras 6 and 9 IS Regs
JSA Schs 6 paras 11 and 12, and 6A para 6 JSA Regs
HB Sch 4 paras 7 and 10 HB Regs
CTB Sch 3 paras 7 and 10 CTB Regs
105 **HB** Sch 4 para 10A HB Regs
CTB Sch 3 para 10A CTB Regs
106 **HB** Sch 4 para 17 HB Regs
CTB Sch 3 para 16 CTB Regs
107 **HB** Regs 27(1)(c) and 28 HB Regs; reg 30(1)(c) HB(SPC) Regs
CTB Regs 17(1)(c) and 18 CTB Regs; reg 20(1)(c) CTB(SPC) Regs
108 **HB** Reg 27(2) HB Regs; reg 30(2) HB(SPC) Regs
CTB Reg 17(2) CTB Regs; reg 20(2) CTB(SPC) Regs
109 **HB** Reg 28(6) HB Regs; reg 31(6) HB(SPC) Regs
CTB Reg 18(6) CTB Regs; reg 21(6) CTB(SPC) Regs
110 **HB** Reg 28(13) HB Regs; reg 31(13) HB(SPC) Regs
CTB Reg 18(13) CTB Regs; reg 21(13) CTB(SPC) Regs
111 **HB** Reg 28(6)-(8) HB Regs; reg 31(6)-(8) HB(SPC) Regs
CTB Reg 18(6)-(8) CTB Regs; reg 21(6)-(8) CTB(SPC) Regs

112 **HB** Reg 28(14) HB Regs; reg 31(14) HB(SPC) Regs
CTB Reg 18(14) CTB Regs; reg 21(14) CTB(SPC) Regs
113 **HB** Reg 28(2)-(4) HB Regs; reg 31(2)-(4) HB(SPC) Regs
CTB Reg 18(2)-(4) CTB Regs; reg 21(2)-(4) CTB(SPC) Regs
114 **HB** Reg 28(11), (12) and (12A) HB Regs; reg 31(11), (12) and (12A) HB(SPC) Regs
CTB Reg 18(11), (12) and (12A) CTB Regs; reg 21(11), (12) and (12A) CTB(SPC) Regs
115 R(IS) 4/05
116 **IS** Reg 40(6) IS Regs
JSA Reg 103(5B) JSA Regs
HB Reg 40(5A) HB Regs
CTB Reg 30(5A) CTB Regs
117 **IS** Reg 35(2) and Sch 9 para 4 IS Regs
JSA Sch 7 para 5 JSA Regs
ESA Reg 95(2) and Sch 8 para 4 ESA Regs
118 **HB** Reg 35(1)(i) HB Regs
CTB Reg 25(1)(i) CTB Regs
119 **HB** Sch 5 para 56 HB Regs
CTB Sch 4 para 56 CTB Regs
120 **IS** Sch 9 para 9 IS Regs
JSA Sch 7 para 10 JSA Regs
ESA Sch 8 para 11 ESA Regs
HB Sch 5 para 9 HB Regs
CTB Sch 4 para 10 CTB Regs
121 **IS** Sch 9 para 5B(2) IS Regs
JSA Sch 7 para 6B(2) JSA Regs
ESA Sch 8 para 7(2) ESA Regs
HB Sch 5 para 65 HB Regs
CTB Sch 4 para 66 CTB Regs
122 **IS** Reg 7(4)-(6) SS(WTCCTC)(CA) Regs
JSA Reg 8(3)-(5) SS(WTCCTC)(CA) Regs
123 **IS** Sch 9 para 5B(1) IS Regs
JSA Sch 7 para 6B(1) JSA Regs
ESA Sch 8 para 7(1) ESA Regs
124 **IS** Sch 9 para 9 IS Regs
JSA Sch 7 para 10 JSA Regs
ESA Sch 8 para 11 ESA Regs
HB Sch 5 paras 6 and 9 HB Regs
CTB Sch 4 paras 7 and 10 CTB Regs
125 **IS** Sch 9 paras 6 and 9 IS Regs
JSA Sch 7 paras 7 and 10 JSA Regs
ESA Sch 8 paras 8 and 11 ESA Regs
HB Sch 5 para 6 HB Regs
CTB Sch 4 para 7 CTB Regs
126 **IS** Sch 9 para 5A(1) IS Regs
JSA Sch 7 para 6A(1) JSA Regs
ESA Sch 8 para 6 ESA Regs
HB Sch 5 para 50 HB Regs
CTB Sch 4 para 51 CTB Regs
127 **IS** Sch 9 para 8 IS Regs
JSA Sch 7 para 9 JSA Regs
ESA Sch 8 para 10 ESA Regs
HB Sch 5 para 8 HB Regs
CTB Sch 4 para 9 CTB Regs
128 **IS** Sch 9 para 33 IS Regs
JSA Sch 7 para 35 JSA Regs
ESA Sch 8 para 37 ESA Regs
HB Sch 5 para 32 HB Regs
CTB Sch 4 para 33 CTB Regs
129 **IS** Sch 9 paras 7 and 8 IS Regs
JSA Sch 7 paras 8 and 9 JSA Regs
ESA Sch 8 paras 9 and 10 ESA Regs
HB Sch 5 paras 7 and 8 HB Regs
CTB Sch 4 paras 8 and 9 CTB Regs
130 **IS** Sch 9 para 31 IS Regs
JSA Sch 7 para 33 JSA Regs
ESA Sch 8 para 35 ESA Regs
HB Sch 5 para 31 HB Regs
CTB Sch 4 para 32 CTB Regs
131 **IS** Sch 10 para 18 IS Regs
JSA Sch 8 para 23 JSA Regs
ESA Sch 9 para 23 ESA Regs
HB Sch 6 para 20 HB Regs
CTB Sch 5 para 20 CTB Regs
132 **IS** Sch 9 paras 5 and 52 IS Regs
JSA Sch 7 paras 6 and 51 JSA Regs
ESA Sch 8 paras 64 and 65 ESA Regs
HB Sch 5 para 51 HB Regs
CTB Sch 4 para 37 CTB Regs
133 **IS** Sch 9 paras 54-56 IS Regs
JSA Sch 7 paras 53-55 JSA Regs
ESA Sch 8 paras 49, 51 and 52 ESA Regs
HB Sch 5 paras 53-55 HB Regs
CTB Sch 4 paras 53-55 CTB Regs
134 **IS** Sch 9 paras 5B(3) and 53 IS Regs
JSA Sch 7 paras 6B(3) and 52 JSA Regs
ESA Sch 8 paras 7(3) and 50 ESA Regs
HB Sch 5 para 52 HB Regs
CTB Sch 4 para 52 CTB Regs
135 **HB** Sch 5 para 4 HB Regs
CTB Sch 4 para 4 CTB Regs
136 **IS** Sch 9 para 40 IS Regs
JSA Sch 7 para 42 JSA Regs
ESA Sch 8 para 42 ESA Regs
HB Sch 5 para 36 HB Regs
CTB Sch 4 para 38 CTB Regs
137 **IS** Sch 9 para 46 IS Regs
JSA Sch 7 para 45 JSA Regs
ESA Sch 8 para 44 ESA Regs
HB Sch 5 para 41 HB Regs
CTB Sch 4 para 43 CTB Regs
138 **HB** Sch 5 para 16 HB Regs
CTB Sch 4 para 17 CTB Regs

139 **IS** Sch 9 para 16 IS Regs
JSA Sch 7 para 17 JSA Regs
ESA Sch 8 para 17 ESA Regs
HB Sch 5 para 15 HB Regs; Sch Part 2 HB&CTB(WPD) Regs
CTB Sch 4 para 16 CTB Regs; Sch Part 2 HB&CTB(WPD) Regs
140 **IS** Sch 9 para 36 IS Regs
ESA Sch 8 para 39 ESA Regs
JSA Sch 7 para 38 JSA Regs
HB Sch 5 para 34 HB Regs
CTB Sch 4 para 35 CTB Regs
141 ss134(8)and 139(6) SSAA 1992
HB Reg 40(3)-(4A) HB Regs
CTB Reg 30(3)-(4A) CTB Regs
142 *R v South Hams District Council ex parte Ash, The Times*, 27 May 1999
143 s74(2) SSAA 1992
144 **HB** Reg 40(6) HB Regs
CTB Reg 30(6) CTB Regs
145 CH/1450/2005
146 **HB** Reg 32 Regs; reg 32 HB(SPC) Regs
CTB Reg 22 CTB Regs; reg 22 CTB(SPC) Regs
147 CIS/1064/2004 seems to lend weight to this approach.
148 CIS/1813/2007, but note CIS/647/2007 and CH/1450/2005, which found the opposite for HB; para 25049 DMG
149 **IS** Sch 9 para 73 IS Regs
JSA Sch 7 para 70 JSA Regs
ESA Sch 8 para 60 ESA Regs
HB Sch 5 para 47A HB Regs
CTB Sch 4 para 48A CTB Regs
150 **HB** Sch 5 para 47 HB Regs
CTB Sch 4 para 48 CTB Regs
151 **IS** Sch 9 para 15(3) IS Regs
JSA Sch 7 para 15(3) JSA Regs
ESA Sch 8 para 16(2) ESA Regs
HB Sch 5 para 14(2) HB Regs
CTB Sch 4 para 15(2) CTB Regs
152 CIS/683/1993
153 **IS** Sch 9 para 25(1)(a) and (1A) IS Regs
JSA Sch 7 para 26(1)(a) and (1A) JSA Regs
ESA Sch 8 para 26(1)(a) and (2) ESA Regs
HB Sch 5 para 25(1)(a) and (2) HB Regs
CTB Sch 4 para 26(1)(a) and (2) CTB Regs
154 **IS** Sch 9 para 25(1A) IS Regs
JSA Sch 7 para 26(1A) JSA Regs
ESA Sch 8 para 26(2) ESA Regs
HB Sch 5 para 25(2) HB Regs
CTB Sch 4 para 26(2) CTB Regs
155 **IS** Reg 42(4)(b) IS Regs
JSA Reg 105(10)(b) JSA Regs
ESA Reg 107(4) ESA Regs
HB Reg 42(6)(c) HB Regs
CTB Reg 32(6)(c) CTB Regs
All para 28174 DMG
156 **IS** Sch 9 para 25(1)(a) and (2)(b) IS Regs
JSA Sch 7 para 26(1)(a) and (2)(b) JSA Regs
HB Sch 5 para 25(1)(a) and (3) HB Regs
CTB Sch 4 para 26(1)(a) and (3) CTB Regs
157 **IS** Sch 9 para 25(2)(a) IS Regs
JSA Sch 7 para 26(2)(a) JSA Regs
Both Reg 1 and Schs 1 para 23(c) and 2 para 23(c) SS(WTCCTC)(CA) Regs
158 That is, under ss23(2)(a) or 59(1)(a) CA 1989 or (in Scotland) s26 C(S)A 1995 or regs 33 or 51 Looked After Children (Scotland) Regulations 2009
159 **IS** Sch 9 para 26 IS Regs
JSA Sch 7 para 27 JSA Regs
ESA Sch 8 para 28 ESA Regs
HB Sch 5 para 26 HB Regs
CTB Sch 4 para 27 CTB Regs
160 **IS** Sch 9 para 25(1)(c) and (2) IS Regs
JSA Sch 7 para 26(1)(c) and (2) JSA Regs
ESA Sch 8 para 26(1)(b) ESA Regs
HB Sch 5 para 25(1)(ba) HB Regs
CTB Sch 4 para 26(1)(ba) CTB Regs
161 **IS** Sch 9 paras 25(1)(ba), 26((a)(iii) and 28(1)(c) IS Regs
JSA Sch 7 paras 26(1)(ba), 27(a)(iii) and 29(1)(c) JSA Regs
ESA Sch 8 paras 26(1)(b), 28(a)(iii) and 30(1)(c) ESA Regs
HB Sch 5 paras 25(1)(ba), 26(a)(iii) and 28 HB Regs
CTB Sch 4 paras 26(1)(ba), 27(a)(iii) and 29 CTB regs
162 **IS** Sch 9 para 25(1)(e) IS Regs; para 28402 DMG
JSA Sch 7 para 26(1)(e) JSA Regs; para 28402 DMG
ESA Sch 8 para 26(1)(d) ESA Regs
HB Sch 5 para 25(1)(d) HB Regs
CTB Sch 4 para 26(1)(d) CTB Regs
163 **IS** Sch 9 para 39 IS Regs
JSA Sch 7 para 41(1) JSA Regs
ESA Sch 8 para 41 ESA Regs
HB Sch 5 para 35 HB Regs
CTB Sch 4 para 36 CTB Regs
164 **IS** Reg 48(9) IS Regs
JSA Reg 110(9) JSA Regs
ESA Reg 112(7) ESA Regs
HB Reg 46(6) HB Regs
CTB Reg 36(6) CTB Regs

165 **IS** Reg 48(10)(a) IS Regs
JSA Reg 110(10) JSA Regs
166 **IS** Sch 9 para 15 IS Regs
JSA Sch 7 para 15 JSA Regs
ESA Sch 8 para 16 ESA Regs
HB Sch 5 para 14 HB Regs
CTB Sch 4 para 15 CTB Regs
167 R(H) 5/05 explains the difference between a loan and a voluntary payment.
168 **IS** Sch 9 para 15(5A) IS Regs
JSA Sch 7 para 15(5A) JSA Regs
ESA Sch 8 para 16(3) ESA Regs
HB Sch 5 para 14 HB Regs
CTB Sch 4 para 15 CTB Regs
169 *Malekout v SSWP* [2010] EWCA Civ 162; [2010] AACR 28
170 para 28102 DMG
171 **IS** Sch 9 para 19 IS Regs
JSA Sch 7 para 20 JSA Regs
ESA Sch 8 para 20 ESA Regs
HB Sch 5 para 22 HB Regs
CTB Sch 4 para 22 CTB Regs
172 **IS** Sch 9 para 18 IS Regs
JSA Sch 7 para 19 JSA Regs
ESA Sch 8 para 19 ESA Regs
HB Sch 5 para 21 HB Regs
CTB Sch 4 para 21 CTB Regs
173 **IS** Sch 9 para 20 IS Regs
JSA Sch 7 para 21 JSA Regs
ESA Sch 8 para 21 ESA Regs
HB Sch 5 para 42 HB Regs
CTB Sch 4 para 23 CTB Regs
174 **IS** Reg 2(1) IS Regs
JSA Reg 1(3) JSA Regs
ESA Reg 2(1) ESA Regs
HB Sch 5 para 42(2) HB Regs
CTB Sch 4 para 23(2) CTB Regs
IS/JSA/HB/CTB definition of 'board and lodging accommodation'
ESA definition of 'board and lodging'
175 CIS/521/2002
176 CIS/13059/1996
177 **IS** Reg 48(4) IS Regs
JSA Reg 110(4) JSA Regs
ESA Reg 112(4) ESA Regs
HB Reg 46(4) HB Regs
CTB Reg 36(4) CTB Regs
All *CAO v Palfrey and Others, The Times*, 17 February 1995; R(IS) 26/95
178 CIS/563/1991
179 **IS** Sch 9 para 22(1) IS Regs
JSA Sch 7 para 23 JSA Regs
ESA Sch 8 para 23(1) ESA Regs
HB Sch 5 para 17(1) HB Regs
CTB Sch 4 para 18(1) CTB Regs
180 **IS** Reg 48(4) IS Regs
JSA Reg 110(4) JSA Regs
ESA Reg 112(4) ESA Regs
HB Reg 46(4) HB Regs
CTB Reg 36(4) CTB Regs
181 **IS** Sch 9 para 22(1) IS Regs
JSA Sch 7 para 23(2) JSA Regs
ESA Sch 8 para 23(2) ESA Regs
HB Sch 5 para 17(1) HB Regs
CTB Sch 4 para 18(1) CTB Regs
182 CFC/13/1993
183 **IS** Sch 9 para 22(2) IS Regs
JSA Sch 7 para 23(2) and (3) JSA Regs
ESA Sch 8 para 23(2) and (3) ESA Regs
HB Sch 5 para 17(2) HB Regs
CTB Sch 4 para 18(2) CTB Regs
184 **IS** Reg 53 IS Regs
JSA Reg 116 JSA Regs
ESA Reg 118 ESA Regs
HB Reg 52 HB Regs
CTB Reg 42 CTB Regs
185 **IS/ESA** Reg 32(1B) SS(C&P) Regs
JSA Reg 24(7) JSA Regs
186 **HB** Reg 88 HB Regs
CTB Reg 74 CTB Regs
187 **IS** Reg 41(1) IS Regs
JSA Reg 104(1) JSA Regs
ESA Reg 105(1) ESA Regs
188 **HB** Reg 41(1) HB Regs
CTB Reg 31(1) CTB Regs
189 **IS** Reg 29(2) IS Regs
JSA Reg 94(2) JSA Regs
ESA Reg 91(2) ESA Regs
HB Reg 33 HB Regs
CTB Reg 23 CTB Regs
190 **IS** Reg 44(1) and (5) IS Regs
JSA Reg 106(1) and (5) JSA Regs
191 **IS** Reg 32(1) IS Regs
JSA Reg 97(1) JSA Regs
192 **IS** Reg 41(2) IS Regs
JSA Reg 104(2) JSA Regs
ESA Reg 105(2) ESA Regs
HB Reg 41(2) HB Regs
CTB Reg 31(2) CTB Regs
193 **IS** Reg 41(6) IS Regs
JSA Reg 104(5) JSA Regs
ESA Reg 105(4) ESA Regs
HB Reg 41(4) HB Regs
CTB Reg 31(4) CTB Regs
194 Regs 41(4) and 48(2) IS Regs
195 **IS** Reg 41(3) IS Regs
JSA Reg 104(3) JSA Regs
196 **IS** Reg 41(7) IS Regs
JSA Reg 104(6) JSA Regs
ESA Reg 105(5) ESA Regs
HB Reg 41(5) HB Regs
CTB Reg 31(5) CTB Regs

197 **IS** Sch 10 para 20 IS Regs
JSA Sch 8 para 25 JSA Regs
ESA Sch 9 para 25 ESA Regs
HB Sch 6 para 22 HB Regs
CTB Sch 5 para 22 CTB Regs
198 *R v SBC ex parte Singer* [1973] 1 All ER 931; *R v Oxford County Council ex parte Jack* [1984] 17 HLR 419; *R v West Dorset DC ex parte Poupard* [1988] 20 HLR 295
199 R(H) 8/08
200 *Leeves v Chief Adjudication Officer* [1998] EWCA 1706, reported as R(IS) 5/99; CIS/2287/2008
201 **IS** Reg 48(2) IS Regs
JSA Reg 110(2) JSA Regs
ESA Reg 112(2) ESA Regs
HB Reg 40(2) HB Regs
CTB Reg 31(2) CTB Regs
202 **IS** s126(5) SSCBA 1992
JSA s5(2)(c) JSA 1995
203 Regs 41(4) and 48(2) IS Regs
204 **IS** Sch 9 para 13 IS Regs
JSA Sch 7 para 14 JSA Regs
ESA Sch 8 para 15 ESA Regs
HB Sch 5 para 13 HB Regs
CTB Sch 4 para 14 CTB Regs
205 **IS** Sch 9 para 1A IS Regs
JSA Sch 7 paras A2 and A3 JSA Regs
ESA Sch 8 para 1A ESA Regs
HB Sch 5 paras A2 and A3 HB Regs
CTB Sch 4 paras A2 and A3 CTB Regs
206 Sch 8 para 15A ESA Regs
207 **IS** Sch 9 para 64 IS Regs
JSA Sch 7 para 62 JSA Regs
ESA Sch 8 para 55 ESA Regs
HB Sch 5 para 58 HB Regs
CTB Sch 4 para 58 CTB Regs
208 **HB** Reg 46(7) HB Regs
CTB Reg 36(7) CTB Regs
209 **IS** Regs 39C and 39D IS Regs
JSA Regs 102C and 102D JSA Regs
ESA Regs 102 and 103 ESA Regs
210 **IS** Reg 40(4) IS Regs
JSA Regs 98(2)(e) and 103(6) JSA Regs
ESA Reg 104(8) ESA Regs
HB Reg 40(10) HB Regs
CTB Reg 30(11) CTB Regs
All definition of 'occupational pension' in reg 2(1) of each of these Regs or reg 1 for JSA
211 **IS** Reg 41(2) and Sch 9 para 17 IS Regs
JSA Reg 104(2) and Sch 7 para 18 JSA Regs
ESA Reg 105(2) and Sch 8 para 18 ESA Regs
HB Reg 41(2) HB Regs
CTB Reg 31(2) CTB Regs
212 **IS** Sch 9 para 29 IS Regs; para 28240 DMG
JSA Sch 7 para 30 JSA Regs
ESA Sch 8 para 31 ESA Regs
213 **IS** Sch 9 para 30 IS Regs
JSA Sch 7 para 31 JSA Regs
ESA Sch 8 para 32 ESA Regs
All R(IS) 13/01
214 **HB** Sch 5 para 29 HB Regs
CTB Sch 4 para 30 CTB Regs
215 **IS** Sch 9 para 30ZA IS Regs
JSA Sch 7 para 31A JSA Regs
ESA Sch 8 para 33 ESA Regs
HB Sch 5 para 29 HB Regs
CTB Sch 4 para 30 CTB Regs
216 **IS** Sch 9 para 28 IS Regs
JSA Sch 7 para 29 JSA Regs
ESA Sch 8 para 30 ESA Regs
HB Sch 5 para 28 HB Regs
CTB Sch 4 para 29 CTB Regs
217 **IS** Sch 9 para 28(2) and (5) IS Regs
JSA Sch 7 para 29(2) and (5) JSA Regs
ESA Sch 8 para 30(2) and (3) ESA Regs
HB Sch 5 para 28A HB Regs
CTB Sch 4 para 29A CTB Regs
218 **IS** Sch 9 para 58 IS Regs
JSA Sch 7 para 56 JSA Regs
ESA Sch 8 para 53 ESA Regs
HB Sch 5 para 57 HB Regs
CTB Sch 4 para 57 CTB Regs
All *Casewell v SSWP* [2008] EWCA Civ 524, reported as R(IS) 7/08
219 **IS** Sch 9 para 27 IS Regs
JSA Sch 7 para 28 JSA Regs
ESA Sch 8 para 29 ESA Regs
HB Sch 5 para 27 HB Regs
CTB Sch 4 para 28 CTB Regs
220 **IS** Sch 9 para 76 IS Regs
JSA Sch 7 para 72 JSA Regs
ESA Sch 8 para 63 ESA Regs
HB Sch 5 para 63 HB Regs
CTB Sch 4 para 63 CTB Regs
221 **IS** Sch 9 paras 15, 30A and 66 IS Regs
JSA Sch 7 paras 15, 32 and 64 JSA Regs
ESA Sch 8 paras 16, 34 and 56 ESA Regs
222 **IS** Sch 10 para 8(b) IS Regs
JSA Sch 8 para 13(b) JSA Regs
ESA Sch 9 para 12(b) ESA Regs
HB Sch 6 para 10(b) HB Regs
CTB Sch 5 para 10(b) CTB Regs
223 **IS** Sch 9 para 11 IS Regs
JSA Sch 7 para 12 JSA Regs
ESA Sch 8 para 13 ESA Regs
HB Sch 5 para 11 HB Regs
CTB Sch 4 para 12 CTB Regs

224 **IS** Sch 9 para 2 IS Regs
JSA Sch 7 para 2 JSA Regs
ESA Sch 8 para 2 ESA Regs
HB Sch 5 para 2 HB Regs
CTB Sch 4 para 2 CTB Regs
225 **IS** Sch 9 para 21 IS Regs
JSA Sch 7 para 22 JSA Regs
ESA Sch 8 para 22 ESA Regs
HB Sch 5 para 23 HB Regs
CTB Sch 4 para 24 CTB Regs
226 para BW2 Annex B para 13 GM
227 **IS** Sch 9 para 51 IS Regs
JSA Sch 7 para 50 JSA Regs
ESA Sch 8 para 48 ESA Regs
HB Sch 5 para 49 HB Regs
CTB Sch 4 para 51 CTB Regs
228 **IS** Sch 9 para 43 IS Regs
JSA Sch 7 para 43 JSA Regs
ESA Sch 8 para 43 ESA Regs
HB Sch 5 para 39 HB Regs
CTB Sch 4 para 41 CTB Regs
229 **IS** Sch 9 para 10 IS Regs
JSA Sch 7 para 11 JSA Regs
ESA Sch 8 para 12 ESA Regs
HB Sch 5 para 10 HB Regs
CTB Sch 4 para 11 CTB Regs
230 **IS** Sch 9 para 23 IS Regs
JSA Sch 7 para 24 JSA Regs
ESA Sch 8 para 24 ESA Regs
HB Sch 5 para 24 HB Regs
CTB Sch 4 para 25 CTB Regs
231 **IS** Sch 9 para 24 IS Regs
JSA Sch 7 para 25 JSA Regs
ESA Sch 8 para 25 ESA Regs
HB Sch 5 para 33 HB Regs
CTB Sch 4 para 34 CTB Regs
232 **IS** Sch 9 para 48 IS Regs
JSA Sch 7 para 47 JSA Regs
ESA Sch 8 para 45 ESA Regs
HB Sch 5 para 44 HB Regs
CTB Sch 4 para 45 CTB Regs
233 **IS** Sch 9 para 49 IS Regs
JSA Sch 7 para 48 JSA Regs
ESA Sch 8 para 46 ESA Regs
HB Sch 5 para 45 HB Regs
CTB Sch 4 para 46 CTB Regs
234 **IS** Sch 9 para 50 IS Regs
JSA Sch 7 para 49 JSA Regs
ESA Sch 8 para 47 ESA Regs
HB Sch 5 para 46 HB Regs
CTB Sch 4 para 47 CTB Regs
235 **HB** Schs 4 para 11 and 5 paras 19 and 20 HB Regs
CTB Schs 3 para 11 and 4 paras 19 and 20 CTB Regs
236 **IS** Sch 9 para 69 IS Regs
JSA Sch 7 para 67 JSA Regs
ESA Sch 8 para 57 ESA Regs
HB Sch 5 para 59 HB Regs
CTB Sch 4 para 59 CTB Regs
237 **IS** Sch 9 para 75 IS Regs
JSA Sch 7 para 71 JSA Regs
ESA Sch 8 para 62 ESA Regs
HB Sch 5 para 62 HB Regs
CTB Sch 4 para 62 CTB Regs
238 **IS** Sch 9 para 2A IS Regs
JSA Sch 7 para 2A JSA Regs
ESA Sch 8 para 2A ESA Regs
HB Sch 5 para 2A HB Regs
CTB Sch 4 para 2A CTB Regs
239 **IS** Reg 42(1) IS Regs
JSA Reg 105(1) JSA Regs
ESA Reg 106(1) ESA Regs
HB Reg 42(1) HB Regs
CTB Reg 32(1) CTB Regs
240 paras 28608-16 DMG; see also CIS/15052/1996
241 Because reg 32(1) CTB Regs refers to HB instead of CTB
242 **IS** Reg 42(2) IS Regs
JSA Reg 105(2) JSA Regs
ESA Reg 106(2) ESA Regs
HB Reg 42(2) HB Regs
CTB Reg 32(2) CTB Regs
243 **IS** Reg 42(2ZA) and (2A) IS Regs
JSA Reg 105((2B) and (3) JSA Regs
ESA Reg 106(3) and (4) ESA Regs
244 **IS** Reg 42(2)(e)-(f) IS Regs
JSA Reg 105(2)(d) JSA Regs
ESA Reg 106(2)(e) and (f) ESA Regs
HB Reg 42(2)(f)-(g) HB Regs
CTB Reg 32(2)(f)-(g) CTB Regs
245 CIS/16271/1996
246 paras 28608-16 DMG
247 **IS** Reg 42(3) IS Regs
JSA Reg 105(6) JSA Regs
ESA Reg 107(1) ESA Regs
248 **IS** Reg 42(3A) and (3B) IS Regs
JSA Reg 105(7)(a), (8) and (9) JSA Regs
ESA Reg 107(2)(a) and (b) ESA Regs
249 **IS** Reg 42(3C) IS Regs
JSA Reg 105(7)(d) JSA Regs
ESA Reg 107(2)(c) ESA Regs
250 CIS/15052/1996, para 10
251 **IS** Reg 42(5) IS Regs
JSA Reg 105(12) JSA Regs
ESA Reg 108(1) ESA Regs
252 Reg 2 SS(PAOR) Regs
253 **IS** Reg 42(4)(a) IS Regs
JSA Reg 105(10)(a) JSA Regs
ESA Reg 107(3) ESA Regs
HB Reg 42(6)(b) HB Regs
CTB Reg 32(6)(b) CTB Regs

254 **IS** Regs 42(4)(b) and (4ZA) IS Regs
JSA Regs 105(10)(b) and (10A) JSA Regs
ESA Regs 107(4) and (5) ESA Regs
HB Regs 42(6)(c) and (7) HB Regs
CTB Regs 32(6)(c) and (7) CTB Regs
255 **IS** Reg 42(6) IS Regs; CIS/191/1991
JSA Reg 105(13) JSA Regs
ESA Reg 108(3) ESA Regs
HB Reg 42(9) HB Regs
CTB Reg 32(9) CTB Regs
256 R(SB) 13/86
257 **IS** Reg 42(6A) IS Regs
JSA Reg 105(13A) JSA Regs
ESA Reg 108(4) ESA Regs
HB Reg 42(10) HB Regs
CTB Reg 32(10) CTB Regs
258 R(SB) 13/86
259 **IS** Reg 42(6A)(a) IS Regs
JSA Reg 105(13A)(a) JSA Regs
ESA Reg 108(4)(a) ESA Regs
HB Reg 42(10)(a) HB Regs
CTB Reg 32(10)(a) CTB Regs
260 CIS/147/1993
261 *Sharrock v CAO*, 26 March 1991 (CA); CIS/93/1991; CIS/422/1992; CIS/701/1994
262 CIS/93/1991
263 **HB** Reg 31 HB Regs
CTB Reg 21 CTB Regs
264 **HB** Reg 29(1)(a) HB Regs
CTB Reg 19(1)(a) CTB Regs
265 **HB** Reg 29(1)(b) HB Regs
CTB Reg 19(1)(b) CTB Regs
Both para BW2.53 GM
266 *R v HBRB of the London Borough of Ealing ex parte Saville* [1986] 18 HLR 349
267 **HB** Reg 29(2) HB Regs
CTB Reg 19(2) CTB Regs
268 **HB** Reg 29(3) HB Regs
CTB Reg 19(3) CTB Regs
269 **IS** Reg 32(1) IS Regs
JSA Reg 97 JSA Regs
ESA Reg 94(1) ESA Regs
HB Reg 33 HB Regs
CTB Reg 23 CTB Regs
270 R(IS) 3/93
271 R(IS) 10/95
272 **IS** Reg 32(6) IS Regs
JSA Reg 97(6) JSA Regs
ESA Reg 94(6) ESA Regs
273 **IS** Reg 32(2) and (3) IS Regs
JSA Reg 97(2) and (3) JSA Regs
ESA Reg 94(2) and (3) ESA Regs
274 **IS** Reg 32(4) IS Regs
JSA Reg 97(4) JSA Regs
ESA Reg 94(4) ESA Regs
275 **IS** Reg 32(5) and Sch 8 para 10 IS Regs
JSA Reg 97(5) and Sch 6 para 13 JSA Regs
ESA Reg 94(5) and Sch 7 para 8 ESA Regs
276 **IS** Reg 29(2) IS Regs
JSA Reg 94(2) JSA Regs
ESA Reg 91(2) ESA Regs
277 **IS** Reg 29(2)(b) IS Regs
JSA Reg 94(2)(b) JSA Regs
ESA Reg 91(2)(c) ESA Regs
278 **IS** Reg 31(1)(a) IS Regs
JSA Reg 96(1)(a) JSA Regs
ESA Reg 93(1)(a) ESA Regs
279 **IS** Reg 31(1)(b) IS Regs
JSA Reg 96(1)(b) JSA Regs
ESA Reg 93(1)(b) ESA Regs
280 **IS** Reg 31(2) IS Regs
JSA Reg 96(2) JSA Regs
ESA Reg 93(2) ESA Regs
281 **IS** Reg 2(1) IS Regs
JSA Reg 1(3) JSA Regs
ESA Reg 2(1) ESA Regs
282 R(SB) 33/83
283 R(SB) 22/84; R(SB) 11/85
284 CIS/590/1993
285 *SSWP v JP (JSA)* [2010] UKUT 90 (AAC)

2. **People over pension credit age**
286 **PC** s5 SPCA 2002
HB/CTB s136(1) SSCBA 1992
287 **HB** Reg 23(3) HB(SPC) Regs
CTB Reg 13(3) CTB(SPC) Regs
288 s15 SPCA 2002; reg 15 SPC Regs
289 **HB** Regs 25 and 26 HB(SPC) Regs
CTB Regs 15 and 16 CTB(SPC) Regs
290 **HB** Reg 27(4) HB(SPC) Regs
CTB Reg 17(4) CTB(SPC) Regs
291 **HB** Reg 24 HB(SPC) Regs
292 **HB** Reg 27(4) HB(SPC) Regs
CTB Reg 17(4) CTB(SPC) Regs
293 **HB** Reg 29 HB(SPC) Regs
CTB Reg 19 CTB(SPC) Regs
294 **PC** Reg 17(10) SPC Regs
HB Reg 33(12) HB(SPC) Regs
CTB Reg 23(12) CTB(SPC) Regs
295 **HB** Reg 34 HB(SPC) Regs
CTB Reg 24 CTB(SPC) Regs
296 **PC** Regs 17(10) and 17A(4A) SPC Regs
HB Reg 36(2) and (4) HB(SPC) Regs
CTB Reg 26(2) and (4) CTB(SPC) Regs
297 **HB** Reg 36(5) HB(SPC) Regs
CTB Reg 26(5) CTB(SPC) Regs
298 **HB** Reg 34 HB(SPC) Regs
CTB Reg 24 CTB(SPC) Regs
299 *Parsons v Hogg* [1985] 2 All ER 897 (CA), appendix to R(FIS) 4/85

300 **PC** Reg 17A(2) SPC Regs
HB Reg 35(1) HB(SPC) Regs
CTB Reg 25(1) CTB(SPC) Regs
301 **PC** Reg 17A(h) and (k) SPC Regs
HB Reg 35(1)(h) and (k) HB(SPC) Regs
CTB Reg 25(1)(h) and (k) CTB(SPC) Regs
302 **PC** Reg 17A(h)-(k) SPC Regs
HB Reg 35(1)(h)-(k) HB(SPC) Regs
CTB Reg 25(1)(h)-(k) CTB(SPC) Regs
303 **PC** Reg 17A(2)(e) SPC Regs
HB Reg 35(1)(e) HB(SPC) Regs
CTB Reg 25(1)(e) CTB(SPC) Regs
304 R(IS) 9/95
305 *Minter v Kingston Upon Hull City Council and Potter v SSWP* [2011] EWCA Civ 1155
306 **PC** Reg 17A(2)(g) SPC Regs
HB Reg 35(1)(g) HB(SPC) Regs
CTB Reg 25(1)(g) CTB(SPC) Regs
307 **PC** Reg 17A(4) SPC Regs
HB Reg 35(3) HB(SPC) Regs
CTB Reg 25(3) CTB(SPC) Regs
308 **PC** Sch 6 para 6 SPC Regs
HB Sch 4 para 8 HB(SPC) Regs
CTB Sch 2 para 8 CTB(SPC) Regs
309 **PC** Reg 17A(3)(a) SPC Regs
HB Reg 35(2)(a) HB(SPC) Regs
CTB Reg 25(2)(a) CTB(SPC) Regs
310 para 86058 DMG
311 para 86054 DMG
312 **PC** Reg 17A(3)(b) SPC Regs
HB Reg 35(2)(b) HB(SPC) Regs
CTB Reg 25(2)(b) CTB(SPC) Regs
313 CIS/77/1993; CIS/89/1989
314 **PC** Sch 6 para 7 SPC Regs
HB Sch 4 para 10 HB(SPC) Regs
CTB Sch 2 para 10 CTB(SPC) Regs
315 **PC** Reg 17A(3)(c) SPC Regs
HB Reg 35(2)(c) HB(SPC) Regs
CTB Reg 25(2)(c) CTB(SPC) Regs
316 **PC** s15(1)(c) SPCA 2002
HB Reg 29(1)(c) HB(SPC) Regs
CTB Reg 19(1)(c) CTB(SPC) Regs
317 **PC** Reg 17A(3)(e) SPC Regs
HB Reg 35(2)(e) HB(SPC) Regs
CTB Reg 25(2)(e) CTB(SPC) Regs
318 **PC** Reg 17A(3)(d) SPC Regs
HB Reg 35(2)(d) HB(SPC) Regs
CTB Reg 25(2)(d) CTB(SPC) Regs
319 para 86162 DMG
320 **PC** Sch 6 para 6 SPC Regs
HB Sch 4 para 8 HB(SPC) Regs
CTB Sch 2 para 8 CTB(SPC) Regs
321 Reg 17ZA SPC Regs
322 **PC** Reg 17B(5) SPC Regs; reg 13(1) and (4) SSB(CE) Regs
HB Reg 39(1)-(3) HB(SPC) Regs
CTB Reg 29(1)-(3) CTB(SPC) Regs
323 **PC** Reg 17B(1) SPC Regs; regs 2 and 13(4) SSB(CE) Regs
HB Regs 2(1) and 39(2) and (11) HB(SPC) Regs
CTB Regs 2(1) and 29(2) and (11) CTB(SPC) Regs
324 Reg 32(3) SS(C&P) Regs
325 **PC** Reg 17B(4)(b) SPC Regs; reg 12(2) SSB(CE) Regs
HB Reg 38(2)(a) HB(SPC) Regs
CTB Reg 28(2)(a) CTB(SPC) Regs
326 **PC** Reg 17B SPC Regs; reg 11(1) SSB(CE) Regs
HB Reg 37(1) HB(SPC) Regs
CTB Reg 27(1) CTB(SPC) Regs
327 **PC** Reg 17B(5)(b) SPC Regs; reg 13(10) SSB(CE) Regs
HB Reg 39(8) HB(SPC) Regs
CTB Reg 29(8) CTB(SPC) Regs
328 **HB** Sch 4 para 2 HB(SPC) Regs
CTB Sch 2 para 2 CTB(SPC) Regs
329 Sch 6 para 1 SPC Regs
330 **PC** Sch 6 para 4(1)(a) SPC Regs
HB Sch 4 para 5(1)(a) HB(SPC) Regs
CTB Sch 2 para 5(1)(a) CTB(SPC) Regs
331 **PC** Sch 6 para 4(1)(b) SPC Regs
HB Sch 4 para 5(1)(b) HB(SPC) Regs
CTB Sch 2 para 5(1)(b) CTB(SPC) Regs
332 **HB** Sch 4 para 5(1)(c) HB(SPC) Regs
CTB Sch 2 para 5(1)(c) CTB(SPC) Regs
333 **HB** Sch 4 para 5(1)(d) HB(SPC) Regs
CTB Sch 2 para 5(1)(d) CTB(SPC) Regs
334 **PC** Sch 6 paras 3 and 4A SPC Regs
HB Sch 4 para 4 HB(SPC) Regs
CTB Sch 2 para 4 CTB(SPC) Regs
335 **PC** Sch 6 para 4(2) SPC Regs
HB Sch 4 para 5(2) HB(SPC) Regs
CTB Sch 2 para 5(2) CTB(SPC) Regs
336 Sch 6 para 4(3) SPC Regs
337 **PC** Sch 6 para 2 SPC Regs
HB Sch 4 para 3 HB(SPC) Regs
CTB Sch 2 para 3 CTB(SPC) Regs
338 **HB** Sch 4 para 5A HB(SPC) Regs
CTB Sch 2 para 5A CTB (SPC) Regs
339 **PC** Sch 6 para 5 SPC Regs
HB Sch 4 para 7 HB(SPC) Regs
CTB Sch 2 para 7 CTB(SPC) Regs
340 **HB** Sch 4 para 9 HB(SPC) Regs
CTB Sch 2 para 9 CTB(SPC) Regs
341 **HB** Reg 30(1)(c) HB(SPC) Regs
CTB Reg 20(1)(c) CTB(SPC) Regs
342 **PC** Reg 15(5)(a) and (ab) SPC Regs
HB Reg 29(1)(h) and (l) HB(SPC) Regs
CTB Reg 19(1)(h) and (l) CTB(SPC) Regs

Notes

343 **PC** Reg 15(3) SPC Regs
HB Reg 29(3) HB(SPC) Regs
CTB Reg 19(3) CTB(SPC) Regs
344 **PC** Reg 17A(2)(h)-(j) SPC Regs
HB Reg 35(1)(h)-(j) HB(SPC) Regs
CTB Reg 25(1)(h)-(j) CTB(SPC) Regs
345 **PC** s15(1)(b) SPCA 2002
HB Sch 5 para 21 HB(SPC) Regs
CTB Sch 3 para 21 CTB(SPC) Regs
346 **PC** Reg 15(2) SPC Regs
HB Reg 29(1)(k) HB(SPC) Regs
CTB Reg 19(1)(k) CTB(SPC) Regs
347 **PC** Reg 15(1) SPC Regs
HB Reg 29(1)(j) HB(SPC) Regs
CTB Reg 19(1)(j) CTB(SPC) Regs
348 **PC** Reg 15(1)(b) SPC Regs
HB Reg 29(1)(j)(ii) HB(SPC) Regs
CTB Reg 19(1)(j)(ii) CTB(SPC) Regs
349 **PC** Reg 15(1)(n) SPC Regs
HB Reg 29(1)(j)(xiii) HB(SPC) Regs
CTB Reg 19(1)(j)(xiii) CTB(SPC) Regs
350 Reg 15(1)(j) SPC Regs
351 s15 SPCA 2002
352 **PC** Reg 15(1)(c) and (e) and Sch 4 para 2 SPC Regs
HB Reg 29(1)(j)(iii) and (v) and Sch 5 para 2 HB(SPC) Regs
CTB Reg 19(1)(j)(iii) and (v) and Sch 3 para 2 CTB(SPC) Regs
353 **PC** Reg 15(1)(a) SPC Regs
HB Reg 29(1)(j)(i) HB(SPC) Regs
CTB Reg 19(1)(j)(i) CTB(SPC) Regs
354 **PC** Reg 15(1)(g) SPC Regs
HB Reg 29(1)(j)(vii) HB(SPC) Regs
CTB Reg 19(1)(j)(vii) CTB(SPC) Regs
355 **PC** Sch 4 para 3 SPC Regs
HB Sch 5 para 3 HB(SPC) Regs
CTB Sch 3 para 3 CTB(SPC) Regs
356 **PC** Reg 15(1)(k) SPC Regs
HB Reg 29(1)(j)(x) HB(SPC) Regs
CTB Reg 19(1)(j)(x) CTB(SPC) Regs
357 **PC** Reg 15(1)(i) SPC Regs
HB Reg 29(1)(j)(ix) HB(SPC) Regs
CTB Reg 19(1)(j)(ix) CTB(SPC) Regs
358 **PC** Reg 15(1)(l) and (m) SPC Regs
HB Reg 29(1)(j)(xi) and (xii) HB(SPC) Regs
CTB Reg 19(1)(j)(xi) and (xii) CTB(SPC) Regs
359 **PC** Sch 4 paras 4-6 SPC Regs
HB Sch 5 paras 4-6 HB(SPC) Regs
CTB Sch 3 paras 4-6 CTB(SPC) Regs
360 **PC** Reg 15(1)(h) SPC Regs
HB Reg 29(1)(j)(viii) HB(SPC) Regs
CTB Reg 19(1)(j)(viii) CTB(SPC) Regs
361 **HB** Sch 5 paras 7 and 8 HB(SPC) Regs
CTB Sch 3 paras 7 and 8 CTB(SPC) Regs
362 Sch 4 paras 7 and 7A SPC Regs
363 **PC** Sch 4 para 1(a) SPC Regs
HB Sch 5 para 1(a) HB(SPC) Regs; Sch Part 1 HB&CTB(WPD) Regs
CTB Sch 3 para 1(a) CTB(SPC) Regs; Sch Part 1 HB&CTB(WPD) Regs
364 **PC** Sch 4 para 1(cc) SPC Regs
HB Sch 5 para 1(d) HB(SPC) Regs
CTB Sch 3 para 1(d) CTB(SPC) Regs
365 **PC** Sch 4 para 1(b), (ba) and (c) SPC Regs
HB Sch 5 para 1(b) and (c) HB(SPC) Regs; Sch Part 1 HB&CTB(WPD) Regs
CTB Sch 3 para 1(b) and (c) CTB(SPC) Regs; Sch Part 1 HB&CTB(WPD) Regs
366 **PC** Sch 4 para 1(d) SPC Regs
HB Sch 5 para 1(e) HB(SPC) Regs
CTB Sch 3 para 1(e) CTB(SPC) Regs
367 **PC** Sch 4 para 1(e) SPC Regs
HB Sch 5 para 1(f) HB(SPC) Regs
CTB Sch 3 para 1(f) CTB(SPC) Regs
368 **PC** Sch 4 para 1(f) SPC Regs
HB Sch 5 para 1(g) HB(SPC) Regs
CTB Sch 3 para 1(g) CTB(SPC) Regs
369 ss134(8) and 139(6) SSAA 1992
370 *R v South Hams District Council ex parte Ash*, *The Times*, 27 May 1999
371 s74(2) SSAA 1992
372 **HB** Sch 5 para 20 HB(SPC) Regs
CTB Sch 3 para 20 CTB(SPC) Regs
373 **HB** Reg 29(1)(o) HB(SPC) Regs
CTB Reg 19(1)(o) CTB(SPC) Regs
374 Reg 15(5)(d) SPC Regs
375 CIS/683/1993
376 **PC** Sch 4 para 9 SPC Regs
HB Sch 5 para 10 HB(SPC) Regs
CTB Sch 3 para 10 CTB(SPC) Regs
377 **PC** Income from capital under s15(1)(i) SPCA 2002 would count but is ignored under regs 15(6) and 17(8), Sch 5 para 1A and Sch 4 para 18 SPC Regs
HB Reg 29(1)(i) HB(SPC) Regs
CTB Reg 19(1)(i) CTB(SPC) Regs
378 **PC** Sch 4 para 8 SPC Regs
HB Sch 5 para 9 HB(SPC) Regs
CTB Sch 3 para 9 CTB(SPC) Regs
379 Reg 15(6) and Sch 4 para 18 SPC Regs
380 **PC** Reg 1(2) SPC Regs
HB Reg 2(1) HB(SPC) Regs
CTB Reg 2(1) CTB(SPC) Regs
All definition of 'board and lodging accommodation'
381 CIS/521/2002
382 **PC** s15(1)(i) SPCA 2002; Sch 4 para 18 SPC Regs
HB Reg 29(1)(i) and Sch 5 para 22 HB(SPC) Regs
CTB Reg 19(1)(i) and Sch 3 para 24 CTB(SPC) Regs

383 **PC** Reg 17(8) SPC Regs
HB Regs 29(1)(i) and 44(2) HB(SPC) Regs
CTB Regs 19(1)(i) and 34(2) CTB(SPC) Regs
384 **PC** Sch 4 para 18 SPC Regs
HB Sch 5 para 22 HB(SPC) Regs
CTB Sch 3 para 24 CTB(SPC) Regs
385 **PC** s15(1)(i) SPCA 2002; reg 15(6) and Sch 4 para 18 SPC Regs
HB Reg 29(1)(i) HB(SPC) Regs
CTB Reg 19(1)(i) CTB(SPC) Regs
386 **HB** Sch 5 para 24 HB(SPC) Regs
CTB Sch 3 para 23 CTB(SPC) Regs
387 s15(2) SPCA 2002; reg 15(6) SPC Regs
388 **HB** Regs 25 and 26 HB(SPC) Regs
CTB Regs 15 and 16 CTB(SPC) Regs
389 **HB** Reg 43 HB(SPC) Regs
CTB Reg 33 CTB(SPC) Regs
390 **HB** Reg 29(2) HB(SPC) Regs
CTB Reg 19(2) CTB(SPC) Regs
391 **PC** ss15(1)(c) and 16(1) SPCA 2002; reg 16 SPC Regs
HB Reg 29(1)(c) HB(SPC) Regs
CTB Reg 19(1)(c) CTB(SPC) Regs
392 **PC** Reg 16 SPC Regs
HB Reg 29(1)(s) HB(SPC) Regs
CTB Reg 19(1)(s) CTB(SPC) Regs
393 **PC** Reg 16 SPC Regs
HB Reg 29(1)(t) HB(SPC) Regs
CTB Reg 19(1)(t) CTB(SPC) Regs
394 **PC** Reg 16 SPC Regs
HB Reg 29(1)(w) HB(SPC) Regs
CTB Reg 19(1)(w) CTB(SPC) Regs
395 para 85136 DMG
396 **PC** Reg 17(9) SPC Regs
HB Reg 33(8) HB(SPC) Regs
CTB Reg 23(8) CTB(SPC) Regs
397 **PC** Sch 4 para 15 SPC Regs
HB Sch 5 para 16 HB(SPC) Regs
CTB Sch 3 para 16 CTB(SPC) Regs
398 **PC** Sch 4 para 16 SPC Regs
HB Sch 5 para 17 HB(SPC) Regs
CTB Sch 3 para 17 CTB(SPC) Regs
399 **PC** Sch 4 para 10 SPC Regs
HB Sch 5 para 11 HB(SPC) Regs
CTB Sch 3 para 11 CTB(SPC) Regs
400 **PC** Sch 4 para 11 SPC Regs
HB Sch 5 para 12 HB(SPC) Regs
CTB Sch 3 para 12 CTB(SPC) Regs
401 **PC** Sch 4 para 11(3)(b) SPC Regs
HB Sch 5 paras 12(3) HB(SPC) Regs
CTB Sch 3 paras 12(3) CTB(SPC) Regs
402 **PC** Sch 4 para 14 SPC Regs
HB Sch 5 para 15 HB(SPC) Regs
CTB Sch 3 para 15 CTB(SPC) Regs
403 **PC** Sch 4 para 13 SPC Regs
HB Sch 5 para 14 HB(SPC) Regs
CTB Sch 3 para 14 CTB(SPC) Regs
404 **PC** Reg 18(6) SPC Regs
HB Reg 41(8) HB(SPC) Regs
CTB Reg 31(8) CTB(SPC) Regs
405 paras 28608-16 DMG; see also CIS/15052/1996
406 **PC** Reg 18(1)-(5) SPC Regs
HB Reg 41(1)-(7) HB(SPC) Regs
CTB Reg 31(1)-(7) CTB(SPC) Regs
407 para 85453 DMG
408 **PC** Reg 18(9) SPC Regs
HB Reg 41(11) HB(SPC) Regs
CTB Reg 31(11) CTB(SPC) Regs
409 **PC** Reg 24 SPC Regs
HB Reg 42 HB(SPC) Regs
CTB Reg 32 CTB(SPC) Regs
410 The rules do not include grants and loans in the definition of 'income'.
411 **HB** Schs 4 para 6 and 5 para 18 HB(SPC) Regs
CTB Schs 2 para 6 and 3 para 18 CTB(SPC) Regs
412 **HB** Sch 5 para 19 HB(SPC) Regs
CTB Sch 3 para 19 CTB(SPC) Regs
413 **PC** s15 SPCA 2002; regs 15 and 17B(4) SPC Regs
HB Regs 29 and 38(2) HB(SPC) Regs
CTB Regs 19 and 28(2) CTB(SPC) Regs
414 **PC** Regs 17A(3)(f), 18(7A) and 24(2) SPC Regs
HB Regs 35(2)(f), 41(8C) and 42(3) HB(SPC) Regs
CTB Regs 25(2)(f), 31(8C) and 32(3) CTB(SPC) Regs
415 **PC** Reg 17(2)(b)(i) SPC Regs
HB Reg 33(2)(b)(i) HB(SPC) Regs
CTB Reg 23(2)(b)(i) CTB(SPC) Regs
416 **PC** Reg 17(2)(b)(ii) SPC Regs
HB Reg 33(2)(b)(ii) HB(SPC) Regs
CTB Reg 23(2)(b)(ii) CTB(SPC) Regs
417 **PC** Reg 17(4) SPC Regs
HB Reg 33(4) HB(SPC) Regs
CTB Reg 23(4) CTB(SPC) Regs
418 **PC** Reg 17(1) SPC Regs
HB Reg 33(1) HB(SPC) Regs
CTB Reg 23(1) CTB(SPC) Regs
419 para 85030 DMG
420 Reg 1(2) SPC Regs
421 Reg 13B SPC Regs
422 Sch 3B para 2 SS&CS(DA) Regs
423 Sch 3B paras 1(b) and 3 SS&CS(DA) Regs

41

Chapter 41

Capital

This chapter covers:

This chapter explains how capital affects your entitlement to income support, income-based jobseeker's allowance (JSA), income-related employment and support allowance, pension credit, housing benefit and council tax benefit. For the capital limits and rules on social fund community care grants and loans, see Chapter 25, and for health benefits, see Chapter 13. There are no capital rules for non-means-tested benefits.

Note: unless otherwise stated, references to income-based JSA also refer to joint-claim JSA.

Key facts

- If you have more than £16,000 capital, you are not entitled to income support (IS), income-based jobseeker's allowance (JSA), income-related employment and support allowance (ESA), housing benefit (HB) or council tax benefit (CTB). There is no capital limit for pension credit (PC) and, if you get the guarantee credit of PC, there is no limit for HB and CTB.
- If you have capital above a lower limit, your benefit is affected because this is assumed to give you a certain income, called 'tariff income'.
- Getting IS, income-based JSA, income-related ESA or the guarantee credit of PC means the amount of your HB or CTB is automatically the maximum, so there is no need to work out your capital again for HB or CTB.

Future changes: April 2013 and after

Major changes are taking place that affect the benefits and tax credits system (see Chapter 2). From October 2013, a new benefit, universal credit (UC), will be introduced which will replace most means-tested benefts. UC will be means tested. You will not be able to get UC if you have capital over £16,000. Capital below £16,000 will be disregarded. The new housing element in PC will also have a capital limit. See CPAG's *Welfare Rights Bulletin* for updates.

1. People under pension credit age

This part applies to:

- income support (IS), including if you are over the qualifying age for pension credit (PC – see p509) and your partner is claiming IS for you;
- income-based jobseeker's allowance (JSA), including for men over the qualifying age for PC but under 65;
- income-related employment and support allowance (ESA), including for men over the qualifying age for PC but under 65;
- housing benefit (HB) and council tax benefit (CTB) if you and your partner (if you have one) are under the qualifying age for PC.

If you get IS, income-based JSA or income-related ESA, you do not need to work out your capital again for HB and CTB because you receive your maximum HB or CTB,[1] less any deductions for non-dependants (see pp123 and 265).

Note: in this part, whenever HB or CTB are referred to, this only applies to the rules for people under the qualifying age for PC.

The capital limits

There is a lower and upper limit:[2]

- the lower limit is £6,000;
- the upper limit is £16,000.

If you have over £16,000 you are not entitled to benefit (but for CTB, see p126 for second adult rebate). The first £6,000 is ignored and does not affect your weekly benefit at all. If you have between £6,000.01 and £16,000 you may be entitled to benefit but some income from your capital is assumed. This is 'tariff income' (see p926), which is assumed to be £1 for every £250, or part of £250, of your capital within those limits. The lower limit is £10,000 if you live in a care home (see below).

Whichever limit applies, some capital is disregarded (see p977), but you may also be treated as having some capital which you do not actually possess (see p985).

Care homes

If you live permanently in a care home (see p687):

- the lower limit is £10,000;
- the upper limit is £16,000.

Tariff income starts above £10,000.

You cannot claim **CTB** if you are permanently in a care home because you are not liable for council tax, so these limits do not apply to CTB.

For **HB**,[3] the £10,000 lower limit applies if you live permanently in one of the limited categories of care home for which HB is payable, referred to on p690. Some temporary absences (see p254) are ignored.

Whose capital counts

Your partner's capital

If you are a member of a couple (see p753), your partner's capital is added to yours.[4]

Your child's capital

Your child's capital is not added to yours and does not affect your benefit, with the following exception.[5]

For **IS and income-based JSA**, if you are still entitled to have amounts for children included in your benefit claim (ie, you have an award that includes a child and which began before 6 April 2004 and you have not yet been awarded child tax credit (CTC)), your child's capital is not added to yours. However, if your child's capital is over £3,000, you cannot get benefit included for her/him (although the family premium is still payable – see p822).[6] If that applies, any income of the child is not counted as yours either.[7]

What counts as capital

The term 'capital' is not defined. In general, it means lump-sum or one-off payments rather than a series of payments – eg, it includes savings, property and statutory redundancy payments (see p907 for how other payments when you stop work are treated).[8]

Capital payments can normally be distinguished from income because they are not payable for any specified period(s) and they are not part of a regular series of payments (although capital can be paid by instalments).[9]

However, some capital is treated as income (see p926) and some income is treated as capital (see p976).

Savings

Your savings generally count as capital – eg, cash you have at home, premium bonds, stocks and shares, unit trusts and money in a bank account or building society.

Your savings from past earnings can only be treated as capital when all relevant debts, including tax liabilities, have been deducted.[10] Savings from other past income (including benefits – see p982) are treated as capital after the period for which the income was paid has lapsed – eg, a weekly payment of child benefit will become capital a week after it is paid and a monthly occupational pension will become capital after a month.[11] There is no provision for disregarding money put aside to pay bills.[12] If you have savings just below the capital limit, it may be best to pay bills by monthly standing order or using a budget account to prevent your capital going above the limit.

Fixed-term investments

Capital held in fixed-term investments counts. However, if it is presently unobtainable it may have little or no value. If you can convert the investment into a realisable form, sell your interest, or raise a loan through a reputable bank using the asset as security, its value counts. If it takes time to produce evidence about the nature and value of the investment, you may be able to get an interim payment of IS, JSA, ESA or HB[13] (see p289), or a crisis loan from the social fund (see p564).

Property and land

Any property or land that you own counts as capital. Many types of property are disregarded (see p977). See also 'proprietary estoppel' on p974.

Loans

A loan to you usually counts as money you possess. In the following situations, you can argue that a loan should not count as your capital:

- a loan granted on condition that you only use the interest but do not touch the capital because the capital element has never been at your disposal;[14]
- money you have been paid to be used for a particular purpose on condition that the money must be returned if not used in that way;[15]
- property you have bought on behalf of someone else who is paying the mortgage;[16]
- money held in your bank account on behalf of another person, which is to be returned to her/him at a future date;[17]
- when you get the loan, you are under an immediate obligation to repay it.[18]

See p926 if you find that a loan is taken into account as income even though it is paid as a lump sum.

If you lend money to someone, it could still count as your 'notional capital' (see p985) depending on your reasons for lending it. You will normally have a legal right to be repaid and that right itself could have a capital value, although the value would normally be less than the amount loaned, and could be nil if you have no expectation of getting the money back.[19]

Trusts

A trust is a way of owning an asset. In theory, the asset is split into two notional parts: the legal title owned by the trustee and the beneficial interest owned by the beneficiary. A trustee (if not also a beneficiary) can never have use of the asset, only the responsibility of looking after it. An adult beneficiary can ask for the asset at any time. Anything can be held on trust – eg, money, houses and shares.

If you are the adult beneficiary of:

- a non-discretionary trust, you can obtain the asset from the trustee at any time. You effectively own the asset and so its market value counts as your capital;
- a discretionary trust, you cannot insist on receiving payments from it. Payments are at the discretion of the trustee within the terms of the trust. Any payments made are treated in full as income or capital depending on the nature of the payment. The trust asset itself does not normally count as your capital because you cannot demand payment (of either income or capital);[20]
- a trust which gives you the right to receive payments in the future (eg, on reaching 25) has a current capital value, unless disregarded (see p981).

If you transfer an asset into a trust in order to increase benefit entitlement, it could still count as yours under the 'notional capital' rules (see p986).

If you only have a life interest (in Scotland, a life rent) in an asset (ie, you have the right to enjoy an asset in your lifetime, but the asset will pass on to someone else when you die), the value of your right to receive income is disregarded[21] (see p981), but not the income itself if you get any.

If the beneficiary is under 18, even with a non-discretionary trust, s/he has no right to payment until s/he is 18 (or later if that is what the trust stipulates). Her/his interest may nevertheless have a current value.[22]

If you hold an asset as a trustee, it is not part of your capital. You are only a trustee either if someone gives you an asset on the express condition that you hold it for someone else (or use it for her/his benefit), or if you have expressed a clear intention that your own asset is for someone else's benefit and renounced its use for yourself.[23] Assets other than money may need to be transferred in a particular way to the trust.

It is not enough only to intend to give someone an asset. However, in the case of property and land, **'proprietary estoppel'** may apply. It could arise if you lead someone to believe that you are transferring your interest in some property to her/him, but fail to do so – eg, it is never properly conveyed. If that person acts on the belief that s/he has ownership (eg, s/he improves or repairs it, or takes on a mortgage), it would then be unfair were s/he to lose out if you insisted that you were still the owner.[24] In this case, you can argue the capital asset has been transferred to her/him and you are like a trustee. Thus, you can insist that it is not your capital asset, but the other person's, when claiming benefit.

If money (or another asset) is given to you to be used for a special purpose, it may be possible to argue that it should not count as your capital. This is called a 'purpose trust'.[25]

Payments of personal injury compensation

A payment that does not come from a trust and is made because of personal injury to you or your partner is disregarded for 52 weeks.[26] This gives you time to spend some or all of the payment, or put it into a trust, before your benefit is affected.

The 52 weeks starts from when you receive the payment. As you spend it, the disregard goes down to the level of the payment you have left. A subsequent payment for the same injury is not disregarded unless it is put into a trust.

If a trust fund has been set up out of money paid because of a personal injury to yourself or your partner, its value is ignored without time limit.[27] The 52-week disregard does not apply to lump-sum payments you then get from the trust (see below for how payments from trust funds are treated).

If the personal injury was to your partner and s/he has since died, you cannot carry over the remainder of the 52-week disregard, or if the payment is in a trust fund, it is no longer ignored.[28] If the personal injury was to a child, income or capital belonging to the child does not count as yours (with one exception), so compensation paid for the child should not affect your benefit. The exception is for IS and JSA if your claim began before 6 April 2004 and you still get amounts for a child included – ie, you have not yet transferred to CTC. In this case, the value of a personal injury trust for a child is not ignored and you should seek advice about whether it is in your interests to transfer to CTC.

For the payment to be disregarded, it is not necessary for the trust to be set up by a formal deed. The important point is that the person who is awarded the compensation should not be able to have any direct access to it.

In this context, **'personal injury'** includes not only accidental and criminal injuries, but also any disease and injury as a result of a disease. Therefore, a trust fund for someone who has had both legs amputated following meningitis and septicaemia could be disregarded.[29] In one case it also included damages from a negligence claim against solicitors who had failed to make a medical negligence claim in time.[30]

Trust funds administered by a court

The value of a trust fund is also ignored if damages are awarded for personal injury (or for children as compensation for the death of a parent) and the money paid into a special fund to be administered by a court – eg, the Court of Protection.[31] As well as ignoring the capital value, income from these funds is also ignored.[32]

Note: the notional income and capital rules (see pp932 and 985) do not apply to trusts or funds administered by a court which have been set up as a result of a personal injury.

Payments from trust funds

Payments made from a trust fund *not* set up from money for a personal injury to you or your partner:

- from a discretionary trust count as income or capital depending on the nature of the payment.[33] Capital payments are taken into account in full, but income from the trust would generally be treated as a voluntary payment and ignored;[34]

- from a non-discretionary trust count in full as capital whatever the nature of the payment.[35]

Payments made to you from a discretionary or non-discretionary trust set up from money for a personal injury to you or your partner are treated either as income or capital depending on the nature of the payment. Income is disregarded but capital payments count in full.[36]

Trustees may have a discretion to use such funds to purchase items that would normally be disregarded as capital, such as personal possessions (eg, a wheelchair, car or new furniture) or to arrange payments that would normally be disregarded as income – eg, ineligible housing costs. Similarly, they may have discretion to clear debts or pay for a holiday, leisure items or educational or medical needs. See p923 for the treatment of voluntary payments and pp923 and 934 for the treatment of payments made to third parties.

Money held by your solicitor

Money held by your solicitor normally counts as your capital. This includes compensation payments, other than for personal injury, before a trust fund has been set up.[37] A payment for personal injury to you or your partner is ignored for 52 weeks from when you receive it (see p974). If it is sent to your solicitor first, it is likely the 52 weeks will start from when the solicitor receives it. If you have had legal aid and your solicitor is holding money back while working out the statutory charge to be deducted for legal costs, it does not count as your capital, as it is not possible to identify the capital which belongs to you until any statutory charge has been quantified and deducted.[38]

Income treated as capital

Certain payments which appear to be income are, nevertheless, treated as capital. These are:[39]

- income from capital (eg, interest on a bank account) and income from property let to tenants (see p924). However, income from the first five disregarded property bullet points listed on p977, trust funds administered by a court (see p975), income from the home of a partner, former partner or relative in the circumstances described on p979, income from the home in which you normally live and income from business assets or personal injury trusts count as income not capital;
- a lump sum or 'bounty' paid to you not more than once a year as a part-time firefighter or part-time member of a lifeboat crew, or as an auxiliary coastguard or member of the Territorial Army;
- *the following payments:*
  - an advance of earnings or loan from your employer;
  - holiday pay which is not payable until more than four weeks after your employment ends or is interrupted;

– income tax refunds;
– irregular (one-off) charitable or voluntary payments.

This does not apply for IS or income-based JSA if you are involved in a trade dispute, or for IS if you are returning to work after a dispute (see p700);

- for IS, income-based JSA and income-related ESA only, a discharge grant paid on release from prison;
- for IS and income-based JSA only, arrears of residence order payments from a local authority;
- for HB and CTB only, any arrears of CTC or working tax credit (WTC);[40]
- for HB and CTB, the gross receipts from work carried out under New Enterprise Allowance.

Disregarded capital

Your home

If you own the home in which you normally live, its value is ignored.[41]

The value of your home

Your '**home**' includes any garage, garden, outbuildings and land, together with any premises that you do not occupy as your home but which it is impractical or unreasonable to sell separately – eg, croft land.[42] This disregard applies to any home in which you are treated as normally living (eg, because you are only temporarily living away from it – see p850), although if you own more than one property, only the value of the one normally occupied is disregarded under this rule.[43] Although the home may consist of more than one unit of accommodation,[44] both units will only count as the home if you (as opposed to a member of your family) normally have to occupy both units – ie, if one unit is treated as an extension or annexe of the other.[45]

Disregards

The value of the property can be disregarded even if you do not normally live in it in the following circumstances.

- **If you have left your former home following a marriage or relationship breakdown**, the value of the property is ignored for 26 weeks from the date you left. It may also be disregarded for longer if any of the steps below are taken. If it is occupied by your former partner who is a lone parent, its value is ignored as long as s/he lives there.[46]
- **If you have sought legal advice or have started legal proceedings in order to occupy property** as your home, its value is ignored for 26 weeks from the date you first took either of these steps.[47] The 26 weeks can be extended if it is reasonable to do so, if you need longer to move into the property.
- **If you are taking reasonable steps to dispose of any property**, its value is ignored for 26 weeks from the date you *first* took such steps (which may start before you claim benefit).[48] The definition of '**property**' here includes land on

its own, even if there are no buildings on it.[49] The steps you take must be 'reasonable' so, for example, advertising at an unrealistic sale price would not count. Placing the property with an estate agent or contacting a possible buyer should count,[50] as might taking ancillary proceedings to resolve financial issues in a divorce.[51] The disregard can continue beyond 26 weeks, even for years if it is reasonable – eg, if a spouse cannot sell because a court orders that the former matrimonial home should not be sold until the children are grown up. Taking a property off the market and putting it on again will not necessarily begin a new 26-week period, but it may do if the second attempt to sell is quite separate.[52]

- **If you are carrying out essential repairs or alterations** which are needed so that you can occupy a property as your home, the value of the property is ignored for 26 weeks from the date you first began to take steps to carry them out.[53] 'Steps' may include applying for planning permission, or a grant or loan to make the property habitable, employing an architect or finding someone to do the work.[54] If you cannot move into the property within that period because the work is not finished, its value can be disregarded for as long as is necessary to allow the work to be carried out.
- **If you have acquired a property for occupation** as your home but have not yet moved in, its value is ignored if you intend to live there within 26 weeks of acquiring it.[55] If you cannot move in by then, the value of the property can be ignored for as long as seems reasonable.
- **If you sell your home** and intend to use the money from the sale to buy another home, the capital is ignored for 26 weeks from the date of the sale.[56] This also applies even if you do not actually own the home but, for a price, you surrender your tenancy rights to a landlord.[57] If you need longer to complete a purchase, your capital can continue to be ignored if it is reasonable to do so. You do not have to have decided within the 26 weeks to buy a *particular* property. It is sufficient if you intend to use the proceeds to buy *some* other home within the 26-week (or extended) period,[58] although your 'intention' must involve more than a mere 'hope' or 'aspiration'.[59] There must be an element of 'certainty' which may be shown by evidence of a practical commitment to another purchase, although this need not involve any binding obligation.[60] If you intend to use only part of the proceeds of sale to buy another home, only that part is disregarded even if, for example, you have put the rest of the money aside to renovate your new home.[61]
- **If your home is damaged or you lose it altogether**, any payment in consequence of that, including compensation, which is to be used for its repair, or for acquiring another home, is ignored for 26 weeks, or longer if it is reasonable to do so.[62]
- If you have taken out a **loan or been given money for the express purpose of essential repairs and improvements** to your home, it is ignored for 26 weeks, or longer if it is reasonable to do so.[63] If it is a condition of the loan that it must

be returned if the improvements are not carried out, you should argue that it should be ignored altogether.[64]

- If you have **deposited money with a housing association as a condition of occupying your home**, this is ignored indefinitely.[65] If money which was deposited for this purpose is now to be used to buy another home, this is ignored for 26 weeks, or longer if reasonable, in order to allow you to complete the purchase.[66]
- **Grants made to local authority tenants to buy a home or do repairs/alterations** to it can be ignored for up to 26 weeks, or longer if reasonable, to allow completion of the purchase or the repairs/alterations. **Note:** the repairs or alterations must be required to make the property fit for occupation as your home.[67]

When considering whether it is reasonable to extend the period of any disregard, all the circumstances should be considered – eg, your personal circumstances, any efforts made by you to use or dispose of the home[68] and the general state of the market. In practice, periods of around 18 months are not considered unusual.

It is possible for property to be ignored under more than one of the above paragraphs in succession.[69]

Some income generated from property which is disregarded is ignored (see p925).

The home of a partner, former partner or relative

The value of a home (see p977) is also ignored if it is occupied wholly or partly as her/his home by:[70]

- *either*
  - your partner[71] (ie, your spouse/civil partner), provided you are both still treated as living in the same household (see p753) or your cohabitee, provided you are still treated as living together as husband and wife or civil partners (see p754); *or*
  - a relative of yours, or any member of your family,

  who in either case, is over the qualifying age for PC (see p509) or is incapacitated (see p979);
- *your former partner* from whom you are not estranged, divorced or out of a civil partnership. This means your husband/wife/civil partner where you are not still treated as living in the same household or your former cohabitee where you are not still treated as living together as husband and wife or civil partners;
- your former partner from whom you are estranged, divorced or out of a civil partnership, if s/he is a lone parent. If your former partner is not a lone parent, the value of the home is ignored for 26 weeks from the date you ceased to live

in the home.[72] You are 'estranged' if you are living apart because your relationship has broken down even if the separation is amicable.[73]

'Incapacitated' is not defined, but guidance suggests it refers to someone who is getting an incapacity or disability benefit, or who is sufficiently incapacitated to qualify for one of those benefits.[74] However, you should argue for a broader interpretation, if necessary.

'Relative' includes: a parent, son, daughter, step-parent/son/daughter (including the civil partner of a parent and the son or daughter of a civil partner), or parent/son/daughter-in-law (including the parent of a civil partner and the civil partner of a son or daughter), brother or sister, or a partner of any of these people, or a grandparent or grandchild, uncle, aunt, nephew or niece.[75] It also includes half-brothers and sisters and adopted children.[76]

Personal possessions

All personal possessions, including jewellery, furniture or a car, are ignored.[77] A personal possession has been defined as any physical asset not used for business purposes, other than land.[78] For example, in one case, a static caravan on a non-residential site was treated as a personal possession. However, a home that you own but do not live in would not normally be a personal possession but would count as capital – see p977. Personal possessions are not ignored if you have bought them in order to be able to claim or get more benefit. In this case, the sale value, rather than the purchase price, is counted as actual capital and the difference is treated as notional capital (see p985).[79]

Compensation for damage to, or the loss of, any personal possessions, which is to be used for their repair or replacement, is ignored for six months, or longer if reasonable.[80]

Business assets

If you are self-employed, your business assets are ignored for as long as you continue to work in that business.[81] If you cannot work because of physical or mental illness, but intend to work in the business when you are able, the disregard runs for 26 weeks from the date of claim, or for longer if reasonable in the circumstances.[82] If you stop working in the business, you are allowed a reasonable time to sell these assets without their value affecting your benefit. It is sometimes difficult to distinguish between personal and business assets. The test is whether the assets are 'part of the fund employed and risked in the business'.[83] If the assets of a business partnership (eg, plant and machinery) have been sold but the partnership has not yet been dissolved, the proceeds of sale can still count as business assets.[84] **Note:** letting a single house does not constitute a business.[85] For the treatment of business assets if you are taking part in New Enterprise Allowance, see p984.

Tax rebates

Tax rebates for the tax relief on interest on a mortgage or loan obtained for buying your home or carrying out repairs or improvements are ignored.[86] For tax refunds, see p927.

Personal pension schemes

The value of a fund held under a personal pension scheme is ignored.[87] Note that the value of the right to receive an occupational or personal pension is also ignored.

Insurance policy and annuity surrender values

The surrender value of any life assurance or endowment policy is ignored.[88] **Note:** the life assurance aspect need not be the sole or even the main aspect of the policy, although the other features of any policy may still be considered under the actual or notional income and capital rules (see pp985 and 987). The surrender value of any annuity is also ignored (see pp926 and 971),[89] as is the value of the right to receive any payment under an annuity (see below). Any actual income the surrender value generates, which is not disregarded as income, can be taken into account as income. Any payment under the annuity counts as income[90] (but see p931 for when this is ignored).

Future interest in property

A future interest in most kinds of property is ignored.[91] A **'future interest'** is one which will only revert to you, or become yours for the first time, when some future event occurs.

However, this does not include a freehold or leasehold interest in property which has been let *by you* to tenants. If you did not let the property to the tenant (eg, because the tenancy was entered into before you bought the property), your interest in the property should be ignored as a future interest in the normal way.

An example of a future interest is where someone else has a life interest in a fund and you are only entitled to it after that person has died.

The right to receive a payment in the future

If you know you will receive a payment in the future, you could sell your right to it at any time so it has a market value and therefore constitutes an actual capital resource. The value of this is ignored if it is a right to receive:

- income under a life interest or, in Scotland, a life rent;[92]
- an occupational or personal pension;[93]
- any rent if you are not the freeholder or leaseholder.[94] Any actual income which this right generates for you and which is not disregarded as income can be taken into account as income;
- any payment under an annuity (see p931).[95] Any actual income generated by this right and which is not disregarded as income can be taken into account as income;

- any earnings or income that is ignored because it is frozen abroad;[96]
- any outstanding instalments where capital is being paid by instalments;[97]
- any payment under a trust fund set up with money paid because of a personal injury to you or your partner.[98]

Benefits and other payments

Arrears of benefits and tax credits

The general rule is that arrears of specified benefits and other payments (see below) are ignored for:[99]

- 52 weeks after they are received by you; *or*
- longer in some cases of official error. If arrears are £5,000 or over and are paid to compensate for an official error (see p1130), they are ignored until the end of your (or your partner's) award. If you or your partner then reclaim the same benefit (ie, IS, income-based JSA, income-related ESA, HB or CTB), or move from IS, income-based JSA or income-related ESA to another of these three benefits, they continue to be ignored for the whole of this next and any subsequent awards if there is no gap between awards.[100]

Arrears of the following benefits are ignored under the above general rule: attendance allowance (AA), mobility supplement, disability living allowance (DLA), income-based JSA, IS, income-related ESA, HB, CTB, CTC, WTC and discretionary housing payments, or concessionary payments instead of any of these.

Also ignored for 52 weeks from the date you receive the payment are:

- arrears of certain war widows', widowers' and surviving civil partners' payments;[101]
- fares to hospital, payments for prescriptions and dental charges;[102]
- payments in lieu of milk tokens, vitamins or Healthy Start food vouchers;[103]
- payments to assist prison visits.[104]

Other payments

The following payments are ignored:

- social fund payments;[105]
- refunds of council tax liability (ignored for 52 weeks from the date you receive the arrears);[106]
- a payment to a disabled person under the Disabled Persons (Employment) Act 1944 (other than a training allowance or training bonus) to assist with employment, or a local authority payment to assist blind homeworkers;[107]
- *any payments made* to holders of the Victoria or George Cross;[108]
- any payments to compensate for the loss of entitlement to HB;[109]
- payments under the Supporting People programme for support services to help you live independently.[110]

Charitable and personal injury payments

Charitable payments

Any payment in kind by a charity is ignored.[111]

Personal injury payments

A personal injury payment can be disregarded for a period of 52 weeks after you first receive it and when it is held in a trust (see p974).

Payments from the Macfarlane Trusts and similar funds

All payments from the Macfarlane Trusts, the Fund, the Skipton Fund, the Caxton Foundation, the Eileen Trust, MFET Ltd and the London Bombings Relief Charitable Fund (see p923) are ignored.[112] Payments from these trusts and funds do not have to be declared for HB and CTB at all or, for all other benefits, if they are kept separately from your other capital and income.[113] Certain payments from money that originally came from them are also ignored. All payments from the Independent Living Funds are ignored.

Creutzfeldt-Jakob disease payments

Payments made to you or your partner out of government trust funds for people with variant Creutzfeldt-Jakob disease (CJD) are ignored for varying periods.[114]

- If you or your partner have CJD or you were the partner of someone with CJD when s/he died, the payment is ignored for life.
- If you are the parent of someone with CJD, the payment is ignored for two years or, if s/he is a dependent child (see p751), until s/he leaves full-time education or reaches 20, whichever is the latest.

You can also give money from your payment to a partner, parent or dependent child or leave them money from the payment after you die, and it is disregarded for their benefit claim for the same varying periods.

World War Two compensation payments

The way these compensation payments are treated is described on p1002. The rules are the same as for people over the qualifying age for PC.[115]

Payments by social services

The following payments for children and families from social services or social work departments are ignored:

- in England and Wales, payments under s17 of the Children Act 1989;
- in Scotland, payments under s12 of the Social Work (Scotland) Act 1968 or, for HB and CTB, under s22 of the Children (Scotland) Act 1995.[116]

Payments made by local authorities to young people who have previously been looked after by social services are also ignored. These are:

- in England and Wales, payments under ss23B, 23C or 24A of the Children Act 1989;
- in Scotland, payments under ss29 or 30 of the Children (Scotland) Act 1995.

Certain payments under s23C of the Children Act 1989 and s29 of the Children (Scotland) Act 1995) are not only ignored as the young person's capital, but also as yours if s/he passes it to you, and s/he was in your care, is still living with you and is aged 18 or over.

However, if you or your partner are involved in a trade dispute or, for IS, it is paid during the first 15 days following your return to work after the dispute, a payment counts as income for IS and income-based JSA.

Also ignored indefinitely are:

- community care or healthcare direct payments;[117]
- special guardianship allowances (payable in England and Wales);[118]
- payments under ss2, 3 or 4 of the Adoption and Children Act 2002.[119]

Employment and training programme payments

Some payments are ignored for 52 weeks from the date they are received:[120]

- payment for travel or other expenses from the Employment, Skills and Enterprise Scheme or Mandatory Work Activity scheme;
- for income-related ESA, payment for travel or other expenses for undertaking required work-related activity;
- payment under s2 of the Employment and Training Act 1973 or s2 of the Enterprise and New Towns (Scotland) Act 1990;
- capital acquired for the purpose of participating under the 'self-employment route' (eg, for income-based JSA, HB and CTB, New Enterprise Allowance).[121] Any capital acquired is ignored for as long as you are receiving assistance for taking part in the programme and, after you have ceased trading, for as long as is reasonable in order to dispose of the assets.[122]

For when employment and training programme payments are treated as income, notional income and notional capital, see pp928, 934 and 990.

Miscellaneous payments

- A sports award made by the Sports Council National Lottery funds, except for any part of the award which is made for ordinary living expenses (see p932), is disreageded for 26 weeks.[123]
- An education maintenance allowance or 16–19 Bursary Fund (paid in England) is ignored indefinitely.[124]
- For IS, income-based JSA and income-related ESA, any payments made to jurors or witnesses for attending at court are ignored, except for payments for loss of earnings or benefit.[125]

- Any payment in a currency other than sterling is taken into account after disregarding banking charges or commission payable on conversion.[126]

Capital treated as income

Some payments which appear to be capital are treated as income (see p926).

Any capital treated as income is ignored as capital.[127]

Notional capital

In certain circumstances, you are treated as having capital that you do not possess. This is called '**notional capital**'.[128] There is a similar rule for notional income (see p932). Notional capital counts in the same way as capital you do possess, except that a 'diminishing notional capital rule' (see p987) may be applied so that the value of the notional capital you are treated as having is considered to reduce over time.

You may be treated as having notional capital if:

- you deliberately deprive yourself of capital in order to claim or increase benefit (see below);
- you fail to apply for capital which is available to you (see p989);
- someone makes a payment of capital to a third party on your behalf or on behalf of a member of your family (see p990);
- you (or a member of your family) receive a payment of capital on behalf of a third party and you (or the member of your family) use or keep the capital (see p991);
- you are a sole trader or a partner in a business which is a limited company (see p991).

Note: the 'diminishing notional capital rule' (see p987) can only apply if you are treated as having notional capital under the first bullet point.

Deprivation of capital in order to claim or increase benefit

If you deliberately get rid of capital in order to claim or increase your benefit, you are treated as still possessing it.[129] The same applies if your partner got rid of capital, even if s/he did so before you became a couple.[130] You are likely to be affected by this rule if, at the time of using up your money, you knew that you might qualify for benefit (or more benefit) as a result, or qualify more quickly. It should not be used if you knew nothing about the effect of using up your capital (eg, you do not know about the capital limit for claiming benefit)[131] or if you have been using up your capital at a rate which is reasonable in the circumstances. Knowledge of capital limits can be inferred from a reasonable familiarity with the benefit system as a claimant,[132] but if you fail to make enquiries about the capital limit, this does not constitute an intention to secure benefit. This is because you cannot have the intention if you do not know about the capital rules.[133]

Why was the capital disposed of?

Even if you did know about the capital limits, it still has to be shown that you intended to obtain, retain or increase your benefit.[134] For example, in one case, a claimant faced repossession of his home and transferred ownership to his daughter (who he feared would otherwise be made homeless), despite having been warned by DWP staff that he would be disqualified from benefit if he did so. It was held that, under the circumstances, he had not disposed of the property with the intention of gaining benefit.[135] The longer the period that has elapsed since the disposal of the capital, the less likely that it was for the purpose of obtaining benefit.[136] However, no matter how long it has been since you may have disposed of an asset, there is no set 'safe' period after which it may be said that benefit can be claimed without the need for further enquiry.[137]

A person who uses up her/his resources may have more than one motive for doing so. Even if qualifying for benefit is only a subsidiary motive for your actions and the predominant motive is something quite different (eg, ensuring your home is in good condition by spending capital to do necessary repairs and improvements), you may still be counted as having deprived yourself of a resource in order to gain benefit.[138]

Examples of the kinds of expenditure that could be caught by the rule are an expensive holiday and putting money in trust.[139] (For IS, income-based JSA and income-related ESA, putting money in trust for yourself does not constitute deprivation if the capital being put in trust came from compensation paid for any personal injury.[140]) The essential test is not the kind of item that the money has been spent on but the intention behind the expenditure.

Paying off debts and bankruptcy

If you pay off a debt which you are required by law to repay immediately, you may not be counted as having deprived yourself of money in order to gain benefit.[141] It is the facts of your case that are important: if you paid off an immediately repayable debt when you thought it would not be recalled for some time, it may be that you will be held to have deprived yourself of money in order to get benefit. However, even if you pay off a debt that you are not required by law to repay immediately, the decision maker must still prove that you did so in order to get benefit – again, it is the facts of your case that are important.[142]

If you are declared bankrupt, you cannot spend your capital without court approval and cannot normally be held to have deprived yourself of it if you do. Capital you have (but cannot spend) does not count for benefit purposes from the date of the bankruptcy order.[143] However, if you deliberately go bankrupt or do not take reasonable steps to discharge the bankruptcy in order to get benefit, your capital can still count as notional capital.

Intention to get benefit

In practice, arguing successfully that you have not deprived yourself of capital to get or increase benefit may depend on whether you can show that you would have spent the money in the way you did (eg, to pay off debts or reduce your mortgage), regardless of the effect on your benefit entitlement. Where this is unclear, the burden of proving that you did it in order to get benefit lies with the decision maker.

In one case, a council house was bought at a discount using a loan from a relative secured by a trust deed over the property. In effect, the relative was being given the value of the discount. When the owner fell ill he had to be rehoused so that the relative acquired the property. A claim for HB was initially refused on the grounds that the claimant had deprived himself of the value of the property he had bought. A court later rejected this decision on the grounds that there was no evidence of intention, as it was clear that the sole purpose of the arrangement was so that the relative would be gifted the discount value.[144]

Calculation of notional capital

Notional capital is calculated in the same way as actual capital and the same disregards usually apply.[145] The only possible exception is that you may not be able to rely on the disregard for the 26 weeks (or longer) you would otherwise be allowed to take steps to dispose of a property, even if the new owner is trying to sell it. However, there is conflicting caselaw on this.[146]

Other points on deprivation of capital

If you have intentionlly deprived yourself of capital in order to get IS, it does not necessarily follow that you also intended to get HB and CTB. Similarly, deprivation to get income-based JSA cannot be treated as a deprivation for IS (although deprivation for IS can be treated as deprivation for income-based JSA, and deprivation for IS or income-based JSA can be treated as deprivation for income-related ESA). Each decision maker must reach her/his own decision on each benefit. Even decisions on deprivation for HB must be made independently of decisions for CTB.[147] This may result in different conclusions being drawn on any disposal for each benefit. Even if intent is found in two different benefits, there may be different views about the amount of capital that has been intentionally disposed of.

However, if you are held to have deprived yourself of capital for the purposes of claiming HB and CTB and you then submit a successful claim for IS, income-based JSA or income-related ESA, the local authority should put the notional capital rules for HB and CTB on hold for as long as the other benefit remains in payment.[148]

The diminishing notional capital rule

This rule provides a calculation for working out how your notional capital may be treated as *spent*.[149] It only applies if you have deliberately deprived yourself of capital.[150] The rule starts to operate from the first week or part-week after the week in which it is first decided that notional capital is to be taken into account.

- **If your benefit has been refused altogetherbecause of your notional capital**, the amount of your notional capital is reduced by the weekly total of any of the following benefits (or the additional amounts of the benefits, unless it is IS, income-based JSA or income-related ESA) to which you would have been entitled but for the notional capital rule.

IS	IS, HB and CTB
Income-based JSA	Income-based JSA, HB and CTB
Income-related ESA	Income-related ESA, HB and CTB
HB	IS, income-based JSA, income-related ESA, HB and CTB
CTB	IS, income-based JSA, income-related ESA, HB and CTB
PC	PC, HB and CTB

  In order to ensure that account is taken of as many other benefits as possible, it is important to claim any of the other benefits as soon as the notional capital rule has been applied. Any notice you are then given of the amount of benefits you have 'lost' can be supplied as evidence of the total weekly aggregate that should be taken into account.

- **If your means-tested benefit is reduced because of tariff income from your notional capital**, that capital is diminished by the amount of that reduction each week (or part-week). For example, if your notional capital is £6,750, giving a tariff income of £3 a week, the reduction is £3 a week until it reaches £6,500, when it will be £2 and so on.

  For HB and CTB, the amount of your notional capital is also reduced by the weekly aggregate of the amount of the following benefits to which you would have been entitled but for the notional capital rule.

HB	IS, income-based JSA, income-related ESA and CTB
CTB	IS, income-based JSA, income-related ESA and HB

- **The reduction in your notional capital is calculated on a weekly basis.** However, if your benefit has been stopped altogether because of the notional capital rule, the weekly amount by which your notional capital is reduced is fixed for a period of at least 26 weeks. Even if the amount of benefit to which you would have been entitled increases during this period, there will be no change in the amount by which the capital is reduced. However, guidance for HB and CTB states that in circumstances not related to capital (eg, you have married or had a baby), a new assessment can be made.[151] If you reclaim benefit 26 weeks or more after your previous claim, the aggregate of your benefit entitlement can be recalculated from the week after your second claim. If it is more than it was before, the weekly amount by which your notional capital is reduced is increased, but the weekly reduction stays the same as in the earlier assessment if the aggregate of your benefit entitlement remains unchanged or is less than it was before. You do not have to reclaim at the end of every 26-week period but there can be no recalculation unless and until you do. However, you cannot reclaim until at least 26 weeks (for IS, income-based JSA, HB and CTB) have passed since the last assessment. Once the amount of reduction has been recalculated in this way, it is again fixed for the same period.

For IS, PC, income-related ESA or income-based JSA, you should ask the DWP for a forecast of when your notional capital will reduce to a point where a further claim might succeed. The onus is on you to reclaim when it is to your advantage to do so – ie, when you may qualify for an increased assessment or because you have requalified for benefit.[152] If you delay, you may lose out, as new assessments cannot take effect before you reclaim. However, if you reclaim too soon, you have to wait until the fixed periods have lapsed before you can apply for a fresh determination.

- **If you have both actual and notional capital**, you may have to draw on your actual capital to meet your living expenses, which may include (and will probably exceed) amounts equivalent to benefits you have 'lost'. There is no reason why this should affect the amount by which your notional capital is diminished, even if this effectively results in double-counting. Any reduction in your actual capital should be taken into account in calculating any tariff income arising from your combined actual and notional capital, unless you have spent it at such a rate and in such a way that it raises questions of intent, when you may find that the notional capital rules are applied all over again.

Failing to apply for capital

The benefit rules treat you as having capital you could get if you applied for it.[153] Examples of failure to apply could be where money is held in court which would be released on application, or even an unclaimed premium bond win. You are only treated as having such capital from the date you could obtain it.

This rule does not apply if you fail to apply for:

- capital from a discretionary trust; *or*
- capital from a trust (or fund administered by a court) set up from money paid as a result of a personal injury; *or*
- capital from a personal pension scheme or, if you are under the qualifying age for PC (see p509), from an occupational pension scheme or payment from the Pension Protection Fund; *or*
- a loan which you could only get if you gave your home or other disregarded capital (see p977) as security; *or*
- for HB and CTB only, CTC or WTC.[154]

Capital payments made to a third party on your behalf

If someone pays an amount to a 'third party' (eg, a fuel company or a building society) for you or your partner (or a child for HB or CTB, or for IS or income-based JSA if children are still included in your claim – see p760), this may count as your capital.

It counts if the payment is to cover:[155]

- certain normal living expenses – ie, food, household fuel, council tax, water charges or ordinary clothing or footwear. School uniforms and sportswear are not ordinary clothing[156] nor are special shoes needed because of a disability.[157] Payments made, for instance, for food or clothes for you or your partner count as yours. However, since a child's capital is not counted as belonging to you, a payment to, for example, a clothes shop for your child should count as the child's notional capital and not yours, and, in most cases, is ignored;
- rent for which HB could be payable (less any non-dependant deductions);
- for IS, income-based JSA and income-related ESA only, housing costs which could be met by IS, income-based JSA or income-related ESA.

Payments to a third party do *not* count as yours if they are:[158]

- for other kinds of expenses (eg, a TV licence or mortgage capital repayments) unless they come from a benefit or pension (see below);
- from the Macfarlane Trusts or similar funds listed on p983;
- for participating in the Employment, Skills and Enterprise Scheme or Mandatory Work Activity.

Payments from an occupational or personal pension scheme or from the Pension Protection Fund to a third party count as yours regardless of whether or not the payments are used, or intended to be used, for ordinary living expenses.[159] They are disregarded, however, if:

- you (or your partner) are bankrupt (or the subject of a sequestration order), the payment is made to the trustee or other person acting on your creditors' behalf and you and your partner (or, for IS or income-based JSA where children are still included in your claim (see p760) and HB and CTB, your family) have no other income other than the payment made;[160] *or*
- the payments do nothing to support you financially (and therefore do not reduce or remove your need to be supported by IS, income-based JSA, income-related ESA, HB or CTB) – eg, deductions from an occupational pension made under an attachment of earnings order.[161]

For IS, income-based JSA and income-related ESA only, payments *derived* from certain social security benefits (including war disablement pensions, war widows' pensions and Armed Forces Compensation Scheme payments) and paid to a third party count:[162]

- as yours if you are entitled to the benefit; *and*
- as your partner's if s/he is entitled to the benefit; *and*
- for IS or income-based JSA where children are still included in your claim (see p760), as a member of your family's, if it is the family member who is entitled to the benefit.

For IS, income-based JSA and income-related ESA, there are different rules if you could be liable to pay maintenance (see p799).

Capital payments made to you for a third party

If you or your partner get a payment for someone not in your family (eg, a relative who does not have a bank account), it only counts as yours if it is kept or used by you.[163] For HB and CTB (and for IS or income-based JSA where children are still included in your claim – see p760), the same also applies to payments received by a member of your family for someone not in the family. Payments from the Macfarlane Trusts and similar funds listed on p983 or the Employment, Skills and Enterprise Scheme or Mandatory Work Activity scheme, do not count at all. Payments from pension schemes paid for a third party are disregarded in the same circumstances as described on p990.

Companies run by sole traders or a few partners

Normally, if you hold shares in a company, their value is taken into account. If, however, your influence in the company is such that you are like a sole trader or like a partner in a small partnership, you are treated accordingly. For IS, income-based JSA and income-related ESA, the value of your shareholding is ignored but you are treated as possessing a proportionate share of the capital of the company.[164] This does not apply while you are doing any work on the company's business,[165] even if you only do a little work for the company – eg, taking messages.[166] It has, however, been held that a 'sleeping partner' in a business managed and worked exclusively by others may not benefit from this disregard. As well as having a financial commitment to the business, you must also be involved or engaged in it in some practical sense as an earner.[167]

For HB and CTB, the local authority has a discretion whether to apply the same rules as for IS. If it decides to, it must apply them all.[168]

How capital is valued

Market value

Your capital is valued at its current market or surrender value.[169] This means the amount of money you could raise by selling it or raising a loan against it. The test is the price that would be paid by a willing buyer to a willing seller on a particular date.[170] So if an asset is difficult or impossible to realise, its market value should be very heavily discounted or even nil.[171]

In the case of a house, an estate agent's figure for a quick sale is a more appropriate valuation than the district valuer's figure for a sale within three months.[172]

It is not uncommon for an unrealistic assessment to be made of the value of your capital. You should consider challenging any decision you disagree with (see Chapters 45 and 46).

Expenses of sale

If there would be expenses involved in selling your capital, 10 per cent is deducted from its value (before any debts are deducted) for the cost of sale.[173]

Debts

Deductions are made from the 'gross' value of your capital for any debt or mortgage secured on it.[174] If a creditor (eg, a bank) holds the land certificate to your property as security for a loan and has registered notice of deposit of the land certificate at the Land Registry, this counts as a debt secured on your property.[175] If a single mortgage is secured on a house and land, and the value of the house is disregarded for benefit purposes, the whole of the mortgage can be deducted when calculating the value of the land.[176]

If you have debts which are not secured against your capital (eg, tax liabilities), these cannot be offset against the value of your capital.[177] However, once you have repaid your debts, your capital may well be reduced. You can be penalised if you deliberately get rid of capital in order to get benefit (see p985).

If you are overdrawn at the bank and have savings in another account at the same bank, the amount of the overdraft should be deducted from your savings if the terms of the accounts allow the bank to make these transfers.[178]

Capital that is jointly owned under a joint tenancy

If you jointly own any capital asset (except as a partner in a company – see p991) under a joint tenancy, you are treated as owning an equal share of the asset with all other owners.[179] For example, if two of you own the asset, you will each be treated as having a 50 per cent share of it. This rule does not apply, however, if you jointly own the capital asset as tenants in common.[180]

The key differences between a joint tenancy and a tenancy in common are that, with a joint tenancy, each co-owner owns the whole of the capital asset jointly and severally. If one of the joint tenants were to die, her/his interest in the asset would pass automatically to the other joint tenant(s). With a tenancy in common, each co-owner owns a discrete share in the asset and this share can be passed on by the deceased on her/his death to whoever s/he wishes.

If the rule does apply, the value of your deemed share should be calculated in the same way as your actual capital. However, it is only the value of your deemed share looked at in isolation which counts, and this will usually be worth less than the same proportion of the value of the whole asset. If the asset is a house, for example, the value of any deemed share may be very small or even worthless, particularly if the house is occupied and there is a possibility that the sale of the property cannot be forced. This is because even a willing buyer could not be expected to pay much for an asset s/he would have difficulty making use of or selling on to someone else.[181] Whether a sale can be forced depends on individual circumstances, and valuations should take into account legal costs and the length of time it could take to gain possession of the property.[182] A valuation should set out details of the valuer's expertise (where relevant), describe the property in sufficient detail to show that all factors relevant to its value have been taken into account, and should state any assumptions on which it is based.[183] You may need to challenge any decision (see Chapters 45 and 46) based on an inadequate valuation.

The rule applies regardless of whether the capital asset in question is in the UK or abroad (see p994 for the rules which apply to assets abroad).[184]

If the rule does not apply to you because you jointly own the capital asset under a tenancy in common, it is your actual share in the asset which has to be valued.

Treatment of assets after a relationship breakdown

When partners separate, assets such as their former home or a bank account may be in joint or sole names. For example, if a bank account is in joint names, under the rule about jointly owned capital, you and your former partner are treated as having a 50 per cent share each (see p992). On the other hand, a former partner may have a right to some, or all, of an asset that is in your sole name – eg, s/he may have deposited most of the money in a bank account in your name. If this is established, you may be treated as not entitled to the whole of the account but as holding part of it as trustee for your former partner.[185] If an asset such as the matrimonial home belongs to your former partner and you have no share in it, you cannot be treated as having any interest in it under the Matrimonial Causes Act 1973 unless you take divorce or separation proceedings and get a property order.[186]

Shares

Shares are valued at their current market value less 10 per cent for the cost of sale and after deducting any 'lien' held by brokers for sums owed for the cost of their acquisition and any commission.[187] Market value should be calculated in accordance with guidance from HM Revenue and Customs, based on the bid price plus a quarter of the difference between this and the offer price.[188] Fluctuations in price between routine reviews of your case are normally ignored. If you have a minority holding of shares in a company, the value of the shares should be based on what you could realise on them, and not by valuing the entire share capital of the company and attributing to you an amount calculated according to the proportion of shares held.[189]

Unit trusts

These are valued on the basis of the 'bid' price quoted in newspapers. No deduction is allowed for the cost of sale because this is already included in the 'bid' price.[190]

The right to receive a payment in the future

The value of any such right that is not ignored (see p981) is its market value – what a willing buyer will pay to a willing seller.[191] For something which is not yet realisable this may be very small.

Overseas assets

If you have assets abroad, and there are no exchange controls or other prohibitions that would prevent you transferring your capital to this country, your assets are valued at their current market or surrender value in that country.[192] If there are problems getting benefit because it is difficult to get the assets valued, you may be able to get an interim payment of IS, income-based JSA or income-related ESA (see p1046), or a 'payment on account' of HB (see p289).

If you are not allowed to transfer the full value of your capital to this country, you are treated as having capital equal to the amount that a willing buyer in this country would give for those assets.[193] It seems likely that the price such a person (if there is one) would be willing to pay may bear little relation to the actual value of the assets.

The same deductions of 10 per cent if there are expenses of sale, and for any debts or mortgage secured on the assets abroad, are made. If the capital is realised in a currency other than sterling, charges payable for converting the payment are also deducted.[194]

2. **People over pension credit age**

This part applies to:

- pension credit (PC);
- housing benefit (HB) and council tax benefit (CTB), if you or your partner (if you have one) are over the qualifying age for PC (see p509) and not getting income support (IS), income-based jobseeker's allowance (JSA) or income-related employment and support allowance (ESA).

This part does not apply to IS, income-based JSA or income-related ESA even if you or your partner are over the qualifying age for PC. See p971 for the rules on how your capital is treated.

Note: in this part, whenever HB or CTB are referred to, this only applies to the rules for people over PC age.

How capital is taken into account

Unlike other benefits, for **PC** there is no upper limit on your capital beyond which you are excluded from benefit. Instead, your capital above the lower limit of £10,000 is taken into account in the assessment as follows.

- Actual income from capital (eg, interest or regular payments) is only taken into account for some specific kinds of capital.[195] This includes the value of the right to receive certain kinds of payment in the future, and capital in a trust unless the trust is set up out of personal injury payments to you or your partner or is a charitable trust (see p950).
- Any other capital, unless it is specifically disregarded, is assumed to provide you with a set rate of income called 'deemed income' (see p951). Some capital can be ignored for a period of time or ignored permanently. This part explains which payments can be disregarded. If deemed income is taken into account, any actual income (eg, interest) is ignored.[196]

If any actual income is taken into account (eg, payments from a trust), the capital is ignored when working out how much deemed income to include.

For **HB and CTB**, there is an upper capital limit. If your capital is over £16,000 you are not eligible for HB or CTB unless you get PC guarantee credit. Capital between the lower limit of £10,000 and the upper limit is taken into account in the assessment in the same way as described above for PC.

The capital limits

Pension credit

For PC, the lower limit is £10,000. There is no upper capital limit.

Capital of £10,000 or less is ignored altogether. If you have capital above £10,000, you are treated as having a deemed income of £1 for every £500, or part of £500, by which your capital exceeds £10,000.[197]

Housing benefit and council tax benefit

For HB and CTB:

- the lower limit is £10,000;
- the upper limit is £16,000.[198]

If you have over £16,000, you are not entitled to benefit. The first £10,000 is ignored. If you have capital above £10,000, you are treated as having a deemed income of £1 for every £500, or part of £500, by which your capital exceeds that amount.[199]

If you get the guarantee credit of PC, all your and your partner's capital (and income) is ignored for HB and CTB.[200] This is because entitlement to PC guarantee credit acts as a passport to maximum HB and CTB. Because PC has no upper capital limit, you can have maximum HB or CTB even with capital above £16,000.

If you get the savings credit of PC but not the guarantee credit, the following applies.[201]

- Your capital for HB and CTB purposes is the capital figure worked out by the DWP for your PC. This is modified to include any capital belonging to your partner which was not taken into account in the PC calculation – eg, if a partner abroad is no longer included for PC but is for HB/CTB. If this is over £16,000, you are not entitled to HB or CTB.
- For PC savings credit during an 'assessed income period', an increase in capital does not affect your PC, but may affect HB and CTB. If capital rises above £16,000 (worked out by the local authority under HB/CTB rules), you are no longer entitled to HB or CTB. If capital goes up but is still less than £16,000, the local authority must continue to use the DWP capital figure.

Whose capital counts

Your partner's capital is added to yours.[202]

The capital of any dependent child does not affect your PC as you cannot claim for any children in your PC (see p510).

For HB and CTB, your child's capital is not added to yours and does not affect your claim.[203] You can get benefit included for your child, including premiums, even though her/his capital is over £3,000.

What counts as capital

The term 'capital' is not defined. In general, it means lump-sum or one-off payments rather than a series of payments – eg, it includes savings, investments and property.[204]

Savings

Your savings generally count as capital – eg, cash you have at home, premium bonds, stocks and shares, unit trusts and money in a bank account.

Savings from past income (including benefits – see p1001) are treated as capital after the period for which the income was paid has lapsed. There is no provision for disregarding money put aside to pay bills.[205] If you have savings just below the capital limit, it may be best to pay bills (eg, for gas, electricity and telephone) by monthly standing order or using a budget account to prevent your capital going above the limit.

Fixed-term investments

Capital held in fixed-term investments counts. However, if it is presently unobtainable, it may have little or no value. If you can convert the investment into a realisable form, sell your interest, or raise a loan through a reputable bank using the asset as security, its value counts. If it takes time to produce evidence about the nature and value of the investment, you may be able to get an interim payment of PC (see p1046), HB[206] (see p289) or a crisis loan from the social fund (see p564).

Property and land

Any property or land that you own counts as capital. Many types of property are disregarded (see p998). See also 'proprietary estoppel' on p974.

Loans

A loan to you usually counts as money you possess. However, in some limited circumstances you can argue that a loan should be disregarded (see p973). If you lend someone money, see p973.

Trusts

Money or property held in a trust for you or your partner is ignored when working out deemed income (see p995). You are not assumed to have a fixed income from the trust.[207] This applies to both discretionary and non-discretionary trusts. However, payments actually made from the trust can be taken into account. If made regularly, payments are treated as income. For discretionary trusts, regular payments are either disregarded in full or in part (see p952). If payments are not made regularly, they are taken into account as capital.

The rules are different if the trust is set up from personal injury payments (see below). Payments made from certain charitable trusts are specifically ignored (see p1002).

Payments of personal injury compensation

Any money paid because of a personal injury to you or your partner is ignored whether or not it has been placed into a trust.[208] Neither deemed income (see p995) nor actual income from the fund is taken into account. The capital value is not ignored if it was paid in respect of someone who is no longer a member of your family – eg, because s/he has died.[209]

Trust funds administered by a court

The value of a trust fund is also ignored where damages are awarded in respect of personal injury and the money paid into a special fund to be administered by a court – eg, the Court of Protection. Payments from these funds are ignored completely, both as capital and income.[210]

Disregarded capital

Some kinds of capital are ignored in the assessment of PC, HB and CTB.

Your home

If you own the home you normally live in, its value is ignored.[211] The value of your home is disregarded for the purposes of the deemed income rule (see p995).[212]

The value of your home

Your **'home'** includes any garage, garden, outbuildings and land, together with any premises that you do not occupy as your home but which it is impractical or unreasonable to sell separately – eg, croft land.[213] This disregard applies to any home in which you are treated as normally living (eg, because you are only temporarily living away from it – see p850), although if you own more than one property, only the value of the one normally occupied is disregarded under this rule.[214] Although the home may consist of more than one unit of accommodation,[215] both units only count as your home if you (as opposed to any member of your family) normally have to occupy both units – ie, if one unit is treated as an extension or annexe of the other.[216]

Disregards

The value of the property can be disregarded, even if you do not normally live in it, in the following circumstances.

- **If you have left your former home following a marriage or relationship breakdown**, the value of the property is ignored for 26 weeks from the date you left. It may also be disregarded for longer if any of the steps below are taken. If it is occupied by your former partner who is a lone parent, its value is ignored as long as s/he lives there.[217]
- **If you have sought legal advice or have started legal proceedings in order to occupy property** as your home, its value is ignored for 26 weeks from the date you first took either of these steps.[218] The 26 weeks can be extended, if it is reasonable to do so, if you need longer to move into the property.
- **If you are taking reasonable steps to dispose of any property**, its value is ignored for 26 weeks from the date you first took such steps (which may start before you claimed benefit).[219] See p977 for more details.
- **If you are carrying out essential repairs or alterations** which are needed so that you can occupy a property as your home, the value of the property is ignored for 26 weeks from the date you first began to take steps to carry them out.[220] See p978 for more details.
- **If you have acquired a property for occupation** as your home but have not yet moved in, its value is ignored if you intend to live there within 26 weeks of aquiring it.[221] If you cannot move in by then, the value of the property can be ignored for as long as seems reasonable.
- **Any amounts paid to you or deposited in your name for the sole purpose of buying a home for you to live in or carrying out essential repairs or alterations to your home or the home you intend to occupy** are ignored for

a year from the date you were paid them.[222] For PC, if there is an assessed income period (p520) that extends beyond the year's disregard, the rules provide for the disregard to last until the end of that period. However, it is not clear how this applies in all cases. For example, it would not apply if your PC entitlement or assessed income period began only after the year's disregard had expired.[223] Arguably, it should apply in other cases where there is an assessed income period.[224]

- **Any compensation paid under an insurance policy because of loss or damage to your home** is ignored for a year from the date it is paid to you.[225] For PC, if there is an assessed income period, it can be disregarded until the end of that period in the same way as explained in the bullet point above.

When considering whether to increase the period of any disregard, all the circumstances should be considered – eg, your personal circumstances, any efforts made by you to use or dispose of the home[226] and the general state of the market. In practice, periods of around 18 months are not considered unusual.

It is possible for property to be ignored under more than one of the above paragraphs in succession.[227]

The home of a former partner or relative

The value of a home (see p998) is also ignored if it is occupied wholly or partly as her/his home by:[228]

- a relative of yours or your partner (see p980 for who this includes) who is over the qualifying age for PC (see below) or is incapacitated (see below);[229]
- your former partner from whom you are not estranged, divorced or out of a civil partnership. This means your husband/wife/civil partner where you are not still treated as living in the same household or your former cohabitee where you are not still treated as living together as husband and wife or civil partners;
- your former partner from whom you are estranged, divorced or out of a civil partnership if s/he is a lone parent. If your former partner is not a lone parent, the value of the home is ignored for 26 weeks from the date you ceased to live in the home.[230]

'Incapacitated' is not defined, but guidance suggests it refers to someone who is getting an incapacity or disability benefit, or who is sufficiently incapacitated to qualify for one of those benefits.[231] However, you should argue for a broader interpretation, if necessary.

Personal possessions

All personal possessions, including items such as jewellery, furniture or a car, are ignored.[232]

Compensation paid under an insurance policy for damage to or loss of your personal possessions is ignored for a year from the date you were paid the compensation or, for PC only, until the end of the assessed income period (if there is one) if that is longer.[233]

Business assets

If you are self-employed, your business assets are ignored for as long as you continue to work in that business.[234] If you cannot work because of physical or mental illness, but intend to work in the business when you are able, the disregard operates for 26 weeks from the date of claim, or for longer if reasonable in the circumstances.[235] For more about this, see p980.

Insurance policy and annuity surrender values

The surrender value of any life assurance or endowment policy is ignored.[236] **Note:** the life assurance aspect need not be the sole or even the main aspect of the policy (although the other features of any policy may still be considered under the actual or notional income and capital rules – see p954).

The surrender value of any annuity is also ignored for the purposes of the deemed income rule (see p951). Any actual income the surrender value generates for you, and which is not disregarded as income, can be taken into account as income.[237] Any payment under the annuity counts as income (but see p952 for when this is ignored).[238]

Future interests in property

A future interest in most kinds of property is ignored.[239] A **'future interest'** is one which will only revert to you, or become yours for the first time, when some future event occurs. For more about this, see below.

The right to receive a payment in the future

If you know you will receive a payment in the future, you could sell your right to that payment at any time so it has a market value and therefore constitutes an actual capital resource. The value of this is ignored if it is a right to receive:

- income under a life interest or, in Scotland, a life rent.[240] However, it is only ignored for the purposes of the deemed income rule (see pp951 and 995);
- an occupational or personal pension;[241]
- any rent if you are not the freeholder or leaseholder.[242] However, it is only ignored for the purposes of the deemed income rule (see pp951 and 995). Any actual income which this right generates for you, and which is not disregarded as income, can be taken into account as income;
- any payment under an annuity (see p952).[243] However, that is only ignored for the purposes of the deemed income rule (see pp951 and 1003). Any actual income generated by this right, and which is not disregarded as income, can be taken into account as income.

Benefits and other payments

Arrears of specified benefits (see below) are ignored for:[244]

- one year after they are received by you; *or*
- for PC if there is an assessed income period that extends beyond the year's disregard (p520), the rules provide for the disregard to last until the end of that period. However, it is not clear how this applies in all cases. For example, it would not apply if your PC entitlement or assessed income period began only after the year's disregard had expired.[245] Arguably, it should apply in other cases where there is an assessed income period;[246] *or*
- for the remainder of the award if the payment is £5,000 or more for arrears or late payment of a specified benefit (see below), which was made to compensate for an official error, and which you received in full since becoming entitled to PC, HB or CTB. If you got the compensation before then, it is still disregarded if your current award follows immediately from a previous award of IS, income-based JSA, income-related ESA, HB or CTB (or PC for current awards of HB and CTB) in which the compensation was disregarded, or it is still being disregarded in an award of one of those benefits.

The **specified benefits** are:

- attendance allowance, disability living allowance, income-based JSA, income-related ESA, IS, PC, HB, CTB, child tax credit, constant attendance allowance and exceptionally severe disablement allowance; *and*
- for PC only, child benefit and social fund payments; *and*
- for HB and CTB only, working tax credit and discretionary housing payments; *or*
- concessionary payments (ie, compensation) made instead of any of the above benefits or payments made in lieu of any of these benefits.

Also ignored for one year (or for PC, to the end of the assessed income period – see above) from when you get the payments are:

- payments under the Supporting People programme for support services to help you live independently;
- arrears of a supplementary pension to war widows, widowers or surviving civil partners for pre-1973 service.

Ignored indefinitely are:[247]

- the lump-sum state retirement pension if you deferred your pension and chose a lump sum rather than increased income;
- community care or health direct payments.

Charitable and personal injury payments

Personal injury payments

Any money paid because of a personal injury to you or your partner is ignored (see p997).

Macfarlane Trusts and similar funds

All payments from the Macfarlane Trusts, the Skipton Fund, the Fund, the Caxton Foundation, the Eileen Trust, MFET Ltd, the London Bombings Relief Charitable Fund and the Independent Living Funds are ignored.[248] Certain payments from money that originally came from any of these trusts and funds, other than the Independent Living Funds, are also ignored.

Creutzfeldt-Jakob disease payments

Payments made out of trust funds established from funds provided by the Secretary of State for people with variant Creutzfeldt-Jakob disease (CJD) are ignored as capital for varying periods.[249] See p983 for details.

World War Two compensation payments

There are two ways in which such compensation payments may be disregarded.

- **Former prisoners of war in Japan:** £10,000 is ignored indefinitely if you received an *ex gratia* payment from the Secretary of State because the Japanese imprisoned or interned you, your partner or a deceased spouse/civil partner during World War Two.[250]
- **Victims of World War Two:** any payment (except for a war pension) made to compensate for the fact that, during World War Two, you, your partner or a deceased spouse/civil partner was a slave or forced labourer, lost property or suffered a personal injury, or was the parent of a child who died, is ignored for an indefinite period.[251]

Funeral plan payments

The value of any funeral plan contract is ignored indefinitely.[252]

A funeral plan contract is a contract under which:

- you make at least one payment to another person;
- that person undertakes to provide, or ensure you are provided with, a funeral in the UK on your death; *and*
- the sole purpose of the plan is to provide, or ensure that you are provided with, a funeral on your death.

Payments in other currencies

Any payment in a currency other than sterling is taken into account after disregarding banking charges or commission payable on conversion.[253]

Notional capital

In certain circumstances, you are treated as having capital which you do not, in fact, possess. This is called **'notional capital'**.[254] There is a similar rule for notional income (see p953). Notional capital counts in the same way as capital you actually do possess except that a 'diminishing notional capital rule' (see p987) may be applied so that the value of the notional capital you are treated as having is considered to reduce over time.

You are treated as having notional capital if you:

- deliberately deprive yourself of capital in order to claim or increase benefit (see below);
- are in a position like a sole trader or a partner in a business (see below).

Note: the 'diminishing notional capital rule' (see p987) can only apply if you are treated as having notional capital under the first bullet point.

Deprivation of capital in order to claim or increase benefit

If you deliberately get rid of capital in order to claim or increase your benefit, you are treated as still possessing it.[255] See p985 for when you are likely to be affected by this rule. It applies in the same way as for people under the qualifying age for PC except that you are not treated as having deprived yourself of capital if:[256]

- you pay off or reduce a debt which you owe; *or*
- you pay for goods or services if the purchase of those goods or services was reasonable in the circumstances of your case.

Companies run by sole traders or a few partners

Normally, if you hold shares in a company, their value is taken into account. If, however, your influence in the company is such that you are like a sole trader or partner in a small partnership, you are treated accordingly. The value of your shareholding is ignored, but you are treated as possessing a proportionate share of the capital of the company.[257] This does not apply while you are doing any work on the company's business,[258] even if you do very little work for the company – eg, taking messages.[259] It has, however, been held that a 'sleeping partner' in a business managed and worked exclusively by others may not benefit from this disregard. As well as having a financial commitment to the business, you must also be involved or engaged in it in some practical sense as an earner.[260]

How capital is valued

There are a number of issues to consider when valuing capital.

- **Market value.** Capital is valued at its current market or surrender value,[261] which could be very low if it is difficult to sell. See p991 for more information.
- **Expenses of sale.** If there would be expenses involved in selling your capital, 10 per cent is deducted from its value for the cost of sale.[262]
- **Debts.** Deductions are made from the 'gross' value of your capital for any debt or mortgage secured on it.[263] For more information, see p992.
- **Capital that is jointly owned under a joint tenancy.** If you jointly own any capital asset (except as a partner in a company, when the rules explained above apply instead) under a joint tenancy, you are treated as owning an

equal share of the asset with all other owners.[264] For example, if two of you own the asset, you are each treated as having a 50 per cent share of it. This rule does not apply, however, if you jointly own the capital asset as tenants in common.[265] For more information, see p992.

- **Treatment of assets after a relationship breakdown.** There are no specific rules about this, but there is some guidance and caselaw. For information, see p993.
- **Shares** are valued at their current market value less 10 per cent for the cost of sale and after deducting any 'lien' held by brokers for sums owed for the cost of their acquisition and any commission.[266] See p993 for more details.
- **Unit trusts** are valued on the basis of the 'bid' price quoted in newspapers. No deduction is allowed for the cost of sale because this is already included in the 'bid' price.[267]
- **The right to receive a payment in the future.** The value of any such right that is not ignored (see p1000) is its market value – what a willing buyer would pay to a willing seller.[268] For something which is not yet realisable, this may be very small.
- **Overseas assets.** If you have assets abroad, and there are no exchange controls or other prohibitions that would prevent you transferring your capital to this country, your assets are valued at their current market or surrender value in that country.[269] If you are not allowed to transfer your capital, you are treated as having capital equal to the amount that a willing buyer in this country would give (which might not be very much).[270] Deduct any debts or mortgage secured on the assets, 10 per cent for any expenses of sale and any charges for converting the payment into sterling.[271]

Notes

1. **People under pension credit age**

1 **HB** Sch 6 para 5 HB Regs
CTB Sch 5 para 5 CTB Regs
2 **IS** Regs 45 and 53 IS Regs
JSA Regs 107 and 116 JSA Regs
ESA Regs 110 and 118 ESA Regs
HB Regs 43 and 52 HB Regs
CTB Regs 33 and 42 CTB Regs
3 Reg 52(3), (4), (5), (8) and (9) HB Regs
4 **IS/HB/CTB** s136(1) SSCBA 1992
JSA s13(2) JSA 1995
ESA Sch 1 para 6(2) WRA 2007
5 **IS** Reg 23(2) IS Regs
JSA Reg 88(2) JSA Regs
ESA Reg 83(2) ESA Regs
HB Reg 25(3) HB Regs
CTB Reg 15(3) CTB Regs
6 **IS** Reg 17(1)(b) IS Regs
JSA Reg 83(b) JSA Regs
7 **IS** Reg 44(5) IS Regs
JSA Reg 106(5) JSA Regs
8 para BW1.71 GM; para 29020 DMG
9 *R v SBC ex parte Singer* [1973] 1 WLR 713
10 R(SB) 2/83; R(SB) 35/83; R(IS) 3/93
11 R(IS) 3/93 para 22
12 R(IS) 3/93
13 **IS/JSA/ESA** Reg 2 SS(PAOR) Regs
HB Reg 93(1) HB Regs
14 R(SB) 12/86
15 R(SB) 53/83; R(SB) 1/85
16 R(SB) 49/83
17 R(SB) 12/86; for how this works in Scotland, see *JK* v SSWP *(JSA)* [2010] UKUT 437 (AAC); [2011] AACR 26
18 CIS/2287/2008
19 *JC v SSWP* [2009] UKUT 22(AAC)
20 *Gartside v Inland Revenue Commissioners* [1968] 1 All ER 121; [1968] AC 553
21 **IS** Sch 10 para 13 IS Regs
JSA Sch 8 para 18 JSA Regs
ESA Sch 9 para 18 ESA Regs
HB Sch 6 para 15 HB Regs
CTB Sch 5 para 15 CTB Regs
22 *Peters v CAO,* reported as appendix to R(SB) 3/89
23 R(IS) 1/90; CSIS/639/2006
24 R(SB) 23/85; CSIS/639/2006
25 *Barclays Bank v Quistclose Investments Ltd* [1970] AC 567; R(SB) 49/83; CFC/21/1989
26 **IS** Sch 10 para 12A IS Regs
JSA Sch 8 para 17A JSA Regs
ESA Sch 9 para 17 ESA Regs
HB Sch 6 para 14A HB Regs
CTB Sch 5 para 14A CTB Regs
27 **IS** Sch 10 para 12 IS Regs
JSA Sch 8 para 18 JSA Regs
ESA Sch 9 para 16 ESA Regs
HB Sch 6 para 14 HB Regs
CTB Sch 5 para 14 CTB Regs
28 R(IS) 3/03
29 R(SB) 2/89
30 *KQ v SSWP (IS)* [2011] UKUT 102 (AAC); [2011] AACR 43
31 **IS** Sch 10 paras 44 and 45 IS Regs
JSA Sch 8 paras 42 and 43 JSA Regs
ESA Sch 9 paras 43 and 44 ESA Regs
HB Sch 6 paras 45 and 46 HB Regs
CTB Sch 5 paras 47 and 48 CTB Regs
All R(IS) 9/04; *CP v SSWP (IS)* [2011] UKUT 157 (AAC)
32 **IS** Sch 9 paras 15 and 22 IS Regs
JSA Sch 7 paras 15 and 23 JSA Regs
ESA Sch 8 paras 16 and 23 ESA Regs
HB Sch 5 paras 14 and 17 HB Regs
CTB Sch 4 paras 15 and 18 CTB Regs
33 CIS/25/1989
34 **IS** Sch 9 para 15 IS Regs
JSA Sch 7 para 15 JSA Regs
ESA Sch 8 para 16 ESA Regs
HB Sch 5 para 14 HB Regs
CTB Sch 4 para 15 CTB Regs
All para 29239 DMG
35 **IS** Reg 48(4) IS Regs
JSA Reg 110(4) JSA Regs
ESA Reg 112(4) ESA Regs
HB Reg 46(4) HB Regs
CTB Reg 36(4) CTB Regs
36 **IS** Sch 9 para 15 IS Regs
JSA Sch 7 para 15 JSA Regs
ESA Sch 8 para 16 ESA Regs
HB Sch 5 para 14 HB Regs
CTB Sch 4 para 15 CTB Regs
37 *Thomas v CAO,* appendix to R(SB) 17/87
38 CIS/984/2002
39 **IS** Reg 48 IS Regs
JSA Reg 110 JSA Regs
ESA Reg 112 ESA Regs
HB Reg 46 HB Regs
CTB Reg 36 CTB Regs

40 **HB** Reg 46(9) HB Regs
CTB Reg 36(9) CTB Regs
41 **IS** Sch 10 para 1 IS Regs
JSA Sch 8 para 1 JSA Regs
ESA Sch 9 para 1 ESA Regs
HB Sch 6 para 1 HB Regs
CTB Sch 5 para 1 CTB Regs
42 **IS** Reg 2(1) IS Regs, definition of 'dwelling occupied as the home'; R(SB) 3/84; CIS/427/1991 and R(IS) 3/96
JSA Reg 1(3) JSA Regs, definition of 'dwelling occupied as the home'
ESA Reg 2(1) ESA Regs, definition of 'dwelling occupied as the home'
HB Sch 6 para 1 HB Regs
CTB Sch 5 para 1 CTB Regs
43 **IS** Sch 10 para 1 IS Regs
JSA Sch 8 para 1 JSA Regs
ESA Sch 9 para 1 ESA Regs
HB Sch 6 para 1 HB Regs
CTB Sch 5 para 1 CTB Regs
44 R(JSA) 9/03
45 R(SB) 10/89
46 **IS** Sch 10 para 25 IS Regs
JSA Sch 8 para 5 JSA Regs
ESA Sch 9 para 5 ESA Regs
HB Sch 6 para 25 HB Regs
CTB Sch 5 para 25 CTB Regs
47 **IS** Sch 10 para 27 IS Regs
JSA Sch 8 para 7 JSA Regs
ESA Sch 9 para 7 ESA Regs
HB Sch 6 para 27 HB Regs
CTB Sch 5 para 27 CTB Regs
48 **IS** Sch 10 para 26 IS Regs
JSA Sch 8 para 6 JSA Regs
ESA Sch 9 para 6 ESA Regs
HB Sch 6 para 26 HB Regs
CTB Sch 5 para 26 CTB Regs
All CIS/6908/1995; R(IS) 4/97
49 R(IS) 4/97
50 R(SB) 32/83
51 R(IS) 5/05
52 *SP v SSWP* [2009] UKUT 255 (AAC)
53 **IS** Sch 10 para 28 IS Regs
JSA Sch 8 para 8 JSA Regs
ESA Sch 9 para 8 ESA Regs
HB Sch 6 para 28 HB Regs
CTB Sch 5 para 28 CTB Regs
54 *R v London Borough of Tower Hamlets Review Board ex parte Kapur*, 12 June 2000, unreported
55 **IS** Sch 10 para 2 IS Regs
JSA Sch 8 para 2 JSA Regs
ESA Sch 9 para 2 ESA Regs
HB Sch 6 para 2 HB Regs
CTB Sch 5 para 2 CTB Regs
56 **IS** Sch 10 para 3 IS Regs
JSA Sch 8 para 3 JSA Regs
ESA Sch 9 para 3 ESA Regs
HB Sch 6 para 3 HB Regs
CTB Sch 5 para 3 CTB Regs
57 R(IS) 6/95
58 R(IS) 7/01
59 CIS/685/1992
60 CIS/8475/1995; CIS/15984/1996
61 R(SB) 14/85
62 **IS** Sch 10 para 8(a) IS Regs
JSA Sch 8 para 13(a) JSA Regs
ESA Sch 9 para 12(a) ESA Regs
HB Sch 6 para 10(a) HB Regs
CTB Sch 5 para 10(a) CTB Regs
63 **IS** Sch 10 para 8(b) IS Regs
JSA Sch 8 para 13(b) JSA Regs
ESA Sch 9 para 12(b) ESA Regs
HB Sch 6 para 10(b) HB Regs
CTB Sch 5 para 10(b) CTB Regs
64 *Barclays Bank v Quistclose Investments Ltd* [1970] AC 567; CSB/975/1985
65 **IS** Sch 10 para 9(a) IS Regs
JSA Sch 8 para 14(a) JSA Regs
ESA Sch 9 para 13(a) ESA Regs
HB Sch 6 para 11(a) HB Regs
CTB Sch 5 para 11(a) CTB Regs
66 **IS** Sch 10 para 9(b) IS Regs
JSA Sch 8 para 14(b) JSA Regs
ESA Sch 9 para 13(b) ESA Regs
HB Sch 6 para 11(b) HB Regs
CTB Sch 5 para 11(b) CTB Regs
67 **IS** Sch 10 para 37 IS Regs
JSA Sch 8 para 9 JSA Regs
ESA Sch 9 para 36 ESA Regs
HB Sch 6 para 38 HB Regs
CTB Sch 5 para 38 CTB Regs
68 CIS/4757/2003
69 CIS/6908/1995
70 **IS** Sch 10 para 4 IS Regs
JSA Sch 8 para 4 JSA Regs
ESA Sch 9 para 4 ESA Regs
HB Sch 6 para 4 HB Regs
CTB Sch 5 para 4 CTB Regs
71 **IS** Reg 2(1) IS Regs
JSA Reg 1(3) JSA Regs
ESA Reg 2(1) ESA Regs
HB Reg 2(1) HB Regs
CTB Reg 2(1) CTB Regs
All definitions of 'partner' and 'couple'
IS/HB/CTB s137(1) SSCBA 1992
JSA s35 JSA 1995, definition of 'couple'
72 **IS** Sch 10 para 25 IS Regs
JSA Sch 8 para 5 JSA Regs
ESA Sch 9 para 5 ESA Regs
HB Sch 6 para 25 HB Regs
CTB Sch 5 para 25 CTB Regs
73 R(IS) 5/05; CH/3777/2007

74 para 29437 DMG
HB/CTB para BW1.Annex A, A1.01 GM
75 **IS** Reg 2(1) IS Regs
JSA Reg 1(3) JSA Regs
ESA Reg 2(1) ESA Regs
HB Reg 2(1) HB Regs
CTB Reg 2(1) CTB Regs
76 CSB/209/1986; CSB/1149/1986; R(SB) 22/87
77 **IS** Sch 10 para 10 IS Regs
JSA Sch 8 para 15 JSA Regs
ESA Sch 9 para 14 ESA Regs
HB Sch 6 para 12 HB Regs
CTB Sch 5 para 12 CTB Regs
78 R(H) 7/08
79 CIS/494/1990 and CIS/2208/2003
80 **IS** Sch 10 para 8(a) IS Regs
JSA Sch 8 para 13(a) JSA Regs
ESA Sch 9 para 12(a) ESA Regs
HB Sch 6 para 10(a) HB Regs
CTB Sch 5 para 10(a) CTB Regs
81 **IS** Sch 10 para 6(1) IS Regs
JSA Sch 8 para 11(1) JSA Regs
ESA Sch 9 para 10(1) ESA Regs
HB Sch 6 para 8(1) HB Regs
CTB Sch 5 para 8(1) CTB Regs
82 **IS** Sch 10 para 6(2) IS Regs
JSA Sch 8 para 11(2) JSA Regs
ESA Sch 9 para 10(2) ESA Regs
HB Sch 6 para 8(2) HB Regs
CTB Sch 5 para 8(2) CTB Regs
83 R(SB) 4/85
84 CIS/5481/1997
85 CFC/15/1990
86 **IS** Sch 10 para 19 IS Regs
JSA Sh 8 para 23 JSA Regs
ESA Sch 9 para 24 ESA Regs
HB Sch 6 para 21 HB Regs
CTB Sch 5 para 21 CTB Regs
87 **IS** Sch 10 para 23A IS Regs
JSA Sch 8 paras 28 and 29 JSA Regs
ESA Sch 9 paras 28 and 29 ESA Regs
HB Sch 6 para 32 HB Regs
CTB Sch 5 para 32 CTB Regs
88 **IS** Sch 10 para 15 IS Regs
JSA Sch 8 para 20 JSA Regs
ESA Sch 9 para 20 ESA Regs
HB Sch 6 para 17 HB Regs
CTB Sch 5 para 12 CTB Regs
All R(IS) 7/98
89 **IS** Sch 10 para 11 IS Regs
JSA Sch 8 para 16 JSA Regs
ESA Sch 9 para 15 ESA Regs
HB Sch 6 para 13 HB Regs
CTB Sch 5 para 13 CTB Regs
90 **IS** Reg 41(2) IS Regs
JSA Reg 104(2) JSA Regs
ESA Reg 105(2) ESA Regs
HB Reg 41(2) HB Regs
CTB Reg 31(2) CTB Regs
All *Beattie v Secretary of State for Social Security* [2001] EWCA Civ 498, *The Times*, 3 May 2001, upholding CIS/114/1999, reported as R(IS) 10/01
91 **IS** Sch 10 para 5 IS Regs
JSA Sch 8 para 10 JSA Regs
ESA Sch 9 para 9 ESA Regs
HB Sch 6 para 7 HB Regs
CTB Sch 5 para 7 CTB Regs
92 **IS** Sch 10 para 13 IS Regs
JSA Sch 8 para 18 JSA Regs
ESA Sch 9 para 18 ESA Regs
HB Sch 6 para 15 HB Regs
CTB Sch 5 para 15 CTB Regs
93 **IS** Sch 10 para 23 IS Regs
JSA Sch 8 para 28 JSA Regs
ESA Sch 9 para 28 ESA Regs
HB Sch 6 para 31 HB Regs
CTB Sch 5 para 31 CTB Regs
94 **IS** Sch 10 para 24 IS Regs
JSA Sch 8 para 30 JSA Regs
ESA Sch 9 para 30 ESA Regs
HB Sch 6 para 33 HB Regs
CTB Sch 5 para 33 CTB Regs
95 **IS** Sch 10 para 11 IS Regs
JSA Sch 8 para 16 JSA Regs
ESA Sch 9 para 15 ESA Regs
HB Sch 6 para 13 HB Regs
CTB Sch 5 para 13 CTB Regs
96 **IS** Sch 10 para 14 IS Regs
JSA Sch 8 para 19 JSA Regs
ESA Sch 9 para 19 ESA Regs
HB Sch 6 para 16 HB Regs
CTB Sch 5 para 16 CTB Regs
97 **IS** Sch 10 para 16 IS Regs
JSA Sch 8 para 21 JSA Regs
ESA Sch 9 para 21 ESA Regs
HB Sch 6 para 18 HB Regs
CTB Sch 5 para 18 CTB Regs
98 **IS** Sch 10 para 12 IS Regs
JSA Sch 8 para 17 JSA Regs
ESA Sch 9 para 16 ESA Regs
HB Sch 6 para 14 HB Regs
CTB Sch 5 para 14 CTB Regs
99 **IS** Sch 10 para 7 IS Regs
JSA Sch 8 para 12 JSA Regs
ESA Sch 9 para 11 ESA Regs
HB Sch 6 para 9 HB Regs
CTB Sch 5 para 9 CTB Regs

Notes

100 **IS** Sch 10 para 7(2) IS Regs
JSA Sch 8 para 12(2) JSA Regs
ESA Sch 9 para 11(2) ESA Regs
HB Sch 6 para 9(2) HB Regs
CTB Sch 5 para 9(2) CTB Regs
101 **IS** Sch 10 para 41 IS Regs
JSA Sch 8 para 39 JSA Regs
ESA Sch 9 para 40 ESA Regs
HB Sch 6 para 9 HB Regs
CTB Sch 5 para 39 CTB Regs
102 **IS** Sch 10 para 38 IS Regs
JSA Sch 8 para 36 JSA Regs
ESA Sch 9 para 37 ESA Regs
HB Sch 6 para 40 HB Regs
CTB Sch 5 para 40 CTB Regs
103 **IS** Sch 10 para 39 IS Regs
JSA Sch 8 para 37 JSA Regs
ESA Sch 9 para 38 ESA Regs
HB Sch 6 para 41 HB Regs
CTB Sch 5 para 41 CTB Regs
104 **IS** Sch 10 para 40 IS Regs
JSA Sch 8 para 38 JSA Regs
ESA Sch 9 para 39 ESA Regs
HB Sch 6 para 42 HB Regs
CTB Sch 5 para 42 CTB Regs
105 **IS** Sch 10 para 18 IS Regs
JSA Sch 8 para 23 JSA Regs
ESA Sch 9 para 23 ESA Regs
HB Sch 6 para 20 HB Regs
CTB Sch 5 para 20 CTB Regs
106 **IS** Sch 10 para 36 IS Regs
JSA Sch 8 para 35 JSA Regs
ESA Sch 9 para 35 ESA Regs
HB Sch 6 para 37 HB Regs
CTB Sch 5 para 37 CTB Regs
107 **IS** Sch 10 paras 42 and 43 IS Regs
JSA Sch 8 paras 40 and 41 JSA Regs
ESA Sch 9 paras 41 and 42 ESA Regs
HB Sch 6 paras 43 and 44 HB Regs
CTB Sch 5 paras 43 and 44 CTB Regs
108 **IS** Sch 10 para 46 IS Regs
JSA Sch 8 para 44 JSA Regs
ESA Sch 9 para 45 ESA Regs
HB Sch 6 para 47 HB Regs
CTB Sch 5 para 49 CTB Regs
109 **IS** Sch 10 para 31 IS Regs
JSA Sch 8 para 33 JSA Regs
ESA Sch 9 para 33 ESA Regs
HB Sch 6 para 30 HB Regs
CTB Sch 5 para 29 CTB Regs
110 **IS** Sch 10 para 66 IS Regs
JSA Sch 8 para 59 JSA Regs
ESA Sch 9 para 55 ESA Regs
HB Sch 6 para 57 HB Regs
CTB Sch 5 para 59 CTB Regs
111 **IS** Sch 10 para 29 IS Regs
JSA Sch 8 para 31 JSA Regs
ESA Sch 9 para 31 ESA Regs
HB Sch 6 para 34 HB Regs
CTB Sch 5 para 34 CTB Regs
112 **IS** Sch 10 para 22 IS Regs
JSA Sch 8 para 27 JSA Regs
ESA Sch 9 para 27 ESA Regs
HB Sch 6 para 24 HB Regs
CTB Sch 5 para 24 CTB Regs
113 **IS** para 29467 DMG
HB Reg 86(1) and (3) HB Regs
CTB Reg 72(1) and (3) CTB Regs
114 **IS** Sch 10 para 64 IS Regs
JSA Sch 8 para 57 JSA Regs
ESA Sch 9 para 53 ESA Regs
PC Sch 5 para 13 SPC Regs
HB Sch 6 para 55 HB Regs; Sch 6 para 14 HB(SPC) Regs
CTB Sch 5 para 57 CTB Regs; Sch 4 para 14 CTB(SPC) Regs
115 **IS** Sch 10 paras 61 and 65 IS Regs
JSA Sch 8 paras 56 and 58 JSA Regs
ESA Sch 9 paras 50 and 54 ESA Regs
HB Sch 6 paras 54 and 56 HB Regs
CTB Sch 5 paras 56 and 58 CTB Regs
116 **IS** Sch 10 para 17 IS Regs
JSA Sch 8 para 22 JSA Regs
ESA Sch 9 para 22 ESA Regs
HB Sch 6 para 19 HB Regs
CTB Sch 5 para 19 CTB Regs
117 **IS** Sch 10 para 67 IS Regs
JSA Sch 8 para 60 JSA Regs
ESA Sch 9 para 56 ESA Regs
HB Sch 6 para 58 HB Regs
CTB Sch 5 para 60 CTB Regs
118 **IS** Sch 10 para 68A IS Regs
JSA Sch 8 para 61A JSA Regs
ESA Sch 9 para 58 ESA Regs
HB Sch 6 para 60 HB Regs
CTB Sch 5 para 62 CTB Regs
119 **IS** Sch 10 para 68 IS Regs
JSA Sch 8 para 61 JSA Regs
ESA Sch 9 para 57 ESA Regs
HB Sch 6 para 59 HB Regs
CTB Sch 5 para 61 CTB Regs
120 **IS** Sch 10 paras 1A and 30 IS Regs
JSA Sch 8 paras A2, A3 and 32 JSA Regs
ESA Sch 9 paras 1A, 32 and 32A ESA Regs
HB Sch 6 paras A2, A3 and 35 HB Regs
CTB Sch 5 paras A2, A3 and 35 CTB Regs
121 **IS** Sch 10 para 52 IS Regs
JSA Sch 8 para 47 JSA Regs
ESA Sch 9 para 46 ESA Regs
HB Sch 6 para 49 HB Regs
CTB Sch 5 para 51 CTB Regs

122 **IS** Sch 10 paras 6(3) and (4) IS Regs
JSA Sch 8 paras 11(3) and (4) JSA Regs
ESA Sch 9 paras 10(3) and (4) ESA Regs
HB Sch 6 paras 8(3) and (4) HB Regs
CTB Sch 5 paras 8(3) and (4) CTB Regs
123 **IS** Sch 10 para 56 IS Regs
JSA Sch 8 para 51 JSA Regs
ESA Sch 9 para 47 ESA Regs
HB Sch 6 para 50 HB Regs
CTB Sch 5 para 52 CTB Regs
124 **IS** Sch 10 para 63 IS Regs
JSA Sch 8 para 52 JSA Regs
ESA Sch 9 para 52 ESA Regs
HB Sch 6 para 51 HB Regs
CTB Sch 5 para 53 CTB Regs
125 **IS** Sch 10 para 34 IS Regs
JSA Sch 8 para 34 JSA Regs
ESA Sch 9 para 34 ESA Regs
126 **IS** Sch 10 para 21 IS Regs
JSA Sch 8 para 26 JSA Regs
ESA Sch 9 para 26 ESA Regs
HB Sch 6 para 23 HB Regs
CTB Sch 5 para 23 CTB Regs
127 **IS** Sch 10 para 20 IS Regs
JSA Sch 8 para 25 JSA Regs
ESA Sch 9 para 25 ESA Regs
HB Sch 6 para 22 HB Regs
CTB Sch 5 para 22 CTB Regs
128 **IS** Reg 51(6) IS Regs
JSA Reg 113(6) JSA Regs
ESA Reg 115(8) ESA Regs
HB Reg 49(6) HB Regs
CTB Reg 39(6) CTB Regs
129 **IS** Reg 51(1) IS Regs
JSA Reg 113(1) JSA Regs
ESA Reg 115(1) ESA Regs
HB Reg 49(1) HB Regs
CTB Reg 39(1) CTB Regs
130 R(IS) 7/07
131 CIS/124/1990; CSB/1198/1989
132 R(SB) 9/91
133 CIS/124/1990
134 CIS/40/1989
135 CIS/621/1991. See also CJSA/3937/2002
136 CIS/264/1989
137 R(IS) 7/98, para 12(3)
138 R(SB) 38/85; R(IS) 1/91; R(H) 1/06
139 para BW1.714 GM
140 **IS** Reg 51(1)(a) IS Regs
JSA Reg 113(1)(a) JSA Regs
ESA Reg 115(1)(a) ESA Regs
141 R(SB) 12/91; *Verna Jones v SSWP* [2003] EWCA Civ 964, 10 July 2003, unreported (CA)
142 CIS/2627/1995; *Verna Jones v SSWP* [2003] EWCA Civ 964, 10 July 2003, unreported (CA)
143 *KS v SSWP* [2009] UKUT 122 (AAC); [2010] AACR3
144 *R v Caerphilly CBC HBRB ex parte Jones*, 1 February 1999, unreported
145 **IS** Reg 51(6) IS Regs
JSA Reg 113(6) JSA Regs
ESA Reg 115(8) ESA Regs
HB Reg 49(7) HB Regs
CTB Reg 39(7) CTB Regs
146 CIS/30/1993, but other commissioners have taken a different view (see for example, CIS/25/1990 and CIS/81/1991)
147 para BW1.870 GM
148 para BW1.831 GM
149 **IS** Reg 51A IS Regs
JSA Reg 114 JSA Regs
ESA Reg 116 ESA Regs
PC Reg 22 SPC Regs
HB Reg 50 HB Regs; reg 48 HB(SPC) Regs
CTB Reg 40 CTB Regs; reg 38(SPC) Regs
150 **IS** Reg 51A(1) IS Regs
JSA Reg 114(1) JSA Regs
ESA Reg 116(1) ESA Regs
PC Reg 22(1) SPC Regs
HB Reg 49(1) HB Regs; reg 48(1) HB(SPC) Regs
CTB Reg 40(1) CTB Regs; reg 38(1) CTB(SPC) Regs
151 para BW1.795 GM
152 R(IS) 9/92
153 **IS** Reg 51(2) IS Regs
JSA Reg 113(2) JSA Regs
ESA Reg 115(2) ESA Regs
HB Reg 49(2) HB Regs
CTB Reg 39(2) CTB Regs
154 **HB** Reg 49(2) HB Regs
CTB Reg 39(2) CTB Regs
155 **IS** Reg 51(3)(a)(ii) and (8) IS Regs
JSA Reg 113(3)(a)(ii) and (8) JSA Regs
ESA Regs 2(1) and 115(3)(c) ESA Regs
HB Reg 49(3)(a) and (7) HB Regs
CTB Reg 39(3)(a) and (7) CTB Regs
156 **IS** Reg 51(8) IS Regs
JSA Reg 113(8) JSA Regs
ESA Reg 2(1) ESA Regs
HB Reg 49(7)(b) HB Regs
CTB Reg 39(7) CTB Regs
157 **IS/JSA** para 29867 DMG

158 **IS** Reg 51(3)(a)(ii), (3A)(a) and (ba) IS Regs
JSA Reg 113(3)(a)(ii), (3A)(a), (bb) and (bc) JSA Regs
ESA Reg 115(3)(c), (5)(a) and (ba) ESA Regs
HB Reg 49(3)(b), (4)(a), (bb) and (bc) HB Regs
CTB Reg 39(3)(b), (4)(a), (bb) and (bc) CTB Regs
159 **IS** Reg 51(3)(a)(ia) IS Regs
JSA Reg 113(3)(a)(ia) JSA Regs
ESA Reg 115(3)(b) ESA Regs
HB Reg 49(3)(a) HB Regs
CTB Reg 39(3)(a) CTB Regs
160 **IS** Reg 51(3A)(c) IS Regs
JSA Reg 113(3A)(c) JSA Regs
ESA Reg 115(5)(c) ESA Regs
HB Reg 49(4)(c) HB Regs
CTB Reg 39(4)(c) CTB Regs
161 R(IS) 4/01
162 **IS** Reg 51(3)(a)(i) IS Regs
JSA Reg 113(3)(a)(i) JSA Regs
ESA Reg 115(3)(a) ESA Regs
163 **IS** Reg 51(3)(b) IS Regs
JSA Reg 113(3)(b) JSA Regs
ESA Reg 115(4) ESA Regs
HB Reg 49(3)(c) HB Regs
CTB Reg 39(3)(c) CTB Regs
164 **IS** Reg 51(4) IS Regs
JSA Reg 113(4) JSA Regs
ESA Reg 115(6) ESA Regs
HB Reg 49(5) HB Regs
CTB Reg 39(5) CTB Regs
165 **IS** Reg 51(5) IS Regs
JSA Reg 113(5) JSA Regs
ESA Reg 115(7) ESA Regs
HB Reg 49(6) HB Regs
CTB Reg 39(6) CTB Regs
166 **IS/JSA** para 29879 DMG; see also R(IS) 13/93
167 R(IS) 14/98
168 **HB** Reg 49(5) HB Regs
CTB Reg 39(5) CTB Regs
169 **IS** Reg 49(a) IS Regs
JSA Reg 111(a) JSA Regs
ESA Reg 113 ESA Regs
HB Reg 47(a) HB Regs
CTB Reg 37(a) CTB Regs
170 R(SB) 57/83; R(SB) 6/84
171 R(SB) 18/83
172 R(SB) 6/84
173 **IS** Reg 49(a) IS Regs
JSA Reg 111(a) JSA Regs
ESA Reg 113(a) ESA Regs
HB Reg 47(a) HB Regs
CTB Reg 37(a) CTB Regs
174 **IS** Reg 49(b) IS Regs
JSA Reg 111(b) JSA Regs
ESA Reg 113(b) ESA Regs
HB Reg 47(b) HB Regs
CTB Reg 37(b) CTB Regs
175 CIS/255/1989
176 R(SB) 27/84
177 R(SB) 2/83; R(SB) 31/83
178 *JRL v SSWP (JSA)* [2011] UKUT 63 (AAC); [2011] AACR 30
179 **IS** Reg 52 IS Regs
JSA Reg 115 JSA Regs
ESA Reg 117 ESA Regs
HB Reg 51 HB Regs
CTB Reg 41 CTB Regs
180 *Hourigan v SSWP* [2002] EWCA Civ 1890 reported as R(IS) 4/03
181 CIS/15936/1996; CIS/263/1997; CIS/3283/1997 (joint decision); R(IS) 26/95
182 R(IS) 3/96
183 R(JSA) 1/02
184 CIS/2575/1997
185 R(IS) 2/93
186 R(IS) 1/03
187 **IS** Reg 49(a) IS Regs
JSA Reg 111(a) JSA Regs
ESA Reg 113 ESA Regs
HB Reg 47(a) HB Regs
CTB Reg 37(a) CTB Regs
188 R(IS) 18/95
189 R(SB) 18/83; R(IS) 2/90
190 **IS/JSA** para 29681 DMG
HB/CTB para BW1.530 GM
191 *Peters v CAO* (appendix to R(SB) 3/89)
192 **IS** Reg 50(a) IS Regs
JSA Reg 112(a) JSA Regs
ESA Reg 114(a) ESA Regs
HB Reg 48(a) HB Regs
CTB Reg 38(a) CTB Regs
193 **IS** Reg 50(b) IS Regs
JSA Reg 112(b) JSA Regs
ESA Reg 114(b) ESA Regs
HB Reg 48(b) HB Regs
CTB Reg 38(b) CTB Regs
194 **IS** Sch 10 para 21 IS Regs
JSA Sch 8 para 26 JSA Regs
ESA Sch 9 para 26 ESA Regs
HB Sch 6 para 23 HB Regs
CTB Sch 5 para 23 CTB Regs

2. **People over pension credit age**

195 **PC** s15 SPCA 2002; Sch 5 paras 24-28 SPC Regs
HB Reg 29(1)(i) and Sch 6 paras 27-30 HB(SPC) Regs
CTB Reg 19(1)(i) and Sch 4 paras 27-30 CTB(SPC) Regs
196 **PC** Sch 4 para 18 SPC Regs
HB Reg 29(2) HB(SPC) Regs
CTB Reg 19(2) CTB(SPC) Regs
197 s15(2) SPCA 2002; reg 15(6) SPC Regs
198 **HB** Reg 43 HB(SPC) Regs
CTB Reg 33 CTB(SPC) Regs
199 **HB** Reg 29(2) HB(SPC) Regs
CTB Reg 19(2) CTB(SPC) Regs
200 **HB** Reg 26 HB(SPC) Regs
CTB Reg 16 CTB(SPC) Regs
201 **HB** Reg 27 HB(SPC) Regs
CTB Reg 17 CTB (SPC) Regs
202 **PC** s5 SPCA 2002
HB/CTB s136(1) SSCBA 1992
203 **HB** Reg 23(3) HB(SPC) Regs
CTB Reg 13(3) CTB(SPC) Regs
204 para BP1.71 GM
205 R(IS) 3/93
206 **PC** Reg 2 SS(PAOR) Regs
HB Reg 74(1) HB(SPC) Regs
207 **PC** Sch 5 para 28 SPC Regs
HB Sch 6 para 30 HB(SPC) Regs
CTB Sch 4 para 30 CTB(SPC) Regs
208 **PC** Sch 5 para 16(1) SPC Regs
HB Sch 6 para 17(1) HB(SPC) Regs
CTB Sch 4 para 17(1) CTB(SPC) Regs
209 R(IS) 3/03
210 **PC** Schs 4 paras 13 and 14, and 5 para 16(2) SPC Regs
HB Schs 5 paras 14 and 15, and 6 para 17(2) HB(SPC) Regs
CTB Schs 3 paras 14 and 15, and 4 para 17(2) CTB(SPC) Regs
211 **PC** Sch 5 para 1A SPC Regs
HB Sch 6 para 26 HB(SPC) Regs
CTB Sch 4 para 26 CTB(SPC) Regs
212 **PC** Reg 17(8) SPC Regs
HB Reg 33(11) HB(SPC) Regs
CTB Reg 23(11) CTB(SPC) Regs
213 **PC** Reg 1(2) SPC Regs
HB Reg 2(1) HB(SPC) Regs
CTB Reg 2(1) CTB(SPC) Regs
All definition of 'dwelling occupied as the home'
214 **PC** Sch 5 para 1A SPC Regs
HB Sch 6 para 26 HB(SPC) Regs
CTB Sch 4 para 26 CTB(SPC) Regs
215 R(JSA) 9/03
216 R(SB) 10/89
217 **PC** Sch 5 para 6(1) SPC Regs
HB Sch 6 para 6(1) HB(SPC) Regs
CTB Sch 4 para 6(1) CTB(SPC) Regs
218 **PC** Sch 5 para 2 SPC Regs
HB Sch 6 para 2 HB(SPC) Regs
CTB Sch 4 para 2 CTB(SPC) Regs
219 **PC** Sch 5 para 7 SPC Regs
HB Sch 6 para 7 HB(SPC) Regs
CTB Sch 4 para 7 CTB(SPC) Regs
All CIS/6908/1995; R(IS) 4/97
220 **PC** Sch 5 para 3 SPC Regs
HB Sch 6 para 3 HB(SPC) Regs
CTB Sch 4 para 3 CTB(SPC) Regs
221 **PC** Sch 5 para 1 SPC Regs
HB Sch 6 para 1 HB(SPC) Regs
CTB Sch 4 para 1 CTB(SPC) Regs
222 **PC** Sch 5 paras 17 and 19 SPC Regs
HB Sch 6 paras 18 and 20 HB(SPC) Regs
CTB Sch 4 paras 18 and 20 CTB(SPC) Regs
223 *DG v SSWP (SPC)* [2010] UKUT 241 (AAC)
224 But see CPC/0206/2005 and CPC/1928/2005, which suggest an assessed income period could be reduced on revision.
225 **PC** Sch 5 paras 17 and 18 SPC Regs
HB Sch 6 paras 18 and 19 HB(SPC) Regs
CTB Sch 4 paras 18 and 19 CTB(SPC) Regs
226 CIS/4757/2003
227 CIS/6908/1995
228 **PC** Sch 5 para 4 SPC Regs
HB Sch 6 para 4 HB(SPC) Regs
CTB Sch 4 para 4 CTB(SPC) Regs
229 **PC** Reg 1(2) SPC Regs
HB Reg 2(1) HB(SPC) Regs
CTB Reg 2(1) CTB(SPC) Regs
All definition of 'close relative'
230 **PC** Sch 5 para 6 SPC Regs
HB Sch 6 para 6 HB(SPC) Regs
CTB Sch 4 para 6 CTB(SPC) Regs
231 **PC** para 84444 DMG
HB/CTB para BP1.Annex A, A1.01 GM
232 **PC** Sch 5 para 8 SPC Regs
HB Sch 6 para 8 HB(SPC) Regs
CTB Sch 4 para 8 CTB(SPC) Regs
233 **PC** Sch 5 paras 17 and 18 SPC Regs
HB Sch 6 paras 18 and 19 HB(SPC) Regs
CTB Sch 4 paras 18 and 19 CTB(SPC) Regs
234 **PC** Sch 5 para 9 SPC Regs
HB Sch 6 para 9 HB(SPC) Regs
CTB Sch 4 para 9 CTB(SPC) Regs
235 **PC** Sch 5 para 9A SPC Regs
HB Sch 6 para 10 HB(SPC) Regs
CTB Sch 4 para 10 CTB(SPC) Regs

236 **PC** Sch 5 para 10 SPC Regs
HB Sch 6 para 11 HB(SPC) Regs
CTB Sch 4 para 11 CTB(SPC) Regs
All R(IS) 7/98
237 **PC** Sch 5 para 26 SPC Regs
HB Sch 6 para 29 HB Regs
CTB Sch 4 para 29 CTB Regs
238 **PC** s15(1)(d) SPCA 2002
HB Reg 29(1)(d) HB(SPC) Regs
CTB Reg 19(1)(d) CTB(SPC) Regs
All R(IS) 10/01
239 **PC** Sch 5 para 5 SPC Regs
HB Sch 6 para 5 HB(SPC) Regs
CTB Sch 4 para 5 CTB(SPC) Regs
240 **PC** Sch 5 para 24 SPC Regs
HB Sch 6 para 27 HB(SPC) Regs
CTB Sch 4 para 27 CTB(SPC) Regs
241 **PC** Sch 5 para 22 SPC Regs
HB Sch 6 para 24 HB(SPC) Regs
CTB Sch 4 para 24 CTB(SPC) Regs
242 **PC** Sch 5 para 25 SPC Regs
HB Sch 6 para 28 HB(SPC) Regs
CTB Sch 4 para 28 CTB(SPC) Regs
243 **PC** Sch 5 para 26 SPC Regs
HB Sch 6 para 29 HB(SPC) Regs
CTB Sch 4 para 29 CTB(SPC) Regs
244 **PC** Sch 5 paras 17, 20, 20A and 20B SPC Regs
HB Sch 6 paras 18, 21, 22 and 26B HB(SPC) Regs
CTB Sch 4 paras 18, 21, 22 and 25A CTB(SPC) Regs
245 *DG v SSWP (SPC)* [2010] UKUT 241 (AAC)
246 But see CPC/0206/2005 and CPC/1928/2005, which suggest that an assessed income period could be reduced on revision in some cases.
247 **PC** Sch 5 paras 23A and 23C SPC Regs
HB Sch 6 paras 26A and 26D HB(SPC) Regs
CTB Sch 4 paras 26C and 26D CTB(SPC) Regs
248 **PC** Sch 5 para 15 SPC Regs
HB Sch 6 para 16 HB(SPC) Regs
CTB Sch 4 para 16 CTB(SPC) Regs
249 **PC** Sch 5 para 13 SPC Regs
HB Sch 6 para 14 HB(SPC) Regs
CTB Sch 4 para 14 CTB(SPC) Regs
250 **PC** Sch 5 para 12 SPC Regs
HB Sch 6 para 13 HB(SPC) Regs
CTB Sch 4 para 13 CTB(SPC) Regs
251 **PC** Sch 5 para 14 SPC Regs
HB *Sch 6 para 15* HB(SPC) Regs
CTB Sch 4 para 15 CTB(SPC) Regs
252 **PC** Sch 5 para 11 SPC Regs
HB Sch 6 para 12 HB(SPC) Regs
CTB Sch 4 para 12 CTB(SPC) Regs
253 **PC** Sch 5 para 21 SPC Regs
HB Sch 6 para 23 HB(SPC) Regs
CTB Sch 4 para 23 CTB(SPC) Regs
254 **PC** Reg 21 SPC Regs
HB Reg 47 HB(SPC) Regs
CTB Reg 37 CTB(SPC) Regs
255 **PC** Reg 21(1) SPC Regs
HB Reg 47(1) HB(SPC) Regs
CTB Reg 37(1) CTB(SPC) Regs
256 **PC** Reg 21 SPC Regs
HB Reg 47(2) HB(SPC) Regs
CTB Reg 37(2) CTB(SPC) Regs
257 **PC** Reg 21(3) SPC Regs
HB Reg 47(3) HB(SPC) Regs
CTB Reg 37(3) CTB(SPC) Regs
258 **PC** Reg 21(4) SPC Regs
HB Reg 42(4) HB(SPC) Regs
CTB Reg 37(4) CTB(SPC) Regs
259 R(IS) 13/93
260 R(IS) 14/98
261 **PC** Reg 19(a) SPC Regs
HB Reg 45(a) HB(SPC) Regs
CTB Reg 35(a) CTB(SPC) Regs
262 **PC** Reg 19(a) SPC Regs
HB Reg 45(a) HB(SPC) Regs
CTB Reg 35(a) CTB(SPC) Regs
263 **PC** Reg 19(b) SPC Regs
HB Reg 45(b) HB(SPC) Regs
CTB Reg 35(b) CTB(SPC) Regs
264 **PC** Reg 23 SPC Regs
HB Reg 49 HB(SPC) Regs
CTB Reg 39 CTB(SPC) Regs
265 R(IS) 4/03
266 **PC** Reg 19(a) SPC Regs
HB Reg 45(a) HB(SPC) Regs
CTB Reg 35(a) CTB(SPC) Regs
267 **PC** para 84772 DMG
HB/CTB para BP1.530 GM
268 *Peters v CAO* (appendix to R(SB) 3/89)
269 **PC** Reg 20(a) SPC Regs
HB Reg 46(a) HB(SPC) Regs
CTB Reg 38(a) CTB(SPC) Regs
270 **PC** Reg 20 SPC Regs
HB Reg 46(b) HB(SPC) Regs
CTB Reg 36(b) CTB(SPC) Regs
271 **PC** Sch 5 para 21 SPC Regs
HB Sch 6 para 23 HB(SPC) Regs
CTB Sch 4 para 23 CTB(SPC) Regs

Part 6

Benefit claims, decisions and challenges

Chapter 42

Claims, backdating and getting paid

This chapter covers:

This chapter describes the rules that apply to most benefits, but some have their own more detailed rules. For claims for payments from the social fund, see pp548 and 573. For most rules on claims for housing benefit and council tax benefit, see pp270 and 128.

Key facts

- To be entitled to a benefit, you must usually make a claim for it.
- Depending on the benefit concerned, claims are made by telephoning a contact centre, using a claim form, using the internet, by telephone, or in person at an office.
- You must usually provide a national insurance number and any other evidence considered reasonable.
- You may have to attend work-focused interviews and undertake work-related activity in order to receive certain benefits.
- You are usually paid by direct credit transfer into a bank or similar account.
- You must report any changes in your circumstances that could affect your benefit.

Future changes: April 2013 and after

Major changes are taking place that affect the benefits and tax credits system (see Chapter 2). From October 2013, universal credit (UC) will replace most means-tested benefits. UC will have its own rules on claims, including new rules on satisfying certain work-related requirements (see Chapter 4). Similar rules will be introduced for existing claimants of means-tested benefits until they are transferred to UC. See CPAG's *Welfare Rights Bulletin* for updates.

1. Who should claim

In most cases, to be entitled to benefit, you must make a claim for it.[1]

You should claim benefit for yourself and any adult or child dependants. If you cannot do so, another person can claim on your behalf – eg, an appointee (see below) or your parent if you are a child claiming disability living allowance.

Couples and children

If you are part of a **couple**, for some non-means-tested benefits you may be the claimant and claiming for an adult dependant (see Chapter 33), although in most cases this is no longer possible if you are not already entitled. For most means-tested benefits you may be assessed as a couple, but still only one of you actually makes the claim (see Chapter 34). If both you and your partner satisfy the qualifying conditions, you can sometimes choose which one of you claims income support, income-based jobseeker's allowance (JSA), income-related employment and support allowance or pension credit for both of you.[2] Check to see how the decision on which one of you claims makes you better or worse off. For JSA, there are special provisions for joint claims by couples. In some cases, if you are a member of a couple, both you and your partner are subject to the jobseeking conditions for entitlement to income-based JSA (see p413) and must make a joint claim (see p413).

If you have **children**, except for housing benefit (HB) and council tax benefit (CTB), they are not included in a new claim for benefit, although in some circumstances they continue to be included in a pre-existing claim (see Chapters 33 and 34). Also, you can claim child benefit, but someone else's claim might have priority over your claim (see p101).

Appointees

Someone else (eg, a friend or relative), called an 'appointee', can be authorised to act on your behalf if you cannot claim for yourself – eg, you are mentally ill.[3] This is not necessary if a court has already appointed someone to look after your affairs. The appointee takes on all your rights and responsibilities as a claimant – eg, s/he must notify changes in your circumstances. Normally, this only applies from the date the appointment is agreed, but if someone acts on your behalf before becoming your official appointee her/his actions can be validated in retrospect by her/his appointment.[4] To become an appointee, a person must normally apply in writing. However, if s/he has already been made an appointee by the local authority for HB or CTB purposes, the DWP can, by agreement, make her/him an appointee without a written application, and *vice versa*.[5] S/he must be over 18.

If you are an appointee for a claimant who dies, you must reapply for appointee status in order to settle any outstanding benefit matters.[6] An executor under a will can also pursue an outstanding claim or appeal on behalf of a deceased claimant even if the decision was made before the formal grant of probate.[7]

2. How to make a claim

To qualify for a benefit you must usually make a claim.[8] There are exceptions to this rule. You do not have to make a claim for retirement allowance (see p384) and certain retirement pensions if you are already receiving certain other pensions or widows' benefits (see p536) or, for bereavement payment, if you are over pension age (see p73).[9] Also, there are rules under which you need not claim a Category A or B retirement pension if you have been notified that you need not do so (see p534). If there is a delay in making a claim, you may be able to get an interim payment of benefit (see p1046).

Starting your claim

You usually need to make your claim in writing eventually, although a number of benefits can also be claimed by telephone and some can be claimed online.[10] However, the DWP prefers that your claim for income support (IS), jobseeker's allowance (JSA) and employment and support allowance (ESA) is *started* by telephone.

There is no rule that you must start your claim by telephone However, in practice it is best to make your claim in the way the DWP prefers, if you can.

If starting your claim by telephone is either impractical or impossible for you, tell the Jobcentre Plus office and ask to claim in an alternative way. For example:

- if speaking in English is difficult, an interpreter can be arranged;
- another person may be able to make the call on your behalf, especially if you are there to help;
- a face-to-face interview could take place at the Jobcentre Plus office;
- a home visit could be arranged;
- if none of the above is suitable, a claim form could be completed and sent.

Claiming from a central or regional unit

The following benefits are usually claimed from central or regional units. Claims can be started in a variety of ways, depending on the benefit concerned:

- attendance allowance (AA – see Chapter 9);
- carer's allowance (CA – see Chapter 6);
- child benefit (see Chapter 7);

- disability living allowance (DLA – see Chapter 9);
- guardian's allowance (see Chapter 12);
- industrial injuries benefits (see Chapter 18);
- pension crediit (PC – see Chapter 22);
- retirement pension (see Chapter 23).

Claiming via a Jobcentre Plus telephone contact centre

You are encouraged to start your claim for IS, JSA and ESA by telephoning a Jobcentre Plus contact centre before being sent either written details to confirm or a claim form to fill in.

Housing benefit (HB) and council tax benefit (CTB) are administered by your local authority at its local offices. However, in some cases, claims for HB and CTB can be made with your claim for IS, JSA, ESA or PC.

Claims for bereavement benefits (via the Bereavement Service on 0845 606 0265, textphone: 0845 606 0285), CA, industrial injuries benefits and maternity allowance (MA) can also be started by telephone, although in practice you are sent a claim form even if you do start your claim via the contact centre.

There is a national **contact centre** number for making your claim (tel: 0800 055 6688, textphone: 0800 023 4888, Welsh language: 0800 012 1888). These numbers are free if you are using a landline, but not always if you are using a mobile telephone.[11] Your local Jobcentre Plus office should have a 'warm phone' that you can use free of charge, although you might need to queue. When you make your call, it is routed to a contact centre which takes the details for your claim and sends you a:

- written statement for you to confirm the details (for IS, JSA and ESA). When you sign it, it becomes your written claim; *or*
- claim form (for other benefits).

Claim forms, the internet and other ways of claiming

You can also claim by filling in and returning a **claim form**. You may be able to get claim forms from your local DWP office or (for child benefit and guardian's allowance) HM Revenue and Customs (HMRC). You can download and print forms for most benefits from www.direct.gov.uk/en/moneytaxandbenefits or, for child benefit and guardian's allowance, from www.hmrc.gov.uk/forms. Some benefits have a special telephone line for registering a claim and ordering a claim form – eg, Benefit Enquiry Line for DLA and AA. See the relevant chapter of this *Handbook* for details.

Claims for DLA and AA can be started **online** at www.dwp.gov.uk/eservice. You can claim retirement pension online at www.direct.gov.uk/en/pensionsandretirementplanning, JSA online at www.directgov.uk/en/moneytaxandbenefits and CA online at www.dwp.gov.uk/carersallowance. **Note**: this may only start your claim; you may need to complete a form or send information in order for your claim to be valid.

Many benefits, including ESA, JSA, IS, PC and retirement pension, may be claimed **by telephone** if a number has been specified for this purpose. See the relevant chapter of this *Handbook* for more details.

You can claim CA, DLA, IS, ESA, PC and retirement pension by attending **in person** to make a written claim at designated DWP offices, designated local authority HB/CTB offices, other 'alternative offices' and, in England only, at designated county councils.[12] If you are of qualifying age for PC (see p509), you can also claim AA, bereavement benefits and winter fuel payments at such offices. The alternative offices include some local advice centres and local authority HB offices identified by the DWP.

If you are reporting a birth or a death to a local authority, it may also include other local authority offices under the '**Tell Us Once**' arrangements. You can also claim child benefit following a birth by submitting a claim form at such an office (see Chapter 7). See the relevant benefit chapter of this *Handbook* for more details.

When to claim

Claim as soon as you think you might be entitled to benefit. See p1024 for further information about your date of claim.

Very occasionally, it may be in your interests to wait for the next 'benefit year' to claim contributory ESA or contribution-based JSA on the basis of a better record of national insurance (NI) contributions (see p788). In some circumstances your claim can be backdated (see p1026).

Amending or withdrawing your claim

You can amend your claim by writing to the office handling your claim.[13] If your letter is received before a decision is made, the decision maker can treat your claim as being amended from the date it was initially made.

You can withdraw your claim at any time before a decision is made.[14] In practice you should be allowed to withdraw a claim in respect of a future period, as there is a principle that you should not be forced to continue receiving benefit when you have indicated that you no longer wish to do so.[15]

Making sure your claim is valid

Your claim must be valid. In general, this means that it must be in writing and properly completed, even if you start the claim by telephoning a contact centre, and must be on an approved form. This is usually the claim form, but can be a written statement sent after the telephone call. There are exceptions:

- ESA and PC do not have to be claimed in writing unless you are specifically required to do so (although, for PC and sometimes for ESA, you are eventually

sent a written statement to sign and return, which you must do for your claim to be valid);[16]
- IS, JSA, bereavement benefits and retirement pension can also be claimed by telephone;[17]
- for IS and JSA, there is also an 'evidence requirement' (see p1021).

The decision maker may decide to treat any letter or other written communication as being a valid written claim, but written claims for IS, JSA or ESA *must* be on the approved form.[18] What is and what is not a claim should not, in general, be decided in an over-technical way.[19] Also, if you just write a letter or send the wrong form, you can be sent the approved form to fill in, or if you do not fill in the form properly, it can be returned to you. If you subsequently return it correctly filled in within a month, you count as having made a valid claim on the date of your first letter or form. You can also be given a month to supply information where you claim by telephone.[20] The decision maker can extend this one-month period if s/he thinks it is reasonable (but not for IS or JSA) – eg, because you were ill. See p1026 for other situations when your claim can be backdated.

A claim on an approved form is accepted as valid if it is completed in accordance with the instructions on the form. For IS and JSA, it must also satisfy the evidence requirement. A claim made by telephone is accepted as valid if all the information required to determine the claim is supplied.[21]

If your claim is valid, it is referred to a decision maker to decide if you are entitled to benefit. The decision maker can ask you to provide further information to support your claim (see p1022) or ask you to attend a medical examination before s/he makes a decision. This should not prevent a decision being made on your claim (but see below). If you are asked to provide information after a decision has been made on your claim, see p1045.

If your claim is not accepted as valid

If your claim is not accepted as valid, the decision maker does not make a decision on your entitlement to benefit.

The DWP or HMRC should tell you that your claim is defective and give you the opportunity to correct the defect (and so make the claim valid). You should be given at least one month from the date you are notified of the defect or (for most benefits) longer if considered reasonable.[22] For IS and JSA, you must correct the defect within one month.[23]

If the DWP or HMRC does not accept that your claim is valid, you should still be given a decision saying so. You have the right of appeal against such decisions.[24] If your claim is finally accepted as valid, the decision maker must make a decision on your entitlement to benefit.[25]

Work-focused interviews and work-related activity

Entitlement to certain benefits depends on your attending interviews about work. In these schemes, the general rule is that you must attend a 'work-focused interview'. If you are in a couple, in some cases your partner may have to attend a work-focused interview as well. Most ESA claimants (except those in the support group and lone parents with a child under one) will also have to undertake 'work-related activity' (see p1031).

Evidence requirement for income support and jobseeker's allowance

It is your responsibility to:[26]

- complete your claim form fully and correctly; *and*
- produce information and evidence to verify your claim.

This is also known as the 'onus of proof' rule. For the information you can be asked to provide, see p1022.

If you do not fill in the form properly or provide all the information and evidence required, the DWP must notify you that your claim is defective and contact you to put things right.[27] It might telephone or write to you or, in the case of IS, visit you to get the information or evidence. However, it might simply return your claim form. You should provide the information or evidence or complete the form and return it to your local office within one month of your initial contact (or that of someone contacting the DWP on your behalf). If you do not, you might lose benefit (see p1026 for when your claim can be backdated). In any case, if the DWP does not accept that your claim is valid, you should be given a decision saying so, and you can appeal against that decision.[28]

Exemptions from the evidence requirement

You are exempt from the evidence requirement if:[29]

- you could not complete the form or get the information or evidence required because of a physical, mental, learning or communication difficulty. You must also show that it is not reasonably practicable for you to find someone to help you complete the form or get the proof on your behalf. However, you can argue that someone else is not expected to take the initiative in offering you assistance;[30] *or*
- the information or evidence required does not exist; *or*
- you could not get the information or evidence required without serious risk of physical or mental harm. You must also show that it is not reasonably practicable to get it in another way; *or*
- you could only get the information or evidence required from a third party and it is not reasonably practicable to get it from her/him; *or*
- the decision maker thinks sufficient proof has been provided to show that you are not entitled to IS or JSA (eg, because your capital or income is too high) so it would be inappropriate to require further information or evidence.

If you are unable to complete your claim form or provide the required information or evidence for one of the reasons listed above, notify your local office as soon as possible, ideally explaining this on the claim form or by telephoning or visiting the office. The DWP says that such notice must be given within one month of the date when you first contacted it. Explain your circumstances fully. You can provide supporting letters – eg, from a social worker or a solicitor. If the DWP accepts you are exempt from the evidence requirement, it might:

- help you to fill in the form; *or*
- give you longer to complete it; *or*
- collect evidence or information on your behalf; *or*
- tell you that you do not have to provide the information after all.

If you are claiming JSA, you are normally required to attend an interview at which a properly completed claim form is signed. Your claim is then treated as being made on the date you first notified your intention to claim (usually when you picked up the form and made the appointment for the interview), or the first date in respect of which your claim is made if this is later.[31] If you fail to attend the interview or hand in a properly completed form, you might lose benefit.

Remember that the decision maker can ask you for further information or evidence even after s/he has accepted your claim as valid. However, this should not change the date from which you can be paid. If s/he eventually decides you are entitled to benefit, you should still be paid from your date of claim (see p1024).

Further information to support your claim

Once your claim has been accepted as valid, you may be required to provide additional documentation and evidence and you can be asked for an interview to discuss your circumstances if this is reasonable.[32] You may be able to claim travelling expenses for this.[33] You must provide the information or evidence within one month of the request (within seven days of the request for JSA only). A decision maker can allow you longer than this if reasonable. If you do not provide the information, the decision maker is likely to decide your claim in the way most adverse to you.

It is best to send evidence and documents to the office handling the claim. For certain benefits, a designated local authority or English county council office or other 'alternative office' (see p1018) may also be able to accept evidence and documents. If a local authority has used information on your claim for HB or CTB and has passed it to the DWP because it is relevant to your claim for another benefit, in most cases the DWP must use that information without checking it further.[34]

If you are asked to provide evidence which you do not have, ask what other evidence would be acceptable. Ask the DWP or HMRC to explain what is required and why, and complain if you think any requests for information are unreasonable.

The national insurance number requirement

When you claim benefit (including HB and CTB) you must usually satisfy the NI number requirement by:[35]

- providing an NI number and information or evidence to show that it is yours; *or*
- providing evidence or information to enable the DWP (or HMRC) to trace your NI number, if you do not know it; *or*
- applying for an NI number if you do not have one and providing enough information and evidence to allow one to be allocated to you (this does not necessarily mean that you must actually be allocated an NI number; in general you will have done enough if you have supplied all the information you could reasonably have been expected to when you made your application).[36]

For a few benefits, you do not need to make a claim (see p1017) and the NI number requirement should not apply. If you cannot satisfy the NI number requirement straight away, you may be able to claim an interim payment of benefit (see p1046). If you are refused benefit because you are held not to have satisifed the NI number requirement, you can appeal against that decision.[37]

Exemptions

You are exempt from the NI number requirement if:

- you are under 16 and the benefit is DLA ;[38]
- the benefit is statutory adoption pay, statutory maternity pay, statutory paternity pay, statutory sick pay or a social fund payment;
- the benefit is HB and you live in a hostel.[39]

Members of your family

If you are claiming a means-tested benefit as a couple (see p753) or an increase for your adult dependant in your non-means-tested benefit (see p740), your partner (or adult dependant) must usually also satisfy the NI number requirement.[40] That is usually the case even if s/he is a 'person subject to immigration control' and no extra benefit will be paid for her/him.[41] However, a special rule is intended to apply in some cases. Specifically, this rule exempts your partner from the NI number requirement if you are the benefit claimant and:[42]

- your partner is a 'person subject to immigration control' because s/he does not have leave to enter or remain in the UK – eg, s/he is an asylum seeker or an overstayer (see p1410); *and*
- s/he has not previously been given an NI number; *and*
- if you are claiming IS, ESA, JSA or PC, your partner is not entitled to the benefit, and if you are claiming HB/CTB, s/he is not 'habitually resident' (see p1431). However, it is unclear how in practice this condition could ever fail to be satisifed.

In practice, information will still be requested about an NI number application for your partner (you are still expected to disclose that you have a partner), but an NI number will be refused.[43] The rule ensures that your benefit claim can still be allowed. **Note:** if your claim includes a 'person subject to immigration control', there can be consequences for her/his immigration status (see Chapter 61).

If you are claiming for a child under the age of 16, s/he does not need to satisfy the NI number requirement.[44]

Proof of identity

In addition to satisfying the NI number requirement, you may be asked to produce further documents or evidence that prove your identity. If you are claiming for your partner or an adult dependant (see p740), you must also prove her/his identity.

You can prove your identity with a passport, a national identity card issued by a European Economic Area member state, or a letter issued by the Home Office acknowledging your application for asylum. You could also produce your birth certificate, full driving licence, a travel pass with a photograph, a local council rent card or tenancy agreement or even paid fuel or telephone bills.

Note:

- It is important to provide details of any other people who can confirm what you have stated – eg, your solicitor or other legal representative or official organisation.
- You should not be refused benefit simply because you do not have any documents, especially where it is unreasonable for you to have or obtain them. Ask the decision maker to make a decision on your claim and you can then appeal.

In some cases, the decision maker may refuse to accept evidence that you are who you say you are. Some claimants may have particular difficulty supplying evidence, or believe they are being discriminated against. Press the decision maker to be clear about what is required and why, and complain if you consider any requests for information are unreasonable (see p1255). Contact your local race equality council if you think you have experienced race discrimination.

3. The date of your claim

You are not usually entitled to benefit for any day before your date of claim. See the chapter in this *Handbook* about the benefit you are claiming for information about this. In addition, remember:

- you might be able to claim in advance if you know you are not entitled now but will be later – eg, you are leaving hospital;
- your claim might be backdated in certain circumstances (see p1026);

- if you claim the wrong benefit, your claim can be treated as one for the right benefit (see below).

If you claim the wrong benefit

If you have claimed the wrong benefit but are in fact entitled to another benefit, your original claim can sometimes be treated as a claim for the right benefit.[45] This might be a way around the strict backdating rules (see p1026). For which claims can interchange, see below. See also information in the chapter about the benefit you should have claimed.

Interchange of claims[46]

Benefit claimed	*May be treated as a claim for*
Incapacity benefit	Severe disablement allowance; maternity allowance
Severe disablement allowance	Incapacity benefit; maternity allowance
Employment and support allowance	Maternity allowance
Maternity allowance	Incapacity benefit; employment and support allowance; severe disablement allowance
Widows' benefits; bereavement benefits	Retirement pension
Retirement pension	Widows' benefits; bereavement benefits
Income support	Carer's allowance
Attendance allowance	Disability living allowance
Disability living allowance	Attendance allowance

In addition, a claim for:

- child benefit can be treated as a claim for guardian's allowance and *vice versa*;[47]
- attendance allowance (AA) or disability living allowance (DLA) can be treated as a claim for an increase in disablement pension where constant attendance is needed (see p380) and *vice versa*.

If you claim a non-means-tested benefit (other than child benefit) but are not entitled to it, your claim may be treated as a claim by someone else for an increase in her/his benefit for you (see p747).

If you claim an increase of a non-means-tested benefit for an adult dependant but are not entitled to it, the claim may be treated as a claim by someone else who is entitled.[48]

The decision maker does not have to accept your claim for one benefit as a claim for another. You cannot appeal if this is refused. Your only remedy is to seek a judicial review (see p1202).[49]

In addition, for all benefits, except income support (IS), income-based jobseeker's allowance (JSA) and employment and support allowance (ESA), there is a general power to treat any written document as a claim for benefit.[50]

Backdating your claim

There are strict time limits formaking a claim.[51] If you miss the time limit, your claim can sometimes be backdated for up to three months (12 months for retirement pension). The backdating period is longer for most benefits if you are reclaiming following the award of a 'qualifying benefit' (see p1029).

- If you want your claim to be backdated you must ask for this to happen, otherwise it will not be considered.[52]
- Some benefits can be backdated without special reasons (see below).
- Claims for IS and JSA can only be backdated in limited circumstances (see p1027).
- Special rules apply if you are claiming backdated JSA because your entitlement ceased when you failed to attend an interview (see p422) or sign on (see p425).
- Extra backdating of most benefits is allowed after awards of qualifying benefits (see p1029).
- Claims for AA and DLA can never be backdated.[53]
- Different rules apply to housing benefit (HB) and council tax benefit (CTB) (see p277).
- If you claim the wrong benefit, your claim can sometimes be treated as a claim for the benefit you should have claimed (see p1025).

If you are prevented from receiving backdated benefit because of an error of the DWP (or, in child benefit and guardian's allowance cases, HM Revenue and Customs), write and request an *ex gratia* payment or extra-statutory payment as compensation (see p1261). The intervention of an MP or the Ombudsman (see p1259) may help.

If you satisfy the conditions for getting benefit, it should be paid from your date of claim. If backdating is refused, you can appeal (see Chapter 46). Payment should not be held up because you are challenging the decision on backdating.

Benefits that can be backdated without special reasons

Claims for the following benefits can be backdated for up to three months (or where stated, for up to 12 months) without the need for special reasons:[54]

- incapacity benefit, although new claims are now only possible in very limited circumstances (see Chapter 16);
- ESA, both contributory and income-related (see Chapter 10);
- industrial injuries benefits (see Chapter 18);
- child benefit (see Chapter 7);
- guardian's allowance (see Chapter 12);

- increase of non-means-tested benefit for an adult, although new claims are now only possible in very limited circumstances (see Chapter 33);
- retirement pension for 12 months (see Chapter 23);
- pension credit (PC – see Chapter 22);
- bereavement benefits, except for bereavement payment which can be backdated for 12 months, but see p536 if you are over pension age (see Chapter 5). The time limit can be extended in some cases – eg, when you did not know your partner had died (see p76);
- maternity allowance(see p498); *and*
- carer's allowance (CA – see Chapter 6).

If you want backdated benefit for a period before your actual date of claim (see p1024), you must show that you would have qualified for the benefit had you claimed at the time. For example, if you want to claim three months' backdated child benefit, you must show that you have been responsible for a child (see p94) for the past three months.

You can only get benefit backdated for up to the maximum allowed.[55]

There are exceptions to the rules:

- If you are claiming backdated child benefit after being awarded refugee status, see p1423.
- If you miss the time limit for claiming disablement benefit for occupational deafness or occupational asthma (see p373) or bereavement payment (see p62), you may lose your right to benefit altogether.

Backdating income support and jobseeker's allowance

For IS or JSA, your claim can be backdated for up to one or three months in particular circumstances, or for longer periods after the award of a qualifying benefit.

If you are claiming late, it is important to explain why. If you can, provide evidence or information that backs this up – eg, a copy of the letter from your adviser or information from your employer which misled you (see p1028). If you have been misled, misinformed or given insufficient advice by an officer of the DWP, explain how and when this happened and, where possible, give the name and a description of the officer concerned. Where relevant, explain why there is no one else who could help you make your claim.

One month's backdating of income support or jobseeker's allowance

The decision maker is required to backdate your claim for up to one month if one or more of the following applies (or has applied) and because of this you could not reasonably have been expected to make your claim any earlier.[56]

- The office where you are supposed to claim was closed (eg, because of a strike) and there were no other arrangements for claims to be made.

- You could not get to the DWP office because there were difficulties with the type of transport you normally use and there was no reasonable alternative.
- There were adverse postal conditions – eg, bad weather, a postal strike, or the post office failed to act under its agreement to deliver under-stamped mail to the DWP.[57]
- You (or your partner) stopped getting another benefit but you (or your partner) were not informed before your entitlement ceased so you could not claim IS or JSA in time.
- You claimed IS or JSA in your own right within one month of separating from your partner.
- A close relative of yours died in the month before your claim. 'Close relative' means your partner, parent, son, daughter, brother or sister.
- You were unable to notify the DWP of your intention to make a claim because the telephone lines to the office were busy or not working.

Three months' backdating of income support or jobseeker's allowance

Your claim can be backdated for up to three months if you can show it was not reasonable to expect you to claim earlier than you did for one of the following reasons.[58] If more than one reason applies to you, the combined effect of all of them must be considered in deciding whether it was reasonable to expect you to claim earlier.[59]

- You were given information by an officer of the DWP and as a result thought your claim would not succeed. This includes if:
  - you were given incorrect information or the wrong claim form and this led you to claim the wrong benefit;
  - someone with authority to act on your behalf was given incorrect information;[60]
  - you were told your claim would not be accepted;[61]
  - you were told you did not have to fill in a claim form;[62]
  - the refusal of, or failure to respond to,[63] an earlier claim for the same[64] or a different[65] benefit led you to believe that you were not entitled;
  - the information was incomplete and had not included advice on claiming when it should have done.[66]

  'Officer' includes anyone carrying out public functions at the benefit office – eg, a security guard.[67] It does not matter if the information you received was correct or reasonable on the basis of any information that you gave to the officer about your circumstances, as long as the officer's advice caused you to think that a claim would fail.[68]
- You were given advice in writing by a Citizens Advice Bureau or other advice worker, a solicitor or other professional adviser (eg, an accountant), a doctor or a local authority and as a result thought your claim would not succeed. 'Advice in writing' includes leaflets, emails[69] or information on a website, provided it is directed at claimants in your position. Your claim should be backdated if you

are given written confirmation of advice that was originally given to you orally,[70] provided this is done before the decision maker decides whether you are entitled to backdating.[71] The written advice must also be given to you; it is not enough for your adviser to record a note of oral advice unless you are provided with a copy.[72]
- You or your partner were given written information about your income or capital by your employer or former employer, or a bank or building society and, as a result, you thought your claim would not succeed.
- You could not get to the DWP office because of bad weather.

In addition, your claim can be backdated if you comply with any of the following conditions and it was not 'reasonably practicable' for you to seek help from anyone else to make your claim.[73] If you are mentally ill, this does not necessarily mean you cannot be expected to seek assistance.[74] However, another person is not expected to take the initiative in offering assistance.[75] The conditions are:
- you have learning, language or literacy difficulties; *or*
- you are deaf or blind *or* were sick or disabled (but not if you are claiming JSA); *or*
- you were caring for someone who is sick or disabled; *or*
- you were dealing with a domestic emergency that affected you.

Even if one of these applies, you might be paid less than three months' arrears if you claim because of a new interpretation of the law (see p1149).

If a person has been formally appointed by a court or the DWP to act on your behalf, it is your appointee (see p1016), not you, who must show that it was not reasonable to expect her/him to claim sooner than s/he did for one of the reasons listed above.[76] If someone is informally acting on your behalf, you must show this. Also show that it was reasonable for you to delegate responsibility for your claim and that you took care to ensure the person helping you did it properly.[77]

Extra backdating after awards of qualifying benefits

If your claim for benefit (except ESA) is refused, it can be backdated if you then reclaim it after an award of a 'qualifying benefit'.

A **'qualifying benefit'** is, in general, any benefit which gives you entitlement to another benefit, or makes another benefit payable at a higher rate.[78] For example, depending on your circumstances, you may not be entitled to income-based JSA or HB until you also become entitled to DLA.

For **CA**, there is a special rule which means that if you claim it within three months of the disabled person being awarded a qualifying benefit (eg, AA) on a new claim, the date of your claim is the first day for which the qualifying benefit is payable. (The qualifying benefit is any of those in the third bullet point on p84.) The general rule is that you can get backdating if:

- your original claim (eg, for income-based JSA) is refused while you (or your dependent child or your partner) are waiting to hear about a qualifying benefit (eg, DLA); *and*
- you claimed that qualifying benefit no later than 10 days after your original claim; *and*
- the qualifying benefit is then awarded; *and*
- you then make a further claim (eg, for income-based JSA), within three months of the decision awarding the qualifying benefit and you are now entitled (eg, to income-based JSA) because of the award of the qualifying benefit.

In these circumstances, benefit is backdated to the date of your original claim or the date on which the qualifying benefit was first payable, whichever is later.[79]

Note:

- The rule also applies if the claim for the qualifying benefit was originally refused, but you were awarded it later on revision, supersession or appeal.
- If you lost entitlement to benefit (eg, CA), or payment of it stopped because your award of a qualifying benefit (eg, DLA) was terminated or reduced, your benefit is backdated if you reclaim within three months of the reinstatement of your qualifying benefit. This also applies if you lost entitlement to a benefit (eg, you lost your IS because your income increased) but a claim for a qualifying benefit had not yet been decided and, had it been awarded, you would have been entitled again. In this case, your benefit is backdated if you claim within three months of the date the qualifying benefit is awarded.[80]
- If you lost entitlement to benefit or payment of it stopped because AA or DLA stopped being paid because you were in hospital, a care home or other special accommodation, your benefit is backdated if you reclaim it within three months of the AA or DLA starting to be paid again.[81]

An additional qualifying benefit rule applies for **IS** and **income-based JSA** only. If you have been awarded either of these benefits but that award is terminated, further claims for IS/income-based JSA are backdated either to the date of the termination, or the date when a qualifying benefit was first awarded (whichever date is the later) if:[82]

- you or a member of your family (or, where applicable, the person being cared for) claim a qualifying benefit; *and*
- you make a further claim for IS/income-based JSA within three months of the qualifying benefit being awarded.

Even if you are already entitled to some IS, JSA or ESA, you might only be entitled to it at a higher rate once you or another member of your family become entitled to another benefit. See p1148 for getting extra backdating in this situation.

4. Work-focused interviews and work-related activity

Entitlement to certain benefits depends on attending '**work-focused interviews**'. These are supposed to help and encourage you to keep in contact with the employment market and eventually to begin full-time work. Claimants who are not required to attend an interview can still take part in the schemes on a voluntary basis. At the interview, job opportunities, training and rehabilitation are discussed. Some employment and support allowance (ESA) claimants may also have to undertake **work-related activity** and, at some point, ESA and income support (IS) claimants will have to accept a '**claimant commitment**'.

Although not all of these rules apply to **jobseeker's allowance** (JSA), this has its own rules under which you are required to attend to sign on, attend interviews and actively seek work and, in some cases, engage in work-related activity, including work experience (see Chapter 20).

Work-focused interview rules apply to you if you are claiming:

- IS;
- ESA;
- incapacity benefit (IB);
- severe disablement allowance (SDA).

In addition, your partner may be required to attend a work-focused interview in certain circumstances – eg, if you are claiming carer's allowance (see p1033).

Currently there are three main sets of rules on work-focused interviews:

- the Jobcentre Plus rules for certain IS claimants and, in some cases, their partners (see p1032);
- the ESA and incapacity benefits rules, for people claiming ESA or benefits for incapacity for work (see p1034);
- the lone parent rules, for lone parents claiming IS (see p1035).

Work-related activity and claimant commitments

Certain ESA claimants who are required to take part in work-focused interviews can also be required to undertake some '**work-related activity**'.[83] You can be required to carry out work-related activity by advisers in the DWP or the Work Programme (an employment initiative that includes back-to-work support for ESA claimants). The main features are as follows.

- Claimants in the 'support group' (see p184) or lone parents with a child aged under five do not have to undertake work-related activity.
- Lone parents responsible for a child who is aged five or over but under 13 can only be required to undertake work-related activity during the child's normal school hours.

- Claimants who are entitled to carer's allowance (p84), or whose ESA includes a carer premium (p834), do not have to undertake work-related activity.
- Any requirement to undertake work-related activity must be 'reasonable', taking into account your circumstances.
- The work-related activity is activity that will make it more likely that you will get a job or remain in work. The exact activity will be at the discretion of the personal advisers conducting the interviews either in the DWP or the Work Programme. You cannot be required to apply for a job, undertake work or undergo medical or surgical treatment, and the requirement can be lifted if it is considered unreasonable at the relevant time.
- All work-related activity must be recorded in an 'action plan', which must be in writing and specify the activity you are required to undertake. An action plan must be reconsidered if you request it, and a written decision issued following the request.

If you are required to undertake work-related activity but the DWP considers that you have failed to do so and do not have a 'good cause', your ESA can be reduced. You must show good cause within five working days of the date you are notified by the DWP that you have failed to undertake the activity. 'Good cause' is not defined, but the DWP must take all the circumstances into account, including your physical or mental health. The benefit penalty is the same as if you had failed without good cause to take part in a work-focused interview, and you can appeal against the decision imposing the penalty in the same way (see p1037). The benefit penalty will stop if you comply with the requirement to undertake work-related activity or if you are no longer required to undertake it.

Probably during 2012, the government will also require people claimingESA andIS to sign a **'claimant commitment'** in order to be entitled to benefit. The claimant committment will replace action plans in these benefits. If you are claiming JSA, you will also usually have to accept a claimant commitment, which will replace the jobseeker's agreement (see p22). The claimant commitment for ESA and IS will include a record of any responsibilities you may have to attend work-focused interviews and undertake work-related activity.[84] It is understood that new benefit penalties or 'sanctions' for not complying with the claimant committment will be introduced for ESA and IS, but at the time this *Handook* was written the details had not been confirmed. From October 2013, when universal credit (UC) is introduced, the claimant commitment will include a record of the work-related requirements that you are required to undertake. It is expected that the claimant commitment and the sanctions will then be very similar to those that will apply to UC (see p50). See CPAG's *Welfare Rights Bulletin* for updates.

Jobcentre Plus rules

The Jobcentre Plus rules apply to most claims for IS, unless you are getting IS on the grounds of incapacity for work or on the basis of being a lone parent and your youngest child is seven or over. **Note:** this age may reduce to five in 2012/13. See CPAG's *Welfare Rights Bulletin* for updates. If you are a member of a couple, similar but not identical rules may apply to your partner (see below).

If you make a new claim for IS, you are required to take part in a work-focused interview as a condition of claiming. This applies, even if you have other responsibilities – eg, you are also a carer getting carer's allowance (CA).[85] You are also required to take part in further work-focused interviews under the Jobcentre Plus scheme as a condition of continuing to receive the full rate of IS. These are triggered by certain events, such as stopping or starting part-time work, but in any case occur at least every three years.[86] For information about the benefit penalties if you do not take part, see p1037. Individual interviews may be waived, or deferred until another time (see p1035).

You **do not have to attend an interview** if you are:[87]

- in remunerative work (ie, at least 16 hours a week). In some circumstances, you can be treated as in or not in remunerative work. The rules are the same as for housing benefit (see Chapter 31); *or*
- claiming or entitled to JSA (but if you are a member of a joint-claim couple and you or your partner fit into one of the exempt groups on p396 this does not apply); *or*
- aged under 16 or at least the qualifying age for pension credit (PC – see p509).

Work-focused interviews for partners

If you are a member of a couple and are entitled to certain benefits, your partner may be required to take part in a work-focused interview as well as you, if you are required to do so. This applies if:[88]

- you and your partner are both aged 18 or over but under the qualifying age for PC (see p509); *and*
- you are getting one of the benefits listed below; *and*
- you have been continuously entitled to the benefit for 26 weeks or more; *and*
- the benefit is paid to you at a higher rate because of your partner (including if you get an increase for an adult dependant).

However, your partner does not have to take part in an interview under these rules if s/he is entitled to one of the benefits listed below, or to contributory ESA, as a claimant in her/his own right, or if you or your partner are responsible for a child aged under one.[89]

The benefits (claimed by you) to which these work-focused interviews for partners rules apply are:

- IS;
- income-based JSA (but not joint-claim JSA);
- income-related ESA;
- IB;

- SDA;
- CA.

If these rules apply, generally your partner must take part in one work-focused interview as a condition of your receiving the full amount of the benefit. However, if you are claiming income-based JSA (but not joint-claim JSA) and you or your partner are responsible for a child aged one or over in your household, your partner must take part in further interviews every six months.[90]

The interviews themselves and the consequences of failing to take part are similar to the work-focused interviews that apply to you as a claimant (see p1035). The main differences are:[91]

- the only consequence of your partner failing to take part in an interview is a reduction in your benefit (of £14.20 a week);
- your partner is not required to draw up an action plan;
- if your benefit is reduced because your partner fails to take part in an interview and you are getting more than one of the benefits in the list above, income-based JSA is the first benefit to be reduced, followed by income-related ESA, IS, IB, SDA and then CA; *and*
- both you and your partner are notified of the decision on failure to take part and on good cause for not taking part, and have the right to appeal against it.

Employment and support allowance and incapacity benefits rules

Usually, you come under these rules if you are claiming ESA, IB, IS on the basis of incapacity for work, or SDA, even if you have other responsibilities – eg, you are also a carer entitled to CA. Under these rules, once entitled to benefit, unless you are exempt, you can be required to attend work-focused interviews in order to continue to receive the full rate.[92] Individual interviews may be deferred until another time (see p1035).

There are no limits on the frequency or timing of the interviews.

For information about the benefit penalties if you do not take part, see p1037.

Incapacity benefit, income support and severe disablement allowance

For IB, IS on the basis of incapacity for work and SDA, the rules described here generally apply if you are already entitled to the benefit. They will also apply if you can make a new claim, although in most cases this is now not usually possible and you must claim ESA instead. However, you do not have to attend interviews (*although you can on a voluntary basis*) if you have reached the qualifying age for PC (see p509), or you are incapable of work because you have a severe condition and are exempt, or you are a lone parent and responsible for a child aged under one.[93]

Employment and support allowance

You can be required to attend work-focused interviews if you are entitled to ESA. This includes if you have claimed and been awarded ESA in advance.[94] However, you do not have to attend an interview (although you can on a voluntary basis) if:[95]

- the decision maker has decided that you have, or are treated as having, limited capability for work-related activity – ie, you are in the support group (see p185);
- you are a lone parent and responsible for a child aged under one;
- you are only entitled to contributory ESA at a nil rate;
- you have reached the qualifying age for PC (see p509).

In certain circumstances, you may be required to engage in work-related activity as well as attend interviews (see p1031).

Work-focused interviews for lone parents

Some lone parents whose youngest child is aged seven or over have to attend work-focused interviews under the Jobcentre Plus rules (see p1032). **Note:** this age may reduce to five in 2012/13. See CPAG's *Welfare Rights Bulletin* for updates. There are also similar rules for other lone parents claiming IS, in which entitlement to IS also depends on attending work-focused interviews.

The requirement to attend interviews under these rules applies if you are a lone parent and are responsible for, and living in the same household as, a child. In general, it applies if you make a new claim for IS and you are already on it, even if you have other responsibilities – eg, you are also a carer on CA. You are required to attend repeat work-focused interviews, usually every six months or, if your youngest child is aged four, five or six, every 13 weeks. If your youngest child is older than six, interviews take place when a certain 'trigger point' occurs, such as stopping or starting part-time work, but, in any event must take place at least every three years.[96] Individual interviews may be waived, or deferred until another time.

You are not required to attend a work-focused interview under these rules if you are a lone parent and :[97]

- you are under 18; *or*
- you are at least the qualifying age for PC (see p509); *or*
- your youngest child is aged under one; *or*
- you are already subject to the Jobcentre Plus or the ESA and incapacity benefits rules.

General rules

You are informed when your interview is to take place. It normally takes place at the local DWP office. However, it can take place in your home if the DWP thinks that going to the office would cause undue inconvenience or endanger your health. There is no right of appeal against this decision.[98]

If they apply to you, interviews are compulsory. In the Jobcentre Plus and lone parent rules, you may have the requirement to attend an interview waived (ie, cancelled) or, in any of the rules, deferred to another date if it is considered that an interview would not be of assistance or appropriate – eg, because you are ill, or need to provide care at the scheduled time.[99] There is no right of appeal about this.

The process has three basic stages.

- Initial contact, where you indicate that you want to claim benefit, forms are issued and basic information is taken.
- Initial work-focused interview.
- Repeat work-focused interviews at various times (called 'trigger points') during your claim.

Usually, at the interview you are first seen by a 'financial assessor' to deal with your benefit claim and other potential benefit entitlement before the work-focused interview itself, which is carried out by a personal adviser.

Taking part in an interview

You must 'take part' in the work-focused interview. If you do not, unless you can show 'good cause', a benefit penalty may be imposed on you.[100]

'Taking part' means that you must:[101]

- turn up at the place and time notified;
- 'participate in discussions' with the personal adviser about your employability, and about any activity you are willing to do (or have done) which may enhance your employment prospects;
- answer questions about your educational qualifications, employment history, any current work and your future hopes for working, vocational training, employment skills and abilities, medical conditions which affect your chances of getting a job, and your caring or childcare responsibilities;
- except for ESA (where action plans are drawn up for your 'work-related activity' – see p1031), discuss and assist in completing an 'action plan'. This includes any action you and the personal adviser agree is reasonable and you are willing to take. If there is nothing you can reasonably do, you have not failed to take part. There is nothing which says you must take the steps in the action plan, although this is likely to change in the future. See CPAG's *Welfare Rights Bulletin* for updates;
- in further interviews, discuss your progress, any action you 'might have taken' under the action plan, how the action plan might be amended and any further support that might be available to you.

In the Jobcentre Plus rules, if you are under 18, 'taking part' also requires you to attend an interview with the local authority youth service or Connexions, Careers Wales, Skills Development Scotland or Careers Scotland.[102]

Benefit penalties for failing to take part

Usually, in the Jobcentre Plus and lone parent rules, when you make a new claim for IS, you are required to attend an initial work-focused interview. If the decision maker decides that you did not take part, unless you have 'good cause' for not doing so (see p1038) in the Jobcentre Plus rules you are treated as not having made a claim and hence are not entitled to benefit, and in the lone parent rules your benefit is reduced, as in the first bullet point below.[103]

In all the schemes, you may be required to attend work-focused interviews while you are entitled to benefit. If you fail to take part without 'good cause' (see p1038), your benefit can be reduced. The benefit reduction is:

- in the Jobcentre Plus and lone parent rules, £14.20;[104]
- in the ESA and incapacity benefits rules, 50 per cent of the value of the ESA work-related activity component for the first four weeks of the reduction (ie, £14.07), then 100 per cent of the value (ie, £28.15) for each following week.[105]

Your weekly benefit cannot be reduced by more than these amounts for failing to take part.

In all the rules, the reduction continues to apply until you take part in an interview.[106]

The reduction also cease to apply if you are no longer required to take part in work-focused interviews of the scheme you are in or if you reach the qualifying age for PC (see p509). For benefits other than ESA, the reduction also ceases to apply if, within a month of the date of the decision that you failed to take part in the interview or that you did not have 'good cause' (see p1038) for not taking part, you:[107]

- notify new facts which show you had good cause; *and*
- you could not reasonably have notified those facts within five working days of the date of the interview.

You have a right of appeal against a decision imposing a benefit penalty, including a decision that you did not take part in an interview and you did not have 'good cause' (see p1038). The rules may have the effect that for an appeal about good cause, you must have tried to show good cause within five working days of the date on which the interview was to take place. However, it is understood that the DWP views this as not necessary.[108] The decision may also be revised or superseded on normal grounds (see Chapter 45).

Note: the government may change the rules on benefit penalties for IS and ESA claimants at some point, including increasing the amounts and introducing hardship payments for ESA. Details had not been confirmed at the time this *Handbook* was written. See CPAG's *Welfare Rights Bulletin* for updates.

Good cause for failing to take part

For **benefits other than ESA**, to avoid a penalty, you must show good cause within five working days following the date on which the interview was to take place.[109] However, you may still be able to demonstrate good cause up to a month after the decision that you did not take part was notified to you, if the facts you rely on could not have been brought to the personal adviser's attention within five days.[110] For **ESA**, you must show good cause within five working days of the date you are notified by the DWP that you failed to attend the interview.[111]

In deciding whether you have good cause, for **ESA** the decision maker takes account of all the circumstances, particularly your physical or mental health. For **benefits other than ESA**, the decision maker considers all the circumstances, but in particular must take the following into account:[112]

- any misunderstanding on your part because of learning, literacy or linguistic difficulties, or misleading information given by the benefit authority;
- attending a doctor or dentist appointment or accompanying a person for whom you are caring, where the appointment could not reasonably have been rearranged;
- difficulties with transport where no reasonable alternative was available;
- the practice of your religion that prevented you attending at the fixed time;
- attending a job interview;
- the need to work in your business if you are trying to become self-employed;
- if you or a person for whom you are caring had an accident, illness or relapse;
- attending the funeral of a close friend or relative;
- a disability that makes attendance impracticable;
- any other relevant matter. This will depend on the facts in your case, but might include things like emergencies and problems with caring arrangements.

5. Getting paid

How, when and how often your benefit is paid depends on the benefit you have claimed.[113] The DWP or HM Revenue and Customs (HMRC) decides how benefit is paid to you. In practice, this normally means that you are paid by 'direct payment' (see p1039). There is no right of appeal about the way in which you are paid. Claimants of attendance allowance (AA), carer's allowance (CA), disability living allowance (DLA), employment and support allowance (ESA), income support (IS) and jobseeker's allowance (JSA) who are registered online with the 'government gateway' should be able to use the benefit enquiry service online (BESOL) to track the progress of their claims, access a breakdown of their benefit award and check their next payment.

Direct payments

Payment by direct credit transfer into a bank account, building society account or similar account is the normal method of payment on new claims for benefit. The government calls this '**direct payment**'. If that is not suitable for you, you may be able to get your benefit paid by cheque or by 'simple payment' (see p1040).

If you experience difficulty getting your money as a result of these arrangements, complain to the DWP or HMRC. You could contact your MP.

Account options

When you are paid by direct payment, your benefit can be paid into:

- an existing bank or building society current or savings account;
- a new current account at a bank or building society;
- a new 'basic bank account' at a bank or building society (sometimes this is called an 'introductory' or 'starter' account);
- a Post Office card account; *or*
- in some cases, a credit union account.

All of these accounts (except some credit unions) are suitable for direct payment, and you can withdraw cash without charge. However, they are not all the same – eg, you cannot access all current accounts at post offices, basic bank accounts and Post Office card accounts do not offer cheque books or overdrafts, and you cannot pay bills by direct debit with a Post Office card account. The DWP or HMRC should write to you with details of your options, including how to open an account.

Direct payment means that you can get your benefit in the way you get other money in your account – eg, by cheque, at a cash machine and at supermarket checkouts with a 'cashback' facility. If you do want to get your money at a post office, the following applies to direct payments.

- You may be able to access your bank or building society current account at a post office. However, not all bank and building societies have this facility – check with your bank, building society or the DWP/HMRC.
- You can use a PIN number at a post office if you have a basic bank account. Not all banks and building societies offer these accounts – check with your bank, building society or the DWP/HMRC.
- You can use a PIN number at a post office if you have a Post Office card account. If you have a card account, you can nominate someone else to collect your benefit for you, in which case that person is issued with a card her/himself.

If someone collects your benefit for you

It should be possible, if necessary, to arrange for someone you trust to be able to access your account in order to collect your benefit for you. If you already have a bank or building society account, ask the bank or building society about this. If you use a Post Office card account, a second card can be issued to the person who collects your benefit.

If you lose or forget your PIN

If you lose or forget your PIN, contact the bank to change the PIN and issue you with a new one as soon as possible. If you cannot access your benefit, contact the benefit office for advice about what to do.

If you use a Post Office card account and you lose or forget your PIN, call the customer service helpline number on 0845 722 3344 (or textphone 0845 722 3355). You will get a replacement PIN within four working days. If you cannot access your benefit in the meantime, contact the benefit office for advice.

If all else fails, you may be invited to claim a crisis loan (see p564) while the problem is sorted out. If you cannot get access to your benefit, and the DWP/HMRC refuses to remedy the situation, seek advice (see Appendix 2).

Payment by cheque or 'simple payment'

If you cannot open or manage an account, it should be possible for you to be paid by a cheque which can be cashed at a post office or, from summer 2013, by a specially issued card at a PayPoint outlet – the DWP calls this 'simple payment'. The DWP is currently phasing out its use of cheques and using 'simple payment' instead.

When you are paid

When and how often your benefit is paid depends on the benefit you have claimed.[114] You are sometimes paid in advance and sometimes in arrears. Some benefits have specific pay days, for others the day you are paid depends on your national insurance number. See the chapter for the benefit you are claiming. [115]

Who is paid

Payment is usually made directly to you, but there are some circumstances in which payments can be made to other people or organisations on your behalf.

- If you are unable to manage your own money or if you die, your benefit is paid to a person appointed to act on your behalf (see p1016).[116]
- If it is in the interests of you or your partner, or any of your children for whom you are getting benefit, the decision maker can pay your benefit to another person.[117] For example, if your partner refuses to support you, all or part of her/his benefit can be paid to you. If you are neglecting your children even though benefit is being paid for them, it might be paid to another person to help look after them.
- If you are claiming IS, income-based JSA, income-related ESA or PC and are getting help with your housing costs (see Chapter 38), these are usually paid directly to your lender on your behalf (see p1050).

- If you are claiming IS, JSA, ESA or PC and are in certain types of debt, payments can be made to your creditors on your behalf (see p1048).[118]

Overlapping benefits

There are rules that mean that sometimes you cannot be paid more than one non-means-tested benefit at the same time. These 'overlapping benfit rules' also apply if more than one person is claiming for the same child or adult dependant (see p1043), if you are getting child benefit, guardian's allowance or an increase in your non-means-tested benefit for your child (see p1043), and if you are entitled to an increase in your non-means-tested benefit for an adult dependant who is getting one or more of certain benefits her/himself (see p1043).

DLA care component and AA overlap with constant attendance allowance.[119] Otherwise AA, DLA, disablement benefit (see p378), reduced earnings allowance (see p380) and retirement allowance (see p384) can be received in addition to any of the other benefits described in this *Handbook* – eg, you can receive IB, both components of DLA and disablement benefit all at once.

Earnings replacement benefits

Some benefits are available to compensate you for your inability to work becasue of unemployment, sickness, pregnancy or old age. These are 'earnings replacement' benefits. You cannot usually receive more than one of the following 'earnings replacement' benefits at a time.

- Contributory benefits:
  - contribution-based JSA;
  - IB;
  - contributory ESA;
  - maternity allowance (MA), which counts as contributory for the purposes of this rule;
  - retirement pension;
  - widow's pension or bereavement allowance;
  - widowed mother's or widowed parent's allowance.
- Non-contributory benefits:
  - SDA;
  - CA.

If you are entitled to more than one of the above benefits the following rules apply.[120]

- A contributory benefit is paid in preference to a non-contributory benefit. However, this is topped up by any balance of a non-contributory benefit due.
- Weekly benefits are paid and topped up by any balance of daily benefit (unless you make an application to receive the daily benefit in full). See the chapter in

this *Handbook* about the benefit you are claiming to see if it is a daily or a weekly benefit.
- The highest rate benefit is paid, or if the rates are the same, one benefit is paid.

Special rules apply if you are entitled to widows' benefits or bereavement benefits and to IB at the same time. See p277 of the 2008/09 edition of this *Handbook* for further information.

Other adjustments

If you are getting a training allowance paid by a government department or training agency, your earnings replacement benefit is reduced by the amount of the training allowance.[121]

If you are getting unemployability supplement under the industrial injuries scheme or war pensions scheme, your earnings replacement benefit (other than MA) is reduced by the amount of the unemployability supplement.

You cannot usually get more than one retirement pension at a time. However, there are special rules if you are a widow or widower entitled to both a Category A (see p527) and a Category B retirement pension (see p527) and your Category A pension would be paid at a reduced rate because you have not paid enough contributions (see p793). In this situation, your basic Category A pension is increased by whichever is less of either:[122]
- the amount of the shortfall between your Category A pension and the full Category A amount of £107.45; *or*
- the amount of your Category B pension,

You are also entitled to an additional pension on your own contribution record and one on your spouse or civil partner's record up to the maximum additional pension a person could theoretically receive on one contribution record.[123]

Earnings-related additions to non-means-tested benefits

Additional pensions under the additional state pension scheme (see p137) and graduated retirement benefit (see p529) do not overlap with non-means-tested benefits. However, if two or more benefits would otherwise be payable with an additional pension and graduated retirement benefit, only the higher or highest total of additional pension and graduated retirement benefit payable in addition to one of those benefits is due.[124]

There are exceptions to this rule if you are a Category B retirement pensioner whose own contribution records would entitle you to a Category A retirement pension or if you are a widow who receives transitional long-term IB (see p278 of the 2008/09 edition of this *Handbook*).

An age addition paid with IB, SDA or retirement pension overlaps with another age addition.[125]

Increases to non-means-tested benefits for adult dependants

Only one person may receive an increase of benefit in respect of the same dependant, except when one of you receives an increase because the dependant is someone employed by you to look after your child(ren) and the dependant does not live with you (in this case, both of you can claim). You can only receive one increase in respect of an adult dependant. If, apart from these rules, more than one increase would be payable, only the higher or highest total is paid.[126]

An increase for an adult dependant also overlaps with certain earnings replacement benefits (see p1041) or training allowances which are payable to that dependant – eg, if you are claiming an increase of retirement pension for your partner, but s/he is claiming IB in her/his own right.[127] If the increase is less than or equal to the benefit payable to your dependant, the increase is not paid. If the increase is greater than the basic benefit, you get the difference. This does not apply if the adult is not residing with you and is employed by you to care for a child.

Increases to non-means-tested benefits for child dependants

Only one person may receive child benefit or an increase in a non-means-tested benefit for a child dependant for the same child (see pp93 and 745).

The standard rate of child benefit (see p105) does not overlap with any other benefit. However, if you receive the higher amount payable for your eldest child (see p105), any other benefit (except guardian's allowance) or increase paid for the same child is reduced by £3.15.[128]

All increases for children and child's special allowance overlap with guardian's allowance and industrial death benefit for children and are reduced by the level of guardian's allowance you get for the child.[129]

Missing payments

If you are entitled to benefit you must be paid it.[130] If your benefit is not paid into your account or you are not issued with a cheque, the DWP or HMRC must rectify that.

If you have lost or forgotten your PIN number, see p1040. If there is a long delay, the DWP/HMRC may refer to a rule (applying to benefits paid by the DWP) that says your entitlement to payment is lost 12 months after the date it was due to be paid into your account. However, this should only apply if you have actually been allocated benefit, not if you have not been paid it.[131] If necessary, seek advice (see Appendix 2).

Suspension of payments of benefit

A decision maker can suspend payment of part or all of your benefit in certain circumstances. In some of these circumstances, s/he can ask you to provide further information or evidence or have a medical examination to help her/him decide if you are still entitled to benefit (or are getting it at the correct rate). It is important that you provide the information that is required and attend the medical examination. Your entitlement to benefit could be terminated if you fail to do so (see p1046).

Local authorities can suspend HB in similar circumstances.[132]

Suspension while an appeal is pending

Your benefit can be suspended if the DWP, HMRC (for child benefit and guardian's allowance) or local authority is appealing (or considering an appeal) against:[133]

- a decision of the First-tier Tribunal, Upper Tribunal or court to award *you* benefit; *or*
- a decision of the Upper Tribunal or court about *someone else's case,* but only if the issue in the appeal could affect your claim (and for HB, only if the other case is about an HB issue).

The DWP, HMRC or the local authority must give you written notice of the intention either to request the statement of reasons for the First-tier Tribunal, to apply for leave to appeal or to appeal, whichever is the first that is yet to be done. It must do this as soon as is 'reasonably practicable'.[134]

The decision maker must then do one of these things within the usual time limits for doing so (see Chapter 46 for the time limits). If s/he does not, the suspended benefit must be paid to you. The suspended benefit must also be paid to you if the decision maker withdraws an application for leave to appeal, withdraws the appeal or is refused leave to appeal and it is not possible for her/him to renew the application for leave to appeal.[135]

Suspension in other circumstances

Your benefit can also be suspended if:[136]

- a question has arisen about your entitlement.[137] In this case, all or part of the benefit due to you can be suspended pending a revision, supersession or appeal of the decision about your entitlement;
- you have been getting JSA and a question has arisen about whether you are meeting your jobseeking conditions. Your JSA must be suspended until this matter is resolved;[138]
- it looks as though your award of benefit should be superseded or revised;[139]
- the DWP/HMRC thinks you are being (or may have been) overpaid.[140] All or part of your benefit may be withheld during an investigation;
- you are not living at the last address you notified;[141]
- for child benefit and guardian's allowance, the bank account or other account details which you have given to HMRC are incorrect;[142]
- for HB, a recoverable overpayment may have occurred.[143]

In some cases, your benefit can also be suspended if you fail to provide information or submit to a medical examination (see p1045).

Providing information and evidence

You can be required to supply information or evidence (including of your incapacity for work or limited capability for work[144]) if the decision maker needs this to determine whether your award of benefit should be revised or superseded (see pp1126 and 1135).

You can be required to provide information and evidence if:[145]
- your benefit has been suspended in the circumstances described above; *or*
- you apply for a revision or supersession (see pp1126 and 1135); *or*
- you fail to provide certificates, documents, evidence and other information about the facts of your case as required;[146] *or*
- your entitlement to benefit is conditional on you being incapable of work or having limited capability for work.

You must be notified in writing if the decision maker wants you to provide information or evidence. Within 14 days (currently one month for child benefit, guardian's allowance, HB and CTB) of being sent the request, you must:
- supply the information or evidence.[147] You can be given more time than this if you satisfy the decision maker that this is necessary; *or*
- satisfy the decision maker that the information does not exist or you cannot obtain it.[148]

If the decision maker has not already done so, your benefit can be suspended if you do not provide the information or evidence within 14 days (currently one month for child benefit guardian's allowance, HB and CTB) of the request.[149] To find out if your entitlement to benefit can be terminated, see p1046.

Medical examinations

Most benefits can be suspended if you fail to submit to a medical examination on two consecutive occasions without 'good cause' (there is no specific rule for child benefit, guardian's allowance, HB or CTB).[150] This applies if:
- the decision maker is looking at whether you should still be getting a benefit (or whether you are getting it at the correct rate); *or*
- you apply for a revision or a supersession and the decision maker thinks a medical examination is necessary in order to make a decision.

This rule does not apply if the issue is whether you have limited capability for work (see p205). To find out if your entitlement to benefit can be terminated, see p1046.

Challenging decisions to suspend benefit

The decision maker may be willing to continue to pay your benefit, or at least some of it, if you can show that you will experience hardship otherwise. If you receive a letter telling you that your benefit has been suspended, write back explaining how the suspension affects you and ask for it to be reconsidered. It may be wise to get advice first (see Appendix 2).

You cannot appeal to the First-tier Tribunal against the decision to suspend your benefit. The only ways to change the decision are to negotiate to get your benefit reinstated or to challenge the decision in the courts by judicial review (see p1202). You could also ask for an interim payment (see p1046). Seek advice (see Appendix 2).

Termination of entitlement to benefit

Your entitlement to benefit can be terminated if:

- your benefit was suspended *in full* in the circumstances described on p1044 and you are required to provide information or evidence and fail to do so within one month of the request;[151]
- your benefit was suspended *in full* because you failed to provide information in the circumstances described on p1045, but only if it is more than 14 days (currently one month for child benefit, guardian's allowance, HB and CTB) since your benefit was suspended.[152]

The termination of entitlement to benefit takes effect from the date payment was suspended (or an earlier date if you ceased to be entitled for another reason).[153]

Your entitlement to most benefits (although there is no specific rule for child benefit, guardian's allowance, HB or CTB) can also be terminated if you fail to submit to a medical examination, but only if it is more than one month since your benefit was suspended on this ground.[154] This is discretionary.

If you disagree with a decision to terminate your benefit, you can seek a revision (see p1126) or appeal (see Chapter 46).[155]

Interim payments

If your claim or payment of your benefit is delayed, you can ask for an interim payment. However, it may be that you cannot get an interim payment pending an appeal unless the DWP considers that there is entitlement to benefit.[156]

An interim payment can be made where it seems that you are or may be entitled to benefit and where:[157]

- there is a delay in your making a claim, including being able to satisfy straight away the national insurance number requirement; *or*
- you have claimed it but not in the correct way (eg, you have filled in the wrong form, or filled in the right form incorrectly or incompletely – see p1021) and you cannot put in a correct claim immediately – eg, because the DWP office is closed; *or*
- you have claimed it correctly, but it is not possible for the claim, or for a revision or supersession which relates to it, to be dealt with immediately; *or*
- you have been awarded benefit, but it is not possible to pay you immediately other than by means of an interim payment.

You cannot appeal to the First-tier Tribunal if you are refused an interim payment. It may be possible to apply for judicial review (see p1202). If you are refused an interim payment, see Chapter 25 to find out if you can get a crisis loan. You could contact your MP to see if s/he can help to get the decision reconsidered. You could also try using the emergency service (see below).

An interim payment can be deducted from any later payment of benefit and if it is more than your actual entitlement, the overpayment can be recovered.[158] You should be notified of this in advance, unless it is an interim payment of:

- IS or income-related ESA made because you have not received child support maintenance (see p800). In this case, any overpayment is recovered from the arrears of maintenance rather than your benefit; *or*
- DLA and you are terminally ill or have an invalid vehicle.

Emergencies

If you have lost all your money or there has been a similar crisis, it is possible to get help at any time. Any local police station should have a contact number for DWP staff on call outside normal office hours.

If you are unable to contact the DWP, your local social services office may be able to help. The police station should have a contact number.

If you need money urgently, it is important that you provide as much information as you can to support your claim. It may help if you can get an advice agency or third party (eg, a health visitor, social worker, doctor or MP) to support you.

Change of circumstances after you claim

You have a duty to report certain changes in your circumstances.

If you do not promptly report any change which you have a duty to notify, any resulting overpayment may be recoverable from you (see Chapter 43).

If you are considered to have acted 'knowingly' or dishonestly, you may also be guilty of an offence (see Chapter 44).

The DWP or HMRC should inform you of the main kinds of changes in your circumstances that you need to report, but might not actually list them all. In any case, it is your duty to report *any* change in your circumstances which you might reasonably be expected to know could affect your right to, the amount of, or the payment of, your benefit. For the rules that apply to HB and CTB, see p290.

Notify changes promptly to the office handling your claim. That office might be at a benefit delivery centre or other benefit processing unit (eg, for IS), a central or regional unit (eg, for DLA) or a local Jobcentre Plus office. Check the information sent to you about your benefit award, but seek advice if you are in doubt. For child benefit and guardian's allowance, the rules say that the office handling your claim includes HMRC child benefit office (see Appendix 1), or any office specified by HMRC.

Except for child benefit and guardian's allowance, there is also a special rule for births and deaths (called 'Tell Us Once'). You can usually report such a change in person at a local authority (and, in England, county council) office specified for that purpose. If the change is a death, you can notify it by telephone if a number has been specified for that purpose.[159] Check with your local authority/registry office for the Tell Us Once arrangements in your area.

You can notify the changes in writing or by telephone.[160] For most benefits (at time of writing, these were AA, CA, DLA, ESA, IS, IB, JSA, PC and retirement pensions) you can also notify the changes online using the 'benefit update service online' (BUSOL) if you are registered for this.[161] In any case, it is best to notify changes in writing so that you have a record of what you have reported. If you do report a change by telephone, note the time and date of your call and confirm what was said in writing. Keep a copy of any letters you send. If you give the original to an officer, ask her/him to stamp your copy to confirm s/he has received the original.

Sanctions for benefit offences

If you accept a penalty or caution or are convicted of one or more benefit offences (ie, in connection with fraud), sanctions may be imposed on certain benefits, with the result that they may be paid at a reduced rate or not at all (see Chapter 44). During 2012/13, the government intends to introduce rules under which working tax credit will not be paid to you if you have committed a benefit offence (see p1391).

6. Deductions and payments to third parties

Your benefits are usually paid directly to you, but there are some circumstances when money can be deducted and paid to a third party on your behalf. The majority of these deductions can usually only be made from income support (IS), income-based jobseeker's allowance (JSA), income-related employment and support allowance (ESA) and pension credit (PC). They can also be made from contribution-based JSA and contributory ESA or from other benefits, but only in limited circumstances.

What deductions can be made

Amounts can be deducted from your IS, income-based JSA, income-related ESA or PC to pay for:[162]

- housing costs paid to your lender under the mortgage payment scheme (see p1050);
- other housing costs (see p1051);
- rent arrears (see p1052);

- residential accommodation charges (see p1052);
- hostel payments (see p1052);
- fuel (see p1053);
- water charges (p1053);
- council tax arrears (see p1053);
- community charge arrears (see p1053);
- fines (see p1053);
- repayment of eligible loans (see p1054);
- child support maintenance (see p1054);
- integration loans paid to refugees and others (see p1054); *and*
- repayment of tax credit overpayment and self-assessment tax debts (see p1055).

Except for council tax and community charge arrears and fines, if you are on IS or PC and the amount of benefit is not enough to cover the deduction, deductions can also be made from your incapacity benefit (IB), severe disablement allowance (SDA) or retirement pension, if they are paid in combination with your IS or PC.

You may also have deductions made for the recovery of social fund loans (see p563) and overpayments (see p1079).

Deductions from contribution-based jobseeker's allowance and contributory employment and support allowance

Deductions can be made from your contribution-based JSA or your contributory ESA for the payments listed above, other than for community charge arrears for contributory ESA, if you have an 'underlying entitlement' to income-based JSA or income-related ESA. This applies if, were you not entitled to contribution-based JSA or contributory ESA, you would be entitled to income-based JSA or income-related ESA at the same rate.[163]

Deductions can also be made from contribution-based JSA and contributory ESA if you have no underlying entitlement to income-based JSA or income-related ESA, but only for council tax arrears, fines and child support maintenance arrears and, for JSA only, community charge arrears.

Deductions can also be made for mortgage payments where your income-based JSA/income-related ESA is not enough to cover the deductions (see p1050).

Deductions from other benefits

Deductions can only be made from other benefits to repay certain loans (see p1054) and child support maintenance that you owe (see p1054).

When deductions can be made

Deductions and direct payments to third parties can only be made if you or your partner are liable to make the payments.[164] If there is a doubt about whether you or your partner are liable, deductions should only be made if there is evidence that you are liable – eg, the bill is in your name or your partner's name.

Do you have to agree to deductions?

Your written consent is required before deductions for tax credit overpayments and self-assessment tax debts can be made. Your consent is required before direct payments are also made for arrears of housing costs, rent arrears, service charges for fuel and water, fuel costs (including arrears), water charges (including arrears), repayment of integration and other loans if:[165]

- you (or your partner) do not get child tax credit (CTC) and the total to be deducted for these payments exceeds 25 per cent of your family's applicable amount (see Chapter 37) or, in the case of PC, 25 per cent of your minimum guarantee (see p510). For benefits other than ESA, housing costs included in your applicable amount (see Chapter 38) should *not* be taken into account when calculating the 25 per cent;
- you (or your partner) get CTC, and the total to be deducted for these payments exceeds 25 per cent of your CTC and child benefit and, for benefits other than ESA, your family's applicable amount (see Chapter 37) or, in the case of PC, your minimum guarantee (see p510). Any housing costs included in your applicable amount (see Chapter 38) should *not* be taken into account when calculating the 25 per cent.

The DWP can make deductions without your agreement if they are made for:

- community charge or council tax arrears;
- fines;
- child support maintenance;
- current housing costs;
- nursing home charges or hostel charges not included in housing benefit (HB).

Consent is not needed for these deductions even if the total amount deducted exceeds the 25 per cent referred to above.[166]

The deductions

Deductions are made at the DWP office before you receive your regular benefit payment. If you want to have deductions made to help you clear any arrears or debts, ask at the DWP office dealing with your claim. If you disagree with a decision about deductions, you can appeal (see Chapter 46).

The mortgage payment scheme

When you claim IS, income-based JSA, income-related ESA or PC you may get help with your housing costs (see Chapter 38). The general rules for payment of housing costs are as follows.

- Once you qualify for help with housing costs, the amount for mortgage interest or interest on loans for repairs and improvements is usually paid directly to your lender for each complete week that you are on benefit.[167]
- The main exceptions to this are where your lender is not covered by, or has opted out of, the mortgage payments scheme.[168] The DWP should tell you if this is the case and you must pay your own mortgage.
- If you receive PC and you are entitled only to the savings credit and not to the guarantee credit, direct payments are only made where a written request has been made and the DWP agrees that it is in the best interests of you or your family.[169]

Your housing costs are deducted from your total IS, income-based JSA, income-related ESA or PC entitlement and you get the balance.[170] If you are on IS or PC and the amount of benefit is not enough to cover the deduction, then deductions can also be made from your IB, SDA or retirement pension, if they are paid in combination with your IS or PC. If you are on JSA or ESA and the amount of your income-based JSA/income-related ESA is not enough to cover the deduction, deductions can be made from your contribution-based JSA/contributory ESA. You have to make up any difference between what the DWP pays to your lender and the amount you owe. If you do not have enough benefit to meet the full cost, all but 10p of your benefit is paid and you must pay the rest yourself.[171]

Payments are made every four weeks in arrears even if your payments are due on a calendar month basis.[172]

If you are in mortgage arrears, no amount towards the arrears can be deducted from your benefit if deductions are made under the mortgage payments scheme.

Except in the case of PC, if you have a mortgage protection policy, the amount of mortgage interest paid directly is reduced. The reduction is the amount of income from the insurance policy which is taken into account.[173]

If an overpayment of mortgage interest is paid to your lender, see p1078.

Other housing costs

The IS, income-based JSA, income-related ESA or PC for your mortgage interest is usually paid directly to your lender under the mortgage payments scheme (see p1050).[174] If this applies to you (or would if your lender had not opted out of the scheme), the deductions under this provision only cover payments for other types of housing costs (see p862).[175]

If your current IS, income-based JSA, income-related ESA or PC includes money for such housing costs and you are in debt for these costs (excluding payments for ground rent or rent charge payments unless paid with your service charges or for a tent[176]), deductions can be made from your IS, JSA, ESA or PC both to clear the debt and to meet current payments. Deductions are made if it would be 'in the interests' of you or your family to do so.

You only qualify for direct deductions if you owe more than half of the annual total of the relevant housing cost. This condition can be waived if it is in the 'overriding interests' of you or your family that deductions start as soon as possible – eg, repossession of your home is imminent.[177]

In the case of mortgage payments, the decision maker must be satisfied there are arrears.[178] You must have paid less than eight weeks' full payments in the last 12 weeks.[179] The amount of mortgage interest taken into account is the amount after deductions for non-dependants (see p869).

Rent arrears and arrears of hostel payments

If you are in arrears with your rent (including any inclusive water, fuel and service charges) while on HB, or are £100 or more in arrears of hostel payments (see below), an amount can be deducted from your IS, JSA, ESA or PC and paid directly to your landlord. This can also apply if you are in approved premises under s13 of the Offender Management Act 2007 and have built up arrears of service charges rather than rent arrears.[180]

Rent arrears do not include the amount of any non-dependant deductions (see above), but can cover any water charges or service charges payable with your rent and not met by HB. Fuel charges included in your rent cannot be covered by direct deductions if they change more than twice a year.

To qualify for direct deductions, your rent arrears must be at least four times your full weekly rent. If you have not paid your full rent for eight weeks or more, direct deductions can be made automatically if your landlord asks the DWP to make them.[181] If your arrears relate to a shorter period, deductions can only be made if it is in the overriding interests of your family to do so.[182] In either case, the decision maker must be satisfied that you are in rent arrears. Even if you are, you can ask her/him not to make direct deductions – eg, if you are claiming compensation from your landlord because of the state of repair of your home.[183] Once your arrears are paid off, direct payments can continue for any fuel and water charges included in your rent.[184]

Residential accommodation charges

Deductions can be made from your IS, JSA, ESA or PC to meet your accommodation charges if you have failed to budget for the charges and it is considered to be in your interests for deductions to be made.[185]

Hostel payments

If you (or your partner) live in a hostel or approved premises under s13 of the Offender Management Act 2007, *and* you have claimed HB to meet your accommodation costs *and* your payments cover fuel, meals, water charges, laundry and/or cleaning of your room, part of your IS, JSA, ESA or PC can be paid directly to the hostel for these items.[186] You do not have to be in arrears for this to apply. These costs are all items which cannot be covered by HB (see p262) and which you must meet from your IS, JSA, ESA or PC. Fuel costs are not paid directly if the charge varies according to actual consumption, unless the charge is altered less than three times a year.

Fuel debts

If you are in debt, an amount can be deducted from your benefit each week and paid to the fuel company (mains gas or mains electricity) in instalments – usually once a quarter.[187] This is **'fuel direct'**. In return, the fuel company agrees not to disconnect you. Deductions can be made if:[188]

- the amount you owe is £71 or more (including reconnection or disconnection charges if you have been disconnected); *and*
- you continue to need the fuel supply; *and*
- it is in your, or your family's, interests to have deductions made.

An amount is deducted for the fuel you use each week (your current consumption) as well as for the arrears you owe. The amount deducted for current consumption is whatever is necessary to meet your current weekly fuel costs. This is adjusted if the cost increases or decreases. Deductions for current consumption can be continued after the debt has been cleared.[189]

Water charges

If you get into debt with charges for water and sewerage, direct deductions might be made.[190] Debt includes any disconnection, reconnection and legal charges. If you pay your landlord for water with your rent, deductions are made under the arrangements for rent arrears (see p1052).[191]

Deductions can be made if you failed to budget and it is in the interests of you or your family to make deductions.[192] If you are in debt to two water companies, you can only have a deduction for arrears made to one at a time. Your debts for water charges should be cleared before your debts for sewerage costs, but the amount paid for current consumption can include both water and sewerage charges.[193]

Council tax and community charge arrears

Deductions for council tax can be made from IS, JSA, ESA or PC and for community charge arrears from IS, JSA or PC if the local authority gets a liability order from a magistrates' court (in Scotland, a summary warrant or decree from a sheriff court) and applies to the DWP for recovery to be made in this way.[194] Deductions can be made for arrears and any unpaid costs or penalties imposed.

Fines, costs and compensation orders

Magistrates' courts (any court in Scotland) can apply to the DWP for a fine, costs or compensation order to be deducted from your IS, JSA, ESA or PC.[195] Only one court application can be dealt with at a time. If a second application is made, it is not dealt with until the first debt is paid.

Deductions from IS, JSA, ESA or PC can only be made if you are 18 or over and you have defaulted on payments. Payments continue until the debt is paid off, or your IS, JSA, ESA or PC stops or is too low to cover the repayments.

Repayment of eligible loans

Deductions can be made from your IS, JSA, ESA, PC and (if necessary) your IB, retirement pension or carer's allowance (CA) towards repaying certain 'eligible' loans if you have not kept up with the repayments.[196] This applies only to loans made by certain not-for-profit lenders, such as community development financial institutions, credit unions and charities. When taking out the loan, you must have given your agreement that, were your repayments to fall behind, your lender could send your details to the DWP so that deductions could be made from your benefit. The loan must be unsecured, not made for business purposes and not made by a credit card.

Deductions can be made if you have failed to make payments for at least 13 weeks and have not started making them again. They can only be made where your lender has agreed that no interest or other charges will be added from the point the deductions start, and if you do not have deductions for repayment of a benefit overpayment or social fund loan. Only one deduction for repayment of certain loans can be made.

Repayment of integration loans

Deductions can be made from your benefit to repay an integration loan – ie, those paid to refugees, people granted humanitarian protection under the Immigration Rules and dependants of such people.[197] You must have been told when repayment will start and that it will be by deduction from your benefit.

Child support maintenance

The rules that apply depend on whether the child support maintenance is payable under the old Child Support Agency (CSA) rules that applied up to 3 March 2003, or the new CSA rules that have applied from that date (see Chapter 36 and CPAG's *Child Support Handbook* for more details).

If a child support assessment made by the CSA remains in force, deductions can be made from the non-resident parent's benefit, as described below.

Under the **old CSA rules**, deductions can be made from a non-resident parent's IS, income-based JSA, income-related ESA or PC as a contribution towards the *maintenance* of her/his child(ren). Currently, the maximum deduction is £7.10 a week. Deductions cannot be made in certain circumstances (see p809) and may be reduced if deductions are also being made for debts of other payments (see p1057).[198]

Under the **new CSA rules**, if you are a non-resident parent on benefit and liable to pay child support maintenance at the flat-rate (see p809) a deduction of £5 a week (this is expected to increase, but it is not clear when this will be – see CPAG's *Welfare Rights Bulletin* for updates) can be made from your:[199]

- bereavement allowance;
- retirement pension;
- IB;
- contributory ESA;
- CA;
- SDA;
- industrial injuries benefit;
- widowed mother's allowance/widowed parent's allowance;
- widow's pension;
- training allowance (other than Work-Based Learning for Young People or Skillseekers);
- contribution-based JSA;
- war widow's or war disablement pension.

A deduction can also be made from any IS, income-based JSA, income-related ESA or PC paid either to you or your partner.[200]

The whole of the maintenance may be deducted from one of the benefits listed above.[201] If more than one partner in a couple or polygamous marriage is liable to pay maintenance at the flat rate, £5 is deducted from any IS, income-based JSA, income-related ESA or PC s/he receives.[202]

Deductions may also be made from some benefits for arrears for child support maintenance.[203] In old rules cases, deductions may be made only from your contribution-based JSA or contributory ESA. In new rules cases (including if the case is converted from the old rules), deductions can be made from any of the above benefits *except* IS, income-based JSA, income-related ESA or PC.

Repayment of tax credit overpayments and self-assessment tax debts

If you have a recoverable overpayment of tax credits, or a debt of income tax arising from a self-assessment, it can be paid to HMRC by deductions from benefit. Your written consent is required. You may withdraw the consent.[204]

How much can be deducted

If deductions are being made from your IS, income-based JSA, income-related ESA or PC (or contribution-based JSA where you have an underlying entitlement to income-based JSA, or contributory ESA where you have an underlying entitlement to income-related ESA – see p1049), the maximum deductions are shown below.

Type of arrears	*Deduction for arrears*	*Deduction for ongoing cost*
Mortgage direct payments*	Nil	Current weekly cost
Housing costs*	£3.55 each housing debt (maximum of £10.65)	Current weekly cost
Rent arrears/hostel payment	£3.55	Nil (met by HB)
Fuel	£3.55 each fuel debt (maximum of £7.10 payable)	Estimated amount of current consumption
Water charges	£3.55 (adjusted every 26 weeks)	Estimated costs
Council tax	£3.55	Nil (met by council tax benefit)
Community charge	£3.55 (single person) £5.60 (couple)	Not applicable
Fines	Nil	£5 (lower amount £3.55)
Repayment of eligible loans	Nil	£3.55
Repayment of integration loans	Nil	£3.55
Child support maintenance	Nil	£5 (new rules) £7.10 (old rules)
Residential accommodation charges	Nil	The accommodation allowance (for those in local authority homes); all but £23.25 of your IS, JSA, ESA or PC (for those in private or voluntary homes)
Repayment of tax credit overpayments and self-assessment tax debts	Nil	Maximum £10.65
Hostel charges	Nil	Weekly amount assessed by local authority

*If you have more than one type of housing cost and these are not met in full because of a restriction on the amount that can be covered (see p867) or a non-dependant deduction (see p869), the direct payment to meet current weekly costs is reduced as follows:[205] Multiply the amount of the restriction and/or deduction by the amount of the item of housing costs to be paid directly and then divide by the amount of total housing costs. This ensures that such reductions are shared proportionately between different housing costs.

More than one debt

For **IS, income-based JSA, income-related ESA** and **PC**, deductions for arrears can be made for more than one debt. However:

- the maximum amount that can be deducted from your benefit for arrears (excluding community charge arrears) and for current child support maintenance under the old rules is £10.65 a week.[206] The *total* amount deducted from benefit may be more than that if you are having deductions made for current costs as well as for arrears. If the total amount of deductions for arrears would exceed £10.20 a week, the deductions are made in a set order of priority (see below);
- if deductions of £7.10 would be due for arrears and for current child support maintenance under the old rules, only half of the child support maintenance deduction is made – ie, £3.55;
- for fuel, rent, water charges, housing costs arrears and repayment of certain loans, if the combined cost of deductions for arrears and current consumption is more than 25 per cent of your total applicable amount (see p814) or, for PC, more than 25 per cent of your minimum guarantee (see p510) before housing costs, the deductions cannot be made without your consent.[207]

If there is no underlying entitlement to income-based JSA or income-related ESA, the maximum amount that can be deducted in total (for debts) from **contribution-based JSA** or **contributory ESA** for council tax, fines and child support maintenance arrears or, for JSA only, community charge arrears, is one-third of the weekly amount of JSA or ESA for a person of your age.

Priority between deductions

If you have more debts or current charges than can be met within the limits for direct payments (see p1055), they are paid in the following order of priority:[208]

- housing costs not covered by the mortgage payment scheme;
- rent arrears (and related charges);
- fuel charges;
- water charges;
- council tax and community charge arrears;
- unpaid fines, costs and compensation orders;
- payments for child support maintenance under the old rules. **Note:** payments due under the new rules are always payable, whatever other deductions are being made;
- repayment of integration loans;
- repayment of eligible loans;
- repayment of tax credit overpayments and self-assessment tax debts.

If you owe both gas and electricity arrears, the DWP chooses which one to pay first, depending on your circumstances. If you have arrears for both council tax and community charge, only one application can be dealt with at a time and the earliest debt should be dealt with first.[209]

If you have been overpaid benefit or given a social fund loan, you may have to repay these through deductions from your benefit.[210] You should argue that these deductions should take a lower priority.

7. Recovery of benefits from compensation payments

If you are seeking compensation from someone (a defendant) through the courts (eg, because you have been unfairly dismissed or because you have had a personal injury), you might be awarded damages to compensate you for your loss. However, if, as the result of a defendant's action, you have had to claim benefit, the amount of damages awarded is reduced by the amount of benefit you received.

Employment cases

In an employment case such as wrongful or unfair dismissal, your claim for compensation for loss of earnings may be reduced by the amount of benefit (eg, jobseeker's allowance – JSA) you received.[211] Seek specialist employment law advice. Also, the DWP is able to recover payments of JSA, income support or income-related employment and support allowance from your employer by deductions from your compensation if it is an unfair dismissal or protective award case dealt with in an employment tribunal. In such cases, the DWP sends a 'recoupment notice' to the employer, and a copy to you, setting out the benefit to be deducted before the compensation is paid to you. You may give notice to the DWP that you do not accept the amount recouped within 21 days of the recoupment notice (or longer if allowed), and can appeal to the First-tier Tribunal against the decision that the DWP makes in response.[212]

Personal injury cases

If you are paid compensation in respect of an accident, injury or disease after 6 October 1997, those compensating you can reduce the amount paid to you when you have received benefit in respect of the same loss. They must then pay the money back to the Compensation Recovery Unit (CRU), which is part of the DWP. It does not matter whether the payment is voluntary, with or without legal proceedings, or by order of a court. A reduction is not made if the compensation is paid for pain and suffering, because benefits are not paid for this.

The CRU can only recover the benefit in the right-hand column of the table on p1059, and only if you were paid it as a consequence of the accident, injury or disease.

Note: the CRU can also recover, under a similar scheme with its own rules, certain lump-sum payments made by the DWP to you or a dependant.[213] The lump-sum payments that can be recovered are those made by the DWP for lung diseases under the Pneumoconiosis etc. (Worker's Compensation Act) 1979 (or as compensation if you have had a claim under that Act rejected) or payments under the Diffuse Mesothelioma Scheme.

Details of the procedures to be followed and other advice can be obtained from the CRU (see Appendix 1). A guide to the procedures, *Recovery of Benefits or Lump-sum Payments and NHS Charges*, is available at www.dwp.gov.uk/cru.

Which benefits can be recovered

The recoverable benefit consists of all benefits paid to you 'in consequence' of the injury or disease from which you have suffered during the 'relevant period' (see p1059).

Before you are paid compensation, those compensating you must apply to the DWP for a 'certificate of recoverable benefits'.[214] This tells them which benefits are recoverable.

Those compensating you become liable to pay the DWP for the total amount of recoverable benefit 14 days after the certificate is issued.[215] It is the compensator's obligation, not yours, and so if the compensator fails to pay, the CRU cannot pursue you for the money. The compensator remains liable even if it fails to apply for a certificate.[216]

The relevant period

The **'relevant period'** is usually the period of five years from the date:[217]

- of your accident or injury if you are claiming compensation for an accident or injury; *or*
- you first claimed a recoverable benefit because of the disease if you are claiming compensation in respect of a disease.

The relevant period ends if those compensating you make a final payment of compensation or an agreement is made under which compensation already paid is accepted as being in final payment.[218]

Offsetting against your compensation

Before the compensator pays your compensation, it is allowed to deduct the recoverable benefits paid during the relevant period from certain types of compensation.[219] The type of compensation is shown in the left-hand column and the relevant benefits in the right-hand column of the table on p1060.

Compensation	*Recoverable benefits*
Loss of earnings	Disability working allowance, disablement benefit, employment and support allowance, incapacity benefit, income support, invalidity pension, jobseeker's allowance, reduced earnings allowance, severe disablement allowance, sickness benefit, statutory sick pay (paid before 6 April 1994), unemployment benefit, unemployability supplement, invalidity allowance
Cost of care	Attendance allowance, disability living allowance care component, disablement benefit paid for constant attendance (see p380) or exceptionally severe disablement (see p380)
Loss of mobility	Mobility allowance, disability living allowance mobility component

Example

Gary receives a £30,000 compensation payment consisting of £15,000 for loss of earnings, £5,000 for pain and suffering, and £10,000 for the cost of care. By the time the award is made he has received £20,000 of incapacity benefit and £5,000 disability living allowance care component. The award for loss of earnings is reduced to nil. Gary will receive the full award for pain and suffering, but his award for the cost of care is reduced by £5,000. The compensator is liable to pay the DWP recoverable benefits of £25,000, and pays Gary a net award of £10,000 (£5,000 pain and suffering plus £5,000 care).

Any compensation reduced by this method is treated as being paid to you. Those compensating you must give you a statement showing how the payment has been calculated, even if the recovery of benefits reduces a particular type of compensation to nil. If the recoverable benefit exceeds the compensation paid to you for a particular loss, those compensating you still have to pay the balance to the DWP.

Exempt payments

The recovery rules apply to all claims, no matter how small. However, certain compensation payments are exempt.[220] These include:

- payments under the Fatal Accident Act 1996, the Vaccine Damage Act 1979 and the NHS industrial injury scheme;
- payments under the Pneumoconiosis Compensation Scheme and certain payments for loss of hearing;

- criminal injuries compensation;
- contractual sick pay and redundancy payments;
- payments from insurance companies from policies agreed before the accident; *and*
- payments from certain trusts – eg, the Macfarlane Trust, Eileen Trust, MFET Ltd, The Caxton Foundation, UK Asbestos Trust and the EL Scheme Trust.

Challenging a recovery decision

A decision maker may look at a certificate of recoverable benefit again if s/he is satisfied that it was issued in ignorance of, or based on a mistake about, a material fact, or if there was an error in its preparation – eg, a miscalculation.[221] You and those compensating you can both appeal against the certificate but not until the compensation payment has been made and the benefit paid back to the DWP. There are only four possible grounds for appeal. These are that the:[222]

- amount, rate, or period of benefit specified on the certificate is wrong; *or*
- benefits specified were not paid at all, or were not paid because of an accident, injury or disease; *or*
- benefits specified were not paid to you during the relevant period (see p1059); *or*
- payment on the basis of which the certificate was issued was not a payment which must be repaid – eg, because it was not paid in consequence of an accident, injury or disease.

Appeals are heard by the First-tier Tribunal (see p1155).[223] Further appeals can be made to the Upper Tribunal in the usual way (see p1181).[224]

Notes

1. Who should claim

1 ss1and 13 SSAA 1992
2 **IS** Reg 4(3) and (4) SS(C&P) Regs
JSA Reg 4(3B) SS(C&P) Regs
ESA Reg 4I(1) and (2) SS(C&P) Regs
PC Reg 4D(7) and (8) SS(C&P) Regs
3 **CB/GA** Reg 28 CB&GA(Admin) Regs
Other benefits Reg 33 SS(C&P) Regs
4 R(SB) 5/90
5 Reg 33(1A) SS(C&P) Regs
HB Reg 82(5) HB Regs; reg 63(5) HB(SPC) Regs
CTB Reg 68(5) CTB Regs; reg 52(5) CTB(SPC) Regs
6 CIS/642/1994
7 CIS/379/1992

2. How to make a claim

8 ss1 and 13 SSAA 1992
9 Reg 3 SS(C&P) Regs
10 **CB/GA** Reg 5 CB&GA(Admin) Regs
Other benefits Reg 4 SS(C&P) Regs
11 DWP Press Release, 15 January 2010
12 Regs 4(6A)-(6CC), 4D and 4H SS(C&P) Regs; Memo Vol 1 06/03 DMG
13 **CB/GA** Reg 8 CB&GA(Admin) Regs
Other benefits Reg 5(1) SS(C&P) Regs
14 **CB/GA** Reg 8 CB&GA(Admin) Regs
Other benefits Reg 5(2) SS(C&P) Regs
15 CJSA/3979/1999; CJSA/1332/2001; CDLA/1589/2005; HB/CTB G10/2008
16 Regs 4D and 4G SS(C&P) Regs
17 Reg 4(11) and (11A) SS(C&P) Regs
18 Regs 4(1) and (1A) and 4H(2) SS(C&P)Regs
19 *Novitskaya v London Borough of Brent and Another* [2009] EWCA Civ 1260
20 Regs 4(7) and (7ZA), 4D and 4(H) SS(C&P) Regs; reg 10 CB&GA(Admin) Regs
21 Regs 4(8) and (9), 4D(6)-(6C), 4G(3), 4H(2) SS(C&P) Regs; reg 10(3) CB&GA(Admin) Regs
22 Regs 4(7), 4D, 4G and 4H SS(C&P) Regs; reg 10 CB&GA(Admin) Regs
23 Regs 4(7A) and (7B), 6(1A), (4A) and (4ZA) SS(C&P) Regs
24 Sch 2 SS&CS(DA) Regs and Sch 2 CB&GA(DA) Regs do not include such decisions in the list of decisions against which no appeal lies.
25 s8 SSA 1998
26 Reg 4(1A) SS(C&P) Regs
27 Reg 4(7A) SS(C&P) Regs
28 Sch 2 SS&CS(DA) Regs and Sch 2 CB&GA(DA) Regs do not include such decisions in the list of decisions against which no appeal lies.
29 Reg 4(1B) SS(C&P) Regs
30 CIS/2057/1998
31 Reg 6(4A) SS(C&P) Regs
32 **CB/GA** Reg 7 CB&GA(Admin) Regs
Other benefits Regs 7 and 8(2) SS(C&P) Regs; regs 23 and 24 JSA Regs
33 ss180 and 180A SSAA 1992
34 The Social Security (Claims and Information) Regulations 2007, No.2911
35 ss1(1A) and (1B) and 12A SSAA 1992
36 CH/4085/2007
37 CH/1231/2004; CH/4085/2007
38 Reg 1A SS(DLA) Regs; reg 5 HPG(A) Regs
39 Reg 4(a) HB Regs; reg 4(a) HB(SPC) Regs
40 s1(1A) SSAA 1992; reg 2A SS(IB) Regs; reg 2A SS(ICA) Regs; reg 1A SS(MA) Regs; reg 1A SS(WB&RP) Regs; reg 2A SS(SDA) Regs
41 *SSWP v Wilson* [2006] EWCA Civ 882, reported as R(H) 7/06
42 **IS** Reg 2A IS Regs
JSA Reg 2A JSA Regs
ESA Reg 2A ESA Regs
PC Reg 1A SPC Regs
HB Reg 4(c) HB Regs; reg 4 HB(SPC) Regs
CTB Reg 4 CTB Regs; reg 4 CTB (SPC) Regs
43 HB/CTB Circular A4/2009
44 Reg 2A IS Regs; reg 2A JSA Regs; reg 2A SS(IB) Regs; reg 2A SS(ICA) Regs; reg 1A SS(MA) Regs; reg 1A SS(WB&RP) Regs; reg 2A SS(SDA) Regs

3. **The date of your claim**

45 **CB/GA** Reg 11 CB&GA(Admin) Regs
Other benefits Reg 9(1) and Sch 1 SS(C&P) Regs; reg 2(3) ESA(TP) Regs
46 Sch 1 SS(C&P) Regs
47 Reg 11 CB&GA(Admin) Regs
48 Reg 9(4) and (5) SS(C&P) Regs
49 R(A) 3/81
50 **CB/GA** Reg 5(1)(b) CB&GA(Admin) Regs
PC Reg 4D(2) SS(C&P) Regs
Other benefits Reg 4(1) SS(C&P) Regs
51 Reg 19 and Sch 4 SS(C&P) Regs
52 R(SB) 9/84
53 ss65(4) and (6) and 76 SSCBA 1992
54 **CB/GA** Reg 6 CB&GA(Admin) Regs
Other benefits Reg 19(2) and (3) and Sch 4 SS(C&P) Regs
55 CJSA/3994/1998
56 Reg 19(6) and (7) SS(C&P) Regs
57 CIS/4901/2002
58 Reg 19(4) and (5) SS(C&P) Regs
59 CIS/2484/1999
60 CJSA/4573/1999
61 CJSA/4066/1998
62 CIS/610/1998
63 CJSA/3084/2004
64 CIS/4354/1999
65 CIS/4490/1999
66 CJSA/0580/2003
67 CIS/610/1998
68 CIS/3994/1998
69 CIS/5430/1999
70 CJSA/1136/1998
71 CIS/5430/1999
72 CIS/5430/1999
73 Reg 19(5) SS(C&P) Regs; C12/98 (IS)
74 C12/98 (IS)
75 CIS/2057/1998
76 R(SB) 17/83; R(IS) 5/91; CIS/812/1992
77 R(P) 2/85
78 Reg 6(22) SS(C&P) Regs
79 Reg 6(16)-(26) SS(C&P) Regs
80 Reg 6(19) SS(C&P) Regs
81 Reg 6(19)-(21A) SS(C&P) Regs
82 Reg 6(30) SS(C&P) Regs

4. **Work-focused interviews and work-related activity**

83 s15 WRA Act 2007; s2 WRA 2009
84 ss54 and 58 WRA 2012
85 Regs 2(1) and 3(1)(a)(i) SS(JPI) Regs
86 Reg 4(1) SS(JPI) Regs
87 Regs 3 and 8 SS(JPI) Regs
88 Reg 2(1) SS(JPIP) Regs
89 Reg 7 SS(JPIP) Regs
90 s2AA SSAA 1992; regs 3, 3A and 4 SS(JPIP) Regs
91 Regs 10, 11 and 14 SS(JPIP) Regs
92 SS(IBWFI) Regs; regs 54-62 ESA Regs
93 Reg 3 SS(IBWFI) Regs ; Memo DMG 46/08; Memo DMG 35/09
94 Reg 54 ESA Regs
95 s24(4) WRA 2007; reg 54(2) ESA Regs
96 Regs 1(3) and 2-2B SS(WFILP) Regs
97 Reg 4 SS(WFILP) Regs
98 Reg 10(2) SS(JPI) Regs; reg 2(3) SS(WFILP) Regs; reg 6(1) SS(IBWFI) Regs; reg 56(2) ESA Regs
99 Regs 6 and 7 SS(JPI) Regs; regs 5 and 6 SS(WFILP) Regs; reg 5(4) SS(IBWFI) Regs; reg 59 ESA Regs
100 Regs 12 and 14 SS(JPI) Regs; regs 3 and 7 SS(WFILP) Regs; regs 10 and 11 SS(IBWFI) Regs; regs 61 and 63 ESA Regs
101 Reg 11(2)-(2B) SS(JPI) Regs; reg 3(2)-(2B) SS(WFILP) Regs; regs 6 and 7 SS(IBWFI) Regs; regs 57 and 58 ESA Regs
102 Reg 3(3) SS(JPI) Regs
103 Reg 12(2)(a) SS(JPI) Regs; reg 7(3)(a) SS(WFILP) Regs
104 Reg 12(2)(c)-(8) SS(JPI) Regs; reg 8 SS(WFILP) Regs
105 Reg 63 ESA Regs; reg 9 SS(IBWFI) Regs
106 Reg 12(9) SS(JPI) Regs; reg 8(3)(c) SS(WFILP) Regs; reg 9(8) SS(IBWFI) Regs; reg 64(2) ESA Regs
107 Regs 12(12) and 13 SS(JPI) Regs; reg 9(11) SS(IBWFI) Regs; reg 8(3)(a) and (b) SS(WFILP) Regs
108 Reg 15 SS(JPI) Regs; reg 9 SS(WFILP) Regs; reg 10 SS(IBWFI) Regs. For ESA there is no specific appeal provision, but the DWP has confirmed there is a normal right of appeal against such a decision and that it is not necessary to have attempted to show good cause within five days: email from DWP to CPAG, 21 January 2008.
109 Reg 11(4) SS(JPI) Regs; reg 7(1)(b) SS(WFILP) Regs; reg 8(3) SS(IBWFI) Regs
110 Regs 12(12) and 15(1) SS(JPI) Regs; reg 7(2) SS(WFILP) Regs; reg 9(11) SS(IBWFI) Regs
111 Reg 61(1) ESA Regs
112 Reg 14 SS(JPI) Regs; reg 7(5) SS(WFILP) Regs; reg 8 SS(IBWFI) Regs; reg 61(2) and (3) ESA Regs

5. **Getting paid**

113 **CG/GA** Regs 16-20 CB&GA(Admin) Regs
Other benefits Regs 22-26C SS(C&P) Regs
114 **CB/GA** Regs 16-20 CB&GA(Admin) Regs
Other benefits Regs 22-26C SS(C&P) Regs
115 The Social Security (Transitional Payments) Regulations 2009, No.609
116 **CB/GA** Regs 27 and 28 CB&GA(Admin) Regs
Other benefits Regs 30 and 33 SS(C&P) Regs
117 **CB/GA** Reg 33 CB&GA(Admin) Regs
Other benefits Reg 34(1) SS(C&P) Regs
118 Reg 35 SS(C&P) Regs
119 Reg 6 SS(OB) Regs
120 Reg 4(5) SS(OB) Regs
121 Reg 6 SS(OB) Regs
122 s52(2) SSCBA 1992
123 s16(1), (2) and (6) SSCBA 1992; reg 2 SS(MAP) Regs
124 Reg 4 (2)(f) and (4) SS(OB) Regs
125 Reg 4(3) SS(OB) Regs
126 Reg 9 SS(OB) Regs
127 Reg 10 SS(OB) Regs
128 Reg 8 SS(OB) Regs
129 Reg 7 SS(OB) Regs
130 **CB/GA** Reg 18 CB&GA(Admin) Regs
Other benefits Reg 20 SS(C&P) Regs
131 Reg 38(1)(bb) SS(C&P) Regs; CDLA/2609/2002 commented on the way a similar rule applied to payment by giro/order book.
132 Reg 11 HB&CTB(DA) Regs
133 **CB/GA** Reg 18(3) CB&GA(DA) Regs
HB/CTB Sch 7 para 13(2) CSPSSA 2000; reg 11(2)(b) HB&CTB(DA) Regs
Other benefits s21(2)(c) and (d) SSA 1998; reg 16(3)(b) SS&CS(DA) Regs
134 **CB/GA** Reg 18(4) and (5) CB&GA(DA) Regs
HB/CTB Reg 11(3) HB&CTB(DA) Regs
Other benefits Reg 16(4) SS&CS(DA) Regs
135 **CB/GA** Reg 21 CB&GA(DA) Regs
Other benefits Reg 20(2) and (3) SS&CS(DA) Regs
136 **CB/GA** Reg 18(2) CB&GA(DA) Regs
HB/CTB Sch 7 para 13(2)(a) CSPSSA *2000*
Other benefits ss21(2)(a) and (b), 22 and 24 SSA 1998
137 **CB/GA** Reg 18(2)(a) CB&GA(DA) Regs
HB/CTB Reg 11(2)(a)(i) HB&CTB(DA) Regs
Other benefits Reg 16(3)(a)(i) SS&CS(DA) Regs
138 Reg 16(2) SS&CS(DA) Regs
139 **CB/GA** Reg 18(2)(b) CB&GA(DA) Regs
HB/CTB Reg 11(2)(a)(ii) HB&CTB(DA) Regs
Other benefits Reg 16(3)(a)(ii) SS&CS(DA) Regs
140 **CB/GA** Reg 18(2)(c) CB&GA(DA) Regs
HB/CTB Reg 11(2)(c)(i) and (ii) HB&CTB(DA) Regs
Other benefits Reg 16(3)(a)(iii) SS&CS(DA) Regs
141 Reg 16(3)(a)(iv) SS&CS(DA) Regs
142 Reg 18(e) CB&GA(DA)Regs
143 Reg 11(2)(c) HB&CTB(DA) Regs
144 Reg 17(6) SS&CS(DA) Regs
145 **CB/GA** Reg 19 CB&GA(DA) Regs
Other benefits Reg 17(2) SS&CS(DA) Regs
146 **CB/GA** Reg 23 CB&GA(Admin) Regs
Other benefits Reg 32(1) SS(C&P) Regs
147 **CB/GA** Reg 19(2) CB&GA(DA) Regs
HB/CTB Reg 13(4)(a) HB&CTB(DA) Regs
Other benefits Reg 17(4)(a) SS&CS(DA) Regs
148 **CB/GA** Reg 19(2)(b) CB&GA(DA) Regs
HB/CTB Reg 13(4)(b) HB&CTB(DA) Regs
Other benefits Reg 17(4)(b) SS&CS(DA) Regs
149 **CB/GA** Reg 19(5) CB&GA(DA) Regs
HB/CTB Reg 13(4) HB&CTB(DA) Regs
Other benefits Reg 17(5) SS&CS(DA) Regs
150 s24 SSA 1998; reg 19(2) SS&CS(DA) Regs
151 **CB/GA** Reg 20(1)(a) CB&GA(DA) Regs
HB/CTB Reg 14(1)(a) HB&CTB(DA) Regs
Other benefits Reg 18(1)(a), (2) and (4) SS&CS(DA) Regs
152 **CB/GA** Reg 20(1)(b) CB&GA(DA) Regs
HB/CTB Reg 14(1)(b) HB&CTB(DA) Regs
Other benefits Reg 18(1)(b), (3) and (4) SS&CS(DA) Regs
153 **CB/GA** Reg 20(2) CB&GA(DA) Regs
HB/CTB Reg 14(1) HB&CTB(DA) Regs
Other benefits Reg 18(1) SS&CS(DA) Regs
154 Reg 19(3) and (4) SS&CS(DA) Regs
155 para 04130 DMG; CH/402/2007

156 Reg 2(1A) SS(PAOR) Regs. It is unclear whether in cases involving EU law there would be a breach in not making an interim payment pending an appeal.
157 Reg 2 SS(PAOR) Regs; reg 22 CB&CA(Admin) Regs
158 Regs 3 and 4 SS(PAOR) Regs
159 Reg 32ZZA SS(C&P) Regs; reg 24 JSA Regs
160 Regs 2, 3 and 5 SS(NCC) Regs, which apply for fraud, allow notification by telephone (unless it is specifically required to be in writing), but under reg 4 notification for these purposes for HB/CTB must be in writing.
161 Reg 32ZA SS(C&P) Regs

6. **Deductions and payments to third parties**

162 Regs 34A and 35 and Sch 9 SS(C&P) Regs; CC(DIS) Regs; CT(DIS) Regs; F(DIS) Regs
163 Sch 9 para 1(2) and (3) SS(C&P) Regs
164 Sch 9 para 2(1) SS(C&P) Regs
165 Sch 9 para 8(2) and (4) SS(C&P) Regs
166 Sch 9 para 8 SS(C&P) Regs
167 Reg 34A and Sch 9A para 2 SS(C&P) Regs
168 Sch 9A paras 8 and 9 SS(C&P) Regs
169 Regs 34A(1A) and 34B and Sch 9A para 2A SS(C&P) Regs
170 Sch 9A para 3 SS(C&P) Regs
171 Sch 9A paras 1 and 3 SS(C&P) Regs
172 Sch 9A para 6 SS(C&P) Regs
173 Sch 9A para 3(4) SS(C&P) Regs
174 Sch 9 para 3 SS(C&P) Regs
175 Sch 9 para 3(5) SS(C&P) Regs
176 Sch 9 para 1 SS(C&P) Regs, definition of 'housing costs'
177 Sch 9 para 3(4) SS(C&P) Regs
178 CIS/15146/1996
179 Sch 9 para 3(4) SS(C&P) Regs
180 Sch 9 para 5 SS(C&P) Regs
181 Sch 9 para 5(1)(c)(i) SS(C&P) Regs
182 Sch 9 para 5(1)(c)(ii) SS(C&P) Regs
183 Sch 9 para 5(6) SS(C&P) Regs; R(IS) 14/95
184 Sch 9 para 5(7) SS(C&P) Regs
185 Sch 9 para 4 SS(C&P) Regs
186 Sch 9 para 4A SS(C&P) Regs
187 Sch 9 para 6 SS(C&P) Regs
188 Sch 9 para 6(1) SS(C&P) Regs
189 Sch 9 para 6(4)(b) SS(C&P) Regs
190 Sch 9 paras 1 and 7 SS(C&P) Regs
191 Sch 9 para 7(1) SS(C&P) Regs
192 Sch 9 para 7(2) SS(C&P) Regs
193 Sch 9 para 7(7) SS(C&P) Regs
194 CC(DIS) Regs; CT(DIS) Regs; CIS/11861/1996
195 F(DIS) Regs
196 Sch 9 para 7C SS(C&P) Regs
197 Sch 9 para 7D SS(C&P) Regs; reg 9 Integration Loans for Refugees and Others Regulations 2007, No.1598
198 s43 CSA 1991; Sch 9 paras 7A and 7B SS(C&P) Regs
199 Sch 1 para 4(l)(b) CSA 1991; reg 4(1) CS(MCSC) Regs; Sch 9B para 2 SS(C&P) Regs
200 Sch 1 para 4(1)(c) CSA 1991; reg 4(2) CS(MCSC) Regs; Sch 9B para 2 SS(C&P) Regs
201 Sch 9B para 2 SS(C&P) Regs
202 Sch 9B paras 4-6 SS(C&P) Regs
203 Schs 9 para 7B and 9B para 3(1) SS(C&P) Regs
204 Sch 9 para 7E SS(C&P) Regs
205 Sch 9 para 3(2A) SS(C&P) Regs
206 Sch 9 para 8(1) SS(C&P) Regs
207 Sch 9 paras 5(5) and (5A), 6(6) and (6A), 7(8) and (9), and 8(2) and (2A) SS(C&P) Regs
208 Sch 9 para 9 SS(C&P) Regs
209 Reg 4 CC(DIS) Regs; reg 8 CT(DIS) Regs
210 Regs 15 and 16 SS(PAOR) Regs; reg 3 SF(RDB) Regs

7. **Recovery of benefits from compensation payments**

211 *Nabi v British Leyland (UK) Ltd* [1980] 1 WLR 529 (CA)
212 The Employment Protection (Recoupment of Jobseeker's Allowance and Income Support) Regulations 1996, No.2349S
213 The Social Security (Recovery of Benefits) (Lump Sum Payments) Regulations 2008, No.1596
214 s4 SS(RB)A 1997
215 s6(4) SS(RB)A 1997
216 s7 SS(RB)A 1997
217 s3 SS(RB)A 1997
218 s3(4) SS(RB)A 1997
219 s8 and Sch 2 SS(RB)A 1997
220 s1 and Sch 1 SS(RB)A 1997; reg 2 SS(RB) Regs
221 s10 SS(RB)A 1997
222 s11 SS(RB)A 1997
223 s12 SS(RB)A 1997
224 s13 SS(RB)A 1997; reg 13 SS(RB)App Regs

Chapter 43

Overpayments

This chapter covers :

For overpayments of tax credits, see Chapter 58. If it is considered that an overpayment was made because of fraud, as well as the overpayment being recovered, you may be prosecuted or offered the option of paying a penalty as an alternative to going to court. See Chapter 44 for further information. For the rules on recovery of overpaid interim payments, see Chapter 42.

Key facts

- If you are paid more benefit than you are entitled to, this is called an overpayment.
- For benefits other than housing benefit (HB) and council tax benefit (CTB), the general rule is that if the overpayment arose because you did not disclose or you misrepresented something, regardless of whether this was your fault, you must repay it.
- There are also situations in which overpaid benefit must be repaid, regardless of what caused it.
- All overpayments of HB and CTB are recoverable, except those which were caused by official error and which you could not have reasonably known were overpayments.
- The DWP has the discretion not to recover a recoverable overpayment in certain situations.
- If you are paid too much income support, income-based jobseeker's allowance, income-related employment support allowance or pension credit, you may also have been paid too much HB and CTB.

Future changes: April 2013 and after

Major changes are taking place that affect the benefits and tax credits system (see Chapter 2). From October 2013, a new benefit, universal credit (UC), will replace most means-tested benefits. The government intends that all overpayments of UC will be recoverable. The rules on the recovery of personal independence payment, which will replace disability living allowance for adults in April 2013, are likely to be similar to the current rules on recovery of ordinary overpayments of benefit. See CPAG's *Welfare Rights Bulletin* for updates.

1. Ordinary overpayments of benefits

Most overpayments are recoverable only in certain circumstances. These are referred to in this *Handbook* as 'ordinary overpayments'. The following are *not* ordinary overpayments and different rules apply.

- You have been paid too much income support (IS), income-based jobseeker's allowance (JSA), income-related employment and support allowance (ESA) or pension credit (PC) because other income was paid late (see p1077).
- Too much mortgage interest has been paid directly to your lender (see p1078).
- Too much benefit has been paid into your bank account by mistake (see p1078).
- You have been paid too much housing benefit (HB) or council tax benefit (CTB) (see pp1082 and 1094).

Benefits covered by these rules

This section covers the rules that allow recovery of overpayments of:

- all the benefits (not tax credits) covered in this *Handbook*, other than HB and CTB;
- Sure Start maternity grants, funeral expenses, cold weather and winter fuel payments (see Chapter 26);
- payments from the discretionary social fund (see Chapter 25) made after 5 October 1998.[1]

Note: the government intends to make all overpayments of JSA and ESA recoverable (as well as the new universal credit and the proposed housing credit in PC when these are introduced). When this happens, this section will no longer apply to those benefits. At the time of writing, it is not known when these changes will take effect. See CPAG's *Welfare Rights Bulletin* for updates.

When an overpayment can be recovered

Before an overpayment can be recovered, a number of conditions must usually be met.[2] Unless it can be shown that all of them are present in your case, the benefit cannot be recovered from you.[3] The conditions are that:

- the decisions awarding you benefit have been changed (see below); *and*
- you failed to disclose or misrepresented a material fact (see p1069); *and*
- as a result of your failure to disclose or your misrepresentation an overpayment was made (see p1074); *and*
- the whole amount is recoverable (see p1074).

Note: the DWP has sometimes claimed that it can recover ordinary overpayments outside these rules under common law, but this has been held not to be correct (see p1081).

The decisions awarding you benefit have been changed

Once you have been awarded benefit, if the decision is then considered to be incorrect, it must be changed before any overpayment is recoverable. Any overpayment from a period for which your benefit award has not been changed is not recoverable.[4] There are, therefore, two decisions. First, there is a decision which alters previous decisions awarding you benefit. Second, there is a decision that the overpayment is recoverable.

If both decisions are not made, it is not possible to recover the overpayment from you.[5] Note, however, that both decisions might be included in one and it is possible that your benefit award for the past period is changed, but this is not notified to you until you are also notified that the overpayment is recoverable.[6] In addtion, during the period for which you were overpaid, there may have been more than one decision awarding you benefit, or setting the amount of benefit to which you are entitled. Unless these are *all* changed, *all* of the overpayment cannot be recovered.[7] The new decision should state the new amount payable (if any).[8]

If this rule is not complied with, or it appears that it may not have been, you should appeal to the First-tier Tribunal (see p1155) against the decision that the overpayment is recoverable. If it has not been complied with, the First-tier Tribunal should decide that the decision that the overpayment is recoverable is of no effect – ie, so that the overpayment cannot be recovered because there is no valid decision. In this case, the DWP/HM Revenue and Customs (HMRC) can usually try again to recover the overpayment by making and notifying the correct decisions.[9] However, sometimes the First-tier Tribunal will go further and say that an overpayment is not recoverable, in which case the First-tier Tribunal's decision will be final (unless the DWP/HMRC appeals or the decision can be altered in some other way – see pp1181 and 1126).

How a decision is changed

A decision to alter your benefit award should have been made by a decision maker. A decision maker can change a decision by carrying out a revision or a supersession of the decision to award you benefit (see pp1126 and 1135).

You failed to disclose or you misrepresented a material fact

You have a duty to report your circumstances correctly when you first claim and to notify the DWP/HMRC when they have changed (see p1137).[10]

Even if you innocently misrepresented your situation or you failed to tell the relevant office certain facts because you did not understand how the benefit scheme works, you can still be required to repay the benefit.[11]

A material fact

Overpayments can only usually be recovered if you failed to disclose (see below) or you misrepresented (see p1072) a 'material fact'. A **'material fact'** is one which would influence how much benefit you should be paid.[12] Sometimes there can be a difference between a statement of your honest opinion and a statement of a material fact.[13] For example, it may well be that a statement about the distance you can walk should be taken merely as your honest opinion of your ability, rather than as a statement of fact.[14] If the decision maker has simply come to a different conclusion about the facts than you, you can argue that an overpayment should not be recovered.[15]

Facts	*Conclusions about the facts*
You have arthritis	You have limited capability for work
A friend of the opposite sex is sharing your flat	You are living together as husband and wife
You have a bad back	Your mobility is severely restricted most of the time

Failure to disclose

Failure to disclose occurs if you do not give the relevant office material facts – eg, you forget to tell it that your or your partner's working hours or pay have increased. You:

- must know of the material fact (see p1071); *and*
- have failed to inform the relevant office about the material fact by making a 'valid disclosure' (see below); *and*
- should have reported the material fact (see p1071).

Have you made a valid disclosure?

Generally, to make a valid disclosure you must disclose the material fact to the 'relevant office' in sufficiently clear terms so that how it affects your claim can be examined.

- If you have been told that you need to report a certain fact, the 'relevant office' is the one that handles the benefit you are claiming.[16] This may be a benefit delivery centre (eg, for IS) or a central office (eg, for disability living allowance – DLA). For special rules on reporting a birth or death (sometimes called 'Tell Us Once'), see p1047.
- If you have not been told to report a certain fact, but could reasonably have been expected to know that your benefit might be affected, the law says that the relevant office is any DWP office or, in JSA cases, a specified DWP office. However, it is always best to tell the office handling your claim if you can. For child benefit and guardian's allowance you can disclose changes in your circumstances to the Child Benefit Office, or any office specified to you by HMRC.[17] Again, it is best to ensure that you tell HMRC, as it administers your claim.
- If the office already knew about the fact and you were aware of this, it is arguable that you have not 'failed to disclose'. Even if you were not aware that the office already knew, it may be possible to argue that its knowledge means that any failure on your part did not actually cause the overpayment. This is especially so if the evidence shows that the office would not have acted any differently even if you had reported the fact to it.[18]
- You can usually notify changes in writing or by telephone, but it is best to do so in writing.[19]
- If you filled in a form while giving information, the First-tier Tribunal should not just look at what you said on the form, but also consider whether you gave the necessary information in another way.[20] If you fail to fill in a form correctly, but give the relevant information in the wrong place, you have disclosed the facts.[21]
- If you have made a statement in person or on the telephone but the decision maker says there is no record of this, the decision maker must show, 'on the balance of probabilities', that there would be a record of the conversation at the local office if it had taken place. In order to do this, the decision maker must give the First-tier Tribunal information on:[22]
  - the instructions which should have applied for recording and attaching information to a claimant's file;
  - whether the appropriate administrative arrangements were in place to enable these instructions to be carried out;
  - to what extent in practice these instructions are carried out.
- You should usually make the disclosure yourself, unless you have an appointee acting for you (see p1016).[23] To be effective, disclosure by someone else on your behalf must be made to the right office with your knowledge and you must think that there is no need to repeat the disclosure yourself. However, if someone else makes the disclosure to an office not handling your claim, but s/he reasonably believes that the information will be passed to the correct office, this may count as disclosure.[24]

- Once you have made a proper disclosure to the office handling your claim, you are not expected to repeat it.[25] However, if you give the information to a different office and subsequently become aware that it has not been acted on, you are obliged to take further steps to make a proper disclosure.[26] A short time may elapse before you can reasonably be expected to realise that the original information has not been acted on.[27]

When you must report a fact

You will have failed to disclose a fact if you did not report it and you:[28]

- were clearly told by the DWP/HMRC that you needed to disclose the fact – eg, in your benefit award letter. The instruction must be clear and leave no room for doubt;[29] *and*
- knew about the material fact; *or*
- were *not* clearly told of the need to disclose the fact, but:
  - you knew about the fact; *and*
  - the fact was a change in your circumstances; *and*
  - it was reasonable to expect you to know that your benefit might be affected; *and*
  - you did not report the change 'as soon as reasonably practicable' after it occurred.

You should, therefore, report anything you have been told you need to report and any changes that might affect your benefit. **Note**: the application of this rule to people who are too ill to comply with it is currently being challenged in the European Court of Human Rights.[30] If this may apply to you, but you have still been requested to repay the overpayment, consider appealing and asking for the appeal to be heard once the challenge has been decided.

If you are alleged to have failed to disclose, note the following.

- You may be able to argue that the test of whether you were clearly informed of your need to report a change of circumstances depends on whether it was reasonable for you to understand the instructions from the DWP/HMRC, including if you were mentally unwell.[31]
- In general, you cannot rely on one DWP/HMRC office telling another about the fact. However, if the office handling your claim already knew about the fact, you can argue that you did not fail to disclose it. If the office should have known about the fact because of an automatic computer interface between it and another DWP office, you may be able to argue that any failure on your part did not cause the overpayment. This is especially so if the evidence shows that the office would not have acted any differently, even if you had reported the fact to it. There is, for example, an automatic computer interface between the offices that deal with DLA and IS. [32] Similarly there is a link between the office that deals with DLA/attendance allowance (AA) and the one that deals with

carer's allowance (CA). However, it appears the link does not work where DLA/AA payment have been combined with PC.[33]

- Sometimes, different sections within the same office deal with different benefits without your knowing about it. If this is the case, you can argue that you fulfilled your duty by telling the office that had been notified to you.[34]
- In any case, remember there is still discretion on whether or not the overpayment should be recovered from you (see p1081).

If you did not know about the fact, whether or not it was a change in your circumstances, you have not 'failed' to disclose it.[35] You cannot have failed to disclose something you did not know about unless:

- there is some reason why you should have been aware of it;[36] *or*
- it was reasonable for you to make enquiries which would have revealed the information to you;[37] *or*
- you had been aware of it, but simply forgot.[38]

If you were not told what to report

If you were not clearly told that you needed to report a certain fact, the overpayment is not recoverable unless the fact was a change in your circumstances and you could reasonably have been expected to know that your benefit might be affected.[39] What is reasonable will depend on the details of your case. For example, if you were told by the DWP or a lawyer that your benefit would not be affected, or if you were too ill to have realised that it might be, arguably you could not reasonably have been expected to have known that your benefit might be affected.[40] If there is no obvious connection between the fact and the overpaid benefit, argue that it was not reasonable to expect you to know your benefit might be affected.

Misrepresentation

Misrepresentation occurs if you have provided information that is inaccurate – eg, you gave an incorrect answer to a specific question on the claim form. It does not apply to a failure to give information, unless you do so deliberately, intending to mislead.[41] The following apply.

- It does not matter whether a reasonable person would have also given the information inaccurately. No 'failure' on your part needs to be shown.[42]
- It does not matter if you honestly believed the information you gave to be correct – once it is shown to be incorrect, you have misrepresented it. However, you have not misrepresented if you added the phrase 'not to my knowledge' to your statement.[43]
- A written misrepresentation may be qualified by an oral one. If you fill in a form incorrectly but explain the situation to an officer when handing in the form, the explanation must be taken into account when deciding whether what is stated on the form is misrepresentation.[44] Similarly, if you give

incorrect information in one document but correct information in another, there may not be misrepresentation.[45] However, if you have declared a fact on a previous claim but inadvertently give incorrect information on a later claim, you have misrepresented it. The decision maker is not required to check back for you.[46]

- If you are incapable of managing your affairs but nevertheless sign a claim form which is incorrectly completed, you cannot argue later that you were not capable of making a true representation of your circumstances.[47] However, it is arguable that benefit cannot be recovered from you on the basis of the misrepresentation if you:[48]
  - had a disability or an incapacity, including non-medical issues such as illiteracy or a poor understanding of English; *and*
  - thought you were signing something different from what you were or you did not understand the effect of your signature; *and*
  - took precautions to understand what you were signing – eg, you checked the form for accuracy before you signed it.[49]

Decision makers often rely on general statements you have signed to argue that a failure to disclose facts can later become a misrepresentation. This can occur:[50]

- when you sign the claim form. Some claim forms end with a statement: 'I declare that the information I have given is correct and complete.' If you gave correct answers but left out relevant information because you were unaware of it, the information is incomplete and you have failed to disclose. Argue that signing the declaration does not convert this into a misrepresentation as the declaration means 'complete insofar as I have knowledge of the material facts';[51]
- when you cashed a giro or an order book (although these are generally no longer used). Each time you did this you signed a declaration that you reported any facts which could affect the amount of your benefit. This is different from a 'failure to disclose'. Arguably, the overpayment is recoverable because of the misrepresentation. However, there is doubt about whether such misrepresentation actually causes the overpayment.[52] This might mean that the overpayment is not recoverable.

However:

- if you did not declare a fact because you were unaware of it, signing the declaration does not amount to a misrepresentation because all you are declaring is that you have correctly disclosed those facts *which were known to you*;[53]
- if you were told by the DWP/HMRC that certain facts are irrelevant to your claim, signing the declaration cannot be a misrepresentation if you fail to disclose those facts;[54]

- if someone else disclosed a fact to an office not handling your claim but s/he reasonably believed it would be passed to the correct office, it may be that disclosure has been made, and therefore your signing the declaration does not amount to a misrepresentation.[55]

Did an overpayment result?

You may be able to argue that the overpayment was not caused by your failure to disclose or your misrepresentation.

- If the relevant office has been given the correct information to decide your claim by someone else, but fails to act on it, you could argue that any overpayment did not arise because of your failure.[56] If one office of the DWP fails to inform another about *other* changes in your circumstances (eg, an increase in your earnings), this does not prevent the overpayment resulting from your failure to disclose the information yourself to the second office.[57]
- If the relevant office has obtained information from another source which leads it to think you might be being overpaid but does not suspend your benefit while it makes enquiries to establish this for certain, it is still possible that the cause of the overpayment is your failure to disclose or your misrepresentation.[58]
- In any case, if you have not disclosed a relevant fact to the relevant office and you then sign a declaration that you have reported the relevant facts (eg, when you sign on), this will be a misrepresentation.
- If what you say on your claim form is obviously incorrect and the decision maker does not check this, the overpayment will have been caused by official error, not your misrepresentation, and you do not have to pay it back.[59]

Is the whole amount recoverable?

Check how the overpayment has been calculated. To calculate the amount of the overpayment, you should:

- determine the dates between which the overpayment is recoverable;
- work out the total amount of benefit you were paid over the period;
- work out the correct amount of benefit you should have received during the period;
- deduct this from the total amount of benefit you were paid.

No interest charges may be added to the amount of the overpayment.

The amount of the overpayment is the difference between what you were paid and what you should have been paid.[60] The decision maker works out what you should have been paid using the information you originally gave her/him, plus any facts you misrepresented or did not disclose.

If you have been overpaid IS, income-based JSA, income-related ESA or PC, the decision maker should deduct from the overpayment any of that benefit (but no other) to which you would have been entitled had it been paid correctly.[61]

If your benefit claim contained sufficient information to alert the decision maker to your potential need, but s/he did not investigate this fully, you can argue that the correct entitlement should be offset against the overpayment. It does not matter if the overpayment was for a different period, provided there was sufficient information to alert the decision maker to your need for extra benefit.[62]

If additional facts are needed to prove you were underpaid IS or income-based JSA, you cannot offset the underpayment of those benefits against the overpayment.[63] However, if you have been getting IS or income-based JSA, you can ask the DWP to revise or supersede your award (see pp1126 and 1135). It could then withhold any arrears owed to you to reduce the overpayment.

If you were overpaid IS, income-based JSA or income-related ESA because you had too much capital (see p971), the overpayment is calculated taking account of the fact that, had you received no benefit, you would have had to use your capital to meet everyday expenses. For each 13-week period, the DWP assumes your capital is reduced by the amount of overpaid benefit.[64] This is known as the 'diminishing capital' rule, and if your capital goes below the capital limit, any subsequent overpayment is not be recoverable. However, if there are any increases or decreases in your actual capital during the overpayment period these are also taken into account.[65]

Example

Nina received IS of £100 a week for a period of 30 weeks. She has capital of £20,000. After 13 weeks, the rule means that she is treated as having spent 13 x 100 = £1,300 and her capital is deemed to be £18,700. After a further 13 weeks, her capital is deemed to be £17,400.

After 26 weeks of the period, Nina paid £5,000 towards credit card arrears after the credit card company threatened her with court proceedings. Provided that obtaining benefit was not a significant purpose for her making that payment (see p985), her capital is then deemed to be £12,400.

Although your capital is treated as reducing for these purposes, if you reclaim benefit your full capital counts (see p987).

Apart from checking that the overpayment has been calculated correctly, you should claim any other benefits or tax credits to which you may be entitled and ask for these to be backdated (see p1026 for benefits and p1355 for tax credits) so you can repay the overpayment. Do not delay in making the claims or you could lose out.

If you were overpaid a benefit which overlaps with another benefit you claimed but were not paid (see p1041), ask for a revision or supersession of that benefit and ask for it to be paid instead (see p1126).

If you were overpaid a benefit but in fact were entitled to another, check whether the claim for the benefit you were overpaid can be treated as a claim for the other (see p1025).

Example

Maxine should not have been receiving IS because her partner is in full-time paid work. However, she is caring for her aunt who is disabled and receiving AA. Maxine should ask the DWP to treat her claim for IS as a claim for CA and offset arrears of CA against the IS she has been overpaid.

From whom can an overpayment be recovered

An overpayment can be recovered from you if it was caused by your failing to disclose or misrepresenting a material fact (see p1068).[66] The DWP/HMRC may try to argue that it can recover the overpayment from you even if you are *not* the claimant or were not otherwise paid the benefit. However, it is arguable that it is only a claimant who can fail to disclose.[67]

If you are an appointee (see p1016), the overpayment can be recovered from you or the claimant, or both of you. From whom the overpayment is recoverable depends on the individual facts of the case – ie, who misrepresented or failed to disclose a material fact. The DWP/HMRC should issue a decision that deals with the liability of both the appointee and the claimant.[68] There are two exceptions to this rule.

- If the overpaid benefit has not been given to the claimant, the overpayment cannot be recovered from her/him, unless s/he contributed to the misrepresentation or s/he failure to disclose a material fact.
- The overpayment cannot be recovered from the appointee if s/he used 'due care and diligence' in making the representation.

Having power of attorney is not the same as being an appointee. Unless you are an appointee, a benefit overpayment caused by your actions cannot be recovered from the claimant. However, such an overpayment may be recoverable from you.[69] Seek advice if you are in this situation.

An overpayment can be recovered from a claimant's estate if s/he dies.[70] Recovery can only begin once a grant either of probate or of letters of administration has been made. [71]

Challenging an overpayment decision

Whether or not you are the claimant, you can appeal if you disagree:[72]

- that an overpayment has occurred; *or*
- that an overpayment can be recovered; *or*
- with the amount to be recovered.

You can also appeal if the decision concerns a payment from the regulated social fund (see Chapter 26). If you have been overpaid a payment from the discretionary social fund (see Chapter 25), you can instead seek a review by a social fund officer and then a further review by a social fund inspector (see pp1232 and 1236).

Do not pay back any of the money until your appeal has been decided. If you do so and then successfully appeal, arguably the DWP should reimburse you. If it does not do so, you may be entitled to recover the money in court proceedings because you repaid the money on the basis of a mistake. Write to the DWP/HMRC and explain that you do not intend to repay any of the money until your appeal has been decided. If the DWP is already making deductions from your benefit (see p563), ask it to stop doing so straight away.

Note: even if the final decision is that an overpayment of a particular amount is recoverable, the decision maker has the discretion not to seek recovery, so it is sometimes still worth asking that nothing be recovered (see p1081).

2. Late receipt of other income

Note: this section only applies to payments of income support (IS), income-based jobseeker's allowance (JSA), income-related employment and support allowance (ESA) and pension credit (PC).

Sometimes you receive too much of these benefits because money owing to you does not arrive on time. When you get your arrears, you must repay the IS, income-based JSA, income-related ESA or PC that you would not have received if the other income had been paid on time.[73] This is to prevent a duplication of payment.

The rule applies to any income that affects the amount of these benefits. This includes:

- other social security benefits (remember though, that arrears of some benefits are treated as capital and ignored for 52 weeks – see Chapter 41);
- arrears of child support maintenance paid to you for the period from your application to the date it is assessed by the Child Support Agency;
- benefits paid by other European Economic Area member states.[74]

The decision to make you pay back the money is discretionary and does not carry the right of appeal. You can still ask the DWP not to recover the overpayment, even though it can (see p1081). See p1079 for how the overpayment can be recovered.

However, you are entitled to appeal about whether an overpayment has occurred and how it has been calculated.[75]

3. Excess benefit credited to your account

Your benefit may be paid by direct credit transfer into a bank or building society account. If you are credited with too much benefit because of the direct credit transfer system itself, the excess benefit can be recovered in certain circumstances.[76] This is the case even if the rules for recovery of ordinary overpayments do not apply.

Recovery under this rule can only happen if the overpayment was caused by the direct credit transfer system itself.

Excess benefit credited to your bank or other account can only be recovered if:[77]

- you were notified in writing before you agreed to your benefit being paid into a bank or other account that excess benefit could be recovered; *and*
- it has been certified that you were paid excess benefit because of the direct credit transfer system itself.

If excess benefit cannot be recovered under the rules described above, it could still be recoverable under the ordinary overpayment rules (see p1067) or those for recovery following late payment of income (see p1077).

You can appeal to the First-tier Tribunal against a decision to recover excess benefit credited to your bank or other account.[78]

4. Mortgage interest paid to a lender

Note: this section only applies to payments of income support (IS), income-based jobseeker's allowance (JSA), income-related employment and support allowance (ESA) and pension credit (PC).

If you are getting help with your housing costs in these benefits (see Chapter 38), your mortgage interest is usually paid directly to your lender. Any overpayment of mortgage interest paid directly to your lender must be returned to the DWP by that lender if it arose because:[79]

- you ceased to be entitled to IS, income-based JSA, income-related ESA or PC, but only if the DWP asks for repayment within four weeks of your entitlement ceasing; *or*
- the DWP failed to reduce your mortgage interest payments, even though you were entitled to less money because there was a reduction in:
  - the amount of your outstanding loan; *or*
  - the standard interest rate (see p865); *or*
  - your actual mortgage interest rate. If you have a deferred interest mortgage, the relevant interest rate is the one that you are liable to pay, not the one charged by your lender. If the Secretary of State pays the latter rate by mistake, there is no power to recover.[80]

In this case, your mortgage account should simply be corrected, but if you come off IS, income-based JSA, income-related ESA or PC and interest is recovered, you will be in arrears unless you have started to make payments yourself.

In practice, the DWP often stops sending your lender your ongoing housing costs until it has recovered the overpayment, rather than asking a lender to return what was overpaid. However, the DWP should not do this if you are put into arrears as a result.[81] If you go into arrears, seek advice immediately to avoid losing your home.

You can appeal to the First-tier Tribunal (see p1156) if, for example, you think the rules do not apply to you, if the DWP has not revised or superseded your benefit properly (see p1155), or if you dispute the amount being recovered.[82] If you are not to blame for the overpayment or you would experience hardship, you can also ask the Secretary of State to use her/his discretion not to ask your lender to repay the overpayment.

The DWP can also recover overpaid mortgage interest under the rules for ordinary overpayments described on p1067.[83] If it tries to do this, make sure these rules apply.

5. Recovery of overpaid benefit

This section does *not* apply to recovery of overpayments of housing benefit (HB) or council tax benefit (CTB). Instead, see pp1082 and 1094.

Note: if an overpayment of benefit was included in a debt relief order, it is not recoverable. Similarly, if you are subject to a bankruptcy order, any overpayment notified to you as recoverable before the order was made is not recoverable.[84]

Note: other than when seeking to recover overpaid benefit through the courts, there is no time limit within which the DWP must begin recovery action.

Methods of recovery

There are a number of different ways in which overpayments can be recovered. **Note:** the government may introduce rules allowing the recovery of overpaid benefit through deductions from earnings.[85] It is not yet known when these rules will be introduced. See CPAG's *Welfare Rights Bulletin* for updates.

Deductions from benefit

Recoverable overpayments can usually be paid back through deductions from most of the benefits in this *Handbook*. Currently overpayments of child benefit and guardian's allowance cannot be recovered in this way. However, this will be possible from 7 May 2012. In addition, no deductions can be made from guardian's allowance (except to recover overpaid guardian's allowance once this is allowed), child benefit (except to recover overpaid child benefit from 7 May

2012, HB or CTB.[86] Remember that recovery is discretionary (see p1081). Except in the case of income support (IS), income-based jobseeker's allowance (JSA), income-related employment and support allowance (ESA) and pension credit (PC), deductions can only be made from the benefit of the person who has to repay the overpayment (see p1067).

Overpayments can also be recovered from arrears of benefit you are owed, except arrears of benefit that has previously been suspended (see p1043).[87]

For IS, income-based JSA, income-related ESA and PC overpayments, as long as a couple are married or living together as husband and wife (or are civil partners or living together as if they were civil partners), the amount overpaid can be recovered from either partner's award.[88]

If an overpayment of IS, income-based JSA, income-related ESA or PC occurred because of a duplication of payment, the DWP normally deducts any overpaid IS, income-based JSA or PC from the arrears owing to you.[89] However, if it fails to do so, you can still be asked to repay even if you have spent the money.

Maximum deductions from benefit

The following are the maximum weekly amounts that can be deducted from IS, income-based JSA, contribution-based JSA (but only if you would be entitled to income-based JSA at the same rate), income-related ESA, contributory ESA (but only if you would be entitled to income-related ESA at the same rate) and PC:[90]

- £14.40 if you have agreed to pay a penalty (see p1109), admitted fraud or been found guilty of fraud; *or*
- £10.65 in any other case.

The deduction can be increased by half of any:[91]

- £5, £10 or £20 earnings disregard (see p912); *or*
- charitable income paid on a regular basis subject to a disregard (see p923); *or*
- benefit subject to a £10 disregard (see p918).

If you have been overpaid contribution-based JSA but are not entitled to income-based JSA, the maximum deduction is one-third of the personal allowance for someone of your age (see p816).[92] However, this depends on whether any other deductions are being made from your JSA.

The above amounts are maximum amounts. The DWP might be persuaded to deduct less, especially if you have other direct deductions made from your benefit.

If you have been overpaid a benefit other than IS, income-based JSA, income-related ESA or PC, the rules limiting the maximum payment that can be deducted do not apply. The DWP usually wants to deduct one-third of your weekly benefit. However, you can argue that your rate of repayment should be less than this.

Overpaid benefit cannot be recovered by withholding tax credits.[93]

Recovery through the courts

Recoverable overpayments of benefit may also be recovered by enforcement proceedings in the county court in England or Wales or the sheriff court in Scotland.[94] The DWP/HM Revenue and Customs (HMRC) may use these proceedings if you are no longer claiming benefit.

Once there is a decision from a decision maker, the First-tier Tribunal or Upper Tribunal, the court must enforce it, unless you persuade it to delay enforcement (known as a 'stay of execution') while you appeal against the relevant decision. If you are in this situation, seek advice.

Note: recovery action through the courts in England and Wales must be taken within six years of the decision to recover or, if later, any written acknowledgement of the overpayment or voluntary repayment.[95] In Scotland, the DWP regards the time limit as being 20 years from the date of the decision to recover (if there was no decision, five years from the decision that there was an overpayment).[96] From 8 March 2012, the law has been amended to put beyond doubt that these limits only apply to recovery action through the courts.[97]

Seek advice about how these limits apply to you.

Recovery under common law

The DWP has claimed in the past to be entitled to recover overpayments of benefit under the 'common law', even if the overpayment was entirely caused by official error.

However, it is now clear that the DWP cannot recover ordinary overpayments under the common law. This means that if the DWP cannot recover an ordinary overpayment under the rules described in this chapter (see p1067) because it was not caused by misrepresentation or a failure to disclose, it cannot reclaim it through the courts.[98] The DWP has said that it will identify those people who repaid overpayments that really were not recoverable and will return the repaid amounts to them.[99]

The discretion to recover

The DWP/HMRC does not have to recover an overpayment even if it is recoverable. It has the discretion not to recover all or part of the overpayment.

There is DWP guidance on cases where recovery will not be made, but this emphasises that it will be only in exceptional cases.[100] However, the DWP can apply discretion, particularly if you acted in good faith and recovery would cause you hardship or be detrimental to your health or the health of your family. If you agree to repay the overpayment or do not ask for recovery not to be made, in almost all cases the DWP will recover the overpayment from you. If an overpayment is recoverable from you, but repaying it is difficult, contact the DWP/HMRC debt management section. The details should be on the letters you received about the overpayment. Each case is decided on its merits, but, for example, you should emphasise that you acted in good faith, any misleading advice you received (particularly from the DWP or HMRC) and how repaying would cause you hardship. To demonstrate hardship on financial grounds, you must normally provide full income and expenditure details for you and your family.

You cannot appeal against a refusal to exercise discretion in your favour. Your only possible legal recourse is judicial review (see p1202), but it may also help to involve your MP. The First-tier Tribunal cannot 'write off' part of the overpayment, even if there are mitigating circumstances. It can only decide if it is recoverable and, if so, how much is repayable.

If you have been underpaid in the past but cannot now get arrears (eg, because of the rules on backdating – see p1026), ask the DWP/HMRC to reduce the amount to be recovered by this sum if it will not write it off altogether.

6. Overpayments of housing benefit and council tax benefit

Although this section refers mainly to housing benefit (HB), the rules on recovery of overpayments of council tax benefit (CTB) are generally the same. The references given cover both HB and CTB. See p1094 for the exceptions to the rules for CTB.

If you have been overpaid income support (IS), income-based jobseeker's allowance (JSA) or income-related employment and support allowance (ESA), you may also have been overpaid HB. This is because your automatic passport to maximum HB ceases when you are no longer entitled to those benefits. If you are in this situation, inform the local authority dealing with your HB claim.

To see from whom an overpayment can be recovered, see p1086.

What is an overpayment

An 'overpayment' is an amount of HB which has been paid and to which the local authority decides you were not entitled under the HB rules.[101] Being 'paid' includes payment to you, your landlord or someone else, including HB credited to your local authority rent account (see p282).[102]

Arrears of benefits and tax credits

In general, if you are paid arrears of income, including benefit income, this is treated as if the income was paid at the time when it was due, and this may lead to a decision that you have been overpaid HB.[103] However, remember that arrears of some benefits are treated as capital and ignored for 52 weeks (see p918).

Arrears of tax credits are treated as capital.[104] They are ignored as capital for 52 weeks (see pp982 and 1001).

If your arrears are treated as capital, unless the arrears mean your capital is increased above a relevant capital limit (see p971), you will not have been overpaid HB.

When an overpayment can be recovered

An overpayment can only be recovered if the local authority has taken all the following five steps. It must:

- decide whether the overpayment is legally recoverable (see below);
- decide from whom recovery of the overpayment can be made, and whether recovery should be made (see p1086);
- work out how much of the overpayment is repayable and for what period (see p1087);
- decide how the overpayment should be recovered and at what rate (see p1088);
- notify you of all the above decisions about the overpayment (see p1092) and give you an opportunity to request further information or a review (see p280).

Step one: is the overpayment recoverable

All overpayments of HB are recoverable except, in certain circumstances, those caused by 'official error' (see p1084). An overpayment may be recoverable even if it was caused by an innocent mistake on your part or was somebody else's fault. Remember that, in most cases, the local authority has the discretion to decide whether or not to recover an overpayment (see p1088).

For the differences for overpayments of CTB, see p1094.

Overpayments that are always recoverable

An overpayment is always recoverable if:

- it is the result of the local authority overestimating your HB when making an interim payment (see p289). When the local authority decides how much HB you should get, it is must recover any excess you were paid from future HB payments.[105] However, if you stop getting HB before the local authority decides, this rule does not apply. In this case, the overpayment can only be recovered under the other rules described in this section;
- it is a future payment that has been credited to your rent account. In this case, the overpayment can be recovered even if it was made as a result of an 'official error' (see p1084).[106] If an overpayment of HB caused by an official error has been credited to your account for a *past* period, see p1084.

Overpayments caused by official error

An overpayment that does not fall into the above category is not recoverable if you can show that:[107]

- it was caused by an official error (see below); *and*
- no 'relevant person' caused the official error to be made (see p1085); *and*
- no 'relevant person' could reasonably have been expected to realise that an overpayment was being made (see p1085).

An **'official error'** is a mistake (either an act or omission) by:

- the appropriate authority; *or*
- an officer of the authority; *or*
- a person acting for that authority; *or*
- an officer of the DWP or HM Revenue and Customs (HMRC) acting as such.[108]

It therefore includes:

- a mistake made by the local authority in calculating your entitlement;
- a failure by the local authority to reduce your HB when you inform it of a change of circumstances. It is always best to notify changes in writing to the office you have been told to report changes to, and keep a copy. If you have reported a move into work to the DWP by telephone under the arrangements where it passes this on to the local authority (see p290), if you have provided all the information and evidence needed, any overpayment that occurs will be due to official error. However, if you have not provided all that is needed, the local authority will not treat any overpayment as official error;[109]
- a failure by a another department of the local authority to pass on details of a change of circumstances, where it promised to do so. This is an official error because the definition does not require the mistake to be made by the HB office. If you have not been given a particular office to report a change to, you may have fulfilled your duty to report a change by reporting it to any office of the local authority, and there may have been an official error if that office failed to pass it to the HB office;[110]
- similar mistakes by someone carrying out HB functions on behalf of the local authority – eg, a private agency to whom work has been contracted;
- a mistake made by the DWP in calculating your entitlement to IS, income-based JSA or income-related ESA which results in an incorrect calculation of your entitlement to HB. However, it is not an official error if the local authority failed to check your entitlement with the DWP, unless it has information that shows the award is wrong or fraudulent;[111]
- a failure by the DWP to pass on information to the local authority;[112]
- incorrect advice given to you by an officer of the local authority, the DWP or HMRC, provided s/he is acting as an officer at the time (rather than, say, as a friend giving you informal advice).

The list on p1084 is not exhaustive. The official error does not have to be the sole cause of the overpayment. However, even if an official error has occurred, if the substantial cause of the overpayment was something that you did or failed to do, the overpayment is likely to be recoverable.[113]

No relevant person caused the official error

An official error does not prevent the overpayment being recoverable if the error was partially or wholly caused by a 'relevant person'. A **'relevant person'** is:

- the HB claimant; *or*
- a person acting on the HB claimant's behalf, either because s/he is unable to deal with her/his affairs or because s/he has asked the authority in writing to deal with you on her/his behalf; *or*
- a person to whom the payment was made, including a different person acting on the HB claimant's behalf or a landlord.

The relevant person must have caused the *error*, not the overpayment.[114]

The local authority might say it only needs to show that *any* relevant person caused the official error but it does not have to pursue that person for the overpayment.[115] If a relevant person caused the official error, the overpayment will be recoverable. However, you may still be able to argue that it is not recoverable from you – eg, it was caused by a failure to disclose a relevant fact, but it was not you who failed to disclose. See p1086 for information about from whom overpayments can be recovered.

No one realised an overpayment was being made

Even if the official error was not caused by a relevant person, an overpayment is still recoverable if any relevant person (see above) knew, or ought reasonably to have known, that an overpayment had been made. The test is whether or not you could reasonably have been be expected to *know* (not merely suspect) that an overpayment had occurred. Much depends on what could reasonably have been expected of you given the information available to you, in particular the extent to which the local authority advised you about the scheme, your duties and obligations (espcially your duty to notify changes of circumstances).[116]

If you or another 'relevant person' could only have realised that there was an overpayment at some point during the period of the overpayment, the overpayment is only recoverable from that date.

The local authority's discretion to recover

Apart from certain interim payments of HB on account (see p289), the local authority has a discretion whether or not to recover an overpayment.[117]

If you think that repaying an overpayment will cause you difficulty, contact your local authority and ask it to consider not recovering it. If appropriate, point out that you acted in good faith, or that recovery will cause you hardship. If the hardship is on financial grounds, you should normally supply details of income and expenditure for you and your family.

However, the decision to recover a recoverable overpayment does not carry the right of appeal. Depending on the facts, it might be challengeable by judicial review in the courts, although such cases are exceptional. A policy of always recovering all recoverable overpayments could be challenged by judicial review (see p1202). If you have been overpaid and you think the overpayment might not be recoverable from you, consider challenging the decision either by asking for a revision (see Chapter 45) or making an appeal (see Chapter 46).

If the overpayment was caused by someone else, you could suggest that recovery is made from her/him (if this is your landlord, see p1093).

You may be asked to repay a non-recoverable overpayment on a voluntary basis. You are under no legal obligation to do so.

Step two: from whom can the overpayment be recovered

General rules

The general rule is that a recoverable overpayment can be recovered from the person to whom it was paid (except some overpayments paid to your landlord – see p1087).[118] However, this does not apply if someone else misrepresented or failed to disclose a material fact, or if someone else should have realised that there was an overpayment at the time.

An overpayment can be recovered from someone other than the person to whom it was paid, including the claimant. This applies if:[119]

- the overpayment was caused by misrepresentation or failure to disclose a material fact. These are not specifically defined for HB/CTB, but are likely to be the same as for ordinary overpayments (see p1067). In this case it must be recovered from the person who misrepresented or failed to disclose the fact not the person to whom it was paid; *or*
- the overpayment was caused by an official error (see p1084) and you as the claimant (or someone acting your behalf) or any other person to whom the HB was paid could reasonably have been expected to realise that there was an overpayment at the time. In this case, it must be recovered from whoever should have realised not the person to whom it was paid; *or*
- neither of the above two bullet points apply, in which case the overpayment is also recoverable from the claimant. In such a case, the overpayment may be recovered from you as the claimant as well as the person to whom it was paid.

If you are the claimant and the overpayment is recoverable from you, no matter how it was caused, the local authority can also recover the overpayment by deducting any HB paid to your partner, provided you were a couple both at the time of the overpayment and when the deduction is made.[120]

If you think you have been wrongly chosen under these rules (eg, because you did not fail to disclose a material fact), you can appeal to the First-tier Tribunal.

However, if the overpayment can be recovered from you under these rules, you cannot appeal simply because you think the local authority should recover from another person instead.[121]

In the event of the death of the person from whom recovery is being sought, the local authority may consider recovering any outstanding overpayment from that person's estate.[122]

For the differences for overpayments of CTB, see p1094.

Recovery from your landlord

If a recoverable overpayment has been paid to your landlord, in general s/he can be required to pay it back, as s/he is the person to whom the overpayment was made. However, this does not apply if someone else misrepresented or failed to disclose a material fact, or if someone else should have realised there was an overpayment at the time (see p1086). If your benefit has been calculated using the local housing allowance, your landlord cannot be required to pay back more than s/he actually received – any amount above that may be recoverable from you.[123]

However, it can be recovered from another person, including you as the claimant, in certain circumstances. In any case, the overpayment cannot be recovered from your landlord if:[124]

- s/he was receiving the payment; *and*
- s/he wrote to the local authority notifying it of the possible overpayment; *and*
- the overpayment was not caused by your ceasing to live in the property as your home; *and*
- there are grounds to take action for fraud (see p1103) or the overpayment was caused by a deliberate failure to report a relevant change of circumstances; *and*
- s/he has not colluded with you or otherwise contributed to the overpayment.

Step three: how much is repayable and for what period

Check the amount of an overpayment to ensure the local authority has calculated it correctly. The local authority should distinguish between parts of an overpayment that are recoverable and those that are not. To calculate the amount of the overpayment, it should:

- determine the dates between which you have been paid too much benefit;
- identify the period(s) over which it is entitled to recover;
- work out the total amount of HB you were paid over the period(s) during which it can recover;
- work out the correct amount of HB you should have received during the period(s) of the overpayment. The local authority must award you the amount of HB you would have received if it had been aware of your true circumstances (this applies even if the overpayment occurred before the rules were changed in October 2000). If necessary, it should ask you for any necessary information or evidence to do this. However, the local authority does not include a change of your address when doing this;[125]

- deduct the HB you should have been paid from what you were paid.[126]

The local authority must not add any interest charges to the amount of the overpayment.[127]

For the differences for overpayments of CTB, see p1094.

Deductions from the overpayment

As well as any amount of HB which you should have been paid, the local authority must consider deducting other amounts from the overpayment (this is known as 'offsetting'). These are:

- if you are a council tenant, extra rent paid into your rent account. If you have been getting HB during the overpayment period and, for some reason, have paid more into your rent account than you should have paid according to your original (incorrect) benefit assessment, the extra rent you paid can be deducted from any overpayment made during that period. The local authority might not apply this rule if you paid extra rent to repay rent arrears;[128]
- reductions under the 'diminishing capital rule' (see below).

No other amounts can be deducted.

If you were overpaid HB because you had too much capital, the overpayment is calculated taking into account the fact that, had you received no HB, you would have used your capital. This is known as the **'diminishing capital rule'**. It only applies if:[129]

- you were overpaid for more than 13 weeks; *and either*
- the overpayment was caused by a misrepresentation of, or a failure to disclose, the amount of your capital (see p1069); *or*
- the overpayment was caused by an error (other than an 'official error' – see p1084) about your capital (or that of a member of your family – see p751).

For each 13-week period, the local authority assumes that your capital is reduced by the amount of overpaid HB.[130] However, although your capital is treated as reducing for these purposes, if you reclaim benefit your full capital counts (see p972).

Step four: how the overpayment is recovered

A local authority can decide how much of a recoverable overpayment it will recover. It can ask for the whole amount or recover it by instalments. When an overpayment is recovered from your landlord, note of how this affects your liability to pay rent (see p1093). Overpayments of HB can be recovered:

- from payments of HB (see p1089);
- from other benefits (see p1090);
- by adjusting your rent account if you are a local authority tenant (see p1091);
- through the courts (see p1091).

The methods used and the rates of recovery should be consistent between groups of claimants. For example, council tenants should not be required to repay an overpayment in a lump sum if private tenants can repay by instalment.

For the differences for overpayments of CTB, see p1094.

If you have a debt relief order and an overpayment of HB or CTB is included in it, it is not recoverable. Similarly, if you are subject to a bankruptcy order, any overpayment that is notified as recoverable before the order was made is not recoverable.[131]

Note: the government may introduce rules allowing the recovery of overpaid HB and CTB through deductions from earnings.[132] It is not yet known when these will be introduced. See CPAG's *Welfare Rights Bulletin* for updates.

Note: other than when seeking to recover overpaid benefit through the courts, there is no time limit within which a local authority must begin recovery action.

Recovery from payments of housing benefit

A local authority is entitled to recover an overpayment by deducting sums from HB payable to any person from whom an overpayment can be recovered (see p1086).[133] As well as yourself, this could be your partner (see below) or your landlord (see p1089). Deductions can be made from both future payments of HB and any arrears of HB that are owing.

Also, if you have moved home, your local authority may be able to recover an overpayment of HB from your previous home by adjusting the HB paid at your new home. It can decide to do this if:[134]

- the overpayment occurred after you moved, and occurred because you were no longer living at your previous home; *and*
- the same local authority that paid you the overpayment is paying your HB at your new home.

In these circumstances, the local authority can deduct all the weekly HB owing to you for your new home to recover the overpayment, for however many weeks you were overpaid at your previous home.

Recovery from your partner

If you are the claimant and the overpayment, no matter how it was caused, is recoverable from you, the local authority can also recover it by deductions from any HB paid to your partner, provided you were a couple at the time of the overpayment and when the deduction is made.[135]

Recovery from a landlord

The local authority may recover the overpayment from:

- HB paid to your landlord personally, as a claimant;[136]

- HB paid directly to your landlord on your behalf.[137] The notification of the overpayment (see p1092) should make it clear from whom the authority is recovering;
- HB paid directly to your landlord on behalf of other claimants.[138]

When HB is recovered from a landlord in this way, there are special rules on how this affects your liability to pay rent (see p1093).

The rate of recovery

The same weekly rates apply as those for IS, income-based JSA and income-related ESA (see p1080), except that the £25 disregard that applies to HB/CTB can also be used.[139] They apply to future entitlement (but not to arrears owed to you). However, you can argue that the rate will cause you hardship and a lesser amount should be recovered instead.

Recovery from other benefits

The local authority can ask the DWP to recover an overpayment from your benefit by making deductions from most of the benefits in this *Handbook* (except guardian's allowance and arguably child benefit).[140] If the overpayment is recoverable from your partner (see p1086), it can be recovered by deductions from her/his IS, income-based JSA, income-related ESA or pension credit. Overpayments of HB cannot be recovered through deductions from CTB (and *vice versa*).[141]

An overpayment can also be recovered from benefits paid to your landlord personally.[142]

Deductions can only be made if:[143]

- a recoverable overpayment has been made as a result of a misrepresentation of or failure to disclose (see p1069) a material fact by you, on your behalf or by or on behalf of another person to whom HB has been paid; *and*
- the local authority is unable to recover that overpayment from any HB; *and*
- the person who is to repay the overpayment is receiving enough of at least one of the relevant benefits to allow deductions to be made.

There are no rules limiting the maximum amount that can be deducted. However, you can argue that your rate of repayment should be reasonable. If you are on IS, income-based JSA or income-related ESA, argue that the weekly maximums for those benefits should apply (see p1080). Ask the DWP to use its discretion to reduce the amounts if the deductions will cause you hardship.

If deductions stop because you are no longer entitled to a particular benefit, or the amount to which you are entitled is insufficient for deductions to be made, the DWP notifies the local authority which, once again, becomes responsible for any further recovery action.

Adjustment of a rent account

If you are a local authority tenant, the local authority can recover an overpayment by adding it as a debt to your rent account. If a local authority recovers overpaid HB by adjusting your rent account, the overpayment should be separately identified and you should be informed that the amount being recovered does not represent rent arrears.[144]

If the local authority is seeking to evict you because you owe rent arrears, you should obtain advice. It cannot argue you owe it rent arrears if you have only been overpaid HB. Local authorities are reminded in DWP guidance that overpayments of HB in respect of their own tenants are not rent arrears and should not be treated as such.[145]

An overpayment cannot be recovered in this way if you have a private or housing association landlord. However, an overpayment can be recovered from your landlord (see p1089). If the local authority recovers from your landlord, you might count as being in rent arrears (see p1072).

Court action

If a local authority cannot use any of the above methods of recovery and you cannot agree on repayments, it can try to recover the money you owe through the county court (sheriff court in Scotland) if it thinks you could afford to make repayments. You have one month to ask for a revision or appeal against a decision that an overpayment is recoverable. This should be borne in mind when local authorities are deciding when to start proceedings.

A local authority should not use court proceedings to recover an overpayment if it has not followed the correct procedure (see p1083) – eg, if it has not issued the correct notification (see p1092).[146]

A local authority may use one of two means of recovering through the courts. It can:

- sue you for the debt created by the overpayment.[147] If the correct procedure (see p1083) has not been followed, you can use this as a defence to the local authority's claim.[148] You may also be able to claim compensation in certain circumstances (see p1083). However, you cannot say that you should have received more HB – you must seek a review instead;[149] *or*
- use the special rules to register the overpayment as a debt which can then be recovered using a court procedure.[150] Seek advice if you think the local authority is not entitled to do this.

Note: there is a principle that recovery action through the courts in England and Wales must be taken within six years of the decision to recover or, if later, any written acknowledgement of the overpayment or voluntary repayment.[151] In Scotland, the DWP regards the time limit as being 20 years from the date of the decision to recover (if there was no such decision, five years from the decision that there was an overpayment). Seek advice about how these limits apply to your case.[152]

If the local authority is successful in its court proceedings against you, you may have to pay legal costs and interest, as well as the overpayment. Remember that court procedures often require you to take action within a very short period of time. If the local authority is threatening to use court proceedings, seek urgent advice.

Step five: notification of overpayments

If the local authority decides that a recoverable overpayment has occurred, it must write to the person from whom recovery is being sought (see p1086) within 14 days if possible, notifying her/him of this.[153] This notification must state:[154]

- the fact that there is an overpayment which is legally recoverable;
- the reason why there is a recoverable overpayment;
- the amount of the recoverable overpayment;
- how the amount of the overpayment was calculated;
- the benefit weeks to which the overpayment relates;
- if recovery is to be made from future benefit, how much the deduction will be;
- if recovery is to be made from your landlord by deduction from direct payments of HB of a claimant other than you (if you were overpaid – see p1089), your identity and the claimant whose HB will be deducted;[155]
- that you have a right to ask for a further written explanation of any of the decisions the local authority has made about the overpayment, how you can do this and the time limit for doing so;
- that you have a right to ask the local authority to reconsider any of the decisions it has made about the overpayment, how you can do this and the time limit for doing so.

It may also include any other relevant matters. Local authority guidance states that it should issue a single notification to all relevant parties (eg, landlord and tenant), saying from whom the overpayment is recoverable and from whom it is not.[156]

If you write and ask the local authority for a more detailed written explanation of any of the decisions it has made about an overpayment, it must send you this within 14 days or, if this is not reasonably practicable, as soon as possible.[157]

If a notification sent to you is a clear decision that there is an overpayment which is recoverable from you, but does not contain all the matters set out in the bullets above, it will only be valid if the omissions do not put you at a disadvantage.[158] If, for example, it does not set out your rights to seek a revision so that you do not do so until it is too late, you will have been put at a disadvantage and so can argue that the overpayment is not recoverable. However, if the decision is not about recoverability at all and is only about the fact that you have been overpaid, you can argue that there is no decision saying that you must repay the overpayment.[159]

No recovery should be sought until after you have been notified and the one-month time period for asking for a revision or appealing has passed.[160]

The effect of recovery from your landlord

If you are a private or housing association tenant, an overpayment of HB recovered from your landlord (see p1089) could leave your landlord claiming money from you. The landlord could claim that you are in rent arrears as a result and could seek possession of your home.

Whether or not HB was paid directly to your landlord, s/he may still try to claim that, even if you owe no rent, you nevertheless owe a debt under common law. This is probably not correct. If s/he threatens to sue you, seek advice straight away.

If you are a local authority tenant, these rules do not apply. However, the local authority can recover an overpayment of HB by making deductions from your rent account (see p1090).

If you were overpaid HB after 4 November 1997 and HB was paid directly to your landlord, the following rules apply.

- If you are overpaid, and the local authority recovers the overpayment from your landlord by making deductions from direct payments of **other tenants' HB** (see p1089), the other tenants are treated as having paid the amount of the deduction towards their rent.[161]
- If you are overpaid, and the local authority recovers the overpayment from your landlord by making deductions from direct payments of **your HB**, you are treated as having paid the amount of the deduction towards your rent if your landlord is convicted of an offence or agrees to pay a penalty (see p1109) in relation to that overpayment.[162]

  If the local authority decides to recover under this rule, it must notify both your landlord and you that you are to be treated as having paid your rent.[163]

In these situations, it is clear that your landlord cannot claim that you are in arrears of rent. It is also much easier to argue that your landlord cannot sue you under common law for a debt.

The law does not make clear what happens in other cases where deductions are made from your HB. If you are in this position, you could argue that the rules do not say what happens in your case and so the same rules apply as before the law was introduced. If this is right, you should be treated as having paid your rent. However, because there is a risk of you losing your home if your landlord were to seek possession, you should seek advice immediately.

If you were overpaid HB before 4 November 1997, see the different rules on pp1119–20 of the *Welfare Benefits Handbook* 2000/01 and seek advice.

Challenging an overpayment decision

You can seek a revision or appeal (see Chapters 45 and 46) if you want to dispute:

- the decision that you have been overpaid;
- the amount of the overpayment;
- the decision that it is a recoverable overpayment;
- that the overpayment is to be recovered from you under the rules set out on p1086 – ie, on the grounds that those rules do not allow recovery from you.

Do not pay back any of the money until your challenge has been dealt with. Local authority guidance states that overpayments should not be recovered while under appeal.[164] If the local authority is already making deductions from your HB (see p1087) or deductions are being made from your other benefits (see p1090), ask it to stop this straight away.

If the local authority thinks an overpayment was made because of fraud, as well as recovering the overpayment it can prosecute you or offer you the option of paying a penalty as an alternative to going to court. Seek advice before agreeing to pay and see Chapter 44 for further information.

Overpayments of council tax benefit

An overpayment of council tax benefit (CTB) is called **'excess benefit'**.[165] The rules about recovery are the same as for HB (see p1082), with the following exceptions.

Is the overpayment recoverable

The criteria for when an overpayment is recoverable are the same as for HB (see p1082), except that an overpayment of CTB is always recoverable if:

- it is credited to your council tax account and relates to a future period, even if it was made as a result of an 'official error' (see p1084);[166]
- it has arisen because you were paid CTB, but then your council tax liability was reduced because of a disability reduction, discount, transitional relief or charge-capping;[167]
- it results from the local authority changing the levels of council tax for the financial year.[168]

The amount of the overpayment

The amount overpaid is the difference between what you were actually paid and what you should have received. However, there are two possible variations of what should have been paid – either a reduced amount of main CTB (see p117), or a second adult rebate (see p118) if you are eligible for this and it would have been higher than the revised amount of main CTB.

When assessing the amount overpaid, the local authority should do both calculations (see pp120 and 126) and can only recover the balance between the higher of the two figures and the amount you received. It is always worth checking that the second adult rebate calculation has been done and that the correct amount is being recovered.

From whom can the overpayment be recovered

A CTB overpayment is recovered in the first instance from the CTB claimant or the person to whom benefit was paid – eg, your partner or an appointee. If it cannot be recovered from such a person and you are the claimant, it can be recovered from certain of your partner's benefits, as for HB (see p1086). Overpayments cannot be recovered from any other person, even if s/he caused the overpayment.[169]

CTB is recoverable by the same methods as HB (see p1088), except that:

- the overpayment can be recovered by increasing your outstanding council tax liability;[170]
- there are no limits for the maximum amount of CTB that can be recovered each week;[171]
- the local authority cannot use the special court procedures for recovering the overpayment (see p1091). If it wishes to recover through the courts, it must sue you instead. It may not start proceedings for 21 days after it notifies you of the amount due.[172]

Notes

1. **Ordinary overpayments of benefits**

1 Arguably, such overpayments caused by failure to disclose might not be covered: see CPAG's *Welfare Rights Bulletin* 154. However, the official intention is that they are: SF Dir 43.
2 s71 SSAA 1992
3 R(SB) 34/83
4 s71(5A) SSAA 1992; CIS/3228/2003; R(IS) 13/05. See CPC/3743/2006 for when not all the overpayment period has been covered by the change of the award.
5 R(SB) 7/91
6 *Hamilton v Department for Social Development* [2010] NICA, but see *SSWP v AD (IS)* [2011] UKUT 184 (AAC)
7 CSIS/45/1990
8 CIS/3228/2003
9 R(SB) 7/91; R(IS) 13/05. But see CIS/3228/2003 in cases where a decision changing the award is defective but has been certified.
10 Reg 32 SS(C&P) Regs; reg 24 JSA Regs
11 *Page and Davis v CAO, The Times*, 4 July 1991 (CA)
12 R(SB) 2/92
13 CDLA/5803/1999
14 CDLA/1823/2004
15 R(S) 4/86; R(I) 3/75
16 R(SB) 15/87; *Hinchy v SSWP*, 3 March 2005 (HL), reported as R(IS) 7/05
17 Reg 23(5) CB&GA(Admin) Regs
18 CG/5631/1999; CIS/1887/2002; *WA v SSWP* [2009] UKUT 132 (AAC); *GJ v SSWP (IS)* [2010] UKUT 107 (AAC)

19 Reg 32(1B) SS(C&P) Regs requires notification in writing or by telephone, unless the DWP specifically requires otherwise.
20 R(SB) 18/85
21 CWSB/2/1985
22 CSB/347/1983; R(SB) 10/85
23 R(SB) 15/87
24 CDLA/6336/1999
25 R(SB) 15/87; CIS/3529/2008
26 R(SB) 54/83
27 CSB/393/1985
28 *B v SSWP* [2005] EWCA Civ 929, reported as R(IS) 9/06. The effect of the decison is that recovery is under reg 32 SS(C&P) Regs and, presumably, under the equivalent rules in reg 24 JSA Regs and reg 23 CB&GA(Admin) Regs.
29 *Hooper v SSWP* [2007] EWCA Civ 495, reported as R(IB) 4/07. See also official guidance in Memo DMG 26/07.
30 *B v SSWP*. Contact CPAG for further advice.
31 CDLA/1823/2004; CDLA/2328/2006 suggests that a claimant's 'mental state' may be relevant, a point apparently accepted in *DG v SSWP* [2009] UKUT 120 (AAC)
32 R(IS) 13/05; CG/5631/1999; CG/2888/2000; CIS/1887/2002; *GJ v SSWP* [2010] UKUT 107 (AAC)
33 *PT v SSWP (CA)* [2011] UKUT 103 (AAC)
34 See for example, CIS/1887/2002
35 R(SB) 21/82
36 R(SB) 54/83; CSB/296/1985
37 CG/190/1999
38 R(SB) 21/82
39 Reg 32(1B) SS(C&P) Regs; reg 24(7) JSA Regs; reg 23(4) CB&GA(Admin) Regs
40 CSB/510/1987; CIS/545/1992; CIS/1769/1999. These decisions arose from the old test of failure to disclose and it is not clear that they apply now. However, the point seems to have been adopted in *DG v SSWP* [2009] UKUT 120 (AAC)
41 CIS/5117/1998
42 R(SB) 9/85
43 *Jones and Sharples v CAO* [1994] 1 All ER 225 (CA); R(SB) 9/85
44 R(SB) 18/85
45 R(SB) 2/91
46 R(SB) 3/90
47 *Sheriff v CAO, The Times*, 10 May 1995 (CA), reported as R(IS) 14/96
48 CG/4494/1999 suggests the principle may apply in social security; R(IS) 4/06 is more doubtful, but does not rule it out.
49 CIS/3846/2001
50 *Jones and Sharples v CAO* [1994] 1 All ER 225 (CA); *Franklin v CAO, The Times*, 29 December 1995 (CA); CIS/674/1994; CIS/583/1994
51 CIS/674/1994
52 This was an *obiter* (not binding) comment by the Court of Appeal in *Hinchy v SSWP* [2003] EWCA Civ 138 (CA). The point was not approved or disapproved by the further decision in *Hinchy v SSWP*, 3 March 2005 (HL), reported as R(IS) 7/05
53 *Franklin v CAO, The Times,* 29 December 1995 (CA)
54 CIS/583/1994
55 CDLA/6336/1999
56 CIS/159/1990; CS/11700/1996; CSIS/7/1994; CG/5631/1999; *GJ v SSWP (IS)* [2010] UKUT 107 (AAC)
57 *Duggan v CAO, The Times*, 18 December 1989 (CA); CG/662/1998; CG/4494/1999; *Hinchy v SSWP* [2003] EWCA Civ 138 (CA)
58 *JM v SSWP (IS)* [2011] UKUT 15 (AAC)
59 CIS/222/1991
60 R(SB) 20/84; R(SB) 24/87
61 Reg 13 SS(PAOR) Regs
62 R(IS) 5/92
63 *Commock v CAO,* reported as an appendix to R(SB) 6/90; CSIS/8/1995
64 Reg 14 SS(PAOR) Regs
65 CIS/5825/1999
66 s71(3) SSAA 1992
67 *B v SSWP* [2005] EWCA Civ 929, reported as R(IS) 9/06, which says that overpayments for failure to disclose are recoverable because of a breach of duty by a claimant of reg 32 SS(C&P) Regs; CIS/1996/2006; CIS/2125/2006
68 R(IS) 5/03. This tribunal of commissioners' decision was intended to resolve the conflict between the earlier CIS/332/1993 and R(IS) 5/00, and preferred the latter.
69 CA/1014/1999; CSDLA/1282/2001
70 *Secretary of State for Social Services v Solly* [1974] 3 All ER 922; R(SB) 21/82
71 CIS/1423/1997
72 s12 SSA 1998

2. **Late receipt of other income**

73 s74 SSAA 1992
74 R(SB) 3/91
75 See for example, the appeals in R(SB) 28/85 and R(IS) 6/02

3. **Excess benefit credited to your account**
76 s71(4) SSAA 1992; reg 11 SS(PAOR) Regs; reg 35 CB&GA(Admin) Regs
77 Reg 11 SS(PAOR) Regs; reg 35 CB&GA(Admin) Regs
78 Sch 2 para 20(d) SS&CS(DA) Regs

4. **Mortgage interest paid to a lender**
79 Sch 9A para 11 SS(C&P) Regs
80 *R v Secretary of State for Social Security ex parte Craigie* [2000] EWCA Civ 329, 15 December (CA)
81 *R v Secretary of State for Social Security ex parte Golding* [1996] 1 July, unreported (CA)
82 CIS/5206/1995
83 CIS/5206/1995

5. **Recovery of overpaid benefit**
84 *SSWP v Payne and Another* [2011] UKSC 60
85 ss71(9A), 71ZA(2A) and 78(3C) SSAA 1992
86 Regs 15 and 16 SS(PAOR) Regs
87 Reg 16(3) SS(PAOR) Regs
88 Reg 17 SS(PAOR) Regs
89 s74(2)(b) SSAA 1992
90 Reg 16(4), (4A), (5) and (6) SS(PAOR) Regs
91 Reg 16(6) SS(PAOR) Regs
92 Reg 16(5A) SS(PAOR) Regs
93 There is no provision allowing this.
94 s71(10) SSAA 1992
95 s9(1) Limitation Act 1980
96 DWP, *Benefit Overpayment Recovery Guide,* based on the provisions of The Prescription and Limitation (Scotland) Act 1973 (draft)
97 s38(11) Limitation Act 1980
98 *CPAG v SSWP* [2010] UKSC 54, 8 December 2010, upholding the decision of the Court of Appeal in *CPAG, R (on the application of) v SSWP* [2009] EWCA Civ 1058, 14 October 2009
99 Letter from DWP to CPAG, 28 January 2011
100 *Guidance on the Application of Secretary of State Discretion* (DWP internal document, but some advice agencies may have a copy); DWP, *Overpayment Recovery Guide* (to be replaced by the *Benefit Overpayment Recovery Guide*)

6. **Overpayments of housing benefit and council tax benefit**
101 **HB** Reg 99 HB Regs; reg 80 HB(SPC) Regs
CTB Reg 82 CTB Regs; reg 67 CTB(SPC) Regs
102 **HB** Reg 99 HB Regs; reg 80 HB(SPC) Regs
CTB Reg 82 CTB Regs; reg 67 CTB(SPC) Regs
103 **HB** Reg 79(7) HB Regs; reg 59(7) HB(SPC) Regs
CTB Reg 67(9) CTB Regs; reg 50(9) CTB(SPC) Regs
104 **HB** Reg 46(9) HB Regs; reg 44(3) HB(SPC) Regs
CTB Reg 36(9) CTB Regs; reg 34(3) CTB(SPC) Regs
105 Reg 93(3) HB Regs; reg 74(3) HB(SPC) Regs
106 Reg 100(4) HB Regs; reg 81(4) HB(SPC) Regs
107 **HB** Reg 100(2) HB Regs; reg 81(2) HB(SPC) Regs
CTB Reg 83(2) CTB Regs; reg 68(2) CTB(SPC) Regs
108 **HB** Reg 100(3) HB Regs; reg 81(3) HB(SPC) Regs
CTB Reg 83(3) CTB Regs; reg 68(3) CTB(SPC) Regs
109 HB/CTB A23/2009
110 CH/2567/2007; HB/CTB A15/2009
111 CH/571/2003; CH/5485/2002
112 CH/939/2004; see also *R on the application of Sier v Cambridge CC* [2001], unreported (QBD), as upheld by the Court of Appeal [2001] EWCA 1523, 8 October 2001; CH/3761/2005
113 *Duggan v CAO, The Times,* 18 December 1989 (CA); *R on the application of Sier v Cambridge CC* [2001] unreported (QBD), as upheld by the Court of Appeal [2001] EWCA 1523, 8 October 2001; CH/571/2003; CH/3761/2005
114 *R on the application of Sier v Cambridge CC* [2001] (QBD), as upheld by the Court of Appeal [2001] EWCA 1523, 8 October 2001
115 *Warwick DC v Freeman* [1994] 27 HLR 616 (CA); CH/4918/2003
116 *R v Liverpool City Council ex parte Griffiths* [1990] 22 HLR 312; CH/2554/2002; CH/2567/2007
117 **HB** s75(1) SSAA 1992
CTB Reg 84 CTB Regs; reg 69 CTB(SPC) Regs
118 s75(3)(a) SSAA 1992

119 Reg 101(2) HB Regs; reg 82(2) HB(SPC) Regs
120 Reg 101(2)(b)(ii) and (4) HB Regs; reg 82(2)(b)(ii) and (4) HB(SPC) Regs
121 RH 6/06
122 HB/CTB *Overpayments Guide*, para 4.115
123 Reg 101(2A) HB Regs; reg 82(2A) HB(SPC) Regs
124 Reg 101(1) HB Regs; reg 82(1) HB(SPC) Regs
125 **HB** Reg 104 HB Regs; reg 85 HB(SPC) Regs
CTB Reg 89 CTB Regs; reg 74 CTB(SPC) Regs
Both *Adan v London Borough of Hounslow and SSWP* [2004] EWCA Civ 101, 19 February 2004, reported as R(H) 5/04; CH/4943/2001; HB/CTB Circular A13/2006
126 **HB** Reg 104(1) HB Regs; reg 85 HB(SPC) Regs
CTB Reg 89(1) CTB Regs; reg 74 CTB(SPC) Regs
127 *R v Kensington and Chelsea RBC ex parte Brandt* [1995] 28 HLR 528 at 537 (QBD)
128 **HB** Reg 104(3) HB Regs; reg 85(3) HB(SPC) Regs
CTB Reg 89(3) CTB Regs; reg 74(3) CTB(SPC) Regs
129 **HB** Reg 103 HB Regs; reg 84 HB(SPC) Regs
CTB Reg 88(1) CTB Regs; reg 73 CTB(SPC) Regs
130 **HB** Reg 103(1)(a) and (b) HB Regs; reg 84(1)(a) and (b) HB(SPC) Regs
CTB Reg 88(1)(a) and (b) CTB Regs; reg 73 CTB(SPC) Regs
131 *SSWP v Payne and Another* [2011] UKSC 60
132 s75(8) SSAA 1992
133 **HB** Reg 102 HB Regs; reg 83 HB(SPC) Regs
CTB Reg 86 CTB Regs; reg 71 CTB(SPC) Regs
Both s75 SSAA 1992
134 Reg 104A HB Regs; reg 85A HB(SPC) Regs
135 Reg 101(2)(b)(ii) and (4) HB Regs; reg 83(2)(b)(ii) and (4) HB(SPC) Regs
136 s75(5)(a) SSAA 1992; reg 106 HB Regs; reg 87 HB(SPC) Regs
137 s75(5)(b) SSAA 1992; reg 106 HB Regs; reg 87 HB(SPC) Regs
138 s75(5)(c) SSAA 1992; reg 106 HB Regs; reg 87 HB(SPC) Regs
139 Reg 102 HB Regs; reg 83 HB(SPC) Regs; HB/CTB Circular A42/00
140 Reg 105(1)(a) HB Regs
141 **HB** Reg 105 HB Regs; reg 86 HB(SPC) Regs
CTB Reg 90 CTB Regs; reg 75 CTB(SPC) Regs
142 s75(5)(a) SSAA 1992; reg 106 HB Regs; reg 87 HB(SPC) Regs
143 **HB** Regs 102 and 105 HB Regs; regs 83 and 86 HB(SPC) Regs
CTB Regs 86(3) and 90 CTB Regs; regs 71 and 75 CTB(SPC) Regs
144 *R v Haringey LBC ex parte Azad Ayub* [1992] 25 HLR 566 (QBD)
145 paras A7.360 GM
146 *Warwick DC v Freeman* [1994] 27 HLR 616 (CA)
147 Reg 87 CTB Regs; reg 72 CTB(SPC) Regs; para A7.361 GM
148 *Warwick DC v Freeman* [1994] 27 HLR 616 (CA)
149 *Plymouth CC v Gigg* [1997] 30 HLR 284 (CA)
150 s75(7) SSAA 1992
151 s9(1) Limitation Act 1980
152 DWP, *Benefit Overpayment Recovery Guide,* based on the provisions of The Prescription and Limitation (Scotland) Act 1973 (draft)
153 **HB** Reg 90(1)(b) HB Regs; reg 71(1)(b) HB(SPC) Regs
CTB Reg 76(1)(b) CTB Regs; reg 61 CTB(SPC) Regs
154 **HB** Sch 9 paras 2, 3, 6 and 15 HB Regs; Sch 8 paras 2, 3, 6 and 15 HB(SPC) Regs; para A7.222 GM
CTB Sch 8 paras 2, 3, 6 and 16 CTB Regs; Sch 7 paras 2, 3, 6 and 16 CTB (SPC) Regs
155 **HB** Sch 9 para 15 HB Regs; Sch 8 para 15 HB(SPC) Regs
CTB Sch 8 para 16 CTB Regs; Sch 7 para 16 CTB(SPC) Regs
156 HB/CTB Circular A13/2006
157 **HB** Reg 90(4) HB Regs; reg 71(4) HB(SPC) Regs
CTB Reg 76(2) and (3) CTB Regs; reg 61 CTB(SPC) Regs
158 *Haringey LBC v Awaritefe* [1999] 32 HLR 517 (CA)
159 CH/1395/2006
160 para A7.230-233 GM; HB/CTB Circular A13/2006
161 s75(6) SSAA 1992
162 s75(6) SSAA 1992; reg 107 HB Regs; reg 88 HB(SPC) Regs
163 Reg 107(3) HB Regs; reg 88(3) HB(SPC) Regs

164 HB/CTB *Overpayments Guide*, paras 4.391 and 6.50; *Housing Benefit and Council Tax Benefit General Information Bulletin* HB/CTB G18/2010
165 Reg 82 CTB Regs; reg 67 CTB(SPC) Regs
166 Reg 83(5) CTB Regs; reg 68 CTB(SPC) Regs
167 Regs 82(a) and 83(4) CTB Regs; regs 67(a) and 68(4) CTB(SPC) Regs
168 Regs 82(b) and 83(4) CTB Regs; regs 68(4) and 76(b) CTB(SPC) Regs
169 Regs 85, 86 and 90 CTB Regs; regs 70, 71 and 75 CTB(SPC) Regs
170 Reg 86(2)(b) CTB Regs; reg 71(2)(b) CTB(SPC) Regs
171 HB/CTB Circular A42/00
172 Reg 87 CTB Regs; reg 72 CTB(SPC) Regs

Chapter 44

Fraud and penalties

This chapter covers:

HM Revenue and Customs (HMRC) makes decisions about child benefit and guardian's allowance. The rules on fraud and penalties for these benefits are included in this chapter. HMRC also makes decision about tax credits. For information on tax credits and fraud, see Chapter 59. This chapter does not cover the rules for statutory sick pay, statutory maternity pay and statutory adoption pay.

Key facts

- When you claim benefit, you must give correct and complete information to the DWP, HM Revenue and Customs (HMRC) or the local authority. You might commit an offence if you deliberately mislead the agency dealing with your claim.
- You must also report changes in your circumstances that could affect your entitlement. You may commit an offence if you do not notify the relevant office of such changes promptly.
- From October 2012, you may receive a fine (known as a 'civil penalty') if you have provided incorrect information and you are considered to have acted negligently, or if you have not notified a change of circumstances and you do not have a reasonable excuse.
- If the DWP, HMRC or local authority believes you have committed fraud, you may be prosecuted. Alternatively, you may be given the option of paying a penalty or accepting a formal caution. Your benefit could be stopped or reduced ('sanctioned'), even if you are not prosecuted.
- If you are accused of fraud, seek urgent advice before taking any action or making any statements.

Future changes: April 2013 and after

Major changes are taking place that affect the benefits and tax credits system (see Chapter 2). In October 2013, a new benefit, universal credit (UC), will replace most means-tested benefits. When UC is introduced, it is likely that the rules on fraud, penalties and loss of benefit will be very similar to those that currently apply to existing benefits. See CPAG's *Welfare Rights Bulletin* for updates.

1. Investigating claims

The DWP, HM Revenue and Customs (HMRC) or local authority may start an investigation into your benefit claim for a variety of reasons. It does not have to tell you straight away about the enquiries it is making. It normally waits until it has gathered more information and then asks you to attend an interview to explain matters.

Powers to supply information

In order to prevent fraud, the DWP can ask for information from a wide variety of sources. Not all information is confidential, but there are special rules allowing the release of information to the DWP from:

- tax authorities;[1]
- government departments (issues about passports, immigration, emigration, nationality and prisoners);[2]
- the Registration Service, which is under an additional duty to report particulars of deaths to the DWP for social security purposes and to HMRC;[3]
- local authorities.[4]

Similarly, local authorities may be supplied with information held by the DWP or HMRC and may share information with other local authorities.[5]

Local authorities, HMRC and the DWP can require information about redirected post and have undelivered social security post returned to them.[6]

All information gathered is confidential to the bodies concerned with administration of benefit, including private companies contracted to carry out such functions. Unauthorised disclosure of this information is a criminal offence.[7]

The **Data Protection Act 1998** restricts the use of accessible personal data held on computer or in a relevant filing system in written form. If a local authority, the DWP or HMRC makes a request for information under either the provisions above or the investigative powers below which is inappropriate or unreasonable, the matter can be referred to the Information Commissioner.

Powers of investigation

As 'authorised officers', fraud investigators have certain special powers to obtain information.[8]

In local authorities, authorised officers normally investigate housing benefit (HB) or council tax benefit (CTB) fraud, but if an investigation into HB or CTB has begun, the local authority also has the power to investigate fraudulent claims for income support, jobseeker's allowance, employment and support allowance, pension credit and incapacity benefit.

'Authorised officers' can be:

- officials of any government department (not just the DWP or HMRC);
- employees of local authorities carrying out HB or CTB functions; *or*
- employees of organisations that perform contracted-out HB and CTB functions.

Authorised officers should use a code of practice when obtaining information.[9] No information can be requested that is the subject of 'legal privilege' – ie, confidential communication between a legal adviser and her/his client.[10]

Authorised officers have powers to enter, at a reasonable time, premises which they have reasonable grounds for suspecting are:[11]

- a person's place of employment;
- where a trade or business is carried out or documents relating to it are kept;
- where a personal or occupational pension scheme is administered or documents relating to it are kept;
- where someone operating a compensatory scheme for an industrial accident or disease may be found;
- where a person on whose behalf a compensatory payment for an industrial accident or disease may be found.

This may include someone's home. The authorised officer must show a certificate of appointment if asked for it. S/he can question anyone on the premises, and require, if reasonable, any documents or copies of documents.

Authorised officers cannot come into your home without your permission (except if your home is also where you run a business) and they cannot detain you. They cannot make you give information or answer questions in such a way as to confess that you, or your partner, are guilty of an offence.[12]

Fraud investigators (not just authorised officers) can use ongoing surveillance to investigate social security fraud – eg, observing people entering or leaving premises. Any surveillance must be authorised by an officer of the appropriate level. Authorisation is only given where surveillance is necessary for the purposes of preventing or detecting crime and where the authorised surveillance activity is proportionate to the outcome the investigator is seeking to achieve.

Fraud investigators (rather than authorised officers) are bound by codes of practice under the Police and Criminal Evidence Act 1984.[13] If the codes are breached, this may restrict the use of evidence they have obtained.[14] If you think the officers have acted unfairly, seek advice.

Interviews

Fraud investigators may carry out interviews to gather information. If you are suspected of fraud, officers should carry out a formal interview, known as an 'interview under caution'. You should always be cautioned before the interview if there are grounds to suspect that you have committed an offence. If the fraud officer fails to do so, the interview may not be admissible in court. If you do not understand the caution, its meaning should be explained to you.

You do not have to answer any questions put to you, but if you fail to answer questions after you have been cautioned this might be taken as a sign of guilt. If you are interviewed under caution and you decide not to answer questions, you could instead prepare a written statement to give to the investigators.

You might not be told why the interview is happening. If you have not been informed of the purpose of a fraud interview, a court may rule that the interview is inadmissible as evidence.

If you think fraud officers may interview you, seek advice before you attend the interview. Free legal advice may be available from a solicitor. Try to take someone (eg, a solicitor, adviser or friend) to the interview with you. Although s/he cannot speak for you, s/he can support you and take notes. Although it can be very distressing to be accused of committing an offence, remain calm and listen carefully to the questions you are asked. If you do not understand anything, ask for clarification. You must answer the questions yourself. Think carefully about the implications of the answers you give.

If you think you can explain why the situation has arisen, you should probably do so, since if you do not mention it at the interview your explanation is less likely to be believed if you are prosecuted.[15] In addition, if you are able to explain matters, your benefit is less likely to be taken away (see p1112). However, do not confess to something that you did not do just to finish the interview or in an attempt to prevent your benefit from being stopped.

A formal interview is taped. A transcript of the tape is produced for use at any trial or appeal hearing.

2. **Prosecution of offences**

Benefit offences can broadly be divided into two categories, based on the severity of the penalty you can potentially be given. For information about:

- false representations for claiming benefit, see p1104; *and*
- dishonest representations for claiming benefit, see p1105.

In more serious cases, you may be charged with an offence under the Theft Act 1968. This includes the possibility of being prosecuted for theft, obtaining property by deception and false accounting.[16]

If found guilty, you can be fined or imprisoned, or both. Any fine that you have to pay is in addition to any overpayment that is found to be recoverable from you (see Chapter 43).

Note: the government intends to introduce rules (probably in 2012/13), under which the DWP will generally conduct prosecutions for benefit offences, including for housing benefit (HB) and council tax benefit (CTB) – ie, not the local authority.[17] See CPAG's *Welfare Rights Bulletin* for updates.

False representations for claiming benefit

False representations for claiming benefit are considered to be the less serious of the benefit offences. You commit these offences if you:

- for the purpose of claiming a benefit or payment for yourself or someone else, or for any other purpose relating to the benefit rules:[18]
  - make a statement which you know to be false; *or*
  - give information or produce documents that you know to be false (or knowingly cause or allow someone else to do so).

  It does not have to be shown that you intended to obtain benefit to which you were not entitled;[19]
- fail to notify the DWP, HM Revenue and Customs (HMRC) or local authority promptly of a change of circumstances and which you know affects your entitlement to benefit or other payment.[20] This also applies to appointees and other third parties receiving benefit on your behalf, and landlords receiving direct payments of HB. You count as notifying a change promptly if you do so as soon as reasonably practicable after the change occurs;[21]
- cause or allow another person to fail to notify a change of circumstances to the DWP, HMRC or local authority promptly and which you know affects her/his entitlement to benefit or other payment.[22]

You do not 'know' something if you are merely careless about whether or not something is true, or if you fail to find out.[23] You will not have committed an offence if you fail to notify a change of circumstance that did not affect your entitlement to benefit or if there was already no entitlement to benefit.[24] The maximum penalty for these offences is a £5,000 fine or three months in prison, or both.[25]

Duty to report a change in circumstances

The rules on fraud and your duty to report a change of circumstances are different from the general rules on reporting a change of circumstances outlined on p1047. For fraud purposes, you will only have committed an offence if you failed to report promptly a change which you knew affected your benefit. However, in order to avoid potential allegations of fraud or prosecution, you must report *all* changes promptly, and in writing or by telephone. **Note:** for most benefits, you may be allowed to report a change other than in writing or by telephone. For some benefits (attendance allowance, carer's allowance, disability living allowance, employment and support allowance, income support and jobseeker's allowance) notification can be accepted online if you have registered with the government gateway to do so. For HB and CTB, although the change must usually be in writing, you may be permitted by the local authority to report a change other than in writing, including by telephone (see p290). For child benefit and guardian's allowance you must report the change in writing unless HMRC says otherwise.[26] In all cases, it is best to report the change in a way that allows you to show that you have done so – eg, in writing. For an offence to have been committed, you must have acted 'knowingly' when failing to report a change of circumstances. To have acted knowingly, you must have been aware of where the change must be reported and the manner in which it must be reported.[27]

Except for child benefit and guardian's allowance, there is a special rule if the change is a birth or a death (sometimes called 'Tell Us Once'). You can report such a change in person at a local authority (and, in England, county council) office, if an office has been specified for reporting these changes. You can notify a death by telephone if a number has been specified for that purpose.[28]

Advisers and other third parties

The offences of allowing or causing a claimant to fail to notify a change of circumstances or knowingly allowing or causing someone to give false information do not place any additional duty on advisers to notify the DWP, HMRC or local authority of a claimant's change of circumstances. In order for an offence to be committed, there must be some sort of implied permission given to the person not to do so.[29] You do not 'allow' someone to do something unless you are able to stop them doing it.[30] If you are an adviser, you should not be liable if you have advised your client fully of the law and the requirement to notify a change of circumstances and provide truthful information. You should do nothing to help facilitate a misrepresentation or failure to notify a change of circumstances – eg, help to complete a claim or review form which you know is inaccurate.

Dishonest representations for claiming benefit

Dishonest representations for claiming benefit are considered to be the more serious of the benefit offences. You commit these offences if you commit any of the acts that fall under the offence of false representations for claiming benefit (see p1104) and you act dishonestly ('knowingly' in Scotland) in doing so.[31] This means that you did something that most people would consider dishonest and that you must have known this was dishonest.[32]

The maximum penalty for these offences if you are convicted in a magistrates' court (sheriff court in Scotland) is a £5,000 fine or six months in prison, or both. If you are convicted in the Crown Court, you can receive an unlimited fine or seven years in prison, or both.[33]

Will you be prosecuted?

Not all cases in which there is evidence to justify a prosecution are taken to court. In some, you may be given the chance to pay a penalty (see p1109) or accept a formal caution instead (see p1111), although it is understood that use of formal cautions is to stop at some point in the near future.[34] In some cases, no fraud action is taken at all. The factors taken into account include the strength of the evidence, the amount of benefit involved, whether an offence was planned and your personal circumstances. **Note:** you may have sanctions imposed on certain benefits not only if you have been prosecuted and convicted, but also if you have accepted a penalty or a formal caution.

There are time limits for prosecutions for false representations for claiming benefit (see p1104). A prosecution must be started either within three months of the date the DWP, HMRC or local authority (or, in Scotland, the Procurator Fiscal) thinks it has sufficient evidence to prosecute you, or within 12 months of the date you committed the offence, whichever is later.[35]

Prosecutions for dishonest representations for claiming benefit (see p1105) may be started at any time.

What to do if you are prosecuted

The most important thing to do if you are prosecuted is to get advice. You may be entitled to free legal help from a solicitor and representation in court. You should check carefully that the DWP, HMRC or local authority is able to prove all the parts of the offence with which you are charged. Do not plead guilty until you have obtained advice.

3. Loss of benefit for benefit offences

You can have sanctions imposed on certain benefits, known as 'sanctionable' benefits (see p1107) if:[36]

- you are convicted of one or more benefit offences; *or*
- there is a recoverable overpayment and you agree to pay a penalty for a benefit offence instead of being prosecuted; *or*
- you accept a formal caution instead of being prosecuted.

This is sometimes referred to as the 'one-strike rule' because it can apply after just one offence – a conviction is not always required. However, if you are convicted of two or more benefit offences within five years, you can have a longer sanction imposed under the 'two-strikes rule' instead. This applies if:[37]

- you are convicted of one or more benefit offences in two separate sets of proceedings; *and*
- the later offence occurs within five years of the date on which you were first convicted of an offence; *and*
- the later offence has not previously been taken into account.

Note: at some point, probably during 2012/13, the government intends to change the rules on the 'two-strikes rule', so that it can also apply if you have been convicted just once, but then commit a subsequent offence, including accepting a penalty for a benefit offence or a formal caution.[38] See CPAG's *Welfare Rights Bulletin* for updates.

The benefit offence(s) must have been committed after 1 April 2010 (for the 'one-strike rule') or 1 April 2002 (for the 'two-strikes rule') and be:[39]

- in connection with a claim for a 'disqualifying' benefit (see below); *or*
- in connection with the receipt or payment of a 'disqualifying' benefit; *or*
- for the purpose of aiding the committing of a benefit offence (whether or not by the same person); *or*
- an attempt or a conspiracy to commit a benefit offence.

Disqualifying benefits

All social security benefits, as well as war pensions, are 'disqualifying' benefits for the purposes listed above, except statutory sick pay, statutory maternity pay, statutory adoption pay, statutory paternity pay and maternity allowance.[40] **Note:** at some point, probably during 2012/13, the government intends to add child tax credit (CTC) and working tax credit (WTC) to the list of disqualifying benefits.[41] See CPAG's *Welfare Rights Bulletin* for updates.

Sanctionable benefits

Sanctions can be imposed on 'sanctionable benefits'. These are all the disqualifying benefits above *except*:

- attendance allowance;
- disability living allowance;
- child benefit;
- guardian's allowance;
- retirement pension;
- graduated retirement benefit;
- social fund payments;
- Christmas bonus.[42]

The above benefits cannot therefore be sanctioned.

Joint-claim jobseeker's allowance (JSA) is also not a sanctionable benefit. However, it can still be removed or reduced.[43] When CTC and WTC become disqualifying benefits, they will not become sanctionable benefits. See CPAG's *Welfare Rights Bulletin* for updates. However, note that under separate rules, you will lose WTC if you have committed a benefit offence on or after 5 April 2012 (see p1391).

The sanctions

If the 'loss of benefit for benefit offences' rules apply, sanctionable benefits are not paid during the sanction period, unless the benefit is income support (IS), income-based JSA, joint-claim JSA, income-related employment and support allowance (ESA) , pension credit (PC), housing benefit (HB) or council tax benefit (CTB).[44] These benefits are usually paid at a reduced rate during the sanction period.[45] The reduction is usually 40 per cent of the appropriate personal allowance for a single person of the offender's age (see p816), or 20 per cent if you or a member of your family (see p751) are pregnant or seriously ill. **Joint-claim JSA** is not paid at all if the loss of benefit for benefit offences rules apply to both of you, or to one of you while the other has been given an employment-, training- or employment programme-related sanction (see Chapter 20). Otherwise, unless you are in a 'vulnerable group' or the decision maker is satisfied that you or your partner would face hardship (see p487), you are not paid **income-based JSA** at a reduced rate until the 15th day of the sanction period. **HB** and **CTB** are unaffected if you or a member of your family are entitled to IS, income-related ESA, PC or income-based JSA during a sanction period.

The **sanction period** is currently four weeks under the 'one-strike rule', and 13 weeks under the 'two-strikes rule'. The 13-week sanction period can be applied to any claim for the sanctionable benefit within a five-year and 28-day period following the later conviction.[46]

Note: under changes due to be introduced in April 2013, the sanction periods under the 'one-strike rule' will be increased to three years if you are convicted for serious fraud or conspiracy to defraud, if the overpayment is at least £50,000, if you are given a sentence of at least a year or if the offence is committed over a period of at least two years. The 'one-strike rule' sanction period will be 13 weeks if you are convicted in less serious cases and four weeks if you pay a penalty or accept a formal caution. Sanction periods under the 'two-strikes rule' will be increased to at least 26 weeks (except for serious fraud, for which the sanction period is three years) or three years if the second or other offence is within five years of the previous one.[47] See CPAG's *Welfare Rights Bulletin* for updates.

While benefits are sanctioned, an underlying entitlement remains in place to ensure the link between benefits and other entitlements (eg, free school lunches and free prescriptions) remains.

4. Penalties for benefit offences

The DWP, HM Revenue and Customs (HMRC) or local authority may offer you the option of paying a financial penalty under civil law instead of being prosecuted under criminal law. However, under the 'one-strike rule', your benefit can still be sanctioned if you accept a penalty. During 2012/13, this is likely to be applied to the 'two-strikes rule' as well (see p1106). **Note**: penalties for offences currently only apply if, because of your actions, you have been overpaid. However, from 8 May 2012, the government intends that penalties will also apply if you have not been overpaid, but had you been overpaid because of your actions, the overpayment would have been recoverable from you.[48] See CPAG's *Welfare Rights Bulletin* for updates.

Currently, the penalty is 30 per cent of the amount of the overpayment that is recoverable from you.[49] The overpayment must have been caused by an offence you committed after 18 December 1997.[50] **Note:** from 8 May 2012, the government intends to change this rule so that the penalty is 50 per cent of the overpayment (or £350 if you were not actually overpaid), subject to a minimum penalty of £350 and a maximum of £2,000.[51] See CPAG's *Welfare Rights Bulletin* for updates.

Currently, the penalty is added to the overpayment of benefit and is recoverable in the same way as the overpayment (see pp1079 and 1088).[52]

The option of paying a penalty

You can *only* be offered the option of paying a penalty if:[53]

- an overpayment has been found to be recoverable from you. The DWP, HMRC or local authority must have gone through the process of revising or superseding your award of benefit and issued a decision that the overpayment is recoverable; *and*
- the overpayment was due to an act or omission on your part. This act or omission must have occurred after 18 December 1997;[54] *and*
- there are grounds for prosecuting you for an offence relating to the overpayment.

The DWP, HMRC or local authority issues you with a notice setting out how the scheme works and giving you information about how you agree to pay a penalty or notify your withdrawal of your agreement.[55] If you are not issued with a proper notice, it may not be possible for the penalty to be enforced.

The notice is sent with an invitation to an interview to discuss accepting the penalty. Under official guidance, the interview should not be carried out by the same officer who gave the interview under caution.[56] The interview is only about whether to offer you a penalty. You cannot use it to add to or alter any statement that you made about the alleged offence in an interview under caution. Guidance states that if you are unable to decide whether or not to accept the penalty at the interview, you should be allowed five days to make up your mind.[57] Remember the following.

- If you agree to pay a penalty, you cannot be prosecuted for any offence relating to the overpayment.[58] However, this does not stop you being prosecuted in the future if you commit another offence or one relating to a different overpayment.
- Your benefit may still be sanctioned, even though you are not prosecuted.
- If it is found on revision, supersession or appeal that the overpayment is not due or not recoverable, any penalty you have paid must be repaid to you.[59] This does not affect the existence of the agreement, so you still cannot be prosecuted.
- If the amount of the overpayment is changed on revision, supersession or appeal, the agreement is cancelled, so you lose your immunity from prosecution and any penalty you have paid must be repaid to you. However, if you make a fresh agreement:
  - you are again immune from prosecution; *and*
  - the amount of penalty you have already paid can be offset against the new penalty rather than being repaid to you.[60]
- If you do not accept the penalty, the DWP, HMRC or local authority considers whether to prosecute you.

Changing your mind

If you agree to pay a penalty, you are entitled to change your mind, provided you notify the DWP, HMRC or local authority within 28 days in the manner specified by the DWP, HMRC or local authority.[61] You lose your immunity from prosecution, but you do not have to pay the penalty and, if you have paid any part of it, it must be refunded to you. At some point, probably during 2012/13, this 'cooling-off' period will be reduced from 28 days to 14 days.[62] See CPAG's *Welfare Rights Bulletin* for updates.

Whether to accept a penalty

It can be difficult to decide whether to accept a penalty or risk facing prosecution. Seek advice and consider your options carefully. Bear the following in mind.

- If you are not prosecuted, your case will not go to court and you cannot get a prison sentence. However, if you accept a penalty your benefit could still be sanctioned.
- You may be invited to pay a penalty when there is insufficient evidence to prosecute you.
- The fraud officer can only recommend that your case be considered for prosecution. The DWP, HMRC or local authority legal department decides whether or not to prosecute (see p1103). You are not automatically prosecuted if you refuse to accept a penalty.

- If you are prosecuted and found guilty, you might be offered community service rather than a fine. On the other hand, you could get a large fine or even a prison sentence.
- A penalty may be a substantial amount of money. For minor offences, a fine could be less than the penalty.

5. Formal cautions

The DWP currently operates a system of 'cautioning' for social security offences. This only applies within the DWP, although some local authorities have similar systems of their own. Scottish local authorities use 'administrative cautions', which are similar in the way they operate to the cautioning system in England and Wales. Although these administrative cautions cannot be cited in the Scottish courts, the Procurator Fiscal can take them into account when deciding whether to prosecute for any later offence. The cautioning system is not in regulations, but is based on guidance for the police.[63] Under the 'one-strike rule' (and from some point probably in 2012/13 under the 'two-strikes rule'), if you accept a caution your benefit can still be subject to a sanction (see p1106). However, the DWP will cease offering cautions for benefit offences at some point in the near future.[64]

A formal caution can only be offered when you have been interviewed under caution (see p1103), an overpayment has been calculated and the fraud investigator believes there is sufficient evidence to prosecute you. Cautions are generally only offered in less serious fraud cases where the value of an overpayment is low.

The procedure is as follows.

- You attend a formal caution interview, where you are asked to sign a record admitting the offence and accepting the caution. If you accept a caution, you cannot be prosecuted for the offence to which you have admitted.
- A caution is recorded by the DWP on a central database. The record is kept initially for five years. It is subject to data protection rules. Information about the caution can be disclosed to other bodies in some circumstances – eg, to local authorities for use in housing benefit (HB) and council tax benefit matters or to the police for use in criminal investigations.
- In England and Wales, a properly recorded formal caution may be cited in court if you are successfully prosecuted for a subsequent offence. It may then become part of a criminal record.
- If you refuse to admit the offence and accept a formal caution, your case is considered for prosecution.

Whether to accept a caution

In can be difficult deciding whether to accept a caution or risk facing prosecution. Seek advice and consider your options carefully. Bear the following in mind.

- If you are not prosecuted, your case will not go to court and you cannot get a prison sentence. However, if you accept a caution, your benefit may still be sanctioned.
- A formal caution may be offered in circumstances where there is insufficient evidence to prosecute you for an offence. You are not necessarily prosecuted just because you refuse to accept a caution. You should not admit to something that you did not do just to avoid the threat of prosecution.
- Accepting a formal caution is an admission of guilt. Once you have accepted a caution you cannot change your mind.
- Although accepting the formal caution means that you cannot be prosecuted for offences specified on the caution certificate, you may be prosecuted for related offences not specified, such as an HB overpayment.
- If you are subsequently found guilty of another benefit offence in court, your formal caution could be cited and may mean that you get a stiffer sentence.

6. The effect of a fraud investigation on benefit

If the DWP, HM Revenue and Customs (HMRC) or local authority have doubts about your entitlement to benefit, other procedures may be applied at the same time as a fraud investigation.

- In some circumstances, your benefit may be suspended (see p1043) – eg, if there are doubts about your entitlement or if there is a possibility that you are being overpaid.
- You may be asked to provide information and evidence about your claim. If you do not do so within a specified time limit, your claim can be terminated (see p1045). If you still believe that you are entitled to benefit, make a new claim.

If a fraud investigation is taking a long time to complete, your benefit may also be suspended for a long time. However, the DWP, HMRC or local authority should not withhold your benefit indefinitely without making a decision on whether or not you are entitled to it. Complain if you think an investigation is taking too long (see p1255). If that brings no results, seek legal advice about forcing the DWP, HMRC or local authority to make a decision.

The decision on whether you should be prosecuted is separate from a decision to recover an overpayment of benefit (see Chapter 43). Whether you are entitled to benefit, and the amount and recoverability of any overpayment, is decided by the DWP, HMRC or local authority decision maker without any regard to your honesty of intention. The two processes are independent and have different tests. Therefore:

- a decision or appeal on your claim does not have to be delayed while you wait for the outcome of a criminal prosecution;[65]
- a court fine does not prevent the DWP, HMRC or local authority from taking action to recover an overpayment. If you have made payments under a compensation order made by a court to the DWP, HMRC or local authority, it cannot also recover that amount as an overpayment.[66]

Acquittal in a fraud case does not necessarily mean that the decision on your benefit entitlement was wrong. Whatever the result of an investigation or prosecution, the DWP, HMRC or local authority may take more time assessing your future claims because it may check out your circumstances thoroughly. Complain if it takes too long to make a decision (see p1255). You should not be prevented from making a fresh claim during a fraud investigation if your circumstances have changed. You could also apply for interim payments (see p1046) or help from the social fund (see Chapter 25).

7. Future changes: civil penalties

At some point, probably during 2012/13, the government intends to introduce civil penalties. These will be different from the penalties for benefit offences (see p1109). Civil penalties cannot apply if you have been sent a notice about a penalty for a benefit offence, or if you have been charged or accepted a formal caution about a benefit offence. Otherwise, the rules will say that a civil penalty may be applied if:[67]

- you have negligently made an incorrect statement or representation, or negligently given incorrect information or evidence about a claim for or an award of a benefit; *and*
  - you fail to take 'reasonable steps' to correct the error; *and*
  - the error results in your being overpaid benefit; *or*
- you have failed to provide information or evidence, or have failed to notify a relevant change of circumstances, you do not have a 'reasonable excuse' and the failure results in your being overpaid.

A 'relevant change of circumstances' means one which affects any entitlement to benefit.

Rules on the amount of the penalty had not been finalised at the time of writing. The penalty may be recovered by deductions from benefit, or via a county court (or, in Scotland, a sheriff court) order. If you are claiming jointly with your partner, if the penalty is for negligently making incorrect statements, representations, information or evidence, it can be recovered from your partner instead of you, unless s/he was not (and could not reasonably be expected to be) aware of the error.

You should be able to appeal against the imposition of a civil penalty – eg, to argue that you did not behave negligently or that you had a 'reasonable excuse' for failing to declare a change in your circumstances. **Note**: if you receive a decison that you have been overpaid because you have failed to disclose a change of circumstances, consider if you also want to appeal against that decision and/or the decision that the overpayment is recoverable from you (see Chapter 43).

See CPAG's *Welfare Rights Bulletin* for updates.

Notes

1. **Investigating claims**
1 ss122 and 122ZA SSAA 1992
2 s122B SSAA 1992
3 ss124 and 125 SSAA 1992
4 ss122D and 122E SSAA 1992
5 ss122C and 122E SSAA 1992
6 ss182A and 182B SSAA 1992
7 s123 and Sch 4 SSAA 1992
8 ss109A, 109B and 109C SSAA 1992
9 *Social Security Fraud Act 2001 Code of Practice on Obtaining Information,* DWP, available from www.dwp.gov.uk/docs/cop-ssfa.pdf
10 s109B(5)(b) SSAA 1992; *Social Security Fraud Act 2001 Code of Practice on Obtaining Information,* DWP, s2.11
11 s109C SSAA 1992
12 ss109B(5) and 109C(6) SSAA 1992
13 s67(9) PACEA 1984
14 s78(1) PACEA 1984; *DHSS v McKee* [1995] 6 *Bulletin of NI Law* 17 (NI Crown Court)
15 s34 CJPOA 1994

2. **Prosecution of offences**
16 *Osinuga v Director of Public Prosecution, The Times,* 26 November 1997 (DC)
17 s112 WRA 2012; s116ZA SSAA 1992
18 s112(1) SSAA 1992
19 *Clear v Smith* [1981] 1 WLR 399 (DC)
20 s112(1A) SSAA 1992
21 s112(1C)-(1F) SSAA 1992
22 s112(1B) and (1F) SSAA 1992
23 *Taylor's Central Garages v Roper* [1951] 115 JPR 445
24 *R v Passmore* [2007] EWCA Crim 2053; *R v Laku* [2008] EWCA Crim 1745
25 s112(2) SSAA 1992
26 Regs 4 and 5 SS(NCC) Regs; reg 4 CB&GA(Admin) Regs
27 *Coventry City Council v Vassell* [2011] EWCH 1542 (Admin)
28 Regs 3(1A), 4(1A) and 5(1ZZA) SS(NCC) Regs
29 *R v Chainey* [1914] 1 KB 137 at 142 (DC)
30 *R v Tilley* [2009] EWCA Crim 1426
31 s111A SSAA 1992
32 *R v Ghosh* [1982] QB 1053 at 1064D-G (CA)
33 s111A(3) SSAA 1992
34 *Tackling Fraud and Error in the Benefit and Tax Credits Systems: fraud and error strategy,* HMRC and DWP, October 2010
35 s116(2), (2A) and (7) SSAA 1992

3. **Loss of benefit for benefit offences**
36 s6B(1) SSFA 2001
37 s7(1) SSFA 2001
38 s119 WRA 2012; ss6B and 7 SSFA 2001
39 ss6B(13) and 7(8), definition of 'benefit offence', SSFA 2001
40 s6A(1), definition of 'disqualifying benefit', SSFA 2001; reg 19A, definition of 'disqualifying benefit', SS(LB) Regs
41 s115 WRA 2012
42 s6A(1), definition of 'sanctionable benefit', SSFA 2001; reg 19 SS(LB) Regs
43 s8 SSFA 2001
44 s7(2)-(5) SSFA 2001
45 ss7, 8 and 9 SSFA 2001; regs 3, 3A, 5-10 and 17-18 SS(LB) Regs

46 ss6B(11)and 7(6) SSFA 2001; reg 2 SS(LB) Regs
47 s118 WRA 2012; s6B(11A) SSFA 2001; *Tackling Fraud and Error in the Benefit and Tax Credits Systems: fraud and error strategy*, HMRC and DWP, October 2010

4. **Penalties for benefit offences**
48 s113 WRA 2012; s115A SSAA 1992
49 s115A(3) SSAA 1992
50 s25(7) SSA(F)A 1997
51 s115 WRA 2012
52 s115A(4)(a) SSAA 1992
53 s115A(1) SSAA 1992
54 s25(7) SSA(F)A 1997; art 2(1)(b) SSA(F)AO No.5
55 s115A(2) SSAA 1992; reg 2(1) and (2) SS(PN) Regs
56 HB Fraud Circular HB/CTB F4/98, para 24. Note: this guidance is no longer easily available.
57 HB Fraud Circular HB/CTB F4/98, para 48. Note: this guidance is no longer easily available.
58 s115A(4)(b) SSAA 1992
59 s115A(6) SSAA 1992
60 s115A(7) SSAA 1992
61 s115A(5) SSAA 1992
62 s115 WRA 2012

5. **Formal cautions**
63 Cautions guidance issued by DWP to local authorities (not currently available in published form)
64 s121 WRA 2012

6. **The effect of a fraud investigation on benefit**
65 *Mote v SSWP and Chichester District Council* [2007] EWCA Civ 1324, 14 December 2007, reported as R(IS) 4/08
66 CIS/683/1994

7. **Future changes: civil penalties**
67 s116 WRA 2012; ss115C-115D SSAA 1992

Chapter 45

Decisions, revisions and supersessions

This chapter covers:

This chapter covers the rules for benefits and the regulated social fund. It does *not* cover the rules for statutory sick pay and statutory maternity, adoption and paternity pay (see Chapter 47), payments from the discretionary social fund (see Chapter 48), the health benefits in Chapter 13 or the other types of financial help on pp14–16, or discretionary housing payments (see p294).

References in this chapter to HM Revenue and Customs (HMRC) only apply to decisions about child benefit and guardian's allowance. HMRC also makes decisions about tax credits. For information about tax credit decisions, see Chapters 57 and 60.

Key facts

- Once you have made a valid claim for benefit, a decision must be made by a decision maker – ie, an officer of the DWP, a local authority or HM Revenue and Customs.
- If you want more information about a decision, you can ask for an explanation.
- In many cases, you can also ask for written reasons for a decision.
- If you think a decision is wrong, you can ask the decision maker to change it by seeking a revision or a supersession. In many cases, you can also challenge a decision by appealing to the First-tier Tribunal. You may also be able to seek a supersession if your circumstances change after a decision is made.

Future changes: April 2013 and after

Major changes are taking place that affect the benefits and tax credits system (see Chapter 2).

- In October 2013, a new benefit, universal credit (UC), will be introduced. The rules described in this chapter will, in general, apply to UC.
- From April 2013, if you disagree with a decision, you will only be able to appeal against it if you have first asked the decision maker to revise the decision. This is unlikely to apply to housing benefit and council tax benefit decisions.

See CPAG's *Welfare Rights Bulletin* for updates.

1. Decisions

In this *Handbook,* those who make decisions about benefits and the social fund are referred to as **'decision makers'**. In practice, decisions about:

- benefits and the social fund (other than child benefit, guardian's allowance, housing benefit (HB) and council tax benefit (CTB)) are made by officers in the DWP;
- child benefit and guardian's allowance are made by officers of HM Revenue and Customs (HMRC);
- HB and CTB are made by officers of the local authority.

Some issues (eg, whether you have or can be treated as having limited capability for work or are terminally ill for benefit purposes) are decided by the DWP, even if the main benefit decision is made by another authority – eg, the local authority.[2]

Employment officers (EOs) work in Jobcentre Plus offices. They are sometimes called personal advisers. If you are claiming jobseeker's allowance (JSA), their job is to agree with you the steps you are willing to take to get back to work, keep a check on those steps, and offer practical help and advice.

If you are claiming a benefit for people of working age, such as JSA or employment and support allowance (ESA), you might be referred to a training or employment scheme provider for support in finding, returning to and maintaining paid employment – eg, the Work Programme. If you are claiming JSA, you might be referred to a provider to do Mandatory Work Activity. Scheme providers can notify you that you are required to participate in a particular scheme, but they *cannot* decide to sanction you if you fail to participate as required.

Rent officers make determinations about rent for HB purposes – eg, they determine the amount of local housing allowances. You cannot challenge a rent officer's determinations (eg, by revision, supersession or appeal), but you may be able to ask for these to be redetermined. For further information, see Chapter 15.

Making a decision

Once you have made a valid claim for benefit, a decision must be made by a decision maker.[1] The decision maker may need further information before making a decision. You can be asked to provide this (see pp272, 275, 1019 and 1022). If you fail to provide information or evidence:

- your claim may be treated as defective. However, you are usually given an opportunity to remedy the defect (see pp272 and 1019). If your claim is for income support (IS) or JSA, it is treated as defective if all required information and evidence is not provided (see p1021);
- the decision maker might draw adverse conclusions and make a decision based on these;
- payment of your benefit could be suspended or your award terminated (see pp1045 and 1046).

In addition, if your claim:

- involves medical issues, the decision maker can refer you to a 'healthcare professional' (see below) for a medical examination and a report.[3] The healthcare professional can ask you to have a medical examination. If you fail to do so without 'good cause', the decision maker must decide against you. Remember that different rules apply if you fail to attend a medical examination about your capability for work or if a decision maker requires you to attend for a medical examination to see if a decision to award you benefit should be revised or superseded (see p1045) or if the First-tier Tribunal refers you to a healthcare professional for a medical examination (see p1174);
- involves issues about your national insurance contributions, the decision maker can refer these to HMRC. See p1119 for further information;
- for disablement benefit involves whether you may have a prescribed disease or have a disablement or the extent of any injury you have from an industrial accident, the decision maker can refer the issue to a healthcare professional for a report. When deciding how to take account of the report, the decision maker must have regard to the experience of the healthcare professional;[4]
- involves a question about the facts where special expertise is needed, the decision maker can get assistance from experts.[5]

Healthcare professionals

A 'healthcare professional' is a registered medical practitioner (eg, a doctor), registered nurse, or registered occupational therapist or physiotherapist, or for disability living allowance mobility component for a severe visual impairment only, a registered optometrist or orthoptist.[6]

A decision maker may withhold making a decision if there is a test case pending (see p1150).

If you think a decision is wrong, you may be able to seek a revision or supersession, or appeal against it. The position is different if you are given wrong advice by an employee of the DWP, local authority or HMRC. See p1261 for information about seeking compensation.

Decisions made with limited information

The decision maker may need more evidence or information to make a decision. S/he can make a decision in the meantime in certain circumstances.

A decision is made on the basis that the evidence or information needed is adverse to you, if:[7]

- for IS, JSA and social fund payments only, it is needed to decide:
  - whether you should be paid benefit (or less benefit) because you (or a member of your family) are involved in a trade dispute (see p700); *or*
  - whether you are in relevant education (see p634);
- for IS, ESA, social fund payments and pension credit (PC) only, it is needed to decide whether you are entitled to a severe disability premium (additional amount for PC).

For retirement pension only, if you deferred claiming your pension, but when you did claim you had not yet elected whether to take a lump sum or an increased pension, the decision maker can choose whether or not to decide your claim immediately.[8] If s/he does make a decision on your claim, s/he must revise it when you make the election (see p1133).

For IS, ESA, PC and social fund payments only, if further evidence or information is needed to decide what housing costs you can be paid (see Chapter 38), a decision is made on the basis of the evidence or information the decision maker already has.[9]

Special procedure

Certain questions are dealt with by a special procedure. These are to do with contributions and a person's employment – eg:[10]

- whether you were an 'employed earner' for the purposes of paying contributions or entitlement to industrial injuries disablement benefit; *or*
- whether you were liable to pay a particular class of contributions or have paid contributions for a particular period; *or*
- the amount of contributions you were liable to pay.

The decision maker refers matters that are HMRC's responsibility to HMRC for a decision, which is then binding on the decision maker.[11] The decision maker can continue to deal with other issues relating to your claim, but can defer making a decision on it. The decision maker should also refer matters to HMRC if s/he decides your claim on the basis of facts which do not appear to be under dispute – eg, if it appears you do not satisfy the contribution conditions for the benefit, but you apply for a revision or supersession of the decision, or appeal against it because, for example, you think your contribution record is wrong.

When HMRC makes a decision, you can appeal against it.[12] The appeals process is similar to appealing against an HMRC decision on your entitlement to statutory payments (see Chapter 47).

The First-tier Tribunal can also require the DWP to refer matters that are HMRC's responsibility, but which are relevant to a benefit appeal, to HMRC for a decision.[13] The Secretary of State may revise the decision on your claim as a result. If not, the matter goes back to the First-tier Tribunal.

Note: the decision maker can also make arrangements for some issues to do with whether you can be credited with earnings or contributions to be decided by HMRC.[14] You can appeal to the First-tier Tribunal against these decisions in the same way as against DWP decisions (see Chapter 46).

Delays

The DWP and HMRC have target times for dealing with claims. Local authorities must make a decision on your claim for HB or CTB within 14 days or, if that is not reasonably practicable, as soon as possible after that.

If you have been waiting more than the relevant time for a decision, check that your claim has been received. If it has not, let the office have a copy or fill out a new form and refer to the claim form you sent earlier. If the DWP, the local authority or HMRC deny receiving your claim, you may have to claim again and ask for it to be backdated if possible.

If your claim has been received but not dealt with, ask why. If you are not satisfied with the explanation for the delay, make a complaint (see Chapter 50). In extreme cases, it might be possible to apply for judicial review (see p1202).

If a decision cannot be made on your claim straight away:

- ask the office to make interim payments (see p1046). If the benefit is HB and you are a private or housing association tenant, in most cases you *must* be given a payment on account (see p289);
- if your claim is for a non-means-tested benefit, you may be able to claim a means-tested benefit in the meantime. The amount paid to you that you would not otherwise have received may be deducted from arrears of social security benefits that you subsequently receive, or you may be asked to repay the amount;[15]
- you may be able to claim a crisis loan from the social fund if you have inadequate resources.

Correcting a decision

Unless the benefit is child benefit or guardian's allowance, if the decision maker makes an accidental error in her/his decision (eg, a typing error or mathematical miscalculation), this can be corrected.[16] You must be sent or given written notice of the correction as soon as it is practicable. To see how the time limit for seeking an 'any grounds' revision of the decision can be extended when a decision has been corrected, see p1128.

Information about decisions

You must be given written notice of a decision against which you have a right of appeal (see p1158 for which decisions). This is sometimes called a 'decision notice'. You must be informed of:[17]

- your right to appeal against the decision; *and*
- your right to a written statement of reasons for the decision (if this is not already included) – see below.

You may want to know more about a decision or want a breakdown of how your benefit has been calculated. To find out more about a decision, you can also ask for an explanation. **Note:** you do *not* have to ask for an explanation or a written statement of reasons in order to seek a revision or a supersession, or to appeal.

Explanations

You can ask for an explanation of any decision maker's decision, in writing, in person or over the telephone. Contact the office that made the decision. Ask about anything that is unclear to you and point out any errors you think the decision maker made.

At the end of the explanation, you should be asked whether you are happy with the decision and whether or not you want it to be looked at again. If you are not happy with a decision, say so. The decision maker should then advise you about your right to seek a revision (see p1126) or to appeal (see Chapter 46). S/he may refer to this as a dispute or a request for a reconsideration but you should use the term 'revision'.

Explanations are usually given orally and it can sometimes be difficult to take in or remember what has been said. You have a right to a written statement of reasons for a decision if it is one against which you can appeal (see below).

The time limit for seeking an 'any grounds' revision or appealing is very strict. It runs from the date you are sent or given the decision with which you disagree, *not* the date of the explanation, and can only be extended in limited circumstances (see pp1128 and 1162). Therefore, ensure you seek a revision or appeal within the time limit even if an explanation for the decision has not yet been given to you.

Written reasons for a decision

Whether or not you asked for an explanation, you may want to see the reasons for a decision in writing. You have a right to a written statement of reasons for a decision against which you have a right of appeal if these have not already been provided with the decision.[18] This is especially useful if you are considering seeking a revision or supersession, or appealing against the decision. You must ask for the written statement of reasons within one month of being notified of the decision. The decision maker must then provide one within 14 days if this is practicable (for HB and CTB) or as soon as practicable afterwards (for other benefits).

Note: your time limit for seeking a revision or appealing is extended if you ask for a written statement of reasons, but only if these have not already been provided. See pp1128 and 1162 for further information.

'Month' means a complete calendar month running from the day after the day you have been sent or given a decision.[19] For example, a decision sent on 24 July has a time limit that expires at the end of 24 August.

The DWP says a written statement of reasons for a decision is provided automatically with a decision about some benefits (see below). Although you may believe a written statement of reasons has not been included with your decision or that what has been provided is inadequate, the DWP, the local authority or HMRC could disagree. In these cases, the decision maker is likely to argue that your time limit for seeking an 'any grounds' revision or appealing cannot be extended.

If you are in any doubt about the situation, you should presume your time limit for seeking an 'any grounds' revision or appealing has *not* been extended. If you miss the time limit in this situation, you should argue that the rules that allow a late application for a revision or a late appeal apply (see pp1128 and 1204). You may also be able to apply for an 'anytime' revision (see p1129).

Automatic statements of reasons

The DWP says that written statements of reasons are automatically provided with decisions about: bereavement benefits, ESA, incapacity benefit, maternity allowance, retirement pension, severe disablement allowance, and social fund funeral payments, cold weather payments and Sure Start maternity grants.

Remember to read and consider the reasons carefully to ensure you understand why the decision maker made her/his decision. You are then better prepared to argue why the decision should be changed if you seek a revision or appeal.

If you disagree with a decision maker's decision

If you think a decision maker's decision is wrong (eg, because the decision maker got the facts or law wrong, or your circumstances have changed), you may be able to:

- seek a revision of the decision (see p1126); *or*
- seek a supersession of the decision (see p1135).

In many cases, you also have a right to appeal to the First-tier Tribunal (see Chapter 46) and you do not have to seek a revision or supersession first.

The time limits for seeking what is known as an 'any grounds' revision or appealing are strict – normally only one month (see pp1128 and 1162). For information about how an application for a revision could affect your appeal rights and the time limit for appealing, see pp1165 and 1162.

You can seek a revision or a supersession of a decision that you cannot appeal to the First-tier Tribunal (see p1159 for which decisions). If you are still dissatisfied, you should seek advice about whether you can apply for judicial review (see p1202).

Checklist for challenging a decision

1. To get more information about a decision, ask for an explanation or a written statement of reasons (if this has not already been provided – see p1121).
2. Decide whether to seek a revision or appeal. Get advice as soon as possible if you need this (see Appendix 2).
3. Ensure you keep within the time limit (see p1128 for revisions and p1162 for appeals).

Note: you cannot challenge a notification that you must participate in a training or employment scheme – eg, the Work Programme or Mandatory Work Activity. However, if you are sanctioned by a decision maker for failing to participate, you can seek a revision or supersession of, or appeal against, the sanction.

If you disagree with an employment officer's decision

You cannot seek a revision or supersession of, or appeal against, an EO's decision. However:

- although you cannot appeal against an EO's decision to issue a jobseeker's direction (see p469), if you are sanctioned by a decision maker for failing to comply with it, you can appeal against the sanction;
- if you cannot reach an agreement with your EO about the terms of your jobseeker's agreement or whether it should be changed, you can ask for it to be referred to a decision maker for a decision. See p454 for details of the procedure. If you disagree with the decision maker's decision, you can seek a revision of, or appeal against, that decision.

Contacting benefit offices

Writing to the DWP, the local authority or HMRC is nearly always the best way to have your case dealt with. It ensures there is a record of what you said and enables you to cover all the points you want to make. Always keep a copy of the letters, forms and other documents you send as well as copies of those sent to you. Such a record may help you or your adviser to challenge decisions.

It is often necessary to telephone the DWP, the local authority or HMRC. If you do this, make a note of the date and what is said. If the information is important, follow up the telephone call with a letter confirming what was said.

If you need to visit an office (eg because your case cannot be dealt with by telephone) and you cannot get there (eg, because of your age, health or a disability), an officer may be able to make a home visit. If you are refused a visit and are not satisfied with the reason you are given, ask to speak to a supervisor or the customer services manager.

2. Getting a decision changed

If you are getting benefit but you cease to satisfy the conditions of entitlement or if the amount of benefit to which you are entitled should be reduced or increased, the decision awarding you benefit can be changed either by a revision or a supersession. In some cases, this can only be done if one of the grounds for revision or supersession applies (see pp1129 and 1136). You can ask for a revision or a supersession, or the decision maker can decide to do one. Claims for benefit or questions about your entitlement can be treated as requests for a revision or a supersession.[20]

If you are trying to get arrears going back several years, it can be difficult to identify the grounds for a revision or supersession. If you are the one who wants the revision or supersession, the onus is on you to show that there are grounds. You can obtain information held by the DWP, the local authority or HM Revenue and Customs (HMRC) by making a 'subject access request' under the Data Protection Act 1998. See the Information Commissioner's website at www.ico.gov.uk for details.

In some cases the DWP, the local authority or HMRC may say it has destroyed old papers relating to your claim. Check to see if your papers have simply been stored (archived), rather than actually destroyed. You can try to argue that missing papers should be presumed to contain information that is favourable to your case. However, this is unlikely to be accepted unless you can show that the papers were destroyed deliberately to thwart your case.[21]

After you seek a revision or supersession

When considering whether to carry out a revision or a supersession on her/his own initiative, the decision maker decides what further evidence is needed in order to come to a decision, and how to collect this. The DWP can ask you to have a medical examination (see p1045).

The decision maker can ask you for more evidence or information if s/he thinks this is needed to consider all the issues raised by your application for a revision or supersession.[22] You must provide this information within one month of the request. The decision maker can allow longer than this. If you do not provide the information, your application is decided on the basis of the information and evidence the decision maker already has.

Remember, in some cases if you fail to provide information in a shorter time period or have a medical examination, payment of your benefit could be suspended and your entitlement terminated (see p1046).

If a decision is changed

If a decision is changed in your favour, you can receive arrears of benefit. You usually get more arrears with a revision than a supersession (see pp1135 and 1141 for when a revision or supersession takes effect). For this reason, it is best to apply for a revision if you can. If you are in any doubt about how you would be better off, seek advice. If you were:

- underpaid benefit because of a clear error by the DWP, the local authority or HMRC, you could apply for compensation as well as getting arrears (see p1261);
- overpaid benefit, the decision maker decides whether or not to recover the overpayment (see Chapter 43). There is no limit on how far back an overpayment can be recovered.

The risks of revision and supersession

Following a revision or a supersession, the original decision may remain the same or be changed to either increase *or* decrease the amount of your benefit, or take away your entitlement altogether. Seek advice before you seek a revision or supersession if you are concerned about what could happen in your case. There are particular issues if you are seeking a revision or supersession of a disability living allowance (DLA) decision (see p1126). However, you must always notify changes in your circumstances that you might reasonably be expected to know might affect your right to, the amount of, or payment of, your benefit. Bear the following in mind.

- Although s/he does not have to do so, the decision maker can consider issues even if these are not raised by your request for a revision or supersession.[23] Thus, you may apply for a revision or supersession in the hope that your benefit will be increased, but the outcome could be that you get less benefit.
- If a revision or supersession reduces the amount of benefit to which you are entitled, it may mean that you have been overpaid. See Chapter 43 for information about overpayments and when they can be recovered.

Disability living allowance

Seek advice if you want to seek a revision or supersession because you have not been awarded one component of DLA when you are already in receipt of the other, or if you are not happy with the rate you have been awarded of one component of DLA when you are satisfied with the rate you have been awarded of the other. In these circumstances, although s/he does not have to do so, the decision maker may consider:

- the component which is not the subject of the revision or supersession;
- reducing the length of the period for which you have been awarded a component, even if it was originally awarded for an indefinite period.

Suggest that s/he should not do so.

3. **Revisions**

If you disagree with a decision maker's decision (including a decision superseding an earlier decision), you can seek a revision.[24] If you seek a revision, the decision maker must look at the decision again to see if it can be changed. The DWP, the local authority and HM Revenue and Customs (HMRC) often refer to your request as a dispute or a request for a reconsideration. However, you should use the term 'revision'. Seeking a revision is only one of the ways of getting a decision changed. See p1160 for help in deciding whether to seek a revision or supersession, or to appeal.

In some cases, if you can show grounds, you can seek a revision even if the decision was made a long time ago (see p1129). Revisions can, therefore, be a way around the strict time limit for appealing to the First-tier Tribunal (see p1162).

Following a revision, your benefit could be increased, but it could also be decreased or stopped altogether. See p1125 for what you should consider before seeking a revision.

For information on how to seek a revision, see p1133. To find out when a revision takes effect, see p1135.

When a decision can be revised

You can ask for a decision maker's decision to be revised or the decision maker can decide to do this.[25] There are two types of revision:

- 'any grounds' revisions where you do not have to show that specific grounds apply (see p1127); *and*
- 'any time' revisions where you must show that specific grounds apply (see p1129).

Note:
- If you want to seek a revision of a decision about employment and support allowance (ESA), attendance allowance (AA) or disability living allowance (DLA) because you (or the person on whose behalf you are claiming) are terminally ill, you must state this explicitly.[26] If you do not do so, the decision maker cannot revise the decision on this ground.
- You cannot seek a revision of a First-tier Tribunal's or an Upper Tribunal's decision. In some cases you can seek a supersession of these. Otherwise you must appeal (see Chapter 46).

'Any grounds' revisions

You can ask for a revision on any grounds if you do so within a strict time limit, normally one month.[27] The decision maker may refer to this as the dispute period. We call these 'any grounds' revisions in this *Handbook*. You do not have to show specific grounds; it is enough if you simply think a decision is wrong. However, you should still explain why you disagree with the decision and provide information and evidence to support this.

In addition, if the decision maker commences action within one month of the date you are sent or given a decision, for benefits other than housing benefit (HB) or council tax benefit (CTB), s/he can decide to revise it her/himself, on any grounds.[28] For HB and CTB, a decision maker can also decide to revise a decision her/himself but only if, within one month of the date you are sent or given it, s/he has information which shows that there was a mistake about the facts of your case or the decision was made in ignorance of relevant facts.[29]

A decision maker can only revise a decision on 'any grounds' on the basis of your circumstances at the time:[30]
- the decision took effect; *or*
- the decision was made, in the case of advance awards for benefits other than HB and CTB. This includes most decisions to convert an award of income support (IS), incapacity benefit (IB) or severe disablement allowance (SDA) to ESA (see p193).

If your circumstances have since changed, you should instead make a fresh claim or ask for the decision to be superseded (see p1135).

You do not have to seek a revision and can appeal to the First-tier Tribunal instead. However, if you seek a revision rather than appealing you get two bites at the cherry, because if your application for a revision is turned down, there are special rules about time limits that allow you to appeal to the First-tier Tribunal against the original decision.

If you are uncertain whether your request for a revision of a decision is being acted on, you should appeal against the decision within the time limit (see p1162). However, your appeal could lapse if the decision maker revises the decision, even if you do not get everything you want.

Time limit for seeking an 'any grounds' revision

If you want an 'any grounds' revision you must ask for one:

- in the case of a **Sure Start maternity grant** or a **social fund funeral expenses payment**, within one month of the date you were sent or given the decision or within the time limit for claiming the payment (see pp575 and 582) if this is later;[31]
- in the case of a **cold weather payment** or a **winter fuel payment**, within one month of the date you were notified of the decision. For these purposes, you are generally assumed to have been notified seven days after the decision was made. There are exceptions, including if you were not awarded a payment and you questioned this. In this case, you are assumed to have been notified on the date the decision maker issued a decision in response to your question;[32]
- in the case of **HB** and **CTB**, within one month of the date you were sent or given the decision.[33] If a written statement of reasons has not already been included with the decision, days between the date your request for the statement is received by the local authority and the date on which it is provided to you are ignored when calculating the one month;[34]
- in all **other cases**:[35]
  - within one month of the date you were sent or given the decision; *or*
  - within one month and 14 days of the date you were sent or given the decision, if you requested a written statement of reasons (see p1121) and it is provided within the month; *or*
  - within 14 days of a written statement of reasons being provided, if you requested one within one month of the date you were sent or given the decision, but it is not provided within that one-month period.

For benefits (other than a Sure Start maternity grant or a social fund funeral expenses payment, child benefit or guardian's allowance), if an accidental error in a decision has been corrected (see p1120), any day falling before the day on which the correction is notified to you is ignored when calculating the one-month period.[36]

Late requests for an 'any grounds' revision

You can ask for an 'any grounds' revision outside the time limit in limited circumstances. You must do so within an absolute time limit of 13 months from the date you were notified of the decision.[37] However, if you requested a written statement of reasons (see p1121):

- for **HB** and **CTB**, days between the date you requested the statement and the date on which it was provided are ignored in calculating the 13 months; *or*
- for **other benefits**, if the statement of reasons is provided:
  - within one month of the date you were notified of the decision, the 13 months are extended by 14 days; *or*

 - during a period later than one month after the date you were notified of the decision, the 13 months are extended by 14 days, plus the number of days in that period.

Your application outside the time limit must contain:[38]

- sufficient details about the decision with which you disagree for it to be identified. You should say which benefit you are disagreeing about and the date the DWP, the local authority or HMRC sent you the decision; *and*
- a summary of your reasons for applying for a revision late. You must show that:[39]
  - it is reasonable to grant your request; *and*
  - your application for a revision has merit; *and*
  - there are special circumstances. The special circumstances must mean that it was not practicable for you to request a revision within the time limit. Any special circumstances can count. The longer you have delayed seeking a revision, the more compelling the special circumstances must be.

When deciding whether it is reasonable to grant your application, the decision maker cannot take account of the fact that:[40]

- a court or the Upper Tribunal has interpreted the law in a different way than previously understood and applied;
- you (or anyone acting for you) misunderstood or were unaware of the relevant law, including the time limits for seeking a revision.

You cannot appeal against the decision maker's refusal to let you seek a revision outside the time limit.[41] The only remedy is judicial review. However, you might be able to make a late appeal against the original decision.

'Any time' revisions

If you can show there are specific grounds (see below), you can ask for a revision at any time (called an 'any time' revision in this *Handbook*). There is no time limit for seeking an 'any time' revision. In practice, if you ask for a revision and it is within one month of your being sent or given the decision, the DWP, the local authority or HMRC treats your application as one for an 'any grounds' revision (see p1127). If a decision maker refuses to do an 'any time' revision, see p1135.

The main grounds for revision

There are a number of grounds for an 'any time' revision. The main ones are where there has been:

- an official error (see p1130);
- a mistake about or ignorance of facts (see p1131);

- an award of a 'qualifying benefit' (see p1132);
- an appeal against a decision (see p1132).

Other grounds for revision are summarised on p1133.

Official error

A decision can be revised at 'any time' if there was an official error.[42] For **benefits, other than child benefit and guardian's allowance**, this means an error made by an officer of the DWP or HMRC or an employee of a local authority (or a person acting on behalf of, and employed by someone providing services to, a local authority).[43] For HB and CTB, it also includes errors made by the local authority. Other than for HB and CTB, it also includes errors made by an officer of the Child Maintenance and Enforcement Commission and also a person employed by someone providing services to the DWP. For **child benefit and guardian's allowance**, it means an error made by an officer of HMRC or a person employed by someone providing services to HMRC.[44]

If the official error was made by an adjudication officer before the Social Security Act 1998 took effect (see CPAG's *Welfare Benefits Handbook* 1999/00, p2:649), you can argue that the decision can be revised.[45]

The following can count as official errors.

- The decision maker made an error of law, ie s/he got the law wrong. If the decision maker was only shown to have made an error of law after a later decision of the Upper Tribunal or a court, this ground does not apply. In this case, you could make a fresh claim (or ask for a supersession), but the 'anti-test case rule' could apply (see p1149).
- There is specific evidence that the decision maker had (or, in the case of HB and CTB, the local authority had), but which s/he failed to take into account even though it was relevant. You should argue this applies even if the evidence does not conclusively prove your entitlement, so long as it raised a strong possibility that you were entitled.
- There is documentary or other written evidence of your entitlement that the DWP, the local authority or HMRC had, but failed to give to the decision maker dealing with your claim when the earlier decision was made.
- The decision maker failed to ask you about something that was relevant to your claim. However, the decision maker is likely to say that it is *not* an official error if s/he fails to keep your claim constantly under review or to raise issues that you should have raised, or if s/he fails to make enquiries into things that do not appear to be at issue.[46]

If someone else (eg, you, your partner or your representative) caused or materially contributed to the error, it does not count as an official error. This includes if the way your claim form was completed contributed to the error.[47]

Mistake about or ignorance of facts

An 'any time' revision can be done if there was a mistake about the facts of your case or the decision was made in ignorance of relevant facts, but only if, as a result of the mistake or ignorance about the facts, the decision was more favourable to you than it would have been – eg, you were awarded too much benefit.[48] If you have been overpaid benefit, the decision maker may seek to recover the overpayment (see Chapter 43). **Note:** there must have been a mistake about or ignorance of facts, not conclusions or opinions about the facts. See p1069 for some examples.

The rules are different if there was a mistake about, or ignorance of, facts relating to a 'disability determination', a 'limited capability for work determination' or an 'incapacity determination'.[49] In this case, it must be shown that, at the time the decision that you were entitled to a benefit was made (eg, DLA or ESA), you (or the person being paid the benefit) knew, or could reasonably have been expected to know, about the fact and that it was relevant to your benefit. If the benefit is a qualifying benefit for another benefit (see p1132) and revision of the decision means your entitlement to the other benefit is affected, the decision about the other benefit takes effect on the same date.[50]

Disability, limited capability for work and incapacity determinations[51]

A **'disability determination'** is a decision about whether you satisfy the disability conditions for AA or DLA, are disabled for the purposes of SDA, or whether the existence or extent of your disablement is sufficient for you to be entitled to industrial injuries disablement benefit or to be paid at the same rate as that paid immediately before the decision that you were entitled to benefit.

A **'limited capability for work determination'** is a decision about whether you have, or can be treated as having, limited capability for work (see Chapter 11).

An **'incapacity determination'** is a decision about your incapacity for work under the personal capability assessment, whether you can be treated as incapable of work, or whether there are exceptional circumstances (see Chapter 32).

Note: if the mistake about or ignorance of facts means you should be entitled to *more* benefit:

- a decision can be superseded on this ground (see p1137), but arrears might be limited;
- a decision can be revised on 'any ground' if you apply in time (see p1127);
- for benefits other than HB and CTB, if the decision maker starts action within one month of the date you are sent a decision, s/he can decide to revise it her/himself, on any grounds;[52]
- for HB and CTB, a decision can be revised if, within one month of your being sent or given it, the local authority has information that shows there was a

mistake about the facts of your case or the decision was made in ignorance of relevant facts.[53]

Awards of a 'qualifying benefit'

A qualifying benefit is, in general, any benefit which gives you entitlement to another benefit, or makes another benefit payable at a higher rate. If you are awarded a benefit (eg, IS, income-related ESA or HB) and for a period which includes the date that award took effect, **you or a member of your family are awarded a 'qualifying benefit'** (eg, DLA or carer's allowance) or the qualifying benefit is increased, the decision awarding you benefit can be revised.[54] See p751 for who counts as your family.

A decision to end your entitlement to HB or CTB because your (or a member of your family's) qualifying benefit ceases can also be revised at any time. This only applies if the qualifying benefit is later reinstated following a revision, supersession or appeal.[55] For other benefits, see p1029 to see how a new claim can be backdated.

For IS, JSA, ESA and pension credit (PC) only, if you have a non-dependant living with you (see p832) and since you were awarded IS, income-based JSA, income-related ESA or PC, **your non-dependant has been awarded a 'qualifying benefit'** for a period that includes the date your award took effect and this means that you are now entitled to a severe disability premium (for IS, JSA or ESA) or a severe disability additional amount (for PC), the decision awarding benefit can be revised.[56]

See p1147 for further information. If you are only entitled to a benefit once a qualifying benefit is awarded, see pp1029 and 277.

A decision that has been appealed

If you appealed against a decision, and you:

- appealed within the time limit or were allowed a late appeal (see pp1162 and 1204) and the appeal has not yet been determined, a decision maker can look at the decision again and carry out a revision.[57] This includes if the First-tier Tribunal has adjourned the hearing or if the Upper Tribunal has sent a case back to the First-tier Tribunal to make a new decision; *or*
- make a fresh claim or seek a supersession when your circumstances change (eg, because the First-tier Tribunal cannot, in general, take changes into account – see p1176) and as a result a new decision about your entitlement is made, a decision maker can revise the new decision once the appeal against the first decision has been determined. This only applies if you appealed against a decision to the First-tier Tribunal (or, for HB and CTB only, to the Upper Tribunal or a court);[58] *and*
  - a fresh claim is decided or the decision is superseded before your appeal is determined; *and*
  - the appeal is then determined; *and*

- the decision maker would have made her/his decision differently if s/he had been aware of the appeal decision at the time her/his decision was made.

Note: if you have appealed against a decision, your appeal could lapse if a decision maker revises the decision, even if you do not get everything you want (see p1165).

Other grounds for revision

There are a large number of other situations when a decision maker can do an 'any time' revision. This includes if the decision is one against which you have no right of appeal (see p1159 for which decisions).[59]

Other decisions that can be revised at 'any time' include those:

- refusing reduced earnings allowance, because of a decision about your entitlement to industrial injuries disablement benefit – eg, you are awarded disablement benefit after an appeal to the First-tier Tribunal;[60]
- to award you ESA if, when you first claimed ESA, you were not entitled because you were treated as not having limited capability for work (eg, because you had failed to a return the ESA50 questionnaire), and you can now be accepted as having limited capability for work for the earlier period;[61]
- about HB, where your maximum rent increases because of a rent officer redetermination, or because a local housing allowance rate or broad rental market area has been amended because of a rent officer's error, or if (in Scotland) an order or notice that your landlord is not entitled to charge rent for your property is revoked following an appeal;[62]
- about retirement pension, PC, HB or CTB, where you or your partner deferred claiming a pension, then change, your option from a higher pension to a lump sum (or, for retirement pension only, *vice versa*); [63]
- about entitlement to a benefit that depends on your national insurance contribution record, where the decision needs to be changed because additional contributions have been added to the record restrospectively.[64]

There are a number of situations in which decisions about your incapacity for work under the personal capability assessment that affect IS and IB decisions can be revised.[65] See pp1109–10 of the 2011/12 edition of this *Handbook* for details.

Note: the list above is not exhaustive. There are other decisions that can be revised at any time.[66]

How to seek a revision

Apply for a revision to the office that sent you the decision with which you disagree or, for JSA, the office where you have to sign on.[67] For benefits (other than child benefit, guardian's allowance, HB and CTB), if you are a person who is, or would be, required to attend a work-focused interview as a condition of getting benefit, you can also apply to the Jobcentre Plus office. The DWP, the local authority or HMRC can treat a request for a supersession as a request for a revision.[68]

For **HB** and **CTB**, you must apply for a revision in writing.[69] A late application for a revision must also be in writing.[70]

For **benefits other than HB and CTB**, you do not have to ask for a revision in writing, although it is always best to do so. This ensures that the decision maker understands that you are asking for a revision, not just seeking an explanation or complaining about the rules.

Example

Stan is awarded IS, but the DWP says he is not entitled to help with his housing costs. He telephones the benefit office and complains that he has not got enough money to live on. The benefit office takes no action because it thinks Stan is simply letting off steam, not seeking a revision. Stan should have made it clear he wanted a revision. He can still ask for one (or appeal) but only if he is within the time limit (see pp1128 and 1162).

A decision maker does not have to consider any issues other than those raised by your application for a revision or which caused her/him to act on her/his own initiative.[71] You should, therefore, ensure you:

- tell the decision maker all the points about the decision with which you disagree;
- provide any information or evidence that supports your case. This includes, for example, medical evidence from a GP, consultant or other health worker if this is relevant. If you are claiming AA or DLA, evidence or information from your carer or a diary of your walking, supervision or care needs over a period may be useful.

The decision maker may ask you for further information or evidence to help her/him make a decision (see p1124). Follow up your request for a revision with the DWP, the local authority or HMRC to check that your application has been received to ensure that you do not miss the time limit for seeking an 'any grounds' revision or for appealing.

The revised decision

After a decision maker considers a revision, s/he can decide there are:

- grounds for revision and that the original decision was correct or should be changed; *or*
- no grounds for revision and refuse to change the original decision.

For information about challenging the decision, see p1135.

When a revision takes effect

The date a revision takes effect is important. This is the date from which you are paid arrears if you are entitled to more benefit, or have been overpaid if you are entitled to less benefit. In all cases, a revision takes effect from:

- the date the decision being revised took (or would have taken) effect[72] – eg, your date of claim or the date a supersession took effect; *or*
- the correct date, if the date on which the decision being revised took effect was found to be wrong.[73]

It is important to make it clear that you want payment for the past period. You might get less backdating if the 'anti-test case rule' applies (see p1149).

Challenging a revision

If a decision is revised or the decision maker refuses to revise a decision, you are notified of this in writing. If the original decision is one against which you have a right of appeal (see p1158 for which decisions), you can appeal to the First-tier Tribunal against the revised decision (or in the case of a refusal to do an 'any grounds' revision, against the original decision). Your time limit for appealing (see p1162) runs from the date you are sent or given the notification.[74]

If a decision maker refuses to do an 'any time' revision (see p1129) (eg, because s/he does not accept that an official error was made), you cannot appeal against the refusal.[75] However, you could make a late request for an 'any grounds' revision or try to make a late appeal against the original decision, if you are still within the absolute time limit for these.

4. Supersessions

If your circumstances have changed since a decision was made, you can seek a supersession.[76] You can also seek a supersession if you think a decision is wrong, but you must show there are grounds (see p1136). You can seek a supersession of an original decision or one superseding an earlier decision.

You can seek a supersession even if the decision was made a long time ago, but the arrears of benefit you are paid can be limited (see p1141 for when a supersession takes effect). It is usually better to try for a revision or appeal.

Following a supersession, your benefit could be increased, but it could also be decreased or stopped altogether. See p1125 for what to consider before seeking a supersession.

For information on how to seek a supersession, see p1140. To find out when a supersession takes effect, see p1141.

When a decision can be superseded

You can ask for a decision maker's decision (and in some cases a First-tier Tribunal's or an Upper Tribunal's decision) to be superseded or the decision maker can decide to do this her/himself.[77] However, there must be grounds for a supersession.

Note:

- If a decision could be revised, it cannot be superseded unless there are grounds for supersession that are not covered by the revision rules.[78]
- You can argue that decisions made by an appeal tribunal or a commissioner before 3 November 2008 cannot be superseded because they are not mentioned in the relevant rules (but these rules are due to be amended).[79]

The main grounds for supersession

There are a large number of grounds for supersession. The main grounds are:

- change of circumstances (see below);
- mistakes about or ignorance of facts (see p1137);
- where a decision is legally wrong (see p1138);
- where there are issues about your capability for work (see p1138);
- where a qualifying benefit has been awarded (see p1139).

Other grounds for supersession are summarised on p1139.

Change of circumstances

A decision can be superseded if:[80]

- your circumstances have changed since it had effect; *or*
- in the case of advance awards (other than for housing benefit (HB) and council tax benefit (CTB)), your circumstances have changed since it was made. This includes most decisions to convert an award of income support (IS), incapacity benefit (IB) or severe disablement allowance (SDA) to employment and support allowance (ESA) (see p193); *or*
- it is anticipated that your circumstances will change.

The change must mean that the decision may no longer be correct. This is what is known as a 'relevant change of circumstances'. If the change means that you could be entitled to more benefit, there is a strict time limit for reporting the change in order to get all the arrears of benefit to which you are entitled (see p1141 for when a supersession takes effect).

The decision maker might say that a change of circumstances you have reported is a change that could not possibly result in a supersession and so refuse to consider a supersession. If this happens, see p1147.

You should bear the following in mind.

- An amendment to the law counts as a change of circumstances, but a decision of a court or the Upper Tribunal that the law has been wrongly interpreted does not.[81]
- A new medical opinion is not a change of circumstances, but a new medical report following an examination might give evidence of such a change.[82]
- For IS, jobseeker's allowance (JSA) and ESA, the repayment of a student loan does not count as a relevant change of circumstance.[83]
- For attendance allowance (AA) and disability living allowance (DLA), you or the person claiming on your behalf must state explicitly that you are terminally ill in the application for a supersession for this to count as a relevant change of circumstances.[84]
- In respect of your assessed income period for pension credit (PC), the only change of circumstances that is relevant for these purposes is that the period has ended for one of the reasons listed on p522.[85]
- In deciding whether there has been a change of circumstances, it is necessary to compare the circumstances as they were at the time the decision took effect and as they were at the time the supersession would take effect. So for example, in considering a supersession of a decision of the First-tier Tribunal to award a benefit, a decision maker may have difficulty showing that there has been a change of circumstances if there is no statement of reasons for the First-tier Tribunal's decision.[86]

Note: you must always report any change in your circumstances which you might reasonably be expected to know might affect your right to, the amount of, or payment of, your benefit (see p1047).

Change of circumstances after benefit is refused

If you were correctly refused benefit but your circumstances are now different, you *cannot* seek a supersession on the grounds of a change of circumstances. You must instead make a fresh claim (unless you are seeking a supersession because there has been a 'recrudescence' of a prescribed disease – see p373).[87] Even if you are appealing against the decision refusing or stopping your benefit, you should make a fresh claim when your circumstances change and appeal if you are still refused. If you do not, you could lose out. This is because if you appeal to the First-tier Tribunal against a decision refusing benefit or terminating your award, the Tribunal cannot take a change of circumstances into account if it happens after the decision with which you disagree (but see p1176).

Mistake about or ignorance of facts

A decision can be superseded if there was a mistake about the facts of your case or if it was made in ignorance of relevant facts, and in the case of a decision maker's decision:[88]

- for HB and CTB, a revision on the same ground cannot be done. Note that the local authority can revise a decision if, within one month of your being sent or given it, it has information that shows that there was a mistake about the facts of your case or the decision was made in ignorance of relevant facts;[89] *or*
- for other benefits, the time limit for seeking an 'any grounds' revision (or any longer period allowed) has passed (see p1128).

In practice, this ground for supersession only applies if, as a result of a mistake or ignorance about the facts, a decision was less favourable to you than it would have been (eg, you were awarded too little benefit) and you have missed the time limit for seeking an 'any grounds' revision. If a decision is more favourable to you than it would have been (ie, you were being overpaid), a decision maker can instead do an 'any time' revision (see p1131).

Note:

- There must have been a mistake about the facts or the decision maker must not have had all the facts, but it does not matter how the mistake came about or whether you could have produced evidence sooner than you did or failed to give the information on your claim form.
- The mistake or ignorance must be in respect of facts, not conclusions or opinions about the facts. See p1069 for some examples.

Decisions that are legally wrong

A decision can be superseded if it was made by a decision maker and was legally wrong (known as an error of law), and:[90]

- for HB and CTB, a revision on the same ground cannot be done; *or*
- for other benefits, the time limit for seeking an 'any grounds' revision (or any longer period allowed) has passed (see p1128).

In many cases, if there has been an error of law, an 'any time' revision on grounds of official error is also possible. If the new decision is to your advantage, revision is the better option as full arrears of benefit are payable.

Note: if you think a decision of the First-tier Tribunal or the Upper Tribunal is legally wrong, you need to appeal against it.

Capability for work

A decision can be superseded if it is a decision to award you ESA or national insurance (NI) credits on the basis that you have, or are treated as having, limited capability for work (see Chapter 11). The decision can be superseded if, since the decision was made:[91]

- a healthcare professional (see p1118 for who counts) approved by the Secretary of State has provided medical evidence on your capability for work – eg, following a work capability assessment; *or*

- the decision maker has decided that you can be treated as having limited capability for work under specified provisions.

The rules allow the decision maker to consider whether you are still entitled to ESA or NI credits. However, your ESA (or NI credits) should only be stopped if s/he decides on the basis of the evidence that you no longer have limited capability for work.[92] If you have told the decision maker that your condition has not improved since your last assessment or you have a variable condition, you can argue that reference should be made to earlier assessments and decisions on your claim.[93]

Note:

- A decision to award you ESA or NI credits might still be superseded on the grounds of a change of circumstances.
- There are similar rules under which a decision about your incapacity for work under the personal capability assessment that affected IS, incapacity benefit or NI credits could be superseded.[94] See pp1115–16 of the 2011/12 edition of this *Handbook* for details.

Awards of qualifying benefits

A qualifying benefit is, in general, any benefit which gives you entitlement to another benefit, or makes another benefit payable at a higher rate. If you are awarded a benefit (eg, IS, ESA or HB) but, from a later date than the entitlement began, **you or a member of your family become entitled to a 'qualifying benefit'** (eg, DLA or carer's allowance (CA)) or the qualifying benefit is increased, the decision awarding you benefit can be superseded.[95] See p751 for who counts as your family.

For IS, JSA, ESA and PC only, if you have a non-dependant living with you (see p832) and since you were awarded IS, income-based JSA, income-related ESA or PC, **your non-dependant has been awarded a 'qualifying benefit'** for a period beginning after the date your award took effect, and this means that you are now entitled to a severe disability premium (for IS, JSA or ESA) or a severe disability additional amount (for PC), the decision awarding you benefit can be superseded.[96]

See p1147 for further information. If you are only entitled to a benefit once a qualifying benefit is awarded, see pp1029 and 277.

Other grounds for supersession

There are a large number of other situations when a decision maker can do a supersession. This includes if the decision is one against which you have no right of appeal (see p1159 for which decisions).[97]

Other decisions that can be superseded include those:

- about HB, where your maximum rent decreases because of a rent officer redetermination. Note that a decrease in your maximum rent because a local

housing allowance rate or a broad rental market area has been amended because of a rent officer's error is dealt with as a change of circumstances;[98]
- about PC, HB and CTB, where you or your partner deferred claiming a pension and you are paid a lump sum or repay it because you change your option to a pension increase;[99]
- about entitlement to a benefit that depends on your NI contribution record, where the decision needs to be changed because additional contributions have been added to the record from a later date;[100]
- of the First-tier Tribunal or the Upper Tribunal while a test case was pending, where the test case is eventually decided in your favour (see p1198).[101]

The list above is not exhaustive. There are many other decisions that can be superseded.[102]

How to seek a supersession

Apply for a supersession to the office that made the decision with which you disagree. The following can be treated as a request for a supersession:[103]
- a request for a revision;
- a notification of a change in circumstances;
- a claim for benefit or a question about your entitlement.

For benefits other than HB and CTB, you do not have to ask for a supersession in writing although it is always best to do so. For HB and CTB, you *must* ask the local authority for a supersession in writing.[104]

The decision maker does not have to consider any issue other than those raised by your application for a supersession or which caused her/him to act on her/his own initiative.[105] You should, therefore, ensure you:
- tell the decision maker all the points about the decision with which you disagree;
- provide any information or evidence that supports your case. This includes medical evidence from a GP or consultant or other health worker if this is relevant. If you are claiming AA or DLA, evidence or information from your carer or a diary of your walking, supervision or care needs over a period may be useful.

The decision maker may ask you for further information or evidence to help her/him make a decision (see p1124).

The new decision

After a decision maker carries out a supersession, s/he makes a new decision. S/he can decide that:

- the original decision should continue; *or*
- the original decision should be replaced and what the new decision should be.

For information about challenging a decision, see p1146. If the decision maker refuses to consider a supersession, see p1147.

When a supersession takes effect

If a decision is superseded, the date a new decision (the supersession) takes effect is important. This is the date from which you are paid arrears if you are entitled to more benefit, or the date from which you have been overpaid if you are entitled to less benefit. It is important to make it clear that you want payment for a past period. **Note:**

- There is a general rule (see below) that applies in many cases.
- There are a large number of exceptions when the general rule does not apply. For these, the date a supersession takes effect depends on the ground for the supersession. For exceptions, see below and the chapter in this *Handbook* about the benefit you are claiming.
- If there has been a mistake about or ignorance of facts, in most cases the general rule applies. However, there are two exceptions (see p1144).

Note: for how the 'anti-test case rule' may affect the amount of backdated benefit you can receive, see p1145.

The general rule

The general rule is that, if a decision is superseded, the new decision takes effect from the date you applied for the supersession.[106] However, if the decision maker decides to do one on her/his own, the new decision takes effect from the date the decision is made.

Changes in your circumstances

If the ground for supersession is a change in your circumstances, when the supersession takes effect usually depends on whether or not it is advantageous to you. For HB or CTB, see below. For other benefits, see p1142. **Note:**

- If a supersession is advantageous to you, you must usually notify the decision maker of the change within one month or you could lose out.
- If a supersession is not advantageous to you, you may have been overpaid. The DWP, the local authority or HMRC might seek to recover the overpayment.

There are exceptions.

- For benefits other than child benefit and guardian's allowance, if there has been a **change in the legislation** that affects your benefit, the supersession takes effect from the date the legislation takes effect.[107]

- For benefits other than HB or CTB, if your **carer** (or your partner's carer) **has stopped being paid CA**, the supersession takes effect from the day after the last day for which CA was paid. This means that if you are now entitled to the severe disability premium with your IS, income-based JSA or income-related ESA (or the severe disability additional amount with PC), this can be backdated to when the carer stopped getting CA for looking after you (or your partner).[108]
- For benefits other than HB or CTB, if your **non-dependant has become entitled to ESA that includes a work-related activity or a support component**, the supersession takes effect from when the component is first paid to the non-dependant.[109]
- For ESA only, if the change is that **you are terminally ill** (you must state this in the application for a supersession), the supersession takes effect from the date you became terminally ill.[110]

Housing benefit and council tax benefit

For HB or CTB, the supersession usually takes effect from the Monday after the week in which the change occurs.[111] However, if the change is one you are required to notify to the local authority (other than, if you get PC, one of the types of change covered by the exceptions to the rules described on p293) and the supersession is *advantageous* to you, the change must be notified within one month of its taking place.[112] The one-month period can be extended in certain circumstances (see p1143). If you notify the change outside the one-month period (or any longer period allowed by the local authority), the supersession usually takes effect from the Monday after the week in which you notify the change.

For further information on when changes in circumstances take effect and exceptions to this rule, see p292.

Other benefits

For benefits other than HB and CTB, if the supersession is *advantageous* to you, it takes effect as follows.

- If the decision maker decides to do a supersession her/himself, it usually takes effect from the start of the benefit week in which s/he first took action with a view to doing a supersession.[113]
- If you apply for the supersession and the decision is about AA or DLA[114] *and*:
  - the change means you are now entitled to a particular rate of benefit, the supersession takes effect from the day you satisfy the conditions of entitlement to that rate. You must notify the DWP of the change within one month of doing so;
  - the change makes a difference to whether benefit is payable to you (eg, you go into, or leave, hospital or a care home), the supersession takes effect from the day of the change. You must notify the DWP of the change within one month of it taking place.

To see if the one-month period can be extended, and when a supersession takes effect if it is not, see p1143.

- If you apply for the supersession and the decision is not about AA or DLA, the supersession takes effect from the date of the change, so long as the DWP or HM Revenue and Customs is notified of the change within one month of its taking place.[115] To see if the one-month period can be extended, and when a supersession takes effect if it is not, see below.

If the decision maker decides to do a supersession her/himself or you apply for a supersession and it is *not advantageous* to you, the supersession usually takes effect from the date of the change of circumstances.[116] This does not apply to certain disability, limited capability for work and incapacity decisions.

A supersession takes effect from the date you (or the person being paid the benefit) ought to have notified the change, if the change related to your disability, limited capability for work or incapacity for work and the decision is:[117]

- a disability decision about AA, DLA, SDA, industrial injuries disablement benefit; *or*
- a decision about your limited capability for work, including whether you can be treated as having limited capability for work (see Chapter 11); *or*
- a decision about your incapacity for work under the personal capability assessment, whether you can be treated as incapable of work or there are exceptional circumstances (see Chapter 32).

This only applies if the change was one you were required to notify and you (or the person being paid the benefit) failed to notify the change when you knew that you should have, or could reasonably be expected to have known that you should have, done so. If this is not the case, the decision is a disability decision and the change related to your disability, the general rule on p1141 applies – ie, the supersession takes effect from the date you applied for it or the date the decision was made.[118] So if your condition is found to have improved in the past, and you could not have been expected to report this, you will not have been overpaid benefit.

If the benefit is a qualifying benefit (see p1139) and the supersession means your entitlement to another benefit is affected, the decision about the other benefit takes effect on the same date.[119]

Late notification of a change of circumstances

If the supersession is *advantageous* and you fail to notify a change within the one-month periods above, you can apply for an extension of time in limited circumstances.[120] The time limit can be extended to 13 months. Your application must contain:[121]

- details of the relevant change of circumstances; *and*
- the reasons why you failed to notify the change in time. You must show that:[122]

- it is reasonable to grant your request; *and*
- the change of circumstances is relevant to the decision you want changed; *and*
- there are special circumstances that mean it was not practicable for you to notify the change within the time limit. The longer you have delayed notifying a change, the more compelling the special circumstances have to be.

When deciding whether it is reasonable to grant your application, the decision maker cannot take account of the fact that:[123]

- a court or the Upper Tribunal has interpreted the law in a different way than previously understood and applied;
- you (or anyone acting for you) misunderstood or were unaware of the relevant law, including the time limits for seeking a supersession.

If your application for an extension of time is refused, arrears are limited. The supersession takes effect:

- for benefits (other than AA, DLA, IS, JSA, ESA, PC, HB and CTB), from when you notified the change;[124] *or*
- for AA or DLA, from the date you applied for the supersession;[125] *or*
- for IS, JSA, ESA and PC:[126]
  - if you are paid in arrears, from the start of the benefit week in which you notified the change; *or*
  - if you are paid in advance and you notifed the change on the first day of the benefit week, from that day. Otherwise it takes effect from the start of the benefit week following the week in which you notified the change; *or*
- for HB and CTB, usually from the Monday after the date when you notified the change (see p292).[127]

Mistake about or ignorance of facts

If there has been a mistake about or ignorance of facts, the general rule on p1141 usually applies. So even if you are entitled to more benefit, arrears are limited.

The general rule does not apply in the following circumstances.

- If the First-tier Tribunal or the Upper Tribunal made a decision in ignorance of relevant facts or made a mistake about the facts and, as a result, the decision was more advantageous to you than it would otherwise have been, the supersession takes effect from the date the Tribunal's decision took effect.[128] If this means that you have been overpaid, the decision maker may seek to recover the overpayment. However, if it is a disability decision about AA, DLA, SDA, industrial injuries disablement benefit or a decision about your incapacity for work under the personal capability assessment or whether you can be treated as incapable of work or there are exceptional circumstances (see Chapter 32), this only happens if you (or the person being paid the benefit) knew, or could reasonably have been expected to know, the fact in question and that it was relevant to the decision. **Note:** this exception was not amended to include decisions about limited capability for work. It is not known if this was an omission or the intention.

- For HB and CTB, if a decision was made in ignorance of facts or there was a mistake about the facts and the new decision is advantageous to you, the supersession takes effect from the start of the benefit week in which:[129]
  - you applied for the supersession; *or*
  - if you did not apply for a supersession, the local authority first had sufficient information to show that the original decision was made in ignorance of, or based on a mistake about, the facts.

Awards of qualifying benefits

If you are entitled to a benefit at a higher rate because you, a member of your family or a non-dependant were awarded a qualifying benefit, the supersession takes effect on the date of entitlement to the qualifying benefit or to an increase in its rate. For IS, JSA, ESA and PC only, if you had a non-dependant living with you while you were waiting for a decision on your claim for a qualifying benefit, and a severe disability premium (additional amount with PC) can now be included, the supersession takes effect from the date the non-dependant can be ignored (or ceased to live with you). See p1147 for further information.[130]

Test cases

If a decision about your benefit is being superseded because of a decision by the Upper Tribunal or a court in another case (a test case), the supersession is effective from the date of the Upper Tribunal's or court's decision, even if you did not realise it was relevant to your case until some time later.[131] This could help you get considerable arrears of benefit. See p1149 for further information about the 'anti-test case rule'. However, if, while an appeal against the initial decision in a test case was pending:

- for benefits other than HB and CTB, a decision was made on your claim for benefit or to make a revision or a supersession, but your benefit was suspended and the test case is eventually decided against you (in whole or in part), the supersession takes effect from the date the earlier decision took effect;[132]
- you appealed to the First-tier Tribunal or the Upper Tribunal, the First-tier Tribunal or the Upper Tribunal determines your appeal as if the test case had been decided in the way most unfavourable to you and the test case eventually goes in your favour (see p1198), the supersession takes effect from the date it would have taken effect had the Tribunal made its decision in accordance with the decision in the test case.[133]

Note: there is a special rule if your award of AA or DLA was terminated on or after 8 March 2001 because you moved, or planned to move, to another European

Economic Area country or to Switzerland. In this case, the decision maker does a supersession of the decision to terminate your award and it takes effect on 18 October 2007.[134]

Other grounds for supersession

There are a large number of other exceptions to the general rule. The main ones are as follows.

- If your award of IS, JSA, ESA or PC is being superseded to include help with **mortgage interest** or **interest on a loan for repairs and improvements** (see Chapter 38), the supersession can be backdated for up to eight weeks. This can only be done if the supersession could not take place sooner because your lender did not supply the DWP with your mortgage details.[135]
- For HB only, if your **maximum rent has decreased** because of a rent officer redetermination, the new decision usually takes effect from the start of the benefit week after the date of the determination.[136]

There are other exceptions to the general rule, including if a decision is superseded:

- for ESA, because a healthcare professional (see p1118 for who counts) approved by the Secretary of State has provided medical evidence on your capability for work or a decision maker has decided that you can be treated as having limited capability for work-related activity;[137]
- for PC, HB and CTB, if you or your partner deferred claiming a pension and you are paid a lump sum or change your option to a pension increase;[138]
- if entitlement to a benefit depends on your NI contribution record, and the decision needed to be changed because additional contributions have been added to the record.[139]

The list above is not exhaustive. There are amany other exceptions to the general rule.[140]

Challenging a supersession

Following your application for a supersession, or a decision maker deciding to do a supersession on her/his own, a new decision is issued in writing. If you do not get all that you wanted from the supersession, you can seek a revision of the new decision. If the decision is one against which you have a right of appeal (see p1158), you can appeal to the First-tier Tribunal. If you have a right of appeal against the decision, you must be told about this.

If the decision maker has said there are no grounds for a supersession, you must show why there are, and say what you think the new decision should be. If the decision maker has done a supersession, but you do not agree that s/he had grounds for this, you should explain why.

If a decision maker refuses to consider a supersession

When you apply for a supersession, a decision maker must make a decision if your application for a supersession contains a ground for supersession that is potentially relevant to the amount of benefit you can be paid or the length of time you can be paid it. There are two possibilities.

- The decision maker agrees that there is a reason to change your award. For example, you are claiming HB and notify the decision maker that your non-dependant has moved out and so are entitled to more benefit. In this situation, the decision maker does a supersession.
- The decision maker does not think there is a reason to change your award. For example, you are getting DLA care component at the lowest rate, feel your condition has deteriorated and want to claim middle rate instead. However, the decision maker thinks you do not qualify for the middle rate. In this situation, the decision maker issues a decision refusing to do a supersession.

In either situation, you can seek a revision of the decision maker's decision or appeal against it.[141] The only situations in which a decision maker does not have to make a decision are if an application has not been made properly and, therefore, cannot possibly lead to a supersession, or if an application is transparently not on a potentially relevant ground for supersession or is otherwise misconceived. In these cases, there is no decision against which you can seek a revision or appeal, but you may be able to apply for a judicial review.

5. Revisions and supersessions after a 'qualifying benefit' award

There are special revision and supersession rules, known as 'qualifying benefit' rules. A qualifying benefit is, in general, any benefit which gives you entitlement to another benefit, or makes another benefit payable at a higher rate. The rules help where, because of delays in assessing entitlement to a qualifying benefit – eg, attendance allowance (AA), disability living allowance (DLA), carer's allowance (CA) or child benefit:

- you did not get certain premiums paid with your means-tested benefit (eg, enhanced disability, severe disability, disabled child or carer premium), or additional amounts paid with your pension credit (PC) or allowances for your children. Other than for housing benefit (HB) or council tax benefit (CTB), this includes where there are delays in assessing your non-dependant's entitlement to a qualifying benefit (see p1148); *or*
- a non-dependant deduction was made from your means-tested benefit.

These rules can help you get arrears of benefit, even if the qualifying benefit was awarded some time ago, and you did not report the change in your circumstances at the time.[142]

Note: you can only ask for a revision or supersession on this ground if you are already entitled to income support (IS), jobseeker's allowance (JSA), employment and support allowance (ESA), PC, HB or CTB.[143] It is, therefore, essential to make a claim for these at the same time as the claim for a qualifying benefit. If you only qualify for one of these when the qualifying benefit is awarded, see p1149.

You or a family member are awarded a qualifying benefit or an increased rate

If you, or a member of your family (see p751 for who counts), are awarded a qualifying benefit or an increase in its rate, and arrears of the qualifying benefit are payable, your award of IS, JSA, ESA, PC, HB or CTB can be increased on revision or supersession and arrears paid for the same length of time.[144] This applies if:

- you are now entitled to premiums/additional amounts (or if the qualifying benefit is child benefit, to allowances for your children paid with your benefit); *or*
- no non-dependant deduction should now be made from your means-tested benefit because you are now entitled to AA or the care component of DLA.

Note: for IS, JSA, ESA and PC only, if you had a non-dependant living with you while you were waiting for a decision on your claim for a qualifying benefit, your IS, ESA or PC award can be superseded to include the severe disability premium (additional amount), from the date s/he can be ignored (or from the date s/he ceased to reside with you) if this is after the date from which the qualifying benefit is payable.[145]

Example

Gus has been getting IS, HB and CTB for two months. His IS does not include any premiums and, because his uncle lives with him and his partner, Tanya, a non-dependant deduction is being made from his HB and CTB. He claims DLA, and Tanya claims carer's allowance (CA) on 15 July. Six months later, Gus is awarded DLA highest rate care component and Tanya is awarded CA, both payable from 15 July. Gus is now entitled to the disability, enhanced disability and carer premiums with his IS and a non-dependant deduction should not be made from his HB and CTB. His IS, HB and CTB awards are superseded and he is paid six months' arrears, backdated to 15 July.

Your non-dependant is awarded a qualifying benefit or an increased rate

For IS, JSA, ESA and PC only, if you have a non-dependant living with you and, but for this, a severe disability premium (additional amount for PC) would be paid, your award of IS, income-based JSA, income-related ESA or PC can be increased on revision or supersession to include this premium (additional amount) from the date the non-dependant is awarded a qualifying benefit – eg, AA or middle or highest rate DLA care component.[146]

If you only qualify when the qualifying benefit is awarded

If you make an unsuccessful claim for IS, JSA, ESA or PC, but only qualify when the qualifying benefit is awarded, you should make a second claim as soon as you hear about the qualifying benefit. See p1029 for further information.

If you only qualify for HB or CTB when the qualifying benefit is awarded, see p277. If you lose benefit because of the way the rules operate, ask the local authority for compensation.

Remember, if you only claim for the first time *after* you hear about the qualifying benefit:

- for IS or JSA, you can only get arrears if you satisfy the backdating rules on p1027;
- for ESA and PC and (if you are at least the qualifying age for PC (see p509) and not getting IS, income-based JSA or income-related ESA) HB and CTB, your claim can only be backdated for up to three months;
- for HB or CTB if you are under the qualifying age for PC or either you or your partner are getting IS, income-based JSA or income-related ESA, your claim can only be backdated for up to six months, and only if you can show 'good cause' for your late claim (see p277).

There are similar rules that help you get extra backdating if your entitlement to incapacity benefit, severe disablement allowance or CA depends on whether you (or in the case of CA, the person for whom you care) are entitled to a qualifying benefit. See p1029 for information.

6. The 'anti-test case rule'

Special rules apply when a case is going through the appeals system that will determine a point of social security law (a test case). A rule (the 'anti-test case rule') says that some court and Upper Tribunal decisions should be ignored when decision makers are considering your entitlement to benefit for periods before the court or the Upper Tribunal decisions were given. If the anti-test case rule applies, you get arrears of benefit backdated only to the date of the decision in the test case.

How the anti-test case rule operates

If the Upper Tribunal or a court decides in an appeal that a decision maker in a totally different case (the test case) has made an error of law (see p1182 for what counts), and you make a claim, or seek a revision or a supersession (whether before or after the test case decision), your decision maker must decide any part of *your* claim (or revision or supersession) which relates to the period *before* the test case decision as if the decision that was under appeal in the test case had been found by the Upper Tribunal or court in question not to have been wrong.[147] The anti-test case rule only applies if the test case is the first authoritative decision on the issue, and not merely a later decision confirming an earlier decision.[148]

The test case decision only has to be disregarded for the period before it was made if it found the decision maker to have been wrong, not if it found her/him to be right.

You can avoid the anti-test case rule by appealing rather than seeking a revision or supersession. This means that in cases where the anti-test case rule might apply, and you are still within the absolute time limit for appealing, it may be better to appeal first (applying for an extension of time to appeal if necessary) and only ask for a revision or supersession if you cannot appeal.

What happens while a test case is pending

If an appeal (a test case) is pending against a decision of the Upper Tribunal or a court, the decision maker can postpone making a decision on your claim or request for a supersession or revision.[149] This prevents you appealing until a decision is made in the test case. If you already have a decision in your favour, the decision maker can suspend payment of your benefit (see p1044).

If you would be entitled to benefit even if the test case were decided against you, the decision maker can make a decision.[150] This is done on the assumption that the test case has been decided in the way that is most unfavourable to you. However, this does mean that you are at least paid something while you wait for the result of the test case. Then, if the decision in the test case is in your favour, the decision maker revises her/his decision.

If the decision on your claim or request for a revision or supersession is postponed, once a decision has been made in the test case, the decision maker makes the decision in your case.[151]

If you have already appealed to the First-tier Tribunal, see p1198.

Notes

1. **Decisions**
  1 R(SB) 29/83; R(SB) 12/89; CIS/807/1992; R(H) 3/05
  2 Reg 11 SS&CS(DA) Regs
  3 s19 SSA 1998
  4 Reg 12 SS&CS(DA) Regs
  5 **HB/CTB** Sch 7 para 5 CSPSSA 2000
  Other benefits s11(2) SSA 1998
  6 s39(1) SSA 1998; reg 3 Social Security (Disability Living Allowance) (Amendment) Regulations 2010, No.1651
  7 Regs 13(2) and (3) and 15 SS&CS(DA) Regs
  8 Reg 13A SS&CS(DA) Regs
  9 Reg 13(1) SS&CS(DA) Regs
  10 s8 SSC(TF)A 1999
  11 s10A SSA 1998; reg 11A SS&CS(DA) Regs
  12 s11 SSC(TF)A 1999
  13 s24A SSA 1998; reg 38A SS&CS(DA) Regs
  14 s17 SSC(TF)A 1999; Sch 3 paras 16 and 17 SSA 1998; the National Insurance Contribution Credits (Transfer of Functions) Order 2009, No.1377
  15 s74 SSAA 1992; regs 7-10 SS(PAOR) Regs
  16 **HB/CTB** Reg 10A HB&CTB(DA) Regs
  Other benefits Reg 9A SS&CS(DA) Regs
  17 **CB/GA** Reg 26(1) CB&GA(DA) Regs
  HB/CTB Reg 10A(1) HB&CTB(DA) Regs
  Other benefits Reg 28(1) SS&CS(DA) Regs
  18 **CB/GA** Regs 3 and 26(1)(b) and (2) CB&GA(DA) Regs
  HB/CTB Reg 10(1)(b) and (2) HB&CTB(DA) Regs
  Other benefits Regs 2 and 28(1)(b) and (2) SS&CS(DA) Regs
  19 R(IB) 4/02

2. **Getting a decision changed**
  20 R(I) 50/56
  21 R(IS) 11/92
  22 **CB/GA** Regs 7(2) and (3) and 14(3) CB&GA(DA) Regs
  HB/CTB Regs 4(5) and 7(5) HB&CTB(DA) Regs
  Other benefits Regs 3(2) and 6(4) SS&CS(DA) Regs
  23 **HB/CTB** Sch 7 paras 3(2) and 4(3) CSPSSA 2000
  Other benefits ss9(2) and 10(2) SSA 1998

3. **Revisions**
  24 **HB/CTB** Sch 7 para 3 CSPSSA 2000
  Other benefits s9 SSA 1998
  25 **CB/GA** s9(1) SSA 1998; regs 5, 8, 10 and 11 CB&GA(DA) Regs
  HB/CTB Sch 7 para 3(1) CSPSSA 2000; reg 4 HB&CTB(DA) Regs
  Other benefits s9(1) SSA 1998; reg 3 SS&CS(DA) Regs
  26 Reg 3(9)(b) and (c) SS&CS(DA) Regs
  27 **CB/GA** Reg 5(2)(b) CB&GA(DA) Regs
  HB/CTB Reg 4(1)(a) HB&CTB(DA) Regs
  Other benefits Reg 3(1)(b) SS&CS(DA) Regs
  28 **CB/GA** Reg 5(2)(a) CB&GA(DA) Regs
  Other benefits Reg 3(1)(a) SS&CS(DA) Regs
  29 Reg 4(1)(b) HB&CTB(DA) Regs
  30 **CB/GA** Reg 5(3) CB&GA(DA) Regs
  HB/CTB Reg 4(10) HB&CTB(DA) Regs
  Other benefits Reg 3(9)(a) SS&CS(DA) Regs; Sch 2 para 25A(1)(b) and (c) ESA(TP)(EA) No.2 Regs
  31 Reg 3(3) SS&CS(DA) Regs
  32 Regs 1(3), definition of 'date of notification', and 3(1)(b) SS&CS(DA) Regs
  33 Regs 2 and 4(1)(a) HB&CTB(DA) Regs
  34 Reg 4(4) HB&CTB(DA) Regs
  35 **CB/GA** Regs 3 and 5(2)(b) CB&GA(DA) Regs
  Other benefits Regs 1(3), 2(b) and 3(1)(b) SS&CS(DA) Regs
  36 **HB/CTB** Reg 10A(3) HB&CTB(DA) Regs
  Other benefits Reg 9A(3) SS&CS(DA) Regs

37 **CB/GA** Reg 6(3)(c) CB&GA(DA) Regs
HB/CTB Regs 4(4) and 5(3)(b) HB&CTB(DA) Regs
Other benefits Reg 4(3)(b) SS&CS(DA) Regs
38 **CB/GA** Regs 5(2)(b) and 6(3)(a) and (b) CB&GA(DA) Regs
HB/CTB Reg 5(3)(a) HB&CTB(DA) Regs
Other benefits Regs 3(1)(b)(iv) and 4(3)(a) SS&CS(DA) Regs
39 **CB/GA** Reg 6(4) and 5) CB&GA(DA) Regs
HB/CTB Reg 5(4) and (6) HB&CTB(DA) Regs
Other benefits Reg 4(4) and (5) SS&CS(DA) Regs
40 **CB/GA** Reg 6(6) CB&GA(DA) Regs
HB/CTB Reg 5(5) HB&CTB(DA) Regs
Other benefits Reg 4(6) SS&CS(DA) Regs
41 R(TC) 1/05
42 **CB/GA** Reg 10(2)(a) CB&GA(DA) Regs
HB/CTB Reg 4(2)(a) HB&CTB(DA) Regs
Other benefits Reg 3(5)(a) SS&CS(DA) Regs
43 **HB/CTB** Reg 1(2) HB&CTB(DA) Regs
Other benefits Reg 1(3) SS&CS(DA) Regs
44 Reg 10(3) CB&GA(DA) Regs
45 R(CS) 3/04; CG/2122/2001
46 CIS/34/2006
47 CDLA/393/2006
48 **CB/GA** Reg 10(2)(b) CB&GA(DA) Regs
HB/CTB Reg 4(2)(b) HB&CTB(DA) Regs
Other benefits Reg 3(5)(b) and (d) SS&CS(DA) Regs
49 Regs 3(5)(c)and 7A(1) SS&CS(DA) Regs
50 Reg 7A(2) SS&CS(DA) Regs
51 Reg 7A SS&CS(DA) Regs
52 **CB/GA** Reg 5(2)(a) CB&GA(DA) Regs
Other benefits Reg 3(1)(a) SS&CS(DA) Regs
53 Reg 4(1)(b) HB&CTB(DA) Regs
54 **CB/GA** Reg 11 CB&GA(DA) Regs
HB/CTB Reg 4(7B) HB&CTB(DA) Regs
Other benefits Reg 3(7) SS&CS(DA) Regs
55 Reg 4(7C) HB&CTB(DA) Regs
56 Reg 3(7ZA) SS&CS(DA) Regs
57 **CB/GA** Reg 8(2) CB&GA(DA) Regs
HB/CTB Reg 4(1)(c) HB&CTB(DA) Regs
Other benefits Reg 3(4A) SS&CS(DA) Regs
58 **CB/GA** Reg 8(3) CB&GA(DA) Regs
HB/CTB Reg 4(7) HB&CTB(DA) Regs
Other benefits Reg 3(5A) SS&CS(DA) Regs
59 **CB/GA** Reg 9 CB&GA(DA) Regs
HB/CTB Reg 4(6) HB&CTB(DA) Regs
Other benefits Reg 3(8) SS&CS(DA) Regs
60 Reg 3(7A) SS&CS(DA) Regs
61 Reg 3(5D) SS&CS(DA) Regs
62 Reg 4(3), (7E) and (7F) HB&CTB(DA) Regs; reg 18A(1) and (3) HB Regs; reg 18A(1) and (3) HB(SPC) Regs
63 **RP** Reg 3(7E) SS&CS(DA) Regs
PC Reg 3(7D) SS&CS(DA) Regs
HB/CTB Reg 4(7D) HB&CTB(DA) Regs
64 Reg 3(8C) and (8D) SS&CS(DA) Regs
65 Reg 3(5B), (7B), (7C), (7CC) and (7F) SS&CS(DA) Regs
66 **HB/CTB** Reg 4(7A) HB&CTB(DA) Regs
Other benefits Reg 3(5C), (5E)-(5H), (6), (6A), (7EA), (7EB) and (8B) SS&CS(DA) Regs
67 **CB/GA** Reg 2(1) CB&GA(DA) Regs, definition of 'appropriate office'
HB/CTB Reg 4(8) HB&CTB(DA) Regs
Other benefits Reg 3(11) SS&CS(DA) Regs
68 **CB/GA** Reg 7(1) CB&GA(DA) Regs
HB/CTB Reg 4(9) HB&CTB(DA) Regs
Other benefits Reg 3(10) SS&CS(DA) Regs
69 Reg 4(8) HB&CTB(DA) Regs
70 Reg 5(2) HB&CTB(DA) Regs
71 **HB/CTB** Sch 7 para 3(2) CSPSSA 2000
Other benefits s9(2) SSA 1998
72 **HB/CTB** Sch 7 para 3(3) CSPSSA 2000
Other benefits s9(3) SSA 1998
73 **CB/GA** Reg 12 CB&GA(DA) Regs
HB/CTB Reg 6 HB&CTB(DA) Regs
Other benefits Reg 5(1) SS&CS(DA) Regs
74 **CB/GA** Reg 28(2) CB&GA(DA) Regs
HB/CTB Sch 7 para 3(5) CSPSSA 2000; r23 and Sch 1 TP(FT) Rules
Other benefits s9(5) SSA 1998; r23 and Sch 1 TP(FT) Rules
75 R(IS) 15/04; *Beltekian v Westminster City Council and Another* [2004] EWCA Civ 1784, 8 December 2004, reported as R(H) 8/05

4. **Supersessions**

76 **HB/CTB** Sch 7 para 4 CSPSSA 2000
Other benefits s10 SSA 1998
77 **CB/GA** Reg 13(1) CB&GA(DA) Regs
HB/CTB Reg 7(2) HB&CTB(DA) Regs
Other benefits Reg 6(2) SS&CS(DA) Regs
78 **CB/GA** Reg 15 CB&GA(DA) Regs
HB/CTB Reg 7(4) HB&CTB(DA) Regs
Other benefits Reg 6(3) SS&CS(DA) Regs

79 *DN v Leicester City Council (HB)* [2010] UKUT 253 (AAC)
80 **CB/GA** Reg 13(2)(a) CB&GA(DA) Regs
HB/CTB Regs 7(2)(a) and (3) and 7A(4) HB&CTB(DA) Regs
Other benefits Reg 6(2)(a) SS&CS(DA) Regs; Sch 2 para 25A(2) ESA(TP)(EA) No.2 Regs
All *Wood v SSWP* [2003] EWCA Civ 53 reported as R(DLA) 1/03; *Saker v Secretary of State for Social Services*, reported as R(I) 2/88; CIB/2338/2000. But note that CIS/3655/2007 decided that *Saker* no longer applies and that a change is only relevant if the decision is no longer correct.
81 *CAO v McKiernon*, 8 July 1993 (CA)
82 *Cooke v The Secretary of State for Social Security* [2001], reported as R(DLA) 6/01; R(S) 4/86; R(IS) 2/98; CIB/7899/1996; CIS/856/1994
83 Reg 6(6)(a) SS&CS(DA) Regs
84 Reg 6(6)(c) SS&CS(DA) Regs
85 Reg 6(8) SS&CS(DA) Regs
86 CSDLA/637/2006; CSDLA/822/2006
87 **HB/CTB** Sch 7 para 2 CSPSSA 2000
Other benefits s8(2) SSA 1998; reg 12A SS&CS(DA) Regs
88 **CB/GA** Reg 13(2)(b) and (c)(i) CB&GA(DA) Regs
HB/CTB Reg 7(2)(b) and (d) HB&CTB(DA) Regs
Other benefits Reg 6(2)(b) and (c) SS&CS(DA) Regs
89 Reg 4(1)(b) HB&CTB(DA) Regs
90 **CB/GA** Reg 13(2)(b) CB&GA(DA) Regs
HB/CTB Reg 7(2)(b) HB&CTB(DA) Regs
Other benefits Reg 6(2)(b) SS&CS(DA) Regs
91 Regs 6(2)(r) and 7A(1) SS&CS(DA) Regs; CIB/4033/2003; R(IB) 2/05
92 CSIB/377/2003; CIB/1509/2004 ; R(IB) 5/05; *JB v SSWP (IB)* [2010] UKUT 246 (AAC)
93 CIB/1972/2000; CIB/3179/2000; CIB/3985/2001
94 Reg 6(2)(g) and (7A)(1) SS&CS(DA) Regs
95 **CB/GA** Reg 13(2)(e) CB&GA(DA) Regs
HB/CTB Reg 7(2)(i) HB&CTB(DA) Regs
Other benefits Reg 6(2)(e) SS&CS(DA) Regs
96 Reg 6(2)(ee) SS&CS(DA) Regs
97 **CB/GA** Reg 13(2)(d) CB&GA(DA) Regs
HB/CTB Reg 7(2)(e) HB&CTB(DA) Regs
Other benefits Reg 6(2)(d) SS&CS(DA) Regs
98 Reg 7(2)(c) HB&CTB(DA) Regs; reg 18A(2) HB Regs; reg 18A(2) HB(SPC) Regs
99 **PC** Reg 6(2)(o) SS&CS(DA) Regs
HB/CTB Reg 7(2)(j) HB&CTB(DA) Regs
100 Reg 6(2)(s) SS&CS(DA) Regs
101 **CB/GA** Reg 13(2)(c)(ii) CB&GA(DA) Regs
HB/CTB Reg 7(2)(d)(ii) HB&CTB(DA) Regs
Other benefits Reg 6(2)(c)(ii) SS&CS(DA) Regs
102 **HB/CTB** Regs 7(2)(g), (h), (q) and (r) and 7A(2) and (3) HB&CTB(DA) Regs
Other benefits Reg 6(2)(f), (fa), (h), (j), (k), (l), (n), (m), (p) and (q) SS&CS(DA) Regs
103 **CB/GA** Reg 14(1) CB&GA(DA) Regs
HB/CTB Reg 7(6) HB&CTB(DA) Regs
Other benefits Reg 6(5) SS&CS(DA) Regs
All R(I) 50/56
104 Reg 7(7) HB&CTB(DA) Regs
105 **HB/CTB** Sch 7 para 4(3) CSPSSA 2000
Other benefits s10(2) SSA 1998
106 **HB/CTB** Sch 7 para 4(5) CSPSSA 2000
Other benefits s10(5) SSA 1998
107 **HB/CTB** Reg 8(10) HB&CTB(DA) Regs
Other benefits Reg 7(9)(a)(ii), (30) and (30A) SS&CS(DA) Regs
108 Reg 7(2)(bc) SS&CS(DA) Regs
109 Reg 7(17H) SS&CS(DA) Regs
110 Reg 7(2)(be) SS&CS(DA) Regs
111 Reg 8(2) HB&CTB(DA) Regs
112 Reg 8(3) HB&CTB(DA) Regs
113 **CB/GA** Reg 16(4) CB&GA(DA) Regs
Other benefits Reg 7(2)(bb) and (9)(a) SS&CS(DA) Regs
114 Reg 7(9) SS&CS(DA) Regs; *SSWP v DA* [2009] UKUT 214 (AAC)
115 **CB/GA** Reg 16(3)(a) CB&GA(DA) Regs
Other benefits Reg 7(2)(a) SS&CS(DA) Regs
116 **CB/GA** Reg 16(5) CB&GA(DA) Regs
Other benefits Reg 7(2)(c)(iv) and (v) SS&CS(DA) Regs
117 Regs 7(2)(c)(ii) and 7A(1) SS&CS(DA) Regs
118 Reg 7(2)(c)(v) SS&CS(DA) Regs
119 Reg 7A(2) SS&CS(DA) Regs
120 **CB/GA** Reg 17 CB&GA(DA) Regs
HB/CTB Reg 9 HB&CTB(DA) Regs
Other benefits Reg 8 SS&CS(DA) Regs
121 **CB/GA** Reg 17(3) CB&GA(DA) Regs
HB/CTB Reg 9(2) HB&CTB(DA) Regs
Other benefits Reg 8(3) SS&CS(DA) Regs

122 **CB/GA** Reg 17(4) and (5) CB&GA(DA) Regs
HB/CTB Reg 9(3) and (4) HB&CTB(DA) Regs
Other benefits Reg 8(4) and (5) SS&CS(DA) Regs
123 **CB/GA** Reg 17(6) CB&GA(DA) Regs
HB/CTB Reg 9(5) HB&CTB(DA) Regs
Other benefits Reg 8(6) SS&CS(DA) Regs
124 **CB/GA** Reg 16(3)(b) CB&GA(DA) Regs
Other benefits Reg 7(2)(b)(iii) SS&CS(DA) Regs
125 Reg 7(9)(d) SS&CS(DA) Regs
126 Reg 7(2)(b)(i) and (ii) SS&CS(DA) Regs
127 Reg 8(3) HB&CTB(DA) Regs
128 **CB/GA** Reg 16(7) CB&GA(DA) Regs
HB/CTB Reg 8(7) HB&CTB(DA) Regs
Other benefits Reg 7(5) SS&CS(DA) Regs
129 Reg 8(4) HB&CTB(DA) Regs
130 **CB/GA** Reg 16(10) CB&GA(DA) Regs
HB/CTB Reg 8(14) HB&CTB(DA) Regs
Other benefits Reg 7(7) SS&CS(DA) Regs
131 **CB/GA** Reg 16(9) CB&GA(DA) Regs
HB/CTB Reg 8(8) HB&CTB(DA) Regs
Other benefits Reg 7(6) SS&CS(DA) Regs
All *MP v SSWP (DLA)* [2010] UKUT 130 (AAC)
132 **CB/GA** Reg 16(9A) CB&GA(DA) Regs
Other benefits Reg 7(6A) SS&CS(DA) Regs
133 **CB/GA** Reg 16(8) CB&GA(DA) Regs
HB/CTB Reg 8(11) HB&CTB(DA) Regs
Other benefits Reg 7(33) SS&CS(DA) Regs
134 Reg 7(9A) SS&CS(DA) Regs
135 Reg 7(12) and (13) SS&CS(DA) Regs
136 Reg 8(2) and (6) HB&CTB(DA) Regs
137 Reg 7(38)-(40) SS&CS(DA) Regs
138 **PC** Reg 7(7A) SS&CS(DA) Regs
HB/CTB Reg 8(14A) HB&CTB(DA) Regs
139 Reg 7(8A) SS&CS(DA) Regs
140 **HB/CTB** Reg 8(6A), (9), (14D), (14C) and (15) HB&CTB(DA) Regs
Other benefits Reg 7(8), (8ZA), (8ZB), (10), (11), (24), (25), (28), (29), (29A)-(29C) and (34)-(37) SS&CS(DA) Regs
141 *Wood v SSWP* [2003] EWCA Civ 53, reported as R(DLA) 1/03

5. **Revisions and supersessions after a 'qualifying benefit' award**
142 *HR v Wakefield DC* [2009] UKUT 72 (AAC)
143 **IS/JSA/ESA/PC** s8(2) SSA 1998
HB/CTB Sch 7 para 2 CSPSSA 2000
144 **IS/JSA/ESA/PC** Regs 3(7), 6(2)(e) and 7(7) SS&CS(DA) Regs
HB/CTB Regs 4(7B) and (7C), 7(2)(i) and 8(14) HB&CTB(DA) Regs; CIS/1178/2001
145 Reg 7(7)(b) SS&CS(DA) Regs
146 Regs 3(7ZA)and 6(2)(ee) and 7(7) SS&CS(DA) Regs

6. **The 'anti-test case rule'**
147 **HB/CTB** Sch 7 para 18 CSPSSA 2000
Other benefits s27 SSA 1998
All *CAO and Another v Bate* [1996] 2 All ER 790 (HL)
148 R(FC) 3/98; R(I) 1/03
149 **HB/CTB** Sch 7 para 16 CSPSSA 2000
Other benefits s25 SSA 1998
150 **CB/GA** s25(3) and (4) SSA 1998; reg 22 CB&GA(DA) Regs
HB/CTB Sch 7 para 16(3) and (4) CSPSSA 2000; reg 15 HB&CTB(DA) Regs
Other benefits s25(3) and (4) SSA 1998; reg 21 SS&CS(DA) Regs
151 **HB/CTB** Sch 7 para 18(2) CSPSSA 2000
Other benefits s27(2) SSA 1998

Chapter 46

Appeals

This chapter covers:

This chapter covers the rules for benefits, the *regulated* social fund and appeals about national insurance (NI) credits. It does *not* cover the rules for statutory sick pay and statutory maternity, adoption and paternity pay (see Chapter 47), payments from the *discretionary* social fund (see Chapter 48), the health benefits in Chapter 13 or the other types of financial help on pp14–16, discretionary housing payments (see p294) or NI contributions. Most appeals about NI contributions are dealt with by the First-tier Tribunal in the Tax Chamber, similar to appealing against an HM Revenue and Customs (HMRC) decision on your entitlement to a statutory payment (see p1225).

References in this chapter to HMRC only apply to decisions about child benefit and guardian's allowance. HMRC also makes decisions about tax credits. For information about challenging tax credits decisions, see Chapters 57 and 60.

Key facts

- If you disagree with certain decisions made by the DWP, the local authority or HM Revenue and Customs (HMRC), you can appeal to the First-tier Tribunal.
- You can seek a revision before appealing to the First-tier Tribunal. There are advantages and disadvantages of doing this.
- If your appeal to the First-tier Tribunal is unsuccessful, you might be able to appeal to the Upper Tribunal. If your appeal to the Upper Tribunal is unsuccessful, you might be able to appeal to a court.
- Occasionally, if you cannot appeal, you may be able to challenge a decision by a judicial review.
- The time limits for appealing are very strict.

- Appeals can take time. If your circumstances change while you are waiting for your appeal to be heard, you may need to make a fresh claim for benefit or seek a supersession.

Future changes: April 2013 and after

Major changes are taking place that affect the benefits and tax credits system (see Chapter 2). From April 2013, if you disagree with a decision, you will only be able to appeal against it if you have first asked the decision maker to revise the decision. This is unlikely to apply to housing benefit and council tax benefit decisions. Also, appeals will be made directly to HM Courts and Tribunals Service. You will not have to submit your appeal to the DWP or HMRC first. See CPAG's *Welfare Rights Bulletin* for updates.

1. Appealing to the First-tier Tribunal

The appeals against decision makers' decisions described in this chapter are dealt with by a judge (and in some cases members) of the First-tier Tribunal (Social Security and Child Support) – referred to as the First-tier Tribunal in this *Handbook*, except in Chapter 47, who has been assigned to its Social Entitlement Chamber (led by the Chamber President). The First-tier Tribunal is organised by region, with a regional judge who is responsible for the recruitment and training of Tribunal members. Details of the regional offices are in Appendix 1.

The administration of the work of all tribunals is the responsibility of HM Courts and Tribunals Service (HMCTS), part of the Ministry of Justice. HMCTS officials deal with the day-to-day work of the First-tier Tribunal.

Procedural rules

There are procedural rules that the First-tier Tribunal must follow (covered on pp1193–99). The overriding objective of the rules is to enable the First-tier Tribunal to deal with cases fairly and justly.[1] The Tribunal can do a number of things, including to:

- extend or shorten time limits (see p1203);
- postpone or adjourn appeal hearings (see p1197);
- issue directions – eg, requiring parties to appeals to do certain things (see p1193);
- strike out appeals in specific circumstances (see p1195);
- bar people from taking part in your appeal (not including you – see p1196).

Appeal rights

You can appeal to the First-tier Tribunal against some decisions of the DWP, the local authority or HM Revenue and Customs (HMRC).

- There is a **strict time limit** for appealing – normally one month (see p1162).
- You must appeal **in writing** and normally on the appropriate form (see p1161).
- Your **appeal must be valid** – ie, contain all the information required. If it is not valid, it might not go ahead (see p1163).

Send or deliver your completed appeal form to the office that made the decision with which you disagree. That office passes your appeal to the First-tier Tribunal along with its response (see p1166). **Note:** a decision maker can ask you to provide further information about your appeal, but it is the First-tier Tribunal that decides if your appeal is valid, *not* the DWP, the local authority or HMRC (see p1164).

Who can appeal

You can appeal to the First-tier Tribunal if you are the claimant. However, certain other people can also appeal.

- If you are appealing about a **benefit other than housing benefit (HB) or council tax benefit (CTB)**, you have a right to appeal if you are:[2]
  - a claimant;
  - an appointee claiming on someone's behalf (see p1016);
  - claiming attendance allowance (AA) or disability living allowance (DLA) on behalf of someone who is terminally ill, even if this is without her/his knowledge;
  - a person from whom an ordinary overpayment of a benefit or a regulated social fund payment or a duplication of payment of income support (IS), income-based jobseeker's allowance (JSA), income-related employment and support allowance (ESA) or pension credit (PC) can be recovered (see Chapter 43). This is the case even if you were not the person who claimed the benefit that was overpaid;[3]
  - the partner of a claimant, if the decision concerns whether *you* failed to take part in a work-focused interview without good cause;[4] *or*
  - a person appointed by the DWP or HMRC to proceed with a claim for benefit made by someone who has since died or to make a claim for (and who has now claimed) benefit for someone who has died.[5]
- If you are appealing about **HB or CTB**, you have a right to appeal if you are a person affected by the decision – ie, your rights, duties or obligations are affected by the decision, and you are:[6]
  - a claimant;
  - someone acting for a claimant who is unable to act for her/himself – eg, an appointee (see p1016);
  - someone from whom the local authority decides an overpayment can be recovered (including a landlord or agent);[7] *or*
  - a landlord or agent, if the decision concerns whether or not to make a direct payment of HB to you.

In all cases, if the person who appealed dies, the DWP, the local authority or HMRC can appoint someone else to proceed with the appeal.[8]

Reasons for the decision maker's decision

You can ask why a decision was made, but remember that there is a strict time limit for making an appeal (normally one month – see p1162). For information about explanations, see p1121, and for written statements of reasons for a decision, see p1121. These could help you decide if it is worth challenging the decision. Bear the following in mind.

- Sometimes it might not be clear whether you have been given a written statement of reasons with your decision, or you might not receive it before your time limit for appealing expires. In both of these situations, appeal within the one-month time limit to protect your position.
- On receiving the written statement of reasons, if there are grounds for a revision or supersession (see pp1126 and 1136), you may decide it is worth asking for one of these rather than appealing immediately (but see p1160 for the disadvantages). In any case, if you appeal, a decision maker should look at the decision again and could decide to revise it.

Time limit for requesting a written statement of reasons

You must ask for a written statement of reasons within one month of being sent or given notice of a decision.[9] The written statement of reasons must then be provided within 14 days, so far as this is practicable (for HB or CTB) or within 14 days or as soon as it is practicable (for benefits other than HB and CTB). See p1162 for information about your time limit for appealing if you ask for a written statement of reasons.

Decisions you can appeal

You can appeal to the First-tier Tribunal against most decisions taken by the Secretary of State for Work and Pensions (the DWP), a local authority officer or an officer of HMRC (known as decision makers – see p1117).[10] You can appeal against an original decision (even if you have first sought a revision) or a decision made after a supersession.

You must be given a written notice of any decision against which you can appeal.[11] The notice must give you information about your right to appeal against the decision and your right to request a written statement of reasons for it if this has not been included.

Sometimes, a decision maker refuses to make a decision on your claim. If this happens, it effectively prevents you having the right to appeal. However, a decision maker must make a decision on every valid claim.[12] See pp1019 and 272 for what counts. You can then appeal and the First-tier Tribunal decides whether the decision is correct. **Note:** if the decision maker does not accept that a claim made on the correct claim form is valid, you should be given a decision saying so. You can appeal to the First-tier Tribunal and ask it to decide if your claim is valid.[13]

A decision maker can sometimes postpone making a decision if there is a test case pending (see p1150).

Examples of decisions against which you can appeal

All benefits:

Whether you are entitled to a benefit.

Whether you have been overpaid benefit and if it is recoverable.

Whether your claim has been validly made or can be backdated.

Whether benefit is payable under the overlapping benefit rules.[14]

Whether a benefit penalty should be applied because you failed to take part in a work-focused interview and whether you had good cause.

Whether you have limited capability for work or limited capability for work-related activity.

Whether you satisfy the habitual residence test.

Whether you satisfy the disability conditions for benefit.

Jobseeker's allowance only:

Whether you are available for or actively seeking work.

Whether you have left a job voluntarily or have lost it through misconduct.

Whether you have given up or lost your place on a training or employment scheme.

Whether you should be sanctioned and how long a sanction should last.

Whether you can be paid hardship payments.

Whether a jobseeker's agreement is reasonable or you had good cause for refusing or failing to carry out a jobseeker's direction.

Note: if you are uncertain whether you can appeal against a decision, seek advice. There is a strict time limit for appealing (see p1162).

Decisions you cannot appeal

You cannot appeal to the First-tier Tribunal against some decisions.[15] You *can* ask for an 'any time' revision or a supersession of a decision against which you do not have a right of appeal, whatever your reason for thinking it is wrong.[16] However, if the decision maker refuses to revise or supersede the decision, your only legal remedy is to apply for judicial review (see p1202).

Examples of decisions against which you cannot appeal

Who should be the claimant when a couple is unable to decide.

Who should be entitled to child benefit when two people whose claims have equal priority cannot agree.

Whether a claim for one benefit can be treated as a claim for (or in addition to) another benefit.

Whether to demand recovery of an overpayment, and the amount of weekly deductions.
Whether to suspend payment of benefit.
Whether to take action against people who are liable to maintain claimants (see p799).
Whether to appoint a person as an appointee (see p1016).
Whether to make an interim payment or payment on account.

Note: if you are uncertain whether you can appeal against a decision, seek advice straight away. If a decision maker says you cannot appeal against a refusal to do an 'any time' revision, or to consider a supersession, see pp1135 and 1147.

Revision, supersession or appeal?

Revisions, supersessions and appeals are all ways of getting decisions changed. If you can seek a revision or supersession as well as appealing, you need to be careful which one you choose. For more information about revisions and supersessions, see Chapter 45.

Advantages

The advantages of applying for an **'any grounds' revision** include that you:

- could receive a decision more quickly if you seek a revision than if you only appeal;
- get two bites at the cherry, because if your application for a revision is turned down, you can still appeal against the original decision.

You do not have to seek a revision and can appeal straight away. However, if the decision maker agrees that a decision is wrong, s/he might revise it anyway and your appeal could lapse (see p1165).

Example

Lindsey fails to satisfy the 'work capability assessment' and her ESA ceases. She asks the DWP to revise the decision because she has a new medical report that shows she cannot walk far without significant discomfort. The DWP considers the new medical evidence but refuses to revise its decision. Lindsey can still appeal to the First-tier Tribunal against the original decision.

An advantage of seeking an **'any time' revision** is that there is no time limit for doing so (see p1129). You can ask for an 'any time' revision even if the time limit for appealing has expired. However, you cannot appeal against a refusal to do an 'any time' revision (see p1135).

An advantage of seeking a **supersession** is that, in most cases, there is no time limit for doing so – eg, if there has been a mistake about the facts or if a test case is decided in your favour but you do not become aware of this until some time after.

Disadvantages

The disadvantages of applying for a **revision** include that the time limit for appealing continues to run while the decision maker considers your application for a revision. If you are unsure if the DWP, the local authority or HMRC has received your request, appeal within the time limit to protect your position.

There is a major disadvantage to applying for a **supersession**. You generally get less arrears of benefit if you seek a supersession rather than a revision or an appeal, even if you are successful. See p1141 for information about when a supersession takes effect. If you think there is a risk that you will not obtain all the arrears you are due, seek a revision or appeal instead of applying for a supersession if you can.

Check whether the 'anti-test case' rule (see p1149) applies to you. If it does, the arrears of benefit you get could be limited.

In some cases, you should seek advice before you **appeal**. Because the First-tier Tribunal looks at your case afresh, there is a risk you could lose benefit. For example, if your appeal is about a benefit that can be paid at different rates (eg, AA, DLA, ESA or industrial injuries disablement benefit), the rate could go down. If you are appealing about an overpayment, the amount could increase.

How to appeal

You must appeal in writing, preferably using the appropriate form.[17] This is called a 'notice of appeal'.

Appeal forms

For **HB and CTB**, use the form approved by your local authority. For **other benefits**, the appeal form is in leaflet GL24 (CH24A for child benefit and guardian's allowance), *If You Think Our Decision is Wrong*. Get the forms from the office that made the decision you want to appeal against. The GL24 is available at www.direct.gov.uk and the CH24A at www.hmrc.gov.uk.

If you do not use the appropriate form, your appeal can be accepted provided it is in writing and includes all the information required (see p1163). There is no guarantee of this, so use the form wherever possible. **Note:** you must appeal within a strict time limit (see p1162).

You must sign the appeal form.[18] It appears that if you have provided written notice that you have appointed a representative, s/he can sign it on your behalf.[19] Send or deliver your appeal to the office of the DWP, the local authority or HMRC that sent you the decision.[20]

If you want the First-tier Tribunal to deal with your appeal quickly, make this clear on your appeal form, explaining why. You could also telephone the DWP, the local authority or HMRC or write to the First-tier Tribunal, asking it to intervene.

The time limit for appealing

For **benefits other than child benefit and guardian's allowance**, your appeal, including all the information described on p1163, must arrive at the relevant office by the latest of the following:[21]

- within one month after the date the written decision was sent to you; *or*
- if you ask for a written statement of reasons for the decision (where one has not already been given to you – see p1121), within 14 days after the latest of:
  - the end of that month – ie, if the written statement of reasons is provided within the one-month period, you get one month plus 14 days to appeal; *or*
  - the date the written statement of reasons is provided.

For **child benefit and guardian's allowance**, your appeal, including all the information described on p1163, must arrive at the relevant office by the latest of the following:[22]

- within one month of the date the written decision was sent to you; *or*
- if you ask for a written statement of reasons for the decision (where one has not already been given to you – see p1121), within 14 days of the latest of:
  - the end of that month – ie, if the written statement of reasons is provided within the one-month period, you get one month plus 14 days to appeal; *or*
  - the date the written statement of reasons is provided.

Remember, you must ask for a written statement of reasons within one month of being given notice of a decision.

If the decision maker revises a decision, the one-month time limit runs from the date you are sent the new decision.[23] If you applied for an 'any grounds' revision and the decision maker refused to do a revision, you must appeal within one month after the date you are sent notice of the refusal.[24] However, if the decision maker refuses to do an 'any time' revision and says you cannot appeal, you should appeal against the original decision within the time limit (if this has not already passed) or if this is not possible, seek advice.

'Month' means a complete calendar month running from the day after the day you have been sent or given a decision.[25] For example, a decision sent on 24 July has an appeal time limit that expires at the end of 24 August.

When **calculating time**, if something has to be done by a certain day, it must be done by 5pm that day. If a time limit ends on a day other than a working day, you have until the next working day to meet the time limit.[26]

If you miss the time limit, your appeal is still treated as made in time if the decision maker does not object.[27] If s/he does object, the First-tier Tribunal can extend your time limit.[28] There is no guarantee that it will do so, so keep within the time limit wherever possible. There is an **absolute time limit** for appealing after which you *cannot* appeal. See p1205 for further information. **Note:** the First-tier Tribunal decides whether your appeal has been made within the time limit, *not* the DWP, the local authority or HMRC. If you think your appeal has been made within the time limit, you should explain why when you appeal.

If you miss the time limit, the decision maker objects to your appeal being treated as made in time and the First-tier Tribunal does not extend it, you could try to make a late application for an 'any grounds' revision in limited circumstances (see p1128). If you can show grounds, you can ask for an 'any time' revision or a supersession. You can also appeal to the Upper Tribunal against the decision not to extend the time limit.[29]

Note:

- The First-tier Tribunal can also shorten time limits, but should only do this if this will enable it to deal with your appeal fairly and justly (see p1204).
- If you are required to provide information you did not include with your appeal, your time limit can be extended under separate rules (see p1164).

Making sure your appeal is valid

For your appeal to be valid, it must contain all the information required. If you do not use the correct appeal form, your appeal can still be valid.[30] The First-tier Tribunal decides whether your appeal is valid, *not* the DWP, the local authority or HMRC.

Your appeal must be in English or Welsh. You must provide:[31]

- your name and address and that of your representative, if you have one;
- the address where documents can be sent or delivered – eg, to you or your representative;
- details about the decision with which you disagree. For example, the DWP appeal form asks you for:
  - the name of the benefit you are appealing about; *and*
  - the date you were sent the decision with which you disagree (this is on the letter notifying you of the decision);
- a summary of your reasons for believing the decision was wrong (your grounds for appeal). Do not simply say you think the decision was wrong, but explain why.

Examples

'The decision says I have been overpaid income-based jobseeker's allowance because I failed to disclose that my wife had started working part time, but I wrote to you as soon as she started work and told you what her take-home pay would be.'

'HMRC says I should not get child benefit for my son because he left school in June. This decision is wrong because my son stayed on at school to do his A levels.'

'You say I cannot get DLA care component. This decision is wrong because you have not taken into account the amount of help I need due to incontinence problems.'

It is also helpful to include information and evidence that supports your appeal because a decision maker looks at the decision again before the appeal hearing and might revise it.

What happens if you do not provide sufficient information

If you do not include the information required on your appeal form or in your appeal letter, a decision maker can ask you to provide the information you left out.[32] If you used an appeal form, this is returned to you to complete. Be sure to provide the information within the time allowed (see below), otherwise you might not count as having made your appeal within the time limit.

Your time limit for appealing (see p1162) is automatically extended if you are asked to complete your appeal form or provide information. The time limit is extended by:[33]

- 14 days from the date your appeal form is returned to you for completion, if the completed form is received back within 14 days;
- 14 days from the date you are asked for further information, if you provide this within 14 days of the request;
- the length of time you are given to complete the form or provide information, if this is longer than 14 days.

If you fail to complete the form properly or provide the information required in time, your appeal, along with any relevant documents and evidence, is forwarded to the First-tier Tribunal. A judge then considers whether your appeal is valid and can go ahead.[34] **Note:** if you complete and return the form or provide the information:

- after the expiry of the time limit, but before your appeal is forwarded to the First-tier Tribunal, the decision maker should accept that your appeal is valid and then consider whether to object to it being treated as made in time (see p1204);[35]
- before the judge makes a decision, any further details you provide must be taken into account.[36]

If your appeal is not accepted as valid, you can try to make a late appeal (see p1204).

What happens after you appeal

After you appeal, a decision maker looks at the decision you are appealing about again and might revise it. Your appeal should not be held up unduly while the decision maker considers whether s/he should carry out a revision. See p1165 for further information about what might happen if the decision is revised.

The DWP, the local authority or HMRC prepares the appeal papers – known as the decision maker's response. See p1166 for what it must contain. It sends a copy to you (and your representative if you have one).[37] A copy is also forwarded to the First-tier Tribunal; this must be done as soon as reasonably practicable.

You might find that your appeal is not dealt with if there is a test case or a lead case pending that deals with the same issues (see p1198).

If the decision maker does not forward your appeal

You are entitled to have your appeal heard within a reasonable period of time, so your appeal should be processed promptly and passed to the First-tier Tribunal without delay.[38] Following a complaint, an Ombudsman said the local authority should forward an appeal to the First-tier Tribunal within 28 days.[39] The decision maker can still consider revising the decision pending the appeal being heard.

You cannot usually bypass the normal procedures. However, if the decision maker does not forward your appeal within a reasonable period, forward a copy of it to the First-tier Tribunal yourself. Although you cannot usually expect the First-tier Tribunal to deal with your appeal before the decision maker has had a chance to prepare her/his response, it is free to allow matters to be handled differently if circumstances require it.[40] The Tribunal can direct the decision maker to provide documents, information and evidence (see p1193).[41] You can apply for a direction requiring the decision maker to do so by a specified date, or a direction setting a hearing date.[42] **Note:** in some circumstances, the First-tier Tribunal can even bar the decision maker from taking further part in the appeal (see p1196), in which case your appeal could be decided without a response being made.

When your appeal can lapse

After you appeal, a decision maker looks again at the decision you are appealing about and might revise it – eg, on the basis of any facts, information or evidence you provided with your appeal form. If this happens, your appeal could lapse, even if you do not get everything you want, and you have to appeal again.[43]

Your appeal lapses if the revised decision is more advantageous to you than the original decision – eg, the decision:[44]

- awards you benefit at a higher rate or for a longer period;
- lifts a refusal or disqualification of benefit or a JSA sanction (in whole or in part);
- reverses a decision to pay benefit to a third party (see p1048);
- means you gain financially from the revised decision;
- says an overpayment of benefit is not recoverable or that less should be recovered; *or*

- reverses a decision that an accident was not an industrial accident.

If the revised decision is not more advantageous to you, your appeal must go ahead, but against the revised decision.[45] You have one month from the date the decision is sent or given to you to make further representations.[46] At the end of that period (or earlier if you agree in writing), your appeal proceeds unless the decision is revised again and is now more advantageous to you.[47] If your appeal lapses, you must make a fresh appeal. Your time limit for appealing (see p1162) runs from the date the revised decision is sent to you.[48]

The decision maker's response

The DWP, the local authority or HMRC must prepare a bundle of papers relevant to your appeal (called the 'decision maker's response') and forward this to the First-tier Tribunal as soon as reasonably practicable.[49] You and your representative (if any) are normally both sent a copy.[50] However, check with your representative as this might not always happen.[51]

The response must include the reasons why the decision maker opposes your appeal.[52] The decision maker must also provide:[53]

- a copy of any written record of, and statement of reasons for, the decision with which you disagree;
- copies of all relevant documents s/he has, unless the First-tier Tribunal directs otherwise. If your appeal involves a medical issue or one about your disability, a record of medical examinations you have had in connection with your claim is usually included; *and*
- a copy of your appeal form (or letter) along with all the documents you provided with it, and unless already provided to the First-tier Tribunal, the name and address of your representative (if any).

Read through the whole response carefully to find out the case being made against you. Be sure to take it with you to the hearing.

The enquiry form

When the HMCTS regional office (see p1156) receives your appeal papers, it sends you a questionnaire (called an enquiry form) asking you whether you want an oral hearing and, if so, when you and your representative (if you have one) are available to attend. If you want an oral hearing, you must state this on the enquiry form. **Note:** you should always consult your representative before completing and returning the form.

You are sent a postage-paid envelope in which to return the enquiry form. You should return it within 14 days. If you do not return the enquiry form in time, the First-tier Tribunal may strike out your appeal (see p1195) or automatically deal with your appeal at a paper hearing (see p1170).

For further information about oral and paper hearings, see p1168. Bear in mind that your appeal must be dealt with at an oral hearing, unless both you and the DWP, the local authority or HMRC have consented or both of you have not objected to the appeal being dealt with without a hearing.

Providing other information

Make sure that everything you want to say in support of your appeal has been put in writing and that there are no other documents which you would like the First-tier Tribunal to see. Note the following.

- You can provide a written submission and additional evidence or information to support your appeal (known as a **'reply'**) – eg, independent medical evidence or supporting statements from witnesses. Otherwise, the bundle of papers prepared by the decision maker is the only written information the First-tier Tribunal has to consider in reaching its decision.
- You (or your representative, if any) must provide your reply within one month after the date you were sent the decision maker's response.[54] The First-tier Tribunal can give you longer (or shorter) than one month.[55] There is no guarantee that you will be given longer, so keep within the time limit wherever possible. See p1203 for further information.

Note: the First-tier Tribunal might issue directions requiring you (or the DWP, the local authority or HMRC) to provide a submission or further information or documents within a specific period. You (or the decision maker) can also apply to the Tribunal and ask it to issue directions. If you are given a direction, it is important that you comply with it. If you do not, your appeal can be struck out (see p1195). See p1193 for further information about directions.

If a test case or lead case is pending

If a test case or lead case is pending that deals with issues raised in your appeal, you may find that your appeal is delayed (see p1198).

Withdrawing an appeal

If you change your mind about appealing, you can withdraw your appeal. If your appeal has:[56]

- not yet been passed to the First-tier Tribunal, write to the DWP, the local authority or HMRC, saying that you do not wish your appeal to go ahead. Your authorised representative can write on your behalf;
- been passed to the First-tier Tribunal, you must give written notice to it before the hearing that you want to withdraw your appeal. You can also withdraw your appeal once the hearing has started, but only if the judge agrees.

If you tell the First-tier Tribunal that you want to withdraw your appeal before the hearing (eg, you telephone the Tribunal office), but then you fail to confirm this in writing, the clerk to the Tribunal can waive the requirement to provide written notice.[57] You can ask the Tribunal to reconsider the clerk's decision – eg, if you did not send written notice because you changed your mind and no longer wanted to withdraw your appeal. You must apply in writing within 14 days after the date you are sent notice of the decision. The First-tier Tribunal can give you longer (or shorter) than this. There is no guarantee you will be given longer, so keep within the time limit wherever possible (see p1203).

If you withdraw your appeal but then decide that you want it to go ahead, you can apply for it to be reinstated.[58] You must apply in writing. Your application must be received by the First-tier Tribunal within one month after the date it received notice that you wanted to withdraw your appeal, or if you withdrew your appeal at an oral hearing, within one month after the date of the hearing. The First-tier Tribunal can give you longer (or shorter) than one month. There is no guarantee that you will be given longer, so keep within the time limit wherever possible (see p1203).

Oral or paper hearings

Your appeal must be dealt with at an **oral hearing**, unless:[59]

- both you and the DWP (or the local authority or HMRC) have consented or both of you have not objected to the appeal being dealt with without an oral hearing; *and*
- the First-tier Tribunal considers it can decide the matter without an oral hearing.

If either you or the DWP (or the local authority or HMRC) have stated that you want an oral hearing, there must be one. If you want an oral hearing, state this on the enquiry form (see p1166). Otherwise, the First-tier Tribunal presumes that you do not object to a paper hearing.

Note: the First-tier Tribunal can decide to strike out your appeal (see p1195) without an oral hearing.[60]

Your appeal could be dealt with at an oral hearing *even if you opt for a paper hearing* – eg, if the DWP (or the local authority or HMRC) wants one. In any case, the First-tier Tribunal may decide there should be an oral hearing because it can only deal with your appeal fairly and justly by doing so (eg, it needs to ask you questions about the facts of your case) or if during a paper hearing it is uncertain whether or not anyone asked for an oral hearing.[61] If you get unexpected notice of an oral hearing, contact HMCTS to check the reasons for this. You should be given an opportunity to attend.

If there is not an oral hearing, the First-tier Tribunal makes its decision by looking at what you said on your appeal form, any evidence or other information you provided to support your appeal and the decision maker's response. This is known as a **paper hearing**.

If you opt for a paper hearing but then decide you want an oral hearing, you may be able to change your mind. You must tell the First-tier Tribunal before it makes its decision.

Why choose an oral hearing?

You may not want to attend an oral hearing – eg, because you are worried about speaking for yourself or about the cost or difficulty in attending. You can seek advice before you decide what to do, but remember the following.

- You are more likely to win your appeal if you attend an oral hearing, particularly if it concerns a medical issue or your disability, or if the facts of your case are in dispute.
- If you attend an oral hearing, you can explain your side of the story.
- You can ask someone to represent you at the hearing (see p1194) – your chances of winning are likely to be higher if you do.[62] You can also take a friend, relative or adviser with you for support.
- The First-tier Tribunal aims to provide a qualified interpreter if you need one. If you do, tell the Tribunal in advance of the hearing – eg, on the enquiry form. If a qualified interpreter is not available, the Tribunal might allow a relative to act as your interpreter if s/he understands that s/he should simply translate accurately and tell your answers in your own words, without comment or explanation.[63]
- You, an interpreter (if needed) and any witnesses may be able to get expenses paid – eg, you can claim for travel (including the extra costs involved for disabled people), meals, loss of earnings and childcare costs.[64]

Note: if you or your representative cannot be physically present at an oral hearing (eg, because of a disability), one might be arranged at a venue where you can (called a 'domiciliary hearing' – see p1170), or you might be able to be present via a video link, telephone or other instantaneous two-way electronic communication.[65] Contact HMCTS to see if this can be arranged.

The oral hearing

You must be given reasonable notice of the oral hearing. You must be given at least 14 days' notice, unless you agree to less notice than this or there are urgent or exceptional circumstances.[66] If you have not been given the correct notice (you can argue that this includes the decision maker's response as well as the time and date of the hearing[67]), you can object to the hearing going ahead. If the First-tier Tribunal decides to proceed with the hearing, you should attend and explain why your case will be prejudiced (eg, you did not have an adequate time to prepare it) and ask for an adjournment (see p1197).

The First-tier Tribunal can go ahead with an the oral hearing even if you are not there if it:[68]

- is satisfied that you were notifed of the hearing, or that reasonable steps have been taken to notify you; *and*
- thinks that it is in the interests of justice.

An appeal is heard in public unless the First-tier Tribunal thinks it should be in private.[69] The First-tier Tribunal can exclude people from hearings in some circumstances. If you want your hearing to be in private, ask the First-tier Tribunal to consider this. In practice, it is extremely rare for members of the public to attend.

The First-tier Tribunal can **postpone or adjourn a hearing** (see p1197). Remember that if you do not attend a hearing, it can hear your appeal without you.

The paper hearing

You are not sent notice of a paper hearing. The First-tier Tribunal makes its decision in your absence and you are then notified of its decision.

If you opt for a paper hearing, think about sending the First-tier Tribunal a written submission on your arguments about your appeal and any information and evidence you can get to support your appeal (called a 'reply'). If you intend to send a reply, state this clearly on the enquiry form and state how long it may take to provide it. See p1207 for information about how to prepare an appeal.

You must provide your reply within one month after the date you were sent the decision maker's response.[70] If you need longer than this to provide a reply, ask HMCTS for an extension. If your paper hearing takes place before the month is up and you could (and would) have provided further evidence within that period, you can challenge the First-tier Tribunal's decision on the ground that it made an error of law.[71]

Domiciliary hearings

Most appeal venues have access for disabled people, and the First-tier Tribunal may meet the cost of special transport to get there or arrange the hearing at another venue. However, if you are unable to attend a hearing at the venue, it is possible to hold the hearing in your home – a 'domiciliary hearing'. Include a letter from your doctor with your request, confirming that you are unable to travel at all – eg, even by taxi. You can argue that you can appeal against a decision to refuse you a domiciliary hearing.[72] Alternatively, if the refusal meant that your appeal was unfair, you may be able to appeal against the First-tier Tribunal's decision on your appeal.[73] **Note:** you may be able to be present via a video link, telephone or other means of instantaneous two-way electronic communication.[74] Contact HMCTS to see if this can be arranged.

At the hearing

A **judge** and up to two other **members** hear and decide your appeal. The judge makes a note of what is said by you, your representative, the DWP (or the local authority or HMRC) and any witnesses. If the First-tier Tribunal has an even number of members, the judge has the casting vote.[75] See p1177 for information about decisions. To see which members decide your appeal, see below.

If the First-tier Tribunal thinks your appeal involves issues that require special expertise not otherwise available to it, it can ask an **expert** (the First-tier Tribunal may call her/him an 'assessor') to assist.[76] The expert can be asked, for example, to attend the hearing and give evidence or provide a written report. Any written report should be sent to every party involved in the appeal. The expert cannot take part in making the decision.

The **clerk to the First-tier Tribunal** is there in an administrative capacity – eg, to pay expenses. The clerk cannot take part in making the decision on your appeal and should not express any views on the case.

A **presenting officer** sometimes attends – eg, when an appeal is considered complicated. S/he represents the decision maker but is not necessarily the person who made the decision you are appealing about. S/he explains the reasons for the decision, but is not there to defend it at all costs and may provide information which helps your case.[77] If there is no presenting officer, the First-tier Tribunal can still consider and decide your appeal, although it might adjourn and request a presenting officer to attend a new hearing. A presenting officer should attend then, but this does not always happen in practice.

You can have a **representative** with you at the hearing.[78] If you have one, see p1194 for information about the notice you must send or give the First-tier Tribunal. You can also be accompanied by someone at the hearing – eg, a friend or relative. The First-tier Tribunal can give permission for her/him to act as your representative or assist you in presenting your case.[79]

Who decides your appeal

Those who decide a particular kind of appeal are as follows.[80]

- **A judge, a doctor and a person with experience of disability** decide DLA and AA appeals. However, if your appeal only raises issues of law, so a doctor and a person with experience of disability are not needed, a judge can hear your appeal (or a judge and a member whose experience and qualifications are needed to make the decision).
- **A judge and a doctor** decide appeals about:
  - whether you are incapable of work under the 'personal capability assessment' or have limited capability for work under the 'work capability assessment' or have limited capability for work-related activity;

  - industrial injuries benefits (see Chapter 18) or severe disablement allowance (SDA), unless the only issue is whether there should be a declaration of an industrial accident.

  However, if your appeal only raises issues of law so a doctor is not needed, a judge can hear your appeal (or a judge and a member whose experience and qualifications are needed to make the decision).
- **A judge** decides all other appeals on her/his own.

The judge must be legally qualified. S/he always acts as the chair of the hearing.

Unless your appeal is a DLA or AA appeal, an accountant may also be included (if the examination of financial accounts is required) or there can be an additional doctor (where there are complex medical issues). However, there can never be more than two members, plus a judge.

If your appeal is meant to be heard by two or more members but some of these are absent, the hearing can still go ahead. This only applies if you and the DWP (or the local authority or HMRC) agree.[81]

If the group deciding your appeal is composed incorrectly, you should appeal to the Upper Tribunal and argue that this was an error of law.[82] This can apply, for example, if your DLA and ESA appeals were heard together at the same time so a person with experience of disability took part when your appeal should have been decided by a judge and a doctor. However, the First-tier Tribunal can hear your DLA and ESA appeals consecutively (one after the other) so long as only the correct members as shown above took part.

Note: you cannot argue that a doctor should not decide your appeal even if s/he regularly provides medical reports about benefit claimants to the DWP.[83] You *can* argue that the First-tier Tribunal should not rely on evidence from a DWP doctor with whom any of the members hearing your appeal sit at other times; this depends on how often and how recently this has happened.[84]

Procedure at an oral hearing

When the First-tier Tribunal is ready to hear your case, you (and your representative if you have one) are taken in with any presenting officer (see p1171). There are no strict rules of procedure. The judge decides how the hearing is conducted.[85] The First-tier Tribunal's overriding objective is that your appeal is dealt with fairly and justly.[86] This includes ensuring that you are able to participate fully.

The judge should introduce everyone present. The judge (and members) often start by asking you (and the presenting officer) questions. The presenting officer, if any, may be asked to summarise the decision maker's case. You should be given the opportunity to explain your case. If you think there are mistakes in the papers, point them out. You can call witnesses and ask questions of the presenting officer's witnesses. See p1207 for information about preparing for your appeal and presenting your case.

The First-tier Tribunal considers all the facts, evidence and law before it makes a decision. It should not bargain with you by 'offering' to allow part of your appeal if you agree to drop other parts – eg, by offering you one component of DLA if you agree not to argue for the other.[87]

Medical examination at the oral hearing

The First-tier Tribunal cannot carry out physical examinations unless your appeal relates to the assessment of your disablement for SDA or industrial injuries disablement benefit, or whether you have a prescribed disease or injury.[88] Studying X-ray evidence does not count as a physical examination, so you can ask the Tribunal to consider this.[89] Although there is no 'walking test' or physical test for the DLA mobility component,[90] the First-tier Tribunal may take its observation of you into account. It should not, however, attach undue weight to its observations[91] and you should be given the opportunity to comment on them. The Tribunal should remember that what it sees may only be relevant to your condition on that day and not in general.[92] It should check, for instance, whether you have just taken medication or have been resting for some time in the waiting area.

The First-tier Tribunal decides whether to carry out a physical examination. It should let you know at the hearing if it thinks one is not necessary so you can make representations.[93] The examination usually takes place after the main hearing in a separate room in the absence of everyone else. You are examined by the medical member(s) of the Tribunal.[94] You can have someone with you as a chaperone or if, for instance, you need help undressing. Make sure you tell the medical member(s) if you are in pain or discomfort. It is also a good idea to provide a full list of any medicines you are taking. After the examination, you should be invited to make further representations to the First-tier Tribunal if you wish.

Appeals about disability, incapacity or limited capability for work

Tell the First-tier Tribunal how your disability or or limited capability for work affects you at work or in your daily life at home. You should be completely straightforward, neither underplaying nor overplaying your symptoms. If you feel better on some days than others, explain how and how often, and say whether you are being seen on a good day or a bad day.

The First-tier Tribunal listens and asks you questions. It considers all of the medical and other relevant evidence, and tries to draw out the evidence about your disabilities, with the help of questioning from the doctor member(s). This may confirm the opinions expressed in medical reports with which you disagree, or it may support your view. See p1209 for information about medical evidence.

The First-tier Tribunal should not feel restricted to accepting the medical evidence about you given in written reports.[95] If there is conflict between what is said in a report and what you have said in writing (eg, on your claim form), the Tribunal should not accept the evidence in the report without first listening to what you have to say about how your condition affects you.[96] Ensure that you explain any inconsistencies. The Tribunal should be particularly careful not to automatically accept the findings in electronically produced medical reports (see p210).[97]

The First-tier Tribunal can adjourn the hearing and refer you to a healthcare professional approved by the DWP (eg, a doctor or a nurse) for a medical examination and report if your appeal concerns:[98]

- whether you are entitled to AA or DLA, the appropriate rate of benefit or the period for which you are entitled; *or*
- whether you are entitled to SDA; *or*
- whether you are incapable of work or have limited capability for work or for work-related activity; *or*
- the extent of your disablement for SDA or industrial injuries disablement benefit purposes; *or*
- whether you have a loss of faculty as a result of an industrial accident (see p374).

A medical examination may take place in your home or at a DWP medical examination centre.

Alternatively, a report may be requested from your GP or other medical adviser. The written decision to adjourn for a report should make clear why the First-tier Tribunal adjourned and what sort of medical evidence is being sought.

Remember that, although you cannot be compelled to undergo a medical examination, the First-tier Tribunal might draw negative conclusions if you refuse.

What the First-tier Tribunal considers

The job of the First-tier Tribunal is to decide whether the decision you are appealing about was correct. It must look at the law and issues afresh, taking into account any new evidence or information you (and the DWP, the local authority or HMRC) provide.

The First-tier Tribunal should consider an issue if it is in the appeal papers or in any representations you make, or if the evidence should lead it to believe it is relevant to your appeal.[99] You (or the DWP, the local authority or HMRC) can even raise an issue at the hearing.[100] However, the First-tier Tribunal might then adjourn to give the other side a chance to meet the point. You do not necessarily have to raise an issue with the Tribunal for it to be something it should consider, even if you have a representative. However, the issue must be one which in some way obviously demands attention.[101] If you have a representative, the First-tier Tribunal may decide not to investigate matters that s/he does not raise on your behalf.[102]

The First-tier Tribunal does not have to consider issues that are 'not raised by' your appeal.[103] However, it can consider issues even if neither you nor the DWP, the local authority or HMRC raises them.[104] The First-tier Tribunal should exercise its discretion fairly.

Difficulties may arise – eg, where you are appealing about not being awarded one component of DLA when you are already in receipt of the other, or against the rate of one component of DLA when you are satisfied with the rate you receive of the other, or where you ask for a higher rate of DLA or AA than you are already getting. In these circumstances, the First-tier Tribunal *does not have to* consider issues which are not the subject of your appeal. However, it may decide to consider both components of DLA, or to consider whether you should get a lower rate of DLA or AA than you are already getting. You should be given notice of this, and:

- a chance to prepare your case properly and make representations or to consider withdrawing your appeal.[105] Ask for the hearing to be adjourned if you need time to do this or want someone to advise or represent you;
- if your appeal is being dealt with at a paper hearing, a chance to attend an oral hearing or to withdraw your appeal;[106]
- an explanation of why the Tribunal decided to use its discretion in this way in the statement of reasons for its decision.[107]

Note: if you are concerned about what might happen in your appeal, you can withdraw it at any time before the First-tier Tribunal makes its decision (see p1167). You need permission if you ask to withdraw your appeal at the hearing.

Faulty revisions and supersessions

If your appeal involves a revision or a supersession decision which is faulty, the First-tier Tribunal can remedy any defect and make any decision that the decision maker could have taken.[108] This includes where the decision maker:

- carried out a supersession but failed to state the grounds or to identify the correct grounds for doing so; *or*
- carried out a supersession when s/he should have conducted a revision (and, in some cases, *vice versa*).

In addition, the First-tier Tribunal can decide that an 'any time' revision should be done where no decision has been made on the matter by a decision maker (either to revise the decision or refuse to do so) – ie, if you are appealing because the decision maker refused to carry out a supersession.[109]

If errors in the decision making are extensive, try to argue that the First-tier Tribunal should adjourn the hearing, point out the errors to the decision maker and invite her/him to reconsider, rather than making any corrections itself.[110]

Changes of circumstances after you appeal

When the First-tier Tribunal hears your appeal, it considers whether the decision with which you disagree was correct down to the date it was made. If your circumstances change after the decision, the Tribunal cannot take this into account.[111] This can include where a change occurs between the date a decision is made on a renewal claim for DLA and the date that decision takes effect.[112]

Any evidence you get after the decision with which you disagree could still be relevant to your appeal. If the evidence relates to the period before the decision you are disputing was made, or to a past event that was relevant to the decision, it must be taken into account.[113] In some situations, events that happen after the date of the decision can throw light on the situation at or before that date, in which case evidence of such events may also be taken into account – eg, if the First-tier Tribunal needs to decide if an improvement in your health was likely to happen.

What to do if circumstances change

It is important as a general rule for you to consider making a fresh claim (or consider seeking a supersession) every time your circumstances change, and appeal if you are unhappy with the subsequent decision. This is particularly so where your appeal is about:

- whether you are incapable of or have limited capability for work, or qualify for AA or DLA or the rate of AA or DLA to which you are entitled and your condition has worsened;
- whether you satisfy the 'habitual residence' test (see Chapter 62); *or*
- how much income or capital you have, and this changes.

If you wait until the First-tier Tribunal makes its decision and this goes against you, you could lose out. You can only get arrears from the date your circumstances changed if you make a fresh claim (or seek a supersession) and ask for benefit to be backdated. This is only possible in limited circumstances.

Example

Ravi has been getting DLA mobility component. A decision maker decides his condition has improved and so he is no longer virtually unable to walk and stops his DLA. He appeals. While waiting for his appeal hearing, his condition deteriorates, he makes a fresh claim and is awarded DLA mobility component. When the First-tier Tribunal hears his appeal against the original decision, it upholds the decision maker's decision. However, because Ravi made a fresh claim when his circumstances changed, he has not lost out.

If you make a fresh claim (or seek a supersession), you can ask the decision maker to wait until your appeal has been determined before making a decision. However, if the decision maker decides the fresh claim (or supersession) and you disagree with the decision:

- you can appeal against the new decision. Consider whether it is in your interests to ask for all of the appeals to be heard together by the First-tier Tribunal;[114] *or*
- whether or not you appeal against the new decision, you can ask the decision maker to revise it once your first appeal is determined (see p1132).

Example

Henry claims PC but the decision maker says he does not satisfy the 'habitual residence test' and refuses his claim. He appeals against the decision and makes a fresh claim for PC on 8 July 2011. The fresh claim is refused. Henry wins his appeal. Because he did not appeal the new decision, the First-tier Tribunal can only award PC up to 8 July 2011. However, the decision maker does an 'any time' revision and awards PC from that date.

The decision

You may be told the First-tier Tribunal's decision at the hearing and you are given a **decision notice** confirming it. If it is not given at the hearing or you opted for a paper hearing, the decision notice is sent to you later. It may include a summary of the First-tier Tribunal's reasons for its decision. You *must* be informed of:[115]

- your right to request a statement of reasons for the First-tier Tribunal's decision (see p1178); *and*
- the conditions for appealing to the Upper Tribunal, including the time limit for doing so.

Note:

- If the First-tier Tribunal is unable to come to a unanimous decision, it makes a majority decision. The judge has the casting vote.
- A decision can be corrected, superseded, reviewed or set aside (see p1179). You (or the DWP, the local authority or HMRC) can also appeal against it to the Upper Tribunal.

Record of proceedings

A record of the First-tier Tribunal proceedings is made by the judge.[116] It must be sufficient to indicate the evidence taken and submissions made, as well as any procedural applications. The judge decides the medium to use – eg, the record might be handwritten (you can apply for a typed copy if the original is difficult ro read) or a digital recording (you can apply for a typed transcript).

The record is kept by the First-tier Tribunal for six months from the date of its decision or for six months from various other specific dates. You must apply in writing for a copy within the six-month period. The First-tier Tribunal can give you longer (or shorter) than this. There is no guarantee that you will be given longer, so keep within the time limit wherever possible (see p1203). Bear in mind that if you apply after the six-month period, the record may have been destroyed.

If you are considering an appeal to the Upper Tribunal, it is a good idea to ask for a copy of the record of proceedings. If you foresee disputes about what happened at the hearing, you should also make and keep your own notes.

The statement of reasons

The First-tier Tribunal may give the reasons for its decision at the oral hearing, or give or send you a written statement of reasons.[117] The written statement of reasons is prepared by the judge. If you are not provided with a written statement of reasons, you have a right to apply for one.[118] If you lose your appeal and want to appeal to the Upper Tribunal, you must generally have one. It may otherwise be difficult to show that the First-tier Tribunal made an error of law (see p1182).

Your request for a statement of reasons must be:[119]

- in writing; *and*
- received by the First-tier Tribunal within one month (see p1162) of your being sent or given its decision notice. The First-tier Tribunal can give you longer (or shorter) than this.[120] There is no guarantee that you will be given longer, so keep within the time limit wherever possible (see p1203).

If you request a written statement of reasons, this must then be sent to you within one month or as soon as it is reasonably practicable after that.[121]

Note:

- If you mistakenly ask the First-tier Tribunal for permission to appeal to the Upper Tribunal instead of asking for a statement of reasons, it should treat this as a request for a statement of reasons.[122]
- If the judge refuses wrongly to provide a statement of reasons, you may have grounds for appeal to the Upper Tribunal.
- If there is a long delay in getting a statement of reasons, you could apply for permission to appeal to the Upper Tribunal. The Upper Tribunal can require the First-tier Tribunal to provide reasons for its decision.[123]

The DWP (or the local authority or HMRC) can also ask for a statement of reasons. If this happens, it usually means it is considering appealing to the Upper Tribunal.

After the hearing

If you have won your appeal, the DWP (or the local authority or HMRC) should carry out the First-tier Tribunal's decision straight away. It can do this on the basis of the decision notice (see p1177). However, if either you or the DWP, the local authority or HMRC apply for permission to appeal to the Upper Tribunal, the First-tier Tribunal can suspend the effect of its decision until the application is determined (either by the First-tier or Upper Tribunal), and then until any review of, or appeal against, the decision is determined.[124] This could be useful – eg, if you are seeking permission to appeal against a decision that an overpayment is recoverable from you.

If the DWP (or the local authority or HMRC) disagrees with the decision, it might consider appealing against it to the Upper Tribunal. In this case, you are not normally paid while it decides what to do. See p1043 for details of what the DWP (or the local authority or HMRC) must do before it can suspend your benefit. If the DWP (or the local authority or HMRC) decides to appeal, you are not normally paid until the Upper Tribunal decides the case.[125] However, you can ask the DWP, the local authority or HMRC to pay you if you are left in financial hardship. You might also be able to get a crisis loan (see p564).

If you disagree with the First-tier Tribunal's decision

If you disagree with the First-tier Tribunal's decision, you cannot simply ask it to look at the decision again – eg, if you have additional evidence. However:

- if the decision contains a **clerical mistake or other accidental slip or omission** this **can be corrected** by the First-tier Tribunal. This only applies if it is a genuine error such as a typing or spelling mistake or a mathematical miscalculation, not an error of law on an important issue in your appeal – eg, a change of the date of onset of an industrial disease. **Note:** the Tribunal cannot use this rule to amend or add to its reasons for the decision, but can amend these if it reviews its decision (see p1186);[126]
- it **can be superseded** by the DWP (or the local authority or HMRC), if there are grounds (see p1135). However, if the First-tier Tribunal made a mistake about the law, you must appeal to the Upper Tribunal;
- you (or the DWP, the local authority or HMRC) can **appeal to the Upper Tribunal** against it (see p1181);
- if you (or the DWP, the local authority or HMRC) seek permission to appeal to the Upper Tribunal against a decision, the First-tier Tribunal can **review** it (see p1186);
- it **can be set aside**, which means the decision is cancelled and your appeal is heard again (see below).

If you are considering an appeal to the Upper Tribunal, remember to ask for the First-tier Tribunal's statement of reasons within the one-month time limit (see p1178). You should do so even if you are first going to apply for the First-tier Tribunal's decision to be set aside.

When a decision can be set aside

A decision of the First-tier Tribunal can only be set aside in limited circumstances. The First-tier Tribunal can set aside a decision if it thinks it is 'in the interests of justice' to do so and:[127]

- you, your representative or the DWP (or the local authority or HMRC) were not sent or did not receive appeal papers or other relevant documents, or the First-tier Tribunal was not sent them, at an appropriate time – eg, in sufficient time before the hearing; *or*
- you, your representative or the DWP, the local authority or HMRC were not present at the hearing. However, if you (or they) chose not to attend, it might not be 'in the interests of justice' to set the decision aside; *or*
- there was some other procedural irregularity.

You must apply in writing to the Tribunal. The application must be received no later than one month after the date you are sent the decision notice (see p1177).[128] The First-tier Tribunal can give you longer (or shorter) than this.[129] There is no guarantee that you will be given longer, so keep within the time limit wherever possible (see p1203). **Note:** the rules do not say what the time limit is if you are given the decision notice at the hearing. It is not known if this was an error.

Bear the following in mind.

- Applications are normally decided without a hearing.[130] Make sure you give a full explanation of your reasons when you apply. If your application is late, explain the reasons for this.
- If the First-tier Tribunal's decision is set aside, your appeal is heard again and a new decision is made. You should be given the opportunity to ask for an oral hearing, even if your appeal was originally decided at a paper hearing.[131]
- If a decision is wrongly set aside, any subsequent rehearing by the First-tier Tribunal is invalid. The First-tier Tribunal could refuse to re-hear the case if there was no power to set aside the previous decision.[132]

Note: in some circumstances, a decision can also be set aside when you (or the DWP, the local authority or HMRC) seek the permission of the First-tier Tribunal to appeal to the Upper Tribunal (see p1181).

If the decision is not set aside

The First-tier Tribunal can treat your application for a decision to be set aside as an application for permission to appeal to the Upper Tribunal, or as an application for a correction of the decision.[133] It can also review its decision when you (or the DWP, the local authority or HMRC) seek permission to appeal to the Upper Tribunal (see p1186).

If the First-tier Tribunal refuses to set aside a decision, you can appeal to the Upper Tribunal against the refusal.[134] It might be better to try to appeal to the Upper Tribunal against the original decision. If your application for the First-tier Tribunal's decision to be set aside is refused, the time limit for appealing to the Upper Tribunal can run from the date you are sent notice of this.[135] However, this only applies where you applied for the decision to be set aside within the one-month time limit (or any longer period allowed by the First-tier Tribunal).

If you seek permission to appeal to the Upper Tribunal

The First-tier Tribunal's decision *must* be set aside if an application is made for permission to appeal to the Upper Tribunal, and you and the DWP (or the local authority or HMRC) agree that the First-tier Tribunal made an 'error of law' (see p1182).[136] Bear in mind that the First-tier Tribunal does not send copies of applications for permission to appeal to the other party. If you think that the DWP (or the local authority or HMRC) might agree that the First-tier Tribunal made an 'error of law', you should send a copy of your application to them. However, there is no guarantee that they will take any action on this.

Note: the First-tier Tribunal can review its decision if you (or the DWP, the local authority or HMRC) seek permission to appeal to the Upper Tribunal (see p1186).

2. Appealing to the Upper Tribunal

You have a right of appeal against any decision of the First-tier Tribunal (other than an excluded decision) to the Administrative Appeals Chamber of the Upper Tribunal (called the Upper Tribunal in this *Handbook*).[137] Your appeal is dealt with by a judge (or judges).

Excluded decisions[138]

Excluded decisions are certain decisions taken by the First-tier Tribunal when it considers a review (see p1186) – ie, decisions:

- to review, or not to review, an earlier decision;
- to take no action, or not to take any particular action, in the light of a review of an earlier decision;
- to set aside an earlier decision on review (the decision that is set aside is also excluded);
- to refer, or not to refer, a matter to the Upper Tribunal.

There is only **one possible ground for appeal**: that the First-tier Tribunal has made an 'error of law' (see p1182).[139] You must first apply for, and obtain, permission to appeal and there is a strict time limit for applying (see p1185). The DWP, the local authority and HM Revenue and Customs (HMRC) have the same right of appeal as you.

If you have evidence, it might enable you to ask the DWP (or the local authority or HMRC) for a supersession of the First-tier Tribunal's decision (see p1135) and you can do so while your appeal is pending. Bear in mind that the amount of arrears you can get with a supersession is usually limited, so you need to continue with your appeal at the same time.

Note: you can also apply for a judicial review by the Upper Tribunal of a decision of the First-tier Tribunal against which you do not have a right of appeal. If you are in any doubt about whether you should appeal against a decision, or apply for a judicial review, see p1192.

Procedural rules

There are procedural rules that the Upper Tribunal must follow (see pp1193–1199). The overriding objective of the rules is to enable the Upper Tribunal to deal with cases fairly and justly.[140] The Upper Tribunal can do a number of things, including to:

- extend or shorten time limits (see p1203);
- adjourn or postpone appeal hearings (see p1197);
- issue directions – eg, requiring parties to appeals to do certain things (see p1193);
- strike out appeals (see p1195);
- bar people from taking part in your appeal, including you if the DWP (or the local authority or HMRC) has appealed (see p1196).

Some Upper Tribunal decisions can be made by approved legally qualified HMCTS staff (called 'registrars').[141] You can ask an Upper Tribunal judge to reconsider a registrar's decision. You must apply in writing within 14 days after the date you are sent notice of the decision. The Upper Tribunal can give you longer (or shorter) than this. There is no guarantee you will be given longer, so keep within the time limit wherever possible (see p1203).

Error of law

The First-tier Tribunal made an error of law if:[142]

- it got the **law wrong** or misinterpreted it – eg, it misunderstood the particular benefit rule concerned. **Note:** if the First-tier Tribunal sets out the reasons for its decision in the decision notice (see p1177) and these indicate that it did not apply the law correctly, the decision notice is likely to be a more reliable statement of the First-tier Tribunal's reasons than a later conflicting explanation in a statement of reasons;[143]
- there is **no evidence** to support its decision;
- it gave you a physical examination when it was not permitted to do so (see p1173), and based its decision on evidence obtained from that examination;[144]
- the **factsit found** are such that, had it acted reasonably and interpreted the law correctly, it could not have made the decision it did. This argument can be used where the facts are inconsistent with the decision – eg, the First-tier Tribunal finds that a man and a woman live in separate households, but decides they are living together as husband and wife;[145]

- it **took things into account which it should not have, or refused or failed to take into account things which it should have** taken into account. However, the First-tier Tribunal has not necessarily made an error of law if it fails to take account of evidence that was not before it at the hearing – ie, if you (or the DWP, the local authority or HMRC) only produce evidence when your appeal is before the Upper Tribunal;
- there is a **breach of the rules of natural justice**. This includes where:
  - the procedure followed by the First-tier Tribunal leads to unfairness. Whether or not this is so depends on the facts of the case, but examples include if:
    - you are not allowed to call witnesses to support you; *or*
    - the First-tier Tribunal has unreasonably refused to postpone or adjourn a hearing (see p1197) even though you notifed it that you could not attend and had a good reason; *or*
    - the standard of interpretation is not adequate and the First-tier Tribunal does not take appropriate action;[146] *or*
    - the First-tier Tribunal pressures you into giving up your right to a fair hearing – eg, it bargains with you by 'offering' you one component of disability living allowance (DLA) if you agree not to argue for the other;[147]
  - you did not get notice of the hearing through no fault of your own and the result is that you lost without having a chance to put your case properly, even if you could have applied for the First-tier Tribunal's decision to be set aside instead;[148]
  - you (or the DWP, the local authority or HMRC) asked for an oral hearing but one did not take place;[149]
  - you did not receive the decision maker's response or receive it in sufficient time before the hearing and were not given an opportunity to read it properly;[150]
  - the First-tier Tribunal removed your entitlement to benefit at a paper hearing without warning you or giving you the chance to make representations;[151]
- it does not give **proper findings of fact**. The First-tier Tribunal must find sufficient facts to support its decision.[152] It can rely on the summary of the facts given in the decision maker's response (see p1166), but only if these are not in dispute and s/he has covered all relevant issues.[153] If you and the DWP (or the local authority or HMRC) disagree about the facts, the First-tier Tribunal must explain which version it prefers and why;
- it does not provide **adequate reasons** for its decision.[154] The First-tier Tribunal must not simply say what its decision was. It must give sufficient reasons so that you can see why, on the evidence, it reached the conclusion it did. It should refer to the main items of evidence on which it has relied. However, the First-tier Tribunal has not necessarily erred in law for failing to mention every item of evidence put forward. If a delay in writing the reasons indicates that

they are unreliable as an accurate statement of the First-tier Tribunal's reasoning, you can argue the reasons are inadequate.[155] **Note:** the First-tier Tribunal does not have to give its reasons for refusing to adjourn an appeal hearing.[156]

Note: the First-tier Tribunal has *not* erred in law simply because a different judge (and members) or the Upper Tribunal might have come to a different conclusion.[157] An appeal to the Upper Tribunal is not another opportunity to argue about the facts of the case.[158]

How to appeal to the Upper Tribunal

You must first obtain permission to appeal to the Upper Tribunal.[159] This means you must show that the First-tier Tribunal has possibly made an error of law (see p1182) and you have the beginnings of a case. There is a strict time limit for applying for permission to appeal. If you wish to appeal you:

- must usually have the First-tier Tribunal's statement of reasons (see p1178). You may find it difficult to show that it made an error of law without one;
- first have to apply for permission to appeal to the First-tier Tribunal. If it refuses (or rejects) your application, you can apply for permission directly to the Upper Tribunal.

Applying to the First-tier Tribunal

You must apply for permission to appeal, in the first instance, to the First-tier Tribunal.[160] You should first apply for a statement of reasons for its decision (see p1178).

Your application for permission to appeal must:[161]

- be in writing; *and*
- contain details of your grounds for appeal (ie, the error(s) of law you think the First-tier Tribunal made) and sufficient information about its decision for it to be identified. If you are making a late application, you must also give your grounds for this; *and*
- state the result you are seeking – eg, say what you think the First-tier Tribunal's decision should have been, or how it should have dealt with your appeal.

Bear in mind that the person considering your application might not be the judge who decided your appeal.[162] Applications for permission to appeal are normally decided without a hearing.[163] You should therefore make sure you give a full explanation of your grounds for appeal when you apply.

You do not have to attach a copy of the First-tier Tribunal's statement of reasons to your application because it already has one. However, if there is no statement of reasons for the First-tier Tribunal's decision – eg, because you did not apply for one, or one has not been provided:[164]

- the First-tier Tribunal must treat your application for permission to appeal as an application for a statement of reasons. Unless the First-tier Tribunal decides to give you permission to appeal, you must seek permission to appeal again – eg, once the statement of reasons is provided. If a statement is refused because you did not apply in time, see below; *and*
- if your application for a statement of reasons is (or has been) refused because of a delay in making the application (ie, you missed the one-month time limit or any longer period allowed), the First-tier Tribunal can admit your application for permission to appeal, but only if it thinks it is in the interests of justice to do so. It then goes on to decide whether or not to give you permission.

You must be sent a record of the decision on your application for permission as soon as practicable.[165] If your application is refused, you must also be sent a statement of reasons for the refusal and notice of your right to apply to the Upper Tribunal for permission to appeal, along with information about how to apply, and the time limit for doing so. If your application for permission to appeal is refused (or rejected), you may make a fresh application to the Upper Tribunal (see p1186). You should study the First-tier Tribunal's reasons for refusing your application carefully; be prepared to re-think your arguments before applying to the Upper Tribunal.

Note:

- If you (or the DWP, the local authority or HMRC) apply for permission to appeal to the Upper Tribunal, the First-tier Tribunal can:
  - review its decision (see p1186); *or*
  - treat the application for permission to appeal as an application for the decision to be corrected or set aside.[166]
- If you and the DWP (or the local authority or HMRC) agree that the First-tier Tribunal made an 'error of law', its decision must be set aside (see p1181).

The time limit for applying

Your application for permission to appeal must be received by the First-tier Tribunal no later than one month (see p1162) after the latest of the following dates – ie, the date you were sent:[167]

- a written statement of reasons (see p1178) for the First-tier Tribunal's decision. See above for how your application is dealt with if you do not have a statement of reasons; *or*
- notice that, following a review, the reasons for the First-tier Tribunal's decision were amended, or the decision was corrected; *or*
- notice that an application for the First-tier Tribunal's decision to be set aside was unsuccessful.

The First-tier Tribunal can extend (or shorten) your time limit for applying for permission to appeal to the Upper Tribunal.[168] There is no guarantee that you will be given longer, so keep within the one-month time limit wherever possible. If your time limit is not extended, the First-tier Tribunal must reject your application.[169] If your application is rejected, you can still apply to the Upper Tribunal for permission, but see p1205 for the special rules that apply.

When the First-tier Tribunal can review its decision

When the First-tier Tribunal receives an application for permission to appeal to the Upper Tribunal (from you or the DWP, the local authority or HMRC), it must first consider whether to review its decision.[170] You do not have a right to apply for a review yourself, but if you do, your application can be treated as an application for permission to appeal.[171]

The First-tier Tribunal can only review a decision if it is satisfied that there was an error of law in the decision (see p1182).[172] If it *does* review the decision, it can:[173]

- correct accidental errors in the decision or the record of the decision; *and*
- amend the reasons given for the decision – eg, if it considered matters, but inadvertently did not include them in the statement of reasons, or if it dealt with a point in the statement of reasons inadequately or unclearly. However, the First-tier Tribunal should not add reasons which it had not fully considered before it made its decision;[174] *and*
- set aside the decision. If it does this, it must either make a new decision or refer your appeal to the Upper Tribunal for it to make a decision.

You must be notifed in writing of the outcome of the review and your right of appeal (if any).[175] If the First-tier Tribunal has taken any action and you were not given an opportunity to comment before the review, you must also be notifed that you can apply for the action to be cancelled and for the decision to be reviewed again.

If the First-tier Tribunal decides not to review its decision, or reviews it but takes no action (or no action on a part of the decision), it must consider whether to give you permission to appeal to the Upper Tribunal against the decision (or the part of the decision on which no action was taken).[176]

Applying to the Upper Tribunal

Before you can apply to the Upper Tribunal, you must first apply to the First-tier Tribunal for permission to appeal.[177] If the First-tier Tribunal refuses you permission to appeal or rejects your application (eg, because your application was late), you may make a fresh application to the Upper Tribunal. You must apply in writing.

Forms

Use Form UT 1 (Social Entitlement), available from the regional office of HM Courts and Tribunals Service (HMCTS), the Upper Tribunal Office (see Appendix 1) or at www.justice.gov.uk/global/forms/hmcts/tribunals/aa/index.htm.

Your application must include:[178]

- your name and address and the name and address of your representative (if any – see p1194). You must also give the address where documents can be sent or delivered;
- details of the decision you want to appeal;
- the grounds for your appeal – ie, the error(s) of law you think the First-tier Tribunal made;
- if your application is late, a request for your time limit for appealing to be extended and the reasons why you are applying late;
- whether you want your application to be dealt with at an oral hearing;
- copies of the First-tier Tribunal's decision, its statement of reasons (if you have one – see below) and the notice of its refusal or rejection of your application for permission. If your application to the First-tier Tribunal was rejected because it (or your application for a statement of reasons) was late, you must also include the reasons why.

The Upper Tribunal can waive any irregularities in your application for permission to appeal.[179]

If your application to the First-tier Tribunal for permission to appeal was rejected, either because it was late or your application for a statement of reasons was late, the Upper Tribunal can only allow your application if it thinks it is in the interests of justice to do so.[180]

If you do not have a statement of reasons

The fact that you do not have a statement of reasons for the First-tier Tribunal's decision does not prevent you from applying to the Upper Tribunal for permission to appeal. However, you must still show that the First-tier Tribunal made an error of law (see p1182) without it – eg, if what is said in the decision notice is sufficient to do so.[181] The failure of the First-tier Tribunal to provide a statement of reasons where it has a duty to do so is, in itself, an error of law.[182]

You can send your application by post, fax or document exchange, or deliver it in person. You can also send it by other methods (eg, email) if you have been given permission in advance by the Upper Tribunal.[183]

The Upper Tribunal Office obtains the file of your appeal papers from the regional office of HMCTS. The Upper Tribunal considers these as well as what you say in your application before reaching a decision. The DWP (or the local authority or HMRC) plays no part in the procedure at this stage.

You are sent a written notice of the Upper Tribunal's decision on your application for permission to appeal, including the reasons for the decision.[184] You cannot appeal against a refusal to grant you permission to appeal to the Upper Tribunal, but you might be able to apply for the decision to be set aside (see p1191) or to a court for judicial review (see p1202).[185]

The time limit for applying

Your application for permission to appeal must be received by the Upper Tribunal no later than one month (see p1162 for the definition) after the date the First-tier Tribunal's refusal (or rejection) was sent to you.[186] The Upper Tribunal can extend (or shorten) your time limit for applying for permission to appeal.[187] There is no guarantee that you will be given longer, so keep within the one-month time limit wherever possible. See p1205 for further information about late appeals to the Upper Tribunal.

When you get permission to appeal

If you have been granted permission to appeal by the First-tier Tribunal, you must send a **'notice of appeal'** to the Upper Tribunal so that it is received within one month after you are sent notice of the permission.[188] You are sent a form on which to do this. The Upper Tribunal can extend (or shorten) the time limit.[189] There is no guarantee that you will be given longer, so keep within the time limit wherever possible (see p1203). **Note:** if you send your notice of appeal late and your time limit is not extended, your appeal is rejected and does not go ahead.

As well as the notice of appeal, you must send a copy of the notice telling you that your application for permission to appeal has been granted, a copy of the First-tier Tribunal's decision and its statement of reasons (if you have one), along with your details and your reasons for appealing against the decision. If you are sending the notice of appeal late, you must also include a request for an extension of time and the reasons why your notice is late.

Where you have applied for permission to appeal directly to the Upper Tribunal on Form UT 1 (see p1186), unless you are told otherwise, your application is treated as a notice of appeal. In this case, you do not have to send in another.[190]

Remember that the Upper Tribunal can suspend the effect of the First-tier Tribunal's decision pending your appeal being decided (see p1193). This can be useful – eg, if you are appealing about whether an overpayment of benefit can be recovered.

If a test case is pending

If a test case is pending that deals with issues raised in your appeal, you may find that your appeal is delayed (see p1198).

Withdrawing an appeal

If you change your mind about appealing, you can withdraw your appeal.[191] However, once you have been given permission to appeal, you must have the consent of the Upper Tribunal. You must give notice to the Upper Tribunal that you want to withdraw your appeal:

- in writing, before a decision is made; *or*
- at an oral hearing.

If you withdraw your appeal but then decide that you want it to go ahead, you can apply for it to be reinstated.[192] You must apply in writing. Your application must be received by the Upper Tribunal within one month after the date it received written notice that you wanted to withdraw your appeal, or if you withdraw your appeal at an oral hearing, within one month after the date of the hearing. The Upper Tribunal can give you longer (or shorter) than one month. There is no guarantee that you will be given longer, so keep within the time limit wherever possible (see p1203).

The written procedure

The Upper Tribunal Office sends you a copy of the appeal file. You and the DWP (or the local authority or HMRC) are asked for responses and are told the timetable for providing them, usually as follows.[193]

- The decision maker is asked to provide a response first.
- You are given the chance to reply. You are usually given one month in which to do so, although the Upper Tribunal may extend (or shorten) the time limit.[194] There is no guarantee that you will be given longer, so keep within the time limit wherever possible (see p1203).

If you have nothing to add and do not want to reply at any stage, tell the Upper Tribunal Office.

You may find the decision maker supports your appeal. In this case, the Upper Tribunal may give its decision without reasons if you consent to this.[195]

The Upper Tribunal decides whether or not there should be an oral hearing of the appeal.[196] It must take your views (and those of the DWP, the local authority or HMRC) into account. It normally only holds an oral hearing if the case involves complicated issues of law that cannot easily be resolved by written argument. It can decide to hold an oral hearing even if you have not asked for one. If there is no oral hearing, the Upper Tribunal reaches a decision on the basis of written responses and other documents.

Note: because of the length of time you usually have to wait before your case is dealt with, you should make a fresh claim for benefit (or seek a supersession) if, for example, your circumstances change. However, see p1176 (the issues are similar to those for appeals to the First-tier Tribunal).

Oral hearings

Oral hearings are usually held in Cardiff, Edinburgh, Leeds, London or Manchester but can be held in other locations, subject to the needs of the case. A hearing closer to your home can exceptionally be held if you have difficulty travelling because of a disability. A judge decides whether or not to hold a local hearing based on, for instance, medical evidence and why a local hearing is needed.

You must be given at least 14 days' notice of the hearing, although you may get less notice than this if you agree, or your appeal is urgent or there are exceptional circumstances.[197] Your fares are paid in advance.

You and your representative may be able to participate in the oral hearing via a video link – eg, if your disability makes it difficult for you to travel, or to avoid travel costs and time.[198] Video conferencing facilities are available in a number of areas outside London. You may also be able to participate in the hearing by telephone or other means of instantaneous two-way electronic communication. Ask the Upper Tribunal Office if this can be arranged.

Usually, one judge hears your appeal. However, if there is a 'question of law of special difficulty', an important point of principle or practice, or it is otherwise appropriate, two or three judges may hear your appeal,[199] but the procedure is the same.

The Upper Tribunal may ask you to provide a summary of the arguments you are going to make (a 'skeleton argument') in advance of the hearing. If it does, you must provide one.[200]

The hearing is more formal than that before the First-tier Tribunal, but the judge lets you say everything you want to. Judges usually intervene a lot and ask questions so you need to be prepared to argue your case without your script. A full set of Upper Tribunal (and commissioners') decisions (see p1212) and the statute law (see p1210) are available for your use. The DWP (or the local authority or HMRC) is usually represented by a lawyer, so you should also consider obtaining representation.

The decision

There are two stages to an Upper Tribunal decision.

- First, the Upper Tribunal decides if the First-tier Tribunal made an error of law. If it decides that it did, the First-tier Tribunal's decision is normally set aside and no longer has any effect.
- Second, the Upper Tribunal decides how to deal with the case.[201]

- If the Upper Tribunal agrees that the First-tier Tribunal's decision was wrong, the case is often sent back to the First-tier Tribunal to hear your appeal again and make a new decision. The Upper Tribunal can give directions on how to reconsider the issues.
- If the Upper Tribunal thinks the First-tier Tribunal's statement of reasons for its decision contains all the material facts, or it has been able to make any necessary extra findings of fact, the Upper Tribunal makes the final decision.

The Upper Tribunal's decision is usually given in writing, but may be given orally at the hearing.[202] Detailed reasons for the decision are given. You must be sent a decision notice as soon as is reasonably practicable, as well as notice of your right of review or appeal (if any), how to seek a review or appeal and the time limits for doing so.

If you disagree with the Upper Tribunal's decision

If you disagree with the Upper Tribunal's decision you cannot simply ask it to look at the decision again – eg, if you have additional points to make. However:

- the Upper Tribunal may **correct** any **clerical mistake or other accidental slip or omission** in a decision or record of a decision;[203]
- the Upper Tribunal may **set aside** its decision.[204] A decision can be set aside if the Upper Tribunal thinks it is in the interests of justice *and*:
  - you, your representative or the DWP (or the local authority or HMRC) were not sent papers or other relevant documents, or did not receive them at an appropriate time, or the Upper Tribunal was not sent them at an appropriate time; *or*
  - you, your representative or the DWP (or the local authority or HMRC) were not present at the hearing; *or*
  - there has been some other procedural irregularity.

  You must apply in writing for a decision to be set aside. Your application must be received by the Upper Tribunal no later than one month after you were sent notice of the decision. The Upper Tribunal can extend (or shorten) this time limit. There is no guarantee that you will be given longer, so keep within the time limit wherever possible (see p1203);[205]
- it can be **superseded** by the DWP (or the local authority or HMRC) if there are grounds – eg, where there was a mistake about, or ignorance of, the facts (see p1135). However, if the Upper Tribunal made a mistake about the law, you must appeal to a court;
- you or the DWP (or the local authority or HMRC) can **appeal** to the Court of Appeal (in Scotland, the Court of Session) – see p1199;
- if you (or the DWP, the local authority or HMRC) seek permission to appeal to the Court of Appeal (or in Scotland, the Court of Session), the Upper Tribunal can **review** its decision (see p1201).

Note: the Upper Tribunal can treat an application for a decision to be corrected, set aside or reviewed, or for permission to appeal against a decision as an application for any other of these.[206]

Judicial review in the Upper Tribunal

Occasionally, you can challenge decisions of the First-tier Tribunal by applying for a judicial review by the Upper Tribunal. You cannot usually apply for a judicial review if you have a right of appeal to the Upper Tribunal against the decision. You need the services of a solicitor or legal advice centre to apply for a judicial review. Before making *any* application, seek advice about whether you could be liable for the other side's costs (see p1214).

In **England and Wales**, you can apply for a judicial review of a First-tier Tribunal decision if it is a decision against which you have no right of appeal to the Upper Tribunal *and*:[207]

- it is a decision made under any of the First-tier Tribunal procedural rules; *or*
- it is a decision to review (or not to review) a decision following an application for permission to appeal to the Upper Tribunal (see p1186) or a decision as to what action to in take in the light of the review.

You must first apply for permission in writing and must include specified information.[208] You can use Form JR1 which is available from the Upper Tribunal office or at www.justice.gov.uk/global/forms/hmcts/tribunals/aa/index.htm. You must apply promptly. In any event, your application must be received by the Upper Tribunal by the latest of the following:[209]

- three months after the date of the decision, action or omission you are seeking to challenge; *or*
- one month after the date you were sent written reasons for the First-tier Tribunal's decision; *or*
- one month after the date you were sent notice that an application to set aside the decision (see p1179) was unsuccessful, so long as the application was made within the time limit (or longer period allowed).

In **Scotland**, you can challenge a decision of the First-tier Tribunal by a judicial review if it is a procedural decision or ruling, including procedural omissions or oversights.[210] You must first apply to the Court of Session. If specified conditions are satisfied, your case is then transferred to the Upper Tribunal.[211] You must apply promptly.

Note: you can only apply for a judicial review of a decision of the First-tier Tribunal if you do not have a right of appeal against it. If you are in any doubt about whether you have a right of appeal against a decision you want to challenge, you can apply both for permission to appeal and for a judicial review. The Upper Tribunal will decide which is the proper route. However, you should seek advice before you do – eg, to ensure you will not be liable for the other side's costs.

3. Procedural rules

There are procedural rules that the First-tier Tribunal and the Upper Tribunal must follow. The overriding objective is to enable both to deal with cases fairly and justly.[212] This includes avoiding delay (provided the issues can be considered properly), avoiding unnecessary formality, seeking flexibility in the proceedings and ensuring that all the parties can participate fully. It also includes dealing with appeals in ways that are proportionate to the importance of the case, the complexity of the issues, the potential costs and the resources of the parties. All parties must help the First-tier Tribunal and the Upper Tribunal further the objective and co-operate with it. This involves ensuring, as far as possible, that your case is ready by the time of the hearing.[213]

Both the First-tier Tribunal and the Upper Tribunal can do a number of things to further the overriding objective.[214] This includes giving directions (see below), striking out an appeal (see p1195) or barring people from taking part (see p1196) and adjourning or postponing a hearing (see p1197). This also includes:

- extending or shortening any time limits (see p1203);
- summonsing witnesses to attend a hearing, answer questions and produce documents. **Note:** you cannot be required to give evidence or produce any document that you could not be compelled to give by a court;[215]
- suspending the effect of its decision while considering an application for permission to appeal, or any appeal against or review of that decision. The Upper Tribunal can also suspend the effect of a decision of the First-tier Tribunal while an application for permission to appeal against the decision is being considered, and pending the appeal being determined.[216]

In addition, the Upper Tribunal can require the First-tier Tribunal to provide reasons for its decision or other information or documents relating to the appeal.[217]

Note:

- If you have a representative, you must notify the First-tier Tribunal or the Upper Tribunal (see p1194).
- If you and the DWP or the local authority or HM Revenue and Customs (HMRC) agree what the solution to your dispute should be, you can ask a judge to make a 'consent order' (but see p1199).

Directions

The First-tier Tribunal and the Upper Tribunal might issue directions requiring you (or the DWP, the local authority or HMRC) to provide a submission, further information or documents.[218] You or the decision maker can also apply to the First-tier Tribunal or the Upper Tribunal to ask it to issue directions. This can be useful, for example, if you are having trouble getting documents or information from the decision maker. You can apply in writing, or orally at the hearing.[219] In either case, you must give reasons for your application. The Tribunal must send you and the decision maker (and anyone affected by the direction) notice of any direction it issues, unless it thinks there is a good reason not to do so.[220] You can challenge a direction (eg, if you think insufficient time has been given to comply with it) by applying for another direction to amend, suspend or set aside the first one.[221]

If you are given a direction, it is important that you comply with it. If you (or the DWP, the local authority or HMRC) fail to comply with a requirement or a direction, the First-tier Tribunal and the Upper Tribunal can take any action it thinks is 'just', including:[222]

- waiving the requirement;
- requiring you (or the DWP, the local authority or HMRC) to remedy the failure;
- striking out the appeal (see p1195) (or barring the DWP, the local authority or HMRC from taking further part – see p1196). *You* can be barred from taking further part in an appeal to the Upper Tribunal if the DWP (or the local authority or HMRC) appealed.

Alternatively, the First-tier Tribunal or the Upper Tribunal might conclude that the information or evidence was adverse to you.

If you miss the deadline in a direction, try to provide what has been requested as soon as possible. The Tribunal may still consider the information or evidence – eg, if you provide it at the hearing.[223] However, remember that the Tribunal can decide *not* to consider evidence if it is late or if it would otherwise be unfair to do so.[224]

Representatives

You can have a representative to help you with your appeal and to be with you at the hearing.[225] S/he can help you understand the procedures, present your case to the First-tier Tribunal or the Upper Tribunal and ensure the Tribunal is aware of all the relevant issues and the law. You must send or give the relevant tribunal written notice of your representative's name and address or s/he must do this on your behalf. For the First-tier Tribunal only, this does not apply if you provide this notice to the DWP (or the local authority or HMRC) before your appeal is forwarded to it. If your representative is providing the notice, s/he should also provide an authorisation signed by you. **Note:**even if your representative acted for you in your appeal to the First-tier Tribunal, you must still authorise her/him to act for you in your appeal to the Upper Tribunal.

Even if you have not previously notified the First-tier Tribunal or Upper Tribunal that you have a representative, someone can attend the hearing with you (eg, a friend or relative) and act as your representative, or assist you at the hearing, if the Tribunal agrees.[226]

Once you have given notice that you have a representative, s/he is presumed to be acting for you unless you give notice in writing that this is no longer the case.[227] Your representative must be sent any documents required to be sent to you; these then do not have to be sent to you.[228] However, do not presume this always happens. If you receive documents, check that your representative has also.

When your appeal can be struck out

Your appeal to the First-tier Tribunal or the Upper Tribunal can be struck out, in whole or in part, but only if you fail to comply with a direction or in a limited number of other circumstances. This cancels your appeal, or part of the appeal, and it does not go ahead. See below for when you can get your appeal reinstated.

If you fail to comply with a direction

If you fail to comply with a direction given to you by the First-tier Tribunal or the Upper Tribunal (see p1193) – eg, you fail to provide information or documents required by the Tribunal:[229]

- your appeal is **struck out automatically** if you were notified in the direction that a failure to comply *would* lead to your appeal being struck out;
- there is **discretion to strike out** your appeal if you were notified in the direction that a failure to comply with it *could* lead to your appeal being struck out.

In both cases, you can apply for your appeal to be reinstated (see below).

Getting your appeal reinstated

If your appeal is struck out because you failed to comply with a direction given to you by the First-tier Tribunal or the Upper Tribunal (see p1193), you may be able to get it reinstated.[230] You must apply in writing. Your application must be received by the relevant tribunal within one month of your being sent notice that your appeal was struck out. The Tribunal can give you longer (or shorter) than one month. There is no guarantee that you will be given longer, so keep within the time limit wherever possible (see p1203). You should explain why you think your appeal should not have been struck out – eg, why you think you did comply with the direction, or why you were unable to do so or to comply in time.

Other circumstances

Your appeal *must* be struck out if **the First-tier Tribunal or the Upper Tribunal does not have 'jurisdiction'** to deal with it – eg, you do not have a right to appeal against the decision or you have appealed to the wrong tribunal.[231] If the Tribunal no longer has jurisdiction because of a change of circumstances, this rule only applies if your appeal has not been transferred to another court or tribunal.

There is discretion to strike out your appeal if:[232]

- you **failed to co-operate with the First-tier Tribunal or the Upper Tribunal** to such an extent that it cannot deal with your appeal fairly and justly; *or*
- for appeals to the First-tier Tribunal only, if it considers your appeal has **no reasonable propect of success.**

In all cases:

- you must be given an opportunity to comment. You should always take this opportunity and explain why you think your appeal should not be struck out – eg, why you had a good reason for failing to co-operate with the Tribunal or why you think you have a chance of winning your appeal;
- you cannot apply for your appeal to be reinstated (but see below).

Challenging a decision

If the First-tier Tribunal strikes out your appeal or refuses to reinstate your appeal after it has been struck out, you may be able to make a fresh appeal against the decision maker's decision.[233] See p1162 for the time limit for appealing and p1203 for late appeals. Otherwise, you can appeal to the Upper Tribunal against the First-tier Tribunal's decision to strike out your appeal or to refuse to reinstate it.[234]

Being barred from taking part in an appeal

The decision maker and any people (other than you) who are taking part in the appeal because they have a right of appeal against the decision you are challenging (see p1157) can be barred from taking a further part in the appeal in the same circumstances in which your appeal can be struck out.[235] In practice, this is likely to apply mainly if the decision maker (or other person with a right of appeal):

- fails to comply with a direction; *or*
- fails to co-operate with the First-tier Tribunal or the Upper Tribunal to such an extent that it cannot deal with your appeal fairly and justly.

The decision maker (or other person) can apply for the bar to be lifted in the same circumstances in which you can apply for an appeal to be reinstated (see p1195). If the decision maker (or other person) is barred from taking a further part in your appeal, and the bar has not been lifted, the First-tier Tribunal or the Upper Tribunal does not have to consider any response or other submission made by her/him.[236] In addition, the Tribunal can decide any or all of the issues against her/him without further consideration.

Note: if the DWP (or the local authority or HMRC) appeals to the Upper Tribunal, *you* could be barred from taking further part in the appeal under the rules above.

Postponements and adjournments

The First-tier Tribunal and the Upper Tribunal can postpone or adjourn a hearing.[237] Remember that if you do not attend a hearing, the Tribunal can hear the appeal without you.[238] Your appeal to the First-tier Tribunal is less likely to succeed if you do not attend. **Note:** oral hearings at the Upper Tribunal are more concerned with legal arguments than evidence of facts, so if you have a representative, an oral hearing is likely to go ahead if s/he can attend, even if you are unable to do so.

Your case might be postponed or adjourned if there is a test case or lead case pending which deals with the same issues as your appeal (see p1198).

Getting a hearing postponed

If the hearing date is inconvenient or you want more time to prepare your case, you can ask for the hearing to be postponed to another date. You should apply in writing to the relevant tribunal before the hearing date, saying why you want your appeal to be postponed. Make it clear that you do not want the hearing to go ahead in your absence. You should apply as soon as you decide that you want a postponement. The Tribunal can postpone your oral hearing even if this is not requested. Bear the following in mind.

- Do *not* presume that a postponement will be granted. Telephone before the hearing is due to take place to check if it has been agreed. Be ready to attend the hearing if it goes ahead. If you have a representative, s/he should warn you that your application might not be successful.[239]
- If you do not attend the hearing, the judge conducting the hearing should consider whether it should be adjourned, even if you have been refused a postponement.[240]

Getting a hearing adjourned

Even if a hearing (either oral or paper) is underway, it can be adjourned – eg, if you or the DWP (or the local authority or HMRC) asks for an adjournment, or if the First-tier Tribunal or the Upper Tribunal itself thinks this is the best course (eg, if more evidence is required or you need time to consider statute law or caselaw). The First-tier Tribunal should consider the benefit of an adjournment (eg whether further evidence would be helpful), why you (or the DWP, the local authority or HMRC) are not ready to go ahead and what the impact of an adjournment would be on the other party and the tribunal system.[241] It should adjourn a hearing:

- if there is doubt about whether you received notice of the oral hearing;[242] *or*
- if you have advised it that you cannot attend, have a good reason for not attending and have asked for another hearing date;[243] *or*
- if you are unable to attend the hearing (eg, you are in prison) but your evidence could be expected to play an important part in it reaching a decision;[244] *or*

- if you want to be represented at the oral hearing, but your representative is not available on the date it has been listed and has made a reasonable request for a postponement. Your representative should explain why s/he cannot attend and why no one else can represent you in her/his place;[245] *or*
- if you need to get a representative – eg, because it is difficult for you to represent yourself or the decision with which you disagree concerns a large overpayment;[246] *or*
- to enable you to get additional evidence which you could not until then have reasonably been expected to realise was needed.[247]

You should consider asking for an adjournment if the First-tier Tribunal says it is going to consider whether you should get a lower rate of benefit than you are getting currently, to allow you to prepare your case and make representations.

If a hearing is not postponed or adjourned

If the hearing is not postponed or adjourned and the First-tier Tribunal makes a decision with which you disagree, you can try to appeal to the Upper Tribunal or, in limited circumstances, apply for the decision to be set aside (see p1179). If the Upper Tribunal makes a decision with which you disagree, you can try to appeal to the Court of Appeal (in Scotland, the Court of Session) or, in limited circumstances, to apply for the decision to be set aside (see p1191).

Test cases and lead cases

Sometimes appeals to the First-tier Tribunal or the Upper Tribunal are made by more than one person about the same issues of fact or law. When this happens, there are procedural rules that can mean appeals dealing with the same issues may be delayed until a decision has been made in a test case or a lead case.

If a **test case** is pending against a decision of the Upper Tribunal or a court that deals with issues raised in your case, the DWP (or the local authority or HMRC) can suspend payment of your benefit or even postpone making a decision about your claim (see p1150). This means you will not be able to appeal until a decision is made about the test case.

However, for benefits other than housing benefit and council tax benefit, if a test case is pending and you have already appealed to the First-tier Tribunal or Upper Tribunal (your appeal is then known as a 'look-alike' case), the decision maker can serve notice requiring the First-tier Tribunal or the Upper Tribunal in *your* appeal:[248]

- not to make a decision and to refer your case back to her/him;
- to deal with your appeal by either:
  - postponing making a decision until the test case is decided; *or*
  - deciding your appeal as if the test case had been decided in the way most unfavourable to you, but only if this is in your interests. If this happens, and the test case eventually goes in your favour, the decision maker has to make

a new decision superseding the decision of the First-tier Tribunal or Upper Tribunal in the light of the decision in the test case.[249]

If the decision on your appeal has been postponed, once a decision has been made in the test case, the decision is made on your appeal.

If appeals are made to the First-tier Tribunal by more than one person about the same issues of fact or law, the First-tier Tribunal can specify one or more of the appeals as a **lead case** and postpone making a decision on all the other related appeals.[250] The decision to treat an appeal as a lead case is made by the Social Entitlement Chamber president.[251] When the Tribunal makes its decision in the lead cases(s), the decision applies to (ie, is binding on) all the other related appeals. You must be sent a copy of the decision. If your appeal is not the lead case, you can apply to the First-tier Tribunal for a direction that the decision does not apply to, and is not binding on, your appeal. You must apply in writing within one month after the date you are sent a copy of the decision. The First-tier Tribunal can give you longer (or shorter) than this. There is no guarantee that you will be given longer, so keep within the time limit wherever possible (see p1203).

Consent orders

If all the parties (eg, you and the DWP, the local authority or HMRC) agree what the solution to your dispute should be, you can ask the judge in the First-tier Tribunal or the Upper Tribunal to make a 'consent order' and to make any other appropriate provision you have agreed.[252] This procedure is unlikely to be relevant in most cases. The Tribunal only deals with your appeal in this way if it considers it appropriate. It may simply make a decision on your appeal in the usual way. In any case, the decision maker can often revise the decision with which you disagree. Note, however, that if you are appealing to the First-tier Tribunal, your appeal could lapse if s/he revises the decision (see p1165).

If a consent order is made, there does not have to be a hearing and no reasons for the order need to be given. Seek independent advice *before* agreeing to a consent order.

4. Appealing to the courts

You might consider taking your case to a court if you want to:

- appeal against a decision of the Upper Tribunal (see below); *or*
- apply for a judicial review (see p1202).

Appeals from the Upper Tribunal

You may appeal against a decision of the Upper Tribunal (other than an excluded decision) to the Court of Appeal (in Scotland, the Court of Session). You can only do this if the Upper Tribunal made an error of law (see p1182 for what might count) and you must first obtain permission to appeal.[253] The DWP, the local authority and HM Revenue and Customs (HMRC) have the same rights of appeal as you.

Excluded decisions[254]

Excluded decisions are decisions taken by the Upper Tribunal refusing to grant permission to appeal against a decision of the First-tier Tribunal and certain decisions taken when it considers a review (see p1201) – ie, decisions:

- to review, or not to review, an earlier decision;
- to take no action, or not to take any particular action, in the light of a review of an earlier decision;
- to set aside an earlier decision on review (the decision that is set aside is also excluded).

Permission to appeal to the Court of Appeal or the Court of Session cannot be given unless the Upper Tribunal or the Court, considers that:[255]

- the appeal would raise some important point of principle or practice; *or*
- there is some other compelling reason for the Court to hear the appeal.

The procedure in the Court is strict, formal and far less flexible than the procedure before the First-tier Tribunal or Upper Tribunal.

The DWP (or the local authority or HMRC) is represented by a solicitor and a barrister. You should consider obtaining legal advice from a solicitor before appealing. See p1203 for information about meeting the cost of going to court. **Note:** before making any application, seek advice about whether you could be liable for the other side's costs.

How to appeal

You apply for permission to appeal, in the first instance, to the Upper Tribunal. Your application must:[256]

- be in writing; *and*
- contain sufficient information about the Upper Tribunal's decision for it to be identified; *and*
- state the error(s) of law you think the Upper Tribunal made. These must be identified clearly;[257] *and*
- if your application is late, include a request for an extension of time and the reasons why the application was not made in time; *and*
- state the result you are seeking – eg, what you think the Upper Tribunal's decision should have been.

Your application must be received by the Upper Tribunal within three months after the date you were sent:[258]

- written notice of the decision; *or*
- notice that the reasons for the decision have been amended, or the decision has been corrected, following a review; *or*
- notice that an application for a set-aside has been refused. This only applies if the application for a set-aside was made within the time limit (or any longer period allowed).

The Upper Tribunal can extend (or shorten) your time limit for applying for permission to appeal to the Court.[259] There is no guarantee that you will be given longer, so keep within the time limit wherever possible (see p1203). If your time limit is not extended, the Upper Tribunal must refuse your application.[260]

You must be sent a record of the decision on your application for permission as soon as practicable.[261] If your application has been refused, you must also be sent a statement of reasons for the refusal and notice of your right to apply to the Court for permission, along with information about how to apply and the time limit for doing so.

When the Upper Tribunal can review its decision

When the Upper Tribunal receives an application for permission to appeal to the Court of Appeal or Court of Session (from you or the DWP, the local authority or HMRC), it can review its decision if:[262]

- when it made the decision, it overlooked a legal provision, or a Court or Upper Tribunal decision it should have followed, which could have had a 'material effect' on the decision; *or*
- since the Upper Tribunal decision, a Court has made a decision which the Upper Tribunal must follow. This only applies if the Court's decision could have had a 'material effect' on the Upper Tribunal's decision had it been made at the time.

If the Upper Tribunal *does* review the decision it can:[263]

- correct accidental errors in the decision or the record of the decison; *and*
- amend the reasons given for the decision; *and*
- set aside the decision. If it does this, it must make a new decision.

You must be notifed in writing of the outcome of the review and your right of appeal (if any).[264] If the Upper Tribunal has taken any action and you were not given an opportunity to comment before the review, you must also be notifed that you can apply for the outcome to be set aside and for the decision to be reviewed again.

If the Upper Tribunal does not review its decision, or reviews it but takes no action (or no action on a part of the decision), it must consider whether to give you permission to appeal to the Court against the decision (or the part of the decision on which no action was taken).[265]

If the Upper Tribunal refuses permission to appeal

If the Upper Tribunal refuses you permission to appeal, you can made a fresh application to the Court of Appeal (in England and Wales) or the Court of Session (in Scotland).[266] The Upper Tribunal's statement of reasons for the refusal tells you the relevant court and the time limit for applying.[267] The time limit is very short so you should lodge your application with the court as soon as possible.

Generally, in **England and Wales**, the Court of Appeal first considers your application for permission to appeal without an oral hearing. If permission is refused, you can ask for the decision to be reconsidered at a hearing by writing to the Court Office, but you must do this within seven days.[268] However, if the Court of Appeal considers that your application is totally without merit, it can make an order stating you cannot do this.[269]

If the Court of Appeal refuses you permission to appeal after an oral hearing, you cannot appeal further, or apply for a judicial review.

In **Scotland**, the procedures for appealing to the Court of Session are similar to those for England and Wales but there are a number of differences. The Court of Session hears applications for permission to appeal in open court rather than making the decision simply by reading the papers. The DWP (or the local authority or HMRC) may agree that the application for permission and the appeal itself are heard at the same time.

When you get permission to appeal

If permission to appeal is granted by the Upper Tribunal or the Court, you must serve a notice of appeal on the relevant parties. There are strict time limits for doing this. Seek advice immediately if you are in this position. The DWP solicitor will accept service on behalf of the DWP. The solicitor to HMRC will accept service on behalf of HMRC (see Appendix 1 for the addresses). Ask your local authority who will accept service on its behalf.

Applying for judicial review

Occasionally it is possible to challenge decisions with which you disagree by a judicial review in the High Court (the Court of Session in Scotland). Judicial review is a means of challenging the decisions of any form of tribunal, government department or local authority. For example, you can apply for a judicial review of a decision:

- made by a decision maker, if it is a decision against which you do not have a right of appeal (see p1159); *or*
- made by the DWP refusing you a payment from the discretionary social fund (see Chapter 25); *or*
- made by a local authority about discretionary housing payments (see p294).

You cannot usually go to the Court for a judicial review if you have another independent means of appeal, such as to the First-tier Tribunal or the Upper Tribunal.

You need the services of a solicitor or legal advice centre to apply for a judicial review. In England and Wales, you must apply to the High Court promptly. In any event, you must apply within three months of the decision you want to challenge. In Scotland, you apply to the Court of Session. There is no time limit but you should make your application as soon as possible.[270]

Note:

- You can apply for judicial review of some decisions of the Upper Tribunal, but only if the case would raise some important point of principle or practice, or there is some other compelling reason for the Court to hear it.[271]
- In some cases, you may be able to apply to the Upper Tribunal for a judicial review instead of the Court (see p1192). In Scotland, you must first apply to the Court of Session and it transfers your case to the Upper Tribunal if relevant criteria are satisfied.

Meeting the cost of going to court

Free legal help from a solicitor is currently available for cases in the Court of Appeal, the High Court and the Court of Session, and you should consider obtaining legal advice and representation for these. If you are not eligible for free legal help, you are likely to have to pay court fees. If you want to be represented by a lawyer, you will also have her/his fees and, if you were to lose your case, your opponent's costs. It may be a worthwhile investment if your claim is worth hundreds of pounds.

Note:

- Before making *any* application to a court, seek advice about whether you could be liable for the other side's costs.
- Free legal help for social security cases is likely to be abolished, although it will still be available for judicial review cases. See CPAG's *Welfare Rights Bulletin* for updates.

5. Time limits

Any of the time limits given to you by the First-tier Tribunal or the Upper Tribunal can be extended or shortened.[272] The rules do not specify when this should (or must) be done. However, the overriding objective of *all* the tribunal rules is to enable the First-tier Tribunal and the Upper Tribunal to deal with appeals fairly and justly (see p1193).[273]

Shortening time limits

The First-tier Tribunal and the Upper Tribunal may shorten your and the DWP's, the local authority's or HM Revenue and Customs' (HMRC's) time limits if it thinks that, for your appeal to be dealt with fairly and justly, delay should be avoided, provided the issues can be considered properly.[274] You might want to ask for the DWP's (or the local authority' s or HMRC's) time limits (eg, to apply for permission to appeal) to be shortened if your situation is urgent or your circumstances are exceptional.

Extending time limits

If you know you have missed (or are going to miss) a time limit, you should ask for it to be extended by the First-tier Tribunal or the Upper Tribunal. Other than if you are appealling to the First-tier Tribunal, there is no limit on how far a time limit can be extended, even if it ran out a long time ago. The First-tier Tribunal and the Upper Tribunal do not have to extend any particular time limit so there is no guarantee that you will be given more time. You should, therefore, keep within the time limits wherever possible. See below for further information about late appeals.

Always ask in writing for a time limit to be extended and apply in advance if you can. Give the reasons why you are (or are going to be) late in meeting the time limit, as well as any special circumstances which mean your time limit should be extended so that your appeal can be dealt with fairly and justly (see p1206 for some ideas).

Late appeals to the First-tier Tribunal

If you miss the time limit for appealing to the First-tier Tribunal (see p1162), but are within the absolute time limit for appealing (see p1205):

- your appeal must be treated as having been made within the time limit if the decision maker does not object.[275]
  See p1205 for what the decision maker considers. If s/he does object, s/he *must* refer your appeal to the First-tier Tribunal immediately;
- if the decision maker objects to your appeal being treated as made within the time limit, the First-tier Tribunal can extend the time limit.[276]
  There is no guarantee that you will be given longer. It might be simpler to ask for a revision or supersession of the decision maker's decision instead of making a late appeal, if there are grounds for doing so and this would give you everything to which you are entitled (see Chapter 45). However, you often get less arrears of benefit if you seek a supersession.

In addition to the information you must provide on your appeal form, you must include the reasons why your appeal is late (see p1161).[277] Also, give details of any special circumstances that mean it would be fair and just for the First-tier Tribunal to extend the time limit (see p1206 for some ideas about what may be relevant).

The absolute time limit for appealing

No appeal to the First-tier Tribunal can be allowed outside an absolute time limit which is 12 months from the date your time limit for appealing expired.[278]

If the decision maker thinks your appeal has been made outside the 12-month limit, s/he must refer your appeal to the First-tier Tribunal immediately.[279] **Note:**

- the First-tier Tribunal decides whether your appeal has been made within the time limit, not the DWP, the local authority or HMRC;[280]
- if the First-tier Tribunal decides that you cannot appeal because your appeal was made outside the absolute time limit for appealing but you think your appeal was made in time, you can appeal to the Upper Tribunal against the decision.[281]

What the decision maker considers

The decision maker does not object to your appeal being treated as having been made in time if s/he is satisfied that it is in the interests of justice to do so.[282] For these purposes, it is not in the interests of justice unless it was not practicable for you to appeal in time because:[283]

- you, your partner or a dependant died or had a serious illness;
- you are not resident in the UK;
- normal postal services were disrupted; *or*
- there are other special circumstances that are 'wholly exceptional' .

The longer you have delayed appealing, the more compelling the special circumstances must be.[284] When deciding whether it is in the interests of justice, account cannot be taken of the fact that:[285]

- a court or the Upper Tribunal has interpreted the law in a different way than was previously understood and applied;
- you (or anyone acting for you) misunderstood or were unaware of the relevant law, including the time limits for appealing.

Late appeals to the Upper Tribunal

The one-month time limit for applying to **the First-tier Tribunal** for permission to appeal to the Upper Tribunal (see p1185) can be extended. There is no absolute time limit for applying.

If your application is refused or rejected, you can apply directly to **the Upper Tribunal** for permission to appeal. If you apply outside the one-month limit for doing so (see p1188), the time limit can be extended. There is no absolute time limit for applying.

Note: if your application to the First-tier Tribunal for permission to appeal was rejected because it was late or your application for a statement of reasons was late, the Upper Tribunal can only allow your application if it thinks it is in the interests of justice to do so.[286]

The decision whether or not to allow a late appeal to the Upper Tribunal must be made bearing in mind the merits of the appeal and the consequences for you (and the DWP, the local authority or HMRC). If you are refused permission, you do not have a right of appeal against the decision, but you might be able to apply for a judicial review.

Reasons and circumstances

The overriding objective of the tribunal rules is to enable the First-tier Tribunal and the Upper Tribunal to deal with appeals fairly and justly (see p1193). Your reasons and circumstances may mean it would be fair and just to extend a time limit. What may or may not be such a reason or circumstance cannot be defined in advance, but the following are all relevant.

- The **reasons for the delay**. Make sure you explain these as clearly and as fully as possible. Do not worry if some or all of the delay is your fault. Almost any explanation is better than none at all. The worst situation is where you knew the time limit, but simply ignored it. Even then it may be possible to say something favourable. Say if things have been difficult at home or you were confused by the rules or just assumed that the DWP (or the local authority or HMRC) were the experts and had got it right until, for example, you were advised otherwise or read an article in a newspaper. Reasons for the delay could include the fact that:
  - you did not receive the decision;
  - you made a reasonable mistake in calculating the time limit;
  - you posted your appeal in time but it went astray in the post;
  - you were ill;
  - a mistake was made by your advisers. It should not make any difference that you might be able to sue them for negligence;
  - you were given wrong advice or otherwise misled by the DWP (or the local authority or HMRC) – eg, you were discouraged from appealing by a decision maker who advised you incorrectly that an appeal would be doomed to fail.

  If you have been badly advised by the DWP (or the local authority or HMRC) and lose money because you are refused a late appeal, you should consider claiming compensation (see Chapter 50).
- The **length of the delay**. Short delays are likely to be easier to justify than long delays. However, the usual approach is that time limits have to be kept to, and there has to be good reason for not doing so. So even a short delay may be difficult to justify without good reason.
- The **merits of your appeal**. The more likely your appeal is to succeed, the greater the injustice in refusing to extend the time limit. A strong case is particularly useful if there has been a very long delay and a time limit is usually

extended where there has been a 'clear error', which would have long-term continuing effects unless corrected.[287]

- The **amount of money at stake**. Even if there has been no clear error, a time limit may be extended if there is a lot of money at stake.[288]
- A **decision in a test case**. A decision in a test case, establishing that an earlier decision was incorrect, can amount to a reason to extend a time limit, in some circumstances.[289] Such appeals often involve large sums of money and (given the test case) a clear error in the decision which is being appealed against.

6. Presenting your case

Appeals to the First-tier Tribunal are taken on all sorts of issues – disputes about facts or the law or both – so the advice given here can only be general. You usually need to think about both the facts and the law because they are connected.

Sorting out the facts

You are likely to know more than anyone else about the facts of your case. Your key task is to pass your knowledge on to the First-tier Tribunal. It rehears your case completely, so fresh facts and arguments can be put by either side.

Remember to:

- check through the appeal papers carefully to work out what evidence the decision maker used in support of the decision. This helps you decide what evidence you need to win your case;
- study the decision maker's evidence and think about your arguments – eg, to show how the decision maker may have got the wrong impression;
- gather evidence to back up your arguments. If you want to give any evidence or information to the First-tier Tribunal, send it to it as soon as possible before your oral hearing. Otherwise, it might decide to adjourn your appeal (see p1197) or even decide not to take the evidence or information into account (see p1193). The First-tier Tribunal sends a copy to the DWP, the local authority or HM Revenue and Customs (HMRC), who might then decide to support your appeal;
- ask any witnesses who support your case to attend the hearing. The First-tier Tribunal has the power to refuse to hear witnesses who are not relevant, but it should always be fair to you and generally allow witnesses to speak, even if it looks like they may have nothing useful to say.[290] Bear in mind that the First-tier Tribunal can summons witnesses.[291]

Evidence

Evidence includes:

- oral evidence – what you (and any witnesses or others) actually say at the hearing; *and*

- written evidence – any documents you (or the DWP, the local authority or HMRC) provide, including medical evidence.

The First-tier Tribunal can issue directions (see p1193) on how you (or the DWP, the local authority or HMRC) should provide evidence or on whether witnesses should give evidence – eg, orally at a hearing, or by making a written submission or a witness statement within a set period of time.[292] It can accept evidence from you (or the DWP, the local authority or HMRC) even if it was not available to a previous decision maker.[293]

The First-tier Tribunal considers all the evidence.[294] It decides what weight the evidence should be given, taking account of any possible deficiencies, when deciding whether the facts are proved.[295] The Tribunal should decide your appeal in an investigative way, but Tribunal members should not make their own enquiries into the facts of your case before the hearing.[296]

The DWP (or the local authority or HMRC) might use video evidence – eg, if you are appealing about entitlement to employment and support allowance or disability living allowance. You cannot prevent the DWP (or the local authority or HMRC) doing so.[297] However, insist you are given proof that the surveillance was properly authorised and time to view and consider the evidence in advance of the hearing and, if relevant, that the person who made the video is called as a witness.

Oral evidence

You are usually expected to give your own oral evidence at the hearing, if you can. Your representative is generally not allowed to give it for you. However, s/he can assist the First-tier Tribunal in gathering evidence from you – eg, by asking you questions,[298] and can give her/his *own* evidence based on her/his observations.[299] The First-tier Tribunal cannot dismiss oral evidence without a proper explanation of why it has done so.[300]

Witnesses can also give oral evidence at the hearing. You or the DWP (or the local authority or HMRC) can call witnesses, although the First-tier Tribunal can limit the number.[301]

You, your representative and the presenting officer can report what other people have said – called **hearsay evidence**. The First-tier Tribunal must carefully weigh up its value, given that the person who originally made the statement is not present at the hearing.[302]

If s/he is at the hearing, the presenting officer (see p1171) puts the DWP's (or the local authority's or HMRC's) case but is not necessarily the person who actually made the decision on your claim. Unless giving her/his own evidence (eg, because s/he was directly involved in the decision on your claim), any factual statements s/he makes are hearsay evidence.[303]

Written evidence

Written evidence includes letters, medical and other reports, wage slips, bank statements, birth certificates and anything else that helps prove the facts. If, for example, the DWP (or the local authority or HMRC) says you failed to disclose an increase in your earnings and you have been overpaid, you could explain to the First-tier Tribunal how and when you did so. It is even better to produce a copy of the letter you sent informing it of the change. It is not unknown for the DWP (or the local authority or HMRC) to fail to include copies of relevant documents in the decision maker's response. Check the response carefully and submit copies of any missing documents to the Tribunal as soon as you can. If you do not have copies, insist that the decision maker provides these. The Tribunal can issue a direction requiring the decision maker to do so (see p1193).

Most evidence relied on by the DWP (or the local authority or HMRC) is written and you can point out that you have not had the opportunity of questioning the witnesses. You are not entitled to insist on the presence of any particular witness,[304] although you could ask the First-tier Tribunal to issue a direction for her/him to attend a hearing. You should argue that the First-tier Tribunal should not place any weight on the written evidence of, for instance, an interviewing officer if you are disputing the interview, or an investigating officer if you are disputing what s/he heard or saw.

Medical evidence

Your medical evidence should deal with the points in dispute and also with the dates relevant to the decision with which you disagree. If your doctor does not know about the effect of your disability on your everyday life, tell her/him about it and ask her/him to confirm that this is consistent with the degree of your disability. Your evidence, or that of a friend or relative, may also be of use.

Where medical evidence might be useful, you can ask your doctor to provide it, or ask an advice agency to write to your doctor. Your doctor may charge for such evidence, but an advice agency or solicitor might be able to get a report free. The report should be sent to the First-tier Tribunal in advance of the hearing, with a copy of the letter to your doctor as this helps to show that s/he is expressing her/his own opinion about your case. You could also ask your doctor to supply a copy of her/his notes about you over the last few years.

Note:

- The First-tier Tribunal can refer you for an examination and obtain a report if it thinks this is necessary (see p1174). If the lack of a report is causing you difficulties at the hearing, you could remind the First-tier Tribunal of its power to obtain one.
- If your opinion about the effect of your ill health or disabilities is contradicted by evidence from a doctor, you should:
  - point out how long the doctor has known you and what s/he knows about your day-to-day living activities or walking ability. If a doctor does not know

you or how you are affected by your condition (for instance, if s/he only gave you a very short examination), this should be taken into account;
- seek further medical evidence to support your view in advance of the hearing if you foresee any conflict of evidence.

- You can argue that the First-tier Tribunal should not rely on evidence from a DWP doctor with whom any of the members hearing your appeal sit at other times. This depends on how often and on how recently this has happened.[305]

Checking the law

If you know what the law says, you know what facts you have to prove. The primary sources of social security law are statute law and caselaw decided by the Upper Tribunal and courts. It is easy to find both, once you know what you are looking for. The footnotes in this *Handbook* point you in the right direction. There are also a number of books that explain the law and refer you to relevant legislation and cases (see Appendix 3).

Look carefully at the decision maker's response (see p1166), as this refers to the statute law and caselaw which s/he thinks is relevant. The DWP (or the local authority or HMRC) does not always get the law right and you should emphasise a point that it has overlooked or got wrong.

Statute law

Statute law consists of Acts of Parliament and regulations (and rules for procedure in the First-tier Tribunal and Upper Tribunal). The Acts set out the main framework and empower the making of regulations and rules covering the details. These regulations and rules are known as statutory instruments .

The best way to look up the relevant statute law is to read one of the annotated volumes of legislation listed in Appendix 3. Remember that, in rare cases, the books do not contain all the regulations and rules that are relevant. You can purchase regulations and rules individually from The Stationery Office. Many Acts, regulations and rules are also available at www.legislation.gov.uk. The Acts, regulations and rules are sometimes amended, so you must confirm that those in the annotated volumes of legislation (or obtained individually or online) are up to date.

If you are trying to discover the current law or chase up a reference, unless your appeal is an old one and the law has changed since the relevant time, you can refer to *The Law Relating to Social Security* – known as the 'Blue Volumes'. These are available at www.dwp.gov.uk/publications/specialist-guides/law-volumes. Make sure it is up to date.

Benefit law is complicated and the staff who administer benefits are issued with guidance manuals and circulars. The DWP (or the local authority or HMRC) and the First-tier Tribunal and Upper Tribunal are only bound by what the law says, not by the guidance. Nevertheless, it is sometimes useful to check the guidance. See Appendix 3 for a list of what is available.

If the statute law is ambiguous

If the statute law is ambiguous, the First-tier Tribunal, the Upper Tribunal and the courts can look at statements made to Parliament by ministers when the law was first made.[306] It may, therefore, be worth checking the House of Commons' and House of Lords' official reports (known as *Hansard*) to see what was said in Parliament when the law was first introduced. You can find *Hansard* at www.parliament.uk/business/publications/hansard. You can also check the transcripts of debates in the Delegated Legislation Committee at www.parliament.uk/business/publications/hansard/commons/gc-debates/delegated-legislation-committee. Other important sources of information are the Social Security Advisory Committee (http://ssac.independent.gov.uk) and the Industrial Injuries Advisory Council (http://iiac.independent.gov.uk).

Caselaw

The decision maker's response often refers to decisions of the Upper Tribunal and the courts (known as 'caselaw'). You should also use caselaw to support your appeal if possible. To help you decide which cases to use, see p1212. **Note:** the most important Upper Tribunal decisions are chosen to be reported. See p1212 for information about identifying decisions.

Precedent

When the Upper Tribunal or a court decides an appeal, the decision sets a precedent, which a decision maker or the First-tier Tribunal deciding a similar case must follow.[307] Unreported decisions must be followed in the same way as reported ones.[308]

Note: before 3 November 2008, decisions now made by the Upper Tribunal were made by social security commissioners. Commissioner's decisions also set a precedent.

Where there is an irreconcilable conflict between two or more decisions, the **First-tier Tribunal** has to choose which decision to follow.[309]

- It normally follows a reported decision of the Upper Tribunal (or a commissioner) in preference to an unreported one.
- It must follow an Upper Tribunal decision made by a three-judge panel (or the decision of a tribunal of commissioners) in preference to a decision of a single judge (or commissioner).
- Decisions of the Supreme Court, House of Lords, the Court of Appeal, the Court of Session or the European Court of Justice take precedence over all decisions of the Upper Tribunal (and commissioners).[310]

The **Upper Tribunal** has more freedom than the First-tier Tribunal.

- It does not have to follow an Upper Tribunal decision made by a single judge (or the decision of a single commissioner) if satisfied that the earlier decision was wrong.[311]

- It must follow an Upper Tribunal decision made by a three-judge panel (and the decision of a tribunal of commissioners) although, if the judge thinks it may be wrong, s/he can ask the President of the Administrative Appeals Chamber for the case to be transferred to another three-judge panel in the Upper Tribunal to reconsider the point.
- If an appeal is being heard by a three-judge panel in the Upper Tribunal, the panel does not have to follow the decision of another similarly composed panel (or tribunal of commissioners), but usually does so.[312]

Which cases to use

Caselaw can seem less precise than statute law, and frequently cases seem to contradict each other. Very often there are small differences in the facts of the cases, which justify the different results. To find cases relevant to your own, you can use the footnotes in this *Handbook* or any of the publications listed in Appendix 3. Bear the following in mind.

- Find cases where the facts are similar to yours. If cases appear to be against you, look at the facts of those cases and see whether any differences justify a different decision in your case (known as 'distinguishing' cases). One distinction may simply be that what seemed reasonable in the 1950s does not seem fair in the 2010s.[313]
- Most appeals before April 1987 were decided when there was a right of appeal to commissioners on questions of fact as well as law, so the First-tier Tribunal may not necessarily be erring in law if it takes a different view from a commissioner in a pre-April 1987 decision.
- Ensure that the caselaw is still relevant to the decision you are appealing. A case might only apply to a previous version of the law – ie, if there have been amendments to the statute law since it was decided.
- Check the decisions referred to in the decision maker's response (see p1166) as sometimes they rely on only part of a decision and fail to mention another part which is more favourable to you.

Identifying Upper Tribunal and commissioners' decisions

All Upper Tribunal decisions have file numbers – eg, CDLA/2195/2008. The last numbers indicate the year in which the appeal was lodged. The second letter(s) indicate(s) the type of benefit involved in the decision. An extra 'S' after the 'C' denotes a Scottish case, as in CSIB/721/2004.

Upper Tribunal decisions that are published on the Upper Tribunal website are given a 'citation number'. First, the parties to the appeal are identified; the DWP, HMRC or the local authority are identified by name and the benefit claimant by initials. The first name (or initials) is the party who appealed and the second, the other party. Next is the year the decision was given (in square brackets). The final number is the appeal number. For example, *Stroud DC v JG* [2009] UKUT 67 (AAC) was an appeal by Stroud District Council decided by the UK Upper Tribunal

(Administrative Appeals Chamber) in 2009. From 2010, citation numbers also include letters to indicate the type of benefit involved in the decision – eg, *SW v SSWP(IB)* [2010] UKUT 73 (AAC) involved incapacity benefit.

Note: commissioners' decisions (ie, decisions made before 3 November 2008) only had file numbers and were not given citation numbers.

Significant decisions are highlighted on the Upper Tribunal website.

Reported decisions are given a new number. All reported decisions:

- from 1951 to 2010 begin with an 'R' – eg, CU/255/1984 became R(U) 3/86. The second letter(s) denote(s) the type of benefit. The last numbers indicate the year in which the decision was published.
- from 2010, begin with the citation number (see above). This is followed by the year the decision is reported (in square brackets), then the letters AACR (meaning Administrative Appeals Chamber Reports) and the reported decision number – eg, *Torbay BC v RF (HB)* [2010] UKUT 7 (AAC); [2010] AACR 26.

Identifying court decisions

Court decisions are identified by the names of the parties involved in the appeal. The first name is usually the party who has appealed and the second name is the other party. In judicial review cases, the case citation begins with 'R'.

Examples of court decisions

Mallinson v Secretary of State for Social Security, 21 April 1994 (HL) is a House of Lords decision.

Hockenjos v Secretary of State for Social Security [2004] EWCA Civ 1749, 21 December 2004 is a Court of Appeal decision.

R v South Tyneside MBC ex parte Tooley [1997] QBD and *R (Reynolds) v Secretary of State for Work and Pensions* [2002] EWHC Admin 426 are decisions following applications for judicial review.

Obtaining Upper Tribunal, commissioners' and court decisions

Many **Upper Tribunal and commissioners' decisions** are available at www.justice.gov.uk/guidance/courts-and-tribunals/tribunals/aa/decisions.htm and on the Rightsnet website at www.rightsnet.org.uk. Decisions may be obtained also from the Upper Tribunal Office (see Appendix 1); some are available free of charge.

All reported decisions from 1991 to December 2009 are available on the DWP website (see Appendix 1). Reported decisions are published from time to time in bound volumes, which are sometimes available in law libraries. The bound volumes of decisions from 2010 onwards are called Administrative Appeal Chamber Reports.

Summaries of reported Upper Tribunal and commissioners' decisions, most highlighted decisions and important court decisions are published in CPAG's

Welfare Rights Bulletin. It is important to use the full decision, not just the summary, at the appeal hearing.

If an unreported decision is to be used at a hearing in the First-tier Tribunal by the DWP (or the local authority or HMRC), a copy should be supplied to you. Similarly, if you wish to use one, you should supply copies to everyone, preferably by sending one to the First-tier Tribunal in advance of the hearing.

Many **court decisions** are now available online. A useful link to these is at www.bailii.org. In addition, where there has been an appeal against an Upper Tribunal (or a commissioner's) decision, it is usually reported.

At the hearing

Each case is different and hearings are informal, so there is no set pattern for presenting cases. If you want to make a presentation on your appeal, make this clear to the First-tier Tribunal as soon as possible – eg, before the hearing starts. Bear the following in mind.

- Send any detailed submissions and medical reports before the hearing.
- You can use a written submission at the hearing and read directly from it. However, the First-tier Tribunal usually asks questions, so be prepared to talk about your case without the script.
- Make it clear at the beginning which parts of the decision maker's response are in dispute and the parts with which you agree. It is then usually best to set out the facts and to call any witnesses before turning to legal arguments.
- It is the First-tier Tribunal's job to help you to say everything you want by putting you at your ease and asking the right questions. However, you must also be prepared for some searching questions. If you forget to say something when it is your turn to speak, do not hesitate to add it at the end of the hearing.

Advice and representation

There are a number of agencies which can advise you and help you prepare your case for the hearing (see Appendix 2). Some can also represent you at hearings if you feel that someone else would put your case better than you. Remember that many non-lawyer advisers know more about social security law than lawyers, and their advice and representation are usually free.

Meeting the costs of going to the First-tier or Upper Tribunal

You might be able to get free advice and free assistance to cover preparatory work for a hearing, such as obtaining medical reports and writing submissions. If you are on income support, income-based jobseeker's allowance, income-related employment and support allowance or the guarantee credit of pension credit or you have a very low income, you might be able to get this free from a solicitor. If you have a solicitor acting for you in an industrial injury or personal injury claim, s/he may have medical and other reports and evidence which you can use for your benefit claim.

You cannot normally get free legal help from a solicitor to cover representation in **appeals to the First-tier Tribunal** (but see p1214 for help from non-lawyers). If you are not eligible for free advice and assistance, or you want to be represented by a lawyer at an oral hearing, you are likely to have to pay. It may be a worthwhile investment if your claim is worth hundreds of pounds.

If you are resident in Scotland, free legal help is available for **appeals to the Upper Tribunal**. This includes help preparing for paper as well as oral hearings. If you are resident in England or Wales, free legal help for appeals to the Upper Tribunal is available in exceptional cases. If you are granted funding, you must send a copy of the funding notice (in Scotland, the legal aid certificate) to the Upper Tribunal Office as soon as practicable.[314] You must also let the other parties involved in your appeal know that you have been granted funding.

Legal aid is available for a **judicial review by the Upper Tribunal** of a decision of the First-tier Tribunal (see p1192).

Note: free advice, assistance and help and legal aid for social security cases is likely to be abolished. See CPAG's *Welfare Rights Bulletin* for updates.

Notes

1. **Appealing to the First-tier Tribunal**

1 r2(2) TP(FT) Rules
2 **CB/GA** Reg 24 CB&GA(DA) Regs
Other benefits s12 SSA 1998; reg 25 SS&CS(DA) Regs
3 s12(4) SSA 1998
4 Reg 14 SS(JPIP) Regs
5 **CB/GA** Regs 29 and 31 CB&GA(A) Regs
Other benefits Reg 30(1), (5) and (6)-(6B) SS(C&P) Regs
6 Sch 7 para 6(3) and (6) CSPSSA 2000; reg 3 HB&CTB(DA) Regs; *Wirral MBC v Salisbury Independent Living Ltd* [2012] EWCA Civ 84
7 R(H) 3/04; R(H) 10/07
8 **CB/GA** Reg 33 CB&GA(DA) Regs
HB/CTB Reg 21 HB&CTB(DA) Regs
Other benefits Reg 34 SS&CS(DA) Regs
9 **HB/CTB** Reg 10(1)(b) and (2) HB&CTB(DA) Regs
CB/GA Reg 26(1)(b) and (2) CB&GA(DA) Regs
Other benefits Reg 28(1)(b) and (2) SS&CS(DA) Regs
10 **CB/GA** s12 and Schs 2 and 3 SSA 1998; reg 25(2) CB&GA(DA) Regs
HB/CTB Sch 7 para 6 CSPSSA 2000
Other benefits s12 and Schs 2 and 3 SSA 1998; reg 26 SS&CS(DA) Regs
11 **CB/GA** Reg 26 CB&GA(DA) Regs
HB/CTB Reg 10 HB&CTB(DA) Regs
Other benefits Reg 28 SS&CS(DA) Regs
12 R(SB) 29/83; R(SB) 12/89; CIS/807/1992; R(H) 3/05
13 R(IS) 6/04
14 *SSWP v Adams* [2003] EWCA Civ 796, 18 June 2003 (EWCA), reported as R(G) 1/03

15 **CB/GA** Sch 2 SSA 1998; reg 25 and Sch 2 CB&GA(DA) Regs
HB/CTB Sch 7 para 6(2) CSPSSA 2000; reg 16 and Sch HB&CTB(DA) Regs
Other benefits Sch 2 SSA 1998; reg 27 and Sch 2 SS&CS(DA) Regs
16 **CA/GA** Regs 9 and 13(2)(d) CB&GA(DA) Regs
HB/CTB Regs 4(6) and 7(2)(e) HB&CTB(DA) Regs
Other benefits Regs 3(8) and 6(2)(d) SS&CG(DA) Regs
17 **CB/GA** Reg 31(1A) CB&GA(DA) Regs
HB/CTB Reg 20(1) HB&CTB (DA) Regs
Other benefits Reg 33(2) SS&CS(DA) Regs
18 r23(6) TP(FT) Rules
19 r11(5) TP(FT) Rules
20 **CB/GA** Reg 31(1A) CB&GA(DA) Regs
HB/CTB Reg 20(1) HB&CTB(DA) Regs
Other benefits Reg 33(2) SS&CS(DA) Regs
21 rr12 and 23(2) and Sch 1 TP(FT) Rules
22 Reg 28(1) and (2) CB&GA(DA) Regs
23 s9(5) SSA 1998; Sch 7 para 3(5) CSPSSA 2000
24 **CB/GA** Reg 28(2) CB&GA(DA) Regs
Other benefits Sch 1 TP(FT) Rules
25 CIB/3937/2000
26 r12 TP(FT) Rules
27 r23(4) TP(FT) Rules
28 r5(3)(a) TP(FT) Rules
29 *LS v London Borough of Lambeth (HB)* [2010] UKUT 461 (AAC); [2011] AACR 27
30 **CB/GA** Reg 31(1A) CB&GA(DA) Regs
HB/CTB Reg 20(1) HB&CTB(DA) Regs
Other benefits Reg 33(2) SS&CS(DA) Regs
31 r23(6) TP(FT) Rules
32 **CB/GA** Reg 31(1B)-(6) CB&GA(DA) Regs
HB/CTB Reg 20(2)-(6) HB&CTB(DA) Regs
Other benefits Reg 33(3)-(7) SS&CS(DA) Regs
33 **CB/GA** Reg 31(6) CB&GA(DA) Regs
HB/CTB Reg 20(6) HB&CTB(DA) Regs
Other benefits Reg 33(7) SS&CS(DA) Regs
34 **CB/GA** Reg 31(7) CB&GA(DA)A Regs
HB/CTB Reg 20(7) HB&CTB(DA) Regs
Other benefits Reg 33(8) SS&CS(DA) Regs
35 paras 06114-16 DMG; para C7/7.128-29 GM
36 **CB/GA** Reg 31(8) CB&GA(DA) Regs
HB/CTB Reg 20(8) HB&CTB(DA) Regs
Other benefits Reg 33(9) SS&CS(DA) Regs
37 r24 TP(FT) Rules
38 r24(1)(b) TP(FT) Rules; Art 6 European Convention on Human Rights; s6 HRA 1998; CH/3497/2005
39 Complaint 01/C/13400 against Scarborough BC
40 R(H) 1/07
41 r5 TP(FT) Rules
42 r6(1)-(3) TP(FT) Rules
43 **HB/CTB** Sch 7 para 3(6) CSPSSA 2000
Other benefits s9(6) SSA 1998
44 **CB/GA** Reg 27(1) and (5) CB&GA(DA) Regs
HB/CTB Reg 17(1) and (2) HB&CTB(DA) Regs
Other benefits Reg 30(1) and (2) SS&CS(DA) Regs
45 **CB/GA** Reg 27(2) CB&GA(DA) Regs
HB/CTB Reg 17(3) HB&CTB(DA) Regs
Other benefits Reg 30(3) SS&CS(DA) Regs
46 **CB/GA** Reg 27(3) CB&GA(DA) Regs
HB/CTB Reg 17(4) HB&CTB(DA) Regs
Other benefits Reg 30(4) SS&CS(DA) Regs
47 **CB/GA** Reg 27(4) CB&GA(DA) Regs
HB/CTB Reg 17(5) HB&CTB(DA) Regs
Other benefits Reg 30(5) SS&CS(DA) Regs
48 **CB/GA** Reg 28(2) CB&GA(DA) Regs
HB/CTB Sch 7 para 3(5) CSPSSA 2000
Other benefits s9(5) SSA 1998
All benefits Sch 1 TP(FT) Rules
49 r24(1)(b) TP(FT) Rules
50 r24(5) TP(FT) Rules
51 r11(6)(a) TP(FT) Rules
52 r24(2) TP(FT) Rules
53 r24(4) TP(FT) Rules
54 r24(6) and (7) TP(FT) Rules
55 r5(3)(a) TP(FT) Rules
56 **CB/GA** Reg 32 CB&GA(DA) Regs
HB/CTB Regs 20(9) HB&CTB(DA) Regs
Other benefits Reg 33(10) SS&CS(DA) Regs
All r17 TP(FT) Rules
57 r4 TP(FT) Rules; Practice Statement, *Delegation of Functions to Staff in Relation to the Social Entitlement Chamber of the First-tier Tribunal on or after 1 December 2010*, 1 December 2010
58 r17(4) and (5) TP(FT) Rules

59 r27(1) TP(FT) Rules; *MH v Pembrokeshire CC (HB)* [2010] UKUT 28 (AAC); *AT v SSWP (ESA)* [2010] UKUT 430 (AAC); *MM v SSWP (ESA)* [2011] UKUT 334 (AAC)
60 r27(3) TP(FT) Rules
61 r5(3)(f) TP(FT) Rules
62 r11 TP(FT) Rules
63 *ZO v SSWP (IB)* [2010] UKUT 143 (AAC)
64 r21 TP(FT) Rules
65 r1 TP(FT) Rules, definition of 'hearing'
66 r29 TP (FT) Rules
67 CH/3594/2002
68 r31 TP(FT) Rules; *WT v SSWP (DLA)* [2011] UKUT 93 (AAC)
69 r30 TP(FT) Rules
70 r24(6) and (7) TP(FT) Rules
71 *MP v SSWP (DLA)* [2010] UKUT 103 (AAC)
72 *LS v Lambeth LB (HB)* [2010] UKUT 461 (AAC); [2011] AACR 27
73 CIB/2751/2002; CDLA/1350/2004
74 r1(3) TP(FT) Rules, definition of 'hearing'
75 Art 8 First-tier Tribunal and Upper Tribunal (Composition of Tribunal) Order 2008, No.2835
76 s28 TCEA 2007
77 para 06430 DMG; para C7/7.31 GM
78 r11 TP(FT) Rules; CIB/1009/2004; CIB/2058/2004
79 r11(7) and (8) TP(FT) Rules
80 Practice Statement, *Composition of Tribunals in Social Security and Child Support Cases in the Social Entitlement Chamber on or after 3 November 2008*, 30 October 2008
81 Sch 4 para 15(6) TCEA 2007
82 *PJ v SSWP (ESA)* [2011] UKUT 224 (AAC)
83 *Gillies v SSWP* [2006] UKHL 2, 26 January 2006, reported as R(DLA) 5/06
84 *SSWP v Cunningham* [2004] 211, 6 August 2004 (ScotCS), reported as R(DLA) 7/04; R(DLA) 3/07
85 Practice Statement, *Composition of Tribunals in Social Security and Child Support Cases in the Social Entitlement Chamber on or after 3 November 2008*, 30 October 2008, para 12
86 r2 TP(FT) Rules
87 CSDLA/606/2003
88 s20(3) SSA 1998; r25(2) TP(FT) Rules; R(DLA) 5/03
89 R(IB) 2/06
90 r25(4) TP(FT) Rules
91 R(DLA) 1/95, qualified by CM/2/1994; *GL v SSWP* [2008] UKUT 36 (AAC)
92 R(DLA) 8/06
93 CI/3384/2006
94 Practice Statement, *Composition of Tribunals in Social Security and Child Support Cases in the Social Entitlement Chamber on or after 3 November 2008*, 30 October 2008, para 14
95 CM/527/1992; CIB/3074/2003
96 CIB/5586/1999
97 CIB/476/2005; CIB/511/2005
98 s20(2) SSA 1998; r25(3) and Sch 2 TP(FT) Rules
99 *Mongan v Department for Social Development* [2005] NICA 16, 13 April 2005, reported as R3/05 (DLA)
100 CH/1229/2002
101 *Mooney v SSWP* [2004] SLT 1141, 23 April 2004, reported as R(DLA) 5/04; *Mongan v Department for Social Development* [2005] NICA 16, 13 April 2005, reported as R3/05 (DLA); *SSWP v Hooper* [2007] EWCA Civ 495, reported as R(IB) 4/07
102 CSDLA/336/2000; CSIB/160/2000; R(H) 1/02
103 **HB/CTB** Sch 7 para 6(9)(a) CSPSSA 2000
Other benefits s12(8)(a) SSA 1998
104 CH/1229/2002; R(IB) 2/04; *AP-H v SSWP (DLA)* [2010] UKUT 183 (AAC)
105 CI/531/2000; CDLA/1000/2001; CH/1229/2002; R(IB) 2/04; CDLA/884/2008
106 CDLA/4184/2004
107 R(IB) 2/04
108 R(IB) 2/04; CH/3009/2002
109 CDLA/1707/2005
110 R(IB) 2/04; R(IB) 7/04; CIS/1675/2004
111 **HB/CTB** Sch 7 para 6(9)(b) CSPSSA 2000
Other benefits s12(8)(b) SSA 1998
112 R(DLA) 4/05
113 R(DLA) 2/01; R(DLA) 3/01; CJSA/2375/2000
114 R(SB) 4/85
115 r33 TP(FT) Rules
116 Practice Statement, *Record of Proceedings in Social Security and Child Support Cases in the Social Entitlement Chamber on or after 3 November 2008*, 30 October 2008
117 r34(2) TP(FT) Rules
118 r34(3) TP(FT) Rules; CCS/1664/2001
119 r34(4) TP(FT) Rules; CIB/3937/2000
120 r5(3)(a) TP(FT) Rules
121 r34(5) TP(FT) Rules
122 r38(7)(a) TP(FT) Rules
123 r5(3)(n) TP(UT) Rules
124 r5(3)(l) TP(FT) Rules

125 **HB/CTB** Sch 7 para 13 CSPSSA 2000; reg 11 HB&CTB(DA) Regs
Other benefits s21 SSA 1998; reg 16 SS&CS(DA) Regs; reg 18 CB&GA(DA) Regs
126 r36 TP(FT) Rules; CI/3887/1999; CSDLA/168/2008; *AS v SSWP (ESA)* [2011] UKUT 159 (AAC)
127 r37(1) and (2) TP(FT) Rules
128 r37(3) TP(FT) Rules
129 r5(3)(a) TP(FT) Rules
130 r27(2) TP(FT) Rules; CSB/172/1990
131 CIB/4193/2003
132 CI/79/1990; CIS/373/1994
133 r41 TP(FT) Rules
134 *LS v London Borough of Lambeth (HB)* [2010] UKUT 461 (AAC)
135 r38(3) and (4) TP(FT) Rules
136 **HB/CTB** Sch 7 para 7(3) CSPSSA 2000
Other benefits s13(3) SSA 1998

2. **Appealing to the Upper Tribunal**

137 s11 TCEA 2007; *LS v Lambeth LB (HB)* [2010] UKUT 461 (AAC); [2011] AACR 27
138 s11(5)(d) and (e) TCEA 2007
139 s11 TCEA 2007
140 r2 TP(UT) Rules
141 r4 TP(UT) Rules; Practice Statement, *Delegation of Functions to Staff on or after 3 November 2008*, 30 October 2008
142 R(A) 1/72; R(SB) 11/83; R(IS) 11/99; R(I) 2/06
143 CIS/2345/2001; CH/4065/2001
144 CDLA/433/1999
145 CDLA/7980/1995; CH/5221/2001; CH/396/2002; CIB/2977/2002
146 CDLA/2748/2002
147 CSDLA/606/2003
148 CS/1939/1995; CDLA/5413/1999; CIB/303/1999
149 CDLA/3224/2001
150 CH/3594/2002
151 CDLA/1480/2006
152 CDLA/2997/2008 [2008] UKUT 6 (AAC)
153 R(IS) 4/93
154 R(DLA) 3/08; *SP v SSWP* [2009] UKUT 97 (AAC)
155 CJSA/322/2001; R(IS) 5/04
156 *Carpenter v SSWP* [2003] EWCA Civ 33, reported as R(IB) 6/03
157 CDLA/1456/2002; R(H) 1/03
158 *Basildon District Council v AM* [2009] UKUT 113 (AAC)
159 s11(3) TCEA 2007
160 s11(4)(a) TCEA 2007; r21(2) TP(UT) Rules. There is disagreement about whether you must always apply to the First-tier Tribunal first (ie, whether the Upper Tribunal can waive this requirement): *HM v SSWP* [2009] UKUT 40 (AAC); *MA v SSD* [2009] UKUT 57 (AAC)
161 r38(2), (5) and (6) TC(FT) Rules
162 para 11 Practice Statement, *Composition of Tribunals in Social Security and Child Support Cases in the Social Entitlement Chamber on or after 3 November 2008*, Tribunals Judiciary, 30 October 2008
163 r27(2) TP(FT) Rules; CSB/172/1990
164 r38(7) TP(FT) Rules
165 r39(3)-(5) TP(FT) Rules
166 r41 TP(FT) Rules
167 r38(3) TP(FT) Rules
168 r5(3)(a) TP(FT) Rules
169 r38(5) TP(FT) Rules
170 s9 TCEA 2007; r39(1) TP(FT) Rules
171 r41 TP(FT) Rules
172 r40(2) TP(FT) Rules
173 s9(4) and (5) TCEA 2007
174 *SE v SSWP* [2009] UKUT 163 (AAC); *AM v SSWP (IB)* [2009] UKUT 224 (AAC)
175 r40(3) and (4) TP(FT) Rules
176 r39(2) TP(FT) Rules
177 s11(4)(a) TCEA 2007; r21(2) TP(UT) Rules. There is disagreement about whether you must always apply to the First-tier Tribunal first (ie, whether the Upper Tribunal can waive this requirement): *HM v SSWP* [2009] UKUT 40 (AAC); *MA v SSD* [2009] UKUT 57 (AAC)
178 r21(4), (5), (6)(a) and (7) TP(UT) Rules; CSDLA/1207/2000
179 r7(1) and (2)(a) TP(UT) Rules
180 r21(7)(b) TP(UT) Rules
181 R(IS) 11/99; CDLA/5793/1997
182 CCS/1664/2001
183 r13(1) TP(UT) Rules
184 r22(1) and (2) TP(UT) Rules
185 s13(8)(c) TCEA 2007; r43 TP(UT) Rules; CDLA/3432/2001
186 r21(3)(b) TP(UT) Rules
187 r5(3)(a) TP(UT) Rules
188 r23 TP(UT) Rules
189 r5(3)(a) TP(UT) Rules
190 r22(2)(b) TP(UT) Rules
191 r17 TP(UT) Rules
192 r17(4) and (5) TP(FT) Rules
193 rr24 and 25 TP(UT) Rules
194 rr5(3)(a) and 25(2) TP(UT) Rules
195 r40(3)(b) TP(UT) Rules
196 r34 TP(UT) Rules

197 r36 TP(UT) Rules
198 r1(3) TP(UT) Rules, definition of hearing
199 Practice Statement, *Composition of Tribunals in Relation to Matters that Fall to be Decided by the Administrative Appeals Chamber of the Upper Tribunal on or after 1 October 2010*, 1 October 2010
200 R(I) 1/03
201 s12 TCEA 2007
202 r40 TP(UT) Rules
203 r42 TP(UT) Rules
204 r43 TP(UT) Rules
205 r5(3)(a) TP(UT) Rules
206 r48 TP(UT) Rules
207 s18 TCEA 2007; Direction, *Classes of Cases Specified Under Section 18(6) of the Tribunals, Courts and Enforcement Act 2007*
208 r28 TP(UT) Rules
209 r28(2) and (3) TP(UT) Rules
210 ss20 and 21 TCEA 2007; Act of Sederunt (Transfer of Judicial Review Applications from the Court of Session) 2008, No.357; *Currie, Petitioner* [2009] CSOH 145, [2010] AACR 8
211 *EF v SSWP* [2009] UKUT 92 (AAC), reported as R(IB) 3/09

3. **Procedural rules**

212 r2 TP(FT) Rules; r2 TP(UT) Rules
213 *MA v SSWP* [2009] UKUT 211 (AAC)
214 rr5, 6, 15 and 16 TP(FT) Rules; rr5-7, 15 and 16 TP(UT) Rules
215 r16(3) TP(FT) Rules; r16(3) TP(UT) Rules
216 r5(3(l) TP(FT) Rules; r5(3(l) TP(UT) Rules
217 r5(3(n) TP(UT) Rules
218 rr5, 6 and 15 TP(FT) Rules; rr5, 6 and 15 TP(UT) Rules; *SR v Bristol City Council* [2008] UKUT 7 (AAC)
219 r6(2) and (3) TP(FT) Rules; r6(2) and (3) TP(UT) Rules
220 r6(4) TP(FT) Rules; r5(4) TP(UT) Rules
221 r6(5) TP(FT) Rules; r6(5) TP(UT) Rules
222 r7 TP(FT) Rules; r7 TP(UT) Rules
223 CIB/4253/2004
224 r15(2)(b) TP(FT) Rules; r15(2)(b) TP(UT) Rules
225 r11 TP(FT) Rules; r11 TP(UT) Rules; CIB/1009/2004; CIB/2058/2004
226 r11(7) and (8) TP(FT) Rules; r11(5) and (6) TP(UT) Rules
227 r11(6)(b) TP(FT) Rules; r11(4)(b) TP(UT) Rules
228 r11(6)(a) TP(FT) Rules; r11(4)(a) TP(UT) Rules; *MP v SSWP (DLA)* [2010] UKUT 103 (AAC)
229 r8(1), (3)(a) and (5) TP(FT) Rules; r8(1), (3)(a) and (5) TP(UT) Rules
230 r8(5) and (6) TP(FT) Rules; r8(5) and (6) TP(UT) Rules
231 r8(2) and (4) TP(FT) Rules; r8(2) and (4) TP(UT) Rules
232 r8(3)(b) and (c) and (4) TP(FT) Rules; r8(3)(b) TP(UT) Rules
233 R(IS) 5/94
234 *LS v London Borough of Lambeth (HB)* [2010] UKUT 461 (AAC)
235 rr1(3), definition of 'respondent', and 8(7) TP(FT) Rules; rr1(3), definition of 'respondent', and 8(7) TP(UT) Rules
236 r8(8) TP(FT) Rules; r8(8) TP(UT) Rules
237 r5(3)(h) TP(FT) Rules; r5(3)(h) TP(UT) Rules; *MA v SSWP* [2009] UKUT 211 (AAC)
238 r31 TP(FT) Rules; r38 TP(UT) Rules
239 CDLA/1290/2004
240 CDLA/3680/1997
241 *MA v SSWP* [2009] UKUT 211 (AAC)
242 CDLA/5413/1999
243 CIS/566/1991; CS/99/1993
244 CIS/2292/2000
245 CIS/6002/1997; *R v Social Security Commissioner ex parte Angora Bibi* [2000] 23 May 2000, unreported (HC); CIB/1009/2004; CIB/2058/2004
246 CIS/3338/2001
247 *MH v Pembrokeshire (HB)* [2010] UKUT 28 (AAC)
248 s26 SSA 1998
249 s26(5) SSA 1998
250 rr5(3)(b) and 18 TP(FT) Rules
251 Practice Statement, *Composition of Tribunals in Social Security and Child Support Cases in the Social Entitlement Chamber on or after 3 November 2008*, 30 October 2008, para 10
252 r32 TP(FT) Rules; r39 TP(UT) Rules

4. **Appealing to the courts**

253 s13 TCEA 2007
254 s13(8)(c)-(e) TCEA 2007
255 s13(6) TCEA 2007; The Appeals from the Upper Tribunal to the Court of Appeal Order 2008, No.2834; r41.59 Rules of the Court of Session 1994
256 r44(1), (6)(a) and (7) TP(UT) Rules
257 *Fryer-Kelsey v SSWP* [2005] EWCA Civ 511, 21 April 2005, reported as R(IB) 6/05
258 r44(2), (3) and (5) TP(UT) Rules
259 r5(3)(a) TP(UT) Rules
260 r44(6) TP(UT) Rules
261 r45(3)-(5) TP(UT) Rules
262 s10 TCEA 2007; r45(1) TP(UT) Rules
263 s10(4) and (5) TCEA 2007
264 r46(2) and (3) TP(UT) Rules

265 r45(2) TP(UT) Rules
266 s13(3)-(5) TCEA 2007
267 r45(4)(b) TP(UT) Rules
268 Practice Direction 52.3
269 r52.3(4A) Civil Procedure Rules
270 See *Hanlon v Traffic Commission* [1988] SLT 802 and *Perfect Swivel v Dundee District Licensing Board* (No.2) [1993] SLT 112
271 *R(Cart) v The Upper Tribunal* [2011] UKSC 28, 22 June 2011; *Eba v Advocate General for Scotland* [2011] UKSC 29, 22 June 2011

5. **Time limits**
272 r5(3)(a) TP(FT) Rules; r5(3)(a) TP(UT) Rules
273 r2 TP(FT) Rules; r2 TP(UT) Rules
274 r2(2)(e) TP(FT) Rules; r2(2)(e) TP(UT) Rules
275 r23(4) TP(FT) Rules
276 r5(3)(a) TP(FT) Rules
277 r23(3) TP(FT) Rules
278 r23(5) and (8) TP(FT) Rules
279 r23(7)(b) TP(FT) Rules
280 **CB/GA** Reg 28(3) CG&GA(DA) Regs
HB/CTB Reg 19(5) HB&CTB(DA) Regs
Other benefits Reg 32(1) SS&CS(DA) Regs
281 *LS v London Borough of Lambeth (HB)* [2010] UKUT 461 (AAC)
282 **CB/GA** Reg 29A CB&GA(DA) Regs
HB/CTB Reg 19(5A) HB&CTB(DA) Regs
Other benefits Reg 32(4) SS&CS(DA) Regs
283 **CB/GA** Reg 30(1) and (2) CB&GA(DA) Regs
HB/CTB Reg 19(6) and (7) HB&CTB(DA) Regs
Other benefits Reg 32(5) and (6) SS&CS(DA) Regs
284 **CB/GA** Reg 30(4) CB&GA(DA) Regs
HB/CTB Reg 19(8) HB&CTB(DA) Regs
Other benefits Reg 32(7) SS&CS(DA) Regs
285 **CB/GA** Reg 30(5) CB&GA(DA) Regs
HB/CTB Reg 19(9) HB&CTB(DA) Regs
Other benefits Reg 32(8) SS&CS(DA) Regs
286 r21(7)(b) TP(UT) Rules
287 R(M) 1/87; R(I) 5/91
288 R(M) 1/87
289 CIS/147/1995

6. **Presenting your case**
290 R(SB) 6/82
291 r16 TP(FT) Rules
292 r15(1)(e) and (f) TP(FT) Rules
293 r15(2) TP(FT) Rules
294 CDLA/2014/2004
295 *Walsall Metropolitan Borough Council v PL* [2009] UKUT 27 (AAC)
296 *GL v SSWP* [2008] UKUT 36 (AAC)
297 R(DLA) 4/02; CIS/1481/2006 ; *DG v SSWP (DLA)* [2011] UKUT 14 (AAC)
298 CIB/2058/2004
299 r11(5) TP(FT) Rules; CDLA/1138/2003; CDLA/2462/2003
300 R(SB) 33/85; R(SB) 12/89
301 r15(1)(d) TP(FT) Rules; CDLA/2014/2004
302 CIS/4901/2002
303 *Walsall Metropolitan Borough Council v PL* [2009] UKUT 27 (AAC)
304 R(SB) 1/81
305 *SSWP v Cunningham* [2004] 6 August, ScotCS 211, reported as R(DLA) 7/04; R(DLA) 3/07
306 *Pepper v Hart* [1992] 3 WLR 1032, *The Times*, 30 November 1992
307 R(I) 12/75; *Dorset Healthcare Trust v MH* [2009] UKUT 4 (AAC)
308 R(SB) 22/86
309 R(I) 12/75; *Dorset Healthcare Trust v MH* [2009] UKUT 4 (AAC)
310 *CSBO v Leary*, reported as R(SB) 6/85; see generally CS/140/1991
311 R(G) 3/62; R(U) 4/88
312 R(U) 4/88
313 *Nancollas v Insurance Officer* [1985] 1 All ER 833 (CA), also reported as R(I) 7/85
314 r18 TP(UT) Rules

Chapter 47

Challenging decisions on statutory payments

This chapter covers:

This chapter explains the rules for challenging decisions on entitlement to statutory sick pay (SSP), statutory maternity pay (SMP), statutory paternity pay (SPP) and statutory adoption pay (SAP). These rules do not apply to challenging decisions on other benefits (except some decisions on national insurance contributions – see p768).

In this chapter, when the term First-tier Tribunal is used, it means the First-tier Tribunal (Tax) and when the term Upper Tribunal is used, it means the Upper Tribunal (Tax and Chancery). When the term SPP is used, it means both ordinary SPP and additional SPP.

Key facts

- Statutory sick pay (SSP), statutory maternity pay (SMP), statutory paternity pay (SPP) and statutory adoption pay (SAP) are normally paid by your employer (in some cases, your ex-employer) and your employer should make the initial decision on your entitlement.
- If you disagree with your employer's decision, or your employer has failed to make a decision, you can ask HM Revenue and Customs (HMRC) to decide whether you are entitled.
- You and your employer have the right to appeal against HMRC's decision on your entitlement. You can request that your appeal be decided either by an HMRC review or by the First-tier Tribunal. If you disagree with the HMRC review decision, you can still ask the First-tier Tribunal to consider your appeal.

- If you disagree with the decision of the First-tier Tribunal, you might be able to appeal to the Upper Tribunal. If you disagree with the Upper Tribunal's decision, you might be able to appeal to a court.
- If you are considering challenging your employer's decision on your entitlement to a statutory payment, consider how this might affect your employment. You may wish to consult an employment adviser to discuss this.

1. Information from your employer

If you have taken the necessary steps to request statutory sick pay (SSP), statutory maternity pay (SMP), statutory paternity pay (SPP) or statutory adoption pay (SAP) from your employer (see pp602 and 624), but your employer decides it is not liable to pay you (or if your employer has been paying you SSP, but it decides your period of entitlement has, or is due to, come to an end), it should provide you with details of its decision and the reasons for it within certain time limits. This also applies to a former employer for SMP, SPP and SAP.[1]

For SSP, your employer should normally provide this information on Form SSP1 or on its own computerised form if it contains the same information. For SMP, ordinary SPP, additional SPP and SAP, it is normally given on Form SMP1, OSPP1, ASPP1 or SAP1 respectively. The employer should also return certain evidence to you, such as your MATB1 form (see p603) or evidence you have provided to establish your SPP or SAP entitlement.

For SSP and SMP, you can also request a written statement from your employer, detailing in respect of the period before your request, its view on the:[2]

- days (or for SMP, weeks) you are entitled to SSP or SMP, and the reason why SSP or SMP is not payable for other days (or for SMP, other weeks);
- daily rate of SSP, or the weekly rate of SMP, to which you are entitled.

For SMP you also have the right to request this information from a former employer. If your request is reasonable, your employer (or former employer) should provide this information within a reasonable time.

2. Involving HM Revenue and Customs

If you disagree with your employer's decision on your entitlement to statutory sick pay (SSP), statutory maternity pay (SMP), statutory paternity pay (SPP) or statutory adoption pay (SAP), or if your employer has failed to make a decision, you can request that HM Revenue and Customs (HMRC) makes a formal decision on your entitlement.[3] There are time limits for doing so (see p1223).

If your employer has failed to make a decision or has not provided you with the information normally contained on Form SSP1, SMP1, OSPP1, ASPP1 or SAP1,

HMRC is likely to attempt to get your employer to provide this before it makes any decision on your entitlement.

It can take some time to get a final decision on your entitlement, so you should consider whether there are other benefits or tax credits which you can claim in the interim (see Chapter 1). If you claim employment and support allowance (ESA – see Chapter 10) while waiting for a decision on your SSP or maternity allowance (MA – see Chapter 21) while waiting for a SMP decision, the DWP will not normally make a decision on your entitlement to ESA or MA until HMRC has made a decision on your entitlement to SSP or SMP (because you will not qualify for ESA if you are entitled to SSP, nor for MA if you are entitled to SMP). For this reason, the DWP can request that HMRC makes a formal decision on your entitlement to SSP or SMP, if you have not already requested this yourself. Despite this, it is important not to delay a claim for ESA or MA or you may lose some weeks' benefit if the final decision is that you do not qualify for SSP or SMP.

Applying for a decision

How to apply for a decision from HM Revenue and Customs

You should normally apply on Form SSP14 (for SSP), SMP14 (for SMP), SPP14 (for ordinary and additional SPP) or SAP14 (for SAP), which can be obtained from the Statutory Payments Disputes Team (see Appendix 1). Send your application to the Statutory Payments Disputes team. Applications made to a local HMRC enquiry centre can also be accepted (for the address, see www.hmrc.gov.uk).

Time limits

Your application to HMRC must be made within six months of the earliest date for which your entitlement to SSP, SMP, SPP or SAP is in dispute.[4]

If you cannot obtain and return the correct form before the six-month deadline, you should apply for a decision by letter. Your letter *must* contain details of the period in respect of which your entitlement to SSP, SMP, SPP or SAP is at issue and the grounds (if any) on which your employer is refusing payment.[5]

If possible, you should send a copy of the SSP1, SMP1, OSPP1, ASPP1 or SAP1 form your employer has given you and evidence of your entitlement – eg, a medical certificate if you have been sick for more than seven days, a MATB1 form, or the 'matching certificate' from the adoption agency. However, do not delay your application if you do not have this information.

Requests for further information

On receiving your application, HMRC may contact you for further information and is likely to send a form to your employer to complete.

HMRC can require your employer to provide certain information and can impose a financial penalty on your employer if your employer fails do so. For example, if your employer has not notified you of its decision on your entitlement to SSP, SMP, SPP or SAP within the time limits, HMRC can impose a penalty, with added penalties for each day it fails to comply. However, in this situation if your employer does not comply, you should press HMRC to make its own decision on your entitlement.

HMRC can also request information from you if it is making a decision on your entitlement to SSP or SMP, or from you or your spouse/partner if it is making a decision on your entitlement to SPP or SAP.[6]

It is only likely to impose a financial penalty on you for not providing information or documents that it reasonably needs to decide your entitlement if you fraudulently or negligently make incorrect statements.[7]

HM Revenue and Customs' decision

HMRC may try to negotiate between you and your employer to settle the dispute. In order to do this, before it issues a formal decision on your application, it may send both you and your employer a written opinion on your entitlement to SSP, SMP, SPP or SAP. If you disagree with the opinion, you should write to HMRC, giving your reasons. HMRC may give you a deadline to object to its written opinion before it issues a formal decision. HMRC considers any new information you or your employer have provided and should then issue a formal decision on your entitlement.

In some cases, HMRC sends the formal decision without first issuing a written opinion. The formal decision is legally binding on the employer (see p1230 for the time limits for complying). However, both you and your employer have a right to appeal against it (see p1225).

Varying or superseding a decision

HMRC can change one of its own decisions by varying or superseding it.[8] It can **vary** its decision if it believes that the decision was wrong at the time it was made. The new decision may take effect from the date that the original decision would have had effect if the reason for the variation had been known. If you or your employer have appealed against a decision, HMRC may vary that decision at any time before the appeal is determined. If HMRC varies its decision, it must notify you and your employer of the new decision in writing.

HMRC can **supersede** an earlier decision if the decision has become incorrect for any reason – eg, if your circumstances have changed. The new decision will take effect from the date of your change in circumstances.

If HMRC varies or supersedes an earlier decision, either you or your employer can appeal against the new decision (see p1225).

3. Appealing against the decision

Who can appeal

Both you and your employer can appeal against a decision by HM Revenue and Customs (HMRC).[9] In this section, the rules are explained as if it is you, not your employer, who are the appellant. The same rules apply to your employer if your employer has appealed.

How to appeal

Your appeal should be made in writing to HMRC and should include your reasons for appealing.[10] Send your appeal to the Statutory Payments Disputes Team (see Appendix 1).

Time limits

Your appeal should reach HMRC within 30 days of the date on which HMRC's decision was issued (but see below).[11]

The 30-day time limit for appealing can be extended by HMRC as long as you request this in writing, you have a reasonable excuse for not having made your appeal within the time limit and your appeal was made without unreasonable delay.[12] If HMRC does not accept your late appeal, you can apply to the First-tier Tribunal for permission to appeal late (see p1228). If the First-tier Tribunal refuses the application, you can appeal to the Upper Tribunal .

You can request that your appeal be decided by either the First-tier Tribunal or by HMRC conducting a review. In addition to sending your written appeal to HMRC, you should notify:[13]

- the First-tier Tribunal in writing, that you want it to consider your appeal (see p1227); *or*
- HMRC in writing, that you want it to conduct a review. (If HMRC conducts a review and you disagree with its decision you can still apply to the First-tier Tribunal for a decision on your appeal, provided you apply within the time limits on p1227).

If, having made your appeal, you do not either ask the First-tier Tribunal to consider your appeal or HMRC to review its decision, HMRC can write to you, offering to review its decision (called an 'HMRC-initiated review' in this chapter). Before HMRC initiates a review it may try to settle the appeal (see below).

Until HMRC has issued a notification offering you a review, you can still notify the First-tier Tribunal that you want it to decide your appeal or request a review by HMRC yourself.

Note:

- In addition to the rules on reviews, HMRC can try to settle an appeal with the consent of all the parties at any time before the determination of the appeal. If, before the appeal is decided, an agreement is reached between HMRC and you (if you have appealed) or your employer (if your employer has appealed), the matter is treated as settled by agreement and the appeal lapses.[14]

- You can withdraw your appeal at any time before it is decided by notifying HMRC and your employer that you wish to do so. Your employer and HMRC have 30 days to object and, if no objection is made, your appeal will lapse.[15]

Review by HM Revenue and Customs

If you have requested that your appeal be decided by an HMRC review or if HMRC has initiated a review, before making its review decision HMRC must first notify you of its initial view on your entitlement. This will not necessarily be the same as its original decision on your entitlement.

Initial view on entitlement

If you have requested that your appeal be decided by an HMRC review, HMRC should send you its initial view on your entitlement within 30 days beginning with the date it receives your written request for a review, or longer if this is reasonable.[16] The same rules apply if it is your employer who has initiated the review.

If HMRC has initiated the review, HMRC should send its initial view on your entitlement with its offer of a review.[17] You then have 30 days starting on the date of HMRC's letter either to inform in writing:[18]

- HMRC that you want it to conduct the review (see below); *or*
- the First-tier Tribunal that you want it to decide your appeal (see p1227).

If this period has ended, an appeal can only be considered by the First-tier Tribunal if it gives permission (see p1228).

If you do not accept the offer of a review or notify the First-tier Tribunal that you want it to consider your appeal within the above time limit, HMRC will proceed as if you have agreed to its initial view on your entitlement and will treat the matter as settled by agreement. Notification of this should be sent to you and your employer, and your appeal will lapse.[19]

The review

After HMRC has issued its initial view on your entitlement (and, for HMRC-initiated reviews, provided you have accepted HMRC's offer of a review), a review should be carried out by an HMRC decision maker who was not involved in making the original decision. If you disagree with HMRC's initial view, it is important to write to explain why.

The decision maker must consider any representations you make, if these are made at a stage that gives her/him a reasonable opportunity to do so.[20]

HMRC should notify you of its review decision and the reasons for it within 45 days beginning with the date it:[21]

- notified you of its initial view of the matter, if you requested the review; *or*
- received your acceptance of its offer of a review, if HMRC initiated the review.

In either case, these time limits can be changed if you agree.

If HMRC does not notify you of its review decision within these time limits, its decision is taken to be the same as its initial view on your entitlement and HMRC must inform you of this.[22]

If you or your employer do not agree with HMRC's review decision, you may notify the First-tier Tribunal that you want it to consider your appeal. The time limit for doing so is 30 days beginning with the date of either:[23]

- HMRC's letter notifying you of its review decision; *or*
- if HMRC did not notify you of its review decision within the time limits, the date of its letter telling you it has adopted its initial view on your entitlement as its decision.

In the latter situation, you can appeal before receiving HMRC's letter, provided your appeal is made after the expiry of the time limits for making the review decision.

If you do not notify the First-tier Tribunal within these time limits, your appeal can only be considered by the First-tier Tribunal if it gives permission (see p1228).[24]

Appeals to the First-tier Tribunal

You can request that the First-tier Tribunal consider your appeal if:[25]

- you have missed the time limit for appealing against HMRC's original decision on your entitlement and HMRC does not agree to accept your late appeal (but see below);
- you want your appeal against HMRC's original decision on your entitlement to be decided by the First-tier Tribunal, rather than by an HMRC review (see p1225). If you do not notify the First-tier Tribunal before HMRC issues its initial view on your entitlement (see p1226) or sends you its offer of an HMRC-initiated review (see p1225), you can still request that the First-tier Tribunal consider your appeal in the followign circumstnaces.
- you have appealed and HMRC has initiated a review as described on p1225. Rather than accept the offer of a review, you can notify the First-tier Tribunal that you want it to decide your appeal. See p1226 for the time limits for doing so, and below if you miss the time limit;
- you requested that your appeal be decided by an HMRC review or accepted HMRC's offer of a review, but either you do not agree with the review decision or HMRC has not notified you of its review decision within the time limits. You can notify the First-tier Tribunal that you want it to determine your appeal. See above for the time limits for notifying the First-tier Tribunal and below if you miss the time limit.

Time limits

If you either miss the time limit for appealing against HMRC's original decision on your entitlement to SSP, SMP, SSP or SAP (and HMRC does not agree to accepting your late appeal), or one of the time limits for notifying the First-tier Tribunal that you want it to determine your appeal, you can still ask the First-tier Tribunal to consider your appeal but it must give its permission for the time limit to be extended. Although there are no specific rules about when the time limit can be extended,[26] the overriding objective of the rules is to enable a tribunal to deal with cases fairly and justly. Whether the First-tier Tribunal extends the time limit will depend on the circumstances of your case. Explain the circumstances when you apply for permission (see p1206 for guidance). As success is not certain, it is important to keep within the time limits if you can.[27]

Notifying the First-tier Tribunal

To request that the First-tier Tribunal considers your appeal, your written notice must contain:[28]

- your name and address, the name and address of anyone representing you and the address where you want the First-tier Tribunal to send any documents;
- the details of the decision you are appealing against;
- the grounds on which you are relying to make the appeal. If you are making a late application, you must also give your grounds for doing so; *and*
- the result you are looking for.

Use the 'Notice of Appeal (tax)' form, available from www.justice.gov.uk (click on link for tax tribunal) or telephone 0845 223 8080 (typetalk: 18001 0845 223 8080). Your notice should be sent to the First-tier Tribunal (Tax) (see Appendix 1). You must include a copy of the written record of the decision which you are appealing against and any statement giving the reasons for that decision (eg, the notification HMRC sent informing you of its decision), unless you do not have this information and cannot reasonably obtain it.

How the First-tier Tribunal decides your case

The First-tier Tribunal allocates your case to be considered in one of four ways: as a 'default paper case' (which is normally decided without a hearing unless you write to the First-tier Tribunal to request one), a 'basic case', a 'standard case' or as a 'complex case'.[29]

Further details of the procedures for each kind of case can be obtained from the First-tier Tribunal (Tax) leaflet *Making an Appeal* available from www.justice.gov.uk (search for 'making an appeal to the tax chamber').

The First-tier Tribunal can confirm the decision of HMRC or change HMRC's decision.[30] The Tribunal must send you a decision notice telling you of its decision and this may include its full written findings and the reasons for its decision.[31] If you disagree with the decision of the First-tier Tribunal, you may be able to appeal against it to the Upper Tribunal (see below).

In certain circumstances, you can apply for the First-tier Tribunal's decision to be set aside (there is a time limit for doing so), or the First-tier Tribunal can correct its own decision.[32] The First-tier Tribunal can also review its decision if you have applied for permission to appeal to the Upper Tribunal.[33]

4. Appeals to the Upper Tribunal

You and your employer can appeal to the Upper Tribunal (Tax and Chancery Chamber) against a decision of the First-tier Tribunal, but only on the grounds that the First-tier Tribunal has made an 'error of law' (see p1182).[34] The rules for making an appeal are almost the same as those for making an appeal to the Upper Tribunal (Administrative Appeals Chamber), described in Chapter 46, (although there are differences in the procedure for lodging an appeal and in the time limit for applying). The application for permission to appeal should be made to the First-tier Tribunal (Tax) and must normally be received no later than 56 days after the latest of the dates listed on p1185 (usually the date the First-tier Tribunal sent you its full written reasons for the decision). In some circumstances the First-tier Tribunal can give permission for you to appeal later than this.[35]

If you have not been sent the First-tier Tribunal's full written findings and reasons, you must obtain these before applying for permission to appeal. Write to the First-tier Tribunal to request these – your request must be received within 28 days of the date it sent you its decision notice. In some circumstances, this time limit can be extended.[36]

If the First-tier Tribunal refuses permission for you to appeal, you can apply to the Upper Tribunal for permission. Use Form FTC1, available from www.justice.gov.uk (search for 'FTC1').

See p1188 for the time limits for applying.[37] If, without a hearing, the Upper Tribunal refuses you permission to appeal, or gives permission subject to conditions or on limited grounds, you may apply for this decision to be reconsidered at a hearing. An application to do so must be made in writing and be received within 14 days of the date the Upper Tribunal sent you notice of its decision, although the Upper Tribunal has discretion to extend this time limit.[38] However, the Upper Tribunal has the power to make an order for costs (expenses in Scotland), so before making any application seek advice about whether you could be liable for costs if you were to lose your case.

See Chapter 46 for information on the procedures of the Upper Tribunal.

5. Appeals to the courts

You and your employer have the right to appeal against the decision of the Upper Tribunal to the Court of Appeal (the Court of Session in Scotland) on the grounds that the Upper Tribunal made an 'error of law' – ie, the Upper Tribunal interpreted the law incorrectly.[39]

Your application for permission to appeal should normally be made to the Upper Tribunal within one month of the date it sent you written reasons for its decision. This time limit can be extended with the permission of the Upper Tribunal.[40] See Chapter 46 for further details on appealing to the courts.

Seek advice from a solicitor, law centre or legal advice centre if you are considering appealing against the decision of the Upper Tribunal.

6. If your challenge is successful

If it is decided that your employer should pay you a statutory payment , your employer should pay you within the time limits detailed below, unless it has appealed against the decision. Your employer does not have to pay you until a final decision is given on appeal.

Time limits for payment

When it is decided by HM Revenue and Customs (HMRC) or on appeal that you are entitled to a statutory payment and no appeal against this decision has been made (or the matter has been finally determined), your employer should pay you on or before the first payday after either:[41]

- the day on which the employer is notified that the appeal has been disposed of; *or*
- the day the employer receives notification that leave to appeal has been refused, and there is no further opportunity to apply for leave; *or*
- in any other case, the day the time limit for appeal expires.

If, because of your employer's payroll methods, it is not practical for you to be paid at this time, your employer should pay you on or before your next payday after this date.

If your employer does not pay

If your employer does not pay you within the above time limits, HMRC should pay you (although HMRC states it will first contact your employer to try to get it to pay).[42] Write to HMRC's Statutory Payments Disputes Team (see Appendix 1) asking for payment. This applies even if your employer is insolvent, but only for payment owed for the period before the date of insolvency. For any period that falls after the date of insolvency, HMRC, rather than your employer, is automatically liable to pay you any statutory payment for which you are eligible.[43]

Notes

1. **Information from your employer**
1 ss130 and 132 SSAA 1992; reg 15 SSP Regs; reg 25A SMP Regs; reg 11 SPPSAP(A) Regs; reg 11 ASPP(BAAO)(A) Regs
2 ss14(3) and 15(2) SSAA 1992

2. **Involving HM Revenue and Customs**
3 s8 SSC(TF)A 1999
4 Reg 3 SSP&SMP(D) Regs; reg 13 SPPSAP(A) Regs; reg 13 ASPP(BAAO)(A) Regs
5 Reg 3 SSP&SMP(D) Regs; reg 13 SPPSAP(A) Regs; reg 13 ASPP(BAAO)(A) Regs
6 Reg 14 SSP Regs; reg 25 SMP Regs; reg 14 SPPSAP(A) Regs; reg 14 ASPP(BAAO)(A) Regs
7 s11(1) and (2) Employment Act 2002; s113A SSAA 1992
8 s10 SSC(TF)A 1999; regs 5 and 6 SSC(DA) Regs

3. **Appealing against the decision**
9 s11(2)(a) SSC(TF)A 1999
10 s12 SSC(TF)A 1999
11 s12(1) SSC(TF)A 1999
12 s49 TMA 1970; reg 9 SSC(DA) Regs
13 ss 49A, 49B, 49D and 49I TMA 1970; reg 7 SSC(DA) Regs
14 s49A(4) TMA 1970; reg 11 SSC(DA) Regs
15 Reg 11(5) SSC(DA) Regs
16 s49B(2) and (5) TMA 1970
17 s49C(2) TMA 1970
18 ss49C(3) and (8)and 49H TMA 1970
19 s49C(4) TMA 1970; reg 11 SSC(DA) Regs
20 s49E(4) TMA 1970
21 s49E(6) and (7) TMA 1970
22 s49E(8) and (9) TMA 1970
23 s49G TMA 1970
24 s49G(3) TMA 1970
25 ss49D, 49G and 49H TMA 1970
26 s49(2)(b) TMA 1970; r20(4) TP(FT)(TC) Rules
27 ss49(2), 49G(3) and (4) and 49H(3) and (4) TMA 1970; r2 TP(FT)(TC) Rules
28 r20 TP(FT)(TC) Rules
29 r23 TP(FT)(TC) Rules
30 Reg 10 SSC(DA) Regs
31 r35 TP(FT)(TC) Rules
32 rr37 and 38 TP(FT)(TC) Rules
33 r41 TP(FT)(TC) Rules

4. **Appeals to the Upper Tribunal**
34 s11 TCEA 2007; reg 12(2) SSC(DA) Regs
35 r39 TP(FT)(TC) Rules
36 rr5(3)(a) and 35(4) and (5) TP(FT)(TC) Rules
37 r21 TP(UT) Rules
38 rr5(3)(a)and 22(3)-(5) TP(UT) Rules

5. **Appeals to the courts**
39 s13(2) TCEA 2007; reg 12(2) SSC(D&A) Regs
40 r44 TP(UT) Rules

6. **If your challenge is successful**
41 Reg 9 SSP Regs; reg 29 SMP Regs; reg 42 SPPSAP(G) Regs; reg 34 ASPP(G) Regs
42 ss151(6), 164(9)(b), 171ZD(3), 171ZED(3) and 171ZM(3) SSCBA 1992; reg 9A SSP Regs; reg 7 SMP Regs; reg 43 SPPSAP(G) Regs; reg 35 ASPP(G) Regs
43 Reg 9B SSP Regs; reg 7(3) and (4) SMP Regs; reg 43(2) and (3) SPPSAP(G) Regs; reg 35(2) and (3) ASPP(G) Regs

Chapter 48

Social fund reviews

This chapter covers:

Key facts

- The social fund review system covers decisions on community care grants, budgeting loans and crisis loans.
- There are two stages: an internal review carried out by the DWP and a further review carried out by a social fund inspector at the Independent Review Service. There is no right of appeal to a tribunal.

Future changes: April 2013 and after

Major changes are taking place that affect the benefits and tax credits system (see Chapter 2). The Independent Review Service will not exist after April 2013, when the discretionary social fund is localised. See CPAG's *Welfare Rights Bulletin* for updates.

1. Internal reviews

Powers of review

The law on internal reviews is set out in legislation and legally binding social fund (SF) directions.[1] All decisions on community care grants (CCGs), budgeting loans (BLs) and crisis loans (CLs) made by decision makers are subject to review,[2] including:

- the refusal of a CCG or loan;
- the amount awarded;
- payment to a third party or in instalments;
- refusal to determine a repeat application (see p548);
- refusal to treat an application for a CL as an application for a CCG;
- overpayment decisions (see p1235).

Decisions about the repayment of loans are not subject to review, but you can ask for them to be reconsidered (see p563).

A reviewing officer *must* review a decision if:

- you apply for a review within the time limit (see below);[3] *or*
- a decision was based on a mistake about the law, the directions or a material fact, or was given in ignorance of a material fact. This can be conducted at any time.[4]

A reviewing officer *may* review a decision:

- if you misrepresented or failed to disclose a material fact, in which case any overpayment is recoverable;[5] *or*
- in such other circumstances as s/he thinks fit.[6]

In both of the above cases, the reviewing officer can conduct a review at any time. The second case offers wide (but discretionary) scope for reviews on any grounds, and at any time (eg, if you have missed the time limit for a mandatory review) with or without an application.

Procedure

Applying for a review

You must apply for a review of a decision by writing to the office where the decision was made within 28 days of the date the decision was issued to you.[7] Your application must include your grounds for requesting a review.[8] If somebody is making an application on your behalf, it must be accompanied by your written authority (unless the person is your appointee – see p1016).[9]

Late applications can be accepted for 'special reasons'.[10] 'Special reasons' are not defined. They could include reasons why the application is late (eg, ill health, domestic crisis or wrong advice) or any other reasons – eg, you will experience hardship without a review. If the DWP does not accept there are special reasons, get advice. You may have to threaten judicial review if its refusal is unreasonable (see p1202).

If your application is out of time, you can also ask a reviewing officer to conduct a discretionary review (see above).

The DWP can ask you to submit further information in connection with your application if reasonably required.[11]

You can withdraw your application in writing at any time.[12]

See p1235 for reviews relating to overpayment decisions.

Review interviews

If a CL or CCG decision is not wholly revised in your favour, you may be offered a phone interview. If this is difficult for you, ask for an interview in person instead.[13] Whichever interview you have, you can have someone with you to help explain your situation. Ask for an interpreter if you need one.

If a BL decision is not wholly revised in your favour, the reviewing officer must either phone or write to you to explain why and ask further questions if necessary.

During an interview you must be given an explanation of the reasons for the review decision and an opportunity to make representations and submit any additional evidence.[14] The reviewing officer must make an accurate written record of the interview, including your representations, which must be agreed with you.[15]

Decisions

You are entitled to a written decision on your application for review (whether or not you have had an interview), which must include notification of your right to request a further review by a social fund inspector (SFI).[16] There are no legal time limits for carrying out reviews and notifying decisions. The SF Independent Review Service has stated that all reviews should be carried out within 10 working days, and a review of a crisis loan decision relating to urgent living expenses should be completed on the day the request is received.[17] If there are unreasonable delays, complain to the SF manager and, if necessary, ask your MP or an advice agency to assist.

How review decisions are made

Community care grants and crisis loans

When carrying out a review about a CCG or CL, a reviewing officer must take into account the same circumstances and priorities that the decision maker does (see pp558 and 568).

The reviewing officer must also:[18]

- check whether the decision was correctly arrived at – eg, sustainable on the evidence, based on all relevant considerations and a correct interpretation of the law;
- check that the decision maker acted fairly and reasonably and exercised discretion properly;
- check that you were given the opportunity to put your case and that there was no bias;
- take into account all the circumstances that existed at the time of the original decision and any new evidence and relevant changes in circumstances since the decision was made.

The reviewing officer does not have to take into account any issue not raised by the application for review.[19]

Budgeting loans

When carrying out a review about a BL decision, a reviewing officer must have regard to the same factors as decision makers (see p561).[20] This means that s/he is bound by the factual criteria set out in the directions (see p547).

The reviewing officer must also take into account:[21]

- whether the decision was correctly arrived at and whether you had sufficient opportunity to put your case;
- your personal circumstances – ie, whether you are single or have a partner and whether you have children;
- any new loan debt you have;
- the district budget and the maximum amounts payable, from the time of the original decision up to the date of the review decision.

The reviewing officer does not have to take into account any issue not raised by the application for review.[22]

The above legal duties and restrictions mean that the scope for revision of a decision is very limited. In practical terms, unless your circumstances have changed or there has been an increase in the district budget and maximum awards, the decision will merely be confirmed by the reviewing officer.

Overpayments

A decision to award you a CCG or a loan can be reviewed at any time if you misrepresented or failed to disclose a material fact (see p1069). Any resulting overpayment is recoverable. An overpayment decision is most likely to be triggered by a decision that you were not entitled to a qualifying benefit when you applied for a CCG or BL. You are entitled to a written decision of any overpayment and can ask for a further review by a reviewing officer.[23]

The reviewing officer must:[24]

- check whether the decision was correctly arrived at and based on the evidence and law; *and*
- take into account all the circumstances of the misrepresentation or non-disclosure and any new evidence which has been produced.

You will then receive a new decision. If you are still dissatisfied, you can request a further review by an SFI (see p1236).[25]

Tactics

- Always consider requesting a review if you are dissatisfied with a decision. Although you could end up with a less favourable decision, any CCG you have received is only recoverable if you misrepresented or failed to disclose a material fact (see p1069), while a review decision to award you a lower loan, or no loan, has no practical effect if you have already been paid.
- Explain, as fully as possible, why you disagree with a decision. Make it clear that your application *is* for one of the allowable purposes (see Chapter 25) and why it should be given high priority. If you are unhappy about the amount awarded, explain and justify the reasonableness of the amount you asked for.
- Be prepared to receive a negative review decision and to pursue your case by requesting a further review by an SFI (see p1236).

2. Social fund inspector reviews

Powers of review

The law relating to reviews by social fund inspectors (SFIs) is set out in legislation and legally binding SFI directions.[26]

All decisions which have been reviewed by a reviewing officer are subject to further review by an SFI.[27]

The SFIs conduct their reviews independently of the DWP. They are part of the Independent Review Service for the social fund (SF) (see Appendix 1).

SFIs can:[28]

- confirm the decision of the reviewing officer; *or*
- substitute their own decision; *or*
- refer the case back to a reviewing officer at the DWP for redetermination (in practice, this happens in very few cases).

Procedure

Applying for a further review

You must apply for a further review in writing within 28 days of the date the review decision was issued to you.[29] You can apply by letter or on Form IRS1, *Did You Get What You Wanted?*, available from your local Jobcentre Plus office or the Independent Review Service website (see Appendix 1). Your application must include your grounds for requesting a further review (see p1237).[30] If somebody is applying on your behalf, you must send your written authority (unless the person is your appointee).[31] You should specifically authorise the person to make an application for further review by an SFI on your behalf. You need to do this even if you supplied written authority when you first applied for an internal review. Late applications can be accepted for 'special reasons' (see p1233).[32] If your case is urgent, state this and explain why.

You must send your application directly to the Independent Review Service office in Birmingham.[33]

Process

Reviews are almost always conducted on the basis of written information (papers received from the local DWP and any new evidence submitted). You have no right to an oral hearing, although an SFI can interview you, if necessary, at a mutually convenient location.[34]

Within a few days of receiving an application, the SFI dealing with your case should write to you setting out the main issues and facts of the case and any additional information s/he needs. You should also be sent copies of your application form, the decisions made by the SF decision maker and reviewing officer, and the local guidance on priorities. You will normally be given eight days to make any further comments or supply further information or evidence to the

SFI (either by telephone or on the reply form provided). It is important to look through the papers carefully and add anything relevant. You can request more time if you need it. The SFI will then decide the case.[35]

Decisions

You should receive a detailed written decision from the SFI. The Independent Review Service says it aims to clear all cases within 12 working days (23 days if further investigation is necessary). Crisis loan (CL) reviews relating to urgent living expenses should be dealt with within 24 hours.[36] If you are unhappy about an SFI decision, get advice. There is no right of appeal, but you can ask an SFI to reconsider her/his decision – eg, because it is unreasonable or wrong in law.[37] You can also apply for a judicial review of the decision (see p1202).

If a case is referred back to the DWP for another internal review, the SFI should identify the factors that need further consideration. A decision maker must redetermine the case and send you a new decision, with a full explanation of how this was reached, taking into account the SFI's comments.[38] If you are dissatisfied with the new decision, you have the right to request a further review by an SFI.

How social fund inspectors' decisions are made

When carrying out a further review, SFIs must take into account the same factors as reviewing officers when conducting internal reviews (see p1232).[39] This means they must exercise individual discretion in community care grant (CCG) and CL reviews, but they are bound by the weighting rules in budgeting loan reviews. See p1234 for reviews of overpayment decisions.

The High Court has ruled that it must be clear from an SFI's decision that s/he has taken the Secretary of State's guidance into account.[40] In another case, the High Court ruled that the SFI must apply the law at the time of the SFI decision, not the law at the time of the original SF officer's decision.[41]

SFI decision making tends to be of a much higher standard. SFIs are more independent and thorough and tend to be less bound by local budgets and guidance. Note, however, that the SFI is primarily concerned with ensuring that the DWP decision was 'reasonable' rather than 'right' – ie, that discretion was exercised reasonably and in accordance with the law.[42] Nevertheless, they overturn approximately half of all CCG and CL decisions.

Notes

1. **Internal reviews**
1 s38 SSA 1998; SF Dirs 31-39
2 s38 SSA 1998
3 s38(1)(a) SSA 1998
4 SF Dir 31
5 s38(1)(b) SSA 1998; s71ZA SSAA 1992; SF Dir 43
6 s38(1)(c) SSA 1998
7 Reg 2(1)(a) and (2)(a) SF(AR) Regs
8 Reg 2(4) SF(AR) Regs
9 Reg 2(6) SF(AR) Regs
10 Reg 2(3) SF(AR) Regs
11 Reg 2(5) SF(AR) Regs
12 SF Dir 37
13 SF Dir 33
14 SF Dir 34
15 SF Dir 35
16 SF Dir 36
17 IRS, *The Journal,* Issue 28, Summer 2004
18 SF Dirs 32 and 39
19 s38 SSA 1998
20 s38(7) SSA 1998
21 SF Dirs 32 and 39
22 s38(6) SSA 1998
23 SF Dir 44
24 SF Dirs 45 and 46
25 SF Dir 47

2. **Social fund inspector reviews**
26 s38 SSA 1998; SFI Dirs
27 s38(3) SSA 1998
28 s38(4) SSA 1998
29 Reg 2(1)(b) and (2)(b) SF(AR) Regs
30 Reg 2(4) SF(AR) Regs
31 Reg 2(6) SF(AR) Regs
32 Reg 2(3) SF(AR) Regs
33 Reg 2(1)(b)(ii)(bb) SF(AR) Regs
34 Part 7 para 14 SFG
35 IRS, *The Journal,* Issue 21, Spring 2002 and Issue 28, Summer 2004
36 IRS, *The Journal,* Issue 28, Summer 2004
37 s38(5) SSA 1998
38 SF Dir 38
39 s38 SSA 1998; SFI Dirs 1-5
40 *R v IRS ex parte Connell,* 3 November 1994, unreported (HC)
41 *R v SFI ex parte Ledicott* [1995] CO/2492/94 (HC)
42 SF Commissioner's Advice on SFI Dirs 1 and 2, 2 January 2002

Chapter 49

Discrimination and human rights

This chapter covers:

Key facts

- If the benefit rules treat you, and others in a similar situation, worse than another group of people, this may be unlawful under European law or under the Human Rights Act 1998.
- If the less favourable treatment is based on your sex, the European Equal Treatment Directive may help you.
- If the less favourable treatment is based on your sex, race, colour, language, religion, political or other opinion, national or social origin, association with a national minority, property, birth or other status, or on another ground, the Human Rights Act may help you.
- The Human Rights Act can help you if the benefit rules breach some of its other provisions, including the right to a fair trial, the right to a private and family life and the right to peaceful enjoyment of your possessions.

1. European law and discrimination between men and women

Social security benefits are not governed by British law alone. There are also regulations and Directives made by the European Union (EU) that apply directly in the UK and throughout the European Economic Area (EEA) (see Chapter 64).

In particular, there are a number of Directives designed to ensure that (subject to limited exceptions) social security benefits, occupational pensions, pay and other benefits from employment are received on an equal basis by both men and women. This chapter deals only with the EU rules that prevent discrimination in social security between men and women, but there are other anti-discrimination provisions in EU law that prevent discrimination on grounds of nationality. See Chapter 64.

British courts (including decision makers, the First-tier Tribunal and the Upper Tribunal) are obliged to apply EU law as well as domestic British law and, although British law has been amended to take these Directives into account, the EU rules override the British rules where the two still conflict.[1] Cases involving points of EU law which are not clear may be referred to the European Court of Justice (ECJ) in Luxembourg for a ruling. The ECJ is not the same as the European Court of Human Rights, which is an institution of the Council of Europe and operates from Strasbourg.

There has been a vast amount of caselaw in the ECJ and national courts on these anti-discrimination provisions and this *Handbook* cannot cover the subject comprehensively.[2] What follows is an outline of the general principles and what they mean in practical terms for people claiming benefits. If you think you may benefit from the principle of equal treatment, seek advice (see Appendix 2).

2. The principle of equal treatment

The 'principle of equal treatment' established by European Union Directive 79/7 is that:

> 'There shall be no discrimination whatsoever on ground of sex either directly, or indirectly by reference in particular to marital or family status.'[3]

'Discrimination' means treating one person less favourably than another. Indirect discrimination occurs when a rule appears to be neutral but, in practice, can be complied with by fewer members of one sex than the other and that rule cannot be justified for reasons other than discrimination based on sex.

For example, a rule which said that applicants for a job have to be at least 1.9m tall would be indirectly discriminatory even though it applied equally to women and men. This is because, in practice, fewer women than men are likely to qualify. Such a rule would be unlawful unless the employer could show a good, non-discriminatory, reason for employing only tall people.

It is often necessary to rely on statistical evidence to prove indirect discrimination. Governments cannot rely on purely financial reasons to justify a discriminatory practice.[4]

The principle of equal treatment only prohibits discrimination 'on ground of sex'. It does not prevent a government from discriminating on the grounds of marital or family status unless that amounts to a form of indirect discrimination on the grounds of sex. So a rule is not necessarily contrary to the Directive just because it differentiates between married (or cohabiting) people and single people.[5] On the other hand, a rule which differentiates between married men and married women or single men and single women is directly discriminatory on grounds of sex.

However, this broad general principle is subject to a number of limitations and exceptions (known as '**derogations**'). This means that you have to ask three questions.

- Is the benefit you are claiming (or your liability to pay contributions) covered by the Directive? Only schemes for benefits that cover certain risks are subject to the principle of equal treatment.
- Does the Directive apply to you? You are only entitled to benefit from the principle of equal treatment if you are a member of the working population (see p1242).
- Does the Directive include a derogation which applies in your case? If so, the government is allowed to discriminate against you.

3. **Which benefits are covered**

Directive 79/7 applies to schemes for state benefits that are designed to protect against:[6]

- sickness;
- invalidity;
- old age;
- accidents at work and occupational diseases;
- unemployment.

Most contributory benefits are covered by the Directive. However, whether or not a benefit is contributory is not the crucial factor in deciding whether it falls within the scope of the Directive. Certain non-contributory benefits, such as carer's allowance, severe disablement allowance and industrial injuries benefits are within its scope.[7]

The Directive can also apply to benefits that are intended to supplement or replace the schemes referred to above.[8] For example, a commissioner decided that income-based jobseeker's allowance (JSA) was covered as it is a benefit that protects against the risk of unemployment.[9] A similar approach has been taken by the Court of Appeal.[10] A commissioner has held that pension credit falls within the scope of the Directive as an old-age benefit.[11] The same principle should apply to all types of employment and support allowance (ESA), which comprise both contributory and non-contributory elements, as well as ESA in youth.

Income support, housing benefit and council tax benefit are not covered by the Directive, so discrimination arguments about these benefits need to be brought under alternative provisions – eg, the Human Rights Act (see p1247).

Certain risks are specifically excluded from the Directive – in particular, positive discrimination for maternity allowances and the different pension ages for men and women. Widows' and widowers' benefits and family benefits (eg, child benefit and child tax credit), are also excluded from the scope of the Directive.

4. **Who is covered**

Directive 79/7 applies to you if you are a member of the working population. There is no requirement to have moved from one member state to another in order to fall within its scope. If you are not a member of the working population, you cannot use the Directive to stop the government discriminating against you, even if the benefit which you are claiming is covered.

The **'working population'** is defined as being:[12]

- workers – ie, people in employment;
- self-employed people;
- people seeking employment;
- workers and self-employed people whose jobs have been interrupted by illness, accident or involuntary unemployment;
- workers and self-employed people who have retired or become unable to work because of invalidity.

This means that to be covered by the Directive you must have been either working or actively looking for work when you became affected by one of the risks set out on p1241.[13] So, for example, the Directive does not apply to you if:

- you have been so ill or disabled since before you reached the age of 16 that you have never been able to contemplate working or looking for work; *or*
- you stopped working for a reason which is not included in the list of risks on p1241 (eg, because you were pregnant) and before you began to look for work again you became too ill to work.

It is not necessary for the risks to be experienced by you personally. In one case, a woman who gave up work to look after her severely disabled mother was held to be a member of the working population because her work had been interrupted by invalidity, even though it was the invalidity of her mother not her own.[14]

5. Exceptions to the principle of equal treatment

The Directive permits member states to adopt or continue discriminatory rules on certain aspects of entitlement to benefits even if they are within its scope.

Discriminatory rules which may be lawful are those which:[15]

- set a different age for men and women to become entitled to retirement pensions. This also covers rules that deal with the possible consequences for other benefits of having different pension ages;
- allow people who have looked after children to claim retirement pensions and other benefits on advantageous terms;
- allow special treatment for people who, before 22 December 1984, opted 'not to acquire rights or incur obligations under a statutory scheme'. This is intended to cover the rules on married women's reduced national insurance contributions (see p772).

European Economic Area states are supposed to keep these discriminatory rules under review to ensure that they are still justified in the light of social developments,[16] and to notify the European Commission of the measures that they have taken to do so.[17]

Perhaps more importantly, the European Court of Justice has repeatedly held that the elimination of sex discrimination is a fundamental right, which it has a duty to protect. Therefore, it will scrutinise any exceptions by member states to ensure that the measures are proportional.[18] This means, in each case, the member state that made the rule must establish that the discriminatory means adopted are an appropriate way of achieving the ends.

6. Equal treatment and benefits

Difference in pension age

In the UK, a lot of the cases that have come before the courts have been related to the derogation that allows different pension ages and any possible consequences arising from this[19] – eg, whether it is lawful to withdraw or reduce earnings-replacement benefits (eg, contribution-based jobseeker's allowance (JSA), incapacity benefit, contributory employment and support allowance (ESA), severe disablement allowance (SDA), carer's allowance (CA) and reduced earnings allowance (REA)), when a claimant reaches pension age. In most cases, the effect of this is that women are denied benefits that are paid to men of the same age.

It is clear that not just any connection between a benefit and pension age is sufficient for the derogation to apply. The question is on how close the link must be before it is covered.

This question has been the subject of a number of European Court of Justice (ECJ) decisions. In the *Thomas* case, the Court ruled that different pension ages for men and women in non-contributory benefits such as CA and SDA were contrary to Directive 79/7 and, therefore, unlawful.[20] As a result, British law was amended to bring the rules on non-contributory benefits into line with the law as declared by the ECJ.

In the *Equal Opportunities Commission (EOC)* case, the ECJ held that the provisions in the UK's state pension scheme which require men to pay national insurance contributions for 44 years and women for 39 years to qualify for the same full basic state retirement pension were authorised by the Directive.[21]

The decision in the *Graham* case was that the DWP could lawfully:[22]

- reduce invalidity benefit (now abolished) to pension rate at 60 for women and 65 for men;
- take invalidity benefit away altogether from women at 60 and men at 65; *and*
- pay extra benefit to men who became incapable of work between the ages of 55 and 60 and not to women in the same position.

A commissioner has considered whether the same discriminatory age rules contravene the Directive.[23] The commissioner held that there was a possible contravention of the Directive in spite of the ECJ judgment in *Graham*. It was significant in the case before the commissioner that incapacity had arisen after pension age. This was important because it may not be lawful to limit the contributions that a claimant has paid to those paid before pension age where that age is different for women from that for men. However, to enforce that right, the claimant would be required to pay outstanding contributions after age 60.

By contrast, in the *Richardson* case, it was held that the discriminatory treatment of men in respect of free prescriptions for those over retirement age unlawfully discriminated against men, since there was no necessary or objective link to pension ages.[24] The Court followed a similar line in the *Taylor* case, in which it was held that the refusal of winter fuel payments to men aged between 60 and 64 was in breach of Directive 79/7, as men were unlawfully discriminated against.[25]

The combined effect of these cases is that, to be covered by the derogation for 'the possible consequences for other benefits' of setting different pension ages for men and women, the discriminatory rule must be necessary *either*:

- to avoid disturbing the financial equilibrium of the social security system; *or*
- to ensure coherence between the retirement pension scheme and other benefit schemes.

Applying these tests, the Court has held (in general terms) that for contributory benefits (*Graham*) or the liability to pay national insurance contributions (*EOC*), a discriminatory link to pension age is lawful, but for non-contributory benefits (*Thomas*) such discrimination is unlawful.

The ECJ has considered the discriminatory rules in respect of REA. REA is not contributory, although the requirement that the claimant must have been an 'employed earner' at the time of the industrial accident or the onset of the prescribed disease means that, in practice, many REA claimants would have been paying, or liable to pay, Class 1 contributions.[26] Although the Advocate General gave an opinion that was favourable, the ECJ held that the discrimination within the REA regulations is objectively justified and, therefore, exempt from the prohibition on discrimination under Directive 79/7.[27]

It may be possible to argue that the UK rule which does not allow a woman to claim JSA beyond pension age is discriminatory. This has become a particularly important issue following the introduction of the 'right to reside test' (see p1447), because in order to have a right to reside and claim certain benefits some people have to sign on.

Shared care

In the case of *Hockenjos* before the Court of Appeal, it was argued that the income-based JSA rules discriminated against a man who had shared care of his two children with his separated partner.[28] Although the children spent equal periods of time with each parent, only the mother received an additional amount of income-based JSA for the children because she was the parent who received child benefit for them. For couples, the child benefit regulations give priority to female claimants. If a couple subsequently separate, it was argued that the rules favour the person already in receipt of child benefit and, therefore, discriminate against men and are contrary to the Directive. The Court of Appeal referred the case back to the commissioner to decide on the discrimination point. The commissioner subsequently held that where a person is able to rely on Directive 79/7, receipt of child benefit should not be the determining factor in deciding who has responsibility for a child.[29] The case was further appealed to the Court of Appeal. The Court held that, in genuine shared care cases, linking increases in JSA to child benefit for dependent children for whom there is shared responsibility is discriminatory and, therefore, contrary to Directive 79/7. Consequently, in such cases, both parents are entitled to the child addition of income-based JSA for their children. The Court further held that a person would be considered to be sharing the care of her/his child if s/he is caring for her/him 104 nights or more a year.

The Secretary of State applied for leave to appeal to the House of Lords but it was refused.

A fresh claim for the addition is not likely to succeed because child additions in income-based JSA have been abolished for claims made after April 2004. Instead, claimants are expected to claim child tax credit (CTC). In theory, it is possible to make a similar argument in respect of CTC, but CTC does not fall under this area of European Union (EU) law and, therefore, the discrimination argument would have to be made by relying on human rights law. This is more difficult and the courts have been largely unsympathetic to human rights' challenges in social security. The Upper Tribunal rejected a similar argument based on Articles 14 and 1 of the European Convention on Human Rights in respect of CTC. The Court of Appeal dismissed the appeal, holding that: 'There may well be a better or fairer way of distributing child tax credit, but a particular policy choice has been made and it cannot in our judgment be characterised as unreasonable or as being manifestly without reasonable foundation.' The Supreme Court was to hear a further appeal in March 2012.[30]

Income-based jobseeker's allowance

Cases have focused on discrimination in the income-based JSA rules. For example, in one case, a woman successfully argued that a student who was pregnant and temporarily gave up her course could claim income-based JSA.[31] The UK regulations that excluded her from benefit were discriminatory as they would have far greater impact on women. However, the decision was subsequently overturned by the Court of Appeal.[32] The Court decided that the JSA regulations were not directly discriminatory against pregnant women or against women generally and were not, for that reason, in breach of the Directive. The regulations make no express distinction between men and women, nor do they seek to deal with whether a woman is pregnant or not. What they do is define student status in such a way that any full-time student who interrupts her/his course will be deemed to remain a student and so be ineligible for JSA until the last day of the course (or an earlier date if s/he abandons it or is dismissed from it). In this case, therefore, the claimant's ineligibility for JSA derived from the fact that she was a student, not from the fact that she was pregnant.

Another case considered whether the requirement to be available for work for 40 hours a week in order to qualify for JSA was indirectly discriminatory. The commissioner found that the rule could not be discriminatory because the JSA regulations allowed certain people to be exempt from this condition. In particular, those with caring responsibilities can be exempt from the 40 hours a week requirement provided the restrictions are reasonable.[33]

A more successful outcome was found in a number of joined cases that looked at the discriminatory effect of the JSA rules on part-time staff employed in schools and colleges. The rules meant that these people were treated as working during periods when they received no pay. Consequently, they were unable to claim income-based JSA. The commissioners found this rule to be incompatible with Article 4 of Directive 79/7 and decided that it should be struck down – ie, that the discriminatory rules could not be applied.[34] The same discriminatory rules operate within the income support (IS) regulations, but as IS is not within the scope of the Directive, it is not possible to challenge them in the same way.

The anti-test case rules

The anti-test case rules in UK law limit backdating of benefit if a claimant relies on a court or Upper Tribunal decision in another case in order to claim (see p1149).

In some cases, this limit may be in breach of EU law. In the case of *Emmott,* the ECJ disapplied a national rule on the time limits for taking judicial review proceedings.[35] However, in *Johnson,* the ECJ ruled that the anti-test case provisions were not in breach of EU law.[36] In another case (*Steenhorst Neerings),* the ECJ held that a domestic law that limits the period prior to a claim for which benefit can be claimed is not inconsistent with EU law.[37] A commissioner has considered the application of UK time limits for claims and the anti-test case rule and held that the anti-test case rules do not breach Directive 79/7.[38]

Gender recognition

There has been a focus on whether the Gender Recognition Act 2004 complies with Directive 79/7. The ECJ held in the case of *Richards* that Article 4 of the Directive prevents legislation that denies a person who has undergone male-to-female gender reassignment her entitlement to a retirement pension purely because she has not reached the age of 65 (and when a woman would be entitled at the age of 60).[39] Commissioners have also considered a number of issues relating to gender recognition and held that a person who has changed gender from male to female can claim retirement pension from the age of 60.[40]

7. The Human Rights Act

Key aspects of the Act

The Human Rights Act 1998 came into effect on 2 October 2000 and applies to decisions made on or after this date.[41] It incorporates into UK law most of the Articles of the European Convention on Human Rights.[42] For social security purposes, all of the relevant provisions of the Convention now form part of our domestic law.

The First-tier Tribunal, Upper Tribunal or court must take account of any relevant caselaw of the European Court of Human Rights (ECtHR) when deciding an appeal in which a human rights issue arises.[43] However, where there is a conflict between a UK court and the ECtHR, the decision of the UK court should generally be followed.[44]

In addition, all legislation must be applied, *so far as it is possible to do so,* in a way which is compatible with the Convention.[45] This duty applies to all social security decision makers (eg, Secretary of State decision makers, the First-tier Tribunal and the Upper Tribunal) and applies regardless of whether the legislation in question was made before October 2000 or after.[46]

This obligation is a strong one. It may require words to be 'read into' the statutory provision concerned in order to remove a breach of the Convention (as long as this stops short of creating a new and different legal rule) and decision makers should strive to find a Convention-compatible reading of the statute or regulations at issue.[47]

Relevant Articles of the Convention

The Articles of the Convention most likely to be relevant in social security are:

- Article 6(1): right to a fair trial;
- Article 8: right to respect for private and family life, home and correspondence;
- Article 1 of the First Protocol: protection of property;
- Article 14: prohibition of discrimination (although you cannot rely on this alone; it must be combined with a breach of another Article).

In addition, Article 2 of the First Protocol (right to education) could be relevant.

Note: Article 14 will often be needed in social security cases to supplement the other Articles because of the difficulty of bringing social security within those Articles.

Key aspects of relevant Articles

Article 6(1)

'In the determination of his civil rights and obligations or any criminal charge against him, everyone is entitled to a fair and public hearing within a reasonable time by an independent and impartial tribunal established by law.'

Article 6 should cover any social security benefit where there is no element of discretion. Whether the benefit is contributory or non-contributory, or means tested or non-means tested, should not matter.[48] Child tax credit and working tax credit fall within Article 6.[49]

The discretionary social fund may be excluded, but this is not certain because the discretion that appropriate officers have is constrained (especially for budgeting loans). *Ex gratia* payments made by the Secretary of State and discretionary housing payments are almost certainly excluded.

The term 'fair … hearing' means that a claimant must:

- have real and effective access to a court. Although access to a court, the First-tier Tribunal or the Upper Tribunal may be restricted in a particular case or class of cases,[50] any restriction must not impair the very essence of the right and must both be proportionate and pursue a legitimate aim;[51]
- have a real opportunity of presenting her/his case;
- be given a reasoned decision; *and*

- have 'equality of arms' with her/his opponent.[52] This includes the right to have a representative. In an appropriate case, there may be a right to paid representation.[53] However, the test here is a broad one. 'Equality of arms' only requires that a claimant is not placed under a substantial disadvantage compared with her/his opponent – eg, the Secretary of State or HM Revenue and Customs.[54] This rule was held to have been breached when the DWP failed to ensure the attendance of one of its staff members as a witness at an appeal hearing[55] and when it failed to provide an appeal tribunal with the claimant's previous personal capability assessments.[56]

'Public hearing' includes the concept of a right to an oral hearing, but this will usually be confined to a hearing by the First-tier Tribunal.[57]

'Within a reasonable time' has not been interpreted very beneficially as far as social security cases are concerned, with the ECtHR only finding breaches of this criterion where there were delays of four years and more.[58] Delays of seven months[59] and one year[60] before an appeal is heard have been found to be reasonable. A delay of five years in processing an appeal and forwarding it to a tribunal was found to breach Article 6, but the claimant was not entitled to have his appeal allowed.[61] Much, therefore, depends on the circumstances and, in particular, the benefit in question.

'Independent and impartial tribunal' includes the *appearance* of impartiality. The test of bias is 'real possibility of bias'.[62] This is an objective test based on the circumstances of the case and whether these would lead a fair-minded observer to conclude that there was a real possibility of bias.[63]

Note: a breach of Article 6 can be reviewed or appealed, if the court itself complies with Article 6.[64]

Article 8

'Everyone has the right to respect for his private and family life, his home and his correspondence.

There shall be no interference by a public authority with the exercise of this right except such as is in accordance with the law and is necessary in a democratic society in the interests of national security, public safety or the economic wellbeing of the country, for the prevention of disorder or crime, for the protection of health or morals, or for the protection of the rights and freedoms of others.'

This Article may impose an obligation on the state to ensure there is effective respect for private or family life – eg, by regulating the conduct of people. This does not extend to an obligation to provide any particular social security benefit.

Benefits that promote respect for family life or the home may be covered by Article 8.[65] However, the income support (IS) and jobseeker's allowance schemes are not, in general, covered by Article 8.[66]

'Family life' extends beyond formal and 'legitimate' relationships – eg, to children whose parents are not married.[67]

'Private life' covers the right to develop personally as well as create relationships with others,[68] and can include protection of a person's physical and psychological integrity.[69] However, it is not a breach of the right to respect for private life to film a disability living allowance claimant in public to check whether s/he is entitled to the benefit.[70] **Note:** wide discretion is given to national governments in deciding how the right in question should be 'respected', and Article 8(2) provides a get-out for governments where there is a *prima facie* breach of Article 8(1).

Article 1 of the First Protocol

'Every natural or legal person is entitled to the peaceful enjoyment of his possessions. No one shall be deprived of his possessions except in the public interest and subject to the conditions provided for by law and by the general principles of international law.

The preceding provisions shall not, however, in any way impair the right of a State to enforce such laws as it deems necessary to control the use of property in accordance with the general interest or to secure the payment of taxes or other contributions or penalties.'

This Article will be breached if:

- the state interferes with the peaceful enjoyment of the claimant's possessions; *or*
- the claimant has been deprived of possessions by the state; *or*
- the claimant's possessions have been subjected to control by the state.

Both contributory and non-contributory benefits which arise as a matter of right are 'possessions' under Article 1.[71]

Even if your benefit is a 'possession', this Article gives no general right to be paid it at a particular rate unless the reduction in your benefit is so substantial that it affects 'the very substance of the right'.[72] In a case concerning the reduction of retirement pension for hospital inpatients, the following factors were listed as helping to determine whether there was deprivation.[73]

- Did the provision in question reduce a benefit previously in payment?
- Was the provision in force throughout the time when the claimant was paying relevant contributions?
- How close was the link between the benefit and payment of contributions?
- The amount of the reduction in benefit.

Note: as with Article 8, states have a wide get-out in accordance with the 'public interest' or 'general interest'.

Article 14

'The enjoyment of the rights and freedoms set forth in this Convention shall be secured without discrimination on any ground such as sex, race, colour, language, religion, political or other opinion, national or social origin, association with a national minority, property, birth or other status.'

It is important to note that this Article only comes into play if one of the other Articles applies, though it is not necessary to demonstrate that the other Article has been breached. It includes a long list of different sorts of discrimination, with a catch-all 'or other status'. This covers 'age',[74] 'residence'[75] and being homeless.[76] It should also cover discrimination on the grounds of disability. The 'status' must amount to a personal characteristic.[77]

It covers indirect, as well as direct, discrimination. The test for indirect discrimination is whether the effect of a rule on a particular group is 'disproportionately prejudicial'.[78]

Only different treatment of people 'placed in an analogous situation' falls within Article 14.

It will be breached if a measure creates differential treatment that does not pursue a legitimate aim, or if it is disproportionate to the aim pursued.[79] Administrative convenience is not a legitimate aim.[80] Although very weighty reasons are needed to justify discrimination based on race or sex,[81] that has to be balanced against the fact that judgements about economic and social strategy are generally for governments to make and so may only be disagreed with by courts or tribunals if the judgement is 'manifestly without reasonable foundation'.[82]

Article 2 of the First Protocol

'No person shall be denied the right to education. In the exercise of any functions which it assumes in relation to education and to teaching, the State shall respect the right of parents to ensure such education and teaching in conformity with their own religious and philosophical convictions.'

This Article applies to both school education and further and higher education, which may provide new scope for arguments in respect of the problems created for students by the IS and housing benefit (HB) rules in particular.[83]

The Article, however, is expressed in the negative, so it probably does not create any duty on a state to subsidise education.

Using the Human Rights Act

For most social security cases, there are no special courts or procedures that need to be used if you want to bring a challenge that relies on the Human Rights Act. Arguments using the Act can, therefore, be used at the First-tier Tribunal, the Upper Tribunal and with social fund inspectors, and the ordinary time limits for bringing such challenges apply (see Chapters 45 and 46).[84] In addition, guidance has been issued concerning social security (and child support) appeals, which recommends the following.

- Any Human Rights Act challenge should be raised at as early an opportunity as possible – eg, in the grounds of the appeal.
- Such grounds of appeal need to:
  - identify the rule, regulation or practice which it is alleged breaches the Act and the Article(s) of the Convention;
  - set out the Articles of the Convention which it is claimed have been breached, and explain why they have been breached; *and*
  - set out the relevant supporting caselaw (and provide copies of the cases).
- Grounds of appeal which fail to do the above and merely state that the decision is in breach of the Convention are unlikely to succeed.
- Raising an argument relying on the Convention for the first time at the hearing, when it could have reasonably been raised in advance, will almost certainly lead to an adjournment of the appeal.[85]

The starting point for any relevant decision-making body considering a Human Rights Act challenge is to decide whether the statute, regulation, rule or practice at issue is compatible with the relevant Articles of the Convention, or whether it can be read 'so far as it is possible to do so' in such a way as to make it compatible with the Convention. However, if the legislation cannot be interpreted in a way which makes it compatible with the Convention, the following apply.

- If the legislation is contained in an Act of Parliament, the First-tier Tribunal, Upper Tribunal or social fund inspector has to apply it as it stands.[86] Even the higher courts (High Court, Court of Appeal, Court of Session in Scotland and House of Lords) are limited to issuing what is known as a 'declaration of incompatibility' in this situation,[87] which does not change the legislation[88] and the government minister may consider amending the legislation.[89]
- If the legislation in question is contained in a regulation, the First-tier Tribunal, the Upper Tribunal or social fund inspector may disapply the (incompatible) regulation,[90] unless the Act under which the regulation was made is so prescriptive that it required an incompatible regulation to be made. In this latter case, the First-tier Tribunal, Upper Tribunal or social fund inspector cannot disapply the regulation,[91] and the remedy here is again limited to seeking a declaration of incompatibility from the higher courts.

Challenges in social security using the Human Rights Act and the Convention are difficult and need specialist input. If you have a case in which a Human Rights Act argument arises, seek specialist advice (see Appendix 2).

Notes

1. **European law and discrimination between men and women**
   1 s2 ECA 1972
   2 For a detailed account see McCrudden (ed), *Equality of Treatment Between Women and Men in Social Security*, Butterworths, 199

2. **The principle of equal treatment**
   3 Art 4(1) Directive 79/7/EEC
   4 *M A De Weerd (née Roks) and Others v Bestuur van de Bedrijfsvereniging voor de Gezondheid, Geestelijke en Maatschappelijke Belangen and Others*, C-343/92 [2004] ECR, unreported
   5 R(SB) 6/91

3. **Which benefits are covered**
   6 Art 3(1)(a) Directive 79/7/EEC
   7 *Thomas v Secretary of State for Social Security*, C-328/91 [1993] ECR, unreported
   8 Art 3(1)(b) Directive 79/7/EEC
   9 R(JSA) 3/02
   10 *Hockenjos v Secretary of State for Social Security* [2001] EWCA Civ 624 (CA)
   11 CPC/4177/2005

4. **Who is covered**
   12 Art 2 Directive 79/7/EEC
   13 *Achterberg-te Riele and Others v Sociale Verzekeringsbank*, C-48/88, C-106-107/88 [1989]
   14 *Drake v CAO*, C-150/85 [1986] ECR, unreported

5. **Exceptions to the principle of equal treatment**
   15 Art 7(1) Directive 79/7/EEC
   16 Art 7(2) Directive 79/7/EEC
   17 Art 8(2) Directive 79/7/EEC
   18 *Johnston v Chief Constable of the Royal Ulster Constabulary* [1986] ECR 723

6. **Equal treatment and benefits**
   19 Art 7(1)(a) Directive 79/7/EEC
   20 *Thomas v Secretary of State for Social Security*, C-328/91 [1993] ECR, unreported
   21 *R v Secretary of State for Social Security ex parte EOC*, C-9/91 [1992] ECR I-04297
   22 *Graham v Secretary of State for Social Security*, C-92/94 [1995] ECR, unreported
   23 R(IB) 5/04
   24 *R v Secretary of State for Health ex parte Richardson*, C-137/94 [1995] ECR, unreported
   25 *R v Secretary of State ex parte Taylor*, C-382/98 [1999] ECR, unreported
   26 It is possible to be an employed earner but not liable to pay NI contributions if you are in part-time or low-paid work and earn less than the lower earnings limit.
   27 *Hepple and Others v CAO*, C-196/98, reported as R(I) 2/00
   28 *Hockenjos v Secretary of State for Social Security* [2001] EWCA Civ 624 (CA)
   29 R(JSA) 1/05; R(JSA) 2/05
   30 CTC/2608 [2009] UKUT 24 (AAC); *Humphreys v HMRC* [2010] EWCA Civ 56, 11 February 2010
   31 R(JSA) 3/02
   32 *Secretary of State for Social Security v Walter* [2001] EWCA Civ 1913 [2002] ICMLR 794, reported as R(JSA) 3/02
   33 R(JSA) 4/02; regs 6 and 13(4) JSA Regs
   34 R(JSA) 4/03
   35 *Emmott v Minister for Social Welfare*, C-208/90 [1991] ECR 1-4569
   36 *Johnson v Chief Adjudication Officer*, C-410/92 [1994] ECR I-5483
   37 *Steenhorst Neerings v Bestuur van de Bedrijfsvereniging voor Detailhandel, Ambachten en Huisvrouwen*, C-338/91 [1993] ECR I-5475
   38 CSP/503/2007; CP/1425/2007; CP/2862/2007
   39 *Richards v SSWP*, C-423/04 [2006], reported as R(P) 1/07
   40 CP/1425/2007; CSP/503/2007; CP/2862/2007

7. **The Human Rights Act**
   41 ss7(1)(b) and 22(4) HRA 1998
   42 s1(2) HRA 1998
   43 s2(1) HRA 1998
   44 *Leeds CC v Price* [2006] UKHL 10
   45 s3(1) HRA 1998

Notes

46 See definition of 'public authority' in s6(3) HRA 1998
47 *Ghaidan v Godin-Mendoza* [2004] UKHL 30, 3 All ER 411
48 *Salesi v Italy* [1998] 26 EHRR 187 (ECtHR); R(IS) 6/04
49 CTC/2162/2005
50 See for example, the categories of non-appealable decisions in Sch 2 SS&CS(DA) Regs
51 *Tolstoy Miloslavsky v United Kingdom* [1995] 20 EHRR 441 (ECtHR); R(IS) 6/04
52 *Neumeister v Austria* [1968] 1 EHRR 91 (ECtHR); CDLA/5413/1999
53 *Airey v Ireland* [1979] 2 EHRR 305 (ECtHR); see also CJSA/5101/2001 which confirmed that there is no general right to (paid) legal representation before an appeal tribunal.
54 *De Haes and Gijsels v Belgium* [1997] 24 EHRR 1 (ECtHR)
55 CJSA/5100/2001
56 CIB/3985/2001
57 *Schuler-Zgraggen v Switzerland* [1993] 16 EHRR 405 (ECtHR)
58 *Deumeland v Germany* [1986] 8 EHRR 448 (ECtHR); *Schouten and Meldrum v Netherlands* [1995] 19 EHRR 432 (ECtHR)
59 R(IS) 1/04
60 R(IS) 2/04
61 CIB/8/2008
62 *Porter and another v Magill* [2001] UKHL 67 [2002] 1 All ER 465 (HL)
63 *Gillies v SSWP* [2006] UKHL 2
64 *Runa Begum v LB Tower Hamlets* [2003] UKHL 5, 1 All ER 731 (HL); but see also *Tsfayo v United Kingdom,* Application No.60860/00, 14 November 2006, unreported (ECtHR)
65 *R (Hooper and others) v SSWP* [2003] EWCA Civ 813, [2003] 3 All ER 673, para 18; *Petrovic v Austria* [2001] 33 EHRR 14 (ECtHR); CH/4574/2003 and *Esfandiari* (R(IS) 11/06). But note, in contrast, CH/663/2003 and *Langley v SSWP* [2004] EWCA Civ 1343
66 *R (Reynolds) v SSWP* [2003] EWCA Civ 797, [2003] All ER 577, para 28
67 *Marckx v Belgium* [1979] 2 EHRR 330 (ECtHR); *X, Y and Z v UK* [1997] 24 EHRR 143 (ECtHR)
68 *Niemietz v Germany* [1992] 16 EHRR 97 (ECtHR)
69 *Botta v Italy* [1998] 26 EHRR 241 (ECtHR)
70 R(DLA) 4/02
71 *Stec and others v UK*, Application Nos.65731/01 and 65900/01, 5 September 2005; *R (RJM) v SSWP* [2008] UKHL 63
72 *Müller v Austria* (Commission) [1975] 3 DR 25
73 CP/5084/2001
74 *R (Reynolds) v SSWP* [2003] EWCA Civ 797, All ER 577, para 28
75 *R (Carson) v SSWP* [2003] EWCA Civ 797, 3 All ER 577
76 *R (RJM) v SSWP* [2008] UKHL 63
77 *R (S) v Chief Constable of the South Yorkshire Police* [2004] 1 WLR 2196; *Carson and Reynolds v SSWP* [2005] UKHL 37
78 *Esfandiari and others v SSWP* [2006] EWCA Civ 282 (R(IS) 11/06)
79 *Belgian Linguistics* [1968] 1 EHRR 252 (ECtHR)
80 *Darby v Sweden* [1990] 13 EHRR 774 (ECtHR)
81 *Schmidt v Germany* [1994] 18 EHRR 513 (ECtHR)
82 *Stec and others v United Kingdom,* Application Nos.65731/01 and 65900/01, final judgment, 12 April 2006 (ECtHR)
83 See *Douglas v North Tyneside MBC* [2003] EWCA Civ 1847; [2004] 1 All ER 709 and *Sahin v Turkey* [2007] 44 EHRR 5 (ECtHR)
84 s7(5) HRA 1998
85 President's Protocol No.6, *Handling Questions Under the Human Rights Act 1998,* 14 July 2000
86 s3(2)(b) HRA 1998
87 s4 HRA 1998
88 s4(6) HRA 1998
89 s10(2) HRA 1998
90 On the basis that the minister acted outside the powers given to him in the Act to make such regulations (referred to as the *ultra vires* rule), following the House of Lords' decision in *CAO v Foster* [1993] 1 All ER 705 (HL).
91 s3(2)(c) HRA 1998

Chapter 50

Complaints

This chapter covers:

Key facts

- Complaints can be made about any goverment or local authority department.
- You can complain about a delay in dealing with your claim, poor administration, behaviour of staff or the way in which a particular policy or practice has impacted on you.
- If the authority does not resolve your complaint, you may be able to complain to the Ombudsman or Adjudicator.
- If your complaint is about an independent adviser such as a Citizens Advice Bureau or law centre, you should seek legal advice about taking action for negligence.

1. Complaining to the DWP

The DWP has separate complaints policies for each of its agencies and each agency has its own complaints procedure.

The individual agencies are:

- the Pension Service;
- Jobcentre Plus;
- the Child Support Agency (CSA);

- the Disability and Carers Service;
- the Debt Management Organisation.

If you want to complain about the CSA, see CPAG's *Child Support Handbook*.

If you want to complain about how a particular DWP agency has dealt with your individual case, you should first contact the office that dealt with your claim. If you are still dissatisfied, you can contact the manager of the agency (or the Complaints Resolution Team in CSA cases). If you remain dissatisfied, you can contact the Chief Executive of the agency (or the Complaints Review Team for CSA cases), who will aim to reply within 15 working days. If you are not satisfied following this, you can complain to the Independent Case Examiner (see below). You may also have grounds to make a complaint to the Ombudsman. Further details on the complaints procedure for each agency (and its target response time) can be found on the directgov website, linked from the DWP website at www.dwp.gov.uk/contact-us/complaints-and-appeals.

Note: the Pension Service and the Disability and Carers Service merged on1 April 2008 to create a new DWP agency, the Pension, Disability and Carers Service. However, for complaint purposes the two remain distinct organisations.

Ask your local office for any written information on the standards and levels of service that you can expect. This may include targets for the time it should take to deal with your claim. You can also visit the DWP, HM Revenue and Customs (HMRC) and HM Courts and Tribunals Service (HMCTS) websites (see Appendix 1) for information about standards and complaints. If the complaint is about the local authority, visit the relevant local authority website. All the agencies should also be able to provide you with written details about how to complain if you are not getting the service you think you should be.

Whenever you write to the DWP, HMRC, HMCTS or local authority, you should quote your national insurance number. You should explain exactly what you are complaining about, any costs you have incurred as a result of this problem and what you would like to see done to resolve your complaint. Always keep a copy of any letters you send or receive and take the name of anyone you speak to on the phone.

2. Complaining to the Independent Case Examiner

The Independent Case Examiner's Office (ICE) deals with complaints about the Child Support Agency and the other agencies of the DWP.

A complaint can only be made to the ICE if you have already completed the complaints procedure of the particular agency concerned. This usually means you have had a response from the Chief Executive or a senior manager or the

Complaints Review Team for CSA cases. Complaints can be made in writing (including online) or by telephone (see Appendix 1). The complaint form can be downloaded from the ICE website at www.ind-case-exam.org.uk. You need to give all relevant information, including the agency you are complaining about.

The ICE will first consider whether or not it can accept the complaint. If it can, it will attempt to settle the complaint by suggesting ways in which the agency concerned and the complainant can come to an agreement. If this fails, the ICE prepares a formal report, setting out how the complaint arose and how it believes it should be settled. The ICE considers whether there has been maladminstration; it cannot deal with matters of law or cases that are subject to judicial review or under appeal.

A complaint should be made no later than six months after the final response from the agency you are complaining about. If you are unhappy with the way the ICE dealt with your case, you can ask your MP to consider referring your concerns to the Parliamentary and Health Service Ombudsman (see p1260).

3. Complaining to HM Revenue and Customs

If you want to complain about how HM Revenue and Customs (HMRC) has dealt with your tax credit, child benefit or guardian's allowance or with your national insurance credits or contributions, it is best to raise the complaint with the office dealing with your case, or the named contact person on the letters you have received, setting out the nature of your complaint. Describe any facts and events relating to it and say what you think HMRC has done wrong. Also include in the complaint any loss that you have incurred as a result.

If you are not happy with the response to your complaint, you can write to the senior court or tribunal manager at the same office and ask for a review. You should receive a response within 10 days. If you think the matter has still not been resolved satisfactorily, you can appeal to the Complaints, Correspondence and Litigation Team (CCLT) at HM Courts and Tribunals Service (see Appendix 1). This is not an independent appeal, but an internal review of how the complaint has been handled. It is the final stage of the internal complaints procedure. HMRC aims to respond within 15 days.

If you are not happy with HMRC's reply, you can ask the independent Adjudicator to look into it (see p1258). HMRC's complaints procedure is set out in its factsheet, *Complaints and Putting Things Right* (C/FS), available on its website at www.hmrc.gov.uk/factsheets/complaints-factsheet.pdf.

4. Complaining to the Adjudicator

The Adjudicator's Office investigates complaints about HM Revenue and Customs (HMRC). The Adjudicator is similar in nature to the Ombudsman (see p1260). Therefore, complaints can be made about delays, inappropriate staff behaviour, misleading advice or any other form of maladministration. The Adjudicator cannot, however, investigate disputes about matters of law. The Adjudicator will only investigate a complaint if you have first exhausted the HMRC internal complaints procedure. A complaint should be made within six months of the final correspondence with HMRC.[1]

The Adjudicator can recommend that compensation is paid, and HMRC has undertaken to follow her/his recommendations in all but exceptional circumstances. If you are unhappy with the Adjudicator's response to your complaint, you can ask your MP to put your complaint to the Parliamentary and Health Service Ombudsman. As well as looking at your complaint about HMRC, the Ombudsman may also look into the way in which the Adjudicator has investigated your complaint.[2] Further information about the Adjudicator can be found at www.adjudicatorsoffice.gov.uk.

5. Complaining to a local authority

Local authorities are required to have an effective complaints procedure, which should be made available to the public. If you are unhappy about the actions of your local authority and wish to make a complaint, you should ask for a copy of its complaints policy. If you are unable to obtain the complaints policy or there is no formal complaints procedure, you should begin by writing to the supervisor of the person dealing with your claim, making it clear why you are dissatisfied. If you do not receive a satisfactory reply, take up the matter with someone more senior in the department and ultimately the principal officer. Send a copy of the letter to your ward councillor and to the councillor who chairs the relevant committee responsible (eg, for housing benefit/council tax benefit) – local authority officers are always accountable to the councillors. If this does not produce results, or if the delay is causing you severe hardship, consider a complaint to the Local Government Ombudsman/Public Services Ombudsman (see p1261) or court action.

Government departments also monitor local authorities, so you could contact your MP or write to the relevant minister – eg, the Secretary of State for Work and Pensions. If a minister believes there is a widespread problem with maladministration in the local authority, s/he can ask the Benefit Fraud Inspectorate to report on the authority's administration.

If you want to make a complaint about an elected member of a council, you must write to the local authority. The Localism Act, which came into force on 15 November 2011, requires all local authorities to promote and maintain high standards of conduct by elected members. However, local authorities are now free to set up standards committees to consider complaints about the conduct of councillors only if they choose to do so. The practice may therefore vary and you should ask your local authority for its procedure for complaints against members.

6. Complaining to HM Courts and Tribunals Service

Complaints about the administration of your appeal

HM Courts and Tribunals Service (HMCTS) provides administrative support to the First-tier Tribunal and Upper Tribunal. If you have a complaint about the administration of your appeal, complain to HMCTS. Raise your complaint initially with the person who has been dealing with your appeal. Her/his name and telephone number should be on all correspondence that you have received. If you are not satisfied with the response, you can ask to be referred to the area manager. If you remain dissatisfied, complain in writing to the Chief Executive of HMCTS.

Complaints about the conduct of panel members

If you are unhappy about the way in which you were treated by a Tribunal member (eg, because s/he was discourteous or racist), raise the matter initially by writing to the Tribunal judge of the region in which the appeal was heard. The judge will then investigate the complaint. You should receive an acknowledgement of your complaint within five working days of the complaint being received. The regional judge will contact all the people involved and then write, telling you whether or not the complaint is upheld and, if so, what action is to be taken.

If the complaint is about the conduct of the regional judge it should be made to the President of HMCTS. If your complaint is about the President it should be made to the Lord Chancellor.

7. Using your MP

If you are not satisfied with the reply from the officers to whom you have written, you may wish to take up the matter with your MP.

Most MPs have 'surgeries' in their areas where they meet constituents to discuss problems. You can get the details from your local library or Citizens Advice Bureau. You can either go to the surgery or write to your MP with details of your complaint. To find out who your MP is, contact the House of Commons information service on 020 7219 4272 or go to www.findyourmp.parliament.uk.

Your MP will probably want to write to the benefit authorities for an explanation of what has happened. If you wish to make a complaint to the relevant Ombudsman, you must usually make the complaint through your MP. This does not apply if you are complaining to the Local Government Ombudsman/Public Services Ombudsman about a local authority.

8. Complaining to the Ombudsman

The role of the Parliamentary and Health Service Ombudsman is to investigate complaints from members of the public who believe they have experienced an injustice because of maladministration by a government department.[3] Maladministration means poor administration and can include avoidable delays, failure to advise about appeal rights, refusal to answer reasonable questions or respond to correspondence, discourteousness, racism or sexism.

There is also a Local Government Ombudsman (in Scotland and Wales, the Public Services Ombudsman), who hears complaints about local government.[4]

The Ombudsman will not usually investigate a complaint unless you have first exhausted the internal complaints procedure. However, if the authority is not acting on your complaint, or there are unreasonable delays, this delay may also form part of your complaint. The time limit for lodging a complaint with the Ombudsman is 12 months from the date you were notified of the matter complained about. However, a delay in bringing a complaint does not necessarily prevent a complaint being heard if there are good reasons for the delay.

A public body, such as the DWP or a local authority, is required to follow the recommendations of a complaints panel unless there are good reasons not to. If a public body has failed to do so, you may have grounds to complain to the Ombudsman and, in some circumstances, may have grounds for a judicial review.

The Parliamentary and Health Service Ombudsman

The Parliamentary and Health Service Ombudsman deals with complaints about all central government departments. This includes the DWP, HM Revenue and Customs, HM Courts and Tribunals Service and any agencies carrying out functions on behalf of these departments. In order to make a complaint, you must write to your MP, who will then refer the complaint to the Ombudsman. To find out who your MP is contact the House of Commons information service on 020 7219 4272 or go to www.findyourmp.parliament.uk. The Ombudsman can only investigate complaints of maladministration and not complaints about entitlement, which should be dealt with by the First-tier Tribunal. The Ombudsman has powers to look at documents held by the benefit authority on your claim. You may be interviewed to check any facts. The Ombudsman can recommend financial compensation if you have been unfairly treated or experienced a loss as a result of the maladministration.

The Local Government Ombudsman/Public Services Ombudsman

If you have tried to sort out your complaint with the local authority but you are still not satisfied with the outcome, you can apply to the Local Government Ombudsman (in Scotland, the Scottish Public Services Ombudsman; in Wales, the Public Services Ombudsman for Wales). The Ombudsman can investigate any cases of maladministration by local authorities, but not matters of entitlement, which can be dealt with by the First-tier Tribunal.

You can complain to the Ombudsman either in writing (including online) or by telephone (see Appendix 1). The Ombudsman has powers to look at documents held by the local authority on your claim. You may be interviewed to check any facts. Straightforward cases can be dealt with in about three months. The Ombudsman can recommend financial compensation if you have been unfairly treated or experienced a loss as a result of the maladministration. A complaint may also make the authority review its procedures, which could benefit other claimants.

One outcome of your complaint may be a 'local settlement'. This is where the local authority agrees to take some action that the Ombudsman considers is a satisfactory response to your complaint and the investigation will be discontinued. If you are unhappy with the way in which the Ombudsman has dealt with your complaint, you should seek legal advice as quickly as possible.

9. Compensation payments

You should expect prompt, courteous and efficient service from staff dealing with your claim. If you are dissatisfied with the way your claim has been administered you can seek compensation.

The DWP, HM Revenue and Customs (HMRC) and local authorities sometimes pay compensation if you can show that you have lost out through their error or delay and the loss cannot be made good by a revision, supersession, appeal or backdating a claim (see Chapters 45 and 46). For instance, if you failed to claim carer's allowance because you were misled by the DWP and you could not have the benefit backdated for more than three months, you could claim compensation.

The DWP uses a guide, *Financial Redress for Injustice Resulting from Maladministration*, to help it decide when and how much compensation (known as an 'extra statutory' or *ex gratia* payment) should be paid. The guide is available from the DWP website (see Appendix 1). HMRC has a code of practice, *Complaints* (C/FS), which sets out when it will make compensatory or consolatory payments.

You should ask for a payment equal to the money you have lost, but you could also ask for additional amounts to cover interest on arrears and extra expenses you had to pay out, and to compensate you for any hardship or distress experienced because of the mistake. Payments are discretionary. If your loss was as a clear result of incorrect advice or negligence on the part of the agency, you may be able to bring a court action for damages.[5] Seek legal advice if this is the case. Tactically, it is probably better to pursue a payment under these schemes before making a complaint to the Ombudsman. This is because if the Ombudsman does not uphold your complaint, the particular benefit authority is likely to resist making a compensation payment.

10. **Delays**

All benefit authorities should act promptly to process a claim. A failure to do so can lead to your making a complaint and possibly obtaining compensation.

Local authorities should process housing benefit and council tax benefit claims within 14 days as long as you have given them all the information they have asked for.[6] Many do not. Complaining may be one way to get your claim processed more quickly, although threatening legal action may be more effective. The Local Government Ombudsman/Public Services Ombudsman often orders compensation to be paid where there have been long delays which are not your fault.

HM Revenue and Customs has no official targets for processing tax credit claims.

DWP offices have target times for dealing with claims, but they are not always able to meet these. If there is a delay that has resulted in or from maladministration, you may be entitled to compensation in the form of interest if the arrears of benefit involved were more than £100 and the compensation would be more than £10.[7]

The DWP should automatically consider whether compensation should be paid if you are owed arrears of benefit. You should still write to your local DWP office and ask. If you do not get a sympathetic response, you could ask your MP to write on your behalf or to take up your case with the social security minister.

11. Legal action

It is not possible to sue a benefit authority for negligence in the way it decides your claim.[8] Instead, if a decision is wrong, you can seek a revision or supersession or appeal against it. However, it is possible to seek compensation through the courts if there has been:

- misadvice – ie, if an employee of a benefit authority or HM Courts and Tribunals Service gives wrong advice which leads to some financial loss for you;
- unpaid benefit – ie, if your benefit claim has been determined but you have not received payment;
- a breach of human rights.

Although it is possible to seek compensation through the courts it should never be the first course of action and should only ever be considered after seeking legal advice.

If a benefit authority refuses to process your claim, you may have grounds for a judicial review – in this case, seek legal advice.

Notes

4. **Complaining to the Adjudicator**
   1 For further details, see CPAG's *Welfare Rights Bulletin* 180
   2 See also CPAG's *Welfare Rights Bulletin* 180

8. **Complaining to the Ombudsman**
   3 s5(1)(a) Parliamentary Commissioner Act 1967
   4 ss23 and 24 Local Government Act 1974

9. **Compensation payments**
   5 *Haringey LBC v Cotter* [1996] 29 HLR 682 (CA)

10. **Delays**
   6 **HB** Reg 89(2) HB Regs; reg 70(2) HB(SPC) Regs
   CTB reg 75(2) CTB Regs; reg 60(1) CTB(SPC) Regs
   7 DWP leaflet, *Financial Redress for Injustice Resulting from Maladministration*, November 2009

11. **Legal action**
   8 *Jones v Department of Employment* [1989] QB 1 (CA)

Part 7

Tax credits

Chapter 51

Child tax credit

This chapter covers:

Key facts

- Child tax credit (CTC) is paid to families with children or qualifying young people.
- You do not have to have paid national insurance contributions to qualify.
- CTC is paid whether or not you are in full-time paid work.
- CTC does not count as income for income support, income-based jobseeker's allowance, income-related employment and support allowance or pension credit purposes and can be paid in addition to these benefits.
- CTC is administered and paid by HM Revenue and Customs.
- If you disagree with a CTC decision, you can apply for a revision, or appeal against it (see Chapter 60).

Future changes: April 2013 and after

Major changes are taking place that affect the benefits and tax credits system (see Chapter 2).

- From April 2013, total benefit payments to many working-age households will be 'capped' (see p25). There will be limited exceptions, including households in which someone is entitled to working tax credit or receives disability living allowance. CTC will be included in the capped amount.
- From October 2013, when universal credit (UC) is introduced, amounts for children will be included in UC. No new claims for CTC will be allowed, probably from April 2014. If you are still getting CTC in April 2014, you will be transferred to UC at some time between April 2014 and October 2017.

See CPAG's *Welfare Rights Bulletin* for updates.

1. Who can claim child tax credit

You qualify for child tax credit (CTC) if:[1]

- you (or your partner) have at least one dependent child (including some qualifying young people) for whom you are responsible (see p1269);
- your income is sufficiently low (see Chapter 55);
- you are 'present' and 'ordinarily resident' in the UK. You can be treated as present and ordinarily resident in the UK in some circumstances – eg, if you are temporarily away. You can be treated as not being in the UK if you claim CTC for the first time on or after 1 May 2004 and do not have a 'right to reside'. See Chapter 62 for further information;
- you are not a 'person subject to immigration control' (see Chapter 61).

2. The rules about your age

You (and your partner) must be aged at least 16 to qualify for child tax credit (CTC).[2] There is no upper age limit. If you are under 16, someone else (eg, your parent or the adult with whom you normally live) may be able to claim CTC for you *and* your child.

3. Who is included in your claim

You can only qualify for child tax credit (CTC) if you are responsible for one or more children. Some qualifying young people continue to count as children until they are 20 (see p1269).

If you are a member of a couple, you must claim CTC jointly with your partner.[3] If you are not a member of a couple, you claim for yourself.[4] For information about who counts as a couple for tax credit purposes, see p1284. The rules are the same as for working tax credit. See Chapter 56 for further information about joint claims for CTC. **Note:** if you claim jointly with your partner, but then cease to count as a couple (or you claim as a single person, but then become a member of a couple), you should report this change in your circumstances and claim tax credits as a single person (or a couple) immediately.

If you are a couple:

- when working out how much CTC you get, your partner's income is added to yours (see Chapter 55);
- CTC is paid to the person who is the main carer for your children (see p1354).

Children

To qualify for CTC, you must be 'responsible' for a child or qualifying young person.[5] The terms 'child' or 'children' in this chapter include these qualifying young people. You do not have to be the child's parent. You could, for example, be the grandparent, sister or brother. See p1271 for when you count as responsible for a child and p1273 for when you do not count as responsible.

If you are entitled to CTC for a child (or would have been had you made a claim) and the child dies, you continue to be entitled to CTC for the child for eight weeks immediately following her/his death (or to the date your child would have turned 20 if this is earlier).[6] After that period, you may still continue to qualify for CTC – ie, if you are responsible for any other child(ren) and still satisfy the means test.

Who counts as a child

Someone counts as a child until her/his 16th birthday.[7] In some circumstances, a young person aged under 20 also counts as a child. HM Revenue and Customs (HMRC) refers to her/him as a **'qualifying young person'**.

A young person counts as a child during any period:[8]

- from her/his 16th birthday until 31 August following that birthday, whether or not s/he is in full-time non-advanced education or 'approved training' (but see p1270 if s/he has started work or has claimed benefit in her/his own right);
- from 1 September following her/his 16th birthday (or from 31 August if s/he turns 16 on that date), while s/he is under 20 and in:
  - full-time non-advanced education (see p1270). This does not apply if s/he is getting the education because of her/his employment. A young person counts as in full-time education during any gaps between the ending of one course and the start of another, if s/he is enrolled on and commences the other course; *or*
  - 'approved training' (see p98 for what counts) or has been enrolled or accepted to undertake approved training. This does not apply if s/he is getting the training by means of a contract of employment.

  The education or training must have begun before s/he reached 19, or s/he must have been enrolled or accepted to undertake the education or training before that age. **Note:** there is no equivalent to the child benefit 'terminal date rule' (see p98), so unless the young person is under 18 and the rule below applies, s/he cannot count as a child once the course or training ends. Therefore, ensure you notify HMRC when the course or training ends;
- from 1 September following her/his 16th birthday (or from 31 August if s/he turns 16 on that date), while s/he is under 18, has ceased full-time education or 'approved training' (see p98) and it is not more than 20 weeks since s/he did so. S/he must notify HMRC within three months of ceasing full-time education or 'approved training' that s/he has registered for work or training with a

qualifying body – eg, the place where your local authority provides careers advice for young people or the Ministry of Defence. This rule can apply again if s/he goes back into full-time education or 'approved training' and ceases again.

When working out whether a young person counts as in full-time education or 'approved training', HMRC ignores:[9]
- an interruption of up to six months, whether it began before or after the young person turned 16; *and*
- an interruption of any length which is due to the young person's illness or disability 'of the mind or body'.

The interruption is only ignored if HMRC thinks it is reasonable to do so.

You should let HMRC know if the above applies to ensure that you continue to get CTC for your child.

Full-time non-advanced education[10]

'**Education**' means education at a school or college or (if receiving the education before the age of 16) elsewhere, if approved by HMRC.

Education counts as **full time** if it is for more than 12 hours a week, on average, in normal term time, including instruction or tuition, supervised study, exams, practical work and experiments or projects provided for in the curriculum but excluding meal breaks and unsupervised study.

For examples of what counts as **non-advanced** education, see p98.

When a young person does not count as a child

A young person cannot count as a child during any period following her/his 16th birthday:[11]
- which includes a week in which, having ceased full-time education or 'approved training', s/he is in full-time paid work. This means work of 24 hours or more per week. For information about:
  - what counts as paid work, see p1297;
  - how the hours are calculated, see p1297;
  - situations when the young person is not treated as in full-time paid work, see p1304.

  The rules are the same as for working tax credit (WTC).

  Remember that, even if a young person has *not* started full-time paid work, s/he cannot count as a child from 1 September after her/his 16th birthday if s/he has ceased full-time education or 'approved training' and has not registered for work or training with a qualifying body – eg, the place where your local authority provides careers advice for young people or the Ministry of Defence (see p1269); *or*

- which includes a period in which s/he gets income support (IS), income-based jobseeker's allowance (JSA) or income-related employment and support allowance (ESA) in her/his own right. **Note:** you might not count as responsible for a child age 16 or over if s/he gets CTC, incapacity benefit (IB) or contributory ESA in her/his own right (see p1273).

Being responsible for a child

For tax credits purposes, a child can only count as the responsibility of one claimant (or joint-claim couple).[12] You are treated as 'responsible' for a child if:[13]

- s/he normally lives with you. HMRC calls this the 'normally living with test'; *or*
- you have the main responsibility for her/him. HMRC calls this the 'main responsibility test'. This test only applies if you and another person (or couple) make competing claims for CTC for the same child.

If a child for whom you are treated as responsible has a child of her/his own who normally lives with her/him, you also count as responsible for that child.[14] This does not apply if your child is 16 or over and is awarded CTC in her/his own right.[15]

The 'normally living with test'

The rules do not define when a child counts as 'normally living with' you. HMRC says it means that your child 'regularly, usually, typically' lives with you and that this allows for temporary or occasional absences.[16] So if your child counts as normally living with you, s/he should also count as doing so even if s/he is away from home – eg, because s/he is away at school or for a temporary period on holiday or in hospital. You can argue that a child is normally living with you if s/he spends more time with you than with anyone else.[17]

Your child can count as normally living with you even if s/he also lives with someone else or only lives with you for part of the week, and lives for part of the week with someone else – eg, her/his other parent. This means that more than one person could claim CTC for the same child. However, CTC can only be paid to one claimant (or joint-claim couple). If more than one claims, see the 'main responsibility' test below.

The 'main responsibility test'

If you (and your partner) and at least one other person (or couple) with whom the child also normally lives claim CTC for the same child, you only qualify for CTC for the child if you can show you have the 'main responsibility' for her/him. The main responsibility test applies if:[18]

- your child normally lives with *both* you *and*:
  - at least one other person in another household – eg, with you and with the child's other parent from whom you have separated; *or*

– someone who is not your partner in the same household – eg, with you and with the child's grandparent where you live together.

It also applies if it is a combination of these situations. 'Household' is not defined. See p754 for ideas about what might count as a household; *and*

- you and at least one of the other people with whom your child normally lives claim CTC.

You and the other CTC claimant(s) can decide which of you should count as having 'main responsibility'. If you cannot agree, a decision maker decides.[19] You can challenge the decision (see p1273). **Note:** if you and another claimant have more than one child, you can each claim CTC for different children – eg, if you have two children, you could claim for one and the other claimant could claim for the other.

'**Main responsibility**' is not defined in the rules. The decision maker is likely to consider things like:[20]

- whether any court orders exist that set out where your child is to live or who is to care for her/him;
- who pays for your child's food and clothes and who is responsible for giving her/him pocket money;
- who your child normally lives with and where the majority of her/his clothes and toys are kept;
- who is the main contact or registered address for the school or college, nursery or childcare provider or for healthcare and who takes most responsiblity for your child when s/he is at school;[21]
- who looks after your child when s/he is ill and who arranges appointments to see a doctor.

Even though you may be sharing responsibility for a child and s/he normally lives with you for part of the week, you might not qualify for CTC because the rules might not treat you as having the main responsibility. There is currently no provision for allowing CTC to be split between parents if a child divides her/his time between their homes. Even if you share actual responsibility for the child (eg, you share responsibility with your ex-partner) and are a 'substantial minority carer' (ie, you have the child with you for at least 104 nights a year), you cannot argue that you should be regarded as responsible for the child.[22] However, see CPAG's *Welfare Rights Bulletin* for updates.

If you share responsibility for your child(ren) equally with the other CTC claimant(s), it may be difficult to decide who has the *main* responsibility. In this case, you might be able to argue that the decision maker should regard you as having the main responsibility if you would be entitled to more CTC than the other claimant(s).[23]

When you do not count as responsible for a child

Even if a child normally lives with you or if the main responsibility test applies, you have the 'main responsibility' for her/him, you do *not* count as responsible for the child and cannot claim CTC for her/him during any period when s/he is:[24]

- provided with or placed in accommodation and the accommodation or the child's maintenance is funded wholly or partly by the local authority under specified provisions or out of other public funds. This includes children staying with foster carers who get foster payments for them from the local authority. This does not apply if your child is staying in certain forms of residential accommodation and this is only necessary because your child has a disability or because her/his health would be significantly impaired or further impaired if s/he were not staying in the accommodation. You must have been treated as responsible for her/him immediately before s/he went into the accommodation;[25] *or*
- being looked after by a local authority and has been placed with you because you want to adopt her/him. This only applies if the local authority is paying for the child's accommodation or maintenance or both under specified provisions ; *or*
- in custody. This only applies if your child:
  - is serving a life or unlimited sentence; *or*
  - is serving a term of more than four months; *or*
  - has been detained 'during Her Majesty's pleasure'; *or*
- at least 16 and:
  - is awarded CTC in her/his own right for a child for whom s/he is responsible; *or*
  - receives WTC in her/his own right (including in a joint claim); *or*
  - is entitled to and receiving IB or contributory ESA in her/his own right; *or*
  - is married, in a civil partnership or living with someone as a couple and her/his partner is not in full-time education or approved training (see pp1270 and 98 for what counts). This does not apply if you were getting CTC for the child and s/he was living with a partner before 1 September 2008; *or*
  - is your partner and and you are living with her/him. This does not apply if you were getting CTC for her/him and living with her/him as a couple before 1 September 2008.

Note: a young person does not count as a child if s/he gets IS, income-based JSA or income-related ESA in her/his own right (see p1270).

Challenging a decision

HMRC might say that:

- your child does not normally live with you or that you are not the person with main responsibility for her/him so you are not entitled to CTC;

- someone else has claimed CTC for your child(ren) and now satisfies the 'main reponsibility test' when you have been getting CTC for the same child(ren). In this case, your entitlement to CTC ends and you may have been overpaid.

If you think a decision is wrong and it affects your tax credits, you can appeal.[26] See Chapter 60 for more information about revisions and appeals.

It is possible that the DWP, the local authority and HMRC might reach different conclusions about whether your child(ren) can be included in your claims. If so, you should appeal *all* the decisions with which you disagree.

4. The amount of child tax credit

The amount of child tax credit (CTC) you get depends on:

- your maximum CTC. This is made up of a combination of 'elements' (see p1275);
- how much income you have; *and*
- the 'income threshold figure' that applies to you.

The elements and thresholds can be increased every April. If you do not qualify for CTC currently, you might qualify if the rates go up.

If you are on a means-tested benefit

Being on income support (IS), income-based jobseeker's allowance (JSA), income-related employment and support allowance (ESA) or pension credit (PC) is an automatic passport to maximum CTC.[27] You, therefore, do not need to work out your income or capital. In these circumstances, CTC equals maximum CTC.

If you are not on a means-tested benefit

If you are not on IS, income-based JSA, income-related ESA or PC, you need to follow the steps below to calculate your CTC.

- **Step one:** work out your 'relevant period' (see pp1308 and 1319).
- **Step two:** work out your maximum entitlement (your maximum CTC) for the relevant period (see p1319).
- **Step three:** work out your relevant income (see p1319).
- **Step four:** compare your income with the 'income threshold figure' for the relevant period. This is currently £15,860 if you are entitled to CTC only, or £6,420 if you are entitled to CTC and your maximum amount of tax credits includes working tax credit (WTC) elements.[28] See p1320 for further information.
- **Step five:** calculate your CTC entitlement for the relevant period (see p1320). If your income is less than the 'income threshold figure', CTC equals maximum

CTC. If your income exceeds the 'income threshold figure', your maximum CTC is reduced by 41 per cent of the excess. See previous editions of this *Handbook* for the percentages before 2012/13. **Note:** in previous tax years, your CTC was not reduced below the level of the family element unless your annual income was higher than £40,000.

You may also be entitled to WTC. Full details of both calculations are in Chapter 54.

Maximum child tax credit

Your maximum CTC is calculated by adding together all of the elements that apply to you.[29] These are:[30]

- child element (£2,690 a year) – one for each child;
- disabled child element (£2,950 a year) – one for each child who qualifies;
- severely disabled child element (£1,190 a year) – one for each child who qualifies;
- family element (£545 a year).

For details of how you qualify for the above elements, see Chapter 54.

Example

Joe and Louise have three children, aged three, 10 and 17. The 17-year-old works 35 hours a week. One of the younger children gets disability living allowance mobility component. Joe and Louise's maximum CTC is made up of the family element, two child elements and one disabled child element. The 17-year-old does not count as a child for CTC purposes.

5. Claims and backdating

The rules on claiming, backdating and how your claim can be be renewed at the end of the year are in Chapter 56. This section gives an outline of the rules on claims for child tax credit (CTC).

Making a claim

Your first claim for CTC must usually be made in writing on the form approved or authorised by HM Revenue and Customs (HMRC).[31] You use the same form for CTC and for working tax credit (WTC). See p1348 for further information. Send the completed form to Comben House, Farriers Way, Netherton, Merseyside or any other office specified in writing by HMRC.[32] You can use the pre-paid envelope provided with the claim form. Keep a copy of your claim form in case queries arise.

You must provide any information and evidence required (see below). You can amend or withdraw your claim before you are given notice of the decision on your claim.[33]

Who should claim

If you are a member of a couple, you must make a joint claim with your partner. If you are not a member of a couple, you claim for yourself. For information about who counts as a couple for tax credit purposes, see p1284. If you cannot make your claim yourself, an 'appointee' (see p1347) can claim on your behalf.

Information to support your claim

When you claim CTC, you must:[34]

- satisfy the national insurance (NI) number requirement (see p1349);
- provide proof of your identity, if required;
- supply information to support your claim (see p1348).

It is important that you provide all the information required. If you do not do so, a decision might not be made on your claim.

When you claim CTC you must provide:

- your child benefit reference number. This can be found on any letters about child benefit that you have received;
- details of your (and your partner's) income for the previous tax year (see Chapter 55);
- details of a bank or building society account into which CTC can be paid. If you do not have an account, you need to open one within four weeks of making your claim. (This is the time limit from 6 April 2012, previously it was eight weeks.) See pp1350 and 1355 for further information.

If you are also claiming WTC, there is other information you must also provide (see p1289). HMRC might need further information before it makes a decision on your claim. See p1350 for details of the time you must be given to provide the information and what happens if you fail to do so.

When to claim

The general rule is that your claim runs from the date it is received by HMRC.[35] You cannot make a claim in advance of the tax year for which you are claiming. See below for information on how and when claims can be backdated.

Awards of CTC are always based on annual income. HMRC bases the initial award of CTC on your (and your partner's) *previous* tax year's income. If you think your income for the current tax year is likely, eventually, to be low enough for you to qualify for CTC (eg, you are self-employed and you do not yet know your previous tax year's income, or your income is going to fall or has fallen because your work is seasonal, you are going on maternity leave or you might be made redundant), you may wish to consider making a claim (including a request for your claim to be backdated if relevant), even if you know you will be given what is known as a 'nil award'. This protects your position because you can then ask HMRC to amend the award on the basis of a change in your income (see p1328). The amended award would run from your original date of claim (or the date to which your claim was backdated). See *Protect Your Right to Tax Credits by Claiming Early,* at www.hmrc.gov.uk/taxcredits/start/claiming/backdate-ahead/protect-claim.htm. However, see pp1365–68 before deciding what to do.

Backdating your claim

It is important to claim in time. A claim for CTC can usually only be backdated for a maximum of 31 days. (This is the time limit from 6 April 2012, previously it was 93 days.)[36] You only need to show that you qualified for CTC during that period. Unlike for most means-tested benefits, you do not have to show any reasons for your delay. See p1355 for further information.

Note: if you are waiting to hear whether your child is entitled to disability living allowance (DLA), you should claim CTC, even if you will not qualify for CTC until the disabled child element or severely disabled child element can be included. If you do not qualify, you are given a 'nil award'. A special rule then allows your entitlement to these elements to be backdated more than one month (see p1365). (This is the time limit from 6 April 2012, previously it was three months.) You must notify HMRC within one month of the date the DLA is awarded.

Renewal awards

At the end of the tax year in which you claimed CTC, you (and your partner), receive a 'final notice' from HMRC asking you to confirm that your income and/or your household circumstances are as stated for the previous tax year (see p1361). You must reply within a strict time limit. HMRC then makes a final decision, based on your actual income during the tax year. It decides whether you were entitled to CTC and, if so, the amount of your award. This is known as the 'annual review'. HMRC also uses the information about your income and household circumstances for the previous tax year to renew your award for the next tax year.[37] **Note:** if you have a 'nil award', you may be given notice that your claim will not be renewed unless you specifically request this.

Example

Joe is a lone parent who is in full-time paid work. He claims CTC in October 2011. His initial award is based on his income during the 2010/11 tax year. In May 2012, he is sent a final notice. He sends HMRC details of his actual income for 2011/12. HMRC uses this information to work out whether his CTC award was correct. Joe's actual income for

2011/12is now the previous year's income for his CTC claim for 2012/13. HMRC uses this income to make an initial decision to award Joe CTC and set payments for 2012/13.

6. Getting paid

This section gives an outline of the rules about payment of child tax credit (CTC). For more information about getting paid, see p1354.

CTC is normally paid by direct credit transfer into the bank (or similar) account of whomever is deemed to be the main carer of your children (see p1354). If you are unable to act for yourself, payment can be made to someone else on your behalf – called your 'appointee' (see p1347).[38]

How often is CTC paid?	CTC is paid every week or every four weeks, whichever is more convenient for you, although HM Revenue and Customs (HMRC) can decide how often.[39]

You can be paid by cheque while your account arrangements are finalised.

If your award of CTC (or the combination of CTC and working tax credit (WTC)) is £2 a week or less, it is paid in a single lump sum into your account to cover the whole year.[40] **Note:** if your entitlement to CTC (or the combination of CTC and WTC) is less than £26 for the whole of the tax year, no award is made and you are not paid at all.[41]

Note:

- Your CTC cannot currently be paid at a reduced rate if you have been sanctioned for benefit offences (see p1106). However, possibly from 2012 or 2013, the government intends to amend the rules and your CTC might not be paid for a set period of time. See CPAG's *Welfare Rights Bulletin* for updates.
- If you have forgotten your PIN, see p1040. The issues are the same as for benefits.
- If payment of your CTC is delayed and this is causing hardship, ask HMRC to make a 'next day/same day payment'. You may also be eligible for a crisis loan (see p564). If you wish to complain about how your claim has been dealt with, see p1257. You might be able to claim compensation (see p1261).
- If payment of your CTC is postponed or suspended, see p1355.
- If you are overpaid CTC, you might have to repay it (see Chapter 58). In some cases, interest can be added to the overpayment. If you have been accused of fraud, see Chapter 59. In some cases you may be given a financial penalty.

Length of award

Your award of CTC runs from the date your claim is received by HMRC (or from the date to which your claim can be backdated) to the end of the tax year.[42] However, changes in your circumstances can be taken into account during the tax year. In some cases, you *must* report changes of circumstances. See below and Chapter 57 for details.

Change of circumstances

Your award of CTC is made on the basis of your (and your partner's) previous year's income and your personal circumstances on the date of your claim. If your current year's income or your personal circumstances change, your award of CTC can be amended. Remember the following.

- There are some changes you *must* report to HMRC (see p1363). If you fail to do so within one month, you might be given a financial penalty. Some of these end your entitlement to CTC and you have to make a fresh claim, including if:
  - you were claiming as a single person and you become part of a couple or you were claiming as a couple and you cease to be a member of a couple; *or*
  - you or your partner lose your right to reside in the UK or no longer count as ordinarily resident.
- Unless it is a change that you must report, it is optional to report changes that affect your maximum entitlement to CTC – eg, when you have a baby or one of your children stops getting disability living allowance (DLA) (see p1364). However, changes that increase your maximum entitlement to CTC can generally only be backdated one month from when you notify HMRC. Changes that decrease your entitlement always take effect from the date of the change, so an overpayment can occur if you delay.
- There is a special rule that allows an increase in your entitlement to CTC to be backdated *more* than one month if your child is awarded DLA and the disabled child or severely disabled child elements should now be included in your CTC entitlement. You must notify HMRC within one month of the date the DLA is awarded (see p1365).
- It is optional to report changes in your income (see p1365). These are always taken into account at the end of the tax year, but you may want to consider reporting these sooner to avoid an overpayment or underpayment of CTC.

7. Tax, tax credits and benefits

Child tax credit (CTC) is not taxable.

Tax credits

If you are in full-time paid work, you might qualify for working tax credit (WTC). WTC can be paid in addition to CTC.

Means-tested benefits

CTC is not taken into account as income for income support (IS), income-based jobseeker's allowance (JSA), income-related employment and support allowance (ESA) or pension credit (PC).

Unless you are on IS, income-based JSA or income-related ESA or are at least the qualifying age for PC (see p509), the amount of CTC you are paid *is* taken into account as income for housing benefit and council tax benefit.

If you get arrears of CTC, these count as capital for means-tested benefits and can be disregarded in some circumstances (see pp982 and 1001).

Non-means-tested benefits

CTC can be paid in addition to any non-means-tested benefits to which you (or your partner) are entitled, including child benefit, but see Chapter 55 for which of these benefits may be taken into account as income for CTC. If your child qualifies for disability living allowance (DLA), you might qualify for the disabled child or severely disabled child elements of CTC and the income from DLA is ignored.

Passports and other sources of help

If you are entitled to CTC, you may also qualify for:

- health benefits such as free prescriptions (see Chapter 13). You do not have to satisfy the means test if you are getting CTC and your gross annual income is no more than a set amount; *and*
- education benefits such as free school lunches (see p14).

You may also qualify for a Sure Start maternity grant or a social fund funeral expenses payment.

Notes

1. **Who can claim child tax credit**
   1 ss3(3) and (7), 8 and 42 TCA 2002; regs 3-5 CTC Regs; reg 3 TC(R) Regs; reg 3 TC(Imm) Regs

2. **The rules about your age**
   2 s3(3) TCA 2002

3. **Who is included in your claim**
   3 s3(3)(a) and (5A) TCA 2002; reg 2(1) CTC Regs; CTC/3864/2004; CSTC/724/2006
   4 s3(3)(b) TCA 2002
   5 s8(1) TCA 2002
   6 s8(5) TCA 2002; reg 6 CTC Regs
   7 s8(3) TCA 2002; reg 2(1) CTC Regs, definition of 'child'
   8 s8(4) TCA 2002; regs 2, definition of 'qualifying young person' and 'full-time education', 4 and 5(1)-(3A) CTC Regs
   9 Reg 5(7) CTC Regs
   10 Regs 2(1), definition of 'advanced education' and 'full-time education', and 5(5) and (6) CTC Regs
   11 Regs 2, definition of 'remunerative work', and 5(4) CTC Regs
   12 Reg 3(1) rule 2.2 CTC Regs
   13 s8(2) TCA 2002; reg 3(1) rules 1 and 2 CTC Regs
   14 Reg 3(2) CTC Regs
   15 Reg 3(1) rule 4 Case D CTC Regs
   16 para 02202 TCTM
   17 CFC/1537/1995
   18 Reg 3(1) rule 2 CTC Regs
   19 Reg 3 rule 3 CTC Regs
   20 para 02204 TCTM
   21 *KN v HMRC* [2009] UKUT 79 (AAC)
   22 *Humphreys v Revenue and Customs* [2010] EWCA Civ 56. Leave to appeal to the Supreme Court has been granted.
   23 CTC/4390/2004. However, the judge in *CM v HMRC (TC)* [2010] UKUT 400 (AAC) disagreed that this was a legitimate consideration.
   24 Reg 3(1) rule 4.1 CTC Regs. Note that the rule does not appear to have been amended when s23 Children Act 1989 was revoked.
   25 Reg 3(1) rule 4.2 CTC Regs; reg 9 CB Regs
   26 CTC/2090/2004

4. **The amount of child tax credit**
   27 ss7(2) and 13 TCA 2002; reg 4 TC(ITDR) Regs
   28 Reg 3(2) and (3) TC(ITDR) Regs
   29 s9(2) TCA 2002
   30 Reg 7 CTC Regs

5. **Claims and backdating**
   31 Reg 5 TC(CN) Regs
   32 Reg 2 TC(CN) Regs, definition of 'appropriate office' and 'relevant authority'
   33 Reg 5(7) TC(CN) Regs; R(IS) 3/05
   34 Reg 5(3)-(6) TC(CN) Regs
   35 s5(2) TCA 2002
   36 Reg 7 TC(CN) Regs
   37 Regs 11 and 12 TC(CN) Regs

6. **Getting paid**
   38 s24(3) TCA 2002; reg 6 TC(PC) Regs
   39 Regs 8 and 13 TC(PC) Regs
   40 Reg 10 TC(PC) Regs
   41 Reg 9 TC(ITDR) Regs
   42 s5(2) TCA 2002

Chapter 52

Working tax credit

This chapter covers:

Key facts

- Working tax credit (WTC) is paid to low-paid workers. It tops up your wages if you are in full-time paid work (known as 'remunerative work').
- You do not have to have paid national insurance contributions to qualify.
- WTC is administered and paid by HM Revenue and Customs.
- If you disagree with a WTC decision, you can apply for a revision, or appeal against it (see Chapter 60).

Future changes: April 2013 and after

Major changes are taking place that affect the benefits and tax credits system (see Chapter 2).

- From April 2013, total benefit payments to many working-age households will 'capped' (see p25). WTC will *not* be included in the capped amount, and a cap will *not* be applied if someone in the household is entitled to WTC.
- From October 2013 when universal credit (UC) is introduced, you will be able to qualify for UC if you are working full or part time and also if you are out of work. No new claims for WTC will be allowed, probably from April 2014. If you are claiming WTC at that point, you will be transferred to UC at some time between April 2014 and October 2017.

See CPAG's *Welfare Rights Bulletin* for updates.

1. Who can claim working tax credit

You qualify for working tax credit (WTC) if:[1]

- you (or your partner) are in full-time paid work (see below);
- your income is sufficiently low (see Chapter 55);
- you are 'present' and 'ordinarily resident' in the UK. You can be treated as present and ordinarily resident in the UK in some circumstances – eg, if you are temporarily away. See Chapter 62 for further information;
- you are not a 'person subject to immigration control' (see Chapter 61).

Full-time paid work

For the purpose of WTC, you count as being in full-time work if any of the following apply.[2]

- You work at least 30 hours a week and you are 25 or over.
- You work at least 16 hours a week and:
  - you have a physical or mental disability which puts you at a disadvantage in getting a job and you qualify for a disabled worker element; *or*
  - you are 60 or over; *or*
  - you are a single claimant and you are are responsible for a child or qualifying young person (see p1271); *or*
  - you are a member of a couple and you (or your partner) are responsible for a child or qualifying young person (see p1271). However, from 6 April 2012, this will only apply if your partner counts as incapacitated for the purposes of the childcare element (see p1314), is entitled to carer's allowance, is a hospital inpatient or is in prison; *or*
  - you are a member of a couple and you (or your partner) are responsible for a child or qualifying young person (see p1271). However, from 6 April 2012, this will only apply if your partner's combined hours of work are at least 24 a week. This means that if you both work, one of you must do 16 hours a week and the other must do at least eight hours a week. If only one of you works, that person must work at least 24 hours a week.

In addition, you must be actually working on the date of your claim or have accepted an offer of work which is expected to start within seven days, and the work must be expected to last for at least four weeks. However, you can continue to count as in full-time paid work for four weeks after you leave work, or your hours reduce to less than the number required. See p1304 for information about what is known as 'WTC run-on'.

In some circumstances you can be treated as in full-time paid work when you are not, or treated as not being in full-time paid work even if you are. For further information about full-time paid work, see Chapter 53.

Note: before April 2012, you also counted as in full-time paid work if you (or your partner) worked at least 16 hours a week, were at least 50 and qualified for a 50-plus element. See the 2011/12 edition of this *Handbook* for details.

2. The rules about your age

You (and your partner) must be aged at least 16 to make a claim for working tax credit.[3] There is no upper age limit.

3. Who is included in your claim

If you are a member of a **couple**, you must claim working tax credit (WTC) jointly with your partner.[4] If you are not a member of a couple, you claim for yourself.[5] For information about who counts as a couple for tax credit purposes, see below. WTC includes elements for you and your partner and for the special needs of either of you (see Chapter 54). When working out how much WTC you get, your partner's income is added to yours (see Chapter 55). See Chapter 56 for further information about joint claims for WTC.

If you are responsible for one or more **children**:

- you (or your partner) need only do paid work of 16 hours a week to qualify for WTC (although if you are a member of a couple, in most cases your combined hours must be at least 24 a week);
- if you are a couple and one of you works at least 16 hours a week, your hours of work can be added to those of your partner to enable you to qualify for the 30-hour element (see p1311);
- you (and your partner) might qualify for the childcare element of WTC if you pay for childcare.

See p1269 for who counts as a child. The rules are the same as for child tax credit (CTC).[6] Some young people can continue to count as children for a period. HM Revenue and Customs (HMRC) calls them 'qualifying young people'. The terms 'child' or 'children' in this chapter include these qualifying young people.

For when you count as responsible for a child, see p1271. HMRC uses the same test as for CTC.[7]

Couples

You and your partner count as a 'couple' if you are:[8]

- a man and woman and are:
  - married, unless you are separated and this is under a court order or is likely to be permanent (see p1285); *or*

  - not married and are 'living together as husband and wife' (see p1285); *or*
- the same sex as your partner and are:
  - registered as civil partners, unless you are separated and this is under a court order or is likely to be permanent (see below); *or*
  - not civil partners and are living together as if you are – ie, you would be regarded as 'living together as husband and wife' if you were a different sex from your partner (see below).[9]

Note: if you claim jointly with your partner but then cease to count as a couple (or you claim as a single person but then become a member of a couple), you should report this change in your circumstances and claim tax credits as a single person (or couple) immediately.

Married couples and civil partners

You must claim tax credits jointly with your partner if you are married to her/him or you are registered as civil partners. You continue to count as a couple while you and your partner are **temporarily separated**. It does not matter how long the temporary separation lasts (but see p1286 if you or your partner go abroad).

If you and your partner are **permanently separated** or are separated under a court order, you can claim tax credits as a single person immediately. This is the case even if you are still living under the same roof and whether or not you are taking steps to divorce your partner or dissolve your civil partnership. The test is whether you are 'separated in circumstances in which the separation is likely to be permanent' and this depends on your (and your partner's) intentions.[10] If you and your partner are having a trial separation and there is at least a 50 per cent chance of reconciliation, HMRC is likely to say you still count as a couple.[11]

You count as a 'polygamous unit' if you are a member of a couple married under a law which permits polygamy and either you or your partner are also married to another person (unless any of you are separated and this is under a court order or is likely to be permanent).[12] Special rules apply if you are a member of a 'polygamous unit'.[13]

Living together as husband and wife

You must claim tax credits jointly with your partner if:

- you are 'living together as husband and wife'; *or*
- you are not civil partners but are living together as if you are, in circumstances where you would be regarded as 'living together as husband and wife' if you were a different sex from your partner.

In determining whether or not you count as living together as husband and wife, HMRC is likely to consider the same factors the DWP does for means-tested benefits.[14] See pp754 and 757 for more information about the situations when you might count as living together as husband and wife.

No one factor is in itself conclusive, as it is your 'general relationship' as a whole which is of paramount importance.[15] As relationships between couples often vary considerably, each case depends on all its own particular facts and circumstances.

People with no sexual relationship who live together might sometimes still be treated as a couple. People who provide mutual support and share household expenses should not necessarily be treated as a couple – this is also the case where friends share a home.[16]

Decision makers often apply too narrow an interpretation of the test. There is no rule, for example, that if your partner stays with you for three nights or more a week you are *automatically* to be treated as a couple living together.

If you and your partner stop living together, you can claim tax credits as a single person immediately. However, if you and your partner are only temporarily living apart (eg, one of you is in hospital or in respite care), you may still be treated as a couple.

If you or your partner go abroad

If you or your partner go abroad, either permanently or for more than a set period of time (see p1495), you cease to satisfy the residence conditions. In this case, you must terminate your joint claim. Failure to do this may result in a penalty (see p1385). The person still in the UK may be able to make a new claim as a single person.

Challenging a decision

In some cases you may have to prove that you are a couple – eg, if you want to claim WTC instead of income support and you are not in full-time paid work yourself, but your partner is. In other cases you may have to prove that you are not a couple – eg, if your former partner's income is being taken into account when working out your tax credits.

If you think a decision about whether or not you count as a couple is wrong and it affects your tax credits, consider appealing. It is possible that the DWP, the local authority and HMRC might reach different conclusions about whether you are a couple. If so, appeal *all* the decisions with which you disagree.

4. The amount of working tax credit

The amount of working tax credit (WTC) you get depends on:

- your maximum WTC. This is made up of a combination of 'elements' (see p1287);
- how much income you have; *and*
- the 'income threshold figure'.

The elements and threshold can be increased every April. If you do not qualify for WTC currently, you might qualify if the rates go up.

If you are on a means-tested benefit

Being on income support (IS), income-based jobseeker's allowance (JSA), income-related employment and support allowance (ESA) or pension credit (PC) is an automatic passport to maximum WTC.[17] You therefore do not need to work out your income and capital. In these circumstances, WTC equals maximum WTC. **Note:** this does not apply while you are getting 'WTC run-on' (see p1304).

In practice, there are not many situations when you can claim IS, income-based JSA or income-related ESA at the same time as WTC. This is because you cannot claim IS or JSA if you or your partner are in full-time paid work for IS/JSA purposes, and you cannot claim income-related ESA if you do *any* work (unless this is work you may do while claiming) or if your partner is in full-time paid work for ESA purposes. However, you might be able to claim both – eg, if you (or your partner) are a 'term-time only' worker or are off sick (see Chapter 31). WTC counts in full as income for IS, income-based JSA, income-related ESA and PC.

If you are not on a means-tested benefit

If you are not on IS, income-based JSA, income-related ESA or PC, you need to follow the steps below to calculate your WTC.

- **Step one:** work out your 'relevant period' (see pp1308 and 1319).
- **Step two:** work out your maximum entitlement (your maximum WTC) for the relevant period (see p1319).
- **Step three:** work out your relevant income (see p1319).
- **Step four:** compare your income with the 'income threshold figure' for the relevant period – currently £6,420 for WTC.[18]
- **Step five:** calculate WTC entitlement for the relevant period (see p1320). If your income is less than the 'income threshold figure', WTC equals maximum WTC. If your income exceeds the 'income threshold figure', your maximum WTC is reduced by 41 per cent of the excess. **Note:** see previous editions of this *Handbook* for the percentages before 2012/13.

You may also be entitled to child tax credit (CTC). Full details of both calculations are in Chapter 54.

Maximum working tax credit

Your maximum WTC is calculated by adding together all the elements that apply to you.[19] These are:[20]

- basic element (£1,920 a year);
- disabled worker element (£2,790 a year);
- lone parent/couple element (£1,950 a year);

- 30-hour element (£790 a year);
- severe disability element (£1,190 a year);
- childcare element (see Chapter 54 for how this is calculated).

If you are a member of a couple, more than one disabled worker element and severe disability element can be included – eg, if both you and your partner qualify, two are included. For details of how you qualify for the above elements, see Chapter 54. **Note:** before April 2012, there was also a 50-plus element. See the 2011/12 edition of this *Handbook* for details.

Example

Glen gets disability living allowance care component at the lowest rate and HM Revenue and Customs accepts that he is at a disadvantage in getting a job. His maximum WTC is made up of the basic element and the disabled worker element.

5. Claims and backdating

The rules on claiming, backdating and how your claim can be renewed at the end of the year are in Chapter 56. This section gives an outline of the rules on claims for working tax credit (WTC).

Making a claim

Your first claim for WTC must usually be made in writing on the form approved or authorised by HM Revenue and Customs (HMRC). You use the same form for WTC and for child tax credit (CTC). See p1348 for further information. Send the completed form to Comben House, Farriers Way, Netherton, Merseyside or any other office specified in writing by HMRC.[21] You can use the pre-paid envelope provided with the claim form.[22] Keep a copy in case queries arise.

You must provide any information and evidence required (see p1289). You can amend or withdraw your claim before you are given notice of the decision on your claim.[23]

Who should claim

If you are a member of a couple, you must make a joint claim with your partner. If you are not a member of a couple, you claim for yourself. For information about who counts as a couple for tax credit purposes, see p1284. If you cannot make your claim yourself, an 'appointee' (see p1347) can claim on your behalf.

Information to support your claim

When you claim WTC, you must:[24]

- satisfy the national insurance number (NI) requirement (see p1349);
- provide proof of your identity, if required;
- supply information to support your claim (see p1348).

It is important that you provide all the information required. If you do not do so, a decision might not be made on your claim.

When you claim WTC you must provide:

- details of your (and your partner's) income for the previous year (see Chapter 55);
- details of the work that you do, including your usual hours;
- if you are employed, your P60 or wage slips for the last tax year you were employed;
- if you are self-employed, your tax reference number and the date you became self-employed;
- details of any childcare payments you make to a registered or approved childcare provider;
- details of a bank or building society account into which your WTC can be paid. If you do not have an account, you need to open one within four weeks of making your claim. (This is the time limit from 6 April, previously it was eight weeks.) See pp1350 and 1355 for further information.

If you are also claiming CTC, you must provide additional information (see p1276).

HMRC might need further information before it makes a decision on your claim. See p1350 for details of the time you must be given to provide the information and what happens if you fail to do so.

When to claim

The general rule is that your claim runs from the date it is received by HMRC.[25] You cannot make a claim in advance of the tax year in which you are claiming, but you *can* claim WTC in advance of starting work, provided you expect to start work within seven days and will be entitled to WTC within seven days of starting work.[26] See p1290 for how and when claims can be backdated.

Awards of WTC are always based on annual income. HMRC bases the initial award of WTC on your (and your partner's) *previous* tax year's income. If you think your income for the current tax year is likely, eventually, to be sufficiently low for you to qualify for WTC (eg, you are self-employed and you do not yet know your previous tax year's income, or your income is going to fall or has fallen because your work is seasonal, you are going on maternity leave or you might be made redundant), you may wish to consider making a claim (including a request for your claim to be backdated if relevant), even if you know you will be given what is known as a 'nil award'. This protects your position because you can then ask HMRC to amend the award on the basis of a change in your income (see p1328). The amended award would then run from your original date of claim (or the date to which your claim was backdated). See *Protect Your Right to Tax Credits by Claiming Early,* at www.hmrc.gov.uk/taxcredits/start/claiming/backdate-ahead/protect-claim.htm. See pp1365–67 before deciding what to do.

Backdating your claim

It is very important to claim in time. A claim for WTC can usually only be backdated for a maximum of 31 days. (This is the time limit from 6 April, previously it was 93 days.)[27] You only need to show that you qualified for WTC during that period. Unlike for most means-tested benefits, you do not have to show any reasons for your delay. See p1355 for further information.

Note: there is a special backdating rule if you claim WTC when you are awarded a qualifying benefit – eg, disability living allowance (see p1355). Under this rule, your WTC can be backdated more than 31 days.

Renewal awards

At the end of the tax year in which you claimed WTC, you (and your partner if you are a member of a couple) receive a 'final notice' from HMRC asking you to confirm that your income and/or your household circumstances are as stated for the previous tax year (see p1361). You must reply within a strict time limit. HMRC then makes a final decision, based on your actual income during the tax year. It decides whether you were entitled to WTC and, if so, the amount of your award. This is known as the 'annual review'. HMRC also uses the information about your income and household circumstances for the previous tax year to renew your award for the next tax year.[28] **Note:** if you have a 'nil award', you may be given notice that your claim will not be renewed unless you specifically request this.

Example

Louise works 30 hours a week. She claims WTC in June 2011. Her initial award is based on her income during the 2010/11 tax year. In May 2012, she is sent a 'final notice'. She sends HMRC details of her actual income for 2011/12. HMRC uses this information to work out whether her WTC award was correct. Louise's actual income for 2011/12 is now the previous year's income for her WTC claim for 2012/13. HMRC uses this income to make an initial decision to award Louise WTC and set payments for 2012/13.

6. Getting paid

This section gives an outline of the rules on payment of working tax credit (WTC). For more information about getting paid, see p1354.

WTC is normally paid by direct credit transfer into your bank (or similar) account. If you make a joint claim, any WTC to which you are entitled towards your childcare expenses is paid to whoever is decided to be the main carer of your child(ren) (see p1354). If you are unable to act for yourself, payment can be made to someone on your behalf – called your 'appointee' (see p1347).[29]

How often is WTC paid?	Every week or every four weeks, whichever is more convenient for you, although HM Revenue and Customs (HMRC) can decide how often.[30]

You can be paid by cheque while your account arrangements are finalised.

If your award of WTC (or the combination of WTC and child tax credit (CTC)) is £2 a week or less, it is paid in a single lump sum into your account to cover the whole year.[31] **Note:** if your entitlement to WTC (or the combination of WTC and CTC) is less than £26 for the whole of the tax year, no award is made and you are not paid at all.[32]

Note:

- Your WTC cannot currently be paid at a reduced rate if you have been sanctioned for benefit offences (see p1106). However, possibly from 2012 or 2013, the government intends to amend the rules and your WTC might not be paid for a set period of time. See CPAG's *Welfare Rights Bulletin* for updates.
- If you have forgotten your PIN, see p1040. The issues are the same as for benefits.
- If payment of your WTC is delayed and this is causing hardship, ask HMRC to make a 'next day/same day payment'. You may also be eligible for a crisis loan (see p564). If you wish to complain about how your claim has been dealt with, see p1257. You might be able to claim compensation (see p1261).
- If payment of your WTC is postponed or suspended, see p1355.
- If you are overpaid WTC, you might have to repay it (see Chapter 58). In some cases, interest can be added to the overpayment. If you have been accused of fraud, see Chapter 59. In some cases you may be given a financial penalty.

Length of award

Your award of WTC runs from the date your claim is received by HMRC (or from the date to which your claim can be backdated) to the end of the tax year.[33] However, changes in your circumstances can be taken into account during the tax year. In some cases, you *must* report changes of circumstance. See below and Chapter 57 for details.

Change of circumstances

Your award of WTC is made on the basis of your (and your partner's) previous year's income and your personal circumstances on the date of your claim. If your current year's income or your personal circumstances change, your award of WTC can be amended. Remember the following.

- Some changes you *must* report to HMRC (see p1363). If you do not do so within one month, you may receive a financial penalty. Some changes end your entitlement to WTC and you have to make a fresh claim, including if:
  - you were claiming as a single person and you become part of a couple or you are claiming as a couple and you cease to be a member of a couple; *or*
  - you or your partner no longer count as ordinarily resident in the UK.
- Unless it is a change that you must report, it is optional to report changes that affect your maximum entitlement to WTC – eg, when your hours increase to 30 or more so you would qualify for a 30-hour element (see p1364). However, changes that increase your maximum entitlement to WTC can generally only be backdated one month from when you notify HMRC. Changes that decrease your entitlement always take effect from the date of the change so an overpayment can occur if you delay.
- There is a special rule that allows an increase in your entitlement to WTC to be backdated more than one month (but see below) if you are awarded a qualifying benefit and the disabled worker element or severe disability elements should be included in your WTC entitlement. You must notify HMRC within one month of the date the qualifying benefit is awarded (see p1365).
- It is optional to report changes in your income (see p1365). These are always taken into account at the end of the tax year, but you may want to consider reporting these sooner to avoid an overpayment or underpayment of WTC.

If you are claiming WTC and you only qualify for the lone parent or childcare element because you (or your partner) are responsible for a child and the child dies, you are paid WTC for a further eight weeks (or to the date your child would have turned 20 if this is earlier) as if this had not happened.[34] This is only the case if you would have continued to qualify for the element but for the child's death. After that period, you may continue to qualify for WTC – eg, if you still satisfy the means test and work sufficient hours to count as in full-time paid work.

7. Tax, tax credits and benefits

Working tax credit (WTC) is not taxable.

Tax credits

If you have dependent children (including a 'qualifying young person'), you might qualify for child tax credit (CTC). CTC can be paid in addition to WTC.

Means-tested benefits

WTC counts as income for income support (IS), income-based jobseeker's allowance (JSA), income-related employment and support allowance (ESA), pension credit (PC), housing benefit (HB) and council tax benefit (CTB). Also note the following.

- You may be able to claim IS/income-based JSA/income-related ESA or WTC, for example, if your partner works more than 16 but less than 24 hours a week. You may be able to claim both IS/income-based JSA/income-related ESA and WTC at the same time in some circumstances (see p729).
- There is no rule that prevents you or your partner doing full-time paid work while claiming PC, so you can claim WTC at the same time as PC.
- In some cases, if you have to pay housing costs (see Chapter 38) you might be better off financially if you claim IS, income-based JSA, income-related ESA or PC.
- If you qualify for HB or CTB, you might get an additional earnings disregard (see p915).

If you get arrears of WTC, these count as capital for means-tested benefits and can be disregarded (see pp982 and 1001).

Non-means-tested benefits

In some situations, while you are receiving WTC you get national insurance credits. See p786 for further details.

WTC can be paid in addition to any non-means-tested benefits to which you (or your partner) are entitled, but see Chapter 55 for which of these benefits may be taken into account as income for WTC. Qualifying for certain non-means-tested benefits means you may also qualify for the disabled worker element or severe disability element of WTC.

Passports and other sources of help

If you are entitled to WTC, you may also qualify for health benefits, such as free prescriptions (see Chapter 13). You do not have to satisfy the means test if your gross annual income is no more than a set amount and you are getting WTC which includes a disabled worker element or a severe disability element, or CTC with your WTC.

You may also qualify for free school lunches (see p14) and a Sure Start maternity grant or a social fund funeral expenses payment.

Notes

1. **Who can claim working tax credit**
   1 ss3(3) and (7), 10 and 42 TCA 2002; regs 4-8 WTC(EMR) Regs; reg 3 TC(R) Regs; reg 3 TC(I) Regs
   2 Reg 4(1) (second condition) WTC(EMR) Regs

2. **The rules about your age**
   3 s3(3) TCA 2002

3. **Who is included in your claim**
   4 s3(3)(a) and (5A) TCA 2002; CTC/3864/2004; R(TC) 1/07
   5 s3(3)(b) TCA 2002
   6 Reg 2 WTC(EMR) Regs, definition of 'child' and 'qualifying young person'
   7 Reg 2(2) WTC(EMR) Regs
   8 s3(5A) TCA 2002; reg 2(1) WTC(EMR) Regs, definition of 'couple'
   9 s48(2) TCA 2002
   10 s3(5A)(a)(ii) and (c)(ii) TCA 2002
   11 R(TC) 2/06
   12 ss3(6A) and 43 TCA 2002; reg 2 TC(PM) Regs
   13 TC(PM) Regs
   14 *Crake and Butterworth v SBC* [1982] 1 All ER 498; R(SB) 17/81; CTC/3864/2004
   15 R(SB) 17/81; R(G) 3/71; CIS/87/1993
   16 CSSB/145/1983

4. **The amount of working tax credit**
   17 ss7(2) and 13 TCA 2002; reg 4 TC(ITDR) Regs
   18 Reg 3(2) TC(ITDR) Regs
   19 s11 TCA 2002
   20 Regs 3 and 20 and Sch 2 WTC(EMR) Regs

5. **Claims and backdating**
   21 Reg 2 TC(CN) Regs, definition of 'appropriate office' and 'relevant authority'
   22 Regs 2, definitions of 'appropriate office' and 'relevant authority', and 5 TC(CN) Regs
   23 Reg 5(7) TC(CN) Regs; R(IS) 5/05
   24 Reg 5(3)-(6) TC(CN) Regs
   25 s5(2) TCA 2002
   26 Reg 10 TC(CN) Regs
   27 Reg 7 TC(CN) Regs
   28 Regs 11 and 12 TC(CN) Regs

6. **Getting paid**
   29 s24(3) TCA 2002; reg 6 TC(PC) Regs
   30 Regs 8 and 13 TC(PC) Regs
   31 Reg 10 TC(PC) Regs
   32 Reg 9 TC(ITDR) Regs
   33 s5(2) TCA 2002
   34 Reg 19 WTC(EMR) Regs; reg 6 CTC Regs

Chapter 53

Work and tax credits

This chapter covers:

Key facts

- To qualify for working tax credit, you or your partner must be in full-time paid work (HM Revenue and Customs calls this 'remunerative work'). You can be treated as in full-time paid work in some circumstances.
- Your entitlement to child tax credit (CTC) does not depend on whether or not you are in full-time paid work. However, you cannot get CTC for a young person who has left education or 'approved training' and is in full-time paid work.
- Earnings affect the amount of your tax credits.

1. The full-time paid work rule

To qualify for working tax credit (WTC), you or your partner must be in full-time paid work. HM Revenue and Customs (HMRC) calls this 'remunerative work'.[1] See p1296 for what counts as full-time work, p1297 for what counts as paid work and p1297 for how your hours are calculated. 'Work' includes self-employment and work which is done from home.

In some circumstances, you may be treated as not being in full-time paid work even if you are (see p1304). In others, you may be treated as if you are in full-time paid work when you are not (see p1302). If you are unsure if you are in full-time paid work, see p1301.

Income from work affects your entitlement to WTC. This means that, although your (or your partner's) hours of work are high enough for you to qualify, you might not satisfy the means test. Although full-time paid workdoes not affect entitlement to child tax credit (CTC), income from work affects the amount you can be paid.

If neither you nor your partner are in full-time paid work, you may be able to claim income support (IS), jobseeker's allowance (JSA) or employment and support allowance (ESA). You may be able to choose whether to claim IS/JSA/ESA or WTC. In some situations, you may be able to claim both IS/JSA/ESA and WTC – eg, if you are a 'term-time only' worker or are off sick and getting statutory sick pay. This is because different rules on what counts as full-time paid work apply for WTC than those that apply for IS/JSA/ESA. See p729 for information about what you should consider.

Note: you cannot get CTC for a qualifying young person for any period that includes a week in which s/he has left full-time education or 'approved training' and is in full-time paid work (24 hours or more).[2] The rules about full-time paid work are the same as for WTC claimants.

What counts as full-time work

For the purpose of WTC, you count as being in full-time work if any of the following apply.[3]

- You work at least 30 hours a week and you are 25 or over.
- You work at least 16 hours a week and:
  - you have a physical or mental disability which puts you at a disadvantage in getting a job and you qualify for a disabled worker element; *or*
  - you are 60 or over; *or*
  - you are a single claimant and are responsible for a child or qualifying young person (see p1271); *or*
  - you are a member of a couple and you (or your partner) are responsible for a child or qualifying young person (see p1271). However, from 6 April 2012, this will only apply if your partner counts as incapacitated for the purposes of the childcare element (see p1314), is entitled to carer's allowance, is a hospital inpatient or is in prison; *or*
  - you are a member of a couple and you (or your partner) are responsible for a child or qualifying young person (see p1271). However, from 6 April 2012, this will only apply if your and your partner's combined hours of work are at least 24 a week. This means that if you both work, one of you must do 16 hours a week and the other must do at least eight hours a week. If only one of you works, that person must work at least 24 hours a week.

If you are under 25, you can only claim WTC if you count as being in full-time work while working at least 16 hours a week.

Note: before 6 April 2012, you also counted as in full-time work if you (or your partner) worked at least 16 hours a week, were at least 50 and qualified for a 50-plus element. See the 2011/12 edition of this *Handbook* for details.

If your circumstances change and you are no longer responsible for a child or qualifying young person, or no longer qualify for a disabled worker element, unless you are 60 or over, you may have to increase your weekly hours to 30 or more to continue to qualify for WTC. See Chapter 57 for more information on changes of circumstances and when you must report them.

Note the following.

- At the date of your claim, you must:[4]
  - be working; *or*
  - have accepted an offer of work which is expected to start within seven days. In this case, you only count as being in full-time paid work when the work begins.
- The work must be expected to continue for at least four weeks after you make your claim (or if you have accepted an offer of work, after the work starts).[5]
- You can continue to count as being in full-time work for four weeks after you leave work, or your hours reduce to less than the number you (or your partner) need to do. See p1304 for information about what is known as 'WTC run-on'.

If you normally work sufficient hours a week, but are off sick or on maternity, paternity or adoption leave, you may be able to claim WTC as you can be treated as in full-time paid work (see p1302). You may also be able to claim IS, JSA or ESA.

What counts as paid work

'Paid work' includes work for which you are paid or expect to be paid.[6] Payment of a benefit (eg, carer's allowance) does not count for these purposes. The information on p719 about what counts as paid work for means-tested benefits also applies to WTC.

How your hours are calculated

How you calculate your hours depends on whether you are employed or self-employed (see below). To work out whether you are in full-time paid work:[7]

- if you are employed, include all the hours:
  - you normally work under your contract, if you are an apprentice or employee; *or*
  - you normally perform in the office in which you are employed, if you are an office holder. This includes elective office, as well as company directors; *or*
  - for which you are normally paid by the employment agency with whom you have a contract, if you are an agency worker; *or*
- if you are self-employed, include all the hours you normally do for payment or for which you expect to be paid.

Paid meal and refreshment breaks count towards the total hours you work.[8] Also included is any time allowed for visits to a hospital, clinic or other establishment, but only if this is for the treatment or monitoring of your disability and if you are paid, or expect to be paid, for the time.[9] Your total hours from more than one job are added together.

Periods when you are on a customary or paid holiday from work are ignored in calculating your hours.[10] Likewise, unpaid meal and refreshment breaks are ignored.

Employed and self-employed[11]

You count as **employed** if you are employed under a contract of service or apprenticeship and your earnings are taxable as employment income under certain provisions of the Income Tax (Earnings and Pensions) Act 2003. You count as **self-employed** if you are carrying out a trade, profession or vocation.

Hours you normally work

Whether you are employed or self-employed, the measure for WTC purposes is the number of hours you normally work.[12] 'Normally' is not defined in the WTC rules. HMRC says you should calculate your hours based on what you 'regularly, usually or typically' do and that the number of hours you normally work might not be the number of hours specified in your contract of employment.[13] The hours that are relevant are those you *actually* work. If you routinely do paid overtime, argue that these are hours you normally work and that they should be included. See below if your hours fluctuate.

Example

Harriet is a cashier in a supermarket. Her partner stays at home to look after their children. She is contracted to work 21 hours a week over a three-day week but she does 3.5 hours overtime almost every week. She gets an unpaid half-hour lunch break. When Harriet and her partner claim WTC, she has just returned from two weeks' paid holiday.

Harriet normally works 21 + 3.5 = 24.5 hours a week. Unpaid lunch breaks and the time she was on paid holiday are not taken into account. As Harriet and her partner are responsible for children, one of them needs to work at least 16 hours a week and between them, they need to work at least 24 hours a week. Harriet therefore counts as being in full-time paid work.

When working out your normal hours if you are self-employed, HMRC says you can include not only the hours you spend providing orders or services but also those that are necessary to your self-employment – eg, trips to wholesalers and retailers, visits to potential clients, time spent on advertising or canvassing, cleaning the business or vehicles used as part of the business, bookkeeping and research work.[14]

If your hours fluctuate

Working out the number of hours you normally work is straightforward if:

- you do the same number of hours each and every week; *or*

- your hours vary, but you always do at least enough hours each week to count as being in full-time paid work.

However, if your weekly hours fluctuate, it can be more complicated. Unless you are a term-time only worker (ie, you have a recognisable 'work cycle' that lasts for a year with periods during which you are not required to work – eg, in an educational establishment – see below, there is no rule on how to average your hours. Working out the number of hours you 'normally work' is a question of judgement. If you have a regular pattern of work (a recognised 'work cycle'), HMRC says the hours you 'normally' work are those that reflect an overall view of the pattern of your hours over a representative period, or over a year.[15] For example, if you always work two weeks on and two weeks off, you can try to argue that your hours should be averaged over a four-week period.

If you are in any doubt about what your normal hours are, contact HMRC and seek advice. If you are unsure whether you are in full-time paid work, see p1301.

Examples

Shane works in a residential project. He works three weeks on and one week off. When he is on, he works 40 hours a week. His average hours are 40 x 3 ÷ 4 = 30 hours a week. Shane can try to argue that he normally works 30 hours or more a week. As Shane is aged 45, does not have a physical or mental disability and has no children, he must work at least 30 hours a week. He therefore counts as being in full-time paid work.

Narindar is contracted to do 15 hours a week. However, she gets regular overtime of three hours every other week. Her average hours are 15 + 18 ÷ 2 = 16.5 hours. Narindar can try to argue that she normally works 16 hours or more a week. As Narindar is a lone parent, she need only work 16 hours or more a week. She therefore counts as being in full-time paid work.

Appeal if you think your average hours have been calculated unfairly. You should first work out whether you are better off claiming IS/JSA/ESA or WTC (see p729).

'Term-time only' workers

If you have a recognisable 'work cycle' that lasts for a year (eg, in a school or an educational establishment where you have periods of school holidays or similar vacations during which you do not work), the 'term-time only' worker rule applies.[16] The periods when you are not working are ignored when deciding whether you are in full-time paid work. Note that this rule can also apply to other seasonal workers. However, if you work casually or intermittently (eg, you are a seasonal worker who works in the summer but you are unemployed the rest of the year), HMRC might say your work cycle is that part of the year in which you are working and that you do not count as in full-time work when you are unemployed.[17]

In practice, if the hours of work you do during term time mean you are in full-time paid work during term time, you also count as being in full-time paid work over the holidays. You should be able to claim WTC during this period if your normal hours of work each week are sufficient during term time. Because the way hours are calculated is different for JSA and ESA, if you are not paid for the holidays, you might also be able to claim JSA (or if you have a partner, s/he might also be able to claim income-related ESA) during these periods if you satisfy the other qualifying conditions (see Chapter 31).

Example

Dee is 35 years old and has no children. She is a cleaner at a local college and works 35 hours a week, 32 weeks of the year. She does not work (and is not paid) when the students are on study leave or on holiday. The periods when Dee does not work are ignored. She is in full-time paid work during term time because she works 30 hours or more a week. She therefore counts as being in full-time paid work throughout the year and can claim WTC.

Sometimes it may not be clear whether you have a 'work cycle' that lasts a year – eg, if you have only started your job recently or have a fixed-term contract that finishes at the end of the school term, or are employed on a casual or relief basis.[18] It can take time before it can be said that you have a yearly work cycle.[19] However, if you have an indefinite contract to work in term time only, you can argue that you have a yearly work cycle from the start.[20]

Students

You are not excluded from claiming WTC simply because you are a student. However, you must count as in full-time paid work under the rules described in this chapter. So if, for example, you do sufficient hours of paid work in addition to your studies or during the holidays, you can qualify for WTC. **Note:** the work must be expected to last for four weeks.

Any work you do in studying for a degree or other qualification does not count as full-time paid work – any grant or loan you receive is for your maintenance and is not paid in return for work done on the course. You are not considered to be in full-time paid work if you are a student nurse because the NHS bursary and other grants or loans you get are not payments for work done on the course and do not count as income for tax credit purposes.[21] However, if you are paid in return for the work you do (eg, you are paid by an employer during a work placement), you can argue that you are in full-time paid work. There are a number of situations in which you do not count as in full-time paid work even if you are – eg, if you are on a government training scheme being paid a training allowance (see p1304).

When calculating how much WTC you can get, student loans and most other student income is disregarded. See p1336 for what income counts.

Foster carers

If you are working sufficient hours as a foster carer, you can qualify for WTC. HMRC generally treats foster carers as self-employed. It says that the hours of work you declare on your claim form should be accepted.[22] If you do more than one job, the total hours are added together, so if you are doing work in addition to foster caring, the hours from the other work can be added to those spent foster caring.

Fostering allowances that qualify for tax relief are generally ignored when calculating your WTC and CTC. See p1341 for further information.

Note: for IS and JSA, if you or your partner are (or for income-related ESA, your partner is) a foster carer (or in Scotland a kinship carer) receiving a payment for looking after a child from a local authority or voluntary organisation, you are (or s/he is) treated as not being in full-time paid work (see p725). You may wish to consider how you would be better off financially.

If you are unsure whether you are in full-time paid work

If you are unsure if the number of hours you normally work are sufficient at the **date of your claim**, contact HMRC and seek advice. Bear in mind that a claim for WTC can be backdated for 31 days automatically (see p1355), so there is scope to postpone claiming WTC until you are certain. If time is running out and you are still uncertain, consider making a claim to protect your position.

If you are refused WTC because neither you nor your partner are in full-time paid work for WTC purposes and within 14 days of that decision you claim IS or JSA, your claim for IS or JSA can be backdated to the date you claimed WTC.[23] This rule does not apply to ESA. However, your ESA claim can be backdated for up to three months (see p190).

If your **circumstances change** while you are claiming WTC, consider the following.

- If you are now uncertain about whether you are still in full-time paid work (eg, your weekly hours change), keep a record of the hours you work each week.
  - If it appears that you no longer normally work sufficient hours a week, you are no longer entitled to WTC.
  - If you have a partner and are getting a childcare element because *both* of you are in full-time paid work and it appears that one of you no longer normally works 16 hours a week, you may no longer be entitled to a childcare element (see p1314).

  In both cases, you must report your change in hours to HMRC within one month. See Chapter 57 for more information on changes of circumstances and when you must report them.

- If you are no longer responsible for a child or qualifying young person (you must report this to HMRC within one month) or no longer qualify for a disabled worker element, unless you are 60 or over you may now have to increase your hours to continue to qualify for WTC.
- If you no longer count as being in full-time paid work, check to see if you (or your partner) qualify for IS, JSA or ESA and make a claim if this is possible. Remember that claims for IS and JSA can only be backdated in limited circumstances (see p1027).
- Whether or not you are in full-time paid work, check to see if you qualify for pension credit (PC). There is no full-time paid work rule for PC, but earnings and WTC count as income.
- If your hours change, but you still count as being in full-time paid work, the amount of WTC to which you are entitled could be affected by:
  - a change in your earnings. If these increase, you may wish to report this to HMRC to avoid an overpayment at the end of the year. If these decrease, you can get increased WTC if you report the change. You may wish to consider waiting until the end of the year (see pp1365–67);
  - whether or not you are entitled to have a 30-hour element included in calculating your WTC. If your entitlement decreases, you must report your change in hours to HMRC within one month. Any increase in your entitlement to WTC can only be backdated one month from the date you notify HMRC of the change (see p1364). (This is the time limit from 6 April 2012, previously it was three months)

2. Treated as being in full-time paid work

You or your partner are treated as being in full-time paid work:

- during any period when:[24]
  - you are being paid statutory maternity pay (SMP), ordinary or additional statutory paternity pay (SPP), statutory adoption pay (SAP) or maternity allowance (MA); *or*
  - you are absent from work during ordinary maternity leave, ordinary paternity leave or ordinary adoption leave, or during the first 13 weeks of additional maternity or adoption leave; *or*
  - you are absent from work during additional paternity leave, but only during the period in which you would have been paid additional SPP had you qualified.

  If you are an employee, you are treated as in full-time paid work from the start of the period, so long as you are in full-time paid work for working tax credit (WTC) purposes immediately before the period begins. However, if this is not the case (eg, you are under 25, or are 25 or over but working less than 30 hours a week and the child you and your partner are having or adopting is your first), you are treated as in full-time paid work from the date of birth (or adoption) so long as you would have counted as in full-time paid work had you been responsible for a child or qualifying young person immediately before the period begins.[25]

If you are self-employed, you count as in full-time paid work during any period when the above would have applied had the work done in the week before the period began been as an employee.

If you do not return to work when your SMP, SPP, SAP or MA ceases or your leave ends, you are no longer treated as being in full-time paid work under this rule; *and*

- during any period when:[26]
  - you are being paid statutory sick pay (SSP) or short-term lower rate incapacity benefit (IB); *or*
  - you are being paid income support (IS) because you are entitled to SSP, are disqualified from IB because of misconduct or failure to accept treatment or are incapable of work because of pregnancy or you are being paid employment and support allowance (ESA), or you are getting national insurance credits because you are incapable of work or have limited capability for work. This only applies for 28 weeks.

  You must have been in full-time paid work for WTC purposes immediately before the period began.

  If you are self-employed, you count as in full-time paid work during any period when the above would have applied had the work done in the week before the period began been as an employee.

  If you do not return to work when your SSP or short-term lower rate IB ceases (or if you are being paid IS or ESA, after 28 weeks), you no longer count as being in full-time paid work under this rule.

Even though you continue to count as in full-time paid work, you should consider letting HMRC know if you are in any of the above situations. This is because any MA and short-term lower rate IB are ignored as income for WTC, as is the first £100 a week of any SMP, SPP and SAP. You are entitled to maximum WTC if you are on IS or income-related ESA although any WTC you receive counts in full as income for those benefits.

You or your partner are also treated as being in full-time paid work:

- if you were in full-time paid work within the past seven days.[27] This means you can make a new claim or continue to qualify for WTC – eg, during a short period between jobs or when you are on jury service;
- during any period when you are on strike or are suspended from work while complaints or allegations against you are investigated, so long as you were in full-time paid work for WTC purposes immediately before the start of the period. You must not be on strike for longer than 10 consecutive days when you should be working.[28]

You and your partner can also be treated as being in full-time paid work during a four-week 'WTC run-on' period (see below).

Working tax credit run-on

If you or your partner stop work or reduce your hours, you can get what is known as 'WTC run-on'. You are treated as being in full-time paid work for the four weeks immediately after you stop work, or your hours reduce to less than the number you (or your partner) must do to count as in full-time paid work.[29] This means you continue to qualify for WTC for the four-week period, even if you would otherwise no longer count as in full-time paid work. It also means that you continue to qualify for all the elements you were previously getting for that period – eg, the 30-hour element and the childcare element, even if the reduction in hours means you would otherwise lose entitlement to these. This applies whether or not you actually count as in full-time paid work. **Note:** you must report the change in your circumstances to HMRC within one month.

3. Treated as not being in full-time paid work

You or your partner are treated as *not* being in full-time paid work during any period during which you are receiving pay in lieu of notice after you stop work, unless you continue to qualify under the four-week 'run-on' rule (see above).[30] In addition, you or your partner are treated as *not* being in full-time work if:[31]

- you are a volunteer, or are working for a charity or voluntary organisation and are giving your services free (except for your expenses);
- you are providing care for someone who is staying with you temporarily but who is not normally a member of your household; *and*
  - the only payment you receive is from a health authority, a local authority, a voluntary organisation, a primary care trust or from the person her/himself for caring for her/him; *and*
  - the payment is disregarded as a tax-free payment under HM Revenue and Customs' 'rent-a-room' scheme (see p1339);

  Note that if you are an adult placement carer who has *not* opted for the 'rent-a-room' scheme, you *can* count as in full-time paid work.[32]
- you are on a specified government scheme – eg:
  - you are working on a training scheme and are being paid a training allowance (see p1305) unless the training allowance or the money you are being paid by the DWP is subject to income tax as a profit from work;[33]
  - the only payment you receive, or expect to receive, is a sports award from the Sports Council.

Note that if you are on any other employment programme and you are paid for your services, if you do sufficient hours you can count as being in full-time paid work;[34]

- you are working while you are a sentenced or remand prisoner. This means you cannot qualify for working tax credit even if the work you do is outside the prison – eg, while you are on temporary release.

Training allowance

A **'training allowance'** is an allowance paid to maintain you or a member of your family:[35]
- by a government department or by or on behalf of the Secretary of State, Scottish Enterprise or the Highlands and Islands Enterprise; *and*
- for the period or part of a period during which you are on a course provided or approved by or under arrangements made by any of these.

Allowances paid to, or in respect of, you by a government department or by the Scottish Executive are not included if these are paid because you are a trainee teacher or on a full-time course of education, unless this is under arrangements made under s2 of the Employment and Training Act 1973.

4. Working tax credit and out-of-work benefits

Sometimes it is difficult to show that you count as being in full-time paid work, and the differences between the rules for working tax credit (WTC) and out-of-work benefits (income support (IS), jobseeker's allowance (JSA) or employment and support allowance (ESA)) mean that in some situations you may have a choice about whether to claim WTC *or* out-of-work benefits. In some situations, you might be able to claim both IS/income-based JSA/income-related ESA and WTC. For example, if you are a single claimant, you might be able to claim IS or income-based JSA and WTC if you are a 'term-time only' worker or are off sick and getting statutory sick pay. If you are a member of a couple, you might be able to claim income-related ESA and WTC if your partner is working 16 or more, but less than 24, hours a week. See p729 for further information.

Notes

1. **The full-time paid work rule**
   1 s10(1) TCA 2002
   2 Regs 2, definition of 'remunerative work', and 5(4)(a) CTC Regs
   3 Reg 4(1) (second condition) WTC(EMR) Regs
   4 Reg 4(1) (first condition) WTC(EMR) Regs
   5 Reg 4(1) (third condition) WTC(EMR) Regs
   6 Reg 4(1) (fourth condition) WTC(EMR) Regs
   7 Reg 4(3) WTC(EMR) Regs
   8 Reg 4(4)(b) WTC(EMR) Regs
   9 Reg 4(5) WTC(EMR) Regs
   10 Reg 4(4)(a) WTC(EMR) Regs
   11 Reg 2(1) WTC(EMR) Regs
   12 Reg 4(3) WTC(EMR) Regs
   13 para 02451-02452 TCTM
   14 para 02453 TCTM
   15 para 02457 TCTM
   16 Reg 7 WTC(EMR) Regs; *Stafford and Banks v CAO* [2001] UKHL 33 (HL), reported as R(IS) 15/01
   17 R(JSA) 1/07
   18 R(JSA) 8/03
   19 CIS/914/1997; CJSA/2759/1998
   20 R(JSA) 5/02
   21 R(FIS) 1/83; R(FIS) 1/86; para 02431 TCTM
   22 para 02440 TCTM
   23 Reg 6(28) SS(C&P) Regs

2. **Treated as being in full-time paid work**
   24 Reg 5 WTC(EMR) Regs
   25 Reg 5A WTC(EMR) Regs
   26 Reg 6 WTC(EMR) Regs
   27 Reg 8 WTC(EMR) Regs
   28 Regs 7A and 7B WTC(EMR) Regs
   29 Reg 7D WTC(EMR) Regs

3. **Treated as not being in full-time paid work**
   30 Reg 7C WTC(EMR) Regs
   31 Reg 4(2) WTC(EMR) Regs
   32 para 02440 TCTM
   33 *Reg 4(2)(c) and (d) and (2A)* WTC(EMR) Regs
   34 para 02440 TCTM
   35 Reg 2(1) WTC(EMR) Regs

Chapter 54

The amount of tax credit

This chapter covers:

Key facts

- The amount of tax credit to which you are entitled depends on your family circumstances and your income.
- There are no limits on the amount of savings or other capital that you can have.
- If you are entitled to income support (IS), income-based jobseeker's allowance (JSA), income-related employment and support allowance (ESA) or pension credit (PC), you are automatically entitled to the maximum amount of tax credit that you could receive.
- If you are not entitled to IS, income-based JSA, income-related ESA or PC, you may receive less than your maximum amount of tax credit, depending on the level of your income.
- Your maximum amount of child tax credit depends on the size of your family, the ages of the children in your family and whether any child in your family has a disability.
- The amount of working tax credit you can get depends on whether you are single with no dependants, a lone parent, or a member of a couple, the hours you work, whether you (or your partner if you have one) are disabled, and whether you have eligible childcare costs.

Future changes: April 2013 and after

Major changes are taking place that affect the benefits and tax credits system (see Chapter 2).

– From April 2013, total benefit payments to many working-age households will be 'capped' (see p25). There will be limited exceptions, including households in which someone is entitled to working tax credit or receives constant attendance

allowance or disability living allowance. Child tax credit will be included in this capped amount.
- From October 2013, a new benefit, universal credit (UC), will be introduced, which will replace tax credits. If you are already getting tax credits in October 2013, you will be able to continue to do so until you are are transferred to UC. The government has said that a transitional amount will be paid to ensure that no one is worse off at the point of transfer.
- No new claims for tax credits will be accepted from 6 April 2014, although it will be possible to renew your claim until you have moved onto UC.

See CPAG's *Welfare Rights Bulletin* for updates.

1. The relevant period

The amount of tax credit you can receive is based on your entitlement during a 'relevant period'. Tax credit awards are calculated using a maximum *annual* amount that you could receive. If you claim at the beginning of the new tax year, your award will usually be calculated on the basis that you will be entitled to tax credit for the whole of that tax year (6 April to 5 April), and your relevant period will, therefore, be one year.[1] Your annual entitlement is calculated and then paid to you over the course of that year.

If you claim a tax credit after the beginning of a tax year, your award is calculated for a period beginning with the date on which you make your claim and ending at the end of that tax year, unless you are able to have your claim backdated to an earlier period (see p1355). Similarly, if your circumstances change in the course of the year, and your award is amended, a new relevant period will begin. The new relevant period is calculated on the basis that it will end at the end of the tax year.[2] In both of these cases, you will be entitled to tax credit for less than a year, and so only a proportion of the annual amount can be paid.

In order to work out your maximum amount of tax credit, therefore, you need to know the length of your relevant period.

A **'relevant period'** is:

- for child tax credit (CTC), a period of an award during which your maximum amount remains the same;[3]
- for working tax credit (WTC), a period during which the elements making up your maximum amount of tax credit (apart from the childcare element) remain the same and your average weekly childcare charge does not change by £10 or more or reduce to nil.[4]

If you are entitled to both CTC and WTC, a relevant period is one during which both of the above conditions are satisfied.[5]

2. The maximum amount of child tax credit

The maximum amount of child tax credit (CTC) you can get is calculated by adding together each of the 'elements' which apply to you.[6] The amount of each element is set at a yearly rate. The annual rate is converted to a daily rate by dividing by the number of days in the tax year (365 in 2012/13) and rounding up to two decimal places. To calculate entitlement, the daily rate of each element is then multiplied by the number of days in the relevant period. The effect of this is that entitlement in a whole year is always slightly higher than the annual rates listed below – eg, the family element (£1.50 x 365) works out as £547.50 in 2012/13. If you are entitled to CTC for a period of less than a year, or if your entitlement changes part way through the year, the amount of each of these elements is adjusted so that the correct proportion of your annual maximum amount is paid to you.[7] How entitlement is calculated when entitlement changes part-way through a tax year is explained on p1323.

The elements are:[8]

Element	*Annual rate*
Family element	£545
Child element	£2,690
Disabled child element	£2,950
Severely disabled child element	£1,190

- One family element is payable for your family, and the amount is not affected by how many children you have, or their ages, or whether you are a single parent or one of a couple (see p1284 for who counts as your family).
- You get a child element for each child in your family (see p1269 for when a child or young person can count as a member of your family).
- You get a disabled child element for any child in your family who gets disability living allowance (DLA), or who is registered blind or who has been taken off the register in the last 28 weeks. The element still applies if DLA has stopped because your child is in hospital.[9] It is paid in addition to the child element for that child.
- You get a severely disabled child element for each child in your family who gets the highest rate of the care component of DLA. The element still applies if DLA has stopped because your child is in hospital.[10] It is paid in addition to the child element and disabled child element for that child.

Note: the legislation only refers to a child element, payable at different annual rates if the child is disabled or severely disabled. In practice, HM Revenue and Customs (HMRC) refers to a disabled child element and a severely disabled child element, paid in addition to the basic child element. This may lead to a slight discrepancy when each element is rounded up to daily rates.

Example

Tracy is a single parent with two children aged five and three. The annual elements used when calculating her maximum amount are as follows:

Family element	£545
Child element for three-year-old child	£2,690
Child element for five-year-old child	£2,690

3. The maximum amount of working tax credit

The maximum amount of working tax credit (WTC) you get is calculated by adding together each of the 'elements' which apply to you.[11] The amount of each element, except the childcare element, is set at a yearly rate. The annual rate is converted to a daily rate by dividing by the number of days in the tax year (365 in 2012/13) and rounding up to two decimal places. To calculate entitlement, the daily rate of each element is then multiplied by the number of days in the relevant period. The effect of this is that entitlement in a whole year is always slightly higher than the annual rates listed below – eg, the basic element works out as £1,923.55 in 2012/13. The amount of the childcare element is set using your average *weekly* childcare costs.[12] See p1314 for how your childcare element is calculated.

If you are entitled to WTC for a period of less than a year, or if your entitlement changes part way through the year, the amount of each of these elements is adjusted so that the correct proportion of your annual maximum amount is paid to you.[13] See p1323 for an explanation of how entitlement is calculated when entitlement changes part way through a tax year.

There are seven elements.[14] An additional element was payable for some claimants aged over 50 in previous tax years. This has been abolished from 6 April 2012. See the 2011/12 edition of this *Handbook* for more information if you were entitled to the 50-plus element in 2011/12.

Element	*Annual rate*
Basic element	£1,920
Lone parent element	£1,950
Couple element	£1,950
30-hour element	£790
Disabled worker element	£2,790
Severe disability element	£1,190

Childcare element:	*Weekly rate*
Maximum eligible cost for two or more children per week	£300
Maximum eligible cost for one child per week	£175
Percentage of eligible costs covered	70%

Basic element

One basic element is paid with each award of WTC. To be entitled to this element, you must be engaged in 'qualifying remunerative work'. In this *Handbook* we call this 'full-time work'.[15] For the definition of full-time work, see Chapter 53. Unless you qualify for the basic element of WTC, you cannot qualify for any of the other elements.[16]

Couple element

You get the couple element if you are one of a couple making a joint claim (see p1347).[17] You cannot get the couple element if your partner is serving a prison sentence of more than 12 months or is a 'person subject to immigration control' (see p1410), unless either you or your partner are responsible for a child or qualifying young person.[18] You can only have one couple element included in your maximum amount.[19] For when you count as a couple, see p1284.

Lone parent element

You get the lone parent element if you claim as a single person and are responsible for a child or qualifying young person.[20]

30-hour element

You get a 30-hour element if you are:[21]

- a single claimant who works for at least 30 hours a week; *or*
- making a joint claim and either or both of you work for at least 30 hours a week; *or*
- making a joint claim, responsible for a child or qualifying young person, and:
  - you are both working; *and*
  - one of you works at least 16 hours a week; *and*
  - your joint hours of work total at least 30 hours a week.

You can only have one 30-hour element included in your maximum amount.[22]

Disabled worker element

You get a disabled worker element if you:[23]

- work at least 16 hours a week; *and*
- have a disability which puts you at a disadvantage in getting a job; *and*
- receive, or have recently received, a qualifying benefit for sickness or disability.

If you are claiming as a couple, at least one of you must satisfy all these conditions.

Having 'a disability which puts you at a disadvantage in getting a job' means you must meet any one of the conditions listed in Appendix 9. For initial claims only (where there has been no entitlement to the disabled worker element in the preceding two years), this can include undergoing a period of rehabilitation as a result of an illness or accident, but only for the remainder of the tax year in which you claim.

In order to count as receiving a 'qualifying benefit', you must satisfy one of the following conditions (referred to in the legislation as Cases A to G). A disabled worker element can be included in your maximum amount in a new claim or added to an existing tax credit award at any time during the tax year if you report a change (see p1323). You must:

- (Case A) for at least one day in the 182 days immediately preceding your claim, have been in receipt of:
  - incapacity benefit (IB) at the long-term or short-term higher rate; *or*
  - severe disablement allowance (SDA); *or*
  - employment and support allowance (ESA) for at least 28 weeks (including linked periods); *or*
  - credits for limited capability for work following the end of the entitlement period of contributory ESA, for at least 28 weeks (including periods on ESA and linked periods); *or*
  - ESA or credits (as above), together with IB, SDA or statutory sick pay (SSP) for at least 28 weeks (including linked periods); *or*
- (Case B) for at least one day in the 182 days immediately preceding your claim, have been in receipt of a disability premium paid for you with income support (IS), income-based jobseeker's allowance (JSA), housing benefit or council tax, or a higher pensioner premium with IS or JSA; *or*
- (Case C) receive disability living allowance (DLA), attendance allowance (AA) or a mobility supplement or constant attendance allowance payable with a war pension or industrial injuries disablement benefit. If your qualifying benefit stops, you are no longer entitled to the disability element on these grounds;[24] *or*
- (Case D) have an invalid carriage or similar vehicle; *or*
- (Case E) have received for at least 140 days forming a single period of incapacity for work (see Chapter 32) or limited capability for work (see Chapter 11) (the last of which must have fallen within the 56 days of the date of the claim) SSP, occupational sick pay, short-term IB at the lower rate, IS on account of incapacity, ESA, or credits for incapacity or for limited capability for work for a period of 20 weeks; *and*
  - have a disability at the date of the claim which is likely to last for at least six months (or for the rest of your life if your death is expected within that time); *and*

  - have gross earnings which are less than they were before the disability began by at least the greater of 20 per cent and £15 a week; *or*
- (Case F) have undertaken 'training for work' for at least one day in the 56 days immediately preceding the claim *and* were receiving one of the benefits or credits listed under Case A within the 56 days before that training started. 'Training for work' means training provided under the Employment and Training Act 1973, or, in Scotland, the Enterprise and New Towns (Scotland) Act 1990, or training which you attend for 16 hours or more a week if its primary purpose is teaching occupational or vocational skills.[25]

Renewals or linked claims

(Case G) If you make a further claim for WTC within 56 days of the day your previous award ended, *and* in that earlier claim you qualified for the disabled worker element under Case A, B, E or F above, you will be treated as though you still met those conditions, and can continue to receive the disabled worker element in your new award. You must also still have a disability which puts you at a disadvantage in getting a job (see Appendix 9 – note that for renewals and new claims within two years of a previous entitlement to the disabled worker element this must be under Part 1[26]).

You can still benefit from this linking rule if your income was too high for you to receive any WTC within the previous 56 days, as long as your maximum amount of WTC would have included the disabled worker element on one of the above grounds.[27]

If both you and your partner meet the above conditions, two disabled worker elements can be paid.[28]

Severe disability element

You get a severe disability element if you receive the highest rate of the care component of DLA or the higher rate of AA, or if payment of either of these has been suspended because you are in hospital.[29] If you have a partner who meets this condition, a severe disability element can be included for her/him, whether or not s/he is in work.

If both you and your partner meet the condition, two severe disability elements can be paid.[30]

Childcare element

If you have 'eligible childcare costs', your maximum amount of WTC can include a childcare element.[31] This is added to the other elements to which you are entitled. For the definition of eligible childcare costs and an explanation of how these are calculated, see pp1315–18.

4. The childcare element of working tax credit

Your maximum amount of working tax credit (WTC) can include a childcare element to help meet the cost of 'relevant childcare' (see p1315).[32] This element is 70 per cent of actual childcare costs of up to £175 a week for one child or £300 a week for two or more children – ie, up to £122.50 or £210 a week.[33]

To get the childcare element of WTC, you or your partner must be 'responsible for' at least one child.[34] You do not have to be the child's parent. 'Responsible for' has the same meaning for WTC as it does for child tax credit (CTC) (see p1271).[35]

The childcare element is part of the maximum WTC calculation and cannot be claimed on its own or as part of CTC.[36]

This element can be included to help meet the costs of childcare if you incur charges for relevant childcare and you are:[37]

- a lone parent working at least 16 hours a week; *or*
- a member of a couple; *and*
  - you are both working at least 16 hours a week; *or*
  - one of you is working at least 16 hours a week and the other is incapacitated (see below); *or*
  - one of you is working at least 16 hours a week and the other is in hospital or in prison (serving a sentence or remanded in custody).

You are still entitled to the childcare element during periods throughout which you are treated as in work for WTC purposes – eg, during the first 39 weeks of maternity leave or the four-week run-on (see p1302).[38]

Incapacitated

You or your partner are treated as incapacitated if you:[39]

- get short-term higher rate or long-term incapacity benefit (IB); *or*
- have been getting contributory employment and support allowance (ESA) for at least 28 weeks or credits for limited capability for work following the end of the entitlement period of contributory ESA; or, provided you satisfied the national insurance (NI) contribution conditions for contributory ESA, a combination of that and statutory sick pay for at least 28 weeks (the 28 weeks can have been in one period or in periods that can be linked together); *or*
- get severe disablement allowance; *or*
- get attendance allowance, disability living allowance (DLA) (or an equivalent award paid as an increase under the war pensions or industrial injuries disablement scheme) or would be getting it but for the fact that you are in hospital; *or*
- get industrial injuries disablement benefit with constant attendance allowance; *or*

- have an award of housing benefit or council tax benefit which includes a disability premium or a higher pensioner premium in respect of incapacity; *or*
- you have an invalid carriage or similar vehicle;[40] *or*
- are entitled to carer's allowance.

You can claim the childcare element for a new baby as well as for any other children for whom you are responsible while you are on statutory maternity, paternity or adoption leave (for the first 39 weeks only), or while you are paid maternity allowance. See p1302 for these and other situations when you are treated as in full-time work.

Relevant childcare charges can be for any child in your family up to the last day of the week in which 1 September falls, following the child's 15th birthday or her/his 16th birthday if s/he is disabled.[41] **'Disabled child'** means a child who:[42]

- receives DLA, or whose DLA has been suspended because s/he is a hospital inpatient; *or*
- has been registered blind; *or*
- ceased to be registered blind in the 28 weeks immediately preceding the WTC claim.

Relevant childcare

In England, in order to be 'relevant childcare' the childcare must be:[43]

- provided by a childcare provider correctly registered by Ofsted, either in the Early Years Register (for children from birth up to the 31 August after their fifth birthday) or the Childcare Register (the compulsory part for children from 1 September after their fifth birthday up to the age of eight, or the voluntary part for children aged eight and over);
- provided to a child between three and four years by a school under the direction of the school's governing body, or an equivalent body, on school premises or premises that may be inspected as part of an inspection of the school by the Chief Inspector;
- out-of-school hours childcare or supervised activity-based childcare provided for a child aged between five and 15 years (16 if disabled) by a school on the school premises or premises that may be inspected as part of an inspection of the school by the Chief Inspector;
- provided by a domiciliary worker or nurse from an agency registered under the Domiciliary Care Agencies Regulations 2002 in the child's home;
- provided by a foster parent who is also registered with Ofsted, but not in respect of the child who is being fostered by that foster parent.

In Wales, in order to be 'relevant childcare', the childcare must be:[44]

- provided by a childcare provider registered by the Care and Social Services Inspectorate Wales;

- provided by an approved foster parent, who is providing daycare or childminding for a child aged eight or over, but not for a child who is being fostered by that foster parent. If the child is under eight, the foster parent must also be registered by the Care and Social Services Inspectorate Wales;
- out-of-school-hours childcare provided by a school on the school premises or by a local authority;
- provided by a person approved under the Tax Credits (Approval of Child Care Providers) (Wales) Scheme 2007 in the child's home or, if several children are being looked after, in one of the children's homes;
- provided by a domiciliary worker or nurse from an agency registered under the Domiciliary Care Agencies (Wales) Regulations 2004 in the child's home.

In Scotland, in order to be 'relevant childcare', the childcare must be:[45]
- provided by a childcare provider registered by the Care Inspectorate;
- in an out-of-school-hours childcare club registered by the Care Inspectorate;
- provided in the child's home by, or introduced through, a childcare agency, sitter service or nanny agency registered by the Care Inspectorate.

For Crown servants working abroad, 'relevant childcare' also includes a childcare provider approved under a Ministry of Defence accreditation scheme abroad.

You cannot claim help with the costs of childcare provided in your own home if that care is provided by a relative of your child. '**Relative**' means parent, grandparent, aunt or uncle, brother or sister, whether related by blood, marriage, civil partnership or 'affinity'.[46] By 'affinity', we understand that HM Revenue and Customs (HMRC) means people who are related through a partner, rather than a spouse or civil partner. For example, if childcare is provided in your home by your partner's mother, she is related to the child by affinity, even if your partner is not the child's parent, and so you cannot claim for the cost of paying her.

You can claim help with the costs of childcare provided by a relative away from your home, but that relative must also be a registered or approved childminder. In practice, it is unlikely that a childminder would be able to remain registered for long if only looking after a child to whom s/he was related – contact the relevant agency for advice in this situation. If approved under the Tax Credits (Approval of Childcare Providers) (Wales) Scheme 2007, s/he must also care for at least one other child who is not related to her/him.[47]

You can only claim for charges that you actually pay. If you receive childcare vouchers from your employer, you cannot claim for the amount covered by the voucher, so you should seek advice on whether you are better off accepting vouchers in exchange for part of your salary. You cannot claim the childcare element for free early years' entitlement or for charges in respect of the child's compulsory education or, in England, for childcare during school hours for a child of compulsory school age. If you will not be making payments for childcare until some time after you have claimed WTC, you cannot receive a childcare element for these until you start making the payments. If you have made an arrangement with a childcare provider to pay childcare costs, you can claim for these up to a week before the childcare is provided.[48]

The amount of the childcare element

Step one: work out your relevant period

Add up the number of days in your relevant period (see p1308). If you are making a claim for tax credits before the beginning of a new tax year, your award is usually based on entitlement at the same rate for a whole tax year, and your relevant period is one year. The tax year 2012/13 has 365 days.

Step two: calculate your relevant childcare charge

Your **'relevant childcare charge'** is your average weekly charge. The way in which your average weekly charge is calculated depends on whether you pay for childcare weekly, monthly or at some other interval, and on whether the amount you pay varies over time.[49]

- If you pay for childcare on a weekly basis and the charge is a fixed weekly amount, add together the charges in the most recent four weeks before the claim and divide by four.
- If you pay for childcare on a weekly basis, have paid for childcare for at least 52 weeks and the charge varies over time, add together the charges in the 52 weeks before the claim and divide by 52.
- If you pay on a monthly basis and the charge is a fixed monthly amount, multiply that monthly amount by 12 and divide the total by 52.
- If you pay on a monthly basis and the charge varies from month to month, add together the charges for the last 12 months and divide the total by 52.
- If there is not sufficient information for HMRC to establish your average weekly charge by any of the above methods, the charge will be calculated by HMRC on the basis of information which you provide about your childcare costs, using any method which, in its opinion, is reasonable.
- If you have entered into an agreement to pay for childcare, which will be provided during the period of your award, your average weekly childcare costs will be calculated on the basis of your own written estimate of these costs. In practice, you provide this estimate on your tax credit claim form.
- If you are only paying childcare costs for a fixed period (eg, over the summer holidays), your relevant childcare charge can be averaged and paid over that period rather than over the whole year.

When you have calculated your average weekly childcare charges by one of these methods, round the figure up to the nearest whole pound.

Step three: calculate your actual childcare costs for the relevant period

The weekly amount found in Step two is now converted to an amount covering your relevant period. Multiply the weekly charge by 52 to calculate the annual amount. Divide this figure by the number of days in the current tax year to find the daily rate, and then multiply this daily rate by the number of days in your relevant period. This gives your childcare costs for the relevant period.[50]

Step four: calculate your maximum eligible childcare costs for the relevant period

Divide the maximum eligible weekly childcare cost which applies to you by seven, to find the daily rate. The maximum eligible weekly cost is £175 for one child, and £300 for two or more children. Round this figure up to the nearest penny and then multiply this daily rate by the number of days in the relevant period.

Step five: calculate the childcare element for the relevant period

Take the lower of the two figures found in Steps three and four, and calculate 70 per cent of that figure. Round the amount up to the nearest penny. This gives your childcare element for the relevant period.

Example

Tracy paid a fixed amount of £200 every week in eligible childcare costs for her two children during each of the four weeks before her application for tax credits was made. She makes an application for WTC in advance of the new tax year. She will continue to pay £200 a week for the same childcare. Her childcare element for the whole of a tax year is calculated as follows.

Step one

Tracy's relevant period is one year (365 days).

Step two

Her relevant childcare charge is £200. (This is her average weekly charge.)

Step three

£200 x 52 = £10,400

(£10,400 ÷ 365) x 365 = £10,400

Step four

The maximum weekly eligible childcare cost for Tracy is £300, as she has two children.

The daily rate is £300 ÷ 7 = £42.86 (rounded up to the nearest penny).

The annual rate is £42.86 x 365 = £15,643.90

Step five

The lower figure from Steps three and four is £10,400.

Childcare element is 70% x £10,400 = £7,280

Tracy's childcare element for the relevant period (in this case, one whole tax year) is £7,280.

5. **How to calculate the amount of tax credit**

If you are receiving certain benefits

If you are entitled to income support (IS), income-based jobseeker's allowance (JSA), income-related employment and support allowance (ESA) or pension credit (PC), you are automatically entitled to the maximum amount of child tax credit (CTC) or working tax credit (WTC) you could receive. **Note:** this does not apply to WTC during the four-week 'run-on' period after stopping work.[51] You calculate this by adding together the elements of each tax credit for which you qualify over your relevant period, as described above. Your maximum amount is not subject to any reduction during the period you are receiving IS, income-based JSA, income-related ESA or PC (but see Chapter 58 if an overpayment is being recovered from your award).

If you are not receiving certain benefits

The following describes how your entitlement is worked out if you are *not* receiving IS, income-based JSA, income-related ESA or PC. **Note**: the rates, taper, disregard and thresholds apply to entitlement in 2012/13. To calculate tax credits entitlement for 2011/12, see the 2011/12 edition of this *Handbook*.

Step one: work out your relevant period

Add up the number of days in your relevant period (see p1308). If you are making a claim for tax credit at the beginning of a new tax year, your award will be based on entitlement at the same rate for a whole tax year, and your relevant period will be one year. The tax year 2012/13 has 365 days.

Step two: your maximum entitlement for the relevant period

First, identify the different elements of each tax credit for which you are eligible. Take the daily rate of each element apart from the childcare element of WTC.

For each element, multiply this daily rate by the number of days in the relevant period. Add the adjusted amounts of each element together. Next, calculate your childcare element for the relevant period as described on p1317.

Add the childcare element for the relevant period to the other elements for the relevant period to find your maximum entitlement for the relevant period.

Step three: your relevant income

The income used in the tax credit calculation is your 'relevant income' (see Chapter 55).

The usual procedure which HM Revenue and Customs (HMRC) uses is to base the calculation on your previous tax year's income. In some cases, it may be to your advantage to have an estimate of your current tax year's income used in the calculation instead (see p1328).

Divide this income by the number of days in the tax year to which your claim for tax credits relates to find the daily rate, then multiply this daily rate by the number of days in the relevant period. Round this amount down to the nearest penny. This is your relevant income.

At the end of the tax year, when determining whether your entitlement during that year should have been based on the current year's income or the previous year's income, HMRC will compare the two amounts. If your income has changed, a prescribed amount is disregarded so that your award continues to be based on the previous year's income. From 6 April 2012, a new disregard is applied to a decrease in income. See p1328 for more on annual income.[52]

- If your income in 2012/13 is more than your income in 2011/12 but the difference is less than £10,000, your 2011/12 income will be used.
- If your income in 2012/13 is more than your income in 2011/12 and the difference is more than £10,000, your 2012/13 income minus £10,000 will be used.
- If your income in 2012/13 is less than your income in 2011/12 but the difference is less than £2,500, your 2011/12 income will be used.
- If your income in 2012/13 is less than your income in 2011/12 and the difference is more than £2,500, your 2012/13 will be used, plus £2,500.

Note: the government has announced that the disregard for an increase in income will be reduced from £10,000 to £5,000 from 6 April 2013.

Step four: compare your income with the threshold for the relevant period

Find the annual threshold which applies to you.

- If you are entitled to WTC only, the annual threshold is £6,420.
- If you are entitled to WTC *and* CTC, the annual threshold is £6,420.
- If you are entitled to CTC only, and not to WTC, the annual threshold is £15,860.

Divide the threshold which applies to you by the number of days in the current tax year, and then multiply this figure by the number of days in the relevant period. Round this amount up to the nearest penny. This figure is your threshold for the relevant period.

Step five: calculate tax credit entitlement for the relevant period

- If your income is less than the threshold that applies to you, you are entitled to receive the maximum amount of tax credit(s).

- If your income is greater than the threshold which applies to you, subtract the threshold figure from your relevant income to find your excess income. Calculate 41 per cent of this excess income and round this figure down to the nearest penny. Finally, reduce your maximum amount of tax credit(s) by this amount.
- The different elements of your maximum tax credit are tapered away in a set order.
  - First, the elements of WTC, except for the childcare element are reduced.
  - Next, the childcare element is reduced.
  - Third, the child elements of CTC plus any disabled or severely disabled child elements for your children are reduced.
  - Finally, the family element is reduced. In previous tax years, this was protected until income reached a second threshold, but from 6 April 2012 this is no longer the case and the family element is reduced immediately after the child elements.

If you are entitled to CTC only, or to WTC only, and the calculation results in entitlement of less than £26, no award of tax credit will be made. If you are entitled to both CTC and WTC and the total entitlement from both adds up to less than £26, no award will be made.[53]

To find out how much your weekly payment will be, divide the above total by the number of days in your relevant period to find the daily rate and then multiply this daily rate by seven. If your tax credit is paid four-weekly, multiply the daily rate by 28 to calculate the amount of your payments.

Example

Tracy claims tax credits at the beginning of the tax year 2012/13. During the tax year 2011/12 she worked 20 hours a week and earned £8 an hour, gross. During the tax year 2012/13, she continues to work the same hours, for the same rate of pay. Tracy's entitlement to tax credits is calculated as follows.

Step one: work out the relevant period

Tracy's relevant period is 365 days.

Step two: maximum entitlement for the relevant period

CTC	Family element	£547.50
	Child element for three-year-old child	£2,690.05
	Child element for five-year-old child	£2,690.05
WTC	Basic element	£1,923.55
	Lone parent element	£1,952.75
	Childcare element	£7,280.00
Total maximum amount of tax credit		£17,083.90

Note: although Tracy's annual period is one year, the figures for each element do not equal the annual amount of each element. For example, the annual amount of the family element is £545, but the calculation above shows Tracy's family element during her relevant period of one year as being £547.50. This is because when the annual amount has been divided by 365 the figure produced is *rounded up* to the nearest penny, before being multiplied by the number of days in the tax year. This rounding up has the effect of increasing Tracy's annual maximum amount.

Step three: relevant income

Tracy earned £8,342.85 during the tax year 2011/12. (She is paid £8 an hour, gross, and works 20 hours a week.) This total is calculated as follows:

((£8 x 20) ÷ 7) x 366 = £8,365.71

She continues to be paid at the same rate during the tax year 2012/13. This total is calculated as follows:

((£8 x 20) ÷ 7) x 365 = £8,342.85

During the year in which tax credits are paid (2012/13), as the decrease is below the disregard, her income for the year 2011/12 is used.

Tracy's income for the relevant period is therefore:

(£8,365.71 ÷ 365) x 365 = £8,365.71, rounded down to the nearest penny.

Step four: compare income with the threshold for the relevant period

As Tracy will receive both WTC and CTC, her annual threshold figure is £6,420.

The threshold for the relevant period is therefore:

(£6,420 ÷ 365) x 365 = £6,420, rounded up to the nearest penny.

Step five: calculate tax credit entitlement for the relevant period

Tracy has excess income of £1,945.71 (income of £8,365.71 minus the threshold figure of £6,420).

Apply the taper of 41 per cent to this excess income:

41% x £1,945.71 = £797.74

Tracy's maximum tax credit (£17,083.90) will be reduced by this amount. Her total tax credit entitlement will be:

£17,083.90 – £797.74= £16,286.16

The reduction is first applied to the elements of her WTC apart from the childcare element – ie, the basic element of £1,923.55 plus the lone parent element of £1,952.75 = £3,876.30:

£3,876.30 – £797.74 = £3,078.56

Tracy's tax credits for the tax year 2012/13 will, therefore, be:

WTC (not including childcare element)	£3,078.56
Childcare element	£7,280.00
CTC	£5,927.60
Total tax credits	**£16,286.16**

To find the weekly rate of payment, this figure is divided by 365 (the number of days in Tracy's relevant period) and multiplied by 7.

(£16,286.16 ÷ 365) x 7 = £312.34

6. **Entitlement after a change of circumstances**

There are three different ways in which your circumstances can change that will affect your entitlement to tax credits.

- If your circumstances change in a way that affects your maximum entitlement, a new relevant period begins. For example, if a disability benefit which gives entitlement to a disability element is awarded to you or someone included in your claim, this changes your maximum amount of tax credit and starts a new relevant period.
- Other changes, such as becoming single or part of a couple, will bring your award to an end, and you will have to make a fresh claim for tax credit, if you remain entitled. This will also start a new relevant period.
- Finally, some changes that do not affect your maximum entitlement and do not bring your existing award to an end will affect the amount of tax credit which is payable to you. For example, if your existing award has been based on your current tax year's income and you have a significant rise in your income during that tax year, you may be overpaid tax credit unless you report the change at once, enabling your award to be recalculated.

See p1363 for more information about how these changes affect your award.

In any of these circumstances, your tax credit award will need to be recalculated. This is done by working through Steps one to five as described on pp1319–20, for each relevant period.

Example

Tracy claims disability living allowance (DLA) for her five-year-old child and this is awarded (middle rate of the care component) from day 201 of the tax year 2012/13. She therefore has two relevant periods during this tax year. The first is 200 days long, and the second, from the date her daughter is awarded DLA, 165 days long.

Her entitlement during the first 200 days is calculated as follows:

Step one: work out the relevant period

The first relevant period is 200 days long.

Step two: maximum entitlement for the relevant period

Maximum entitlement to all of the elements of tax credits for the relevant period of 200 days, apart from the childcare element, is calculated.

Child tax credit (CTC)	Family element	£300
	Child element for three-year-old child	£1,474
	Child element for five-year-old child	£1,474
Working tax credit (WTC)	Basic element	£1,054
	Lone parent element	£1,070
	Total	**£5,372**

Next, the childcare element for the relevant period is calculated, as described above.

Childcare element	£3,989.05

Tracy's total maximum amount of tax credit for this relevant period is therefore £9,361.05 (£5,372 + £3,989.05).

Step three: relevant income

Tracy's annual income is £8,365.71. This is adjusted for the relevant period by dividing by the number of days in the tax year, and multiplying by the number of days in the relevant period.

(£8,365.71 ÷ 365) x 200 = £4,583.95

Step four: compare income with the threshold for the relevant period

As Tracy receives both WTC and CTC, her annual threshold figure is £6,420. The threshold figure is also adjusted to cover the relevant period.

(£6,420 ÷ 365) x 200 = £3,517.81

Step five: calculate tax credit entitlement for the relevant period

Tracy has excess income of £1,066.14 (relevant income of £4,583.95 minus the threshold figure of £3,517.81).

Apply the taper of 41 per cent to this excess income:

41% x £1,066.14 = £437.11

Tracy's maximum tax credit (£9,361.05) will be reduced by this amount. Her total tax credit entitlement will be:

£9,361.05 – £437.11 = £8,923.94

This reduction of £437.11 is first applied to the elements of her WTC apart from the childcare element – ie, the basic element of £1,054 plus the lone parent element of £1,070 = £2,124.

£2,124 – £437.11 = £1,686.89

Tracy's tax credits for the first 200 days will be made up as follows:

WTC	£1,686.89
Childcare element	£3,989.05
CTC	£3,248.00
Total tax credits	**£8,923.94**

Tracy's total tax credit entitlement for the first 200 days is therefore £8,923.94.

To find the weekly rate of payment, this figure is divided by 200 and multiplied by 7.

(£8,923.94 ÷ 200) x 7 = £312.34

Her entitlement for the second relevant period is calculated as follows:

Step one: work out relevant period

The second relevant period is 165 days long.

Step two: maximum entitlement for the relevant period

Maximum entitlement to all of the elements of tax credits for the relevant period of 165 days, apart from the childcare element, is calculated:

CTC	Family element	£247.50
	Child element for three-year-old child	£1,216.05

	Child element for five-year-old child	£1,216.05
	Disabled child element for five-year-old child	£1,334.85
WTC	Basic element	£869.55
	Lone parent element	£882.75
Total		£5,766.75

Next, the childcare element for the relevant period is calculated, as described above.

	Childcare element	£3,290.96

Tracy's total maximum amount of tax credit for this relevant period is therefore £9,057.71 (£5,766.75 + £3,290.96).

Step three: relevant income

Tracy's annual income is £8,365.71. This is adjusted for the relevant period by dividing by the number of days in the tax year, and multiplying by the number of days in the relevant period.

(£8,365.71 ÷ 365) x 165 = £3,781.76

Step four: compare income with the threshold for the relevant period

As Tracy receives both WTC and CTC, her annual threshold figure is £6,420. The threshold figure is also adjusted to cover the relevant period.

(£6,420 ÷ 365) x 165 = £2,902.19

Step five: calculate tax credit entitlement for the relevant period

Tracy has excess income of £879.57 (relevant income of £3,781.76 minus the threshold figure of £2,902.19).

Apply the taper of 41 per cent to this excess income.

41% x £879.57 = £360.62

Tracy's maximum tax credit (£9,057.71) will be reduced by this amount. Her total tax credit entitlement will be:

£9,057.71 – £360.62 = £8,697.09

The reduction is first applied to the elements of her WTC apart from the childcare element – ie, the basic element of £869.55 plus the lone parent element of £882.75 = £1,752.30.

£1,752.30 – £360.62 = £1,391.68

Tracy's tax credits for the second 165 days will be made up as follows:

WTC	£1,391.68
Childcare element	£3,290.96
CTC	£4,014.45
Total tax credits	**£8,697.09**

Tracy's total tax credit entitlement for the second 165 days is therefore £8,697.09.

To find the weekly rate of payment, this figure is divided by 165 and multiplied by 7.

(£8,697.09 ÷ 165) x 7 = £368.97

Notes

1. **The relevant period**
   1 s5(1) TCA 2002
   2 s5(2) TCA 2002
   3 Reg 8(2) TC(ITDR) Regs
   4 Reg 7(2) TC(ITDR) Regs
   5 Reg 8(2) TC(ITDR) Regs

2. **The maximum amount of child tax credit**
   6 Reg 7 CTC Regs
   7 Regs 7 and 8 TC(ITDR) Regs
   8 Reg 7 CTC Regs
   9 Reg 8(1) and (2) CTC Regs
   10 Reg 8(1) and (3) CTC Regs

3. **The maximum amount of working tax credit**
   11 Reg 20 WTC(EMR) Regs
   12 Reg 15 WTC(EMR) Regs
   13 Regs 7 and 8 TC(ITDR) Regs
   14 Reg 20 WTC(EMR) Regs
   15 Reg 4 WTC(EMR) Regs
   16 Reg 3(2) WTC(EMR) Regs
   17 Reg 11(1) WTC(EMR) Regs
   18 Reg 11 WTC(EMR) Regs
   19 Reg 3 WTC(EMR) Regs
   20 Reg 12 WTC(EMR) Regs
   21 Reg 10 WTC(EMR) Regs
   22 Reg 3 WTC(EMR) Regs
   23 Reg 9 WTC(EMR) Regs
   24 R(TC) 1/06
   25 Reg 9B WTC(EMR) Regs
   26 Reg 9A WTC(EMR) Regs
   27 Reg 9(8) WTC(EMR) Regs
   28 Reg 3(3) WTC(EMR) Regs
   29 Reg 17 WTC(EMR) Regs
   30 Reg 3(3) WTC(EMR) Regs
   31 Reg 13 WTC(EMR) Regs

4. **The childcare element of working tax credit**
   32 Regs 3 and 13 WTC(EMR) Regs
   33 Reg 20(3) WTC(EMR)Regs
   34 Reg 14(1) WTC(EMR) Regs
   35 Reg 14(1) WTC(EMR) Regs
   36 Reg 20 WTC(EMR) Regs
   37 Reg 13(1) WTC(EMR) Regs
   38 Regs 5-8 WTC(EMR) Regs; Explanatory Note to The Working Tax Credit (Entitlement and Maximum Rate) (Amendment) Regulations 2009, No.1829
   39 Reg 13(4) WTC(EMR) Regs
   40 Reg 13(8) WTC(EMR) Regs
   41 Reg 14(3) WTC(EMR) Regs
   42 Reg 14(4) WTC(EMR) Regs
   43 Reg 14(2) WTC(EMR) Regs; see also HMRC leaflet (WTC5), June 2010
   44 Reg 14(2)(f) WTC(EMR) Regs
   45 Reg 14(2)(b) WTC(EMR) Regs
   46 Reg 14(1A)(a) and (1B)(a) WTC(EMR) Regs
   47 Reg 14(1A)(d) WTC(EMR) Regs
   48 Reg 27(2A) and (5B) TC(CN) Regs
   49 Reg 15 WTC(EMR) Regs
   50 Reg 7(3) TC(ITDR) Regs, steps 7-10

5. **How to calculate the amount of tax credit**
   51 ss7(2) and 13 TCA 2002; reg 4 TC(ITDR) Regs
   52 s7(3) TCA 2002; reg 5 TC(ITDR) Regs
   53 Reg 9 TC(ITDR) Regs

Chapter 55

Income: tax credits

This chapter covers:

This chapter explains what kind of income is taken into account and what is disregarded when working out your child tax credit and working tax credit. Chapter 54 explains how income affects the amount of tax credit you get.

Note: in this chapter, unless otherwise stated, references to income-based jobseeker's allowance (JSA) also refer to joint-claim JSA.

Key facts

- The amount of tax credit to which you are entitled depends on how much income you have.
- In general, most taxable income is taken into account, while non-taxable income is ignored, but there are exceptions.
- The assessment is based on income for a full tax year, 6 April to 5 April.
- The amount to which you are entitled changes if your income increases or decreases by more than a certain amount in the current year compared with the previous year. To avoid overpayments or underpayments of tax credits, you should tell the Tax Credit Office if your income changes.
- Your savings or other capital are not taken into account, and you are eligible for tax credits whatever the level of your capital. However, interest and other income earned from savings or capital does count.

Future changes: April 2013 and after

Major changes are taking place that affect the benefits and tax credits system (see Chapter 2). From 2013/14, the disregard in tax credits for increases in income is expected to decrease from £10,000 to £5,000.[1] This means that your tax credit award will be affected if your income increases by more than £5,000 in the year. See CPAG's *Welfare Rights Bulletin* for updates.

1. Annual income

The assessment is always based on income over a full tax year (6 April to 5 April) except during a time when you are getting income support (IS), income-based jobseeker's allowance (JSA), income-related employment and support allowance (ESA) or pension credit (PC). If the tax credit award only runs for part of the year, the full year's income is reduced on a *pro rata* basis (see p1319).

Note: while you are on IS, income-based JSA, income-related ESA or PC, you are entitled to maximum tax credits without any income test, so the level of your income in the previous or current year is not relevant. When your benefit stops, the tax credit award is again based on annual income.

When you claim

When claiming for all or part of the tax year 6 April 2012 to 5 April 2013, your award is based initially on your income for the previous year, 6 April 2011 to 5 April 2012. This is the case even if you know at the outset that your income during the year of the award will be different. If your income in the previous year is too high to qualify for tax credits, but you satisfy the other qualifying conditions, the decision will be to award tax credits at a nil rate. If you think your income will be lower or significantly higher in the current year, you can ask for the award, including a nil-rate award, to be revised.

If your income has changed since the previous year

Your income can decrease by up to £2,500 compared with the previous year or increase by up to £10,000 without it affecting your final entitlement. Changes less than these disregarded amounts do not affect your award until the following year.

Before 2012/13, any decrease in income affected entitlement and the disregard for increases depended on the year of the award:

- awards in 2011/12 – £10,000 disregarded;
- awards in 2006/07 to 2010/11 – £25,000 disregarded;
- awards up to 2005/06 – £2,500 disregarded.

If you do not tell HM Revenue and Customs (HMRC) about your change in income, your award continues at the same rate until the end of the tax year if other circumstances stay the same. At that point, you must give full details when HMRC sends you the annual review pack and it will recalculate your final entitlement for that year. This can take some months, so if your income has gone up, you should tell HMRC by 6 April to avoid being overpaid from the start of your renewed award. You should do this even if the increase is not enough to affect your award this year. If you have not given up-to-date income details by 6

April, HMRC starts your renewed award assuming your income increased in line with average earnings.

If you tell HMRC during the year about an increase in income of more than £10,000 compared with the previous year, your award can be revised based on an estimate of the current year's income less a disregard of £10,000. This is advisable if you want to reduce the risk of overpayments at the end of the year.

If you expect your income in the current year to decrease by more than £2,500 compared with the previous year, tell HMRC. It will adjust your award basing it on your estimate plus £2,500. Tell HMRC quickly if you later think your estimate was too low so it can readjust your award. If you do not, you could end up with an overpayment.

You can phone the Tax Credit Helpline or write to the Tax Credit Office with details of your current year's income. There is no special form to fill in so make sure you provide full details of *all* your (and your partner's) relevant income for the current year.

At the end of the tax year

At the end of the tax year, HMRC finalises your entitlement. It sends you an annual review form to see whether your income in the current year is any different from that in the previous year and to decide the amount of income on which to base your final entitlement.

Note: the previous year means the tax year that ended immediately before the year of the award – eg, 6 April 2011 to 5 April 2012 for awards in the tax year 6 April 2012 to 5 April 2013.

If your income in the current year:[2]

- has not changed since the previous year, the previous year's income is used;
- has fallen by £2,500 or less, the previous year's income is used;
- has fallen by more than £2,500, the current year's income plus £2,500 is used;
- has increased by £10,000 or less, the previous year's income is used;
- has increased by more than £10,000, the current year's income minus £10,000 is used.

See p1328 for the disregards before 2012/13.

Examples

From 6 April 2011 to 5 April 2012 Izzy worked part time and earned a total of £5,000. Since then she has worked full time and earned £12,500 in the current year of the award, from 6 April 2012 to 5 April 2013. Her tax credit award is initially based on income of £5,000. Because her income went up by just £7,500 in the current year – below the £10,000 threshold – her final entitlement is also based on income of £5,000.

From 6 April 2011 to 5 April 2012, Marsha and Bill, who are claiming as a couple, had total income of £27,000. In the current year of the award, from 6 April 2012 to 5 April 2013,

Marsha stopped work and they earned £11,000 between them. Their tax credit award is initially based on the previous year's income of £27,000. Because their income went down by £16,000 in the current year (£27,000 – £11,000), their final entitlement is based on income of £13,500 (£11,000 + £2,500). For the next year, 6 April 2013 to 5 April 2014, their award will be based on income of £11,000.

Estimating income

There are no special rules for how to estimate income. Using, for instance, payslips and benefit award letters, work out how much income you have already received in the current year and estimate how much you will receive for the remainder of the year. Tax credits are always worked out using annual income, so you must include all income received or estimated for the whole tax year, 6 April to 5 April, even if you are asking for an award to be adjusted part way through the year.

If you are self-employed, HMRC's Self Assessment Helpline (tel: 0845 900 0444) can advise you how to work out your business profits. You need to estimate your profits for the accounting period that ends in the current tax year. This might be different from your current earnings, particularly if your accounting year-end is early in the tax year.

2. Whose income counts

If you are a member of a couple (see p1284), your partner's income is added to yours.[3] Otherwise, only your own income counts.

If you were previously part of a couple, but now are single or a lone parent, only your income counts in your new award, not that of your former partner, even if the previous year's income is used in the assessment. In your previous award as a couple, your joint income counts, even if the current year's income is used in the assessment – ie, including the remainder of the tax year after you separated.

If you were single or a lone parent but are now in a couple, your joint income is assessed, whether or not entitlement is based on the current or previous tax year.

Children's income

Children's income is ignored. However, if you have transferred money under a trust to your child and tax rules treat that income as still belonging to you, it may also be treated as yours for tax credits.[4]

3. What income counts

In general, taxable social security benefits are taken into account, and gross earnings (before tax and national insurance (NI)) and business profits are taken into account less your pension contributions. Most other income, such as pensions and interest on savings, is added together and taken into account only to the extent that the total exceeds £300 a year. The rules specify what income must be taken into account and what is disregarded.

If you have a special exemption from income tax, your income is calculated as though you were liable for tax.[5] People such as foreign military personnel, officials of international organisations or consular staff may have such an exemption.

Types of income

Income to be taken into account falls into certain categories and within each category certain amounts may be disregarded. There is also a general list of income that is disregarded (see p1340).

The income taken into account in the assessment is worked out as follows.[6]

Add together your income, or your joint income if you are a couple, from:

- social security benefits (see p1332);
- income from employment (see p1333);
- taxable profits from self-employment (see p1335);
- student income (see p1336);
- miscellaneous income (see p1337).

Add together your income, or your joint income if you are a couple, from:

- pension income (see p1337);
- income from investments (see p1338);
- income from property (see p1339);
- foreign income (see p1339);
- notional income (see p1342).

If the total income in the last group of five categories is £300 or less, it is ignored completely; otherwise deduct £300 and add the remainder to your income under the first group of five categories. **Note:** couples share one £300 disregard.[7]

This gives you the total income that is taken into account – subject to any disregards described later in this chapter.

Example

Mr and Mrs Killean renew their claim for child tax credit (CTC) and working tax credit (WTC) from April 2012. HM Revenue and Customs (HMRC) assesses their claim on their joint income for the year 6 April 2011 to 5 April 2012. In 2011/12 Mrs Killean earned £13,500 before tax and NI contributions. Mr Killean received contributory employment

and support allowance (ESA) totalling £4,700 and an occupational pension of £500.
Income taken into account is:
Employment income = £13,500
ESA = £4,700
Occupational pension = £200 (ie, £500 less £300 disregard)
Total income = £18,400

Benefits

Generally, benefits are taken into account if they are taxable, and ignored if they are not.

Disregarded benefits

The following benefits are disregarded:[8]

- attendance allowance;
- bereavement payment;
- child benefit;
- Christmas bonus;
- council tax benefit;
- disability living allowance;
- discretionary housing payment;
- guardian's allowance;
- housing benefit (HB);
- income support (IS), except to strikers;
- income-based jobseeker's allowance (JSA);
- income-related ESA including a transitional addition;[9]
- industrial injuries benefit (except industrial death benefit);
- maternity allowance;
- pension credit (guarantee and savings credit);[10]
- severe disablement allowance;
- short-term lower rate incapacity benefit (IB);
- social fund payments;
- transitional long-term IB (paid if you transferred from invalidity benefit in 1995);
- any payment to compensate for the loss of IS, JSA or HB;
- any payment in lieu of milk tokens or vitamins;
- increases for a child[11] or adult dependant[12] paid with any of the above.

Tax credits *themselves* are disregarded. Statutory sick pay (SSP), statutory maternity pay (SMP), statutory adoption pay (SAP) and statutory paternity pay (SPP) are treated as employment income (see p1333). Retirement pensions, widowed mother's allowance, widowed parent's allowance, widow's pension, industrial death benefit and war pensions are treated as pension income (see p1337).

Benefits taken into account

Any benefits not in the list above are taken into account in full. This includes:

- bereavement allowance;
- carer's allowance (CA);
- contribution-based JSA;[13]
- contributory ESA including a transitional addition;
- long-term IB (except the non-taxable transitional long-term IB – see p1332);
- short-term higher rate IB;
- increases for a child or adult dependant (even if not taxable) paid with any of the above.

It is the amount of benefit payable that is taken into account. Arrears of benefit or any *ex gratia* payment in connection with a benefit are taken into account as income for the year in which the payment of arrears is made.[14]

Each year the DWP should give you a statement of the taxable benefits you received in the previous tax year. You can ask the local benefit office for a replacement if you did not get one. If you get any increase for a child dependant paid with CA or IB (or widowed mother's or widowed parent's allowance), this will not be included in the statement but it is taken into account as income, so you should include it when completing your tax credit claim form.

Employment income

For tax credits, it is your **'gross'** pay that is taken into account.[15] This means your pay before any income tax or NI contributions are deducted.

Income counts whether received in the UK or elsewhere.[16]

What counts as employment income

'Employment income' means the following income received in the tax year:[17]

- any earnings from an office or employment, including:[18]
  - wages;
  - fees;
  - bonuses;
  - commission;
  - overtime pay;
  - tips or gratuities;
  - goods or assets that can be converted into money – eg, gifts of drink, clothes and fuel;
  - payments made on your behalf – eg, rent paid by your employer directly to your landlord;
- taxable expenses (see p1334 for expenses that do not count as earnings);[19]

- any taxable cash voucher, non-cash voucher or credit token – eg, company credit card.[20] Vouchers spent on allowable expenses are ignored.[21] Disregard 15p a day from meals vouchers;[22]
- taxable payments in connection with the termination of your employment or with a change in your duties or wages, including non-statutory and statutory redundancy payments, pay in lieu of notice and employment tribunal awards for unfair dismissal. With the exception of pay in lieu of notice (except in some cases involving damages for breach of contract or practice),[23] the first £30,000 of the total of such payments is ignored;[24]
- SSP;[25]
- SMP above £100 a week. The first £100 a week is ignored;[26]
- ordinary and additional SPP and SAP above £100 a week;[27]
- strike pay from your trade union (even though this is non-taxable);[28]
- the cash equivalent of the benefit of a company car for private use and car fuel benefits if you earn £8,500 or more or you are a company director.[29] Other expenses in connection with the car are ignored.[30] However, if you are a disabled employee with an adapted or automatic company car, the car is exempt from income tax and ignored for tax credits;[31]
- payments for agreeing to restrict your future conduct or activities;[32]
- taxable income from an employee share scheme;[33]
- payment for work done while sentenced or on remand in prison.[34]

The taxable value of goods and vouchers is shown on Form P9D or P11D, given to you by your employer at the end of the tax year.

Payments not counted as earnings

Some payments do not count as earnings and are disregarded in the tax credits assessment. Insofar as they are exempt from income tax, ignore the following:[35]

- expenses incurred 'wholly, exclusively and necessarily' in the course of your employment.[36] **Note:** if you are a volunteer with a charity or voluntary organisation, all your expenses are ignored.[37] If you earn less than £8,500 a year, generally all your expenses are ignored.[38] However, any that are taxable would be taken into account – eg, 'round-sum' expense allowances payable irrespective of how you might spend it;[39]
- certain other expenses – eg, for travel and subsistence, mileage allowance, car parking expenses, fixed deductions for work tools and tax-free mobile phone;[40]
- homeworkers' additional household expenses and salary given up under the home computer initiative;[41]
- childcare vouchers or credit tokens for 'relevant childcare' (see p1315) (but any childcare element in your WTC is based on the lower subsidised childcare costs);[42]
- certain other vouchers – eg, for staff canteens, sports and recreation facilities and small gifts;[43]

- certain professional fees – eg, to approved professional bodies, for indemnity insurance or registration under the protection of vulnerable groups scheme;[44]
- any charity payments under a payroll giving scheme[45] (deduct from earnings or from a benefit or pension);[46]
- payment for work-related training, individual learning account training and retraining expenses when leaving employment;[47]
- job grant, return-to-work credit, in-work credit and DWP payments from certain former employment schemes.[48]

Some groups of workers have special income tax exemptions. The following are ignored as earnings for tax credits:
- certain armed forces' allowances – eg, for travel to and from leave, food, certain operational allowances, council tax relief, continuity of education and reserve forces' training;[49]
- free coal to miners, or former miners, or cash in lieu;[50]
- if you are an actor or performer, the tax-free amount of agents' fees;[51]
- expenses for mainland transfers for offshore oil and gas workers;[52]
- Crown employees' foreign service allowance;[53]
- expenses of a minister of religion, including a rent deduction;[54]
- European Commission daily subsistence allowance to seconded national experts.[55]

Deduct pension contributions

Deduct any contributions you make to a personal or occupational pension that is approved by HMRC.[56]

If you pay contributions through your employer, your P60 or P45 should show your wages after the contributions have been deducted, so there is no further deduction to make.

If you pay the pension contributions directly, deduct the gross annual contributions. Because tax relief is given on personal pension contributions, your actual contributions are less than the gross amount included in the pension plan. It is the higher gross amount that you should deduct from your employment income. Your pension provider should supply you with annual statements of contributions received.

If you have no income from employment but are still making pension contributions, deduct the contributions from any other income you may have.

Income from self-employment

Your taxable profits from any 'trade', 'profession' or 'vocation' are taken into account for the relevant year.[57] If you have a business partner, it is taxable profits from your share of the business income that count.[58] This includes trading outside the UK. It also includes profits from renting out property if this is conducted as a business. (If property income comes from a 'trade', income counts without the

£300 disregard that would otherwise apply to such income.) If renting property is not conducted as a business, see p1339.

Taxable profits are shown on your tax return for the relevant year. If you have not yet submitted a tax return, the notes that accompany the tax credit claim form (TC600) explain how to work out your profit. You should deduct allowable business expenses from annual turnover to arrive at a profit figure. HMRC's Self Assessment Helpline (tel: 0845 900 0444) should be able to give advice. See also p1330. **Note:** the provision allowing artists, farmers and market gardeners to average out fluctuating profits across two tax years does not apply; it is the actual taxable profit in the relevant year that counts.[59]

Business losses

If your business is run on a commercial basis and has made a loss, your income is nil for that tax year unless you have other income that counts in the assessment. If you do have other income, you should deduct the amount of the loss from that income (from joint income if you are claiming as a couple).[60] If you do not have enough income to offset the full amount, any left over can be carried forward and deducted from profits of the same trade in the next and later tax years.

Deduct pension contributions

Deduct the gross amount of any contributions you make to an approved personal pension scheme or a retirement annuity (see p1335).

Student income

The following income is taken into account:[61]

- adult dependants' grant;
- in Scotland, lone parents' grant;
- professional and career development loan, but only any amount applied for or paid in respect of living expenses for the period supported by the loan.[62]

Other kinds of student support are disregarded – eg:

- student loans;
- supplementary grants (other than those above);
- tuition fees;
- postgraduate maintenance grant;
- young student's bursary, health bursary, social work bursary, English opportunity bursary and other bursaries;
- education maintenance allowance;[63]
- hardship funds;
- learning grants;
- care to learn grant;
- childcare grant;
- parents' learning allowance.

Note: unlike means-tested benefits, students are not excluded from WTC and CTC. So long as you satisfy the eligibility rules, you can qualify.

Miscellaneous income

Any income that does not fit into any of the other nine categories on p1331 is taken into account if it is taxable under the HMRC 'sweep-up' provisions in Part 5 of the Income Tax (Trading and Other Income) Act 2005.[64] This includes copyright royalties if your writing does not amount to a trade or profession.

Pension income

Pension income taken into account

The following pension income is taken into account. The first £300 a year is ignored from the total of your pension and any income from savings, investments, property or foreign or notional income.

- **State retirement pensions** and **graduated retirement benefit.**[65] (**Note:** the Christmas bonus and winter fuel payment are ignored.) HMRC says that, as well as your pension, it takes into account any additional state pension, adult dependant addition and child dependant addition paid with your pension.[66] Include as income any lump sum to which you become entitled through deferring your state pension.
- **Personal and occupational pensions.**[67] It is the gross amount before tax is deducted that counts. Your pension provider should give you a certificate each year showing how much pension was paid and how much tax taken off. If you retired because of work-related illness or disability caused by injury on duty, only count the amount of pension that you would have been paid if you had retired on non-work-related ill-health grounds. Any extra amount paid is ignored.[68] Tax-free lump sums paid under a personal pension scheme, retirement annuity contract or tax-exempt pension scheme are ignored completely.[69] If you cash in a small pension or the fund is too small to pay a pension (within the 'trivial commutation' limit – your pension provider can advise on this), the lump sum you get counts. If you get a winding-up lump sum when your occupational pension scheme winds up, this counts.
- **Widow's pension**, **widowed mother's** and **widowed parent's allowance**, including any increases for a child or adult dependant.[70]
- **Industrial death benefit.**[71]
- **Survivor's guaranteed income payment** and **child's payment** under the Armed Forces Compensation Scheme.[72]

Pension income disregarded

Ignore the following **war pensions**:[73]

- war disablement pension including constant attendance allowance and mobility supplement;

- annuity or additional pension to holders of the Victoria Cross, George Cross and certain other medals;
- wounds, injury or disablement pensions to members of the armed forces – eg, guaranteed income payment;
- death in service pensions for service in the armed forces or war injuries. If the death in service pension is overlapped by another pension, ignore an equivalent amount from the other pension.

Investment income

There is no capital limit in the tax credit assessment as there is with means-tested benefits. The value of your savings is ignored completely. However, taxable *income* from savings and investments is taken into account. For example, the amount of savings in a bank account is ignored, but the interest on those savings is taken into account.

Investment income is taken into account as described below. The first £300 a year is ignored from the total of your investment income and any income from pensions or property, or foreign or notional income.

Investment income taken into account

Take into account the following amounts before tax is deducted:[74]

- interest on invested money, including outside the UK – eg, interest on savings in a bank account;[75]
- dividends from shares of a company resident in the UK (including the tax credit payable by the company with the dividend);[76]
- income from government stocks and bonds;[77]
- taxable payments from a life assurance policy, life annuity contract or capital redemption policy;[78]
- discounts on securities – ie, the profit from trading in securities such as government stocks and bonds;[79]
- payments from a trust;[80]
- payments from the estate of a deceased person;[81]
- interest arising from a debt owed to you.[82]

Investment income disregarded

Certain investment income is disregarded:

- interest, dividend or bonus from an individual savings account (ISA);[83]
- interest under a certified Save As You Earn (SAYE) scheme;[84]
- income from savings certificates and tax reserve certificates;[85]
- £70 per tax year of interest on deposits with National Savings and Investments;[86]
- investment income from tax-exempt annual payments – eg, from a covenant;[87]
- winnings from betting, pools, lotteries and games with prizes;[88]
- certain compensation payments to World War Two victims;[89]

- interest on damages awarded through the courts for personal injuries, or periodical payments of personal injury damages or from the Thalidomide Trust;[90]
- annuity payments under a Criminal Injuries Compensation Scheme award;[91]
- interest on the first £30,000 of a home income plan loan taken out before 9 March 1999 to buy a life annuity;[92]
- interest on compensation to a child under 18 for the loss of a parent;[93]
- payments from the variant Creutzfeldt-Jakob disease government-funded trust, the Macfarlane Trusts, Independent Living Funds and the Eileen Trust. These are disregarded for the lifetime of the disabled person or a partner who receives the payment or inherits from the estate, or for two years if paid to or inherited by a parent;[94]
- capital element of a purchased life annuity;[95]
- tax-free health and employment insurance or immediate-needs annuity payments.

Property income

The capital value of the property is ignored but rental income from the property is taken into account unless this is exempt from tax under the 'rent-a-room' scheme.[96] This scheme allows you to rent furnished accommodation in your own home earning up to £4,250 a year tax free.[97]

If you are not within the 'rent-a-room' scheme (eg, you rent out a property that you do not live in yourself), the amount of rent taken into account is the same as that agreed for income tax purposes. You can deduct from the rent received expenses wholly and exclusively incurred in running the property – eg, repairs, council tax (if you, rather than your tenant, are liable to pay), water charges, insurance premiums and mortgage interest (but not capital repayments of a mortgage).[98] You can offset any losses against property income in the following tax year.

The first £300 a year is ignored from the total of your property income and any pensions, investment income, foreign or notional income.

If you rent property as a business (eg, you run a hotel or guesthouse), count this as income from self-employment (see p1335).[99]

Income from property outside the UK counts as 'foreign income' (see below).

Income from outside the UK

Although earnings from abroad are taken into account in the same way as UK earnings, other 'foreign income' (eg, from pensions, property or investments, other than taxable gains from an overseas insurer, which fall within the definition of 'investment income') is taken into account subject to the following rules.[100]

The following are disregarded:[101]

- a banking charge or commission for converting currency to sterling;[102]

- social security payments from outside the UK that are equivalent to tax-free UK benefits (see p1332);
- certain pensions or compensation for victims of Nazi persecution;
- one-tenth of the amount of any overseas pension or of a pension payable in the UK by the governments of certain countries;
- tax-free lump-sum payments under an overseas pension scheme;
- personal injury damages from a court outside the UK;
- certain education allowances payable to workers in the public sector of some countries outside the UK;
- property losses in one tax year that can be offset against property income in the following year;[103]
- maintenance payments;
- income that you are prevented from transferring to the UK by law or by the government of the country where the income arises or because you cannot get foreign currency in that country; other income that remains abroad is counted.[104]

The first £300 a year is disregarded from the total of your 'foreign income' and any pensions, investment, property or notional income.

Income from outside the UK is still taken into account even if you would normally have tax relief on that income in the UK to avoid double taxation in both countries (such income is treated as though it were taxable in the UK in the normal way).[105]

Converting currency

If your income is in another currency, HMRC converts it to sterling using a 12-month average of exchange rates for the tax year in which the income is paid.[106] If your tax credit award is based on an estimate of current year's income, the rate of conversion will be adjusted once the exchange rate average is available at the end of the tax year. These rates are published on the HMRC website (see Appendix 1).

General income disregards

All of the following income is disregarded in the tax credit assessment.[107]

Employment and training programmes

Ignore the following income:

- travelling expenses, a living away from home allowance and a training grant if you are participating in training under s2 of the Employment and Training Act 1973 or, in Scotland, under s2 of the Enterprise and New Towns (Scotland) Act 1990, or attending a course at an employment rehabilitation centre (where these are not taxable as profits);[108]
- if you are aged 25 or over and getting jobseeker's allowance while on a 'qualifying course', a discretionary payment to help meet your special needs;[109]

- a payment to a disabled person under s2 of the Employment and Training Act 1973 or s15 of the Disabled Persons (Employment) Act 1944 to assist disabled people to get or keep employment;[110]
- education maintenance allowance;[111]
- certain DWP payments from former employment programmes.

See also p1335 for other disregarded payments.

Maintenance and children

Any maintenance you receive from an ex-partner is ignored, whether it is paid under a court order or not. Any child support you receive from your child's other parent is ignored.[112]

If you *pay* maintenance, you cannot deduct this from income.

If you foster a child placed with you by a local authority or independent fostering provider, all your income from foster care (eg, the fostering allowance) is ignored, provided the annual amount is no more than £10,000 plus £200 a week for each child under 11 and £250 a week for each child aged 11 or over. If your fostering income is over this limit, only the taxable amount is taken into account – ie, the amount above this limit or the actual net profit.[113] There is a similar disregard for local authority payments if a child or adult is placed with you under an adult placement scheme or staying put care for care leavers, or you are a kinship carer of a looked-after child.[114]

Note: a foster child may not count as a member of your family for tax credits, so you may not get CTC for her/him (see p1273).

An adoption allowance,[115] or special guardianship payment for a child who is a member of your household is ignored completely. For a child who lives with you under a residence order, a residence order allowance and any payments made by a local authority under s17 of the Children Act 1989 or, in Scotland, under s22 of the Children (Scotland) Act 1995 or s50 of the Children Act 1975 are ignored.[116]

Other income

The following is ignored from your income:

- any contribution you make to an approved personal or occupational pension scheme (see p1335);[117]
- payments for fares to hospital;[118]
- payments to assist prison visits;[119]
- community care direct payments;[120]
- payments under the Supporting People programme;[121]
- asylum support payments or vouchers for a former asylum seeker or dependant;[122]
- trade union provident benefits – eg, sickness or accident benefit or funeral payment;[123]

- payment for expenses incurred if you are an unpaid volunteer with a charity or voluntary organisation;[124]
- jury or witness payments if this is not compensation for loss of earnings or loss of benefit;[125]
- a payment to you for someone you are caring for temporarily made by a health authority, local authority, voluntary organisation, primary care trust or by the person themselves under the local authority's financial assessment. This disregard only applies if the payment would be tax free under HMRC's 'rent-a-room' scheme (see p1339);[126]
- any payment under an insurance policy taken out to insure against the risk of being unable to maintain mortgage repayments or other payments on a loan secured on your home. However, any payment you get above the amount you use to maintain the repayments, plus the premiums on that policy or buildings insurance premiums required as a condition of the mortgage, counts as your income;[127]
- any payment under an insurance policy taken out to insure against the risk of being unable to maintain repayments under a hire purchase, regulated or conditional sale agreement. However, any payment above the amount you use to maintain the repayments and the premiums on that policy counts as your income;[128]
- the gross amount of any 'gift aid' donation to charity;[129]
- a sports award for anything other than living expenses. Living expenses count as your income. Ignore parts of the award for dietary supplements and living-away-from-home accommodation costs.[130]

4. Notional income

Sometimes you are treated as though you have income that you do not actually have. This is called **'notional income'**.[131] There are four kinds of notional income:
- income you have deprived yourself of to get or increase tax credits;
- income that would be available to you if you applied for it;
- a reasonable rate for work you have done for less than the going rate;
- income you are treated as having through certain provisions for preventing tax avoidance or when tax law treats capital as income and charges it to income tax.

Deprivation of income

You are treated as having income you have deprived yourself of for the purpose of getting a tax credit or a higher tax credit.[132] See p985 for details of when this rule might affect you (the basic rules are similar to those that apply to deprivation of capital for benefits).

Failing to apply for income

You are treated as having income that would become available to you if you applied for it.[133] This does not include:

- income under a trust set up from a personal injury payment;
- income from a personal pension scheme;
- interest on damages awarded through the courts for personal injury;
- a rehabilitation allowance;
- Category A or B retirement pension;
- graduated retirement benefit;
- shared additional pension.

Cheap or unpaid labour

If you work or provide a service for less than the going rate, you are treated as getting a reasonable rate for the job if the person has the means to pay.[134]

This does not affect you if you are a volunteer and HM Revenue and Customs is satisfied that it is reasonable for you to provide your services free of charge. Nor does it apply if you are on an employment or training programme under s2 of the Employment and Training Act 1973 where no training allowance is payable (with the exception of the intensive activity period).

Sometimes carers looking after disabled people have been expected to charge the person they care for under a similar provision affecting means-tested benefits. If you are in this position, see p935 for more details.

Preventing tax avoidance and treatment of capital as income

If income is treated as yours under certain prevention of tax avoidance provisions or where tax law treats capital as income, it also counts as your income for tax credits.[135]

Notes

1 *Budget* 2010, para 2.42

1. Annual income

2 s7(3)(a), (b) and (e) TCA 2002; reg 5 TC(ITDR) Regs

2. Whose income counts

3 s7(5) TCA 2002
4 Reg 14(2)(b)(vii) TC(DCI) Regs

3. What income counts

5 Reg 3(6) TC(DCI) Regs
6 Reg 3(1) TC(DCI) Regs
7 Reg 3(1) Step 1 TC(DCI) Regs
8 Reg 7(3) TC(DCI) Regs
9 A transitional addition is part of the ESA applicable amount under reg 67(1)(d) ESA Regs, inserted by Sch 2 para 52 ESA (TP)(EA)(No.2) Regs
10 PC paid under SPCA 2002 is by definition not counted as social security income under reg 7(1) TC(DCI) Regs
11 Reg 7(4) TC(DCI) Regs
12 Regulations make no mention of the treatment of increases for adults. However, these are non-taxable if paid with a non-taxable benefit and the intention is that tax credits follow suit. See HMRC *Employment Income Manual*, para 76102.
13 s674 IT(EP)A 2003
14 Reg 7(1)(c) and (d) TC(DCI) Regs
15 Reg 4 TC(DCI) Regs
16 Reg 4(1) TC(DCI) Regs
17 Reg 4 TC(DCI) Regs
18 Regs 2(2) and 4(1)(a) TC(DCI) Regs; HMRC, *Employment Income Manual*, para 00520
19 Reg 4(1)(b) TC(DCI) Regs
20 Reg 4(1)(c)-(e) TC(DCI) Regs
21 ss362 and 363 IT(EP)A 2003; reg 4(4) Table 1 para 11D and (5) TC(DCI) Regs
22 Reg 4(4) Table 1 para 8 TC(DCI) Regs
23 HMRC, *Employment Income Manual*, paras 12975-79
24 Reg 4(1)(f) TC(DCI) Regs
25 Reg 4(1)(g) TC(DCI) Regs
26 Reg 4(1)(h) TC(DCI) Regs
27 Reg 4(1)(h) TC(DCI) Regs
28 Reg 4(1)(k) TC(DCI) Regs
29 Reg 4(1)(i) TC(DCI) Regs
30 Reg 4(4) Table 1 paras 14B, 14C and 14D TC(DCI) Regs
31 Reg 4(4) Table 1 para 2B TC(DCI) Regs
32 Reg 4(1)(j) TC(DCI) Regs
33 Reg 4(1)(l) TC(DCI) Regs
34 Reg 4(1)(m) TC(DCI) Regs
35 Reg 4(4) TC(DCI) Regs; for a full list see para 04200 TCTM
36 Reg 4(5) TC(DCI) Regs; s336 IT(EP)A 2003
37 Reg 19 Table 7 para 1 TC(DCI) Regs
38 ss216 and 217 IT(EP)A 2003
39 Reg 4(1)(b) TC(DCI) Regs
40 Regs 4(4) Table 1 paras 1, 2A, 2C, 4, 6, 11F, 13, and 20, and 4(5) TC(DCI) Regs; ss231, 337, 338, 367, 370, 371, 373, 376 and 377 IT(EP)A 2003
41 Reg 4(4) Table 1 paras 17 and 19 TC(DCI) Regs
42 Reg 4(4) Table 1 para 15 TC(DCI) Regs
43 Reg 4(4) Table 1 paras 5, 8, 11E and 14 TC(DCI) Regs
44 Regs 4(4) Table 1 para 21 and 4(5) TC(DCI) Regs; ss343 and 346 IT(EP)A 2003
45 Reg 4(5) TC(DCI) Regs; s713 IT(EP)A 2003
46 Regs 5(3) and 7(5A) TC(DCI) Regs
47 Reg 4(4) Table 1 paras 11C and 18 TC(DCI) Regs
48 Reg 4(4) Table 1 para 16 TC(DCI) Regs
49 Reg 4(4) Table 1 paras 3, 3A, 3B, 3C and 7 TC(DCI) Regs
50 Regs 4(4) Table 1 para 9 and 5(2) Table 2 para 11 TC(DCI) Regs
51 Reg 4(5) TC(DCI) Regs; s352 IT(EP)A 2003
52 Reg 4(4) Table 1 para 11A TC(DCI) Regs
53 Reg 4(4) Table 1 para 11B TC(DCI) Regs
54 Reg 4(5) TC(DCI) Regs; s351 IT(EP)A 2003
55 Reg 4(4) Table 1 para 11 TC(DCI) Regs
56 Reg 3(7)(c) TC(DCI) Regs
57 Reg 6(a) TC(DCI) Regs
58 Reg 6(b) TC(DCI) Regs
59 Reg 6 TC(DCI) Regs
60 Reg 3(1) Step 4 TC(DCI) Regs
61 Reg 8 TC(DCI) Regs
62 Reg 19(c) Table 8 para 2 TC(DCI) Regs

63 Reg 19 Table 6 para 5(a) TC(DCI) Regs
64 Reg 18 TC(DCI) Regs
65 Reg 5(1)(a) TC(DCI) Regs
66 para 04301 TCTM; HMRC, *Employment Income Manual,* para 76102
67 Reg 5(1)(b)-(o) TC(DCI) Regs
68 Reg 5(2) Table 2 para 9 TC(DCI) Regs
69 Reg 5(2) Table 2 para 10 TC(DCI) Regs
70 Reg 5(1)(a) TC(DCI) Regs
71 Reg 5(1)(a) TC(DCI) Regs
72 Reg 5(1)(b) TC(DCI) Regs
73 Reg 5(2) Table 2 paras 1-8 TC(DCI) Regs
74 Reg 10(1) TC(DCI) Regs
75 Reg 10(1)(a) TC(DCI) Regs
76 Reg 10(1)(d) TC(DCI) Regs
77 Reg 10(1)(c) TC(DCI) Regs
78 Reg 10(1)(e) TC(DCI) Regs
79 Reg 10(1)(b) TC(DCI) Regs
80 Reg 10(1)(a) TC(DCI) Regs
81 Reg 10(1)(a) TC(DCI) Regs
82 Reg 10(1)(a) TC(DCI) Regs
83 Reg 10(2)(a) Table 4 paras 1(a), (b) and 2 TC(DCI) Regs
84 Reg 10(2)(a) Table 4 para 3 TC(DCI) Regs
85 Reg 10(2)(c) TC(DCI) Regs
86 Reg 10(2)(d) TC(DCI) Regs
87 Reg 10(2)(e) TC(DCI) Regs
88 Reg 10(2)(a) Table 4 para 4 TC(DCI) Regs
89 Reg 10(2)(a) Table 4 paras 5-7 TC(DCI) Regs
90 Reg 10(2)(a) Table 4 para 8 TC(DCI) Regs; para 4608 TCTM
91 Reg 10(2)(a) Table 4 para 9 TC(DCI) Regs
92 Reg 10(2)(a) Table 4 para 10 TC(DCI) Regs
93 Reg 10(2)(a) Table 4 para 11 TC(DCI) Regs
94 Reg 10(2)(b) Table 5 TC(DCI) Regs
95 Reg 10(2)(a) Table 4 para 12 TC(DCI) Regs
96 Reg 11 TC(DCI) Regs
97 See HMRC Help Sheet HS 223
98 para 04006 TCTM; HMRC, *Property Income Manual*, paras 2020-40 and 2105
99 para 04006 TCTM
100 Reg 12(1) TC(DCI) Regs
101 Reg 12(3) TC(DCI) Regs
102 Reg 3(7)(a) TC(DCI) Regs
103 Reg 12(4) TC(DCI) Regs
104 Reg 3(3) TC(DCI) Regs
105 Reg 3(5A) TC(DCI) Regs
106 Reg 3(6A) TC(DCI) Regs
107 Reg 19 TC(DCI) Regs
108 Reg 19 Table 7 para 2(a)-(c) TC(DCI) Regs
109 Reg 19 Table 8 para 1 TC(DCI) Regs
110 Reg 19 Table 6 para 2 TC(DCI) Regs
111 Reg 19 Table 6 para 5 TC(DCI) Regs
112 Reg 19 Table 6 para 10 TC(DCI) Regs
113 Reg 19 Table 6 para 9 TC(DCI) Regs
114 The Qualifying Care Relief (Specified Social Care Schemes) Order 2011
115 Reg 19 Table 6 para 11(a) TC(DCI) Regs
116 Reg 19 Table 6 para 11(a) and (b) TC(DCI) Regs
117 Reg 3(7)(c) TC(DCI) Regs
118 Reg 19 Table 6 para 12 TC(DCI) Regs
119 Reg 19 Table 6 para 13 TC(DCI) Regs
120 Reg 19 Table 6 para 14 TC(DCI) Regs
121 Reg 19 Table 6 para 14A TC(DCI) Regs
122 Reg 19 Table 6 para 15 TC(DCI) Regs
123 Reg 19 Table 6 para 16 TC(DCI) Regs
124 Reg 19 Table 7 para 1 TC(DCI) Regs
125 Reg 19 Table 8 para 6 TC(DCI) Regs
126 Reg 19 Table 8 paras 3 and 4 TC(DCI) Regs
127 Reg 19 Table 8 para 5(a) TC(DCI) Regs
128 Reg 19 Table 8 para 5(b) TC(DCI) Regs
129 Reg 3(7)(b) TC(DCI) Regs
130 Reg 19 Table 8 para 7 TC(DCI) Regs

4. **Notional income**

131 Reg 13 TC(DCI) Regs
132 Reg 15 TC(DCI) Regs
133 Reg 16 TC(DCI) Regs
134 Reg 17 TC(DCI) Regs
135 Reg 14 TC(DCI) Regs

Chapter 56

Claims, backdating and getting paid: tax credits

This chapter covers:

Key facts

- Tax credits are administered and paid by HM Revenue and Customs. Claims are dealt with by the Tax Credit Office.
- Tax credit claims are dealt with differently from social security benefits. Tax credits are dealt with over a tax year, using annual income, and entitlement is finalised at the end of the tax year.
- Tax credit claims are reviewed between April and July each year. This process also acts as a renewal claim for the new tax year.
- From April 2012, tax credit claims can usually only be backdated for 31 days.

Future changes: April 2013 and after

Major changes are taking place that affect the benefits and tax credits system (see Chapter 2).

- From October 2013, a new benefit, universal credit (UC), will be introduced, which will replace tax credits. If you are already getting tax credits in October 2013, you will continue to do so until you are transferred onto UC.
- No new claims for tax credits will be accepted from 6 April 2014, although it will be possible to renew a claim until the point when you are transferred to UC.

See CPAG's *Welfare Rights Bulletin* for updates.

1. Who should claim

You must be at least 16 years old to claim tax credits.[1]

If you are a member of a married couple or registered civil partnership, or live with someone as if you were married or civil partners, you must claim jointly with your partner. This is known as a 'joint claim'.[2] See p1284 for when you count as a member of a married or unmarried couple, as registered civil partners, or are treated as someone's civil partner. Both partners must claim the tax credits jointly, but there are special rules about who receives payment of the different tax credits. HM Revenue and Customs (HMRC) can treat a claim by one member of a couple as having been made by the other member.[3] Note, however, that if you or your partner leave the UK and are no longer treated as being in the UK (see p1495), you cannot make a joint claim. Instead, the partner in the UK must make a new claim as a single person. Failure to notify the Tax Credit Office (TCO) of this may result in a penalty (see p1385).

If you are a single person, you make a single claim. If you made a joint claim and are no longer part of a couple, or if you made a single claim and are now part of a couple, your award stops. You must make a new claim.[4] You should tell the TCO as soon as possible. If you do not, you could be overpaid. You could also incur a financial penalty if you fail to notify the change within one month.[5] When you contact the TCO to report the fact that your couple claim has ended, your new single claim can be made in the same telephone call without the need to fill in a new claim form.[6] If you report that a single claim has ended and you are now part of a couple, you will need to complete a new claim form and request backdating or you will lose out on tax credits. In either case, your new claim can only be backdated for 31 days. (This is the time limit from 6 April 2012, previously it was 93 days.)

Appointees

The following people can make a claim on your behalf if you are unable to make the claim yourself:[7]

- a receiver appointed by the Court of Protection with power to make a claim for tax credits on your behalf;
- in Scotland, a tutor, curator or other guardian acting or appointed in terms of the law who is administering your estate;
- in Northern Ireland, a controller appointed by the High Court with power to make a tax credit claim on your behalf;
- a person who is your 'appointee' (see p1016) for social security purposes; *or*
- if there is no one who satisfies the above, a person aged 18 or over who applies to HMRC in writing to act on your behalf and is appointed by HMRC in that capacity.

2. How to make a claim

You have no entitlement to tax credits unless you make a claim.[8] You claim both child tax credit (CTC) and working tax credit (WTC) on one claim form. If you have been getting additional amounts for your children in your income support (IS) and your entitlement to IS ends because of the changes to the rules on lone parents (see p347), the DWP can pass the required information to HM Revenue and Customs (HMRC) to allow a 'deemed claim' for CTC and you do not have to fill in a separate claim form.[9] If you are starting work after being on jobseeker's allowance (JSA) or IS as a lone parent, you can claim tax credits at your local Jobcentre Plus office as part of the 'In and Out of Work Project', which can also include telephone claims.

You must claim tax credits in writing on Form TC600, unless the above exceptions apply or you are renewing a claim (see p1350). In practice, HMRC only accepts written applications not on a claim form in a few exceptional circumstances, although it has discretion on this.[10] You can get a claim form by contacting the Tax Credit Helpline on 0345 300 3900 (textphone: 0345 300 3909), which can also answer questions about tax credits. Citizens Advice Bureaux, Jobcentre Plus offices and HMRC enquiry centres may also have a supply of claim forms. Even if you are advised by the helpline that you are not entitled to tax credits, still request a claim form and make a claim if you think you are eligible. There will then be a decision on which to base an appeal or ask for a revision later.

If you cannot complete all the details asked for on the claim form, phone the Tax Credits Helpline for further advice. Send the completed claim form directly to the Tax Credit Office (TCO) in the pre-paid envelope provided with the claim form (the address is Comben House, Farriers Way, Netherton, Merseyside) or to any other office specified in writing by HMRC (such as the TCO address in Appendix 1).[11] Keep a copy of your claim form in case queries arise.

If you have sent your claim form to the TCO and you later realise that the details on it need to be amended, you should contact the TCO as soon as possible. You can amend or withdraw your claim at any time before the claim has been decided.[12] Even if your claim has been decided, there are certain circumstances when your entitlement to tax credits can be amended. Once your claim has been decided and an award made, however, you cannot withdraw it until the annual review.[13] For more details of when these changes in circumstances apply, see Chapter 57.

Information to support your claim

Your claim must contain all of the information requested on the claim form, unless HMRC decides otherwise.[14] If you do not supply all the requested information, a decision may not be made on your claim until the required information is provided. If you need advice about the information required, contact the helpline (see p1348).

National insurance number requirement

Your claim must include the following in respect of each person for whom a claim is made:[15]

- her/his national insurance (NI) number plus information or evidence establishing that it is her/his NI number; *or*
- information or evidence to enable HMRC to find her/his NI number; *or*
- an application for an NI number, with the necessary evidence or information to allow one to be allocated.

You do not need to meet the NI number requirement if HMRC believes you have a 'reasonable excuse'.[16] 'Reasonable excuse' is not defined, but HMRC says it will vary from case to case and discretion must be used fairly.[17] The NI number requirement does not need to be satisfied for someone (usually one member of a couple) who is a 'person subject to immigration control' because s/he does not have leave to enter or remain in the UK and who has not been given an NI number.[18] However, the NI number requirement does apply in other cases where a person has limited leave to enter or remain in the UK but is still subject to immigration to control, although if s/he has not been given an NI number, you can argue this is a reasonable excuse. **Note:** there is an immigration status condition for entitlement to tax credits (see p1410).

Income

If you are receiving IS, income-based JSA, income-related employment and support allowance (ESA) or pension credit (PC) when you claim tax credits, you only need to inform the TCO of this; you do not need to provide any other income details.[19] HMRC expects you to know which type of JSA or ESA you are getting.[20]

Otherwise, when you make a claim for tax credits, you must provide details of your income during the previous tax year. If you are part of a couple and making a joint claim, your award is based on your joint income during the previous tax year. This applies even in situations in which you may not have been living as a couple in the previous year, so income before the relationship began still counts as joint income.[21] For details of what counts as income, see Chapter 55.

If you think that your current tax year's income is going to be substantially different to the previous tax year's income, you should still complete the claim form with details of your previous tax year's income. When HMRC makes a decision on your claim, you will be sent an award notice which tells you how to notify it of your estimated income for the current year. You can also request that your award be adjusted at any time during the year of the award. Where appropriate, HMRC will then adjust your award of tax credits, using your estimated figure of your current year's income (see p1365 for more information).

If you worked as an employee throughout the previous tax year, your P60 for that year will have details of your taxable income. If you received any payments in kind from your employer, you should have details of these on Form P9D or P11D, which your employer should give you. If you were self-employed throughout the previous tax year, you can use your tax return as the basis for your taxable income. If you were in receipt of taxable social security benefits, you should be able to get a statement of taxable benefit income from the DWP.

If your previous year's income was too high to receive tax credits, you should still claim tax credits if you meet the qualifying conditions and think your current year's income may be less than that in the previous year. This is referred to by HMRC as a 'protective claim' and can result in a 'nil award', but tax credits may become payable when your current year's income is known.

Bank account details

You are required to provide details of a bank, building society or Post Office card account into which the tax credits can be paid. This is because entitlement depends on having a bank or other account.[22] See p1355 if you do not have a bank or similar account.

Further information and evidence

HMRC might need further information or evidence before making a decision (including one on a claim or revision). The information or evidence can be required from you or from your employer or childcare provider. If material is required, HMRC gives notice to provide it within a specified time limit. In all cases, this must be at least 30 days.[23] The basic rule is that you can be required to provide any further information or evidence that HMRC considers necessary. If you do not provide the material requested, you might be refused tax credits. If you provide incorrect information or fail to comply with requirements to provide information or evidence, you may be subject to a financial penalty or, if you are considered to have acted fraudulently, a fine or imprisonment, or both (see Chapter 59).

Renewing your claim

From 6 April HMRC reviews all tax credit awards, including nil awards and awards that ended before 5 April. This review process and your response form the basis of the renewal of your claim for the following year. Your response to the annual review is treated as a claim for the new tax year, unless you state that you wish to withdraw your claim. Your claim may be renewed automatically if you have been on IS, income-based JSA, income-related ESA or PC throughout the previous tax year and are still in receipt of one of these benefits. In some cases where income is too high for an award to be made, HMRC may write to you at least 35 days before the annual review to notify you that your claim will not be renewed unless you respond within 30 days that you want your claim to continue.[24] However, renewing a nil award may prove valuable if income drops unexpectedly later in the year.[25] HMRC sends you an annual review pack. You can give the information asked for in the pack by returning the forms in the envelope provided or by phoning the Tax Credit Helpline (see p1360).

During the annual review process, tax credits continue to be paid on a provisional basis.[26] If HMRC does not have up-to-date income details, these payments are based on the assumption that your income for the tax year just ended increased in line with average earnings.[27] If your income increased by more than this, you may be overpaid until the review is complete. Therefore, it is best to provide income details as soon as possible and not wait for the forms.

Annual review

If you claimed tax credits for the tax year 2011/12, HMRC should write to you between April and July 2012, enclosing an annual review form (TC603R). This is referred to in the legislation as the 'final notice'.[28] Unless you have been on IS, income-based JSA, income-related ESA or PC throughout 2011/12, or have a nil award, you should also receive an annual declaration form (TC603D – see p1352).

If you made more than one claim for tax credits during the previous tax year (eg, because you separated from your partner during that year and had to make a new claim for tax credits as a single person), you will receive a separate annual review form and annual declaration form, if required, for each claim. If you are sent more than one set of forms covering different claims, you should reply to each separately, even if they ask for the same information. If an annual declaration is required, one member of a couple can make a declaration by telephone on behalf of her/his partner, but if it is in writing both partners must sign it.[29] If a couple separate during the renewal period, a declaration by one partner will allow the claim to be renewed up to the date of separation.[30] Both members of a separated couple are expected to make signed declarations for the previous year to allow the award for that year to be finalised. However, if only one signs the declaration, the award can be finalised, based on the information held by HMRC about the other member.[31]

If you are sent an annual review form, but not an annual declaration form, you are asked to check that all the details on this form about your claim for the previous year are correct and to notify the TCO of any changes in your circumstances. You will then be deemed to have confirmed that all the details in the form are correct.[32] The final decision on the award for 2011/12 and an initial decision on the award for 2012/13 are as set out on the annual review form. However, you should always check the form and the notes accompanying it carefully to see whether you need to return the forms or report a change or error.

If you need to reply to the annual review form, you must do so by the date specified on the form. This is 31 July, unless the form is sent to you after 1 July, in which case you must be given at least 30 days to reply.[33]

If the details on the forms sent to you about your claim and income are not correct and you fail to reply within the time allowed, you may not receive the correct amount of tax credit. If you are overpaid as a result, you may have to repay the overpayment. If you fail to notify certain changes of circumstances promptly, you may have to make a penalty payment(s) (see p1363).

Annual declaration

You may receive an annual declaration form (TC603D) that asks for details of your income in the previous tax year. Anyone who was not on IS, income-based JSA, income-related ESA or PC throughout 2011/12 and who does not have a nil award should get an annual declaration form.

If you are sent an annual declaration form, you must always complete and return it by the date specified in the accompanying annual review form – usually 31 July. If you do not, your tax credit payments will stop, you may have to repay any tax credit paid since 6 April and you may have to pay a penalty payment(s). You must also tell the TCO of any changes in personal circumstances from those set out in the annual review form.

If, before this date, you do not know your total income for the period in question, you should not delay returning your forms. Instead, provide an estimate and send details of your actual income as soon as you can. You must do this before the deadline given on the form or you may lose out on backdating (see below).

If you return your annual declaration form before the 31 July deadline, your renewal claim will be backdated to 6 April 2012. If you do not return it before 31 July but, having been sent a notice that your payments of tax credits have ceased, return it within 30 days following the date on the notice, your renewal claim will be backdated to 6 April 2012. If neither of these apply, but you return your annual declaration form before 31 January 2013 and you have 'good cause' for returning it late, your renewal claim will be backdated to 6 April 2012.[34] 'Good cause' is not defined, but HMRC says it will look at each case on its individual merits. It will consider whether you were not able to complete the form because of exceptional circumstances and could not make arrangements for someone else to handle your affairs.[35] If you are not accepted as having good cause, HMRC's view is that there is no right of appeal against this decision, but as this is disputed you should appeal and ask the First-tier Tribunal to accept your appeal. It is strongly arguable that you do have the right of appeal in this situation.[36] If you return your annual declaration late without good cause, or after 31 January in any case, this should be treated as a new claim and it can only be backdated for 31 days.[37] (This is the time limit from 6 April 2012, previously it was 93 days.)

However, these rules allowing late return of your declaration do not apply if:

- your previous claim was on the basis that you were single and you are now a member of a couple; *or*
- your previous claim was made on the basis that you were a member of a couple and you are now single.[38]

Final decision

HMRC aims to process your completed forms within 30 days of receiving them. You should receive a final decision confirming whether your award for 2011/12 was correct. If you did not have an annual declaration form to complete, the final decision is as set out in your annual review form (unless, having read your annual review form, you find that you have a change of circumstances to report, in which case HMRC will send you details of your new award after it has dealt with the reported change).

HMRC will also send you an initial decision notice (TC602) setting out your award for the tax year 2012/13.

If you are notified that you have been overpaid tax credits, see Chapter 58.

3. When to claim

You cannot make a claim for tax credits in advance of the tax year for which you are claiming.[39] The general rule is that a claim for tax credits runs from the date it is received by the Tax Credit Office (TCO) until the end of the tax year in which the claim is made.[40] If you were entitled to tax credits before the date your claim is received by the TCO, your claim can be backdated for a period of up to 31 days. (This is the time limit expected from 6 April 2012, previously it was 93 days.) Backdating of working tax credit (WTC) is possible for a longer period if you only become entitled to WTC following an award of disability living allowance or another qualifying benefit (see p1355).

Once a claim for tax credits has been made, it can be renewed at the end of that tax year (see p1350).

4. How your claim is dealt with

Once you have made your claim for tax credits, HM Revenue and Customs (HMRC) must make a decision on whether you are entitled to either of the tax credits and, if so, at what rate.[41] HMRC may first require you, or your partner if you are making a joint claim, to provide any information or evidence that it needs to make a decision.[42]

You are notified of your award on Form TC602. You are asked to check the details on your award notice using a checklist (TC602(SN)). You should contact the Tax Credit Office if any of the details shown on the award notice are wrong or have changed. If you do not and an overpayment results, HMRC may expect you to pay it back (see p1374).

The first decision made after your claim is called the 'initial decision'. You can amend, either verbally or in writing, the details you provided when making your claim at any time until HMRC makes its initial decision and your date of claim will remain the same.

The initial decision is usually made on the basis of your circumstances at the date you make your claim and on your previous tax year's income. If your income or circumstances do not change, the award runs at the amount awarded on the initial decision until the end of the tax year. Your payments can continue on a provisional basis at the start of the new tax year while you are waiting to renew your claim and have not had a final decision on the previous year, or if you have renewed your claim but not yet received an initial decision on the new tax year. For more details on renewing your claim and provisional payments, see p1350.[43]

Certain changes in circumstances can mean that the initial decision will be changed. For more information on decisions and changes in circumstances, see Chapter 57.

5. **Getting paid**

Who is paid

If you make a joint claim, child tax credit (CTC) and the childcare element of working tax credit (WTC) is paid to whoever is the 'main carer' of the children.[44] The **'main carer'** can be either you or your partner, depending on who you both agree should be paid CTC. If you and your partner are living at the same address and either you do not identify who should be paid, or you cannot agree, HM Revenue and Customs (HMRC) decides. If you and your partner are not currently living at the same address or one of you is temporarily absent, HMRC decides which of you will be paid.[45] If the main carer changes following an award of tax credits, HMRC can make the payments to that person instead if it considers it reasonable.[46]

If you claim WTC as part of a joint claim and one of you is working, the payment (apart from any childcare amount payable) is made to the person who is engaged in full-time paid work (see Chapter 53). If you are both in full-time paid work, you can decide who will receive the payment between you. If you cannot agree, HMRC will decide. If you both agree, you can write to the Tax Credit Office (TCO) requesting that payment be made to the other person.[47]

If you make a joint claim and your partner subsequently dies, you receive any outstanding amount of tax credits that would have been paid to your partner.[48]

If an appointee (see p1016) has claimed tax credits on your behalf, payment is made to the appointee.

How and when payments are made

HMRC makes payments of tax credits by direct credit transfer into a bank, building society (or similar) or Post Office card account.[49] You can request that the payments are made into your account every week or every four weeks, but HMRC has the discretion to make payments weekly or four-weekly as it sees fit. CTC and the childcare element of WTC must be paid at the same time and at the same intervals.[50] If you are entitled to less than £2 tax credits a week, your award may be paid as a lump sum.[51]

If it is not considered appropriate for payments to be made into an account, HMRC can decide on the manner and timing of payment by other means.[52] If you do not provide account details, HMRC should write to you, requesting that you supply the information within four weeks, after which your payments may be postponed.[53] (This is the time limit expected from 6 April 2012, previously it was eight weeks.) If you then require an authority from HMRC to open an account, you have three weeks from the date it supplies you with this to provide details of your account. If you do not provide details of an account within three months of your payments being postponed (or by the end of the relevant tax year if this is earlier), your entitlement may cease from the date that payments were postponed. These periods can be extended if there are exceptional circumstances or you have a 'reasonable excuse' for not being able to provide the details within the time limits.[54] If you lose or forget your PIN, see p1040.

Postponement of payment

Payment of tax credits may be postponed if:[55]

- there is an appeal pending against a decision of the First-tier Tribunal, Upper Tribunal or a court either in your case or in another case that may affect your award (including if HMRC is waiting for a receipt of a decision or statement of reasons, or considering whether to make a further appeal or request a statement of reasons);
- you have failed to provide account details;
- details of your account or address appear to be incorrect; *or*
- you have failed to respond to a request for information or evidence by a specified date.

6. Backdating your claim

Note: the time limit for backdating new claims was previously 93 days, but is 31 days from 6 April 2012.

In general, your claim for tax credits can be backdated for up to 31 days (but see below), provided you would have satisfied the rules of entitlement throughout the 31-day period.[56] HM Revenue and Customs looks at your claim form for evidence of possible backdating. However, it is best to ask for your claim to be backdated to when you think your entitlement began (subject to the 31-day limit).

If you were awarded tax credits but no payment was made because you failed to provide sufficient details of an account into which tax credits could be paid and you subsequently provide the necessary details, your award can be backdated for up to three months from the date you supply the information.[57]

A new claim for working tax credit (WTC) can be backdated for more than 31 days if it includes the disabled worker element and you claim within 31 days of being awarded a qualifying disability benefit. For this to apply, your WTC entitlement in the backdating period must have depended on a qualifying disability benefit being awarded.[58] If you have an existing award of WTC or child tax credit and want to be awarded the disability or severe disability elements following an award of a qualifying disability benefit, see p1365.

See p1423 for backdating if you are granted refugee status.

Notes

1. **Who should claim**

1 s3(3) TCA 2002
2 s3(3)(a) and (8) TCA 2002
3 Reg 13(3) TC(CN) Regs
4 s3(4) TCA 2002
5 Reg 21(2)(a) TC(CN) Regs; s32(3) TCA 2002
6 HMRC, *Departmental Report 2008*, p38
7 Regs 17 and 18 TC(CN) Regs

2. **How to make a claim**

8 S3(1) TCA 2002
9 Reg 2 TCA(TP)O
10 Reg 5(2) TC(CN) Regs
11 Reg 2 TC(CN) Regs
12 Reg 5(7) TC(CN) Regs
13 R(IS) 3/05; reg 12(7)(c) TC(CN) Regs
14 Reg 5(3) TC(CN) Regs
15 Reg 5(4) TC(CN) Regs
16 Reg 5(6) TC(CN) Regs
17 para 06110 TCTM
18 Reg 5(8) TC(CN) Regs
19 ss7(2) TCA 2002; Form TC600, Part 5
20 HMRC leaflet, *Why Do Overpayments Happen* (WTC8), pp4-5
21 CTC/2270/2007
22 Reg 14 TC(PC) Regs
23 ss14, 15, 16, 17, 18, 19 and 22 TCA 2002; regs 30-33 TC(CN) Regs
24 Reg 12(8) TC(CN) Regs
25 s14(3) TCA 2002
26 s24(4) TCA 2002; reg 7 TC(PC) Regs
27 Reg 12(4) TC(PC) Regs
28 s17(1) TCA 2002
29 Reg 34 TC(CN) Regs
30 Reg 13 TC(CN) Regs
31 s18(3) TCA 2002
32 s17(2)(b) and (6)(b) TCA 2002
33 Reg 33 TC(CN) Regs
34 Reg 11 TC(CN) Regs
35 para 0136160 TCM
36 *SG v HMRC (TC)* [2011] UKUT 199 (AAC), 16 May 2011, in particular para 84
37 Reg 11(3) TC(CN) Regs
38 Reg 11(4) TC(CN) Regs

3. **When to claim**
39 Reg 9 TC(CN) Regs
40 s5(2) TCA 2002

4. **How your claim is dealt with**
41 s14(1) TCA 2002
42 s14(2) TCA 2002
43 s24(4) TCA; reg 7 TC(PC) Regs

5. **Getting paid**
44 Reg 3 TC(PC) Regs
45 Reg 3(3) TC(PC) Regs
46 Reg 3(6) TC(PC) Regs
47 Reg 4 TC(PC) Regs
48 Reg 5 TC(PC) Regs
49 Reg 13(1) TC(PC) Regs
50 Reg 8(2), (2A) and (2B) TC(PC) Regs
51 Reg 10 TC(PC) Regs
52 Reg 9 TC(PC) Regs
53 Reg 11(2A) TC(PC) Regs
54 Reg 14 (3) & (4A-4E) TC(PC) Regs; para 06110 TCTM
55 Reg 11 (1) to (4) TC(PC) Regs

6. **Backdating your claim**
56 Reg 7 TC(CN) Regs
57 Reg 14(2) TC(PC) Regs
58 Reg 8 TC(CN) Regs

Chapter 57

Decisions and changes in circumstances: tax credits

This chapter covers:

Key facts

- The tax credit decision-making process is different from that for social security benefits, as tax credits are dealt with over a tax year.
- An 'initial decision' is made following your claim and is an estimate of your award for the year. It may be changed during the year.
- A 'final decision' is made at the end of the tax year and is your actual entitlement for the year. It may only be changed in limited circumstances.
- Your award of tax credits may be affected by changes in your circumstances.

Future changes: April 2013 and after

Major changes are taking place that affect the benefits and tax credits system (see Chapter 2).

- From October 2013, a new benefit, universal credit (UC), will be introduced, which will replace tax credits. If you are already getting tax credits in October 2013, you will continue to do so until you are transferred onto UC.
- No new claims for tax credits will be accepted from 6 April 2014, although it will be possible to renew a claim until the point when you are transferred to UC.

See CPAG's *Welfare Rights Bulletin* for updates.

1. Making a decision

Once you have made a valid claim for tax credits (see p1348), a decision must be made by the commissioners for Her Majesty's Revenue and Customs (HMRC).[1] In practice, decisions are made by civil servants in HMRC.

An '**initial decision**' is made at the start of your claim and is based on an estimate of your tax credit entitlement in the coming tax year (6 April to 5 April). You are then sent a tax credits award notice setting out your award. A '**final decision**' is made after the end of the tax year in which your claim was made. It is based on your actual circumstances during the year and is the decision that confirms what your entitlement actually was. Again, you are sent a tax credits award notice.

Unless the decision on your entitlement is changed, either on revision or on appeal, the initial decision and the final decision are the only decisions on your claim that you will get.

Information and evidence

HMRC can require you to provide certain information and evidence for making a decision (see p1348). If you provide incorrect information or fail to comply with requirements to provide information or evidence, you may be subject to a financial penalty or, if you are considered to have acted fraudulently, a fine or imprisonment, or both (see Chapter 59).

Delays, negligence and complaints

It is not possible to sue HMRC for negligence in the way in which your claim is decided.[2] If a decision is wrong, you can seek a revision or appeal against it. If you are given wrong advice by an employee of HMRC, you may be able to seek compensation either through the courts or through the internal complaints procedure (see p1261). If you are given wrong information by HMRC or the DWP which led to an overpayment, this may be grounds for recovery to be waived (see Chapter 58).

If your claim has been received but not dealt with, ask why. If you are not satisfied with the explanation for the delay, make a complaint to HMRC (see Chapter 50). You can also complain if, for example, you have been treated badly or your case has been mishandled. In some cases, you can seek a judicial review (see p1202). If there are unreasonable delays in processing your claim, you may be able to make a complaint to the Ombudsman.

If you disagree with a decision or your circumstances change

Most decisions about your entitlement to tax credits can be revised or appealed. If you think a decision is wrong, you can seek a revision, or appeal to the First-tier Tribunal (see Chapter 60).

If you want to seek a revision or appeal against a decision, you should not delay. The time limit for appeals in particular is strict – normally 30 days. Some changes in your circumstances must be notified to HMRC within one month. If you want your tax credit entitlement increased in full because of a change in your circumstances (other than a fall in your expected income), you should report the change within one month (see p1363).

2. Contacting HM Revenue and Customs

Telephoning the Tax Credit Helpline (tel: 0345 300 3900; textphone: 0345 300 3909) is HM Revenue and Customs's (HMRC's) preferred method of contact. Be ready to give your name, address and national insurance (NI) number. Always keep a note of the date and time of your call, with a brief note of what is said and, if possible, the name and title of the person you speak to. It is best to follow up your call with a letter confirming the information you have provided and the advice given by the Helpline. Write to the Tax Credit Office at the address on the award notice and include your name, address, NI number and the date. Always keep a copy of your letter. If you are appealing, disputing recovery of an overpayment or making a complaint, it is best to use the relevant form or put it in writing.

If you notify a change of circumstances, HMRC should send you a new award notice (if the change affected your award) within 30 days.[3] If you do not receive an award notice within 30 days of reporting a change, HMRC asks you to call the Helpline again. However, provided you can prove the original notification was made, this is not part of your responsibilities (see p1374).

3. Initial decisions

On receiving an application for tax credits, HM Revenue and Customs (HMRC) must make an initial decision on whether an award should be made and, if so, the amount.[4] The claim form does not distinguish between child tax credit and working tax credit, so HMRC must decide your entitlement to both types of credit.

The main evidence on which this decision is based is that on your claim form, unless you supply further evidence before the decision is made. You can be required to provide extra information or evidence (see p1348).

The evidence used normally relates to your income in the tax year *previous* to the year in which you are claiming and to your circumstances (eg, if you have a partner and/or children) in the *current* tax year – ie, the one in which you are claiming. So, for an initial decision for 2012/13, the current year is 2012/13 and the previous year is 2011/12. See Chapter 55 for more details about income.

You must be notified of the initial decision. The notice must include the date on which it is given and your right of appeal against it.[5] If you had already claimed tax credits in the previous year, your initial decision for the coming year may be included in the final notice (see below).[6] The initial decision sets the amount of tax credit you are due to receive until the final decision is made, unless it is changed on revision or appeal.

4. Final decisions

After the end of the tax year in which you claimed, HM Revenue and Customs (HMRC) must make a final decision on whether you were entitled to tax credits and, if so, the amount of your award.[7] Therefore, the final decision can establish that:

- the initial decision was correct;
- you were underpaid tax credit;
- you were overpaid tax credit.

Underpayments established in a final decision must be paid to you as a lump sum.[8] **Overpayments** are usually recovered from you (see Chapter 58). **Note:** you do not have the right of appeal against a decision that an overpayment is to be recovered from you (although you can ask HMRC not to recover it – see p1374).

If you do not agree that you have been paid too much tax credit, it is important that you appeal against the lower award notified to you in the final decision.

The final decision is made in two main stages.

- A final notice is issued to gather information and evidence about what your income and circumstances were in the year.
- The information from the final notice is used to make a final decision on your entitlement for the year.

Final notice

At the end of the tax year in which you claimed, a final notice is sent to you.[9] Your response to the final notice forms the basis of the renewal of your claim for the new tax year (unless you specify that you wish to withdraw your claim or HMRC notifies you that it will not be renewed unless you request it).[10] HMRC refers to this process as 'annual review' and 'annual declaration' (see p1350). The notice either:

- requires you to confirm that the circumstances taken into account by HMRC in your award were correct. If they were not correct, you must specify in what way they were not correct; *or*
- informs you that, unless you reply within the time allowed, you will be deemed to have confirmed that the circumstances were correct.[11]

The notice also asks about your income (see p1362). You are required to respond by 31 July (or at least 30 days after the date on the notice, if it was sent after 1

July).[12] Replying in time is important, not only to ensure your entitlement for the previous year is correct but also to renew your claim. If you reply after 31 July, but before 31 January 2013, you can still be treated as having replied in time for the purpose of renewing your claim. For more details, see p1350.[13]

Current year's income

The final notice asks about your actual income for the tax year just ended. In the assessment of tax credits for that year, this was referred to as '**current year's income**'. So, for a final notice for 2011/12, the current year is 2011/12. The initial decision for that year was based on income in the previous year, or may have been revised according to an estimate of your current year's income. For the final decision, HMRC needs to compare that figure with your actual income. It is, therefore, very important that you tell the Tax Credit Office if your current year's income was different from that used to make the initial decision or any subsequent revision.

Sometimes you may only be able to provide an estimate of what your actual income was in the tax year just ended. The final notice allows for this. If you use an estimate of your current year's income, the final notice must inform you that your estimate will be treated as the actual amount of your current year's income, unless you state what it actually was within the time allowed.[14]

You may be asked to provide information about, or make a declaration about, your current year's income, or be informed that unless you respond you will be treated as having confirmed your income.[15]

Previous year's income

The final notice may ask you to confirm your actual income for the tax year before the one that has just ended. This is referred to as '**previous year's income**'. So, for a final notice for 2011/12, the previous year was 2010/11. When making a decision, HMRC may have used an estimate of previous year's income, or confirmation that it fell within a specified range. If so, you are either required to make a declaration, or are informed that the amount given in the final notice will be used unless you respond within the time allowed.[16]

Responding to the final notice

Responses to the final notice must usually be on a form provided by HMRC. Alternatively, you can call the Tax Credit Helpline. If you are unable to respond to the final notice (eg, because of illness), responses can be accepted from receivers and people who are appointees for tax credit or benefit purposes.[17]

Final decision

Once a final notice has been issued, HMRC must make a decision on your actual entitlement to tax credits for the year. A final decision cannot be made before you have responded to the final notice, unless the time allowed for you to make such a response has passed. Once this decision is made, it is usually the final decision on your entitlement for the tax year concerned, unless it is changed either on revision or appeal (see Chapter 60). However, if you have responded to a final notice and a final decision has been made, the final decision can be revised if you make a new response, as long as that new response is made on or before the final date you were given for your original response.[18]

You must be notified of a final decision.[19] However, your final notice may have said what the final decision will be and the date on which it will be made, unless you respond and say that the circumstances or income on which the decision is based are incorrect. If you did not reply to such a final notice, HMRC need not send you a separate notice of the final decision.[20] For more information about the way in which a final decision is made on your claim, see Chapter 56.

5. Change of circumstances after a claim

Changes in your family circumstances, childcare charges or income during your award may lead to changes in your entitlement. If changes do affect your entitlement, this can be altered either soon after the change has occurred, or at the end of the year when the final decision is made and HM Revenue and Customs (HMRC) makes a final check on your details. However, certain changes must be notified to the Tax Credit Office (TCO) within one month or you may incur a penalty. Some other changes which *increase* your entitlement should be notified within one month if your increased award is to be backdated in full.

Once an initial decision has been made, there are three types of change which can affect your entitlement to tax credits:

- changes which must be notified to the TCO;
- changes which affect your maximum entitlement to tax credits;
- changes in income.

Changes that must be notified to the Tax Credit Office

Some changes must be notified to the TCO within one month of the date of the change or the date you became aware of the change, if this was later. The notification must be is 'given' to the appropriate office (see p1368).[21] If you do not do this, HMRC may impose a financial penalty on you (see p1385). You must notify the TCO within one month if:

- you were claiming as a single person but are now part of a couple. Your tax credit entitlement comes to an end from the time the change occurred, and you must make a new claim;
- you were claiming as a couple but are no longer part of that couple. Your entitlement comes to an end from the date the change occurred, and you must make a new claim;

- you or your partner leave the UK permanently or for more than eight weeks (12 if due to illness or bereavement) and cannot be treated as being in the UK (see p1495). Entitlement comes to an end and you must make a new claim. If your partner is not treated as being in the UK, you must make a new claim as a single person (and when s/he comes back, claim again as a couple);
- for child tax credit (CTC) only, you lose your right to reside in the UK (see p1447);
- there has been a decrease of £10 a week or more over four consecutive weeks in your or your partner's average weekly childcare charge (as calculated on p1317) or the childcare costs have stopped. This change takes effect the day after the four consecutive weeks. If you have been awarded childcare costs for a fixed period that was known when the costs were awarded, the change takes effect from the week following the end of the period of the award, instead of the usual four-week period;[22]
- you or your partner stop normally working at least 16 or 30 hours a week (see p1295 for rules about work). You can still count as being in work in some situations – eg, in some cases of illness or maternity. If you stop work, you may get a four-week run-on of working tax credit (WTC – see p1304);
- you are a couple with children, and you and your partner stop normally working a combined total of 24 or 30 hours a week;
- you or your partner cease to be responsible for one or more of your children (see p1271 for when you count as responsible);
- a child for whom you or your partner are responsible dies (see p1271 for who counts as a child);
- a child for whom you or your partner are responsible stops counting as a child or qualifying young person, other than by reaching age 20 (see p1269 for who counts as a child). In this case, you must notify the TCO within one month of the date the change actually occurred, rather than when you became aware of the change.

Changes that affect your maximum entitlement

Note: the time limit for backdating increases was previously three months, but is one month from 6 April 2012. There are certain other changes in circumstances which affect your maximum entitlement to tax credits – ie, they affect the tax credit elements to which you are entitled (see Chapter 54).

You do not have to notify the TCO of these changes when they occur. Some changes can be notified up to a week in advance (see p1368). However, most changes which *increase* your entitlement are only backdated for a maximum of one month from the time that you make the notification.[23] The only exception concerns the disability and severe disability elements (see p1365). Changes that *decrease* your entitlement always take effect from the date of change, no matter when you notify the TCO of them. Delaying notifying these changes can, therefore, lead to your being underpaid or overpaid. Note that overpayments will usually be recovered from you (see Chapter 58).

The sorts of changes to which these rules apply include:

- if you have a new baby, or another child joins your family;
- if you or your partner start normally working at least 16, 24 or 30 hours a week;
- if your childcare costs increase by £10 or more a week for at least four weeks in a row. The change takes effect from the first week in which your costs increase.[24] You can report an increase of £10 or more a week as soon as one occurs, as long as you expect it to last for at least four weeks. For how your childcare costs are calculated, see p1314.

Changes in entitlement to the disability or severe disability elements

The disabled worker and severe disability elements of WTC can be backdated for more than one month if the TCO is notified that you have been awarded a qualifying disability benefit within one month of that award being made.[25] If the award means that you are entitled to backdated WTC on a new claim, see p1355.

A similar rule applies to CTC entitlement. If a child for whom you are responsible is awarded disability living allowance (DLA), you will be entitled to the disabled child element and, if awarded the highest rate care component, the severely disabled child element in your award of CTC. The elements can be backdated for more than one month if the TCO is notified of the award of DLA within one month of the DLA decision.[26] See p1396 for revisions.

New relevant period

Following any of the changes of circumstance that must be notified or changes that affect your maximum entitlement, the way your tax credits are calculated changes.[27] All such changes mean that either your entitlement to tax credit has ceased or that a new 'relevant period' is started from the time the change is treated as taking effect. A new relevant period means that a new calculation of your entitlement is made. For example, an increase in your childcare costs of the sort described above results in a new relevant period, so there will be a new calculation of your entitlement for the new period in which your childcare element may be increased. See p1323 for details of the calculation.

Changes in income

The initial decision on your award of tax credit is usually based on your previous year's income. Your award can be changed to reflect:

- an expected fall in your annual income of more than £2,500 compared with the previous year – eg, if your earnings fall during the year; *and*

- an expected rise in your annual income of more than £10,000 compared with the previous year – eg, if your earnings increase during the year. A rise of less than £10,000 is disregarded during the year. **Note:** the government has announced that this disregard will be reduced to £5,000 from 2013/14.

Example

Rekha and Sophie work in the same job for the same salary. They are both lone parents, each with one child, born a few months apart.

Rekha had her baby in April 2011 and her 2011/12 income was £4,000 after the disregard applied to statutory maternity pay (SMP). She returned to work in April 2012 on a salary of £12,000. Rekha received maximum tax credits while on maternity leave in 2011/12 because her income was below the £6,420 threshold. She also receives maximum tax credits when she returns to work in 2012, because her 2012/13 income will not increase by more than the disregard of £10,000, so her entitlement is still based on 2011/12 income.

Sophie had her baby in January 2012 and her 2011/12 income was £9,000 (after the disregard applied to SMP). She expects to return to work in October 2012 and earn approximately £7,000 in 2012/13. Sophie's award for 2012/13 will continue to be based on her 2011/12 income of £9,000 because her income has not fallen by more than £2,500.

The £10,000 disregard only applies to increases in annual income in the current year (2012/13) compared with the previous year (2011/12). If you ask the TCO to base your award on the current year's income because of an expected decrease of more than £2,500, any subsequent increase in your current year's income is not disregarded and will affect your award. See Chapter 55 for how income affects your award.

Consider carefully whether to notify the TCO during the year of changes in income. Whether or not you are better off doing so depends on your circumstances, and it is worth seeking advice. Consider the general points in the following two sections. However, if you have not done so already, tell the TCO about an increase in income before the end of the tax year so that provisional payments for the new tax year starting in April will be accurate. Payment of tax credits continues during the renewal process on the assumption that your income has increased in line with average earnings.[28] If your income increased by more than this, you may be overpaid.

If you expect your annual income to fall by more than £2,500

- If you notify the TCO of an estimated decrease in your annual income of more than £2,500 during the year, your tax credit payments may be increased. However, the first £2,500 of the decrease is disregarded, so it is only any decrease over that amount that makes a difference. In effect, HMRC adds

£2,500 onto the current year's income and bases your award on the result. For example, if your 2011/12 income was £10,000 and your 2012/13 income will be £6,000, your tax credits award will be based on £8,500. If, at the end of the year, your 2012/13 income turns out to be £7,000, your award is based on £9,500 and you will have been overpaid.[29]

- An increase in tax credits means that if you get housing benefit (HB) or council tax benefit (CTB), the amount of these could be reduced as tax credits count as income (see Chapter 40). If your income later increases, you are not protected by the £10,000 disregard and any increase in income may produce an overpayment if your award was based on the lower current year estimate.
- At the end of the year, it may be that your income did not fall as you predicted and, as a result, you have been overpaid tax credits, which you may have to repay. HB and CTB are based on the amount of tax credits you actually *receive*. In these circumstances, HB and CTB are *not* increased for the period during which you were overpaid tax credits. Not only will you have been overpaid tax credits, you may have lost out on the additional HB and CTB which you would have been able to claim had you been receiving a lower award of tax credits.
- If you do *not* notify the TCO of a fall in income of more than £2,500 during the year, your tax credit entitlement is not adjusted until the final decision at the end of the year. In this instance, you will have been underpaid tax credits for the year, and this should be paid to you as a lump sum. This lump sum counts as capital and is ignored for 52 weeks after you have received it.[30] You will not, therefore, have been overpaid HB or CTB as a result of receiving these arrears.

If you expect your annual income to rise by more than £10,000

- If you notify the TCO that you expect your income to increase by more than £10,000 during the year, your tax credit award is decreased. This may mean that you prevent an overpayment of tax credits building up further during the year (see Chapter 58). Your HB and CTB (if you are entitled to any) can then be increased to take account of the lower award of tax credits.
- If you do *not* notify the TCO of an expected rise in your income during the year, you will keep being paid the 'extra' tax credits during the year and will incur an overpayment. The overpaid tax credit is usually recoverable from you by a reduction in the tax credits you are paid in the following year, in which case your HB and CTB in that year are likely to increase.
- There is no penalty for incurring an overpayment of tax credits on the basis of an increase in income.
- All this, however, does not mean that you are always better off building up such an overpayment. You will not know for sure exactly how much you have been overpaid and at what rate it will be recovered from you until the final decision at the end of the year. Although the reduced tax credit entitlement in the following year may increase your HB and CTB, your increased earnings will

also have the effect of reducing these benefits, and any further fluctuations in your income could complicate matters further.

- Ultimately, whether you are better off not notifying the TCO of such an expected rise during the year depends on the amount of the likely overpayment, how recovery is likely to affect your HB and CTB in the next year, whether your income is likely to rise or fall again and how comfortable you feel about building up a recoverable overpayment.

Notifying changes in circumstances

You can notify any changes in your circumstances either orally or in writing. The notification must be given to an 'appropriate office', defined as the TCO in Preston (see Appendix 1) or any other office specified in writing by HMRC – eg, the TCO address shown on your award notice.[31] This may include the Jobcentre Plus office dealing with your tax credits claim as part of the 'In and Out of Work Project' (see p1348) or the Child Benefit Office as part of the 'Tell Us Once' initiative, but only if this has been specified in writing by HMRC. If you did notify the DWP or another part of HMRC of a change which affects your tax credit entitlement and this was not passed on and resulted in an overpayment, you should raise this in your dispute. In practice, to be safe, you should ensure that the TCO has been informed. HMRC encourages claimants to telephone the Helpline with queries or to report a change (see p1360). In practice, however, it is advisable to confirm the notification in writing to the TCO and to keep a copy so you have a record of what you have said and when you said it.

Notification must be given by the person who claimed the tax credit. In joint claim cases, it can be given by either member of the couple.[32]

Some changes of circumstances can be notified up to a week in advance. These are if:[33]

- you have accepted an offer of work and expect to start work within seven days;
- you have arranged childcare and will incur childcare costs during the current tax year;
- your weekly childcare costs are going to change by £10 a week or more.

You can also notify in advance if you expect your child to stay on in full-time, non-advanced education or approved training from 1 September after her/his 16th birthday.

You can amend the notification at any time before the initial award is revised, in which case the amended notification is taken as being notified at the time that your original notification was sent.[34]

Notes

1. **Making a decision**
   1 ss2and 14 TCA 2002
   2 *Jones v Department of Employment* [1989] QB 1 (CA)

2. **Contacting HM Revenue and Customs**
   3 HMRC leaflet, *What Happens if We've Paid You Too Much Tax Credit?* (COP26)

3. **Initial decisions**
   4 s14(1) TCA 2002
   5 s23 TCA 2002
   6 s23(3) TCA 2002

4. **Final decisions**
   7 s18 TCA 2002
   8 s30 TCA 2002
   9 s17(1) TCA 2002
   10 Regs 11 and 12 TC(CN) Regs
   11 s17(2) TCA 2002
   12 Reg 33 TC(CN) Regs
   13 Reg 11 TC(CN) Regs
   14 s17(8) TCA 2002
   15 s17(4) TCA 2002
   16 s17(6) TCA 2002
   17 Regs 34-36 TC(CN) Regs
   18 s18 TCA 2002
   19 s23 TCA 2002
   20 s23(3) TCA 2002

5. **Change of circumstances after a claim**
   21 ss6(3) and 32(3) TCA 2002; regs 2, 21 and 22 TC(CN) Regs
   22 Reg 16(5) WTC(EMR) Regs
   23 Regs 20 and 25 TC(CN) Regs
   24 Reg 16(5)(a) WTC(EMR) Regs
   25 Reg 26 TC(CN) Regs
   26 Reg 26A TC(CN) Regs
   27 Regs 7(2) and 8(2) TC(ITDR) Regs
   28 Reg 12(4) TC(PC) Regs
   29 s7(3)(d) TCA 2002; reg 5(b) TC(ITOR) Regs
   30 **HB** Sch 6(9) HB Regs
   CTB Sch 5(9) CTB Regs
   31 Regs 2 and 22 TC(CN) Regs
   32 Reg 23 TC(CN) Regs
   33 Reg 27 TC(CN) Regs
   34 Reg 24 TC(CN) Regs

Chapter 58

Overpayments of tax credits

This chapter covers:

For the rules on overpayments of benefits, see Chapter 43.

Key facts

- The rules on the recovery of tax credit overpayments are different from those that apply to social security benefits.
- All tax credit overpayments are recoverable, however they are caused, but HM Revenue and Customs (HMRC) has the discretion to decide whether or not to recover.
- There are rules on the amount that may be recovered and guidance on the way in which HMRC should recover an overpayment of tax credits.
- There is no right of appeal to an independent tribunal about a decision on whether or not to recover an overpayment of tax credits. However, if you disagree with a decision, you can ask HMRC to consider whether or not the overpayment should be recovered.
- If you do not accept that you were overpaid, you can appeal.
- Interest may also be added to overpayments and there is a right of appeal against this decision.

1. What is an overpayment of tax credits

The main rules are the same for child tax credit (CTC) and working tax credit (WTC).[1] If you (and your partner, if you are making a joint claim) are paid more tax credit for a tax year than you are entitled to, the extra amount is regarded as an overpayment. HM Revenue and Customs (HMRC) can decide to adjust your award during the year of your current tax credit award to prevent an overpayment building up (an **'in-year overpayment'**) and/or recover all or some of the overpayment from you after the end of the tax year (an **'end-of-year overpayment'**). There is no right of appeal against the decison to recover the overpayment, although you can appeal against a decision that your entitlement to tax credit has changed. This means that by challenging the new decision on your entitlement, you can, in effect, challenge the finding that there is an overpayment or challenge the amount of the overpayment.

When an overpayment occurs

The most likely cause of an overpayment is if:

- your income rose by more than the disregarded amount (see p1365) in the current year, compared with the previous tax year – eg, your income rises by more than £10,000 in 2012/13, compared with 2011/12;[2]
- you did not tell the Tax Credit Office (TCO) in time about a change of circumstances that reduces your entitlement (see p1363);
- the information you gave to the TCO was incorrect;
- HMRC failed to act on information you provided, or made a mistake – ie, an 'official error';
- none of the above applies, but an overpayment occurred anyway because of the way the rules on income and changes in circumstances work.

In-year overpayments

In-year overpayments arise during the year of your current tax credit award. Decisions on in-year overpayments can be made during the course of the tax year concerned in the following circumstances.[3]

- If HMRC thinks that there is likely to be an overpayment, it can adjust the award (or an award of another tax credit) to reduce or wipe out the overpayment. This may mean that your award is reduced for the rest of the year.
- If an award is terminated on the grounds that you did not satisfy the basic conditions for entitlement, HMRC may decide that the amount already paid to you, or some of it, is to be regarded as an overpayment. The basic conditions of entitlement are, for CTC, that you are responsible for a child (see p1269) and, for WTC, that you are engaged in full-time work (see p1296).

End-of-year overpayments

End-of-year overpayments are overpayments that are identified at or after the end of the tax year concerned – ie, after your award for that year has been finalised. HMRC can decide that there has been an end-of-year overpayment when it makes:[4]

- a final decision (see p1361);
- an enquiry decision (see p1398);
- a decision on discovery (see p1398).

Notification of overpayments

HMRC must change the decision on your entitlement and notify you of the new decision.[5] Remember that you have the right of appeal against any decision about the amount of your entitlement to tax credit (see p1400). If you think that the new decision on your entitlement is wrong and that, therefore, you have not been overpaid as much as HMRC says, or that you have not been overpaid at all, appeal against the new decision on your entitlement. If your appeal against the new decision on your entitlement is outside the 30-day time limit because you did not realise that you needed to appeal until you received a detailed calculation, argue that this is a reasonable excuse for the appeal being late.[6]

You may only find out about an **in-year overpayment** when HMRC writes to you to say that your entitlement has changed and your payment has been adjusted. If HMRC is going to recover an **end-of-year overpayment** from you, it must also give you notice of that, how much it is and how it is to be recovered from you. It usually does this at the same time as it writes to you about the final decision on your entitlement for the tax year. There is no right of appeal against the decision to recover an overpayment.[7] For what you can do, see p1374.

2. Recovery of overpayments

The basic rule is that HM Revenue and Customs (HMRC) can recover all or part of any overpayment.[8] It usually recovers the overpayment by:

- adjusting (ie, reducing) your current award; *or*
- requiring you to repay the overpayment.

However, it does not have to recover an overpayment and should exercise discretion. The official policy is in the HMRC leaflet *What Happens if We've Paid You Too Much Tax Credit* (COP26), which can be obtained by telephoning the Tax Credits Helpline on 0345 300 3900 or from www.hmrc.gov.uk. An overpayment may be written off, in whole or in part, if HMRC has made a mistake or failed to act, and you have acted correctly in connection with your claim.[9] The guidance also allows for recovery to be waived in exceptional circumstances or if it would cause hardship (see p1374). HMRC will suspend recovery of overpayments on receipt of the completed dispute form (TC846), which can be obtained by telephoning 0345 300 3900 or from www.hmrc.gov.uk.[10]

You must be given notice that you must repay an end-of-year overpayment. The notice must also say how much the overpayment is, and how it is to be recovered from you.[11]

HMRC does not ask you if recovering an overpayment will cause you hardship or if you think the overpayment should not be recovered from you. Instead, you have to tell it about such things. It is, therefore, important to contact the Tax Credit Office (TCO) as soon as possible.

Overpayments and award notices

For every overpayment, there should be a revised decision on your entitlement, which is sent as an award notice. The tax credit award notices can be very complicated. You should be sent a checklist (Form TC602(SN)) with your award notice with information used in the calculation for you to check. You can request an award calculation notice (Form TC647) from HMRC, which gives more details about how your payment has been worked out. If it is still unclear, you can write to the TCO (its address will be at the top of the award notice) requesting an individual explanation. However, you should not delay sending in your dispute form while you are waiting for the explanation, as recovery may start unless you have registered a dispute. You can send further details once you have received the full explanation.

If you still do not receive a satisfactory response, consider taking up the matter with your MP or making a complaint (see Chapter 50).

From whom can an overpayment be recovered

In-year overpayments are recovered from you by reducing the ongoing tax credit award. An end-of-year overpayment can be recovered from the person(s) to whom the tax credit award was made. This means:[12]

- if you made a claim as a single person, the overpayment can be recovered from you;
- if you made a joint claim with your partner, the overpayment can be recovered from one or both of you. If you have separated from your partner, HMRC's practice is first to ask you both to repay the overpayment equally. If you wish, you and your ex-partner may agree to each pay different amounts. Although HMRC has the power to ask one person to repay the whole amount, guidance states that usually each person will be asked to repay a maximum of half the overpayment, unless one partner has acted fraudulently or negligently and the other is seen to be an 'innocent partner'.[13]

Reducing the overpayment

According to official guidance, HMRC may reduce ('offset') the amount of the overpayment by the amount of any tax credit to which you would have been entitled had you claimed correctly – ie, by your 'notional entitlement'. This is referred to in HMRC guidance as 'offsetting notional entitlement' and will be applied if the overpayment was caused by: [14]

- your ceasing to count as a single claimant and becoming part of a couple (you will need details of your partner's income); *or*

- your ceasing to count as part of a couple and claiming instead as a single claimant.

In either case, you must have some tax credit entitlement following the change in your status.

HMRC may contact you about this but, as this cannot be guaranteed, you should contact it yourself if you think you may benefit from offsetting. Offsetting can be applied to in-year or end-of-year overpayments. It is understood that HMRC will not refund overpayments already repaid, but may offset notional entitlement on old cases if there is still an overpayment outstanding, or if you still have a review, dispute or complaint outstanding about the overpayment. Offsetting may not be applied in some cases if you did not report the change. In such cases, HMRC may also consider imposing a penalty. If HMRC refuses to offset your overpayment, ask it to consider any factors you think are relevant, including if there has been no actual loss to the public purse and whether you made a 'genuine error' or not. Although the guidance only refers to single/couple claims, you should request offsetting notional entitlement in other circumstances – eg, if you were overpaid because you left the UK for more than the permitted period but you would have been entitled to tax credits on your return. In some cases, refusals by HMRC to offset may be challenged by judicial review in the courts. Seek further advice.[15]

Disputing recovery

You can 'dispute' HMRC's decision to recover an overpayment if you think HMRC failed to meet its responsibilities or if there were exceptional circumstances why you were unable to meet your responsibilities as set out in HMRC leaflet *What Happens if We've Paid You Too Much Tax Credit?* (COP26). To dispute recovery, complete Form TC846 (available at www.hmrc.gov.uk or by contacting the helpline), or write to the TCO. HMRC will not recover all or part of the overpayment if it accepts that it has not fulfilled its responsibilities (see below) and you have met yours. Recovery of the overpayment will be suspended on receipt of a completed TC846 or other correspondence, while the dispute is considered. If your dispute is rejected and you provide new information, recovery should be suspended again while this is considered.[16] There is no official time limit for disputing recovery, but you should do so as soon as possible; if you leave it for a long time, HMRC will be less likely to allow your dispute.

Official errors and responsibilities

The way in which HMRC exercises its discretion whether or not to recover tax credit overpayments is set out in its leaflet *What Happens if We've Paid You Too Much Tax Credit?* (COP26), which is used if you dispute recovery. If an overpayment has been caused by an official error or failure to act by

HMRC (referred to as failing to meet its 'responsibilities'), it may decide not to recover all or part of the overpayment.

However, for the overpayment not to be recovered, you must also show that you have acted correctly in relation to your claim for tax credits – ie, you have met your 'responsibilities'. Your **'responsibilities'** are not used or defined in the law, but the official guidance is that HMRC will not ask you to repay an overpayment if it accepts that:[17]

- the overpayment was caused by HMRC failing to meet its responsibilities; *and*
- you have met all of your responsibilities.

If HMRC thinks it has met all its responsibilities but you have not met all of yours, it will normally recover the overpayment. If it thinks that both itself and you have failed to meet responsibilities, it will look at the circumstances and may write off parts of the overpayment. An overpayment can still occur even though both you and HMRC have met these reponsibilities, in which case HMRC is still likely to seek recovery.

HMRC regards its responsibilities as:

- giving you correct advice based on your information;
- accurately recording your information and paying the correct amount;
- putting right mistakes you tell it about and sending you a corrected award notice;
- accurately recording your notification of changes in your circumstances;
- sending you a new award notice within 30 days of having all the necessary information.

HMRC regards your responsibilities as:

- providing accurate, complete and up-to-date information;
- reporting changes of circumstances throughout the year;
- using the checklist (TC602(SN)) sent with your award notice to tell it if anything is wrong or incomplete;
- checking that your payments match the amount given on the award notice;
- reporting any errors on your award notice, normally within one month.

If there were exceptional circumstances which meant that you were unable to meet your responsibilities at the time, such as illness, you should explain this and HMRC may write off the overpayment. Remember that if you want recovery suspended while HMRC considers the matter, it is best to dispute the decision to recover the overpayment on Form TC846 (see p1377).

Hardship and mental health

Hardship is not defined, but HMRC leaflet *What Happens if We've Paid You Too Much Tax Credit* (COP26) refers to financial hardship in terms of family circumstances that lead to extra living costs, such as looking after someone who is chronically ill or disabled, and inability to pay for essential living expenses such as rent, gas or electricity. In cases of hardship, HMRC may put recovery on hold, reduce the amount being recovered by extending the period over which the overpayment is repaid, partially remit or, in exceptional circumstances, write off the overpayment altogether. Other guidance suggests that consideration will also be given to reducing or writing off your overpayment if you are unemployed and have no savings or assets, or if you are on incapacity benefit (IB) or employment and support allowance (ESA) and have little prospect of gaining employment.[18]

The situation may be kept under review, depending on your circumstances – ie, if there is a chance that your ability to repay will increase. It is in your interest to show how repayment will leave you in hardship.

The guidance also states that if you have a mental health problem, HMRC will deal with your case carefully and sympathetically to avoid causing you distress. It may require a letter from a healthcare professional or mental health social worker explaining the nature of your illness, prognosis and prospects for recovery. If your mental health problem existed at the time the overpayment occurred, this may be considered to be exceptional circumstances and so HMRC should consider writing off the overpayment. If you have a mental health problem at the time the overpayment is being recovered, HMRC may decide not to continue with the recovery.[19]

These decisions are discretionary and there is no right of appeal against them. Explain your circumstances and ask HMRC to exercise its discretion in your favour. The guidance on hardship and mental health applies whether you are repaying directly or by deductions from an ongoing award, but it may not be commonly known to all helpline staff. There is a special payment helpline on 0845 302 1429 to discuss hardship. You may also write with a financial statement to the HMRC office dealing with repayment. You should not use Form TC846 (see p1377) if you want more time to repay. If you remain unhappy with the decision, see p1378 for what you can do.

How the overpayment is recovered

You must be notified of the new decision on your entitlement that gave rise to the overpayment.[20] For **end-of-year overpayments**, HMRC must notify you (and your partner, if it is a joint overpayment) of the amount to be repaid, and how the overpayment is to be repaid.[21]

There are four ways in which HMRC can require you to repay:[22]

- deductions from ongoing payments of any tax credit (see p1377). This is HMRC's preferred method of repayment. The amount that is deducted is usually limited;
- directly to HMRC. You should receive a notice showing the full amount to be repaid. You are offered a standard repayment period of 12 monthly instalments, although up to 10 years may be negotiated;

- with your agreement, by deductions from certain benefits paid by the DWP (see p1055);[23]
- with your agreement, via PAYE by altering your tax code to allow deductions from your wages.[24]

Deductions from ongoing awards

HMRC can adjust your payments so that you receive less money and so, in effect, repay the overpayment. It will only do this if you have an ongoing award as the same household in which the overpayment arose. For example, it will not make a deduction from an ongoing award if you were overpaid as a single person and are now claiming as a couple. You should be notified of the amount being deducted. The amount by which HMRC can reduce your payments is limited by law. The law only deals with end-of-year overpayments but, in practice, HMRC takes the same approach with in-year overpayments. The *maximum* amounts by which HMRC can reduce your tax credit award are:[25]

- 10 per cent of the award if you are receiving the maximum tax credits to which you could be entitled – ie, with no reduction for income;
- 100 per cent of the award if you receive only the family element of child tax credit (CTC);
- 25 per cent of the award if neither of the above apply.

Note: these are maximum amounts, although HMRC applies them automatically. If you accept that you should repay but cannot afford to repay at these rates, contact HMRC and ask it to accept repayment at a lower rate. In order to persuade HMRC, you may need to show why it would cause you hardship (see p1374) to pay at the maximum rate.

Revised notices of overpayments, changing the method of recovery, can be issued at any time.[26]

Direct payment to HM Revenue and Customs

If you are no longer entitled to tax credits, or one tax credit award has ended and another started because of a change in your household (eg, you started or stopped being part of a couple), you must repay your overpayment by direct payments to HMRC. HMRC will suspend direct recovery if you are already repaying another overpayment (at the 10 per cent or 25 per cent rate described above) through your current tax credit award – but you may need to ask for this.[27] The notice to pay (TC610) asks you to contact HMRC to pay in full or negotiate repayment. If the overpayment has not been repaid and you have not contacted HMRC within 42 days, a reminder letter will be sent, followed by a more strongly worded warning letter. Failure to respond to this letter may mean that HMRC starts legal proceedings to recover the debt.

Other methods of recovery

HMRC may recover tax credit overpayments by deductions from specified benefits with your written consent.[28] See p1055 for more information. It may recover tax credit from your wages via PAYE, but only with your agreement.[29] If HMRC is not satisfied with recovery using the methods described above, it will consider taking legal action. Further action will follow if HMRC considers that you are refusing to repay, or neglecting to keep to an agreement to repay. All the circumstances will be taken into account before taking such action, but HMRC may:[30]

- seize and sell your personal possessions. However, we understand that this power is generally not used, and unless you let HMRC officials or agents into your property, they cannot enter your home and seize your personal possessions without a warrant from the court; *or*
- take court action against you, including bankruptcy proceedings.

Negotiating repayment

If you have difficulty repaying, HMRC may agree to your repaying the overpayment over a longer period than normal by making an instalment plan. In cases of hardship or if your mental health is a factor (see p1374), the overpayment may be written off. Contact the Tax Credit Payment Helpline on 0845 302 1429 (textphone 0845 300 3909), or write to HMRC at the address on the Notice to Pay. Usually you will be asked to pay something straight away, and the rest over a later period. HMRC will take into account all the relevant circumstances, including your income, savings, other debts and outgoings. Usually you must show how the repayments will cause you hardship by providing evidence of your income and expenditure and showing, for example, how you will be unable to meet your essential living expenses, or providing evidence of your mental health problems.

What to do

There is no right of appeal against a decision to recover an overpayment, although you can dispute it with HMRC, or negotiate repayment. However, you do have the right of appeal against a decision on your entitlement to tax credits, including the amount of your entitlement. Do not assume that HMRC always gets decisions on your entitlement right. If you have been overpaid and are unclear why, check the decisions about your entitlement (see p1373). For more on appeals, see p1400.

HMRC is only likely not to recover an overpayment following a dispute or negotiation about repayment in cases involving offsetting, mental health or hardship, or if it has failed to meet its responsibilities.

The only legal challenge to a decision to insist on recovering an overpayment (ie, either after a dispute or an attempt to negotiate repayment) is by judicial review in the courts. Usually, this is only possible in extreme cases – eg, if HMRC insists on you repaying an overpayment that was clearly caused by an error or failure by HMRC, you met all your responsibilities and it is urgent that HMRC changes its decision. For more about judicial review, see p1202.

The only other way of making HMRC change its mind is by making a complaint. You first need to use the HMRC's own complaints procedure. If you remain dissatisfied, you can complain to the Independent Adjudicator or to the Parliamentary Ombudsman (see Appendix 1 for the addresses and Chapter 50 for details about making a complaint). They can recommend action and order financial compensation, but both are likely to take time to complete their investigations. Both the Adjudicator and the Ombudsman can deal with complaints about tax credits, but it may be most appropriate to complain to the Adjudicator about HMRC's use of discretion (eg, on whether to recover an overpayment) and to the Ombudsman about maladministration – eg, if there have been severe delays.

3. Interest on overpayments

In certain circumstances, HM Revenue and Customs (HMRC) can add interest to the overpayment, with the effect of increasing the amount you have to repay.

When interest is added

Interest may be added to an overpayment being recovered from you (and/or your partner, if you have a joint claim) if HMRC considers that the overpayment is due to 'fraud or neglect' on the part of you (and/or your partner).[31]

If interest is added, it is added from 30 days after whichever of the following dates apply:[32]

- if you (or your partner) were treated during the tax year concerned as being overpaid as a result of your award being terminated because you did not satisfy the basic conditions of entitlement (see p1371), the date of the decision terminating the award; *or*
- if the above did not apply, the date in the final notice that you were given to confirm your actual income for the tax year.

When added to the overpayment, the interest is treated as if it were part of the overpayment. This means that it is subject to the same rules as the overpayment itself.[33]

How much interest is added

The amount of interest added to the penalty is 6.5 per cent a year or, if it is different from the average lending rate of the main banks, the bank lending rate plus 2.5 per cent.[34]

Challenging an interest decision

Decisions adding interest to an overpayment carry the right of appeal (see Chapter 60). For example, you might wish to argue on appeal that you did not act fraudulently or negligently, or that the amount of the interest is wrong. You (and/ or your partner, if s/he is subject to the decision) must be given notice of a decision adding interest to an overpayment. The notice must be dated and include details of your right of appeal against the decision.[35]

Notes

1. **What is an overpayment of tax credits**

1 s28 TCA 2002
2 Reg 5 TC(ITDR) Regs
3 s28(5) and (6) TCA 2002
4 s28(1) TCA 2002
5 s23 TCA 2002
6 HMRC stated it would regard this as a reasonable excuse in pre-March 2006 versions of its leaflet, *What Happens if We've Paid You Too Much Tax Credit?* (COP 26)
7 ss29(1) and (2) and 38 TCA 2002

2. **Recovery of overpayments**

8 s28(1) TCA 2002
9 HMRC leaflet, *What Happens if We've Paid You Too Much Tax Credit?* (COP26)
10 HMRC leaflets, *How HMRC Handle Tax Credits Overpayments* and *What Happens if We've Paid You Too Much Tax Credit?* (COP 26)
11 ss28(1) and 29 TCA 2002
12 s28(3) and (4) TCA 2002
13 HMRC leaflets, *How HMRC Handle Tax Credits Overpayments* and *What Happens if We've Paid You Too Much Tax Credit?* (COP 26), p11; CCM 8290
14 *Pre-Budget Report 2009*, chapter five; HMRC statement at www.hmrc.gov.uk/pbr2009/ individuals.htm; HMRC leaflet, *What Happens if We've Paid You Too Much Tax Credit?* (COP 26), p2
15 For the pre-January 2010 position, see CPAG's *Welfare Rights Bulletin* 211, p4. See also draft standard letters at www.cpag.org.uk/cro
16 www.hmrc.gov.uk/taxcredits/things-go-wrong/overpayments/ dispute.htm#4
17 HMRC leaflet, *What Happens if We've Paid You Too Much Tax Credit?* (COP 26)
18 HMRC leaflet, *How HMRC Handle Tax Credits Overpayments*
19 HMRC leaflet, *How HMRC Handle Tax Credits Overpayments*
20 S23 TCA 2002
21 s29 TCA 2002
22 s29(3)-(5) TCA 2002
23 Sch 9 (7E) SS(C&P) Regs
24 S29(5) TCA 2002
25 Reg 12A TC(PC) Regs; HMRC leaflet, *What Happens if We've Paid You Too Much Tax Credit?* (COP 26)
26 s29(2) TCA 2002
27 HMRC leaflets, *How HMRC Handle Tax Credits Overpayments* and *What Happens if We've Paid You Too Much Tax Credit?* (COP 26), p9
28 Sch 9 (7E)(3) SS(C&P) Regs
29 s684 (7A) IT(EP)A 2003
30 s29(3) TCA 2002 (overpayment of tax credits may be treated as if it were outstanding tax); HMRC leaflet, *How HMRC Handle Tax Credits Overpayments*

3. **Interest on overpayments**

31 s37(1) TCA 2002
32 s37(2)-(3) TCA 2002
33 s37(6) TCA 2002
34 Reg 4 TC(IR) Regs
35 ss37(4) and 38(1)(d) TCA 2002

Chapter 59

Investigations, penalties and fraud: tax credits

This chapter covers:

Key facts

- HM Revenue and Customs has wide powers to investigate your tax credits claim and require information from you.
- In certain circumstances, including if you supply incorrect information or do not comply with other requirements, a financial penalty may be imposed on you.
- If you have committed a benefit offence, you will be disqualified from receiving working tax credit for a set period.
- If you are considered to have acted fraudulently, you may be fined, imprisoned, or both.

1. Investigation of claims

HM Revenue and Customs (HMRC) has powers to require you to supply information and evidence to help it check whether your claim is correct, and to investigate fraud. HMRC refers to investigations into the accuracy of awards as 'examinations' and 'enquiries'. Examinations are carried out on some claims *during* the year in order to check that they are correct. Enquiries may be carried out *after* the year concerned to check that you were paid the correct amount. More serious investigations into fraud may also be carried out.

HMRC might ask you to provide things like bank statements or your rent book. It will usually explain why it needs these and give you reasonable time to produce them. You can seek professional advice (eg, from a welfare rights adviser or a solicitor) and can be accompanied at meetings you have with HMRC.

Not all investigations are fraud investigations. Fraud investigations tend only to happen in the more serious cases and, in such cases, HMRC has additional powers (see p1384).

Examinations

During the course of your award, or sometimes before your claim is decided, HMRC may telephone or write to you requiring information or evidence. It may request a meeting with you in connection with your claim. Normally, it will write to you to say that it is examining your claim. HMRC's leaflet, WTC/FS2, gives a basic outline of the procedure.[1] If the examination is started before your claim is decided, normally you will not be paid before the examination is complete. If it starts while you are already receiving tax credits, normally you will continue to be paid while the examination is being carried out.

If you prefer, HMRC will deal with someone else on your behalf – eg, an adviser, accountant or a relative. HMRC will need a short signed letter from you to confirm that that is what you want, or use Form TC689. However, you will still be treated as personally responsible for the information provided.

HMRC may request a meeting to discuss the examination with you. A short leaflet, WTC/FS4, giving a basic description of meetings, is available. You do not have to attend, but remember that HMRC has powers to seek information or evidence (see p1384). HMRC says that it will always arrange for an interpreter for a meeting if required.[2] At the meeting, HMRC will take notes – it should let you have a typed copy later. If you do not co-operate with the examination (eg, you refuse to provide information), your claim might be refused or your award stopped, and you may be subject to a penalty (see p1385).

In some cases, HMRC may ask you to sign the notes as an accurate record of the meeting. You do not have to sign this. Such signed notes may be used by HMRC as evidence, so be very sure that you point out anything you disagree with in the notes before signing. If HMRC finds your claim is incorrect or that you have not notified a change of circumstances that you must report, it might ask you to confirm the information by signing a certificate of full disclosure. Be sure you are satisfied of the accuracy of information in this, as HMRC takes a very serious view if you sign it when you know it is wrong.

You cannot stop an examination taking place, but if you are unhappy with the way you are being treated, you can make a complaint (see Chapter 50).

Enquiries

After your tax credit award is finalised at the end of the tax year, HMRC may carry out an enquiry into the award. Normally, this will not be until the following May or June, at the earliest. There is a deadline by which HMRC must have initiated the enquiry – see p1398. HMRC must write to you about this. HMRC leaflet WTC/FS1 has a basic outline of the procedure.[3]

If you prefer, HMRC will deal with someone else on your behalf – eg, an adviser, accountant or a relative. HMRC will need a short signed letter from you to confirm that that is what you want. However, you will still be treated as personally responsible for the information provided.

HMRC may request a meeting with you. The same points apply as they do to meetings in connection with examinations (see p1383).

You can stop the enquiry by requesting HMRC to complete it by making a decision on your tax credit entitlement for the year in question. If HMRC wishes to continue making the enquiry, it will pass your request to the First-tier Tribunal. You can also appeal to the First-tier Tribunal if you are unhappy with the decision following the enquiry. For more on when the First-tier Tribunal deals with requests and decisions about enquiries, see p1398.

Powers to seek information

HMRC can require you (and/or your partner if you have a joint claim) to provide information or evidence during the course of your award, if it believes your award may be wrong (for an examination). It can also require information or evidence after your award has been finalised (for an enquiry).

It can also do this if it is necessary for a decision relating to an initial claim (see Chapter 56), a revision during an award (see Chapter 60), or a final notice and final decision (see Chapter 57).[4] You must be given at least 30 days to provide the information.[5] HMRC does not have to suspect you of fraud in order to require information or evidence from you.

It is important that you co-operate with requests for information or evidence as far as you can. Even though you may not be the subject of a fraud investigation, HMRC might refuse your claim, suspend your payments or reduce your award (possibly to nil), and there are a number of circumstances in which you can be given a financial penalty or even prosecuted if you refuse to supply information and evidence, or supply material which you know is incorrect (see p1385). It is important that you are as truthful as possible when responding.

HMRC can also require your employer or childcare provider to provide information. They must be given at least 30 days to provide it. If they are subject to these requirements, they can also be subject to penalties (see p1385). They can be required to provide information and evidence relating to your claim or, for the purpose of a revision during an award or an enquiry (see pp1395 and 1400), your award.[6]

If fraud is suspected

If you are suspected of fraud, HMRC may undertake a civil investigation, with a view to charging a financial penalty (see below). In serious cases it will undertake a criminal investigation, with a view to prosecuting you (see p1389). Fraud investigations in serious cases are normally carried out by the Special Compliance

Office of HMRC. If fraud is suspected, HMRC will usually explain to you why your claim is being investigated and that you can seek professional advice from someone who can attend any meetings you have with HMRC. It is advisable to seek professional advice (eg, from a solicitor) if you are investigated on suspicion of fraud. If you are being investigated, seek advice as quickly as possible. You are likely to be interviewed under caution.

In addition to the powers described above, HMRC has specific powers when investigating fraud.[7] If HMRC has 'reasonable grounds' for suspecting fraud, a court can make an order requiring that documents containing relevant evidence be delivered by you (or any other person who has them) to HMRC within the time specified in the court order.

If a court is satisfied that there is 'reasonable ground' for suspecting serious fraud, it can issue a warrant giving HMRC authority to enter and search premises for evidence within 14 days. HMRC can only apply for a warrant if it is satisfied that asking the person in possession of the evidence to deliver it might 'seriously prejudice' the investigation. Under the warrant, HMRC can remove anything that there is 'reasonable cause' to believe may be required as evidence, and search any person on the premises where there is 'reasonable cause' to believe s/he is in possession of such evidence.[8]

2. **Penalties**

HM Revenue and Customs (HMRC) can impose a financial penalty on you if you have:[9]

- fraudulently or negligently made an incorrect statement or declaration, or supplied incorrect information or evidence; *or*
- failed to comply with requirements.

Despite the use of the word 'fraudulently', these penalties are civil penalties; you do not have to be prosecuted for a criminal offence. If you do not think a penalty should be imposed on you (eg, because you had a reasonable excuse for not declaring a change in circumstances or you could not obtain the information asked for), tell HMRC. If a penalty is imposed, HMRC will contact you.[10] You have the right of appeal against the imposition of a penalty (see p1405).

In making its decision, HMRC will consider things like how much you have co-operated (it may reduce the amount of your penalty if you have co-operated in the investigation) and the seriousness of the changes that need to be made. In certain circumstances, these rules can also apply in the same way to your employer or your childcare provider (see p1384).

Incorrect statements and information

HMRC can impose a financial penalty of up to £3,000 (it does not have to impose the maximum) on you if you have acted fraudulently or negligently and you have:[11]

- made an incorrect statement or declaration in connection with a claim, or a notification of a change of circumstances (see p1363) or in a response to a final notice (see p1361); *or*
- given incorrect information or evidence in connection with an initial decision (see p1360), a requirement to provide information or evidence during the course of your award, a revision during an award (see p1395), a final decision (see p1361) or an enquiry (see p1398) .

HMRC regards 'negligence' as not taking 'reasonable care'.[12] If you think you have acted with reasonable care, tell HMRC and ask for a penalty not to be imposed.

Penalties for incorrect statements and information

The maximum penalty is £3,000 (HMRC does not have to impose the maximum). You must be notified of the penalty, including the date on which it is given, and your right of appeal. The penalty is payable 30 days after the date you were notified of it.[13] The amount of the penalty may be increased by the addition of interest (see p1388).

If you are a member of a joint-claim couple (see p1347), the penalty may be imposed or partly imposed on your partner, unless s/he could not reasonably have been expected to have been aware that you had fraudulently or negligently made an incorrect statement or provided incorrect information or evidence. However, even if the penalty is imposed or partly imposed on your partner, the total penalty for the same incorrect statement cannot amount to more than £3,000.

If you are acting for someone else in connection with her/his claim and you fraudulently or negligently make an incorrect statement, the penalty applies to you.

Failure to comply

HMRC can impose a financial penalty on you of up to £300 (it does not have to impose the maximum):[14]

- if you fail to provide information or evidence for a decision on an initial claim (see p1360), a requirement to provide information or evidence during the course of your award, a revision during an award (see p1395), a final decision (see p1361) or for an enquiry (see p1398); *or*
- if you fail to comply with a requirement regarding a final notice (see p1361); *or*

- if you fail to notify a specified change of circumstances within one month of the change or, except in the last case below, of the date you became aware of the change if that is later.[15] These are if:
  - there is a decrease of £10 a week or more over four consecutive weeks in your or your partner's childcare costs, or if the childcare costs have stopped; *or*
  - you have stopped being counted as a single claimant; *or*
  - you were claiming as a couple but are no longer part of that couple. This includes if you or your partner leave the UK permanently or go abroad for more than a set period (see p1495); *or*
  - you (or your partner) lose your right to reside in the UK or stop being regarded as being in the UK; *or*
  - your (or your partner's) hours of work fall to less than 16 or 30 hours a week. **Note:** the government may introduce a rule to say that a couple must report their change of circumstances if their total hours fall below 24 hours a week. See CPAG's *Welfare Rights Bulletin* for updates; *or*
  - you have a joint claim and get the 30-hour element of working tax credit because your joint hours total at least 30 hours a week, but these have now fallen to less than 30 hours a week; *or*
  - you or your partner cease to be responsible for one or more of your children (see p1271 for when you count as responsible); *or*
  - a child for whom you (or your partner) are responsible dies (see p1271 for when you count as responsible for a child); *or*
  - a child for whom you (or your partner) are responsible stops being counted as a child (other than by reaching her/his 20th birthday), including if s/he were due to continue counting as a child by remaining in full-time education or training, but did not do so (see p1269 for who counts as a child).

HMRC says that it will not impose a penalty if you had 'reasonable excuse' for not telling it about the change. Tell HMRC if you think this applies. However, HMRC will not accept the fact that you did not know you had to inform it as a reasonable excuse.[16]

Penalties for failure to comply

The maximum penalty for this is £300. If the penalty is for failure to provide information or evidence, there is a further daily penalty of up to £60 a day for each further day you continue to fail to comply. You must be notified of the penalty, including the date on which it is given, and your right of appeal. The penalty is payable 30 days after the date you were notified of it.[17] The amount of the penalty may be increased by the addition of interest (see p1388).

However, if the penalty is for failure to provide information or evidence, or for a failure regarding a final notice, HMRC cannot apply the penalty itself. Instead, it must write to the HM Courts and Tribunals Service, which will then summons you to the First-tier Tribunal to decide whether the penalty should be applied.[18] You can appeal against the First-tier Tribunal's decision to the Upper Tribunal (see p1404).

Once you have provided the information or evidence, a penalty cannot be imposed on you. You have not failed to provide information or evidence if you did so within any time that HMRC has allowed you to, or if you had a 'reasonable excuse' for the failure, or if, having had a reasonable excuse, you later provided the information or evidence without unreasonable delay.

If you are a member of a couple and a £300 penalty has been imposed for failure to comply with a requirement regarding a final notice or for failure to report the specified change of circumstances, the total of that penalty applied to either or both of you is a maximum of £300.

Interest added to penalties

If a penalty is imposed on you, HMRC has the power to apply interest to it. Although HMRC does not have to apply interest, it can do so even if you are not considered to have acted fraudulently or negligently – ie, if the penalty is for failure to comply. The amount of the interest becomes part of the penalty and is recoverable in the same way as the penalty itself. [19]

The amount of interest added to the penalty is 6.5 per cent per annum or, if that is different from the average lending rate of the main banks, the bank lending rate plus 2.5 per cent.[20]

You can appeal against the penalty itself and the amount of the penalty. However, the way the law is written suggests that there is no right of appeal about the addition of interest.[21]

Separately from the above rules, if HMRC considers that an overpayment has arisen because of 'fraud or neglect' on your part (or, if you are a member of a couple, on the part of one or both of you), it can decide to apply interest to all or some of the overpayment (see p1379).

Recovery of penalties

HMRC has discretion about whether to impose a penalty and, subject to the maximum amounts, the amount. Also, although the penalty itself can only be altered on appeal, HMRC has discretion about whether to insist that you pay all or some of the penalty.[22] If you tried your best to fulfil all your obligations, or if the penalty would cause you hardship, tell HMRC and ask it to exercise its discretion not to recover all or some of the penalty.

If HMRC does decide that a penalty may be imposed upon you, it will try to come to an agreement with you which involves your offering to pay the agreed amount. If you agree, it will send you a final letter setting out the agreement, which HMRC regards as a legally binding contract.[23] It may be best to try to come to an agreement, because if HMRC is not able to reach such an agreement with you, it may use its legal powers to recover the penalty. However, if you think you may want to challenge the penalty (see below), check to see if the contract means that HMRC will not actually issue a decision imposing the penalty. If you do not have a decision, you will not be able to challenge it on an appeal. If HMRC uses its legal powers to recover a penalty, it can:

- seize and sell your personal possessions. However, unless you let them into your property or they are are otherwise easily able to get in, authorised officers cannot enter your home and seize your personal possessions unless they have a warrant from the court; *or*
- take court action against you, including bankruptcy proceedings.[24]

Challenging a penalty

You can tell HMRC that you disagree with the penalty and/or the addition of interest to it – eg, when it contacts you to tell you that you are liable for a penalty. It can remove the penalty and/or the interest. HMRC will decide whether to issue a formal decision, so that you can appeal if you still disagree.[25] Once a formal penalty decision has been made, it cannot be altered except on appeal. You have the right of appeal against all penalties. The appeal right includes the right of appeal against the determination that a penalty has been incurred and the amount of the penalty, although not against any addition of interest.

Note: subject to the maximum, the First-tier Tribunal can increase as well as decrease the amount.

For more information on appeals, see p1400 and for more on penalty appeals, see p1405.

3. **Fraud and criminal prosecution**

You are regarded as having committed the offence of fraud if you knowingly take part in fraudulent activity in order to get a tax credit for you or anyone else. If you are prosecuted and then convicted by a court, you are liable to be fined or imprisoned, or both.[26]

Fines or imprisonment for fraud

If a court convicts you of fraud in connection with tax credits and:[27]

- you are convicted in a moderately serious case, usually in a magistrates' court (sheriff court in Scotland), you are liable to a maximum of six months' imprisonment or a maximum fine of £5,000, or both; *or*
- you are convicted in a very serious case, usually in the Crown Court (High Court in Scotland), you are liable to a maximum of seven years' imprisonment or a fine of an unlimited amount, or both.

Future changes

At some point, probably during 2012/13, the government will change the above rules, so that:[28]

– if your offence is in connection with no more than £20,000 of tax credits, you may be tried only in the magistrates' court (sheriff court in Scotland). If you are convicted, you will be liable to a maximum of 51 weeks' (England and Wales) or six months' (Scotland and Northern Ireland) imprisonment, or a maximum fine of £5,000;

– if the offence is in connection with more than £20,000 of tax credits, you may be tried in either the magistrates' court/sheriff court or the Crown Court (High Court in Scotland). If you are convicted in the magistrates' court/sheriff court, you are liable to a maximum of 12 months' imprisonment (six months in Northern Ireland) or a maximum fine of £5,000, or both. If you are convicted in the Crown Court/High Court, you are liable to a maximum of seven years' imprisonment or a fine of an unlimited amount, or both.

See CPAG's *Welfare Rights Bulletin* for updates.

Will you be prosecuted?

Whether or not you will be prosecuted is a discretionary decision. Not all cases of fraud end in prosecution. HM Revenue and Customs (HMRC) may investigate your claim under civil investigation procedures – ie, without a view to prosecuting you, but with a view to charging a penalty (see p1385). If you are being investigated by the Special Compliance Office *without* a view to prosecuting you, you are normally told about this. However, this does not mean that HMRC cannot change its mind and decide that a prosecution should be made.

The factors that it may take into account are likely to include the strength of the evidence, the amount of tax credits involved, whether an offence was planned and your personal circumstances.

Official HMRC policy indicates that criminal investigations are more likely if:[29]

- there is organised or systematic fraud, including conspiracy;
- false statements are made or false documents given during a civil investigation;
- deliberate concealment, deception, conspiracy or corruption is suspected;
- false or forged documents have been used;
- the person involved has committed previous offences or there is a repeated course of unlawful conduct or previous civil action;
- there is a link to suspected wider criminality.

Note: this is not a complete list and ultimately everything depends on the circumstances of your case.

What to do if you are prosecuted

The most important thing to do is to get advice. You may be entitled to legal help and have a solicitor or barrister represent you in court. You should check carefully that HMRC is able to prove all the parts of the offence you are charged with. Do not plead guilty until you have obtained advice.

4. The effect of an investigation on tax credits

There is nothing to stop payment of your tax credits specifically because an investigation, whether for fraud or not, is underway. However, HM Revenue and Customs (HMRC) can:

- revise a current award if it has 'reasonable grounds' for believing it is wrong (see p1395). **Note:** HMRC might do this if you do not provide the information or evidence that it has requested;
- change an award at the end of the tax year for which the award was made, when the final decision is made (see p1397);
- revise an award via an 'enquiry' or a 'decision on discovery' after the end of the tax year for which the award was made (see pp1398 and 1398);
- postpone payment if an appeal is pending on your claim or a similar claim, or if you have not provided information that has been requested, or it appears that your address or bank account details are incorrect (see p1355).

5. Future changes: loss of working tax credit

At some point, probably during 2012/13, the government will introduce rules that will disqualify you from being paid working tax credit (WTC) for a set period of time if you have committed a benefit offence.[30] See CPAG's *Welfare Rights Bulletin* for updates.

Under these rules, you will be disqualified from WTC if:

- on or after 5 April 2012, you commit a 'benefit offence' (see p1103) concerning a 'disqualifying benefit' (see p1107); *and*
- you would be entitled to WTC if it were not for this rule, whether that is as a single person or as part of a joint claim. If you have a joint claim, WTC is not paid to you or your partner.

The offence must be in connection with a claim for, or payment or receipt of, a disqualifying benefit, or for aiding, attempting or planning such an offence. Note that disqualifying benefits include both WTC and child tax credit (CTC), as well as many other benefits. However, you will not be disqualified from being paid CTC.

You do not need to have been convicted. As part of a 'one-strike' rule, you will be regarded as having committed an offence, including a first offence, even if you have accepted a penalty for a benefit offence (see p1109) or a formal caution (p1111) instead.

Under the one-strike rule, if you are convicted of a serious offence (conspiracy to defraud, overpayment of at least £50,000, a sentence of at least a year or an offence commited over a period of at least two years), you are disqualified from receiving WTC for three years. If you are convicted of a less serious offence, you are disqualified for 13 weeks. If you have accepted a penalty for a benefit offence or a formal caution, you are disqualified for four weeks.

If you commit a subsequent offence (or offences), longer periods of disqualification apply under a 'two-strike' rule. This applies if you have been convicted of one or more benefit offences, and then commit another benefit offence (including if you accept a penalty or a formal caution) within five years of the first. In this situation, you are disqualified from receiving WTC for three years. If this does not apply, but you have commited a repeat offence, you are disqualified for 26 weeks (unless the repeat offence is a serious one, in which case the disqualification is for three years).

Notes

1. **Investigation of claims**

1 ss14(2), 15(2) and 16(2) and (3) TCA 2002; leaflet available at www.hmrc.gov.uk/taxcredits/forms-and-leaflets/leaflets.htm. Note: this may be reissued as *Tax Credits Checks* (WTC/FS10)

2 HMRC leaflet WTC/FS4, available at www.hmrc.gov.uk/taxcredits/forms-and-leaflets/leaflets.htm. Note: this may be reissued as *Tax Credits Checks* (WTC/FS10)

3 s19 TCA 2002; leaflet available at www.hmrc.gov.uk/taxcredits/forms-and-leaflets/leaflets.htm. Note: this may be reissued as *Tax Credits Checks* (WTC/FS10)

4 ss14(2), 15(2), 16(3), 17, 19(2) and 22 TCA 2002

5 Reg 32 TC(CN) Regs

6 ss14(2)(b), 15(2)(b), 16(3)(b) and 19(2)(b) TCA 2002; regs 30 and 31 TC(CN) Regs

7 s36 TCA 2002

8 s36(2) TCA 2002

2. **Penalties**

9 ss31 and 32 TCA 2002

10 HMRC leaflet, *Tax Credits Penalties* (WTC7), available at www.hmrc.gov.uk/taxcredits/forms-and-leaflets/leaflets.htm

11 s31 TCA 2002

12 HMRC leaflet, *Tax Credits Penalties* (WTC7), available at www.hmrc.gov.uk/taxcredits/forms-and-leaflets/leaflets.htm

13 Sch 2 para 1 TCA 2002

14 s32 TCA 2002

15 ss3(4), 6(3) and 32(3) TCA 2002; reg 21(2) TC(CN) Regs

16 HMRC leaflet, *Tax Credits Penalties* (WTC7), available at www.hmrc.gov.uk/taxcredits/forms-and-leaflets/leaflets.htm
17 Sch 2 para 1 TCA 2002
18 Sch 2 paras 1 and 3 TCA 2002
19 s37(5) and (6) TCA 2002
20 Reg 4 TC(IR) Regs
21 ss37(5)-(6) and 38 TCA 2002
22 Sch 2 paras 1 and 5 TCA 2002
23 HMRC leaflet, *Tax Credits Penalties* (WTC7), available at www.hmrc.gov.uk/taxcredits/forms-and-leaflets/leaflets.htm
24 Sch 2 para 7 TCA 2002
25 HMRC leaflet, *Tax Credits Penalties* (WTC7), available at www.hmrc.gov.uk/taxcredits/forms-and-leaflets/leaflets.htm

3. **Fraud and criminal prosecution**

26 s35(1) TCA 2002
27 s35(2) TCA 2002
28 s124 WRA 2012; s35(2) TCA 2002
29 HMRC criminal investigation policy, available at www.hmrc.gov.uk/prosecutions/crim-inv-policy.htm

5. **Future changes: loss of working tax credit**

30 s120 WRA 2012; ss36A-36B TCA 2002

60

Chapter 60

Revisions and appeals: tax credits

This chapter covers:

Rules for revising tax credit decisions are different from those for social security benefits (see Chapter 45).

Tax credit appeals are heard by the First-tier Tribunal Social Entitlement Chamber, which also deals with social security benefits, and are administered by HM Courts and Tribunals Service. Many of the appeal rules are the same for tax credits as they are for social security benefits. Chapter 46 covers appeals for social security benefits. This chapter refers you to Chapter 46 when the tax credit rules are the same as the benefit rules.

Key facts

- Decisions on tax credit entitlement can be changed by revision by HM Revenue and Customs (HMRC) or by appeal to an independent tribunal (the First-tier Tribunal).
- If you are overpaid tax credits, the decision on your entitlement can be changed by revision or appeal, but the decision to recover an overpayment cannot be changed in this way. Instead, you can ask HMRC to use its discretion not to recover all or part of the overpayment and use the complaints procedures if necessary.
- HMRC can only revise your tax credit award if certain grounds are met.
- You must appeal within 30 days after the date of the decision, although you can appeal late in limited circumstances.
- When you appeal, HMRC will usually want to 'settle' the appeal with you. If it is not settled, your appeal will go forward to the First-tier Tribunal.

1. Revisions

If you disagree with a decision, you may be able to have it revised by HM Revenue and Customs (HMRC). The circumstances in which a revision can be made depend on whether the decision with which you disagree is:

- an 'initial decision' on a claim (see below);
- a 'final decision' after the tax year has ended following an annual review (see p1397); *or*
- a decision of the First-tier Tribunal (see p1404).

Most decisions also carry a right of appeal within 30 days after the date on which notice of the decision was given. Unless you are simply reporting a change in circumstances, it is generally better to appeal than ask for a revision. You could be at a disadvantage if you ask for a revision before asking for an appeal because if HMRC does not revise the award, you may have missed the deadline for appeal.

Revising an initial decision during an award

When you claim a tax credit, HMRC must decide whether to make an award and the rate at which to award it.[1] This is called an 'initial decision'. If you disagree with it, you have the right to appeal (see p1400) or you may be able to ask HMRC to revise the decision as described below. Your award can also be revised if your circumstances change.

Your claim is refused or award stopped

If your claim has been turned down altogether or your award has been terminated, you do not have the option to ask for the decision to be revised. You must appeal within 30 days if you want the decision to be changed. If you do not appeal or your appeal is unsuccessful, you need to make a fresh claim to get any further tax credit in that tax year.[2]

No award because your income is too high

If your income in the previous year is too high to qualify for a tax credit, but you satisfy the other qualifying conditions, you are awarded a tax credit at a nil rate. This nil-rate award can be revised if your income is estimated to be lower in the current year.[3]

You disagree with an award

If you have been awarded a tax credit but you disagree with the amount, the initial decision can be revised if:

- your **circumstances have changed** so that you should get an additional or higher element (see p1396); *or*

- HMRC has **reasonable grounds** for believing that you are entitled to a different rate of tax credit or that you are not entitled to a tax credit at all (see p1396); *or*
- there has been an **official error** (see p1397).

Changes in circumstances that increase entitlement to a tax credit element

If your circumstances change so that you should be getting an element you were not getting before, or a higher rate of an element, your award may be revised.[4] For example, if you have a new baby, your child tax credit (CTC) award can be revised to include another child element.

Note: the time limits below were previously three months, but are one month from 6 April 2012.

If you notify the Tax Credit Office (TCO) of the change within one month, the increase in the award can be fully backdated .[5] There are specific rules dealing with the date from when an award is recalculated if there is a change in childcare charges or childcare provided (see p1364).

The increase in the award cannot be backdated for more than one month before the date you provide notification of the change, except in the following cases relating to the disabled and severely disabled child elements of CTC and the disabled worker and severe disability elements of working tax credit (WTC).

- If you claim and are awarded disability living allowance (DLA) for a child, tell the TCO within one month of the decision that DLA has been awarded so that the disabled child element or severely disabled child element of CTC is fully backdated.[6] The same should apply if you get DLA highest rate care component for a child on a supersession or appeal.[7]
- If you are already getting WTC when you claim one of the benefits that would entitle you to a disabled worker element or severe disability element in WTC (eg, DLA – see p1311), if you are awarded the benefit notify the TCO within one month, so that the element can be fully backdated.[8]

If you disagree with a revised decision, you have the right of appeal within 30 days to the First-tier Tribunal (see p1400) or to ask for another revision on 'reasonable grounds' (see below) or because of official error (see p1399).

Reasonable grounds

HMRC has the power to amend or terminate an award on its own initiative. It can do this if it has 'reasonable grounds for believing' that you are:[9]

- entitled to a different rate of tax credit; *or*
- not entitled to WTC or not entitled to CTC.

This could happen, for example, because you tell the TCO about an income change or wrong information is used in deciding your claim. Or it could happen because it has decided to examine your claim and has found errors (see p1383).

If the rate of tax credit is changed, HMRC revises your award, taking into account any change in circumstances from the date it arose unless:

- it is a change that increases entitlement to tax credit elements, which can only be backdated for up to one month (see p1396);
- childcare charges go down by £10 a week or more. In this case, there is a four-week run-on at the same rate before the award is reduced (see p1363);[10]
- there is a four-week run-on because you stop work or reduce your hours below 16, 24 or 30 a week (see p1304).

Decisions can only be revised in this way during the period of the award, not after an award has been terminated, nor after a final decision has been made.[11]

Example

Pauline provides an estimate of her income for the current year and this has decreased by more than £2,500 compared with the previous year's income on which the award was based. The initial decision can be revised and her award recalculated based on the current year's income plus £2,500. The estimate she provides must be sufficient to give HMRC 'reasonable grounds for believing' that her entitlement should change.

HMRC is not obliged to revise even when there are grounds. It could leave changes to be dealt with at the annual review – eg, if it is late in the year and the change is minor.[12]

If you disagree with the revised rate of tax credit, you can appeal within 30 days to the First-tier Tribunal (see p1400) or ask for another revision. However, if you disagree with a decision to end your tax credit entitlement, you have the right to appeal, but not to a further revision.

Official error

An initial award can be revised in your favour if it is incorrect because of an official error (see p1399).[13]

Annual review

After 5 April, HMRC reviews your tax credit award for the year just ended and makes a final decision on your entitlement for that year. It sends you an annual review form which details the circumstances on which the award was based and usually an annual declaration form, giving your income for the tax year just passed (see p1351).

If HMRC sends you an annual declaration form, you must complete and return it by the deadline given (31 July in most cases). HMRC finalises your entitlement for the year just passed.

A final decision is conclusive unless it is changed on appeal or in the following circumstances.

- If you **change your statement** about your income or circumstances before the deadline (see p1398), the final decision can be changed.

- Once a final decision is made, there is a period during which HMRC can enquire into your entitlement. See below for details of **revision on enquiry**.
- Outside the period of enquiry, a final decision can be revised on 'discovery' of certain information about your tax liability or in relation to fraud or neglect. There is a deadline for such revisions. See below for details of **revision on discovery**.
- A final decision can be revised in your favour because of **official error** (see p1399).

Changing your statement

If you reply to the annual review notice but then wish to change your statement, you may do so. If it is before the deadline given in the notice for replying (31 July in most cases), but HMRC has already made a final decision, the final decision may be revised.[14]

If HMRC only had an estimate of your income for the current year (eg, because you are self-employed and have not yet finalised your accounts), you will have a later deadline (usually 31 January) in which to give details of your actual income for that year. If you do so, HMRC must make a new final decision.[15] It can revise the new decision if you change your statement before the later deadline.[16] If you do not give further details of actual income, HMRC must nevertheless make a new final decision once the later deadline is passed.

Revision on enquiry

HMRC can enquire into entitlement for any reason,[17] but it must begin its enquiry by giving you notice by a certain date. That is a year after the deadline by which you were to reply to the annual review notice, or a year after the later deadline for self-employed people or others to supply actual income details where only an estimate had been provided.[18] If you are required to submit an income tax return, the enquiry must begin by the day your tax return becomes final.

When the enquiry is completed, HMRC makes a fresh decision on whether you are entitled and how much the award should be.

Only one enquiry into entitlement can be conducted for any one tax year.[19]

For more details, see p1383.

If you disagree with an enquiry decision

If you disagree with the decision, you have the right to appeal within 30 days to the First-tier Tribunal (see p1400). Alternatively, it may be revised if it is incorrect because of an official error (see p1399).[20] HMRC may also revise an enquiry decision by a 'revision on discovery' (see below).

Revision on discovery

If it is too late to 'enquire' into your entitlement, HMRC can still revise a final decision, but only in specific circumstances, and there are further time limits by when such a revision must take place. A final decision or an enquiry decision may be revised outside the period allowed for an enquiry if HMRC has 'reasonable grounds for believing' that tax credit entitlement is wrong:

- because of a revision of your income tax liability. The revision of your tax credit entitlement must take place within a year of your income tax liability being revised;[21] *or*
- for reasons attributable to fraud or neglect (see below).

There is nothing to stop HMRC going through this process more than once.[22] If a final decision, enquiry decision or discovery decision has been revised for official error, that too can be further revised in this way.[23]

Fraud or neglect

A decision can be revised if HMRC has reasonable grounds for believing that an incorrect decision on tax credit entitlement is attributable to fraud or neglect.[24] The fraud or neglect may be on your part, or your partner's if it is a joint claim, or on the part of anyone acting for you (see p1347 for when a person may act for you).

Your tax credit entitlement in a tax year cannot be revised on this ground after five years from the end of the tax year – eg, a tax credit award for 2006/07 cannot be revised after 5 April 2012.[25]

If you disagree with a discovery decision

You have the right of appeal within 30 days to the First-tier Tribunal (see p1400). Alternatively, the decision may be revised if it is incorrect because of an official error (see below).

Official error

An initial decision, final decision, enquiry decision or discovery decision can be revised in your favour if it is incorrect because of an official error.[26] The decision can be revised at any time up to five years after the date of the decision.

'Official error' means an error relating to a tax credit made by an HMRC or DWP officer or a person providing tax credit services for them. If you, or someone acting for you, contributed to the error, it does not count as an official error. An error of law can count as an official error. It does not count, however, if it is only shown to be an error of law because of a later decision of the Upper Tribunal or court.

How to seek a revision

If your circumstances change, there are rules on how HMRC should be notified. In other cases, there are no set rules to follow.

You, or your partner if you have a joint claim, must make the notification.[27] In some circumstances another person can act for you. If you have an appointee, either for tax credits or benefits, or someone legally appointed to act for you (see p1347), s/he can provide notification of the change on your behalf if you are unable to do it yourself.[28]

You should notify the TCO in writing or by telephone.[29]

The date on which you notify HMRC may be important – eg, for changes in circumstances that you are obliged to tell HMRC about, or if the award can only be backdated for one month from the date of notification. The **'date of notification'** is the date on which notification is given to HMRC.[30] If you want to change any of the details, you can do so at any time before HMRC has made a decision.[31] Your notification will still be taken as made on the original date.[32]

Keep a copy of any letter you send to HMRC. If you call the Tax Credit Helpline, it is advisable to keep a log of your calls: the date and time you made the call, the information provided and what was agreed.

Normally, you must provide notification of the change in circumstance after it has happened, but there are some changes you can notify in advance (see p1368).

What happens after you seek a revision

Before making its decision, HMRC may ask you to provide more information or evidence if it considers it needs this to help with the decision.[33] HMRC may contact your employer if it also needs information from her/him.[34]

It is important that you respond to a request for information by the date given in the letter. If you do not provide the required information, you may have to pay a penalty of up to £300 and, if you still do not comply, a further daily penalty of up to £60 a day could be imposed. See p1385 for how these penalties are applied.

HMRC must give notice of the decision to you, and to your partner if it is a joint claim. This must include details of your right to appeal.[35]

2. Appealing to the First-tier Tribunal

Tax credit appeals are heard by the same First-tier Tribunal that deals with social security benefits and are administered by HM Courts and Tribunals Service (HMCTS).[36]

Many of the tax credit appeal rules are the same as those for social security benefits (see Chapter 46). This chapter refers you to Chapter 46 where the tax credit rules are the same as the benefit rules.

Who can appeal

The following people have the right of appeal:[37]

- you, the tax credit claimant. For joint claimants, both or either of you can make the appeal. If only one appeals, the First-tier Tribunal decision still applies to both, provided you are both given the right to a hearing;[38]

- for appeals about penalties, the person subject to the penalty;
- an appointee, if you are unable to make the appeal yourself (see p1347). If you do not have an appointee, the person (who must be 18 or over) who is to act on your behalf in the appeal should write to HM Revenue and Customs (HMRC) asking to be appointed;
- another person with the power to make a tax credit claim for you – ie, a receiver appointed by the Court of Protection, a judicial factor or guardian.[39]

Decisions you can appeal

You can appeal against:[40]

- an initial decision;
- a final decision;
- a revised decision (for change in circumstances, on reasonable grounds or for official error);
- an enquiry decision;
- a discovery decision;
- a decision imposing a penalty;
- a decision charging interest on an overpayment.

If HMRC decides you have been overpaid tax credits, it can recover all or part of it at its discretion, and you cannot appeal against the decision. You can, however, appeal against the amount of the award. In some cases, HMRC may use its discretion not to recover an overpayment, or to reduce the amount – eg, if recovery would cause hardship (see p1374). Complain to HMRC if you are unhappy with the way your claim has been handled, and if your complaint is not resolved to your satisfaction you can ask the Adjudicator to look into it (see p1257).

Time limit for appealing

Your appeal, including the details specified below, must be given to HMRC within 30 days after the date given on the decision letter.[41]

You may not get a separate initial or final decision notice where the annual review notice states what the decision will be and the date on which it will be made, usually 31 July. This may apply where your award is made up of just the family element of child tax credit (CTC) and your circumstances have not changed. In this case, your appeal must be made within 30 days after the date the annual review notice gives as the date on which the decision is made – eg, by 30 August if the decision date is given as 31 July.

Late appeals

You can appeal outside this 30-day time limit in limited circumstances. These circumstances are the same for tax credits as they are for benefits. You must appeal within an absolute time limit. This is one year after the date the 30-day time limit expired. See p1203 for details of late appeals, but note that where the benefit rules refer to a one-month limit, for tax credits that should be taken to be 30 days.

There is no provision to ask for written reasons for a decision or to extend the time limit if you do. Nor is the time limit extended if you try unsuccessfully to get the decision revised by HMRC before making an appeal.

How to appeal

You can appeal on the form inside HMRC leaflet WTC/AP, *What To Do If You Think Our Decision Is Wrong*. Alternatively, you can write a letter, but you must include:[42]

- sufficient information to identify you – eg, your name and national insurance number;
- sufficient information to identify the decision being appealed – eg, the date of the decision and whether it is CTC or working tax credit (WTC);
- the grounds of your appeal – ie, why the decision is wrong;
- your signature (or a signature on your behalf – eg, from an appointee).

Send your appeal to HMRC at the address given on the decision notice.

What happens after you appeal

Settling the appeal

HMRC will usually want to settle the appeal without going to the First-tier Tribunal. You can point out to HMRC where you think its decision is wrong and supply information or arguments you want it to consider. HMRC may offer you terms on which to settle the appeal. Your appeal can only be settled with your consent. If you do not agree, the appeal must proceed to the First-tier Tribunal.

If you agree to settle the appeal, HMRC must write to you setting out the terms of the agreement – eg, giving a new amount for your award. Your appeal then lapses unless you write to HMRC within 30 days from the date of the written notice of agreement saying you have changed your mind and wish to proceed with your appeal.[43]

If you are asked to settle the appeal, check first whether the proposed agreement gives you everything to which you think you are entitled. Seek advice if you are not sure whether to agree. If in doubt, you should exercise your right to continue with the appeal.

Asking for a hearing

If your appeal is not settled, HMRC prepares the appeal papers (its 'submission'). It sends a copy to you and a copy to your representative and forwards your appeal to HMCTS. HMCTS sends you an enquiry form asking whether you want an oral hearing or not. You should return the form within 14 days of the date it was issued.

For information and issues to consider when deciding whether to opt for an oral hearing, see p1168.

You are entitled to have your appeal heard within a reasonable period of time.

If HMRC does not forward your appeal, you can forward a copy of the appeal yourself. Although the First-tier Tribunal does not normally accept an appeal made directly in this way, it can do so and can require HMRC to produce a submission.[44] You can also complain to HMRC (see p1257) and consider taking up the issue with your MP (see p1259). Before you do, check that the decision is one that carries a right of appeal.

Appeal not heard by the end of the year

If your appeal has not been heard by the time you get HMRC's final decision on your entitlement after the end of the year, you should put in another appeal against the final decision.[45]

When your appeal can be struck out

Your appeal may be struck out in certain circumstances. The rules are the same as those for benefits, explained on p1195.

Withdrawing an appeal

You can ask to withdraw the appeal if you decide not to go ahead with it. You can tell HMRC in writing or telphone the Helpline or, if your appeal has already been forwarded, by writing to HMCTS. See p1167 for more details of withdrawing and reinstating an appeal if you change your mind.

The hearing

The First-tier Tribunal holds an oral hearing if you have asked for one. Otherwise there is a paper hearing in your absence. For details of these, see p1168. For information on asking for the hearing to be postponed or adjourned to a later date, see p1197. The tax credit rules are the same as those for benefits, except that there are no special 'test case' provisions for tax credits that can block your appeal or affect its outcome (although payment can be postponed while there is an appeal pending in another case that could affect your own award).[46] The rules on 'lead cases' described on p1199 do apply to tax credits.

First-tier Tribunal procedures

Chapter 46 describes First-tier Tribunal procedures for benefits and looks at:

- who is present at the hearing;
- who decides your appeal;
- what happens at an oral hearing;
- domiciliary hearings (hearings at home);

- what the First-tier Tribunal can consider;
- changes in circumstances after you appeal;
- the First-tier Tribunal decision;
- after the hearing;
- if you disagree with the First-tier Tribunal's decision;
- procedural rules.

See pp1171–81 and pp1193–99 for details. The tax credit rules are the same, with the following exceptions.

- **Medical examination.** The First-tier Tribunal cannot refer you to a doctor for a medical examination.[47] However, if your appeal concerns a disability question it may be important to get your own medical evidence (see p1209).
- **Change in circumstances after you appeal.** These rules apply to tax credits in the same way as they do to benefits except:
  - wherever Chapter 46 refers to 'supersession' this should read 'revision' for tax credits;
  - if you reclaim or ask for a revision because of a change in circumstances after you appeal, there is no specific provision for a decision maker to revisit her/his decision on that claim/revision once the appeal has been heard on the grounds that s/he would have made a different decision had s/he known what the First-tier Tribunal's decision would be.
- **After the hearing.** If HMRC is considering an appeal to the Upper Tribunal or has decided to appeal, you are normally not paid until the Upper Tribunal decides the case. HMRC can 'postpone' payment in these circumstances, without notifying you of its intention.[48]
- **If you disagree with the First-tier Tribunal's decision.** The First-tier Tribunal decision cannot be 'superseded' (because supersessions do not apply to tax credits) but it can be revised in any of the ways described in this chapter except for official error (see p1395).

  If the First-tier Tribunal made an error of law, you can appeal to the Upper Tribunal as you can in benefit appeals. For tax credits, HMRC is not prevented from revising the First-tier Tribunal's decision on 'reasonable grounds', which could also include an error of law (if it is still within the tax year of the award).
- When a decision can be set aside. If you appeal to the Upper Tribunal, there is no provision obliging the First-tier Tribunal to set aside the decision if both you and HMRC agree the First-tier Tribunal made an error of law.[49]

3. Appealing to the Upper Tribunal

You can appeal to the Upper Tribunal against a decision of the First-tier Tribunal if the First-tier Tribunal made an error of law. In some penalty appeals, you can also appeal about the amount of the penalty (see p1405).

Chapter 46 explains what an error of law is and how to appeal (see p1182). The rules for tax credits are the same as those for benefits described in Chapter 46, except that if you disagree with the Upper Tribunal decision it cannot be 'superseded', but it can be revised in any of the ways described above, except for revision because of official error (see p1395).

4. Appealing to the courts

You can appeal to the Court of Appeal (in England and Wales) or to the Court of Session (in Scotland) against a decision of the Upper Tribunal, but only if there has been an error of law (see Chapter 46).

5. How to prepare an appeal

Suggestions for how to prepare your appeal and present your case are given in Chapter 46. Information in that chapter applies equally to tax credit appeals.

6. Penalty appeals

You have the right to appeal against a decision imposing a penalty. For information on penalties, see p1385.

For most types of penalty, HM Revenue and Customs (HMRC) has the power to make its own decision on imposing one. You can appeal against this decision to the First-tier Tribunal in the normal way, with any further appeal going to the Upper Tribunal under the usual rules.[50] However, to impose a penalty of up to £300 for failing to provide required information or evidence, HMRC cannot make the decision itself but must take 'proceedings' to the First-tier Tribunal. You have an opportunity to attend a hearing where the First-tier Tribunal decides whether to apply a penalty. Your right of appeal then lies with the Upper Tribunal.[51]

In these penalty appeals to the Upper Tribunal (ie, where the decision was made by the First-tier Tribunal under penalty proceedings), you can appeal on a question of law *or* on the amount of the penalty.[52] The usual time limits and procedures for applying for permission to appeal apply.

Notes

1. **Revisions**

1 s14(1) TCA 2002
2 s3(2) TCA 2002
3 s14(3) TCA 2002
4 s15(1) TCA 2002
5 Reg 25 TC(CN) Regs; reg 16(5)(a) WTC(EMR) Regs
6 Reg 26A TC(CN) Regs
7 Email to CPAG from HMRC, 8 February 2010
8 Reg 26(3) TC(CN) Regs
9 s16(1) TCA 2002
10 Reg 16(5)(b) WTC(EMR) Regs
11 s16(1) TCA 2002
12 CTC/2662/2005; CTC/3981/2005
13 s21 TCA 2002
14 s18(5) TCA 2002
15 s18(6) TCA 2002
16 s18(9) TCA 2002
17 s19(1) TCA 2002
18 s19(4) TCA 2002
19 s19(11) TCA 2002
20 s21 TCA 2002
21 s20(1) and (3) TCA 2002
22 s20(6)(a) TCA 2002
23 s20(6)(b) TCA 2002
24 s20(4) TCA 2002
25 s20(5) TCA 2002
26 s21 TCA 2002; reg 3 TC(OE) Regs
27 Reg 23 TC(CN) Regs
28 Regs 28 and 29 TC(CN) Regs
29 Reg 22(3) TC(CN) Regs
30 Reg 19 TC(CN) Regs
31 Reg 22(4) TC(CN) Regs
32 Reg 24 TC(CN) Regs
33 ss15(2)(b), 16(3)(b) and 19(2)(b) TCA 2002
34 Reg 30 TC(CN) Regs
35 s23 TCA 2002

2. **Appealing to the First-tier Tribunal**

36 s63(2) TCA 2002
37 s12 SSA 1998, as applied by reg 4 TC(A) Regs under the power in s63(8) TCA 2002
38 CTC/2612/2005
39 Reg 3 TC(A)(No.2) Regs
40 s38 TCA 2002
41 ss23(2) and 39(1) TCA 2002
42 Reg 2 TC(NA) Regs
43 s54 TMA 1970, as applied by reg 3 TC(A) Regs
44 rr2, 5 and 7 TP(FT) Rules
45 CTC/2662/2005; CTC/3981/2005
46 Reg 11 TC(PC) Regs
47 The power to refer to a doctor in s20 SSA 1998 does not apply to tax credits.
48 Reg 11 TC(PC) Regs
49 s13(3) SSA 1998, as applied by reg 5(2) TC(A) Regs under the power in s63(8) TCA 2002

6. **Penalty appeals**

50 s38 TCA 2002
51 s63 and Sch 2 para 4(1) TCA 2002
52 Sch 2 para 4(1) TCA 2002

Part 8

Immigration and residence rules for benefits and tax credits

Chapter 61

Coming from abroad: immigration status

This chapter covers:

You should check this chapter if you, your partner and child are *not* all European Economic Area (EEA) nationals. If you *are* all EEA nationals, the rules in this chapter do not apply to you. In either case, you must satisfy the residence requirements in Chapter 62.

Key facts

- Your immigration status may mean that you are not entitled to some benefits and tax credits, although there are limited exceptions.
- The immigration status of your partner can affect the amount you are paid. If your partner's or child's leave in the UK is subject to the condition that s/he does not have 'recourse to public funds', your claim could affect her/his right to remain in the UK.

Future changes: April 2013 and after

Major changes are taking place that affect the benefits and tax credits system (see Chapter 2). From April 2013, personal independence payment (PIP) will replace disability living allowance for adults and, from October 2013, universal credit (UC) will replace most means-tested benefits. In order to be entitled to PIP and UC, you must not be a 'person subject to immigration control'. At the time of writing, it is not known which people subject to immigration control will still be able to get these new benefits. See CPAG's *Welfare Rights Bulletin* for updates.

1. Immigration status

It is important to know your immigration status before making a claim for a benefit or tax credit. This is because your immigration status affects your right to benefits and tax credits and a claim can sometimes affect your right to remain in the UK. If you are unsure about your immigration status, you should seek specialist advice from your local law centre, Citizens Advice Bureau or other advice agency that gives immigration advice.

Most people, apart from British citizens, are subject to immigration control. However, for benefit and tax credit purposes, the term 'person subject to immigration control' has a specific meaning (see below). It is this meaning that is referred to when the phrase 'person subject to immigration control' is used in this *Handbook*.

Who is a 'person subject to immigration control'

You are defined as a **'person subject to immigration control'** if you are not a European Economic Area (EEA) national and you:[1]

- require leave to enter or remain in the UK, but do not have it (see p1411);
- have leave to enter or remain which is subject to a condition that you do not have recourse to public funds (see p1411);
- have leave to enter or remain given as a result of a maintenance undertaking (see p1413).

If you are defined as a 'person subject to immigration control', you are (with some limited exceptions) excluded from many benefits and tax credits (see p1413).

Note: you cannot be a 'person subject to immigration control' if you are an EEA national (this includes British citizens) as the definition only applies to non-EEA nationals. See p1501 for a list of EEA states.

Note: if you are *not* an EEA national but you have a 'right to reside' under European Union (EU) law (see p1447), you cannot be denied benefit on the basis of your immigration status. If this applies to you, you do not require leave to enter or remain.[2] If you have been given leave to enter or remain subject to a condition that you do not have recourse to public funds, or as a result of a maintenance undertaking, but you have a right to reside under EU law, you should not be excluded from benefits.

You require leave to enter or remain, but do not have it

You are a 'person subject to immigration control' if you require leave to enter or remain but do not have it.[3]

If you are not an EEA national, you require leave to enter or remain in the UK unless you are:

- a person with the right of abode or certificate of partiality;
- a person with a right of residence in EU law. This will apply if, for example, you are:
  - a family member of an EEA or Swiss national who has a right to reside in the UK (see p1447);[4]
  - a Swiss national with a right to reside. As a result of an agreement between Switzerland and the EU, Swiss nationals, in general, have the same residence rights as EEA nationals and do not require leave to enter or, if they have a right to reside, leave to remain in the UK;[5]
  - the primary carer and/or family member of a UK national who is dependent on you and it is necessary for you to have a right to reside in the UK so that s/he is not deprived of her/his rights as an EU citizen – eg, if your dependent child is a UK national and would have to leave the EU if you were not given a right of residence in the UK (see p1470).[6]

You require leave to enter or remain but do not have it if, for example, you:

- are an asylum seeker with temporary admission;
- have overstayed your limited leave to enter or remain;
- have entered the UK illegally;
- are subject to a deportation order.

Note: there are close links between the benefit authorities and the Home Office UK Border Agency. Making a claim for benefit could alert the immigration authorities to your presence and status in the UK. It is important, therefore, to get specialist immigration advice before claiming if you are unsure about your immigration status.

You have leave to enter or remain which is subject to a condition that you do not have recourse to public funds

You are a 'person subject to immigration control' if you have leave to enter or remain in the UK which is subject to a condition that you do not have recourse to 'public funds'.[7]

Most people admitted to the UK with time-limited leave, such as spouses/civil partners, students or visitors, are given limited leave to stay on condition they do not have recourse to public funds.

'Public funds' are defined in the Immigration Rules as:[8]

- attendance allowance;
- carer's allowance;

- child benefit;
- child tax credit;
- council tax benefit (CTB);
- disability living allowance;
- income-related employment and support allowance;
- housing benefit (HB);
- income support;
- income-based jobseeker's allowance;
- pension credit;
- severe disablement allowance;
- social fund payments;
- working tax credit.

Homelessness assistance and housing provided under specific provisions are also defined as public funds.

Only the benefits and tax credits in the above list are public funds. Therefore, a person with a public funds restriction can claim any other benefit that is not on the list without breaching the condition that they do not have recourse to public funds.

If you have recourse to public funds when your leave is subject to a condition that you do not do so, you will have breached one of the conditions of your leave. This may affect your right to remain in the UK, you could be liable to be deported, have further leave refused and/or be prosecuted for committing a criminal offence.[9] Always seek advice before claiming a benefit which is a public fund.

Having a no recourse to public funds condition attached to your leave means you are a 'person subject to immigration control'. Unless you fall within the limited exceptions (see pp1414, 1415 and 1416), you are not entitled to any of the benefits or tax credits defined as public funds (see p1413). However, if you *are* able to claim because you come within one of the limited exceptions, you will not be regarded as having had recourse to public funds.[10] You can therefore claim a public fund benefit and there will be no problem with your receiving it.

However, you *will* be regarded as having recourse to public funds if someone else's benefit is increased because of your presence. For example, HB and CTB include allowances for all members of a claimant's family and this can result in additional benefit being paid for a family member who is subject to a no recourse to public funds condition. Similarly, the maximum amount of HB payable may be greater under the size criteria (see p321) than it would otherwise have been because of the inclusion of such a family member(s). If the amount of HB or CTB payable is more than it would have been had the family member(s) not been included in the claim, no claim should be made.

You have leave to enter or remain given as a result of a maintenance undertaking

If you have leave to enter or remain given as a result of a maintenance undertaking, you are a 'person subject to immigration control'.[11] For example, if an elderly relative is seeking to join family in the UK, it is usual to require a maintenance undertaking.

A 'maintenance undertaking' means a written undertaking given by another person under the Immigration Rules to be responsible for your maintenance and accommodation.[12] There are specific Home Office forms on which an undertaking can be given. However, no official form need be used, provided the undertaking is sufficiently formal and definite.[13] The document must contain a promise or agreement that the other person will maintain and accommodate you in the future. If it merely contains a statement about her/his present abilities and intentions, it will not amount to an undertaking.[14] Your leave will be considered to be 'as a result of a maintenance undertaking' if this was a factor in granting it. It does not need to have been the only, or even a major, factor.[15] However, if the maintenance undertaking was not relevant to your being granted leave, its existence does not make you a 'person subject to immigration control'. If in doubt about whether you have leave given as a result of an undertaking, seek specialist advice.

2. Benefits and tax credits affected by immigration status

The general rule is that you are excluded from the following benefits and tax credits if you are defined as a 'person subject to immigration control' (see p1410). However, see pp1414, 1415 and 1416 for who can still claim particular benefits and tax credits despite being a 'person subject to immigration control'.

The following benefits are affected by your immigration status:[16]

- attendance allowance;
- carer's allowance;
- child benefit;
- child tax credit;
- council tax benefit;
- disability living allowance;
- income-related employment and support allowance (ESA);
- ESA in youth;[17]
- housing benefit;
- incapacity benefit for incapacity in youth;[18]
- income-based jobseeker's allowance (JSA);
- income support;

- pension credit;
- severe disablement allowance;
- social fund payments;
- working tax credit.

A 'person subject to immigration control' is only excluded from the benefits and tax credits in the above list and can therefore claim any other benefit. For example, if you are a 'person subject to immigration control' and have paid sufficient national insurance contributions, you can claim any of the contributory benefits – eg, retirement pensions, contribution-based JSA and contributory ESA. You can also claim benefits that depend on previous employment – eg, maternity allowance or industrial injuries benefits.

Although the general rule is that a 'person subject to immigration control' is excluded from the benefits in the list above, there are some limited exceptions. The groups of people subject to immigration control who can claim benefits are different for means-tested benefits (see below), non-means-tested benefits (see p1415) and tax credits (see p1416).

3. People subject to immigration control who can get means-tested benefits

The relevant benefits are:

- income support (IS);
- income-based jobseeker's allowance (JSA);
- income-related employment and support allowance;
- pension credit;
- housing benefit (HB);
- council tax benefit (CTB).

If you are a 'person subject to immigration control' (see p1410), this does not exclude you from entitlement to the means-tested benefits listed above if you:[19]

- are a national of Croatia, Macedonia or Turkey and you are lawfully present in the UK. This is most likely to enable you to get benefits if you have leave to enter or remain as you are lawfully present during that period of leave. Asylum seekers with temporary admission have been accepted as being lawfully present.[20] However, in order to be entitled to means-tested benefits, you still need to satisfy the residence tests, and having temporary admission does not give you a right to reside (see p1447);[21] *or*
- have leave to enter or remain given as a result of a maintenance undertaking and have been resident in the UK for at least five years (beginning on either the date of your entry to the UK or the signing of the maintenance undertaking,

whichever is later). If there are gaps in your residence as a result of your going to live for a period in another country, the periods of residency in the UK can be added together to make the five years.[22] However, depending on your circumstances, you may not have ceased to be resident during the short periods of absence and each absence must be considered individually (see p1430);[23] *or*

- have leave to enter or remain given as a result of a maintenance undertaking and the person (or, if more than one, all the people) who gave the undertaking has died; *or*
- have limited leave with the condition that you do not have recourse to public funds, you have not yet had such recourse (other than under this provision) and you depend on funds from abroad that are temporarily disrupted, but which are reasonably expected to resume. You are entitled to a maximum of 42 days' benefit during one period of leave; *or*
- applied for asylum before 3 April 2000 and you have not abandoned your application or been notified of a decision on it (or on an appeal if it was against a decision made before 5 February 1996) and you are covered by the transitional protection rules.[24] See Chapter 58 of the 2010/11 edition of the *Welfare Benefits and Tax Credits Handbook* for these.

Social fund payments

If you are defined as a 'person subject to immigration control', this does not exclude you from entitlement to social fund payments if you are in any of the exempt categories listed above.[25] However, you must meet the other conditions of entitlement, including (except for crisis loans and winter fuel payments) being in receipt of a qualifying benefit.

4. People subject to immigration control who can get non-means-tested benefits

The relevant benefits are:

- attendance allowance (AA);
- carer's allowance;
- child benefit;
- disability living allowance (DLA);
- employment and support allowance in youth;
- incapacity benefit for incapacity in youth;
- severe disablement allowance.

Contributory benefits are not affected by your or your partner's or child's immigration status.

If you are a 'person subject to immigration control' (see p1410), this does not exclude you from the non-contributory benefits listed above if:[26]

- you are a member of a European Economic Area national's (including a UK national's) family (see p1501); *or*
- you are a national of Algeria, Morocco, San Marino, Tunisia or Turkey and either you are currently lawfully working in Great Britain, or you have ceased lawfully working in Great Britain for a reason such as pregnancy, childcare, illness or accident, or because you have reached retirement age.[27] You are lawfully working if your work does not breach any conditions attached to your leave or, if you are an asylum seeker, you have permission to work from the UK Border Agency; *or*
- you are living with a family member (see p1465) who is someone listed in the above bullet point; *or*
- you have leave to enter or remain given as a result of a maintenance undertaking; *or*
- for DLA, AA, and child benefit only, you are covered by a reciprocal agreement. In practice, this is most helpful for child benefit and, in particular, if you are covered by the agreements with Bosnia-Herzegovina, Croatia, Kosovo, Macedonia, Montenegro, Serbia and Slovenia. See p1480 for more information about reciprocal agreements; *or*
- you were in receipt of the benefit immediately before 5 February 1996 (or 7 October 1996 for child benefit). Your entitlement ends if:
  - your benefit is revised or superseded. This means that, if you are receiving your benefit because you have been getting it since 4 February 1996 (6 October 1996 for child benefit) you should not request a revision or supersession of your award or you will bring your entitlement to an end. **Note:** claiming child benefit for an additional child does *not* mean your existing entitlement will be revised or superseded; *or*
  - you break your claim, or your fixed period award comes to an end; *or*
  - your application for asylum (if any) is recorded as having been decided or abandoned.

5. People subject to immigration control who can get tax credits

If you are a 'person subject to immigration control' (see p1410), this does not exclude you from getting child tax credit (CTC) or working tax credit (WTC) if:[28]

- you have leave to enter or remain given as a result of a maintenance undertaking and you have been resident in the UK for at least five years (beginning on the date of either your entry to the UK or the signing of the maintenance undertaking, whichever is later); *or*

- you have leave to enter or remain given as a result of a maintenance undertaking and the person (or, if more than one, all the people) who gave the undertaking has died; *or*
- you are in the UK with limited leave on condition that you do not have recourse to 'public funds', you have not had such recourse (other than under this provision) and you are temporarily without funds because your funds from abroad have been disrupted,but they are reasonably expected to resume. You are entitled to a maximum of 42 days' tax credits in your period of leave; *or*
- (CTC only) you are a national of Algeria, Morocco, San Marino, Tunisia or Turkey and either you are lawfully working in the UK, or you have ceased lawfully working for a reason such as pregnancy, childcare, illness or accident, or because you have reached retirement age. You are lawfully working if your work does not breach any conditions attached to your leave, or, if you are an asylum seeker, you have permission to work from the UK Border Agency; *or*
- (WTC only) you are a national of Croatia, Macedonia or Turkey and you are lawfully present in the UK. This is most likely to enable you to get benefits if you have leave to enter or remain as you are lawfully present during that period of leave. Asylum seekers with temporary admission have been accepted as being lawfully present,[29] but in order to be entitled to CTC, you still need to satisfy the residence tests, and having temporary admission does not give you a right to reside (see p1447);[30] *or*
- (CTC only) you claim CTC on or after 6 April 2004 and immediately before this you were entitled to an increase in your income support (IS) or income-based jobseeker's allowance (JSA) for a child because you fell into either the group of people in the first bullet point or the last bullet point on p1414 as not excluded from means-tested benefits – ie, you are Turkish or Croatian and lawfully present, or you claimed asylum before 3 April 2000 and are covered by the transitional protection rules.[31] This only applies if you are 'transferring' to CTC from an IS or JSA claim that included amounts for a child. It does not assist if you have not been receiving IS or income-based JSA for a child.

Note: if you are a 'person subject to immigration control', but your partner is not (or s/he falls into one of the above groups), you can make a joint claim for tax credits (see p1419).

6. **Partners and children**

Some benefits and tax credits have special rules that apply if any partner or child who lives with you is subject to immigration control. These rules vary, so you need to check the rules for the benefit or tax credit you want to claim.

Means-tested benefits

Income support, income-based jobseeker's allowance and income-related employment and support allowance

If your partner is a 'person subject to immigration control' (see p1410), s/he is included in your claim for income support (IS), income-based jobseeker's allowance (including if you are a joint-claim couple – see p414) or income-related employment and support allowance. However, you are only paid a personal allowance at the single person's rate, *unless* s/he falls into one of the groups that can get the means-tested benefits listed on p1414. If s/he does fall into one of those groups, you are paid at the couple rate.[32]

In all cases, your partner is still treated as part of your household and part of your claim. Therefore, your partner's work, income and capital can all affect your benefit entitlement. Her/his presence means you cannot claim IS as a lone parent (see p347) and may mean you are not entitled to a severe disability premium (see p830).

Premiums are payable in respect of those eligible for benefit. If you qualify for a premium, this should still be paid at the couple rate even if your partner is a 'person subject to immigration control' and not in one of the groups that can get the means-tested benefits on p1414.

Note: if your partner's leave to enter or remain in the UK is subject to a condition that s/he does not have recourse to public funds, you should be aware that receiving the couple rate of a premium could affect her/his right to remain in the UK. Seek specialist advice before making a claim. However, we have no experience of claimants being refused further leave because of this.

Pension credit

If your partner is a 'person subject to immigration control' (whether or not s/he is in one of the exempt groups listed on p1414), s/he is treated as *not* being part of your household.[33] This means that you are paid as a single person and your partner's income and capital do not affect your claim. In general, you cannot get the additional amount for severe disability if you have a partner who is not getting a qualifying benefit or who is not registered blind (see p830). However, if your partner is a 'person subject to immigration control', you should arguably be treated as if you have no partner. This is because 'partner' is not defined and so it should be given its everyday meaning ('the other member of a couple'). The definition of 'couple' requires the two people to be in the same household[34] and the rules state that if your partner is a 'person subject to immigration control' s/he is treated as *not* part of your household.[35] If you are refused the additional amount for severe disability in these circumstances, seek specialist advice.

Housing benefit and council tax benefit

If your partner and/or child for whom you are responsible is a 'person subject to immigration control', this does not affect the amount you are paid. Your partner is included in your claim and your applicable amount includes the couple rate of the personal allowance and any premiums to which either of you are entitled. Similarly, your child is included in your claim and your applicable amount includes a personal allowance for each child together with any premiums for which s/he qualifies.

If your partner comes to live with you in the UK, this may affect your council tax liability even if s/he is a 'person subject to immigration control'. For example, you may lose a single person's discount. If your council tax liability increases, your council tax benefit (CTB) will potentially increase too depending on your circumstances.

Note: if your partner's and/or child's leave is subject to a condition that s/he does not have recourse to public funds, you should be aware that a claim for housing benefit and/or CTB could (depending on your circumstances) result in additional public funds being paid as a result of her/his presence. This could affect her/his right to remain in the UK (see p1411). Seek specialist advice before making a claim.

Non-means-tested benefits

Contributory benefits are not affected by your or your partner's or child's immigration status.

Only the claimant's immigration status affects entitlement to non-contributory benefits. Therefore, for **child benefit,** if you are not a 'person subject to immigration control' or you are but you fall into one of the exempt groups (see p1415), you can claim for any child for whom you are responsible, regardless of the child's immigration status.

Similarly, for **disability living allowance**, if your child is the claimant and s/he is not a 'person subject to immigration control', or s/he is but s/he falls into one of the exempt groups on p1415, s/he can claim even if you are a 'person subject to immigration control'.

Tax credits

If your partner is a 'person subject to immigration control' and you are not, or you are but are in one of the exempt groups on p1416, your joint claim for tax credits (see p1347) is treated as if your partner were not subject to immigration control. You are therefore entitled to working tax credit (WTC) and child tax credit (CTC).[36] However, unless you or your partner are responsible for a child, or your partner is a national of Croatia, Macedonia or Turkey and is lawfully present in the UK, your WTC does not include the couple element.[37]

If your partner's leave is subject to a condition that s/he does not have recourse to public funds, the Immigration Rules state that s/he will not be regarded as having such recourse by making a joint tax credits claim. This means that you and your partner can make the joint claim without it affecting her/his right to remain in the UK. Similarly, if your claim includes a child whose leave is subject to a condition that s/he does not have recourse to public funds, any tax credits awarded in respect of the child will not be regarded as such recourse.[38]

There are no immigration status conditions for children for tax credits. Consequently, any child for whom you are responsible is included in your claim and your CTC and/or WTC includes amounts for her/him.

Note: if your child's leave is subject to a condition that s/he does not have recourse to public funds, a claim for CTC or WTC (other than a joint claim in which one partner is a 'person subject to immigration control' and the other is not or is in one of the exempt groups on p1416) that results in additional public funds being paid because of the child's presence could affect her/his right to remain in the UK. Seek specialist advice before making a claim. However, we have no experience of children being refused further leave because of this.

7. National insurance numbers and contributions

The national insurance number requirement

In general, in order to be entitled to any social security benefit or tax credit, you (and any partner who is included in your claim) must satisfy the national insurance (NI) number requirement (see p1023). The requirement applies when you make a claim for benefit. It also applies if someone who will be included in an existing award of benefit joins your family – eg, if your spouse joins you from abroad. Your partner must, unless s/he is exempt (see below), satisfy the NI number requirement even if you are not going to receive any extra benefit for her/him because s/he is a 'person subject to immigration control' (see p1410). For the rules on when you are paid for your partner, see p1417.

Any child or young person who is included in your housing benefit (HB) or council tax benefit (CTB) claim does not have to satisfy the NI number requirement.[39]

Who is exempt

If you are the benefit claimant, your partner does not have to satisfy the NI number requirement if:[40]

- s/he is a 'person subject to immigration control' because s/he requires leave to enter or remain in the UK, but does not have it (see p1411); *and*
- s/he has not previously been given an NI number; *and*
- you are claiming income support, income-based jobseeker's allowance, income-related employment and support allowance or pension credit and your partner is not entitled to that benefit her/himself; or you are claiming housing benefit or council tax benefit and your partner fails the

'habitual residence test' (see p1442). However, in practice it is difficult to see who could satisfy the first bullet point and not satisfy this bullet point.

Information will still be requested from you about an NI number application for your partner, even though s/he is exempt. An NI number will be refused, but this will not prevent you from being entitled to benefits or tax credits. For the rules on when you are paid for your partner, see p1417.

Tax credits

The NI number requirement for tax credits is similar to the requirement for benefits (and includes the same exemption for partners) except that the requirement does not apply if the Tax Credit Office is satisfied that you (and/or your partner if it is a joint claim) have 'reasonable excuse' for not complying with the requirement.[41] For example, if you are unable to prove your identity because the Home Office has all your documents and you can prove this (eg, with a letter from your solicitor), HM Revenue and Customs should accept that you have reasonable excuse.

National insurance contributions

If you have worked and paid contributions in a country with which the UK has a reciprocal agreement (see p1480), these can be taken into account when working out your entitlement to UK contributory benefits.[42] You may also be able to make up a shortfall in your contribution record by making voluntary contributions. Seek advice to check if this will be worth doing. See p776 for more information on voluntary contributions.

8. Asylum seekers and refugees

Asylum seekers

You are referred to as an **'asylum seeker'** while you are waiting for a Home Office decision on an application for refugee status. If you are a non-European Economic Area national seeking asylum in the UK, unless you have leave on some other basis or you do not require it (eg, because you are joining your family member who has a right to reside in the UK), you fall within the definition of a 'person subject to immigration control'. This is because you are someone who requires leave but does not have it (see p1411). You are therefore excluded from the social security benefits listed on p1413 unless you fall into one of the exempt groups on pp1414, 1415 or 1416. **Note:** in practice, the exemption that prevents you from being excluded from means-tested benefits if you applied for asylum before 3 April 2000 (or you appealed a decision made before 5 February 1996) and your application/appeal is still outstanding, is unlikely to assist as there are now very few such applications or appeals outstanding and you still must have a 'right to reside' to get benefit. However, you may fall into one of the other exempt groups that can apply to asylum seekers as well as other people subject to immigration control.

If benefit can be paid for you because either you are entitled because you are in an exempt group or your partner can include you in her/his claim and receive extra money for you, this will not affect your application for asylum. For example, you can receive any benefit defined as a 'public fund' (see p1411) because asylum seekers are not subject to a 'no recourse to public funds' restriction.

If you are excluded from claiming social security benefits because you are a 'person subject to immigration control', you may be entitled to alternative forms of state support. If you are a destitute asylum seeker, you may be eligible for asylum support from the UK Home Office Border Agency. **Note:** asylum support is taken into account as income when calculating any housing benefit or council tax benefit your partner claims, but it is not taken into account as income for income support (IS), income-based jobseeker's allowance (JSA) or income-related employment and support allowance (ESA).[43] However, any IS, income-based JSA or income-related ESA your partner receives is taken into account as income when calculating your asylum support.

If you are not eligible for asylum support or benefits, ask your local authority for help. If you have children, you may be eligible for support under the Children Act 1989 or Children (Scotland) Act 1995. If you are sick or disabled, you may be eligible for help under the National Assistance Act 1948. Seek independent legal advice if you are refused.

For more information about asylum support and other support for asylum seekers, see CPAG's *Benefits for Migrants Handbook*.

Decisions on asylum applications

When the Home Office makes a decision on your asylum application, it can:

- grant you refugee status. This is also known as granting asylum or refugee leave. This is given initially for five years and you can apply for indefinite leave just before the five-year period expires. Before 30 August 2005, refugees were granted indefinite leave straight away; *or*
- refuse you refugee status; *or*
- refuse you refugee status, but grant you humanitarian protection. This is granted for five years and you can apply for indefinite leave just before the five-year period expires; *or*
- refuse you refugee status or humanitarian protection, but grant you discretionary leave. This is usually granted initially for a period up to three years. You can apply to renew your discretionary leave just before it expires and then, in most cases, apply for indefinite leave after six years of discretionary leave.

In addition to the above, the Home Office can also decide to grant leave exceptionally outside the Immigration Rules – eg, the 'case resolution exercise', established to clear the backlog of outstanding asylum applications from before 5 March 2007. Applications were decided on the basis of the individual's circumstances with indefinite leave to remain being granted to those that qualified.

Refugees and people granted humanitarian protection, discretionary leave or indefinite leave

If you are granted either refugee leave, humanitarian protection, discretionary leave or indefinite leave granted under the 'case resolution exercise, you are no longer a 'person subject to immigration control'. Therefore, during this period of leave, your immigration status does not affect your entitlement to benefit and you can claim all benefits subject to the normal rules of entitlement.

If you are granted refugee leave or humanitarian protection, you have the right to be joined by certain family members under family reunion provisions. A family member who comes to the UK under these provisions is not, during her/his period of leave, a 'person subject to immigration control' and can claim all benefits subject to the normal rules of entitlement.

If you are granted refugee status, humanitarian protection, or exceptional leave (including discretionary leave, or indefinite leave granted under the 'case resolution exercise'), you are exempt from the habitual residence test (see p1442).

Who can get income support

One of the groups of people who are entitled to IS are refugees who are studying English (see p350). If you have been granted refugee leave (not humanitarian protection or discretionary leave), you can claim IS for up to nine months while you are studying if you:[44]

- attend, for more than 15 hours a week, a course for the purpose of learning English so you may obtain employment; *and*
- have been in Great Britain for not more than 12 months on the date the course began.

Backdating tax credits, child benefit and guardian's allowance

If you have been granted refugee leave (not humanitarian protection or discretionary leave), you can claim tax credits, child benefit and guardian's allowance and have them backdated to the date of your asylum application (or, for tax credits, 6 April 2003 if this is later).[45] Generally, with tax credits you are required to reclaim each year. However, under the special backdating rules for refugees, the claim is treated as having been renewed each April.[46]

You must claim backdated tax credits, child benefit and guardian's allowance within three months of receiving the Home Office letter granting you leave as a refugee. If the Home Office letter is sent to a solicitor who is acting for you, the three-month period starts from the date your solicitor receives the letter.[47]

The amount of tax credits paid is reduced by the amount of asylum support you received for your essential living needs over the period.[48]

In many cases, the amount of asylum support is greater than the rate of tax credits and therefore entirely cancels out any entitlement to tax credits over the backdated period. However, there are circumstances when your tax credit entitlement will exceed the amount of asylum support paid and you can claim backdated tax credits – eg, if you worked sufficient hours to qualify for working tax credit.

The amount of child benefit and guardian's allowance paid is *not* reduced by any asylum support you may have received.

Integration loans

If you (or someone of whom you are a dependant) were granted refugee leave or humanitarian protection after 11 June 2007 and you are aged 18 or over, you may be eligible for an integration loan.[49] This is a discretionary loan of between £100 and £1,000 paid for expenses associated with your integration into UK society, including for employment, education and housing. Claims are decided by the UK Border Agency and so these loans are not covered in this *Handbook*. Details and an application form are available on the UK Border Agency website (www.ukba.homeoffice.gov.uk). You should consider applying for a community care grant (see p550) before applying for an integration loan.

Notes

1. Immigration status

1 s115 IAA 1999
2 s7 IA 1988
3 s115(9)(a) IAA 1999
4 s7 IA 1988
5 *The Agreement Between the European Community and its Member States, of the one part, and the Swiss Confederation, of the other, on the Free Movement of Persons*, Luxembourg, 21 June 1999, Cm 5639; reg 2 EEA Regs defines Switzerland as an EEA state; reg 11 provides that no EEA national requires leave to enter the UK.
6 *Zambrano*, C-34/09 [2011] ECR, not yet reported; *Dereci and Others*, C-256/11 [2011] ECR, not yet reported
7 s115(9)(b) IAA 1999
8 para 6 Immigration Rules, HC395
9 s24(1)(b)(ii) IA 1971
10 para 6B Immigration Rules, HC395
11 s115(9)(c) IAA 1999
12 s115(10) IAA 1999
13 *R (Begum) v Social Security Commissioner* [2003] EWHC 3380 (Admin)
14 *Ahmed v SSWP* [2005] EWCA Civ 535
15 CIS/3508/2001

2. **Benefits and tax credits affected by immigration status**
16 s115 IAA 1999; s42 TCA 2002; reg 3 TC(Imm) Regs
17 Reg 11(1)(b) ESA Regs
18 Reg 16(1)(b) SS(IB) Regs

3. **People subject to immigration control who can get means-tested benefits**
19 Reg 2(1) and Part 1 of Sch SS(IA)CA Regs
20 *Szoma v SSWP* [2005] UKHL 64, 27 October 2005
21 *Yesiloz v London Borough of Camden Anor* [2009] EWCA Civ 415
22 R(IS) 2/02
23 CPC/1305/2005
24 Reg 12 SS(IA) Regs; reg 12 SS(PFA)MA Regs
25 Reg 2 SS(IA)CA Regs

4. **People subject to immigration control who can get non-means-tested benefits**
26 Reg 2(2), (3) and (4)(b) and Sch Part II SS(IA)CA Regs; reg 11(1)(b) and (3) ESA Regs; reg 16(1)(b) and (5) SS(IB) Regs
27 *Zoulika Krid v Caisse Nationale d'Assurance Vieillesse des Travailleurs Salariés (CNAVTS),* C-103/94 [1995] ECR I-00719, para 26

5. **People subject to immigration control who can get tax credits**
28 Reg 3 TC(Imm) Regs
29 *Szoma v SSWP* [2005] UKHL 64
30 *Yesiloz v London Borough of Camden and Another* [2009] EWCA Civ 415
31 Reg 5 TC(Imm) Regs. Macedonia is not listed here as it only ratified the European Social Charter on 31 March 2005 – ie, after 6 March 2005

6. **Partners and children**
32 **IS** Reg 21(3) and Sch 7 para 16A IS Regs
JSA Reg 85(4) and Sch 5 para 13A JSA Regs
ESA Reg 69 and Sch 5 para 10 ESA Regs
33 Reg 5(1)(h) SPC Regs
34 s17 SPCA 2002
35 Reg 5(1)(h) SPC Regs
36 Reg 3(2) TC(Imm) Regs
37 Reg 11(4) and (5) WTC(EMR) Regs
38 Para 6B Immigration Rules, HC395. The TC(Imm) Regs are made under s42 TCA 2002.

7. **National insurance numbers and contributions**
39 **HB** Reg 4(b) HB Regs; reg 4(b) HB(SPC) Regs
CTB Reg 4(a) CTB Regs; reg 4(a) CTB(SPC) Regs
40 **IS** Reg 2A IS Regs
JSA Reg 2A JSA Regs
ESA Reg 2A ESA Regs
PC Reg 1A SPC Regs
HB Reg 4(c) HB Regs; reg 4(c) HB(SPC) Regs
CTB Reg 4(b) CTB Regs; reg 4(b) CTB(SPC) Regs
TC Reg 5(8) TC(CN) Regs
41 Reg 5(6) TC(CN) Regs
42 Under orders made in powers conferred by s179 SSAA 1992

8. **Asylum seekers and refugees**
43 **IS** Sch 9 para 21 IS Regs
JSA Sch 7 para 22 JSA Regs
ESA Sch 8 para 22 ESA Regs
HB Sch 5 para 23 HB Regs
CTB Sch 4 para 24 CTB Regs
44 Reg 4ZA(3)(b) and Sch 1B para 18 IS Regs
45 **CB/GA** Reg 6(d) CB&GA(Admin) Regs
TC Regs 3(4)-(9) and 4 TC(Imm) Regs
46 Reg 3(6)(b) TC(Imm) Regs
47 *Tkachuk v SSWP* [2007] EWCA Civ 515; CIS/3797/2003
48 Reg 3(9) TC(Imm) Regs
49 s13 The Asylum and Immigration (Treatment of Claimants, etc) Act 2004, No.19; The Integration Loans for Refugees and Others Regulations 2007, No.1598

Chapter 62

Coming from abroad: residence rules

This chapter covers:

This chapter describes the residence and presence rules that affect your entitlement while you are in Great Britain. It does not cover the rules that affect your entitlement if you go abroad. These are covered in Chapter 63.

See Chapter 61 for information on how your immigration status can affect your entitlement to benefits and tax credits. If you are *not* a European Economic Area (EEA) national, you should check Chapter 61 first as your immigration status may exclude you from the benefit or tax credit you want to claim.

If you *are* an EEA national, the European Union (EU) co-ordination rules may help you to satisfy the residence and presents tests when you are in the UK. An overview of the EU co-ordination rules is provided in Chapter 64.

Key facts

- Different types of residence conditions apply to many (but not all) benefits and tax credits. These are: **residence**, **ordinary residence**, **right to reside** and **habitual residence**.
- Entitlement to some benefits and tax credits also depends on your being present in Great Britain and/or having been present for a certain period of time (known as 'past presence').
- The rules on residence and presence vary between different benefits and tax credits. If you satisfy the conditions for one benefit or tax credit, it does not mean you will necessarily satisfy the conditions for another.

Future changes: April 2013 and after

Major changes are taking place that affect the benefits and tax credits system (see Chapter 2).

- From April 2013, personal independence payment (PIP) will replace disability living allowance (DLA) for adults and, from October 2013, universal credit (UC) will replace most means-tested benefits.
- In order to be entitled to UC, you will need to satisfy the habitual residence test and probably the right to reside test. At the time of writing, it is not yet known how these tests will operate.
- You must also satisfy the residence and presence rules to be entitled to PIP but, at the time of writing, it is not yet known what these will be. However, the government has suggested that they may be different from the current rules for DLA.

See CPAG's *Welfare Rights Bulletin* for updates.

1. Introduction

Many benefits have residence and/or presence conditions. The rules vary between different benefits and tax credits. Whether or not you meet the conditions can depend on how long you have been living in Great Britain, your nationality, your immigration status, and whether you are covered by the provisions of European law.

Although many presence and residence rules refer to Great Britain rather than the UK, there is a reciprocal agreement between Britain and Northern Ireland, which means that, generally, you can satisfy the residence conditions if you move between Great Britain and Northern Ireland.

There are residence conditions for the following benefits and tax credits:

- attendance allowance (see p1433);
- carer's allowance (see p1433);
- child benefit (see p1435);
- child tax credit (see p1440);
- council tax benefit (see p1432);
- disability living allowance (see p1433);
- contributory employment and support allowance (ESA) in youth (see p1433);
- income-related ESA (see p1432);
- guardian's allowance (see p1437);
- housing benefit (see p1432);
- incapacity benefit in youth (see p1433);
- income support (see p1432);
- income-based jobseeker's allowance (JSA) (see p1432);
- pension credit (see p1432);
- Category D retirement pension (see p1439);

- severe disablement allowance (see p1433);
- working tax credit (see p1440).

Contributory benefits, such as contributory ESA, contribution-based JSA and retirement pension (except Category D), as well as the employment-related benefits (maternity allowance and industrial injuries benefits) do not have residence conditions. However, they do have presence requirements, which mean that if you go abroad, some benefits will cease and others will not be increased unless exceptions apply (see Chapter 63). Industrial injuries benefits also have conditions related to your presence in Great Britain at the time you had your accident or contracted your disease. There are no residence or presence requirements for statutory sick pay, statutory maternity pay, statutory paternity pay or statutory adoption pay paid by your employer.

Which rules apply

If you are covered by European Union (EU) law, these more generous provisions will apply. If they do not apply, but you are covered by a reciprocal agreement, those provisions will apply. If you are not covered by either the EU law provisions or a reciprocal agreement, the UK law provisions apply.

UK law

The UK benefits and tax credits legislation contains rules about the residence and presence entitlement conditions that you must satisfy. These rules are set out in this chapter.

European Union law

EU legislation and caselaw apply in the UK and throughout the European Economic Area (EEA). EU law plays an increasingly important role in the UK benefits system, particularly since the introduction of the right to reside test (see p1447). In general, for EU law to apply, you must be an EEA national (see p1501) or the family member of an EEA national.

There are two main areas of EU law which affect benefit and tax credit entitlement that are covered in this *Handbook*:

- residence rights. If you or your family member are an EEA national, EU law may give you a right of residence that enables you to satisfy the right to reside requirement (see p1447);
- the co-ordination rules. These are covered in Chapter 64. These can help you get benefits or tax credits in the UK – eg, by enabling you to count periods of residence, insurance and employment in any EEA state towards your entitlement to UK benefits under the principle of 'aggregation' (see

p1511). See p1432 for the way in which these rules can assist your entitlement to individual benefits and tax credits.

It is not usually necessary, however, to understand how the co-ordination rules may affect you in order to know whether you have a right of residence in EU law, or *vice versa*.

Reciprocal agreements

Reciprocal agreements exist between the UK and some other countries and can assist in similar ways to EU law.

The UK has agreements with the following EEA member states: Austria, Belgium, Cyprus, Denmark, Finland, France, Germany, Iceland, Ireland, Italy, Luxembourg, Malta, Netherlands, Norway, Portugal, Slovenia, Spain and Sweden.

The UK has agreements with the following non-EEA member states: Barbados, Bermuda, Bosnia-Herzegovina, Canada, Croatia, Guernsey, Isle of Man, Israel, Jamaica, Jersey, Kosova, Macedonia, Mauritius, Montenegro, New Zealand, Philippines, Serbia, Turkey and the United States of America.

There are 'association' and 'co-operation' agreements with Algeria, Morocco, San Marino, Slovenia, Tunisia and Turkey.

The scope of the reciprocal agreements differs greatly, in terms of the people covered, the benefits covered and the provisions made. It is therefore crucial to check the individual agreement. You can find the agreements in the *Law Relating to Social Security* at www.dwp.gov.uk. See also CPAG's *Benefits for Migrants Handbook* for more details.

2. The different residence and presence tests

The presence and residence conditions you are required to satisfy vary between the different benefits and tax credits. You may be required to satisfy tests for your:

- presence (see below);
- past presence (see p1430);
- residence (see p1430);
- ordinary residence (see p1430);
- habitual residence (see p1431);
- right to reside (see p1431).

Presence

You must usually be present in Great Britain at the time you make your benefit or tax credit claim, and continue to be present. There are specific rules that allow you to be treated as present during temporary absences (see Chapter 63). Being present means being physically present in Great Britain. If a benefit authority (ie, the DWP, HM Revenue and Customs or local authority) wants to disqualify you from benefit because you were absent from Great Britain, it must show you were absent throughout that day. This means that on the day you leave Great Britain and the day you arrive in Great Britain you count as present.

Past presence

In addition to being present at the time you make your claim, for some benefits you must also have been present for a period of time before you become entitled. The requirement for each benefit is broadly the same: you must have been present for a total of not less than 26 weeks in the preceding 52 weeks before claiming. There are some exceptions to this general rule. If you are covered by the European Union co-ordination rules (see p1503), periods of time in another European Economic Area state can be counted to satisfy this requirement. See the rules for the specific benefits below and Chapter 64.

The benefits that have a past presence requirement are:

- attendance allowance (AA);
- carer's allowance (CA);
- disability living allowance (DLA);
- employment and support allowance (ESA) in youth;
- incapacity benefit (IB) in youth;
- severe disablement allowance (SDA).

Residence

The requirement to be simply resident, rather than ordinarily resident or habitually resident, is only a condition for Category D retirement pension. However, it is a necessary part of being ordinarily resident (see below) or habitually resident (see p1431). Residence is more than mere physical presence in a country and you can be resident without being present – eg, if you are away for a short holiday. You will usually be resident in the country in which you have your home for the time being.[1] You can remain resident during a temporary absence, but it will depend on your circumstances, including the length of your absence, your intentions to return, your accommodation, and where your family and your personal belongs are.

Ordinary residence

The benefits and tax credits that have an ordinary residence requirement are:

- AA;
- CA;
- child benefit;
- child tax credit (CTC);
- DLA;

- ESA in youth;
- IB in youth;
- Category D retirement pension;
- SDA;
- social fund funeral payment;
- working tax credit.

The term **'ordinary residence'** is not defined in legislation, and caselaw has confirmed that the words should have their natural and ordinary meaning.[2] You are ordinary residence in a country if you have a home there that you have adopted for a settled purpose and where you live for the time being (whether for a short or long duration).[3] In practice, ordinary residence is rarely a problem. If you receive a decision that you are not entitled to a benefit or tax credit because you are not ordinarily resident, you should appeal and seek specialist advice. For more information on ordinary residence, see CPAG's *Benefits for Migrants Handbook*.

Habitual residence

The benefits and that have a habitual residence requirement are:

- council tax benefit (CTB);
- housing benefit (HB);
- income-based jobseeker's allowance (JSA);
- income-related ESA;
- income support (IS);
- pension credit (PC).

For the means-tested benefits listed above, you need to satisfy (or be in a group that is exempt from) the habitual residence test. For details on how this test operates, see p1442.

In addition, you cannot get a social fund crisis loan if you would not pass (or you are not exempt from), the habitual residence test for IS, income-based JSA, income-related ESA or PC if you were to claim one of these benefits, unless it is to alleviate the consequences of a disaster (see p564).[4]

Right to reside

The benefits and tax credits that have a right to reside requirement are:

- child benefit;
- CTC;
- CTB;
- income-related ESA;
- HB;

- income-based JSA;
- IS;
- PC.

For the benefits and tax credits listed above, you need to satisfy the right to reside requirement, unless you are in group that is exempt from the habitual residence test (see p1443). For details on how the right to reside test operates, see p1447.

3. Residence and presence rules for individual benefits

This section explains the individual residence and presence rules for each benefit. These include:
- which, if any, residence and presence tests apply;
- how entitlement is affected if your partner or child is absent while you remain in Great Britain; *and*
- how, if you are resident in the UK, you may be assisted by the European Union (EU) co-ordination rules.

This section does not explain the rules on being paid while you are abroad – these are covered in Chapter 63.

Means-tested benefits

To be entitled **to income support (IS), income-based jobseeker's allowance (JSA), income-related employment and support allowance (ESA)** and **pension credit (PC)**, you must:
- be present in Great Britain (see p1429);[5] *and*
- be habitually resident (see p1442), including having a right to reside (see p1447), in the 'common travel area' – ie, the UK, Republic of Ireland, Channel Islands and the Isle of Man (unless you are in a group that is exempt).[6]

In certain circumstances, the rules treat you as present in Great Britain during a temporary absence, so you can continue to receive these benefits while you are abroad for limited periods (see Chapter 63).

To be entitled to **housing benefit (HB)** or **council tax benefit (CTB)**, you must be habitually resident (see p1442), including having a right to reside (see p1447), in the 'common travel area'.[7]

There is no requirement to be present in Great Britain for HB or CTB. However, for HB, you must be liable to make payments in respect of a dwelling in Great Britain which you occupy as your home.[8] There are rules that treat you as occupying your home, including during a temporary absence from it.[9] If you are going abroad, these rules determine whether you can be entitled to HB while you are away (see p254).

For CTB, you must be liable to pay council tax in respect of a dwelling where you are resident.[10] There are rules that treat you as resident during a temporary absence.[11] If you are going abroad, these rules determine whether you can be entitled to CTB while you are away (see p119).

If your partner is abroad

If you have a partner who is abroad, you can continue to receive benefit that includes an amount for her/him for a limited period depending on the circumstances (see Chapter 63).

If this does not apply, or at the end of the limited period, your applicable amount for IS, income-based JSA and income-related ESA will cease to include an amount for your partner. However, each of your means-tested benefits may still be affected by her/his capital, income and work as s/he will be treated as part of your household, despite being temporarily living away from you, unless you are in any of the situations listed on p758.[12]

Your partner's absence is from *you*, not from the family home, so these rules can apply even if your partner has never lived in your current home. The length of the absence is worked out from when it started to when it is likely to finish.

Where questions of 'intention' are involved (eg, when deciding whether you or your partner intend to resume living with your family), the intention must be 'unqualified'. This means it must not depend on a factor over which you have no control – eg, the right of entry to the UK being granted by the Home Office[13] or the offer of a suitable job.[14]

If your child is abroad

If you have a child who is abroad, your benefit entitlement could be affected as s/he will be treated as part of your household, despite temporarily living away from you, unless s/he is does not count as being a member of your household because of one of the reasons on p762.[15]

For IS and income-based JSA, you can only have your child included in your applicable amount for a limited period while s/he is abroad (see Chapter 63).

Attendance allowance, carer's allowance, disability living allowance, employment and support allowance in youth, incapacity benefit in youth and severe disablement allowance

For attendance allowance (AA), carer's allowance (CA), disability living allowance (DLA), ESA in youth, incapacity benefit (IB) in youth and severe disablement allowance (SDA), you must satisfy the presence, past presence and ordinary residence tests. This means to be entitled to each of these benefits you must:[16]

- be present in Great Britain at the time of claim (see p1429);

- have been present in Great Britain for not less than 26 weeks in the last 52 weeks (the 'past presence' test). See p1430, but see also below;
- be ordinarily resident in Great Britain (see p1430).

For ESA in youth, IB in youth and SDA, once you pass the residence and presence tests, you do not need to satisfy them again while you are in the same period of limited capability for work or incapacity for work.[17]

When you can be treated as present

You are treated as present during certain absences (see p1480). Any period when you are treated as present can be counted to satisfy both the presence and the past presence tests.

Exceptions to the 26-week past presence test

If you are claiming the DLA care component for a baby under six months old, there is a shorter 13-week past presence test. If covered by the 13-week presence test, it continues to apply until your child's first birthday. If your child becomes entitled to DLA after reaching six months, the 26-week test applies.

For AA and DLA, the 26-week (or 13-week) past presence test does not apply if you are terminally ill (see p157).[18]

European Union co-ordination rules

AA, CA and the care component of DLA are classed as 'sickness benefits' under the EU co-ordination rules (see p1505).[19] If these rules apply to you (see p1503), you may be able to count periods of residence in another European Economic Area (EEA) member state to satisfy the past presence test for these benefits (and for ESA in youth). If you have a permanent or long-term disability and a sufficient connection with the UK, you may be able to make a new claim for these benefits while resident in another EEA state.[20] **Note:** at the time this *Handbook* was written, the government intended to abolish new claims for ESA in youth.

At present, the UK classes the mobility component of DLA as a 'special non-contributory benefit' (see p1507). You should therefore be entitled to receive this benefit in the state in which you are accepted as 'resident' under the EU co-ordination rules (see p1508).[21]

See Chapter 64 for more details.

Bereavement benefits

You do not need to satisfy any residence or presence rules in order to be entitled to bereavement benefits. There is one exception, which only applies to a bereavement payment.

If you are absent from Great Britain when you claim a bereavement payment, you can only be entitled if:[22]

- your late spouse/civil partner was in Great Britain when s/he died; *or*

- you were in Great Britain on the date of your spouse/civil partner's death; *or*
- neither of the above two bullets apply, but you returned to Great Britain within four weeks of your late spouse/civil partner's death; *or*
- your late spouse/civil partner's national insurance (NI) contribution record is sufficient for you to satisfy the contribution conditions for widowed parent's allowance and bereavement allowance; *or*
- your spouse/civil partner died while abroad in another EEA state and the EU co-ordination rules apply to you (see p1503);
- your spouse/civil partner died while abroad in a state which has a reciprocal agreement with the UK that covers your entitlement to a bereavement payment.

According to official guidance, the DWP takes the view that if you and your late spouse/civil partner were outside Great Britain when s/he died and you do not return to Great Britain within four weeks of the death (and none of the last three bullets above apply), you will be disqualified from a bereavement payment, even if you make your claim within the necessary time limit (see p62) when you are back in Great Britain.[23] It is arguable that this approach is incorrect and you should only be disqualified if you are absent from Great Britain when you make your claim (and none of the above bullets apply). Seek advice if this affects you.

European Union co-ordination rules

Bereavement benefits are classed as 'survivors' benefits' under the EU co-ordination rules (see p1505). If these rules apply to you (see p1503) and the UK is your 'competent state' (see p1508 for what this means) you can, if necessary, rely on NI contributions paid by your late spouse/civil partner in other EEA states (including A8 or A2 states) to calculate your entitlement to bereavement benefits. See p1511 for more information.

If the co-ordination rules apply to you (see p1503) and your late spouse/civil partner died in another EEA state, s/he should be treated as having died in the UK for the purposes of entitlement to a bereavement payment.[24]

Reciprocal agreements

If you have lived and worked in a country with which the UK has a reciprocal agreement (see p1480), you may be able to count periods of insurance paid in that country towards your bereavement benefit entitlement.

Child benefit

To be entitled to child benefit, you and your child(ren) must be present in Great Britain (see p1429).[25]

You are treated as not present and, therefore, not eligible for child benefit if:[26]

- you are not ordinarily resident in the UK (see p1430); *or*

- you do not have a right to reside in the UK (see p1431) and your claim for child benefit was made after 1 May 2004.

Note: you do not need to have a right to reside if you claimed child benefit before 1 May 2004 and you have been receiving it since that date.

You are teated as present if you are:[27]

- a Crown servant posted overseas; *and*
  - you are, or immediately before your posting abroad you were, ordinarily resident in the UK; *or*
  - immediately before your posting you were in the UK in connection with that posting; *or*
- the partner of a Crown servant posted overseas and in the same country as her/him or temporarily absent from that country under the same exceptions that enable child benefit to continue during a temporary absence from Great Britain (see p1482);
- a person who is in the UK as a result of your being deported or legally removed from another country.

You and your child can be treated as present for limited periods during a temporary absence (see p1482).

While you are treated as present, you continue to satisfy that condition of entitlement. This means that you can continue to receive child benefit if it is already being paid and you can also make a fresh claim during your, or your child's, absence. If you, or your child, spend longer abroad than the permitted periods (see p1482), you (or s/he) will cease to satisfy the presence condition and your entitlement to child benefit will end.

European Union co-ordination rules

Child benefit is classed as a 'family benefit' under the EU co-ordination rules (see p1505). If these rules apply to you (see p1503), you may be able to be paid child benefit for a child resident in another EEA country without her/him needing to satisfy the rules on temporary absences. See Chapter 64 for more details.

Contributory employment and support allowance

To be entitled to contributory ESA, you must be in Great Britain.[28] The rules on when you can be paid during a temporary absence are covered in Chapter 63. There are no residence conditions, unless you are claiming contributory ESA in youth (see p1433).

European Union co-ordination rules

If the EU co-ordination rules apply to you (see p1503) and the UK is your 'competent state' (see p1508 for what this means), you can, if necessary, rely on

NI contributions paid in another EEA state (including an A8 or A2 state) to entitle you to contributory ESA in the UK. See p1511 for more information.

You maybe able to continue to receive a sickness or invalidity benefit from another EEA state if the EU co-ordination rules apply to you (see p1503).

Reciprocal agreements

If you have lived and worked in a country with which the UK has a reciprocal agreement (see p1480), you may be able to count periods of insurance paid in that country towards your entitlement to contributory ESA in the UK.

Guardian's allowance

Entitlement to guardian's allowance depends on entitlement to child benefit, so you must meet the conditions for child benefit set out on p1435.

A further condition of entitlement to guardian's allowance is that at least one of the child's parents must:[29]
- have been born in the UK; *or*
- have, at some time after reaching the age of 16, spent a total of 52 weeks in any two-year period in Great Britain.

In order to satisfy the second condition above, you will be treated as being present in Great Britain during any absence abroad which is due to your employment as a serving member of the forces, an airman or airwoman, mariner or continental shelf worker.

European Union co-ordination rules

Guardian's allowance is classed as a 'family benefit' under the EU co-ordination rules (see p1505). If these rules apply to you (see p1503), you may be able to be paid guardian's allowance for a child resident in another EEA country.

If the EU co-ordination rules apply to you (see p1503), time spent in other EEA states (including the A8 and A2 states) can count toward the time spent in Great Britain to help meet the second of the two conditions above (see p1511).

Industrial injuries benefits

Industrial injuries benefits are:
- industrial injuries disablement benefit;
- reduced earnings allowance;
- retirement allowance;
- constant attendance allowance;
- exceptionally severe disablement allowance.

To be entitled to any of these benefits, you must have:
- been in Great Britain when the accident at work happened;[30] *or*

- been engaged in Great Britain in the employment that caused the disease (even if you have also been engaged outside Great Britain in that employment);[31] *or*
- been paying UK NI contributions, either at Class 1 rate or at Class 2 rate as a volunteer development worker when the accident at work happened or you contracted the disease. Benefit is not payable until you return to Great Britain.[32]

There are exceptions to these rules which mean you can qualify for benefit in respect of an accident which happens, or a disease which is contracted, outside Great Britain while you are:[33]

- employed as a mariner or airman or airwoman;
- employed as an apprentice pilot on board a ship or vessel;
- on board an aircraft on a test flight starting in Great Britain in the course of your employment.

In these cases, there are also more generous rules for defining when accidents arise out of and in the course of your employment, and for complying with time limits under benefit rules.[34]

European Union co-ordination rules

Industrial injuries benefits, except retirement allowance, are classed as 'benefits for accidents at work and occupational diseases' under the EU co-ordination rules (see p1505). If these rules apply to you (see p1503) and the UK is your 'competent state' (see p1508 for what this means), you can, if necessary, rely on periods of employment and NI paid in other EEA states (including A8 or A2 states) in order to qualify for industrial injuries benefits in the UK (see p1511).

If you have an accident while travelling abroad in another member state, this can be deemed to have occurred in the state liable to pay industrial injuries benefits.[35] If you have worked in two or more EEA states in a job that gave you a prescribed industrial disease, you will only get benefit from the member state in which you last worked in that job.[36]

Contribution-based jobseeker's allowance

To be entitled to contribution-based JSA, you must be in Great Britain.[37] The rules on when you can be paid during a temporary absence are covered in Chapter 63. There are no residence conditions.

European Union co-ordination rules

Contribution-based JSA is classed as an 'unemployment benefit' under the EU co-ordination rules (see p1505). If these rules apply to you (see p1503) and the UK is your 'competent state' (see p1508), you can, if necessary, rely on NI contributions paid in another EEA state (including an A8 or A2 state) to entitle you to contribution-based JSA in the UK. See Chapter 64 for more details.

If you are coming to, or returning to, the UK to look for work and have been insured in another EEA member state, you may be able to get the other member state's unemployment benefit for up to three months if:[38]

- you were getting that member state's unemployment benefit immediately before coming to the UK;
- you have been registered as available for work for four weeks (or less if the member state's rules allow) in the other member state;
- you claim JSA within seven days after you were last registered in the other member state; *and*
- you satisfy the JSA labour market conditions (see p433).

This can be extended to a maximum of six months if the state from which you are claiming the unemployment benefit agrees.[39] See Chapter 64.

Reciprocal agreements

If you have lived and worked in a country with which the UK has a reciprocal agreement (see p1429), you may be able to count periods of insurance paid in that country towards your entitlement to contribution-based JSA.

Maternity allowance

Entitlement to maternity allowance (MA) is based on past employment. There are no residence requirements, but you are disqualified if you are absent from Great Britain.[40] See p1486 for the rules allowing you to be paid during a temporary absence.

European Union co-ordination rules

MA is classed as a 'maternity benefit' under the EU co-ordination rules (see p1505). If these rules apply to you (see p1503) and the UK is your 'competent state' (see p1508), you can, if necessary, rely on periods of employment in other EEA states (including A8 or A2 states) in order to qualify for MA in the UK. See Chapter 64 for more details.

Retirement pensions

Retirement pensions, other than Category D retirement pension, do not have any residence or presence conditions.[41] They can be paid without time limit whether or not you are present in Great Britain. The exception to this is the annual uprating, which is only paid while you are abroad in certain circumstances (see p1494).

To be entitled to Category D retirement pension, you must:

- have been resident in Great Britain for at least 10 years in any continuous period of 20 years ending on or after your 80th birthday; *and*
- have been ordinarily resident (see p1430) in Great Britain on either:

- your 80th birthday; *or*
- the date on which you claimed Category D pension, if later.

European Union co-ordination rules

Retirement pensions are classed as 'old age benefits' under the EU co-ordination rules (see p1505). If these rules apply to you (see p1503) and the UK is your 'competent state' (see p1508), you can, if necessary, rely on NI contributions paid in other EEA states (including A8 or A2 states) to calculate your entitlement to retirement pensions in the UK. Similarly, for Category D retirement pension, periods of residence in other EEA states can be counted to meet the residence requirement. See Chapter 64 for more details.

Reciprocal agreements

If you have lived and worked in a country with which the UK has a reciprocal agreement (see p1429), you may be able to count periods of residence or insurance paid in that country towards your UK retirement pension entitlement.

Social fund payments

You cannot get a crisis loan, unless it is to alleviate the consequences of a disaster (see p567) if you would not meet (or be in a group that is exempt from) the habitual residence test for IS, income-based JSA, income-related ESA or PC.[42]

A community care grant and crisis loan cannot be awarded for a need that occurs outside the UK.[43]

To qualify for a funeral payment:

- the deceased must have been ordinarily resident (see p1430) in the UK;[44]
- the funeral must take place in the UK. However, it can take place in any EEA state if you or your partner are: [45]
  - an EEA national and a 'worker', including if you have retained this status (see p1456);
  - an EEA national and a 'self-employed person', including if you have retained this status (see p1460);
  - a 'family member' of one of the above (see p1465);
  - an EEA national with a permanent right of residence as a retired or permanently incapacitated worker or self-employed person, or you are the family member of such a person (see p1464);
  - a person with any other right of residence in the UK under EU law – eg, with a permanent right of residence following five years' residence (see p1462).[46]

Tax credits

To be entitled to **child tax credit** (CTC), you (and your partner if you are making a joint claim) must:[47]

- be present in the UK (see p1429); *and*
- be ordinarily resident in the UK (see p1430); *and*
- have a right to reside in the UK (see p1431).

To be entitled to **working tax credit** (WTC), you (and your partner if you are making a joint claim) must be:[48]

- present in the UK (see p1429); *and*
- ordinarily resident in the UK (see p1430).

There are, however, some exceptions.[49]

You do not need to have a right to reside for CTC if you claimed CTC before 1 May 2004 and you have been receiving it since that date.

You do not need to be ordinarily resident in the UK for CTC or WTC if you have been legally removed from another country to the UK.

For WTC, you are treated as being ordinarily resident in the UK if you are exercising your rights as an EEA worker (see p1456) or if you have some other right to reside under EU Directive 2004/38 (see p1449). In practice, being accepted as ordinarily resident is rarely a problem in any case (see p1430).

For the rules on when you can be treated as present for either eight or 12 weeks during a temporary absence, or while you or your partner are a Crown servant posted overseas, see p1495.

While you are treated as present, you continue to satisfy the conditions of entitlement to tax credits. This means that you can continue to receive tax credits that are already in payment and can make a fresh or renewal claim during your absence. If you spend longer abroad than the permitted periods, you will cease to satisfy the presence condition and your tax credit entitlement will end.

Being absent (other than a temporary absence of less than eight or 12 weeks – see p1495) or losing your right to reside are both changes that you must notify to HM Revenue and Customs (HMRC) within one month. If you do not, HMRC may impose a penalty (see Chapter 59), and may also recover any overpaid tax credits (see Chapter 58).

Couples

If you are a member of a couple and make a joint tax credit claim, you must both satisfy the residence requirements. Your entitlement to tax credits as a couple will end if either you or your partner:

- are abroad for longer than a permitted temporary absence;
- (for CTC only) lose the right to reside;
- cease to be ordinarily resident.

The person who continues to satisfy the residence rules can make a fresh claim for CTC and/or WTC as a single person if s/he is entitled on that basis.

You must notify HMRC if you or your partner have ceased to satisfy the residence or presence requirements within one month (see p1363). If you fail to notify HMRC, you may be overpaid (see Chapter 58) and could be subject to a penalty (see Chapter 59). When the partner returns to the UK, or becomes ordinarily resident or acquires a right to reside, you must terminate the single person claim and claim again as a couple.

If you or your partner are abroad (even for a temporary absence of less than eight or 12 weeks) and you (or s/he) were the only partner in full-time work, you may lose entitlement to WTC if the requirement to be in full-time work is no longer satisfied (see p1296). This is a change that you must notify to HMRC within one month. If you do not, HMRC may impose a penalty as well as recovering any overpaid tax credits.

European Union co-ordination rules

CTC is classed as a 'family benefit' under the EU co-ordination rules (see p1505). If these rules apply to you (see p1503), you may be able to be paid CTC for a partner or child resident in another EEA country. See p1512 for more details.

4. **Habitual residence**

The requirement to be habitually resident applies to:[50]

- income support (IS);
- income-based jobseeker's allowance (JSA);
- income-related employment and support allowance (ESA);
- pension credit (PC);
- housing benefit (HB);
- council tax benefit (CTB).

In addition, you cannot get a social fund crisis loan if you would not pass the habitual residence test for IS, income-based JSA, income-related ESA or PC if you were to claim one of these benefits, unless it is to alleviate the consequences of a disaster (see p564).[51]

To be entitled to one of the above benefits, you must either be in one of the groups that is exempt from the habitual residence test or be habitually resident in the **'common travel area'** – ie, the UK, Ireland, the Channel Islands and the Isle of Man.

The habitual residence test

To satisfy the habitual residence test, you must:

- have a right to reside (see p1447); *and*
- be 'habitually resident in fact' (see p1444).

There are some groups of people who are exempt from the habitual residence test (see p1443). If you are in one of these groups, you are treated as if you satisfy both parts of the habitual residence test. If this is accepted, your residence is not subject to any further examination and, provided you meet the other conditions of entitlement, you will be eligible for benefit.

In practice, the DWP or local authority first considers your right to reside and, only if it accepts you satisfy this requirement, does it go on to consider if you are 'habitually resident in fact'. Whether or not you are in a group that is exempt from the habitual residence test is not always considered. If you are in one of these groups, it is worth making it clear to the DWP or local authority that you are exempt, particularly if you might otherwise not be accepted as 'habitually resident in fact' – eg, if you claimed benefit shortly after arriving in the UK. Most people who are exempt have a right to reside, which means that this element of the test is satisfied.

If you fail the habitual residence test

If you fail the habitual residence test, you are not paid any benefit. However, the way the test operates differs slightly between the different benefits concerned.

If you fail the habitual residence test:

- for IS, income-based JSA, income-related ESA, HB and CTB, you are classed as a 'person from abroad'. This means:
  - for IS, income-based JSA and income-related ESA, you have an applicable amount of nil;[52]
  - for HB, you are treated as not liable for rent;[53]
  - for CTB, you are a prescribed person excluded from CTB.[54]
- for PC, you are treated as not present in Great Britain.[55]

The habitual residence test only applies to the benefit claimant. If you are the claimant and you satisfy (or are exempt from) the habitual residence test, whether or not your partner would satisfy the habitual residence test does not affect your entitlement. The exception to this is if you are a joint-claim couple for JSA and you satisfy the habitual residence test but your partner does not. In this case, you can be entitled to JSA without your partner making a joint claim with you and you will be paid as a couple (see p414).

Who is exempt from the habitual residence test

You are exempt from the habitual residence test if you:[56]

- are a European Economic Area (EEA) national who is a 'worker' (see p1456), including if you have retained this status;
- are an EEA national who is 'self-employed person' (see p1460), including if you have retained this status;
- are the family member (see p1465) of an EEA national who is in either of the above two groups;

- are an EEA national with a permanent right of residence as a retired or permanently incapacitated worker or self-employed person, or you are the family member of such a person (see p1464);
- are an A2 national subject to worker authorisation working in accordance with the conditions of your worker authorisation document;
- are a refugee;
- have exceptional leave to enter or remain in the UK granted outside the Immigration Rules (this includes discretionary leave);
- have humanitarian protection granted under the Immigration Rules;
- have been deported, expelled or otherwise legally removed from another country to the UK and you are not a 'person subject to immigration control' – see p1410);
- left Montserrat after 1 November 1995 because of the volcanic eruption;
- left Zimbabwe to come to the UK after 28 February 2009 but before 18 March 2011 and you have received assistance from the UK government to settle in the UK;
- (for HB and CTB only) receive IS, income-related ESA, income-based JSA, or PC;
- (for income-related ESA only) are being transferred from an award of IS which is part of a continuous period of entitlement to one or more of IS, income-based JSA, PC, HB or CTB that included 30 April 2004 (see p1447).

If you are not in one of the above groups, you must have a right to reside (see p1447) and establish that you are 'habitually resident in fact' (see below).

Establishing you are 'habitually resident in fact'

There is no definition of 'habitual residence' in the legislation. However, there is now a considerable amount of caselaw on the meaning of habitual residence and from this certain principles have emerged.

- There is no comprehensive list of factors that are relevant, so all the facts of your situation should be considered.[57]
- To be habitually resident, you must be resident (see p1430). It is not enough merely to intend to reside in the future.[58]
- You must have a settled intention to reside in the common travel area. You do not need to intend to reside permanently; it is enough if you intend to make the common travel area your home for the time being.[59] You must provide evidence of your intention, which can include your reasons for coming to the common travel area, the strength of your ties (or your 'centre of interest') and the viability of your residence here. Factors that could be relevant include arranging or seeking employment, education or training, joining and/or bringing your family, arranging accommodation, bringing possessions, registering with a doctor, joining clubs and associations, and breaking ties

with the place of your previous residence. The viability of your continued residence, although a relevant factor, is not an additional requirement.[60]

- In most cases, you will need an appreciable period of actual residence. How long this period must be is not fixed and depends on your circumstances.[61] Benefit authorities must not set a standard period of time for which all claimants must be resident before they can become habitually resident and any such policy should be challenged by judicial review (see p1202). There is an extensive body of caselaw on what constitutes an appreciable period of residence. Periods of between one and three months are frequently cited,[62] but too much weight should not be put on any one decision, nor should any general rule about a specific time period be derived from it.[63] There is an inter-relationship between your settled intention and your appreciable period, so that the stronger your settled intention to make your home in the common travel area for the time being, the shorter your period of actual residence needs to be before you can be accepted as habitually resident (and *vice versa*).[64]

  You may not need an appreciable period of actual residence, or the period may be very short, if you are:
  - a returning resident. This applies if you have been habitually resident in the common travel area previously, you left in circumstances which meant you ceased to be habitually resident (see below) and you then return to live in the common travel area again. The decision on how long a period of residence you need in order to resume your previous habitual residence depends on the circumstances in which you left, your links with the common travel area while you were away and the circumstances of your return.[65] You can be found to be habitually resident on the day of your return;
  - covered by the co-ordination rules (see p1503) and are claiming IS, income-based JSA, PC or income-related ESA (since the first three of these are listed as special non-contributory benefits and the DWP also considers that income-related ESA is as well – see p1507). If this applies, you cannot be denied benefit solely because you have not satisfied an 'appreciable period' of residence. Your period of residence is one of the factors that should be taken into account in assessing habitual residence, but it is not an absolute requirement, and may be outweighed by other factors.[66]
- A temporary absence, such as to go on holiday, should not mean that you cease to be habitually resident. This should be accepted if you have a definite date of return.[67]
- When deciding whether you are habitually resident, benefit authorities must consider the whole period up to the date the decision is made since the time between the date of your claim and the decision may mean you have been resident for an appreciable period.[68]

Tactics if you fail the habitual residence test

- If you are refused benefit because you have failed the habitual residence test, you should consider challenging this decision (see Chapters 45 and 46). You may want to contact a local advice agency for help with this.
- While challenging the decision, you should make a further claim. If that claim is refused, you should also challenge that decision and make another further claim and so on. This is because when the decision refusing your initial claim is looked at again, the decision maker (or First-tier Tribunal) cannot take account of things that have changed since the decision was made. Thus, if the decision maker considers that you were not habitually resident at the time benefit was originally refused, but you would now be habitually resident (as you have now been resident for an appreciable period of time), s/he cannot take that into account when looking again at the decision in your case. However, s/he would be able to take it into account if you had completed an appreciable period of residence before the date of decision on your second, or subsequent, claim. Sometimes, the benefit authorities say you cannot make another claim while your appeal or request to look again at the first decision is pending. This is wrong. Seek specialist advice if you are in this situation.
- Check to see if you fall into one of the exempt categories (see p1443).
- Establish whether the decision maker considers you do not have a right to reside or you are not habitually resident in fact. However, if you are not in an exempt group, you should demonstrate that you have a right to reside and are also habitually resident in fact.
- Remember that the habitual residence test only applies to the claimant, so if you have a partner who is potentially entitled to the benefit (or an alternative means-tested benefit) and would more easily satisfy the habitual residence test, s/he should make a claim (and you can still challenge the refusal of your claim).
- If your HB or CTB claim is refused, remember that if you were receiving IS, income-based JSA, income-related ESA or PC at the time the decision was made, you are exempt from the habitual residence test for HB and CTB. If the DWP decides that you are not habitually resident, the local authority must consider the issue for itself when it makes its own decision and not just follow the DWP's decision.
- Although the onus of proof is on the benefit authorities to establish that you are *not* habitually resident,[69] it is vital that you produce as much evidence as possible to show that you have a right to reside and are habitually resident in fact.

5. Right to reside

The right to reside requirement applies to:
- income support (IS);
- income-based jobseeker's allowance (JSA);
- income-related employment and support allowance (ESA);
- pension credit (PC);
- housing benefit (HB);
- council tax benefit (CTB);
- child benefit;
- child tax credit (CTC).

In addition, you cannot get a social fund crisis loan if you would not pass (or you are exempt from) the habitual residence test for IS, income-based JSA, income-related ESA or PC, unless it is to alleviate the consequences of a disaster (see p564).[70]

Means-tested benefits

The right to reside requirement was introduced as part of the habitual residence test on 1 May 2004. You must have a right to reside in order to satisfy the habitual residence test for IS, income-based JSA, income-related ESA, PC, HB and CTB.

Transitional protection

If you have been receiving IS, income-based JSA, PC, HB or CTB since 30 April 2004, you do not need a right to reside in order to continue to receive that benefit.[71] You also do not need a right to reside for a new claim for one of these benefits (or, from 31 October 2011, a new claim for income-related ESA), provided the periods of entitlement are continuous since 30 April 2004. You also do not need a right to reside for a new claim for income-related ESA if it is linked to a previous period of entitlement by the 12-week linking rule (see p213), provided this earlier period of entitlement began on or after 31 October 2011.

Example

Delphine is French. She came to the UK in 2003 and claimed IS on incapacity grounds while living with friends. In 2006 she moved into a rented flat and made a new claim for HB/CTB. In 2009 she started work and so her IS stopped, but she continued to get HB/CTB as she had a low income. In 2010, she left her job to have a baby and claimed IS as a lone parent. In November 2011 she became sick and claimed income-related ESA instead of IS. Delphine does not need to pass the right to reside test for any of these new claims because she has been receiving one of the five benefits for each day from 30 April 2004.

In February 2012 her partner, who works full time, moved in with her and so Delphine stopped claiming income-related ESA, HB and CTB. After eight weeks her partner moved out and so Delphine made a new claim for income-related ESA.

She does not need to show a right to reside for this new claim because it is linked by less than 12 weeks to her previous transitionally protected award of ESA.

If you have been receiving transitionally protected IS on grounds of disability and then get transferred to income-related ESA (see p193), you are exempt from the habitual residence test.[72]

The type of right to reside you need

Any right of residence in the common travel area (see p1442) will enable you to satisfy the requirement for each of the means-tested benefits *except:*

- for **IS, income-related ESA, PC, HB and CTB**, you will not satisfy the right to reside test if your *only* right of residence is as:[73]
  - a European Economic Area (EEA) national with the right of residence, during your first three months in the UK;
  - a family member of the above;
  - an EEA jobseeker (but see note below for income-related ESA);
  - a family member of an EEA jobseeker;
- for **income-based JSA**, you will not satisfy the right to reside test if your *only* right of residence is as:[74]
  - an EEA national with the right of residence during your first three months in the UK;
  - a family member of the above.

This means that if your only right to reside is as an EEA jobseeker, this will not satisfy the right to reside test for any of the means-tested benefits *except* income-based JSA. However, if you receive income-based JSA, you can then get HB and CTB since you will be exempt from the habitual residence test for these two benefits (see p1443).

Note: it may be arguable that income-related ESA is a benefit designed to facilitate access to the labour market and that it is therefore unlawful to exclude from this benefit people whose only right to reside is as a jobseeker.[75] Seek specialist advice if this affects you.

Child benefit and child tax credit

For child benefit and CTC, if you do not have a right to reside, you are treated as not present in Great Britain and, therefore, are not entitled to these benefits.[76] If you are making a joint claim for CTC, you and your partner must both have a right to reside. If only one of you has a right to reside that person can make a single claim.

The right to reside requirement was introduced on 1 May 2004. You do not need a right to reside to continue to receive child benefit or CTC if you have been receiving it since this date.

There are no restrictions on what type of right to reside you need to have. This means that if you have any right to reside, you will satisfy the requirement.

If you are claiming CTC and you (or your partner if it is a joint claim) lose your right to reside, this is a change of circumstances that you must notify HM Revenue and Customs of within one month (see p1363). If you have a joint claim for CTC and you or your partner loses the right to reside, the other partner can make a single claim, if entitled.

Who has a right to reside

Whether or not you have a right to reside can be complex. It can depend on your nationality, immigration status, and the circumstances of you and your family members. You may have a right of residence under UK law or one that stems directly from European Union (EU) law. You may have more than one right of residence or you may not have any.

Any residence right is sufficient to satisfy the right to reside requirement except, for means-tested benefits, the residence rights you have as an EEA national during your initial three months in the UK or as a jobseeker (unless you are claiming income-based JSA). These two rights are specified as being insufficient to satisfy the test (see p1448).

You have a right to reside if you are:

- a British citizen;
- an Irish citizen. Irish citizens have a right to reside in Ireland, which is part of the common travel area. Therefore, they satisfy the right to reside requirement for means-tested benefits;
- a Commonwealth citizen with a right of abode;
- a person with leave to enter or remain. You have a right to reside during your period of leave. Any form of leave counts. Examples include indefinite leave, refugee leave, humanitarian protection, discretionary leave and limited leave granted under the Immigration Rules, such as a spouse or a visitor. Note that if you have limited leave which is subject to a condition that you do not have recourse to public funds, or indefinite leave given as the result of a maintenance undertaking, you are a 'person subject to immigration control' and, therefore, likely to be excluded from benefits on that basis (see p1410).

These are just examples of some people whose right to reside is clear. It is not an exhaustive list.

Residence rights of European Economic Area nationals and their family members

The right to reside requirement mainly affects EEA nationals. The residence rights of EEA nationals are complex, as both EU law and UK law must be considered, and both are subject to a considerable amount of interpretation through caselaw.

EU Directive 2004/38 sets out many (but not all) situations in which an EU national or her/his family member has a right to reside in the UK. This Directive has been in force since 30 April 2006 and replaces many of the previous EU Directives and EU Regulations.

The Immigration (European Economic Area) Regulations 2006 ('the EEA Regulations') set out in UK law similar rights of residence to those contained in the Directive. Where these rules conflict with, or do not completely incorporate, Directive 2004/38, you can rely on whichever is more favourable to you.

Nationals of Norway, Iceland, Liechenstein and Switzerland

The EEA Regulations apply to all EEA and Swiss nationals (see p1501),[77] but EU Directive 2004/38 only applies to EU nationals (see p1500). Therefore, if you are a national of Norway, Iceland, Liechtenstein or Switzerland and do not have a right to reside under the EEA Regulations, seek advice since there are agreements with these states which may assist you.[78]

UK nationals

If you are a UK national, you do not have the same rights under EU Directive 2004/38 as other EEA nationals residing in the UK, since the Directive applies to EEA nationals who move to, or reside in, an EU state other than their own.[79] Similarly, the EEA Regulations exclude UK nationals from the definition of EEA national.[80] This is relevant to your family members (since, as a UK national *you* have an automatic right to reside in the UK). If you are the family member of a UK national, you have a right to reside on the basis of EU law as her/his family member (see p1465) if:

- the UK national has lived with a right to reside (eg, as a worker) in *another* EEA state. On her/his return to the UK s/he has the same rights as other EEA nationals. S/he should have a right to reside and you have residence rights as her/his family member, even if s/he is not economically active on her/his return to the UK;[81]
- you are the parent and primary carer of a child who is a UK national and who is dependent on you. You have a right of residence in EU law in order to look after her/him (see p1465).[82]

If you are British and have dual nationality with another EEA state, you do not have rights under EU Directive 2004/38 if you have lived all your life in the UK,[83] but you do have rights under the EEA Regulations in the same way as other EEA nationals,[84] even if you have not moved between EEA states.[85]

A8 and A2 nationals

A8 and A2 states

The A8 states are: Czech Republic, Estonia, Hungary, Latvia, Lithuania, Poland, Slovakia and Slovenia.

These states joined the EU on 1 May 2004.
The restrictions only applied until 30 April 2011.

The A2 states are: Bulgaria and Romania.
These states joined the EU on 1 January 2007.
The restrictions are in force until 31 December 2013.

When the A8 and A2 states joined the EU, the treaties under which they joined allowed existing member states to limit the access to their labour markets by nationals of these 'accession states'. The limitations the UK government chose to impose restricted the residence rights of workers and jobseekers from the A8 states and, later, the A2 states. These restrictions are time-limited for a maximum of seven years from the date the states joined the EU.

Most A8 nationals had and A2 nationals have, for a limited period, certain restrictions on their right to reside as jobseekers, workers or people who retain worker status. For A8 nationals, these restrictions applied between 1 May 2004 and 30 April 2011. The restrictions apply to A2 nationals between 1 January 2007 and 31 December 2013. Although the restrictions on A8 nationals ended on 30 April 2011, the rules are included in this chapter because, in certain circumstances, you may still need to know what the restrictions were and how they operated. This is because the residence rights you or your family member had in the past can affect your current or future residence rights. In particular, they could affect whether you or your family members acquire a right of permanent residence or have a right as a primary carer of a former worker's child in education (see p1469).

While in force, the restrictions on p1450 applied/apply to all A8 and A2 nationals *unless* you fell/fall within one of the exempt groups listed below. If you are an A8 national who was subject to restrictions, you had to work for an 'authorised employer'.[86] Broadly speaking, this meant you had to register each job you took with the Worker Registration Scheme (but see p1452 for the precise meaning as it can affect your residence rights). If you are an A2 national subject to restrictions, you must obtain an accession worker authorisation document (in most cases, an accession worker card specifying the employer you can work for) before you take up employment and then work in accordance with it.[87]

Restrictions on A8 and A2 nationals' residence rights

If you are an A2 national subject to worker authorisation, your residence rights are restricted until 31 December 2013 as follows.[88]

- You do not have a right to reside as ajobseeker.
- You are only defined as a 'worker' if you have an accession worker authorisation document and are working in accordance with it.
- You cannot retain your worker status when you cease work in the ways other workers can (see p1457).[89]

If you are an A8 national whose work had to be registered, your residence rights were restricted between 1 May 2004 and 30 April 2011 as follows.

- You did not have a right to reside as ajobseeker.
- You were only defined as a 'worker' if you were working for an authorised employer.
- You could notretain your worker status when you ceased work in the ways other workers can (see p1457). However, if you lost your job within the first month of employment, you could retain your status until the end of the month.[90]

The restrictions do not affect other residence rights you may have as an EEA national – eg, as a self-employed or self-sufficient person.[91]

A8 nationals: working for an authorised employer

If you are an A8 national, you were working for an 'authorised employer' if you:[92]

- were within the first month of employment;
- applied for a registration certificate within the first month of work, but did not yet have a certificate or refusal;
- had a valid registration certificate for that employer;
- had been legally working (see p1454) for that employer since 30 April 2004;
- began work at an agricultural camp between 1 May 2004 and 31 December 2004 and before 1 May 2004 you had been issued with leave under the Immigration Act 1971 as a seasonal worker at such a camp.

If you only applied for a registration certificate after the first month of work, you only count as working for an authorised employer from the date it was issued; it does not apply retrospectively. However, the Court of Appeal is currently considering this point.[93] See CPAG's *Welfare Rights Bulletin* for updates and seek specialist advice if this may affect you.

A8 nationals who were not required to register

If you are an A8 national, you were not required to register if you:[94]

- had leave to enter or remain on 30 April 2004 which had no restriction on employment;
- were legally working (see p1454) in the UK for 12 months, without breaks of more than 30 days (in total), up to and including 30 April 2004;
- had legally worked for 12 months (beginning before or after 30 April 2004), disregarding any breaks of less than 30 days (in total);
- were the spouse/civil partner or child under 18 of a person with leave to enter or remain in the UK that allowed employment;
- had dual nationality with the UK or another (non-A8/A2) EEA state or Switzerland;

- were a family member of another EEA or Swiss national who had a right to reside under the EEA Regulations (other than an A8/A2 national subject to registration/authorisation if her/his only right to reside was for the first three months in the UK);
- were the member of a diplomatic mission, or the family member of such a person, or a person otherwise entitled to diplomatic immunity;
- were a posted worker – ie, you were working in the UK providing services on behalf of an employer who is not established in the UK.

A2 nationals who are not subject to worker authorisation

If you are an A2 national, you are not subject to worker authorisation if you:[95]

- have (or had on 31 December 2006) leave to enter or remain with no restriction on employment;
- were legally working (see p1454) in the UK for 12 months, without breaks of more than 30 days (in total), up to and including 31 December 2006;
- have legally worked for 12 months (beginning before or after 31 December 2006), disregarding any breaks of less than 30 days (in total);
- are a posted worker – ie, you are working in the UK providing services on behalf of an employer who is not established in the UK;
- are a member of a diplomatic mission, or the family member of such a person, or a person otherwise entitled to diplomatic immunity;
- have dual nationality with the UK or another (non-A2) EEA state;
- are the spouse/civil partner of a UK national or of a person settled in the UK;
- are the spouse/civil partner or child under 18 of a person with leave to enter/remain in the UK that allows employment;
- have a permanent right of residence (see p1462);
- are a student with a registration certificate, which includes a statement that you shall not work more than 20 hours a week (unless it is part of vocational training or during vacations) and you comply with this. If the certificate confirms you can work during the four months after the course ends, the exemption continues for this period;
- are a family member of an EEA national who has a right to reside, unless the EEA national is an A2 national subject to worker authorisation (or the only reason s/he is not an A2 national subject to worker authorisation is because s/he is covered by the group below);
- are a family member of an A2 national subject to worker authorisation who has a right to reside as a worker, student, self-employed or self-sufficient person;
- are a 'highly skilled person'. You are a 'highly skilled person' if you:[96]
  - met the Immigration Rules that applied on 1 January 2007 for entering the UK on this basis, other than English language proficiency; *or*
  - have been awarded a qualification at degree level or higher in the UK, or Higher National Diploma in Scotland and, within 12 months of this award,

you apply for a registration certificate confirming your unconditional access to the labour market.

Legally working

If you are an A2 national you are 'legally working' if:[97]

- you are working in accordance with your worker authorisation document;
- you are working during a period when you are within one of the exempt groups above (other than posted workers);
- the work was done before 1 January 2007 either in accordance with any leave you had under the Immigration Act 1971 or when you did not require leave. The Court of Appeal has held that this does not apply to work done with permission from the Home Office while you were an asylum seeker.[98]

If you are an A8 national you were 'legally working' between 1 May 2004 and 30 April 2011 if:

- you were working for an authorised employer (see p1452);
- you were working during a period when you were within one of the exempt groups above (other than if you were the spouse/civil partner or child of a person whose leave to enter or remain in the UK allowed employment);
- the work was done before 1 May 2004 and was done either in accordance with any leave you had under the Immigration Act 1971 or when you did not require leave. The Court of Appeal has held that this does not apply to work done with permission from the Home Office while you were an asylum seeker.[99]

If you are an A2 national and your employment ends, you cease to be 'legally working', cease to be a 'worker' and, unless you are in an exempt group at that time, you cannot retain your worker status. However, while you are still under a contract of employment, you continue to be legally working and a worker – eg, if you are on maternity leave, holiday leave, sick leave or compassionate leave (including if the leave is unpaid).[100]

The same applied to A8 nationals between 1 May 2004 and 30 April 2011. If you cease working after 30 April 2011, your rights are the same as for other non-accession state EEA nationals and the relevant question is whether you have ceased to be a 'worker'. However, it may still be relevant to know whether you were legally working before 1 May 2011 (to establish if you either had completed your 12 months of legal work that exempted you from restrictions or were a 'worker' at a particular time) as it can affect your residence rights and those of your family members after this date.

Residence rights: summary

If you are an EEA national you have a right to reside in the UK (under both EU Directive 2004/38 and the EEA Regulations) if you :

- are within the first three months of residing in the UK (see below);
- are a 'qualified person'.[101] The term 'qualified person' appears in the EEA Regulations and is used by the benefit authorities. The term does not appear in the Directive, but the same groups of people are covered.[102] You are a **'qualified person'** if you are a:[103]
  - jobseeker (see p1456); *or*
  - worker (seep1456); *or*
  - self-employed person (see p1460); *or*
  - self-sufficient person (see p1461); *or*
  - student (see p1462);
- have a permanent right of residence (see p1462). This will normally be after five years of legal residence but, in limited circumstances, can be acquired before five years.

You also have a right to reside if you are:

- a family member of someone in one of the groups above even if you are not an EEA national yourself. 'Family member' has a specific meaning (see p1465);
- the primary carer of a child of a (former) worker if the child is in education (see p1469);
- a family member or primary carer of a dependent UK national who would otherwise be deprived of her/his rights as an EU national (see p1470).

Note: you can have more than one right to reside at a time.[104] For example, you may be both a self-employed person and also the family member of someone with a permanent right of residence.

Right of residence for the first three months

All EEA nationals have an unconditional right to enter any member state. EEA nationals also have an initial right of residence in any member state for the first three months of their stay.[105] This initial right of residence is given whether or not you are working or seeking work. However, it is subject to your not becoming an unreasonable burden on the social assistance system of the UK.[106]

You also have a right of residence if you are not an EEA national but are the family member of an EEA national who has an initial right of residence for three months.[107]

Note: you can have one or more rights of residence (eg, as the family member of a worker and/or as a jobseeker) *in addition to* your initial right of residence – ie, you do not have to wait for the three months to end before you have another right of residence.

The benefit rules exclude you from entitlement to **IS, income-based JSA, income-related ESA, PC, HB and CTB** if your *only* right of residence is on the basis of the initial three-month residence of your family member. If you have a right of residence on *another* basis during your initial three months in the UK, you can (provided it is not a residence right as a jobseeker unless you claim income-based JSA) satisfy the right to reside requirement and are therefore entitled to benefit (see p1447).

There are no restrictions on what type of right to reside you need for **child benefit and CTC**. This means that if you (or your family member) are an EEA national and you are within your initial three-month period of residence in the UK, you can claim child benefit and CTC. However, you will not be entitled after the first three months, unless you have some other right of residence.

Jobseekers

You have a right to reside as a jobseeker if you are an EEA national, and you can provide evidence that you are looking for work and have a 'genuine chance of being engaged'.[108] You should be accepted as being a jobseeker if you are 'signing on' and are awarded either JSA or national insurance credits (see p779), since both show you have been accepted as being available for work (see p434) and actively seeking work (see p447). It is only in a very small number of cases that you would satisfy these conditions and not have a genuine chance of being engaged.[109]

There is no time limit on how long you can have a right to reside as a jobseeker and it continues for as long as you can provide evidence that you are looking for work and have a genuine chance of being engaged.[110]

Having a right to reside as a jobseeker will satisfy the right to reside requirement for income-based JSA (which, in turn, can 'passport' you to HB and CTB) and also for child benefit and CTC. It does not enable you to satisfy the right to reside requirement for IS, income-related ESA, PC, HB or CTB. You need some other right to reside for these benefits.

If you are an A2 national who is subject to worker authorisation (see p1451), you do not have a right to reside as a jobseeker. Similarly, before 1 May 2011, if you were an A8 national who was required to register your work (see p1451), you did not have a right to reside as a jobseeker (see p1451).

If you are the family member (see p1465) of a jobseeker, you have a right to reside. However, this is only sufficient to satisfy the right to reside requirement for income-based JSA (which, in turn can 'passport' you to HB and CTB), child benefit and CTC.

Workers

If you are a EEA national and a 'worker', you have a right to reside.[111] You therefore satisfy the right to reside requirement for the relevant benefits and you are also exempt from the habitual residence test (see p1443).

If you are an A2 national who must have worker authorisation (see p1451), you only count as a 'worker' if you have an accession worker authorisation document and are working in accordance with it. Similarly, before 1 May 2011, if you were an A8 national who was required to register (see p1451), you only counted as a 'worker' if you were working for an authorised employer.

You count as a 'worker' if:

- you are in an employment relationship. This means you must:[112]
  - provide services;
  - work in return for remuneration;
  - work under the direction of another person;
- the work you do entails activities that are 'genuine and effective' rather than 'marginal and ancillary.' All the relevant factors must be taken into account, including:
  - the duration of the employment. The longer the period of time the employment lasts, the more likely it is that worker status has been established. However, someone working as a steward at Wimbledon for two weeks was held to be a worker;[113]
  - the number of hours worked. There is no minimum threshold. Someone working 10 hours a week was held to be a worker,[114] as was an au pair working 13 hours a week for a modest wage plus board and lodging.[115] The European Court of Justice (ECJ) held that 5.5 hours work was potentially capable of making someone a worker;[116]
  - the level of earnings. There must be some remuneration (although it can be in kind, such as board and lodgings[117]) and voluntary work will not result in worker status.[118] The work can be low paid. If it is so low that you need to subsidise your wages with benefits, this is irrelevant to the question of whether or not you are a worker;[119]
  - the regularity of the work. The more regular and less erratic the work, the more likely it is that worker status will be established. Agency work is not necessarily marginal and ancillary. It is possible to be a worker while undertaking work through an agency.[120]

You only cease to be a worker when the employment relationship ends. While you are still under a contract of employment, you continue to be a worker. Consequently, you are still a worker if you are a woman on maternity leave (including unpaid maternity leave),[121] or if you are on holiday leave or sick leave (including if it is unpaid).[122]

If you have ceased to be a worker, you may retain your worker status in certain circumstances (see below).

Retaining worker status

You can retain the status of worker, even though you are no longer working if:[123]

- you are involuntarily unemployed (see p1458);
- you are temporarily unable to work because of an illness or accident (see p1458);
- you are undertaking vocational training (see p1458).

However, before arguing that you have retained your worker status, you should check whether you have ceased to be a worker (see above). For example, if you are off work on unpaid sick leave but you can return to your job when you are better, you are still a worker so you do not need to argue that you have retained your worker status.

You are involuntarily unemployed

You are 'involuntarily unemployed' if you are seeking and are available to take up a job. This depends on your remaining in the labour market and not on the circumstances in which you left your last job.[124]

You must also register as a jobseeker with Jobcentre Plus. In *all circumstances*, the best way to do this is to claim JSA and keep signing on even if you are not entitled to receive any JSA. However, if you are looking for work but you claim IS, income-related ESA or PC, you should be accepted as having registered as a jobseeker if you have declared that you are looking for work – eg, on your claim form or habitual residence questionnaire.[125] If you previously had a claim refused in these circumstances, seek specialist advice on the possibility of challenging this decision.

You can retain your worker status while registered as a jobseeker indefinitely if you have already been employed for more than a year.[126] If you have worked for a shorter period, you can retain your worker status while registered as a jobseeker for at least six months.[127] You can retain worker status for more than six months if you can provide evidence that you are seeking work and you have a 'genuine chance of being engaged' (see p1456).[128]

You are temporarily unable to work because of an illness or accident

To retain your worker status, your inability to work must be temporary. This can apply if you have a permanent health condition that fluctuates and causes temporary periods when you are unable to work.[129] You do not need to have claimed ESA or another benefit on grounds of incapacity, nor do you need to pass the test of incapacity for work or limited capability for work. The test is whether you are unable to do the work you were doing or, if it follows a period in which you were seeking work, the sort of work you were seeking.[130] Your inability to work must be caused by an illness or accident which you have – ie, you are not covered if you are unable to work because you are looking after a child who is ill.[131]

If you are unable to work because of pregnancy, see p1459.

You are undertaking vocational training

You retain your worker status if you are undertaking a vocational training course. Unless you are involuntarily unemployed, the training must be related to your previous employment. If it is not, you must be accepted as 'involuntarily unemployed'. You should be accepted as 'involuntarily unemployed' if there is no employment available to you that is equivalent to your last employment.[132]

Moving between groups and gaps

You can retain your worker status if you are in one of the groups specified on p1458 and continue to do so if you move into another category.[133] For example, you may have been involuntarily unemployed and registered as a jobseeker, then you became ill and were temporarily unable to work, and then you got better and embarked on vocational training. You retain your worker status throughout.

You may be able to retain your worker status if there is a gap between ceasing work and registering as a jobseeker by claiming JSA.[134] The reasons for the gap and your circumstances will need to be considered to establish if you withdrew from the labour market during that period.[135] Arguably, you should also be able to retain your worker status if there is a gap between ceasing work and being temporarily unable to work because of illness or an accident since there is no requirement that the illness or accident be the reason for your ceasing work. You should also still retain your worker status during a short gap between two different circumstances applying, provided you remain in the labour market during that time.

A2 and A8 nationals

If you are an A2 national who must have worker authorisation, you cannot retain your worker status in the ways described in this section. Similarly, before 1 May 2011, if you were an A8 national who was required to register, you could not could retain your worker status in the ways described in this section. The exception was that, if you were an A8 national required to register and you stopped working during the first month of employment, you could retain your worker status in the ways described in this section for the remainder of that month.[136]

Pregnancy and childbirth

If you have established worker (or self-employed) status and you are now not working because of pregnancy or childbirth, you may still count as a worker or self-employed person, or you may be able to retain your worker or self employed status.

You do not cease to be a worker while you are still under a contract of employment. You are still a worker while on maternity leave, whether or not it is paid. This also applies to A2 nationals and A8 nationals (including before 1 May 2011) who have established worker status.[137] You can still be a self-employed person if you stop work for a period of maternity leave, but intend to resume your self-employment.[138]

You may also be able to retain your worker or self-employed status if you have a pregnancy-related illness that prevents you from working (see p1457).[139]

The Court of Appeal has ruled that an agency worker who was not entitled to maternity leave but who was unable to work because she was in the late stages of pregnancy did *not* retain worker status.[140] However, permission to appeal to the

Supreme Court has been granted. See CPAG's *Welfare Rights Bulletin* for updates. If your circumstances are similar, seek advice.

Self-employed people

If you are an EEA national and a 'self-employed person', you have a right to reside and therefore satisfy the right to reside requirement for each of the relevant benefits. You are also exempt from the habitual residence test (see p1443).

If you are an A2 national (see p1501) and you are self-employed, you have the same rights as other EEA nationals; there are no additional restrictions. This was also true of A8 nationals who were self-employed between 1 May 2004 and 30 April 2011.

You are a self-employed person if you provide ervices in return for remuneration, but not under the direction of another person. The work you do must entail activities that are 'genuine and effective' rather than 'marginal and ancillary'. The same considerations apply when determining this as apply to workers (see p1456).[141]

You count as self-employed when you are establishing yourself in order to pursue your self-employed activity.[142] You must provide evidence of the steps you have taken or the ways in which you have set yourself up as self-employed. It will help if you have registered with HM Revenue and Customs as self-employed. However, if you have not registered this will not necessarily mean you cannot be accepted as self-employed.[143]

If you stop working, you do not necessarily cease to be self-employed. You may be in a temporary lull and it is accepted that you can continue to be self-employed during such times. However, it will depend on your particular circumstances and the evidence you provide. The amount of work you have coming in will be one factor, but other relevant factors include any steps you are taking to develop your business or find new work, marketing and business administration. Account must also be taken of your motives and intentions.[144] You continue to be self-employed if you take a period of maternity leave, but intend to return to work afterwards.[145]

If you have ceased to be self-employed, you may be able to retain your self-employed status in certain circumstances (see below). If you have ceased to be self-employed because of your pregnancy, see p1459.

Retaining self-employed status

If you have established self-employed status, you can retain it when you have stopped working if you are temporarily unable to work as the result of an illness or accident.[146] The same considerations apply as for those retaining worker status when temporarily unable to work (see p1457), except that there are no restrictions on retaining your self-employed status if you are an A2 national (or an A8 national before 1 May 2011).

If you have ceased self-employment because of pregnancy, you may be able to retain your self-employed status (see p1459).

You do not retain self-employed status if you are involuntarily unemployed and registered as a jobseeker or if you are doing vocational training.[147] This may be challenged in the future. See CPAG's *Welfare Rights Bulletin* for updates.

Before arguing that you have retained your self-employed status, check whether you could still count as self-employed. If this applies, the question of whether you retain that status does not arise.

Remember that even if you cannot retain your status as a self-employed person, unless you are an A2 national subject to worker authorisation, you may have a right to reside as a jobseeker and be able to get JSA, child benefit and child tax credit on that basis (see p1456).

Self-sufficient people

You have a right of residence as a self-sufficient person if you have:[148]

- sufficient resources for yourself, and any family members who do not have an independent right to reside, so that you will not become an unreasonable burden on the social assistance system of the UK; *and*
- comprehensive sickness insurance.

If you did count as self-sufficient under the above rules and you have ceased to do so, you may still be treated as satisfying the right to reside test. This will depend on whether or not your benefit claim is regarded as an unreasonable burden on the social assistance system of the UK. If your need to claim benefits is likely only to exist for a short time, it may not amount to an unreasonable burden.[149] If you are in this situation, seek specialist advice.

'Sufficient resources'

The UK government cannot set a fixed amount that will be regarded as 'sufficient resources' and must take account of your personal situation.[150] You will have 'sufficient resources' if your resources:[151]

- exceed the maximum level you (and your family) can have to be eligible for 'social assistance' (see below); *or*
- do not exceed that level, but the decison maker considers that you still have sufficient resources taking into account your (and your family's) personal situation.[152]

The 'maximum level' is the equivalent of your means-tested benefit applicable amount, including any premiums. Your resources also include your accommodation, so if your resources are more than your applicable amount plus your rent, you should be self-sufficient. You may also be self-sufficient if your resources are more than your applicable amount and you are provided with free and stable accommodation by friends or family.[153]

The source of the resources does not matter.[154]

Comprehensive sickness insurance

The requirement to have comprehensive sickness insurance cover is satisfied if you have private health insurance.[155] It may also be satisfied if you are covered by EU Regulation 883/2004 or 1408/71 (see p1503) and the UK is not the 'competent state' for the purposes of those Regulations (see p1508 for what this means). The state which is the competent state is required to reimburse the UK for any NHS costs you incur while in the UK.[156]

If you did count as self-sufficient under the above rules and you have ceased to do so, you may still be treated as satisfying the right to reside test. This will depend on whether or not your benefit claim is regarded as an unreasonable burden on the social assistance system of the UK. If your need to claim benefits is likely only to exist for a short time, it may not amount to an unreasonable burden.[157] If you are in this situation, seek specialist advice.

Students

You have a right to reside as a student if you are an EEA national and you:[158]

- are enrolled as a student in a government-accredited college;
- provide an assurance at the start of your studies that you have sufficient resources for yourself and your family members not to become a burden on the UK social assistance system during your period of residence (see p1461);
- have comprehensive sickness insurance (see above).

People with a permanent right of residence

You have a permanent right of residence if you have 'resided legally' (see below) in the UK for a 'continuous period of five years' (see below).[159] This is a new right that has existed since 30 April 2006. Once you have this permanent right of residence, you do not need to satisfy any other conditions – eg, you do not need to also be a worker or other qualified person.

What counts as 'resided legally'

You have 'resided legally' in any period during which you had a right of residence as a:

- worker (including if you retain your worker status);
- self-employed person (including if you retain your self-employed status);
- self-sufficient person;
- student;
- family member of any of the above.

If you have a continuous period of five years' residence in one or more of these groups, you will have a right of permanent residence under both Directive 2004/38 and the EEA Regulations. However, if you do not and need to rely on periods when you were not in one of these groups, the specific provisions under Directive 2004/38 and the EEA Regulations are relevant.

Under the EEA Regulations, you acquire the right to reside permanently in the UK if you have 'resided in accordance with these Regulations for a continuous period of five years'.[160] Residence in accordance with the previous EEA Regulations 2000 also counts.[161] The significant difference with these earlier Regulations was that they did not provide residence rights for jobseekers and therefore periods of residence as a jobseeker can only be used towards your five years from 30 April 2006.

Directive 2004/38 requires that you have 'resided legally' for a continuous period of five years. This means that you either have a residence right provided under the Directive or under any of the earlier EU legislation which the Directive replaced.[162] This covers all the five groups listed on p1462. Caselaw has held that it does not cover other residence rights not provided under the Directive, such as the right to reside as the primary carer of a worker's child in education.[163] However, this may change as further cases on this question are pending.[164] See CPAG's *Welfare Rights Bulletin* for updates and seek specialist advice if this affects you.

You are not counted as having 'resided legally' during periods when your right of residence was only in accordance with UK law – eg, a period during which you have leave to remain under the UK Immigration Rules.[165]

If you are an A8 or A2 national, you count as having 'resided legally' during periods before your state joined the EU if, during these periods, you would have fallen into one of the five groups above were it not for the fact that you were not an EU national.[166] Once your state joined the EU, you count as having resided legally during any period in which you were in one of the goups above. See p1451 for the additional restrictions for A8 and A2 nationals.[167]

Family members

If you are the family member (see p1465) of a person with a permanent right of residence, you have a right to reside for as long as you remain a family member.[168] After five years of being the family member of an EEA national with a permanent right of residence, you acquire a permanent right of residence yourself. Alternatively, you can add periods as a family member of a person with a permanent right of residence to other periods of residence in accordance with the EEA Regulations (see p1454) to make up your five years and so acquire a permanent right of residence.[169]

Continuous five years

To obtain the permanent right of residence, you must reside legally for a continuous period of five years.

Your continuity of residence is not affected by temporary absences from the UK:[170]

- not exceeding a total of six months a year; *or*

- one absence of up to 12 consecutive months for important reasons – eg, pregnancy and childbirth, serious illness, study or vocational training, or a posting abroad; *or*
- compulsory military service.

Although these periods relate to absences from the UK, it is arguable that temporary gaps between periods of legal residence when you remain in the UK should be treated in the same way.[171] If you have one or more of these temporary absences from the UK, you can link the periods of legal residence on either side when calculating your five continuous years and should also be able to count the time spent abroad.[172]

When you lose permanent residence

Once acquired, you only lose your permanent right of residence if you are absent from the UK for more than two consecutive years.[173] If you resided legally in the UK for a five-year period before 30 April 2006, you acquired a permanent right of residence on 30 April 2006 if before this date you:

- were absent from the UK for less than two years;[174] *or*
- remained in the UK but you were not 'residing legally' for a period of less than two years.[175]

The law is currently unclear about the consequences if these periods were more than two years. Seek specialist advice if this affects you.

Retired and permanently incapacitated workers and self-employed people

If you are a worker or self-employed person and either retired or permanently incapacitated, you can acquire a permanent right of residence before five years in the following circumstances. If you are covered, you are exempt from the habitual residence test (see p1443).

You have a permanent right to reside if you:[176]

- are a worker or self-employed person and you:
  - have reached retirement age or taken early retirement and you either:
    - have a spouse or civil partner who is a UK national (or who lost that nationality by marrying you); *or*
    - have worked in the UK for the preceding year and resided in the UK continuously for more than three years; *or*
  - stopped working in the UK because of a permanent incapacity; *and*
    - you have a spouse or civil partner who is a UK national (or who lost that nationality by marrying you); *or*
    - you have resided in the UK continuously for more than two years; *or*
    - the incapacity was because of an accident at work or occupational disease that resulted in benefit entitlement; *or*

- have worked and resided in the UK continuously for three years and then work in another member state and return to the UK at least once a week; *or*
- are the family member of, and live with, a worker or self-employed person in any of the above groups; *or*
- are the family member of a worker or self-employed person who died while still working and who had not acquired a permanent right of residence under one of the above groups; *and*
  - the worker or self-employed person had lived in the UK for two years; *or*
  - the death resulted from an accident at work or an occupational disease; *or*
  - you lost your UK nationality as a result of marrying the worker or self-employed person.

For the purposes of calculating your period of employment in order to get a permanent right of residence in less than five years, periods when you were involuntarily unemployed (but only for the first month of employment before 1 May 2011 if you are an A8 national whose work had to be registered) or not working because of illness or accident are counted as periods of employment.[177]

Family members of European Economic Area nationals

You have a right to reside if you are a family member of an EEA national who has a right to reside. This applies to all family members, whether or not you are an EEA national youself. You have a right to reside for as long as the EEA national has a right to reside and for as long as you remain her/his family member.

If your *only* right to reside is as the family member of an EEA national who has a right to reside on the basis of being in the UK for less than three months, this will not enable you to satisfy the right to reside requirement for IS, income-related ESA, income-based JSA, PC, HB and CTB (see p1448).

If your *only* right to reside is as the family member of an EEA national who has a right to reside as a jobseeker, this will not enable you to satisfy the right to reside requirement for IS, income-related ESA, PC, HB and CTB (see p1447).

Family member[178]

You are a family member if you are the:
- spouse or civil partner of an EEA national;
- child (or grandchild or great-grandchild) of an EEA national, or her/his spouse/civil partner and you are under 21;
- child (or grandchild or great-grandchild) of an EEA national, or her/his spouse/civil partner and you are her/his dependant;
- parent (or grandparent or great-grandparent) of an EEA national or her/his spouse/civil partner and you are her/his dependant.

If your right to reside depends on your counting as a family member of a person who has a right to reside her/himself, but you are not able to prove what that person is doing (eg, you have no evidence that your spouse from whom you have separated is a worker), you should ask the benefit authority to establish these facts – eg, by finding out whether your spouse is working by looking at the database of NI contributions. If it does not do so and you appeal, you can argue that the benefit authority has not shown that you do not have a right to reside.[179]

Extended family members

If you do not count as a family member under the above rules but you have another relative in the UK who is an EEA national, you may count as her/his 'extended family member'. You are treated as a 'family member' if you are an 'extended family member' and you have been issued with an EEA family permit, a registration certificate or a residence card (see p1471). If you do not have this documentation, you are not treated as a family member.[180]

Extended family member[181]

You are an extended family member if you are the:

- partner of an EEA national and you are in a durable relationship with her/him;
- relative of an EEA national and would satisfy the requirements of the Immigration Rules for indefinite leave as her/his dependent relative if s/he were present and settled in the UK;
- relative of an EEA national or her/his spouse/civil partner and:
  - you have serious health problems that require her/his care; *or*
  - you previously lived with or were dependent on the EEA national in a country other than the UK and you are accompanying her/him to the UK *or* wish to join her/him in the UK, *or* have joined her/him in the UK and are dependent on her/him or a member of her/his household.

You remain a spouse or civil partner even if you are separated. You only cease to be a spouse or civil partner on divorce or termination of the civil partnership.[182]

'Dependence' is not defined in the legislation, but caselaw has established a number of principles.[183]

- To be dependent, you must receive support from the other person.
- It is irrelevant if there are alternative sources of support available.
- The support must be 'material', although not necessarily financial, and must contribute towards your basic necessities.

If you only became dependent on the EEA national in the UK, this will not prevent you from being classed as a family member, unless you are an extended family member, in which case you will need to have already been dependent in the country from where you have come.[184]

Family members of UK nationals

UK nationals do not automatically give residence rights to their family members.

If you are a family member of a UK national, **the EEA Regulations** treats the UK national as an EEA national if:[185]

- s/he is working or self-employed in another EEA state (or was before returning to the UK); *and*
- you are her/his spouse/civil partner. **The EEA Regulations** state that you must have lived together in the other EEA state. However, the ECJ has held that you can have residence rights as a family member whether you became a family member before or after entering the member state.[186] Seek specialist advice if this applies to you.

In these circumstances, the EEA Regulations give you a right to reside if the UK national, being treated as an EEA national, has a right to reside under the Regulations – ie, s/he is within her/his first three months of residence, s/he is a qualified person or s/he has a permanent right of residence. However, the ECJ found that it was not necessary for someone who had been a worker in another EEA state and then returned to her/his own state to carry out an economic activity in order for her/his family member to have a right of residence.[187] Seek specialist advice if this applies to you.

Additionally, if you are the primary carer of a UK national who is dependent on you, or if you are the family member of a UK national (it is likely that s/he will also need to be dependent on you), you have a right to reside if this is necessary for the UK national to enjoy her/his rights as an EU citizen.[188]

If you are the family member of someone who has dual nationality of the UK and another EEA state, you should have rights under the **EEA Regulations** in the same way as family members of other EEA nationals.[189] This should apply even if the dual national has not moved between EEA states.[190] The dual national will not, however, have rights under **EU Directive 2004/38** if s/he has lived all her/his life in the UK and you will not be able to derive any rights from her/him under that Directive.[191]

Family members who retain their right to reside

In general, if you are the family member of an EEA national who has a right to reside, you will lose your right to reside if s/he ceases to be your family member or to have a right to reside. However, there are some exceptions which mean you can retain your right to reside if the EEA national dies or leaves the UK, or if your marriage or civil partnership ends. These rights are provided for in EU Directive

2004/38, but they are not exactly reproduced in the EEA Regulations. The benefit authorities accept the rights set out in the EEA Regulations (the list below), but do not always accept those in the Directive (the list on p1469). If you only have a right to reside under the Directive and are refused benefit or CTC, you should appeal and seek specialist advice.

You retain your right to reside under the EEA Regulations if you are a family member of a qualified person (see p1454), *and:*[192]

- the qualified person dies and you are:
  - not an EEA national, but if you were you would be a worker, or a self-employed or self-sufficient person (or you are the family member of such a non-EEA national) and you resided in the UK with a right to reside under the Regulations for at least a year immediately before s/he died; *or*
  - the child or grandchild of the qualified person (or her/his spouse or civil partner) and in education immediately before the death and you remain in education; *or*
  - a parent with custody of a child in education immediately before the death and who remains in education; *or*
- the qualified person leaves the UK and you are:
  - the child or grandchild of the qualified person (or her/his spouse or civil partner) and in education immediately before the death and you remain in education; *or*
  - a parent with custody of a child in education immediately before the death and who remains in education; *or*
- your marriage or civil partnership to the qualified person is terminated and you are not an EEA national, but if you were you would be a worker, or a self-employed or self-sufficient person (or you are the family member of such a non-EEA national) and you were residing in the UK with a right to reside under the Regulations at the date of the termination; *and*
  - the marriage/civil partnership had, prior to the termination, lasted for at least three years with you both residing in the UK for at least one of those years; *or*
  - you have custody of the qualified person's child; *or*
  - you have a right of access to the qualified person's child which a court has said must take place in the UK; *or*
  - your continued right of residence in the UK is warranted by particularly difficult circumstances, such as your (or another family member) being subject to domestic violence during the period of the marriage/civil partnership.

You have a right to reside on this basis for as long as the conditions apply to you,[193] until you can acquire a permanent right of residence (see p1462).[194]

It is arguable that you retain your right to reside under EU Directive 2004/38 if you are a family member of an EU national with a right to reside, *and*:

- the EU national dies and you:[195]
  - are an EU national; *or*
  - have lived in the UK as her/his family member for at least a year before her/his death and you are a non-EU national; *or*
- the EU national leaves the UK and you are:[196]
  - an EU national; *or*
  - the child or grandchild of the EU national and in education; *or*
  - the parent with custody of a child in education; *or*
- your marriage or civil partnership to the EU national is terminated and:[197]
  - you are an EU national; *or*
  - the marriage/civil partnership had, prior to the termination, lasted for at least three years with you both residing in the UK for at least one of those years; *or*
  - you have custody of the EU national's child; *or*
  - you have a right of access to the EU national's child, which a court has said must take place in the UK; *or*
  - your continued right of residence in the UK is warranted by particularly difficult circumstances, such as your being subject to domestic violence during the period of the marriage/civil partnership.

Before acquiring a permanent right to reside following your retaining your right to reside under the Directive, you must show that you are a worker, or a self-employed or self-sufficient person, or you are the family member of such a person.[198]

Note: you may have a right to reside if you are the family member of someone who has acquired a permanent right of residence either following five years' legal residence (see p1463) or of certain workers or self-employed people who have retired or become permanently incapacitated (see p1464).

Primary carers of children in education

You have a right to reside if you are the primary carer of a child receiving education if one of the parents of the child was an EEA 'worker'.[199] The child must have been in the UK while the parent was a worker in the UK, but it is not necessary for the child to have entered education while the parent was a worker.[200] This also applies if the worker was an A8 national working for an authorised employer, but for less than 12 months.[201] As the first month of work A8 nationals did was always for authorised employers, it should therefore apply to the child in education of any A8 national who has done some work. Similarly, it applies in the same way if the worker was an A2 national working in accordance with her/his worker authorisation document.

Your right to reside as a primary carer ends when the child reaches 18 unless s/he continues to need your care in order to be able to pursue and complete her/his education.[202] 'Education' does not include nursery education[203] or pre-school education since the rights arise when a child enters compulsory education at around the age of five.[204]

This right of residence is provided by Article 10 of EU Regulation 492/11 (before 16 June 2011, by Article 12 of EU Regulation 1612/68) rather than EU Directive 2004/38 or the EEA Regulations. This is relevant when determining whether periods when you have a right to reside on this basis count towards the five-year period of legal residence you need to acquire a right of permanent residency (see p1462). Under Article 10, a child of an EU national employed in a member state has the right to be educated in that member state and it has been accepted that the child therefore has a right to reside in order to complete her/his education. As s/he is a child, her/his primary carer also has a right to reside to enable the child to exercise this right.[205]

You should have a right to reside if you are the spouse of the primary carer of the child in education.[206]

Arguably, the primary carer of the child of a self-employed EEA national should have a right to reside in the same way as the primary carer of the child of an EEA worker and a reference has been made to the ECJ on this question.[207] Seek specialist advice if this affects you.

Primary carers and family members of UK nationals

You have a right to reside if you are either the primary carer of a UK national who is dependent on you, or a family member of a UK national (it is likely s/he will also need to be dependent on you) and, were you to be denied a right to reside, the UK national would be deprived of 'the genuine enjoyment of the substance of her/his rights as an EU national'.[208]

This should apply if you are a non-EU national and if you were denied the right to reside in the UK your dependent child who is a UK national would have to leave the territory of the EU. [209]

Periods of residence on this basis may not count towards the five years' legal residence required to acquire a right of permanent residence (see p1462) as this right of residence comes from Article 20 of the Treaty on the Functioning of the European Union, rather than EU Directive 2004/38 or the EEA Regulations. However, amendments to the EEA Regulations to incorporate these rights are expected, as well as further caselaw developments. See CPAG's *Welfare Rights Bulletin* for updates.

Other rights of residence under European Union law

The usual ways in which you may have a right of residence under EU law in the UK are set out on pp1450–70. If none of these categories apply to you, it may be possible to argue that you should still have a right of residence despite not meeting any of the specific conditions set out above. This only applies if you are an EU national, since your argument is that you have a right to reside directly under Article 21 of the Treaty on the Functioning of the European Union, which only applies to EU nationals.

Article 18 of this Treaty makes all EU nationals 'citizens' of the EU and Article 21 provides that all citizens have the right to reside anywhere in the EU. However, this right is subject to limitations and conditions that require you also to fulfil the conditions that would result in you having a right to reside – eg, as a qualified person (see p1454) or family member of a qualified person.

Nonetheless, in some cases, even if you do not satisfy these conditions, you may nonetheless be able to argue that you should have a right of residence under Article 21 in any event. The cases in which such an argument will be successful are limited.

The only examples of such cases so far have been the following.

- A French national was married to a Cameroonian, both of whom had been working. The Cameroonian developed bowel cancer and had to stop work. The French national had to stop work to look after him. The French national did not have a right of residence as a person retaining her worker status in this situation. The Cameroonian national's right of residence depended on the French national's right and so could not assist. It was decided that the French national, nonetheless, should have a right of residence in these circumstances.[210]
- A German national who had been a worker for several years was then self-sufficient, with the exception that he did not have comprehensive sickness insurance (see p1462). It was decided that, because his family lived in the UK and because he was not a burden on the UK 'social assistance system', he should have a right to reside, despite not meeting the full requirement to have comprehensive sickness insurance.[211]

Arguments that you have a right of residence despite not meeting the usual conditions are complex and you should seek specialist advice. You should always check whether you have a right of residence under one of the other routes first.

Residence documents

To have a right of residence as an 'extended family member' (see p1466) you must have a residence document. If you have some other right of residence, you can also obtain a residence document as detailed below. However, unless your right to reside is as an extended family member, it is not necessary to have a residence document in order to have a right of residence: you have a right of residence simply by being in one of the groups with a right to reside. Note that a residence document does not, in itself, give you a right to reside if, for instance, your right to reside has ended.[212]

You can be issued with the following residence documents.

- A **registration certificate** if you are an EEA national with a right of residence provided under the EEA Regulations.[213]

- A **residence card** if you are a non-EEA national and you have a right to reside as the family member of an EEA qualified person or an EEA national with a permanent right of residence.[214]
- A **document certifying permanent right of residence** if you are an EEA national with a permanent right of residence, or a **permanent residence card** if you are a non-EEA national with a permanent right of residence.[215]
- Before 30 April 2006, EEA nationals and their family members may have been issued with **residence permits**. These were valid for a five-year period. From 30 April 2006, these documents should be treated as if they were the equivalent type of document issued after that date – eg, one of the first three documents in the above bullet points.[216]
- **Family permits** are only issued for entry to the UK if you are a non-EEA family member of an EEA national and do not have any of the other residence documentation.

The time limits within which the above documents should be issued are different if you are applying on the basis that you are an extended family member. In this case, the rules do not specify a period of time within which the documents should be issued.

Note that applications for all these residence documents can be made free of charge. Forms and further information are available on the UK Border Agency website.

Notes

2. **The different residence and presence tests**
   1 R(IS) 6/96 (para 19); R(P) 2/67
   2 R(M)1/85
   3 *R v Barnet London Borough Council ex parte Shah* [1983] 2 AC 309
   4 SF Dir 16

3. **Residence and presence rules for individual benefits**
   5 **IS** s124(1) SSCBA 1992
   JSA s1(2)(i) JSA 1995
   ESA s1(3)(d) WRA 2007
   PC s1(2)(a) SPCA 2002
   6 **IS** Regs 21-21AA IS Regs
   JSA Regs 85-85A JSA Regs
   ESA Regs 69-70 ESA Regs
   PC Reg 2 SPC Regs
   7 **HB** Reg 10 HB Regs; reg 10 HB(SPC) Regs
   CTB Reg 7 CTB Regs; reg 7 CTB(SPC) Regs
   8 s130(1)(a) SSCBA 1992
   9 Reg 7 HB Regs; reg 7 HB(SPC) Regs
   10 s131(3)(a) SSCBA 1992
   11 Reg 8 CTB Regs; reg 8 CTB(SPC) Regs

12 **IS** Reg 16 IS Regs
JSA Reg 78 JSA Regs
ESA Reg 156 ESA Regs
PC Reg 5 SPC Regs
HB Reg 21 HB Regs; reg 21 HB(SPC) Regs
13 CIS/508/1992; CIS/13805/1996
14 CIS/484/1993
15 **IS** Reg 16 IS Regs
JSA Reg 78 JSA regs
ESA Reg 156 ESA Regs
PC Reg 5 SPC Regs
HB Reg 21 HB Regs; reg 21 HB(SPC) Regs
16 **AA** Reg 2 SS(AA) Regs
DLA Reg 2 SS(DLA) Regs
CA Reg 9 SS(ICA) Regs
ESA Reg 11 ESA Regs
IB Reg 16 SS(IB) Regs
SDA Reg 3 SS(SDA) Regs
17 **ESA** Reg 11(4) ESA Regs
IB Reg 16(6) SS(IB) Regs
SDA Reg 3(3) SS(SDA) Regs
18 **AA** Reg 2(3) SS(AA) Regs
DLA Reg 2(4) SS(DLA) Regs
19 *Commission of the European Communities v the European Parliament & the Council of the European Union,* C-299/05 [2007] ECR I-08695
20 *Stewart v SSWP,* C-503/09 [2011] ECR, not yet reported
21 Art 70 EU Reg 883/04; Art 10a EU Reg 1408/71; *Robin Swaddling v Adjudication Officer,* C-90/97 [1999] ECR I-01075
22 s113 SSCBA 1992; reg 4(1) and (2B) SSB(PA) Regs
23 para 073081 DMG, Example 2
24 Arts 5 and 42 EU Reg 883/04; Art 65 EU Reg 1408/71
25 s146 SSCBA 1992
26 Reg 23 CB Regs
27 Regs 23, 30 and 31 CB Regs
28 ss1(3)(d)and 18(4)(a) WRA 2007
29 Reg 9 GA(Gen) Regs
30 s94(5) SSCBA 1992
31 Reg 14 SS(IIPD) Regs
32 Reg 10C(5) and (6) SSB(PA) Regs
33 Reg 2 SS(II)(AB) Regs 1975; SS(II)(MB) Regs
34 Regs 3, 4, 6 and 8 SS(II)(MB) Regs; regs 3 and 6 SS(II)(AB) Regs
35 Art 5 EU Reg 883/04; Art 56 EU Reg 1408/71
36 Art 38 EU Reg 883/04; Art 57 EU Reg 1408/71
37 s1(2)(i) JSA 1995
38 Art 64 EU Reg 883/04; Art 69 EU Reg 1408/71
39 Art 64(3) EU Reg 883/04
40 s113(1) SSCBA 1992
41 s113 SSCBA 1992; reg 4(1) SSB(PA) Regs
42 SF Dir 16
43 SF Dirs 23(1) and 29
44 Reg 7(5) SFM&FE Regs
45 Reg 7(9) and (10) SFM&FE Regs
46 *John O'Flynn v Adjudication Officer,* C-237/94 [1996] ECR I-02617 (R(IS)4/98)
47 s3(3) TCA 2002; reg 3(1) and (5) TC(R) Regs
48 s3(3)TCA 2002; reg 3(1) TC(R) Regs
49 Reg 3 TC(R) Regs

4. **Habitual residence**

50 **IS** Regs 21 and 21AA IS Regs
JSA Regs 85 and 85A JSA Regs
ESA Regs 69 and 70 ESA Regs
PC Reg 2 SPC Regs
HB Reg 10 HB Regs; reg 10 HB(SPC) Regs
CTB Reg 7 CTB Regs; reg 7 CTB(SPC) Regs
51 SF Dir 16
52 **IS** Regs 21 and 21AA and Sch 7 para 17 IS Regs
JSA Regs 85 and 85A and Sch 5 para 14 JSA Regs
ESA Regs 69 and 70 and Sch 5 para 11 ESA Regs
53 Reg 10(1) HB Regs; reg 10(1) HB(SPC) Regs
54 Reg 7 CTB Regs; reg 7 CTB(SPC) Regs; s131(3)(b) SSCBA 1992
55 Reg 2 SPC Regs
56 **IS** Reg 21AA(4) IS Regs
JSA Reg 85A(4) JSA Regs
ESA Reg 70(4) ESA Regs
PC Reg 2(4) SPC Regs
HB Reg 10(3B) HB Regs; reg 10(4A) HB(SPC) Regs
CTB Reg 7(4A) CTB Regs; reg 7(4A) CTB(SPC) Regs
57 R(IS) 6/96, paras 17 and 20; CIS/13498/96, para 17
58 CIS/15927/1996
59 *R v Barnet London Borough Council ex parte Shah* [1983] 2 AC 309, at 344; CIS/13498/1996
60 R(IS) 2/00; CIS/4474/2003
61 *Nessa v Chief Adjudication Officer* [1999] UKHL 41
62 CIS/4474/2003
63 CIS/1972/2003
64 CIS 1304/97; CJSA 5394/98
65 CIS/1304/1997; CJSA/5394/1998

66 Art 70 EU Reg 883/04; Art 10a EU Reg 1408/71; *Robin Swaddling v Adjudication Officer*, C-90/97 [1999] ECR I-01075
67 CIS/12703/1996
68 R(IS) 2/00; CIS/11481/1995
69 R(IS) 6/96

5. **Right to reside**
70 SF Dir 16
71 Reg 6 SS(HR)A Regs; reg 11 SS(PA)A Regs
72 Reg 70(4)(l) ESA Regs
73 **IS** Reg 21AA(2) and (3) IS Regs
ESA Reg 70(2) and (3) ESA Regs
PC Reg 2(2) and (3) SPC Regs
HB Reg 10(3) and (3A) HB Regs; reg 10(3) and (4) HB(SPC) Regs
CTB Reg 7(3) and (4) CTB Regs; reg 7(3) and (4) CTB(SPC) Regs
74 Reg 85A(2) and (3) JSA Regs
75 *Vatsouras* (C-22/08) *and Koupatantze* (C-23/08) *v Arbeitsgemeinschaft (ARGE) Nürnberg 900* [2009] ECR I-04585
76 **CB** Reg 23(4) CB Regs
HPG Reg 4 HPG(EA) Regs
TC Reg 3(5) TC(R) Regs
77 Reg 2(1) EEA Regs
78 **Swiss nationals**: *Agreement between the European Community and its Member States, of the one part, and the Swiss Confederation, of the other, on the Free Movement of Persons*, 21 June 1999, Cm5639
Non-EU/EEA nationals: *Agreement on the European Economic Area*, 2 May 1992 OJ No. L1, 3 January 1994, p3
79 Art 3(1) EU Dir 2004/38
80 Reg 2(1) EEA Regs
81 *Minister voor Vreemdelingenzaken en Integratie v Eind*, C-291/05 [2007] ECR I-10719
82 *Zambrano*, C-34/09 [2011] ECR, not yet reported
83 *McCarthy v SSHD*, C-434/09 [2011] ECR, not yet reported
84 *AA v SSWP* [2009] UKUT 249 (AAC); *HG v SSWP (SPC)* [2011] UKUT 382 (AAC)
85 *MAH (dual nationality – permanent residence) Canada* [2010] UKUT 445 (IAC)
86 Reg 7 A(IWR) Regs
87 Reg 9 A(IWA) Regs
88 Reg 5 A(IWR) Regs; reg 6 A(IWA) Regs
89 Reg 5(4) A(IWR) Regs
90 Reg 5(4) A(IWR) Regs; reg 7A(4) EEA Regs
91 CIS/1042/2008; *SSWP v JB* [2011] UKUT 96 (AAC)
92 Reg 7 A(IWR) Regs
93 *SSWP v ZA* [2009] UKUT 294 (AAC); *MS v SSWP* [2011] UKUT 452 (AAC) (permission granted to appeal)
94 Reg 2 A(IWR) Regs
95 Reg 2 A(IWA) Regs
96 Reg 46 A(IWA) Regs
99 *Miskovic and Another v SSWP* [2011] EWCA Civ 16
100 *BS v SSWP* [2009] UKUT 16 (AAC)
97 Reg 2(7) A(IWR) Regs; reg 2(12) A(IWA) Regs
101 Reg 14(1) EEA Regs
102 Arts 7 and 14 EU Dir 2004/38
103 Reg 6 EEA Regs
104 *SSWP v JB (JSA)* [2011] UKUT 96 (AAC)
105 Reg 13(1) EEA Regs; Art 6(1) EU Dir 2004/38
106 Reg 13(3)(b); Art 14(1) EU Dir 2004/38
107 Reg 13(2) EEA Regs; Art 6(2) EU Dir 2004/38
108 Reg 6(4) EEA Regs; Art 45 TFEU; Arts 14 and 24 EU Dir 2004/38
109 R(IS) 8/08
110 *The Queen v Immigration Appeal Tribunal, ex parte Gustaff Desiderius Antonissen*, C-292/89 [1991] ECR I-00745
111 Regs 6(1) and 14 EEA Regs; Arts 7(1) and 14 EU Dir 2004/38
112 *Deborah Lawrie-Blum v Land Baden-Württemberg*, 66/86 [1986] ECR 02121
113 *Barry v London Borough of Southwark* [2008] EWCA Civ 1440
114 *Ingrid Rinner-Kühn v FWW Spezial-Gebäudereinigung GmbH & Co. KG*, 171/88 [1989] ECR 02743
115 R(IS) 12/98
116 *Hava Genc v Land Berlin*, C-14/09 [2010] ECR I-00931
117 *Udo Steymann v Staatssecretaris van Justitie*, 196/87 [1988] ECR 06159
118 CIS/1837/2006; CIS/868/2008
119 *I Bettray v Staatssecretaris van Justitie*, 344/87 [1989] ECR 01621; *Hava Genc v Land Berlin*, C-14/09 [2010] ECR I-00931
120 CIS/1502/2007
121 CIS/4237/2007
122 *BS v SSWP* [2009] UKUT 16 (AAC)
123 Art 7(3) EU Dir 2004/38; reg 6(2) EEA Regs
124 CH/3314/2005, para 11
125 *SSWP v Elmi* [2011] EWCA Civ 1403
126 Art 7(3)(b) EU Dir 2004/38; reg 6(2)(b)(i) EEA Regs
127 Art 7(3)(c) EU Dir 2004/38; reg 6(2)(b)(ii) EEA Regs
128 Reg 6(2)(b)(iii) EEA Regs

129 CIS/3890/2005
130 CIS/4304/2007
131 CIS/3182/2005
132 *SSWP v EM* [2009] UKUT 146 (AAC)
133 CIS/4304/2007; *SSWP v IR* [2009] UKUT 11 (AAC)
134 CIS/1934/2006
135 *SSWP v IR* [2009] UKUT 11 (AAC)
136 Reg 5(4) A(IWR) Regs; reg 7A(4) EEA Regs
137 CIS/4237/2007
138 CIS/1042/2008
139 CIS/731/2007
140 *JS v SSWP* [2011] EWCA Civ 806
141 *Aldona Malgorzata Jany and Others v Staatssecretaris van Justitie*, C-268/99 [2001] ECR I-08615
142 Reg 4(1)(b) EEA Regs; R(IS) 6/00
143 *TG v SSWP* [2009] UKUT 58 (AAC)
144 *SSWP v JS (IS)* [2010] UKUT 240 (AAC)
145 CIS/1042/2008
146 Art 7(3) EU Dir 2004/38; reg 6(3) EEA Regs
147 *Tilianu v SSWP* [2010] EWCA Civ 1397
148 Art 7(1) EU Dir 2004/38; regs 4(1)(c), 6(1) and 14(1) EEA Regs
149 *SG v Tameside Metropolitan Borough Council* (HB) [2010] UKUT 243 (AAC)
150 Art 8(4) EU Dir 2004/38
151 Reg 4(4) EEA Regs
152 With effect from 2 June 2011
153 *SG v Tameside Metropolitan Borough Council* (HB) [2010] UKUT 243 (AAC)
154 *Commission of the European Communities v Kingdom Belgium*, C-408/03 [2006] ECR I-02647; *Kunqian Catherine Zhu, Man Lavette Chen v Secretary of State for the Home Department*, C-200/02 [2004] ECR I-09925
155 *W(China) and Another v SSHD* [2006] EWCA Civ 1494
156 *SG v Tameside Metropolitan Borough Council (HB)* [2010] UKUT 243 (AAC)
157 *SG v Tameside Metropolitan Borough Council (HB)* [2010] UKUT 243 (AAC)
158 Art 7(1) EU Dir 2004/38; regs 4(1)(d), 6(1) and 14(1) EEA Regs
159 Art 16 EU Dir 2004/38; reg 15 EEA Regs
160 Regs 7A(5) and 15(1) EEA Regs
161 Sch 4 para 6 EEA Regs
162 *SSWP v Taous Lassal*, C-162/09 [2010] ECR, not yet reported
163 *Oakafor and others v SSHD* [2011] EWCA Civ 499
164 *Alarape and Tijani v SSHD* [2011] UKUT 413 (IAC) be heard in the ECJ as Case C-529/11
165 *Ziolkowski* (C-425/10) *and Szeja* (C-425/10) *v Land Berlin* [2011] ECR, not yet reported
166 *Ziolkowski* (C-425/10) *and Szeja* (C-425/10) *v Land Berlin* [2011] ECR, not yet reported
167 Reg 7A(5) EEA Regs
168 Reg 14(2) EEA Regs
169 Reg 15(1)(a) and (b) EEA Regs
170 Art 16(3) EU Dir 2004/38
171 Following *SSWP v Dias*, C-325/09 [2011] ECR, not yet reported
172 *Idezuna v SSHD* [2011] UKUT 474 (IAC), but see CIS/2258/2008 which held the opposite
173 Art 16(4) EU Dir 2004/38; reg 15(2) EEA Regs
174 *SSWP v Lassal*, C-162/09 [2011] ECR, not yet reported
175 *SSWP v Dias*, C-325-09 [2011] ECR, not yet reported
176 Regs 5 and 15 EEA Regs; Art 17 EU Dir 2004/38
177 Regs 5(7) and 7A(3) EEA Regs
178 Art 2(2) EU Dir 2004/38; reg 7(1) EEA Regs
179 *Kerr v DSDNI* [2004] UKHL 23, paras 62-65
180 CPC/3588/2006; *SS v SSWP (ESA)* [2010] UKUT 8 (AAC)
181 Regs 7(3) and 8 EEA Regs. The same groups are covered in Art 3 EU Dir 2004/38, but the term is not used.
182 *Aissatou Diatta v Land Berlin*, 267/83 [1985] ECR 00567
183 CIS/2100/2007which considers the findings of *Centre Public d'Aide Sociale de Courcelles v Lebon*, 316/85 [1987] ECR 02811, *Kunqian Catherine Zhu and Man Lavette Chen v SSHD*, C-200/02 [2004] ECR I-09925 and *Yunying Jia v Migrationsverket*, C-1/05 [2007] ECR I-00001
184 *Pedro v SSWP* [2009] EWCA Civ 1358; *Yunying Jia v Migrationsverket*, C-1/05 [2007] ECR I-00001
185 Reg 9 EEA Regs
186 *Blaise Baheten Metock and Others v Minister for Justice, Equality and Law Reform*, C-127/08 [2008] ECR I-06241
187 *Minister voor Vreemdelingenzaken en Integratie v Eind*, C-291/05 [2007] ECR I-10719
188 *Ruiz Zambrano*, C-34/09 [2011] ECR, not yet reported; *Dereci*, C-256/11 [2011] ECR, not yet reported
189 *AA v SSWP* [2009] UKUT 249 (AAC); *HG v SSWP (SPC)* [2011] UKUT 382 (AAC)

190 *MAH (dual nationality – permanent residence) Canada* [2010] UKUT 445 (IAC)
191 *McCarthy v SSHD*, C-434-09 [2011] ECR, not yet reported
192 Reg 10 EEA Regs
193 Reg 14(3) EEA Regs
194 Reg 10(8) EEA Regs
195 Art 12 EU Dir 2004/38
196 Art 12 EU Dir 2004/38
197 Art 13 EU Dir 2004/38
198 Arts 12(2) and 13(1) EU Dir 2004/38
199 *London Borough of Harrow v Nimco Hassan Ibrahim and SSHD*, C-310/08 [2010] ECR I-01065; *Maria Teixeira v London Borough of Lambeth and SSHD*, C-480/08 [2010] ECR I-01107
200 *Maria Teixeira v London Borough of Lambeth and SSHD*, C-480/08 [2010] ECR I-01107, para 74
201 *SSWP v JS (IS)* [2010] UKUT 347 (AAC)
202 *Maria Teixeira v London Borough of Lambeth and SSHD*, C-480/08 [2010] ECR I-01107, para 87; see also *Alarpe and Tijani v SSHD and AIRE Centre* [2011] UKUT 413 (IAC) for questions referred to the ECJ clarifying the extent of relationship required with the adult child.
203 CIS/3960/2007
204 *SSWP v IM (IS)* [2011] UKUT 231 AAC
205 *GBC Echternach and A Moritz v Minister van Onderwijs en Wetenschappen*, joined cases 389/87 and 390/87 [1989] ECR 00723; *Baumbast and R v Secretary of State for the Home Department*, C-413/99 [2002] ECR I-07091; *London Borough of Harrow v Nimco Hassan Ibrahim and SSHD*, C-310/08 [2010] ECR I-01065; *Maria Teixeira v London Borough of Lambeth and SSHD*, C-480/08 [2010] ECR I-01107
206 *MA v DSD (JSA)* [2011] NICom 205
207 *SSWP v MP (IS)* [2011] UKUT 109 (AAC); *Punakova*, C-148/11 (pending) and joined case *SSWP v LC (IS)* [2011] UKUT 108 (AAC); *Czop* C-147/11 (pending)
208 *Zambrano*, C-34/09 [2011] ECR, not yet reported; *Dereci and Others*, C-256/11 [2011] ECR, not yet reported
209 *SSWP v RR (IS)* [2011] UKUT 451 (AAC)
210 R(IS) 4/09
211 *Baumbast and R v SSHD*, C-413/99 [2002] ECR I-07091
212 *SSWP v Dias*, C-325/09 [2011] ECR, not yet reported; *EM and KN v SSWP* [2009] UKUT 44 (AAC)
213 Reg 16 EEA Regs
214 Reg 17 EEA Regs
215 Reg 18 EEA Regs
216 Reg 31(2) and Sch 4 para 2 EEA Regs

Chapter 63

Going abroad

This chapter covers:

This chapter describes the way your entitlement to benefits and tax credits is affected if you go abroad. It covers the way European Union co-ordination rules can help you take individual UK benefits and tax credits with you when you go to another European Economic Area state. For an overview of the way these rules operate, see Chapter 64. This chapter does not cover the residence and presence conditions that affect your entitlement while you are in the UK (see Chapter 62) nor the way your immigration status can affect your entitlement to benefits and tax credits (see Chapter 61).

Key facts

- Most benefits and tax credits are affected if you, your partner or child go abroad.
- In certain circumstances, you can continue to receive benefit for a set number of weeks while you are away for a temporary period.
- You may be entitled to receive UK benefits for a longer (or indefinite) period if you go to another European Economic Area state.

Future changes: April 2013 and after

Major changes are taking place that affect the benefits and tax credits system (see Chapter 2).

- From April 2013, personal independence payment (PIP) will replace disability living allowance for adults and, from October 2013, universal credit (UC) will replace most means-tested benefits.
- It will be a condition of entitlement for UC and PIP that you are present in Great Britain. At the time of writing, it is not yet known when you might be able to be paid either benefit when abroad.

See CPAG's *Welfare Rights Bulletin* for updates.

1. Introduction

Most benefits and tax credits are affected if you, or your partner or child, go abroad. The rules vary between different benefits and tax credits. Some can always be paid abroad, some can only be paid in certain circumstances and for limited periods, and some benefits have rules affecting the amount that can be paid if you are abroad.

Your entitlement while you are abroad depends on:

- the benefit or tax credit you are claiming (see p1480);
- the reason why you are going abroad;
- whether your absence is temporary or permanent;
- the length of time you are going abroad for;
- the country you are going to;
- whether you are covered by the European Union (EU) co-ordination rules;
- whether you are covered by a reciprocal agreement.

Which rules apply

The UK **benefit and tax credit legislation** contains rules about how your absence affects your entitlement (see below).

The **EU co-ordination rules** can be more generous if you are going to another European Economic Area (EEA) member state. In particular, they can enable you to 'export' certain benefits to other EEA member states and also to claim for family members who are in another EEA state while you remain in the UK. The ways that these EU co-ordination rules can help are covered in this chapter (see p1480). For an overview of the way these rules operate, see Chapter 64.

Reciprocal agreements exist between the UK and some other countries and can assist in similar ways to the EU co-ordination rules.

If you are covered by the EU co-ordination rules, these more generous provisions apply. If they do not apply, but you are covered by a reciprocal agreement, those provisions apply. If you are not covered by either the provisions of the EU co-ordination rules or a reciprocal agreement, you must rely on UK law.

2. UK law

Ordinary residence

In order to receive some benefits and tax credits, you are required to be ordinarily resident in Great Britain (see p1430). If, by going abroad, you cease to be ordinarily resident, your entitlement to the benefits and tax credits listed on p1430 will cease. However, if your absence abroad is temporary and you intend to return to the UK, your ordinary residence is not usually affected.[1] It is very rare that ceasing to be ordinarily resident is the reason why your entitlement ends when you go abroad. It is more likely that your entitlement will end simply because you are absent (see below). If you receive a decision that your entitlement to a benefit or tax credit has ended because you have ceased to be ordinarily resident, you should appeal and seek specialist advice.

Presence and absence

Most benefits require you to be present in Great Britain (or, for tax credits, the UK). There are rules that allow you to be treated as present and, therefore, continue to be entitled to the benefit or tax credit, during a temporary absence in specified circumstances. Some benefits also have a rule that you are disqualified from entitlement if you are absent from Great Britain. There are specified exemptions to this rule for each benefit.

'**Presence**' means being physically present in Great Britain and '**absence**' means 'not physically present' in Great Britain. If the DWP, HM Revenue and Customs or a local authority wants to disqualify you from benefit because you were absent from Great Britain, it must show you were absent throughout that day. This means that, on the day you leave Great Britain and the day you arrive in Great Britain, you count as present.

Temporary absence

The tax credit and child benefit regulations specify that you will be temporarily absent from the UK if, at the beginning of the period of absence, it is unlikely to exceed 52 weeks.[2]

For all other benefits, temporary absence is not defined. It is your responsibility to demonstrate that your absence is going to be temporary[3] and you should therefore provide full details of why you are going abroad, how long you intend to be abroad, and what you intend to do while you are abroad. However, note that while your intentions are relevant, they are not decisive.[4] Note also that the nature of an absence can change over time. If an absence is found to be temporary at the beginning of the period, it does not mean that it will always remain temporary. If your circumstances change while you are abroad (eg, you go abroad for one reason and decide to stay abroad for a different purpose), your absence may cease to be regarded as temporary.[5] There is no set period for a temporary absence. However, as a general rule, absences of more than 12 months are not temporary unless there are exceptional circumstances.[6] If the purpose of the trip abroad is obviously temporary (eg, for a holiday, to visit friends or relatives or for a particular course of medical treatment) and you buy a return ticket, your absence should be viewed as temporary.

3. European Union co-ordination rules and reciprocal agreements

European Union co-ordination rules

If you are a European Economic Area (EEA) national (see p1501) (including a UK national) or a family member of an EEA national and you are travelling to another EEA state, you may be able to benefit from the European Union (EU) co-ordination rules. EU legislation and caselaw apply directly in the UK and throughout the EEA. The EU law that is of most assistance if you or your family member are going to another EEA state is the social security co-ordination rules (see p1502). These can help you to be paid your benefits or tax credits when you go abroad for longer than would be the case under UK law. The EU co-ordination rules can also enable you to be paid benefit for a family member living in another EEA state. See p1480 for information on individual benefits and tax credits and Chapter 64 for further information.

Reciprocal agreements

The UK has agreements with several EEA and non-EEA countries. For a list of these and further information, see p1429.

4. Rules for individual benefits and tax credits

Attendance allowance and disability living allowance

As long as you remain 'ordinarily resident' (see p1478) in Great Britain, you are treated as present and therefore can continue to receive attendance allowance (AA) or disability living allowance (DLA) during an absence from Great Britain if:[7]

- the absence is, and was when it began, for a temporary purpose and does not exceed 26 weeks; *or*
- the absence is temporary and for the specific purpose of being treated for an illness or disability that began before you left Great Britain, and the DWP has agreed you should be treated as present; *or*
- you are abroad as a serving member of the armed forces, or you are living with your spouse, civil partner, son, daughter, stepson, stepdaughter, father, father-in-law, stepfather, mother, mother-in-law or stepmother who is a serving member of the armed forces;
- you are abroad as an airman or airwoman or mariner or continental shelf worker.

European Union co-ordination rules

If the co-ordination rules apply to you (see p1503), you may be able to take your AA and DLA (and carer's allowance – CA) with you, without any time limit, if you go to live or stay in another European Economic Area (EEA) state. AA, DLA and CA have been categorised in different ways under the co-ordination rules at different times. Before 1 June 1992, they were classed as 'invalidity benefits' (see p1505). If your entitlement began before this date, you have the right to export your benefit without any time limit to any EEA state.

From 1 June 1992, the UK government categorised AA, DLA and CA as 'special non-contributory benefits' (see p1507). These are not exportable. However, the European Court of Justice (ECJ) declared that this was wrong and that these benefits are sickness benefits.[8] This means they *are* exportable. You should continue to receive the benefit for as long as the UK remains the competent state (see p1508).[9]

If you had an award of one of these benefits on or after 8 March 2001 and a decision was made to stop your entitlement because you went to another EEA state, the DWP has said that it accepts that decision was wrong and will restore your entitlement and pay arrears from 18 October 2007 (or the date your payment was stopped if this is later).[10] Seek specialist advice if this applies to you.

DLA mobility component continues to be treated by the DWP as a special non-contributory benefit and is therefore considered not to be exportable. This has now been confirmed as lawful by the ECJ.[11]

You should always try to establish your entitlement to benefit before you leave the UK, but if you are covered by the European Union (EU) co-ordination rules, you may be able to make a new claim while resident in another EEA state if you have a permanent or long-term disability and have a sufficient connection with the UK.[12]

Bereavement benefits

In general, bereavement benefits are payable while you are abroad (see the exception for bereavement payment below). However, your benefit is not uprated each year if you have ceased to be ordinarily resident in Great Britain on the day before the annual uprating takes place,[13] unless you have gone to another EEA state and you are covered by the EU co-ordination rules (see p1503) or can rely on a reciprocal agreement.

If you are absent from Great Britain when you claim a bereavement payment, you are only entitled in limited circumstances.

European Union co-ordination rules

Bereavement benefits are classed as 'survivors' benefits' under the EU co-ordination rules (see p1505) and are therefore fully exportable. If these rules apply to you (see p1503) and you go to stay or live in another EEA state, you can be paid your bereavement benefits without a time limit and they will be fully uprated each year. See Chapter 64 for more information.

If the co-ordination rules apply to you and your late spouse/civil partner died in another EEA state, s/he should be treated as having died in the UK for the purposes of entitlement to a bereavement payment.[14]

Carer's allowance

Provided you remain 'ordinarily resident' (see p1478) in Great Britain, you are treated as present and therefore can continue to receive CA during an absence from Great Britain if:[15]

- the absence is, and was when it began, for a temporary purpose and does not exceed four weeks. You must be accompanied by the disabled person for whom you are caring, although you can have a break from caring of up to four weeks (see p85 for the rules on this);
- the absence is temporary and for the specific purpose of caring for the disabled person who is also absent from Great Britain and who remains entitled while absent to AA, DLA care component at the highest or middle rate or constant attendance allowance; *or*
- you are abroad as a serving member of the armed forces, or you are living with your spouse, civil partner, son, daughter, stepson, stepdaughter, father, father-in-law, stepfather, mother, mother-in-law or stepmother who is a serving member of the armed forces;
- you are abroad as an airman or airwoman or mariner or continental shelf worker.

You can continue to be paid an adult dependant increase in your CA for your spouse/civil partner or dependent adult while s/he is abroad if:[16]

- you are entitled to CA; *and*
- you are residing with her/him. **Note:** you can be treated as residing together during a temporary absence from each other.[17]

European Union co-ordination rules

The rules for getting your CA paid in another EEA state under the co-ordination rules are the same as for AA and DLA (see p1480).

If the EU co-ordination rules apply to you (see p1503) and you remain in the UK, you may be able to continue to be paid a dependant's addition for your adult or child dependant if s/he goes to stay or live in another EEA state. See Chapter 64 for more information.

Child benefit

You and your child can be treated as present in Great Britain and therefore you can continue to be entitled to child benefit for limited periods during a temporary absence.

You are treated as present during a temporary absence, provided you are ordinarily resident, for:[18]

- the first eight weeks; *or*
- the first 12 weeks of any period of absence, or any extension to that period of absence, which is in connection with:
  - the treatment of an illness or disability of you, your partner, a child for whom you are responsible, or another relative of either you or your partner; *or*
  - the death of your partner, a child or qualifying young person for whom you or your partner are responsible, or another relative of you or your partner.

'Relative' means brother, sister, parent, grandparent, great-grandparent or child, grandchild or great-grandchild.[19]

You will be 'temporarily absent' from Great Britain if, at the beginning of the period of absence, it is unlikely to exceed 52 weeks.[20]

Your child is treated as present during a temporary absence for:[21]

- the first 12 weeks of any period of absence; *or*
- any period during which s/he is absent for the specific purpose of being treated for an illness or disability which began before her/his absence began; *or*
- any period when s/he is in Northern Ireland; *or*
- any period during which s/he is absent only because s/he is:
  - receiving full-time education at a school or college in another EEA member state (including the A8 and A2 states) or in Switzerland; *or*
  - engaged in an educational exchange or visit made with the written approval of the school or college which s/he normally attends; *or*
  - a child who normally lives with a Crown servant posted overseas who is either in the same country as her/him or is absent from that country for one of the reasons in the above two bullet points.[22]

If a child is born outside the UK during the eight- or 12-week period in which you could be treated as present in Great Britain, s/he will be treated as being in the UK for up to 12 weeks from the start of your absence.[23]

While you and your child are present, or treated as present, you satisfy that condition of entitlement. This means that you can continue to receive child benefit that was already in payment and can also make a fresh claim during your, or her/his, absence.

European Union co-ordination rules

Child benefit is classed as a 'family benefit' under the EU co-ordination rules (see p1505). If these rules apply to you (see p1503):

- you can be paid child benefit for a child resident in another EEA country. The child does not have to be in education; *and/or*

- you can be paid child benefit if you are an EU national and you go to stay or live in another EU country and your benefit will be uprated in the normal way;
- if you are only within the personal scope of Regulation 1408/71 (see p1503) and you go to stay or live in another EEA country, you can only be paid child benefit beyond the limited periods listed on p1483 if you are receiving a UK pension. This can include retirement pension and contributory employment and support allowance (ESA).

See Chapter 64 for more information.

Employment and support allowance

You cannot normally get ESA if you are not in Great Britain.[24] However, contributory ESA and income-related ESA can both be paid when you are temporarily absent from Great Britain in the circumstances listed below, provided you meet the other conditions of entitlement.

If you were entitled to ESA immediately before leaving Great Britain and are temporarily absent from Great Britain, you can continue to be entitled:[25]

- **indefinitely** if:
  - your absence is for NHS treatment at a hospital or other institution outside Great Britain; *or*
  - you are living with your spouse, civil partner, son, daughter, stepson, stepdaughter, father, father-in-law, stepfather, mother, mother-in-law or stepmother who is a serving member of the armed forces;
- for the first **four weeks** if the absence is unlikely to exceed 52 weeks;
- for the first **26 weeks** if the absence is unlikely to exceed 52 weeks and is solely in connection with arrangements made for the treatment of:
  - your disease or disablement which is directly related to your limited capability for work which began before you left Great Britain; *or*
  - the disease or disablement of a dependent child who you are accompanying.

The treatment must be carried out by, or under the supervision of, a person qualified to provide medical treatment, physiotherapy or similar treatment.

If your partner is abroad

If you are the claimant and you stay in Great Britain, your income-related ESA will include an amount for your partner for:[26]

- the first four weeks; *or*
- the first 26 weeks if your partner is accompanying a child abroad for treatment in line with the 26-week rule above.

If you are the claimant and both you and your partner are abroad, your income-related ESA will include an amount for your partner for the first 26 weeks if both you and your partner are accompanying a child abroad for treatment in line with the 26-week rule above.[27]

After this four- or 26-week period, your benefit will be reduced because your applicable amount will be calculated as if you have no partner. However, your partner will still be treated as part of your household and therefore her/his work, income and capital will affect your income-related ESA entitlement unless you are no longer treated as a couple (see p758).[28]

European Union co-ordination rules

If the co-ordination rules apply to you (see p1503), the UK is your competent state (see p1508) and your ESA is classed as an exportable benefit (see below), you should be able to be take your ESA with you if you go to another EEA state.

Contributory ESA is classed under the EU co-ordination rules as a 'sickness benefit' during the assessment phase and as an 'invalidity benefit' after the assessment phase. In cases of long-term or permanent disability, contributory ESA in youth during the assessment phase and arguably all contributory ESA in the assessment phase should be regarded as an 'invalidity benefit' (see p1505).[29]

Income-related ESA is considered by the DWP to be a 'special non-contributory benefit' (see p1507). However, although it is arguable that it should be categorised as a 'sickness benefit' in the assessment phase and an 'invalidity benefit' in the main phase, this has not yet been successful.

If the DWP says that your income-related ESA is a 'special non-contributory benefit' and cannot be paid in another EEA state, seek specialist advice.

Under EU Regulation 883/04 (see p1503), it is arguable that sickness benefits can be exported in similar circumstances to invalidity benefits. Therefore, if you are covered by these rules, the distinction should not matter in the way it does under EU Regulation 1408/71 (see p1511).

See Chapter 64 for more details.

You should always try to establish your entitlement to benefit before you leave the UK, but if you are covered by the EU co-ordination rules, you may be able to make a new claim for contributory ESA in youth while resident in another EEA state if you have a permanent or long-term disability and have a sufficient connection with the UK.[30] Note, however, that the government intends to abolish new claims for contributory ESA in youth from some time in April 2012.

Guardian's allowance

Entitlement to guardian's allowance depends on entitlement to child benefit, so you can be paid guardian's allowance abroad for the same period as child benefit (see p1482).

However, guardian's allowance is not uprated each year if you have ceased to be ordinarily resident in Great Britain on the day before the annual uprating takes place,[31] unless you have gone to another EEA state and you are covered by the EU co-ordination rules (see p1486) or you can rely on a reciprocal agreement.

European Union co-ordination rules

Guardian's allowance is classed as a 'family benefit' under the EU co-ordination rules (see p1505). If these rules apply to you (see p1503):

- you may be able to be paid guardian's allowance for a child resident in another EEA country; *and/or*
- you may be able to be paid guardian's allowance if you are an EU national and you go to stay or live in another EU country and your benefit will be uprated in the normal way;
- if you are only within the personal scope of Regulation 1408/71 (see p1503) and you go to stay or live in another EEA country, you can only be paid guardian's allowance beyond the periods allowed under UK law on p1482 if you are receiving a UK pension (this includes retirement pension or contributory ESA).

See Chapter 64 for more details.

Housing benefit and council tax benefit

There is no requirement to be present in Great Britain to be entitled to **housing benefit** (HB). However, you must be liable to make payments in respect of a dwelling in Great Britain which you occupy as your home.[32] There are rules that treat you as occupying your home,[33] including during a temporary absence from it. If you are going abroad, these rules determine whether you can be entitled to HB while you are away (see p254).

There is no requirement to be present in Great Britain to be entitled to **council tax benefit** (CTB). However, you must be liable to pay council tax in respect of a dwelling of which you are resident.[34] There are rules that treat you as resident during a temporary absence.[35] If you are going abroad, these rules determine whether you can be entitled to CTB while you are away (see p119).

If your partner or child is abroad

Whether or not you have amounts included in your HB or CTB for your partner or child who is abroad depends on whether s/he is treated as part of your household (see pp758 and 762).

Incapacity benefit, severe disablement allowance and maternity allowance

If you are temporarily absent from Great Britain, you can continue to be paid incapacity benefit (IB) or severe disablement allowance (SDA) and maternity allowance (MA) if:[36]

- you are receiving DLA or AA (for when these can be paid abroad, see p1480); *or*
- the DWP agrees. You can then receive the benefit for the first 26 weeks of your temporary absence; *or*

- you are the spouse, civil partner, son, stepson, daughter, stepdaughter, father, stepfather, father-in-law, mother, stepmother, or mother-in-law of a serving member of the forces and you are abroad only because you are living with her/him.

In addition:
- when you left Great Britain you must have been continuously incapable of work for six months and have been continuously incapable since your departure; *or*
- your absence from Great Britain must be for the specific purpose of being treated for an incapacity which began before you left Great Britain; *or*
- for IB only, the incapacity for work is the result of a personal injury caused by an accident at work (see p368) and your absence from Great Britain is for the specific purpose of receiving treatment for that injury.

If you are due to have a medical examination, this can be arranged abroad.

Note: IB and SDA are being replaced by ESA. If you are getting IB or SDA and go abroad for more than 26 weeks, you will not requalify on your return to Great Britain. You may qualify for contributory ESA if you satisfy all the conditions of entitlement including the national insurance (NI) contribution conditions. If you did not lose entitlement to IB or SDA through going abroad, you will at some future point be reassessed for ESA. Under the transfer rules (see p193), you will *not* need to resatisfy the NI contribution conditions. Losing entitlement now could therefore result in a loss of potential future benefit.

You can continue to be paid an **adult dependent increase** within your IB or SDA for your spouse/civil partner or dependent adult while s/he is abroad if:[37]
- you are entitled to IB/SDA;
- you are residing with her/him. **Note:** you can be treated as residing together during a temporary absence from each other.[38]

European Union co-ordination rules

Long-term IB and, if you have a long-term or permanent disability, short-term IB in youth (but note that you cannot currently be entitled to short-term IB) and SDA are classed as 'invalidity benefits' under the EU co-ordination rules (see p1505).[39] If these rules apply to you (see p1503) and the UK is your 'competent state' (see p1508), you can export your IB and SDA if you go to live in another EEA state. Provided you continue to satisfy the rules of entitlement, benefit will be paid without any time limit and at the same rate as if you were still in the UK, including your annual uprating.

The state from which you claim benefit is the one that determines your degree of invalidity, but any checks and medicals take place in the state in which you are living, rather than the one that pays you benefit. The reports are then sent to the paying state. There are special rules that apply if your condition worsens.[40]

If the EU co-ordination rules apply to you and you remain in the UK, you may be able to continue to be paid a dependant's addition for your adult or child dependant if s/he goes to stay or live in another EEA state. See Chapter 64 for more details.

MA is classed as a 'maternity benefit' under the EU co-ordination rules (see p1505). If these rules apply to you (see p1503) and the UK is your 'competent state' (see p1508), you can be paid MA if you go to live or stay in another EEA country.[41] See Chapter 64 for more details.

Income support

You cannot normally get income support (IS) if you are not in Great Britain.[42] However, IS can be paid when you are temporarily absent from Great Britain in the circumstances listed below, provided you meet the other conditions of entitlement.

If you were entitled to IS immediately before leaving Great Britain and are temporarily absent from Great Britain, your entitlement can continue:[43]

- **indefinitely** if your absence is for NHS treatment at a hospital or other institution outside Great Britain;
- during the first **four weeks** of your absence if it is unlikely to exceed 52 weeks and either:
  - you are in Northern Ireland; *or*
  - you and your partner are both abroad and s/he satisfies the conditions for one of the pensioner premiums, a disability premium or a severe disability premium (see p820); *or*
  - you are claiming IS on the grounds of being incapable of work and are abroad for the sole purpose of receiving treatment for that incapacity. The treatment must be carried out by, or under the supervision of, a person qualified to provide medical treatment, physiotherapy or similar treatment; *or*
  - you are incapable of work; *and*
    - you have been continuously incapable for the previous 28 weeks and you are terminally ill or receiving the highest rate of DLA care component; *or*
    - you have been continuously incapable for 364 days; *or*
  - you fall within one of the groups of people who can claim IS (see p346) *other than* if you are:
    - a person in 'relevant education'; *or*
    - involved in a trade dispute, or have returned to work for 15 days or less following the dispute; *or*
    - a 'person subject to immigration control' (see p1410), but you are not excluded from IS because you have limited leave with the condition that you do not have recourse to 'public funds', and you have not yet had such recourse other than under this provision, and you depend on funds from

abroad that are temporarily disrupted, but which are reasonably expected to resume; *or*
  - entitled to statutory sick pay; *or*
  - appealing a decision that you are not incapable of work; *or*
  - incapable of work and not covered by one of the groups of people incapable of work listed above;
- during the first **eight weeks** of your absence if it is unlikely to exceed 52 weeks and is solely in connection with arrangements made for the treatment of a disease or disablement of a child or qualifying young person. The treatment must be carried out by, or under the supervision of, a person qualified to provide medical treatment, physiotherapy or similar treatment and the child or young person must be a member of your family (see p759).

If your partner is abroad

If you are the IS claimant and you stay in Great Britain, your IS applicable amount will include an amount for your partner who is abroad for:[44]
- the first four weeks; *or*
- the first eight weeks if your partner meets the conditions of the eight-week rule above.

If you are the IS claimant and both you and your partner are abroad, your IS will include amounts for your partner for the first eight weeks if both you and your partner meet the conditions of the eight-week rule above.[45]

After this four- or eight-week period, your benefit will be reduced because your applicable amount will be calculated as if you have no partner. However, your partner will still be treated as part of your household and therefore her/his work, income and capital will affect your IS entitlement unless you are no longer treated as a couple (see p758).[46]

If your child is abroad

If you were getting an amount in your IS for your child before s/he went abroad, you can continue to be paid for her/him for:[47]
- the first four weeks; *or*
- the first eight weeks if your child meets the conditions of the eight-week rule above.

European Union co-ordination rules

IS is classed as a 'special non-contributory benefit' under the EU co-ordination rules (see p1507) and therefore cannot be exported. This means that the EU co-ordination rules cannot assist you. You can only be paid IS abroad under the UK rules above.

Industrial injuries benefits

Industrial injuries benefits are:

- disablement benefit;
- reduced earnings allowance (REA);
- retirement allowance;
- constant attendance allowance;
- exceptionally severe disablement allowance.

Disablement benefit and retirement allowance are not affected if you go abroad.[48]

Constant attendance allowance and exceptionally severe disablement allowance are payable for the first six months of a temporary absence, or a longer period that the DWP may allow.[49]

REA can be paid while you are temporarily absent abroad for the first three months or longer if the DWP allows; *and*:[50]

- your absence from Great Britain is *not* in connection with employment, trade or business; *and*
- your claim was made before you leave Great Britain; *and*
- you were entitled to REA before going abroad.

Note: REA has now been abolished. If you break your claim, you will no longer be eligible for benefit.

European Union co-ordination rules

Industrial injuries benefits, with the exception of retirement allowance, are classed as 'benefits for accidents at work and occupational diseases' under the EU co-ordination rules (see p1505) and are therefore fully exportable. If these rules apply to you (see p1503) and you go to stay or live in another EEA state, you can be paid without any time limit and they will be fully uprated each year. See Chapter 64 for more details.

Jobseeker's allowance

You cannot normally get jobseeker's allowance (JSA) if you are not in Great Britain.[51] However, JSA can be paid when you are temporarily absent from Great Britain in the circumstances listed below, provided you meet the other conditions of entitlement. You can be treated as available for work and actively seeking work during certain temporary absences abroad which are similar to those listed below (see pp437 and 450).[52]

If you are temporarily absent from Great Britain, you are treated as being in Great Britain and can therefore be paid JSA:[53]

- **indefinitely** if you are entitled to JSA immediately before leaving Great Britain and your absence is for NHS treatment at a hospital or other institution outside Great Britain;

- for up to **four weeks** if you are entitled to JSA immediately before leaving Great Britain and either:
  - the absence is unlikely to exceed 52 weeks, you continue to satisfy the conditions of entitlement and your partner satisfies the conditions for one of the pensioner premiums, a disability premium or a severe disability premium (see p820); *or*
  - the absence is unlikely to exceed 52 weeks, you continue to satisfy the conditions of entitlement, and you are in Northern Ireland; *or*
  - you are in receipt of a training allowance in the circumstances set out on p434;[54]
- for up to **eight weeks** if you are entitled to JSA immediately before leaving Great Britain and the absence is unlikely to exceed 52 weeks and is solely in connection with arrangements made for the treatment of a disease or disablement of a child or qualifying young person. The treatment must be carried out by, or under the supervision of, a person qualified to provide medical treatment, physiotherapy or similar treatment and the child or young person must be a member of your family (see p759);
- for an absence of up to **seven days** if you are attending a job interview and you notified the employment officer (EO) before you left (in writing if required). On your return, you must satisfy the EO that you attended the interview as stated.

In addition, for contribution-based JSA only, you can be treated as present in Great Britain and therefore entitled to benefit if you are outside Great Britain because you are a continental shelf worker in certain circumstances.[55]

Joint-claim jobseeker's allowance if your partner is abroad

If you are a joint-claim couple (see p413) and your partner is temporarily absent from Great Britain **on the date you make your claim**, you are paid as a couple for:[56]

- an absence of up to **seven days** if your partner is attending a job interview;
- up to **four weeks** if your partner is:
  - in Northern Ireland and the absence is unlikely to exceed 52 weeks; *or*
  - in receipt of a training allowance in the circumstances set out on p434.

After this period, your JSA will be reduced because your applicable amount will be calculated as if you have no partner.[57] However, your partner will still be treated as part of your household, and therefore her/his work, income and capital will affect your income-based JSA entitlement unless you are no longer treated as a couple (see p758).[58]

If you are a joint-claim couple and your partner goes abroad **after you claimed JSA**, you continue to be paid as a joint-claim couple:[59]

- for up to **four weeks** if you are entitled to joint-claim JSA immediately before s/he leaves Great Britain and either:
  - the absence is unlikely to exceed 52 weeks, and you continue to satisfy the conditions of entitlement, and your partner satisfies the conditions for one of the pensioner premiums, a disability premium or a severe disability premium (see p820); *or*
  - the absence is unlikely to exceed 52 weeks, and you both continue to satisfy the conditions of entitlement, and your partner is in Northern Ireland; *or*
  - your partner is in receipt of a training allowance in the circumstances set out on p434;[60]
- for an absence of up to **seven days** if your partner is attending a job interview and has notified the EO before leaving (in writing if required). On her/his return, s/he must satisfy the EO at Jobcentre Plus that s/he attended the interview as stated.

Income-based jobseeker's allowance if your partner is abroad

If you are the income-based JSA claimant and you stay in Great Britain, your applicable amount includes an amount for your partner while s/he is abroad for:[61]

- the first **four weeks** of a temporary absence; *or*
- the first **eight weeks** if your partner meets the conditions of the eight-week rule on p1490.

If you are the income-based JSA claimant and both you and your partner are abroad, your applicable amount will include an amount for your partner for the first eight weeks if both you and your partner meet the conditions of the eight-week rule on p1490.[62]

After this four- or eight-week period, your benefit will be reduced because your applicable amount will be calculated as if you have no partner. However, your partner will still be treated as part of your household, and therefore her/his work, income and capital will affect your income-based JSA entitlement unless you are no longer treated as a couple (see p758).[63]

Income-based jobseeker's allowance if your child is abroad

If you were getting JSA for your child before s/he went abroad, you can continue to be paid for her/him for:[64]

- the **first four weeks**; *or*
- the **first eight weeks** if your child meets the conditions of the eight-week rule on p1490.

European Union co-ordination rules

Contribution-based JSA is classed as an unemployment benefit under the EU co-ordination rules (see p1505). If these rules apply to you (see p1503) and the UK is your 'competent state' (see p1508), you can be paid contribution-based JSA if:[65]

- you satisfied the conditions for contribution-based JSA before you leave the UK for at least four weeks unless authorised by the DWP to go abroad before you have claimed for four weeks; *and*
- you register as unemployed in the EEA state you go to within seven days and comply with its procedures.

You can receive contribution-based JSA for up to three months.

Under Regulation 1408/71 (see p1503), you can export your contribution-based JSA only once in any period of unemployment.[66] This restriction does not apply within Regulation 883/04.

Income-based JSA is classed as a 'special non-contributory benefit' under the EU co-ordination rules (see p1507) and therefore cannot be exported. This means that the EU co-ordination rules cannot assist you. You can only be paid income-based JSA abroad under the UK rules on p1490.

However, it is arguable that income-based JSA should, like contribution-based JSA, be classed as an unemployment benefit and therefore be payable abroad in the same circumstances as contribution-based JSA. Seek specialist advice if this is relevant to you.

Pension credit

You cannot normally get pension credit (PC) if you are not in Great Britain.[67] However, PC can be paid when you are temporarily absent from Great Britain in the circumstances listed below, provided you meet the other conditions of entitlement.

If you were entitled to PC immediately before leaving Great Britain and are temporarily absent from Great Britain, your entitlement can continue:[68]

- **indefinitely** if your absence is for NHS treatment at a hospital or other institution outside Great Britain; *or*
- **for up to 13 weeks** if your absence is unlikely to exceed 52 weeks.

If your partner is abroad

If you are entitled to PC, either while in Great Britain or while abroad but covered by one of the groups above and your partner is abroad, your PC will only include an amount for her/him if s/he is covered by one of the groups above. After this, s/he will not be treated as part of your household and you will be paid as a single person.[69] Your partner can also cease to be treated as part of your household in the circumstances on p758.[70]

European Union co-ordination rules

PC is classed as a 'special non-contributory benefit' under the EU co-ordination rules (see p1507) and therefore cannot be exported. This means that the EU co-ordination rules cannot assist you. You can only be paid PC abroad under the UK rules above.

Retirement pension

With the exception of Category D retirement pension, all retirement pensions are payable without time limit while you are abroad.[71] However, your benefit is not uprated each year if you have ceased to be ordinarily resident on the day before the annual uprating takes place,[72] unless you have gone to another EEA state and you are covered by the EU co-ordination rules (see below) or you can rely on a reciprocal agreement.

For the residence requirements for Category D retirement pension, see p1439.

Note: you cannot 'de-retire' if you are not ordinarily resident in Great Britain (see p1430).[73]

You can continue to be paid an adult dependant increase in your Category A retirement pension for your spouse/civil partner or dependent adult while s/he is abroad if:[74]

- you are entitled to the pension; *and*
- you are residing with her/him. You can be treated as residing together during a temporary absence from each other.[75]

European Union co-ordination rules

Retirement pensions are classed as 'old age benefits' under the EU co-ordination rules (see p1505). If these rules apply to you (see p1503) and the UK is your 'competent state' (see p1508), you can export your retirement pension if you go to live in another EEA state. It will be paid without time limit and at the same rate as if you were still in the UK, including your annual uprating.

If the EU co-ordination rules apply and you remain in the UK, you may be able to continue to be paid a dependant's addition for your adult or child dependant if s/he goes to stay or live in another EEA state. See Chapter 64 for more details.

Statutory maternity, paternity, adoption and sick pay

There are no presence or residence rules for statutory maternity pay (SMP), statutory paternity pay (SPP), statutory adoption pay (SAP) or statutory sick pay (SSP). You remain entitled to these benefits if you go abroad, provided you meet the normal rules of entitlement, including being an employee (see Chapter 27 and 28.[76]

Even while employed abroad, you count as an employee in certain circumstances, including if:[77]

- your employer is required to pay secondary Class 1 NI contributions for you; *or*
- you are a continental shelf worker or, in certain circumstances, an airman or airwoman or mariner; *or*
- you are employed in another EEA state and, had you been employed in Great Britain, you would have been considered an employee, and the UK is the competent state under the EU co-ordination rules (see p1508).

Your employer is not required to pay you SSP, SMP, SPP or SAP if:[78]

- your employer is not required by law to pay employer's Class 1 NI contributions (even if those contributions are in fact made) because, at the time they become payable, your employer:
  - is not resident or present in Great Britain; *or*
  - has (or is treated as having) a place of business in Great Britain; *or*
- because of an international treaty or convention your employer is exempt from the Social Security Acts or those Acts are not enforceable against your employer.

European Union co-ordination rules

It is arguable that SSP is a sickness benefit and SPP and SMP are maternity/ paternity benefits under the co-ordination rules (see p1505). However, given the generosity of the above UK rules, it is unlikely that you will need to rely on the EU co-ordination rules directly.

Tax credits

You can be treated as present and, therefore, entitled to child tax credit (CTC) and working tax credit (WTC) for limited periods during a temporary absence.

You are treated as present for both CTC and WTC during a temporary absence, provided you are ordinarily resident, for:[79]

- the first eight weeks; *or*
- the first 12 weeks of any period of absence, or any extension to that period of absence, which is in connection with:
  - the treatment of an illness or disability of you, your partner, a child for whom you are responsible, or another relative of either you or your partner; *or*
  - the death of your partner, a child or qualifying young person for whom you or your partner are responsible, or another relative (see below) of you or your partner.

'Relative' means brother, sister, parent, grandparent, great-grandparent or child, grandchild, great-grandchild.[80]

You will be 'temporarily absent' from Great Britain if, at the beginning of the period of absence, it is unlikely to exceed 52 weeks.[81]

You are also treated as present if you are:[82]

- a Crown servant posted overseas; *and*
  - you are, or immediately before your posting abroad you were, ordinarily resident in the UK; *or*
  - immediately before your posting you were in the UK in connection with that posting; *or*

- the partner of a Crown servant posted overseas and in the same country as her/him or temporarily absent from that country under the same exceptions that enable tax credits to continue during a temporary absence from Great Britain.

While you are treated as present in any of the ways above, you continue to satisfy that condition of entitlement. This means you can continue to receive any tax credits that are already in payment and can make a fresh or renewal claim during your absence.

If you (or your partner if you are making a joint claim) spend longer abroad than the permitted periods, you will cease to satisfy the presence condition and therefore your tax credit entitlement will end. If you fail to notify this to HM Revenue and Customs within one month (see p1363), you may be overpaid (see Chapter 58) and could be subject to a penalty (see Chapter 59).

For additional considerations if you are making a joint claim as a couple, see p1441.

European Union co-ordination rules

CTC is classed as a 'family benefit' under the EU co-ordination rules (see p1505). If these rules apply, you can be paid CTC:

- for a child resident in another EEA country; *and/or*
- if you are an EU national and you go to stay or live in another EU country.

If you are only within the personal scope of Regulation 1408/71 (see p1503), these co-ordination rules do not generally allow you to export CTC (see p1512). See Chapter 64 for more details.

Notes

2. **UK law**
   1 *R v Barnet LBC ex parte Shah* [1983] 2 AC 309, HL, Lord Scarman at p342D
   2 Reg 4(2) TC(R) Regs; reg 24(2) CB Regs
   3 *Chief Adjudication Officer v Ahmed and others*, 16 March 1994, CA, *The Guardian*, 15 April 1994, reported as R(S)1/96
   4 *Chief Adjudication Officer v Ahmed and others*, 16 March 1994, CA, *The Guardian*, 15 April 1994, reported as R(S)1/96
   5 R(S) 1/85
   6 R(U) 16/62

4. **Rules for individual benefits and tax credits**
   7 **AA** Reg 2(2) SS(AA) Regs
   DLA Reg 2(2) SS(DLA) Regs
   8 *Commission of the European Communities v European Parliament and Council of the European Union*, C-299/05 [2007] ECR I-08695, 18 October 2007
   9 ss65(7), 70(4A) and 72(7B) SSCBA
   10 SS(DLA etc)MA Regs
   11 *Bartlett and others v SSWP*, C-537/09 [2011] ECR, not yet reported
   12 *Stewart v SSWP*, C-503/09 [2011] ECR, not yet reported
   13 Reg 5 SSB(PA) Regs
   14 Arts 5 and 42 Reg 883/04; Art 65 Reg 1408/71
   15 Reg 9(2) and (3) SS(ICA) Regs
   16 Reg 13 SSB(PA) Regs; Sch 2 para 7 SSB(Dep) Regs
   17 Reg 2(4) SSB(PRT) Regs
   18 Reg 24 CB Regs
   19 Reg 24 (1) CB Regs
   20 Reg 24(2) CB Regs
   21 Reg 21 CB Regs
   22 Reg 32 CB Regs
   23 Reg 21(2) CB Regs
   24 ss1(3)(d) and 18(4)(a) WRA 2007
   25 Regs 151-55 ESA Regs
   26 Reg 156 and Sch 5 paras 6 and 7 ESA Regs
   27 Reg 156 and Sch 5 para 7 ESA Regs
   28 Reg 156 ESA Regs
   29 *Stewart v SSWP*, C-503/09 [2011] ECR, not yet reported
   30 *Stewart v SSWP*, C-503/09 [2011] ECR, not yet reported
   31 Reg 5 SSB(PA) Regs
   32 s130(1)(a) SSCBA 1992
   33 Reg 7 HB Regs; reg 7 HB(SPC) Regs
   34 s131(3)(a) SSCBA 1992
   35 Reg 8 CTB Regs; reg 8 CTB(SPC) Regs
   36 Reg 2 SSB(PA) Regs
   37 Reg 13 SSB(PA) Regs; reg 14 SS(IB-ID) Regs
   38 Reg 2(4) SSB(PRT) Regs
   39 *Stewart v SSWP*, C-503/09 [2011] ECR, not yet reported
   40 Arts 5 and 46 EU Reg 883/04; Arts 40 and 41 EU Reg 1408/71; Art 87 EU Reg 987/2009
   41 Arts 7 and 21 Reg 883/04; Art 19 Reg 1408/71
   42 s124(1) SSCBA 1992
   43 Reg 4 IS Regs
   44 Reg 21 and Sch 7 paras 11 and 11A IS Regs
   45 Reg 21 and Sch 7 para 11A IS Regs
   46 Reg 16 IS Regs
   47 Reg 16(5) IS Regs
   48 Reg 9(3) SSB(PA) Regs
   49 Reg 9(4) SSB(PA) Regs
   50 Reg 9(5) SSB(PA) Regs
   51 s1(2)(i) JSA 1995
   52 Regs 14 and 19 JSA Regs
   53 s21 and Sch 1 para 11 JSA 1995; reg 50 JSA Regs
   54 Regs 50(4) and 170 JSA Regs
   55 Reg 11 SSB(PA) Regs
   56 Regs 50(6B), 86C and 170 and Sch 5A para 7 JSA Regs
   57 Sch 5A para 7 JSA Regs
   58 Reg 78 JSA Regs
   59 Reg 50(3) and (6C) and Sch 5A para 7 JSA Regs
   60 Regs 50(4) and 170 JSA Regs
   61 Reg 85 and Sch 5 paras 10 and 11 JSA Regs
   62 Reg 85 and Sch 5 para 11 JSA Regs
   63 Reg 78 JSA Regs
   64 Reg 78(5) JSA Regs
   65 Art 64 EU Reg 883/04; Art 69 EU Reg 1408/71
   66 Art 69(3) EU Reg 1408/71
   67 s1(2)(a) SPCA 2002

68 Regs 3 and 4 SPC Regs
69 Regs 4 and 5 SPC Regs
70 Reg 5 SPC Regs
71 s113 SSCBA; reg 4(1) SSB(PA) Regs
72 Reg 4(3) SSB(PA) Regs
73 Reg 6 SSB(PA) Regs
74 Reg 13 SSB(PA) Regs; reg 10 SSB(Dep) Regs
75 Reg 2(4) SSB(PRT) Regs
76 **SMP** Reg 2A SMP(PAM) Regs
SAP/SPP Reg 4 SPPSAP(PAM) Regs
SSP Reg 10 SSP(MAPA) Regs
77 Art 6 EU Reg 883/04
SMP s171(1) SSCBA 1992; regs 2, 2A, 7 and 8 SMP(PAM) Regs
SAP/SPP ss171ZJ(2) and 171ZS(2) SSCBA 1992; regs 3, 4, 8 and 9 SPPSAP(PAM) Regs
SSP s163(1) SSCBA 1992; reg 16 SSP Regs; regs 5-10 SSP(MAPA) Regs
78 **SMP** Reg 3 SMP(PAM) Regs; reg 17(3) SMP Regs
SAP/SPP Reg 2 SPPSAP(PAM) Regs; reg 32(3) SPPSAP(G) Regs; reg 24(4) ASPP(G) Regs
SSP Reg 16(2) SSP Regs
79 Reg 4 TC(R) Regs
80 Reg 2(1) TC(R) Regs
81 Reg 4(2) TC(R) Regs
82 Reg 3, 5 and 6 TC(R) Regs

Chapter 64

European Union co-ordination rules

This chapter covers:

This chapter describes the ways that the European Union co-ordination rules may assist you to satisfy the entitlement conditions for UK benefits and tax credits if you have moved from another European Economic Area (EEA) state to the UK, and to be paid benefits and tax credits when you or a family member go to live in another EEA state.

The residence and presence conditions for the individual benefits that affect your entitlement while you are in Great Britain are covered in Chapter 62 and the rules that affect your entitlement to benefits and tax credits if you go abroad are covered in Chapter 63.

If you are *not* an EEA national, check Chapter 61 first as your immigration status may exclude you from the benefit or tax credit you want to claim.

Key facts

- If you are a European Economic Area (EEA) national or the family member of an EEA national, you may be able to benefit from the European Union co-ordination rules.
- The co-ordination rules can help you qualify for benefits in the UK. You can count periods of residence and employment in another EEA state and insurance contributions paid in another EEA state to help you meet the conditions of entitlement of the benefit you want to claim.
- The co-ordination rules also allow you to be paid a UK benefit in another EEA state for longer than the UK rules allow, and to be paid a benefit by another EEA state while you are in the UK.

Future changes: April 2013 and after

Major changes are taking place that affect the benefits and tax credits system (see Chapter 2). From April 2013, personal independence payment (PIP) will replace disability living allowance for adults and, from October 2013, universal credit will replace most means-tested benefits. At the time of writing, it is not yet known how these benefits will be categorised, although the government has said that the daily living component of PIP will be classed as a sickness benefit. See CPAG's *Welfare Rights Bulletin* for updates.

1. Introduction

If you are a European Economic Area (EEA) national (see p1501) or a family member of an EEA national, you may be able to benefit from European Union (EU) law. EU legislation and caselaw applies directly in the UK and throughout the EEA. There are two main parts of EU law which affect benefit and tax credit entitlement that are covered in this *Handbook*: the residence rights which enable you to satisfy the right to reside requirement outlined in Chapter 62 and the social security co-ordination rules, which are summarised in this chapter. In general, you will not need to know whether you have a right to reside in order to understand how the co-ordination rules affect you.

The co-ordination rules can help you qualify for benefits in the UK (eg, by enabling you to count periods of residence, insurance and employment in any EEA state to meet the conditions of entitlement) and can help you take benefit to another EEA state for longer than you would be able to do under UK law alone.

European Union law

EU legislation and caselaw apply in the UK and throughout the EEA. In general, for EU law to apply, you must be an EEA national (see below) or the family member of an EEA national.

Member states of the European Union

Austria	Germany	The Netherlands
Belgium	Greece	Poland
Bulgaria	Hungary	Portugal
Cyprus	Ireland	Romania
Czech Republic	Italy	Slovakia
Denmark	Latvia	Slovenia
Estonia	Lithuania	Spain
Finland	Luxembourg	Sweden
France	Malta	United Kingdom

EU law has been extended to countries outside the EU which are covered by the EEA Agreement (see below). The EEA Agreement came into force in January 1994, when the EU joined the European Free Trade Area. In general, EEA nationals are covered by EU law to much the same extent as nationals of EU states. There are slight differences, however, in that EEA nationals cannot rely on the EU Treaty and the Agreement does not have equivalent provisions for all the areas covered by the Treaty.

Member states of the European Economic Area

The EEA consists of the EU countries plus Iceland, Liechtenstein and Norway.

From 1 June 2002, an agreement with Switzerland means that, in general, Swiss nationals are treated the same as EEA nationals. Any references to EEA nationals should therefore be interpreted as including Swiss nationals.[1]

EU law applies in all the above countries, but it extends beyond the actual territory of the member states. It also applies to countries 'for whose external relations a member state is responsible'. Therefore, Spain includes not only the mainland, but also the Balearic and the Canary Islands. Portugal includes Madeira and the Azores. However, there are certain exceptions to this general rule. In particular, in the UK, Gibraltar is covered, but not the Isle of Man and the Channel Islands.

Restricted rights for A8 and A2 nationals

The UK has restricted, for a limited time, the employment and residence rights of most nationals of states that joined the EU in 2004 (the 'A8 states') and in 2007 (the 'A2 states'). These restrictions only affect your entitlement to benefits and tax credits which have a right to reside requirement (see p1447). Other provisions of EU law, including the co-ordination rules, apply to A8 and A2 nationals in the same way as they apply to other EEA nationals.

A8 and A2 states

The A8 states are: Czech Republic, Estonia, Hungary, Latvia, Lithuania, Poland, Slovakia and Slovenia.

These states joined the EU on 1 May 2004.

The restrictions only applied until 30 April 2011.

The A2 states are: Bulgaria and Romania.

These states joined the EU on 1 January 2007.

The restrictions are in force until 31 December 2013.

The co-ordination rules

In order to secure and promote freedom of movement, EU law co-ordinates all the social security systems within the EEA. The intention is that people should not lose out on social security protection simply because they move to another member state.

The current co-ordination rules (EU Regulation 883/04) were introduced on 1 May 2010. These are intended eventually to replace the co-ordination rules in EU Regulation 1408/71. The new rules do not completely repeal the old co-ordination rules and, for the foreseeable future, both will be in force. A benefit claim is determined under the rules applicable at the time it is made (but see p1504).

The co-ordination rules contain the following principles.

- **The single state principle**. You can generally only claim benefit from one member state (see p1508).
- **Equal treatment of people.** Discrimination on nationality grounds in terms of access to, or the rate of, payment of the benefits that are covered is prohibited (see p1510).
- **Equal treatment of benefits, income, facts or events.** If receipt of a benefit or a fact or an event has a legal consequence in one member state, this must be recognised in the same way by other member states (see p1510).
- **Aggregation.** Periods of residence, insurance and employment in any EEA state can be used towards entitlement to benefit in another (see p1511).
- **Exportability of certain benefits**. The co-ordination rules allow you to take certain benefits abroad with you if you go to another member state. These rules generally mean you can take benefit abroad for longer than under UK rules (see p1511).
- **Administrative co-operation.** Member states undertake to co-operate in the administration of the co-ordination rules.

The co-ordination rules set out the above general principles, exceptions to these that apply in certain circumstances, and more detailed provisions on how the principle should apply in certain circumstances. See Chapter 62 for how they can assist you to claim benefits and tax credits in the UK and Chapter 63 for how they can assist you to be paid benefits and tax credits when you go to another EEA state. For further information on the co-ordination rules, see CPAG's *Benefits for Migrants Handbook*.

Where to start

In order to establish whether you are able to rely on the co-ordination rules, you must do the following.

- Check whether you fall under Regulation 883/04 or Regulation 1408/71 (see p1503).

- Check whether you are within the 'personal scope' of the co-ordination rules (see below).
- Check whether the particular benefit you want to claim is covered by the co-ordination rules and into which category it falls (see p1505).
- Check which state is the 'competent state' (see p1508).
- Check the principle you want to apply – eg, exporting benefit or aggregating periods of insurance (see pp1510–11).
- Check the individual benefit and tax credit rules in Chapter 62 if you want to check entitlement in the UK, and in Chapter 63 if you want to be paid when you or your family are in another EEA state.

2. **Who is covered**

In order to be covered by the co-ordination rules, you must fall within their '**personal scope**'. This simply means the range of people to whom the rules apply.

You are within the personal scope of **Regulation 883/04** if:[2]

- you have been 'subject to the legislation of one or more member states'; *and*
- you are:
  - a European Union national; *or*
  - a refugee; *or*
  - a stateless person; *or*
  - a family member (see p1504) or a survivor (as defined in national law, which in the UK means a widow, widower or surviving civil partner[3]) of one of the above.

If you are a national of Iceland, Liechtenstein, Norway or Switzerland, Regulation 883/04 does not yet apply to you, and you remain potentially within the personal scope of Regulation 1408/71. However, Regulation 883/04 is expected to be extended to these four states in 2012, but the UK government is challenging this. See CPAG's *Welfare Rights Bulletin* for updates.

You are within the personal scope of **Regulation 1408/71** if:

- you have been employed or self-employed and have been subject to the legislation of a member state because you have paid (or should have paid) national insurance (NI) in an European Economic Area (EEA) country or you have been a student in an EEA state; *and*
- you are:
  - a national of Iceland, Liechtenstein, Norway or Switzerland; *or*
  - a 'third-country national' – ie, a person with indefinite leave to remain in the UK who is not an EEA national her/himself. A third-country national who is resident in a member state continues to be covered by the co-ordination rules in Regulation 1408/71 rather than Regulation 883/04. This

is because the UK has obtained an opt-out, allowing it to restrict third-country nationals' access to the co-ordination rules.

'Subject to the legislation of a member state'

EEA nationals who are, or have been, subject to the legislation of one or more member states are covered by the co-ordination rules.

Under **Regulation 1408/71** you could not be subject to the legislation of a member state unless you had worked and paid (or should have paid) NI contributions. The only exception was for students and family members.

Under **Regulation 883/04**, the personal scope has been expanded to include more people who have never worked. Therefore, if you are potentially eligible for any social security benefit or special non-contributory benefit (see p1505) in the UK, you should be covered by the new co-ordination rules.

Regulation 883/004 states that: 'Legislation means, in respect of each Member State, laws regulations and other statutory provisions and all other implementing measures relating to the social security branches covered by Article 3(1) of the Regulation.'[4]

The 'social security branches' referred to in this definition include UK benefits which are intended to assist you in the event of one of the risks on p1505 affecting you. Examples include attendance allowance, disability living allowance, carer's allowance, child benefit and child tax credit. None of these depend on your being an employee or self-employed at any time. Potentially, therefore, even if you have never worked, you can be covered by the co-ordination rules. See p1505 for a full list of benefits considered to be social security benefits under Regulation 883/04.

Transitional protection

If you have been in receipt of a benefit because you were assisted under Regulation 1408/71, you remain subject to the legislation of a member state determined in accordance with the rules in Regulation 1408/71 rather than in Regulation 883/04 during a transitional period of a maximum of 10 years. This applies, provided your circumstances do not change. This transitional period is intended to protect anyone who might otherwise have lost benefit under the new Regulation. However, you can ask to be transferred and considered under the new rules if this would be better for you, and the new rules take effect from the start of the following month.[5]

Family members

Family members of a person covered by Regulation 883/04 (and also Regulation 1408/71) can rely on the co-ordination rules that cover that person.

Note: as economically inactive people are now covered under the new rules, a person may not need to rely on being a family member to be covered.

You are a '**family member**' under the co-ordination rules if you are:[6]

- a person defined or recognised as a member of the family or designated as a member of the family or the household by the legislation under which benefits are provided. In general, this means the definition in the UK social security regulations applies – ie, a partner who is a member of your household and a child aged up to 20 for whom you are responsible (see Chapter 33); *or*
- another family member who does not fall within the above definition, but you are mainly dependent on the person who is covered.

3. **Which benefits are covered**

The benefits to which the co-ordination rules apply are referred to as being within the '**material scope**' of the rules. Regulation 883/04 applies to all the benefits to which Regulation 1408/71 applies, as well as to 'paternity benefits' and 'pre-retirement benefits'. The UK currently has no pre-retirement benefits.

Individual social security benefits are not directly referred to. Instead, the Regulations have broad categories of benefits such as 'old age' or 'maternity'. The Regulations refer to these broad categories as benefits designed to cover certain 'risks'. Any social security benefit in a member state designed to provide assistance in the event of a particular risk will fall into that particular category of benefit. Each member state must then list the benefits it considers are designed to assist for that risk.

Benefits are also divided into three different types depending on the conditions of eligibility. These are:

- social security benefits (see below);
- special non-contributory benefits (see p1507);
- social and medical assistance (see p1508).

Those benefits deemed to be social security benefits have the most rights; special non-contributory benefits provide fewer rights; and social and medical assistance are not covered at all.

Social security benefits

These are categorised according to the risk against which they are designed to provide financial protection.[7]

Risk	*UK benefit*
Sickness	Attendance allowance (AA) (but see below)
	Carer's allowance (CA) (but see below)
	Disability living allowance (DLA) care component (but see below)
	Contributory employment and support allowance (ESA) in the assessment phase (but see below)
	Arguably, income-related ESA in the assessment phase (see below)
	Statutory sick pay (SSP)
Maternity	Maternity allowance (MA)
	Statutory maternity pay (SMP)
Paternity	Statutory paternity pay (SPP)
Invalidity	AA, DLA care and mobility component and CA if you were in receipt of benefit before 1 June 1992. If you claimed after this date, see the note below
	Long-term incapacity benefit (IB)
	Severe disablement allowance (SDA)
	Contributory ESA after the assessment phase
	Arguably, contributory ESA during the assessment phase (see below)
	Arguably, income-related ESA (see below)
	Additional pension
Old age	Graduated retirement benefit
	Winter fuel payments
	Increments – eg, to pensions
	Adult dependants' increases of retirement pension
	Age addition in pensions
Pre-retirement	None
Survivors	Bereavement benefits
Accidents at work and occupational diseases	Industrial injuries disablement benefit
	Constant attendance allowance
	Exceptionally severe disablement allowance
	Reduced earnings allowance

Unemployment	Contribution-based jobseeker's allowance (JSA) is the only benefit the UK accepts as being an unemployment benefit. However, it is arguable that income-based JSA may also be an unemployment benefit. This is not accepted by the DWP and needs to be tested by the courts.
Family benefits (see p1512)	Child benefit Child tax credit Dependants' additions in other benefits Guardian's allowance
Family allowances (under Regulation 1408/71 only)	Child benefit Dependants' additions in other benefits

Note: AA, CA and DLA care component have been categorised as assisting with different risks at different times. Until 1 June 1992 they were categorised as invalidity benefits. They were then categorised as special non-contributory benefits until this was held to be wrong[8] and they were then re-categorised as sickness benefits. For the relevance of this if you want to export one of these benefits to another EEA state, see p1481.

Note: it is arguable that income-related ESA is a sickness benefit in the assessment phase and an invalidity benefit after the assessment phase but this argument has not yet been successful and the DWP maintains it is a special non-contributory benefit (see below). If this affects you, seek specialist advice.

Note: if you have a long-term or permanent disability, contributory ESA in youth during the assessment phase should be regarded as an invalidity benefit. Arguably, all contributory ESA during the assessment phase should be regarded as an invalidity benefit.[9]

For rules on exporting family benefits and family allowances see p1512.

Special non-contributory benefits

These are benefits which are:[10]

- intended to provide supplementary or ancillary cover against the risks covered above or solely specific protection for disabled people closely linked to a person's social environment in the state concerned; *and*
- are funded solely from general taxation and do not depend on making contributions as a condition of entitlement; *and*
- are listed as being such in the relevant co-ordination Regulation.

The last criterion above requires each member state to list in an annex to the relevant regulations the benefits it considers to be 'special non-contributory benefits'. The UK government has only listed the four benefits below.[11] However, the DWP considers that income-related ESA is also a special non-contributory benefit. If you are affected by a decision which states that income-related ESA is a special non-contributory benefit, seek specialist advice.

Special non-contributory benefits	DLA mobility component Income support (IS) Income-based JSA Pension credit

Social and medical assistance

The UK does not specify which benefits it considers to be social assistance and consequently excluded from the co-ordination rules. It is likely that social fund crisis loans and community care grants fall into this category.

4. Principles of co-ordination

The single competent state

If you have been subject to the legislation of any member state, you are covered by the co-ordination rules. Under these rules you are generally only able to claim a particular type of benefit from one member state and you are only liable to pay national insurance (NI) contributions to one member state. You can be subject to the legislation of a single member state only.[12]

The **'competent state'** is the state in which the competent institution (see below) is situated.[13] It is the state that is responsible for paying your benefit and to which you are liable to pay NI contributions.

The **'competent institution'** is broadly the institution which is responsible for paying your benefit and to which you are liable to pay NI contributions.[14] The DWP is the UK's primary competent institution.

Under Regulation 883/04, the competent state is the state in which you are:[15]

- employed or self-employed;
- resident and from which you are receiving an unemployment benefit;
- a conscripted member of the armed forces or a person doing compulsory civilian service;
- a civil servant.

If you work simultaneously in two or more member states, you are subject to the legislation of the member state of residence if you pursue a substantial part of your activities in that member state.[16]

If your employer's business is normally in one member state but you are sent to another state to work there, and it is anticipated the posting will last for no more than 24 months, you remain subject to the legislation of the first member state. Similarly, if you are self-employed in one member state and go to another state to provide similar services as a self-employed person, you remain subject to the legislation of the first member state, provided the anticipated duration of your time abroad is two years or less.[17]

If none of these apply, the competent state is the state in which you are resident.

Residence in this context means habitually resident. If there is a difference of views between two states or institutions about where you are resident, a set of factors are provided for deciding this for the purpose of Regulation 883/04. There is no equivalent provision under Regulation 1408/71.

The following factors may be used to help determine your place of habitual residence for the purposes of Regulation 883/04:[18]

- the duration and continuity of presence in the state(s) concerned;
- your personal situation including:
  - the nature and specific characteristics of any activity pursued, in particular the place where such activity is habitually pursued, the stability of the activity, and the duration of any work contract;
  - your family status and family ties;
  - any unpaid activity such as voluntary work;
  - if you are a student, the source of your income;
  - your housing situation, in particular how permanent it is;
  - the member state in which you are deemed to reside for tax purposes.

If there is still a dispute about your place of residence, consideration must be given to your intentions, especially the reasons that led you to move. This will be decisive in establishing your actual place of residence.

If you are subject to the legislation of the UK, either because you last worked in the UK or you are resident in the UK, you remain subject to the legislation of the UK until:[19]

- you start to work in another European Economic Area (EEA) member state;
- you start to receive a pension from another EEA member state and request that the UK cease to be your competent state;
- you move to another EEA member state and become resident there.

Note: the question of when the UK ceases to be responsible for paying your benefits if you move to another state, but do not start working or claiming benefits there, is currently being considered by the Upper Tribunal.[20] See CPAG's *Welfare Rights Bulletin* for updates.

Under Regulation 1408/71, the general rule is that competent state is the one where you were last employed or self-employed and paid (or should have paid) NI contributions. However, there are many exceptions to this.[21]

Equal treatment

If you are covered by the co-ordination rules, you are entitled to the same benefits under the legislation of the 'competent state' (see p1508) as a national of that state. Equal treatment is one of the fundamental rights of European Union (EU) law, and the principle of non-discrimination prohibits discrimination based on your nationality. Both direct discriminataion and, if it cannot be justified as proportionate and in pursuit of a legitimate aim, indirect discrimination are prohibited.

Direct discrimination arises when one person is treated less favourably than another. Indirect discrimination arises when rules which, although apparently neutral and non-discriminatory, have, in practice, a greater adverse impact on some (eg, non-nationals of the competent state) than others – eg, nationals of the competent state. For example, the right to reside test in UK law would appear to apply equally to all EEA nationals. However, British and Irish citizens will always have a right to reside in the common travel area and therefore satisfy the test for means-tested benefits, whereas other EEA nationals will only satisfy it in certain circumstances. Therefore, the test is indirectly discriminatory. Although the Supreme Court has decided that this discrimination is justified and therefore legal,[22] the European Commission's opinion is that this indirect discrimination is not justified and may refer the UK to the European Court of Justice (ECJ) for continuing to apply the right to reside test to EU nationals who habitually reside in the UK.[23]

There is also provision to ensure the 'equal treatment of benefits, income, facts or events'.[24] This rule is designed to ensure that if the competent state regards the receipt of a particular benefit or income, or the occurrence of certain facts or events, as producing certain legal effects, it should regard the receipt of an equivalent benefit or income from another state, or the occurrence of particular facts or events in another state, as producing the same effect. For example, a person getting long-term incapacity benefit (IB) is entitled to have a disability premium included in her/his applicable amount for housing benefit. Therefore, a person getting a benefit equivalent to long-term IB from another state but who is resident in the UK should also receive a disability premium. Similarly, a person receiving an equivalent benefit to disability living allowance from another state who claims working tax credit can argue that s/he should get the disability element addition.

Aggregation

The principle of aggregation for the purpose of acquiring and calculating entitlement to benefits is a key co-ordinating principle.[25]

'Aggregation' means adding together periods of NI contributions, residence or employment/self-employment in all the member states in which you have lived or worked and using this total to calculate your benefit entitlement. This may be necessary if your entitlement to, or retention of, benefits depends on your fulfilling a certain period of residence, employment or insurance. For example, if you want to claim a UK contribution-based benefit such as contributory employment and support allowance, but you have not paid sufficient NI contributions, you can rely on contributions that you have paid in other EEA states in order to satisfy the UK contribution rules. What constitutes a period of residence, employment or insurance is determined by the legislation of the member state in which it took place.[26]

The principle is that you should not lose out if you choose to exercise your rights to move within the EEA. If you were to be at a disadvantage should you need to claim benefit, this may deter you from moving.

Example

Sancha is a Portuguese national who worked for many years in Portugal. She moves to the UK to be with her disabled cousin. Sancha works for two weeks and then claims carer's allowance. Sancha can be paid from her date of claim because she can rely on her periods of residence in Portugal to satisfy the 26-week past presence test.

Apportionment

Although a benefit you claim based on NI contributions is administered and paid by the 'competent state' (see p1508), sometimes all the states in which you have been insured will contribute a proportion of your benefit based on the proportion of your working life that you actually worked in that state.

Exporting benefits

European co-ordination rules allow you to 'export' certain social security benefits to another state if you cease to be resident in the member state in which the entitlement arose.

This means that certain benefits may not be reduced, modified, suspended, withdrawn or confiscated just because you go to live in a different member state.[27] The rules for exporting vary according to the benefit concerned: some are fully exportable, some may be exportable on a temporary basis, and some are not exportable at all. The rules also vary between Regulation 883/04 and Regulation 1408/71.

You should check the individual benefit rules in Chapter 63 to see whether that benefit can be exported. If it can, you should contact the office that pays your benefit well in advance so that arrangements can be made to pay you in the EEA state you are going to.

Under Regulation 883/04, all benefits covered by this Regulation, other than those deemed special non-contributory benefits are exportable. See p1505 for a list of the UK benefits covered.

The following benefits are **fully exportable** and can be exported indefinitely:

- invalidity benefits;
- old age benefits;
- survivors' cash benefits;
- pensions for accidents at work or occupational diseases;
- death grants.

The following benefits can be **exported for a limited period** or subject to certain restrictions:

- unemployment benefits;
- sickness and maternity benefits under Regulation 1408/71.

Under Regulation 883/04 sickness, maternity and paternity benefits should arguably be exportable in a similar way to the fully exportable benefits.[28] However, the DWP may not regard them as fully exportable. Seek specialist advice if this affects you.

Special non-contributory benefits **cannot be exported**. They are paid only in the state in which you are resident.[29]

Family benefits

Under Regulation 883/04, family benefits include child benefit, child tax credit (CTC), guardian's allowance and child dependants' additions in other benefits. Under Regulation 883/04, you can export family benefits without time limit[30] and you can also claim family benefits for family members who are living apart from you in another EU state.[31] This is an improvement on the provisions of Regulation 1408/71 and means that child benefit and CTC can now be exported in the same circumstances.

Under Regulation 1408/71, family benefits include child benefit, CTC, guardian's allowance and child dependents' additions in other benefits. However, under Regulation 1408/71, you cannot export family benefits, but you can claim family benefits for family members who are living apart from you in another EEA state. Regulation 1408/71 also has a category of family allowances, which includes child benefit. These family allowances can be exported if you receive a pension (which can include retirement pension or contributory employment and support allowance). Since child benefit is classified as both a family benefit and a family allowance it can, in limited circumstances, be exported under Regulation 1408/71.

CTC is not a family allowance and so it cannot be exported on that basis under Regulation 1408/71. However, if you receive another UK benefit when living abroad, you may be able to argue that CTC is a supplement to that benefit and can be exported in that capacity.[32]

There are detailed rules in Regulation 883/04 on establishing priority between family members who are each entitled in separate states and when different states have different conditions for benefits (some based on residence, some on employment, others on contributions). These rules are to prevent you claiming family benefits from more than one state for the same family member. If you are entitled to family benefits under the legislation of more than one state, you will receive the highest amount provided for, topped up if necessary by the paying state.

If you are entitled to benefits from more than one state on the same basis, the priority is:[33]

- if family benefits are based on employment/self-employment in both states, the state where the child resides if the parent works there, otherwise the state that pays the highest amount;
- if family benefits are based on receipt of a pension in both states, the state where the child resides if that state also pays the pension, otherwise the state where you have been insured or resided for the longest period;
- if family benefits are based on residence, the state where the child resides.

Overlapping benefit rules

A general principle of the EU rules on co-ordination is that a claimant should not use one period of compulsory insurance to obtain more than one benefit derived from that period of insurance.[34] In general, you are only insured in one EEA member state for any one period, so you cannot use insurance from that one period to obtain entitlement to benefits of the same kind from two member states. Usually, benefits are adjusted to ensure that either only one state (the 'competent state' – see p1508) pays the benefit, taking into account periods of insurance in other EEA member states, or that the benefit is paid *pro rata* according to the lengths of periods of insurance in different member states. Aggregation or exportability provisions apply, but not both.

In certain cases, however, you may be paid both the full level of a UK benefit and a proportion of the benefit from another member state, accrued as a result of having paid insurance contributions there. Member states are not allowed to apply provisions preventing the overlapping of their own benefits with those of other member states if it would have the effect of reducing what you would have received from your years of contributions in the first member state alone.[35]

Notes

1. **Introduction**

1 *The Agreement between the European Community and its Member States, of the one part, and the Swiss Confederation, of the other, on the Free Movement of Persons*, Luxembourg, 21 June 1999, Cm5639 (in force 1 June 2002). Note also that reg 2 EEA Regs defines Switzerland as an EEA state.

2. **Who is covered**

2 Art 2 EU Reg 883/04
3 Art 1(g) EU Reg 1408/71
4 Art 1(l) EU Reg 883/04
5 Art 87(8) EU Reg 883/04
6 Art 1(i) EU Reg 883/04; Art 1(f) EU Reg 1408/71

3. **Which benefits are covered**

7 Art 3 EU Reg 883/04; Art 4(1) EU Reg 1408/71
8 *Commission of the European Communities v European Parliament and Council of the European Union*, C-299/05 [2007] ECR I-08695
9 *Stewart v SSWP*, C-503/09 [2011] ECR, not yet reported
10 Art 70(1) and (2) and Annex 10 EU Reg 883/04; Art 4(2a) EU Reg 1408/71
11 Annex X EU Reg 883/04

4. **Principles of co-ordination**

12 Art 11 EU Reg 883/04; Art 13 EU Reg 1408/71
13 Art 1(s) EU Reg 883/04; Art 1(q) EU Reg 1408/71
14 Art 1(q) EU Reg 883/04; Art 1(o) EU Reg 1408/71
15 Art 11 EU Reg 883/04
16 Art 13 EU Reg 883/04
17 Art 12 EU Reg 883/04
18 Art 11 EU Reg 987/09
19 Arts 11-16 EU Reg 883/04
20 CDLA/735/2009
21 Arts 13-17a EU Reg 1408/71
22 *Patmalniece v SSWP* [2011] UKSC 11
23 European Commission Press Release IP/11/1118, 29 September 2011
24 Art 5 EU Reg 883/04
25 Art 6 EU Reg 883/04
26 *Fonds national de retraite des ouvriers mineurs v Giovanni Mura*, 22-77 [1977] ECR 01699; but see also *Maria Frangiamore v Office National de l'Emploi*, 126/77 [1978] 00725 and *Bestuur van de Nieuwe Algemene Bedrijfsvereniging v WFJM Warmerdam-Steggerda*, 388/87 [1989] ECR 01203
27 Art 7 EU Reg 883/04; Art 10 EU Reg 1408/71
28 Art 7 Reg 883/04 is not limited in the same way as Art 10 Reg 1408/71
29 Art 70 Reg 883/04; Art 10a EU Reg 1408/71
30 *EM v HMRC (TC)* [2010] UKUT 323 AAC
31 Art 67 EU Reg 883/04
32 Art 77(1) EU Reg 1408/1 and *EM v HMRC (TC)* [2010] UKUT 323 (AAC) and *AW v HMRC (TC)* [2011] UKUT 322 (AAC)
33 Art 68(1) EU Reg 883/04
34 Art 10 EU Reg 883/04; Art 12 EU Reg 1408/71
35 *Teresa and Silvana Petroni v Office National des Pensions Pour Travailleurs Salariés (ONPTS), Bruxelles* 24-75 [1975] ECR 01149

Appendices

Appendix 1

Useful addresses

The President and areas of the Tribunals Service

The President of the Social Entitlement Chamber
5th Floor
Fox Court
14 Grays Inn Road
London WC1X 8HN
Tel: 0203 206 0619
www.tribunals.gov.uk

The President (Northern Ireland)
Cleaver House
3 Donegall Square North
Belfast BT1 5GA
Tel: 028 9051 8518

Tribunal areas

Birmingham
Admin Support Centre
PO Box 14620
Birmingham B16 6FR
Tel: 0845 408 3500
Textphone: 0121 634 7218
Fax: 0121 450 6392
ASCBirmingham@tribunals.gsi.gov.uk

Cardiff
Eastgate House
Newport Road
Cardiff CF24 0YP
Tel: 0300 123 1142
Textphone: 0300 123 1264
Fax: 02920 440 596
SSCSA-Cardiff@tribunals.gsi.gov.uk

Glasgow
Wellington House
134–136 Wellington Street
Glasgow G2 2XL
Tel: 0141 354 8400
Textphone: 0141 354 8413
Fax: 0141 354 8463
SSCSA-Glasgow@tribunals.gsi.gov.uk

Leeds
York House
York Place
Leeds LS1 2ED
Tel: 0300 123 1142
Textphone: 0300 123 1264
Fax: 0113 389 6001
SSCSA-Leeds@tribunals.gsi.gov.uk

Liverpool
36 Dale Street
Liverpool L2 5UZ
Tel: 0300 123 1142
Textphone: 0300 123 1264
Fax: 0151 243 1401
SSCSA-Liverpool@tribunals.gsi.gov.uk

Newcastle
Manorview House
Kings Manor
Newcastle upon Tyne NE1 6PA
Tel: 0300 123 1264
Textphone: 0300 123 1264
Fax: 0191 201 2357
SSCSA-Newcastle@tribunals.gsi.gov.uk

Sutton
Copthall House
9 The Pavement
Grove Road
Sutton SM1 1DA
Tel: 0300 123 1142
Textphone: 0300 123 1264
Fax: 020 8652 2301
SSCSA-Sutton@tribunals.gsi.gov.uk

First-Tier Tribunal (Tax)

Tribunals Service
2nd Floor
54 Hagley Road
Birmingham B16 8PE
Tel: 0845 223 8080
www.tribunals.gov.uk/tax
taxappeals@tribunals.gsi.gov.uk

The Upper Tribunal (Administrative Appeals Chamber)

England
5th Floor
7 Rolls Building
Fetter Lane
London EC4A 1NL
Tel: 020 7071 5562
Fax: 020 7071 5663
adminappeals@tribunals.gsi.gov.uk
www.administrativeappeals.tribunals.gov.uk

Scotland
George House
126 George Street
Edinburgh EH2 4HH
Tel: 0131 271 4310
ossc@ossc-scotland.org.uk

Northern Ireland
3rd Floor, Bedford House
16–22 Bedford Street
Belfast BT2 7FD
Tel: 028 9072 8736

Wales
Civil Justice Centre
2 Park Street
Cardiff CF10 1ET
Tel: 029 2066 2257

The Upper Tribunal (Tax and Chancery Chamber)

England and Wales
45 Bedford Square
London WC1B 3DN
Tel: 020 7612 9700

Scotland
George House
126 George Street
Edinburgh EH2 4HH

HM Revenue and Customs (tax credits)

England, Scotland and Wales
Tax Credit Office
Preston PR1 4AT
www.hmrc.gov.uk/taxcredits

Northern Ireland
Tax Credit Office
Dorchester House
52-58 Great Victoria Street
Belfast BT2 7WF

Tax Credit Helpline
Tel: 0345 300 3900
Textphone: 0345 300 3909

HM Revenue and Customs (child benefit and guardian's allowance)

England, Scotland and Wales
Child Benefit Office
PO Box 1
Newcastle upon Tyne NE88 1AA
Tel: 0845 302 1444
Textphone: 0845 302 1474
www.hmrc.gov.uk/childbenefit

HM Revenue and Customs (Solicitor's Office)

South West Wing
Bush House
Strand
London WC2B 4RD
www.hmrc.gov.uk/solicitors

HM Revenue and Customs

National Insurance Contributions Office
Benton Park View
Newcastle upon Tyne NE98 1ZZ
Tel: 0845 302 1479
Textphone: 0845 915 3296
www.hmrc.gov.uk/nic

HM Revenue and Customs (Statutory Payments Disputes Team)

Room BP2OO2
Benton Park View
Longbenton
Newcastle upon Tyne NE98 1YS
Tel: 0191 225 5221

Department for Work and Pensions (benefits)

Quarry House
Quarry Hill
Leeds LS2 7UA
Tel: 0113 232 4000
www.dwp.gov.uk

Department for Work and Pensions (policy)

The Adelphi
1–11 John Adam Street
London WC2N 6HT
Tel: 020 7962 8000

Department for Work and Pensions (Office of the Solicitor)

The Adelphi
1–11 John Adam Street
London WC2N 6HT
Tel: 020 7962 8000

Department for Work and Pensions (Decision Making and Appeals Unit)

Quarry House
Quarry Hill
Leeds LS2 7UB
Tel: 0113 232 4855

Department for Work and Pensions (Overseas Medical Benefits Section)

Tyneview Park
Newcastle upon Tyne NE98 1BA
Tel: 0191 218 1999

Disability and Carers Service

5th Floor
Whitehall 2
Whitehall Quay
Leeds LS1 4HR

Benefit Enquiry Line
Tel: 0800 88 22 00
Textphone: 0800 24 33 55
BEL-customer-services@dwp.gsi.gov.uk

Disability Contact and Processing Unit
Attendance Allowance Unit and Disability Living Allowance Unit
Warbreck House
Warbreck Hill
Blackpool FY2 0YE
Tel: 08457 12 34 56
Textphone: 08457 22 44 33
dcpu.customer-services@dwp.gsi.gov.uk

Carer's Allowance Unit
Palatine House
Lancaster Road
Preston PR1 1HB
Tel: 0845 608 4321
Textphone: 0845 604 5312
cau.customer-services@dwp.gsi.gov.uk

Exporting benefits overseas
Warbreck House
Warbreck Hill Road
Blackpool FY2 0YE
exportability.team@dwp.gsi.gov.uk

Child Support Agency
National Helpline
PO Box 55
Brierly Hill DY5 1YL
Tel: 08457 133 133
Textphone: 08457 138 924
www.direct.gov.uk

Child Maintenance Enforcement Commission
Child Maintenance Options
Tel: 0800 988 0988 (Great Britain)
www.cmoptions.org

Tel: 0800 028 7439 (Northern Ireland)
www.nidirect.gov.uk/choices

Jobcentre Plus
Caxton House
Tothill Street
London SW1H 9NA
Tel: 020 7962 8000
www.direct.gov.uk

The Pension Service
PO Box 50101
London SW1P 2WU
Tel: 0845 60 60 265
Textphone: 0845 60 60 285
www.direct.gov.uk/en/pensionsandretirementplanning

Winter Fuel Payments Helpline
PO Box 10142
Annesley
Nottingham NG15 5WY
Tel: 08459 15 15 15
Textphone: 0845 601 5613
www.thepensionservice.gov.uk

International Pension Centre
Tyneview Park
Whitley Road
Newcastle NE98 1BA
Tel: 0191 218 7777
Textphone: 0191 218 7280

NHS Business Services Authority (help with health costs)

Sandyford House
Archbold Terrace
Newcastle upon Tyne NE2 1DB
Tel: 0845 850 1166
Textphone: 18001 0845 850 1166
www.nhsbsa.nhs.uk/
helpwithhealthcosts.aspx

Department for Education

Sanctuary Buildings
Great Smith Street
London SW1P 3BT
Tel: 0370 000 2288
www.education.gov.uk

Compensation Recovery Unit

England, Scotland and Wales

Durham House
Washington NE38 7SF
Tel: 0191 213 5000
Textphone: 0191 225 2003
www.dwp.gov.uk/cru

Northern Ireland

Magnet House
81-93 York Street
Belfast BT15 1SS
Tel: 028 9054 5890
www.dsdni.gov.uk/ssa_cru

Independent Review Service for the Social Fund

4th Floor
Centre City Podium
5 Hill Street
Birmingham B5 4UB
Freephone: 0800 096 1926
Textphone: 0800 096 1929
Fax: 0121 606 2172/2186
sfc@irs-review.org.uk
www.irs-review.org.uk

Local Government Ombudsman

England

LGO Advice Team
PO Box 4771
Coventry CV4 0EH
Tel: 0300 061 0614
advice@lgo.org.uk
www.lgo.org.uk

Scottish Public Services Ombudsman

4 Melville Street
Edinburgh EH3 7NS
Tel: 0800 377 7330
www.spso.org.uk

Public Services Ombudsman for Wales

1 Ffordd yr Hen Gae
Pencoed CF35 5LJ
Tel: 0845 601 0987
Fax: 01656 641 199
www.ombudsman-wales.org.uk

The Parliamentary and Health Service Ombudsman

Millbank Tower
Millbank
London SW1P 4QP
Tel: 0345 015 4033
Fax: 0300 661 4000
phso.enquiries@ombudsman.org.uk
www.ombudsman.org.uk

The Independent Adjudicator

Judy Clements OBE
Adjudicator's Office
8th Floor, Euston Tower
286 Euston Road
London NW1 3US
Tel: 0300 057 1111
Fax: 020 7667 1830
www.adjudicatorsoffice.gov.uk

Appendix 2

Information and advice

Independent advice and representation

If you want advice or information on a benefit or tax credit issue, the following may be able to assist.

- Citizens Advice Bureaux (CABx). You can find out where your local CAB is from the Citizens Advice website at www.citizensadvice.org.uk (England and Wales) or www.cas.org.uk (Scotland).
- Law centres. You can find your nearest law centre at www.lawcentres.org.uk.
- Other independent advice centres.
- Local authority welfare rights services.
- Local organisations for particular groups of claimants may offer help. For instance, there are unemployed centres, pensioners' groups and centres for people with disabilities.
- Solicitors can give free legal advice to people on low incomes under the 'Legal Help' scheme. This does not cover the cost of representation at an appeal hearing but can cover the cost of preparing written submissions and obtaining evidence such as medical reports.

You can find details of advice centres and lawyers in the phone book either under 'advice' or in the 'community' section at the front of the book. Your library or community centre may have details of where to get advice in your area. Community Legal Advice has a list of many organisations which provide advice in different areas of law, including welfare benefits. You can phone them on 0845 345 4345 or visit http://legaladviserfinder.justice.gov.uk.

Advice from CPAG

Unfortunately, CPAG is unable to deal with enquiries directly from members of the public, but if you are an adviser you can phone for advice from 2pm to 4pm, Monday to Friday on 020 7833 4627.

Organisations based in Scotland can contact CPAG in Scotland at Unit 9, Ladywell, 94 Duke Street, Glasgow G4 0UW or email advice@cpagscotland.org.uk. A phone line is open for advisers in Scotland Monday to Friday from 10am to 12 noon on 0141 552 0552.

Advice from the DWP

The phone book should list contact details for your local DWP office. See also Appendix 1 of this *Handbook* for contact details for the DWP and HM Revenue and Customs (HMRC). If you are disabled, you can obtain free telephone advice on benefits on 0800 882 200; minicom: 0800 243 355 (in Northern Ireland 0800 220 674; minicom: 0800 243 787). This is for general advice and not specific queries on individual claims.

Finding help on the internet

Some information about benefits and tax credits, including a selection of leaflets and forms is available on the DWP website at www.dwp.gov.uk and the HMRC website at www.hmrc.gov.uk. The DWP website also has links to the executive agencies of the DWP. You may also find some useful information at www.direct.gov.uk.

CPAG's website (www.cpag.org.uk) has some articles and briefings, and information about its publications, training and campaigning activities.

The rightsnet website (aimed at advisers) at www.rightsnet.org.uk has details of new legislation, some caselaw and guidance. It also has links to other useful sites.

Most Acts and regulations can be found on the government information website at www.legislation.gov.uk.

You can find commssioners' and Upper Tribunal decisions at www.justice.gov.uk.

Appendix 3

Useful publications

Many of the books listed here will be in your local public library. Stationery Office books are available from Stationery Office bookshops or ordered by post, telephone, fax, email or online from from TSO Orders, PO Box 29, Norwich NR3 1GN (tel: 0870 600 5522; fax: 0870 600 5533; email: customer.services@tso.co.uk; web: www.tsoshop.co.uk). Many publications listed are available from CPAG. See below for order details, or order from http://www.cpag.org.uk/bookshop.

1. Caselaw and legislation

Social Security Case Law – Digest of Commissioners' Decisions
D Neligan (Stationery Office, looseleaf in two vols).

CPAG's Welfare Benefits and Tax Credits Law Online
Includes all social security and tax credits legislation updated and consolidated throughout the year; decisions of the courts and Upper Tribunal, some with commentary; the full text of the *Welfare Benefits and Tax Credits Handbook* updated throughout the year with links to the relevant legislation, Upper Tribunal decisions and caselaw. Annual subscription £53 + VAT per user (bulk discounts available). More information at www.cpag.org.uk/bookshop.

CPAG's Child Support Law Online
Includes all child support legislation updated and consolidated throughout the year; commentary from *Child Support: the legislation* (Jacobs); the *Child Support Handbook* updated once a year in line with the print edition, with links to the relevant legislation, Upper Tribunal decisions and caselaw. Annual subscription £65 + VAT per concurrent user (bulk discounts available). More information at www.cpag.org.uk/bookshop.

CPAG's Housing Benefit and Council Tax Benefit Law Online
Includes complete housing benefit and council tax benefit legislation, updated and consolidated throughout the year; commentary from CPAG's *Housing Benefit & Council Tax Benefit Legislation* (Findlay), updated twice a year in line with the print edition, with links to Upper Tribunal decisions, court cases and other relevant material. Annual subscription £110 + VAT per concurrent user (bulk discounts

available). More information at www.cpag.org.uk/bookshop.

CPAG's Benefits for Migrants Law Online
This service includes the full text of the *Benefits for Migrants Handbook*, updated throughout the year, with links to external databases of UK and European law, and to CPAG's own consolidated social security legislation and caselaw. Annual subscription £30 + VAT per concurrent user (bulk discounts available). More information at www.cpag.org.uk/bookshop.

The Law Relating to Social Security
(Stationery Office, looseleaf, 12 vols)
All the legislation but without any commentary. Known as the 'Blue Book'. Also available at www.dwp.gov.uk/publications/specilaist-guides/law-volumes.

Social Security Legislation, Volume I: Non-Means-Tested Benefits
D Bonner, I Hooker and R White (Sweet & Maxwell)
Legislation with commentary. 2012/13 edition (October 2012): £98 for the main volume, reduced to £92 if you are a CPAG member and order from CPAG before 30 June 2012, or at full price from July.

Social Security Legislation, Volume II: Income Support, Jobseeker's Allowance and the Social Fund
J Mesher, P Wood, R Poynter, N Wikeley and D Bonner (Sweet & Maxwell)
Legislation with commentary. 2012/13 edition (October 2012): £98 for the main volume, reduced to £92 if you are a CPAG member and order from CPAG before 30 June 2012, or at full price from July.

Social Security Legislation, Volume III: Administration, Adjudication and the European Dimension
M Rowland and R White (Sweet & Maxwell)
Legislation with commentary. 2012/13 edition (October 2012): £98 for the main volume, reduced to £92 if you are a CPAG member and order from CPAG before 30 June 2012, or at full price from July.

Social Security Legislation, Volume IV: Tax Credits, Child Trust Funds and HMRC-Administered Social Security Benefits
N Wikeley and D Williams (Sweet & Maxwell)
Legislation with commentary. 2012/13 edition (October 2012): £98 for the main volume, reduced to £92 if you are a CPAG member and order from CPAG before 30 June 2012, or at full price from July.

Social Security Legislation – updating supplement to Volumes I, II, III & IV
(Sweet & Maxwell)
The spring 2012 update to the 2011/12 main volumes: £60 reduced to £55 if you are a CPAG member and order from CPAG before 30 June 2012, or at full price from July.

CPAG's Housing Benefit and Council Tax Benefit Legislation
L Findlay, R Poynter, S Wright, C George and M Williams (CPAG)
Legislation with detailed commentary. 2012/13 (25th) edition (autumn 2012): £105 including Supplement. Reduced to £99 per set if ordered before 30 June 2012. The 24th edition (2011/12) is still available, £100 per set. Available as part of *CPAG's Housing Benefit and Council Tax Law Online*.

2. Official guidance
Decision Makers Guide
(14 volumes, memos and letters)
Available at www.dwp.gov.uk/publications/specialist-guides/decision-makers-guide

Housing Benefit and Council Tax Benefit Guidance Manual
(Stationery Office, looseleaf)
Available at www.dwp.gov.uk/local-authoritystaff/housing-benefit/claims-processing/operational-manuals

DWP Health and Work Guidance
Available at www.dwp.gov.uk/healthcare-professional/guidance

Work Capability Assessment (WCA) Handbook
Available at www.dwp.gov.uk/docs/wca-handbook.pdf

Tax Credit Technical Manual
Available at www.hmrc.gov.uk/manuals/

The Social Fund Guide
(Stationery Office, looseleaf 2 vols)
Available at www.dwp.gov.uk/publications/specialist-guides

3. Leaflets
The DWP publishes many leaflets available free from your local DWP or Jobcentre Plus office. To order large numbers of leaflets, or receive information about new leaflets, contact ION Contact Centre, 2nd Floor, One City West, Gelderd Road, Leeds LS12 6NT, tel: 0845 850 0479, email: ion-pass@xerox.com. Leaflets on HB/CTB are available from your local council.

4. Periodicals
Welfare Rights Bulletin (CPAG, bi-monthly)
Covers developments in social security law, including Upper Tribunal decisions, and updates this *Handbook* between editions. The annual subscription is £34 but it is sent automatically to some categories of CPAG member (contact CPAG for details).

Articles on social security can also be found in *Legal Action* (Legal Action Group), *The Adviser* (Citizens Advice) and the *Journal of Social Security Law* (Sweet & Maxwell).

5. Other publications – general
Universal Credit: what you need to know
£10 (1st edition, spring 2012)
£11 (2nd edition, spring 2013)

Child Support Handbook
£28 (20th edition, summer 2012) (£8.50 for claimants). Also available

as part of *CPAG's Child Support Law Online.*

Debt Advice Handbook
£22 (10th edition, autumn 2012)

Fuel Rights Handbook
£21 (16th edition, autumn 2012)

Personal Finance Handbook
£16.50 (3rd edition, November 2009)

Paying for Care Handbook
£19.50 (6th edition, March 2009)

Student Support and Benefits Handbook: England, Wales and Northern Ireland
£13.50 (9th edition, February 2012)

Benefits for Students in Scotland Handbook
£15 (10th edition, autumn 2012)
Available free online at: http://scottishhandbooks.cpag.org.uk

Council Tax Handbook
£17 (9th edition, November 2011)

Benefits for Migrants Handbook
£25 (6th edition, winter 2012)

Children's Handbook Scotland: a benefits guide for children living away from their parents
£15 (5th edition, autumn 2012)
Available free online at: http://scottishhandbooks.cpag.org.uk

Guide to Housing Benefit and Council Tax Benefit
£30 (summer 2012)

Disability Rights Handbook
£29.50 (May 2012)

ESA: Employment and Support Allowance
£10 (2nd edition, March 2011)

Children in Need: local authority support for children and families
£45 (1st edition, April 2011)

Disabled Children: a legal handbook
£45 (2nd edition, summer 2012)

Tribunal Practice and Procedure
£50 (2nd edition, June 2011)

For CPAG publications and most of those in Sections 1 and 5 contact:
CPAG, 94 White Lion Street, London N1 9PF, tel: 020 7837 7979, fax: 020 7837 6414. Enquiries: email: bookorders@cpag.org.uk. Order forms are available at www.cpag.org.uk/publications. Postage and packing: free for online subscriptions and orders up to £10 in value; for order value £10.01–£100 add a flat rate charge of £3.99; for order value £100.01–£400 add £5.99; for order value £400+ add £9.99.

Appendix 4

Statutory maternity pay, statutory paternity pay (birth) and maternity allowance

Baby is expected during the week beginning Sunday	*Latest start date of employment for SMP*	*15th week before the EWC begins Sunday+*	*Earliest week for SMP or MA begins Sunday++*	*66-week test period for MA begins Sunday*
1.1.12	2.4.11	18.9.11	16.10.11	26.9.10
8.1.12	9.4.11	25.9.11	23.10.11	3.10.10
15.1.12	16.4.11	2.10.11	30.10.11	10.10.10
22.1.12	23.4.11	9.10.11	6.11.11	17.10.10
29.1.12	30.4.11	16.10.11	13.11.11	24.10.10
5.2.12	7.5.11	23.10.11	20.11.11	31.10.10
12.2.12	14.5.11	30.10.11	27.11.11	7.11.10
19.2.12	21.5.11	6.11.11	4.12.11	14.11.10
26.2.12	28.5.11	13.11.11	11.12.11	21.11.10
4.3.12	4.6.11	20.11.11	18.12.11	28.11.10
11.3.12	11.6.11	27.11.11	25.12.11	5.12.10
18.3.12	18.6.11	4.12.11	1.1.12	12.12.10
25.3.12	25.6.11	11.12.11	8.1.12	19.12.10
1.4.12	2.7.11	18.12.11	15.1.12	26.12.10
8.4.12	9.7.11	25.12.11	22.1.12	2.1.11
15.4.12	16.7.11	1.1.12	29.1.12	9.1.11
22.4.12	23.7.11	8.1.12	5.2.12	16.1.11
29.4.12	30.7.11	15.1.12	12.2.12	23.1.11
6.5.12	6.8.11	22.1.12	19.2.12	30.1.11
13.5.12	13.8.11	29.1.12	26.2.12	6.2.11
20.5.12	20.8.11	5.2.12	4.3.12	13.2.11
27.5.12	27.8.11	12.2.12	11.3.12	20.2.11
3.6.12	3.9.11	19.2.12	18.3.12	27.2.11
10.6.12	10.9.11	26.2.12	25.3.12	6.3.11
17.6.12	17.9.11	4.3.12	1.4.12	13.3.11
24.6.12	24.9.11	11.3.12	8.4.12	20.3.11

Baby is expected during the week beginning Sunday	*Latest start date of employment for SMP*	*15th week before the EWC begins Sunday+*	*Earliest week for SMP or MA begins Sunday++*	*66-week test period for MA begins Sunday*
1.7.12	1.10.11	18.3.12	15.4.12	27.3.11
8.7.12	8.10.11	25.3.12	22.4.12	3.4.11
15.7.12	15.10.11	1.4.12	29.4.12	10.4.11
22.7.12	22.10.11	8.4.12	6.5.12	17.4.11
29.7.12	29.10.11	15.4.12	13.5.12	24.4.11
5.8.12	5.11.11	22.4.12	20.5.12	1.5.11
12.8.12	12.11.11	29.4.12	27.5.12	8.5.11
19.8.12	19.11.11	6.5.12	3.6.12	15.5.11
26.8.12	26.11.11	13.5.12	10.6.12	22.5.11
2.9.12	3.12.11	20.5.12	17.6.12	29.5.11
9.9.12	10.12.11	27.5.12	24.6.12	5.6.11
16.9.12	17.12.11	3.6.12	1.7.12	12.6.11
23.9.12	24.12.11	10.6.12	8.7.12	19.6.11
30.9.12	31.12.11	17.6.12	15.7.12	26.6.11
7.10.12	7.1.12	24.6.12	22.7.12	3.7.11
14.10.12	14.1.12	1.7.12	29.7.12	10.7.11
21.10.12	21.1.12	8.7.12	5.8.12	17.7.11
28.10.12	28.1.12	15.7.12	12.8.12	24.7.11
4.11.12	4.2.12	22.7.12	19.8.12	31.7.11
11.11.12	11.2.12	29.7.12	26.8.12	7.8.11
18.11.12	18.2.12	5.8.12	2.9.12	14.8.11
25.11.12	25.2.12	12.8.12	9.9.12	21.8.11
2.12.12	3.3.12	19.8.12	16.9.12	28.8.11
9.12.12	10.3.12	26.8.12	23.9.12	4.9.11
16.12.12	17.3.12	2.9.12	30.9.12	11.9.11
23.12.12	24.3.12	9.9.12	7.10.12	18.9.11
30.12.12	31.3.12	16.9.12	14.10.12	25.9.11
6.1.13	7.4.12	23.9.12	21.10.12	2.10.11
13.1.13	14.4.12	30.9.12	28.10.12	9.10.11
20.1.13	21.4.12	7.10.12	4.11.12	16.10.11
27.1.13	28.4.12	14.10.12	11.11.12	23.10.11
3.2.13	5.5.12	21.10.12	18.11.12	30.10.11
10.2.13	12.5.12	28.10.12	25.11.12	6.11.11
17.2.13	19.5.12	4.11.12	2.12.12	13.11.11
24.2.13	26.5.12	11.11.12	9.12.12	20.11.11
3.3.13	2.6.12	18.11.12	16.12.12	27.11.11
10.3.13	9.6.12	25.11.12	23.12.12	4.12.11
17.3.13	16.6.12	2.12.12	30.12.12	11.12.11
24.3.13	23.6.12	9.12.12	6.1.13	18.12.11
31.3.13	30.6.12	16.12.12	13.1.13	25.12.11

Baby is expected during the week beginning Sunday	*Latest start date of employment for SMP*	*15th week before the EWC begins Sunday+*	*Earliest week for SMP or MA begins Sunday++*	*66-week test period for MA begins Sunday*
7.4.13	7.7.12	23.12.12	20.1.13	1.1.12
14.4.13	14.7.12	30.12.12	27.1.13	8.1.12
21.4.13	21.7.12	6.1.13	3.2.13	15.1.12
28.4.13	28.7.12	13.1.13	10.2.13	22.1.12
5.5.13	4.8.12	20.1.13	17.2.13	29.1.12
12.5.13	11.8.12	27.1.13	24.2.13	5.2.12
19.5.13	18.8.12	3.2.13	3.3.13	12.2.12
26.5.13	25.8.12	10.2.13	10.3.13	19.2.12
2.6.13	1.9.12	17.2.13	17.3.13	26.2.12
9.6.13	8.9.12	24.2.13	24.3.13	4.3.12
16.6.13	15.9.12	3.3.13	31.3.13	11.3.12
23.6.13	22.9.12	10.3.13	7.4.13	18.3.12
30.6.13	29.9.12	17.3.13	14.4.13	25.3.12
7.7.13	6.10.12	24.3.13	21.4.13	1.4.12
14.7.13	13.10.12	31.3.13	28.4.13	8.4.12
21.7.13	20.10.12	7.4.13	5.5.13	15.4.12
28.7.13	27.10.12	14.4.13	12.5.13	22.4.12
4.8.13	3.11.12	21.4.13	19.5.13	29.4.12
11.8.13	10.11.12	28.4.13	26.5.13	6.5.12
18.8.13	17.11.12	5.5.13	2.6.13	13.5.12
25.8.13	24.11.12	12.5.13	9.6.13	20.5.12
1.9.13	1.12.12	19.5.13	16.6.13	27.5.12
8.9.13	8.12.12	26.5.13	23.6.13	3.6.12
15.9.13	15.12.12	2.6.13	30.6.13	10.6.12
22.9.13	22.12.12	9.6.13	7.7.13	17.6.12
29.9.13	29.12.12	16.6.13	14.7.13	24.6.12
6.10.13	5.1.13	23.6.13	21.7.13	1.7.12
13.10.13	12.1.13	30.6.13	28.7.13	8.7.12
20.10.13	19.1.13	7.7.13	4.8.13	15.7.12
27.10.13	26.1.13	14.7.13	11.8.13	22.7.12
3.11.13	2.2.13	21.7.13	18.8.13	29.7.12
10.11.13	9.2.13	28.7.13	25.8.13	5.8.12
17.11.13	16.2.13	4.8.13	1.9.13	12.8.12
24.11.13	23.2.13	11.8.13	8.9.13	19.8.12
1.12.13	2.3.13	18.8.13	15.9.13	26.8.12
8.12.13	9.3.13	25.8.13	22.9.13	2.9.12
15.12.13	16.3.13	1.9.13	29.9.13	9.9.12
22.12.13	23.3.13	8.9.13	6.10.13	16.9.12
29.12.13	30.3.13	15.9.13	13.10.13	23.9.12
5.1.14	6.4.13	22.9.13	20.10.13	30.9.12

Baby is expected during the week beginning Sunday	*Latest start date of employment for SMP*	*15th week before the EWC begins Sunday+*	*Earliest week for SMP or MA begins Sunday++*	*66-week test period for MA begins Sunday*
12.1.14	13.4.13	29.9.13	27.10.13	7.10.12
19.1.14	20.4.13	6.10.13	3.11.13	14.10.12
26.1.14	27.4.13	13.10.13	10.11.13	21.10.12
2.2.14	4.5.13	20.10.13	17.11.13	28.10.12
9.2.14	11.5.13	27.10.13	24.11.13	4.11.12

+ EWC is the expected week of childbirth. The 15th week before the EWC is relevant to the continuous employment rule and the earnings condition for SMP and SPP (birth). See Chapter 27.

++ This is the 11th week before the baby is due (unless your baby is born earlier. See Chapters 21 and 27 for possible exceptions).

Appendix 5

Pension age for women born between 6 April 1950 and 5 December 1953

Date of birth	*Pension age (in years/months)**	*Date pension age reached*
06.04.50 – 05.05.50	60.1 – 60.0	06.05.2010
06.05.50 – 05.06.50	60.2 – 60.1	06.07.2010
06.06.50 – 05.07.50	60.3 – 60.2	06.09.2010
06.07.50 – 05.08.50	60.4 – 60.3	06.11.2010
06.08.50 – 05.09.50	60.5 – 60.4	06.01.2011
06.09.50 – 05.10.50	60.6 – 60.5	06.03.2011
06.10.50 – 05.11.50	60.7 – 60.6	06.05.2011
06.11.50 – 05.12.50	60.8 – 60.7	06.07.2011
06.12.50 – 05.01.51	60.9 – 60.8	06.09.2011
06.01.51 – 05.02.51	60.10 – 60.9	06.11.2011
06.02.51 – 05.03.51	60.11 – 60.10	06.01.2012
06.03.51 – 05.04.51	61.0 – 60.11	06.03.2012
06.04.51 – 05.05.51	61.1 – 61.0	06.05.2012
06.05.51 – 05.06.51	61.2 – 61.1	06.07.2012
06.06.51 – 05.07.51	61.3 – 61.2	06.09.2012
06.07.51 – 05.08.51	61.4 – 61.3	06.11.2012
06.08.51 – 05.09.51	61.5 – 61.4	06.01.2013
06.09.51 – 05.10.51	61.6 – 61.5	06.03.2013
06.10.51 – 05.11.51	61.7 – 61.6	06.05.2013
06.11.51 – 05.12.51	61.8 – 61.7	06.07.2013
06.12.51 – 05.01.52	61.9 – 61.8	06.09.2013
06.01.52 – 05.02.52	61.10 – 61.9	06.11.2013
06.02.52 – 05.03.52	61.11 – 61.10	06.01.2014
06.03.52 – 05.04.52	62.0 – 61.11	06.03.2014
06.04.52 – 05.05.52	62.1 – 62.0	06.05.2014
06.05.52 – 05.06.52	62.2 – 62.1	06.07.2014
06.06.52 – 05.07.52	62.3 – 62.2	06.09.2014
06.07.52 – 05.08.52	62.4 – 62.3	06.11.2014

Date of birth	*Pension age (in years/months)**	*Date pension age reached*
06.08.52 – 05.09.52	62.5 – 62.4	06.01.2015
06.09.52 – 05.10.52	62.6 – 62.5	06.03.2015
06.10.52 – 05.11.52	62.7 – 62.6	06.05.2015
06.11.52 – 05.12.52	62.8 – 62.7	06.07.2015
06.12.52 – 05.01.53	62.9 – 62.8	06.09.2015
06.01.53 – 05.02.53	62.10 – 62.9	06.11.2015
06.02.53 – 05.03.53	62.11 – 62.10	06.01.2016
06.03.53 – 05.04.53	63.0 – 62.11	06.03.2016
06.04.53 – 05.05.53	63.3 – 63.2	06.07.2016
06.05.53 – 05.06.53	63.6 – 63.5	06.11.2016
06.06.53 – 05.07.53	63.9 – 63.8	06.03.2017
06.07.53 – 05.08.53	64.0 – 63.11	06.07.2017
06.08.53 – 05.09.53	64.3 – 64.2	06.11.2017
06.09.53 – 05.10.53	64.6 – 64.5	06.03.2018
06.10.53 – 05.11.53	64.9 – 64.8	06.07.2018
06.11.53 – 05.12.53	65.0 – 64.11	06.11.2018

* For example, '60.1–60.0' means you would be aged between 60 and 60 years and one month, depending on your date of birth, when you reach pension age.

Appendix 6

Prescribed degrees of disablement

Schedule 2 to the Social Security (General Benefit) Regulations 1982 SI No.1408

Description of injury		*Degree of disablement %*
1	Loss of both hands or amputation at higher sites	100
2	Loss of a hand and a foot	100
3	Double amputation through leg or thigh, or amputation through leg or thigh on one side and loss of other foot	100
4	Loss of sight to such an extent as to render the claimant unable to perform any work for which eyesight is essential	100
5	Very severe facial disfiguration	100
6	Absolute deafness	100
7	Forequarter or hindquarter amputation	100
Amputation cases – upper limbs (either arm)		
8	Amputation through shoulder joint	90
9	Amputation below shoulder with stump less than 20.5 cms from tip of acromion	80
10	Amputation from 20.5 cms from tip of acromion to less than 11.5 cms below tip of olecranon	70
11	Loss of a hand or of the thumb and 4 fingers of 1 hand or amputation from 11.5 cms below tip of olecranon	60
12	Loss of thumb	30
13	Loss of thumb and its metacarpal bone	40
14	Loss of 4 fingers of 1 hand	50
15	Loss of 3 fingers of 1 hand	30
16	Loss of 2 fingers of 1 hand	20
17	Loss of terminal phalanx of thumb	20
Amputation cases – lower limbs		
18	Amputation of both feet resulting in end-bearing stumps	90
19	Amputation through both feet proximal to the metatarso-phalangeal joint	80
20	Loss of all toes to both feet through the metatarso-phalangeal joint	40
21	Loss of all toes of both feet proximal to the proximal inter-phalangeal joint	30
22	Loss of all toes of both feet distal to the proximal inter-phalangeal joint	20
23	Amputation at hip	90
24	Amputation below hip with stump not exceeding 13 cms in length measured from tip of great trochanter	80

Description of injury		Degree of disablement %
25	Amputation below hip and above knee with stump exceeding 13 cms in length measured from tip of great trochanter, or at knee not resulting in end-bearing stump	70
26	Amputation at knee resulting in end-bearing stump or below knee with stump not exceeding 9 cms	60
27	Amputation below knee with stump exceeding 9 cms but not exceeding 13 cms	50
28	Amputation below knee with stump exceeding 13 cms	40
29	Amputation of 1 foot resulting in end-bearing stump	30
30	Amputation through 1 foot proximal to the metatarso-phalangeal joint	30
31	Loss of all toes of 1 foot through the metatarso- phalangeal joint	20
Other injuries		
32	Loss of 1 eye, without complications, the other being normal	40
33	Loss of vision of 1 eye, without complications or disfigurement of the eyeball, the other being normal	30
Loss of fingers of right or left hand		
	Index finger:	
34	Whole	14
35	2 phalanges	11
36	1 phalanx	9
37	Guillotine amputation of tip without loss of bone	5
	Middle finger:	
38	Whole	12
39	2 phalanges	9
40	1 phalanx	7
41	Guillotine amputation of tip without loss of bone	4
	Ring or little finger:	
42	Whole	7
43	2 phalanges	6
44	1 phalanx	5
45	Guillotine amputation of tip without loss of bone	2
Loss of toes of right or left foot		
	Great toe:	
46	Through metatarso-phalangeal joint	14
47	Part, with some loss of bone	3
	Any other toe:	
48	Through metatarso-phalangeal joint	3
49	Part, with some loss of bone	1
	2 toes of 1 foot, excluding great toe:	
50	Through metatarso-phalangeal joint	5
51	Part, with some loss of bone	2
	3 toes of 1 foot, excluding great toe:	
52	Through metatarso-phalangeal joint	6
53	Part, with some loss of bone	3
	4 toes of 1 foot, excluding great toe:	
54	Through metatarso-phalangeal joint	9
55	Part, with some loss of bone	3

The degree of disablement due to occupational deafness is assessed using tables and a formula to be found in reg 34 and Sch 3 Social Security (Industrial Injuries) (Prescribed Diseases) Regulations 1985, as amended.

Appendix 7

Prescribed industrial diseases

Part I of Schedule 1 to the Social Security (Industrial Injuries) (Prescribed Diseases) Regulations 1985 as amended

Prescribed disease or injury	*Occupation*
A – Conditions due to physical agents	**Any occupation involving:**
A1 Leukaemia (other than chronic lymphatic leukaemia) or cancer of the bone, female breast, testis or thyroid.	Exposure to electro-magnetic radiations (other than radiant heat), or to ionising particles, where the dose is sufficient to double the condition.
A2 Cataract.	Frequent or prolonged exposure to radiation from red-hot or white-hot material.
A3 Dysbarism, including decompression sickness, barotrauma and osteonecrosis.	Subjection to compressed or rarified air or from molten or red-hot material.
A4 Task-specific focal dystonia of the hand or forearm.	Prolonged periods of handwriting, typing or other repetitive movements of the fingers, hand or arm.
A5 Subcutaneous cellulitis of the hand.	Manual labour causing severe or prolonged friction or pressure on the hand.
A6 Bursitis or subcutaneous cellulites arising at or about the knee due to severe or prolonged external friction or pressure at or about the knee.	Manual labour causing severe or prolonged external friction or pressure at or about the knee.
A7 Bursitis or subcutaneous cellulites arising at or about the elbow due to severe or prolonged external friction or pressure at or about the elbow (beat elbow).	Manual labour causing severe or prolonged external friction or pressure at or about the elbow.
A8 Traumatic inflammation of the tendons of the hand or forearm, or of the associated tendon sheaths.	Manual labour, or frequent or repeated movements of the hand or wrist.

Prescribed disease or injury	*Occupation*
A10 Sensorineural hearing loss amounting to at least 50dB in each ear, being the average of hearing losses at 1, 2 and 3 kHz frequencies, and being due in the case of at least one ear to occupational noise (occupational deafness).	Any occupation involving the use of, or work wholly or mainly in the immediate vicinity of the use of, a: *(a)* band saw, circular saw or cutting disc to cut metal in the metal founding or forging industries, circular saw to cut products in the manufacture of steel, powered (other than hand powered) grinding tool on metal (other than sheet metal or plate metal, pneumatic percussive tool on metal, pressurised air arc tool to gouge metal, burner or torch to cut or dress steel based products, skid transfer bank, knock out and shake out grid in a foundry, machine (other than a power press machine) to forge metal including a machine used to drop stamp metal by means of closed or open dies or drop hammers, machine to cut or shape or clean metal nails, or plasma spray gun to spray molten metal; *(b)* pneumatic percussive tool to drill rock in a quarry, on stone in a quarry works, used underground, for mining coal, for sinking a shaft, or for tunnelling in civil engineering works; *(c)* vibrating metal moulding box in the concrete products industry, or circular saw to cut concrete masonry blocks; *(d)* machine in the manufacture of textiles for weaving man-made or natural fibres (including mineral fibres), high speed false twisting of fibres, or the mechanical cleaning of bobbins; *(e)* multi-cutter moulding machine on wood, planing machine on wood, automatic or semi-automatic lathe on wood, multiple cross-cut machine on wood, automatic shaping machine on wood, double-end tenoning machine on wood, vertical spindle moulding machine (including a high speed routing machine) on wood, edge banding machine on wood, bandsawing machine (with a blade width of not less than 75 millimetres) on wood including one operated by moving the blade towards the material being cut, or chain saw on wood;

Prescribed disease or injury	*Occupation*
	(f) jet of water (or a mixture of water and abrasive material) at a pressure above 680 bar, or jet channelling process to burn stone in a quarry; *(g)* machine in a ship's engine room, or gas turbine for performance testing on a test bed, installation testing of a replacement engine in an aircraft, or acceptance testing of an Armed Service fixed wing combat aircraft; *(h)* machine in the manufacture of glass containers or hollow ware for automatic moulding, automatic blow moulding, or automatic glass pressing and forming; *(i)* spinning machine using compressed air to produce glass wool or mineral wool; *(j)* continuous glass toughening furnace; *(k)* firearm by a police firearms training officer; *(l)* shot-blaster to carry abrasives in air for cleaning.
A11 *(a)* Intense blanching of the skin, with a sharp demarcation line between affected and non-affected skin, where the blanching is cold-induced, episodic, occurs throughout the year and affects the skin of the distal with the middle and proximal phalanges, or distal with the middle phalanx (or in the case of a thumb the distal with the proximal phalanx), of— *(i)* in the case of a person with 5 fingers (including thumb) on one hand, any 3 of those fingers, or *(ii)* in the case of a person with only 4 such fingers, any 2 of those fingers, or *(iii)* in the case of a person with less than 4 such fingers, any one of them or, as the case may be, the one remaining finger, where none of the person's fingers was subject to any degree of cold-induced, episodic blanching of the skin prior to the person's employment in an occupation described in the second column in relation to this paragraph, or	

Prescribed disease or injury	*Occupation*
(b) significant, demonstrable reduction in both sensory perception and manipulative dexterity with continuous numbness or continuous tingling all present at the same time in the distal phalanx of any finger (including thumb) where none of the person's fingers was subject to any degree of reduction in sensory perception, manipulative dexterity, numbness or tingling prior to the person's employment in an occupation described in the second column in relation to this paragraph, where the symptoms in paragraph (a) or paragraph (b) were caused by vibration.	*(a)* The use of hand-held chain saws on wood; *or* *(b)* the use of hand-held rotary tools in grinding or in the sanding or polishing of metal, or the holding of material being ground, or metal being sanded or polished by rotary tools; *or* *(c)* the use of hand-held percussive metal-working tools, or the holding of metal being worked upon by percussive tools, in riveting, caulking, chipping, hammering, fettling or swaging; *or* *(d)* the use of hand-held powered percussive drills or hand-held powered percussive hammers in mining, quarrying, demolition, or on roads or footpaths, including road construction; *or* *(e)* the holding of material being worked upon by pounding machines in shoe manufacture.
A12 Carpal tunnel syndrome.	*(a)* The use, at the time the symptoms first develop, of hand-held powered tools whose internal parts vibrate so as to transmit that vibration to the hand; *or* *(b)* repeated palmar flexion and dorsiflexion of the wrist for at least 20 hours per week for a period or periods amounting in aggregate to at least 12 months in the 24 months prior to the onset of the symptoms, where 'repeated' means once or more often in every 30 seconds.
A13 Osteoarthritis of the hip.	Work in agriculture as a farmer or farm worker for a period of, or periods which amount in aggregate to, 10 years or more.

Prescribed disease or injury	*Occupation*
A14 Oesteoarthritis of the knee	Work underground in a coal mine for a period of, or periods which amount in aggregate to, at least 10 years in any one or more of the following occupations: *(a)* before 1 January 1986 as a coal miner; or *(b)* on or after 1 January 1986 as a– *(i)* face worker working on a non-mechanised coal face;* *(ii)* development worker; *(iii)* face-salvage worker; *(iv)* conveyor belt cleaner; or *(v)* conveyor belt attendant. *'A non-mechanised coal face' means a coal face without either powered roof supports or a power loader machine which simultaneously cuts and loads the coal or without both. Work wholly or mainly fitting or laying carpets or floors (other than concrete floors) for a period of, or periods which amount in aggregate to, 20 years or more.
B – Conditions due to biological agents	**Any occupation involving:**
B1 Anthrax.	*(a)* Contact with anthrax spores, including contact with animals infected by anthrax; *or* *(b)* handling, loading, unloading or transport of animals of a type susceptible to infection with anthrax or of the products or residues of such animals.
B2 Glanders.	Contact with equine animals or their carcasses.
B3 Infection by leptospira.	*(a)* Work in places which are, or are liable to be, infested by rats, field mice or voles, or other small mammals; *or* *(b)* work at dog kennels or the care or handling of dogs; *or* *(c)* contact with bovine animals or pigs or their meat products.
B4 Ankylostomiasis.	Contact with a source of ankylostomiasis.
B5 Tuberculosis.	Contact with a source of tuberculous infection.
B6 Extrinsic allergic alveolitis (including farmer's lung).	Exposure to moulds or fungal spores or heterologous proteins by reason of employment in: *(a)* agriculture, horticulture, forestry, cultivation of edible fungi or malt-working; *or* *(b)* loading or unloading or handling in storage mouldy vegetable matter or edible fungi; *or* *(c)* caring for or handling birds; *or* *(d)* handling bagasse.

Prescribed disease or injury	*Occupation*
B7 Infection by organisms of the genus brucella.	Contact with: *(a)* animals infected by brucella, or their carcasses or parts thereof, or their untreated products; *or* *(b)* laboratory specimens or vaccines of, or containing, brucella.
B8 *(a)* Infection by hepatitis A virus.	Contact with raw sewage.
(b) Infection by hepatitis B or C virus.	Contact with: *(a)* human blood or human blood products; *or* *(b)* any other source of hepatitis B or C virus.
B9 Infection by Streptococcus suis.	Contact with pigs infected by Streptococcus suis, or with the carcasses, products or residues of pigs so infected.
B10 *(a)* Avian chlamydiosis.	Contact with birds infected with chlamydia psittaci, or with the remains or untreated products of such birds.
(b) Ovine chlamydiosis.	Contact with sheep infected with chlamydia psittaci, or with the remains or untreated products of such sheep.
B11 Q fever.	Contact with animals, their remains or their untreated products.
B12 Orf.	Contact with sheep, goats or with the carcasses of sheep or goats.
B13 Hydatidosis.	Contact with dogs.
B14 Lyme disease.	Exposure to deer or other mammals of a type liable to harbour ticks harbouring Borrelia bacteria.
B15 Anaphylaxis.	Employment as a healthcare worker having contact with products made with natural rubber latex.
C – Conditions due to chemical agents	**Any occupation involving:**
C1 *(a)* Anaemia with a haemoglobin concentration of 9g/dl or less, and a blood film showing punctate basophilia. *(b)* Peripheral neuropathy. *(c)* Central nervous system toxicity.	The use or handling of, or exposure to the fumes, dust or vapour of, lead or a compound of lead, or a substance containing lead.
C2 Central nervous system toxicity characterised by parkinsonism.	The use or handling of, or exposure to the fumes, dust or vapour of, manganese or a compound of manganese, or a substance containing manganese.
C3 *(a)* Phossy Jaw.	Work involving the use or handling of, or exposure to, white phosphorus.
(b) Peripheral polyneuropathy or peripheral polyneuropathy with pyramidal involvement of the central nervous system, caused by organic compounds of phosphorus which inhibit the enzyme neuropathy target esterase.	Work involving the use or handling of, or exposure to, organic compounds of phosphorus.

Prescribed disease or injury	*Occupation*
C4 Primary carcinoma of the bronchus or lung.	Exposure to the fumes, dust or vapour of arsenic, a compound of arsenic or a substance containing arsenic.
C5 *(a)* Central nervous system toxicity characterised by tremor and neuropsychiatric disease.	Exposure to mercury or inorganic compounds of mercury for a period of, or periods which amount in aggregate to, 10 years or more.
(b) Central nervous system toxicity characterised by combined cerebellar and cortical degeneration.	Exposure to methylmercury.
C6 Peripheral neuropathy.	The use or handling of, or exposure to carbon disulphide (also called carbon disulfide).
C7 Acute non-lymphatic leukaemia.	Exposure to benzene.
C12 *(a)* Peripheral neuropathy. *(b)* Central nervous system toxicity.	Exposure to methyl bromide (also called bromomethane).
C13 Cirrhosis of the liver.	Exposure to chlorinated naphthalene.
C16 *(a)* Neurotoxicity. *(b)* Cardiotoxicity.	Exposure to the dust of gonioma kamassi.
C17 Chronic beryllium disease.	Inhalation of beryllium or a compound of beryllium.
C18 Emphysema.	Inhalation of cadmium fumes for a period of, or periods which amount in aggregate to, 20 years or more.
C19 *(a)* Peripheral neuropath. *(b)* Central nervous system toxicity.	Exposure to acrylamide.
C20 Dystrophy of the cornea (including ulceration of the corneal surface) of the eye.	Exposure to quinone or hydroquinone.
C21 Primary carcinoma of the skin.	Exposure to arsenic or arsenic compounds, tar, pitch, bitumen, mineral oil (including paraffin) or soot.
C22 *(a)* Primary carcinoma of the mucous membrane of the nose or paranasal sinuses. *(b)* Primary carcinoma of a bronchus or lung.	Work before 1950 in the refining of nickel involving exposure to oxides, sulphides or water-soluble compounds of nickel.
C23 Primary neoplasm of the epithelial lining of the urinary tract (renal pelvis, ureter, bladder and urethra), including papilloma carcinoma-in-situ and invasive carcinoma.	*(a)* The manufacture of 1-naphtylamine, 2-naphthylamine, benzidine, auramine, magenta or 4 aminobiphenyl (also called biphenyl-4-ylamine); *(b)* work in the process of manufacturing methylenebis-orthochloroanile (also called MbOCA) for a period of, or periods which amount in aggregate to, 12 months or more;

Prescribed disease or injury	*Occupation*
	(c) exposure to 2-naphtylamine, benzidine, 4-aminobiphenyl (also called MbOCA) for a period of, or periods which amount in aggregate to, 12 months or more; *(d)* exposure to orthotoluidine, 4-chloro-2-methylaniline or salts of those compounds; *or* *(e)* exposure for a period of, or periods which amount in aggregate to, 5 years or more, to coal tar pitch volatiles produced in aluminium smelting involving the Sodeberg process (that is to say, the method of producing aluminium by electrolysis in which the anode consists of a paste of petroleum coke and mineral oil which is baked in situ).
C24 *(a)* Angiosarcoma of the liver. *(b)* Osteolysis of the terminal phalanges of the fingers. *(c)* Sclerodermatous thickening of the skin of the hand. *(d)* Liver fibrosis, due to exposure to vinyl chloride monomer.	Exposure to vinyl chloride monomer in the manufacture of polyvinyl chloride.
C24A Raynaud's phenomenon due to exposure to vinyl chloride monomer.	Exposure to vinyl chloride monomer in the manufacture of polyvinyl chloride before 1st January 1984.
C25 Vitiligo.	The use or handling of, or exposure to, para-tertiary-butylphenol (also called 4-tert-butylphenol), para-tertiary-butylcatechol (also called 4-tert-butylcatechol), para-amyl-phenol (also called p-pentyl phenol isomers), hydroquinone monobenzyl ether of hydroquinone (also called 4-benzyloxy-phenol), mono-benzyl ether of hydroquinone (also called 4-benzyloxyphenol) or mono-butyl ether of hydroquinone (also called 4-butoxyphenol).
C26 *(a)* Liver toxicity. *(b)* Kidney toxicity.	The use of or handling of, or exposure to, carbon tetrachloride (also called tetrachloromethane).
C27 Liver toxicity.	The use of or handling of, or exposure to the fumes of, or vapour containing, trichloromethane (also called chloroform).
C29 Peripheral neuropathy.	The use of or handling of, or exposure to, n-hexane or n-butyl methyl ketone.
C30 *(a)* Dermatitis. *(b)* Ulceration of the mucous membrane or the epidermis.	The use or handling of, or exposure to, chromic acid, chromates or dichromates.

Prescribed disease or injury	*Occupation*
C31 Bronchiolitis obliterans.	The use or handling of, or exposure to, diacetyl (also called butanedione or 2,3-butanedione) in the manufacture of– *(a)* diacetyl; or *(b)* food favouring containing diacetyl; or *(c)* food to which food flavouring containing diacetyl is added.
C32 Carcinoma of the nasal cavity or associated air sinuses (nasal carcinoma).	*(a)* The manufacture of inorganic chromates; or *(b)* work in hexavalent chrome plating.
D – Miscellaneous conditions	**Any occupation involving:**
D1 Pneumoconiosis.	[Occupations specified in reg 2(b) of, and Part II of Schedule 1 to, the Social Security (Industrial Injuries) (Prescribed Diseases) Regulations 1985 which are too numerous to set out here. They are all occupations involving exposure to dust, such as mining, quarrying, sand blasting, grinding, making china or earthenware, boiler-sealing and other work involving the use of stone, asbestos, etc.]
D2 Byssinosis.	Work in any room where any process up to and including the weaving process is performed in a factory in which the spinning or manipulation of raw or waste cotton or of flax, or the weaving of cotton or flax, is carried on.
D3 Diffuse mesothelioma (primary neoplasm of the mesothelium of the pleura or of the pericardium or of the peritoneum).	Exposure to asbestos, asbestos dust or any admixture of asbestos at a level above that commonly found in the environment at large.
D4 Allergic rhinitis which is due to exposure to any of the following agents: *(a)* isocyanates; *(b)* platinum salts; *(c)* fumes or dusts arising from the manufacture, transport or use of hardening agents (including epoxy resin curing agents) based on phthalic anhydride, tetrachlorophthalic anhydride, trimellitic anhydride or triethylenetetramine; *(d)* fumes arising from the use of rosin as a soldering flux; *(e)* proteolytic enzymes; *(f)* animals including insects and other anthropods used for the purposes of research or education or in laboratories;	

Prescribed disease or injury	*Occupation*
(g) dusts arising from the sowing, cultivation, harvesting, drying, handling, milling, transport or storage of barley, oats, rye, wheat or maize, or the handling, milling, transport or storage of meal or flour made therefrom; *(h)* antibiotics; *(i)* cimetidine; *(j)* wood dust; *(k)* ispaghula; *(l)* castor bean dust; *(m)* ipecacuanha; *(n)* azodice-bonamide; *(o)* animals including insects and other arthropods or their larval forms, used for the purposes of pest control or fruit cultivation, or the larval forms of animals used for the purposes of research, education or in laboratories; *(p)* glutaraldehyde; *(q)* persulphate salts or henna; *(r)* crustaceans or fish or products arising from these in the food processing industry; *(s)* reactive dyes; *(t)* soya bean; *(u)* tea dust; *(v)* green coffee bean dust; *(w)* fumes from stainless steel welding; *(x)* products made with natural rubber latex.	Exposure to any of the agents set out in column 1 of this paragraph.
D5 Non-infective dermatitis of external origin (excluding dermatitis due to ionising particles or electro-magnetic radiant heat).	Exposure to dust, liquid or vapour or any other external agent except chromic acid, chromates or bi-chromates capable of irritating the skin (including friction or heat but excluding ionising particles or electro-magnetic radiations other than radiant heat).
D6 Carcinoma of the nasal cavity or associated air sinuses (nasal carcinoma).	*(a)* Attendance for work in or about a building where wooden goods are; *or* *(b)* attendance for work in a building used for the manufacture of footwear or components of footwear made wholly or partly of leather or fibre board; *or* *(c)* attendance for work at a place used wholly or mainly for the repair of footwear made wholly or partly of leather or fibre board.

Prescribed disease or injury	*Occupation*
D7 Asthma which is due to exposure to any of the following agents: *(a)* isocyanates; *(b)* platinum salts; *(c)* fumes or dusts arising from the manufacture, transport or use of hardening agents (including epoxy resin curing agents) based on phthalic anhydride, tetrachlorophthalic anhydride, trimellitic anhydride or triethylenetetramine; *(d)* fumes arising from the use of rosin as a soldering flux; *(e)* proteolytic enzymes; *(f)* animals including insects and other anthropods used for the purposes of research or education or in laboratories; *(g)* dusts arising from the sowing, cultivation, harvesting, drying, handling, milling, transport or storage of barley, oats, rye, wheat or maize, or the handling, milling, transport or storage of meal or flour made therefrom; *(h)* antibiotics; *(i)* cimetidine; *(j)* wood dust; *(k)* ispaghula; *(l)* castor bean dust; *(m)* ipecacuanha; *(n)* azodicarbonamide; *(o)* animals including insects and other arthropods or their larval forms, used for the purposes of pest control or fruit cultivation, or the larval forms of animals used for the purposes of research, education or in laboratories; *(p)* glutaraldehyde; *(q)* persulphate salts or henna; *(r)* crustaceans or fish or products arising from these in the food processing industry; *(s)* reactive dyes; *(t)* soya bean; *(u)* tea dust; *(v)* green coffee bean dust; *(w)* fumes from stainless steel welding; *(wa)* products made with natural rubber latex; *(x)* any other sensitising agent (occupational asthma).	Exposure to any of the agents set out in column 1 of this paragraph.

Prescribed disease or injury	*Occupation*
D8 Primary carcinoma of the lung where there is accompanying evidence of asbestosis.	*(a)* The working or handling of asbestos or any admixture of asbestos; *or* *(b)* the manufacture or repair of asbestos textiles or other articles containing or composed of asbestos; *or* *(c)* the cleaning of any machinery or plant used in any of the foregoing operations and of any chambers, fixtures and appliances for the collection of asbestos dust; *or* *(d)* substantial exposure to the dust arising from any of the foregoing operations.
D8A Primary carcinoma of the lung.	Exposure to asbestos in the course of– *(a)* the manufacture of asbestos textiles; *or* *(b)* spraying asbestos; *or* *(c)* asbestos insulation work; *or* *(d)* applying or removing materials containing asbestos in the course of shipbuilding, where all or any of the exposure occurs before 1st January 1975, for a period of, or periods which amount in aggregate to, five years or more, or otherwise, for a period of, or periods which amount in aggregate to, ten years or more.
D9 Unilateral or bilateral diffuse pleural thickening with obliteration of the costophrenic angle.	*(a)* The working or handling of asbestos; or any admixture of asbestos; *or* *(b)* the manufacture or repair of asbestos textiles or other articles containing or composed of asbestos; *or* *(c)* the cleaning of any machinery or plant used in any of the foregoing operations and appliances for the collection of asbestos dust; *or* *(d)* substantial exposure to the dust arising from any of the foregoing operations.
D10 Primary carcinoma of the lung.	*(a)* Work underground in a tin mine; *or* *(b)* exposure to bis(chloromethyl) ether produced during the manufacture of chloromethyl methyl ether; *or* *(c)* exposure to zinc chromate, calcium chromate or strontium chromate in their pure forms.

Prescribed disease or injury	*Occupation*
D11 Primary carcinoma of the lung where there is accompanying evidence of silicosis.	Exposure to silica dust in the course of: *(a)* the manufacture of glass or pottery; *(b)* tunnelling in or quarrying sandstone or granite; *(c)* mining metal ores; *(d)* slate quarrying or the manufacture of artefacts from slate; *(e)* mining clay; *(f)* using silicous materials as abrasives; *(g)* cutting stone; *(h)* stone masonry; *or* *(i)* work in a foundry.
D12 Except in the circumstances specified in regulation 2(d): *(a)* chronic bronchitis; *or* *(b)* emphysema; *or* *(c)* both, where there is evidence of a forced expiratory volume in one second (measured from the position of maximum inspiration with the claimant making maximum effort) of: *i)* at least one litre below the mean value predicted, obtained from the following prediction formulae which give the mean values predicted in litres: For a man, where the measurement is made without back-extrapolation, (3.62 x Height in metres) – (0.031 x Age in years) – 1.41; or, where the measurement is made with back-extrapolation, (3.71 x Height in metres) – (0.032 x Age in years) – 1.44. For a woman, where the measurement is made without back-extrapolation, (3.29 x Height in metres) – (0.029 x Age in years) – 1.42; or where the measurement is made with back-extrapolation, (3.37 x Height in metres) – (0.030 x Age in years) – 1.46; or *ii)* less than one litre.	Exposure to coal dust (whether before or after 5th July 1948) by reason of working – (a) underground in a coal mine for a period or periods amounting in aggregate to at east 20 years; (b) on the surface of a coal mine as a screen worker for a period or periods amounting in aggregate to at least 40 years before 1st January 1983; or (c) both underground in a coal mine, and on the surface as a screen worker before 1st January 1983, where 2 years working as a surface screen worker is equivalent to 1 year working underground, amounting in aggregate to at least the equivalent of 20 years underground. Any such period or periods shall include a period or periods of incapacity while engaged in such an occupation.
D13 Primary cacinoma of the nasopharynx	Exposure to wood dust in the course of the processing of wood or the manufacture or repair of wood products, for a period or periods which amount in aggregate to at least 10 years.

Appendix 8

Upper and lower earnings limits

Year	*Lower earnings limit (£)*	*Primary threshold (£) (introduced April 2000)*	*Upper earnings limit (£)*
1975/76	11.00		69.00
1976/77	13.00		95.00
1977/78	15.00		105.00
1978/79	17.50		120.00
1979/80	19.50		135.00
1980/81	23.00		165.00
1981/82	27.00		200.00
1982/83	29.50		220.00
1983/84	32.50		235.00
1984/85	34.00		250.00
1985/86	35.50		265.00
1986/87	38.00		285.00
1987/88	39.00		295.00
1988/89	41.00		305.00
1989/90	43.00		325.00
1990/91	46.00		350.00
1991/92	52.00		390.00
1992/93	54.00		405.00
1993/94	56.00		420.00
1994/95	57.00		430.00
1995/96	58.00		440.00
1996/97	61.00		455.00
1997/98	62.00		465.00
1998/99	64.00		485.00
1999/00	66.00		500.00
2000/01	67.00	76.00	535.00
2001/02	72.00	87.00	575.00
2002/03	75.00	89.00	585.00
2003/04	77.00	89.00	595.00

Year	*Lower earnings limit (£)*	*Primary threshold (£) (introduced April 2000)*	*Upper earnings limit (£)*
2004/05	79.00	91.00	610.00
2005/06	82.00	94.00	630.00
2006/07	84.00	97.00	645.00
2007/08	87.00	100.00	670.00
2008/09	90.00	105.00	770.00
2009/10	95.00	110.00	844.00
2010/11	97.00	110.00	844.00
2011/12	102.00	139.00	817.00
2012/13	107.00	146.00	817.00

Appendix 9

Disability which puts a person at a disadvantage in getting a job

Schedule 1 Regulation 9(1) to the Working Tax Credit (Entitlement and Maximum Rate) Regulations 2002

PART 1

1. When standing he cannot keep his balance unless he continually holds onto something.

2. Using any crutches, walking frame, walking stick, prosthesis or similar walking aid which he habitually uses, he cannot walk a continuous distance of 100 metres along level ground without stopping or without suffering severe pain.

3. He can use neither of his hands behind his back as in the process of putting on a jacket or of tucking a shirt into trousers.

4. He can extend neither of his arms in front of him so as to shake hands with another person without difficulty.

5. He can put neither of his hands up to his head without difficulty so as to put on a hat.

6. Due to lack of manual dexterity he cannot, with one hand, pick up a coin which is not more than $2\frac{1}{2}$ centimetres in diameter.

7. He is not able to use his hands or arms to pick up a full jug of 1 litre capacity and pour from it into a cup, without difficulty.

8. He can turn neither of his hands sideways through 180 degrees.

9. He–

(a) is registered as blind or registered as partially sighted in a register compiled by a local authority under section 24(9)(g) of the National Assistance Act 1948;

(b) has been certified as blind or as partially sighted and, in consequence, registered as blind or partially sighted in a register maintained by or on behalf of a council constituted under section 2 of the Local Government etc. (Scotland) Act 1994; or

(c) has been certified as blind or partially sighted and in consequence is registered as blind or partially sighted in a register maintained by or on behalf of a Health and Social Services Board in Northern Ireland.

10. He cannot see to read 16 point print at a distance greater than 20 centimetres, if appropriate, wearing the glasses he normally uses.

11. He cannot hear a telephone ring when he is in the same room as the telephone, if appropriate, using a hearing aid he normally uses.

12. In a quiet room he has difficulty in hearing what someone talking in a loud voice at a distance of 2 metres says, if appropriate, using a hearing aid he normally uses.

13. People who know him well have difficulty in understanding what he says.

14. When a person he knows well speaks to him, he has difficulty in understanding what that person says.

15. At least once a year during waking hours he is in a coma or has a fit in which he loses consciousness.

16. He has a mental illness for which he receives regular treatment under the supervision of a medically qualified person.

17. Due to mental disability he is often confused or forgetful.

18. He cannot do the simplest addition and subtraction.

19. Due to mental disability he strikes people or damages property or is unable to form normal social relationships.

20. He cannot normally sustain an 8 hour working day or a five day working week due to a medical condition or intermittent or continuous severe pain.

PART 2 (INITIAL CLAIMS ONLY)

21. As a result of an illness or accident he is undergoing a period of habilitation or rehabilitation.

Appendix 10

Limited capability for work assessment

Schedule 2 to the Employment and Support Allowance Regulations 2008

(1) Activity	(2) Descriptors	(3) Points
Part 1: Physical disabilities		
1. Mobilising unaided by another person with or without a walking stick, manual wheelchair or other aid if such aid can reasonably be used.	(a) Cannot either (i) mobilise more than 50 metres on level ground without stopping in order to avoid significant discomfort or exhaustion; or (ii) repeatedly mobilise 50 metres within a reasonable timescale because of significant discomfort or exhaustion.	15
:	(b) Cannot mount or descend two steps unaided by another person even with the support of a handrail.	9
	(c) Cannot either (i) mobilise more than 100 metres on level ground without stopping in order to avoid significant discomfort or exhaustion; or (ii) repeatedly mobilise 100 metres within a reasonable timescale because of significant discomfort or exhaustion.	9

(1) Activity	(2) Descriptors	(3) Points
	(d) Cannot either (i) mobilise more than 200 metres on level ground without stopping in order to avoid significant discomfort or exhaustion; or (ii) repeatedly mobilise 200 metres within a reasonable timescale because of significant discomfort or exhaustion.	6
	(e) None of the above apply.	0
2. Standing and sitting.	(a) Cannot move between one seated position and another seated position located next to one another without receiving physical assistance from another person.	15
	(b) Cannot, for the majority of the time, remain at a work station, either: (i) standing unassisted by another person (even if free to move around); or (ii) sitting (even in an adjustable chair) for more than 30 minutes, before needing to move away in order to avoid significant discomfort or exhaustion.	9
	(c) Cannot, for the majority of the time, remain at a work station, either: (i) standing unassisted by another person (even if free to move around); or (ii) sitting (even in an adjustable chair) for more than an hour before needing to move away in order to avoid significant discomfort or exhaustion.	6
	(d) None of the above apply	0
3. Reaching.	(a) Cannot raise either arm as if to put something in the top pocket of a coat or jacket.	15
	(b) Cannot raise either arm to top of head as if to put on a hat.	9
	(c) Cannot raise either arm above head height as if to reach for something.	6
	(d) None of the above apply.	0

(1) Activity	(2) Descriptors	(3) Points
4. Picking up and moving or transferring by the use of the upper body and arms.	(a) Cannot pick up and move a 0.5 litre carton full of liquid.	15
	(b) Cannot pick up and move a one litre carton full of liquid.	9
	(c) Cannot transfer a light but bulky object such as an empty cardboard box.	6
	(d) None of the above apply.	0
5. Manual dexterity.	(a) Cannot either: (i) press a button, such as a telephone keypad; or (ii) turn the pages of a book with either hand.	15
	(b) Cannot pick up a £1 coin or equivalent with either hand.	15
	(c) Cannot use a pen or pencil to make a meaningful mark.	9
	(d) Cannot use a suitable keyboard or mouse.	9
	(e) None of the above apply.	0
6. Making self understood through speaking, writing, typing, or other means normally used, unaided by another person.	(a) Cannot convey a simple message, such as the presence of a hazard.	15
	(b) Has significant difficulty conveying a simple message to strangers.	15
	(c) Has some difficulty conveying a simple message to strangers.	6
	(d) None of the above apply.	0
7. Understanding communication by both verbal means (such as hearing or lip reading) and non-verbal means (such as reading 16 point print) using any aid it is reasonable to expect them to use, unaided by another person.	(a) Cannot understand a simple message due to sensory impairment, such as the location of a fire escape.	15
	(b) Has significant difficulty understanding a simple message from a stranger due to sensory impairment.	15
	(c) Has some difficulty understanding a simple message from a stranger due to sensory impairment.	6
	(d) None of the above apply.	0

(1) Activity	(2) Descriptors		(3) Points
8. Navigation and maintaining safety, using a guide dog or other aid if normally used.	(a)	Unable to navigate around familiar surroundings, without being accompanied by another person, due to sensory impairment.	15
	(b)	Cannot safely complete a potentially hazardous task such as crossing the road, without being accompanied by another person, due to sensory impairment.	15
	(c)	Unable to navigate around unfamiliar surroundings, without being accompanied by another person, due to sensory impairment.	9
	(d)	None of the above apply.	0
9. Absence or loss of control leading to extensive evacuation of the bowel and/or bladder, other than enuresis (bed-wetting) despite the presence of any aids or adaptations normally used.	(a)	At least once a month experiences: (i) loss of control leading to extensive evacuation of the bowel and/or voiding of the bladder; or (ii) substantial leakage of the contents of a collecting device sufficient to require cleaning and a change in clothing.	15
	(b)	At risk of loss of control leading to extensive evacuation of the bowel and/or voiding of the bladder, sufficient to require cleaning and a change in clothing, if not able to reach a toilet quickly.	6
	(c)	None of the above apply.	0
10. Consciousness during waking moments.	(a)	At least once a week, has an involuntary episode of lost or altered consciousness resulting in significantly disrupted awareness or concentration.	15
	(b)	At least once a month, has an involuntary episode of lost or altered consciousness resulting in significantly disrupted awareness or concentration.	6
	(c)	None of the above apply.	0
Part 2: Mental, cognitive and intellectual function assessment			
11. Learning tasks.	(a)	Cannot learn how to complete a simple task, such as setting an alarm clock.	15
	(b)	Cannot learn anything beyond a simple task, such as setting an alarm clock.	9
	(c)	Cannot learn anything beyond a moderately complex task, such as the steps involved in operating a washing machine to clean clothes.	6

(1) Activity	(2) Descriptors	(3) Points
	(d) None of the above apply.	0
12. Awareness of everyday hazards (such as boiling water or sharp objects).	(a) Reduced awareness of everyday hazards leads to a significant risk of: (i) injury to self or others; or (ii) damage to property or possessions such that they require supervision for the majority of the time to maintain safety.	15
	(b) Reduced awareness of everyday hazards leads to a significant risk of (i) injury to self or others; or (ii) damage to property or possessions such that they frequently require supervision to maintain safety.	9
	(c) Reduced awareness of everyday hazards leads to a significant risk of: (i) injury to self or others; or (ii) damage to property or possessions such that they occasionally require supervision to maintain safety.	6
	(d) None of the above apply.	0
13. Initiating and completing personal action (which means planning, organisation, problem solving, prioritising or switching tasks).	(a) Cannot, due to impaired mental function, reliably initiate or complete at least 2 sequential personal actions.	15
	(b) Cannot, due to impaired mental function, reliably initiate or complete at least 2 personal actions for the majority of the time.	9
	(c) Frequently cannot, due to impaired mental function, reliably initiate or complete at least 2 personal actions.	6
	(d) None of the above apply.	0
14. Coping with change.	(a) Cannot cope with any change to the extent that day to day life cannot be managed.	15
	(b) Cannot cope with minor planned change (such as a pre-arranged change to the routine time scheduled for a lunch break), to the extent that overall day to day life is made significantly more difficult.	9

(1) Activity	(2) Descriptors		(3) Points
	(c)	Cannot cope with minor unplanned change (such as the timing of an appointment on the day it is due to occur), to the extent that overall, day to day life is made significantly more difficult.	6
	(d)	None of the above apply.	0
15. Getting about.	(a)	Cannot get to any specified place with which the claimant is familiar.	15
	(b)	Is unable to get to a specified place with which the claimant is familiar, without being accompanied by another person.	9
	(c)	Is unable to get to a specified place with which the claimant is unfamiliar without being accompanied by another person.	6
	(d)	None of the above apply.	0
16. Coping with social engagement due to cognitive impairment or mental disorder.	(a)	Engagement in social contact is always precluded due to difficulty relating to others or significant distress experienced by the individual.	15
	(b)	Engagement in social contact with someone unfamiliar to the claimant is always precluded due to difficulty relating to others or significant distress experienced by the individual.	9
	(c)	Engagement in social contact with someone unfamiliar to the claimant is not possible for the majority of the time due to difficulty relating to others or significant distress experienced by the individual.	6
	(d)	None of the above apply.	0
17. Appropriateness of behaviour with other people, due to cognitive impairment or mental disorder.	(a)	Has, on a daily basis, uncontrollable episodes of aggressive or disinhibited behaviour that would be unreasonable in any workplace.	15
	(b)	Frequently has uncontrollable episodes of aggressive or disinhibited behaviour that would be unreasonable in any workplace.	15
	(c)	Occasionally has uncontrollable episodes of aggressive or disinhibited behaviour that would be unreasonable in any workplace.	9
	(d)	None of the above apply.	0

Appendix 11

Limited capability for work-related activity assessment

Schedule 3 to the Employment and Support Allowance Regulations 2008

Activity	*Descriptors*
1. Mobilising unaided by another person with or without a walking stick, manual wheelchair or other aid if such aid can reasonably be used.	Cannot either: (a) mobilise more than 50 metres on level ground without stopping in order to avoid significant discomfort or exhaustion; or (b) repeatedly mobilise 50 metres within a reasonable timescale because of significant discomfort or exhaustion.
2. Transferring from one seated position to another.	Cannot move between one seated position and another seated position located next to one another without receiving physical assistance from another person.
3. Reaching.	Cannot raise either arm as if to put something in the top pocket of a coat or jacket.
4. Picking up and moving or transferring by the use of the upper body and arms (excluding standing, sitting, bending or kneeling and all other activities specified in this Schedule).	Cannot pick up and move a 0.5 litre carton full of liquid.
5. Manual dexterity.	Cannot either: (a) press a button, such as a telephone keypad; or (b) turn the pages of a book with either hand.

Activity	*Descriptors*
6. Making self understood through speaking, writing, typing, or other means normally used.	Cannot convey a simple message, such as the presence of a hazard.
7. Understanding communication by hearing, lip reading, reading 16 point print or using any aid if reasonably used.	Cannot understand a simple message due to sensory impairment, such as the location of a fire escape.
8. Absence or loss of control over extensive evacuation of the bowel and/or voiding of the bladder, other than enuresis (bed-wetting), despite the presence of any aids or adaptations normally used.	At least once a week experiences (a) loss of control leading to extensive evacuation of the bowel and/or voiding of the bladder; or (b) substantial leakage of the contents of a collecting device sufficient to require the individual to clean themselves and change clothing.
9. Learning tasks.	Cannot learn how to complete a simple task, such as setting an alarm clock, due to cognitive impairment or mental disorder.
10. Awareness of hazard.	Reduced awareness of everyday hazards, due to cognitive impairment or mental disorder, leads to a significant risk of (a) injury to self or others; or (b) damage to property or possessions such that they require supervision for the majority of the time to maintain safety.
11. Initiating and completing personal action (which means planning, organisation, problem solving, prioritising or switching tasks).	Cannot, due to impaired mental function, reliably initiate or complete at least 2 sequential personal actions.
12. Coping with change.	Cannot cope with any change, due to cognitive impairment or mental disorder, to the extent that day to day life cannot be managed.
13. Coping with social engagement, due to cognitive impairment or mental disorder.	Engagement in social contact is always precluded due to difficulty relating to others or significant distress experienced by the individual.
14. Appropriateness of behaviour with other people, due to cognitive impairment or mental disorder.	Has, on a daily basis, uncontrollable episodes of aggressive or disinhibited behaviour that would be unreasonable in any workplace.

Activity	*Descriptors*
15. Conveying food or drink to the mouth.	(a) Cannot convey food or drink to the claimant's own mouth without receiving physical assistance from someone else; (b) Cannot convey food or drink to the claimant's own mouth without repeatedly stopping, experiencing breathlessness or severe discomfort; (c) Cannot convey food or drink to the claimant's own mouth without receiving regular prompting given by someone else in the claimant's physical presence; or (d) Owing to a severe disorder of mood or behaviour, fails to convey food or drink to the claimant's own mouth without receiving: (i) physical assistance from someone else; or (ii) regular prompting given by someone else in the claimant's presence.
16. Chewing or swallowing food or drink.	(a) Cannot chew or swallow food or drink; (b) Cannot chew or swallow food or drink without repeatedly stopping, experiencing breathlessness or severe discomfort; (c) Cannot chew or swallow food or drink without repeatedly receiving regular prompting given by someone else in the claimant's presence; or (d) Owing to a severe disorder of mood or behaviour, fails to: (i) chew or swallow food or drink; or (ii) chew or swallow food or drink without regular prompting given by someone else in the claimant's presence.

Appendix 12

Abbreviations used in the notes

AAC	Administrative Appeals Chamber
AC	Appeal Cases
AG	Advocate General
All ER	All England Reports
Art(s)	Article(s)
CA	Court of Appeal
CC	County Council
CCLR	Community Care Law Reports
CS	Court of Session
DC	Divisional Court
E	England
ECJ	European Court of Justice
ECR	European Court Reports
ECtHR	European Court of Human Rights
EHRR	European Human Rights Reports
ELR	Education Law Reports
EU	European Union
EWCA	England and Wales Court of Appeal
EWHC	England and Wales High Court
FLR	Family Law Reports
HC	High Court
HL	House of Lords
HLR	Housing Law Reports
ICR	Industrial Cases Reports
IRS	Independent Review Service for the Social Fund
JPR	Justice of the Peace Reports
NICA	Northern Ireland Court of Appeal
MBC	Metropolitan Borough Council
para(s)	paragraph(s)
QB	Queen's Bench Reports
QBD	Queen's Bench Division
r(r)	rule(s)
Reg(s)	Regulation(s)
S	Scotland
s(s)	section(s)
Sch(s)	Schedule(s)
SLT	Scots Law Times
SSWP	Secretary of State for Work and Pensions
UKHL	United Kingdom House of Lords
UKSC	United Kingdom Supreme Court
UKUT	United Kingdom Upper Tibunal
W	Wales
WLR	Weekly Law Reports

Acts of Parliament

CA 1989	Children Act 1989
C(LC)A 2000	Children (Leaving Care) Act 2000
C(S)A 1995	Children (Scotland) Act 1995
CJPOA 1994	Criminal Justice and Public Order Act 1994
CMOPA 2008	Child Maintenance and Other Payments Act 2008
CPA 2004	Civil Partnership Act 2004

CSA 1991	Child Support Act 1991
CSA 1995	Child Support Act 1995
CSPSSA 2000	Child Support, Pensions and Social Security Act 2000
GRA 2004	Gender Recognition Act 2004
HSCA 2008	Health and Social Care Act 2008
HRA 1998	Human Rights Act 1998
IA 1971	Immigration Act 1971
IA 1988	Immigration Act 1988
IAA 1999	Immigration and Asylum Act 1999
ICTA 1988	Income and Corporation Taxes Act 1988
IT(EP)A 2003	Income Tax (Earnings and Pensions) Act 2003
JSA 1995	Jobseekers Act 1995
LGFA 1992	Local Government Finance Act 1992
MCA 1973	Matrimonial Causes Act 1973
NAA 1948	National Assistance Act 1948
NHSA 2006	National Health Service Act 2006
NHS(S)A 1978	National Health Service (Scotland) Act 1978
NHS(W)A 2006	National Health Service (Wales) Act 2006
NHSCCA 1990	National Health Service and Community Care Act 1990
NIA 1965	National Insurance Act 1965
PA 1995	Pensions Act 1995
PA 2007	Pensions Act 2007
PSA 1993	Pension Schemes Act 1993
SPCA 2002	State Pension Credit Act 2002
SSA 1998	Social Security Act 1998
SSA(F)A 1997	Social Security Administration (Fraud) Act 1997
SSAA 1992	Social Security Administration Act 1992
SSCBA 1992	Social Security Contributions and Benefits Act 1992
SSFA 2001	Social Security Fraud Act 2001
TCA 1999	Tax Credits Act 1999
TCA 2002	Tax Credits Act 2002
TCEA 2007	Tribunals, Courts and Enforcement Act 2007
TMA 1970	Taxes Management Act 1970
WRA 2007	Welfare Reform Act 2007
WRA 2009	Welfare Reform Act 2009
WRA 2012	Welfare Reform Act 2012
WRPA 1999	Welfare Reform and Pensions Act 1999

Regulations and other statutory instruments

Each set of regulations has a statutory instrument (SI) number and a date. You ask for them by giving their date and number.

A(IWR) Regs	The Accession (Immigration and Worker Registration) Regulations 2004 No.1219
ASPP(AO) Regs	The Additional Statutory Paternity Pay (Adoptions from Overseas) Regulations 2010 No.1057
ASPP(BAAO)(A) Regs	The Additional Statutory Paternity Pay (Birth, Adoption and Adoptions from Overseas)(Administration) Regulations 2010 No.154

ASPP(G) Regs	The Additional Statutory Paternity Pay (General) Regulations 2010 No.1056
ASPP(WR) Regs	The Additional Statutory Paternity Pay (Weekly Rates) Regulations 2010 No.1060
C(LC)SSB Regs	The Children (Leaving Care) Social Security Benefits Regulations 2001 No.3074
C(LC)SSB(S) Regs	The Children (Leaving Care) Social Security Benefits (Scotland) Regulations 2004 No.747
C(LC)(W) Regs	The Children (Leaving Care) (Wales) Regulations 2001 No.2189 (W151)
CB Regs	The Child Benefit (General) Regulations 2006 No.223
CB(R) Regs	The Child Benefit (Rates) Regulations 2006 No.965
CB&GA(AA) Regs	The Child Benefit and Guardian's Allowance (Administrative Arrangements) Regulations 2003 No.494
CB&GA(Admin) Regs	The Child Benefit and Guardian's Allowance (Administration) Regulations 2003 No.492
CB&GA(DA) Regs	The Child Benefit and Guardian's Allowance (Decisions and Appeals) Regulations 2003 No.916
CL(E) Regs	The Care Leavers (England) Regulations 2010 No.2571
CPP&CR(E) Regs	The Care Planning, Placement and Case Review (England) Regulations 2010 No.959
CS(MCP) Regs	The Child Support (Maintenance Calculation Procedure) Regulations 2000 No.2001/157
CS(MCSC) Regs	The Child Support (Maintenance Calculations and Special Cases) Regulations 2000 No.2001/155
CT(DD)O	The Council Tax (Discount Disregards) Order 1992 No.548
CT(DIS) Regs	The Council Tax (Deductions from Income Support) Regulations 1993 No.494
CTB Regs	The Council Tax Benefit Regulations 2006 No.215
CTB(SPC) Regs	The Council Tax Benefit (Persons who have Attained the Qualifying Age for State Pension Credit) Regulations 2006 No.216
CTC Regs	The Child Tax Credit Regulations 2002 No.2007
EE(A) Regs	The Employment Equality (Age) Regulations 2006 No.1031
EP(RUB&SB) Regs	The Employment Protection (Recoupment of Unemployment Benefit and Supplementary Benefit) Regulations 1977 No.674
ESA Regs	The Employment and Support Allowance Regulations 2008 No.794
ESA(CP) Regs	The Employment and Support Allowance (Consequential Provisions) Regulations 2008 No.1082
ESA(LCW and LCWRA)A Regs	The Employment and Support Allowance (Limited Capability for Work and Limited Capability for Work-Related Activity)(Amendment) Regulations 2011 No.228

ESA(TP) Regs	The Employment and Support Allowance (Transitional Provisions) Regulations 2008 No.795
ESA(TP)(EA)(No.2) Regs	The Employment and Support Allowance (Transitional Provisions, Housing Benefit and Council Tax Benefit) (Existing Awards) (No.2) Regulations 2010 No.1907
ESA(WRA) Regs	The Employment and Support Allowance (Work-Related Activity) Regulations 2011 No.1349
F(DIS) Regs	The Fines (Deductions from Income Support) Regulations 1992 No.2182
GA(Gen) Regs	The Guardian's Allowance (General) Regulations 2003 No.495
HB Regs	The Housing Benefit Regulations 2006 No.213
HB(LHA&IS)A Regs	The Housing Benefit (Local Housing Allowance and Information Sharing) Amendment Regulations 2007 No.2868
HB(LHA,M&C)A Regs	The Housing Benefit (Local Housing Allowance, Miscellaneous and Consequential) Amendment Regulations 2007 No.2870
HB(SPC) Regs	The Housing Benefit (Persons who have Attained the Qualifying Age for State Pension Credit) Regulations 2006 No.214
HB(SPC)(LHA&IS)A Regs	The Housing Benefit (State Pension Credit)(Local Housing Allowance and Information Sharing) Amendment Regulations 2007 No.2869
HB&CTB(CP) Regs	The Housing Benefit and Council Tax Benefit (Consquential Provisions) Regulations 2006 No.217
HB&CTB(DA) Regs	The Housing Benefit and Council Tax Benefit (Decisions and Appeals) Regulations 2001 No.1002
HB&CTB(WPD) Regs	The Housing Benefit and Council Tax Benefit (War Pension Disregards) Regulations 2007 No.1619
HPG(A) Regs	The Health in Pregnancy (Administration) Regulations 2008 No.3109
HPG(EA) Regs	The Health in Pregnancy (Entitlement and Amount) Regulations 2008 No.3108
HPG(NRA) Regs	The Health in Pregnancy Grant (Notices, Revisions and Appeals) (No.2) Regulations 2009 No.751
HSS(DHSF)(W)	The Healthy Start Scheme (Description of Healthy Start Food)(Wales) Regulations 2006 No.3108
HSS&WF(A) Regs	The Healthy Start Scheme and Welfare Food (Amendment) Regulations 2005 No.3262
I(EEA) Regs	The Immigration (European Economic Area) Regulations 2006 No.1003
IS Regs	The Income Support (General) Regulations 1987 No.1967
IS(JSACA) Regs	The Income Support (General)(Jobseeker's Allowance Consequential Amendments) Regulations 1996 No.206
IS(PCP) Regs	The Income Support (Prescribed Categories of Person) Regulations 2009 No.3152
JSA Regs	The Jobseeker's Allowance Regulations 1996 No.207

JSA(DV)(A) Regs	The Jobseeker's Allowance (Domestic Violence)(Amendment) Regulations 2012, draft
JSA(ES&ES) Regs	The Jobseeker's Allowance (Employment, Skills and Enterprise Scheme) Regulations 2011 No.917
JSA(MWAS) Regs	The Jobseeker's Allowance (Mandatory Work Activity Scheme) Regulations 2011 No.688
NHS(CDA) Regs	The National Health Service (Charges for Drugs and Appliances) Regulations 2000 No.620
NHS(DC) Regs	The National Health Service (Dental Charges) Regulations 2005 No.3477
NHS(DC)(S) Regs	The National Health Service (Dental Charges) (Scotland) Regulations 2003 No.158
NHS(DC)(W) Regs	The National Health Service (Dental Charges) (Wales) Regulations 2006 No.491
NHS(FP&CDA)(S) Regs	The National Health Service (Free Prescriptions and Charges for Drugs and Appliances) (Scotland) Regulations 2011 No.55
NHS(FP&CDA)(W) Regs	The National Health Service (Free Prescriptions and Charges for Drugs and Appliances) (Wales) Regulations 2007 No.121
NHS(GOS) Regs	The National Health Service (General Ophthalmic Services) Regulations 1986 No.975
NHS(OCP) Regs	The National Health Service (Optical Charges and Payments) Regulations 1997 No.818
NHS(OCP)(S) Regs	The National Health Service (Optical Charges and Payments) (Scotland) Regulations 1998 No.642
NHS(TERC) Regs	The National Health Service (Travelling Expenses and Remission of Charges) Regulations 2003 No.2382
NHS(TERC)(S) Regs	The National Health Service (Travelling Expenses and Remission of Charges) (Scotland) (No.2) Regulations 2003 No.460
NHS(TERC)(W) Regs	The National Health Service (Travelling Expenses and Remission of Charges Regulations) (Wales) 2007 No.1104
OSPP(A)ASPP(A) & SAP(AO)(PAM) Regs	The Ordinary Statutory Paternity Pay (Adoption), Additional Statutory Paternity Pay (Adoption) and Statutory Adoption Pay (Adoptions from Overseas) (Persons Abroad and Mariners) Regulations 2010 No.150
PAL Regs	The Paternity and Adoption Leave Regulations 2002 No.2788
PIPA Regs	The Social Security (Personal Independence Payment) (Assessment) Regulations 2011, draft
POS Regs	The Primary Ophthalmic Services Regulations 2008 No.1186
RO(HBF)AO	The Rent Officers (Housing Benefit Functions) Amendment Order 2007 No.2871
RO(HBF)O	The Rent Officers (Housing Benefit Functions) Order 1997 No.1984

RO(HBF)(S)O	The Rent Officers (Housing Benefit Functions) (Scotland) Order 1997 No.144
RR(CA)O	The Regulatory Reform (Carer's Allowance) Order 2002 No.1457
SF(AM) Regs	The Social Fund (Applications and Miscellaneous Provisions) Regulations 2008 No.2265
SF(AR) Regs	The Social Fund (Application for Review) Regulations 1988 No.34
SF(RDB) Regs	The Social Fund (Recovery by Deductions from Benefits) Regulations 1988 No.35
SFCWP Regs	The Social Fund Cold Weather Payments (General) Regulations 1988 No.1724
SFM&FE Regs	The Social Fund Maternity and Funeral Expenses (General) Regulations 2005 No.3061
SFWFP Regs	The Social Fund Winter Fuel Payment Regulations 2000 No.729
SMP Regs	The Statutory Maternity Pay(General) Regulations 1986 No.1960
SMP(ME) Regs	The Statutory Maternity Pay (Medical Evidence) Regulations 1987 No.235
SMP(PAM) Regs	The Statutory Maternity Pay (Persons Abroad and Mariners) Regulations 1987 No.418
SMPSS(MA) Regs	The Statutory Maternity Pay, Social Security (Maternity Allowance) and Social Security (Overlapping Benefits) (Amendment) Regulations 2006 No.2379
SPC Regs	The State Pension Credit Regulations 2002 No.1792
SPC(CTMP) Regs	The State Pension Credit (Consequential, Transitional and Miscellaneous Provisions) Regulations 2002 No.3019
SPP(A)&SAP(AO)(No.2) Regs	The Statutory Paternity Pay (Adoption) and Statutory Adoption Pay (Adoptions from Overseas) (No.2) Regulations 2003 No.1194
SPPSAP(A) Regs	The Statutory Paternity Pay and Statutory Adoption Pay (Administration) Regulations 2002 No.2820
SPPSAP(G) Regs	The Statutory Paternity Pay and Statutory Adoption Pay (General) Regulations 2002 No.2822
SPPSAP(G)(A) Regs	The Statutory Paternity Pay and Statutory Adoption Pay (General) and the Statutory Paternity Pay and Statutory Adoption Pay (Weekly Rates) (Amendment) Regulations 2006 No.2236
SPPSAP(PAM) Regs	The Statutory Paternity Pay and Statutory Adoption Pay (Persons Abroad and Mariners) Regulations 2002 No.2821
SPPSAP(WR) Regs	The Statutory Paternity Pay and Statutory Adoption Pay (Weekly Rates) Regulations 2002 No.2818
SS(AA) Regs	The Social Security (Attendance Allowance) Regulations 1991 No.2740
SS(BCO) Regs	The Social Security (Breach of Community Order) Regulations 2001 No.1395

SS(CatE) Regs	The Social Security (Categorisation of Earners) Regulations 1978 No.1689
SS(CCPC) Regs	Social Security (Contribution Credits for Parents and Carers) Regulations 2009 No.19
SS(CMB) Regs	The Social Security (Child Maintenance Bonus) Regulations 1996 No.3195
SS(Con) Regs	The Social Security (Contributions) Regulations 2001 No.1004
SS(C&P) Regs	The Social Security (Claims and Payments) Regulations 1987 No.1968
SS(Cr) Regs	The Social Security (Credits) Regulations 1975 No.556
SS(CTCNIN)Regs	The Social Security (Crediting and Treatment of Contributions, and National Insurance Numbers) Regulations 2001 No.769
SS(DLA) Regs	The Social Security (Disability Living Allowance) Regulations 1991 No.2890
SS(DLA etc)MA Regs	The Social Security (Disability Living Allowance, Attendance Allowance and Carer's Allowance) (Miscellaneous Amendments) Regulations 2011 No.2426
SS(DRPSAPGRB)(MP) Regs	The Social Security (Deferral of Retirement Pension, Shared Additional Pension and Graduated Retirement Benefit)(Miscellaneous Provisions) Regulations 2005 No.2677
SS(EEEIIP) Regs	The Social Security (Employed Earners' Employment for Industrial Injuries Purposes) Regulations 1975 No.467
SS(EF) Regs	The Social Security (Earnings Factor) Regulations 1979 No.676
SS(GA) Regs	The Social Security (Guardian's Allowance) Regulations 1975 No.515
SS(GB) Regs	The Social Security (General Benefits) Regulations 1982 No.1408
SS(GRB) No.2 Regs	The Social Security (Graduated Retirement Benefit) (No.2) Regulations 1978 No.393
SS(HCSA)(A&M) Regs	The Social Security (Housing Costs Special Arrangements)(Amendment and Modification) Regulations 2008 No.3195
SS(HIP) Regs	The Social Security (Hospital In-Patients) Regulations 2005 No.3360
SS(IA)CA Regs	The Social Security (Immigration and Asylum) Consequential Amendments Regulations 2000 No.636
SS(IB) Regs	The Social Security (Incapacity Benefit) Regulations 1994 No.2946
SS(IB)MA Regs	The Social Security (Incapacity Benefit) Miscellaneous Amendments Regulations 2000 No.3120
SS(IB)(T) Regs	The Social Security (Incapacity Benefit) (Transitional) Regulations 1995 No.310
SS(IB-ID) Regs	The Social Security (Incapacity Benefit – Increases for Dependants) Regulations 1994 No.2945

SS(IBWFI) Regs	The Social Security (Incapacity Benefit Work-focused Interviews) Regulations 2008 No.2928
SS(ICA) Regs	The Social Security (Invalid Care Allowance) Regulations 1976 No.409
SS(IFW) Regs	The Social Security (Incapacity for Work) (General) Regulations 1995 No.311
SS(II)(AB) Regs	The Social Security (Industrial Injuries) (Airmen's Benefits) Regulations 1975 No.469
SS(II)(MB) Regs	The Social Security (Industrial Injuries) (Mariners' Benefits) Regulations 1975 No.470
SS(II&D)MP Regs	The Social Security (Industrial Injuries and Diseases) Miscellaneous Provisions Regulations 1986 No.1561
SS(IIPD) Regs	The Social Security (Industrial Injuries) (Prescribed Diseases) Regulations 1985 No.967
SS(IIRE) Regs	The Social Security (Industrial Injuries) (Regular Employment) Regulations 1990 No.256
SS(IoM)O	The Social Security (Isle of Man) Order 1977 No.2150
SS(J&G)O	The Social Security (Jersey and Guernsey) Order 1992 No.1735
SS(JPI) Regs	The Social Security (Jobcentre Plus Interviews) Regulations 2002 No.1703
SS(JPIP) Regs	Social Security (Jobcentre Plus Interviews for Partners) Regulations 2003 No.1886
SS(LAIP) Regs	Social Security (Local Authority Investigations and Prosecutions) Regulations 2008 No.463
SS(LB) Regs	The Social Security (Loss of Benefit) Regulations 2001 No.4022
SS(LPMA) Regs	The Social Security (Lone Parents and Miscellaneous Amendments) Regulations 2008 No.3051
SS(MA)(No.5) Regs 2009	The Social Security (Miscellaneous Amendments)(No.5) Regulations 2009 No.3228
SS(MA)(No.5) Regs 2010	The Social Security (Miscellaneous Amendments) (No.5) Regulations 2010 No.2429
SS(MatA) Regs	The Social Security (Maternity Allowance) Regulations 1987 No.416
SS(MatA)(E) Regs	The Social Security (Maternity Allowance) (Earnings) Regulations 2000 No.688
SS(MatA)(WA) Regs	The Social Security (Maternity Allowance) (Work Abroad) Regulations 1987 No.417
SS(ME) Regs	The Social Security (Medical Evidence) Regulations 1976 No.615
SS(NCC) Regs	The Social Security (Notification of Change of Circumstances) Regulations 2001 No.3252
SS(NDP) Regs	The Social Security (New Deal Pilot) Regulations 2000 No.3134
SS(NIRA) Regs	The Social Security (Northern Ireland Reciprocal Arrangements) Regulations 1976 No.1003
SS(OB) Regs	The Social Security (Overlapping Benefits) Regulations 1979 No.597

SS(PAOR) Regs	The Social Security (Payments on Account, Overpayments and Recovery) Regulations 1988 No.664
SS(RB) Regs	The Social Security (Recovery of Benefits) Regulations 1997 No.2205
SS(RB)App Regs	The Social Security (Recovery of Benefits) (Appeals) Regulations 1997 No.2237
SS(SDA) Regs	The Social Security (Severe Disablement Allowances) Regulations 1984
SS(STB)(T) Regs	The Social Security (Short-term Benefits) (Transitional) Regulations 1974 No.2192
SS(TC)A Regs	The Social Security (Tax Credits) Amendment Regulations 2005 No.2294
SS(WB&RP) Regs	The Social Security (Widow's Benefit and Retirement Pensions) Regulations 1979 No.642
SS(WBRP&OB)(T) Regs	The Social Security (Widow's Benefit, Retirement Pensions and Other Benefits) (Transitional) Regulations 1979 No.643
SS(WFILP) Regs	The Social Security (Work-focused Interviews for Lone Parents) and Miscellaneous Amendments Regulations 2000 No.1926
SS(WTCCTC)(CA) Regs	The Social Security (Working Tax Credit and Child Tax Credit)(Consequential Amendments) Regulations 2003 No.455
SSA(F)AO No.5	The Social Security Administration (Fraud) Act 1997 (Commencement No.5) Order 1997 No.2766
SSB(CE) Regs	The Social Security Benefit (Computation of Earnings) Regulations 1996 No.2745
SSB(Dep) Regs	The Social Security Benefit (Dependency) Regulations 1977 No.343
SSB(MW&WSP) Regs	The Social Security (Benefit) (Married Women and Widows' Special Provisions) Regulations 1974 No.2010
SSB(PA) Regs	The Social Security Benefit (Persons Abroad) Regulations 1975 No.563
SSB(PRT) Regs	The Social Security Benefit (Persons Residing Together) Regulations 1977 No.956
SSC(DA) Regs	The Social Security Contributions (Decisions and Appeals) Regulations 1999 No.1027
SSC(NPPC1C)	The Social Security Contributions (Notional Payment of Primary Class 1 Contributions) Regulations 2000 No.747
SSCBA(AAO) Regs	The Social Security Contributions and Benefits Act 1992 (Application of Parts 12ZA and 12ZB to Adoptions from Overseas) Regulations 2003 No.499
SSCBA(MHMFIB) Regs	The Social Security Contributions and Benefits Act 1992 (Modifications for Her Majesty's Forces and Incapacity Benefit) Regulations 2003 No.737
SSCP(TCA) Regs	The Social Security Commissioners (Procedure) (Tax Credit Appeals) Regulations 2002 No.3237

SS&CS(DA) Regs	The Social Security and Child Support (Decisions and Appeals) Regulations 1999 No.991
SSFA(PM) Regs	The Social Security and Family Allowances (Polygamous Marriages) Regulations 1975 No.561
SSP Regs	The Statutory Sick Pay (General) Regulations 1982 No.894
SSP(HR) Regs	The Social Security Pensions (Home Responsibilities) Regulations 1994 No.704
SSP(MAPA) Regs	The Statutory Sick Pay (Mariners, Airmen and Persons Abroad) Regulations 1982 No.1349
SSP(ME) Regs	The Statutory Sick Pay (Medical Evidence) Regulations 1985 No.1604
SSP&SMP(D) Regs	The Statutory Sick Pay and Statutory Maternity Pay (Decisions) Regulations 1999 No.776
TC(A) Regs	The Tax Credits (Appeals) Regulations 2002 No.2926
TC(A)(No.2) Regs	The Tax Credits (Appeals) (No.2) Regulations 2002 No.3196
TC(ACCP)S	The Tax Credits (Approval of Child Care Providers) Scheme 2005 No.93
TC(CN) Regs	The Tax Credits (Claims and Notifications) Regulations 2002 No.2014
TC(DCI) Regs	The Tax Credits (Definition and Calculation of Income) Regulations 2002 No.2006
TC(Imm) Regs	The Tax Credits (Immigration) Regulations 2003 No.653
TC(IR) Regs	The Tax Credits (Interest Rate) Regulations 2003 No.123
TC(ITDR) Regs	The Tax Credits (Income Thresholds and Determination of Rates) Regulations 2002 No.2008
TC(NA)Regs	The Tax Credits (Notice of Appeal) Regulations 2002 No.3119
TC(OE) Regs	The Tax Credits (Official Error) Regulations 2003 No.692
TC(PC) Regs	The Tax Credits (Payments by the Board) Regulations 2002 No.2173
TC(PM) Regs	The Tax Credits (Polygamous Marriages) Regulations 2003 No.742
TC(R) Regs	The Tax Credits (Residence) Regulations 2003 No.654
TCA(No.3)O	The Tax Credits Act 2002 (Commencement No.3 and Transitional Provisions and Savings) Order 2003 No.938
TCA(TP)O	The Tax Credits Act 2002 (Transitional Provisions) Order 2008 No.3151
TP(FT) Rules	The Tribunal Procedure (First-tier Tribunal) (Social Entitlement Chamber) Rules 2008 No.2685
TP(FT)(TC) Rules	The Tribunal Procedure (First-tier Tribunal) (Tax Chamber) Rules 2009 No.273
TP(UT) Rules	The Tribunal Procedure (Upper Tribunal) Rules 2008 No.2698
WF Regs	The Welfare Food Regulations 1996 No.1434

WRP(PABWW) Regs	The Welfare Reform and Pensions (Persons Abroad: Benefits for Widows and Widowers) (Consequential Amendments) Regulations 2001 No.2618
WRPA(No.9)O	The Welfare Reform and Pensions Act 1999 (Commencement No.9, Transitional Provisions and Savings) Order 2000 No.2958
WTC(EMR) Regs	The Working Tax Credit (Entitlement and Maximum Rate) Regulations 2002 No.2005

Other information

CBTM	*Child Benefit Technical Manual*
CCM	*Claimant Compliance Manual* (HMRC guidance on investigation of tax credit claims)
DMG	*Decision Makers Guide*, vols 1-14
GM	*Housing Benefit/Council Tax Benefit Guidance Manual*
HB/CTB G10/2008	Housing benefit and council tax benefit guidance
GAP	*Guidance and Procedures Volume*
SF Dir/SFI Dir	Direction(s) on the discretionary social fund. They are available in the *Social Fund Guide,* Sweet and Maxwell's *Social Security Legislation* and on the DWP website.
SFG	*The Social Fund Guide*
TCM	*Tax Credits Manual*
TCTM	*Tax Credits Technical Manual*

References like CIS/142/1990 and R(IS) 1/07 are references to commissioners' decisions.
References like CH/426/2008 [2009] UKUT 34(AAC) are references to decisions of the Upper Tribunal

Index

How to use this Index

Because the Handbook is divided into separate sections covering the different benefits, many entries in the index have several references, each to a different section. Where this occurs, we use the following abbreviations to show to which benefit each reference relates.

AA	Attendance allowance
CA	Carer's allowance
C-ESA	Contributory employment and support allowance
C-JSA	Contribution-based jobseeker's allowance
CTB	Council tax benefit
CTC	Child tax credit
DLA	Disability living allowance
ESA	Employment and support allowance
HB	Housing benefit
IB	Incapacity benefit
IIDB	Industrial injuries disablement benefit
IS	Income support
I-ESA	Income-related employment and support allowance
I-JSA	Income-based jobseeker's allowance
JSA	Jobseeker's allowance
MA	Maternity allowance
NI	National insurance
PC	Pension credit
PIP	Personal independence payment
SAP	Statutory adoption pay
SDA	Severe disablement allowance
SF	Social fund
SMP	Statutory maternity pay
SPP	Statutory paternity pay
SSP	Statutory sick pay
UC	Universal credit
WTC	Working tax credit

Entries against the bold headings direct you to the general information on the subject, or where the subject is covered most fully. Sub-entries are listed alphabetically and direct you to specific aspects of the subject.